ANCIENT HISTORY

FROM THE FIRST CIVILIZATIONS TO THE RENAISSANCE

Ancient History

This edition first published in Great Britain in 2004

Duncan Baird Publishers Ltd
Sixth Floor
Castle House
75–76 Wells Street
London W1T 3QH

This fourth revised edition of the text was first published as *The New Penguin History of the World* by Penguin Press/Allen Lane in 2002

DUNCAN BAIRD PUBLISHERS
Managing editor: Christopher Westhorp
Editor: Joanne Clay
Managing designer: Manisha Patel
Designer: Justin Ford
Picture researcher: Julia Ruxton
Map artwork: Russell Bell
Commissioned artwork: Gillie Newman, Stephen Conlin
Decorative borders: Lorraine Harrison

British Library Cataloguing-in-Publication Data.
A catalogue record for this book is available from the British Library.

10 9 8 7 6 5 4 3 2 1

ISBN 1-84483-060-8

Typeset in Sabon 11/15 pt
Colour reproduction by Colourscan, Singapore
Printed in Singapore by Imago

NOTE
The abbreviations CE and BCE are used throughout this book:
CE Common Era (the equivalent of AD)
BCE Before Common Era (the equivalent of BC)

CONTENTS

INTRODUCTION

PEOPLE HAVE very varied ideas not only over what actually happened in history, but over what historians should say about it, and universal agreement about what a history of the world should contain is too much to hope for. All history has to be a selection, and here that is very evident. There is nothing alarming about that. To specify every fact that shaped our past would be to relive it, a logical impossibility. At best, history can only be what one generation thinks important about the past. Sometimes the state of the evidence determines the selection; making the selection is usually the historian's business, though.

Among the things which have helped shape the particular viewpoint from which this book has been written is a certain criterion of historical importance. In one sense, it could be thought a very democratic one, for I have tried to set out the events, movements, determining facts and circumstances which have shaped most human lives. Some people might have preferred a criterion based on something else, but I have chosen to write about the things which seem to me to have had the greatest effect on human behaviour in the long run. One result has been my decision to tell the story of the great civilizations which laid down the foundations of human beliefs and institutions in different parts of the world for many centuries, rather than (for example) to list all countries and their rulers for their own sake. The proper place for such factual detail is an encyclopedia or historical dictionary, not a narrative history. That word "narrative" is another clue to my criteria: it has always seemed to me that chronology is the foundation of history and that historians should extract a story from the welter of fact. The story of this history is of an evolving humanity. It tries to set out interconnexions and relationships between places and individuals often distant from one another in both time and space, so that their contribution to the whole becomes apparent.

That meaningful story is one of the gradual assertion of humanity's ability to manage nature. Nowadays we are often told that human beings have failed; history, some people say, is a catalogue of follies – or worse. Because of

The Great Sphinx of the Giza necropolis, the first and most famous of dynastic Egypt's numerous sphinxes, reclines before the pyramid of Cephren (Khafre), 2555–2532BCE, whose face it bears atop its leonine body. The Great Sphinx has been silent witness to more than 1,660,000 sunrises during the course of four and a half millennia.

Entitled *Cognoscenti in a Room hung with Pictures*, this 17th-century painting from the Flemish School probably depicts European art experts, historians and scholars of the day, although the collection of pictures, instruments and *objets d'art* is likely to be imaginary.

it, they go on, we now face over-population, the destruction of the natural environment and barely contained violence. There is, indeed, a case to be made for such views, but they are easily overdone. Gloom and pessimism are not justified by a considered look backward at humanity's immense achievements. History reveals an increasing and astonishing display of human power to overcome obstacles and bring about conscious change (which is not to say that all the resultant changes have been wise or desirable). Our species has shown a unique ability; other living creatures have survived with more or less success by finding their niche in nature, but humanity has from the start adapted nature to suit itself. From its tiny beginnings in repeated struggles to master nature, for instance, by shaping a stone or an antler into a tool, or by striving to light or merely keep alive a fire, human history is a story of change brought about by human manipulation of the natural world. Such a success story is just as impressive as that of many disasters encountered *en route*.

The great Swiss historian Burckhardt once pointed out, very wisely, that in history you can never begin at the beginning. World history is about human beings, but we do not know who the first human being was. In the usual sense the era of history is the era of literacy, where there are documents for us to use as sources, but we have to start before that, with what we call "prehistory". We must not spend too much precious space on it, but most of humanity's existence has been lived in prehistoric times. For tens of thousands of years before civilization was possible, people much like ourselves in physique were exploiting the earth and changing it slowly. Earlier still, for hundreds of thousands, even millions, of years when nothing like a human being existed on earth, things were happening which shaped our later development and much of later history in very broad and important ways. So we must start there. But the main body of what follows is the story of civilization, a unique achievement, and a very rich and varied one. To tell its story in a way which puts it in a perspective which illuminates our own situation and difficulties has been my deepest ambition in writing this book. I now welcome with enthusiasm the possibility of presenting it to an even wider audience than hitherto. The original text has been thoroughly revised and up-dated, and enhanced by the wealth of illustrations, feature boxes, time charts and maps now made available by its imaginative publishers.

J.M. Roberts

BEFORE HISTORY

WHEN DOES History begin? It is tempting to reply "In the beginning", but like many obvious answers, this soon turns out to be unhelpful. As a great Swiss historian once pointed out, history is the one subject where you cannot begin at the beginning. We can trace the chain of human descent back to the appearance of vertebrates, or even to the photosynthetic cells and other basic structures which lie at the start of life itself. We can go back further, to almost unimaginable upheavals which formed this planet and even to the origins of the universe. Yet this is not "history".

Commonsense helps here: history is the story of humankind, of what it has done, suffered or enjoyed. We all know that dogs and cats do not have histories, while human beings do. Even when historians write about a natural process beyond human control, such as the ups and downs of climate, or the spread of a disease, they do so only because it helps us to understand why people have lived (and died) in some ways rather than others.

This suggests that all we have to do is to identify the moment at which the first human beings step out from the shadows of the remote past. It is not quite as simple as that, though. First, we have to know what we are looking for, but most attempts to define humanity on the basis of observable characteristics prove in the end arbitrary and cramping, as long arguments about "ape-men" and "missing links" have shown. Physiological tests help us to classify data but do not identify what is or is not human. That is a matter of a definition about which disagreement is possible. Some people have suggested that human uniqueness lies in language, yet other primates possess vocal equipment similar to our own; when noises are made with it which are signals, at what point do they become speech? Another famous definition is that man is a tool-maker, but observation has cast doubt on our uniqueness in this respect, too, long after Dr Johnson scoffed at Boswell for quoting it to him.

What is surely and identifiably unique about the human species is not its possession of certain faculties or physical characteristics, but what it has done with them. That, of course, is its history. Humanity's unique achievement is its remarkably intense level of activity and creativity, its cumulative capacity to create change. All animals have ways of living, some complex enough to be called cultures. Human culture alone is progressive; it has been increasingly built by conscious choice and selection within it as well as by accident and natural pressure, by the accumulation of a capital of experience and knowledge which humans have exploited. Human history began when the inheritance of genetics and behaviour which had until then provided the only way of dominating the environment was first broken through by conscious choice. Of course, human beings have always only been able to make their history within limits. Those limits are now very wide indeed, but they were once so narrow that it is impossible to identify the first step which took human evolution away from the determination of nature. We have for a long time only a blurred story, obscure both because the evidence is fragmentary and because we cannot be sure exactly what we are looking for.

In the middle of the Sahara desert, there are thousands of images painted or etched onto the rock that portray a lost world of swollen river beds and fertile wooded plains. The most spectacular examples of prehistoric imagery from the central Sahara date from the period between 6000 and 1500 BCE, when the livestock farmers who inhabited the region painted scenes such as these onto the rocks of the Tassili ni'Ajjer mountains.

1 THE FOUNDATIONS

THE ROOTS OF HISTORY lie in the prehuman past and it is hard (but important) to grasp just how long ago that was. If we think of a century on our calendar as a minute on some great clock recording the passage of time, then white Europeans began to settle in the Americas only about five minutes ago. Slightly less than fifteen minutes before that, Christianity appeared. Rather more than an hour ago people settled in southern Mesopotamia who were soon to evolve the oldest civilization known to us. This is already well beyond the furthest margin of written record; according to our clock people began writing down the past much less than an hour ago, too. Some six or seven hours further back on our scale and much more remote, we can discern the first recognizable human beings of a modern physiological type already established in western Europe. Behind them, anything from a fortnight to three weeks earlier, appear the first traces of creatures with some human characteristics whose contribution to the evolution which followed is still in debate.

THE ORIGINS OF HUMANKIND

HOW FAR BACK into a growing darkness we need go in order to understand human origins is debatable, but it is worth considering for a moment even larger tracts of time simply because so much happened in them which, even if we cannot say anything very precise about it, shaped what followed. This is because humanity was to carry forward into historical times certain possibilities and limitations, and they were settled long ago, in a part even more remote than the much shorter period of time – four and a half million years or so – in which creatures with at least some claim to human qualities are known to have existed. Though it is not our direct concern, we need to try to understand what was in the baggage of advantages and disadvantages with which humans alone among the primates emerged after these huge tracts of time as change-makers. Virtually all the physical and much of the mental formation we still take for granted was by

The continents, which were joined for a time as so-called Pangaea, began to drift around 200 million years ago. South America separated from Africa, as did India, which later moulded itself to Asia. Australia and the Antarctic slowly moved apart from one another.

The evolution of the hominids

The evolution of hominids – the superfamily in which zoologists classify both humans and their closest relations (chimpanzees, gorillas, orang-utans and gibbons) – started at the beginning of the Miocene era, some 24 million years ago. The first known members of our family (the hominids) lived 4 million years ago and have been classified as the *Australopithecus* genus. The first members of our genus (*Homo*) lived 2 million years ago and have been classified in the species *Homo habilis*. Our own species (*Homo sapiens*) appeared some 200,000 years ago. Although some of its earliest members, such as the Neanderthals, had features which distinguished them from us, the skeletons of those who lived in Cro-Magnon 30,000 years ago could easily be mistaken for ours.

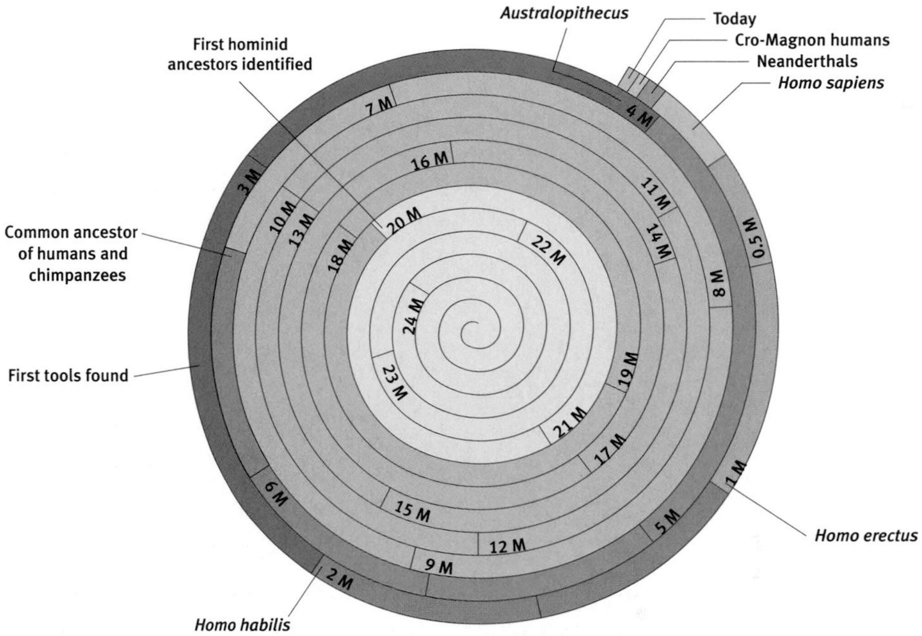

This spiral shows the number of millions of years since the main events in the evolution of hominids took place.

then determined, fixed in the sense that some possibilities were excluded and others were not. The crucial process is the evolution of creatures resembling humans as a distinct branch among the primates, for it is at this fork in the line, as it were, that we begin to look out for the station at which we get off for History. It is here that we can hope to find the first signs of that positive, conscious, impact upon environment which marks the first stage of human achievement.

THE CHANGING EARTH

The bedrock of the story is the earth itself. Changes recorded in fossils of flora and fauna, in geographical forms and geological strata, narrate a drama of epic scale lasting hundreds of millions of years. The shape of the world changed out of recognition many times. Great rifts opened and closed in its surface, coasts rose and fell; at times huge areas were covered with a long-since vanished vegetation. Many species of plants and animals emerged and proliferated. Most died out. Yet these "dramatic" events happened with almost unimaginable slowness. Some lasted millions of years; even the most rapid took centuries. The creatures who lived while they were going on could no more have perceived them than a twenty-first-century butterfly, in its three weeks or so of life, could sense the rhythm of the seasons. Yet the earth was taking shape as a collection of habitats permitting different strains to survive. Meanwhile, biological evolution inched forwards with almost inconceivable slowness.

THE CHANGING CLIMATE

Climate was the first great pace-maker of change. About forty million years ago – an

The development of animals

Vertebrates appeared in the Cambrian, the first period of the primary or Palaeozoic era. They were water animals, from which amphibians would later emerge, the first vertebrates to venture out onto dry land. Many species of fish and amphibians became extinct at the end of the Permian period. After this the secondary or Mesozoic era began, characterized by a predominance of reptiles, including dinosaurs. Birds evolved from dinosaurs and began to frequent the skies during the Cretaceous period. Mammals, however, did not become widespread until the Cenozoic era (Tertiary and Quaternary periods).

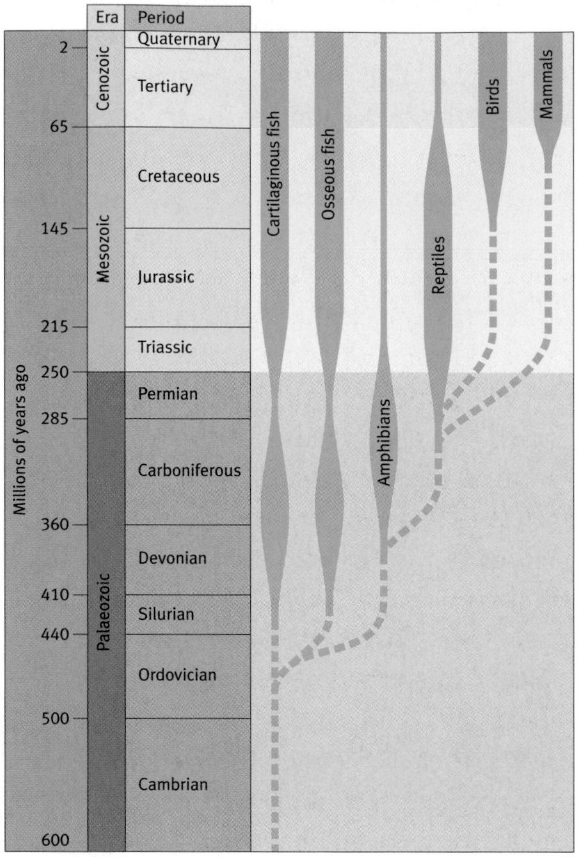

This chart represents the development of animals from the Palaeolithic to Cenozoic eras.

early enough point at which to begin to grapple with our story – a long warm climatic phase began to draw to a close. It had favoured the great reptiles and during it Antarctica had separated from Australia. There were no ice-fields then in any part of the globe. As the world grew colder and the new climatic conditions restricted their habitat, the great reptiles disappeared (though some argue that the impact of a giant meteorite was the crucial fact). But the new conditions suited other animal strains which were already about, among them some mammals whose tiny ancestors had appeared two hundred million years or so earlier. They now inherited the earth, or a considerable part of it. With many breaks in sequence and accidents of selection on the way, these strains were themselves to evolve into the mammals which occupy our own world – ourselves included.

Crudely summarized, the main lines of this evolution were probably determined for millions of years by astronomical cycles. As the earth's position changed in relation to the sun, so did climate. A huge pattern emerges, of recurrent swings of temperature. The extremes which resulted, of climatic cooling on the one hand and aridity on the other, choked off some possible lines of development. Conversely, in other times, and in certain places, the onset of appropriately benign conditions allowed certain species to flourish and encouraged their spread into new habitats. The only major sub-division of this immensely long process which concerns us comes very recently (in prehistoric terms), slightly less than four million years ago. There then began a period of climatic changes which we believe to have been more rapid and violent than any observed in earlier times. "Rapid", we must again remind ourselves, is a comparative term; these changes took tens of thousands of years. Such a pace of change, though, looks very different from the millions of years of much steadier conditions which lay in the past.

THE ICE AGES

SCHOLARS HAVE LONG talked about "Ice Ages", each lasting between fifty and a hundred thousand years, which covered big areas of the northern hemisphere (including much of Europe, and America as far south as modern New York) with great ice sheets, sometimes a mile or more thick. They have now distinguished some seventeen to nineteen (there is argument about the exact number) such "glaciations" since the onset of the first, over three million years ago. We live in a warm period following the most recent of them, which came to an end some ten thousand years ago. Evidence about these glaciations and their effects is now available from all oceans and continents and they provide the backbone for prehistoric chronology. To the external scale which the Ice Ages provide we can relate such clues as we have to the evolution of humanity.

THE EFFECTS OF GLACIATION

The Ice Ages make it easy to see how climate determined life and its evolution in prehistoric times, but to emphasize their dramatic direct effects is misleading. No doubt the slow onset of the ice was decisive and often disastrous for what lay in its path. Many of us still live in landscapes shaped by its scouring and gougings thousands of centuries ago. The huge inundations which followed the retreat of the ice as it melted must also have been locally catastrophic, destroying the habitats of creatures which had adapted to the challenge of arctic conditions. Yet they also created new opportunities. After each glaciation new species spread into the areas uncovered by the thaw. Beyond regions directly affected, though, the effects of the glaciations may have been even more important for the global story of evolution. Changes in environment followed cooling and warming thousands of miles from the ice itself; and the outcome had its own determining force. Both aridification and the spread of grassland, for instance, changed the possibilities of species spreading themselves into new areas, especially if they could stand upright and move on two feet. Some of those species form part of the human evolutionary story, and all the most important stages in that evolution – so far observed – have been located in Africa, far from the ice-fields.

Climate can still be very important today, as contemplation of the disasters brought by drought can show. But such effects, even when they affect millions of people, are not so

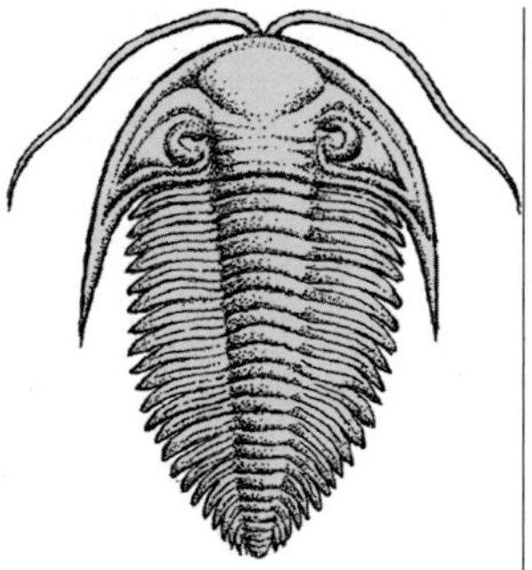

The origins of many of the types of animals that would later inhabit the planet were already present around 550 million years ago, even though animal life at that time was completely aquatic. The Trilobites, a subtype of marine arthropods of which more than 1,000 genera have been classified, were characteristic of such animal groups.

Glaciation

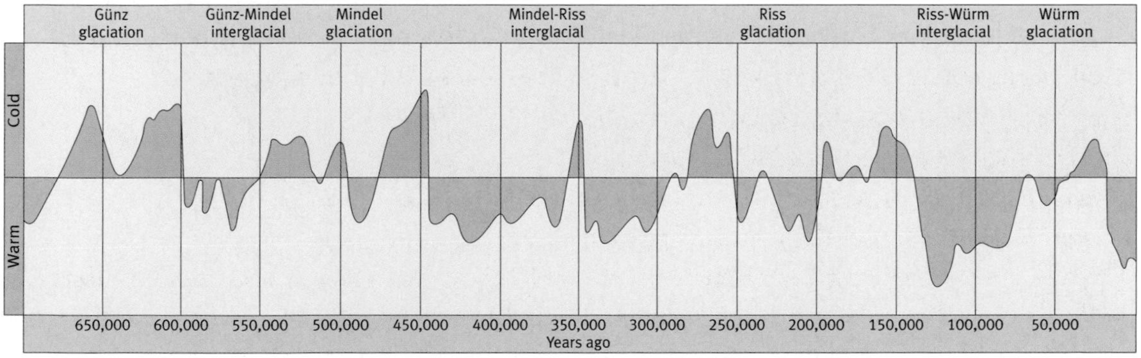

The major glaciations the earth has experienced are charted on this diagram, which also shows the interglacial periods.

A number of studies have managed to determine heat variations in the Quaternary (the last period of the Cenozoic era), which began two million years ago. During the coldest stages, there was an increase in the number of glaciers covering large areas of land. This was accompanied by a decrease in sea-level due to the retention of water masses, in the form of ice, on the continents. The last glaciations that occurred in the Alps have been named Günz, Mindel, Riss and Würm. Each glaciation was followed by a warmer period, known as an interglacial. Glaciations and interglacial periods can only be dated approximately.

fundamental as the slow transformation of the basic geography of the world and its supplies of food which climate wrought in prehistoric times. Until very recently climate determined where and how people lived. It made technique very important (and still does): the possession in early times of a skill such as fishing or fire-making could make new environments available to branches of the human family fortunate enough to possess such skills, or able to discover and learn them. Different food-gathering possibilities in different habitats meant different chances of a varied diet and, eventually, of progressing from gathering to hunting, and then to growing. Long before the Ice Ages, though, and even before the appearance of the creatures from which humanity was to evolve, climate was setting the stage for humanity and thus shaping, by selection, the eventual genetic inheritance of humanity itself.

PROSIMIANS INTO PRIMATES

ONE MORE BACKWARD GLANCE is useful before plunging into the still shallow (though gradually deepening) pool of evidence. Fifty-five million or so years ago, primitive mammals were of two main sorts. One, rodent-like, remained on the ground; the other took to the trees. In this way the competition of the two families for resources was lessened and strains of each survived to people the world with the creatures we know today. The second group were the prosimians. We are among their descendants, for they were the ancestors of the first primates.

The genealogical tree of mammals

Mammals first appeared in the Triassic period, at the beginning of the Mesozoic era, but there were relatively few of these animals in existence during the great age of dinosaurs (Jurassic and Cretaceous periods). It was only after dinosaurs became extinct, around 65 million years ago, that mammals became dominant. In the Jurassic period they were divided into three large groups: prototherians (such as modern-day montotremes, which lay eggs), metatherians (such as modern-day marsupials, whose offspring continue to develop inside the mother's pouch after birth) and eutherians (which comprise all the other classes of modern-day mammals). The oldest fossils of most classes of modern-day mammals, including primates, date back to the beginning of the Tertiary period.

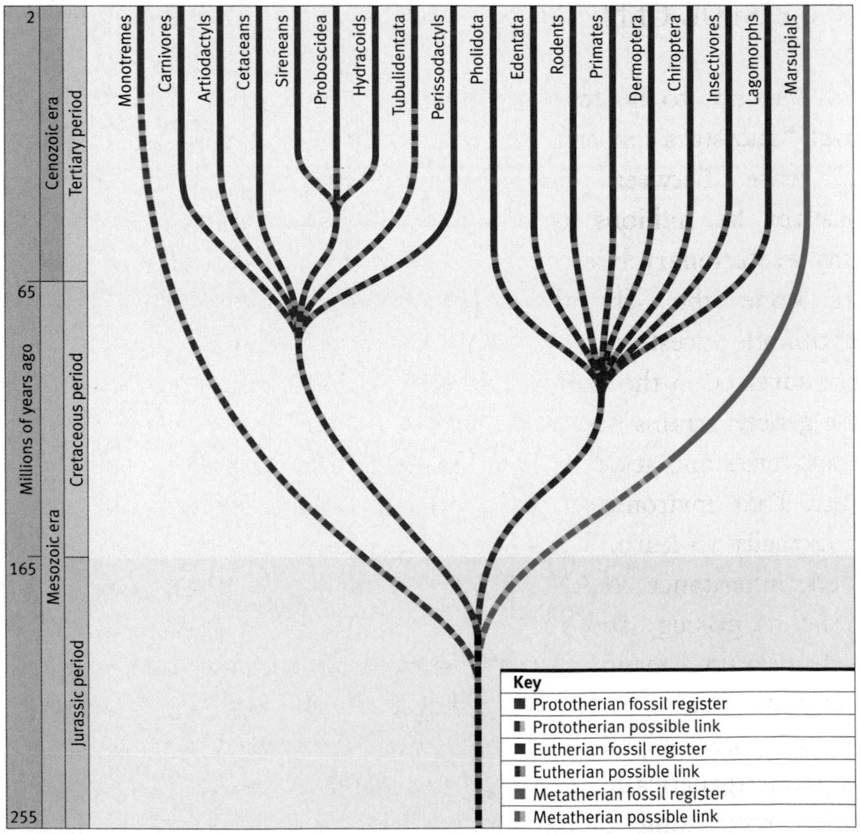

The division of mammals into three main groups is illustrated by this diagram.

The savannah, a landscape characterized by the predominance of herbaceous plants, covers large areas of Africa today. It was one of the environments in which the first hominids evolved.

SUCCESSFUL GENETIC STRAINS

It is best not to be too impressed by talk about "ancestors" in any but the most general sense. Between the prosimians and ourselves lie millions of generations and many evolutionary blind alleys. It is important none the less that our remotest identifiable ancestors lived in trees because what survived in the next phase of evolution were genetic strains best suited to the special uncertainties and accidental challenges of the forest. That environment put a premium on the capacity to learn. Those survived whose genetic inheritance could respond and adapt to the surprising, sudden danger of deep shade, confused visual patterns, treacherous handholds. Strains prone to accident in such conditions were wiped out. Among those that prospered (genetically speaking) were some species with long digits which were to develop into fingers and, eventually, the oppositional thumb, and other forerunners of the apes already embarked upon an evolution towards three-dimensional vision and the decreasing importance of the sense of smell.

The prosimians were little creatures. Tree-shrews still exist which give us some idea of what they were like; they were far from being monkeys, let alone human beings. Yet for millions of years they carried the traits which made humanity possible. During this time geography counted for much in their evolution, by imposing limits on contact between different strains, sometimes effectively isolating them, and thus increasing differentiation. Changes would not happen quickly but it is likely that fragmentations of the environment caused by geographical disturbance led to the isolation of zones in which, little by little, the recognizable ancestors of many modern mammals appeared. Among them are the first monkeys and apes. They do not seem to go back more than thirty-five million years or so.

The more we study chimpanzees, the more similarities we discover between these intelligent creatures and human beings. Although anatomically chimpanzees have more in common with gorillas than they do with humans, genetically, they appear to be closer to us.

MONKEYS AND APES

Monkeys and apes represent a great evolutionary stride. Both families had much greater manipulative dexterity than any predecessor. Within them, species distinct in size or acrobatic quality began to evolve. Physiological and psychological evolution blur in such matters. Like the development of better and stereoscopic vision, the growth of manipulative power seems to imply a growth of consciousness. Perhaps some of these creatures could distinguish different colours. The brains of the first primates were already much more complex than those of any of their predecessors; they were bigger, too. Somewhere the brain of one or more of these strains became complex enough and its physical powers sufficiently developed for the animal to cross the line at which the world as a mass of undifferentiated sensations becomes at least in part a world of objects. Whenever this happened it was a decisive step towards mastering the world by using it, instead of reacting automatically to it.

Some twenty-five or thirty million years ago, as desiccation began to reduce the area of the forests, competition for diminishing forest resources became fiercer. Environmental challenge and opportunity

The Proconsul

The 18-million-year-old Proconsul is one of the first known hominids. A member of the *Dryopithecus* family, which originated in Africa, it probably lived in the trees. Some of its features, such as its large cranium, are similar to those of modern-day hominids, including chimpanzees and gorillas.

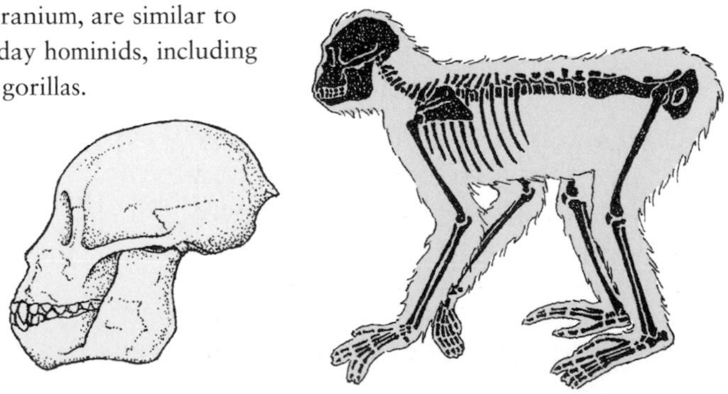

The cranium and skeleton of the Proconsul.

The evolution of anthropoids

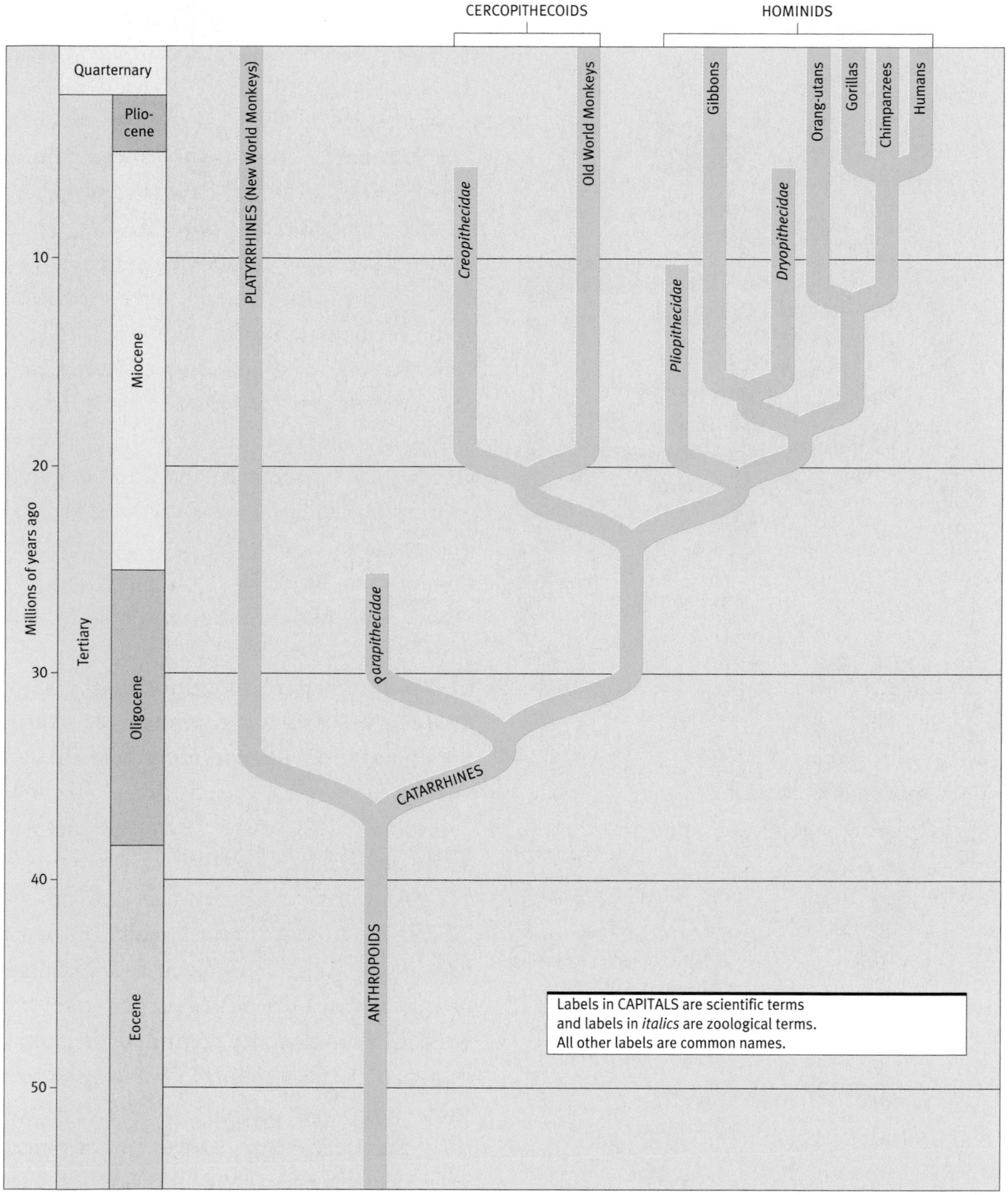

Anthropoids or apes (their zoological name is *Anthropoidea*) is one of the sub-classes into which primates are divided. In the Oligocene period, the second period of the Cenozoic era, they were divided into two branches: catarrhines, or Old World Monkeys, and platyrrhines, or New World Monkeys. At the beginning of the Miocene, the catarrhines were also divided into two branches, the cercopithecoids and the hominids. The oldest order of the hominid family to have been identified is the *Dryopithecus*, which became extinct at the end of the Miocene. Today there are four different hominid families: Hylobate (gibbon), Pongid (orang-utan), Pan (chimpanzee and gorilla) and Hominid (human). The separation between the ancestors of humans and chimpanzees is believed to have occurred five million years ago.

In 1970 CE a team of French and American investigators working in Hadar, Ethiopia, discovered this near-complete skeleton of a hominid female. Nick-named "Lucy", she is believed to have lived 3.2 million years ago. Lucy's pelvis shows that she walked upright, standing 3 ft 7 in (1.2 m) tall. She has been classified as a member of the species *Australopithecus afarensis.*

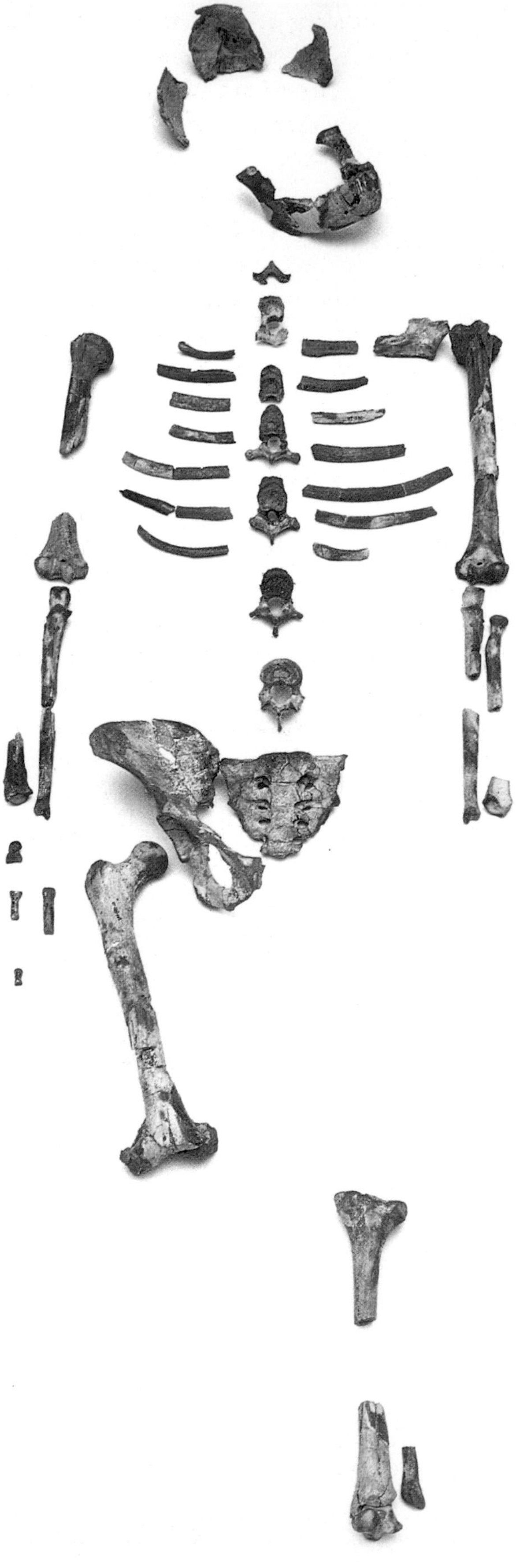

appeared where the trees and the grasslands met. Some primates, not powerful enough to hold on to their forest homes, were able, because of some genetic quality, to penetrate the savannahs in search of food and could meet the challenge and exploit the opportunities. Probably they had a posture and movement marginally more like that of humans than, say, that of the gorillas or chimpanzees. An upright stance and the capacity to move easily on two feet make it possible to carry burdens, among them food. The dangerous open savannah could then be explored and its resources withdrawn from it to a safer home base. Most animals consume their food where they find it; humans do not. Freedom to use the forelimbs for something other than locomotion or fighting also suggests other possibilities. We cannot confirm what the first "tool" was, but primates other than humans have been seen to pick up objects which come to hand and wave them as a deterrent, use them as weapons, or investigate and expose possible sources of food with their aid.

THE HOMINIDS

THE NEXT STEP in the argument is enormous, for it takes us to the first glimpse of a member of the biological family to which both humans and the great apes belong. The evidence is fragmentary, but suggests that some fifteen or sixteen million years ago a successful species was widespread throughout Africa, Europe and Asia. Probably he was a tree-dweller and certainly he was not very large – he may have weighed about 40 pounds. Unfortunately, the evidence is such as to leave him isolated in time. We have no direct knowledge of his immediate forebears or descendants, but some kind of fork in the road of primate evolution had occurred. While one branch was to lead to the great apes and chimpanzees, the other led to human beings. This line has been named "hominid". But the first hominid fossils (found in Kenya and Ethiopia) are dated to only some four and a half to five million years ago, so that for about ten million years the record is obscure. During that time big geological and geographical changes must have favoured and disfavoured many new evolutionary patterns.

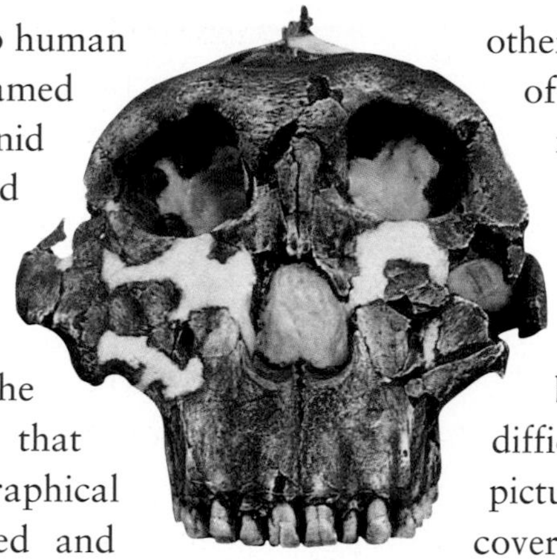

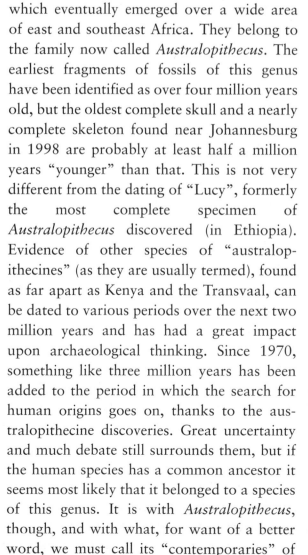

Skull of a *Paranthropus boisei*, discovered in the Olduvai Gorge.

The earliest surviving hominid fossils belong to a species which may or may not provide the ancestors for the small hominids which eventually emerged over a wide area of east and southeast Africa. They belong to the family now called *Australopithecus*. The earliest fragments of fossils of this genus have been identified as over four million years old, but the oldest complete skull and a nearly complete skeleton found near Johannesburg in 1998 are probably at least half a million years "younger" than that. This is not very different from the dating of "Lucy", formerly the most complete specimen of *Australopithecus* discovered (in Ethiopia). Evidence of other species of "australopithecines" (as they are usually termed), found as far apart as Kenya and the Transvaal, can be dated to various periods over the next two million years and has had a great impact upon archaeological thinking. Since 1970, something like three million years has been added to the period in which the search for human origins goes on, thanks to the australopithecine discoveries. Great uncertainty and much debate still surrounds them, but if the human species has a common ancestor it seems most likely that it belonged to a species of this genus. It is with *Australopithecus*, though, and with what, for want of a better word, we must call its "contemporaries" of other species, that the difficulties of distinguishing between apes, near-human apes and other creatures with some human characteristics first appear in their full complexity. The questions raised are still becoming in some ways more difficult to deal with. No simple picture has yet emerged and discoveries are still being made.

THE GENUS *HOMO*

We possess most evidence about *Australopithecus*. But there came to live contemporaneously with some australopithecine species other creatures, to whom the genus name *Homo* has been given. *Homo* was no doubt related to *Australopithecus*, but is first clearly identifiable as distinct about two million years ago on certain African sites; remains attributed to one of his species,

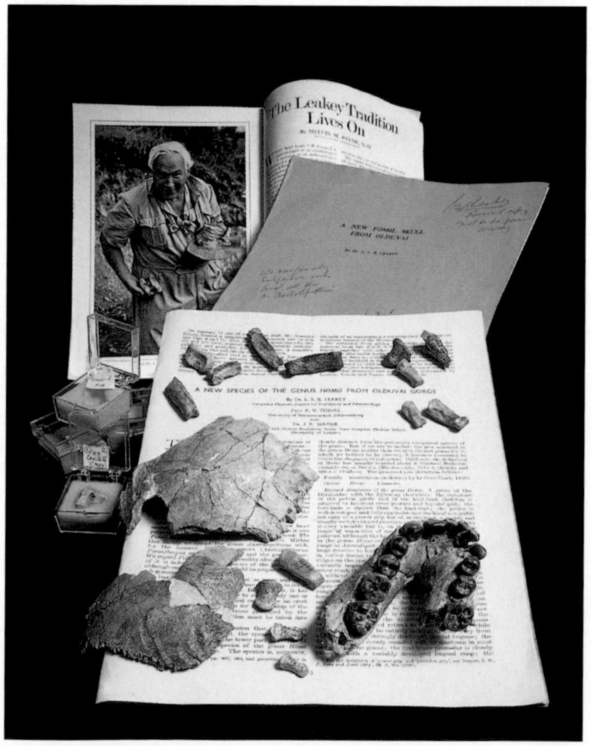

Palaeontologist Louis Leakey (1903–1972 CE) is pictured with one of his major discoveries, the first remains of the species *Homo habilis*, which he found in the Olduvai Gorge in 1960. These bone fragments from the cranium, jaw and fingers provided proof that, 1.7 million years ago, a species of our own genus lived alongside the *Paranthropus boisei*.

The first hominids

All the oldest hominid remains have been discovered in northeastern and southern Africa, which suggests that it was there that the evolution of the human family began. *Australopithecus afarensis* (the oldest known species) and *Paranthropus boisei* lived in northeastern Africa, where most *Homo habilis* remains have also been found. *Australopithecus africanus* and *Paranthropus robustus* lived in southern Africa. A number of experts believe that some of the fossil remains of African hominids should be classified in separate species from those mentioned above. However, because the species mentioned above are the most clearly identified at present, only they feature on this map.

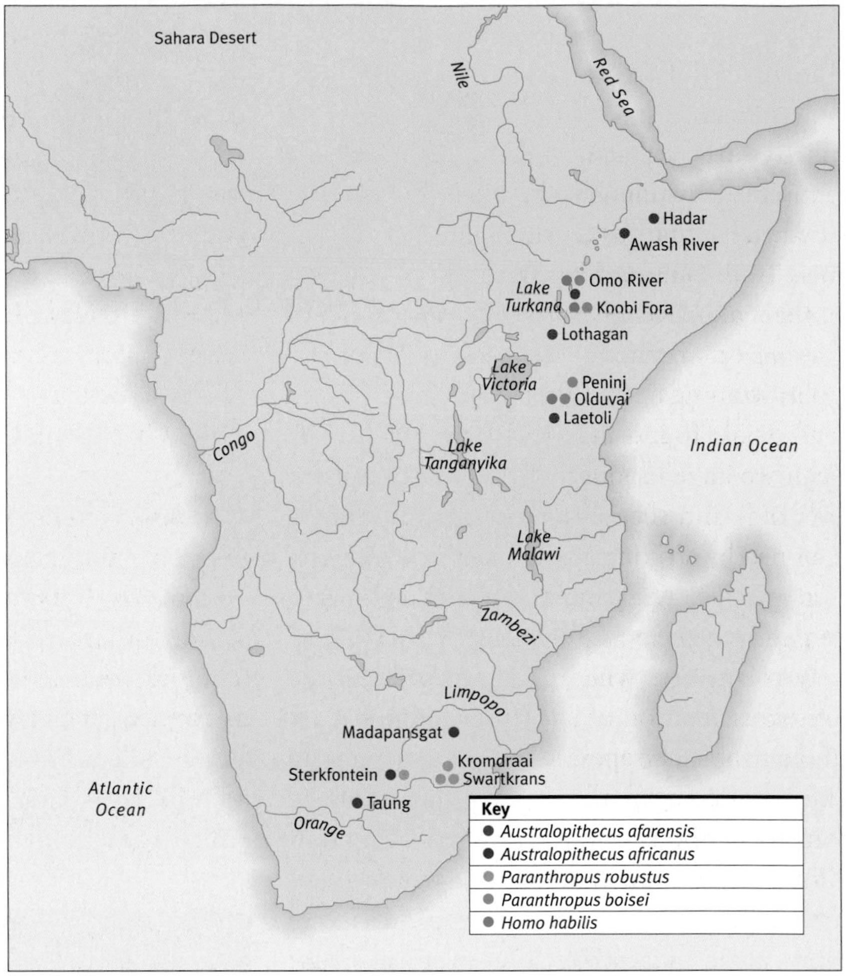

though, have been dated by radioactivity to some million and a half years before that. But, to make confusion worse, the remains of an even bigger hominid have turned up near Lake Rudolf in northern Kenya. About five feet tall, with a brain approximately twice the size of a modern chimpanzee's, he has the undignified name of "1470 man", that being the number attached to his relics in the catalogue of the Kenya museum where they are to be found.

Where specialists disagree and may go on arguing about such fragmentary evidence as we have (all that is left of two million or so years of hominid life could be put on a big table), laymen had better not dogmatize. Yet it is clear enough that we can be fairly certain about the extent to which some characteristics later observable in humans already existed more than two million years ago. We know, for instance, that the australopithecines, though smaller than modern humans, had leg-bones and feet which resembled those of humans more than apes. They walked upright and could run and carry loads for long distances as apes could not. Their hands showed a flattening at the fingertips characteristic of those of humans. These are stages far advanced on the road of human physique, even if the actual descent of our species is from some other branch of the hominid tree.

THE FIRST TOOLS

It is to early members of the genus *Homo* (sometimes distinguished as *Homo habilis*) nonetheless, that we owe our first relics of tools. Tool-using is not confined to humans, but the making of tools has long been thought of as a human characteristic. It is a notable step in winning a livelihood from the environment. Tools found in Ethiopia are the oldest which we have (about two and a half million years old) and they consist of stones crudely fashioned by striking flakes off pebbles to give them an edge. The pebbles seem often to have been carried purposefully and perhaps selectively to the site where they were prepared. Conscious creation of implements had begun. Simple pebble choppers of the same type from later times turn up all over the Old World of prehistory; about one million years ago, for example, they were in use in the Jordan valley. In Africa, therefore, begins the flow of what was to prove the biggest single body of evidence about prehistoric human beings and their precursors and the one which has provided most information about their distribution and cultures. A site at the Olduvai Gorge in Tanzania has provided the traces of the first identified building, a windbreak of stones which has been dated 1.9 million years ago, as well as evidence that its inhabitants were meat-eaters, in the form of bones smashed to enable the marrow and brains to be got at and eaten raw.

THE OLDUVAI EVIDENCE

Olduvai prompts a tempting speculation. The bringing of stones and meat to the site combines with other evidence to suggest that the children of early hominids could not easily cling to their mother for long foraging expeditions as do the offspring of other primates. It may be that this is the first trace of the human institution of the home base. Among primates, only humans have them: places where females and children normally stay while the males search for food to bring back to them. Such a base also implies the shady outlines of sexual differentiation in economic roles. It might even register the achievement of some degree of forethought and planning, in that food was not devoured to gratify the immediate appetite on the spot where it was taken, but reserved for family consumption elsewhere. Whether hunting, as opposed to scavenging from carcasses (now known to have been done by australopithecines), took place is another question, but it is clear that the meat of large animals was consumed at a very early date at Olduvai.

The discoveries at Olduvai

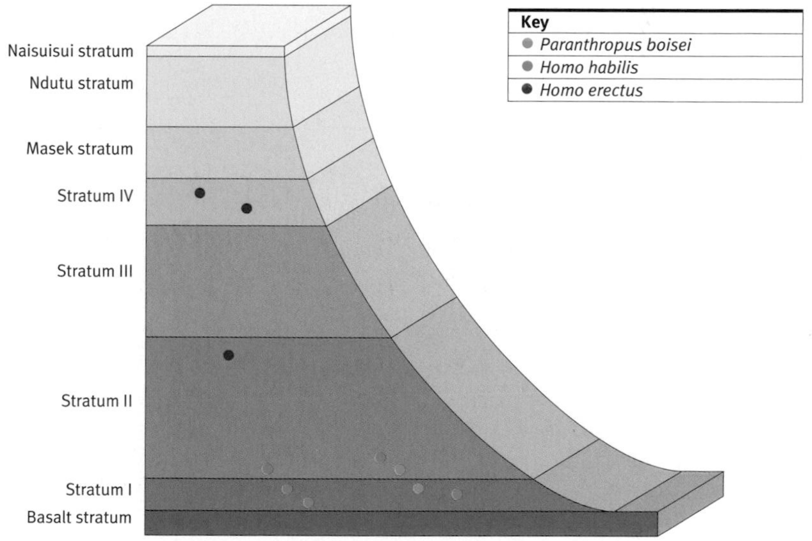

The Olduvai Gorge has supplied a vast amount of information about human origins. As the diagram shows, fossils of both *Paranthropus boisei* and *Homo habilis*, who lived 1.5–2 million years ago, have been uncovered in the oldest layers (on the lower part of the hillside). In more recent layers (on the upper part of the hillside) remains of *Homo erectus* have been found.

Yet such exciting evidence only provides tiny and isolated islands of hard fact. It cannot be presumed that the East African sites were necessarily typical of those which sheltered and made possible the emergence of humanity; we know about them only because conditions there allowed the survival and subsequent discovery of early hominid remains. Nor, though the evidence may incline that way, can we be sure that any of these hominids is a direct ancestor of humanity; they may all only be precursors. What can be said is that these creatures show remarkable evolutionary efficiency in the creative manner we associate with human beings, and suggest the uselessness of categories such as ape-men – and that few scholars would now be prepared to say categorically that we are not directly descended from *Homo habilis*, the species first identified with tool-using.

THE DIFFUSION OF THE GENUS *HOMO*

It is also easy to believe that the invention of the home base made biological survival easier. It would have made possible brief periods of rest and recovery from the hazards posed by sickness and accident, thus sidestepping, however slightly, the process of evolution by physical selection. Together with their other advantages,

The dispersion of *Homo erectus* beyond Africa

Homo erectus is the oldest species to definitely belong to the genus *Homo*. The earliest African remains of the species may be the ones found at Olduvai, which are known to be 1.2 million years old. (Remains found in Koobi Fora and Nariokotome, next to Lake Rudolf, which are 1.6 million years old, are also believed by some experts to belong to the species.) *Homo erectus* is the first species of hominids of which fossil remains have been discovered outside Africa. For a long time it was widely believed that *Homo erectus* began to spread beyond Africa around one million years ago. However, in 1989 CE a jaw was found in Dmanisi, Georgia, which may be 1.6 million years old. As a result of this discovery, the debate has been reopened.

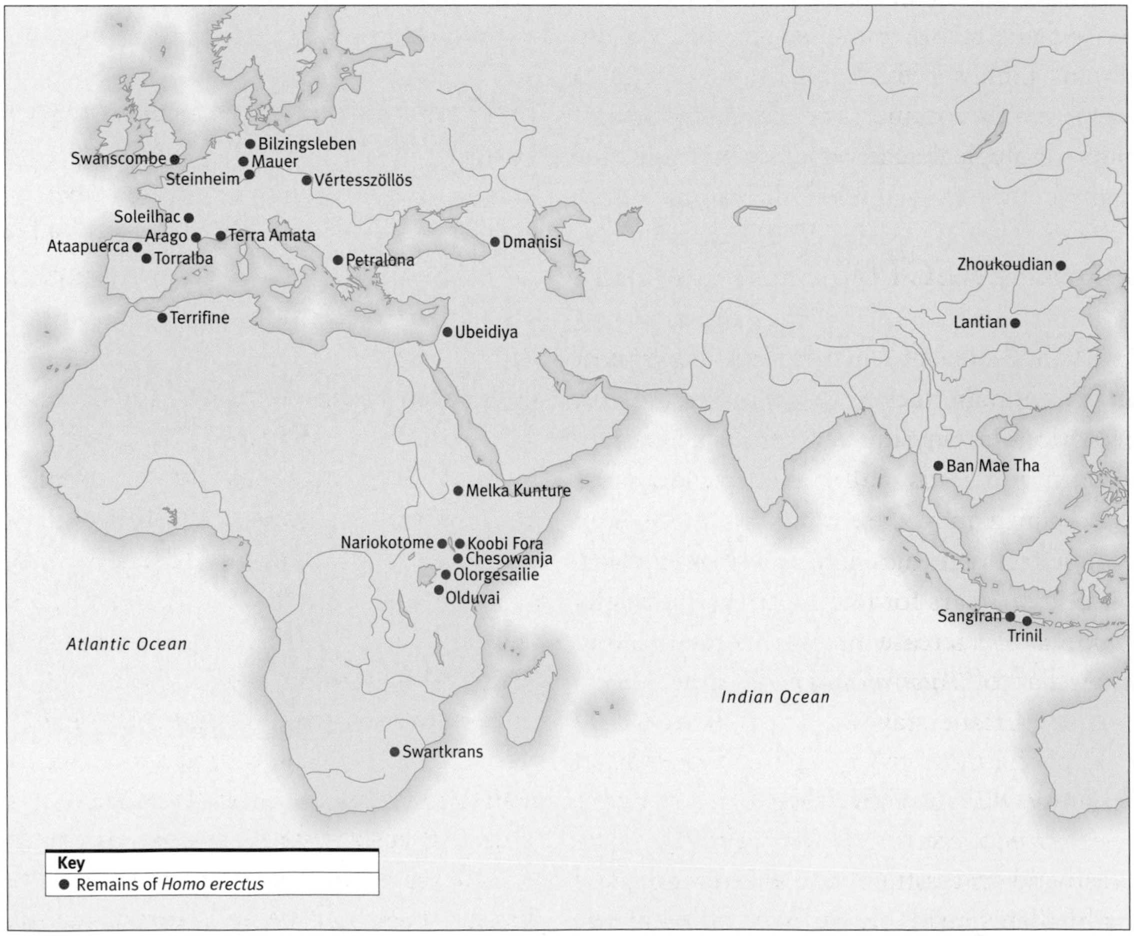

it may help to explain how examples of the genus *Homo* were able to leave traces of themselves throughout most of the world outside the Americas and Australasia in the next million or so years. But we do not know for certain whether this was through the spread of one stock, or because similar creatures evolved in different places. It is generally held, though, that tool-making was carried to Asia and India (and perhaps to Europe) by migrants originally from East Africa. The establishment and survival in so many different places of these hominids must show a superior capacity to grapple with changing conditions, but in the end we do not know what was the behavioural secret which suddenly (speaking once more in terms of prehistoric time) released that capacity and enabled them to spread over the landmass of Africa and Asia. No other mammal settled so widely and successfully before our own branch of the human family, which was eventually to occupy every continent except Antarctica, a unique biological achievement.

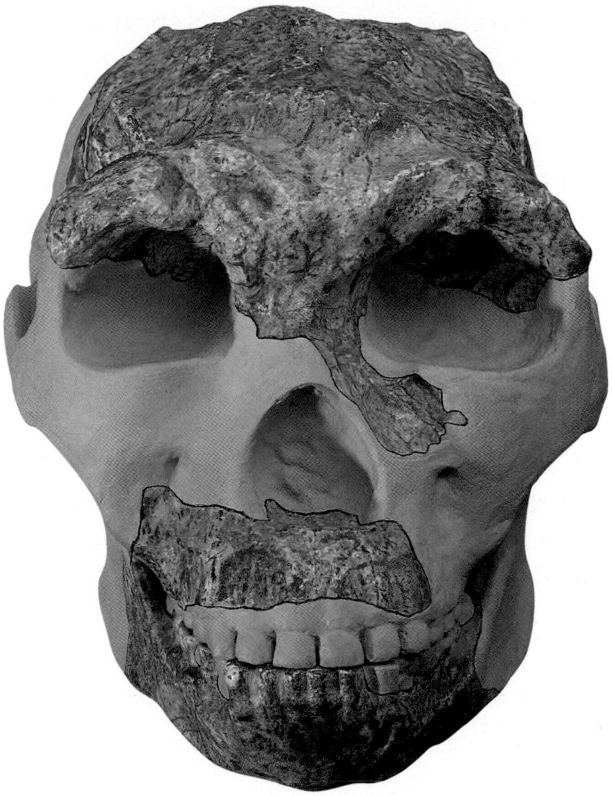

Casts of the skull and lower jawbone of the Lan-t'ien Ape-Man, found during excavations in Lan-t'ien, China, in 1963 and 1964 CE. This find demonstrates the diffusion of *Homo erectus* beyond Africa.

HOMO ERECTUS

THE NEXT CLEAR STAGE in the evolution of the human race is nothing less than a revolution in physique. After a divergence between hominids and more apelike creatures, which may have occurred more than four million years ago, it took rather less than two million years for one successful family of hominids to increase its brain size to about twice that of *Australopithecus*. One of the most important stages of this process and some of the most crucial in the evolution of humanity were already reached in a species called *Homo erectus*. It was already widespread and successful a million years ago, and had by then spread into Europe and Asia. The oldest specimen of the species so far found may be about half a million years older than that, while the last evidence for its survival (from Java) suggests its last members were living between thirty and fifty thousand years ago. *Homo erectus* therefore unsuccessfully exploited a much bigger environment than *Homo habilis* and did so for much longer than has *Homo sapiens*, the branch of hominids to which we belong. Many signs once more point to an African origin and thence to a spread through Europe and Asia (where *Homo erectus* was first found). Apart from fossils, a special tool helps to plot the distribution of the new species by defining areas into which *Homo erectus* did not spread as well as those into which he did. This is the so-called "hand-axe" of stone whose main use seems to have been for skinning and cutting up large animals (its use as an axe seems unlikely, but the name is established). There can be no doubt of the success of *Homo erectus* as a genetic product.

Cranial sizes

There can be no doubt that one of the fundamental landmarks in the evolution of the hominids has been the increase in cranial size needed to house the extraordinary human brain. As the illustration shows, *Australopithecus* had a larger cranial size, in relation to its body size, than either chimpanzees or gorillas. Examinations carried out on archaeological remains belonging to the species *Homo habilis* and *Homo erectus* also show, in this and in various other respects, progress towards the physiology of modern humans.

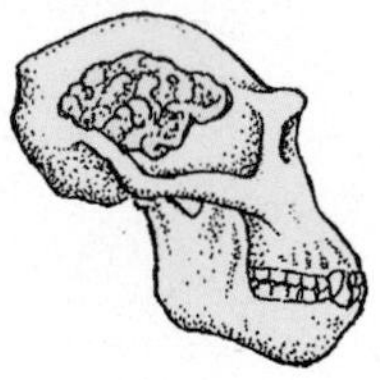

Chimpanzee cranium

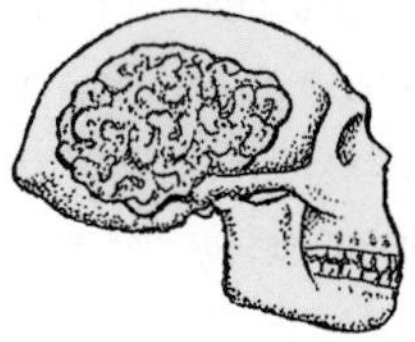

Australopithecus *cranium*

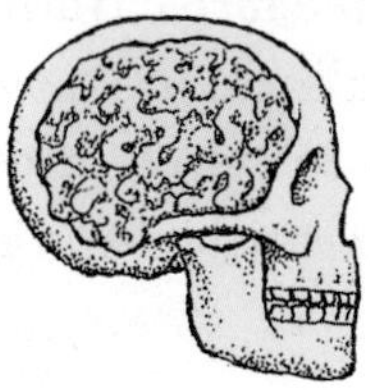

Modern human cranium

PHYSIOLOGICAL CHANGE

When we finish with *Homo erectus* there is no precise dividing line (there never is in human prehistory, a fact it is only too easy to overlook or forget), but we are already dealing with a creature who has added to the upright stance of his predecessors a brain approaching that of modern humans in magnitude. Though we still know little of the way in which the brain is organized, there is, allowing for body size, a rough correlation between size and intelligence. It is reasonable, therefore, to attribute great importance to the selection of strains with bigger brains and to reckon this a huge advance in the story of the slow accumulation of human characteristics.

PROLONGED INFANCY

Bigger brains meant bigger skulls and other changes, too. An increase in antenatal size requires changes in the female pelvis to permit the birth of offspring with larger heads, and another consequence was a longer period of growth after birth; physiological evolution in the female was not sufficient to provide antenatal accommodation to any point approaching physical maturity. Human children need maternal care long after birth. Prolonged infancy and immaturity in their turn imply prolonged dependency: it is a long time before such infants gather their own food. It may be with the offspring of *Homo erectus* that there began that long extension of tolerated immaturity whose latest manifestation is the maintenance of young people by society during periods of higher education.

Biological change also meant that care and nurture came gradually to count for more than large litters in ensuring the survival of the species. This in turn implied further and sharper differentiation in the roles of the sexes. Females were being pinned down much more by maternity at a time when food-gathering techniques seem to have become more elaborate and to demand arduous and prolonged cooperative action by males – perhaps because bigger creatures needed more and better food. Psychologically, too, the change may be significant. A new emphasis on the individual is one concomitant of prolonged infancy. Perhaps it was intensified by a social situation in which the importance of learning and memory was increasing and skills were becoming more complex. About this point the mechanics of what is going forward begin to slip from our grasp (if, indeed, they were ever in it). We are close to the area in which the genetic programming of the hominids is infringed by learning. This is the start of the great change from the natural physical endowment to tradition and culture – and eventually to conscious control – as evolutionary selectors, though we may never know where precisely this change occurs.

THE LOSS OF OESTRUS IN FEMALES

The loss of oestrus by the female hominid is another important physiological change. We do not know when this happened, but after it had been completed her sexual rhythm was importantly differentiated from that of other animals. Humans are the only animals in which the mechanism of the oestrus (the restriction of the female's sexual attractiveness and receptivity to the limited periods in which she is on heat) has entirely disappeared. It is easy to see the evolutionary connection between this and the prolongation of infancy: if female hominids had undergone the violent disruption of their ordinary routine which the oestrus imposes, their offspring would have been periodically exposed to a neglect which would have made their survival impossible.

Carefully placed rocks and the traces of holes in which posts had been set were discovered at the Terra Amata site in France in 1959 CE. The evidence seems to suggest that a hut of the kind shown in this illustration existed at the site 230,000 years ago. However, some experts question whether *Homo erectus* was capable of building such a dwelling.

The selection of a genetic strain which dispensed with oestrus, therefore, was essential to the survival of the species; such a strain must have been available, though the process in which it emerged may have taken a million or a million and a half years because it cannot have been effected consciously.

Such a change has radical implications. The increasing attractiveness and receptivity of females to males make individual choice much more significant in mating. The selection of a partner is less shaped by the rhythm of nature; we are at the start of a very long and obscure road which leads to the idea of sexual love. Together with prolonged infant

Childbirth

The evolutive advantage provided by a larger brain compensated for the drawbacks caused by the increasing difficulty of giving birth. The pelvic girdle of a female chimpanzee is wide enough to allow the head of its offspring to pass through. In humans this process is pushed to the limit, despite the fact that human infants are delivered at a much earlier stage of development than those of any other primate.

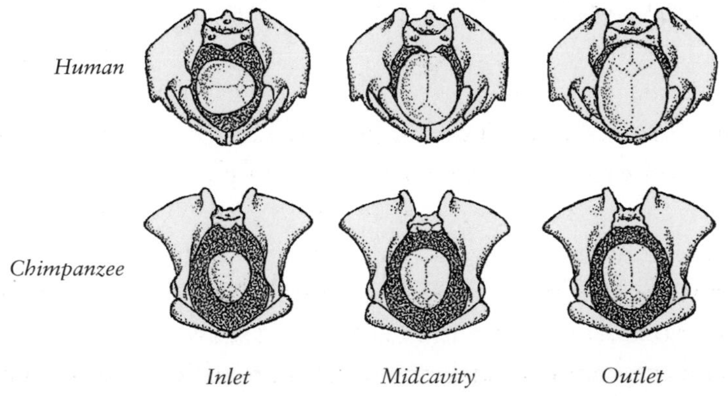

Hand-axes such as this one were made in large areas of Africa, Europe and western Asia over a long period of time, lasting from 1.5 million to 150,000 years ago. Like this one, many axes were carved on both sides.

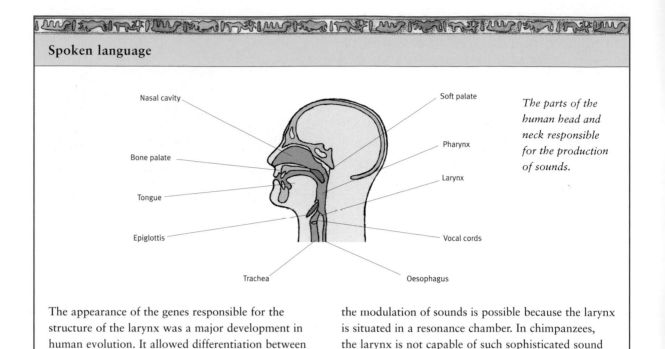

Spoken language

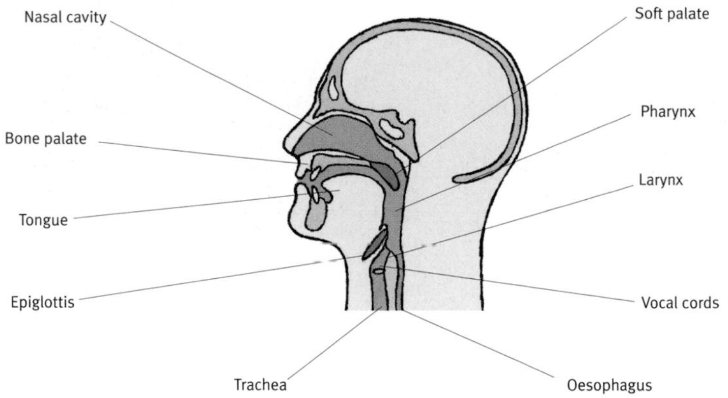

The parts of the human head and neck responsible for the production of sounds.

The appearance of the genes responsible for the structure of the larynx was a major development in human evolution. It allowed differentiation between dozens of different sounds instead of just a few and led to the creation of spoken language. In humans, the modulation of sounds is possible because the larynx is situated in a resonance chamber. In chimpanzees, the larynx is not capable of such sophisticated sound modulation and is therefore not able to produce the wide range of noises required for speech.

dependency, the new possibilities of individual selection point ahead also to the stable and enduring family unit of father, mother and offspring, an institution unique to humanity. Some have even speculated that incest taboos (which are in practice well-nigh universal, however much the precise identification of the prohibited relationships may vary) originate in the recognition of the dangers presented by socially immature but sexually adult young males for long periods in close association with females who are always potentially sexually receptive.

SIGNIFICANT ACHIEVEMENTS OF *HOMO ERECTUS*

In sexual matters it is best to be cautious. The evidence takes us only a very little way. Moreover, it is drawn from a very long span of time, a huge period allowing for considerable physical, psychological and technological evolution. The earliest forms of *Homo erectus* may not have been much like the last, some of whom have been classified by some scientists as archaic forms of the next evolutionary stage of the hominid line. Yet all reflections support the general hypothesis that the changes in hominids observable while *Homo erectus* occupies the centre of our stage were especially important in defining the arcs within which humanity was to evolve. He had unprecedented capacity to manipulate his environment, feeble though his handhold on it may seem to us. Besides the hand-axes which make possible the observation of his cultural traditions, late forms of *Homo erectus* left behind the earliest surviving traces of constructed dwellings (huts, sometimes fifty feet long, built of branches, with stone-slab or skin floors), the earliest worked wood, the first wooden spear and the earliest container, a wooden bowl. Creation on such a scale hints strongly at a new level of mentality, at a conception of the object formed before

Tools

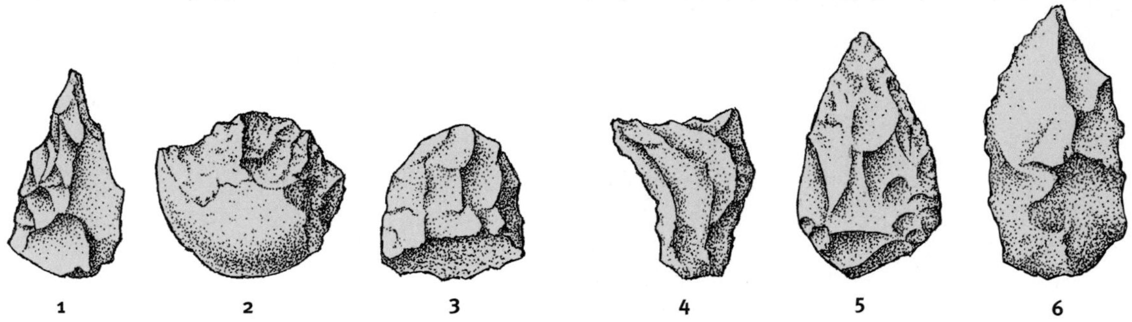

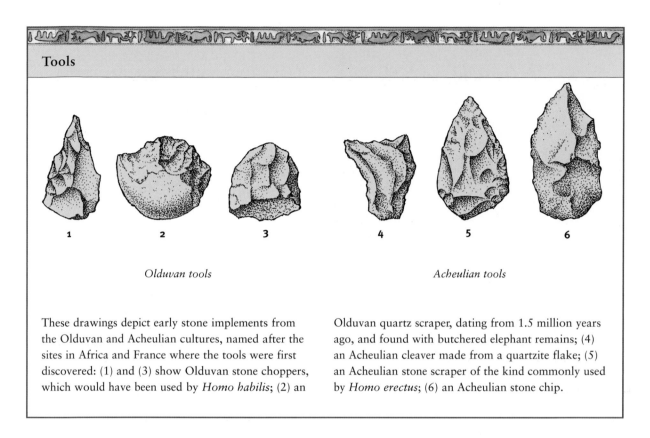

Olduvan tools *Acheulian tools*

These drawings depict early stone implements from the Olduvan and Acheulian cultures, named after the sites in Africa and France where the tools were first discovered: (1) and (3) show Olduvan stone choppers, which would have been used by *Homo habilis*; (2) an Olduvan quartz scraper, dating from 1.5 million years ago, and found with butchered elephant remains; (4) an Acheulian cleaver made from a quartzite flake; (5) an Acheulian stone scraper of the kind commonly used by *Homo erectus*; (6) an Acheulian stone chip.

manufacture is begun, and perhaps an idea of process. Some have argued far more. In the repetition of simple forms, triangles, ellipses and ovals, in huge numbers of examples of stone tools, there has been discerned intense care to produce regular shapes which does not appear to be proportionate to any small gain in efficiency which may have been achieved. Can there perhaps be discerned in this the first tiny budding of the aesthetic sense?

FIRE

THE GREATEST OF PREHISTORIC technical and cultural advances was made when some of these creatures learnt how to manage fire. Until recently, the earliest available evidence of the use of fire had been found in China, and probably dated from between three and five hundred thousand years ago. But very recent discoveries in the Transvaal have provided evidence, convincing to many scholars, that hominids there were using fire well before that. It remains fairly certain that *Homo erectus* never learnt how to *make* fire and that even his successors did not for a long time possess this skill. That he knew how to use it, on the other hand, is indisputable. The importance of this knowledge is attested by the folklore of many later peoples; in almost all of them a heroic figure or magical beast first seizes fire. A violation of the supernatural order is implied: in the Greek legend Prometheus steals the fire of the gods. This is suggestive, not solid, but perhaps the first fire was taken from outbreaks of natural gas or volcanic activity.

Culturally, economically, socially and technologically, fire was a revolutionary instrument – if we remember that a prehistoric "revolution" took thousands of years. It brought the possibility of warmth and light and therefore of a double extension of the habitable environment, into the cold and into the dark. In physical terms one obvious expression of this was the occupation of

The discovery of the use of fire by *Homo erectus* had a huge impact on all subsequent human communities and played a fundamental role in the communal activities of the Neanderthals, a later group depicted in this artist's impression.

caves. Animals could now be driven out and kept out by fire (and perhaps the seed lies here of the use of fire to drive big game in hunting). Technology could move forward: spears could be hardened in fires and cooking became possible, indigestible substances such as seeds becoming sources of food and distasteful or bitter plants edible. This must have stimulated attention to the variety and availability of plant life; the science of botany was stirring without anyone knowing it.

SOCIAL CONSEQUENCES OF FIRE

Fire must have influenced mentality more directly, too. It was another factor strengthening the tendency to conscious inhibition and restraint, and therefore their evolutionary importance. The focus of the cooking fire as the source of light and warmth had also the deep psychological power which it still retains. Around the hearths after dark gathered a community almost certainly already aware of itself as a small and meaningful unit against a chaotic and unfriendly background. Language – of whose origins we as yet know nothing – would have been sharpened by a new kind of group intercourse. The group itself would be elaborated, too, in its structure. At some point, fire-bearers and fire specialists appeared, beings of awesome and mysterious importance, for on them depended life and death. They carried and guarded the great liberating tool, and the need to guard it must sometimes have made them masters. Yet the deepest tendency of this new power always ran towards the liberation of early humans. Fire began to break up the iron rigidity of night and day and even the discipline of the seasons. It thus carried further the breakdown of the great objective natural rhythms which bound our fireless ancestors. Behaviour could now be less routine and automatic. There is even a discernible possibility of leisure, as a direct result of the use of fire.

BIG-GAME HUNTING

BIG-GAME HUNTING was the other great achievement of *Homo erectus*. Its origins must lie far back in the scavenging which turned vegetarian hominids into omnivores. Meat-eating provided concentrated protein. It released meat-eaters from the incessant nibbling of so many vegetarian creatures, and so permitted economies of effort. It is one of the first signs that the capacity for conscious restraint is at work when food is being carried home to be shared tomorrow rather than consumed on the spot today. At the beginning of the archaeological record, an elephant and perhaps a few giraffes and buffaloes were among the beasts whose scavenged meat was

At the Torralba and Ambrona sites in Spain, numerous elephant remains have been found in areas once inhabited by *Homo erectus*. The hominids may have hunted big game, although it is also possible that they were scavengers, taking meat from dead animals.

consumed at Olduvai, but for a long time the bones of smaller animals vastly preponderate in the rubbish. By about three hundred thousand years ago the picture is wholly altered.

This may be where we can find a clue to the way by which *Australopithecus* and his relatives were replaced by the bigger, more efficient *Homo erectus*. A new food supply permits larger consumption but also imposes new environments: game has to be followed if meat-eating becomes general. As the hominids become more or less parasitic upon other species there follows further exploration of territory and new settlements,

San people in the Kalahari desert, Botswana, Africa. Their living conditions are similar to those of their ancestors, who inhabited Africa 10,000 years ago.

Only meticulous excavation work, involving successive campaigns over several years, can reveal most of the information that an archaeological site contains. The excavations shown here are at Atapuerca, Spain, an exceptionally important site at which the remains of numerous hominids have been uncovered.

too, as sites particularly favoured by the mammoth or woolly rhinoceros are identified. Knowledge of such facts has to be learnt and passed on; technique has to be transmitted and guarded, for the skills required to trap, kill and dismember the huge beasts of antiquity were enormous in relation to anything which preceded them. What is more, they were cooperative skills: only large numbers could carry out so complex an operation as the driving – perhaps by fire – of game to a killing-ground favourable because of bogs in which a weighty creature would flounder, or because of a precipice, well-placed vantage points, or secure platforms for the hunters. Few weapons were available to supplement natural traps and, once dead, the victims presented further problems. With only wood, stone and flint, they had to be cut up and removed to the home base. Once carried home, the new supplies of meat mark another step towards the provision of leisure as the consumer is released for a time from the drudgery of ceaselessly rummaging in his environment for small, but continuously available, quantities of nourishment.

CULTURE AND TRADITION

It is difficult not to feel that this is an epoch of crucial significance. Considered against a background of millions of years of evolution, the pace of change, though still unbelievably slow in terms of later societies, is quickening. These are not humans as we know them, but they are beginning to be approximate to them: the greatest race of predators is stirring in its cradle. Something like a true society, too, is dimly discernible, not merely in the complicated cooperative hunting enterprises, but in what this implies in passing on knowledge from generation to generation. Culture and tradition are slowly taking over from genetic mutation and natural selection as the primary sources of change among the hominids. It is the groups with the best "memories" of effective techniques which will carry forward evolution. The importance of experience was very great, for knowledge of methods which were likely to succeed rested upon it, not (as increasingly in modern society) on experiment and analysis. This fact alone would have given new importance to the older and more experienced. They knew how things were done and what methods worked and they did so at a time when the home base and big-game hunting made their maintenance by the group easier. They would not have been very old, of course. Very few can have lived more than forty years.

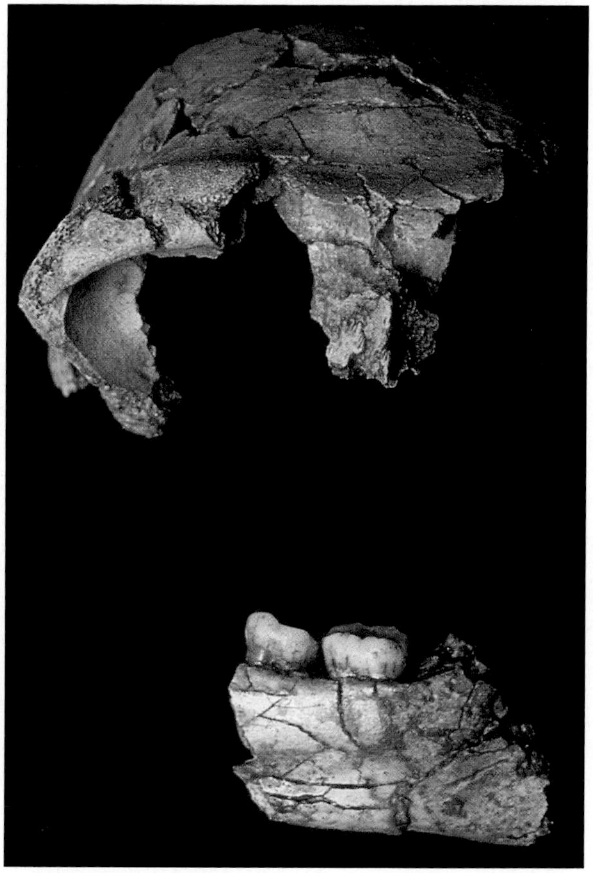

These are fragments of the cranium of a 780,000-year-old hominid – the oldest ever found in Europe. The cranium was discovered in Atapuerca, Spain, by a team of Spanish palaeontologists.

EARLY LANGUAGE

Selection also favoured those groups whose members not only had good memories but the increasing power to reflect upon it given by speech. We know very little about the prehistory of language. Modern types of language can only have appeared long after *Homo erectus* disappeared. Yet some sort of communication must have been used in big-game hunting, and all primates make meaningful signals. How early hominids communicated may never be known, but one plausible suggestion is that they began by breaking up calls akin to those of other animals into particular sounds capable of rearrangement. This would give the possibility of different messages and may be the remote taproot of grammar. What is certain is that a great acceleration of evolution would follow the appearance of groups able to pool experience, to practise and refine skills, to elaborate ideas through language. Once more, we cannot separate one process from others: better vision, an increased physical capacity to deal with the world as a set of discrete objects and the multiplication of artifacts by using tools were all going on simultaneously over the hundreds of thousands of years in which language was evolving. Together they contributed to a growing extension of mental capacity until one day conceptualization became possible and abstract thought appeared.

WAS *HOMO ERECTUS* HUMAN?

It remains true, though, that if nothing very general can be confidently said about the behaviour of hominids before humans, still less can anything very precise be confirmed. We move in a fog, dimly apprehending for a moment creatures now more, now less, like human beings. Their minds, we can be sure, are almost inconceivably unlike our own as instruments for the registration of the outside world. Yet when we look at the range of the attributes of *Homo erectus* it is his human, not pre-human, characteristics which are

Dating methods

Various techniques are used to ascertain the age of archaeological remains. Stratigraphy, for example, involves the analysis of the order in which the strata in the ground and rock within a specific region are found. There are also several physical and biological techniques available to researchers, but the most commonly used dating methods involve chemical techniques, which are based on the radioactive properties of elements such as carbon 14, potassium and uranium. Of these chemical methods, the most widely employed, and often the most reliable, is the carbon dating method. The element carbon 14 converts to nitrogen 14 at a constant rate and is not affected by fluctuations in temperature. It takes 5,730 years for the number of atoms in a sample to be reduced by half, which means that carbon dating provides a relatively accurate means of measuring time.

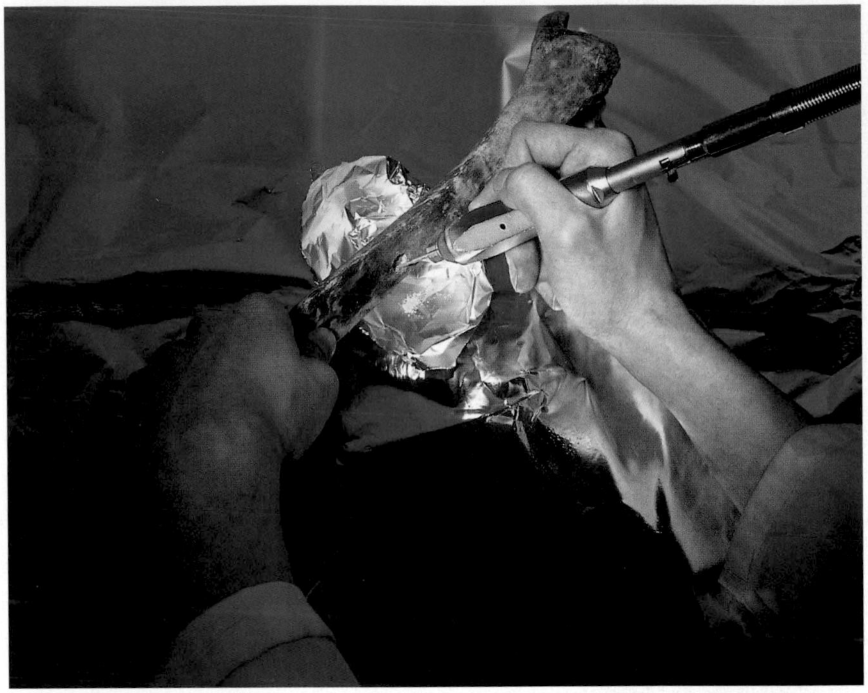

A researcher extracts a sample from an archaeological find – the sample will be tested by the carbon dating method to determine the object's age.

most striking. Physically, he has a brain of an order of magnitude comparable to our own. He makes tools (and does so within more than one technical tradition), builds shelters, takes over natural refuges by exploiting fire, and sallies out of them to hunt and gather his food. He does this in groups with a discipline which can sustain complicated operations; he therefore has some ability to exchange ideas by speech. The basic biological units of his hunting groups probably prefigure the human nuclear family, being founded on the institutions of the home base and a sexual differentiation of activity. There may even be some complexity of social organization in so far as fire-bearers and gatherers or old creatures whose memories made them the data banks of their "societies" could be supported by the labour of others. There has to be some social organization to permit the sharing of cooperatively obtained food, too. There is nothing to be usefully added to an account such as this by pretending to say where exactly can be found a prehistorical point or dividing line at which such things had come to be, but subsequent human history is unimaginable without them. When a sub-species of *Homo erectus*, perhaps possessing slightly larger and more complex brains than others, evolved into *Homo sapiens* it did so with an enormous achievement and heritage already secure in its grasp. Whether we choose to call it human or not hardly matters.

A team of archaeologists at work at the La Brea site in Los Angeles, USA. Excavations carried out at the site uncovered the world's richest fossil deposits.

2 HOMO SAPIENS

THE APPEARANCE of *Homo sapiens* is momentous: here, at last, is recognizable humanity, however raw in form. Yet this evolutionary step is another abstraction. It is the beginning of the main drama and the end of the prologue, but we cannot usefully ask precisely when this happens. It is a process, not a point in time, and it is not a process occurring everywhere at the same rate. All we have to date it are a few physical relics of early humans of types recognizably modern or closely related to the modern. Some of them may well overlap by thousands of years the continuing life of earlier hominids. Some may represent false starts and dead ends, for human evolution must have continued to be highly selective. Though much faster than in earlier times, this evolution is still very slow: we are dealing with something that took place over perhaps two hundred thousand years in which we do not know when our first true "ancestor" appeared (though the place was almost certainly Africa). It is not ever easy to pose the right questions; the physiological and technical and mental lines at which we leave *Homo erectus* behind are matters of definition.

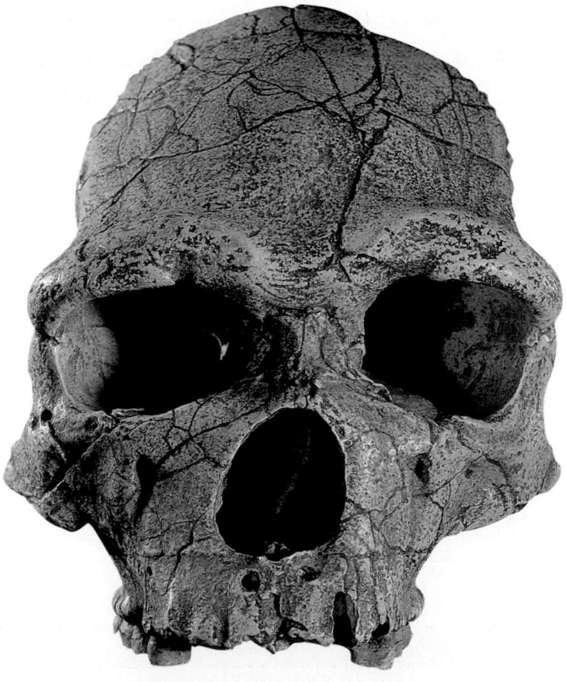

This cranium, found in the French Pyrenees, is more than 200,000 years old and shows the intermediate features of a stage between *Homo erectus* and *Homo sapiens neanderthalis*. The existence of intermediate fossils adds strength to the generally accepted theory that *Homo sapiens* evolved from colonies of *Homo erectus*.

EARLY HUMAN REMAINS

The few early human fossils have provoked much argument. Two famous European skulls seem to belong to the period between two Ice Ages about two hundred thousand years ago, an age climatically so different from ours that elephants browsed in a semitropical Thames valley and the ancestors of lions prowled in what would one day be Yorkshire. The "Swanscombe" skull, named after the place where it was found, shows its possessor to have had a big brain (about 1300 cc) but in other ways not much to resemble modern humans: if "Swanscombe man" was *Homo sapiens*, then he represents a very early version. The other skull, that of "Steinheim man", differs in shape from that of *Homo sapiens* but again held a big brain. Perhaps they are best regarded as the forerunners of early prototypes of *Homo sapiens*, though creatures still living (as their tools show) much like *Homo erectus*.

The next Ice Age then brings down the curtain. When it lifts, a hundred and thirty thousand or so years ago, in the next warm period, human remains again appear. There has been much argument about what they show but it is indisputable that there has been a great step forward. At this point we are entering a period where there is a fairly dense

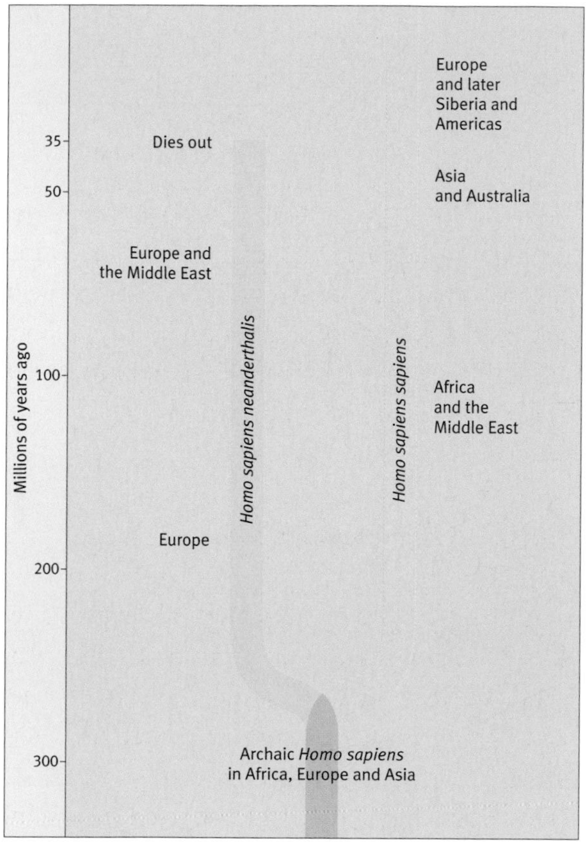

Origins of Homo sapiens neanderthalis *and* Homo sapiens sapiens.

though broken record. Creatures we must now call humans lived in Europe just over a hundred thousand years ago. There are caves in the Dordogne area which were occupied on and off for some fifty thousand years. The cultures of these peoples therefore survived a period of huge climatic change; the first traces of them belong to a warm interglacial period and the last run out in the middle of the last Ice Age. This is an impressive continuity to set against what must have been great variation in the animal population and vegetation near these sites; to survive so long, such cultures must have been resourceful and adaptive.

THE NEANDERTHALS

FOR ALL THEIR ESSENTIAL SIMILARITY to ourselves, the peoples who created the early cultures in Europe are still physiologically distinguishable from modern humans. The first discovery of their remains was at Neanderthal in Germany (because of this, humans of this type are usually called Neanderthals) and it was of a skull so curiously shaped that it was for a long time thought to be that of a modern idiot. Scientific analysis still leaves much about it unexplained. But it is now suggested that *Homo sapiens neanderthalis* (as the Neanderthal is scientifically classified) has its ultimate origin in an early expansion out of Africa of advanced forms of *Homo erectus*, possibly a million years ago. Across many intervening genetic stages, there emerged a population of pre-Neanderthals, from which, in turn, the extreme form evolved whose striking remains were found in Europe (and, so far, nowhere else). This special development has been interpreted by some as a Neanderthal sub-species, perhaps cut off by some accident of glaciation. Evidence of other Neanderthalers has turned up in Morocco, in the northern Sahara, at Mount Carmel in Palestine and elsewhere in the Near East and

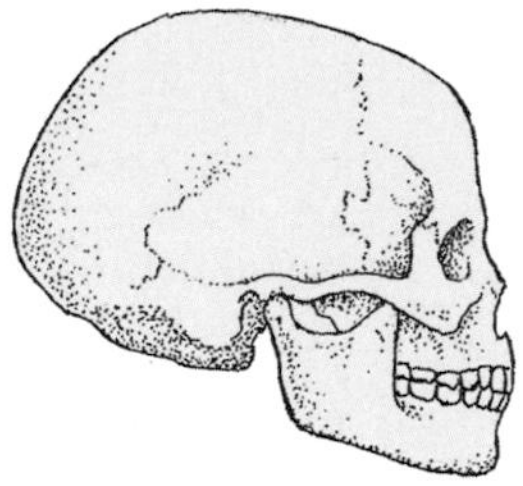

Homo sapiens

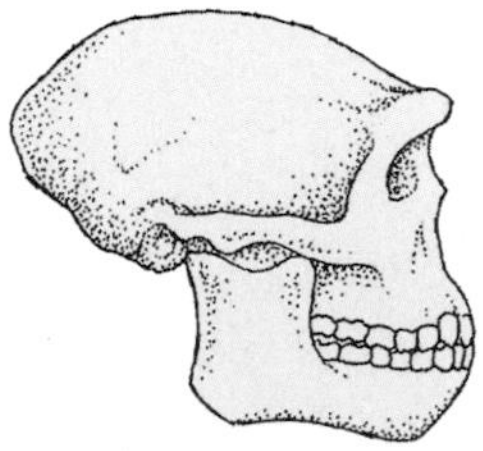

Homo erectus

These illustrations, which depict the craniums of a *Homo erectus* from Java and of a late Palaeolithic *Homo sapiens* from Europe, demonstrate the differences between the two species. *Homo sapiens* has a larger cranium, a higher forehead (without the marked supraorbital arch), a shorter jaw, smaller teeth and a pronounced chin.

Time chart (4,000,000 BCE–100,000 BCE)

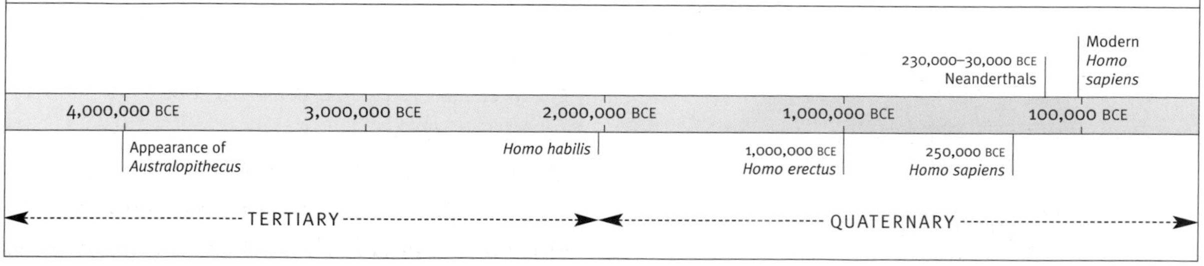

Discoveries of Neanderthal remains

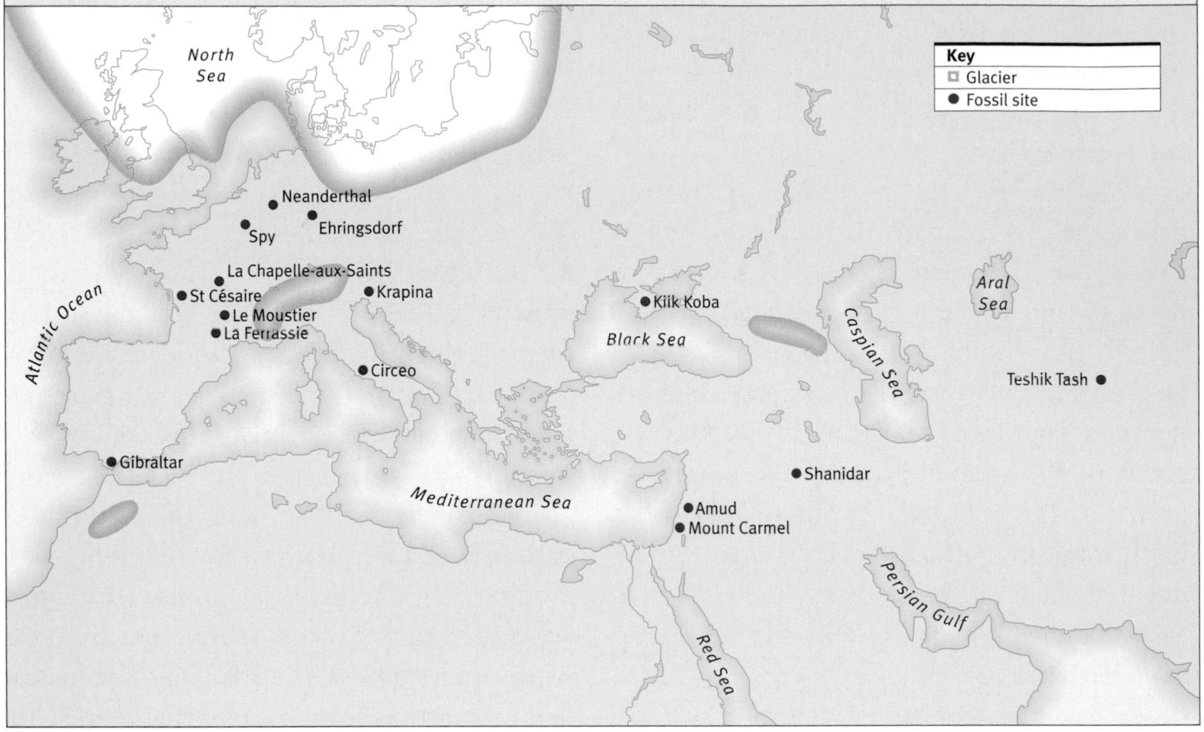

The flint implements made by the Neanderthals have been called Mousterian tools, after the French site at Le Moustier where they were discovered. Large numbers of these tools have been found.

Iran. They have also been traced in Central Asia and China, where the earliest specimens may go back something like two hundred millennia. Evidently, this was for a long time a highly successful species.

Eighty thousand years ago, the artifacts of the Neanderthals had spread all over Eurasia, and they show differences of technique and form. But technology from over a hundred thousand years ago and associated with other forms of "anatomically modern humans", as scholars term other creatures evolved from advanced forms of *Homo erectus*, has been identified in parts of Africa. Moreover, it was more widely spread than that of the Neanderthals. The primeval cultural unity had thus already fragmented, and distinct cultural traditions were beginning to emerge. From the start, there is a kind of provincialism within a young humanity.

The Neanderthals, like the different species which specialists refer to as anatomically modern, walked erect and had big brains. Though in other ways more primitive than the sub-species to which we belong, *Homo sapiens sapiens* (as the guess about the first skull suggests), they represent none the less a great evolutionary stride and show a new mental sophistication we can still hardly grasp, let alone measure. One striking example is their use of technology to overcome environment: we know from the evidence of skin-scrapers they used to dress skins and pelts that Neanderthals wore clothes (though none have survived; the oldest clothed body yet discovered, in Russia, has been dated to about thirty-five thousand years ago). This was an important advance in the manipulation of environment.

RITUALIZED BURIAL

One of the most startling phenomena of the Neanderthal period was the appearance of formal burial. The act of burial itself is momentous for archaeology; graves are of enormous importance because of the artifacts of ancient society they preserve. Yet the Neanderthal graves provide more than this: they may also contain the first evidence of ritual or ceremony.

It is very difficult to control speculation, and some has outrun the evidence. Perhaps some early totemism explains the ring of horns within which a Neanderthal child was buried near Samarkand. Some have suggested, too, that careful burial may reflect a new concern for the individual which was one result of the greater interdependence of the group in the renewed Ice Ages. This could have intensified the sense of loss when a member died and might also point to something more. A skeleton of a Neanderthal man who had lost his right arm years before his death has been found. He must have been very dependent on others, and was sustained by his group in spite of his handicap.

It is tempting but more hazardous to suggest that ritualized burial implies some view of an after-life. If true, though, this would testify to a huge power of abstraction in the hominids and the origins of one of the greatest and most enduring myths, that life is an illusion, that reality lies invisible elsewhere, that things are not what they seem. Without going so far, it is at least possible to agree that a momentous change is under way. Like the hints of rituals involving animals which Neanderthal caves also offer here and there, careful burial may mark a new attempt to dominate the environment. The human brain must already have been capable of

The skeleton of a Neanderthal man, who was found in the Shanidar Cave surrounded by traces of pollen. It is thought that flowers may have been buried with the man's body. However, it is also possible that the ceiling fell onto the body, showering it in earth containing pollen.

Comparison of cranium sizes

One of the first remains of the Neanderthal type to be found was a female cranium, which was discovered in a quarry in Gibraltar in 1848. In 1856, a find in the Neander river valley in Germany gave the Neanderthal variety of *Homo sapiens* its name. Palaeontologists did not immediately realize the significance of their discovery. The findings in La Chapelle-aux-Saints (1908) and La Ferrassie (1909), however, confirmed that the remains found in Neanderthal were not those of a deformed individual, as had been suggested in some quarters, but of a primitive human type. Today the remains of almost 500 Neanderthal specimens have been found. We now know that this race populated Europe and western Asia from 230,000 to 30,000 years ago. Neanderthal humans were short and stocky – a body shape well adapted to life in a cold climate.

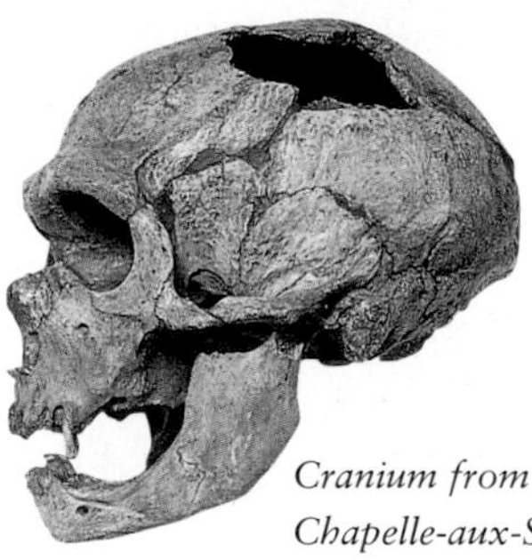

Cranium from La Chapelle-aux-Saints

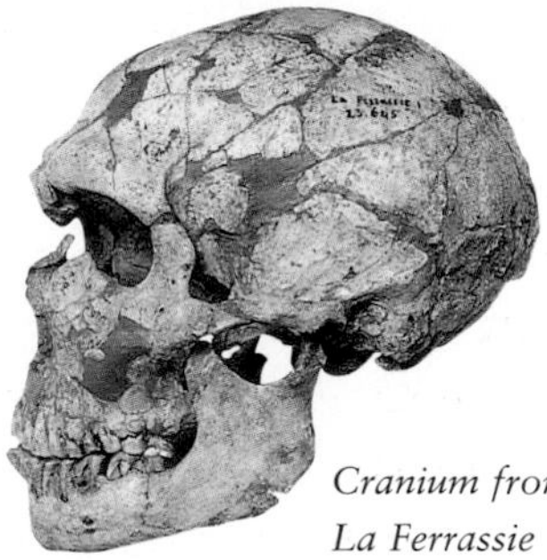

Cranium from La Ferrassie

discerning questions it wanted to answer and perhaps of providing answers in the shape of rituals. Slightly, tentatively, clumsily – however we describe it and still in the shallows though it may be – the human mind is afloat; the greatest voyage of exploration has begun.

THE NEANDERTHALS DISAPPEAR

Neanderthals provide our first evidence of another great institution, warfare. It may have been practised in connection with cannibalism, which was directed apparently to the eating of the brains of victims. Analogy with later societies suggests that here again we have the start of some conceptualizing about a soul or spirit; such acts are sometimes directed to acquiring the magical or spiritual power of the vanquished.

Whatever the magnitude of the evolutionary step which the Neanderthals represent, however, they failed in the end as a species. After long and widespread success they were not in the end to be the inheritors of the earth. Effectively, Neanderthal survivors were to be genetically "vanquished" by another strain of *Homo sapiens*, and about the reasons for this we know nothing. Nor can we know to what extent, if at all, it was mitigated by some genetic transmission through the mingling of stocks.

In the 1930s the remains of a number of *Homo sapiens* were discovered in the Skhul Cave, Mount Carmel, Israel. This photograph shows the reconstructed cranium and various bones of an adult male called Skhul 4. According to the latest research, the inhabitants of Skhul Cave lived 100,000 years ago, which means that their remains are three times older than those of the Cro-Magnon man and contemporaries of classic Neanderthals. However, these remains are anatomically modern.

HOMO SAPIENS SAPIENS

THE SUCCESSOR BOTH TO the Neanderthals and to the archaic human forms among whom they first appeared was *Homo sapiens sapiens*, the species to which we all belong. Biologically it has been outstandingly successful, spreading all over Eurasia within a hundred thousand or so years of its first appearances in Africa (they are dated to about 137,000 years ago) and eventually all over the world. Its members are from the start anatomically identifiable modern humans, with smaller faces, a lighter skull and straighter limbs than the Neanderthals. From Africa they entered the Levant and the Middle East, duly progressing to central and further Asia, and eventually reaching Australasia in about 40,000 BCE. By then, they were beginning to colonize Europe, where they were to live for thousands of years beside the Neanderthals. In about 15,000 BCE they crossed a land bridge across what was to be the Bering Strait to enter the Americas.

THE PALAEOLITHIC

Much remains speculative in assessing the reasons for the timing and pattern of the diffusion of *Homo sapiens sapiens* and palaeoanthropologists remain cautious about the fossil record. Some of them do not like to assert without qualification that remains

Modern *Homo sapiens*

In 1868 CE the remains of an anatomically modern man (now thought to be 30,000 years old) were found in Cro-Magnon, France. More recent discoveries suggest that modern *Homo sapiens* emerged, probably in Africa, more than 100,000 years ago. The map shows some of the places where the earliest specimens of modern *Homo sapiens* were found, and the possible routes they took to spread to Europe. If this hypothesis is correct, the Neanderthals are not direct ancestors of modern humans, who descended from one ancient African community.

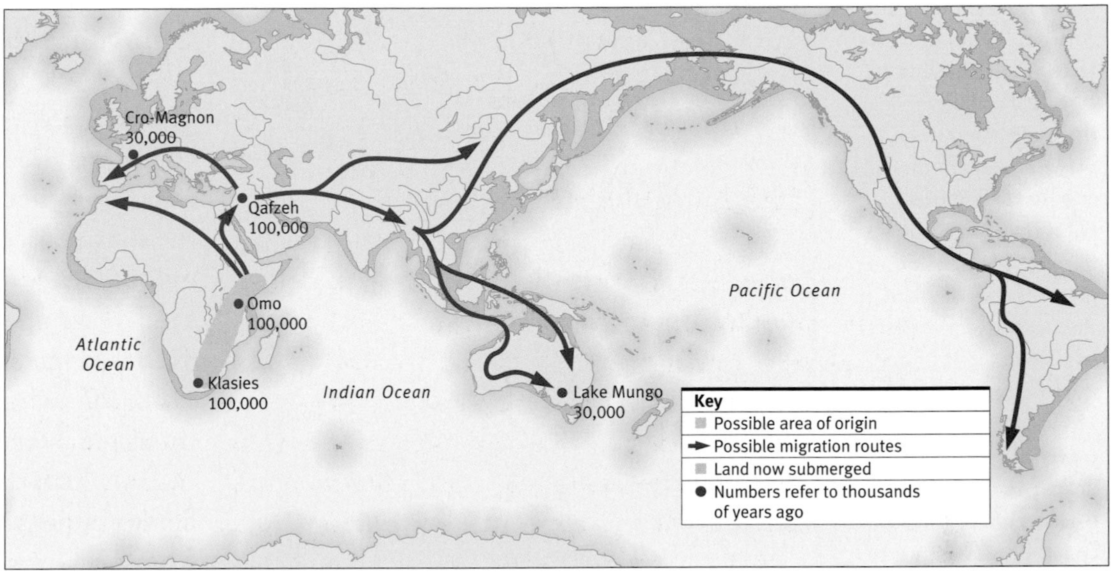

Sites where the remains of early modern Homo sapiens *have been found.*

more than thirty thousand years or so old are indeed those of our species. Nevertheless, it is clear that from about fifty thousand years ago to the end of the last Ice Age in about 9000 BCE we are at last considering plentiful evidence of humans of modern type. This period is normally referred to as the "Upper" Palaeolithic, a name derived from the Greek for "old stones". It corresponds, roughly, to the more familiar term "Stone Age", but, like other contributions to the terminology of prehistory, there are difficulties in using such words without careful qualification.

To separate "Upper" and "Lower" Palaeolithic is easy; the division represents the physical fact that the topmost layers of geological strata are the most recent and that, therefore, fossils and artifacts found among them are later than those found at lower levels. The Lower Palaeolithic is therefore the designation of an age more ancient than the Upper. Almost all the artifacts which survive from the Palaeolithic are made from stone; none is made from metal, whose appearance made it possible to follow a terminology used by the Roman poet Lucretius by labelling what comes after the Stone Age as the Bronze and Iron Ages.

These are, of course, cultural and technological labels; their great merit is that they direct attention to human activities. At one time tools and weapons are made of stone, then of bronze, then of iron. None the less, these terms have disadvantages, too. The obvious one is that within the huge tracts of time in which stone artifacts provide the largest significant body of evidence, we are dealing for the most part with hominids. They had, in varying degree, some, but not all, human characteristics; many stone tools were not made by human beings. Increasingly, too, the fact that this terminology originated in European archaeology created difficulties as more and more evidence accumulated about the rest of the world which did not really fit in. A final disadvantage is that it blurs important

The colonization of America

Many of the facts about the colonization of America by humans remain unclear, but the evidence points towards the main migrations originating from north-east Asia. The first colonization is thought to have occurred during glacial periods, when the decrease in sea-level exposed a land bridge now named Beringia. Human communities travelled from Alaska deeper into the continent, either along the coast, or along a narrow ice-free passage between two glaciers. Some finds in South America seem to indicate that the arrival of *Homo sapiens* in America happened perhaps 40,000 years ago – much earlier than was previously believed.

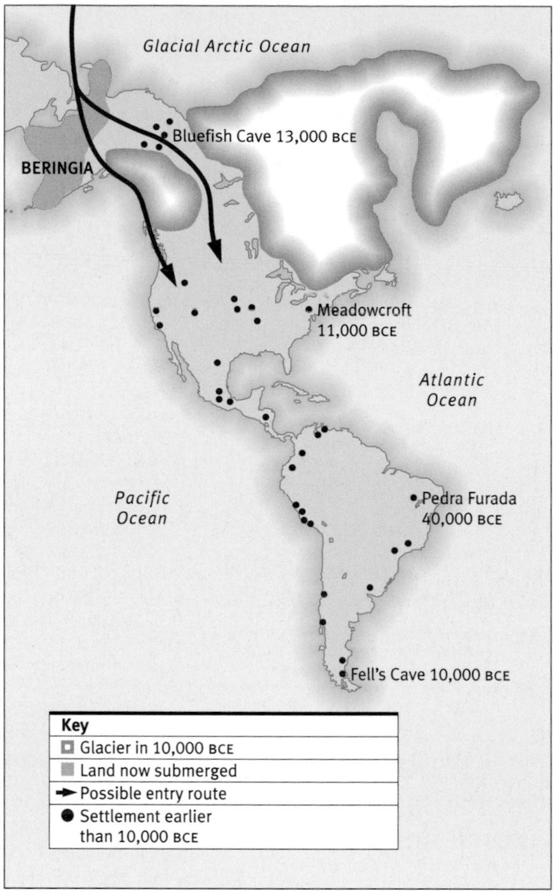

distinctions within periods even in Europe. The result has been its further refinement. Within the Stone Age scholars have distinguished (in sequence) the Lower, Middle and Upper Palaeolithic and then the Mesolithic and the Neolithic (the last of which blurs the division attributed by the older schemes to the coming of metallurgy). The period down to the end of the last Ice Age in Europe is also sometimes called the Old Stone Age, another complication, because here we have yet another principle of classification, simply that provided by chronology. *Homo sapiens sapiens* appears in Europe roughly at the beginning of the Upper Palaeolithic. It is in Europe, though, that the largest quantity of skeletal remains has been found, and it is on this evidence that the distinction of the species has long been based.

CLIMATIC FLUCTUATIONS

The climate of human prehistory was not constant; though usually cold, there were important fluctuations, probably including the sharp onset of the coldest conditions for a million years somewhere about twenty thousand years ago. Such climatic variations still exercised great determinative force on the evolution of society. It was perhaps thirty thousand years ago that the climate changes began which later made it possible for human beings either to enter the Americas, crossing from Asia by a link provided by ice or by land left exposed because the ice-caps contained so much of what is now sea-water and the sea-level was much lower. They moved southwards for thousands of years as they followed the game which had drawn them to the last uninhabited continent. The Americas were from the start peopled by immigrants. But when the ice sheets retreated, huge transformations occurred to coasts, routes and food supplies. This was all as it had been for ages, but this time there was a crucial difference. Humans were present. A new order of intelligence was available to use new and growing resources in order to cope with environmental change. The change to history, when conscious human action to control environment will increasingly be effective, is underway.

NEW IMPLEMENTS

For this period in Europe much has been done to classify cultures identified by their implements. To talk of a change to history may seem a big claim in the light of early humans' resources, judging by their tool kits and weaponry. Yet they already represent a huge range of capacities if we compare them with their predecessors'. The basic tools of *Homo sapiens* were stone, but they were made to serve many more precise purposes than earlier tools and were made in a different way, by striking flakes from a carefully prepared core. Their variety and elaboration are another sign of the growing acceleration of human evolution. New materials came into use in the Upper Palaeolithic, too, as bone and antler were added to the wood and flint of earlier workshops and armouries. These provided new possibilities of manufacture; the bone needle was a great step in the elaboration of clothing, pressure flaking enabled some skilled workmen to carry the refinement of their flint blades to a point at which it seems non-utilitarian, so delicately thinned have they become. The first man-made material, a mixture of clay with powdered bone, also makes its appearance. Weapons especially are improved. The tendency, which can be seen towards the end of the Upper Palaeolithic, for small flint implements to appear more frequently and for them to be more regularly geometrical suggests the making of more complex weapon points. In the same era come the invention and spread of the spear-thrower, the bow and arrow, and the barbed harpoon, used first on mammals and later to catch fish. The last shows an extension of hunting – and therefore of resources – to water. Long before this, perhaps six hundred thousand years ago, hominids had gathered molluscs for food in China and doubtless elsewhere. With harpoons and perhaps more perishable implements such as nets and lines, new and richer aquatic sources of food (some created by the temperature changes of the last Ice Ages) could now be exploited, and this led to achievements in hunting, possibly connected with the growth of forests in post-glacial phases and with a new dependence on and knowledge of the movements of reindeer and wild cattle.

The colonization of Australia

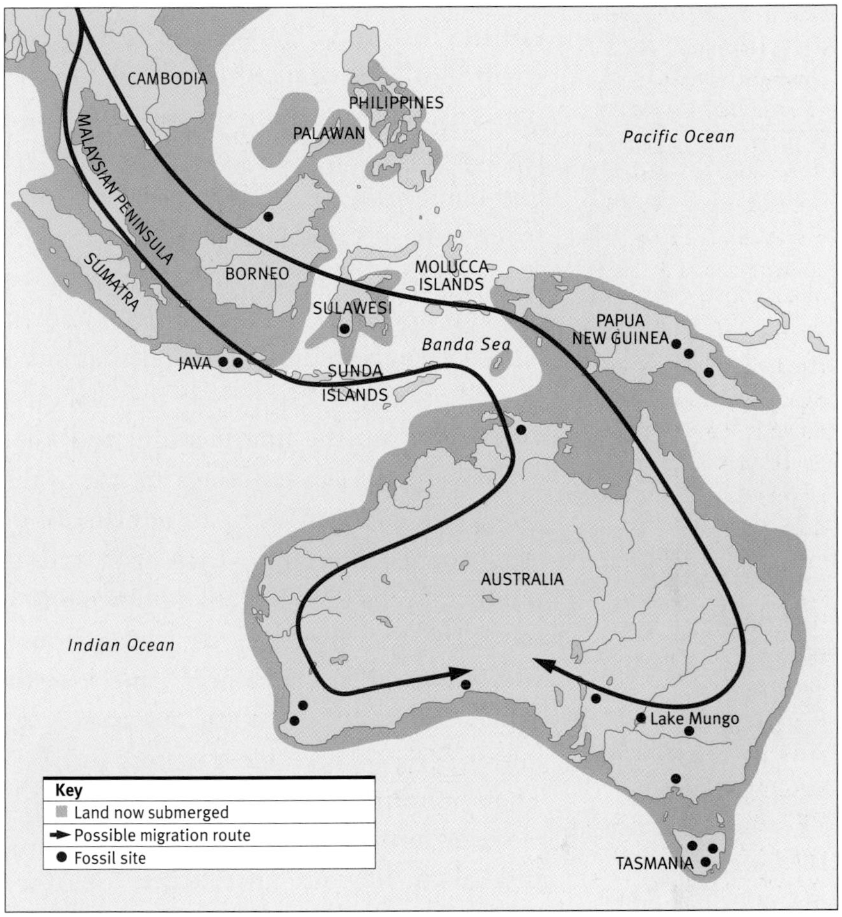

The arrival of *Homo sapiens* in Australia occurred around 55,000 years ago, probably after a journey across the Banda Sea. The remains of those who inhabited Australia 30,000 years ago belong to two kinds of *Homo sapiens*. This fact has led some experts to believe that there were two separate migrations to the continent. However, it is also possible that the difference between the two *Homo sapiens* groups was produced within Australia.

EARLY ART

THE MOST REMARKABLE and mysterious evidence of all which has survived the peoples of the Upper Palaeolithic is their art.

These tools are characteristic of the late Palaeolithic. The flint point (left), which is finely carved, is typical of the Solutrean culture. The bone harpoon is from the Magdalenian culture.

It is the first of its kind of whose existence we can be sure. Earlier humans or even humanoid creatures may have scratched patterns in the mud, daubed their bodies, moved rhythmically in dance or spread flowers in patterns, but of such things we know nothing, because of them, if they ever happened, nothing has survived. Some creature took the trouble to accumulate little hoards of red ochre some forty or sixty thousand years ago, but the purpose of doing so is unknown. It has been suggested that two indentations on a Neanderthal gravestone are the earliest surviving art, but the first plentiful and assured evidence comes in paintings on the walls of European caves. The first were made more than thirty thousand years ago, and their number swells dramatically until we find ourselves in the presence of a conscious art whose greatest technical and aesthetic achievements appear, without warning or forerunner, almost mature. They continue so for thousands of years until this art vanishes. Just as it has no ancestor, it leaves no descendant, though it seems to have employed many of the basic processes of the visual arts still in use today.

Its concentration in space and time must be grounds for suspicion that there is more to be discovered. Caves in Africa abound with prehistoric paintings and carvings dated as far back as twenty-seven thousand years ago and continuing to be added to well into the reign of England's Queen Victoria; in Australia there was cave-painting at least twenty thousand years ago. Palaeolithic art is not, therefore, confined to Europe, but what has been discovered outside Europe has, so far, been studied much more intermittently. We do not yet know enough about the dating of cave paintings in other parts of the world, nor about the uniqueness of the conditions which led to the preservation in Europe of objects which may have had parallels elsewhere. Nor do we know what may have disappeared; there is a vast field of possibilities of what may have been produced in gesture, sound or perishable materials which cannot be explored. None the less, the art of western Europe in the Upper Palaeolithic, all qualifications made, has a colossal and solid impressiveness which is unique.

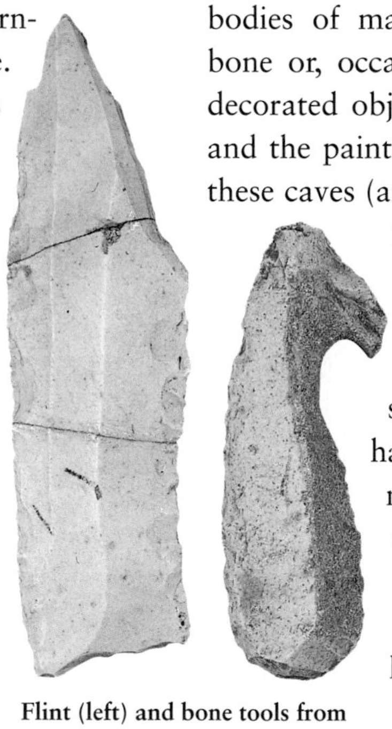

Flint (left) and bone tools from the Aurignacian tradition of the late Palaeolithic.

INTERPRETATION

Most early art has been found in a relatively small area of southwestern France and northern Spain and consists of three main bodies of material: small figures of stone, bone or, occasionally, clay (usually female), decorated objects (often tools and weapons) and the painted walls and roofs of caves. In these caves (and in the decoration of objects) there is an overwhelming preponderance of animal themes. The meaning of these designs, above all in the elaborate sequences of the cave paintings, has intrigued scholars. Obviously, many of the beasts so carefully observed were central to a hunting economy. At least in the French caves, too, it now seems highly probable that a conscious order exists in the sequences in which they are shown. But to go further in the argument is still very hard. Clearly, art in Upper Palaeolithic times has to carry much of a burden later carried by writing, but what its messages mean is still obscure. It seems likely that the paintings were connected with religious or magical

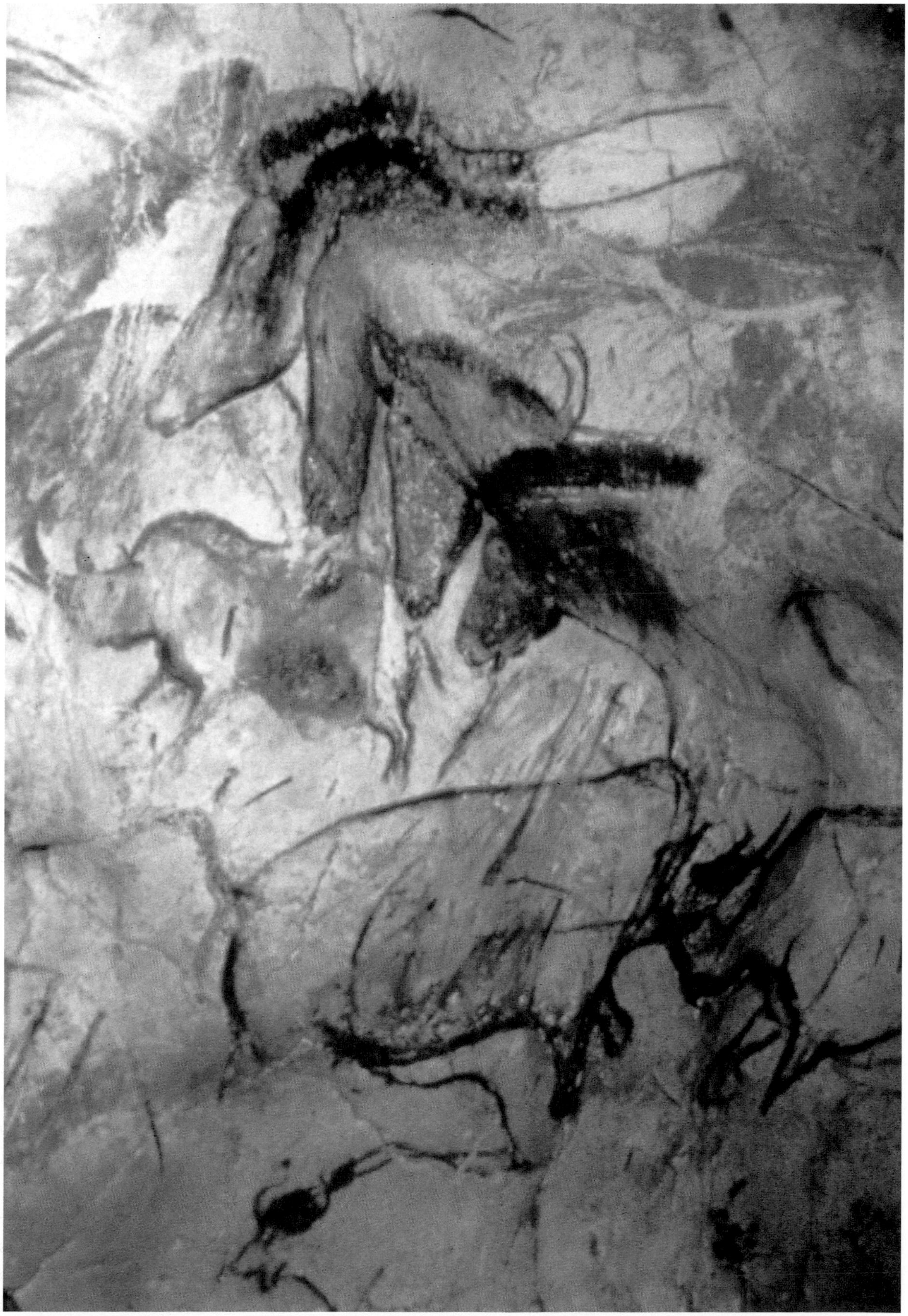

In December 1994 CE, explorers discovered the Chauvet Cave in the Ardèche valley. Inside the cave, more than 300 painted and engraved images of animals were found. Radio carbon tests show that the drawings are more than 30,000 years old. They are, therefore, the oldest paintings yet found and are remarkably well executed, as these beautiful horses' heads show.

This statuette from Lespugue, France, is 23,000 years old and possesses the characteristic features of Palaeolithic Venuses. It has been suggested that her buttocks reveal steatopygia – an accumulation of fat in the hips which acts as a calorie reserve during long periods without food.

practice: African rock painting has been convincingly shown to be linked to magic and shamanism and the selection of such remote and difficult corners of caves as those in which the European paintings have been traced is by itself strongly suggestive that some special rite was carried out when they were painted or gazed upon. (Artificial light, of course, was needed in these dark corners.) The origins of religion have been hinted at in Neanderthal burials and appear even more strongly in those of the Upper Palaeolithic peoples which are often elaborate; here, in their art, is something where inferences are even harder to resist. Perhaps it provides the first surviving relics of organized religion.

THE DEVELOPMENT OF EARLY ART

The birth, maturity and death of the earliest artistic achievement of humankind in Europe occupies a very long period. Somewhere about thirty-five thousand years ago appear decorated and coloured objects, often of bone and ivory. Then, three or four millennia later, we reach the first figurative art. Soon after that we reach the peak of the prehistoric aesthetic achievement, the great painted and incised cave "sanctuaries" (as they have been called), with their processions of animals and mysterious repeated symbolic shapes. This high phase lasted about five thousand years, a startlingly long time for the maintenance of so consistent a style and content. So long a period – almost as long as the whole history of civilization on this planet – illustrates the slowness with which tradition changed in ancient times and its imperviousness to outside influence. Perhaps it is an index, too, of the geographical isolation of prehistoric cultures.

The last phase of this art which has been discerned takes the story down to about 9000 BCE; in it, the stag more and more replaces other animals as subject matter (no doubt thus reflecting the disappearance of the reindeer and the mammoth as the ice retreated) before a final burst of richly decorated tools and weapons brings Europe's first great artistic achievement to an end. The age which followed produced nothing approaching it in scale or quality; its best surviving relics are a few decorated pebbles. Six thousand years were to pass before the next great art.

THE DISAPPEARANCE OF EARLY ART

We know little about the collapse of this great human achievement. The light is never more than dim in the Upper Palaeolithic and the darkness closes in rapidly – which is to say, of course, over thousands of years. Nevertheless, the impression left by the violence of the contrast between what was before and what came after produces a sense of shock. So relatively sudden an extinction is a mystery. We have no precise dates or even precise sequences: nothing ended in one year or

The Palaeolithic Venuses

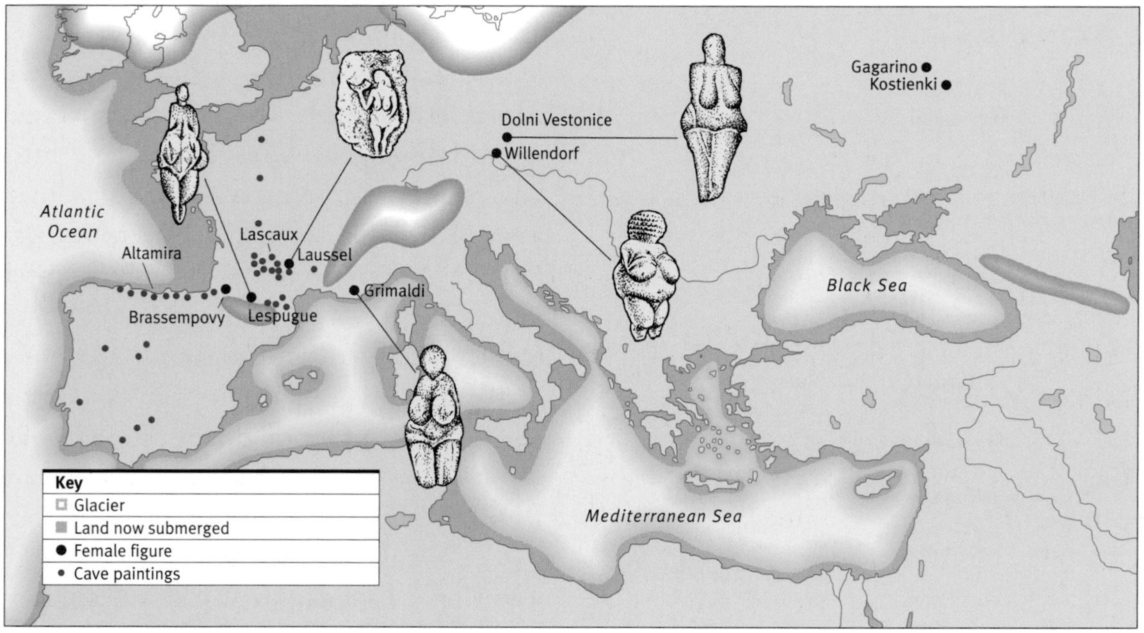

These small statues of women, which are commonly known as the Palaeolithic Venuses, have been discovered at sites all over Europe, from the Pyrenees to Russia, and are between 21,000 and 29,000 years old. They depict partially or completely naked women, with large breasts and buttocks, some of whom may be pregnant. The figures' heads and limbs are given only summary treatment, as though they were less interesting. The statues are thought to be associated with a fertility ritual. Their remarkably widespread geographical distribution demonstrates that they were cultural symbols shared by communities that lived for thousands of years in a territory which extended over a vast area.

another. There was only a gradual closing down of artistic activity over a long time which seems in the end to have been absolute. Some scholars have blamed climate. Perhaps, they argue, the whole phenomenon of cave art was linked to efforts to influence the movements or abundance of the great game herds on which the hunting peoples relied. As the last Ice Age ebbed and each year the reindeer retreated a little, new and magical techniques were sought to manipulate them, but gradually as the ice sheets withdrew more and more, an environment to which earlier humans had successfully adapted disappeared. So did the hope of influencing nature. *Homo sapiens* was not powerless; far from it, it could adapt, and did, to a new challenge. But for a time one cultural impoverishment at least, the abandonment of the first art, was a consequence of adaptation.

It is easy to see much that is fanciful in such speculation, but difficult to restrain excitement over such an astonishing achievement. People have spoken of the great cave sequences as "cathedrals" of the Palaeolithic world and such metaphors are justified if the level of achievement and the scale of the work undertaken is measured against what evidence we have of the earlier triumphs of man. With the first great art, the hominids are now left far behind and we have unequivocal evidence of the power of the human mind.

Our ancestors

DNA studies of diverse human communities suggest that present-day humankind descends from one line. That line began to subdivide about 100,000 years ago and continued to do so throughout the late Palaeolithic (Quaternary period). This diagram, based on studies carried out by Luigi Luca Cavalli-Sforza and his team, shows how the first division separates African communities from the rest of the world.

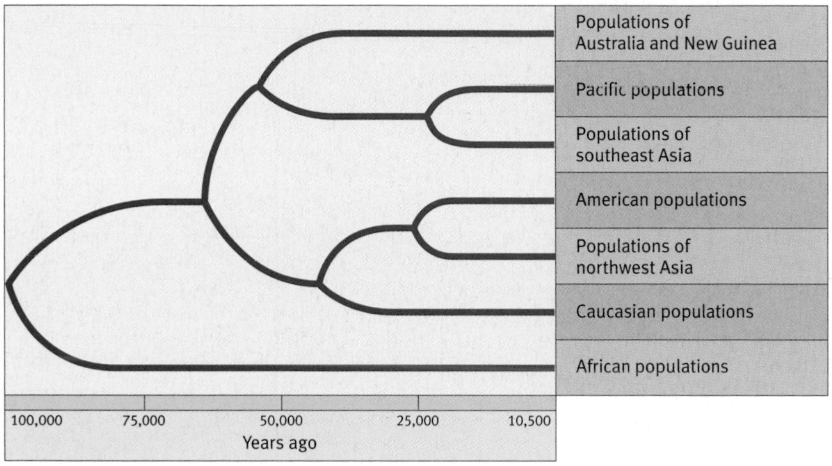

RACIAL DIFFERENTIATION

Much that is known of the Upper Palaeolithic confirms the sense that the crucial genetic changes are behind and that evolution is now a mental and social phenomenon. The distribution of major racial divisions in the world which last down to early modern times appears already broadly fixed by the end of the Upper Palaeolithic. Geographical and climatic divisions had produced specializations in skin pigment, hair characteristics, the shape of the skull and the bone structure of the face. In the earliest Chinese relics of *Homo sapiens* the Mongoloid characteristics are discernible. All the main racial groups are established by 10,000 BCE, broadly speaking in the areas they dominated until the great resettlement of the Caucasian stocks, which was one aspect of the rise of European civilization to world domination after 1500 CE. The world was filling up during the Old Stone Age. Human beings at last penetrated the virgin continents. Mongoloid peoples spread over the Americas and had arrived in Patagonia by 6000 BCE. Twenty thousand or so years earlier, humans had spread widely through Australia, reaching that continent by a combination of island-hopping sea voyages and land bridges which later disappeared. *Homo sapiens* was already a venturesome fellow at the end of the last Ice Age, it seems, with only Antarctica among the continents still awaiting his arrival (as it would wait until the year 1895 of our own era).

POPULATION SIZE

The Upper Palaeolithic world was still a very empty place. Calculations suggest that just twenty thousand humans lived in France in Neanderthal times; this becomes possibly fifty thousand out of perhaps ten million humans in the whole world twenty thousand years ago. "A human desert swarming with game" is one scholar's description of it. They lived by hunting and gathering, and a lot of land was needed to support a family.

However questionable such figures may be, if they are agreed to be of this order of magnitude it is not hard to see that they still mean very slow cultural change. Greatly accelerated though human beings' progress in the Old Stone Age may be and much more versatile though they are becoming, they are

Many figures in a similar style to the Palaeolithic cave paintings have been discovered carved in bone, horn and stone. This carved shoulder blade, for example, comes from the Castillo Cave in Cantabria, Spain.

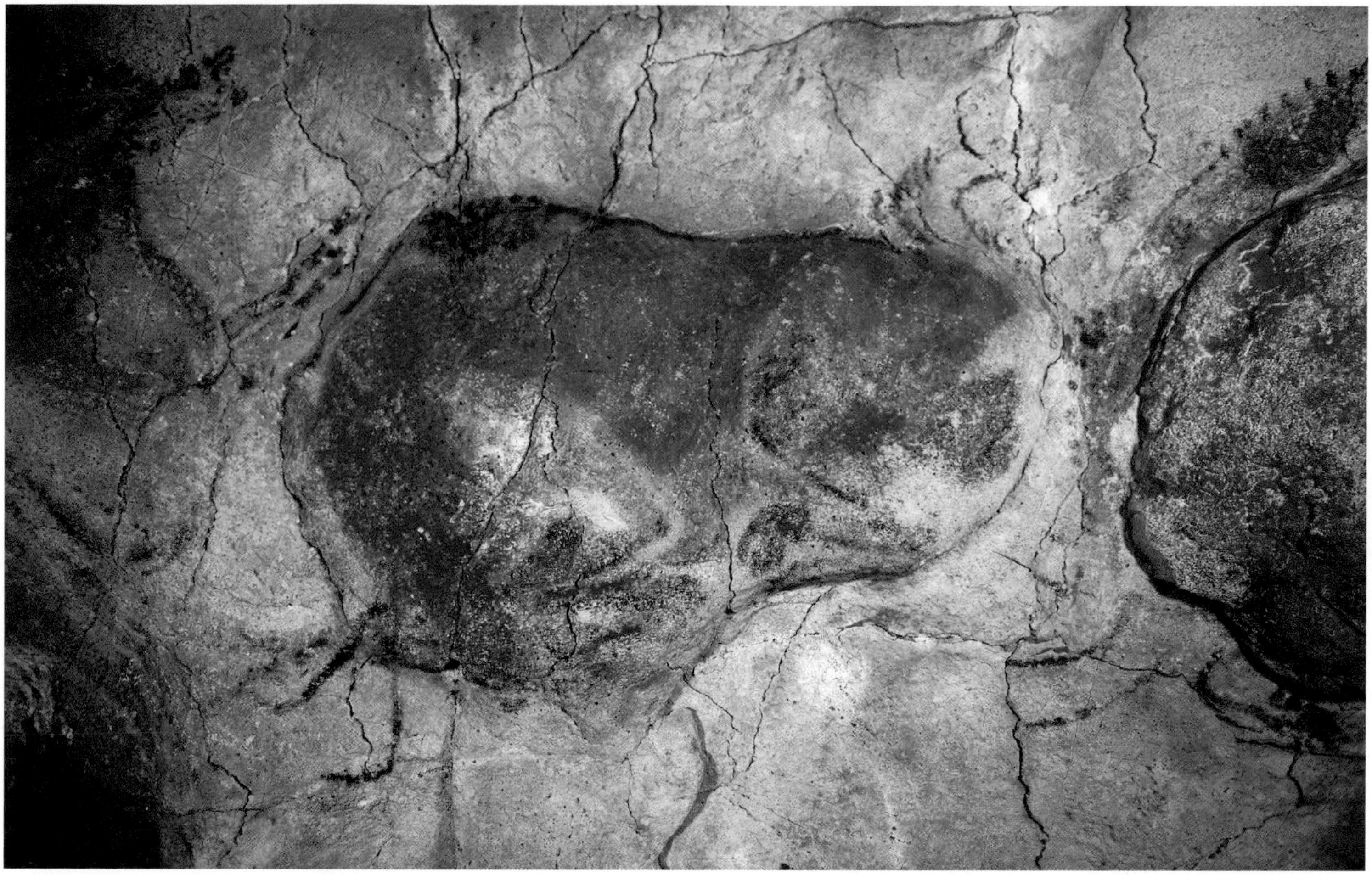

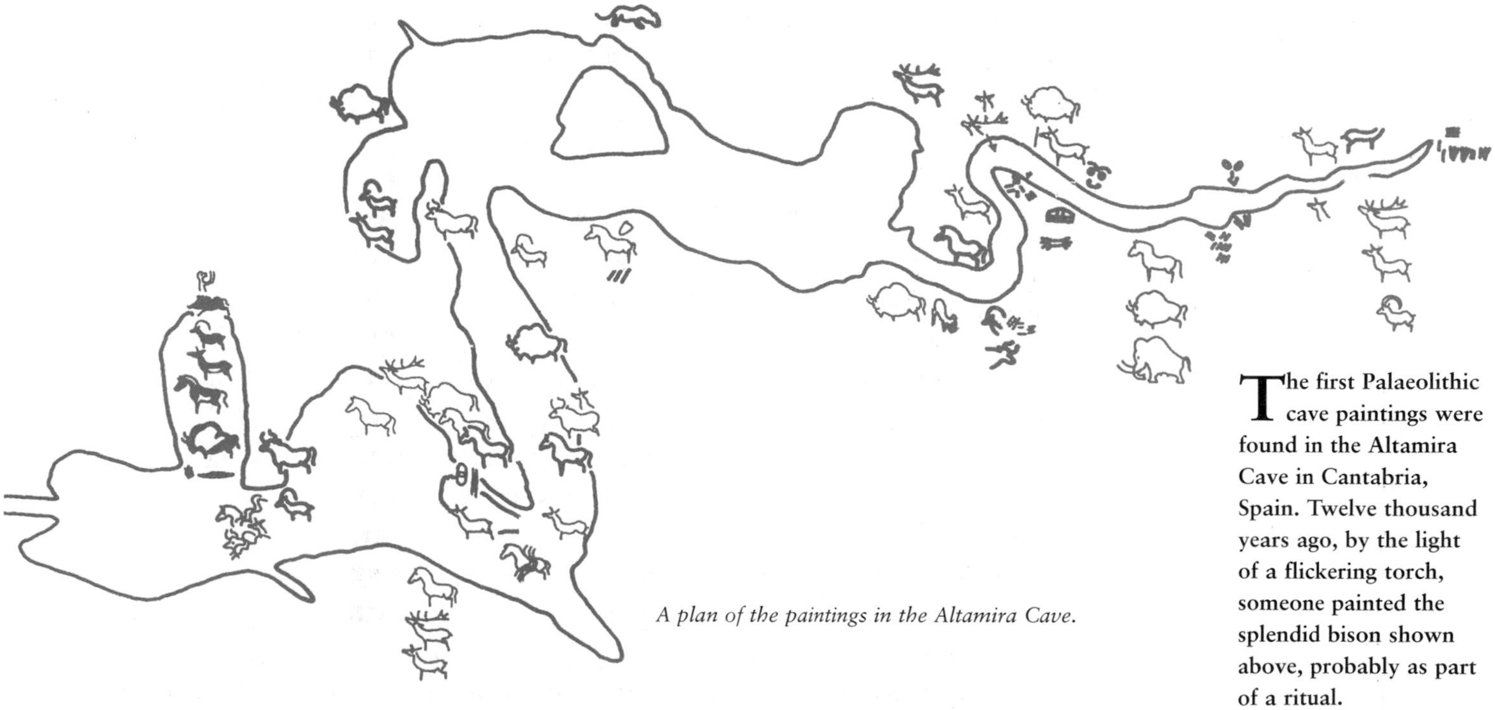

A plan of the paintings in the Altamira Cave.

The first Palaeolithic cave paintings were found in the Altamira Cave in Cantabria, Spain. Twelve thousand years ago, by the light of a flickering torch, someone painted the splendid bison shown above, probably as part of a ritual.

still taking thousands of years to transmit learning across the barriers of geography and social division. A person might, after all, live all his or her life without meeting anyone from another group or tribe, let alone another culture. The divisions which already existed between different groups of *Homo sapiens* open a historical era whose whole tendency was towards the cultural distinction, if not isolation, of one group from another, and this was to increase human diversity until reversed by technical and political forces in very recent times.

About the groups in which Upper Palaeolithic humans lived there is still much unknown. What is clear is that they were both larger in size than in former times and also more settled. The earliest remains of buildings come from the hunters of the Upper Palaeolithic who inhabited what are now the Czech and Slovak Republics and southern Russia. In about 10,000 BCE in parts of France some clusters of shelters seem to have contained anything from four to six hundred people, but judging by the archaeological record, this was unusual. Something like the tribe probably existed, therefore, though about its organization and hierarchies it is virtually impossible to speak. All that is clear is that there was a continuing sexual specialization in the Old Stone Age as hunting grew more elaborate and its skills more demanding, while settlements provided new possibilities of vegetable gathering by women.

At the Princevent site in the Seine valley, France, a number of circles have been found on the ground. The circles have a fireplace at one end and indications that they were inhabited by reindeer hunters, who lived some 10,000 years ago. There are no traces of any posts, which suggests that the hunters built lightweight tents similar to the ones in this drawing. A frame of sticks was probably covered with animal skins.

THE END OF THE PALAEOLITHIC

Cloudy though its picture is, none the less, the earth at the end of the Old Stone Age is in important respects one we can recognize. There were still to be geological changes (the English Channel was only to make its latest appearance in about 7000 BCE, for example) but we have lived in a period of comparative topographical stability which has preserved the major shapes of the world of about 9000 BCE. That world was by then firmly the world of *Homo sapiens*. The descendants of the primates who came out of the trees had, by the acquisition of their tool-making skills, by using natural materials to make shelters and by domesticating fire, by hunting and exploiting other animals, long achieved an important measure of independence of some of nature's rhythms. This had brought them to a high enough level of social organization to undertake important cooperative works.

Homo sapiens' needs had provoked economic differentiation between the sexes. Grappling with these and other material problems had led to the transmission of ideas by speech, to the invention of ritual practices and ideas which lie at the roots of religion, and, eventually, to a great art. It has even been argued that Upper Palaeolithic societies had a lunar calendar. Humans as they leave prehistory are already conceptualizing creatures, equipped with intellect, with the power to objectify and abstract. It is very difficult not to believe that it is this new strength which explains humanity's capacity to make the last and greatest stride in prehistory, the invention of agriculture.

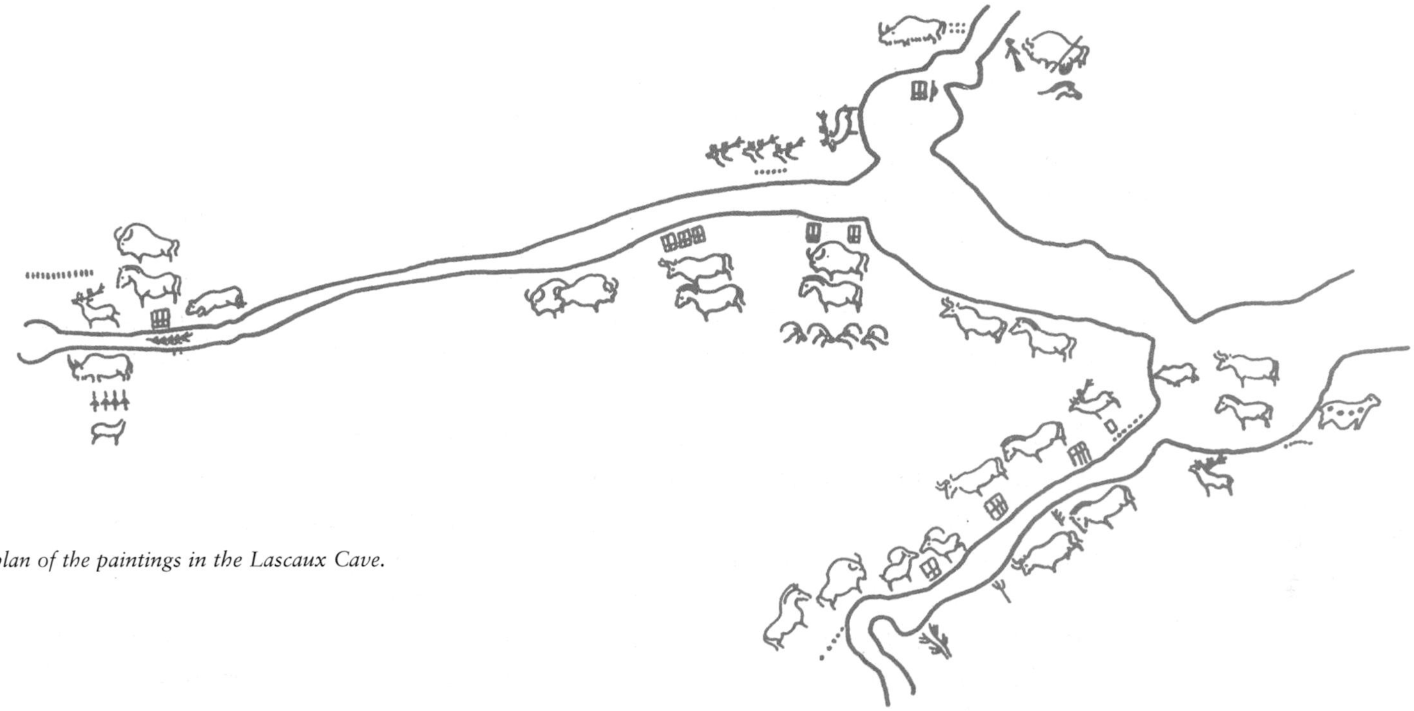

A plan of the paintings in the Lascaux Cave.

Currently, we know of the existence of more than 200 caves in Europe containing Palaeolithic paintings. Most of the images date from the Magdalenian cultural period, which lasted from 15,000 to 10,000 BCE, and 90 per cent of them can be found in France and Spain. This photograph shows one of the most impressive paintings ever discovered, from the Lascaux Cave, in the Dordogne, France.

3 THE POSSIBILITY OF CIVILIZATION

THE SPECIES *Homo sapiens* has existed for at least ten and perhaps twenty times as long as the civilization it has created. The waning of the last Ice Age allowed the long march to civilization to be completed and is the immediate prelude to History. Within five or six thousand years a succession of momentous changes took place of which unquestionably the most important was an increase in food supply. Nothing so sharply accelerated human development or had such widespread results until the changes called industrialization which have gone on over the last three centuries.

THE NEOLITHIC CULTURE

ONE SCHOLAR SUMMED UP these changes which mark the end of prehistory as the "Neolithic revolution". Here begins another tangle of potentially misleading terminology,

Many cave paintings from the Mesolithic cultural age have been found in eastern Spain. This scene, from the Roca del Moros in Cogull, depicts human figures.

This painting of deer running at full speed was found on the rocks of the Gasullo ravine in the Castellón region. It is just one example of the many animal paintings that have been found in the east of Spain.

though the last we need consider in prehistory. Archaeologists follow the Palaeolithic era by the Mesolithic and that by the Neolithic (some add a fourth, the Chalcolithic, by which they mean a phase of society in which artifacts of stone and copper are in simultaneous use). The distinction between the first two is really of interest only to the specialist, but all these terms describe cultural facts; they identify sequences of artifacts which show growing resources and capacities. Only the term "Neolithic" need concern us. It means, at its narrowest and most precise, a culture in which ground or polished stone tools replace chipped ones (though other criteria are sometimes added to this). This may not seem so startling a change as to justify the excitement over the Neolithic which has been shown by some prehistorians, far less talk of a "Neolithic revolution". In fact, though the phrase is still sometimes used it is unsatisfactory because it has had to cover too many different ideas. None the less, it was an attempt to pin down an important and complex change which took place with many local variations. It is still worthwhile, therefore, to try to understand what made the Neolithic so important.

REGIONAL DIFFERENCES

Even in the narrowest technological sense, the Neolithic phase of human development does not begin, flower or end everywhere at the same time. In one place it may last thousands of years longer than in another and its beginnings are separated from what went before, not by a clear line but by a mysterious zone of cultural change. Then, within it, not all societies possess the same range of skills and resources; some discover how to make pottery, as well as polished stone tools, others go on to domesticate animals and begin to gather or raise cereal crops. Slow evolution is the rule and not all societies had reached the same level by the time literate civilization appears. Nevertheless, Neolithic culture is the matrix from which civilization appears and provides the preconditions on which it rests, and they are by no means limited to the production of the highly finished stone tools

Spanish cave paintings provide the first evidence of the use of bows and arrows.

Neolithic cultures are characterized by the existence of polished stone tools, which were rubbed until they had a smooth surface. These polished Neolithic axeheads were used to cut down trees in order to make clearings in forests.

which gave the phase its name.

We must also qualify the word "revolution" when discussing this change. Though we leave behind the slow evolutions of the Pleistocene and move into an accelerating era of prehistory, there are still no clear-cut divisions. They are pretty rare in later history; even when they try to do so, few societies ever wholly break with their past. What we can see is a slow but radical transformation of human behaviour and organization over more and more of the world, not a sudden new departure. It is made up of several crucial changes which make the last period of prehistory identifiable as a unity, whatever we call it.

PHYSIOLOGICAL CHANGE

At the end of the Upper Palaeolithic, humans existed physically much as we know them. They were, of course, still to change somewhat in height and weight, most obviously in those areas of the world where they gained in stature and life expectancy as nutrition improved. In the Old Stone Age it was still unlikely that a man or a woman would reach the age of forty and if they did then they were likely to live pretty miserable lives, in our eyes prematurely aged, tormented by arthritis, rheumatism and the casual accidents of broken bones or rotting teeth. This would only slowly improve. The shape of the human face would go on evolving, too, as diet altered. (It seems to be only after 1066 CE that the edge-to-edgc bite gave way among Anglo-Saxons to the overbite which was the ultimate consequence of a shift to more starch and carbohydrate, a development of some importance for the later appearance of the English.)

This Neolithic flaked spearhead dates from between 4400 and 3300 BCE.

Human physical types differed in different continents, but we cannot presume that capacities did. In all parts of the world *Homo sapiens sapiens* was showing great versatility in adapting his heritage to the climatic and geographical upheavals of the ebbing phase of the last Ice Age. In the beginnings of settlements of some size and permanence, in the elaboration of technology and in the growth of language and the dawn of characterization in art lay some of the rudimentary elements of the compound which was eventually to crystallize as civilization. But much more than these were needed. Above all, there had to be the possibility of some sort of economic surplus to daily requirements.

This was hardly conceivable except in occasional, specially favourable areas of the hunting and gathering economy which sustained all human life and was the only one known to human beings until about ten thousand years ago.

EARLY AGRICULTURE

WHAT MADE CIVILIZATION POSSIBLE was the invention of agriculture. The importance of this was so great that it does seem to justify a strong metaphor and "farming revolution" or "food-gathering revolution" are terms whose meaning is readily clear. They single out the fact which explains why the Neolithic era could provide the circumstances in which civilizations could appear. Even a knowledge of metallurgy, which was spreading in some societies during their Neolithic phases, is not so fundamental. Farming truly revolutionized the conditions of human existence and it is the main thing to bear in mind when considering the meaning of Neolithic, a meaning concisely summarized by a leading archaeologist as "not a time phase falling between exact dates, but ... a period between the end of the hunting way of life and the beginning of a full metal-using economy, when the practice of farming arose and spread through most of Europe, Asia and North Africa like a slow-moving wave".

In the western Sahara, which was far more humid a few thousand years ago than it is today, many small, engraved stone plaques depicting various animals have been found. These provide evidence of the gradual change from hunting to the domestication of livestock. This plaque comes from the Saguia el-Hamra region.

The essentials of agriculture are the growing of crops and the practice of animal husbandry. How these came about and at what places and times is more mysterious. Some environments must have helped more than others; while some peoples pursued game across plains uncovered by the retreating ice, others were intensifying the skills needed to exploit the new, prolific river valleys and coastal inlets rich in edible plants and fish. The same must be true of cultivation and herding. On the whole, the Old World of Africa and Eurasia was better off in domesticable animals than what would later be called the Americas. Not surprisingly, then, agriculture began in more than one place and in different forms. It has been claimed that the earliest instance, based on the cultivation of primitive forms of millet and rice, occurred in the Near East, somewhere about 10,000 BCE.

AGRICULTURE IN THE NEAR EAST

For thousands of years, and until only a couple of centuries ago, the increase of human food supply was to come from methods already available in prehistoric times. New land could be broken in for crops, elementary observation and selection began the conscious modification of species, plant forms were transferred to new locations, and labour was applied to cultivation, through digging, draining and irrigating. These made possible a growth in food production which could sustain a slow, steady rise in human numbers until the great changes brought by chemical

Time chart (10,000 BCE–c.3500 BCE)

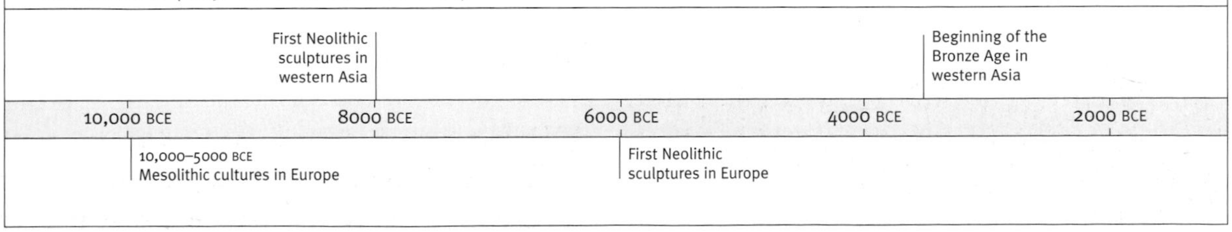

Agricultural tools from the Neolithic: a grinding stone (above) and flint blades (right), which may have been used for reaping.

fertilizers and modern genetic science.

The accidents of survival and the direction of scholarly effort have meant until recently that much more was known about early agriculture in the Near East than about its possible precursors in further Asia. Rice may have been cultivated in the Yangtze valley as early as 7000 BCE. Nonetheless, there is good reason to regard the Near East as a crucial zone. Both the predisposing conditions and the evidence point to the region later called the "Fertile Crescent" as especially significant; this is the arc of territory running northward from Egypt through Palestine and the Levant, through Anatolia to the hills between Iran and the south Caspian to enclose the river valleys of Mesopotamia. Much of it now looks very different from the same area's lush landscape when the climate was at its best, five thousand or so years ago. Wild barley and a wheatlike cereal then grew in southern Turkey and emmer, a wild wheat, in the Jordan valley. Egypt enjoyed enough rain for the hunting of big game well into historical times, and elephants were still to be found in Syrian forests in 1000 BCE.

The region today is still fertile by comparison with the deserts which encircle it, but in prehistoric times it was even more favoured. The cereal grasses which are the ancestors of later crops have been traced back furthest in these lands. There is evidence of the harvesting, though not necessarily of the cultivating, of wild grasses in Asia Minor in about 9500 BCE. There, too, thc afforestation which followed the end of the last Ice Age seems to have presented a manageable challenge; population pressure might well have stimulated attempts to extend living-space by clearing and planting when hunting-gathering areas became overcrowded. From this region the new foods and the techniques for planting and harvesting them seem to have spread into Europe in about 7000 BCE. Within the region, of course, contacts were relatively easier than outside it; a date as early as 8000 BCE has been given to discoveries of bladed tools found in southwest Iran but made from obsidian which came from Anatolia. But diffusion was not the only process at work. Agriculture later appeared in the Americas, seemingly without any import of techniques from outside.

THE DOMESTICATION OF ANIMALS

The jump from gathering wild cereals to planting and harvesting them seems marginally greater than that from driving game for hunting to herding, but the domestication of animals was almost as momentous. The first traces of the keeping of sheep come from northern Iraq, in about 9000 BCE. Over such hilly, grassy areas the wild forebears of the Jersey cow and the Gloucester Old Spot pig roamed untroubled for thousands of years except by occasional contact with their hunters. Pigs, it is true, could be found all

The beginnings of agriculture

The cultivation of plants and the domestication of animals, both of which brought about a radical transformation in the way human beings lived, did not begin in one place. There is a great deal of evidence to suggest that different agrarian traditions developed independently at different times from a number of distinct places of origin, at least eight of which have been identified (see map, right, above). The earliest of agricultural developments appear to have taken place in the Near East area, where farming villages are known to have existed some 10,000 years ago. Agriculture and livestock farming gradually spread from these early centres into new regions. The European farming tradition, for example, was probably disseminated from the Near East into Europe along two main routes: through the Balkans and along the River Danube (from around 6500 BCE) and along the Mediterranean coast (reaching southern France around 5000 BCE).

The map depicting the diffusion of agriculture in Europe (right, below) shows how closely the spread of farming was linked to the spread of pottery manufacture. The typical pottery found in the Mediterranean region is known as cardial pottery, after its *cardium*, or "cockle-shell", decoration. So-called band pottery, named after its incised linear decorations, has been found north of the Alps and across central Europe. Through the discovery of objects belonging to these two groups of pottery, it is possible to chart the locations of early farming communities.

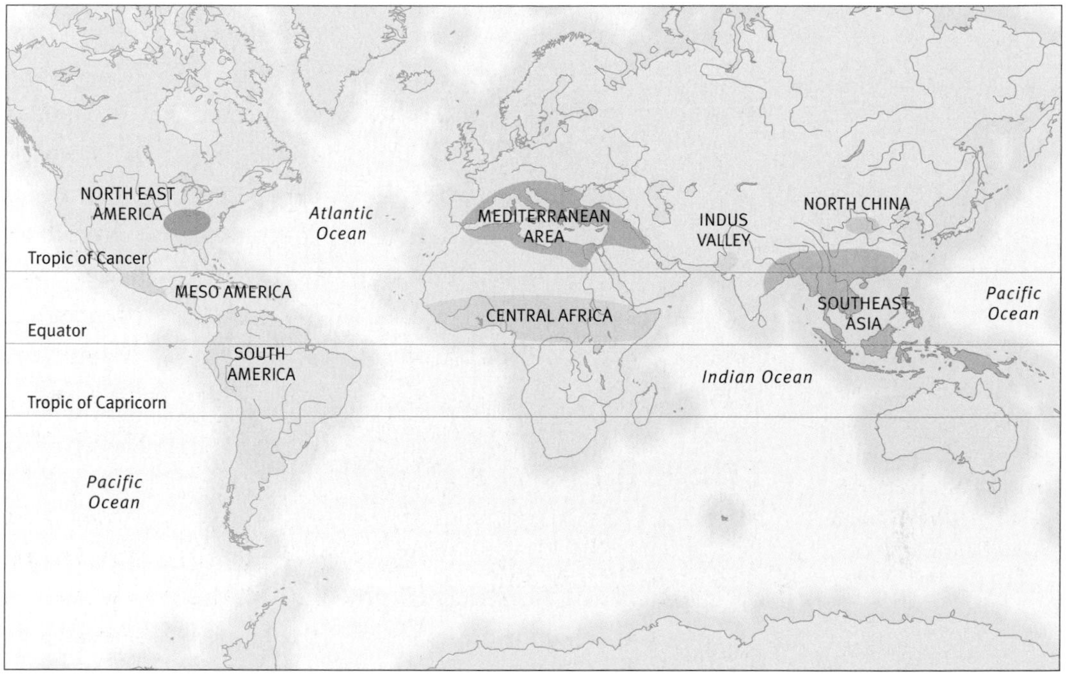

Regions where agriculture developed independently.

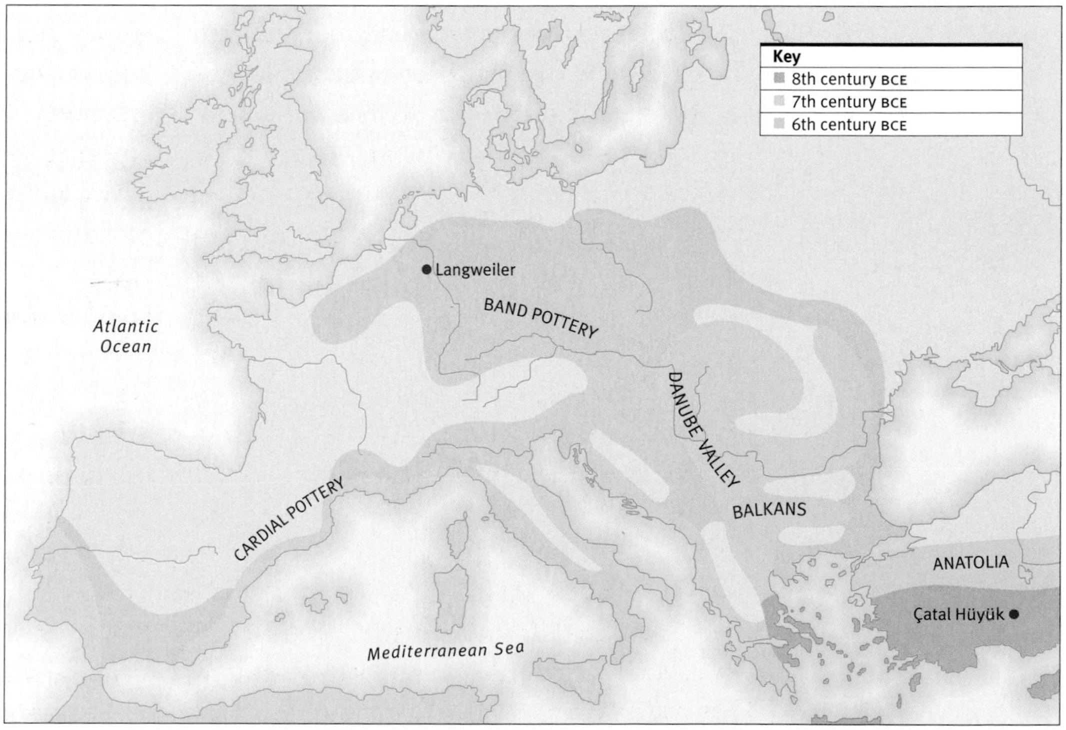

The diffusion of agricultural and cultural traditions in Europe.

Various Neolithic cultural traditions can be identified by their distinct pottery styles. The object pictured above, found in Andalusia in Spain, is an example of the cardial pottery that was characteristic of the western Mediterranean region during the early Neolithic period.

over the Old World, but sheep and goats were especially plentiful in Asia Minor and a region running across much of Asia itself. From their systematic exploitation would follow the control of their breeding and other economic and technological innovations. The use of skins and wool opened new possibilities; the taking of milk launched dairying. Riding and the use of animals for traction would come later. So would domestic poultry.

THE IMPLICATIONS OF SURPLUSES

THE STORY OF HUMANITY is now far past the point at which the impact of such changes can be easily grasped. Suddenly, with the coming of agriculture, the whole material fabric on which subsequent human history was to be based flashes into view, though not yet into existence. It was the beginning of the greatest of humanity's transformations of the environment. In a hunting-gathering society thousands of acres are needed to support a family, whereas in primitive agricultural society about twenty-five acres is enough. In terms of population growth, a huge acceleration became possible. An assured or virtually assured food surplus also meant settlements of a new solidity. Bigger populations could live on smaller areas and true villages could appear. Specialists not engaged in food production could be tolerated and fed more easily while they practised their own skills. Before 9000 BCE there was a village (and perhaps a shrine) at Jericho. A thousand years later it had grown to some eight to ten acres of mud-brick houses.

SOCIAL CHANGES

It is a long time before we can discern much of the social organization and behaviour of early farming communities. It seems possible that at this time, as much as at any other, local divisions were decisive. Physically, humans were more uniform than ever, but culturally they were diversifying as they grappled with different problems and appropriated different resources. The adaptability of different branches of *Homo sapiens* in the conditions left behind after the retreat of the last Ice Age is very striking and produced variations in experience unlike those following earlier glaciations. They lived for the most part in isolated, settled traditions, in which the importance of routine was overwhelming. This would give new stability to the divisions of culture and race which had appeared so slowly throughout Palaeolithic times. It would take much less time in the historical future which lay ahead for these local peculiarities to crumble under the impact of population growth, speedier communication

Basket-making is thought to have begun during the final stages of the Neolithic. These amazingly well-preserved grass baskets were found in Cueva de los Murciélagos in Granada, Spain.

Excavations at the Jericho site, West Bank, have revealed this spectacular circular stone tower. The tower is 30 ft (9 m) high and dates from 8000 BCE. This suggests that some of the earliest Neolithic farming communities were already using complex systems of fortification to defend themselves against enemy incursions.

and the coming of trade – a mere ten thousand years, at most. Within the new farming communities it seems likely that distinctions of role multiplied and new collective disciplines had to be accepted. For some people there must have been more leisure (though for others actually engaged in the production of food, leisure may well have diminished). It is likely that social distinctions became more marked. This may be connected with new possibilities as surpluses became available for barter which led eventually to trade.

This plaster model of a human head was found in Jericho. Carved in bas-relief, it dates from the 7th millennium BCE.

NEW GROUNDS FOR CONFLICT

The surpluses may also have encouraged humanity's oldest sport after hunting – warfare. Hunting was long to be the sport of kings and mastery of the animal world was an attribute of the first heroes of whose exploits we have records in sculpture and legend. Yet the possibility of human and material prizes must have made raids and conquest more tempting. Perhaps, too, a conflict, which was to have centuries of vitality before it, finds its origins here – that between nomads and settlers. Political power may have an origin in the need to organize protection for crops and stock from human predators. We may even speculate that the dim roots of the notion of aristocracy are to be sought in the successes (which must have been frequent) of hunter-gatherers, representatives of an older social order, in exploiting the vulnerability of the settlers, tied to their areas of cultivation, by enslaving them. None the less, though much of the just prehistoric world must have been lawless and violent, it is worth remembering that there was an offsetting factor: the world was still not very full. The replacement of hunter-gatherers by farmers did not have to be a violent process. The ample space and thin populations of Europe on the eve of the introduction of farming may explain the lack of archaeological evidence of violent struggle. It was only slowly that growing populations and pressure on the new farming resources increased the likelihood of competition.

An early-Bronze Age flat axe (far right) and a late-Bronze Age axe (right). The high price of bronze restricted its use – it was mainly employed for making weapons.

EARLY METALLURGY

In the long run metallurgy changed things as much as did farming, but it was to be a very much longer run. Immediately, it made a less rapid and fundamental difference. This is probably because the deposits of ore first discovered were few and scattered: for a long time there was just not much metal around. The first of whose use we find evidence is copper (which rather weakens the attractiveness of the old term "Bronze Age" for the beginning of metal-using culture). At some time between 7000 and 6000 BCE it was first being hammered into shape without heating and smelted at Çatal Hüyük, in Anatolia, though the earliest known metal artifacts date from about 4000 BCE and are beaten copper pins found in Egypt. Once the technique of blending copper with tin to produce bronze was discovered, a metal was available which was both relatively easy to cast and retained a much better cutting edge. It was in use in Mesopotamia soon after 3000 BCE. On bronze much was to be built; from it, too, much derived, among other results the quite new importance of ore-bearing areas. In its turn, this was to give a new twist to trade, to markets and to routes. Still further complications, of course, followed the coming of iron, which appeared after some cultures had indisputably evolved into civilizations – another reflection of the way in which the historical and prehistoric eras run so untidily into one another. Its obvious military value springs to the eye, but it had just as much importance when turned into agricultural tools. This is looking a long way ahead, but it made possible a huge extension of living space and food-producing soil: however successfully they burned woodland and scrub, Neolithic peoples could only scratch at heavy soils with an antler or wooden pick. Turning them over and digging deep began to be possible only when the invention of ploughing (in the Near East in about 3000 BCE) brought animal muscle-power to the assistance of human, and when iron tools became common.

Stone moulds were used to cast various bronze objects. This needle-casting mould was found in Switzerland.

CENTRES OF DEVELOPMENT

It is already clear how quickly – the term is legitimate against the background of earlier prehistory, even if it takes thousands of years in some places – interpenetration and interplay begin to influence the pace and direction of change. Long before these processes have exhausted their effects in some areas, too, the first civilizations are in being. Prehistorians used to argue whether innovations were diffused from a single source or appeared spontaneously and independently in different places, but so complex a background has made this seem a waste of time and energy. Both views, if put forward in an unqualified way, seem somewhat implausible. To say that in one place, and in one place only, all the conditions for the appearance of new phenomena existed and that these were then simply diffused elsewhere is as implausible as saying that in widely differing circumstances of geography, climate and cultural inheritance exactly the same inventions could be thrown up, as it were, time and time again. What we can observe is a concentration of factors in the Near East which made it at one crucial moment immeasurably the most concentrated, active and important centre of new developments. It does not mean that similar individual developments may not have occurred elsewhere: pottery, it seems, was first produced in Japan in about 10,000 BCE, and agriculture evolved in America perhaps as early as 5000 BCE in complete isolation from the Old World.

THE EVE OF CIVILIZATION

Human prehistory thus comes to a ragged, untidy end; once again, there is no neat dividing line from history. At the end of prehistory and on the eve of the first civilizations we confront a world of human societies more differentiated than ever before and more successful than ever in mastering different environments and surviving. Some will continue into history. It is only within the last century or so that the Ainus of northern Japan have disappeared, taking with them a life that is said to have been very similar to one they lived fifteen thousand years ago. Englishmen and Frenchmen who went to

This stone mould (below, left), found in Switzerland, was used to cast bronze needles such as the one shown below, right.

North America in the sixteenth century CE found hunter-gatherers there who must have lived much as their own ancestors had done ten thousand years before. Plato and Aristotle were to live and die before prehistory in America gave way to the appearance of the great Mayan civilization of Yucatán, and prehistory lasted for Eskimos and Australian Aborigines until the nineteenth century.

This figure, found at Çatal Hüyük, dates from 8000–7000 BCE.

THE PACE OF CHANGE

No crude divisions of chronology will help in unravelling so interwoven a pattern of peoples and cultures. But its most important feature is clear enough: by 6000 or 5000 BCE, there existed in one area of the Old World all the essential constituents of civilized life. Their deepest roots lay hundreds of thousands of years further back, in ages dominated by the slow rhythm of genetic evolution. Through the Upper Palaeolithic eras the pace of change had quickened by a huge factor as culture slowly became more important, but this was as nothing to what was to follow. Civilization was to bring conscious attempts on a quite new scale to control and organize humans and their environment. Civilization builds on a basis of cumulative mental and technological resources and the feedback from its own transformations further accelerates the process of change. Ahead lies faster development in every field, in the

An artist's reconstruction of part of the Çatal Hüyük Neolithic site, discovered in 1958 CE in Anatolia. The site's 1,000 dwellings date from around 6000 BCE. They had remarkably regular ground plans, were made of sun-dried bricks and mud and measured around 270 sq ft (25 sq m). The entrance to each house was through a low door from a roof terrace. Wall paintings, statues of a mother goddess and the figure of a bull were found inside some of the buildings, which suggests that they were used as sanctuaries.

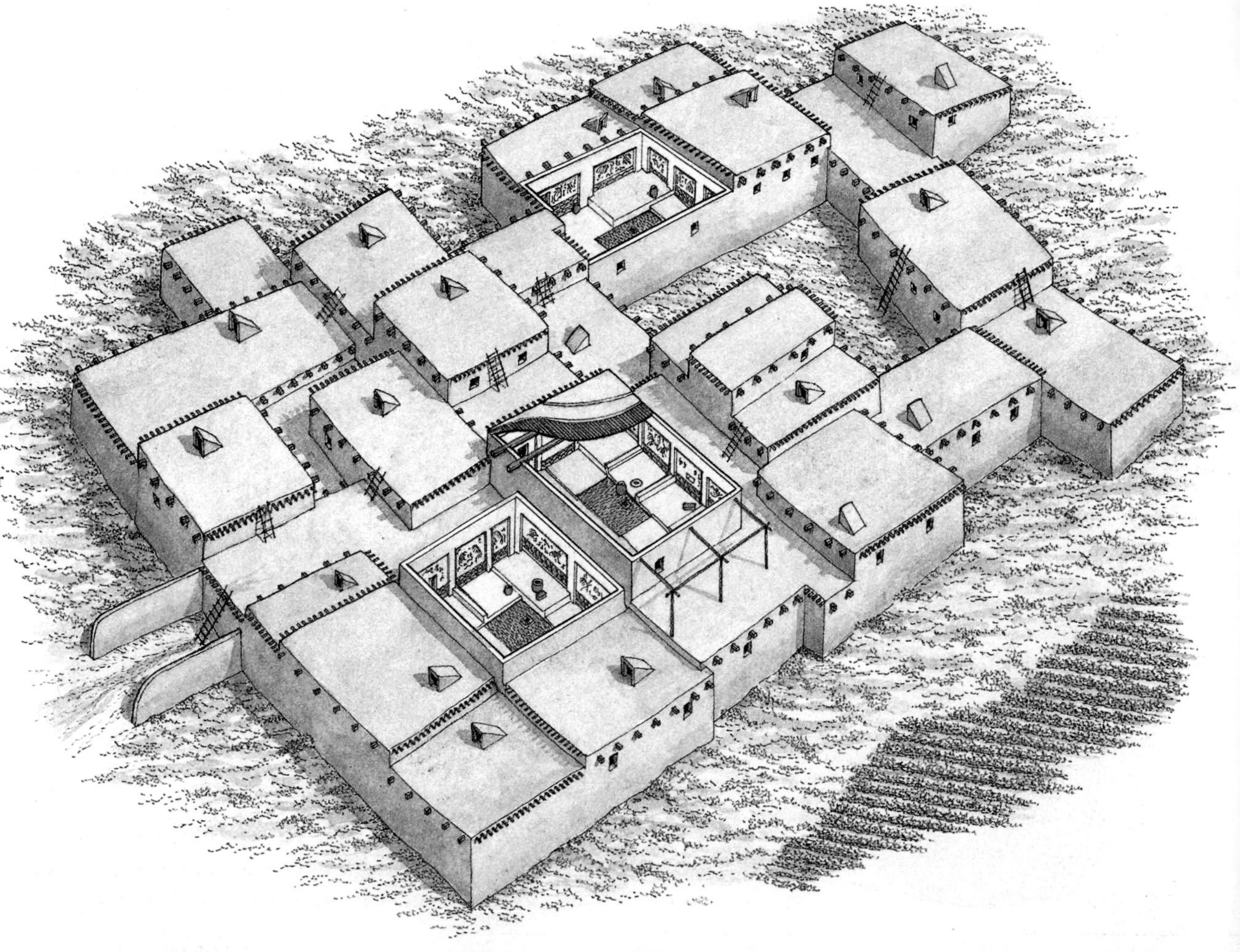

This building, 36 ft (11 m) x 33 ft (10 m), was erected in the 4th millennium BCE at the centre of a small village in Banpo, south of the Yellow River, China. This was the main building in the village, which was inhabited by people from the Yangshao Neolithic culture.

technical control of environment, in the elaboration of mental patterns, in the changing of social organization, in the accumulation of wealth, in the growth of population.

It is important that we get our perspective in this matter right. From some modern points of view the centuries of the European Middle Ages look like a long slumber. No medievalist would agree, of course, but a modern reader who is impressed by the rapidity of the change which encompasses him or her and the relative immobility of medieval society ought to reflect that the art which develops from the Romanesque of Charlemagne's Aachen to the Flamboyant of fifteenth-century France was revolutionized in five or six centuries; in a period about ten times as long, the first known art, that of Upper Palaeolithic Europe, shows, by comparison, insignificant stylistic change.

Further back, the pace is even slower as the long persistence of early tool types shows. Still more fundamental changes are even less easy to comprehend. So far as we know, the last twelve thousand years register nothing new in human physiology comparable to the colossal transformations of the early Pleistocene which are registered for us in a handful of fossil relics of a few of nature's experiments, yet those took hundreds of thousands of years.

THE ROLE OF HUMAN CONSCIOUSNESS

In part, the contrast in the rate of change is the one with which we began, that between Nature and humanity as makers of change.

Found at the Çatal Hüyük site, this terracotta sculpture dates from 6000 BCE and represents the Hittite mother goddess giving birth between two lions or leopards.

The Langweiler 2 site (above) is characteristic of the band pottery culture of the middle of the 6th millennium BCE. These early European farmers lived in villages that consisted of a few very large buildings of up to 483 sq ft (45 sq m), divided into three areas. The central area was used by the family, another space was set aside for livestock and a third probably served as a grain store. The villagers grew cereals and vegetables, bred cattle and pigs and hunted in the large forests nearby.

Humans increasingly choose for themselves and even in prehistory the story of change is therefore increasingly one of conscious adaptation. So the story will continue into historical times, more intensively still. This is why the most important part of the story of humanity is the story of consciousness; when, long ago, it broke the genetic slow march, it made everything else possible. Nature and nurture are there from the moment that humans can first be discerned; perhaps they can never be quite disentangled, but man-made culture and tradition are increasingly the determinants of change.

HUMANKIND'S INHERITANCE

Two reflections ought to be made to balance the indisputable fact that humans have some control over their own destiny. The first is that they have almost certainly not shown any improvement in innate capacity since the Upper Palaeolithic. Their physique has not changed fundamentally in forty thousand years or so and it would be surprising if their mental capacity had done so. So short a time could hardly suffice for genetic changes comparable to those of earlier eras. The rapidity with which humanity has achieved so much since prehistoric times can be accounted for quite simply: there are many more of us upon whose talents humanity can draw and, more important still, human achievements are essentially cumulative. They rest upon a heritage itself accumulating at, as it were, compound interest. Primitive societies had far less inherited advantage in the bank. This makes the magnitude of their greatest steps forward all the more amazing.

If this is speculative, the second reflection need not be: our genetic inheritance not only enables us to make conscious change, to undertake an unprecedented kind of evolution, but also controls and limits us. The irrationalities of the times we live in show the narrow limits of our capacity for conscious control of our destiny. To this extent, we are still determined, still unfree, still a part of a nature which produced our unique qualities in the first place only by evolutionary selection. It is not easy to separate this part of our inheritance, either, from the emotional shaping we have received from the processes through which we evolved. That shaping still lies deep at the heart of all our aesthetic and affective life. Humans must live with an inbuilt dualism. To deal with it has been the aim of most of the great philosophies and religions and the mythologies by which we still live, but they are themselves moulded by it. As we move from prehistory to history it is important not to forget that its determining effect still proves much more resistant to control than those blind prehistoric forces of geography and climate which were so quickly overcome. Nevertheless, human beings at the edge of history are already the creatures we know, change-makers.

A San man in the Kalahari desert in Africa quenches his thirst by extracting the sap from a root. Like today's traditional communities, our prehistoric ancestors managed to survive thanks to a wealth of knowledge about their environment.

THE FIRST CIVILIZATIONS

TEN THOUSAND YEARS AGO, the physical shape of the world was much what it is today. The outlines of the continents were broadly those we know and the major natural barriers and channels of communication have remained constant ever since. By comparison with the upheavals of the hundreds of millennia preceding the end of the last Ice Age, climate, too, was from this time stable; from this point the historian need only regard its short-term fluctuations. Ahead lay the age (in which we still live) in which most change was to be man-made.

Civilization has been one of the great accelerators of such change. It began at least seven times according to one historian, meaning by that that he could distinguish at least seven occasions on which particular mixes of human skills and natural facts came together to make possible a new order of life based on the exploitation of nature. Though all these beginnings fell within a span of three thousand years or so – barely a moment by comparison with the vast scale of prehistory – they were neither simultaneous, nor equally successful. They turned out very differently, some of them racing ahead to lasting achievements while others declined or disappeared, even if after spectacular flowerings. Yet all of them signified an increase in the rate and scale of change dramatic by comparison with anything achieved in earlier times.

Some of these early civilizations are still real foundations of our own world. Some of them, on the other hand, now exercise little or no influence, except perhaps upon our imaginations and emotions when we contemplate the relics which are all that is now left of them. None the less, together they determined much of the cultural map of the world down to this day because of the power of the traditions which sprang from them even when their achievements in ideas, social organization or technology had long been forgotten. The establishment of the first civilizations took place between about 3500 BCE and 500 BCE and provides the first of the major chronological divisions of world history.

Egypt's exceptional artistic heritage has captured the world's imagination since its rediscovery by the archaeologists and scholars who went there with Napoleon Bonaparte in 1798 CE. This remarkable temple in Luxor (the name given to the southern part of Thebes) was built by Amenhotep III (1411–1375 BCE) and was one of the most important temples in Egypt during the New Kingdom period.

1 EARLY CIVILIZED LIFE

FOR AS LONG AS WE KNOW there has been at Jericho a never-failing spring, feeding what is still a sizeable oasis. No doubt it explains why people have lived there on and off for about ten thousand years. Farmers clustered about it in late prehistoric times; its population may then have numbered two or three thousand. Before 6000 BCE it had great water tanks which suggest provision for big needs, possibly for irrigation, and there was a massive stone tower which was part of elaborate defences long kept in repair. Clearly its inhabitants thought they had something worth defending; they had property. Jericho was a considerable place. For all that, it was not the beginnings of a civilization; too much was still lacking.

THE FOUNDATIONS OF CIVILIZATION

It is worth considering for a moment at the outset of the era of civilization just what it is

Sites of the first civilizations

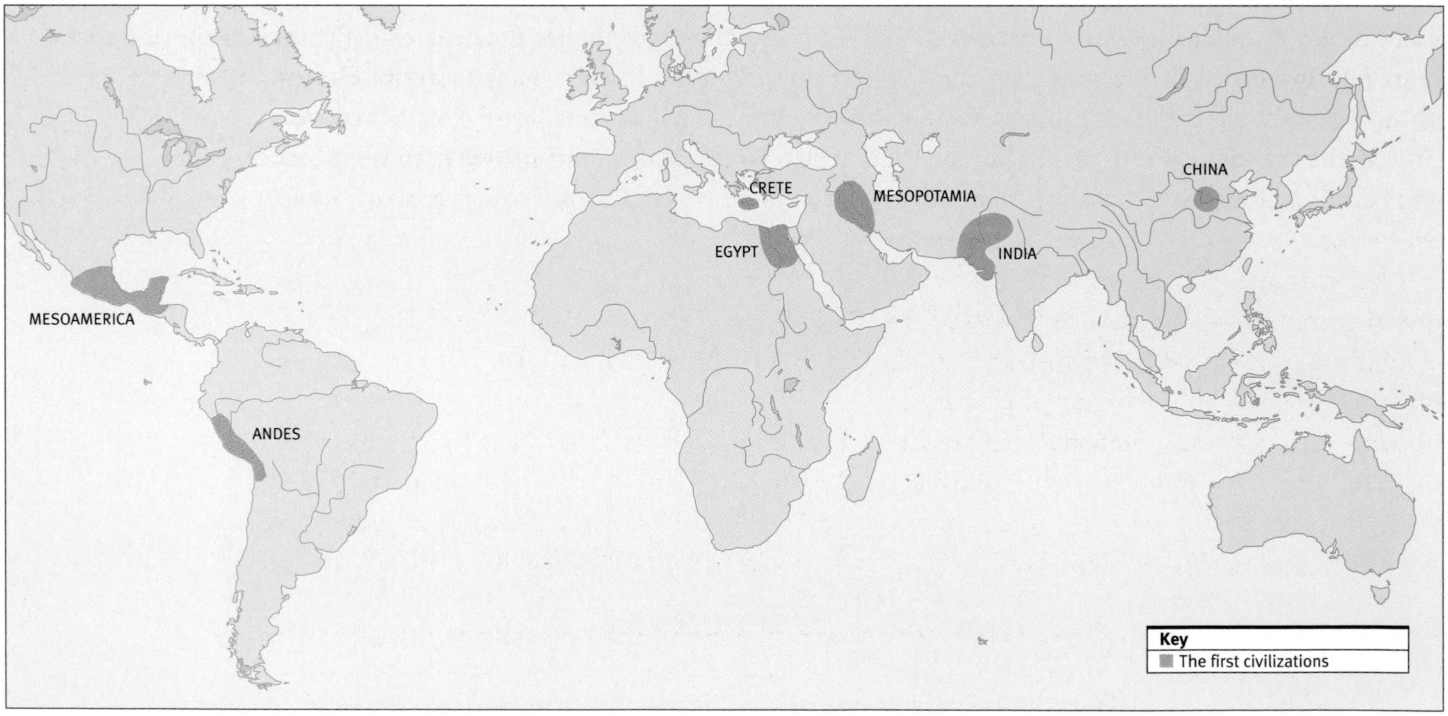

This map shows the areas of the world where ancient civilizations appeared. The fact that each civilization possesses distinguishing features suggests that they all had independent origins. However, those civilizations that were located close to each other, such as Mesopotamia and Egypt, soon came into contact as their respective rulers explored the land around them. Each civilization sought to learn as much as possible about the present or potential resources to be found in its neighbours' territories.

A page from the papyrus Book of the Dead of the ancient Egyptian scribe Ani. The larger figures represent the deceased and his wife.

we are looking for. It is a little like the problem of pinning down in time the first human beings. There is a shaded area in which we know the change occurs, but we can still disagree about the point at which a line has been crossed. All over the Near East around 5000 BCE farming villages provided the agricultural surpluses on which civilization could eventually be raised. Some of them have left behind evidence of complex religious practice and elaborate painted pottery, one of the most widespread forms of art in the Neolithic era. Somewhere about 6000 BCE brick building was going on in Turkey at Çatal Hüyük, a site only slightly younger than Jericho. But by civilization we usually mean something more than ritual, art or the presence of a certain technology, and certainly something more than the mere agglomeration of human beings in the same place.

WHAT IS CIVILIZATION?

Defining civilization is a little like speaking of "an educated man": everyone can recognize one when they see him, but not all educated men are recognized as such by all observers,

Time chart (3500 BCE–c.1000 BCE)

3100 BCE
Egyptian civilization appears

Minoan civilization in Crete

Mesoamerican civilizations

3500 BCE | 3000 BCE | 2500 BCE | 2000 BCE | 1500 BCE

First recognizable civilization in Mesopotamia

Appearance of the first civilization in India

First Chinese civilization

nor is a formal qualification (a university degree, for example) either a necessary or infallible indicator. Dictionary definitions are of no help in pinning down "civilization", either. That of the *Oxford English Dictionary* is indisputable but so cautious as to be useless: "a developed or advanced state of human society". What we have still to decide about is how far developed or advanced and along what lines.

Some have said that a civilized society is different from an uncivilized society because it has a certain attribute – writing, cities, monumental building have all been suggested.

But agreement is difficult and it seems safer not to rely on any such single test. If, instead, we look at examples of what everyone has agreed to call civilizations and not at the marginal and doubtful cases, then it is obvious that what they have in common is complexity. They have all reached a level of elaboration which allows much more variety of human action and experience than even a well-off primitive community. Civilization is the name we give to the interaction of human beings in a very creative way, when a critical mass of cultural potential and a certain surplus of resources have been built up. In civilization this releases human capacities for development at quite a new level and in large measure the development which follows is self-sustaining.

This earthenware female figurine with a reptile head was found in Ur in Mesopotamia and dates from the 5th millennium BCE.

EARLY CIVILIZATIONS

SOMEWHERE IN the fourth millennium BCE is the starting-point of the story of civilizations and it will be helpful to set out a rough overall chronology right at the start. We begin with the first recognizable civilization in Mesopotamia. The next example is in Egypt, where civilization is observable at a slightly later date, perhaps about 3100 BCE. Another marker in the Near East is "Minoan" civilization, which appears in Crete in about 2000 BCE, and from that time we can disregard questions of priorities in this part of the world: it is already a complex of civilizations in interplay with one another. Meanwhile, further east, and perhaps around 2500 BCE, another civilization has appeared in India and it is at least to some degree literate. China's first civilization starts later, toward the middle of the second millennium BCE. Later still come the Mesoamericans. Once we are past about 1500 BCE, though, only this last example is sufficiently isolated for interaction not to be a big part of explaining what happens. From that time, there are no civilizations to be explained which appear without the stimulus, shock or inheritance provided by others which have appeared earlier. For the moment, then, our preliminary sketch is complete enough at this point.

About these first civilizations (whose appearance and shaping is the subject matter of the next few chapters) it is very difficult to generalize.

Of course they all show a low level of technological achievement, even if it is astonishingly high by comparison with that of their uncivilized predecessors. To this extent their shape and development were still determined much more than those of our own civilization by their setting. Yet they had begun to nibble at the restraints of geography. The topography of the world was already much as it is today; the continents were set in the forms they now have and the barriers and channels to communication they supplied were to be constants, but there was a growing technological ability to exploit and transcend them. The currents of wind and water which directed early maritime travel have not changed much, and even in the second millennium BCE human beings were learning to use them and to escape from their determining force.

The city of Tiahuanaco, located on the shores of Lake Titicaca in Peru, is one of the most impressive cities erected by the ancient Andean civilizations. The city's heyday lasted from 500 to 1000 CE and its monumental ruins, such as this monolithic statue, are still standing today.

This suggests, correctly, that at a very early date the possibilities of human interchange were considerable. It is therefore unwise to dogmatize about civilization appearing in any standard way in different places. Arguments have been put forward about favourable environments, river valleys for example: obviously, their rich and easily cultivated soils could support fairly dense populations of farmers in villages which would slowly grow into the first cities. This happened in Mesopotamia, Egypt, the Indus valley and China. But cities and civilizations have also arisen away from river valleys, in Mesoamerica, Minoan Crete and, later, in Greece. With the last two, there is the strong likelihood of important influence from the outside, but Egypt and the Indus valley, too, were in touch with Mesopotamia at a very early date in their evolution. Evidence of such contact led at one time to the view put forward a few years ago that we should look for one central source of civilization from which all others came. This idea is not now very popular. There is not only the awkward case of civilization in the isolated Americas to deal with, but great difficulty in getting the timetable of the supposed diffusion right as more and more knowledge of early chronology is acquired by the techniques of radio-carbon dating.

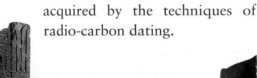

The Shang Dynasty, which appeared in the Yellow River valley in the 18th century BCE, gives its name to the first stage of Chinese civilization. Its important archaeological legacy includes bronze objects, such as this receptacle decorated with images of human faces.

DETERMINING FACTORS

The most satisfactory theory appears to be that civilization was likely always to result from the coming together of a number of factors predisposing a particular area to throw up something dense enough to be recognized later as civilization, but that different environments, different influences from outside and different cultural inheritances from the past mean that humanity did not move in all parts of the world at the same pace or even towards the same goals. The idea of a standard pattern of social "evolution" was discredited even before the idea of "diffusion" from a common civilizing source. Clearly, a favourable geographical setting was essential; in the first civilizations everything rested on the existence of an agricultural surplus. But another factor was just as important – the capacity of the peoples on the spot to take advantage of an environment or rise to a challenge, and here external contacts may be as important as tradition. China seems at first sight almost insulated from the outside, but even there possibilities of contact existed. The way in which different societies generate the critical mass of elements necessary to civilization therefore remains very hard to pin down.

It is easier to say something generally true about the marks of early civilization than about the way it happened. Again, no absolute and universal statements are plausible. Civilizations have existed without writing, useful as it is for storing and using experience. More mechanical skills have

Early systems of writing

Almost all early civilizations developed their own systems of writing, whose marked differences make the possibility of a common origin unlikely. The following examples are illustrated: (1) a 4,300-year-old inscription on a small stamp from Mohenjo Daro, in the undeciphered writing of the Indus valley civilization; (2) a 4,000-year-old Sumerian philosophical text on an earthenware tablet in cuneiform writing; (3) an example of Egyptian hieroglyphs from the temple of the pharaoh Mentuhotep II, in Deir el-Bahari, dating from the same period.

1

2

3

This oracle was engraved on a turtle's shell 3,300 years ago during the Shang period in ancient China.

been very unevenly distributed, too: the Mesoamericans carried out major building operations with neither draught animals nor the wheel, and the Chinese knew how to cast iron nearly fifteen hundred years before Europeans. Nor have all civilizations followed the same patterns of growth; there are wide disparities between their staying power, let alone their successes.

URBANIZATION

Early civilizations, like later ones, seem to have a common positive characteristic in that they change the human scale of things. They bring together the cooperative efforts of more men and women than in earlier societies and usually do this by physically bringing them together in larger agglomerations, too. Our word "civilization" suggests, in its Latin roots, a connection with urbanization. Admittedly, it would be a bold man or woman who was willing to draw a precise line at the moment when the balance tipped from a dense pattern of agricultural villages clustered around a religious centre or a market to reveal the first true city. Yet it is perfectly reasonable to say that more than any other institution the city has provided the critical mass which produces civilization and that it has fostered innovation better than any other environment so far. Inside the city the surpluses of wealth produced by agriculture made possible other things characteristic of civilized life. They provided for the upkeep of a priestly class which elaborated a complex religious structure, leading to the construction of great buildings with more than merely economic functions, and eventually to the writing down of literature. Much bigger resources than in earlier times were thus allocated to something other than immediate consumption and this meant a storing of enterprise and experience in new forms. The accumulated culture gradually became a more and more effective instrument for changing the world.

CULTURAL DIFFERENCES

One of the changes resulting from the birth of civilization is quickly apparent: in different parts of the world human beings grew more rapidly more unlike one another. The most obvious fact about early civilizations is that they are startlingly different in style, but because it is so obvious we usually overlook it. The coming of civilization opens an era of ever more rapid differentiation – of dress, architecture, technology, behaviour, social forms and thought. The roots of this obviously lie in prehistory, when there already existed peoples with different lifestyles, different patterns of existence, different mentalities, as well as different physical characteristics. But this was no longer merely the product of the natural endowment of environment, but of the creative power of civilization itself. Only with the rise to dominance of Western technology in the twentieth century has this variety begun to diminish. From the first civilizations to our own day there have always been alternative models of society available, even if they knew little of one another.

Much of this variety is very hard to recover. All that we can do in some instances is to be aware that it is there. At the beginning there is still little evidence about the life of the mind except institutions so far as we can recover them, symbols in art and ideas embodied in literature. In them lie presuppositions which are the great coordinates around which a view of the world is built – even when the people holding that view do not know they are there (history is often the discovery of what people did not know about themselves). Many such ideas are irrecoverable, and even when we can begin to grasp the shapes which defined the world of the people living in the old civilizations, a constant effort of imagination must be made to avoid the danger of falling into anachronism which surrounds us on every side. Even literacy does not reveal very much of the minds of creatures who were so like and yet so unlike ourselves.

THE NEAR EAST

IT IS IN THE NEAR EAST that the stimulating effects of different cultures upon one another first become obvious and no doubt it is much of the story of the appearance of the earliest civilizations there. A turmoil of racial comings and goings for three or four thousand years both enriched and disrupted this area, where our history must begin. The Fertile Crescent was to be for most of historic times a great crucible of cultures, a zone not only of settlement but of transit, through which poured an ebb and flow of people and

The Fertile Crescent: birthplace of civilization

The oldest civilizations appeared more than 5,000 years ago in a region known as the Fertile Crescent. This consists of a succession of fertile, arable plains that spread out in the shape of a crescent moon from the mouth of the Tigris and Euphrates rivers to the mouth of the Nile, through Mesopotamia, Syria, Palestine and Egypt. To the north and the east of the Fertile Crescent lie mountainous areas. To the south and west lie the vast deserts of Arabia and Libya.

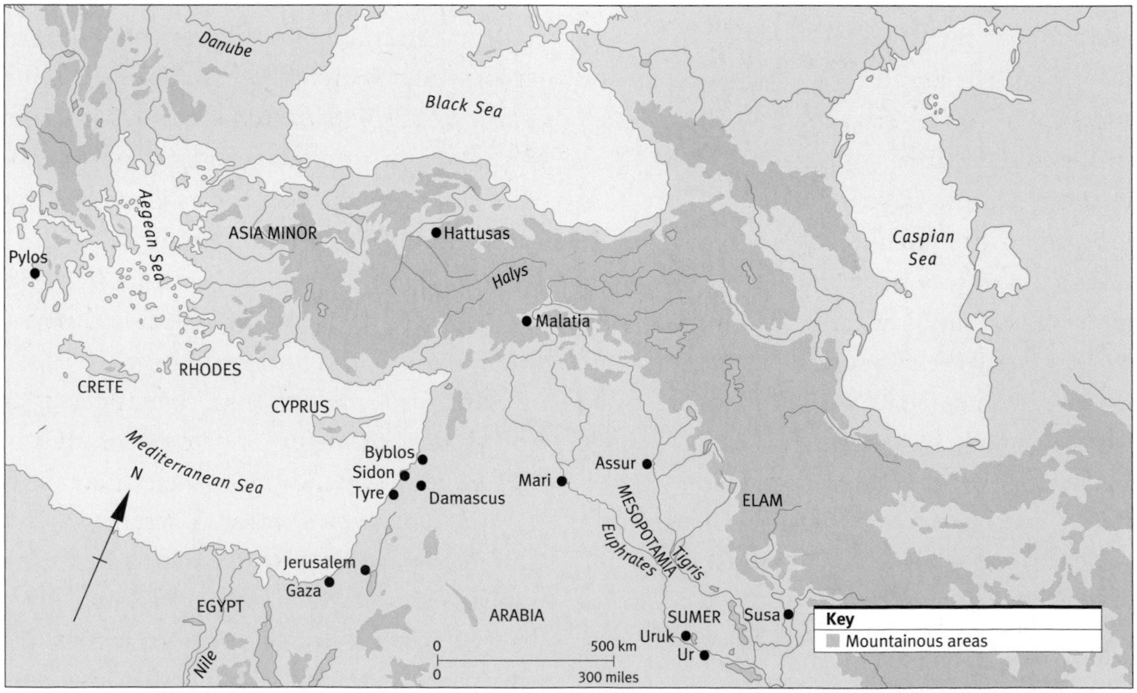

The northern part of the Fertile Crescent.

ideas. In the end this produced a fertile interchange of institutions, language and belief from which stems much of human thought and custom even today.

THE EFFECTS OF OVER-POPULATION

Why so many people came to the Fertile Crescent cannot exactly be explained, but the overwhelming presumption must be that the root cause was over-population in the lands from which the intruders came. Over-population may seem a paradoxical notion to apply to a world whose whole population in about 4000 BCE has been estimated only at between eighty and ninety millions, that is, about the same as Germany's today. In the next four thousand years it grew by about fifty per cent to about one hundred and thirty millions; this implies an annual increase almost imperceptible by comparison with what we now take for granted. It shows both the relative slowness with which our species added to its power and how much and how soon the new possibilities of civilization had already reinforced the human propensity to multiply and prosper by comparison with prehistoric times.

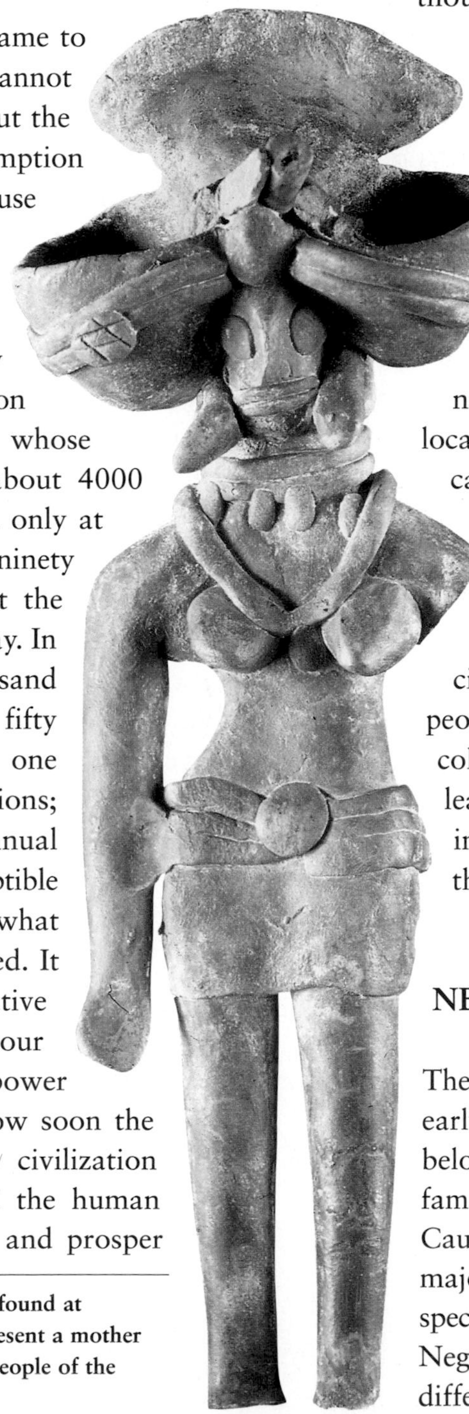

This earthenware figurine, found at Mohenjo-Daro, may represent a mother goddess. It was produced by people of the Indus valley civilization.

Such growth was still slight by later standards because it was always based on a very fragile margin of resources and it is this fragility which justifies talk of over-population. Drought or desiccation could dramatically and suddenly destroy an area's capacity to feed itself and it was to be thousands of years before food could easily be brought from elsewhere. The immediate results must often have been famine, but in the longer run there were others more important. The disturbances which resulted were the prime movers of early history; climatic change was still at work as a determinant, though now in much more local and specific ways. Droughts, catastrophic storms, even a few decades of marginally lower or higher temperatures, could force peoples to get on the move and so help to bring on civilization by throwing together peoples of different tradition. In collision and cooperation they learnt from one another and so increased the total potential of their societies.

This is an illustration of an ivory handle from Yebel el-Arak, in northern Egypt. Made around 3400 BCE, the handle clearly shows the Mesopotamian influence on the Nile valley. It depicts battles on land and sea; the ships at the base of the handle appear to be Egyptian in origin, while those shown in the centre are thought to be Mesopotamian.

NEAR EASTERN PEOPLES

The peoples who are the actors of early history in the Near East all belonged to the light-skinned human family (sometimes confusingly termed Caucasian) which is one of the three major ethnic classifications of the species *Homo sapiens* (the others being Negroid and Mongoloid). Linguistic differences have led to other attempts to distinguish them. All the peoples in the Fertile Crescent of early civilized times have been assigned on philological grounds either to "Hamitic" stocks who evolved in Africa north and north-east of the Sahara, to the Semitic language speakers of the Arabian peninsula, to the peoples of "Indo-European" language who, from southern Russia, had spread also by 4000 BCE into Europe and Iran, or to the true "Caucasians" of Georgia. These have been identified as the *dramatis personae* of early Near Eastern history. Their historic centres all lay around the zone in which agriculture and civilization appear at an early date. The wealth of so well-settled an area must have attracted peripheral peoples.

THE MOVEMENT OF PEOPLES IN THE NEAR EAST

By about 4000 BCE most of the Fertile Crescent was occupied and we can begin there to attempt a summary of the next three thousand years which will provide a framework for the earliest civilizations. Probably Semitic peoples had already begun to penetrate it by then; their pressure grew until by the middle of the third millennium BCE (long after the appearance of civilization) they would be well established in central Mesopotamia, across the middle sections of the Tigris and Euphrates. The interplay and rivalry of the Semitic peoples with the Caucasians, who were able to hang on to the higher lands which enclosed Mesopotamia from the north-east, is one continuing theme some scholars have discerned in the early history of the area. By 2000 BCE the peoples whose languages were the Indo-European group have also entered on the scene, and from two directions. One of these peoples, the Hittites, pushed into Anatolia from Europe, while their advance was matched from the east by that of the Iranians. Between 2000 BCE and 1500 BCE branches of these sub-units dispute and mingle with the Semitic and Caucasian peoples in the Crescent itself, while the contacts of the Hamites and Semites lie behind much of the political history of old Egypt. This scenario is, of course, highly impressionistic. Its value is only that it helps to indicate the basic dynamism and rhythms of the history of the ancient Near East. Much of its detail is still highly uncertain (as will appear) and little can be said about what maintained this fluidity. None the less, whatever its cause, this wandering of peoples was the background against which the first civilization appeared and prospered.

This colossal statue of Ramses II with a princess at his feet was placed in the temple of Karnak 33 centuries ago. The statue still stands, but the inscription bearing the name of Ramses II has been replaced by that of another Egyptian pharaoh.

2 ANCIENT MESOPOTAMIA

A lush, fertile valley in the mountains of northeastern Mesopotamia, one of the original centres of agriculture.

THE BEST CASE for the first appearance of something which is recognizably civilization has been made for the southern part of Mesopotamia, the seven-hundred-mile-long land formed by the two river valleys of the Tigris and Euphrates. This end of the Fertile Crescent was thickly studded with farming villages in Neolithic times. Some of the oldest settlements of all seem to have been in the extreme south, where deposits from centuries of drainage from up-country and annual floodings had built up a soil of great richness. It must always have been much easier to grow crops there than elsewhere provided that the water supply could be made continuously and safely available; this was possible, for though rain was slight and irregular, the river bed was often above the level of the surrounding plain. A calculation has been made that in about 2500 BCE the yield of grain in southern Mesopotamia compared favourably with that of the best Canadian wheat-fields today. Here, at an early date, was the possibility of growing more than was needed for daily consumption, the surplus indispensable to the appearance of town life. Furthermore, fish could be taken from the nearby sea.

IRRIGATION AND RECLAMATION

The setting of southern Mesopotamia was a challenge, as well as an opportunity. The Tigris and Euphrates could suddenly and violently change their beds: the marshy, low-lying land of the delta had to be raised above flood level by banking and ditching and canals had to be built to carry water away. Thousands of years later, techniques could still be seen in use in Mesopotamia which were probably those first employed long ago to form the platforms of reed and mud on which were built the first homesteads of the area. These patches of cultivation would be grouped where the soil was richest. The drains and irrigation channels they needed could be managed properly only if they were managed collectively. No doubt the social organization of reclamation was another result. However it happened, the seemingly unprecedented achievement of making land from watery marsh must have been the forcing house of a new complexity in the way human beings lived together.

This alabaster vase, dating from c.3000 BCE, was found in Uruk and depicts an offering ceremony to the goddess Inanna. The scene may be a reference to a sacred wedding during which the priest, representing the god Dumuzi, was united with the priestess, representing Inanna, in order to renew the fertility of the land.

An illustration of a Sumerian stamp from Uruk depicting a boat. Shipping played an important role in ancient Sumer, now southern Iraq.

COLLECTIVE ORGANIZATION

As the number of Mesopotamians increased, more land was taken to grow food. Sooner or later men of different villages would have come face to face with others intent on reclaiming marsh which had previously separated them from one another. Different irrigation needs may even have brought them into contact before this. There was a choice: to fight or to cooperate. Each meant further collective organization and a new agglomeration of power. Somewhere along this path it made sense for people to band together in bigger units than hitherto for self-protection or management of the environment. One physical result is the town, mud-walled at first to keep out floods and enemies, raised above the waters on a platform. It was logical for the local deity's shrine to be the place chosen: he stood behind the community's authority. It would be exercised by his chief priest, who became the ruler of a little theocracy competing with others.

Something like this – we cannot know what – may explain the difference between southern Mesopotamia in the third and fourth millennia BCE and the other zones of Neolithic culture with which it had already long been in contact. The evidence of pottery and characteristic shrines shows that there were links between Mesopotamia and the Neolithic cultures of Anatolia, Assyria and Iran. They all had much

Towering above the ruins of the city of Uruk are the remains of one of the oldest ziggurats (stepped temples) of Mesopotamia. The ziggurat was built in the 21st century BCE by Ur Nammu, King of Ur, in honour of Inanna, the goddess of fertility.

in common. But only in one relatively small area did a pattern of village life common to much of the Near East begin to grow faster and harden into something else. From that background emerges the first true urbanism – that of Sumer – and the first observable civilization.

THE SUMERIAN CIVILIZATION

SUMER IS AN ANCIENT NAME for southern Mesopotamia, which then extended about a hundred miles less to the south than the present coast. The people who lived there may have been Caucasians, unlike their Semitic neighbours to the south-west and like their northern neighbours, the Elamites who lived on the other side of the Tigris. Scholars are still divided about when the Sumerians – that is, those who spoke the language later called Sumerian – arrived in the area: they may have been there since about 4000 BCE. But since we know the population of civilized Sumer to be a mixture of races, perhaps including the earlier inhabitants of the region, with a culture which mixed foreign and local elements, it does not much matter.

Time chart (3300 BCE–1154 BCE)

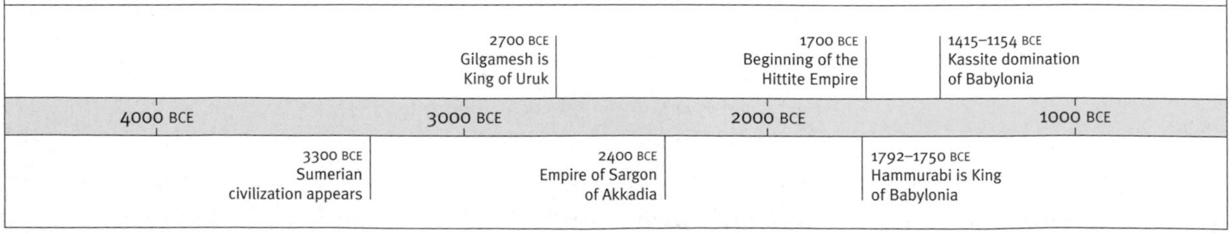

EARLY CULT CENTRES

Sumerian civilization had deep roots. The people had long shared a way of life not very different from that of their neighbours. They lived in villages and had a few important cult centres which were continuously occupied. One of these, at a place called Eridu, probably originated in about 5000 BCE. It grew steadily well into historic times and by the middle of the fourth millennium there was a temple there which some have thought to have provided the original model for Mesopotamian monumental architecture, though nothing is now left of it but the platform on which it rested. Such cult centres began by serving those who lived near them. They were not true cities, but places of devotion and pilgrimage. They may have had no considerable resident populations, but they were usually the centres around which cities later crystallized and this helps to explain the close relationship religion and government always had in ancient Mesopotamia. Well before 3000 BCE some such sites had very big temples indeed; at Uruk (which is called Erech in the Bible) there was an especially splendid one, with elaborate decoration and impressive pillars of mud brick, eight feet in diameter.

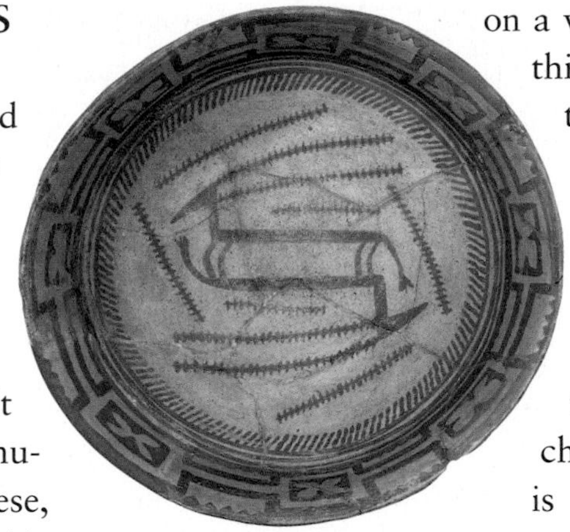

This pottery bowl from Ur dates from the 5th century BCE.

Pottery is among the most important evidence linking pre-civilized Mesopotamia with historic times. It provides one of the first clues that something culturally important is going forward which is qualitatively different from the evolutions of the Neolithic. The so-called Uruk pots (the name is derived from the site where they were found) are often duller, less exciting than earlier ones. They are, in fact, mass-produced, made in standard form on a wheel (which first appears in this role). The implication of this is strong that when they came to be produced there already existed a population of specialized craftsmen; it must have been maintained by an agriculture rich enough to produce a surplus exchanged for their creations. It is with this change that the story of Sumerian civilization can conveniently be begun.

THE INVENTION OF CUNEIFORM

The Sumerian civilization lasts about thirteen hundred years (roughly from 3300 to 2000 BCE), which is approximately as much time as separates us from the age of Charlemagne. At the beginning comes the invention of writing, possibly the only invention of comparable importance to the invention of agriculture before the age of steam. Writing

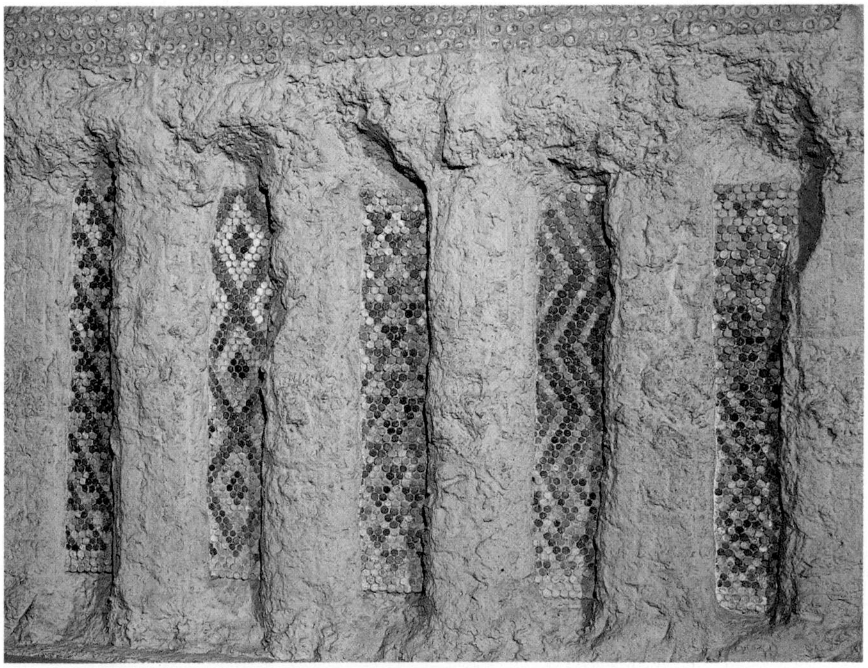

The most important of the early Sumerian cities was Ur, home of the legendary hero Gilgamesh. Excavations have revealed the remains of enormous constructions that are more than 5,000 years old. These pillars, decorated with mosaics, were found in the sanctuary of the goddess Inanna and have been reconstructed at the Berlin Museum.

The origins of writing

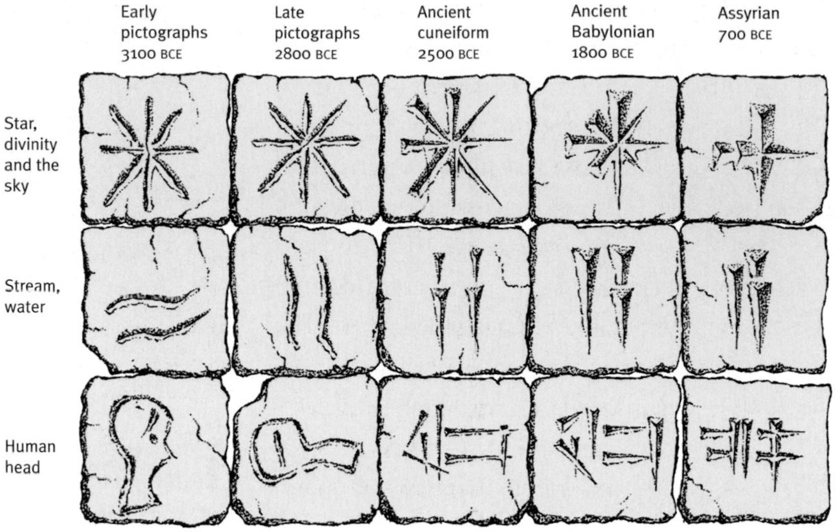

The above examples demonstrate the gradual development of cuneiform writing. Cuneiform characters were originally simplified drawings (pictograms), but later became completely abstract, based on a combination of horizontal, vertical and diagonal wedges.

had in fact been preceded by the invention of cylinder seals, on which little pictures were incised to be rolled on to clay; pottery may have degenerated, but these seals were one of the great Mesopotamian artistic achievements. The earliest writings followed in the form of pictograms or simplified pictures (a step towards non-representative communication), on clay tablets usually baked after they had been inscribed with a reed stalk. The earliest are in Sumerian and it can be seen that they are memoranda, lists of goods, receipts; their emphasis is economic and they cannot be read as continuous prose. The writing on these early notebooks and ledgers evolved slowly towards cuneiform, a way of arranging impressions stamped on clay by the wedge-like section of a chopped-off reed. With this the break with the pictogram form is complete. Signs and groups of signs come at this stage to stand for phonetic and possibly syllabic elements and are all made up of combinations of the same basic wedge shape. It was more flexible as a form of communication by signs than anything used hitherto and Sumer reached it soon after 3000 BCE.

HOW WRITING WAS USED

A fair amount is therefore known about the Sumerian language. A few of its words have survived to this day; one of them is the original form of the word "alcohol" (and the first recipe for beer), which is suggestive. But the language's greatest interest is its appearance in written forms at all. Literacy must have been both unsettling and stabilizing. On the one hand it offered huge new possibilities of communicating; on the other it stabilized practice because the consultation of a record as well as oral tradition became possible. It made much easier the complex operations of irrigating lands, harvesting and storing crops, which were fundamental to a growing society. Writing made for more efficient exploitation of resources. It also immensely strengthened government and emphasized its links with the priestly castes who at first monopolized literacy. Interestingly, one of the earliest uses of seals appears to be connected with this, since they were used somehow to certify the size of crops at their receipt in the temple. Perhaps they record at first the operations of an economy of centralized redistribution, where people brought their due produce to the temple and received there the food or materials they themselves needed.

THE EPIC OF GILGAMESH

The invention of writing opens more of the past to historians. Not only can they study administrative records, but they can at last begin to deal in hard currency when talking about mentality because writing preserves literature. The oldest story in the world is the Epic of Gilgamesh. Its most complete version, it is true, goes back only to the seventh century BCE, but the tale itself appears in Sumerian times and is known to have been written down soon after 2000 BCE.

Gilgamesh was a real person, ruling at Uruk. He became also the first individual and hero in world literature, appearing in other poems, too. His is the first name which must appear in this book. To a modern reader the most striking part of the Epic may be the coming of a great flood which obliterates humankind except for a favoured family who survive by building an ark; from them springs a new race to people the world after the flood has subsided. This was not part of the Epic's oldest versions, but came from a separate poem telling a story which turns up in many Near Eastern forms, though its incorporation is easily understandable. Lower Mesopotamia must always have had much trouble with flooding, which would undoubtedly put a heavy strain on the fragile system of irrigation on which its prosperity depended. Floods were the type, perhaps, of general disaster, and must have helped to foster the pessimistic fatalism which some scholars have seen as the key to Sumerian religion.

The image on this stamp depicts Gilgamesh overpowering a buffalo.

This sombre mood dominates the Epic. Gilgamesh does great things in his restless search to assert himself against the iron laws of the gods which ensure human failure, but they triumph in the end. Gilgamesh, too, must die:

The heroes, the wise men, like the new moon have their waxing and waning. Men will say, "Who has ever ruled with might and with power like him?" As in the dark month, the month of shadows, so without him there is no

The legend of Gilgamesh

The Epic of Gilgamesh consists of a series of mythical verses concerning the Sumerian hero Gilgamesh, King of Uruk, who lived around 2700 BCE. The verses were written down on early earthenware tablets and were eventually collated to form a complete story.

According to the legend, Gilgamesh ruled in the city of Uruk more than 4,000 years ago. As time passed he became a tyrant and his subjects appealed to the gods to keep him in check. The gods created Enkidu, the wild man of the woods, to confront the king. Hearing of Enkidu's existence, Gilgamesh sent a prostitute out to tempt the wild man into the city. In the city, Enkidu and Gilgamesh began to fight but eventually became friends. They decided to combine their strengths to combat the dragon of the woods. The goddess Ishtar, who was infatuated with Gilgamesh, was very jealous of his friendship with Enkidu. Gilgamesh, however, rejected Ishtar, and Enkidu even reproached the goddess for her whimsical nature. Ishtar and the gods could not forgive Enkidu for this insult and killed him. Gilgamesh was stunned – he had lost his friend and he had been made aware of human mortality. He decided to search for the fountain of eternal youth and set off to find Utnapishtim, the sole survivor of the Great Flood. On his journey, Gilgamesh met Sidri. She asked him, "Why are you searching for the fountain of eternal youth? The gods say that the fate of men is to die ... enjoy your days and nights, because that too is man's fate."

Gilgamesh continued his journey until he found Utnapishtim, but came to realize that immortality was impossible. Gilgamesh then returned to his city and resigned himself to the inevitability of death.

This 8th-century BCE Assyrian bas-relief from Jorabad shows Gilgamesh wrestling with a lion.

These images of men in prayer (see above and right) are typical of much Sumerian statuary. Most such figurines were made between 3000 and 2500 BCE and are shown wearing Sumerian sheepskin skirts.

light. O Gilgamesh, this was the meaning of your dream. You were given the kingship, such was your destiny; everlasting life was not your destiny.

Apart from this mood and its revelation of the religious temperament of a civilization, there is much information about the gods of ancient Mesopotamia in the Epic. But it is hard to get at history through it, let alone relate it to the historical Gilgamesh. In particular, attempts to identify a single, cataclysmic flood by archaeological means have not been convincing, though plentiful evidence of recurrent flooding is available. From the water eventually emerges the land: perhaps, then, what we are being given is an account of the creation of the world, of genesis. In the Hebrew Bible earth emerges from the waters at God's will and that account satisfied most educated Europeans for a thousand years. It is fascinating to speculate that we may owe so much of our own intellectual ancestry to a mythical reconstruction by the Sumerians of their own pre-history when farming land had been created out of the morass of the Mesopotamian delta. But it is only speculation; caution suggests we remain satisfied merely to note the undeniable close parallels between the Epic and one of the best of the Bible stories, that of Noah's Ark.

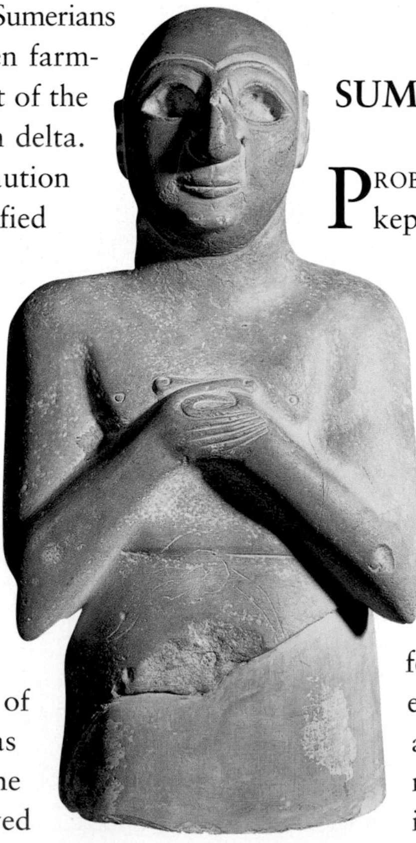

THE DIFFUSION OF THE EPIC

The story of Gilgamesh hints at the possible importance of the diffusion of Sumerian ideas in the Near East long after the focus of its history had moved away to upper Mesopotamia. Versions and parts of the Epic – to stick to that text alone for a moment – have turned up in the archives and relics of many peoples who dominated parts of this region in the second millennium BCE. Though later to be lost until rediscovery in modern times, Gilgamesh was for two thousand years or so a name to which literature in many languages could knowingly refer, somewhat in the way, say, that European authors until recently could take it for granted that an allusion to classical Greece would be understood by their readers. The Sumerian language lived on for centuries in temples and scribal schools, much as Latin lived on for the learned in the muddle of vernacular cultures in Europe after the collapse of the western classical world of Rome. The comparison is suggestive, because literary and linguistic tradition embodies ideas and images which impose, permit and limit different ways of seeing the world; they have, that is to say, historic weight.

SUMERIAN RELIGION

PROBABLY THE MOST important ideas kept alive by the Sumerian language were religious. Cities like Ur and Uruk were the seedbed of ideas which, after transmutation into other religions in the Near East during the first and second millennia BCE, were four thousand years later to be influential worldwide, albeit in almost unrecognizably different forms. There is, for example, in the Gilgamesh Epic an ideal creature of nature, the man Enkidu; his fall from his innocence is sexual, a seduction by a harlot, and thereafter, though the outcome for him is civilization, he loses his happy association with the natural world. Literature makes it possible to observe such hints at the mythologies of other and later societies. In literature, the writers begin to make explicit the meanings earlier hidden in obscure relics of sacrificial offerings, clay figures and the groundplans of shrines and temples. In earliest Sumer these already reveal an organization of human discourse with the supernatural much more complex and elaborate than anything elsewhere at so early a date. Temples had been the focus of the early cities and they grew bigger and more splendid (in part, because of a tradition of building new ones on mounds enclosing their predecessors). Sacrifices were offered in them to ensure good crops. Later their cults elaborated, temples of still greater magnificence were built as far north as Assur, three hundred miles away up the Tigris, and we hear of one built with cedars brought from the Lebanon and copper from Anatolia.

No other ancient society at that time gave religion quite so prominent a place or diverted so much of its collective resources to its support. It has been suggested that this was because no other ancient society left humans feeling so utterly dependent on the will of the gods. Lower Mesopotamia in ancient times was a flat, monotonous landscape of mudflats, marsh and water. There were no mountains for the gods to dwell in,

The biblical myth of the Tower of Babel is probably based on the terraced temples of Mesopotamia, the ziggurats. The Dur-Kurigalzu ziggurat, pictured below, was built for a Kassite king in the 14th century BCE. Early explorers mistook it for the ruins of the Tower of Babel.

This statue, called the Goddess of the Flowing Cup, was found at Mari. It represents a goddess of fertility, who was believed to provide the fields with water.

only the empty heavens above, the remorseless summer sun, the overturning winds against which there was no protection, the irresistible power of flood-water, the blighting attacks of drought. The gods dwelt in these elemental forces, or in the "high places" which alone dominated the plains, the brick-built towers and ziggurats remembered in the biblical Tower of Babel. The Sumerians, not surprisingly, saw themselves as a people created to labour for the gods.

THE SUMERIAN GODS

By about 2250 BCE a pantheon of gods more or less personifying the elements and natural forces had emerged in Sumer. It was to provide the backbone of Mesopotamian religion and the beginning of theology. Originally, each city had its particular god. Possibly helped by political changes in the relations of the cities, they were in the end organized into a kind of hierarchy which both reflected and affected people's views of human society. The gods of Mesopotamia in the developed scheme are depicted in human form. To each of them was given a special activity or role; there was a god of the air, another of the water, another of the plough. Ishtar (as she was later known under her Semitic name) was the goddess of love and procreation, but also of war. At the top of the hierarchy were three great male gods, whose roles are not easy to disentangle, Anu, Enlil and Enki. Anu was father of the gods. Enlil was at first the most prominent; he was "Lord Air", without whom nothing could be done. Enki, god of wisdom and of the sweet waters that literally meant life to Sumer, was a teacher and life-giver, who maintained the order Enlil had shaped.

These gods demanded propitiation and submission in elaborate ritual. In return for this and for living a good life they would grant prosperity and length of days, but not more. In the midst of the uncertainties of Mesopotamian life, some feeling that a possible access to protection existed was essential. Human beings depended on the gods for reassurance in a capricious universe. The gods – though no Mesopotamian could have put it in these terms – were conceptualizations of elementary attempts to control environment, to resist the sudden disasters of flood and dust-storm, to assure the continuation of the cycle of the seasons by the repetition of the great spring festival when the gods were again married and the drama of creation was re-enacted. After that, the world's existence was assured for another year.

Discovered in the ancient city of Nippur, this relief depicts an offering ceremony being carried out in honour of Enlil, god of earth and air, who is seated on the bottom right. The figure's size symbolizes the god's great importance.

Ziggurats were erected in many Mesopotamian cities. They consisted of brick platforms, built one on top of the other and linked by stairways, and were crowned by a temple. The first ziggurats were built by Ur Nammu (2112–2095 BCE), founder of the third dynasty of Ur. The above illustration is a reconstruction of the Ur ziggurat, based on its remains.

DEATH AND THE AFTERLIFE

One of the great demands which humans later came to make of religion was that it should help them to deal with the inevitable horror of death. The Sumerians and those who inherited their religious ideas can hardly have derived much comfort from their beliefs, in so far as we can apprehend them; they seem to have seen the world of life after death as a gloomy, sad place. It was "The house where they sit in darkness, where dust is their food and clay their meat, they are clothed like birds with wings for garments, over bolt and door lie dust and silence." In it lies the origin of the later notions of Sheol, of Hell. Yet at least one ritual involved virtual suicide, for a Sumerian king and queen of the middle of the third millennium were followed to their tombs by their attendants who were then buried with them, perhaps after taking some soporific drink. This could suggest that the dead were going somewhere where a great retinue and gorgeous jewellery would be as important as on earth.

RELIGION AND POLITICS

There were important political aspects to Sumerian religion. All land belonged ultimately to the gods; the king, probably a king-priest as much as a warrior-leader in origin, was but their vicar. No human tribunal, of course, existed to call him to account. The vicariate also meant the emergence of a priestly class, specialists whose importance justified economic privilege which could permit the cultivation of special skills and knowledge. In this respect, too, Sumer was the origin of a tradition, that of the seers, soothsayers, wise men of the East. They also had charge of the first organized system of education, based on memorizing and copying in the cuneiform script.

SUMERIAN ART

Among the by-products of Sumerian religion were the first true likenesses of human beings in art. In particular at one religious centre,

This plaster statuette, which was found in the Temple of Inanna in Nippur, shows a Sumerian couple in an affectionate pose.

Mari, there seems to have been something of a fondness for portraying human figures engaged in ritual acts. Sometimes they are grouped in processions; thus is established one of the great themes of pictorial art. Two others are also prominent: war and the animal world. Some have detected in the early portraiture of the Sumerians a deeper significance. They have seen in them the psychological qualities which made the astonishing achievements of their civilization possible, a drive for pre-eminence and success. This, again, is speculative. What we can also see for the first time in Sumerian art is much of a daily life in earlier times hidden from us. Given the widespread contacts of Sumer and its basic similarity of structure to other, neighbouring peoples, it is not too much to infer that we can begin to see something of life much as it was lived over a large area of the ancient Near East.

Seals, statuary and painting reveal a people often clad in a kind of furry – goatskin or sheepskin? – skirt, the women sometimes throwing a fold of it over one shoulder. The men are often, but not always, clean-shaven. Soldiers wear the same costume and are only distinguishable because they carry weapons and sometimes wear a pointed leather cap. Luxury seems to have consisted in leisure and possessions other than dress, except for jewellery, of which quantities have survived. Its purpose often seems to be the indication of status and it symptomizes a society of growing complexity. There survives, too, a picture of a drinking-party; a group of men sit in armchairs with cups in their hands while a musician entertains them. At such moments Sumer seems less remote.

MARRIAGE

Sumerian marriage had much about it which would have been familiar to later societies. The crux of the matter was the consent of the bride's family. Once arranged to their satisfaction, a new monogamous family unit was established by the marriage which was recorded in a sealed contract. Its head was the patriarchal husband, who presided over both his relatives and his slaves. It is a pattern which was until very recently observable in most parts of the world. Yet there are interesting nuances. Legal and literary evidence suggest that even in early times Sumerian women were less downtrodden than their sisters in many later

A Sumerian statuette portraying a man with a shaved head. He is wearing the long sheep-skin skirt that was typical of Sumerian dress.

Near-Eastern societies. Semitic and non-Semitic traditions may diverge in this. Sumerian stories about their gods suggest a society that was extremely conscious of the dangerous and even awe-inspiring power of female sexuality; the Sumerians were the very first people to write about passion.

This plaster representation of a woman's head was found in Mari next to the Temple of Ishtar.

WOMEN IN SUMER

It is not always easy to relate attitudes to institutions, but Sumerian law did not regard women as mere chattels, but gave them important rights. Even the slave mother of a free man's children had a certain protection at law. Divorce arrangements provided for women as well as men to seek separations and for the equitable treatment of divorced wives. Though a wife's adultery was punishable by death, while a husband's was not, this difference is to be understood in the light of concern over inheritance and property. It was not until long after Sumerian times that Mesopotamian law began to emphasize the importance of virginity and to impose the veil on respectable women. Both were signs of a hardening and more cramping role for them.

TECHNOLOGY

The Sumerians demonstrated great technical inventiveness. Other peoples would be much in their debt. The influence of the Sumerians' laws can be traced well into post-Sumerian times. Sumerians, too, laid the foundations of mathematics, establishing the technique of expressing number by position as well as by sign (as we, for example, can reckon the figure 1 as one, one-tenth, ten or several other values, according to its relation to the decimal point), and they

The Standard of Ur, a mosaic made of shell and lapis lazuli and depicting scenes of war and peace, was found in one of the royal tombs. In this detail, the Sumerian army's foot soldiers and charioteers are shown going into battle.

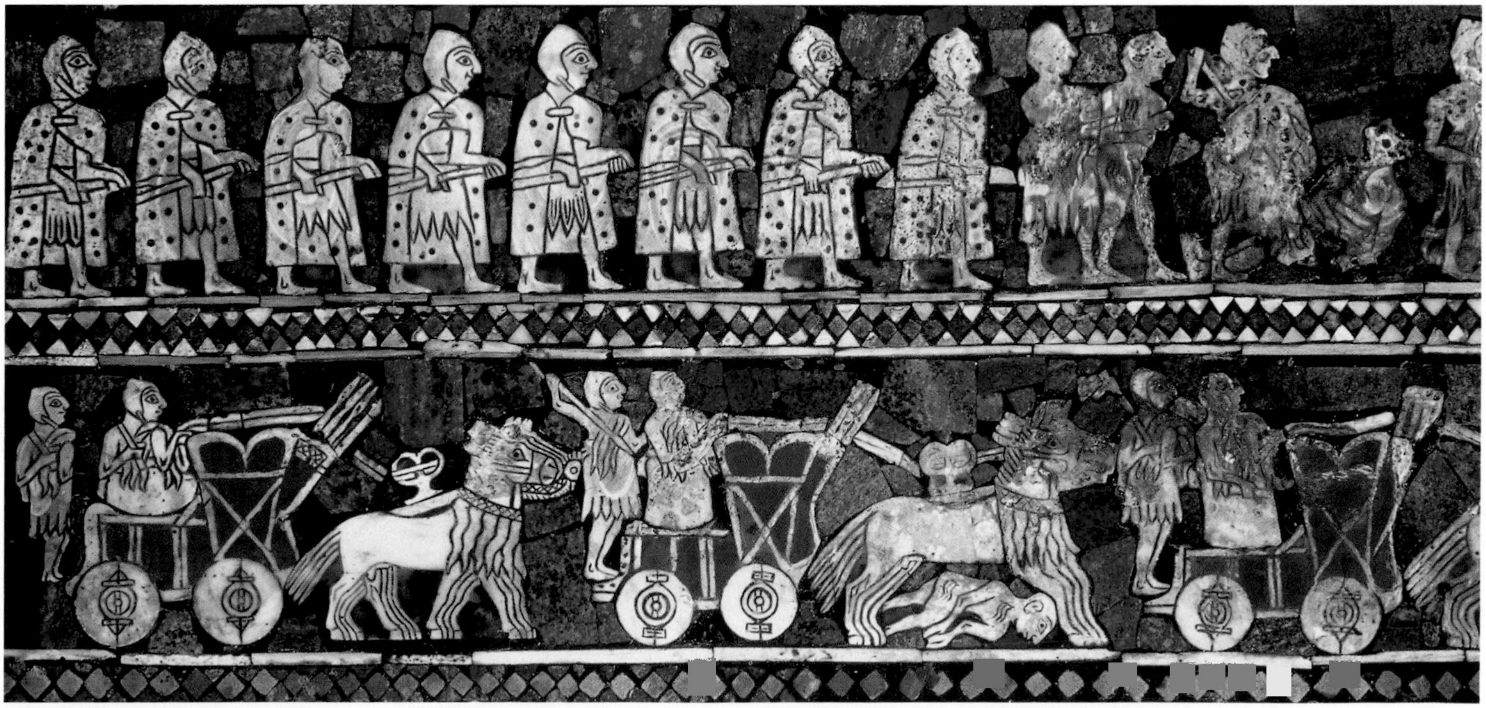

The Ur ziggurat after being partially reconstructed. It was originally built in the 21st century BCE.

arrived at a method of dividing the circle into six equal segments. They knew about the decimal system, too, though they did not exploit it.

By the end of their history as an independent civilization the Sumerians had learnt to live in big groups; one city alone is said to have had thirty-six thousand males. This made big demands on building skill, and even more were made by the large monumental structures. Lacking stone, southern Mesopotamians had first built in reeds plastered with mud, then with bricks made from the mud and dried in the sun. Their brick technology was advanced enough by the end of the Sumerian period to make possible very large buildings with columns and terraces; the greatest of its monuments, the Ziggurat of Ur, had an upper stage over a hundred feet high and a base two hundred feet by a hundred and fifty. The earliest surviving potter's wheel was found at Ur; this was the first way in which use was made of rotary motion. On it rested the large scale production of pottery which made it a man's trade and not, like earlier pottery, a woman's. Soon, by 3000 BCE, the wheel was being used for transport. Another invention of the Sumerians was glass, and specialized craftsmen were casting in bronze early in the third millennium BCE.

The city of Ur (today called Tell al-Muqayyar) was one of the most important cities in Sumer. Because it was located close to what was then the coast, Ur was a major port.

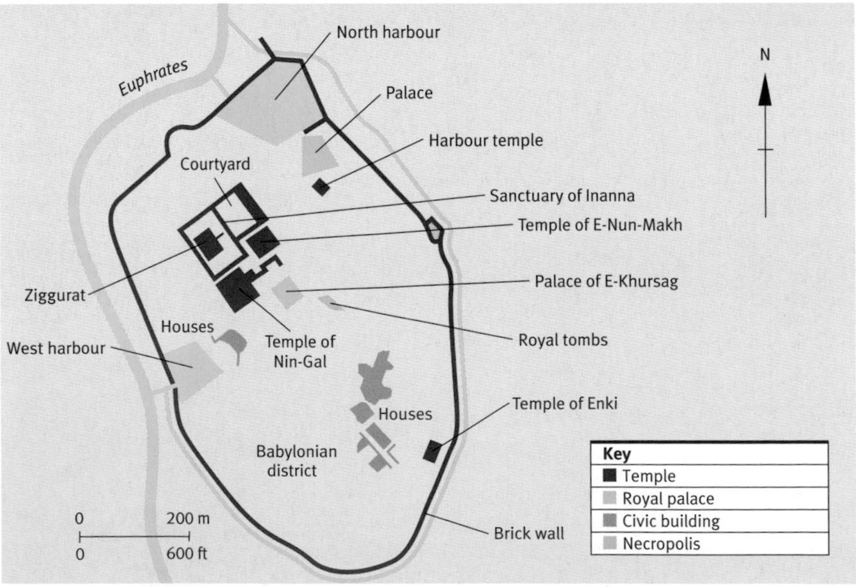

TRADE

Sumerian innovation raises further questions: where did the raw material come from? There is no metal in southern Mesopotamia.

Moreover, even in earlier times, during the Neolithic, the region must have obtained from elsewhere the flint and obsidian it needed to produce the first agricultural implements. Clearly a widespread network of contacts abroad is in the background, above all with the Levant and Syria, huge distances away, but also with Iran and Bahrein, down the Persian Gulf. Before 2000 BCE Mesopotamia was obtaining goods – though possibly indirectly – from the Indus valley. Together with the evidence of documentation (which reveals contacts with India before 2000 BCE), it makes an impression of a dimly emerging international trading system already creating important patterns of interdependence. When, in the middle of the third millennium, supplies of tin from the Near East dried up, Mesopotamian bronze weapons had to give way to unalloyed copper ones.

This bull's head, made of gold and lapis lazuli, once adorned a lyre.

AGRICULTURE

The whole economy was sustained on an agriculture which was from an early date complicated and even rich. Barley, wheat, millet and sesame were grains grown in quantity; the first may have been the main crop, and no doubt explains the frequent evidence of the presence of alcohol in ancient Mesopotamia. In the easy soil of the flood beds iron tools were not needed to achieve intensive cultivation; the great contribution of technology here was in the practice of irrigation and the growth of government. Such skills accumulated slowly; the evidence of Sumerian civilization has been left to us by fifteen hundred years of history.

MESOPOTAMIAN HISTORY

SO FAR THIS HUGE stretch of time has been discussed almost as if nothing happened during it, as if it were an unchanging whole. Of course it was not. Whatever reservations are made about the slowness of change in the ancient world and though it may now seem to us very static, these were fifteen centuries of great change for the Mesopotamians – history, in the truest sense. Scholars have recovered much of the story, but this is not the place to set it out in detail, especially as much of it is still debated, much of it remains obscure and even its dating is for much of the time only approximate. All that is needed here is to relate the first age of Mesopotamian civilization to its successors and to what was going on elsewhere at the same time.

Three broad phases can be marked out in the history of Sumer. The first, lasting from about 3360 BCE to 2400 BCE, has been called its archaic period. Its narrative content is a matter of wars between city states, their waxings and wanings. Fortified cities and the application of the wheel to military technology in clumsy four-wheeled chariots are some of the evidence of this. Towards the middle of this nine-hundred-year phase, local dynasties begin to establish themselves with some success. Originally, Sumerian society seems to have had some representative, even democratic basis, but a growth of scale led to the emergence of kings distinct from the first priestly rulers; probably they began as warlords appointed by cities to command their

Many tombs from the 26th and 25th centuries BCE have been unearthed in Ur. Of these, 17 are thought to have been created for royalty because of their elaborate design and precious contents. This statue of a male goat is made from gold, lapis lazuli, silver and shell. It was found in a tomb where a retinue of 74 people were sacrificed to accompany their lord and master in death.

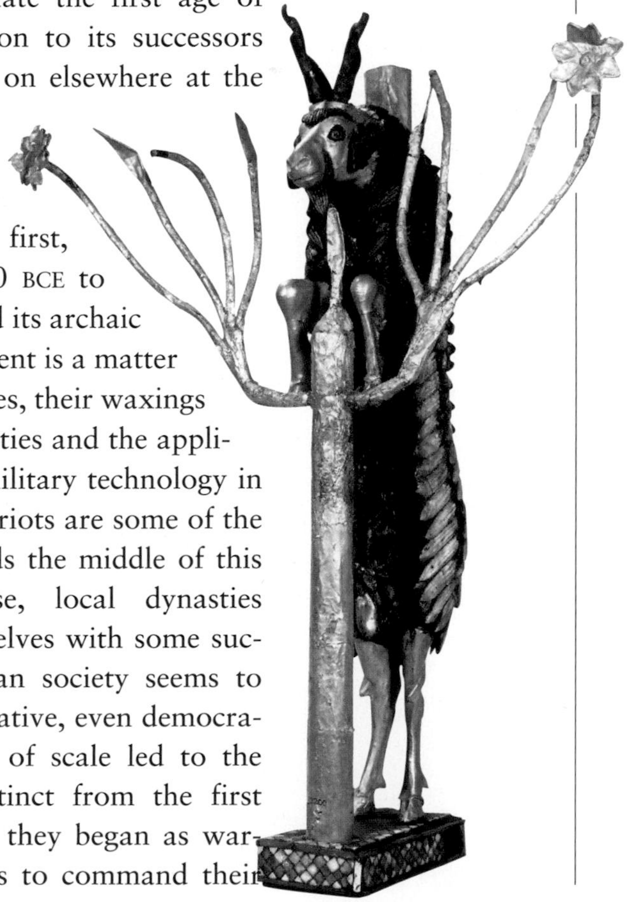

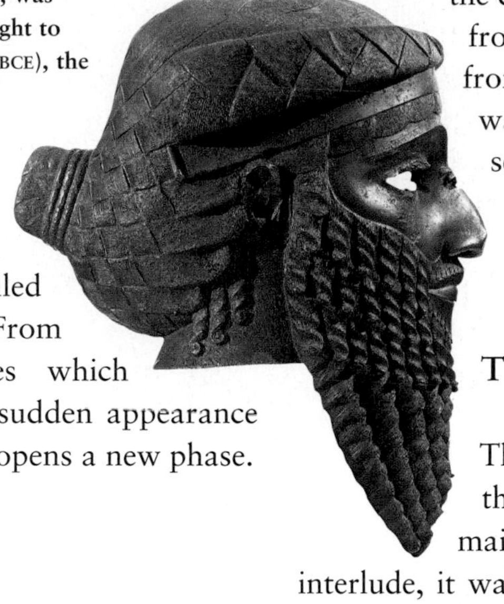

This head, made of cast copper, was found in Nineveh and is thought to represent Naram Sin (2254–2218 BCE), the grandson of Sargon of Akkadia.

forces who did not give up their power when the emergency which called them forth had passed. From them stemmed dynasties which fought one another. The sudden appearance of a great individual then opens a new phase.

SARGON I

Sargon I was a king of the Semitic city of Akkad, who conquered Mesopotamia in 2334 BCE and inaugurated an Akkadian supremacy. There exists a sculpted head which is probably of him; if it is, it is one of the first royal portraits. He was the first of a long line of empire-builders; he has been thought to have sent his troops as far as Egypt and Ethiopia and he drew Sumer into a wider world. Akkadian took cuneiform from Sumer and Sargon's rule was not based on the relative superiority of one city state to another. His regime achieved some degree of integration. His people were among those which for thousands of years pressed in on the civilizations of the river valleys from outside. They took over from its culture what they wanted as they imposed themselves. This left behind a new style of Sumerian art marked by the theme of royal victory.

Rimush, the son and heir of Sargon, had his military victories recorded on a stele, of which this is a fragment.

THE AKKADIAN EMPIRE

The Akkadian empire was not the end of Sumer, but its second main phase. Though itself an interlude, it was important as an expression of a new level of organization. By Sargon's time a true state has appeared. The division between secular and religious authority which had appeared in old Sumer was fundamental. Though the supernatural still penetrated daily life at every level, lay and priestly authority had diverged. The evidence is physically apparent in the appearance of palaces beside the temples in the Sumerian cities; the authority of the gods lay behind their occupants, too.

Obscure though the turning of the notables of early cities into kings remains, the evolution of professional soldiery probably played a part in it. Disciplined infantry, moving in a phalanx with overlapping shields and levelled spears, appear on monuments from Ur. In Akkadia there is something of a climax to early militarism. Sargon, it was boasted, had 5,400 soldiers eating before him in his palace. This, no doubt, was the end of a process which built power on power; conquest provided the resources to maintain such a force. But the beginnings may again have lain originally in the special challenges and needs of Mesopotamia. As population rose, one chief duty of the ruler must have been to mobilize labour for big works of irrigation and flood control. The power to do this could also provide soldiers and as weapons became more complex and

This detail from the Standard of Ur depicts a Sumerian chariot of 4,500 years ago. Each chariot carried two men, one holding the reins and the other ready for combat. The chariot had a compartment designed to hold spears and its wheels were solid pieces.

expensive, professionalism would be more likely. One source of Akkadian success was that they used a new weapon, the composite bow made of strips of wood and horn.

The Akkadian hegemony was relatively short. After two hundred years, under Sargon's great-grandson, it was overthrown, apparently by mountain peoples called Gutians, and the last phase of Sumer, called "neo-Sumerian" by scholars, began. For another two hundred years or so, until 2000 BCE, hegemony again passed to the native Sumerians. This time its centre was Ur and, though it is hard to see what it meant in practice, the first king of the Third Dynasty of Ur who exercised this ascendancy called himself King of Sumer and Akkad. Sumerian art in this phase showed a new tendency to exalt the power of the prince; the tradition of popular portraiture of the archaic period almost vanished. The temples were built again, bigger and better, and the kings seem to have sought to embody their grandeur in the ziggurats. Administrative documents show that the Akkadian legacy was strong, too; neo-Sumerian culture shows many Semitic traits and perhaps the aspiration to wider kingship reflects this inheritance. The provinces which paid tribute to the last successful kings of Ur stretched from Susa, on the frontiers of Elam on the lower Tigris, to Byblos on the coast of Lebanon.

Prisoners are shown being led naked and bound in this detail from the stele of Sharrumkin, King of Akkadia. Sharrumkin, the Sargon of the Bible, was the founder of the first empire to include all Mesopotamia. He is thought to have reigned during the 24th century BCE.

THE SUMERIAN LEGACY

This was the sunset of the first people to achieve civilization. Of course they did not disappear, but their individuality was about to be merged in the general history of Mesopotamia and the Near East. Their great creative era was behind them and has focused our attention on a relatively small area; the horizons of history are about to expand. Enemies abounded on the frontiers. In about 2000 BCE, the Elamites came and Ur fell to them. Why, we do not know. There had been intermittent hostility between the peoples for a thousand years and some have seen in this the outcome of a struggle to control the routes of Iran which could guarantee access to the highlands where lay minerals the Mesopotamians needed. At all events, it was the end of Ur. With it disappeared the distinctive Sumerian tradition, now merged in the swirling currents of a world of more than one civilization. It would now be only visible occasionally in patterns made by others. For fifteen centuries or so Sumer had built up the subsoil of civilization in Mesopotamia, just as its precivilized forerunners had built up the physical subsoil on which it itself rested. It left behind writing, mathematics, monumental buildings, an idea of justice and legalism and the beginnings of a great religious tradition. It is a considerable record and the seed of much else. The Mesopotamian tradition had a long life ahead of it and every side of it was touched by the Sumerian legacy.

NEW PEOPLES IN THE NEAR EAST

While the Sumerians had been building up their civilization, their influence had contributed to changes elsewhere. All over the Fertile Crescent new kingdoms and peoples had been appearing. They were stimulated or taught by what they saw in the south and by the empire of Ur, as well as by their own needs. The diffusion of civilized ways was already rapid. This makes it very hard to

In the inner courtyard of the grand palace of Mari, fragments of paintings dating from the beginning of the 28th century BCE have been discovered. This section probably represents a sacrificial scene. The gigantic figure – only his arm and the bottom of his clothes can be seen – is thought to be the king.

delineate and categorize the main processes of these centuries in a clear-cut way. Worse still, the Near East was for long periods a great confusion of peoples, moving about for reasons we often do not understand. The Akkadians themselves had been one of them, pushing up originally from the great Semitic reservoir of Arabia to finish in Mesopotamia.

The Gutians, who took part in the Akkadians' overthrow, were Caucasians. The most successful of all of these peoples were the Amorites, a Semitic stock which had spread far and wide and joined the Elamites to overthrow the armies of Ur and destroy its supremacy. They had established themselves in Assyria, or upper Mesopotamia, in Damascus, and in Babylon in a series of kingdoms which stretched as far as the coast of Palestine. Southern Mesopotamia, old Sumer, they continued to dispute with the Elamites. In Anatolia their neighbours were the Hittites, an Indo-European people which crossed from the Balkans in the third millennium. At the edges of this huge confusion stood another old civilization, Egypt, and the vigorous Indo-European peoples who had filled up Iran. The picture is a chaos; the area is a maelstrom of races pushing into it from all sides. Patterns grow hard to distinguish.

THE BABYLONIAN EMPIRE

One convenient landmark is provided by the appearance of a new empire in Mesopotamia, one which has left behind a famous name: Babylon. Another famous name is inseparably linked to it, that of one of its kings, Hammurabi. He would have a secure place in history if we knew nothing of him except his reputation as a law-giver; his code is the oldest statement of the legal principle of an eye for an eye. He was also the first ruler to unify the whole of Mesopotamia, and though the empire was short-lived the city of Babylon was to be from his time the symbolic centre of the Semitic peoples of the

Many statues have been found of Gudea, who was king of Lagash in the 21st century BCE. Gudea ruled during the neo-Sumerian age, which followed the decline of the Akkadian empire.

This 19th-century BCE bronze statuette depicts Warad-Sin, sovereign of Larsa, carrying a basket. For centuries this was the traditional style for votive figures, which were buried in the foundations of the temples.

south. It began with the triumph of one Amorite tribe over its rivals in the confused period following the collapse of Ur. Hammurabi may have become ruler in 1792 BCE; his successors held things together until sometime after 1600 BCE, when the Hittites destroyed Babylon and Mesopotamia was once more divided between rival peoples who flowed into it from all sides.

At its height the first Babylonian empire ran from Sumeria and the Persian Gulf north to Assyria, the upper part of Mesopotamia. Hammurabi ruled the cities of Nineveh and Nimrud on the Tigris, Mari high on the Euphrates, and controlled that river up to the point at which it is nearest to Aleppo. Seven hundred or so miles long and about a hundred miles wide, this was a great state, the greatest, indeed, to appear in the region up to this time, for the empire of Ur had been a looser, tributary affair.

This diorite bust shows a headdress typical of those worn by Mesopotamian kings at the beginning of the 2nd millennium BCE.

HAMMURABI'S CODE OF LAWS

The empire had an elaborate administrative structure, and Hammurabi's code of laws is justly famous, though it owes something of its pre-eminence to chance. As probably happened to earlier collections of judgements and rules which have only survived in fragments, Hammurabi's was cut in stone and set up in the courtyard of temples for the public to consult. But at greater length and in a more ordered way than earlier collections it assembled some 282 articles, dealing comprehensively with a wide range of questions: wages, divorce, fees for medical attention and many other matters. This was not legislation, but a declaration of existing law, and to speak of a "code" may be misleading unless this is remembered. Hammurabi assembled rules already current; he did not create those laws *de novo*. This body of "common law" provided one of the major continuities of Mesopotamian history.

The family, land and commerce seem to be the main concerns of this compilation of rules. It gives a picture of a society already far beyond regulation by the ties of kindred, local community and the government of village headmen. By Hammurabi's time the judicial process had emerged from the temple and non-priestly courts were the rule. In them sat the local town notables and from them appeals lay to Babylon and the king himself. Hammurabi's stele (the stone pillar on which his code was carved) stated that its aim was to assure justice by publishing the law:

Let the oppressed man who has a cause
Come into the presence of my statue
And read carefully my inscribed stele.

The first written laws

The oldest known system of laws was created by King Hammurabi of Babylonia and dates from the 18th century BCE. It is thought that the articles are based on a common law tradition that began during the Sumerian period. The laws were engraved on a monolith that is now kept in the Louvre museum in Paris. Its articles regulate a number of issues, including property, slavery, family, trade, prices and wages, loans and the payment of interest, and crimes and their punishments. At the top of the monolith on which the Laws of Hammurabi are engraved, the King added his own image. He is depicted listening respectfully to Shamash, the god of justice, who is seated on his throne with the attributes of power held in his right hand and flames blazing around his shoulders. Shamash is ordering Hammurabi to carry out his wishes, in much the same way as Moses receives instructions from Yahweh in the Bible.

A detail from the stone monolith on which the Laws of Hammurabi are inscribed.

Sadly, perhaps, its penalties seem to have harshened, by comparison with older Sumerian practice, but in other respects, such as the laws affecting women, Sumerian tradition survived in Babylon.

SLAVERY AND LUXURY

The provisions of Hammurabi's code in respect of property included laws about slaves. Babylon, like every other ancient civilization and many of modern times, rested on slavery. Very possibly the origin of slavery is conquest; certainly slavery was the fate which probably awaited the loser of any of the wars of early history and his women and children, too. But by the time of the first Babylonian empire, regular slave-markets existed and there was a steadiness of price which indicates a fairly regular trade. Slaves from certain districts were especially prized for their reliable qualities. Though the master's hold on the slave was virtually absolute, some Babylonian slaves enjoyed remarkable independence, engaging in business and even owning slaves on their own account. They had legal rights, if narrow ones.

It is hard to assess what slavery meant in practice in a world lacking the assumption which we take for granted that chattel slavery cannot be justified. Generalities dissolve in the light of evidence about the diversity of things slaves might do; if most lived hard lives, then so, probably, did most people who were free. Yet it is hard to feel anything but pity for the lives of captives being led away to slavery before conquering kings on scores of memorials from the "golden standard" of Ur in the middle of the third millennium to the stone reliefs of Assyrian conquests fifteen hundred years later. The ancient world rested civilization on a great exploitation of man by man; if it was not felt to be very cruel, this is only to say that no other possible way of running things was conceivable.

Babylonian civilization in due time became a legend of magnificence. The survival of one of the great images of city life – the worldly, wicked city of pleasure and consumption – in the name "Babylon" was a legacy which speaks of the scale and richness of its civilization, though it owes most to a later period. Yet enough remains, too, to see the reality behind this myth, even for the first Babylonian empire. The great palace of Mari is an outstanding example; walls in places forty feet thick surrounded courtyards, three hundred or so rooms forming a complex drained by bitumen-lined pipes running thirty feet deep. It covered an area measuring 150 by over 200 yards and is the finest evidence of the authority the monarch had come to enjoy. In this palace, too, were found great quantities of clay tablets whose writing reveals the business and detail which government embraces by this period.

CULTURE AND SCIENCE

Many more tablets survive from the first Babylonian empire than from its predecessors or immediate successors. They provide the

The city of Mari (today Tell Hariri, Syria) was founded beside the Euphrates River nearly 5,000 years ago. Mari was deserted after it was sacked by Hammurabi in the 18th century BCE.

Numerous clay plaques evoke different aspects of life in Mesopotamia almost 4,000 years ago. Here a carpenter is depicted at work.

detail which enables us to know this civilization better, it has been pointed out, than we know some European countries of a thousand years ago. They contribute evidence of the life of the mind in Babylon, too. It was then that the Epic of Gilgamesh took the shape in which we know it. The Babylonians gave cuneiform script a syllabic form, thus enormously increasing its flexibility and usefulness. Their astrology pushed forward the observation of nature and left another myth behind, that of the wisdom of the Chaldeans, a name sometimes misleadingly given to the Babylonians. Hoping to understand their destinies by scanning the stars, the Babylonians built up a science, astronomy, and established an important series of observations which was another major legacy of their culture. It took centuries to accumulate after its beginnings in Ur but by 1000 BCE the prediction of lunar eclipses was possible and within another two or three centuries the path of the sun and some of the planets had been plotted with remarkable accuracy against the positions of the apparently fixed stars. This was a scientific tradition reflected in Babylonian mathematics, which has passed on to us the sexagesimal system of Sumer in our circle of 360 degrees and the hour of sixty minutes. The Babylonians also worked out mathematical tables and an algebraic geometry of great practical utility.

BABYLONIAN RELIGION

Astronomy began in the temple, in the contemplation of celestial movements announcing the advent of festivals of fertility and sowing, and Babylonian religion held close to the Sumerian tradition. Like the old cities, Babylon had a civic god, Marduk; gradually he elbowed his way to the front among his Mesopotamian rivals. This took a

In this clay plaque a musician is shown strumming a harp.

long time. Hammurabi said (significantly) that Anu and Enlil, the Sumerian gods, had conferred the headship of the Mesopotamian pantheon upon Marduk, much as they had bidden him to rule over all men for their good. Subsequent vicissitudes (sometimes accompanied by the abduction of his statue by invaders) obscured Marduk's status, but after the twelfth century BCE it was usually unquestioned. Meanwhile, Sumerian tradition remained alive well into the first millennium BCE in the use of Sumerian in the Babylonian liturgies, in the names of the gods and the attributions they enjoyed. Babylonian cosmogony began, like that of Sumer, with the creation of the world from watery waste (the name of one god meant "silt") and the eventual fabrication of humans as the slaves of the gods. In one version, gods turned people out like bricks, from clay moulds. It was a world picture suited to absolute monarchy, where kings exercised power like that of gods over the slaves who toiled to build their palaces and sustained a hierarchy of officials and great men which mirrored that of the heavens.

This statue depicts Ishtulilum, who ruled Mari in the year 2100 BCE. The expression on his face is noticeably stern.

THE FALL OF BABYLON

The achievement of Hammurabi did not long survive him. Events in northern Mesopotamia indicated the appearance of a new power even before he formed his empire. Hammurabi had overthrown an Amorite kingdom which had established itself in Assyria at the end of the hegemony of Ur. This was a temporary success. There followed nearly a thousand years during which Assyria was to be a battleground and prize, eventually overshadowing a Babylon from which it was separated; the centre of gravity of Mesopotamian history had decisively moved northwards from old Sumer. The Hittites, who were establishing themselves in Anatolia in the last quarter of the third millennium BCE, were pushing slowly forwards in the next few centuries; during this time they took up the cuneiform script, which they adapted to their own Indo-European language. By 1700 BCE they ruled the lands between Syria and the Black Sea. Then, one of their kings turned southwards against a Babylonia already weakened and shrunken to the old land of Akkad. His successor carried the advance to completion; Babylon was taken and plundered and Hammurabi's dynasty and achievement finally came to an end. But then the Hittites withdrew and other peoples ruled and disputed Mesopotamia for a mysterious four centuries of which we know little except that during them the separation of Assyria and Babylonia which was to be so important in the next millennium was made final.

In 1162 BCE the statue of Marduk was again taken away from Babylon by Elamite conquerors. By that time, a very confused era has opened and the focus of world history has shifted away from Mesopotamia. The story of the Assyrian empire still lies ahead, but its background is a new wave of migrations in the thirteenth and twelfth centuries BCE which involve other civilizations far more directly and deeply than the successors of the Sumerians. Those successors, their conquerors and displacers, none the less built on the foundations laid in Sumer. Technically, intellectually, legally, theologically, the Near East, which by 1000 BCE was sucked into the vortex of world politics – the term is by then not too strong – still bore the stamp of the makers of the first civilization. Their heritage would pass in strangely transmuted forms to others in turn.

Excavations at Ebla, Syria, have revealed temples, palaces and walls dating from 2600 to 1600 BCE. The most important find was that of the palace archives. Thousands of tablets remained intact, having been baked during the fire that destroyed most of the city.

3 ANCIENT EGYPT

MESOPOTAMIA WAS NOT the only great river valley to cradle a civilization, but the only early example to rival it in the antiquity and staying power of what was created was that of Egypt. For thousands of years after it had died, the physical remains of the first civilization in the Nile valley fascinated people and stirred their imaginations; even the Greeks were bemused by the legend of the occult wisdom of a land where gods were half human, half beast, and people still waste their time trying to discern a supernatural significance in the arrangement of the pyramids. Ancient Egypt has always been our greatest visible inheritance from antiquity.

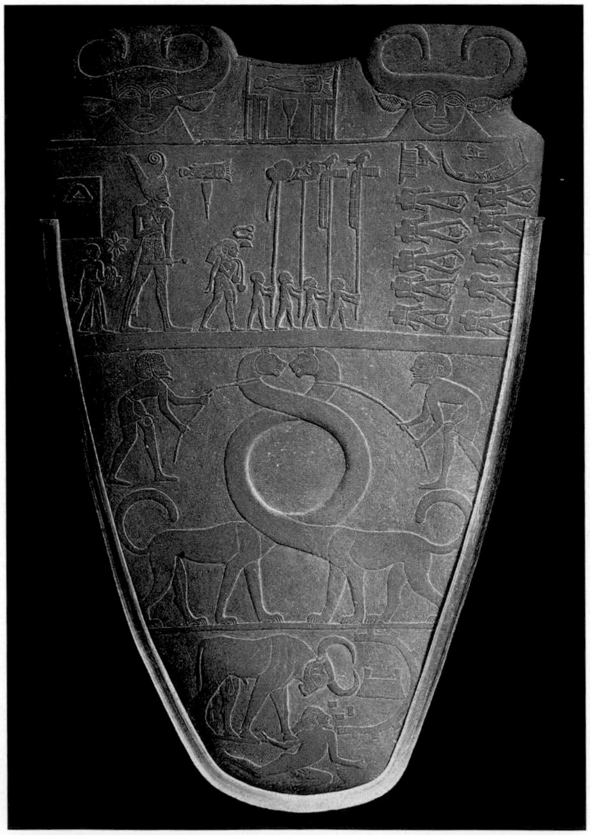

The palette of King Narmer, found in Hieraconpolis in 1898 CE, dates from 5,000 years ago. At the top of the palette, the king's name appears in hieroglyphics, framed by two humanized cows' heads representing the goddess Hathor. Below this, the king, wearing the crown of Lower Egypt, inspects a battlefield.

MESOPOTAMIAN INFLUENCE

The richness of its remains is one reason why we know more about Egyptian than about much of Mesopotamian history. In another way, too, there is an important difference between these civilizations: because Sumerian civilization appeared first, Egypt could benefit from its experience and example. Exactly what this meant has been much debated. Mesopotamian contributions have been seen in the motifs of early Egyptian art, in the presence of cylinder seals at the outset of Egyptian records, in similar techniques of monumental building in brick and in the debt of hieroglyph, the pictorial writing of Egypt, to early Sumerian script. That there were important and fruitful connections between early Egypt and Sumer seems incontestable, but how and when the first encounter of the Nile peoples with Sumer came about will probably never be known. It seems at least likely that when it came, Sumerian influence was transmitted by way of the peoples of the delta and lower Nile. In any case, these influences operated in a setting which always radically differentiated Egyptian experience from that of any other centre of civilization. This was provided by the Nile itself, the heart of Egypt's prehistory, as of its history.

THE ROLE OF THE NILE

Egypt was defined by the Nile and the deserts which flanked it; it was the country the river watered, one drawn-out straggling oasis. In prehistoric times it must also have been one great marsh, six hundred miles long, and, except in the delta, never more than a few miles wide. From the start the annual floods of the river were the basic mechanism of the economy and set the rhythm of life on its banks. Farming gradually took root in the beds of mud deposited higher and higher year by year, but the first communities must have been precarious and their environment semi-aquatic; much of their life has been irrecoverably swept away to the delta silt-beds. What remain of the earliest times are things made and used by the peoples who lived on the edge of the flood areas or on occasional rocky projections within it or at the valley sides. Before 4000 BCE they began to feel the impact of an important climatic change. Sand drifted in from the deserts and desiccation set in. Armed with elementary agricultural techniques, these people could move down to work the rich soils of the flood-plain.

The river was, therefore, from the start the bringer of life to Egypt. It was a benevolent deity whose never-failing bounty was to be thankfully received, rather than the dangerous, menacing source of sudden, ruinous inundations, like those in which the people of Sumer struggled to make land out of a watery waste. It was a setting in which agriculture (though introduced later than in the Levant or Anatolia) gave a quick and rich return and perhaps made possible a population "explosion" which released its human and natural resources. Although, as signs of contact in the fourth millennium BCE show, Sumerian experience may have been available as a fertilizing element, it cannot be said that it was decisive; there always existed a potential for civilization in the Nile valley and it may have needed no external stimulus to discharge it. It is at least obvious, when Egyptian civilization finally emerged, that it is unique, unlike anything we can find elsewhere.

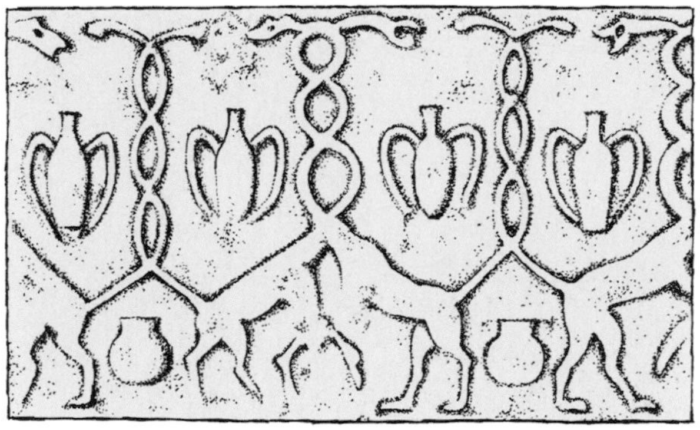

This drawing represents the markings on a Sumerian cylinder. The appearance of similar Mesopotamian subjects on King Narmer's palette indicates Mesopotamia's cultural influence on the early Egyptian civilization.

In the middle of the desert, the Nile valley forms a long and narrow oasis. In ancient Egypt, as there were no bridges over the main section of the river, ferries constantly crossed the water, linking communities on opposite banks. Larger sail and rowing boats travelled north and south, linking Lower and Upper Egypt.

Shallow Egyptian ships, such as the one depicted on this pre-dynastic pottery vase, were powered by oars or by sail, depending on the direction of the journey. Because the wind in Egypt blew consistently from the north, sail could only be used on the Nile to travel southwards.

THE NEOLITHIC HAMITIC PEOPLES

The deepest roots of this civilization have to be pieced together from archaeology and later tradition. They reveal Hamitic peoples in Upper Egypt (the south, that is, up the Nile) in Neolithic times. From about 5000 BCE such peoples were hunting, fishing, gathering crops and finally embarking on purposeful cultivation in the valley. They lived in villages grouped around market centres and seem to have belonged to clans which had animals as symbols or totems; these they copied on their pottery. This was the basis of the eventual political organization of Egypt, which began with the emergence of clan chiefs controlling the regions inhabited by their followers.

At an early stage these peoples already had several important technological accomplishments to their credit, though they do not seem such advanced farmers as those of other parts of the ancient Near East. They knew how to make papyrus boats, how to work hard materials such as basalt, and how to hammer copper into small articles for daily use. They were, that is to say, pretty accomplished well before the dawn of written record, with specialist craftsmen and, to judge by their jewels, well-marked distinctions of class or status. Then, somewhere about the middle of the fourth millennium BCE, there is an intensification of foreign influences, apparent first in the north, the delta. Signs of trade and contact with other regions multiply,

There are no obstacles to shipping on the Nile from its mouth to what ancient Egyptians called "the first waterfall" (a stretch of cataracts, or rapids, that marked the traditional border between Egypt and Nubia).

notably with Mesopotamia, whose influence is shown in the art of this era. Meanwhile, hunting and occasional farming give way to a more intense cultivation. In art, the bas-relief appears which is to be so important later in the Egyptian tradition; copper goods become more plentiful. Everything seems suddenly to be emerging at once, almost without antecedents, and to this epoch belongs the basic political structure of the future kingdom.

UPPER AND LOWER EGYPT

At some time in the fourth millennium BCE there solidified two kingdoms, one northern, one southern, one of Lower and one of Upper Egypt. This is interestingly different from Sumer; there were no city states. Egypt seems to move straight from pre-civilization to the government of large areas. There was no era of city states. Egypt's early "towns" were the market-places of agriculturalists; the agricultural communities and clans coalesced into groups which were the foundation of later provinces. Egypt was to be a united political whole seven hundred years before Mesopotamia, and even later she would have only a restricted experience of city life.

Of the kings of the two Egypts we know little until about 3200 BCE, but we may guess that they were the eventual winners in centuries of struggles to consolidate power over larger and larger groups of people. It is about the same time that the written record begins and because writing is already there at the beginning of the Egyptian story, a much more historical account of the development of its civilization can be put together than in the case of Sumer. In Egypt, writing was used from its first appearance not merely as an administrative and economic convenience but to record events on monuments and relics intended to survive.

Arable land in ancient Egypt

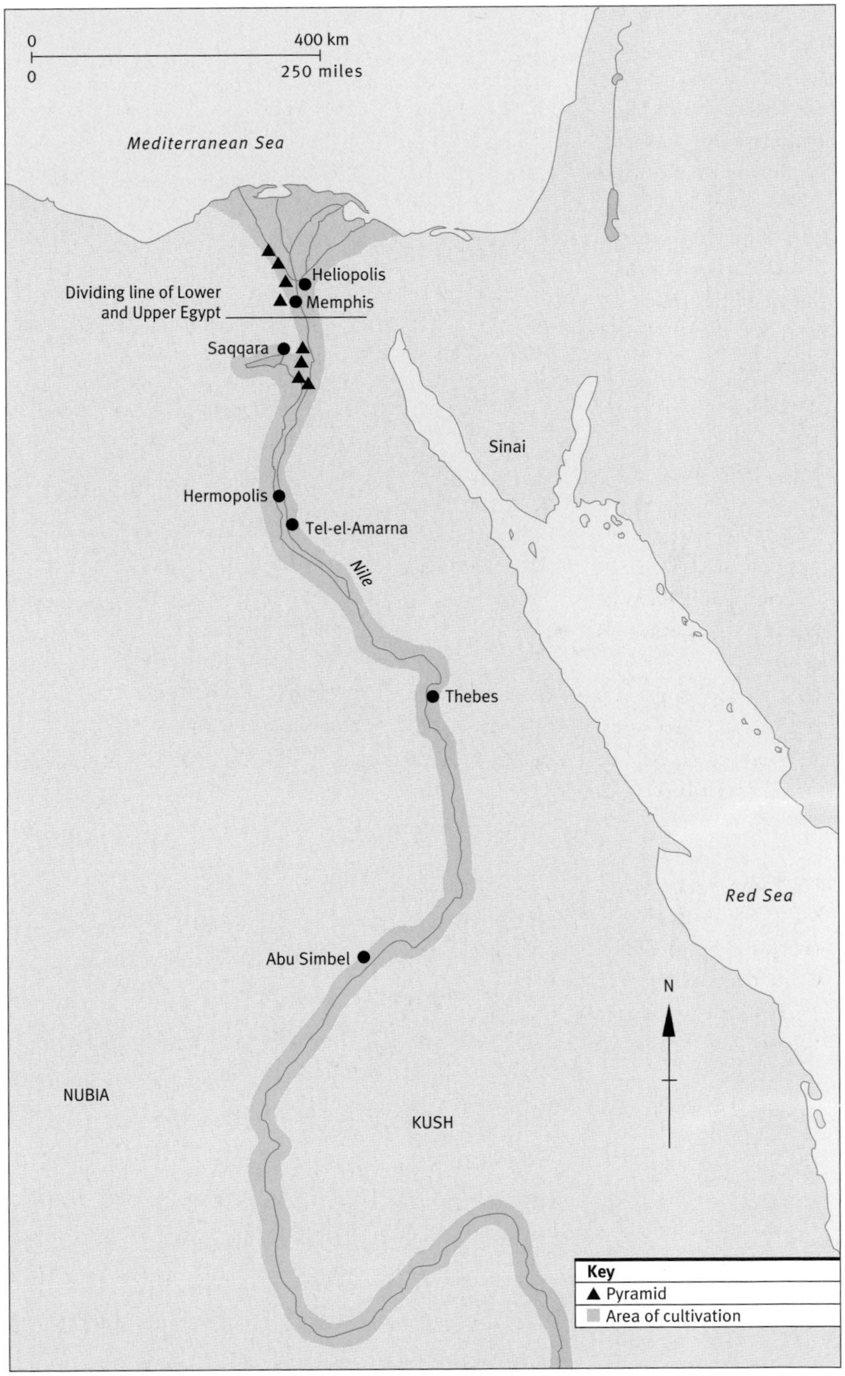

The above map shows the location of arable land in ancient Egypt. Land that could be cultivated was limited to areas that could be watered from the River Nile – a long narrow strip of land in Upper Egypt and a wide triangular area in the delta region in Lower Egypt. During the summer months, the Nile, swelled by rainwater in the south, swept northwards, flooding the plains. When it receded, it left behind a rich belt of fertile silt, which was capable of sustaining two successive crops each year.

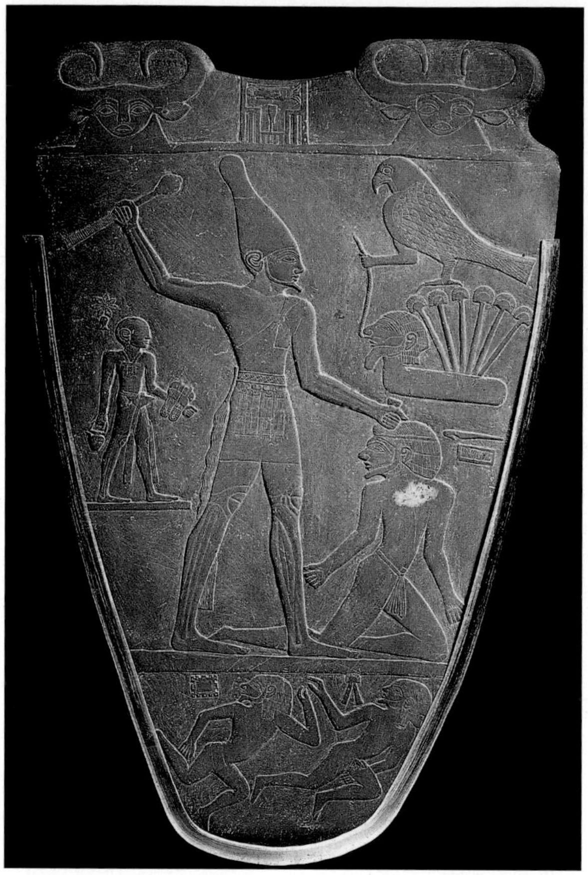

A verse from King Narmer's palette, in which the king, wearing the crown of Upper Egypt, prepares to strike down an enemy. To the right, the hawk god Horus, symbol of royalty, holds a hieroglyph representing the territory of the delta. The scene refers to the battles that preceded the unification of Egypt.

UNIFICATION

In about 3200 BCE, the records tell us, a great king of Upper Egypt, Menes, conquered the north. Egypt was thus unified in a huge state six hundred miles long, running up the river as far as Abu Simbel. It was to be even bigger and to extend even further up the great river which was its heart, and it was also to undergo disruption from time to time, but this is effectively the beginning of a civilization which was to survive into the age of classical Greece and Rome. For nearly three thousand years – one and a half times the life of Christianity – Egypt was a historical entity, for much of it a source of wonder and focus of admiration. In so long a period much happened and we by no means know all of it. Yet it is the stability and conservative power of Egyptian civilization which is the most striking thing about it, not its vicissitudes.

CHRONOLOGY

Roughly speaking, that civilization's greatest days were over by about 1000 BCE. Before that date, Egyptian history can most easily be visualized in five big divisions. Three of these are called respectively the Old, Middle and New Kingdoms; they are separated by two others called the First and Second Intermediate periods. Very roughly, the three "kingdoms" are periods of success or at least of consolidated government; the two intermediate stages are interludes of weakness and disruption from external and internal causes. The whole scheme can be envisaged as a kind of layer cake, with three tiers of different flavours separated by two layers of somewhat formless jam.

This is by no means the only way of understanding Egyptian history, nor for all purposes the best. Many scholars use an alternative way of setting out ancient Egyptian chronology in terms of more than thirty dynasties of kings, a system which has the great advantage of being related to objective criteria; it avoids perfectly proper but awkward disagreements about whether (for example) the first dynasties should be put in the "Old Kingdom" or distinguished as a separate "archaic" period, or about the line to be drawn at the beginning or end of the intermediate era. None the less, a five-part scheme, if we also distinguish an archaic prelude, is sufficient to make sense of ancient Egyptian history, as set out in the accompanying table.

In the first millennium BCE, as in Mesopotamian history, there is something of a break as Egypt is caught up in a great series of upheavals originating outside its own boundaries to which the overworked word "crisis" can reasonably be applied. True, it is not until several more centuries have passed that the old Egyptian tradition really comes to an end. Some modern Egyptians insist on a continuing sense of identity among Egyptians since the days of the pharaohs. None the less, somewhere about the beginning of the first millennium BCE is one of the most convenient places at which to break the story, if only because the greatest achievements of the Egyptians were by then behind them.

THE MONARCHICAL STATE

EGYPT'S GREAT ACHIEVEMENTS were above all the work of and centred in the monarchical state. The state form itself was the expression of Egyptian civilization. It was focused first at Memphis whose building was

Chronology of the Egyptian Dynasties

1 2 3 4 5 6 7 8

The chronology of ancient Egypt poses many problems, in that there is a margin of doubt of some 150 years as to when the first dynasty began. Exact dates are only available after the year 664 BCE, which was the date of the beginning of the 26th Dynasty. The dynastic lists were established in ancient times and used in the history written in Greek, by Manetho, in the 3rd century BCE. Some dynasties reigned simultaneously over different parts of Egypt. One widely accepted current dating system, together with the dynastic synchronization, is as follows:

Early Dynastic Period 3000–2625 BCE
1st Dynasty 3000–2800
2nd Dynasty 2800–2675
3rd Dynasty 2675–2625

Old Kingdom 2625–2130 BCE
4th Dynasty 2625–2500
5th Dynasty 2500–2350
6th Dynasty 2350–2170
7th and 8th Dynasties 2170–2130

First Intermediate Period 2130–1980 BCE
9th and 10th Dynasties (Heracleopolis) 2130–1980
11th Dynasty (Thebes) 2081–1938

Middle Kingdom 1980–1630 BCE
11th Dynasty (all Egypt) 2040–1991
12th Dynasty 1938–1759
13th and 14th Dynasties 1759–c.1630

Second Intermediate Period 1630–1523/39 BCE
15th and 16th Dynasties (Hyksos) 1630–1523
17th Dynasty (Thebes) 1630–1539

New Kingdom 1539–1075 BCE
18th Dynasty 1539–1292
19th Dynasty 1292–1190
20th Dynasty 1190–1075

Third Intermediate Period 1075–656 BCE
21st Dynasty 1075–945
22nd Dynasty 945–712
23rd Dynasty 838–712
24th Dynasty (Saïs) 727–712
25th Dynasty (Nubian) 760–756

Late Period 664–332 BCE
26th Dynasty 664–525
27th Dynasty (Persian) 525–405
28th Dynasty 409–399
29th Dynasty 399–380
30th Dynasty 381–343
31st Dynasty (Persian) 343–332

Hellenistic Period 332–30 BCE
32nd Dynasty (Macedonian) 332–305
33rd Dynasty (Ptolemaic) 305–30

The names of some of the most important pharaohs, the statues and funerary masks of whom are illustrated above, are as follows:

1 Djoser, 2630–2611
2 Cheops (Khufu), 2585–2560
3 Cephren (Khafre), 2555–2532
4 Mycerinus (Menkaure), 2532–2510
5 Ahmose I, 1539–1514
6 Tuthmosis III (Thutmose), 1479–1425
7 Amenhotep IV (Akhnaton), 1353–1336
8 Rameses II, 1279–1213

This sculpture was discovered in the temple built for King Mycerinus of the 4th Dynasty. The king is shown with the goddess Hathor on his right and the personification of a province on his left.

begun during the lifetime of Menes and which was the capital of the Old Kingdom. Later, under the New Kingdom, the capital was normally at Thebes, though there were also periods of uncertainty about where it was. Memphis and Thebes were great religious centres and palace complexes; they did not really progress beyond this to true urbanism. The absence of cities earlier was politically important, too. Egypt's kings had not emerged like Sumer's as the "big men" in a city-state community which originally deputed them to act for it. Nor were they simply men who like others were subject to gods who ruled all men, great or small. The tension of palace with temple was missing in Egypt and when Egyptian kingship emerges it is unrivalled. The pharaohs were to be gods, not servants of gods.

THE PHARAOHS

It was only under the New Kingdom that the title "pharaoh" came to be applied personally to the king. Before that it indicated the king's residence and his court. None the less, at a much earlier stage Egyptian monarchs already had the authority which was so to impress the ancient world. It is expressed in the size with which they are depicted on the earliest monuments. This they inherited ultimately from prehistoric kings who had a special sanctity because of their power to assure prosperity through successful agriculture. Such powers are enjoyed by some African rainmaker-kings even today; in ancient Egypt they focused upon the Nile. The pharaohs were believed to control its annual rise and fall: life itself, no less, to the riparian communities. The first rituals of Egyptian kingship which are known to us are concerned with fertility, irrigation and land reclamation. The earliest representations of Menes show him excavating a canal.

Under the Old Kingdom the idea appears that the king is the absolute lord of the land. Soon he is venerated as a descendant of the gods, the original lords of the land. He becomes a god, Horus, son of Osiris, and takes on the mighty and terrible attributes of the divine maker of order; the bodies of his enemies are depicted hanging in rows like dead gamebirds, or kneeling in supplication lest (like less fortunate enemies) their brains be ritually dashed out. Justice is "what Pharaoh loves", evil "what Pharaoh hates"; he is divinely omniscient and so needs no code of law to guide him. Later, under the New Kingdom, the pharaohs were to be depicted with the heroic stature of the great warriors of other contemporary cultures; they are shown in their chariots, mighty men of war, trampling down their enemies and confidently slaughtering beasts of prey. Perhaps a measure of secularization can be inferred in this change, but it does not remove Egyptian kingship from the region of the sacred and awesome. "He is a god by whose dealings one lives, the father and mother of all men, alone by himself, without an equal", wrote one of the chief civil servants of the pharaoh as late as about 1500 BCE. Until the Middle Kingdom, only he had an afterlife to look forward to. Egypt, more than any other Bronze Age state, always stressed the incarnation of the god in the king, even when that idea was increasingly exposed by the realities of life in the New Kingdom and the coming of iron. Then, the disasters which befell Egypt at the hands of foreigners would make it impossible to continue to believe that Pharaoh was god of all the world.

BUREAUCRACY

Long before the New Kingdom, the Egyptian state had acquired another institutional embodiment and armature, an elaborate and

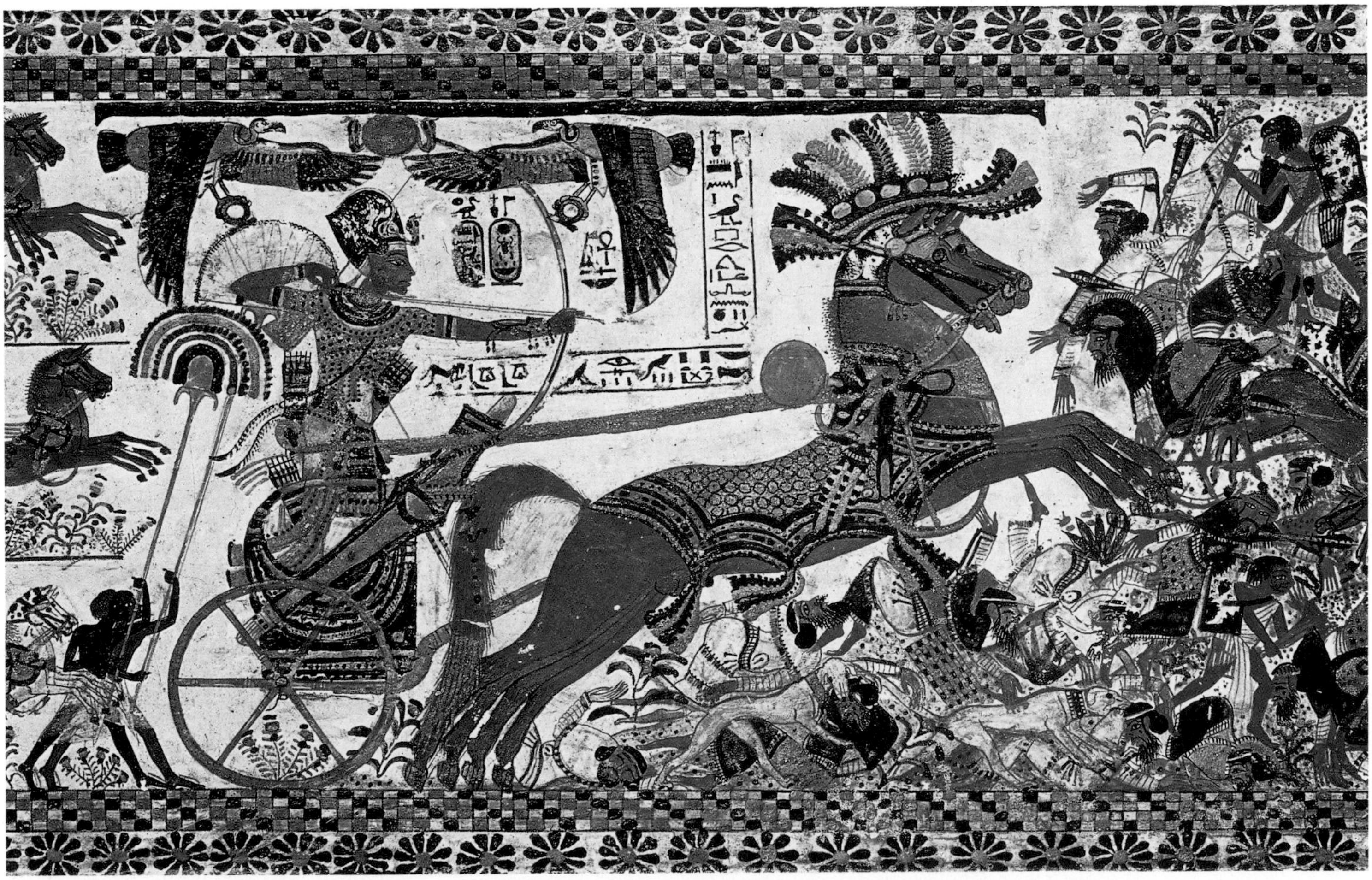

The heroic image of a pharaoh in his war chariot, shooting arrows at the enemy, often appears in Egyptian art. In this case, Tutankhamon is shown leading his troops in an attack against an Asian army.

impressive hierarchy of bureaucrats. At its apex were viziers, provincial governors and senior officials who came mainly from the nobility; a few of the greatest of these were buried with a pomp that rivalled that of the pharaohs. Less eminent families provided the thousands of scribes needed to staff and service an elaborate government directed by the chief civil servants. The ethos of this bureaucracy can be sensed through the literary texts which list the virtues needed to succeed as a scribe: application to study, self-control, prudence, respect for superiors, scrupulous regard for the sanctity of weights, measures, landed property and legal forms. The scribes were trained in a special school at Thebes, where not only the traditional history and literature and command of various scripts were taught, but, it seems, surveying, architecture and accountancy also.

AGRICULTURE

The bureaucracy directed a country most of whose inhabitants were peasants. They cannot have lived wholly comfortable lives, for they provided both the labour for the great public works of the monarchy and the surplus upon which a noble class, the bureaucracy and a great religious establishment could subsist. Yet the land was rich and was increasingly mastered by irrigation techniques established in a pre-dynastic period; these were probably one of the earliest manifestations of the unsurpassed capacity to mobilize collective effort which was to be one of the hallmarks of Egyptian government. Vegetables, barley, emmer were the main crops of the fields laid out along the irrigation channels; the diet they made possible was supplemented by poultry, fish and game (all of which figure plentifully in Egyptian art). Cattle were in use for traction and ploughing at least as early as the Old Kingdom. With little change this agriculture remained the basis of life in Egypt until modern times; it was sufficient to make her the granary of the Romans.

MONUMENTAL BUILDINGS IN EGYPT

On the surplus of this agriculture there also rested Egypt's own spectacular form of conspicuous consumption, a range of great public works in stone unsurpassed in antiquity. Houses and farm buildings in ancient Egypt were built in the mud brick already used before dynastic times: they were not meant to outface eternity. The palaces, tombs and memorials of the pharaohs were a different matter; they were

This 5th-dynasty seated scribe is one of the finest surviving examples of Egyptian sculpture.

built of the stone abundantly available in some parts of the Nile valley. Though they were carefully dressed with first copper and then bronze tools and often elaborately incised and painted, the technology of utilizing this material was far from complicated. Egyptians invented the stone column, but their great building achievement was not so much architectural and technical as social and administrative. What they did was based on an unprecedented and almost unsurpassed concentration of human labour. Under the direction of a scribe, thousands of slaves and sometimes regiments of soldiers were deployed to cut and manhandle into position the huge masses of Egyptian building. With only such elementary assistance as was available from levers and sleds – no winches, pulleys, blocks or tackle existed – and by the building of colossal ramps of earth, a succession of still-startling buildings was produced.

THE PYRAMIDS

The first were put up under the Third Dynasty. The most famous are the pyramids, the tombs of kings, at Saqqara, near Memphis. One of these, the "Step Pyramid", was the masterpiece of the first architect whose name is recorded, Imhotep, chancellor to the king. His work was so impressive that he was later to be deified – as the god of medicine – as well as being revered as astronomer, priest and sage. The beginning of building in stone was attributed to him and it is easy to believe that the building of something so unprecedented as the two-hundred-foot-high pyramid was seen as evidence of godlike power. It and its companions rose without peer over a civilization which until then lived only in dwellings of mud. A century or so later, blocks of stone of fifteen tons apiece were used for the Pyramid of Cheops, and it

This wooden statue dates from the 5th Dynasty. The Egyptian workers who found it in 1860 CE, amazed at its realism, nicknamed it "the town mayor" (Sheik el-beled). The statue stands more than 3 ft (1 m) tall and can be seen in the Museum of Egypt in Cairo.

was at this time (during the Fourth Dynasty) that the greatest pyramids were completed at Giza. Cheops' pyramid was twenty years in the building; the legend that 100,000 men were employed upon it is now thought to be an exaggeration but many thousands must have been and the huge quantities of stone (between five and six million tons) were brought from as far as 500 miles away. This colossal construction is perfectly orientated and its sides, 750 feet long, vary by less than eight inches – only about 0.09 per cent. It is not surprising that the pyramids later figured among the Seven Wonders of the World, nor that they alone from those Wonders survive. They were the greatest evidence of the power and self-confidence of the pharaonic state. Nor, of course, were they the only great monuments of Egypt. Each of them was only the dominant feature of a great complex of buildings which made up together the residence of the king after death. At other sites there were great temples, palaces, the tombs of the Valley of the Kings.

TECHNOLOGICAL LIMITATIONS

These huge public works were in both the real and figurative sense the biggest things the Egyptians left to posterity. They make it less surprising that the Egyptians were later also

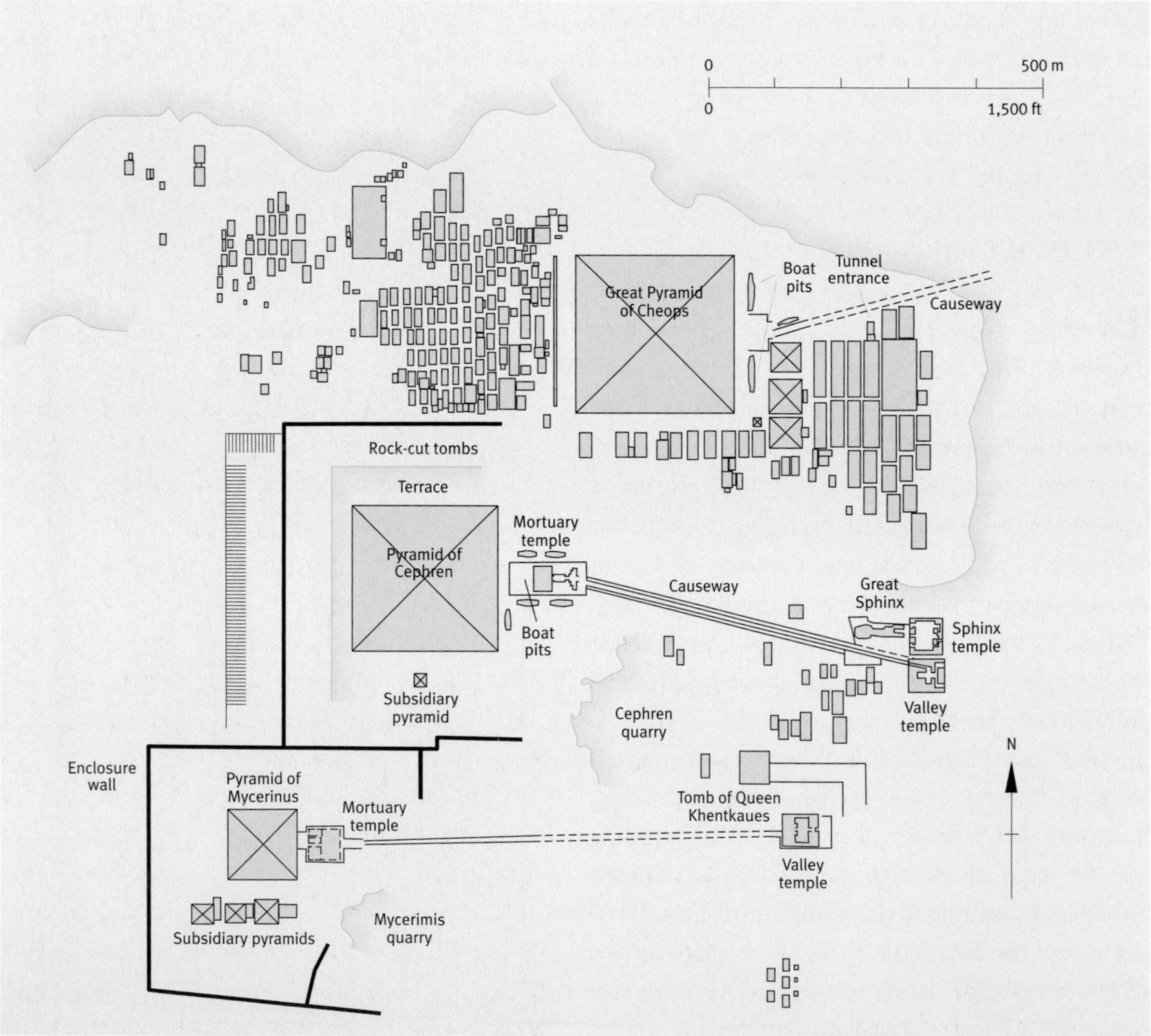

On a low plateau above the Nile valley, near Cairo, the spectacular Giza funeral buildings can be seen. The group is made up of the pyramids of three 4th-dynasty pharaohs and other secondary buildings. Built at the feet of the great pyramids of Cheops (Khufu), Cephren (Khafre) and Mycerinus (Menkaure) were funereal temples, which were linked by a series of pathways to other temples in the valley.

The pyramid of Cephren (Khafre), a pharaoh of the 4th Dynasty, who probably died in the year 2532 BCE. This is the only pyramid in Giza to retain part of the surface that originally covered the whole structure. The huge mortuary chamber, excavated in the rock under the pyramid, had already been sacked when a large, empty granite sarcophagus was discovered in 1818 CE.

to be reputed to have been great scientists: people could not believe that these huge monuments did not rest on the most refined mathematical and scientific skills. Yet this is an invalid inference and in fact untrue. Though Egyptian surveying was highly skilled, it was not until modern times that a more than elementary mathematical skill became necessary to engineering; it was certainly not needed for the erection of the pyramids. What was requisite was outstanding competence in mensuration and the manipulation of certain formulae for calculating volumes and weights, and this was as far as Egyptian mathematics went, whatever later admirers believed.

Modern mathematicians do not think much of the Egyptians' theoretical achievement and they certainly did not match the Babylonians in this art. They worked with a decimal numeration which at first sight looks modern, but it may be that their only significant contribution to later mathematics was the invention of unit fractions.

EGYPTIAN ASTRONOMY

No doubt a primitive mathematics is a part of the explanation of the sterility of the Egyptians' astronomical endeavours – another field in which posterity, paradoxically, was to credit them with great things. Their observations were accurate enough to permit the forecasting of the rise of the Nile and the ritual alignment of buildings, it is true, but their theoretical astronomy was valueless. Here again they were left far behind by the Babylonians. The inscriptions in which Egyptian astronomical science was recorded were to command centuries of respect from astrologers, but their scientific value was low and their predictive quality relatively short-term. The one solid work which rested on the Egyptians' astronomy was the calendar. They were the first people to establish the solar year of 365¼ days and they divided it into twelve months, each of three "weeks" of ten days, with five extra days at the end of the year. This arrangement, it may be remarked, was revived in 1793 CE when the French revolutionaries sought to replace the Christian calendar by one more rational.

The calendar, though it owed much to the observation of stars, must have reflected also in its remoter origins observation of the great pulse at the heart of Egyptian life, the flooding of the Nile. This gave the Egyptian farmer a year of three seasons, each of approximately four months, one of planting, one of flood, one of harvest. But the Nile's endless cycle also influenced Egypt at deeper levels.

RELIGION

THE STRUCTURE AND SOLIDITY of the religious life of ancient Egypt greatly struck other peoples. Herodotus believed that the Greeks had acquired the names of their gods from Egypt; he was wrong, but it is interesting that he should have thought so. Later, the cults of Egyptian gods were seen as a threat by the Roman emperors; they were forbidden, but the Romans had eventually to tolerate them, such was their appeal. Mumbo-jumbo and charlatanry with an Egyptian flavour could still take in cultivated Europeans in the eighteenth century CE; a more amusing and innocent expression of the fascination of the myth of ancient Egypt can still be seen in the rituals of the Shriners, the fraternities of respectable American businessmen who parade about the streets of small towns improbably attired in fezzes and baggy trousers on great occasions. There was, indeed, a continuing vigour in Egyptian religion which, like other sides of Egyptian civilization, long outlived the political forms that had sustained and sheltered it.

Yet it remains something with which it is peculiarly difficult to come to grips. Words like "vigour" can be misleading; religion in ancient Egypt was much more a matter of an

Egyptian religion

The numerous archaeological remains and written documents that have been preserved make the Egyptian religion one of the best-documented ancient religions. The many Egyptian gods were often personified by animals such as a hawk (Horus), or by natural elements, including the sky (Nut). However, some aspects of Egyptian religion point towards the belief in a superior god. This is noticeable in the fundamental role that Osiris played in the afterlife, essential for the Egyptians. State gods also existed, associated with successive capital cities. Amon, for example, was the ram god of Thebes, who during the New Kingdom united with the sun god Re (supreme god of the Old Kingdom) to become Amon-Re. The religious head of the Egyptians was the pharaoh, son of Re, identified as Horus. Beneath him there was a hierarchical class of priests.

The grand temple of Abu Simbel, which houses statues of several Egyptian gods, is designed in such a way that twice a year it is illuminated by the rays of the rising sun.

all-pervasive framework, as much taken for granted as the circulatory system of the human body, than of an independent structure such as what later came to be understood as a church. It was not consciously seen as a growing, lively force: it was, rather, one aspect of reality, a description of an unchanging cosmos. But this, too, may be a misleading way of putting it. An important book about the world outlook of early Mesopotamians and Egyptians had the suggestive title *Before Philosophy*; we have to remember that concepts and distinctions which we take for granted in assessing (and even talking about) the mentalities of other ages did not exist for the people whose minds we seek to penetrate. The boundary between religion and magic, for example, hardly mattered for the ancient Egyptian, though he might be well aware that each had its proper efficacy. It has been said that magic was always present as a kind of cancer in Egyptian religion; the image is too evaluative, but expresses the intimacy of the link. Another distinction lacking in ancient Egypt was the one most of us make automatically between the name and the thing. For the ancient Egyptian, the name was the thing; the real object we separate from its designation was identical with it. So might be other images. The Egyptians lived in symbolism as fishes do in water, taking it for granted, and we have to break through the assumptions of a profoundly unsymbolic culture in order to understand them.

DEATH AND BURIAL RITUALS

A whole world view is involved in appreciating the meaning and role of religion in ancient Egypt. At the outset there is overwhelming evidence of its importance; for almost the whole duration of their civilization, the ancient Egyptians show a remarkably uniform tendency to seek through religion a way of penetrating the variety of the flow of ordinary experience so as to reach a changeless world most easily understood through the life the dead lived there. Perhaps the pulse of the Nile is to be detected here, too; each year it swept away and made new, but its cycle was ever recurring, changeless, the embodiment of a cosmic rhythm. The supreme change threatening people was death, the greatest expression of the decay and flux which was their common experience. Egyptian religion seems from the start obsessed with it: its most familiar embodiments, after all, are

Dating from the 12th Dynasty, this is one of the splendid sarcophagi in which the mummies of important Egyptians were placed.

the mummy and the grave-goods from funeral chambers preserved in our museums. Under the Middle Kingdom it came to be believed that all Egyptians, not just the king, could expect life in another world. Accordingly, through ritual and symbol, through preparation of the case they would have to put to their judges in the afterworld, people might prepare for the afterlife with a reasonable confidence that they would achieve the changeless well-being it offered in principle. The Egyptian view of the afterlife was, therefore, unlike the gloomy version of the Mesopotamians; people could be happy in it.

The struggle to assure this outcome for so many people across so many centuries gives Egyptian religion a heroic quality. It is the explanation, too, of the obsessively elaborate care shown in preparing tombs and conducting the deceased to his eternal resting-place. Its most celebrated expression is the building of the pyramids and the practice of mummification. It took seventy days to carry out the funerary rites and mummification of a king under the Middle Kingdom.

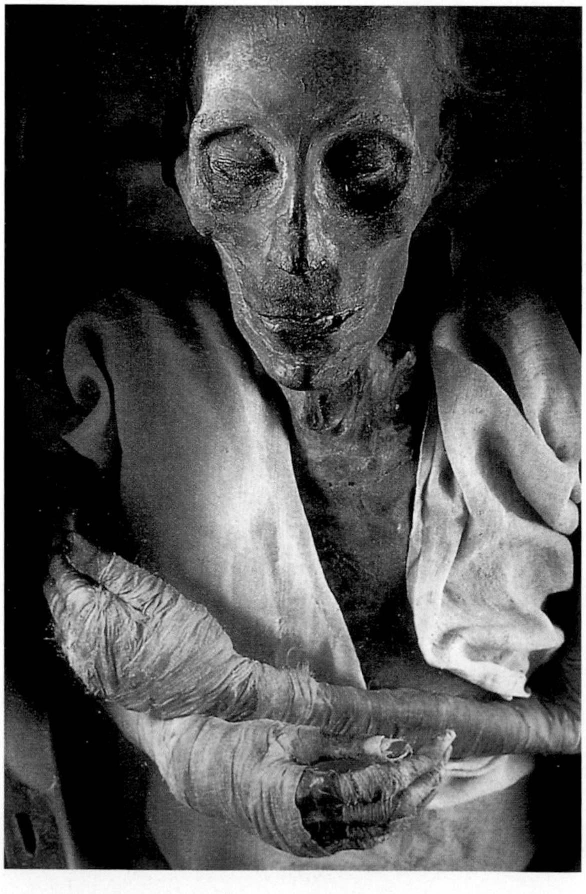

Medical examinations carried out on the mummy of Rameses II, the powerful pharaoh of the 19th Dynasty, have revealed that he suffered from heart disease, dental problems and arthritis.

The Egyptians believed that after death people could expect judgement before Osiris; if the verdict was favourable, they would live in Osiris's kingdom, if not, they were abandoned to a monstrous destroyer, part crocodile, part hippopotamus. This did not mean, though, that in life human beings need do no more than placate Osiris, for the Egyptian pantheon was huge. About two thousand gods existed and there were several important cults. Many of them originated in the prehistoric animal deities. Horus, the falcon god, was also god of the dynasty and probably arrived with the mysterious invaders of the fourth millennium BCE. These animals underwent a slow but incomplete humanization; artists stick their animal heads on to human bodies. These totemlike creatures were rearranged in fresh patterns as the pharaohs sought through the consolidation of their cults to achieve political ends. In this way the cult of Horus was consolidated with that of Amon-Re, the sun-god, of whom the pharaoh came to be regarded as the incarnation. This was the official cult of the great age of pyramid-building and by no means the end of the story.

Horus was later to undergo another transformation, to appear as the offspring of Osiris, the central figure of a national cult, and his consort Isis. This goddess of creation and love was probably the most ancient of all – her origins, like those of other Egyptian deities, go back to the pre-dynastic era, and she is one development of the ubiquitous mother-goddess of whom evidence survives from all over the Neolithic Near East. She was long to endure, her image, the infant Horus in her arms, surviving into the Christian iconography of the Virgin Mary.

RELIGIOUS DIVERSITY AND THE PRIESTLY CLASS

The theme of Egyptian religion is immensely complicated. Different places had different cults and there were even occasional variations of a doctrinal and speculative kind. The most famous of these was the attempt of a fourteenth-century pharaoh to establish the cult of Aton, another manifestation of the sun, in which has been discerned the first monotheistic religion. Yet there is a recurring sense of a striving after synthesis, even if it is often the expression of dynastic or political interest. Much of the history of Egyptian religion must be, if we could only decipher it, the story of ebbings and flowings about the major cults: politics, in fact, rather than religion.

Not only the pharaohs were interested in religious issues. The institutions which maintained these beliefs were in the hands of a hereditary priestly class, initiated into the rituals to whose inner sancta the ordinary worshipper almost never penetrated. The cult statues at the shrine of the temple were rarely seen except by the priests. As time passed, they acquired important vested interests in the popularity and well-being of their cults.

EGYPTIAN ART

The gods loom large in the subject-matter of ancient Egyptian art, but it contains much more besides. It was based on a fundamental naturalism of representation which, however restrained by conventions of expression and gesture, gives two millennia of classical Egyptian art at first a beautiful simplicity and later, in a more decadent period, an endearing charm and approachability. It permitted a realistic portrayal of scenes of everyday life. The rural themes of farming, fishing and hunting are displayed in them; craftsmen are shown at work on their products and scribes at their duties. Yet neither content nor technique is in the end the most striking characteristic of Egyptian art, but its enduring style. For some two thousand years, artists were able to work satisfyingly within the same classical tradition. Its origins may owe something to Sumer and it showed itself later able to borrow other foreign influences yet the strength and solidity of the central and native tradition never wavers. It must have been one of the most

A large amount of ancient Egyptian furniture – such as this painted wooden funeral cask – has been preserved. This is due to the dry atmosphere of the tombs.

Queen Ahmose, from the 18th Dynasty, shown in a bas-relief at the Temple of Hatshepsut, in Deir-el-Bahari.

impressive visual features of Egypt to a visitor in ancient times; what he saw was all of a piece. If we exempt the work of the Upper Palaeolithic, of which we know so very little, it is the longest and strongest continuous tradition in the whole history of art.

It did not prove to be transplantable. Perhaps the Greeks took the column from ancient Egypt, where it had its origins in the mud-plastered bundle of reeds of which a reminiscence survives in fluting. What is clear apart from this is that although the monuments of Egypt continuously fascinated artists and architects of other lands, the result, even when they exploited them successfully for their own purposes, was always superficial and exotic. Egyptian style never took root anywhere else; it pops up from time to time down the ages as decoration and embellishment – sphinxes and serpents on furniture, an obelisk here, a cinema there. Only one great integral contribution was made by Egyptian art to the future, the establishment – for the purposes of the huge incised and painted figures on the walls of tombs and temples – of the classical canons of proportion of the human body which were to pass through the Greeks to western art. Artists were still to be fascinated by these as late as Leonardo, although by now the contribution was theoretical, not stylistic.

HIEROGLYPHIC WRITING

Another great artistic achievement confined to Egypt, though exceptionally important there, was calligraphy. It seems that Egyptians deliberately took the Sumerian invention of representing sounds rather than things, but rejected cuneiform. They invented, instead, hieroglyphic writing. Instead of the device of arranging the same basic shape in different ways which had been evolved in Mesopotamia, they deliberately chose lifelike little pictures or near-pictures. It was much more decorative than cuneiform, but also much harder to master. The first hieroglyphs appear before 3000 BCE; the last example of which we know was written in 394 CE. Nearly 4,000 years is an impressively long life for a calligraphy. But the uninitiated could still not read it for another fourteen and a half centuries after its disappearance, until a French scholar deciphered the inscription on the "Rosetta stone" brought back to France after its discovery by scientists accompanying a French army in Egypt. None of the classical writers of antiquity who wrote about Egypt ever learnt to read hieroglyph, it seems, though enormous interest was shown in it. Yet it now seems likely that hieroglyph had importance in world as well as in Egyptian history because it was a model for Semitic scripts of the second millennium BCE and thus came to be a remote ancestor of the modern Latin alphabet, which has spread around the world in our own times.

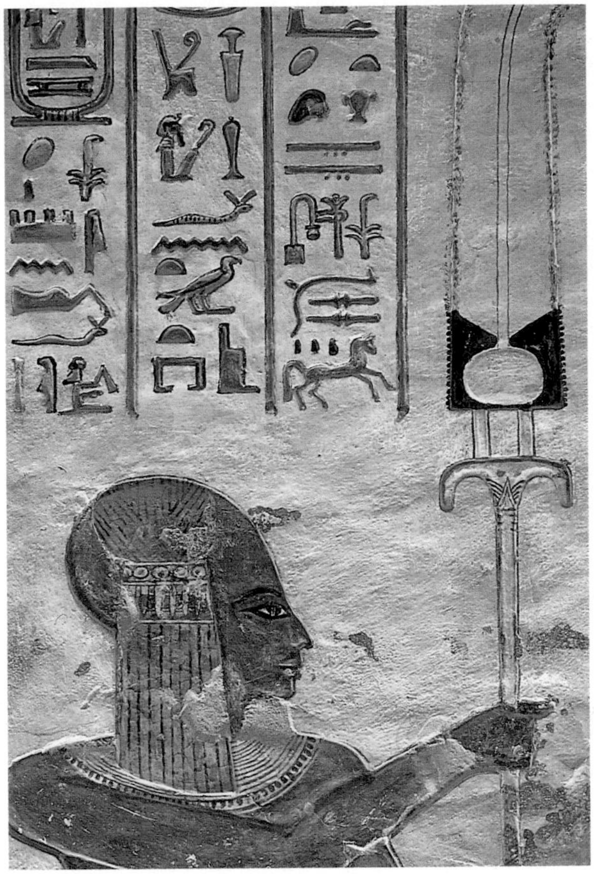

Hieroglyphic writing in a wall painting from a tomb in the Valley of the Kings. Below the hieroglyphs, Prince Amon-hir-Khopshep, son of Rameses II, is depicted.

THE INVENTION OF PAPYRUS

In the ancient world the ability to read hieroglyph was the key to the position of the priestly caste and, accordingly, a closely guarded professional secret. From pre-dynastic times it was used for historical record and as early as the First Dynasty the invention of papyrus – strips of reed-pith, laid criss-cross and pounded together into a homogeneous sheet – provided a convenient medium for its multiplication. Here was a real contribution to the progress of humankind. This invention had much greater importance for the world than hieroglyph; cheaper than skin (from which parchment was made) and more convenient (though more perishable) than clay tablets or slates of stone, it was the most general basis of correspondence and record in the Near East until well into the Common Era, when the invention of paper reached the Mediterranean world from the Far East (and even paper took its name from papyrus). Soon after the appearance of papyrus, writers began to paste sheets of it together into a long roll: thus the Egyptians invented the book, as well as the material on which it could first be written and a script which is an ancestor of our own. It may be our greatest debt to the

A papyrus vignette from the Book of the Dead of Nakhte, an important scribe. The dead man and his wife stand before the god Osiris in the garden of their house. Abundant sycamore trees and date palms surround the garden pool.

Egyptians, for a huge proportion of what we know of antiquity comes to us directly or indirectly via papyrus.

EGYPTIAN ACHIEVEMENT

Undoubtedly, the rumoured prowess of her religious and magical practitioners and the spectacular embodiment of a political achievement in art and architecture largely explain Egypt's continuing prestige. Yet if her civilization is looked at comparatively, it seems neither very fertile nor very responsive. Technology is by no means an infallible test – nor one easy to interpret – but it suggests a people slow to adopt new skills, reluctant to innovate once the creative jump to civilization had been made. Stone architecture is the only major innovation for a long time after the coming of literacy. Though papyrus and the wheel were known under the First Dynasty, Egypt had been in contact with Mesopotamia for getting on for two thousand years before she adopted the well-sweep, by then long in use to irrigate land in the other river valley.

Perhaps the weight of routine was insuperable, given the background of the unchanging reassurance provided by the Nile. Though Egyptian art records workmen organized in teams for the subdivision of manufacturing processes down to a point which faintly suggests the modern factory, many important devices came to Egypt only much later than elsewhere. There is no definite evidence of the presence of the potter's wheel before the Old Kingdom; for all the skill of the goldsmith and coppersmith, bronze-making does not appear until well into the second millennium BCE and the lathe has to wait for the Hellenistic age. The bow-drill was almost the only tool for the multiplication and transmission of energy available to the mass of Egyptian craftsmen.

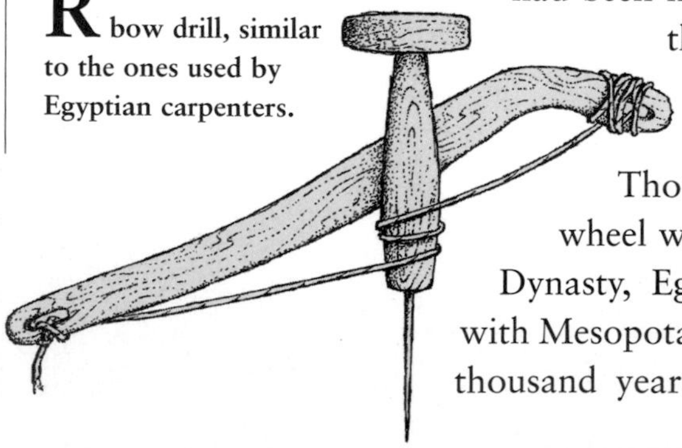

Reconstruction of a bow drill, similar to the ones used by Egyptian carpenters.

MEDICINE

Only in medicine is there indisputable originality and achievement and it can be traced back at least as far as the Old Kingdom. By 1000 BCE Egyptian pre-eminence in this art was internationally and justifiably recognized. While Egyptian medicine was never wholly separable from magic (magical prescriptions and amulets survive in great numbers), it had an appreciable content of rationality and pure empirical observation. It extended as far as a knowledge of contraceptive techniques. Its indirect contribution to subsequent history was great, too, whatever its efficiency in its own day; much of our knowledge of drugs and of plants furnishing *materia medica* was first established by the Egyptians and passed from them, eventually, through the Greeks to the scientists of medieval Europe. It is a considerable thing to have initiated the use of a remedy effective as as long as castor oil has been. Here Egypt left Mesopotamia far behind.

What can be concluded about the health of the ancient Egyptians is another matter. They do not seem to have been so worried about alcoholic over-indulgence as the Mesopotamians, but it is not easy to infer anything from that. Some scholars have said there was an exceptionally high rate of infant mortality and hard evidence of a negative kind exists for some diseases of adults; whatever the explanation, the many mummified bodies surviving reveal no instance of cancer, rickets, or syphilis. On the other hand, the debilitating disease called schistosomiasis, carried by blood flukes and so prevalent in Egypt today, seems to have been prevalent there already in the second millennium BCE. Of course, none of this throws much light on ancient Egyptian medical practice. Nevertheless, Egypt provides our oldest surviving medical treatises, and their prescriptions and recommended cures suggest that Egyptian practitioners could offer a mixed bag of remedies, no better and no worse than most of those deployed in other great centres of civilization at any time before the present. Considerable preservative skill was attributed to the practitioners of mummification, though unjustifiably, since the climate was on their side. Curiously, the products of their art were later themselves regarded as of therapeutic value; powdered mummy was for centuries a sovereign cure for many ills in Europe.

A large number of labourers were expected to serve their master in the afterlife as they had done in real life, as is shown in the paintings and engravings in Egyptian tombs.

PEASANT LIFE

Most Egyptians were peasants, a consequence of Egypt remaining non-urbanized where Mesopotamia did not. The picture of Egyptian life presented by its literature and art reveals a population living in the countryside, using little towns and temples as service centres rather than dwelling places. Egypt was for most of antiquity a country of a few great cult and administrative centres such as Thebes or Memphis and the rest nothing more than villages and markets. Life for the poor was hard, but not unremittingly so. The major burden must have been conscript labour services. When these were not exacted by Pharaoh, then peasants would have considerable leisure at those times when they waited for the flooding Nile to do its work for them. The agricultural base was rich enough, too, to sustain a complex and variegated society with a wide range of craftsmen. About their activities we know more than of those of their Mesopotamian equivalents, thanks to stone-carvings and paintings. The great division of this society was between the educated, who could enter the state service, and the rest. Slavery was important, but, it appears, less fundamental an institution than elsewhere in the ancient Near East.

Ancient Egyptian field workers are depicted in this tomb painting.

Detail from a painting in Thebes showing a woman gathering flax.

Daily life in ancient Egypt

The Egyptians believed firmly in the afterlife and hoped to enjoy the same pleasures there as they had in real life. To this end, they placed symbolic images of servants and objects in their tombs. Because such objects have been excellently preserved by the dry atmosphere, they have provided archaeologists with a vast collection of images. Thanks to them, we are able to visualize daily life in the Egypt of the pharaohs with much greater precision than we can that of any other ancient civilization. We can see peasants working the land or tending their livestock, craftsmen at work, servants serving their masters and musicians and dancers performing. However, in Egyptian burial paintings everything is made to appear perfect, which tends to give an over-idealized impression of Egyptian life. It also is interesting to note that the average life expectancy for ancient Egyptians was just 20 years.

This 18th-dynasty sculpture from Thebes shows a married couple, who clearly wished to depict themselves as united for eternity.

A painting from a 7th-dynasty tomb. This youth, who is depicted smelling a flower, is wearing Middle Kingdom-style dress: a close-fitting white tunic with braces. True to the conventions of Egyptian art, the figure's torso and shoulders are shown front-on while the face is shown in profile.

THE STATUS OF WOMEN

Tradition in later times remarked upon the seductiveness and accessibility of Egyptian women. With other evidence it helps to give an impression of a society in which women were more independent and enjoyed higher status than elsewhere. Some weight must be given to an art which depicts court women clad in the fine and revealing linens which the Egyptians came to weave, exquisitely coiffured and jewelled, wearing the carefully applied cosmetics to whose provision Egyptian commerce gave much attention. We should not lean too strongly on this, but our impression of the way in which women of the Egyptian ruling class were treated is important, and it is one of dignity and independence. The pharaohs and their consorts – and other noble couples – are sometimes depicted, too, with an intimacy of mood found nowhere else in the art of the ancient Near East before the first millennium BCE and suggestive of a real emotional equality; it can hardly be accidental that this is so.

The beautiful and charming women who appear in many of the paintings and sculptures may reflect also a certain political importance for their sex which was lacking elsewhere. The throne theoretically and often in practice descended through the female line. An heiress brought to her husband the right of succession; hence there was much anxiety about the marriage of princesses. Many royal marriages were of brother and sister, without apparently unsatisfactory genetic effects; some pharaohs married their daughters, but perhaps to prevent anyone else marrying them rather than to ensure the continuity of the divine blood. Such a standing must have made royal women influential personages in their own right. Some exercised important power and one even occupied the throne, being willing to appear ritually bearded and in a man's clothes, and taking the title of Pharaoh. True, it was an innovation which seems not to have been wholly approved.

There is also much femininity about the Egyptian pantheon, notably in the cult of Isis, which is suggestive. Literature and art stress a respect for the wife and mother which goes beyond the confines of the circle of the notabilities. Both love stories and scenes of family life reveal what was at least thought to be an ideal standard for society as a whole and it emphasizes a tender eroticism, relaxation and informality, and something of an emotional equality of men and women. Some women were literate and there is even an Egyptian word for a female scribe, but there were, of course, not many occupations open to women except those of priestess or prostitute. If they were well-off, however, they could own property and their legal rights seem in most respects to have been akin to those of women in the Sumerian tradition. It is not easy to generalize over so long a period as

A scene from an 18th-dynasty tomb in Thebes. Servants, wearing only belts and costly jewels, attend to the guests at a banquet. The guests, dressed in the transparent, pleated tunics that were typical of New Kingdom high society, are being entertained by dancers and musicians.

A painting from Sobketpe's tomb depicts Syrians arriving at the Egyptian court to present tributes.

that of Egyptian civilization but such evidence as we have from ancient Egypt leaves an impression of a society with a potential for personal expression by women not found among many later peoples until modern times.

THE OLD KINGDOM

So impressive is the solidity and material richness of Egyptian civilization in retrospect, so apparently unchanging, that it is even more difficult than in the case of Mesopotamia to keep in perspective what were its relations with the world outside or the ebb and flow of authority within the Nile valley. There are huge tracts of time to account for – the Old Kingdom alone, on the shortest reckoning, has a history two and a half times as long as that of the United States – and much happened under the Old Kingdom. The difficulty is to be sure exactly what it was that was going on and what was its importance. For nearly a thousand years after Menes, Egypt's history can be considered in virtual isolation. It was to be looked back upon as a time of stability when pharaohs were impregnable. Yet under the Old Kingdom there has been detected a decentralization of authority; provincial officers show increasing importance and independence. The pharaoh, too, still had to wear two crowns and was twice buried, once in Upper and once in Lower Egypt; this division was still real. Relations with neighbours were not remarkable, though a series of expeditions was mounted against the peoples of Palestine towards the end of the Old Kingdom. The First Intermediate period which followed saw the position reversed and Egypt was invaded, rather than the invader. No doubt weakness and division helped Asian invaders to establish themselves in the valley of the lower Nile; there is a strange comment that "the high born are full of lamentation but the poor are jubilant ... squalor is throughout the land ... strangers have come into Egypt". Rival dynasties appeared near modern Cairo; the grasp of Memphis flagged.

A group of painted wooden soldiers from a tomb in Asyut, probably from the 12th Dynasty. This was the period in which the conquest of Nubia drove the pharaohs to organize permanent military units. The most commonly used weapons were bows, spears, axes and shields. War chariots were introduced in Egypt later by foreign invaders, the Hyksos.

THE MIDDLE KINGDOM

The next great period of Egyptian history was the Middle Kingdom, effectively inaugurated by the powerful Amenemhet I who reunified the kingdom from his capital at Thebes. For about a quarter-millennium after 2000 BCE, Egypt enjoyed a period of recovery whose repute may owe much to the impression (which comes to us through the records) of the horrors of the Intermediate period. Under the Middle Kingdom there was a new emphasis on order and social cohesion. The divine status of the pharaoh subtly changes: not only is he God, but it is emphasized that he is descended from gods and will be followed by gods. The eternal order will continue unshaken after bad times have made men doubt. It is certain, too, that there was expansion and material growth. Great reclamation work was achieved in the marshes of the Nile. Nubia, to the south, between the first and third cataracts, was conquered and its gold-mines fully exploited.

Egyptian settlements were founded even further south, too, in what was later to be a mysterious kingdom called Kush. Trade leaves more elaborate traces than ever before and the copper mines of the Sinai were now exploited again. Theological change also followed – there was something of a consolidation of cults under the god Amon-Re which reflected political consolidation. Yet the Middle Kingdom ended in political upheaval and dynastic competition.

The Second Intermediate period of roughly two hundred years was marked by another and far more dangerous incursion of foreigners. These were the Hyksos, possibly a Semitic people, who used the military advantage of the iron-fitted chariot to establish themselves in the Nile delta as overlords to whom the Theban dynasties paid tribute. Not much is known about them. Seemingly, they took over Egyptian conventions and methods, and even maintained the existing bureaucrats at first, but this did not lead to assimilation. Under the Eighteenth Dynasty the Egyptians evicted the Hyksos in a war of peoples; this

This statue of the 18th-dynasty queen Hatshepsut shows her holding two vases containing offerings of wine and milk. The statue was found in Hatshepsut's mortuary temple and dates from c.1490–70 BCE.

was the start of the New Kingdom, whose first great success was to follow up victory in the years after 1570 BCE by pursuing the Hyksos into their strongholds in south Canaan. In the end, the Egyptians occupied much of Syria and Palestine.

THE NEW KINGDOM

The New Kingdom in its prime was so successful internationally and has left such rich physical memorials that it is difficult not to think that the Hyksos domination must have had a cathartic or fertilizing effect. There was under the Eighteenth Dynasty almost a renaissance of the arts, a transformation of military techniques by the adoption of Asiatic devices such as the chariot, and, above all, a huge consolidation of royal authority. It was then that a female, Hatshepsut, for the first time occupied the throne in a reign notable for the expansion of Egyptian commerce, or so her mortuary temple seems to show. The next century or so brought further imperial and military glory, with Hatshepsut's consort and successor, Tuthmosis III, carrying the limits of Egyptian empire to the Euphrates. Monuments recording the arrival of tribute and slaves and marriages with Asiatic princesses testify to an Egyptian pre-eminence matched at home by a new richness of decoration in the temples and the appearance of a sculpture in the round which produced busts and statues generally regarded as the peak of Egyptian artistic achievement. Foreign influences also touched Egyptian art at this time; they came from Crete.

Imperial expansion began in the 18th Dynasty, drawing Egypt into a conflict over power in the Near East. Great battles were fought in Nubia, to the south, and in Syria and Palestine, to the north-east. In this painting, Nubian and Syrian envoys prostrate themselves before the Egyptian pharaoh.

THE END OF ISOLATION

Towards the end of the New Kingdom, the evidence of multiplied foreign contacts begins to show something else: the context of Egyptian power had already changed importantly. The crucial area was the Levant coast which even Tuthmosis III had taken seventeen years to subdue. He had to leave unconquered a huge empire ruled by the Mitanni, a people who dominated eastern Syria and northern Mesopotamia. His successors changed tack. A Mitanni princess married a pharaoh and to protect Egyptian interests in this area the New Kingdom came to rely on the friendship of her people. Egypt was being forced out of the isolation which had long protected her. But the Mitanni were under growing pressure from the Hittites, to the north, one of the most important of the peoples whose ambitions and movements break up the world of the Near East more and more in the second half of the second millennium BCE.

We know a lot about the preoccupations of the New Kingdom at an early stage in this process because they are recorded in one of the earliest collections of diplomatic correspondence, for the reigns of Amenhotep III and IV (c.1400–1362 BCE). Under the first of these kings, Egypt reached its peak of prestige and prosperity. It was the greatest era of Thebes. Amenhotep was fittingly buried there in a tomb which was the largest ever prepared for a king, though nothing of it remains but the fragments of the huge statues the Greeks later called the colossi of Memnon (a legendary hero, whom they supposed to be Ethiopian).

THE REIGN OF AKHNATON

Amenhotep IV succeeded his father in 1379 BCE. He attempted a religious revolution, the substitution of a monotheistic cult of the sun-god Aton for the ancient religion. To mark his seriousness, he changed his name to Akhnaton and founded a new city at Amarna, 300 miles north of Thebes, where a temple with a roofless sanctuary open to the sun's rays was the centre of the new religion. Although there can be no doubt of Akhnaton's seriousness of purpose and personal piety, his attempt must have been doomed from the start, given the religious conservatism of Egypt, but there may have been political motives for his persistence. Perhaps he was trying to recover power usurped by the priests of Amon-Re. Whatever the explanation, the opposition Akhnaton provoked by this religious revolution helped to cripple him on other fronts. Meanwhile, Hittite pressure was producing clear signs of strain in the Egyptian dependencies; Akhnaton could not save the Mitanni who lost all their lands west of the Euphrates to the Hittites in 1372 BCE and dissolved in civil war which foreshadowed their kingdom's disappearance

Akhnaton and his wife Nefertiti depicted with their daughters, under the beneficial rays of Aton. During this period, Egyptian art departed from many of its conventions and showed figures in relaxed postures. This strongly contrasted with the rigid style that had been the norm, and which would later become common practice once again.

thirty years or so later. The Egyptian sphere was crumbling. There were other motives, perhaps, than religious outrage for the later exclusion of Akhnaton's name from the official list of kings.

TUTANKHAMON

Akhnaton's successor bore a name which is possibly the most widely known of those of ancient Egypt. Amenhotep IV had changed his own name to Akhnaton because he wished to erase the reminiscence of the cult of the old god Amon; his successor and son-in-law changed his name from Tutankhaton to Tutankhamon to mark the restoration of the old cult of Amon and the collapse of the attempted religious reform. It may have been gratitude for this that led to the magnificent burial in the Valley of the Kings, which was given to Tutankhamon after only a short and otherwise unremarkable reign.

THE DECLINE OF EGYPT

When Tutankhamon died, the New Kingdom had two centuries of life ahead, but their atmosphere is one of only occasionally interrupted and steadily accelerating decline. Symptomatically, Tutankhamon's widow arranged to marry a Hittite prince (though he was murdered before the ceremony could take place). Later kings made efforts to recover lost ground and sometimes succeeded; the waves of conquest rolled back and forth over Palestine and at one time a pharaoh took a Hittite princess as a bride as his predecessors had taken princesses from

A relief from a stele depicting servants presenting gifts of gold to the 18th-dynasty ruler Ay (1352–1348 BCE) as a token of Akhnaton's esteem. The stele was found in the tomb built for Ay at Al-Amarmah.

other peoples. But there were yet more new enemies appearing; even a Hittite alliance was no longer a safeguard. The Aegean was in uproar, the islands "poured out their people all together" and "no land stood before them", say the Egyptian records. These sea peoples were eventually beaten off, but the struggle was hard.

At some time during these turbulent years a small Semitic people, called by the Egyptians "Hebrews", left the delta and (according to their later tradition) followed their leader Moses out of Egypt into the deserts of Sinai. From about 1150 BCE the signs of internal disorganization, too, are plentiful. One king, Rameses III, died as a result of a conspiracy in the harem; he was the last to achieve some measure of success in offsetting the swelling tide of disaster. We hear of strikes and economic troubles under his successors; there is the ominous symptom of sacrilege in a generation of looting of the royal tombs at Thebes. The pharaoh is losing his power to priests and officials and the last of the Twentieth Dynasty, Rameses XI, was in effect a prisoner in his own palace. The age of Egypt's imperial power was over. So, in fact, was that of the Hittites, and of other empires of the end of the second millennium. Not only Egypt's power, but the world which was the setting of her glories, was passing away.

A fragment from a bas-relief in the temple of Abu Simbel, depicting the battle of Qadesh between Rameses II and Muwatallis, King of the Hittites.

THE EGYPTIAN LEGACY

Undoubtedly, it is in changes affecting the whole ancient world that much of the explanation of the decline of Egypt must be sought, yet it is impossible to resist the feeling that the last centuries of the New Kingdom expose weaknesses present in Egyptian civilization from the beginning. These are not easy to discern at first sight; the spectacular heritage of Egypt's monuments and a history counted not in centuries but in millennia stagger the critical sense and stifle scepticism. Yet the creative quality of Egyptian civilization seems, in the end, strangely to miscarry. Colossal resources of labour are massed under the direction of men who, by the standards of any age, must have been outstanding civil servants, and the end is the creation of the greatest tombstones the world has ever seen. Craftsmanship of exquisite quality is employed, and its masterpieces are grave-goods. A highly literate elite, utilizing a complex and subtle language and a material of unsurpassed convenience, uses them copiously, but has no philosophical or religious idea comparable to those of Greek or Jew to give to the world. It is difficult not to sense an ultimate sterility, a nothingness, at the heart of this glittering *tour de force*.

In the other scale must be placed the sheer staying power of ancient Egyptian civilization; after all, it worked for a very long time, a spectacular fact. Though it underwent at least two phases of considerable eclipse, it recovered from them, seemingly unchanged.

A painted, stuccoed, wooden stele dating from the 21st or 22nd Dynasty. A musician strums his harp in respect for Re-Harakhty, god of Heliopolis, who is depicted with a hawk's head crowned by a sun disk. He is holding a staff and a whip, both of which are symbols of Egyptian royalty.

Survival on such a scale is a great material and historical success; what remains obscure is why it should have stopped there. Egypt's military and economic power in the end made little permanent difference to the world. Her civilization was never successfully spread abroad. Perhaps this is because its survival owed much to its setting. If it was a positive success to create so rapidly institutions which with little fundamental change could last so long, this could probably have been done by any ancient civilization enjoying such a degree of immunity from intrusion. China was to show impressive continuity, too.

It is important also to remember once more how slow and imperceptible all social and cultural change was in early times. Because we are used to change, we must find it difficult to sense the huge inertia possessed by any successful social system (one, that is, which enables people to grapple effectively with their physical and mental environment) in almost any age before the most recent.

In the ancient world the sources of innovation were far fewer and far more occasional than now. The pace of history is rapid in ancient Egypt if we think of prehistoric times; it seems glacially slow if we reflect how little daily life must have changed between Menes and Tuthmosis III, a period of more than fifteen hundred years and therefore comparable to that which separates us from the end of Roman Britain. Marked change could only come from sudden and overwhelming natural disaster (and the Nile was a reliable safeguard), or invasion or conquest (and Egypt long stood at the edge of the battleground of peoples in the Near East, affected only occasionally by their comings and goings). Only very slowly could technology or economic forces exert such pressures for change as we take for granted. As for intellectual stimuli, these could hardly be strong in a society where the whole apparatus of a cultural tradition was directed to the inculcation of routine.

Speculation about the nature of Egyptian history tends always to revert to the great natural image of the Nile. It was always present to the Egyptian eyes, so prominent, perhaps, that it could not be seen for the colossal and unique influence it was, for no context broader than its valley needed consideration. While in the background the incomprehensible (but in the end world-shaping) wars of the Fertile Crescent rage across the centuries, the history of Old Egypt goes on for thousands of years, virtually a function of the remorseless, beneficent flooding and subsidence of the Nile. On its banks a grateful and passive people gathers the richness it bestows. From it could be set aside what they thought necessary for the real business of living: the proper preparation for death.

The last journey: a boat carrying the sarcophagus of a dead Egyptian sails along the Nile.

4 INTRUDERS AND INVADERS: THE DARK AGES OF THE ANCIENT NEAR EAST

MESOPOTAMIA AND EGYPT are the twin foundation stones of written history. For a long time the first two great centres of civilization dominate chronology and may conveniently be dealt with more or less in isolation. But obviously their story is not the whole story of the ancient Near East, let alone that of the ancient world. Soon after 2000 BCE the movements of other peoples were already breaking it up into new patterns. A thousand years later, other centres of civilization were in existence elsewhere and we are well into the historical era.

Unfortunately for the historian, there is no simple and obvious unity to this story even in the Fertile Crescent, which for a long time continued to show more creativity and dynamism than any other part of the world. There is only a muddle of changes whose beginnings lie far back in the second millennium and which go on until the first of a new succession of empires emerges in the ninth century BCE. The sweeping upheavals and re-arrangements which stud this confusion are hard even to map in outline, let alone to explain; fortunately, their details do not need to be unravelled here. History was speeding up and civilization was providing human beings with new opportunities. Rather than submerge ourselves in the flood of events, we can more usefully try to grasp some of the change-making forces at work.

A COMPLICATING WORLD

The most obvious change-making force continues to be great migrations. Their fundamental pattern does not change much for a

Assyrian bas-reliefs show many scenes of cities under siege. In this bas-relief from the palace of Nimrud (Kalaj), the Assyrians are depicted using an armour-plated siege tower mounted on wheels. The siege tower has a battering ram attached, which would have been used to breach the enemy walls.

thousand years or so after 2000 BCE, nor does the ethnic cast of the drama. The basic dynamic was provided by the pressure of peoples of Indo-European linguistic stock on the Fertile Crescent from both east and west. Their variety and numbers grow, but their names need not be remembered here, even if some of them bring us to the remote origins of Greece. Meanwhile, Semitic peoples dispute with the Indo-Europeans the Mesopotamian valleys; with Egypt and the mysterious "Peoples of the Sea" they fight over Sinai, Palestine and the Levant. Another branch of the Indo-European race is established in Iran – and from it will eventually come the greatest of all the empires of the ancient past, that of sixth-century Persia. Still another branch of these peoples pushes out into India. These movements must explain much of what lies behind a shifting pattern of empires and kingdoms stretching across the centuries. By standards of modern times some of them were quite long-lived; from about 1600 BCE a people called Kassites from Caucasia ruled in Babylon for four and a half centuries, which is a duration comparable to that of the entire history of the British empire. Yet, by the standards of Egypt, such polities are the creatures of a moment, born today and swept away tomorrow.

MILITARY TECHNIQUES

It would indeed be surprising if the old empires and kingdoms had not proved fragile in the end, for many other new forces were also at work which multiplied the revolutionary effects of the wanderings of peoples. One of them which has left deep traces is improvement in military technique. Fortification and, presumably, siege-craft had already reached a fairly high level in Mesopotamia by 2000 BCE. Among the Indo-European peoples who nibbled at the civilization these skills protected were some with recent nomadic origins; perhaps for that reason they were able to revolutionize warfare in the field, though they long remained unskilled in siege-craft. Their introduction of the two-wheeled war chariot and the cavalryman transformed operations in open country. The soldiers of Sumer are depicted trundling about in clumsy four-wheeled carts, drawn by asses; probably these

Four warriors in a two-wheeled Assyrian war chariot. Mounted warriors began to take part in battles in the Near East during the 2nd millennium BCE.

Time chart (2200 BCE–562 BCE)

2000 BCE Knossos Palace built in Crete
1700–1200 BCE Hittite Empire
965–928 BCE Reign of Solomon
883–859 BCE Reign of Ashurnasirpal, Assyrian emperor

2000 BCE — 1500 BCE — 1000 BCE — 500 BCE

2200 BCE Minoan civilization in Crete
1600 BCE Mycenaean civilization
604–562 BCE Reign of Nebuchadnezzar II of Babylon

The 7th-century BCE Assyrian king Ashurbanipal, depicted taking part in a hunt near his palace in Nineveh. With neither saddle nor stirrups, it was difficult for horse-riders to keep their balance.

were simply a means of moving generals about or getting a leader into the mêlée, so that spear and axe could be brought to bear. The true chariot is a two-wheeled fighting vehicle drawn by horses, the usual crew being two, one man driving, the other using it as a platform for missile weapons, especially the composite bow formed of strips of horn. The Kassites were probably the first people to exploit the horse in this way and their rulers seem to have been of Indo-European stock. Access to the high pastures to the north and east of the Fertile Crescent opened to them a reserve of horses in the lands of the nomads. In the river valleys horses were at first rare, the prized possessions of kings or great leaders, and the barbarians therefore enjoyed a great military and psychological superiority. Eventually, though, chariots were used in the armies of all the great kingdoms of the Near East; they were too valuable a weapon to be ignored. When the Egyptians expelled the Hyksos, they did so by, among other things, using this weapon against those who had conquered them with it.

THE USE OF CAVALRY

Warfare was changed by riding horses. A cavalryman proper not only moves about in the saddle but fights from horseback; it took a long time for this art to be developed, for managing a horse and a bow or a spear at the same time is a complex matter. Horse-riding came from the Iranian highlands, where it may have been practised as early as 2000 BCE. It spread through the Near East and Aegean well before the end of the next millennium. Later, after 1000 BCE, there appeared the armoured horseman, charging home and dominating foot-soldiers by sheer weight and impetus. This was the beginning of a long era in which heavy cavalry were a key weapon, though their full value could only be exploited centuries later, when the invention of the stirrup gave the rider more control.

THE IMPORTANCE OF IRON

During the second millennium BCE chariots came to have parts made of iron; soon they had hooped wheels. The military advantages of this metal are obvious and it is not surprising to find its uses spreading rapidly through the Near East and far beyond, in spite of attempts by those who had iron to restrict it. At first, these were the Hittites. After their decline iron-working spread rapidly, not only because it was a more effective metal for making arms, but because iron ore, though scarce, was more plentiful than copper or tin. It was a great stimulus to economic as well as military change. In agriculture, iron-using peoples could till heavy soils which had remained impervious to wood or flint. But there was no rapid general transfer to the new metal; iron supplemented bronze, as bronze and copper had supplemented stone and flint in the human tool-kit, and did so in some places more rapidly than others. Already in the eleventh century BCE iron was used for weaponry in Cyprus (some have argued that steel was produced there, too) and from that island iron spread to the Aegean soon after 1000 BCE. That date can serve as a rough division between the Bronze and Iron Ages, but is no more than a helpful prop to memory. Though iron implements became more plentiful after it, parts of what we may call the "civilized world" long went on living in a Bronze Age culture. Together with the "Neolithic" elsewhere, the Bronze Age lives on well into the first millenium BCE, fading away only slowly like the smile on the face of the Cheshire cat. For a long time, after all, there was very little iron to go round.

LONG-DISTANCE TRADE

Metallurgical demand helps to explain another innovation, a new and increasingly complex inter-regional and long-distance trade. It is one of those complicating inter-reactions

From copper to iron

The natural resources of copper and gold, which were easy to work, were the first metals to be used in western Asia. The discovery that it was possible to extract metals from various minerals using heat appears to have been made in western Asia and southeastern Europe in the 7th millennium BCE and in eastern Asia in the 3rd millennium BCE. Bronze, made from an alloy of copper and tin, was discovered in the 4th millennium BCE in western Asia and in the 3rd millennium BCE in eastern Asia. It was widely used for producing weapons and tools. Iron, which was more difficult to work, was used in western Asia from the beginning of the 2nd millennium BCE. Iron gradually replaced bronze for making weapons and tools – it was in plentiful supply and, when coal was added to the metal compound, it produced weapons that could be sharpened. Very high temperatures are needed to forge iron, a practice which started in China during the 6th century BCE. In the rest of the world, however, cast iron continued to be used for another 1,000 years.

Assyrian bronze and iron mace heads dating from around the 9th century BCE.

which seem to be giving the ancient world a certain unity just before its disruption at the end of the second millennium BCE. Tin, for example, had to be brought from Mesopotamia and Afghanistan, as well as Anatolia, to what we should now call "manufacturing" centres. The copper of Cyprus was another widely traded commodity and the search for more of it gave Europe, at the margins of ancient history though she was, a new importance. Mine-shafts in what is now the Federal Republic of Yugoslavia were sunk sixty and seventy feet below ground to get at copper even before 4000 BCE. Perhaps it is not surprising that some European peoples later came to display high levels of metallurgical skill, notably in the beating of large sheets of bronze and in the shaping of iron (a much more difficult material to work than bronze until temperatures high enough to cast it were available).

NEW METHODS OF TRANSPORT

The growth of long-range commerce depends on transport. At first, the carriage of goods was a matter of asses and donkeys; the domestication of camels in the middle of the second millennium BCE made possible the caravan trade of Asia and the Arabian peninsula which was later to seem to be of ageless antiquity, and opened an environment hitherto almost impenetrable, the desert. Except among nomadic peoples, wheeled transport probably had only local importance, given the poor quality of early roads. Early carts were drawn by oxen or asses; they may have been in service in Mesopotamia about 3000 BCE, in Syria around 2250 BCE, in Anatolia two or three hundred years later and in mainland Greece about 1500 BCE.

A 7th-century BCE bas-relief from Nineveh showing an Assyrian camp outside the walls of a city. Two dromedaries are shown. These animals were probably introduced into Mesopotamia from Arabia during the latter half of the 2nd millennium BCE. Camels were used for transport, but not for combat.

A detail from the 16th-century BCE wall paintings found at the Akrotiri settlement, on the island of Thera (Santorini). A coastal city is depicted surrounded by mountains.

WATER TRANSPORT

For goods in quantity, water transport was already likely to be cheaper and simpler than transport by land in the second millennium BCE; this was to be a constant of economic life until the coming of the steam railway. Long before caravans began to bring up to Mesopotamia and Egypt the gums and resins of the south Arabian coasts, ships were carrying them up the Red Sea and merchants were moving back and forth in trading vessels across the Aegean. Understandably, it was in maritime technology that some of the most important advances in transport were made.

We know that Neolithic peoples could make long journeys by sea in dug-out canoes and there is even some evidence of navigation from the seventh millennium. The Egyptians of the Third Dynasty had put a sail on a sea-going ship; the central mast and square sail were the beginning of seamanship relying on anything but human energy. Improvements of rigging came slowly over the next two millennia. It has been thought that these made some approach to the fore-and-aft rigging which was necessary if ships were to sail closer to the wind, but for the most part the ships of antiquity were square-rigged. Because of this, the direction of prevailing winds was decisive in setting patterns of sea-borne communication. The only other source of energy was human: the invention of the oar is an early one and it provided the motive power for long sea crossings as well as for close handling. It seems likely, though, that oars were used more frequently in warships, and sail in what it is at a very early date possible to call merchantmen. By the thirteenth century BCE, ships capable of carrying more than 200 copper ingots were sailing about the eastern Mediterranean, and within a few centuries more, some of these ships were being fitted with watertight decks.

THE INVENTION OF MONEY

Even in recent times goods have been exchanged or bartered and no doubt this was what trade meant for most of antiquity. Yet a great step was taken when money was invented. This seems to have happened in Mesopotamia, where values of account were being given in measures of grain or silver before 2000 BCE. Copper ingots seem to have been treated as monetary units throughout the Mediterranean in the late Bronze Age. The first officially sealed means of exchange which survives comes from Cappadocia in the form of ingots of silver of the late third millennium BCE: this was a true metal currency. Yet though money is an important invention and one which was to spread, we have to wait until the eighth century BCE for the Assyrians to have a silver standard for the first coins. Refined monetary devices (and Mesopotamia had a credit system and bills of

Trading and storing goods

There is evidence to suggest that trade acquired growing importance in the Near East during the 2nd millennium BCE, although this does not mean that a real market economy operated at that time. It was only in the 7th century BCE that money began to be minted; before this, trade had been carried out by exchanging goods, including metal ingots. Bartering and the sending of diplomatic gifts or tributes were also common practices.

In Egypt, the storage of surplus cereals, controlled by the pharaohs' scribes and the temples, allowed Egyptians to survive years of bad harvests, such as those described in the biblical story of Joseph.

Scenes from an 11th-dynasty Egyptian burial painting, showing some of the processes involved in the storage of food.

A detail from an 18th-dynasty wall painting shows Nubian envoys bearing gifts for the Egyptian pharaoh. Such gifts explain why archaeologists have discovered many objects far from their original place of manufacture, although the presence of some may be the result of long-distance trade.

exchange in early times) may help to promote trade, but they are not indispensable. Peoples in the ancient world could get along without them. The Phoenicians, a trading people of legendary skill and acumen, did not have a currency until the sixth century BCE; Egypt, a centrally controlled economy and of legendary wealth, did not adopt a coinage until two centuries after that, and Celtic Europe, for all its trade in metal goods, did not coin money until two centuries later still.

TRADING WITHOUT MONEY

Meanwhile, goods were exchanged without money, though it is hard to be sure quite what this means. Although there was an important rise in the volume of goods moved about the world, by 1000 BCE or so, not all of this was what would now be termed "trade". Economic organization in ancient times is for a long time obscure. Any specialized function – pottery-making, for example – implies machinery which on the one hand distributes its products and, on the other, ensures subsistence to the specialist by redistributing to him and his fellows the food they need to survive, and perhaps other goods. But this does not require "trade", even in the form of barter. Many peoples in historic times have been observed operating such distribution through their chiefs: these men presided over a common store, "owning", in a sense, everything the community possessed, and doling out such shares from it as were required to keep society working smoothly. This may be what lay behind the centralization of goods and supplies in Sumerian temples; it would also explain the importance of the recording and sealing of consignments deposited there and hence the early association of writing with accounting.

As for economic exchange between communities, confident generalization about its earliest stages is even more hazardous. Once into the era of historical record, we can see many activities going on which involve the transfer of commodities, not all of them aimed at monetary gain. Payment of tribute, symbolic or diplomatic gifts between rulers, votive offerings, were some of the forms it took. We should not rush to be over-definite; right down to the nineteenth century CE the Chinese empire conceived its foreign trade in terms of tribute from the outside world and the pharaohs had a way of translating trade with the Aegean into similar notions, to judge by tomb paintings. In the ancient world, such transactions might include the transfer of standard objects such as tripods or vessels of a certain weight or rings of uniform size which therefore present at an early date some of the characteristics of currency. Sometimes such things were useful; sometimes they were merely tokens. All that is wholly certain is that the movement of commodities increased and that much of this increase in the end took the form of the profitable exchanges we now think of as commerce.

New towns must have helped such changes. They sprang up all over the old Near East no doubt in part because of population growth. They register the successful exploitation of agricultural possibilities but also a growing parasitism. The literary tradition of the alienation of countrymen from the city is already there in the Old Testament. Yet city life also offered a new intensity of cultural creativity, a new acceleration of civilization.

THE ROLE OF LITERACY

One sign of accelerating civilization is the spreading of literacy. In about 2000 BCE, literacy was still largely confined to the river-valley civilizations and the areas they influenced. Cuneiform had spread throughout Mesopotamia where two or three languages were written in it; in Egypt the monumental inscriptions were hieroglyphic and day-to-day writing was done on papyrus in a simplified form called hieratic. A thousand years or so later, the picture had changed. Literate peoples were then to be found all over the Near East, and in Crete and Greece, too. Cuneiform had been adapted to yet more languages with great success; even the Egyptian government adopted it for its diplomacy. Other scripts were being invented, too. One, in Crete, takes us to the edge of modernity, for it reveals a people in about 1500 BCE whose language was basically Greek. With the adoption of a Semitic alphabet, the Phoenician, the medium of the first western literature was in existence by about 800 BCE, and so, perhaps, was its first surviving expression, in what were later called the works of Homer.

A lion hunt is depicted on this gold-encrusted copper dagger. The weapon was found in a Mycenaean tomb dating from the 16th century BCE.

Pictographic and alphabetic systems of writing

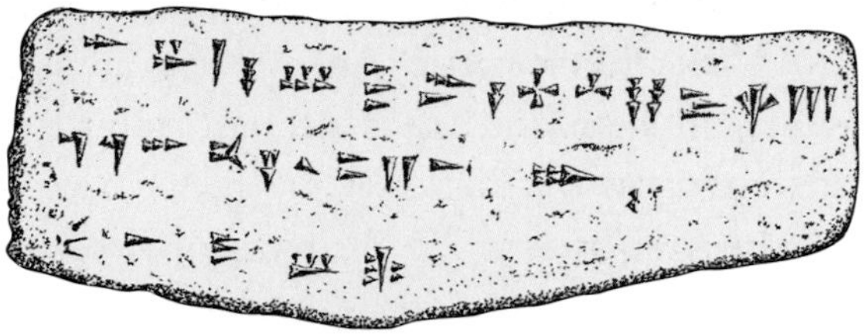

Ugarit tablet

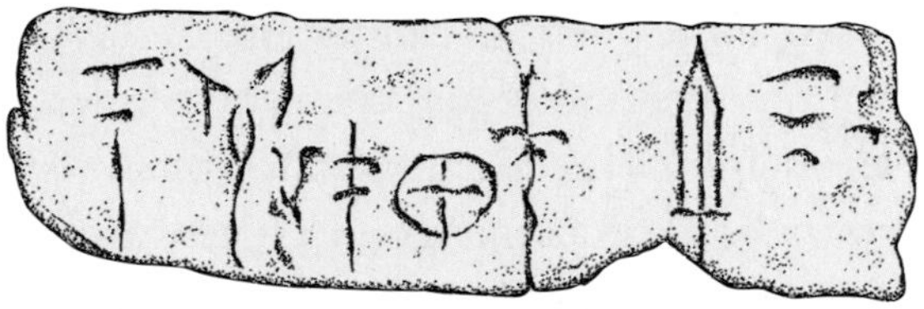

Cretan tablet ("Linear A")

Classical Greek tablet

From the middle of the 2nd millennium BCE, writing became much more widespread in the ancient world. In Crete, in the Mediterranean, two types of pictographic writing, derived from Egyptian hieroglyphics, were used. They were called "Linear A" and "Linear B" (only the latter has so far been deciphered).

An important breakthrough came with the appearance of the first alphabetic writing, which was probably Canaanite. Other alphabetic writing systems were derived from this one, including Ugarit, on which the Greek alphabet was based, and from which Latin was later developed.

STATEHOOD AND POWER

Localized themes make nonsense of chronology; they register changes lost to sight if history is pinned too closely to specific countries. Yet individual countries and their peoples, though subject to general forces and in more and more frequent contact, also become increasingly distinct. Literacy pins down tradition; in its turn, tradition expresses communal self-consciousness. Presumably tribes and peoples have always felt their identity; such awareness is much strengthened when states take on more continuing and institutionalized forms. The dissolution of empires into more viable units is a familiar story from Sumer to modern times, but some areas emerge time and time again as enduring nuclei of tradition. Even in the second millennium BCE, states are getting more solid and show greater staying power. They were still far from achieving that extensive and continuing control of their peoples whose possibilities have only fully been revealed in modern times.

Yet even in the most ancient records there seems to be an unchecked trend towards a greater regularity in government and greater institutionalizing of power. Kings surround themselves with bureaucracies and tax-collectors find the resources for larger and larger enterprises. Law becomes a widely accepted idea; wherever it penetrates, there is a limitation, even if at first only implicit, of the power of the individual and an increase of that of the law-giver. Above all, the state expresses itself through its military power; the considerable problem of feeding, equipping and administering standing professional armies is solved by 1000 BCE.

CULTURAL DIFFERENTIATION

When states become powerful, the story of governmental and social institutions begins to escape from the general categories of early civilization. In spite of a new cosmopolitanism made possible by easier intercourse and cross-fertilizing, societies take very diverse paths. In the life of the mind, the most conspicuous expression of diversity is religion. While some have discerned in the pre-classical era a tendency towards simpler, monotheistic systems, the most obvious fact is a huge and varied pantheon of local and specialized deities, mostly coexisting tolerantly, with only an occasional indication that one god is jealous of his distinction.

There is a new scope for differentiation in other expressions of culture, too. Before civilization began, art had already established itself as an autonomous activity not necessarily linked to religion or magic (often so linked though it continued to be). The first literature has already been mentioned and of other sides of the mind we also begin to see something. There is the possibility of play; gaming-boards appear in Mesopotamia, Egypt, Crete. Perhaps people were already gambling. Kings and noblemen hunted with passion, and in their palaces were entertained by musicians and dancers. Among sports, boxing seems to go back into Bronze Age Crete, an island where the unique sport of bull-leaping was also practised.

In such matters it is more obvious than anywhere else that we need not pay much heed to chronology, far less to particular dates, even when we can be sure of them. The notion of an individual civilization is less and less helpful over the area with which we have so far been concerned, too. There is too much interplay for it to bear the weight it can do in Egypt and Sumer.

Somewhere between about 1500 and 800 BCE big changes took place which ought not to be allowed to slip through the mesh of a net woven to catch the history of the first two great civilizations. In the confused, turbulent Near East and eastern Mediterranean of the centuries around 1000 BCE a new world different from that of Sumer and the Old Kingdom was in the making.

A games table, made of ebony and ivory, from the tomb of the 18th-dynasty pharaoh Tutankhamon.

EARLY AEGEAN CIVILIZATION

A NEW INTERPLAY OF CULTURES brought many changes to peoples on the fringe of the Near East but civilization in the Aegean islands was rooted in the Neolithic as it was elsewhere. The first metal object found in Greece – a copper bead – has been dated to about 4700 BCE, and European as well as Asian stimuli may have been at work. Crete is the largest of the Greek islands. Several centuries before 2000 BCE, towns with a regular layout were being built there by an advanced people which had been there through Neolithic times. They may have had contacts with Anatolia which spurred them to exceptional achievements, but the evidence is

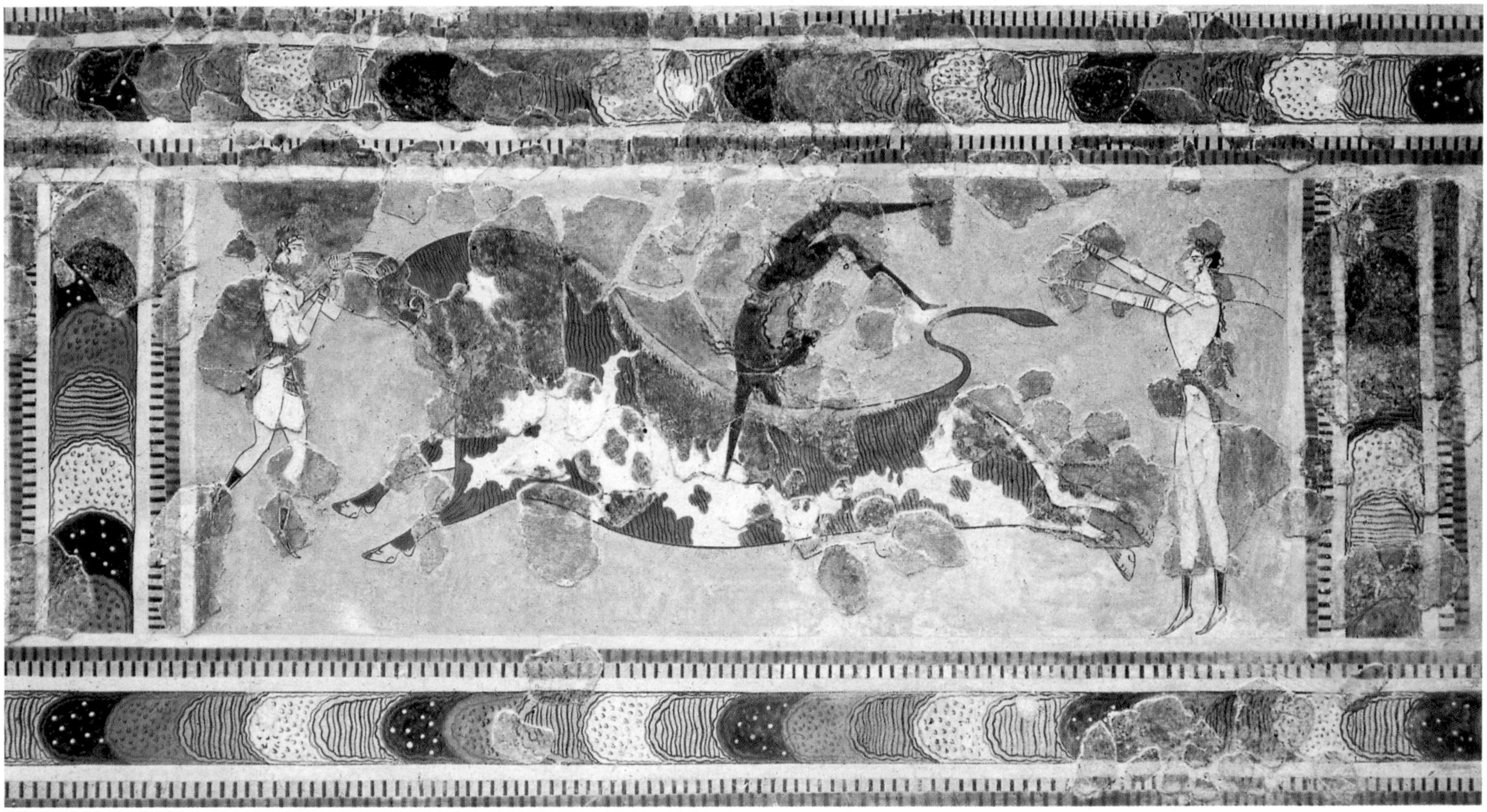

This magnificent fresco at the palace of Knossos in Crete is around 3,500 years old. It depicts the sport of bull-leaping.

indecisive. They could well have arrived at civilization for themselves. At any rate, for about a thousand years they built the houses and tombs by which their culture is distinguished and these did not change much in style. By about 2500 BCE there were important towns and villages on the coasts, built of stone and brick; their inhabitants practised metal-working and made attractive seals and jewels. At this stage, that is to say, the Cretans shared much of the culture of mainland Greece and Asia Minor. They exchanged goods with other Aegean communities. There then came a change. About five hundred years later they began to build the series of great palaces which are the monuments of what we call "Minoan" civilization; the greatest of them, Knossos, was first built about 1900 BCE. Nothing quite as impressive appears anywhere else among the islands and it exercised a cultural hegemony over more or less the whole of the Aegean.

MINOAN CRETE

Minoan is a curious name; it is taken from the name of a King Minos who, although celebrated in legend, may never have existed. Much later, the Greeks believed – or said – that he was a great king in Crete who lived at Knossos, parleyed with the gods, and married Pasiphae, the daughter of the sun. Her monstrous offspring, the Minotaur, devoured sacrificial youths and maids sent as tribute from Greece at the heart of a labyrinth eventually penetrated successfully by the hero Theseus, who slew him. This is a rich and suggestive theme and has excited scholars, who believe it can throw light on Cretan civilization, but there is no proof that King Minos ever existed. It may be that, as legend suggests, there was more than one of that name, or that his name was a titular identification of several Cretan rulers. He is one of those fascinating figures who, like King

Arthur, remain just beyond the borders of history but inside those of mythology.

Minoan, then, simply means the civilization of people who lived in Bronze Age Crete; it has no other connotation. This civilization lasted some six hundred years, but only the outlines of a history can be put together. They reveal a people living in towns linked in some dependence on a monarchy at Knossos. For three or four centuries they prosper, exchanging goods with Egypt, Asia Minor and the Greek mainland, and subsisting on a native agriculture. It may have been this which explains Minoan civilization's leap forward. Crete seems then, as today, to have been better for the production of olives and vines than either the other islands or mainland Greece. It seems likely, too, that she raised large numbers of sheep and exported wool. Whatever its precise forms, Crete experienced an important agricultural advance in late Neolithic times, which led not only to better cereal-growing but, above all, to the cultivation of the other two great staples of Mediterranean agriculture, the olive and vine. They could be grown where grains could not and their discovery changed the possibilities of Mediterranean life. Immediately they permitted a larger population. On this much else could then be built because new human resources were available, but it also made new demands, for organization and government, for the regulation of a more complex agriculture and the handling of its produce.

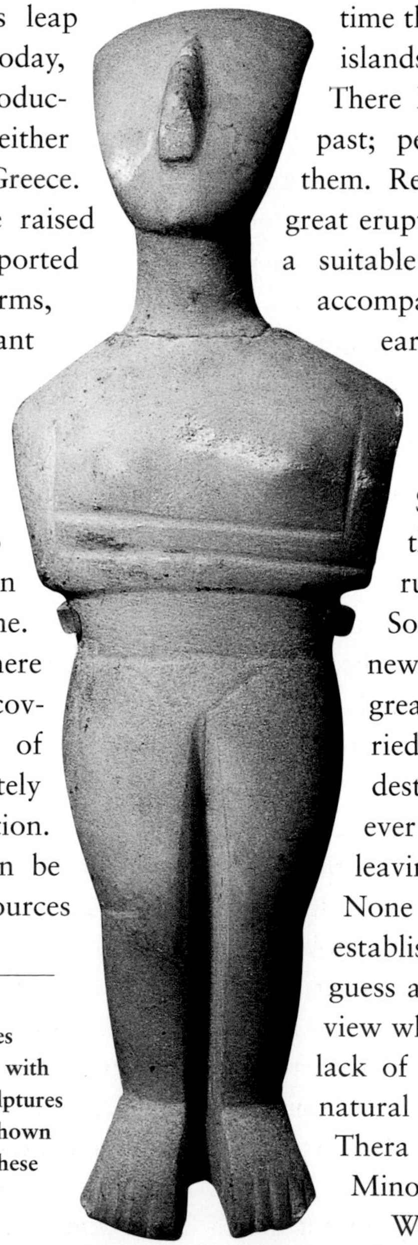

In the 3rd millennium BCE, the Cyclades formed a bridge linking western Asia with the rest of the Greek world. Marble sculptures of naked female idols, such as the one shown here, were often made on the islands. These sculptures are remarkable for their geometrical stylization.

THE END OF MINOAN CIVILIZATION

The peak of Minoan civilization came about 1600 BCE. A century or so later, the Minoan palaces were destroyed. The mystery of this end is tantalizing. At about the same time the major towns of the Aegean islands were destroyed by fire, too. There had been earthquakes in the past; perhaps this was another of them. Recent scholarship identifies a great eruption in the island of Thera at a suitable time; it could have been accompanied by tidal waves and earthquakes in Crete, seventy miles away, and followed by the descent of clouds of ash which blighted Cretan fields. Some people have preferred to think of a rising against the rulers who lived in the palaces. Some have discerned signs of a new invasion, or postulated some great raid from the sea which carried off booty and prisoners, destroying a political power for ever by the damage it inflicted, by leaving no new settlers behind. None of these can be conclusively established. It is only possible to guess about what happened and the view which does least violence to the lack of evidence is that there was a natural cataclysm originating in Thera which broke the back of Minoan civilization.

Whatever the cause, this was

not the end of early civilization in Crete, for Knossos was occupied for another century or so by people from the mainland. Never the less, though there were still some fairly prosperous times to come, the ascendancy of the indigenous civilization of Crete was, in effect, over. For a time, it seems, Knossos still prospered. Then, early in the fourteenth century BCE it, too, was destroyed by fire. This had happened before, but this time it was not rebuilt. So ends the story of early Cretan civilization.

CRETAN SEA POWER

Fortunately, the salient characteristics of Cretan civilization are easier to understand than the detail of its history. The most obvious is its close relationship with the sea. More than a thousand years later, Greek tradition said that Minoan Crete was a great naval power exercising political hegemony in the Aegean through her fleet. This idea has been much blown upon by modern scholars anxious to reduce what they believe to be an anachronistic conception to more plausible proportions and it certainly seems misleading to see behind this tradition the sort of political power later exercised through their navies by such states as fifth-century Athens or nineteenth-century Great Britain. The Minoans may have had a lot of ships, but they were unlikely to be specialized at this early date and there is no hope in the Bronze Age of drawing a line between trade, piracy and counter-piracy in their employment. Probably there was no permanent Cretan "navy" in a public sense at all. Nevertheless, the Minoans felt sufficiently sure of the protection the sea gave them – and this must have implied some confidence in their ability to dominate the approaches to the natural harbours, most of which are on the north coast – to live in towns without fortifications, built near to the shore on only slightly elevated ground. We do not have to look for a Cretan Nelson among their defenders; that would be silly. But we can envisage a Cretan Hawkins or Drake, trading, freebooting and protecting the home base.

The Minoans thus exploited the sea as other peoples exploited their natural environments. The result was an interchange of products and ideas which shows once more how civilization can accelerate where there is the possibility of cross-fertilization. Minoans had close connections with Syria before 1550 BCE and traded as far west as Sicily, perhaps further. Someone took their goods up the Adriatic coasts. Even more important was

The sea was a recurring theme in the art of Minoan Crete, reflecting the important role that it played in the everyday lives of the people. Octopus motifs, such as the one shown here, were often used to decorate vases.

their penetration of Greece. The Minoans may well have been the most important single conduit through which the goods and ideas of the earliest civilizations reached Bronze Age Europe. Certain Cretan products begin to turn up in Egypt in the second millennium BCE and this was a major outlet; the art of the New Kingdom shows Cretan influence. There was even, some scholars think, an Egyptian resident for some time at Knossos, presumably to watch over well-established interests, and it has been argued that Minoans fought with the Egyptians against the Hyksos. Cretan vases and metal goods have been found at several places in Asia Minor: these are the things which survive, but it has been argued that a wide range of other products – timber, grapes, oil, wood, metal vases and even opium – were supplied by the Minoans to the mainland. In return, they took metal from Asia Minor, alabaster from Egypt, ostrich eggs from Libya. It was already a complex trading world.

CULTURAL ACHIEVEMENTS

Together with a prosperous agriculture, trade made possible a civilization of considerable solidity, long able to recover from natural disaster, as the repeated rebuilding of the palace at Knossos seems to show. The palaces are the finest relics of Minoan civilization, but the towns were well built too, and had elaborate piped drains and sewers. This was technical achievement of a high order; early in the sequence of palaces at Knossos the bathing and lavatory provision is on a scale unsurpassed before Roman times. Other cultural achievement was less practical, though artistic rather than intellectual; Minoans seem to have taken their mathematics from Egypt and left it at that. Their religion went under with them, apparently leaving nothing to the future, but the Minoans had an important contribution to make to the style of another civilization on the Greek mainland. Art embodied Minoan civilization at its highest

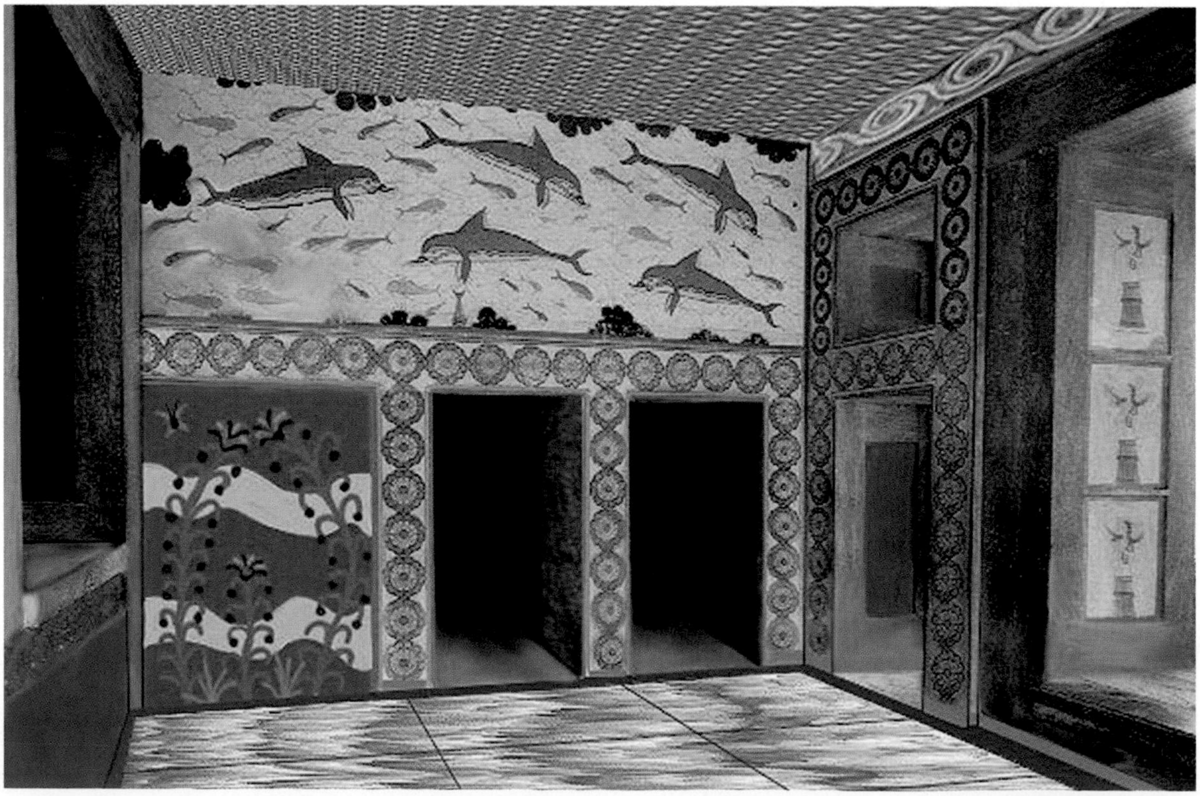

Reconstruction of a chamber in the royal apartments at Knossos. The famous dolphin fresco, which decorates one of the walls, reflects a taste for joyful, colourful imagery that appears to have been typical of Minoan artists.

The palace of Knossos

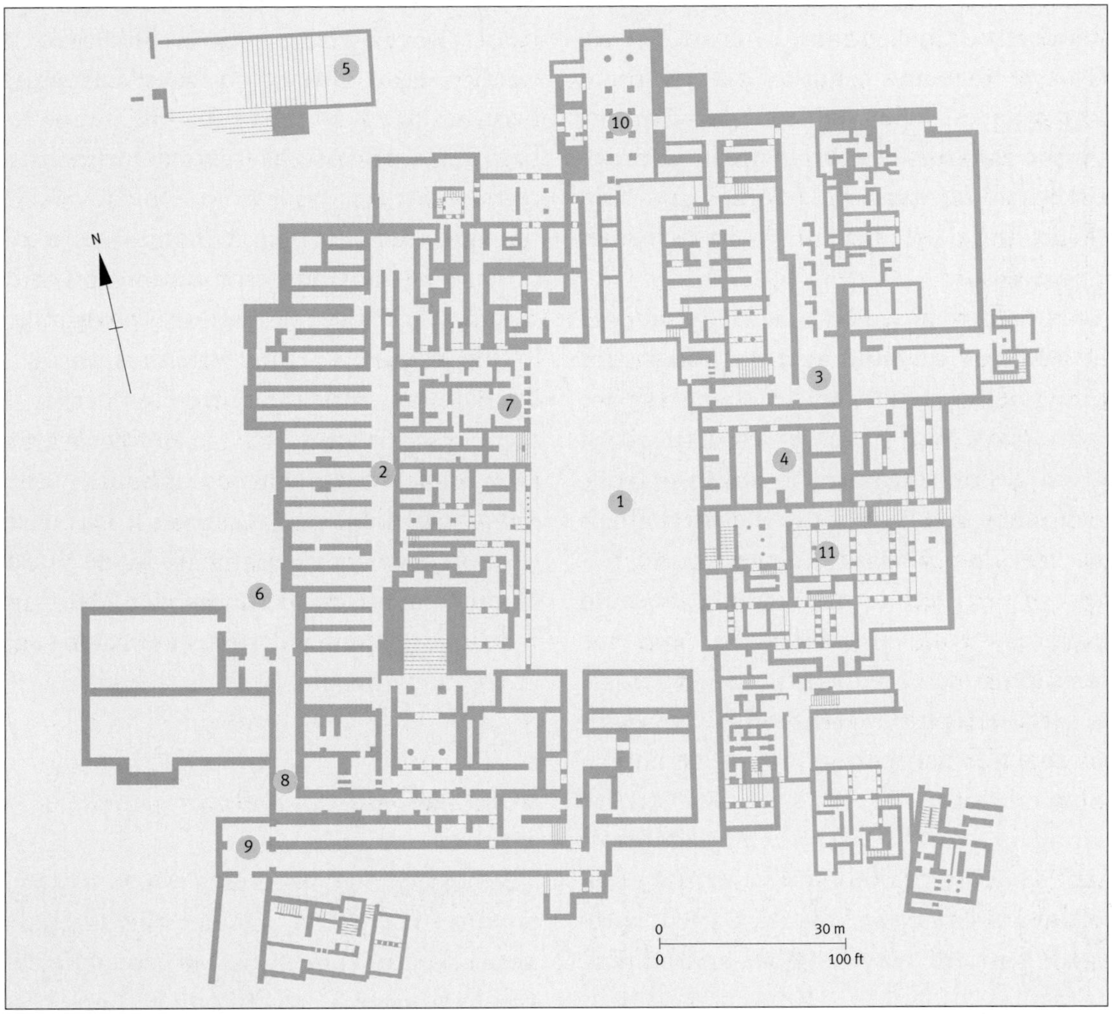

Key	
1	Central courtyard
2	Main floor
3	Workshop area
4	Royal domestic quarters
5	Theatre
6	Main entrance
7	Throne room
8	Procession corridor
9	Stepped causeway
10	Hall of pillars
11	Hall of the double axes

Plan of the palace of Knossos.

For ancient Greeks, Knossos was the capital from which Minos, King of Crete, ruled. Perhaps the extensive ruins of the palace gave rise to the legend about the labyrinth and the Minotaur. Knossos was certainly the most important of all the Minoan palaces on Crete. Archaeological excavations were begun in 1900 CE by Arthur Evans and revealed large archives full of baked-clay tablets. The writing on them, called "Linear B", took 50 years to decipher. Using the information provided by the tablets, we are able to reconstruct many aspects of life in Minoan Crete. Built in about 1900 BCE on a hill which had long been inhabited, the palace reached the zenith of its splendour half a millennium later.

and remains its most spectacular legacy. Its genius was pictorial and reached a climax in palace frescoes of startling liveliness and movement. Here is a really original style, influential across the seas, in Egypt and in Greece. Through other palatial arts, too, notably the working of gems and precious metals, it was to shape fashion elsewhere.

THE MINOAN LIFESTYLE

Representative art provides a little evidence about the Cretans' style of life. They seem to have dressed scantily, the women often being depicted bare-breasted; the men are beardless. There is an abundance of flowers and plants to suggest a people deeply and readily appreciative of nature's gifts; they do not give the impression that the Minoans found the world an unfriendly place. Their relative wealth – given the standards of ancient times – is attested by the rows of huge and beautiful oil-jars found in their palaces. Their concern for comfort and what cannot but be termed elegance comes clearly through the dolphins and lilies which decorate the apartments of a former Minoan queen.

Archaeology has also provided evidence of the Minoan religious world, though this does not, perhaps, take us very far since we have no texts. We have representations of gods and goddesses, but it is not easy to be sure who they are. Nor can we penetrate their rituals very far, beyond registering the frequency of sacrificial altars, sanctuaries in high places, double-headed axes, and the apparent centring of Minoan cults in a female figure (though her relationship to other deities remains a mystery). She is perhaps a Neolithic fertility figure such as was to appear again and again as the embodiment of female sexuality: the later Astarte and Aphrodite. In Crete she appears skirted, bare-breasted, standing between lions and holding snakes. Whether there was a male god, too, is less clear. But the appearance of bulls' horns in many places and of frescoes of these noble beasts is suggestive if it is linked to later Greek legend (Minos' mother, Europa, had been seduced by Zeus in the shape of a bull; his wife Pasiphae enjoyed a monstrous coition with a bull from which was born the half-bull, half-man Minotaur), and to the obscure but obviously important rites of bull-leaping. Sacrifice, it is clear, was important in the Minoans' ritual attempts to achieve communion with their deity or deities, and there is evidence which, it has been argued, even points to its inclusion of human victims. Yet it is striking that whatever it was, Cretan religion does not seem to have made Minoans gloomy; pictures of sports and dancing or delicate frescoes and pottery do not suggest an unhappy people.

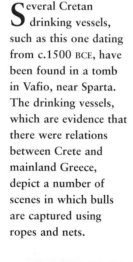

Several Cretan drinking vessels, such as this one dating from c.1500 BCE, have been found in a tomb in Vafio, near Sparta. The drinking vessels, which are evidence that there were relations between Crete and mainland Greece, depict a number of scenes in which bulls are captured using ropes and nets.

MINOAN POLITICS

The political arrangements of this society are obscure. The palace was not only a royal residence, but in some sense an economic centre – a great store – which may perhaps best be understood as the apex of an advanced form of exchange based on redistribution by the ruler. The palace was also a temple, but not a fortress. In its maturity it was the centre of a highly organized structure whose inspiration may have been Asian; knowledge of the literate empires of Egypt and Mesopotamia was available to a trading people. One source of our knowledge of what Minoan government was trying to do is a huge collection of thousands of tablets which are its administrative records. They indicate rigid hierarchy and systematized administration, but not how this worked in practice. However effective government was, the only thing the records certainly show is what it aspired to, a supervision far

A detail from one of the frescoes at the palace of Akrotiri, on the island of Thera, dating from the middle of the 2nd millennium BCE. The style of the frescoes is reminiscent of those discovered in Minoan palaces in Crete.

closer and more elaborate than anything conceivable by the later Greek world. If there are any analogies, they are again with the Asian empires and Egypt.

At present, the tablets tell us only of the last phase of Minoan civilization because many of them cannot be read. The weight of scholarly opinion now inclines to the view put forward a few years ago that the script of a great mass of them found at Knossos is used to write Greek and that they date from about 1450 to 1375 BCE. The script in which they are written has been termed "Linear B". The earlier written records are found at first in hieroglyph, with some symbols borrowed from Egypt, and then in another script (not yet deciphered) termed "Linear A" and used from perhaps as early as 1700 BCE. Almost certainly it was wholly non-Greek. Some have argued that the incoming Greeks took over pre-existing Minoan administrative practice and put down records, such as were already kept, in their own tongue. The earlier tablets probably contain information which is very like that in the later, but, if so, it is about Crete before the coming of whoever presided over the last phase and mysterious end of Minoan civilization.

THE END OF THE CRETAN CULTURE

Successful invasion from the European mainland would itself have been a sign that the conditions which had made this civilization possible were crumbling away in the troubled times of the closing Bronze Age. Crete for a long time had no rival to threaten her coasts. Perhaps the Egyptians had been too busy; in the north there had long been no possible threat. Gradually, the second of these conditions had ceased to hold. Stirring on the mainland were others of those "Indo-European" peoples who have already cropped up in so many places in this story. Some of them penetrated Crete again after the final collapse of Knossos; they were apparently successful colonists who exploited the lowlands and drove away the Minoans and their shattered culture to lonely little towns of refuge where they disappear from the stage of world history.

Ironically, only two or three centuries before this, Cretan culture had exercised something like hegemony in Greece, and Crete was always to hang about mysteriously at the back of the Greek mind, a lost and golden land. A direct transfusion of Minoan culture to the mainland had taken place through the first Achaean peoples (the name usually given to these early Greek-speakers) who came down into Attica and the Peloponnese and established towns and cities there in the eighteenth and seventeenth centuries BCE. They entered a land long in contact with Asia, whose inhabitants had already contributed to the future one enduring symbol of Greek life, the fortification of the high place of the town, or acropolis. The new arrivals were culturally hardly superior to those they conquered, though they brought

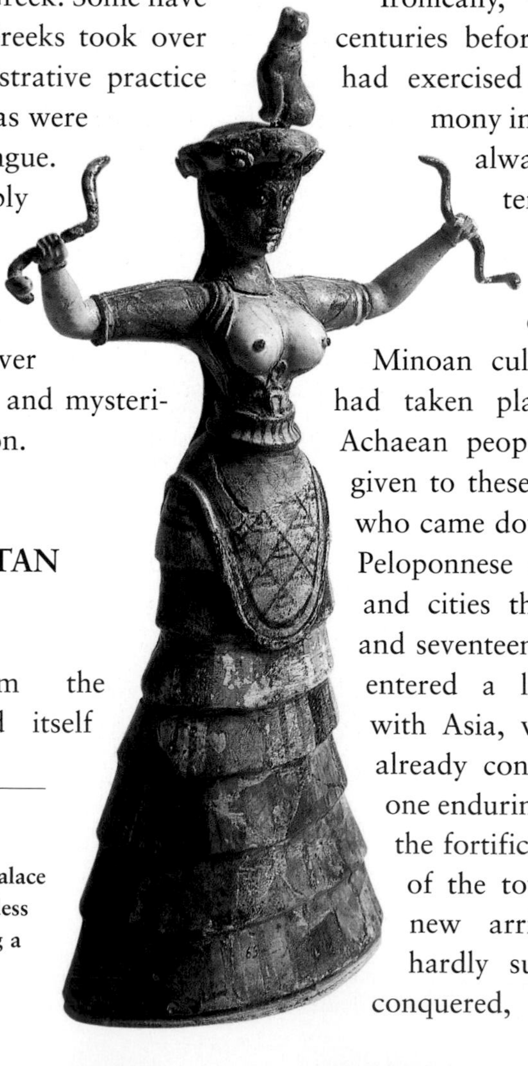

This polychrome ivory Minoan statuette was discovered in the palace of Knossos in Crete. It depicts a goddess or priestess – she is portrayed holding a snake in each hand and has a cat on her head.

with them the horse and the war chariot. They were barbarians by comparison with the Cretans, with no art of their own. More aware of the role of violence and war in society than were the islanders (no doubt because they did not enjoy the protection of the sea and had a sense of continuing pressure from the homelands from which they had come), they fortified their cities heavily and built castles. Their civilization had a military style. Sometimes they picked sites which were to be the later centres of Greek city-states; Athens and Pylos were among them. They were not very large, the biggest containing at most not more than a few thousand people. One of the most important was at Mycenae, which gave its name to the civilization that finally spread over Bronze Age Greece in the middle of the second millennium BCE.

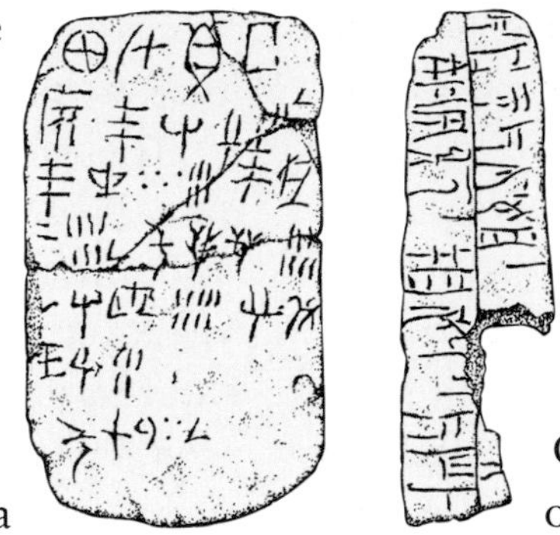

Cretan clay tablets bearing inscriptions.

MYCENAEAN GREECE

The Mycenaean civilization left some splendid relics, for it was very rich in gold; strongly influenced by Minoan art, it was also a true synthesis of Greek and indigenous cultures on the mainland. Its institutional basis seems to have been rooted in patriarchal ideas, but there is more to it than that. The bureaucratic aspiration revealed by the Knossos tablets and by others from Pylos in the western Peloponnese of about 1200 BCE suggests currents of change flowing back from Crete towards the mainland. Each considerable city had a king. The king at Mycenae, presiding over a society of warrior landowners whose tenants and slaves were the aboriginal peoples, may have been at an early date the head of some sort of federation of kings. There is suggestive evidence in

A painted Minoan sarcophagus, from Hagia Triada in Crete. The painting depicts religious burial ceremonies. On the left, women pour wine over an altar. On the right, men present a variety of offerings to an image made in the likeness of the deceased.

Hittite diplomatic records which points to some political unity in Mycenaean Greece. Below the kings, the Pylos tablets show a close supervision and control of community life and also important distinctions between officials and, more fundamentally, between slave and free. What cannot be known is just what such differences meant in practice. Nor can we see much of the economic life that lay at the root of Mycenaean culture, beyond its centralization in the royal household, as in Crete.

Whatever its material basis, the culture represented most spectacularly at Mycenae had by 1400 BCE spread all over mainland Greece and to many of the islands. It was a coherent whole, though well-established differences of Greek dialect persisted and distinguished one people from another down to classical times. Mycenae replaced the Cretan trading supremacy in the Mediterranean with its own. It had trading posts in the Levant and was treated as a power by Hittite kings. Sometimes Mycenaean pottery exports replaced Minoan, and there are even some examples of Minoan settlements being followed by Mycenaean.

The Mycenaean empire, if the term is permissible, was at its height in the fifteenth and fourteenth centuries BCE. For a while, the weakness of Egypt and the crumbling of the Hittite power favoured it; for a time a small people enriched by trade had disproportionate importance while great powers waned. Mycenaean colonies were established on the shores of Asia Minor; trade with other Asian towns, notably Troy, at the entrance to the Black Sea, prospered. But there are some signs of flagging from about 1300 BCE. War seems to have been one answer; Achaeans took important parts in attacks on Egypt at the end of the century and it now seems that a great raid by them which was immortalized as the Siege of Troy took place about 1200 BCE. The troubled background to these events was a series of dynastic upheavals in the Mycenaean cities.

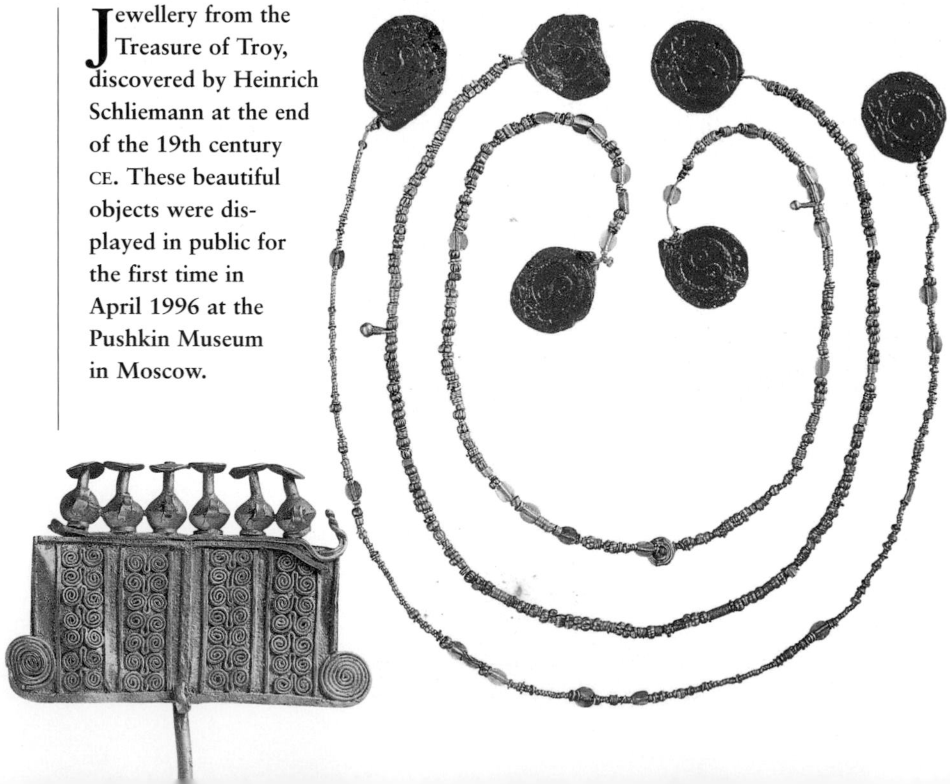

Jewellery from the Treasure of Troy, discovered by Heinrich Schliemann at the end of the 19th century CE. These beautiful objects were displayed in public for the first time in April 1996 at the Pushkin Museum in Moscow.

THE DARK AGES OF THE AEGEAN

What can be called the Dark Ages of the Aegean were about to close in and they are as obscure as what was happening in the Near East at about the same time. When Troy fell, new barbarian invasions of mainland Greece had already begun. At the very end of the thirteenth century the great Mycenaean centres were destroyed perhaps by earthquakes and the first Greece broke up into disconnected settlements. As an entity Mycenaean civilization collapsed, but not all the Mycenaean sites were abandoned, though their life continued at a lower level of achievement. The kingly treasures disappeared, the palaces were not rebuilt.

In some places the established resident peoples hung on successfully for centuries; elsewhere they were ruled as serfs or driven out by new conquerors from the north, who had been on the move from about a century before the fall of Troy. It does not seem likely that these new peoples always settled the lands they ravaged, but they swept away the existing political structures and the future would be built on their kinships, not on the Mycenaean institutions. There is a picture of confusion as the Aegean Dark Age deepens; only just before 1000 BCE are there a few signs that a new pattern – the ground plan of classical Greece – was emerging.

THE DORIANS AND IONIANS

Legendary accounts of this period attribute much to one particular group among the newcomers, the Dorians. Vigorous and bold, they were to be remembered as the descendants of Heracles. Though it is very dangerous to argue back from the presence of later Greek dialects to identifiable and compact groups of early invaders, tradition makes them the speakers of a tongue, Doric, which lived on into the classical age as a dialect setting them apart. In this case, tradition has been thought by scholars to be justified. In Sparta and Argos, Dorian communities which would be future city-states established themselves. But other peoples also helped to crystallize a new civilization in this obscure period. The most successful were those later identified as speakers of "Ionic" Greek, the Ionians of the Dark Age. Setting out from Attica (where Athens had either survived or assimilated the invaders who followed Mycenae), they took root in the Cyclades and

The entrance to "Agamemnon's tomb", or the so-called Treasury of Atreus, seen from inside the burial place. It was built in the 13th century BCE and discovered in 1874 CE by Heinrich Schliemann, an amateur archaeologist who believed in the veracity of Homer and who set out to find the burial places of his heroes.

Agamemnon, King of Mycenae, appears in the *Iliad* as the most powerful of the Greeks. Even today, the ruins of his capital are evidence of its importance in the 15th and 14th centuries BCE. These photographs show the city walls (above) and its monumental entrance, the Gate of Lions (right).

Ionia, the present Turkish coast of the Aegean. Here, as migrants and pirates, they seized or founded towns, if not on islands, almost always on or near the coast, which were the future city-states of a seafaring race. Often the sites they chose had already been occupied by the Mycenaeans. Sometimes – at Smyrna, for example – they displaced earlier Greek settlers.

This is a confusing picture at best and for much of it there is only fragmentary evidence. Yet from this turmoil there would slowly re-emerge the unity of civilization enjoyed by the Bronze Age Aegean. At first, though, there were centuries of disruption and particularism, a new period of provincialism in a once cosmopolitan world. Trade flagged and ties with Asia languished. What replaced them was the physical transference of people, sometimes taking centuries to establish new settled patterns, but in the end setting out the ground-plan of a future Greek world.

DEPOPULATION IN THE AEGEAN REGION

There occurred a colossal setback in civilized life which should remind us how fragile it could be in ancient times. Its most obvious sign was a depopulation between 1100 and 1000 BCE so widespread and violent that some scholars have sought explanations in a sudden cataclysm – plague, perhaps, or a climatic change such as might have suddenly and terribly reduced the small cultivable area of the Balkan and Aegean hillsides. Whatever the cause, the effects are to be seen also in a waning of elegance and skill; the carving of hard gems, the painting of frescoes and the making of the fine pottery all come to a stop. Such cultural continuity as the age permitted must have been largely mental, a matter of songs, myths and religious ideas.

HOMERIC GREECE

Of this troubled time a very little is dimly and remotely reflected in the bardic epics later set down in writing in the *Iliad* and the *Odyssey*. They include material transmitted for generations by recitation, whose origins lie in tradition near-contemporary with the events they purport to describe, though later attributed to one poet, Homer. Exactly what is reflected, though, is much harder to agree about; the consensus has recently been that it is hardly anything for Mycenaean times, and little more for what immediately followed them. The central episode of the *Iliad*, the attack on Troy, is not what matters here, though the account probably reflects a real preponderance of Achaean initiative in the settlement of Asia Minor. What survives is a little social and conceptual information carried incidentally by the poems. Though Homer gives an impression of some special pre-eminence enjoyed by the Mycenaean king, this is information about the post-Mycenaean Aegean of the eighth century, when recovery from the Dark Ages begins. It reveals a society whose assumptions are those of barbarian warlords rather than those of rulers commanding regular armies or supervising bureaucracies like those of Asia. Homer's kings are the greatest of great nobles, the heads of large households, their acknowledged authority tempered by the real power of truculent near-equals and measured by their ability to impose themselves; their lives are troubled and exacting. The atmosphere is individualistic and anarchic: they are more like a band of Viking leaders than the rulers who ran their affairs with instruments like the Mycenaean tablets. Whatever reminiscences of detail may survive from earlier times (and these have sometimes been confirmed in their accuracy by excavation) and however many reflections of later society they eventually contained, the poems only fitfully illuminate a primitive society, still in confusion, settling

A coat of armour made of bronze and a helmet with metallic ear plates, found in a Mycenaean burial place in Dendra (c.1400 BCE). Achaean warriors wore metal plates to protect themselves and proved invincible against enemies who did not have such sophisticated armour – the *Iliad* bears testament to this.

The Trojan wars

Greek literature begins with two epic poems by Homer, the *Iliad* and the *Odyssey*. The first narrates the siege of Troy (Ilium) by the Greeks and the second the homecoming of one of the Greek heroes, Ulysses. These poems, written in the 8th century BCE (centuries after the events to which they refer had taken place), are full of legendary elements, which in turn gave rise to the idea that Troy was also merely a legend.

The first excavations took place on a mound next to the mouth of the Dardanelles straits, where Heinrich Schliemann believed Troy might have been located, and were begun in 1870. Schliemann found a 3rd-millennium treasure which he immediately attributed to the Trojan king Priam. Subsequent excavations have revealed that Troy was a major city throughout the 3rd and 2nd millennia BCE. On the level of excavation work known as Troy VII, traces of a fire that destroyed the city in the 13th century BCE have been discovered. The fire was probably started by the Greek invaders whose deeds were recounted by Homer. Troy was abandoned in about 1100 BCE. In 700 BCE, it regained importance as a Greek city, which also disappeared many years later.

Classical Greek literature and art contain many references to the Trojan wars. On this vase, Achilles dresses the wounds of a fellow warrior.

This marble bas-relief, dating from the 8th century BCE, was found in Nimrud, Assyria. However, its design is Phoenician and depicts an unmistakably Egyptian motif: the winged sphinx with the royal headdress of the pharaohs.

down perhaps, but neither so advanced as Mycenae had been, nor even dimly foreshadowing what Greece was to become.

The new civilization which was at last to emerge from the centuries of confusion owed much to the resumption of intercourse with the East. It was very important that the Hellenes (the name by which the invaders of Greece came to be distinguished from their predecessors) had spread out into the islands and on to the Asian mainland; they provided many points of contact between two cultural worlds. But they were not the only links between Asia and Europe. Seeds of civilization were always carried about by the go-betweens of world history, the great trading peoples.

THE PHOENICIANS

One of the trading peoples, another seafaring race, had a long and troubled history, though not so long as its legends said; the Phoenicians claimed that they had arrived in Tyre in about 2700 BCE. This may be treated like stories about the descent of the Dorian kings from Heracles. None the less, they were already settled on the coast of the modern Lebanon in the second millennium BCE, when the Egyptians were getting their supplies of cedar-wood from them. The Phoenicians were a Semitic people. Like the Arabs of the Red Sea, they became seafarers because geography urged them to look outwards rather than inland. They lived in the narrow coastal strip which was the historic channel of communication between Africa and Asia. Behind them was a shallow hinterland, poor in agricultural resources, cut up by hills running down from the mountains to the sea so that the coastal settlements found it difficult to unite. There were parallels with the experience of later Greek states tempted to the sea in similar circumstances and in each case the result was not only trade but colonization.

Weak at home – they came under the sway of Hebrew, Egyptian and Hittite in turn – it cannot be entirely coincidental that the Phoenicians emerge from the historical shadows only after the great days of Egypt, Mycenae and the Hittite empire. They, too, prospered in others' decline. It was after 1000 BCE, when the great era of Minoan trade was long past, that the Phoenician cities of Byblos, Tyre and Sidon had their brief golden age. Their importance then is attested by the biblical account of their part in the building of Solomon's Temple; "thou knowest", says Solomon, "that there is not among us any that can skill to hew timber like unto the Sidonians", and he paid up appropriately (1 Kings v, 6). This is perhaps evidence of a uniquely large and spectacular public works contract in ancient times, but there is copious later evidence to show the continuing importance of Phoenician enterprise. Ancient writers often stressed their reputation as traders and colonizers. They may have traded with the savages of Atlantic Europe, and must have been navigators of some skill to get so far. Phoenician dyes were long famous and much sought after down to classical times. No doubt commercial need stimulated their inventiveness; it was at Byblos (from which the Greeks were to take their name for a book) that the alphabet later adopted by the Greeks was invented. This was a great step, making a more widespread literacy possible. Yet no remarkable Phoenician literature survives, while Phoenician art tends to reflect their role of the middleman, borrowing and copying from Asian and Egyptian models, perhaps as the customer demanded.

PHOENICIAN TRADING STATIONS

Trade was the Phoenician occupation and did not at first require settlement overseas. Yet they came to base themselves more and more on colonies or trading stations, sometimes where Mycenaeans had traded before them. There were in the end some twenty-five such ports scattered up and down the Mediterranean, the earliest set up at Kition (the modern Larnaca) in Cyprus at the end of the ninth century BCE. Sometimes colonies followed earlier Phoenician commercial activity on the spot. They might also reflect the time of troubles which overtook the Phoenician cities after a brief phase of independence at the beginning of the first millennium. In the seventh century BCE Sidon was razed to the ground and the daughters of the king of Tyre were carried off to the harem of the Assyrian Ashurbanipal. Phoenicia was then reduced to its colonies elsewhere in the Mediterranean and little else. Yet their establishment may also have reflected anxiety at a wave of Greek colonization in the west which threatened the supply of metal, especially of British tin and Spanish silver. This could

A Phoenician war ship from the 1st millennium BCE, shown in an Assyrian bas-relief. The ship has a pointed ram, designed to make a hole in the hull of an enemy vessel. One of the two lines of oarsmen and the shields of the soldiers on board are visible. From the start of the 1st millennium BCE, Phoenician ships dominated the shipping routes of the western Mediterranean.

explain the Phoenician foundation of Carthage a century earlier; it was to become the seat of a power more formidable by far than Tyre and Sidon had ever been and went on to establish its own chain of colonies. Further west, beyond the Straits of Gibraltar, Cadiz was already known to Phoenicians who called there while looking for an Atlantic trade further north.

The Phoenicians were among the most important traffickers in civilization but so, willy-nilly, had been others, the Mycenaeans by their diffusion of a culture and the Hellenes by their stirring up of the ethnic world of the Aegean. The Cretans had been something more; true originators, they not only took from the great established centres of culture, but remade what they took before diffusing it again. These peoples help to shape a more rapidly changing world. One important side-effect, of which little has yet been said, was the stimulation of continental Europe. The search for minerals would take explorers and prospectors further and further into that unknown. Already in the second millennium BCE there are the first signs of a complicated future; beads found at Mycenae were manufactured in Britain from Baltic amber. Trade was always slowly at work, eating away isolation, changing peoples' relations with one another, imposing new shapes on the world. But it is hard to relate this story to the stirring of the ethnic pot in the Aegean, let alone to the troubled history of the Asian mainland from the second millennium BCE.

This terracotta mask depicts the face of a Phoenician god.

THE NEAR EAST IN THE AGES OF CONFUSION

"Confusion" is a matter of perspective. For about eight hundred years from, say, the end of Knossos, the history of the Near East is indeed very confused if our standpoint is that of world history. What was essentially going on were disputes about control of the slowly-growing wealth of the best-defined agricultural region of the ancient world (the empires which came and went could not find resources in the desert and steppe area on the borders of the Near East which could justify their conquest) and in that story it is hard to find any continuing thread. Invaders came and went rapidly, some of them leaving new communities behind them, some setting up new institutions to replace those they overthrew. This could hardly have been grasped by those to whom these events would only have come home occasionally, and suddenly, when (for instance) their homes were burned, their wives and daughters raped, their sons carried off to slavery – or, less dramatically, when they discovered that a new governor was going to levy higher taxes. Such events would be upsetting enough – if a stronger word is not required. On the other hand, millions of people must also have lived out their lives unaware of any change more dramatic than the arrival in their village one day of the first iron sword or sickle; hundreds of communities lived within a pattern of ideas and institutions unchanged for many generations. This is an important reservation. It must not be forgotten when we stress the dynamism and violence of the Near East's history during the transition from the Bronze to Iron Ages, an era already considered from the standpoint of the peoples of the Aegean.

On the mainland, wandering peoples moved about in a zone where there were long-established centres of government and population, powerful and long-lasting political structures, and numerous hierarchies of specialists in administration, religion and learning. These partly explain why the coming of new peoples obliterates less of what had already been achieved than in the Aegean. Another conservative force was the contact many of the barbarians had already had with civilization in this region. It left them wanting not to destroy it but to enjoy its fruits themselves. These two forces helped in the long run to diffuse civilization further and to produce the increasing cosmopolitanism of a large and confused, but civilized and interconnected, Near East.

The Phoenicians were quick to recognize Ibiza's strategic position in Mediterranean trade routes. One of the most outstanding examples of Ibizan architecture is the spectacular necropolis at Puig de Molin. This terracotta votive statue is one of the objects discovered at the necropolis.

THE HITTITES

The story of the civilized Near East begins very early, somewhere back towards the beginning of the second millennium BCE, with the arrival in Asia Minor of the Hittites. Perhaps they belonged to the same group of peoples as those of Minoan Crete, at any rate they were established in Anatolia at about the same time that Minoan civilization was rising to its greatest triumphs. They were far from being primitive barbarians. They had a legal system of their own and absorbed much of what Babylon could teach. They had enjoyed a virtual monopoly of iron in Asia; this not only had great agricultural importance but, together with their mastery of fortification and the chariot, gave the Hittites a military superiority which was the scourge of Egypt and Mesopotamia. The raid which cut down Babylon in about 1590 BCE was something like the high-water mark of the first Hittite "empire". A period of eclipse and obscurity followed. Then, in the first half of the fourteenth century, came a renaissance of power. This second and even more splendid era saw a Hittite hegemony which stretched at one brief moment from the shores of the Mediterranean to the Persian Gulf. It dominated all of the Fertile Crescent except Egypt and successfully

The Hittite Empire

This map shows the Hittite Empire at the height of its expansion, during the 14th to 12th centuries BCE. Little is known about Hittite geography. The empire's first nucleus was located on the Anatolia plateau, where its capital, Hattusas, was built. In the year 1300 BCE, a battle between the Hittites (under King Muwatallis) and the Egyptians (under Ramses II) was fought in Qadesh, beside the Orontes River.

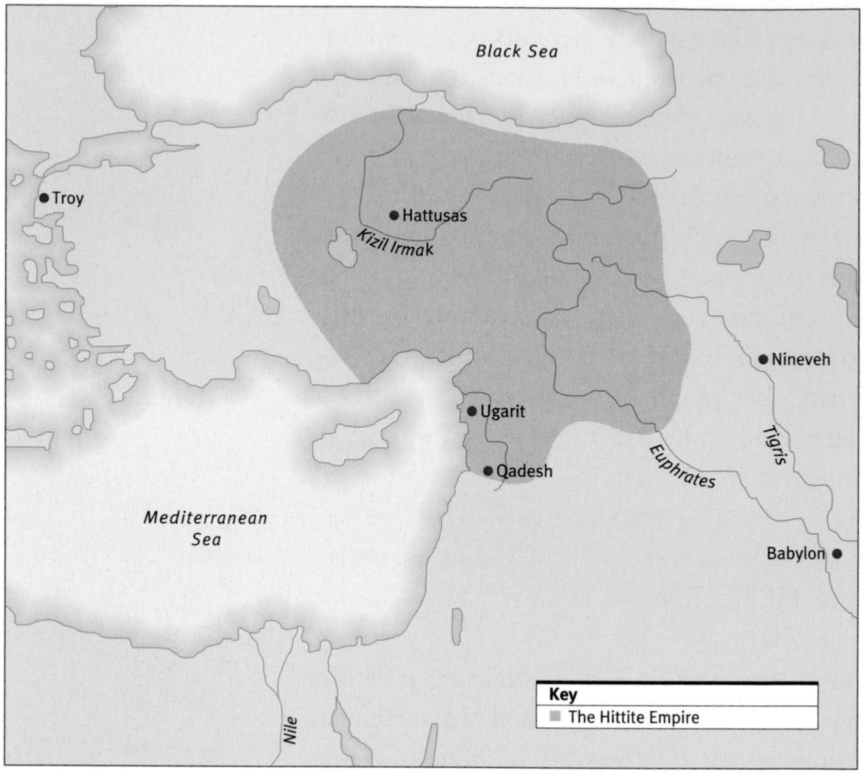

challenged even that great military power while being almost ceaselessly at war with the Mycenaeans. But, like other empires, it crumbled after a century or so, the end coming in about 1200 BCE.

THE END OF THE HITTITE EMPIRE

The culmination and collapse of the great organizing effort at the beginning of "dark ages" for Greece and the Aegean has two interesting features. The first is that the Hittites by this time no longer enjoyed a monopoly of iron; by about 1000 BCE it is to be found in use all over the Near East and its diffusion must surely be part of the story of the swing of power against the Hittites.

The other interesting feature is a coincidence with the rhythm of migrations, for it seems that the great diffusers of iron technology were the Indo-European peoples who from about 1200 BCE were throwing so much into turmoil. The disappearance of Troy, which never recovered from the Achaean destruction, has been thought of great strategic importance in this respect; the city seems to have played until this time a leading role in an alliance of powers of

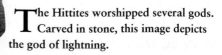

The Hittites worshipped several gods. Carved in stone, this image depicts the god of lightning.

Asia Minor, who had held the line against the barbarians from the north. After its overthrow, no other focus for resistance appeared. There is a closeness of timing which some have thought too pronounced to be merely coincidental between the collapse of the last Hittite power and the attacks of "sea peoples" recorded in the Egyptian records. The particular conquerors of the Hittites were a people who were from the race called the Phrygians.

A Hittite warrior depicted in the rigid and slightly rough style that is characteristic of most Hittite sculpture.

THE SEA PEOPLES

The "sea peoples" were yet another indicator of the great folk movements of the era. Armed with iron, from the beginning of the twelfth century BCE they were raiding the mainland of the East Mediterranean basin, ravaging Syrian and Levantine cities. Some of them may have been "refugees" from the Mycenaean cities who moved first to the Dodecanese and then to Cyprus. One group among them, the Philistines, settled in Canaan in about 1175 BCE and are commemorated still by a modern name derived from their own: Palestine. But Egyptians were the major victim of the sea peoples. Like the Vikings of the northern seas two thousand years later, sea-borne invaders and raiders plunged down on the delta again and again, undeterred by occasional defeat, at one time even wresting it from Pharaoh's control. Egypt was under great strain. In the early eleventh century, she broke apart and was disputed between two kingdoms. Nor were the sea peoples Egypt's only enemies. At one point, a Libyan fleet appears to have raided the delta, though it was drawn off. In the south, the Nubian frontier did not yet present a problem, but around 1000 BCE an independent kingdom emerged in the Sudan which would later be troublesome. The tidal surge of barbarian peoples was wearing away the old structures of the Near East just as it had worn away Mycenaean Greece.

HEBREW ORIGINS

This is far enough into the welter of events to make it clear that we have entered an age both too complex and too obscure for straightforward narration. Mercifully, there soon appear two threads through the turmoil. One is an old theme renewed, that of the continuing Mesopotamian tradition about to enter its last phase. The other is quite new. It begins with an event we cannot date and know only through tradition recorded centuries later, but which probably occurred during the testing time imposed on Egypt by the sea peoples. Whenever and however it happened, a turning-point had been reached in world history when there went out of Egypt people whom the Egyptians called Hebrews and the world later called Jews.

For many people over many centuries, humanity's history before the coming of Christianity was the history of the Jews and what they recounted of the history of others. Both were written down in the books called the Old Testament, the sacred writings of the Jewish people, subsequently diffused worldwide in many languages by the Christian missionary impulse and the invention of printing. They were to be the first people to arrive at an abstract notion of God and to forbid his representation by images. No people has produced a greater historical impact from such comparatively insignificant origins and resources, origins so insignificant indeed that it is still difficult to be sure of very much about them.

SEMITIC PEOPLES

Jewish origins lie among the Semitic, nomadic peoples of Arabia, whose prehistoric and historic tendency was to press into the richer lands of the Fertile Crescent nearest to their original homes. The first stage

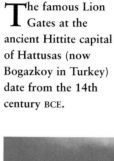

The famous Lion Gates at the ancient Hittite capital of Hattusas (now Bogazkoy in Turkey) date from the 14th century BCE.

of their story of which history must take notice is the age of the patriarchs, whose traditions are embodied in the biblical accounts of Abraham, Isaac and Jacob. There do not seem to be good grounds for denying that men who were the origins of these gigantic and legendary figures actually existed. If they did, it was in about 1800 BCE and their story is a part of the confusion following the end of Ur. The Bible states that Abraham came from Ur to Canaan; this is quite plausible and would not conflict with what we know of the dispersal of Amorite and other tribes in the next four hundred years. Those among them who were to be remembered as the descendants of Abraham became known in the end as "Hebrews", a word meaning "wanderer", which does not appear before Egyptian writings and inscriptions of the fourteenth or thirteenth centuries BCE, long after their first settlement in Canaan. Though this word is not wholly satisfactory, it is probably the best name to give the tribes with which we are concerned at this time. It is a better term to identify this group than "Jews", and for all the traditional associations gathered around that word by centuries of popular usage it is best to reserve it (as scholars usually do) for a much later era than that of the patriarchs.

CANAAN

It is in Canaan that Abraham's people are first distinguishable in the Bible. They are depicted as pastoralists, organized tribally, quarrelling with neighbours and kinsmen over wells and grazing, still liable to be pushed about the Near East by the pressures of drought and hunger. One group among them went down into Egypt, we are told, perhaps in the early seventeenth century BCE; it was to appear in the Bible as the family of Jacob. As the story unfolds in the Old Testament, we learn of Joseph, the great son of Jacob, rising high in Pharaoh's service. At this point we might hope for help from Egyptian records. It has been suggested that this happened during the Hyksos ascendancy, since only a period of large-scale disturbance could explain the improbable pre-eminence of a foreigner in the Egyptian bureaucracy. It may be so, but there is no evidence to confirm or disprove it. There is only tradition, as there is only tradition for all Hebrew history until about 1200 BCE. This tradition is embodied in the Old Testament; its texts only took this present form in the seventh century BCE, perhaps eight hundred years after the story of Joseph, though older elements can be and have been distinguished in them. As evidence, it stands in something like the relation to Jewish origins in which Homer stands to those of Greece.

None of this would matter very much, and certainly would not interest anyone except professional scholars, were it not for events which occurred from one to three thousand years later. Then, the destinies of the whole world were swayed by the Christian and Islamic civilizations whose roots lay in the religious tradition of a tiny, not very easily identifiable Semitic people, for centuries hardly distinguishable from many similar wanderers by the rulers of the great empires of Mesopotamia and Egypt. This was because the Hebrews somehow arrived at a unique religious vision.

THE COMING OF MONOTHEISM

THROUGHOUT THE WORLD of the ancient Near East it is possible to see at work forces which were likely to make monotheistic religious views more appealing. The power of

These inscriptions, which were carved into the rock of Mount Sinai during the 2nd millennium BCE, can be traced to the western Semites. Such inscriptions, later developed in Canaan, Phoenicia and Greece, form the distant roots of the Latin alphabet.

local deities was likely to be questioned after contemplation of the great upheavals and disasters which regularly swept across the region after the first Babylonian empire. The religious innovations of Akhnaton and the growing assertiveness of the cult of Marduk have both been seen as responses to such a challenge. Yet only the Hebrews and those who came to share their beliefs were able to push the process home, transcending polytheism and localism to arrive at a coherent and uncompromising monotheism.

YAHWEH AND THE HEBREW COVENANT

The timing of the process of monotheism is very difficult to establish but its essential steps were not complete before the eighth century BCE. In the earliest times at which Hebrew religion could be distinguished it was probably polytheistic, but also monolatrous – that is to say, that like other Semitic peoples, the tribes who were the forerunners of the Jews believed that there were many gods, but worshipped only one, their own. The first stage of refinement was the idea that the people of Israel (as the descendants of Jacob came to be called) owed exclusive allegiance to Yahweh, the tribal deity, a jealous god, who had made a covenant with his people to bring them again to the promised land, the Canaan to which Yahweh had already brought Abraham out of Ur, and which remains a focus of racial passion right down to the present day. The covenant was a master idea. Israel was assured that if it did something, then something desirable would follow. This was very unlike the religious atmosphere of Mesopotamia or Egypt.

The exclusive demands of Yahweh opened the way to monotheism, for when the time came for this the Israelites felt no respect for other gods which might be an obstacle for such evolution. Nor was this all. At an early date Yahweh's nature was already different from that of other tribal gods. That no graven image was to be made of him was the most distinctive feature of his cult. At times, he appears as other gods, in an immanent dwelling place, such as a temple made with hands, or even in manifestations of nature, but, as the Israelite religion developed, he could be seen as transcendent deity:

"the LORD is in his holy temple, the LORD's throne is in heaven"
Psalm xi, 4.

says a hymn. He had created everything, but existed independently of his creation, a universal being.

"Whither shall I go from thy spirit? or whither shall I flee from thy presence?" asked the Psalmist.
Psalm cxxxix, 7.

The creative power of Yahweh was something else differentiating the Jewish from the Mesopotamian tradition. Both saw human origins in a watery chaos; "the earth was

The Hebrew rulers

The enormous influence that the Hebrew tradition, as depicted in the Bible, has had on our culture has inspired many researchers to attempt to unravel the history of that ancient nation. But the scarcity of the archaeological evidence makes it impossible to verify the historical truth of the biblical stories. We may never know for certain whether Abraham, Isaac, Jacob and Joshua really existed. Perhaps one day a palace archive will be found, which will provide concrete information about the Hebrew monarchy. At present, the chronology of the Hebrew kings before the reign of David is wholly conjectural.

Chronological table showing prophets, kings, dynasties and major events of biblical times

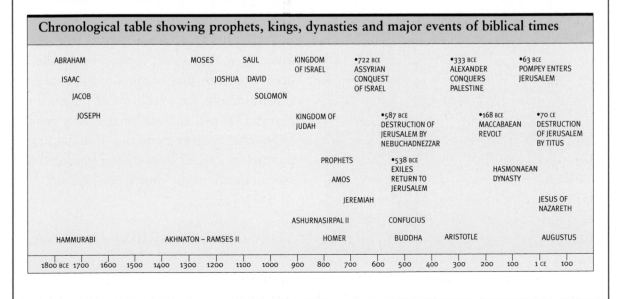

ABRAHAM
ISAAC
JACOB
JOSEPH
MOSES
JOSHUA
SAUL
DAVID
SOLOMON
KINGDOM OF ISRAEL
KINGDOM OF JUDAH
•722 BCE ASSYRIAN CONQUEST OF ISRAEL
•587 BCE DESTRUCTION OF JERUSALEM BY NEBUCHADNEZZAR
PROPHETS
AMOS
JEREMIAH
•538 BCE EXILES RETURN TO JERUSALEM
•333 BCE ALEXANDER CONQUERS PALESTINE
•168 BCE MACCABAEAN REVOLT
HASMONAEAN DYNASTY
•63 BCE POMPEY ENTERS JERUSALEM
•70 CE DESTRUCTION OF JERUSALEM BY TITUS
JESUS OF NAZARETH
ASHURNASIRPAL II
CONFUCIUS
HAMMURABI
AKHNATON – RAMSES II
HOMER
BUDDHA
ARISTOTLE
AUGUSTUS

1800 BCE 1700 1600 1500 1400 1300 1200 1100 1000 900 800 700 600 500 400 300 200 100 1 CE 100

without form, and void; and darkness was upon the face of the deep", says the book of Genesis. For the Mesopotamian, no pure creation was involved; somehow, matter of some sort had always been there and the gods only arranged it. It was different for the Hebrew; Yahweh had already created the chaos itself. He was for Israel what was later described in the Christian creed, "maker of all things, by whom all things are made". Moreover, He made man in His own image, as a companion, not as a slave; man was the culmination and supreme revelation of His creative power, a creature able to know good from evil, as did Yahweh Himself. Finally, humans moved in a moral world set by Yahweh's own nature. Only He was just; laws made by humans might or might not reflect His will, but He was the sole author of right and justice.

MOSES

The implications of the founding Hebrew ideas were to take centuries to clarify and millennia to demonstrate their full weight. At first, they were well wrapped up in the assumptions of a tribal society looking for a god's favour in war. Much in them reflected the special experience of a desert-dwelling people. Later Jewish tradition placed great emphasis on its origins in the exodus from Egypt, a story dominated by the gigantic and mysterious figure of Moses. Clearly, when the Hebrews came to Canaan, they were already consciously a people, grouped round the cult of Yahweh. The biblical account of the wanderings in Sinai probably reports the crucial time when this national consciousness was forged. But the biblical tradition is again all that there is to depend upon and it was only recorded much later. It is certainly credible that the Hebrews should at last have fled from harsh oppression in a foreign land – an oppression which could, for example, reflect burdens imposed by the mobilizing of labour for huge building operations. Moses is an Egyptian name and it is likely that there existed a historical original of the great leader who dominates the biblical story by managing the exodus and holding the Hebrews together in the wilderness. In the traditional account, he founded the Law by bringing down the Ten Commandments from his encounter with Yahweh. This was the occasion of the renewal of the covenant by Yahweh and his people at Mount Sinai, and it may be seen as a formal return to its traditions by a nomadic people whose cult had been eroded by long sojourn in the Nile delta. Unfortunately, the exact role of the great religious reformer and national leader remains impossible to define and the Commandments themselves cannot be convincingly dated until much later than the time when he lived.

A reconstruction of how the temple Solomon built in Jerusalem may have looked. According to the detailed description in the Bible, the temple was a long building at the end of which was the sanctuary containing the Ark of the Covenant. No traces of the temple remain, but the description matches the design of a number of contemporary temples that have been discovered in Syria.

THE HEBREWS ARRIVE IN CANAAN

Though the biblical account cannot be accepted as it stands, it should be treated with

The Gebel Musa, located in the south of the Sinai peninsula, has traditionally been identified as the mountain where Moses received the Ten Commandments from Yahweh. However, we have no proof that Hebrew tribes actually went to the mountain during their exodus from Egypt.

respect as our only evidence for much of Jewish history. It contains much that can be related to what is known or inferred from other sources. Archaeology comes to the historians' help only with the arrival of the Hebrews in Canaan. The story of conquest told in the book of Joshua fits evidence of destruction in the Canaanite cities in the thirteenth century BCE. What we know of Canaanite culture and religion also fits the Bible's account of Hebrew struggles against local cult practice and a pervasive polytheism. Palestine was disputed between two religious traditions and two peoples throughout the twelfth century and this, of course, again illustrates the collapse of Egyptian power, since this crucial area could not have been left to be the prey of minor Semitic peoples had the monarchy's power still been effective. It now seems likely that the Hebrews attracted to their support other nomadic tribes, the touchstone of alliance being adherence to Yahweh. After settlement, although the tribes quarrelled with one another, they continued to worship Yahweh and this was for some time the only uniting force among them, for tribal divisions formed Israel's only political institution.

The Hebrews took as well as destroyed. They were clearly in many ways less advanced culturally than the Canaanites and they took over their script. They borrowed their building practice, too, though without always achieving the same level of town life as their predecessors. Jerusalem was for a long time a little place of filth and confusion, not within striking-distance of the level reached by the town life of the Minoans long before. Yet in Israel lay the seeds of much of the future history of the human race.

The Twelve Tribes of Israel

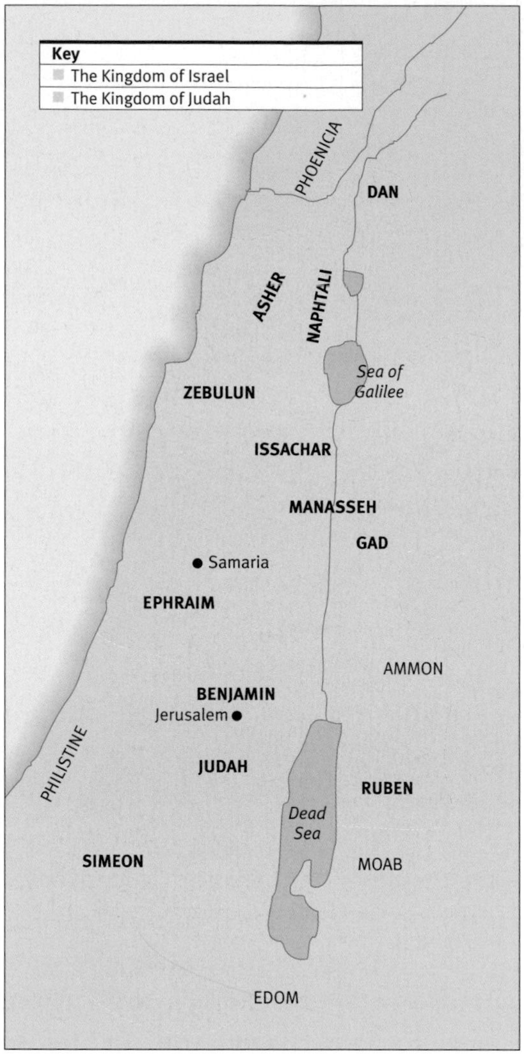

The two Hebrew kingdoms and the territories of the Twelve Tribes.

When Solomon died, in about 928 BCE, only the two southernmost Hebrew tribes, Judah and Simeon, accepted his son Roboam as their king. As is shown on the above map, the Hebrew nation was thus divided into two separate kingdoms: the Kingdom of Judah in the south, whose capital was in Jerusalem, and the Kingdom of Israel in the north, whose first capital was Siquem. The Kingdom of Israel disappeared when, in about 722 BCE, the Assyrians conquered Samaria, its last capital. The Kingdom of Judah survived until 587 BCE, the year in which Jerusalem was conquered and destroyed by Nebuchadnezzar, King of Babylonia, who deported its inhabitants.

HEBREW KINGSHIP

SETTLEMENT IN PALESTINE had been essentially a military operation and military necessity provoked the next stage in the consolidation of a nation. It seems to have been the challenge from the Philistines (who were obviously more formidable opponents than the Canaanites) which stimulated the emergence of the Hebrew kingship at some time about 1000 BCE. With it appears another institution, that of the special distinction of the prophets, for it was the prophet Samuel who anointed (and thus, in effect, designated) both Saul, the first king, and his successor, David. When Saul reigned, the Bible tells us, Israel had no iron weapons, for the Philistines took care not to endanger their supremacy by permitting them. None the less, the Jews learnt the management of iron from their enemies; the Hebrew words for "knife" and "helmet" both have Philistine roots. Ploughshares did not exist, but if they had they could have been beaten into swords.

KING DAVID

Saul won victories, but died at last by his own hand and his work was completed by David. Of all Old Testament individuals, David is outstandingly credible both for his strengths and weaknesses. Although there is no archaeological evidence that he existed, he lives still as one of the great figures of world literature and was a model for kings for two thousand years. The literary account, confused though it is, is irresistibly convincing. It tells of a noble-hearted but flawed and all-too-human hero who ended the Philistine peril and reunited the kingdom which had split at Saul's death. Jerusalem became Israel's capital and David then imposed himself upon the neighbouring peoples. Among them were the

The image of only one Hebrew king has survived – that of Jehu, King of Israel (842–814 BCE). On the monument known as the Black Obelisk of Salmanazar, Jehu appears prostrated before the Assyrian king Salmanazar III.

Phoenicians who had helped him against the Philistines, and this was the end of Tyre as an important independent state.

KING SOLOMON

David's son and successor, Solomon, was the first king of Israel to achieve major international standing. He gave his army a chariot arm, launched expeditions against the Edomites, allied with Phoenicia and built a navy. Conquest and prosperity followed.

"Solomon reigned over all kingdoms from the river [Euphrates] unto the land of the Philistines, and unto the border of Egypt . . . and Judah and Israel dwelt safely, every man under his vine and under his fig tree, from Dan even to Beersheba, all the days of Solomon."

1 Kings iv, 21, 25.

Again, this sounds like the exploitation of possibilities available to the weak when the great are in decline; the success of Israel under Solomon is further evidence of the eclipse of the older empires and it was matched by the successes of other now-forgotten peoples of Syria and the Levant who constituted the political world depicted in the obscure struggles recorded in the Old Testament. Most of them were descendants of the old Amorite expansion. Solomon was a king of great energy and drive and the economic and technical advances of the period were also notable. He was an entrepreneur ruler of the first rank. The legendary "King Solomon's Mines" have been said to reflect the activity of the first copper refinery of which there is evidence in the Near East, but this is disputed. Certainly the building of the Temple (after Phoenician models) was only one of many public works, though perhaps the most important. David had given Israel a capital, thus increasing the tendency to political centralization. He had planned a temple and when Solomon built it the worship of Yahweh was given a more splendid form than ever before and an enduring focus.

THE PROPHETS

A tribal religion had successfully resisted the early dangers of contamination by the fertility rites and polytheism of the agriculturalists among whom the Hebrews had settled in Canaan. But there was always a threat of backsliding which would compromise the covenant. With success came other dangers, too. A kingdom meant a court, foreign contacts and – in Solomon's day – foreign wives who cherished the cults of their own gods. Denunciation of the evils of departing from the law by going a-whoring after the fertility gods of the Philistines had been the first role of the prophets; a new luxury gave them a social theme as well.

The prophets brought to its height the Israelite idea of God. They were not soothsayers such as the Near East already knew (though this is probably the tradition which formed the first two great prophets, Samuel and Elijah), but preachers, poets, political and moral critics. Their status depended essentially on the conviction they could generate in themselves and others, that God spoke through them. Few preachers have had such success. Israel would be remembered in the end not

A city under siege, a scene often repeated on Assyrian bas-reliefs such as this one. Samaria, the capital of Israel, was conquered in c.722 BCE following a long siege by Assyrian troops.

A recurring scene in Assyrian art – people being sent from their own land into exile. This is the fate that befell the inhabitants of the kingdom of Judah after Jerusalem was conquered by Nebuchadnezzar in 587 BCE.

for the great deeds of her kings but for the ethical standards announced by her prophets. They shaped the connections of religion with morality which were to dominate not only Judaism but Christianity and Islam.

The prophets evolved the cult of Yahweh into the worship of a universal God, just and merciful, stern to punish sin but ready to welcome the sinner who repented. This was the climax of religious culture in the Near East, a point after which religion could be separated from locality and tribe. The prophets also bitterly attacked social injustice. Amos, Isaiah and Jeremiah went behind the privileged priestly caste to do so, denouncing religious officialdom directly to the people. They announced that all humans were equal in the sight of God, that kings might not simply do what they would; they proclaimed a moral code which was a given fact, independent of human authority. Thus the preaching of adherence to a moral law which Israel believed was god-given became also a basis for a criticism of existing political power. Since the law was not made by a human agency it did not ostensibly emerge from that power; the prophets could always appeal to it as well as to their divine inspiration against king or priest. It is not too much to say that, if the heart of political liberalism is the belief that power must be used within a moral framework independent of it, then its taproot is the teaching of the prophets.

THE EXILE

Most of the prophets after Samuel spoke against a troubled background, which they called in evidence as signs of backsliding and corruption. Israel had prospered in the eclipse of paramount powers, when kingdoms came and went with great rapidity. After Solomon's death, Hebrew history had ups as well as

The Assyrian king Tiglathpileser III (744–727 BCE), seated on the throne and surrounded by dignitaries and servants. This scene is part of an enormous group of wall paintings found in an Assyrian palace in the ancient city of Til Barsib.

downs, but broadly took a turn for the worse. There had already been revolts; soon the kingdom split. Israel became a northern kingdom, built on ten tribes gathered together around a capital at Samaria; in the south the tribes of Benjamin and Judah still held Jerusalem, capital of the kingdom of Judah. The Assyrians obliterated Israel in 722 BCE and the ten tribes disappeared from history in mass deportations. Judah lasted longer. It was more compact and somewhat less in the path of great states; it survived until 587 BCE, when Jerusalem's walls and Temple were razed by a Babylonian army. The Judaeans, too, then suffered deportations, many of them being carried away to Babylon, to the great experience of the Exile, a period so important and formative that after it we may properly speak of "the Jews", the inheritors and transmitters of a tradition still alive and easily traced. Once more great empires had established their grip in Mesopotamia and gave its civilization its last flowering. The circumstances which had favoured the appearance of a Jewish state had disappeared. Fortunately for the Jews, the religion of Judah now ensured that this did not mean that their national identity was doomed too.

TURMOIL IN MESOPOTAMIA

Since the days of Hammurabi, the peoples of the Mesopotamian valley had been squeezed in a vice of migratory peoples. For a long time its opposing jaws had been the Hittites and the Mitanni, but from time to time others had ruled in Assur and Babylon. When, in due course, the Hittites also crumbled, ancient Mesopotamia was the seat of no great military power until the ninth century BCE, though such a sentence conceals much. One Assyrian king briefly conquered Syria and Babylon early in the eleventh century; he was soon swept away by a cluster of pushful Semitic tribes whom scholars call Aramaeans, followers of the old tradition of expansion into the fertile lands from the desert. Together with a new line of Kassite kings in Babylon they were the awkward and touchy neighbours of the reduced kings of Assyria for two hundred years or so – for about as long as the

United States has existed. Though one of these Semitic peoples was called the Chaldees and therefore subsequently gave its name somewhat misleadingly to Babylonia, there is not much to be remarked in this story except further evidence of the fragility of the political constructions of the ancient world.

THE ASSYRIAN EMPIRE

SHAPE ONLY BEGINS to reappear in the turmoil of events in the ninth century BCE when Mesopotamia recovered. Then, the Old Testament tells us, Assyrian armies were once more on the move against the Syrian and Jewish kingdoms. After some successful resistance the Assyrians came back again and again, and they conquered. This was the beginning of a new, important and unpleasant phase of Near Eastern history. A new Assyrian empire was in the making. In the eighth century it was moving to its apogee, and Nineveh, the capital high up the Tigris, which had replaced the ancient centre of Assur, became the focus of Mesopotamian history as Babylon had once been. Assyrian empire was unified in a way that other great empires were not; it did not rely on the vassalization of kings and the creation of tributaries. Instead, it swept native rulers away and installed Assyrian governors. Often, too, it swept away peoples. One of its characteristic techniques was mass deportation; the Ten Tribes of Israel are the best-remembered victims.

Assyrian expansion was carried forward by repeated and crushing victory. Its greatest successes followed 729 BCE, when Babylon was seized. Soon after, Assyrian armies destroyed Israel, Egypt was invaded, its kings were confined to Upper Egypt and the delta was annexed. By then Cyprus had submitted, Cilicia and Syria had been conquered. Finally, in 646 BCE, Assyria made its last important conquest, part of the land of Elam, whose kings dragged the Assyrian conqueror's chariot through the streets of Nineveh. The consequences were of great importance for the whole Near East. A standardized system of government and law spanned the whole area. Conscript soldiers and deported populations were moved about within it, sapping its provincialism. Aramaic spread widely as a common language. A new cosmopolitanism was possible after the Assyrian age.

The Assyrian Empire

The Assyrian Empire lasted for more than a millennium. Researchers have identified three stages in its development – the Old Empire, the Middle Empire and the New Empire. The Old Empire lasted from the 18th to 14th centuries BCE. The Middle Empire brought a new era of Assyrian expansion that came to an end in the 9th century BCE with the advance of the Ramians. However, the greatest moment for the Assyrian civilization came during the New Empire, founded by King Ashurnasirpal I (883–859 BCE). From the 9th to 7th centuries BCE, the Assyrians terrorized the communities of the Fertile Crescent. Assyrian military campaigns are recorded on the walls of their palaces. In about 612 BCE, the Assyrian Empire was defeated by a coalition of the Babylonians and the Medes.

A 7th-century BCE relief in the palace of Nineveh depicting the Assyrian king Ashurbanipal taking part in the regal sport of lion hunting.

ASSYRIAN MONUMENTS

The great formative power of the Assyrians is commemorated in monuments of undeniable impressiveness. Sargon II (721–705 BCE) built a great palace at Khorsabad, near Nineveh, which covered half a square mile of land and was embellished with more than a mile of sculpted reliefs. The profits of conquest financed a rich and splendid court. Ashurbanipal (668–626 BCE) also left his monuments (including obelisks carried off to Nineveh from Thebes), but he was a man with a taste for learning and antiquities and his finest relic is what survives of the great collection of tablets he made for his library. In it he accumulated copies of all that he could discover of the records and literature of ancient Mesopotamia. It is to these copies that we owe much of our knowledge of Mesopotamian literature, among them the Epic of Gilgamesh in its fullest edition, a translation made from Sumerian.

The ideas that moved this civilization are thus fairly accessible from literature as well as from other sources. The frequent representation of Assyrian kings as hunters may be a part of the image of the warrior-king, but may also form part of a conscious identification of the king with legendary conquerors of nature who had been the heroes of a remote Sumerian past.

The stone reliefs which commemorate the great deeds of Assyrian kings also repeat, monotonously, another tale, that of sacking, enslavement, impalement, torture and the final solution of mass deportation. The Assyrian empire had a brutal foundation of conquest and intimidation. It was made possible by the creation of the best army up to this

Extent of the Assyrian Empire

The decisive push for Assyrian imperial expansion took place during the reigns of Tiglathpileser III (744–727 BCE) and Sargon II (721–705 BCE). Moving outwards from the nucleus of their original settlement in the high basin of the Tigris, the Assyrians eventually controlled the whole of the Fertile Crescent. This expansion culminated in the conquest of Egypt during the reign of Ashurbanipal.

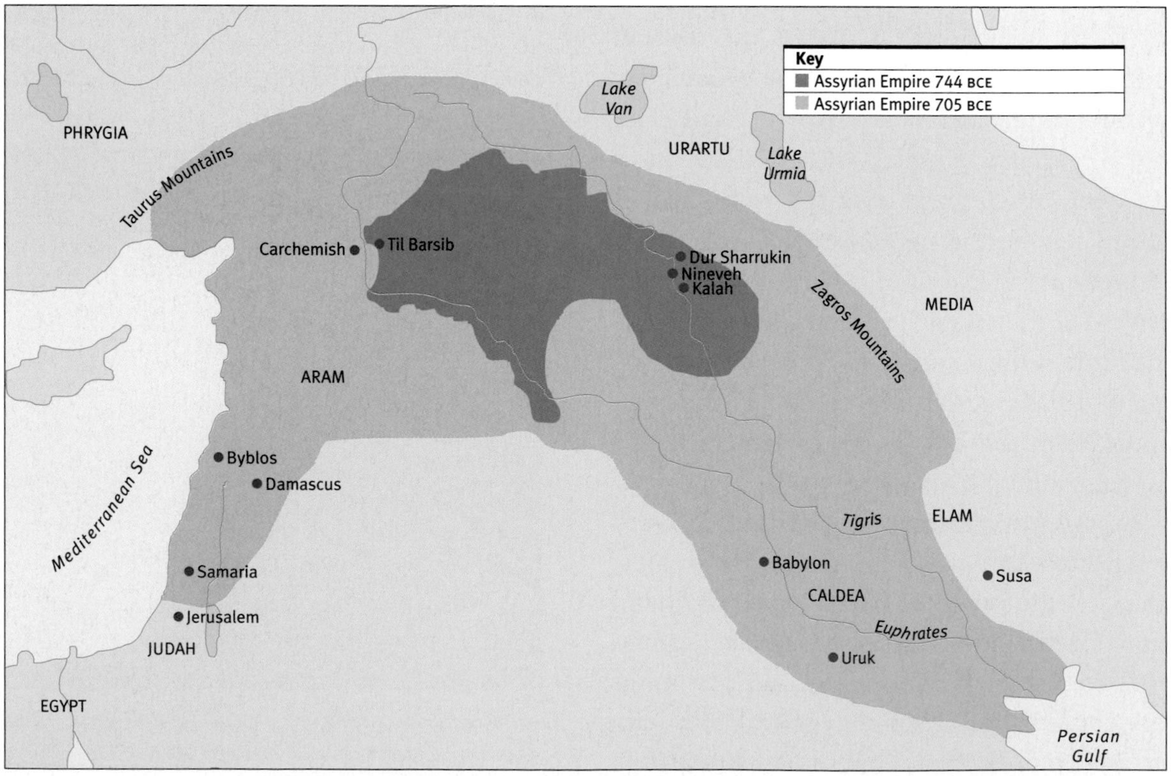

Map showing the expansion of the Assyrian Empire, 744–705 BCE.

time. Fed by conscription of all males and armed with iron weapons, it also had siege artillery able to breach walls until this time impregnable, and even some mailed cavalry. It was a coordinated force of all arms. Perhaps, too, it had a special religious fervour. The god Assur is shown hovering over the armies as they go to battle and to him kings reported their victories over unbelievers.

THE ASSYRIAN EMPIRE DISAPPEARS

Whatever the fundamental explanation of Assyrian success, it quickly waned. Possibly, empire put too great a strain on Assyrian numbers. The year after Ashurbanipal died, the empire began to crumble, the first sign being a revolt in Babylon. The rebels were supported by the Chaldeans and also by a great new neighbour, the kingdom of the Medes, now the leading Iranian people. Their entrance as a major power on the stage of history marks an important change; for a long time the Medes had been distracted by having to deal with yet another wave of barbarian invaders from the north, the Scythians, who poured down into Iran from the Caucasus (and at the same time down the Black Sea coast towards Europe). They were light cavalrymen, fighting with the bow from horseback, and it took time to come to terms with them in the seventh century. This was, in fact, the first major eruption into western Asia of a new force in world history, nomadic peoples straight from Central Asia. Like all other great invasions, the Scythian advance pushed other peoples before them (the kingdom of Phrygia was overrun by one of these). Meanwhile, the last of the political units of

The formidable Assyrian war machine combined the use of chariots, cavalry and infantry, as depicted on this bas-relief.

the Near East based on the original Caucasian inhabitants was gobbled up by Scyths, Medes or Assyrians. All this took a century and more, but amounted to a great clearing of the stage. The instability and fragmentation of the periphery of the Fertile Crescent had long favoured Assyria; it ceased to do so when Scyths and Medes joined forces. This pushed Assyria over the edge and gave the Babylonians independence again; Assyria passes from history with the sack of Nineveh by the Medes in 612 BCE.

The sacking of Nineveh was not quite the end of the Mesopotamian tradition. Assyria's collapse left the Fertile Crescent open to new masters. The north was seized by the Medes, who pushed across Anatolia until halted at the borders of Lydia and at last drove the Scyths back into Russia. An Egyptian pharaoh made a grab at the south and the Levant, but was defeated by a Babylonian king, Nebuchadnezzar, who gave Mesopotamian civilization an Indian summer of grandeur and a last Babylonian empire, which more than any other captured the imagination of posterity. It ran from Suez, the Red Sea and Syria across the border of Mesopotamia and the old kingdom of Elam (by then ruled by a minor Iranian dynasty called the Achaemenids). If for nothing else, Nebuchadnezzar would be remembered as a great conqueror. He destroyed Jerusalem in 587 BCE after a Jewish revolt and carried off the tribes of Judah into captivity, using them as he used other captives, to carry out the embellishment of his capital, whose "hanging gardens" or terraces were to be remembered as one of the Seven Wonders of the World. He was the greatest king of his time, perhaps of any time until his own.

THE CULT OF MARDUK

The glory of the empire came to a focus in the cult of Marduk, which was now at its zenith. At a great New Year festival held each year all the Mesopotamian gods – the idols and statues of provincial shrines – came down the rivers and canals to take counsel with Marduk at his temple and acknowledge his supremacy. Borne down a processional way three-quarters of a mile long (which was, we are told, probably the most magnificent street of antiquity) or landed from the Euphrates nearer to the temple, they were taken into the

This bas-relief from the palace of King Ashurbanipal shows the monarch resting under a vine arbour with the queen beside him. The royal couple are drinking, while the servants fan them.

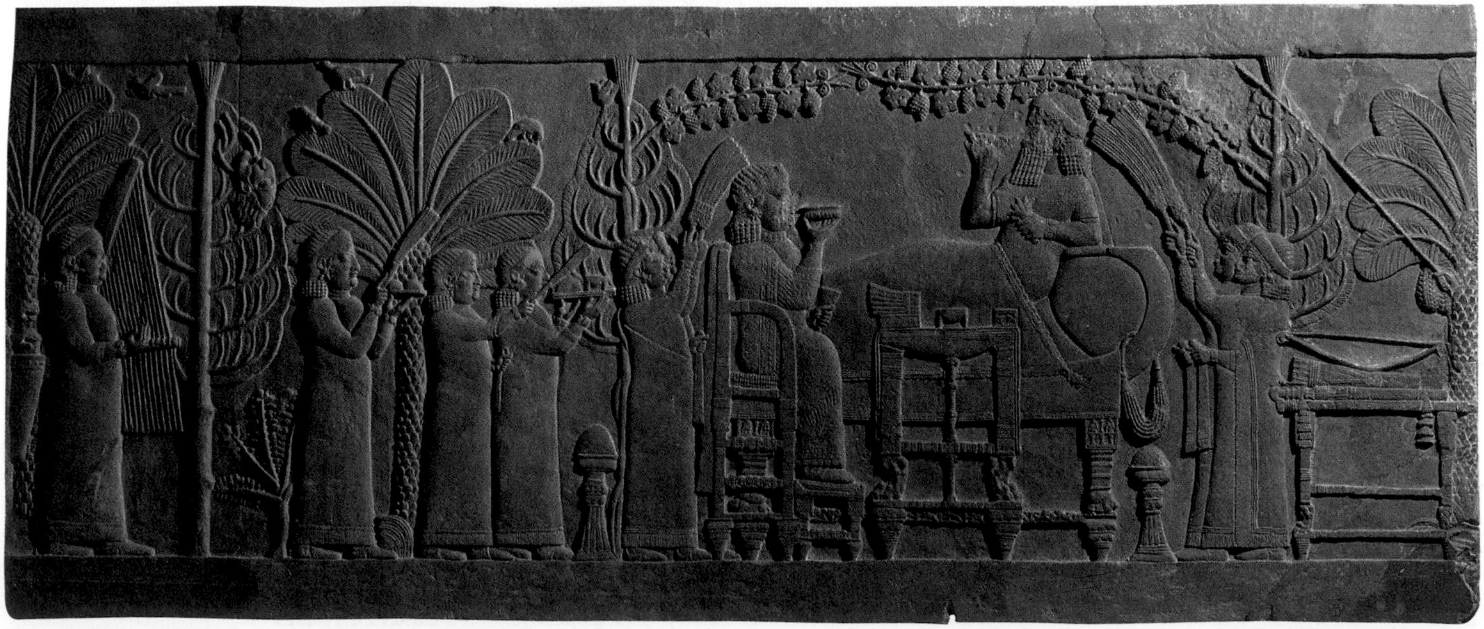

A detail from one of the bas-reliefs that decorated the walls of a chamber in the palace of Sargon II (721–705 BCE) in Dur Sharrukin (Jorsabad). This bas-relief depicts the transportation of wood that was used to construct the palace.

presence of a statue of the god which, Herodotus reported two centuries later, was made of two and a quarter tons of gold. No doubt he exaggerated, but it was indisputably magnificent. The destinies of the whole world, whose centre was this temple, were then debated by the gods and determined for another year. Thus theology reflected political reality. The re-enacting of the drama of creation was the endorsement of Marduk's eternal authority, and this was an endorsement of the absolute monarchy of Babylon, to which was delegated responsibility to assure the order of the world.

THE END OF INDEPENDENT MESOPOTAMIAN TRADITION

The cult of Marduk was the last flowering of the Mesopotamian tradition and was soon to end. More and more provinces were lost under Nebuchadnezzar's successors. Then came an invasion in 539 BCE by new conquerors from the east, the Persians, led by the Achaemenids. The passage from worldly pomp and splendour to destruction had been swift. The book of Daniel telescopes it in a magnificent closing scene, Belshazzar's feast. "In that night," we read, "was Belshazzar the

Babylon, which had been the most important city in southern Mesopotamia in the first centuries of the 2nd millennium BCE, would enjoy another moment of splendour after the fall of the Assyrian Empire. This detail is taken from a glazed brickwork wall in Nebuchadnezzar II's throne room in his Babylon palace.

king of the Chaldeans slain. And Darius the Median took the kingdom" (Daniel v, 30–31). Unfortunately, this account was only written three hundred years later and it was not quite like that. Belshazzar was neither Nebuchadnezzar's son nor his successor, as the book of Daniel says, and the king who took Babylon was called Cyrus. None the less, the emphasis of the Jewish tradition has a dramatic and psychological truth. In so far as the story of antiquity has a turning-point, this is it. An independent Mesopotamian tradition going back to Sumer was over. We are at the edge of a new world. A Jewish poet summed it up exultantly in the book of Isaiah, where Cyrus appears as a deliverer to the Jews:

"Sit thou silent, and get thee into darkness, O daughter of the Chaldeans: for thou shalt no more be called, The lady of kingdoms."

Isaiah xlvii, 5.

A reconstruction in the Berlin Museum of glazed brickwork ornamentation from the throne room of the palace of Babylon (7th–6th centuries BCE).

THE BEGINNINGS OF CIVILIZATION IN EASTERN ASIA

As contacts between them multiplied, the isolation of the oldest civilizations in the Near East was steadily broken down. From that interplay emerged a more cosmopolitan, if still highly differentiated, world of cultural traditions. Yet at the same time areas of the world in which other civilizations had appeared (only a little later, in the timescales of early history) remained almost untouched by what happened in the area delimited by the Aegean, Egypt and Iran. There is no need to look further than distance and topography for explanations. Yet the consequences of remoteness and inaccessibility were very important. What took place in northern China and the Indian sub-continent was to shape cultural traditions in remote places for thousands of years. As centres for the diffusion of civilized life they long remained impervious to outside cultural influence; little more than peripheral and occasional contact with other zones of civilization was possible until a very long time had gone by. The outcome was the establishment of cultural traditions over large areas which contained elements which would be strong enough to endure even through periods of intimate connection with other traditions; even in this century, the institution of caste long dominated Indian thinking about society, and Confucian ideas once enshrined in the curriculum for the imperial examinations system still shaped the ideas of the Chinese literati. The influence of China and India was also to spread far beyond their own physical limits or later political frontiers and the spheres of influence they created are still visible today. The influence of these traditions was widespread and powerful. From the standpoint of world history they were of vast importance.

During the 3rd century BCE, the first Buddhist *stupas* (commemorative burial mounds) were constructed in India. The Great Stupa in Sanchi (right) was built in around 220 BCE, almost three centuries after the Buddha's death. Its domed shape symbolizes both the master's tomb and the cosmic egg, which represents the original universe in Indian scriptures. The enormous carved gateway was erected in the 1st century CE.

1 ANCIENT INDIA

EVEN NOW, ANCIENT INDIA is still visible and accessible to us in a very direct sense. At the beginning of the twentieth century, some Indian communities still lived as all our primeval ancestors must once have lived, by hunting and gathering. The bullock cart and the potter's wheel of many villages today are, as far as can be seen, identical with those used four thousand years ago. A caste system whose main lines were set by about 1000 BCE still regulates the lives of millions, and even of some Indian Christians and Muslims. Gods and goddesses whose cults can be traced to the Stone Age are still worshipped at village shrines.

INDIAN DIVERSITY

In some ways ancient India is with us still as is no other ancient civilization. Yet although such examples of the conservatism of Indian

The Indus valley

The first Indian civilization emerged more than 4,000 years ago in the valley carved by the great Indus River, which is fed by snow and glacial meltwater from its source in the Himalayas. On the Punjab Plains, the Indus is further swollen by tributaries such as the Sutlej and the Jhelum, bringing water from the mighty Punjab River to the east.

The remains of many ancient settlements have been discovered in the Indus valley region, including those of the cities of Mohenjo-Daro in the south and Harappa in the north.

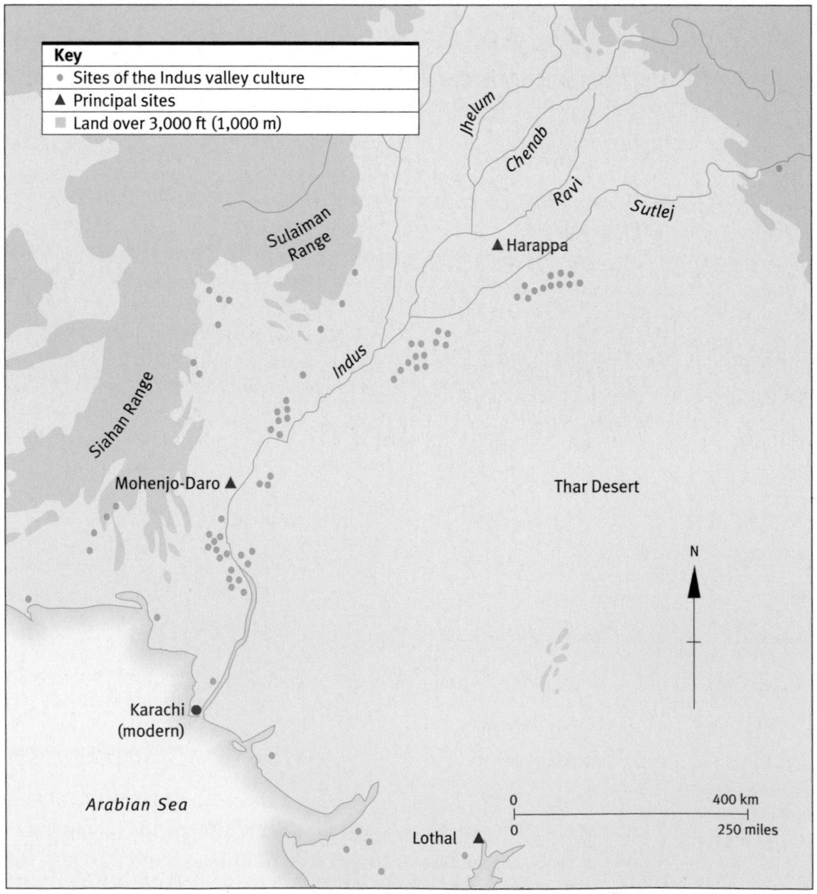

Map showing the cities of the early Indus valley civilization.

The Khyber Pass is the most famous of the routes through the mountains along India's northwestern border, linking the highlands of Afghanistan and the fertile Indus valley. The route has frequently been used to invade India.

life are commonplace, the country that contains them contains many other things too. The hunter-gatherers of the early twentieth century were the contemporaries of other Indians used to travelling in railway trains. The diversity of Indian life is enormous, but wholly comprehensible given the size and variety of its setting. The sub-continent is, after all, about the size of Europe and is divided into regions that are clearly distinguished by climate, terrain and crops. There are two great river valleys, the Indus and Ganges systems, in the north; between them lie desert and arid plains, and to the south the highlands of the Deccan, largely forested. When written history begins, India's racial complexity, too, is already very great: scholars identify six main ethnic groups. Many others were to arrive later and make themselves at home in the Indian sub-continent and society, too. All this makes it hard to find a focus.

This small limestone bust found at Mohenjo-Daro is one of the most famous archaeological pieces from the first Indian civilization, that of the Indus valley. Thought to represent a priest or a king, the bearded figure has a band tied around his forehead. His dress – a tunic covering one shoulder – is similar to that of contemporary Mesopotamian figures of kings.

GEOGRAPHICAL INSULATION

Indian history has a unity in the fact of its enormous power to absorb and transform forces playing on it from the outside. This provides a thread to guide us through the patchy and uncertain illumination of its early stages which is provided by archaeology and texts long transmitted only by word of mouth. Its basis is to be found in another fact: India's large measure of insulation from the outside world by geography. In spite of her size and variety, until the oceans began to be opened up in the sixteenth and seventeenth centuries CE, India had only to grapple with occasional, though often irresistible, incursions by alien peoples. To the north and northwest she was protected by some of the highest mountains in the world; to the east lay belts of jungle. The other two sides of the sub-continent's great triangle opened out into the huge expanses of the Indian ocean. This natural definition not only channelled and restricted communication with the outside world; it also gave India a distinctive climate. Much of India does not lie in the tropics, but none the less that climate is tropical. The mountains keep away the icy winds of Central Asia; the long coasts open themselves to the rain-laden clouds which roll in from the oceans and cannot go beyond the northern ranges. The climatic clock is the annual monsoon, bringing the rain during the hottest months of the year. It is still the central prop of an agricultural economy.

INFLUENCES FROM THE NORTH

Protected in some measure from external forces though she has always been before modern times, India's northwestern frontier is more open than her others to the outside world. Baluchistan and the frontier passes were the most important zones of encounter between India and other peoples right down to the seventeenth century CE; in civilized

Time chart (2250 BCE–185 BCE)

2250–1750 BCE Zenith of the Harappan civilization

700–500 BCE Upanishads composed

321–185 BCE Maurya Dynasty: first Indian empire

2000 BCE | 1500 BCE | 1000 BCE | 500 BCE

1750 BCE Aryan invasion begins

1500–1000 BCE Vedic hymns composed

563–483 BCE Life of the Buddha

times even India's contacts with China were first made by this roundabout route (though it is not quite as roundabout as Mercator's familiar projection makes it appear). At times, this northwestern region has fallen directly under foreign sway, which is suggestive when we consider the first Indian civilizations; we do not know much about the way in which they arose but we know that Sumer and Egypt antedated them. Mesopotamian records of Sargon I of Akkad report contacts with a "Meluhha" which scholars have believed to be the Indus valley, the alluvial plains forming the first natural region encountered by travellers once they have entered India. It was there, in rich, heavily forested countryside, that the first Indian civilizations appeared at the time when, further west, the great movements of Indo-European peoples were beginning to act as the levers of history. There may have been more than one stimulus at work.

The evidence also shows that agriculture came later to India than to the Near East. It, too, can first be traced in the sub-continent in its northwest corner. There is archaeological evidence of farming in Baluchistan in about 6000 BCE. Three thousand years later, there are signs of settled life on the alluvial plains and parallels with other river-valley cultures begin to appear. Wheel-thrown pottery and copper implements begin to be found. All the signs are of a gradual build-up in intensity of agricultural settlements until true civilization appears as it did in Egypt and Sumer. But there is the possibility of direct Mesopotamian influence in the background and, finally, there is at least a reasonable inference that already India's future was being shaped by the coming of new peoples from the north. At a very early date the complex racial composition of India's population suggests this, though it would be rash to be assertive about it.

When at last indisputable evidence of civilized life is available, the change is startling.

Archaeological excavations have revealed the advanced town planning that characterized the cities of the Harappan culture built more than 4,000 years ago. The Mohenjo-Daro citadel's Great Bath, pictured here, had a fountain and a drainage system. The pool was rendered watertight by a thick layer of bitumen.

One scholar speaks of a cultural "explosion". There may have been one crucial technological step, the invention of burnt brick (as opposed to the sun-baked mud brick of Mesopotamia) which made flood control possible in a flat plain lacking natural stone. Whatever the process, the outcome was a remarkable civilization which stretched over a half-million square miles of the Indus valley, an area greater than either the Sumerian or Egyptian.

Among the objects discovered during excavations at the ancient city of Harappa, in the north of present-day Pakistan, was this stone gaming board.

THE HARAPPAN CIVILIZATION

This figurine from the Harappa culture, found at Mohenjo-Daro, represents a slender, naked young woman, adorned with a necklace and numerous bracelets. It is thought that the girl was probably a dancer.

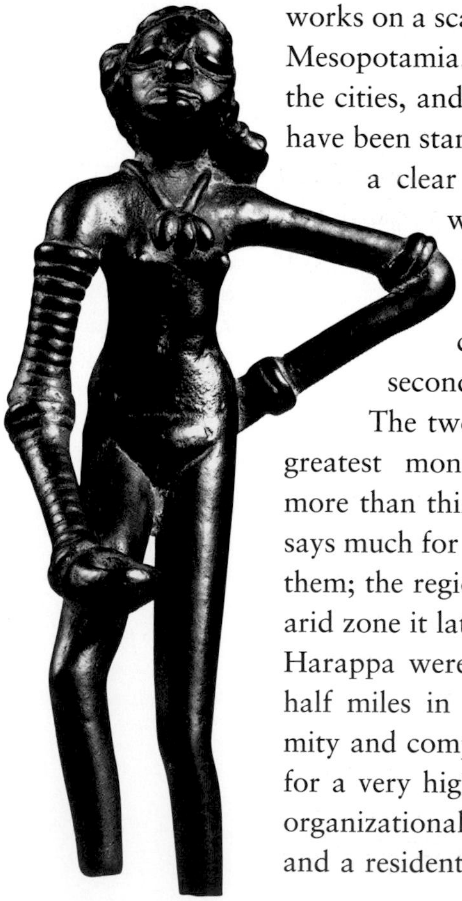

SOME HAVE CALLED INDUS civilization "Harappan", because one of its great sites is the city of Harappa on a tributary of the Indus. There is another such site at Mohenjo-Daro; three others are known. Together they reveal human beings highly organized and capable of carefully regulated collective works on a scale equalling those of Egypt and Mesopotamia. There were large granaries in the cities, and weights and measures seem to have been standardized over a large area. It is a clear that a well-developed culture was established by 2600 BCE and lasted for something like six hundred years with very little change before declining in the second millennium BCE.

The two cities which are this culture's greatest monuments may have contained more than thirty thousand people each. This says much for the agriculture which sustained them; the region was then far from being the arid zone it later became. Mohenjo-Daro and Harappa were between two and two and a half miles in circumference and the uniformity and complexity of their building speaks for a very high degree of administrative and organizational skill. They each had a citadel and a residential area; streets of houses were laid out on rectangular grid plans and made of bricks of standardized sizes. Both the elaborate and effective drainage systems and the internal layout of the houses show a strong concern for bathing and cleanliness; in some streets of Harappa nearly every house has a bathroom. Perhaps it is not fanciful to see in this some of the first manifestations of what has become an enduring feature of Indian religion, the bathing and ritual ablutions still so important to Hindus.

HARAPPAN CULTURE

The inhabitants of both Mohenjo-Daro and Harappa traded far afield and lived an economic life of some complexity. A great dockyard, connected by a mile-long canal to the sea at Lothal, four hundred miles south of Mohenjo-Daro, suggests the importance of external exchanges which reached, through the Persian Gulf, as far north as Mesopotamia. In the Harappan cities themselves evidence survives of specialized craftsmen drawing their materials from a wide area and subsequently sending out again across its length and breadth the products of

Thousands of small, square Harappan seals have been found. Mainly made of soapstone, most of the stamps depict animal figures, including unicorns, bulls, buffaloes and tigers. Most of the stamps are inscribed; although some 2,000 different inscriptions have been discovered, they have yet to be deciphered.

their skills. This civilization had cotton cloth (the first of which we have evidence) which was plentiful enough to wrap bales of goods for export whose cordage was sealed with seals found at Lothal. These seals are part of our evidence for Harappan literacy; a few inscriptions on fragments of pottery are all that supplements them and provides the first traces of Indian writing. The seals, of which about 2,500 survive, provide some of our best clues to Harappan ideas. The pictographs on the seals run from right to left. Animals often appear on them and may represent six seasons into which the year was divided. Many "words" on the seals remain unreadable, but it now seems at least likely that they are part of a language akin to the Dravidian tongues still used in southern India.

THE DIFFUSION OF HARAPPAN CIVILIZATION

Ideas and techniques from the Indus spread throughout Sind and the Punjab, and down the west coast of Gujarat. The process took centuries and the picture revealed by archaeology is too confused for a consistent pattern to emerge. Where its influence did not reach – the Ganges valley, the other great silt-rich area where large populations could live, and the southeast – different cultural processes were at work, but they have left nothing so spectacular behind them. Some of India's culture must derive from other sources; there are traces elsewhere of Chinese influence. But it is hard to be positive. Rice, for example, began to be grown in India in the Ganges valley; we simply do not know where it came from, but one possibility is China or South-East Asia, on whose coasts it was grown from about 3000 BCE. Two thousand years later, this crucial item in Indian diet was used over most of the north.

THE END OF HARAPPAN CIVILIZATION

We do not know why the first Indian civilizations began to decline, although their passing can be roughly dated. The devastating floods of the Indus or uncontrollable alterations of its course may have wrecked the delicate balance of the agriculture on its banks. The forests may have been destroyed by tree-felling to provide fuel for the brick-kilns on which Harappan building depended. But perhaps there were also other agencies at work. Skeletons, possibly those of men killed where they fell, were found in the streets of Mohenjo-Daro. Harappan civilization seems to end in the Indus valley about 1750 BCE and this coincides strikingly with the irruption into Indian history of one of its great creative forces, invading "Aryans", though scholars do not favour the idea that invaders destroyed the Indian valley cities. Perhaps the newcomers entered a land already devastated by over-exploitation and natural disasters.

A clay figurine from Mohenjo-Daro. Scholars think this woman, who is wearing a short skirt, a belt, abundant long necklaces and a tall headdress, may have been a dancer.

ARYAN INVASION

Strictly speaking, "Aryan" is a linguistic term, like "Indo-European". None the less, it has customarily and conveniently been used to identify one group of those peoples whose movements make up so much of the dynamic of ancient history in other parts of the Old World after 2000 BCE. At about the time when other Indo-Europeans were flowing into Iran, somewhere about 1750 BCE, a great influx began to enter India from the Hindu Kush. This was the beginning of centuries during which waves of these migrants washed deeper and deeper into the Indus valley and the Punjab and eventually reached the upper Ganges. They did not obliterate the native peoples, though the Indus valley civilization crumbled. No doubt much violence marked their coming, for the Aryans were warriors and nomads, armed with bronze weapons, bringing horses and chariots, but they settled and there are plenty of signs that the native populations lived on with them, keeping their own beliefs and practices alive. There is a great deal of archaeological evidence of the fusion of Harappan with later ways. However qualified, this was an early example of the assimilation of cultures which was always to characterize Indian society and which was eventually to underly classical Hinduism's remarkable digestive power.

A number of Harappan clay figurines depicting a cart being pulled by two oxen have been found. The imprints of ancient wheels have also been discovered, and evidence suggests that the Harappan carts were very similar to the ones still used in the region today.

ARYAN CULTURE

It seems clear that the Aryans brought to India no culture so advanced as that of the Harappans. It is a little like the story of the coming of Indo-Europeans in the Aegean. Writing, for example, disappears and does not emerge again until the middle of the first millennium BCE; cities, too, have to be re-invented and when they are again to be found they lack the elaboration and order of their Indus valley predecessors. Instead, the Aryans appear to have slowly given up their pastoral habits and settled into agricultural life, spreading east and south from their original settlement areas in a sprawl of villages. This took centuries. Not until the coming of iron was it complete and the Ganges valley colonized; iron implements made cultivation easier. Meanwhile, together with this physical opening up of the northern plains, the invaders had made two decisive contributions to Indian history, in its religious and in its social institutions.

ARYAN RELIGION

The Aryans laid the foundations of the religion which has been the heart of Indian civilization. This centred on sacrificial concepts; through sacrifice the process of creation which the gods achieved at the beginning of time was to be endlessly repeated. Agni, the god of fire, was very important, because it was through his sacrificial flames that people could reach the gods. Great importance and standing was given to the *brahmans*, the priests who presided over these ceremonies. There was a pantheon of gods of whom two of the most important were Varuna, god of the heavens, controller of natural order and the embodiment of justice, and Indra, the warrior god who, year after year, slew a dragon and thus released again the heavenly waters which came with the breaking of the monsoon. We learn about them from the *Rig-Veda*, a collection of more than a thousand hymns performed during sacrifice, collected for the first time in about 1000 BCE but certainly accumulated over centuries. It is one of our most important sources for the history not only of Indian religion but also of Aryan society.

THE *RIG-VEDA*

The *Rig-Veda* seems to reflect an Aryan culture as it has been shaped by settlement in India and not as it had existed at earlier times or with original form. It is, like Homer, the eventual written form of a body of oral tradition, but quite different in being much less difficult to use as a historical source, since its status is much more certain. Its sanctity made its memorization in exact form essential, and though the *Rig-Veda* was not to be written down until after 1300 CE, it was then still almost certainly largely uncorrupted from its original form. Together with later Vedic hymns and

Harappan streets followed very regular grid-plan layouts, as can be seen in this street in Mohenjo-Daro's lower city. Most of the houses in this part of the town had bathrooms and remarkably advanced drainage and sanitary systems.

Agni, the Vedic god of fire, is depicted on this bas-relief. He is surrounded by a halo of flames and his mount, a goat, appears at his feet. Agni was the most commonly invoked Vedic god – a beneficial figure who brought light and warmth. His flames were also believed to purify sacrifices, making them acceptable to other divinities.

prose works, it is our best source for Aryan India, whose archaeology is cramped for a long time because building materials less durable than the brick of the Indus valley cities were used in its towns and temples.

There is a suggestion again of the world of Homer in the world revealed by the *Rig-Veda*, which is one of Bronze Age barbarians. Some archaeologists now believe they can identify in the hymns references to the destruction of the Harappan cities. Iron is not mentioned and appears only to have come to India after 1000 BCE (there is argument about how late and from what source). The setting of the hymns is a land which stretches from the western banks of the Indus to the Ganges, inhabited by Aryan peoples and dark-skinned native inhabitants. These formed societies whose fundamental units were families and tribes. What these left behind, though, was less enduring than the pattern of Aryan social organization which gradually emerged, to which the Portuguese later gave the name we use, "caste".

THE CASTE SYSTEM

About the early history of the vast and complicated subject of the caste system and its implications it is impossible to speak with assurance. Once the rules of caste were written down, they appeared as a hard and solid structure, incapable of variation. Yet this did not happen until caste had been in existence for hundreds of years, during which it was still flexible and evolving. Its root appears to be a recognition of the fundamental class divisions of a settled agricultural society, a warrior-aristocracy (*kshatriyas*), priestly *brahmans* and the ordinary peasant-farmers (*vaishyas*). These are the earliest divisions of Aryan society which can be observed and seem not to have been exclusive; movement between them was possible. The only unleapable barrier in early times seems to have been that between non-Aryans and Aryans; one of the words used to denote the aboriginal inhabitants of India by Aryans was *dasa*, which came eventually to denote "slave". To the occupational categories was soon added a fourth category for non-Aryans. Clearly it rested on a wish to preserve racial integrity. These were the *shudras*, or "unclean", who might not study or hear the Vedic hymns.

This structure has been elaborated almost ever since. Further divisions and subdivisions appeared as society became more complex and movements within the original threefold structure took place. In this the *brahmans*, the highest class, played a crucial role.

This 13th-century CE bas-relief portrays Varuna, the Vedic god of justice. He carries a coil of rope for tying up criminals.

Landowners and merchants came to be distinguished from farmers; the first were called *vaishyas*, and *shudras* became cultivators. Marriage and eating taboos were codified. This process gradually led to the appearance of the caste system as we know it. A vast number of castes and sub-castes slowly inserted themselves into the system. Their obligations and demands eventually became a primary regulator of Indian society, perhaps the only significant one in many Indians' lives. By modern times there were thousands of *jatis* – local castes with members restricted to marrying within them, eating only food cooked by fellow-members, and obeying their regulations. Usually, too, a caste limited those who belonged to it to the practice of one craft or profession. For this reason (as well as because of the traditional ties of tribe, family and locality and the distribution of wealth) the structure of power in Indian society right down to the present day has had much more to it than formal political institutions and central authority.

On this bas-relief Indra, the Vedic warrior god, rides an elephant and brandishes his favourite weapon, the thunderbolt, or *vajra*. Indra was believed to be an invincible fighter and the Aryans invoked his protection in battle.

POLITICAL SYSTEMS

In early times Aryan tribal society threw up kings, who emerged, no doubt, because of military skill. Gradually, some of them acquired something like divine sanction, though this must always have depended on a nice balance of relations with the *brahman* caste. But this was not the only political pattern. Not all Aryans accepted this evolution. By about 600 BCE, when some of the detail of early Indian political history at last begins to be dimly discernible through a mass of legend and myth, two sorts of political communities can be discerned, one non-monarchical, tending to survive in the hilly north, and one monarchical, established in the Ganges valley. This reflected centuries of steady pressure by the Aryans towards the east and south during which peaceful settlement and intermarriage seem to have played as big a part as conquest. Gradually, during this era, the centre of gravity of Aryan India had shifted from the Punjab to the Ganges valley as Aryan culture was adopted by the peoples already there.

THE GANGES VALLEY

As we emerge from the twilight zone of the Vedic kingdoms, it is clear that they established something like a cultural unity in northern India. The Ganges valley was by the seventh century BCE the great centre of Indian population. It may be that the cultivation of rice made this possible. A second age of Indian cities began there, the first of them market-places and centres of manufacture, to judge by the way they brought together specialized craftsmen. The great plains, together with the development of armies on a larger and better-equipped scale (we hear of the use of elephants), favoured the consolidation of larger political units. At the end of the seventh century BCE, northern India was organized in sixteen kingdoms, though how this happened and how they were related to one another is still hard to disentangle from their mythology. None the less, the existence of coinage and the beginnings of writing make it likely that they had governments of growing solidity and regularity.

The processes in which they emerged are touched on in some of the earliest literary sources for Indian history, the *Brahmanas*, texts composed during the period when Aryan culture came to dominate the Ganges valley (c.800–600 BCE). But more about them and the great names involved can be found in later documents, above all in two great Indian epics, the *Ramayana* and the *Mahabharata*. The present texts are the result of constant revision from about 400 BCE to 400 CE, when they were written down as we know them for the first time, so their interpretation is not easy. In consequence, it remains hard to get at the political and administrative reality behind, say, the kingdom of Magadha, based on southern Bihar, which emerged eventually as the preponderant power and was to be the core of the first historical empires of India. On the other hand (and possibly more importantly), the evidence is clear that the Ganges valley was already what it was to remain, the seat of empire, its cultural domination assured as the centre of Indian civilization, the future Hindustan.

This small terracotta plaque, dating from the 2nd century BCE, was found in Kaushambi and is a fine example of early Indian sculpture. The sumptuous throne upon which the two lovers are seated suggests that the work may represent a prince and his bride, perhaps on their wedding night.

THE NORTH–SOUTH DIVIDE

The later Vedic texts and the general richness of the Aryan literary record make it all too easy to forget the existence of half the subcontinent. Written evidence tends to confine Indian history down to this point (and even after) to the history of the north. The state of archaeological and historical scholarship also reflects and further explains the concentration of attention on northern India. There is just much more known about it in ancient times than about the south. But there are also better and less accidental justifications for such an emphasis. The archaeological evidence shows, for example, a clear and continuing cultural lag in this early period between the area of the Indus system and the rest of India (to which, it may be remarked, the river was to give its name). Enlightenment (if it may be so expressed) came from the north. In the south, near modern Mysore,

This 3rd-century BCE capital originally crowned a polished stone pillar inscribed with the precepts of the Maurya emperor of India, Asoka (264–228 BCE). The four lions, standing back-to-back on the wheel of law, are now the symbol of the modern-day Indian Union.

settlements roughly contemporaneous with Harappa show no trace of metal, though there is evidence of domesticated cattle and goats. Bronze and copper only begin to appear at some time after the Aryan arrival in the north. Once outside the Indus system, too, there are no contemporary metal sculptures, no seals and fewer terracotta figures. In Kashmir and eastern Bengal there are strong evidences of Stone Age cultures with affinities with those of south China, but it is at least clear that, whatever the local characteristics of the Indian cultures with which they were in contact and within the limits imposed by geography, first Harappan and then Aryan civilization was dominant. They gradually asserted themselves towards Bengal and the Ganges valley, down the west coast towards Gujarat, and in the central highlands of the sub-continent. This is the pattern of the Dark Age, and when we reach that of history, there is not much additional light. The survival of Dravidian languages in the south shows the region's persistent isolation.

TOPOGRAPHICAL DIFFERENTIATION

Topography explains much of this isolation. The Deccan has always been cut off from the north by jungle-clad mountains, the Vindhya. Internally, too, the south is broken and hilly, and this did not favour the building of large states as did the open plains of the north. Instead, south India remained fragmented, some of its peoples persisting, thanks to their inaccessibility, in the hunting and gathering cultures of a tribal age. Others, by a different accident of geography, turned to the

Indian epic literature

The two oldest known epic texts of Hindu literature are the *Mahabharata* and the *Ramayana*. Although originally written in about 400 BCE, they relate events that took place in India between the years 1400 and 1000 BCE. The first text consists of various legendary subjects that surround a central theme: the fight for power between two families, the Kauravas and the Pandavas. But, most importantly, the *Mahabharata* is an exposition of *dharma*, a moral code governing how a warrior, a king, or anyone who wants to be included in the cycle of rebirth, should act. One of the most beautiful passages, the *Bhagavad Gita* (*The Song of the Lord*), constitutes (along with the Upanishads) the basic religious scriptures for Hinduism. The second poem, the *Ramayana*, narrates the life of Rama, the incarnation of Vishnu, who is hailed as the perfect king and man.

Hanuman, the flying monkey-god, features in the Ramayana *as one of Rama's loyal generals.*

A scene from the *Ramayana* is depicted in this 18th-century manuscript illustration: Rama, the poem's protagonist, and his younger brother Laksmana are wandering in search of Rama's wife, Sita. In the poem, Rama shows himself to be a virtuous warrior, completely loyal to the aristocratic code of honour.

seas – another contrast with the predominantly agrarian empires of the north.

INDIAN RELIGIONS

MILLIONS OF PEOPLE must have been affected by the changes so far described. Estimates of ancient populations are notoriously unreliable. India's has been put at about 25 millions in 400 BCE, which would be roughly a quarter of the whole population of the world at that time. The importance of India's early history never the less lies in the way it laid down patterns still shaping the lives of even larger numbers today, rather than in its impact on big populations in antiquity. This is above all true of religion. Classical Hinduism crystallized in the first millennium BCE. As it did, India also gave birth to another great world religion – Buddhism; it eventually dominated wide areas of Asia. What people do is shaped by what they believe they can do; it is the making of a culture that is the pulse of Indian history, not the making of a nation or an economy, and to this culture religion was central.

SHIVA

The deepest roots of the Indian religious and philosophical synthesis go very deep indeed. One of the great popular cult figures of the Hindu pantheon today is Shiva, in whose worship many early fertility cults have been brought together. A seal from Mohenjo-Daro already shows a figure who looks like an early Shiva, and stones like the *lingam* found in modern temples, the phallic cult-object which is his emblem, have been found in the Harappan cities. There is some presumptive evidence therefore for speculating that the worship of Shiva may be the oldest surviving

The central element of the *Mahabharata* is the struggle of the five Pandavas brothers against their cousins, the hundred Kauravas princes. In this scene, the Kauravas armies are attacking the army of Abhimanyu, the son of Arjuna.

Mysticism and mythology in ancient India

Vedic and *Brahman* literature, which is the oldest source of knowledge of Hindu mythology and mysticism, encompasses a range of works, from the *Rig-Veda* to the Upanishads.

The great historian of Indian philosophy, Surendranath Dasgupta, distinguishes four different types of mysticism. The first type is gathered in Vedic and *Brahman* literature (the *Vedas*, 1500–1000 BCE) and focuses on the control of nature and the gods through ritual. The second type of mysticism, gathered in the texts called Upanishads (1000–500 BCE), contains a number of philosophical speculations about the nature of the universe and the position of man within it. The third, the *yoga*, is related to control of the body and the mind. The fourth, the Buddhist, dates from the 6th century BCE and uses control of the body and the mind for the realization of the four Truths (the existence of pain, the causes of pain, the cessation of pain and how to arrive at these truths) and the achievement of *nirvana* (freedom from all desires). These types of mysticism have several common elements: all are based on experience and can be communicated, all aim to free the spirit from matter, all state that in order to achieve this, control over the body and mind are vital. They also all state that knowledge does not consist of analysis, but of directly approaching one's inner self.

This 12th-century CE *bas-relief depicts, from left to right, the three main gods of the classical Hindu pantheon: Brahma, first being to be created and creator of all things; Vishnu, a social and good god, preserver of the world; and Shiva, the contradictory god of destruction, asceticism and procreation.*

religious cult in the world. Though he has assimilated many important Aryan characteristics, he is pre-Aryan and survives in all his multi-faceted power, still an object of veneration today. Nor is Shiva the only possible survival from the remote past of Indus civilization. Other Harappan seals seem to suggest a religious world centred about a mother-goddess and a bull. The bull survives to this day, the Nandi of countless village shrines all over Hindu India (and newly vigorous in his modern incarnation, as the electoral symbol of the Congress Party).

VISHNU

Vishnu, another focus of modern popular Hindu devotion, is much more an Aryan. Vishnu joined hundreds of local gods and goddesses still worshipped today to form the Hindu pantheon. Yet his cult is far from being either the only or the best evidence of the Aryan contribution to Hinduism. Whatever survived from the Harappan (or even pre-Harappan) past, the major philosophical and speculative traditions of Hinduism stem from Vedic religion. These are the Aryan legacy. To this day, Sanskrit is the language of religious learning; it transcends ethnic divisions, being used in the Dravidian-speaking south as much as in the north by the *brahman*. It was a great cultural adhesive and so was the religion it carried. The Vedic hymns provided the nucleus for a system of religious thought more abstract and philosophical than primitive animism. Out of Aryan notions of hell and paradise, the House of Clay and the

World of the Fathers, there gradually evolved the belief that action in life determined human destiny. An immense, all-embracing structure of thought slowly emerged, a world view in which all things are linked in a huge web of being. Souls might pass through different forms in this immense whole; they might move up or down the scale of being, between castes, for example, or even between the human and animal worlds. The idea of transmigration from life to life, its forms determined by proper behaviour, was linked to the idea of purgation and renewal, to the trust in liberation from the transitory, accidental and apparent, and to belief in the eventual indentity of soul and absolute being in *Brahma*, the creative principle. The duty of the believer was the observation of *Dharma* – a virtually untranslatable concept, but one which embodies something of the western ideas of a natural law of justice and something of the idea that people owed respect and obedience to the duties of their station.

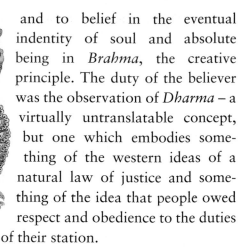

Brahma, creator of the universe, was a focus of early worship. His prestige began to decline as Vishnu and Shiva became more popular. Here he appears riding a wild goose, whose flight symbolizes the soul's efforts to free itself.

THE *BRAHMANS*

These developments took a long time. The steps by which the original Vedic tradition began its transformation into classical Hinduism are obscure and complicated. At the centre of the early evolution had been the *brahmans* who long controlled religious thought because of their key role in the sacrificial rites of Vedic religion. The brahmanical class appears to have used its religious authority to emphasize its seclusion and privilege. To kill a *brahman* soon became the gravest of crimes; even kings could not contend with their powers. Yet they seem to have come to terms with the gods of an older world in early times; it has been suggested that it may have been the infiltration of the brahmanical class by priests of the non-Aryan cults which ensured the survival and later popularity of the cult of Shiva.

Shiva is a complex and contradictory god, destroyer and restorer, ascetic and sensual. He represents the Hindu idea of combining complementary qualities in one personality. In this bronze statue from the Chola kingdom (9th to 12th centuries CE), he is depicted as the lord of dance.

THE UPANISHADS

The sacred Upanishads, texts dating from about 700 BCE, mark the next important evolution towards a more philosophical religion.

They are a mixed bag of about two hundred and fifty devotional utterances, hymns, aphorisms and reflexions of holy men pointing to the inner meaning of the traditional religious truths. They give much less emphasis to personal gods and goddesses than earlier texts and also include some of the earliest ascetic teachings which were to be so visible and striking a feature of Indian religion, even if only practised by a small minority. The Upanishads met the need felt by some to look outside the traditional structure for religious satisfaction. Doubt appears to have been felt about the sacrificial principle. New patterns of thought had begun to appear at the beginning of the historical period and uncertainty about traditional beliefs is already expressed in the later hymns of the *Rig-Veda*. It is convenient to mention such developments here because they cannot be understood apart from the Aryan and pre-Aryan past. Classical Hinduism was to embody a synthesis of ideas like those in the Upanishads (pointing to a monistic conception of the universe) with the more polytheistic popular tradition represented by the *brahmans*.

This detail from a 19th-century CE painting portrays Vishnu riding his mount Garuda, the magical eagle. Garuda, whose mission was to defend humanity against demons, was also revered as a god.

JAINISM

Abstract speculation and asceticism were often favoured by the existence of monasticism, a stepping-aside from material concerns to practise devotion and contemplation. The practice appeared in Vedic times. Some monks threw themselves into ascetic experiment, others pressed speculation very far and we have records of intellectual systems which rested on outright determinism and materialism. One very successful cult which did not require belief in gods and expressed a reaction against the formalism of the brahmanical religion was Jainism, a creation of a sixth-century teacher who, among other things, preached a respect for animal life which made agriculture or animal husbandry impossible. Jains therefore tended to become merchants, with the result that in modern times the Jain community is one of the wealthiest in India.

The Chandogya Upanishad

"That hidden essence you do not see, dear one,
From that a whole nyagrodha tree will grow.
There is nothing that does not come from him.
Of everything he is the inmost Self.
He is the truth; he is the Self supreme.
You are that, Shvetaketu; you are that."
"Please, Father, tell me more about this Self."
"Yes, dear one, I will," Uddalaka said.
"Place this salt in water and bring it here
Tomorrow morning." The boy did.
"Where is that salt?" his father asked.
"I do not see it."
"Sip here. How does it taste?"
"Salty, Father."
"And here? And there?"
"I taste salt everywhere."
"It *is* everywhere, though we see it not.
Just so, dear one, the Self is everywhere,
Within all things, although we see him not.
There is nothing that does not come from him.
Of everything he is the inmost Self.
He is the truth; he is the Self supreme.
You are that, Shvetaketu; you are that."

An extract from the Chandogya Upanishad, translated by Eknath Easwaran.

THE BUDDHA

The first images of the Buddha were carved at the beginning of the Common Era. Some of the most impressive of these sculptures are situated in the caves at Ajanta, in central India. From the 2nd century BCE to the 7th century CE, communities of Buddhist monks inhabited the caves, using them as temples.

By far the most important of the innovating systems was the teaching of the Buddha, the "enlightened one" or "aware one" as his name may be translated.

It has been thought significant that the Buddha, like some other religious innovators, was born in one of the states to the northern edge of the Ganges plain where the orthodox, monarchical pattern emerging elsewhere did not establish itself. This was early in the sixth century BCE. Siddhartha Gautama was not a *brahman*, but a prince of the warrior class.

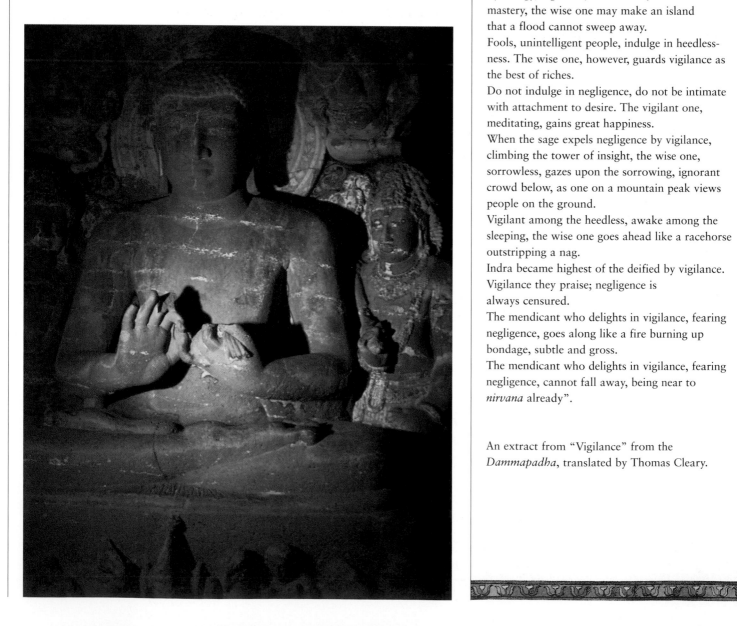

The *Dammapadha*

"Vigilance is the realm of immortality; negligence is the realm of death. People who are vigilant do not die; people who are negligent are as if dead.
The wise, with thorough knowledge of vigilance, enjoy being vigilant and delight in the realm of the noble.
Meditative, persevering, always striving diligently, the wise attain *nirvana*, supreme peace.
Energetic, alert, pure in deed, careful in action, self-controlled, living in accord with truth the vigilant one will rise in repute.
By energy, vigilance, self-control, and self-mastery, the wise one may make an island that a flood cannot sweep away.
Fools, unintelligent people, indulge in heedlessness. The wise one, however, guards vigilance as the best of riches.
Do not indulge in negligence, do not be intimate with attachment to desire. The vigilant one, meditating, gains great happiness.
When the sage expels negligence by vigilance, climbing the tower of insight, the wise one, sorrowless, gazes upon the sorrowing, ignorant crowd below, as one on a mountain peak views people on the ground.
Vigilant among the heedless, awake among the sleeping, the wise one goes ahead like a racehorse outstripping a nag.
Indra became highest of the deified by vigilance. Vigilance they praise; negligence is always censured.
The mendicant who delights in vigilance, fearing negligence, goes along like a fire burning up bondage, subtle and gross.
The mendicant who delights in vigilance, fearing negligence, cannot fall away, being near to *nirvana* already".

An extract from "Vigilance" from the *Dammapadha*, translated by Thomas Cleary.

After a comfortable and gentlemanly upbringing he found his life unsatisfying and left home. His first recourse was asceticism. Seven years of this proved to him that he was on the wrong road. He began instead to preach and teach. His reflections led him to propound an austere and ethical doctrine, whose aim was liberation from suffering by achieving higher states of consciousness. This was not without parallels in the teaching of the Upanishads.

BUDDHIST PHILOSOPHY

An important part in Buddhism was to be played by *yoga*, which was to become one of what were termed the "Six Systems" of Hindu philosophy. The word has many meanings but in this context is roughly translatable as "method" or "technique". It sought to achieve truth through meditation after a complete and perfect control of the body had been attained. Such control was supposed to reveal the illusion of personality which, like all else in the created world, is mere flux, the passage of events, not identity. This system, too, had already been sketched in the Upanishads and was to become one of the aspects of Indian religion which struck visitors from Europe most forcibly. The Buddha taught his disciples to discipline and shed the demands of the flesh so that no obstacle should prevent the soul from attaining the blessed state of *nirvana* or self-annihilation, freedom from the endless cycle of rebirth and transmigration, a doctrine urging people not to do something, but to be something – in order not to be anything. The way to achieve this was to follow an Eightfold path of moral and spiritual improvement. All this amounts to a great ethical and humanitarian revolution.

THE LEGACY OF THE BUDDHA

The Buddha apparently had great practical and organizing ability. Together with his unquestionable personal quality, it must have helped to make him a popular and successful

Monastic communities transformed these natural caves, at Ajanta in the Maharashtra state in western India, into one of the country's most important and most richly decorated monuments. After its heyday in the 5th and 6th centuries CE, the site was abandoned and was not rediscovered until the early 19th century CE.

Although there are no early Indian images of the Buddha as a man, several representations of his footprints exist. This pair, surrounded by a lotus-petal motif symbolizing purity and wisdom, is from Bodh Gaya, where the enlightenment of the Buddha took place.

teacher. He sidestepped, rather than opposed, the brahmanical religion and this must have smoothed his path. The appearance of communities of Buddhist monks gave his work an institutional form which would outlive him. He also offered a role to those not satisfied by traditional practice, in particular to women and to low-caste followers, for caste was irrelevant in his eyes. Finally, Buddhism was non-ritualistic, simple and atheistic. It soon underwent elaboration and, some would say, speculative contamination, and like all great religions it assimilated much pre-existing belief and practice, but by doing so it retained great popularity.

Yet Buddhism did not supplant brahmanical religion and for two centuries or so was confined to a relatively small part of the Ganges valley. In the end, too – though not until well into the Common Era – Hinduism was to be the victor and Buddhism would dwindle to a minority belief in India. But it was to become the most widespread religion in Asia and a potent force in world history. It is the first world religion to spread beyond the society in which it was born, for the older tradition of Israel had to wait for the Common Era before it could assume a world role. In its native India, Buddhism was to be important until the coming of Islam. The teaching of the

This figure, which adorned the doorway of the Great Stupa at Sanchi, depicts a *yakshi*, one of the benign deities who made trees blossom and were incorporated into the Buddhist creed. The *yakshi*'s headdress and jewellery are similar to those of figurines found at Mohenjo-Daro, suggesting the continuation of a cultural heritage begun 2,000 years previously.

Buddha marks, therefore, a recognizable epoch in Indian history; it justifies a break in its exposition. By his day, an Indian civilization still living today and still capable of enormous assimilative feats stood complete in its essentials. This was a huge fact; it would separate India from the rest of the world.

CONTINUITY OF EARLY INDIAN CIVILIZATION

Much of the achievement of early civilization in India remains intangible. There is a famous figure of a beautiful dancing-girl from Mohenjo-Daro, but ancient India before the Buddha's time did not produce great art on the scale of Mesopotamia, Egypt or Minoan Crete, far less their great monuments. Marginal in its technology, India came late – though how much later than other civilizations cannot be exactly said – to literacy, too. Yet the uncertainties of much of India's early history cannot obscure the fact that its social system and religions have lasted longer than any other great creations of the human mind. Even to guess at what influence they exercised through the attitudes they encouraged, diffused through centuries in pure or impure forms, is rash. Only a negative dogmatism is safe; so comprehending a set of world views, institutions so careless of the individual, philosophy so assertive of the relentless cycles of being, so lacking in any easy ascription of responsibility for good and evil, cannot but have made a history very different from that of human beings reared in the great Semitic traditions. And these attitudes were formed and settled for the most part a thousand years before Christ.

2 ANCIENT CHINA

Although the original Great Wall was built at the end of the 3rd century BCE, the wall sections that are still standing mainly date back to the Ming Dynasty (14th to 17th century CE).

THE MOST STRIKING FACT of China's history is that it has gone on for so long. For about two and a half thousand years there has been a Chinese nation using a Chinese language. Its government, at least in name, as a single unit has long been taken to be normal, in spite of periods of grievous division and confusion. China has had a continuing experience of civilization rivalled in duration only by that of ancient Egypt and this is the key to Chinese historical identity. China's nationhood is as much cultural as political. The example of India shows how much more important culture can be than government, and China makes the same point in a different way; there, culture made unified government easier. Somehow, at a very early date, it crystallized certain institutions and attitudes which were to endure because they suited its circumstances. Some of them seem even to transcend the revolution of the twentieth century.

TOPOGRAPHY

We must begin with the land itself, and at first sight it does not suggest much that makes for unity. The physical theatre of Chinese history is vast. China is bigger than the United States and now contains five times as many people. The Great Wall which came to guard the northern frontier was in the end made up of between 2,500 and 3,000 miles of fortifications and has never been completely surveyed. From Peking to Hong Kong, more or less due south, is 1,200 miles as the crow flies. This huge expanse contains many climates and many regions. One great distinction stands out among them, that between northern and southern China. In summer the north is scorching and arid while the south is humid and used to floods; the north looks bare and dustblown in the winter, while the south is always green. This is not all that this distinction implies. One of the major themes of early Chinese history is of the spread of civilization, sometimes by migration, sometimes by diffusion, from north to south, of the tendency of conquest and political unification to take the same broad direction, and of the continual stimulation and irrigation of northern civilization by currents from the outside, from Mongolia and Central Asia.

China's major internal divisions are set by mountains and rivers. There are three great river valleys which drain the interior and run across the country roughly from west to east. They are, from north to south, the Hwang-Ho,

Physical map of China

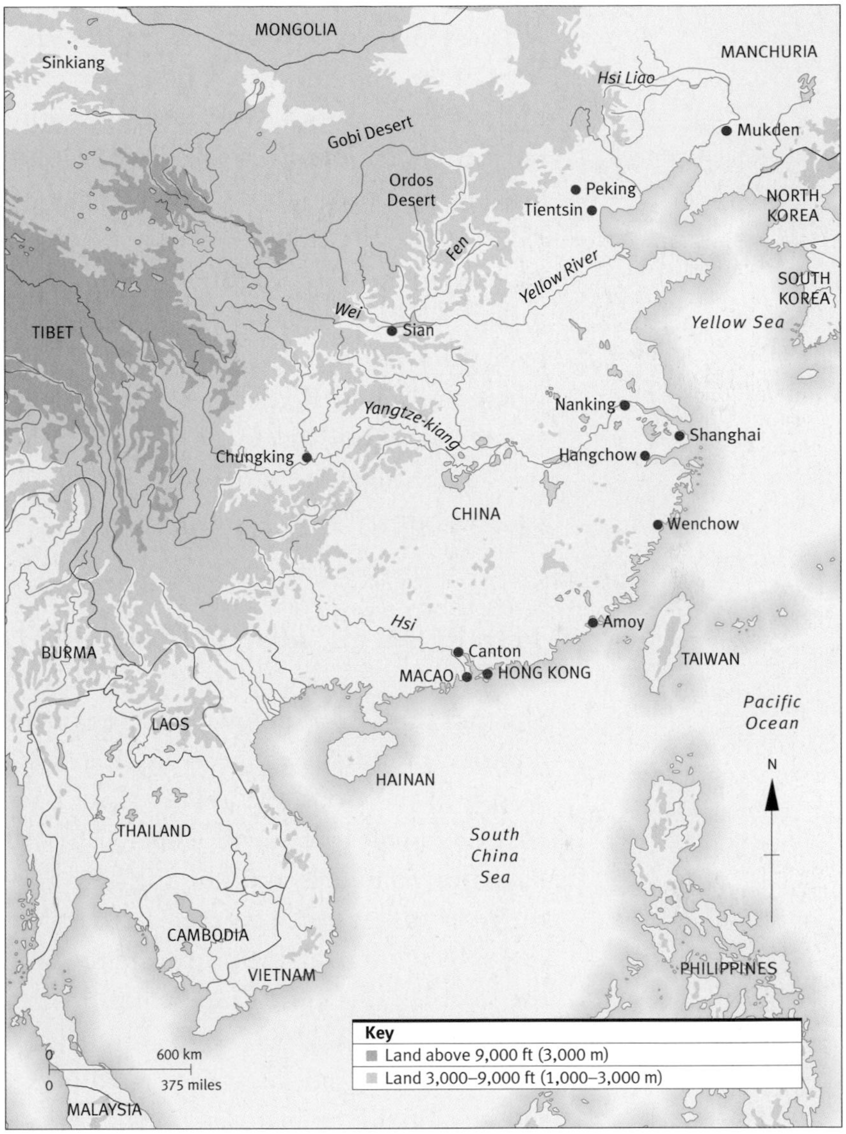

Chinese civilization emerged more than 3,000 years ago in the Yellow River valley, cold in winter but with fertile loess lands. From this area, civilization began to extend gradually southwards. By the 6th century BCE, it had reached the Yangtze valley and under the Han Dynasty (202 BCE–220 CE) the Chinese world also included the tropical lands that reach the sea in southern China.

Time chart (1700 BCE–221 BCE)

- c.1700–1050 BCE: Shang period
- 1050–771 BCE: Western Chou period
- 900 BCE
- 722–481 BCE: Period of the Springs and Autumns
- 600 BCE
- 403–221 BCE: Period of the Warring States
- 300 BCE
- 221 BCE: Unification of China by Shih-Huang-ti, First Emperor

or Yellow River, the Yangtze and the Hsi. It is surprising that a country so vast and thus divided should form a unity at all. Yet China is isolated, too, a world by itself since the start of the Pliocene. Much of China is mountainous and except in the extreme south and northeast her frontiers still sprawl across and along great ranges and plateaux. The headwaters of the Yangtze, like those of the Mekong, lie in the high Kunlun, north of Tibet. These highland frontiers are great insulators. The arc they form is broken only where the Yellow River flows south into China from inner Mongolia and it is on the banks of this river that the story of civilization in China begins.

THE ROLE OF THE YELLOW RIVER

Skirting the Ordos desert, itself separated by another mountain range from the desolate wastes of the Gobi, the Yellow River opens a sort of funnel into north China. Through it have flowed people and soil; the loess beds of the river valley, easily worked and fertile, laid down by wind from the north, are the basis of the first Chinese agriculture. Once this region was richly forested and well watered, but it became colder and more desiccated in one of those climatic transformations which are behind so much primeval social change. To Chinese pre-history overall, of course, there is a bigger setting than one river valley. "Peking man", a version of *Homo erectus*, turns up as a fire-user about six hundred thousand years ago, and there are Neanderthal traces in all three of the great river basins. The trail from these forerunners to the dimly discernible cultures which are their successors in early Neolithic times, leads us to a China already divided into two cultural zones, with a meeting place and mixing area on the Yellow River. It is impossible to separate the tangle of cultural

This curve lies in the stretch of the great Yellow River that crosses the Ordos desert, to the north of the fertile lands where Chinese civilization first emerged.

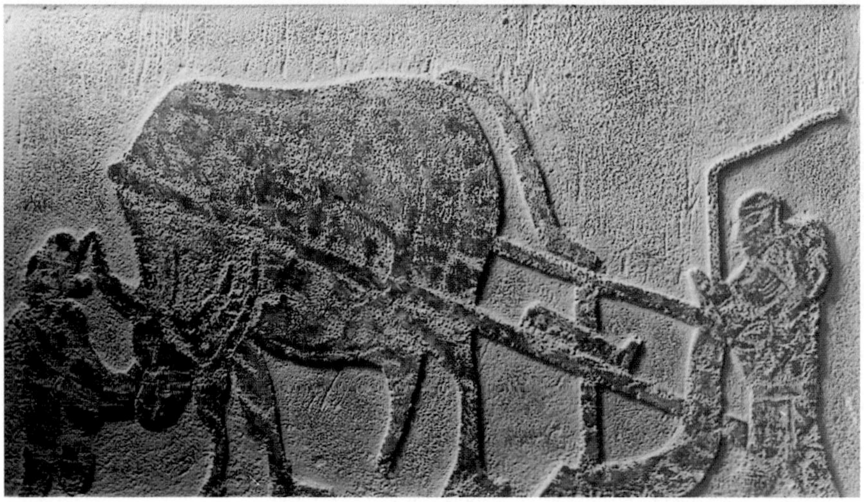

An image of a man using an ox-drawn plough was found on this brick from a Han-period tomb in China's Szechwan province.

interconnections already detectable by that time. But there was no even progress towards a uniform or united culture; even in early historical times, we are told, "the whole of China ... was teeming with Neolithic survivals". Against this varied background emerged settled agriculture; nomads and settlers were to coexist in China until our own day. Rhinoceros and elephant were still hunted in the north not long before 1000 BCE.

THE IMPACT OF AGRICULTURE

As in other parts of the world, the coming of agriculture meant a revolution. It has been argued that peoples who lived in the semi-tropical coastal areas of South-East Asia and south China were clearing forests to make fields as far back as 10,000 BCE. Certainly they exploited vegetation to provide themselves with fibres and food. But this is still a topic about which much more needs to be known. Rice was being farmed along the Yangtze in the seventh millennium BCE and ground just above the flood level of the Yellow River begins to yield evidence of agriculture (probably the growing of millet) from about 5800 BCE. Somewhat like that of early Egypt, the first Chinese agriculture seems to have been exhaustive or semi-exhaustive. The land was cleared, used for a few years, and then left to revert to nature while the cultivators turned attention elsewhere. From what has been called the "nuclear area of North China", agriculture can be seen later to spread both north to Manchuria and to the south. Within it there soon appeared complex cultures which combined with agriculture the use of jade and wood for carving, the domestication of silk-worms, the making of ceremonial vessels in forms which were to become traditional and perhaps even the use of chopsticks. In other words, this was in Neolithic times already the home of much that is characteristic of the Chinese tradition of historic times.

A pottery vase from the Neolithic culture of Longshan, which flourished in southern China in the 3rd millennium BCE. The strange shapes of many of these vases, painstakingly made with very thin sides, suggest that they were designed for ritual rather than everyday use.

This highly decorative cooking vessel is made of bronze and dates from Chinese Shang Ding period (c.16th–11th centuries BCE).

EARLY SOCIETY

Ancient writers recognized the importance of this revolutionary social change and legends identified a specific inventor of agriculture, yet very little can be inferred confidently or clearly about social organization at this stage. Perhaps because of this there has been a persistent tendency among Chinese to idealize it. Long after private property had become widespread it was assumed that "under heaven every spot is the sovereign's ground" and this may reflect early ideas that all land belonged to the community as a whole. Chinese Marxists later upheld this tradition, discerning in the archaeological evidence a golden age of primitive Communism preceding a descent into slave and feudal society. Argument is unlikely to convince those interested in the question one way or the other. Ground seems to be firmer in attributing to these times the appearance of a clan structure and totems, with prohibitions on marriage within the clan. Kinship in this form is almost the first institution which can be seen to have survived to be important in historical times. The evidence of the pottery, too, suggests some new complexity in social roles. Already things were being made which cannot have been intended for the rough and tumble of everyday use; a stratified society seems to be emerging before we reach the historical era.

One material sign of a future China already obvious at this stage is the widespread use of millet, a grain well adapted to the sometimes arid farming of the north. It was to be the basic staple of Chinese diet until about a thousand years ago and sustained a society which in due course arrived at literacy, at a great art of bronze-casting based on a difficult and advanced technology, at the means of making exquisite pottery far finer than anything made anywhere else in the world and, above all, at an ordered political and social system which identifies the first major age of Chinese history. But it must be remembered once more that the agriculture which made this possible was for a long time confined to north China and that many parts of this huge country only took up farming when historical times had already begun.

Bronze ritual axes, such as this one from the Shang period, were used to decapitate victims during sacred ceremonies. Human sacrifice was common in Shang-period China. Often hundreds of people were sacrificed during the burial ceremonies that accompanied the funerals of kings.

THE SHANG DYNASTY

The narrative of early times is very hard to recover, but can be outlined with some confidence. It has been agreed that the story of civilization in China begins under rulers from a people called the Shang, the first name with independent evidence to support it in the traditional list of dynasties which was for a long time the basis of Chinese chronology. From the late eighth century BCE we have better dates, but we still have no chronology for early Chinese history as well founded as, say, that of Egypt. It is more certain that somewhere about 1700 BCE (and a century each way is an acceptable margin of approximation) a tribe called the Shang, which enjoyed the military advantage of the chariot, imposed itself on its neighbours over a sizeable stretch of the Yellow River valley. Eventually, the Shang domain was a matter of about 40,000 square miles in northern Honan; this made it somewhat smaller than modern England, though its cultural influences reached far beyond its periphery, as evidence from as far away as south China, Chinese Turkestan and the northeastern coast shows.

Shang kings lived and died in some state; slaves and human sacrificial victims were

This bronze lid from a ritual vase dates from the period of the Western Chou and depicts a stylized animal head.

buried with them in deep and lavish tombs. Their courts had archivists and scribes, for this was the first truly literate culture east of Mesopotamia. This is one reason for distinguishing between Shang civilization and Shang dynastic paramountcy; this people showed a cultural influence which certainly extended far beyond any area they could have dominated politically. The political arrangements of the Shang domains themselves seem to have depended on the uniting of landholding with obligations to a king; the warrior landlords who were the key figures were the leading members of aristocratic lineages with semi-mythical origins. Yet Shang government was advanced enough to use scribes and had a standardized currency. What it could do when at full stretch is shown in its ability to mobilize large amounts of labour for the building of fortifications and cities.

THE CHOU DYNASTY

Shang China succumbed in the end to another tribe from the west of the valley, the Chou. A probable date is between 1120 and 1150 BCE. Under the Chou, many of the already elaborate governmental and social structures inherited from the Shang were preserved and further refined. Burial rites, bronze-working techniques and decorative art also survived in hardly altered forms. The great work of the Chou period was the consolidation and diffusion of this heritage. In it can be discerned the hardening of the institutions of a future Imperial China which would last two thousand years.

The Chou thought of themselves as surrounded by barbarian peoples, waiting for the benevolent effects of Chou tranquillization (an idea, it may be remarked, which still underlay the persistent refusal of Chinese officials two thousand years later to regard diplomatic missions from Europe as anything but respectful bearers of tribute). Chou supremacy in fact rested on war, but from it flowed great cultural consequences. As under the Shang, there was no truly unitary state and Chou government represented a change of degree rather than kind. It was usually a matter of a group of notables and vassals, some more dependent on the dynasty than others, offering in good times at least a formal acknowledgement of its supremacy and all increasingly sharing in a common culture. Political China (if it is reasonable to use such a term) rested upon big estates which had

Jade was a much prized material in ancient China. This ritual dagger dates from the beginning of the Shang period in the 2nd millennium BCE and has a jade blade.

This 17th-century CE watercolour is entitled "Don't gamble with danger" and illustrates the story of King You of the Chou Dynasty, who lost the empire because he wanted to make the queen laugh.

sufficient cohesion to have powers of long survival and in this process their original lords turned into rulers who could be called kings, served by elementary bureaucracies.

THE PERIOD OF WARRING STATES

The Chou system collapsed from about 700 BCE, when a barbarian incursion drove the Chou from their ancestral centre to a new home further east, in Honan. The dynasty did not end until 256 BCE, but the next distinguishable epoch dates from 403 to 221 BCE and is significantly known as the Period of the Warring States. In it, historical selection by conflict grew fierce. Big fish ate little fish until one only was left and all the Chinese lands were for the first time ruled by one great empire, the Ch'in, from which the country was

Tang "the Victorious", founder of the Shang Dynasty, is shown walking in the country-side in this 17th-century CE watercolour. According to legend, Tang came across people catching birds and persuaded them to let the birds go free, a gesture which won him great popularity.

to get its name. This is matter for discussion elsewhere; here it is enough to register an epoch in Chinese history.

Reading about these events in the traditional Chinese historical accounts can produce a slight feeling of beating the air, and historians who are not experts in Chinese studies may perhaps be forgiven if they cannot trace over this period of some fifteen hundred years or so any helpful narrative thread in the dimly discernible struggles of kings and over-mighty subjects. They should be; after all, scholars have not yet provided one. Nevertheless, two basic processes were going on for most of this time, which were very important for the future and which give the period some unity, though their detail is elusive. The first of these was a continuing diffusion of culture outwards from the Yellow River basin.

These two jade figures date from the middle Western Chou period (10th century BCE). Because figures are rarely found in Shang or early Chou art, it is thought that these may have been imported or inspired by similar objects from southern or south-western China.

To begin with, Chinese civilization was a matter of tiny islands in a sea of barbarism. Yet by 500 BCE it was the common possession of scores, perhaps hundreds, of what have been termed "states" scattered across the north, and it had also been carried into the Yangtze valley. This had long been a swampy, heavily forested region, very different from the north and inhabited by far more primitive peoples. Chou influence – in part thanks to military expansion – irradiated this area and helped to produce the first major culture and state of the Yangtze valley, the Ch'u civilization. Although owing much to the Chou, it had many distinctive linguistic, calligraphic, artistic and religious traits of its own. By the end of the Period of Warring States we have reached the point at which the stage of Chinese history is about to be much enlarged.

LANDOWNERS AND PEASANTS

The second of the fundamental and continuing processes that took place under both Shang and Chou was the establishment of landmarks in institutions which were to survive until modern times. Among them was a fundamental division of Chinese society into a landowning nobility and the common people. Most of these were peasants, making up the vast majority of the population and paying for all that China produced in the way of civilization and state power. What little we know of their countless lives can be quickly said; even less can be discovered than about the anonymous masses of toilers at the base of every other ancient civilization. There is one good physical reason for this: the life of the Chinese peasant was an alternation between his mud hovel in the winter and an encampment where he lived during the summer months to guard and tend his growing crops. Neither has left much trace. For the rest, he appears sunk in the anonymity of his community (he does not belong to a clan), tied to the soil, occasionally taken from it to carry out other duties and to serve his lord in war or hunting. His depressed state is expressed by the classification of modern Chinese communist historiography which lumps Shang and Chou together as "Slavery Society" preceding the "Feudal Society" which comes next.

THE NOBILITY

Although Chinese society was to grow much more complex by the end of the Warring States period, the distinction of common people from the nobly born remained. There were important practical consequences: the nobility, for example, were not subject to punishments – such as mutilation – inflicted on the commoner; it was a survival of this in later times that the gentry were exempt from the beatings which might be visited on the commoner (though, of course, they might suffer appropriate and even dire punishment for more serious crimes). The nobility long enjoyed a virtual monopoly of wealth, too, which outlasted its earlier monopoly of metal weapons. None the less, these were not the crucial distinctions of status, which lay elsewhere, in the nobleman's special religious standing through a monopoly of certain ritual practices. Only noblemen could share in the cults which were the heart of the Chinese notion of kinship. Only the nobleman belonged to a family – which meant that he had ancestors. Reverence for ancestors and propitiation of their spirits had existed before the Shang, though it does not seem that in early times many ancestors were thought likely to survive into the spirit world. Possibly the only ones lucky enough to do so would be the spirits of particularly important persons; the most likely, of course, were the rulers themselves, whose ultimate origin, it was claimed, was itself godly.

THE CLAN AND THE FAMILY

The family emerged as a legal refinement and subdivision of the clan, and the Chou period was the most important one in its clarification. There were about a hundred clans, within each of which marriage was forbidden. Each was supposed to be founded by a hero or a god. The patriarchal heads of the clan's families and houses exercised special authority over its members and were all qualified to carry out its rituals and thus influence spirits to act as intermediaries with the powers which controlled the universe on the clan's behalf. These practices came to identify persons entitled to possess land or hold office.

This bronze male figure on a base stands 8.5 ft (2.62 m) high and dates from the 12th century BCE (Shang period). Found in one of two sacrificial pits in the Szechwan province of China, the figure clearly once held an object – probably an elephant tusk – in his hands. His long robe is decorated with small figures.

The clan offered a sort of democracy of opportunity at this level: any of its members could be appointed to the highest place in it, for they were all qualified by the essential virtue of a descent whose origins were godlike. In this sense, a king was only *primus inter pares*, a patrician outstanding among all patricians.

RELIGION

THE FAMILY ABSORBED enormous quantities of religious feeling and psychic energy; its rituals were exacting and time-consuming. The common people, not sharing in this, found a religious outlet in maintaining the worship of nature gods. These always got some attention from the élite, too, the worship of mountains and rivers and the propitiating of their spirits being an important imperial duty from early times, but they were to influence the central developments of Chinese thought less than similar notions in other religions.

RELIGION AND POLITICAL FORMS

Religion had considerable repercussions on political forms. The heart of the ruling house's claim to obedience was its religious superiority. Through the maintenance of ritual, it had access to the goodwill of unseen powers, whose intentions might be known from the oracles. When these had been interpreted, the ordering of the agricultural life of the community was possible, for they regulated such matters as the time of sowing or harvesting. Much turned, therefore, on the religious standing of the king; it was of the first importance to the state. This was reflected in the fact that the Chou displacement of the Shang was religious as well as military. The idea was introduced that there existed a god superior to the ancestral god of the dynasty and that from him there was derived a mandate to rule. Now, it was claimed, he had decreed that the mandate should pass to other hands. This was the introduction of another idea fundamental to the Chinese conception of government and it

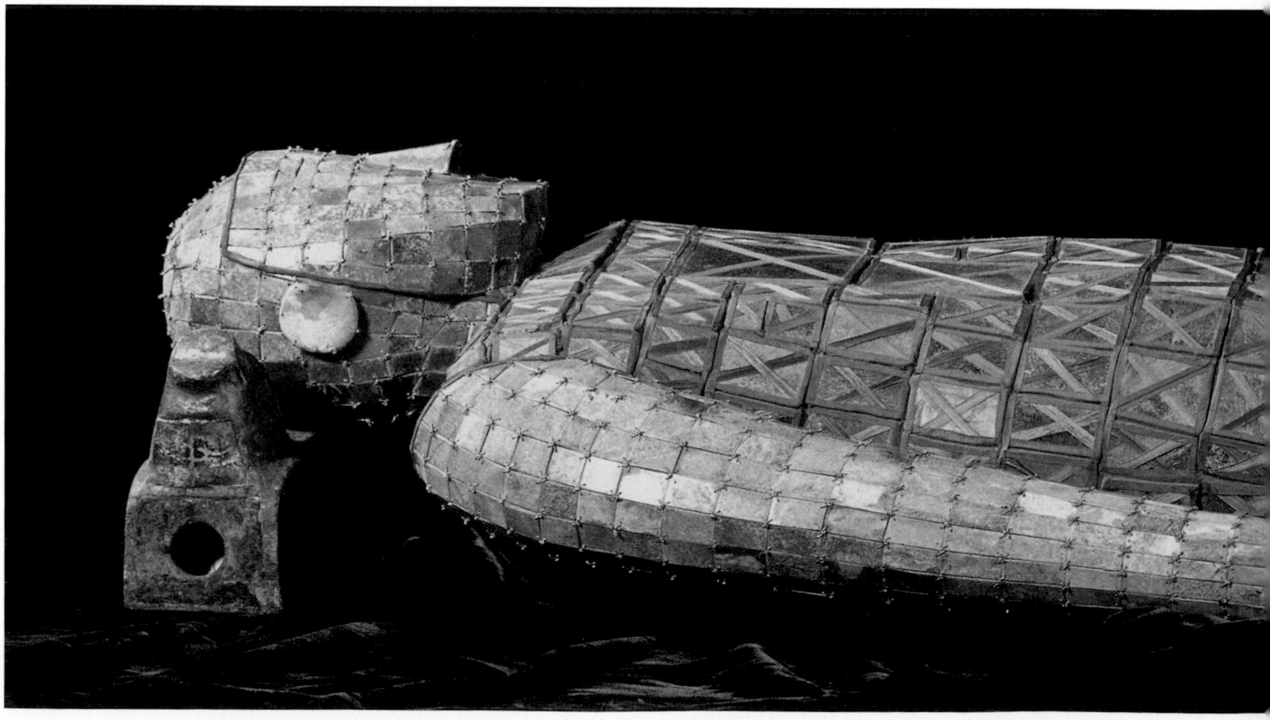

was to be closely linked to the notion of a cyclic history, marked by the repeated rise and fall of dynasties. Inevitably, it provoked speculation about what might be the signs by which the recipient of the new mandate should be recognized. Filial piety was one, and to this extent, a conservative principle was implicit. But the Chou writers also introduced an idea rendered not very comfortably into English by the word "virtue". Clearly, its content remained fluid; disagreement and discussion were therefore possible.

THE ROLE OF THE MONARCH

In its earliest forms the Chinese "state" – and over long periods one must think of more than one authority coexisting – seems little more than an abstraction from the idea of the ruler's estate and the necessity to maintain the rituals and sacrifices. The records do not leave an impression of a very busy monarchy. Apart from the extraordinary decisions of peace or war, the king seems to have had little to do except fulfil his religious duties, hunt, and initiate building projects in the palace complexes which appear as early as Shang times, though there are indications of Chou kings also undertaking (with the labour of prisoners) extensive agricultural colonization. For a long time the early Chinese rulers did without any very considerable bureaucracy. Gradually a hierarchy of ministers emerged who regulated court life, but the king was a landowner who for the most part needed only bailiffs, overseers and a few scribes. No doubt much of his life was spent on the move about his lands.

The only other aspect of the king's activity which needed expert support was the supernatural. Out of this much was to grow, not least the intimate connection between rule in China and the determination of time and the calendar, both very important in agricultural societies. These were based on astronomy, and though this came to have a respectable basis in observation and calculation, its origins were magical and religious.

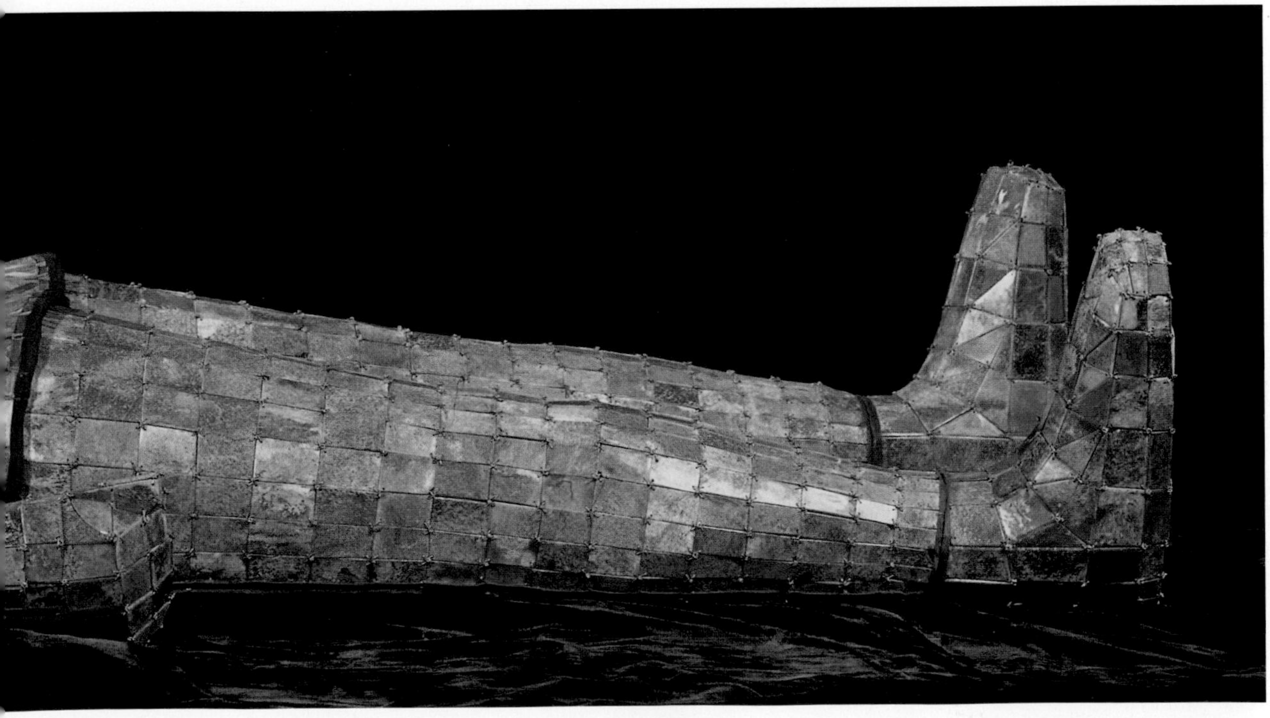

Prince Tou Wan's 2nd-century BCE burial suit, pictured here, is made of more than 2,000 small jade plates. The remains of 10 of these fantastic cocoons have been discovered – jade was believed to be a key to immortality. This practice reached the zenith of its popularity under the Han Dynasty. Expensive burials were later banned by an emperor who considered them to be a lure for grave robbers.

This bone oracle dates from the Shang period. The oldest Chinese inscriptions, of which several thousand exist, date from this period and have been found engraved on bone or on tortoise shells. The oracle was heated until it began to crack. The cracks were then interpreted to divine the spirits' answers to the questions posed.

THE USE OF ORACLES

In Shang times all the great decisions of state, and many lesser ones, were taken by consulting oracles. This was done by engraving turtle shells or the shoulder-blades of certain animals with written characters and then applying to them a heated bronze pin so as to produce cracks on the reverse side. The direction and length of these cracks in relation to the characters would then be considered and the oracle read accordingly by the king. This was an enormously important practice from the point of view of historians, for such oracles were kept, presumably as records. They also provide us with evidence for the foundation of Chinese language, as the characters on the oracle bones (and some early bronzes) are basically those of classical Chinese. The Shang had about 5000 such characters, though not all can be read. Nevertheless, the principles of this writing show a unique consistency; while other civilizations gave up pictographic characterization in favour of phonetic systems, the Chinese language grew and evolved, but remained essentially within the pictographic framework. Already under the Shang, moreover, the structure of the language was that of modern Chinese – monosyllabic and depending on word order, not on the inflection of words, to convey meaning. The Shang, in fact, already used a form of Chinese.

THE IMPORTANCE OF WRITING IN ANCIENT CHINA

Writing was to remain high on the scale of Chinese arts and has always retained some trace of the religious respect given to the first characters. Only a few years ago, examples of Mao Zedong's calligraphy were widely reproduced and were used to enhance his prestige during his ascendancy. This reflects the centuries during which writing remained the jealously guarded privilege of the élite. The readers of the oracles, the so-called *shih*, were the primitive form of the later scholar-gentry class; they were indispensable experts, the possessors of hieratic and arcane skills. Their monopoly was to pass to the much larger class of the scholar-gentry in later times. The language thus remained the form of communication of a relatively small élite, which not only found its privileges rooted in its possession but also had an interest in preserving it against corruption or variation. It was of enormous importance as a unifying and stabilizing force because written Chinese became a language of government and culture transcending divisions of dialect, religion and region. Its use by the élite tied the vast country together.

THE FIRST IRON CASTING

Several great determinants of future Chinese history had thus been settled in outline by the end of the Chou period. That end came after increasing signs of social changes which were affecting the operation of the major institutions. This is not surprising; China long remained basically agricultural, and change was often initiated by the pressure of population upon resources. This accounts for the impact of the introduction of iron, probably in use by about 500 BCE. As elsewhere a sharp rise in agricultural production (and therefore in population) followed. The first tools which have been found come from the fifth century BCE; iron weapons came later. At an early date, too, tools were made by casting, as iron moulds for sickle blades have been found dating from the fourth or fifth centuries. Chinese technique in handling the new metal was thus advanced in very early

Language and writing in China

The Chinese language, which the Chinese call *Han*, is part of a large family that linguists have classified as Sino-Tibetan, to which the languages of Tibet and Burma also belong. The numerous Chinese dialects that exist today are completely different from one another in spoken form and can thus be treated as independent languages. However, they are linked by a common literary tradition, which originated in the Shang period, in the 2nd millennium BCE. Literary Chinese (*wen-yen*), in which the texts that are considered to be the country's classical culture have been written, is different from the spoken dialects and has traditionally acted as a point of contact between all of them, preventing any of them being transformed into a written language.

Throughout Chinese history there has been a strong continuity in both the spoken language and writing. The latter has retained a large number of letters, as it did not adopt a phonetic system. In 1953 an official system of transcription into the Latin alphabet was agreed upon, known as *pinyin*. The older Wade-Giles transcription system was devised in 1859 and revised in 1892. Although the Wade-Giles system was abolished by the Chinese government in 1979, it is still the one that is most widely used in the rest of the world.

These are pictographic signs used during the Shang period (2nd millennium BCE). The images shown above are easily recognizable: each one shows a man using a different system to carry a load. Although, over time, the letters became gradually more abstract, the Shang pictograms represent the starting point of Chinese writing and they were used to transcribe a language that was already recognizable as Chinese.

times. Whether by development from bronze casting or by experiments with pottery furnaces, which could produce high temperatures, China somehow arrived at the casting of iron at about the same time as knowledge of how to forge it. Exact precedence is unimportant; what is noteworthy is that sufficiently high temperatures for casting were not available elsewhere for another nineteen hundred years or so.

URBANIZATION

Another important change under the later Chou was a great growth of cities. They tended to be sited on plains near rivers, but the first of them had probably taken their shape and location from the use of landowners' temples as centres of administration for their estates. This drew to them other temples, those of the popular nature gods, as communities collected about them. Then, under the Shang, a new scale of government begins to make itself felt; we find stamped-earth ramparts, specialized aristocratic and court quarters and the remains of large buildings. At Anyang, a Shang capital in about 1300 BCE, there were metal foundries and potters' kilns as well as palaces and a royal graveyard. By late Chou times, the capital Wang Ch'eng is surrounded by a rectangle of earth walls each nearly three kilometres long.

There were scores of cities by 500 BCE and their prevalence implies an increasingly varied society. Many of them had three well-defined areas: a small enclosure where the aristocracy lived, a larger one inhabited by

This 19th-century CE engraving depicts Confucius surrounded by his disciples. The master said, "Yu, do you want me to teach you what knowledge is? If you know something, you must state what you know. If you do not know something, you must confess that you do not know. That is knowledge." (***The Analects of Confucius***, **II, 17**)

specialized craftsmen and merchants, and the fields outside the walls which fed the city. A merchant class was another important development. It may not have been much regarded by the landowners but well before 1000 BCE a cowry shell currency was used which shows a new complexity of economic life and the presence of specialists in trade. Their quarters and those of the craftsmen were distinguished from those of the nobility by walls and ramparts around the latter, but they, too, fell within the walls of the city – a sign of a growing need for defence. In the commercial streets of cities of the Warring States Period could be found shops selling jewellery, curios, food and clothing, as well as taverns, gambling houses and brothels.

THE GROWING INDEPENDENCE OF THE NOBILITY

The heart of Chinese society, none the less, still beat to the slow rhythms of the countryside. The privileged class which presided over the land system showed unmistakable signs of a growing independence of its kings as the Chou period came to an end. Landowners originally had the responsibility of providing soldiers to the king and development in the art of war helped to increase their independence. The nobleman had always had a monopoly of arms; this was already significant when, in Shang times, Chinese weaponry was limited for the most part to the bow and the bronze halberd. As time passed, only noblemen could afford the more expensive weapons, armour and horses which increasingly came into use.

The warrior using a chariot as a platform for archery, before descending to fight the last stage of the battle on foot with bronze weapons, evolved in the last centuries of the pre-Common Era into a member of a team of two or three armoured warriors, moving with a company of sixty or seventy attendants and supporters, accompanied by a battle-wagon carrying the heavy armour and new weapons like the cross-bow and long iron sword, which were needed at the scene of action. The nobleman remained the key figure under this system as in earlier times.

As historical records become clearer, it can be seen that economic supremacy was rooted in customary tenure which was very potent and far reaching. Ownership of estates – theoretically all granted by the king – extended not only to land but to carts, livestock, implements and, above all, people. Labourers could be sold, exchanged, or left by will. This was another basis of a growing independence for the nobility, but it also gave fresh importance to distinctions within the landowning class. In principle, estates were held by them in concentric circles about the king's own demesne, according to their closeness to the royal line and, therefore, according to the degree of closeness of their relations with the spirit world. By about 600 BCE, it seems clear that this had effectively reduced the king to dependence on the greatest princes. There appear a succession of protectors of the royal house; kings could only resist the encroachments of these oriental Bolingbrokes and Warwicks in so far as the success of any one of them inevitably provoked the jealousy of others, and because of the kingly religious prestige which still counted for much with the lesser nobility. The whole late Chou period was marked by grave disorder and growing scepticism, though, about the criteria by which the right to rule was recognizable. The price of survival for the princes who disputed China was the elaboration of more effective governments and armed forces, and often they welcomed innovators prepared to set aside tradition.

From the 1st millennium BCE, circular coins with a hole in the centre were common (see above), and they are still the standard type of coin used by the Chinese.

THE HUNDRED SCHOOLS ERA

In the profound and prolonged social and political crisis of the last decaying centuries of the Chou and the Warring States period (433–221 BCE), there was a burst of speculation about the foundations of government and ethics. The era was to remain famous as the time of the "Hundred Schools", when wandering scholars moved about from patron to patron, expounding their teachings.

One sign of this new development was the appearance of a school of writers known as the "Legalists". They are said to have urged that law-making power should replace ritual observances as the principle of organization of the state; there should be one law for all, ordained and vigorously applied by one ruler. The aim of this was the creation of a wealthy and powerful state. This seemed to many of their opponents to be little more than a cynical doctrine of power, but the Legalists were to have important successes in the next few centuries because kings, at least, liked their ideas. The debate went on for a long time.

CONFUCIUS

IN THE DEBATE about the organization of the state, the main opponents of the Legalists were the followers of the teacher who is the most famous of all Chinese thinkers, Confucius. It is convenient to call him by that name, though it is only a latinized version of his Chinese name, K'ung-fu-tzu, and was given to him by Europeans in the seventeenth century CE, more than two thousand years after his birth in the middle of the sixth century BCE. He was to be more profoundly respected in China than any other philosopher. What he said – or was said to have said – shaped his countrymen's thinking for two thousand years

Dating from the 3rd century BCE, these ancient Chinese bronze coins are in the shapes of a hoe and a knife.

and was to be paid the compliment of bitter attack by the first post-Confucian Chinese state, the Marxist republic of the twentieth century CE.

THE PRECEPTS OF CONFUCIUS

Confucius came from a *shih* family. He was a member of the lesser nobility who may have spent some time as a minister of state and an overseer of granaries and probably never rose above a minor official rank. When he could not find a ruler to put into practice his recommendations for just government he turned to meditation and teaching; his aim was to present a purified and more abstract version of the doctrine he believed to lie at the heart of the traditional practices and thus to revive personal integrity and disinterested service in the governing class. He was a reforming conservative, seeking to teach his pupils the essential truths of ancient ways (*Tao*) materialized and obscured by routine. Somewhere in the past, he thought, lay a mythical age when everyone knew his or her place and duty; to return to that was Confucius's ethical goal. He advocated the principle of order – the attribution to everything of its correct place in the great gamut of experience. The practical expression of this was the strong Confucian predisposition to support the institutions likely to ensure order – the family, hierarchy, seniority – and due reverence for the many nicely graded obligations between people.

This 16th-century CE ivory statue portrays Confucius. Even though sacred ceremonies were held in his honour, the great Chinese master considered himself to be a secular thinker, as opposed to a religious prophet. On one occasion he said, "If we know nothing about life how can we know anything about death?" (*The Analects of Confucius*, XI, 11)

This was teaching likely to produce individuals who would respect the traditional culture, emphasize the value of good form and regular behaviour, and seek to realize their moral obligations in the scrupulous discharge of duties. It was immediately successful in that many of Confucius's pupils won fame and worldly success (though his teaching deplored the conscious pursuit of such goals, urging, rather, a gentlemanly self-effacement). But it was also successful in a much more fundamental sense, since generations of Chinese civil servants were later to be drilled in the precepts of behaviour and government which he laid down. "Documents, conduct, loyalty and faithfulness", four precepts attributed to him as his guidance on government, helped to form reliable, sometimes disinterested and even humane civil servants for hundreds of years.

The style of the teachings of Confucius, who is depicted in this 18th-century CE portrait, is reflected in the maxim, "To learn without thinking is fatal but to think without learning is just as bad." (*The Analects of Confucius*, II, 15)

Mysticism and philosophy in ancient China

Various archaeological finds provide evidence that, at the time of the Shang and Chou dynasties, members of the royal family and the aristocracy believed in the power of dead ancestors and that this belief lay at the heart of their religion. The 6th century BCE, however, saw the appearance of the two philosophical trends that have dominated Chinese thinking to the present day: Confucianism and Taoism. Confucianism was the philosophy of social organisation, of common sense and practical knowledge. Taoism was the philosophy of the contemplation of nature, of tranquillity, and of eternal rebirth.

CONFUCIUS

Confucianism derives its name from K'ung-fu-tzu or Confucius (551–479 BCE). He was a social and moral reformer rather than a religious leader. His ideology was adopted by the ruling classes for 2,000 years and became the basis of Chinese philosophy.

Later, Meng-tzu or Mencius (4th century BCE) was to add to this doctrine the idea of humanity's benevolence and natural goodness. Hsün-tzu (3rd century BCE) attacked the doctrine of Mencius with its opposite, stating that human beings are evil and must be taught to follow the path of morality.

LAO TZU

Taoists believe Lao Tzu was the creator of Taoism. Thought to be a contemporary of Confucius, he was the legendary author of a book of aphorisms called *Tao-te Ching* (*The Classic of the Way and its Power*).

The philosophies of Confucianism, Taoism and Buddhism are often collectively referred to as the "three teachings".

THE THIRTEEN CLASSICS

Confucian texts were later to be treated with something like religious awe. His name gave great prestige to anything with which it was associated. He was said to have compiled some of the texts later known as the Thirteen Classics, a collection which only took its final form in the thirteenth century CE. Rather like the Old Testament, they were a somewhat miscellaneous collection of old poems, chronicles, early state documents, moral sayings and an early cosmogony called the Book of Changes, but they were used for centuries in a unified and creative way to mould generations of China's civil servants and rulers in the precepts which were believed to be those approved by Confucius (the parallel with the use of the Bible, at least in Protestant countries, is striking here, too). The stamp of authority was set upon this collection by the tradition that Confucius had selected it and that it must therefore contain doctrine which digested his teaching. Almost incidentally it also reinforced still more the use of the Chinese in which these texts were written as the common language of China's intellectuals; the collection was another tie pulling a huge and varied country together in a common culture.

It is striking that Confucius had so little to say about the supernatural. In the ordinary sense of the word he was not a "religious" teacher (which probably explains why other teachers had greater success with the masses). He was essentially concerned with practical duties, an emphasis he shared with several other Chinese teachers of the fourth and fifth centuries BCE. Possibly because the stamp was then so firmly taken, Chinese thought seems less troubled by agonized uncertainties over the reality of the actual or the possibility of personal salvation than other, more tormented, traditions. The lessons of the past, the wisdom of former times and the maintenance of good order came to have more importance in it than pondering theological enigmas or seeking reassurance in the arms of the dark gods.

CHINESE THOUGHT

For all his great influence, and his later promotion as the focus of an official cult, Confucius was not the only maker of Chinese intellectual tradition. Indeed, the tone of Chinese intellectual life is perhaps not attributable to any individual's teaching. It shares something with other oriental philosophies in its emphasis upon the meditative and reflective mode rather than the methodical and interrogatory which is more familiar to Europeans. The mapping of knowledge by systematic questioning of the mind about the nature and extent of its own powers was not to be a characteristic activity of Chinese philosophers. This does not mean they inclined to otherworldliness and fantasy, for Confucianism was emphatically practical. Unlike the ethical sages of Judaism, Christianity and Islam, those of China tended always to turn to the here and now, to pragmatic and secular questions, rather than to theology and metaphysics.

This can also be said of systems rivalling Confucianism which were evolved to satisfy Chinese needs. One was the teaching of Mo-Tzu, a fifth-century thinker, who preached an active creed of universal altruism; people were to love strangers like their own kin. Some of his followers stressed this side of his teaching, others a religious fervour which encouraged the worship of spirits and had greater popular appeal.

TAOISM

Lao Tzu, another great teacher (though one whose vast fame obscures the fact that we know virtually nothing about him), was supposed to be the author of the text which is the key document of the philosophical system later called Taoism. This was much more obviously competitive with Confucianism, for it advocated the positive neglect of much that Confucianism upheld; respect for the established order, decorum and scrupulous observance of tradition and ceremonial, for example. Taoism urged submission to a conception already available in Chinese thought and familiar to Confucius, that of the Tao or "way", the cosmic principle which runs through and sustains the harmoniously ordered universe. The practical results of this were likely to be political quietism and non-attachment; one ideal held up to its practitioners was that a village should know that other villages existed because it would hear their cockerels crowing in the mornings, but should have no further interest in them, no commerce with them and no political order binding them together. Such an idealization of simplicity and poverty was the very opposite of the empire and prosperity Confucianism upheld.

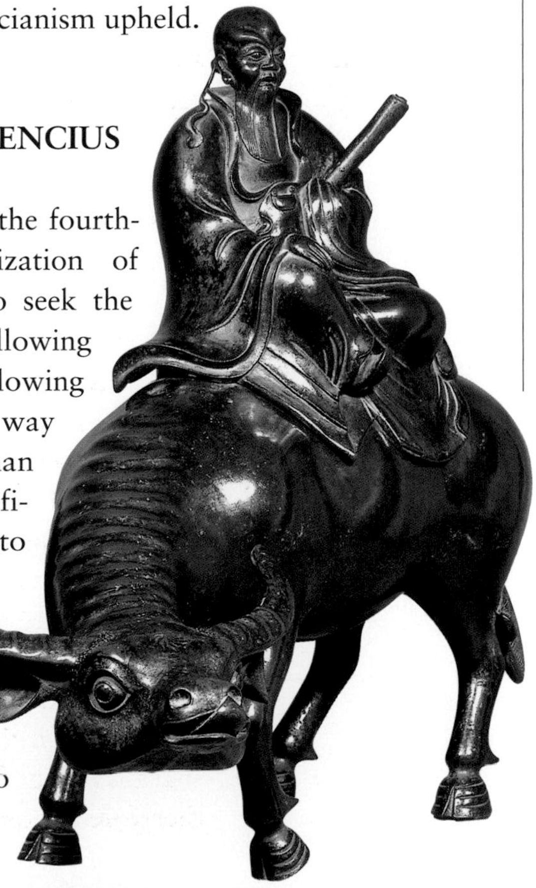

This statuette depicts Lao Tzu, the legendary founder of Taoism, riding a buffalo.

THE TEACHINGS OF MENCIUS

Still another and later sage, the fourth-century Mencius (a latinization of Meng-tzu), taught people to seek the welfare of humanity in following Confucian teaching. The following of a moral code in this way would assure that human beings' fundamentally beneficent natures would be able to operate. Moreover, a ruler following Confucian principles would come to rule all China. But all schools of Chinese philosophy had to take account of Confucian teaching, so great was its prestige and influence. Eventually, with Buddhism (which had not reached China by the end of the Warring States period) and Taoism, Confucianism was habitually referred to as one of the "three teachings" which were the basis of Chinese culture.

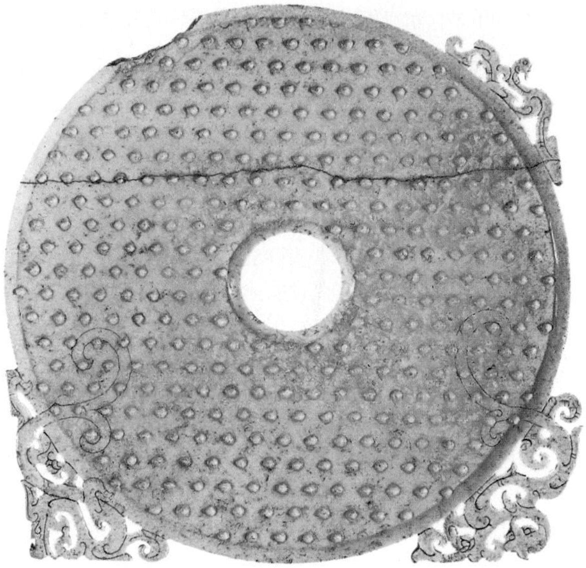

From the dawn of Chinese civilization jade disks, perhaps symbolizing the sky, have been produced. This example, carved in the 4th century BCE, demonstrates the masterful technique that Chinese craftsmen had acquired in working this precious material. The disk is pierced by a central hole representing an entrance to the void of timelessness.

THE IMPORTANCE OF CONFUCIANISM

The total effect of the sages' teachings is imponderable, but probably enormous. It is hard to say how many people were directly affected by such doctrines, and in the case of Confucianism its great period of influence lay still in the remote future at the time of Confucius' death. Yet Confucianism's importance for the directing élites of China was to be immense. It set standards and ideals to China's leaders and rulers whose eradication was to prove impossible even in our own day.

Moreover, some of its precepts – filial piety, for example – filtered down to popular culture through stories and the traditional motifs of art. It thus further solidified a civilization many of whose most striking features were well entrenched by the third century BCE. Certainly Confucianism's teachings accentuated the preoccupation with the past among China's rulers which was to give a characteristic bias to Chinese historiography, and it may also have had a damaging effect on scientific enquiry. Evidence suggests that after the fifth century BCE a tradition of astronomical observation which had permitted the prediction of lunar eclipses fell into decline. Some scholars have seen the influence of Confucianism as part of the explanation of this.

A 3rd-century BCE terracotta figure, discovered near the mausoleum of the Qin emperor Shih Huang-ti. This is one of the few female effigies to have survived from that period, although thousands of male terracotta figures, forming the emperor's burial army, have been found.

ART AND ARCHITECTURE

China's great schools of ethics are one striking example of the way in which almost all the categories of her civilization differ from those of our own tradition and, indeed, from those of any other civilization of which we have knowledge. Its uniqueness is not only a sign of its comparative isolation, but also of its vigour. Both are displayed in its art, which is what now remains of ancient China that is most immediately appealing and

This bronze ritual vase dates from the late Shang period and was used to hold the fragrant wine that was offered to ancestors during sacred ceremonies. Thought to be from a Shang royal tomb, the vase is decorated with magical symbols, including dragon-like birds and animals and a large mask.

accessible. Of the architecture of the Shang and Chou, not much survives; their building was often in wood, and the tombs do not reveal very much. Excavation of cities, on the other hand, reveals a capacity for massive construction; the wall of one Chou capital was made of pounded earth thirty feet high and forty thick.

Smaller objects survive much more plentifully and they reveal a civilization which even in Shang times is capable of exquisite work, above all in its ceramics, unsurpassed in the ancient world. A tradition going back to Neolithic times lay behind them. Pride of place must be given none the less to the great series of bronzes which begin in early Shang times and continue thereafter uninterruptedly. The skill of casting sacrificial containers, pots, wine-jars, weapons, tripods was already at its peak as early as 1600 BCE. And it is argued by some scholars that the "lost-wax" method, which made new triumphs possible, was also known in the Shang era. Bronze casting appears so suddenly and at such a high level of achievement that people long sought to explain it by transmission of the technique from outside. But there is no evidence for this and the most likely origin of Chinese metallurgy is from locally evolved techniques in several centres in the late Neolithic.

None of the bronzes reached the outside world in early times, or at least there has been no discovery of them elsewhere, which can be dated before the middle of the first millennium BCE. Nor are there many discoveries outside China at earlier dates of the other things to which Chinese artists turned their attention, to the carving of stone or the appallingly hard jade, for example, into beautiful and intricate designs. Apart from what she absorbed from her barbaric nomadic neighbours, China not only had little to learn from the outside until well into the historical era, it seems, but had no reason to think that the outside world – if she knew of it – wanted to learn much from her.

Thousands of life-size terracotta figures, such as this one, were found at the mausoleum of Shih Huang-ti, the Qin First Emperor. The figures are copies of the Chinese imperial army's soldiers at the end of the 3rd century BCE. This is a model of a rearguard archer in battle position. A cuirass of bronze plates protects his chest, shoulders and back.

3 THE OTHER WORLDS OF THE ANCIENT PAST

A herd of cattle, led by a drover, is depicted in this cave fresco in the Tassili mountains of the central Sahara. The image demonstrates that what is now a sun-scorched desert was a fertile region 6,000 years ago.

SO FAR IN THIS ACCOUNT huge areas of the world have still hardly been mentioned. Although Africa has priority in the story of the evolution and spread of humanity and though the entry of humankind to the Americas and Australasia calls for remark, once those remote events have been touched upon, the beginnings of history focus attention elsewhere. The homes of the creative cultures which have dominated the story of civilization were the Near East and Aegean, India and China. In all these areas some meaningful break in rhythm can be seen somewhere in the first millennium BCE; there are no neat divisions, but there is a certain rough synchrony which makes it reasonable to divide their histories in this era. But for the great areas of which nothing has so far been said, such a chronology would be wholly unrevealing.

This is, in the main, because none of them had achieved levels of civilization comparable to those already reached in the Mediterranean and Asia by 1000 BCE. Remarkable things had been done by then in

western Europe and the Americas, but when they are given due weight there still remains a qualitative gap between the complexity and resources of the societies which produced them and those of the ancient civilizations which were to found durable traditions. The interest in the ancient history of these areas lies more in the way they illustrate that varied roads might lead towards civilization and that different responses might be demanded by different environmental challenges than in what they left as their heritage. In one or two instances they may allow us to reopen arguments about what constitutes "civilization", but for the period of which we have so far spoken the story of Africa, of the Pacific peoples, of the Americas and western Europe is not history but still prehistory. There is little or no correspondence between its rhythms and what was going on in the Near East or Asia, even when there were (as in the case of Africa and Europe though not of the Americas) contacts with them.

A giraffe has been discovered etched onto this rock wall in Twifelfontein, Namibia. Many similar examples of cave art, all of which are difficult to date, have been found in southwest Africa.

AFRICA

AFRICA IS A GOOD PLACE TO START, because that is where the human story first began. Historians of Africa, sensitive to any slighting or imagined slighting of their subject, like to dwell upon Africa's importance in pre-history. As things earlier in this book have shown, they are quite right to do so; most of the evidence for the life of the earliest hominids is African; they spread from it into Eurasia and beyond, and the first humans in due course followed them. Then, though, in the Upper Palaeolithic and the Neolithic the focus moves elsewhere. Much was still to happen in Africa but the period of its greatest creative influence on the rest of the world was over.

CLIMATIC CHANGE

Why Africa's influence dwindles we cannot say, but one primary force may well have been a change of climate. Even recently, say in about 3000 BCE, the Sahara supported animals such as elephants and hippopotami, which have

Time chart (3500 BCE–450 BCE)

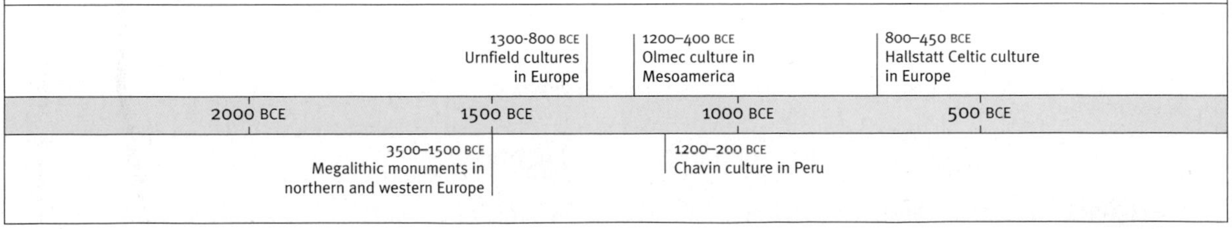

long since disappeared there; more remarkably, it was the home of pastoral peoples herding cattle, sheep and goats. In those days, what is now desert and arid canyon was fertile savannah intersected and drained by rivers running down to the Niger and by another system seven hundred and fifty miles long, running into Lake Chad. The peoples who lived in the hills where these rivers rose have left a record of their life in rock painting and engraving very different from the earlier cave art of Europe which depicted little but animal life and only an occasional human. This record also suggests that the Sahara was then a meeting place of Negroid and what some have called "Europoid" peoples, those who were, perhaps, the ancestors of later Berbers and Tuaregs. One of these peoples seems to have made its way down from Tripoli with horses and chariots and perhaps to have conquered the pastoralists. Whether they did so or not, their presence, like that of the Negroid peoples of the Sahara, shows that Africa's vegetation was once very different from that of later times: horses need grazing. Yet when we reach historical times the Sahara is already desiccated, the sites of a once prosperous people are abandoned, the animals have gone.

THE PEOPLES OF AFRICA

It may be climatic change in the rest of Africa which drives us back upon Egypt as the beginning of African history. Yet Egypt exercised little creative influence beyond the limits of the Nile valley. Though there were contacts with other cultures, it is not easy to penetrate them. Presumably the Libyans of Egyptian records were the sort of people who are shown with their chariots in the Sahara cave-paintings, but we do not certainly know. When the Greek historian Herodotus came to write about Africa in the fifth century BCE, he found little to say about what went on outside Egypt. His Africa (which he called Libya) was a land defined by the Nile, which he took to run south, roughly parallel to the Red Sea, and then to swing westwards. South of the Nile there lay for him in the east the Ethiopians, in the west a land of deserts, without inhabitants. He could obtain no information about

Climatic changes in the Sahara

Ten thousand years ago, Mediterranean-type flora flourished in the Sahara desert region. The remains of several settlements reveal that fishing communities once existed on the shores of vast lakes. Tribes of farming settlers are also known to have lived in the central Sahara until c.2000 BCE. Progressive desertification brought an end to these ways of life.

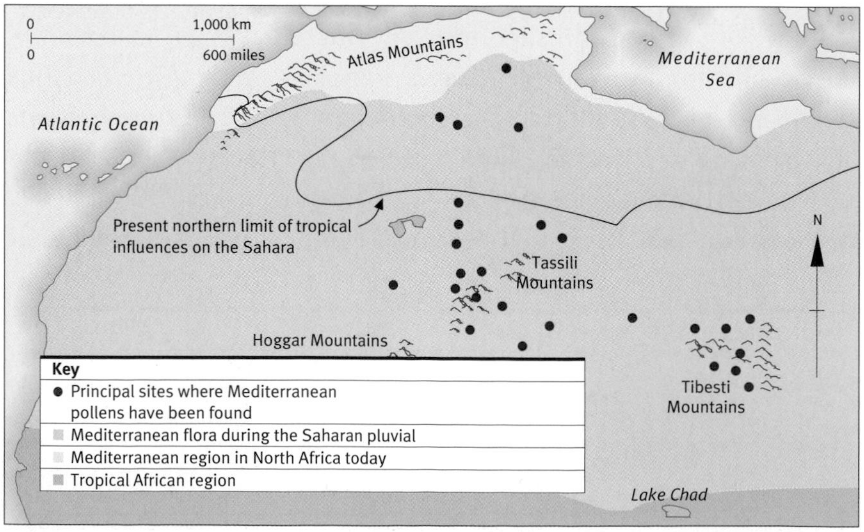

it, though a travellers' tale spoke of a dwarfish people who were sorcerers. Given his sources, this was topographically by no means an unintelligent construction, but Herodotus had grasped only a small part of the ethnic truth. The Ethiopians, like the old inhabitants of Upper Egypt, were members of the Hamitic peoples who make up one of three racial groups in Africa at the end of the Stone Age later distinguished by anthropologists. The other two were the ancestors of the modern San people (once derogatorily known as "Bushmen"), inhabiting, roughly, the open areas running from the Sahara south to the Cape, and the Negroid group, eventually dominant in the central forests and West Africa. (Opinion is divided about the origin and distinctiveness of a fourth group, the Pygmies.) To judge by the stone tools, cultures associated with Hamitic or proto-Hamitic peoples seem to have been the most advanced in Africa before the coming of farming. This was, except in Egypt, a slow evolution and in Africa the hunting and gathering cultures of prehistory have coexisted with agriculture down to modern times.

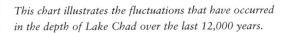

Rainfall is vital for the San who live in the Kalahari desert today, where for 10 months a year there may be no surface water. Like earlier African communities affected by the increasing aridity of their territory, the San are being forced to adapt to a changing environment. Their ancestors inhabited a large part of southern and eastern Africa 10,000 years ago.

Fluctuations in the depth of Lake Chad

The changes that have taken place in the depth of Lake Chad in Africa from 10,000 BCE to the present demonstrate that levels of precipitation in the Sahara were much higher during the period 10,000–4000 BCE than they are today.

As the chart clearly shows, precipitation in the region reached its highest level 6,000 years ago. By the beginning of the Common Era, the volume of water contained in Lake Chad was little different from that to be found there now.

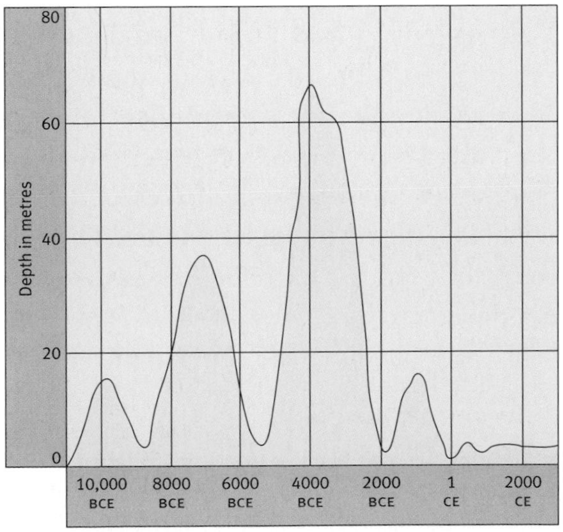

This chart illustrates the fluctuations that have occurred in the depth of Lake Chad over the last 12,000 years.

THE SPREAD OF AGRICULTURE

The same growth which occurred elsewhere when food began to be produced in quantity soon changed African population patterns, first by permitting the dense settlements of the Nile valley, which were the preliminary to Egyptian civilization, then by building up the Negroid population south of the Sahara, along the grasslands separating desert and equatorial forest in the second and first millennia BCE. This seems to reflect a spread of agriculture southwards from the north. It also reflects the discovery of nutritious crops better suited to tropical conditions and other soils than the wheat and barley which flourished in the Nile valley. These were the millets and rice of the savannahs. The forest areas could not be exploited until the coming of other plants suitable to them from Southeast Asia and eventually America. None of this happened before the birth of Christ. Thus was established one of the major characteristics of African history, a divergence of cultural trends within the continent.

THE KUSHITES

By the time of Christ's birth, iron had come to Africa and it had already produced the first exploitation of African ores. This occurred in the first independent African state other than Egypt of which we have information, the kingdom of Kush, high up the Nile, in the region of Khartoum. This had originally been the extreme frontier zone of Egyptian activity. After Nubia had been absorbed, the Sudanese principality which

This rock painting from Tassili in the Sahara desert depicts wounded warriors returning to camp and collapsing from pain and exhaustion. Various figures are shown going to their aid.

existed to its south was garrisoned by the Egyptians, but in about 1000 BCE it emerged as an independent kingdom, showing itself deeply marked by Egyptian civilization. Probably its inhabitants were Hamitic people and its capital was at Napata, just below the Fourth Cataract. By 730 BCE Kush was strong enough to conquer Egypt and five of its kings ruled as the pharaohs known to history as the Twenty-Fifth or "Ethiopian" Dynasty. None the less, they could not arrest the Egyptian decline. When the Assyrians fell on Egypt, the Kushite dynasty ended. Though Egyptian civilization continued in the kingdom of Kush, a pharaoh of the next dynasty invaded it in the early sixth century BCE. After this, the Kushites, too, began to push their frontiers further to the south and in so doing their kingdom underwent two important changes. It became more Negroid, its language and literature reflecting a weakening of Egyptian trends, and it extended its reach over new territories which contained both iron ore and the fuel needed to smelt it. The technique of smelting had been learnt from the Assyrians. The new Kushite capital at Meroë became the metallurgical centre of Africa. Iron weapons gave the Kushites the advantage over their neighbours which northern peoples had enjoyed in the past over Egypt, and iron tools extended the area which could be cultivated. On this basis was to rest some three hundred years of prosperity and civilization in the Sudan, though later than the age we are now considering.

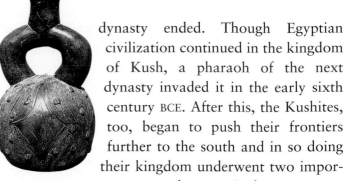

This decorative jug, with handles and a spout, demonstrates the highly artistic quality of Chavin pottery.

THE AMERICAS

IT IS CLEAR THAT THE HISTORY of humankind in the Americas is much shorter than that in Africa or, indeed, that anywhere else. About twenty thousand years ago, after Mongoloid peoples had crossed into North America from Asia, they filtered slowly southwards for thousands of years. Cave-dwellers have been traced in the Peruvian Andes as many as fifteen thousand years ago.

This head is one of eight such colossal figures that have been found at a site at San Lorenzo, in Mexico. Between 1200 and 900 BCE, the site was an important Olmec ceremonial centre. These extraordinary heads, which are carved in basalt and weigh more than 20 tons each, are thought to depict Olmec rulers.

The Americas contain very varied climates and environments; it is scarcely surprising, therefore, that archaeological evidence shows that they threw up almost equally varied patterns of life, based on different opportunities for hunting, food-gathering and fishing. What they learnt from one another is probably undiscoverable. What is indisputable is that some of these cultures arrived at the invention of agriculture independently of the Old World.

AGRICULTURE IN THE AMERICAS

Disagreement is still possible about when precisely the invention of agriculture happened in the Americas because, paradoxically, a great deal is known about the early cultivation of plants at a time when the scale on which this took place cannot reasonably be called agriculture. It is, nevertheless, a change which comes later than in the Fertile Crescent. Maize began to be cultivated in Mexico in about 2700 BCE, but had been improved by 2000 BCE in Mesoamerica into something like the plant we know today. This is the sort of change which made possible the establishment of large settled communities. Further south, potatoes and manioc (another starchy root vegetable) also begin to appear at about this time and a little later there are signs that maize has spread southwards from Mexico. Everywhere, though, change is gradual: to talk of an "agricultural revolution" is even less appropriate in the Americas than in the Near East.

The Chavin culture was the first major Andean culture. Its most important ceremonial centre was located at the site of the present-day Peruvian city of Chavin de Huantar. Supernatural creatures, such as the one shown above, decorated the outer walls of the site's ancient temple.

THE OLMECS

Farming, villages, weaving and pottery all appear in Central America before the second millennium BCE and towards the end of it come the first stirrings of the culture which produced the first recognized American civilization, that of the Olmecs of the eastern Mexican coast. It was focused, it seems, on important ceremonial sites with large earth pyramids. At these sites have been found colossal monumental sculpture and fine carvings of figures in jade. The style of this work is highly individual. It concentrates on human and jaguar-like images, sometimes fusing them. For several centuries after 800 BCE it seems to have prevailed right across Central America as far south as what is now El Salvador. It appears apparently without antecedents or warning in a swampy, forested region which makes it hard to explain in economic terms, except that maize could be harvested four times a year where there was open land in the tropics supplying reliable rainfall and warmth all year. Yet we do not know much else which helps explain why civilization, which elsewhere required the relative plenty of the great river valleys, should in the Americas have sprung from such unpromising soil.

Olmec civilization transmitted something to the future, for the gods of the later Aztecs were to be descendants of those of the Olmecs. It may also be that the early hieroglyphic systems of Central America

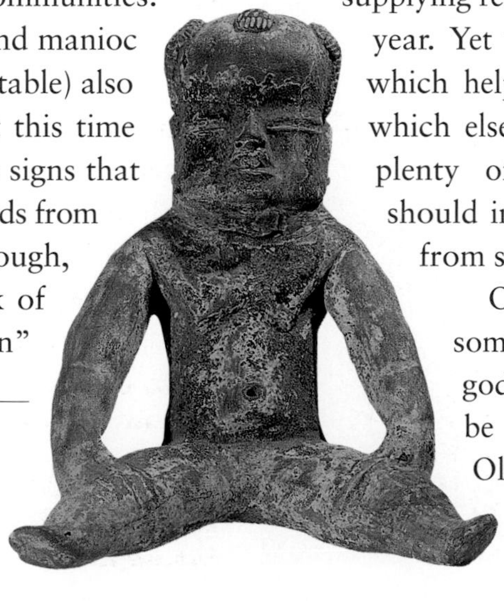

A 1st-millennium BCE Olmec figure. The Mesoamerican artistic tradition began with the Olmec culture.

originate in Olmec times, though the first survivals of the characters of these systems follow only a century or so after the disappearance of Olmec culture in about 400 BCE. Again, we do not know why or how this happened. Much further south, in Peru, a culture called Chavin (after a great ceremonial site) also appeared and survived a little later than Olmec civilization to the north. It, too, had a high level of skill in working stone and spread vigorously only to dry up mysteriously.

What should be thought of these early lunges in the direction of civilization is very hard to see. Whatever their significance for the future, they are millennia behind the appearance of civilization elsewhere, whatever the cause of that may be. When the Spanish landed in the New World nearly two thousand years after the disappearance of Olmec culture they would still find most of its inhabitants working with stone tools. They would also find complicated societies (and the relics of others) which had achieved prodigies of building and organization far outrunning, for example, anything Africa could offer after the decline of ancient Egypt. All that is clear is that there are no unbreakable sequences in these matters.

This intricately decorated gold *lunula* (a crescent moon-shaped necklace) was found in Blessington in County Wicklow, Ireland. It dates from around 2000 BCE.

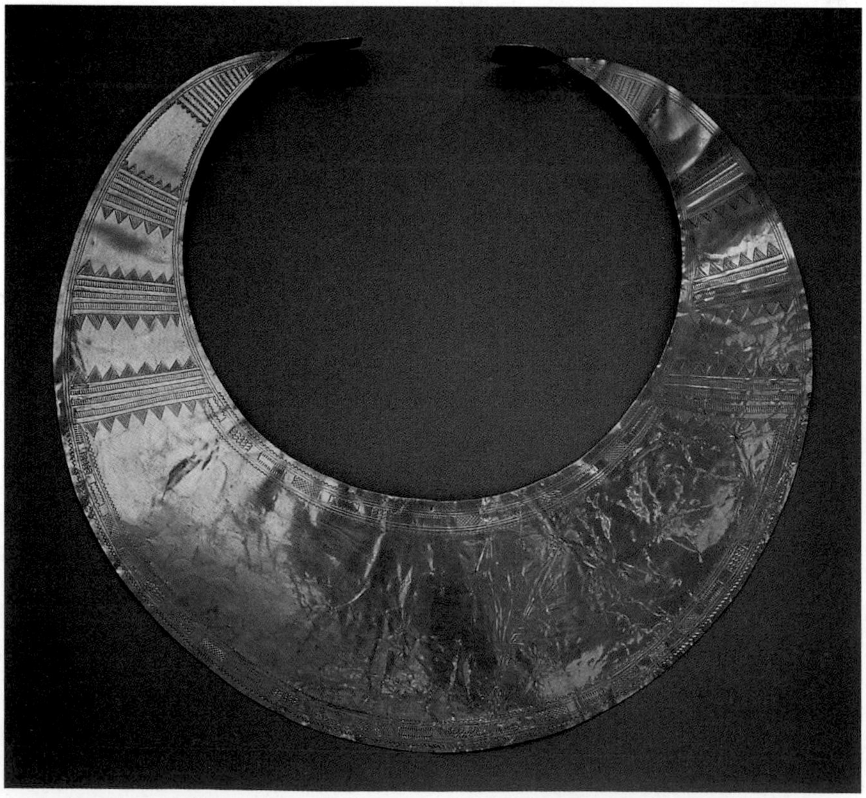

EUROPE

THE ONLY OTHER AREA where a startlingly high level of achievement in stoneworking was reached was western Europe. This has led enthusiasts to claim it as another seat of early "civilization", almost as if its inhabitants were some sort of depressed class needing historical rehabilitation. Europe has already been touched upon as a supplier of metals to the ancient Near East. Yet, though much that we now find interesting was happening there in prehistoric times, it does not provide a very impressive or striking story. In the history of the world, prehistoric Europe has little except illustrative importance. To the great civilizations which rose and fell in the river valleys of the Near East, Europe was largely an irrelevance. It sometimes received the impress of the outside world but contributed only marginally and fitfully to the process of historic change. A parallel might be Africa at a later date, interesting for its own sake, but not for any special and positive contribution to world history. It was to be a very long time before men would even be able to conceive that there existed a geographical, let alone a cultural, unity corresponding to the later idea of Europe. To the ancient world, the northern lands where the barbarians came from before they appeared in Thrace were irrelevant (and most of them probably came from further east anyway). The northwestern hinterland was only important because it occasionally disgorged commodities wanted in Asia and the Aegean.

This figure, from Trudholm on the Danish island of Seeland, is one of the most important archaeological pieces from Bronze Age Europe. The figure represents a horse on a wheeled base pulling a disk, which is gold-plated on one side. It is thought that the object represents a mythical chariot carrying the sun across the sky.

THE TWO REGIONS WITHIN PREHISTORIC EUROPE

There is not much to say about prehistoric Europe, but in order to get a correct perspective, one more point should be made. Two Europes must be separated. One is that of the Mediterranean coasts and their peoples. Its rough boundary is the line which delimits the cultivation of the olive. South of this line, literate, urban civilization comes fairly quickly once we are into the Iron Age, and apparently comes after direct contact with more advanced areas. By 800 BCE the coasts of the western Mediterranean were already beginning to experience fairly continuous intercourse with the East. The Europe north and west of this line is a different matter. In this area literacy was never achieved in antiquity, but was imposed much later by conquerors. It long resisted cultural influences from the south and east – or at least did not offer a favourable reception to them – and it is for two thousand years important not for its own sake but because of its relationship to other areas. Its role was not entirely passive: the movements of its peoples, its natural resources and skills all at times impinged marginally on events elsewhere. But in 1000 BCE – to take an arbitrary date – or even at the beginning of the Common Era, Europe has little of its own to offer the world except its minerals, and nothing which represents cultural achievement on the scale reached by the Near East, India or China. Europe's age was still to come; hers would be the last great civilization to appear.

EARLY FARMING METHODS IN EUROPE

Civilization did not appear later in Europe than elsewhere because the continent's natural endowment was unfavourable. It contains a disproportionately large area of the world's land naturally suitable for cultivation. It would be surprising if this had not favoured an early development of agriculture and the archaeological evidence demonstrates this. The relative ease of simple agriculture in Europe may have had a negative effect on social evolution; in the great river valleys men had to work collectively to

One of the earliest European images of a plough appears in this cave etching from the Val Camonica region in the Italian Alps. The etching, which dates from c.3000 BCE, also depicts copper daggers, axes, animals and a solar disk.

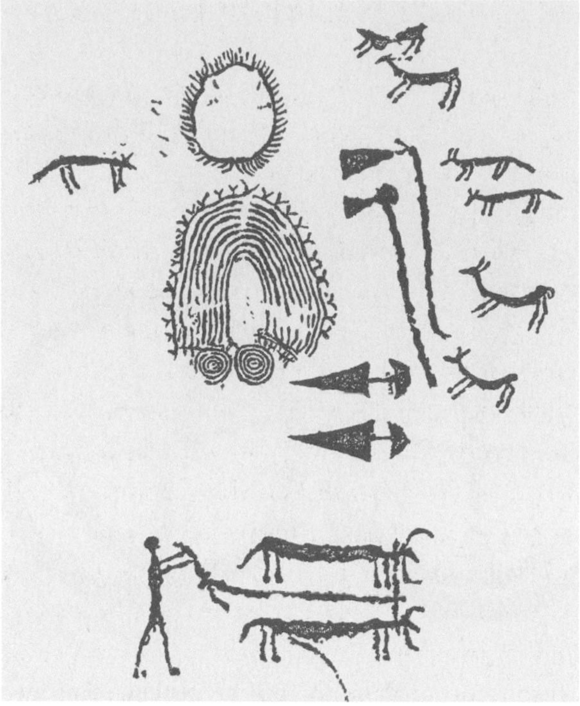

control irrigation and exploit the soil if they were to survive, while in much of Europe an individual family could scratch a living on its own. There is no need to fall into extravagant speculation about the origins of western individualism in order to recognize that there is something very distinctive and potentially very important.

Scholarly consensus now accepts that both agriculture and copper-working (the earliest form of metallurgy) made their way into and across Europe from Anatolia and the Near East. Thessaly and northern Greece had farming communities a little after 7000 BCE. By 5000 BCE others existed as far west as northern France and the Netherlands, and soon after appeared in the British Isles. The main routes by which this spread occurred had been the Balkans and their river valleys, but at the same time farming had been taken up on Mediterranean islands and along the coasts of southern Europe as far west as Andalucia. By 4000 BCE copper was being worked in the Balkans. It no longer seems likely, then, that either this technique or agriculture arose spontaneously among Europeans, though they quickly imitated others who brought these skills with them as migrants. It took thousands of years, though, for Europe to acquire the major cereals from the Near East.

THE DIVERSE PEOPLES OF EUROPE

Most of the northwestern and western parts of Europe were occupied in about 3000 BCE by peoples sometimes termed western Mediterranean, who were gradually squeezed out during the third millennium by others from the east. By about 1800 BCE the resulting cultures seem to have fragmented sufficiently distinctly for us to identify among them the ancestors of the Celts, the most important of prehistoric European peoples, a society of warriors rather than traders or prospectors. They had wheeled transport. One enterprising group had reached the British Isles. There is much disagreement about how far Celtic influence is to be traced, but it will not much disfigure the truth if we think of Europe divided in about 1800 BCE into three groups of peoples. The ancestors of the Celts then occupied most of modern France, Germany, the Low Countries and upper Austria. To their east were the future Slavs, to their north (in Scandinavia) the future Teutonic tribes. Outside Europe, in northern Scandinavia and northern Russia, were the Finns, who were linguistically non-Indo-European.

Except in the Balkans and Thrace, the movements of these peoples affected the older centres of civilization only in so far as they affected access to the resources of the areas into which they moved. This was above all a matter of minerals and skills. As the demands of the Near Eastern civilizations grew, so did Europe's importance. The first centres of metallurgy to develop there had been in the Balkans. Developments in southern Spain, Greece and the Aegean and central Italy had followed by 2000 BCE. In the later Bronze Age, metal-working was advanced to high levels even in places where no local ores were available. We have here one of the earliest examples of the emergence of crucial economic areas based on the possession of special resources. Copper and tin shaped the penetration of Europe and also its coastal and river navigation because these commodities were needed and were only available in the Near East in small quantities. Europe was the major primary producer of the ancient metallurgical world, as well as a major manufacturer. Metal-working was carried to a high level and produced beautiful objects long before that of the Aegean, but it is possibly an argument against exaggerated awe about material factors in history that this skill, even when combined with a bigger supply of metals after the collapse of Mycenaean demand, did not release European culture for the achievement of a full and complex civilization.

MEGALITHIC MONUMENTS

ANCIENT EUROPE HAD, OF COURSE, another art form which remains indisputably impressive. It is preserved in the thousands of megalithic monuments to be found stretching in a broad arc from Malta, Sardinia and Corsica, around through Spain and Brittany to the British Isles and Scandinavia. They are not peculiar to Europe but are more plentiful there, and appear to have been erected earlier in Europe than in other continents. "Megalith" is a word derived from the Greek for "large stone" and many of the stones used are very large indeed. Some of these monuments are tombs, roofed and lined with slabs of stone, some are stones standing singly, or in groups. Some of them are laid out in patterns which run for miles across country; others enclose small areas like groves of trees. The most complete and striking megalithic site is Stonehenge, in southern England, whose erection is now thought to have taken about nine hundred years to its completion in around 2100 BCE. What such places originally looked like is hard to guess

Megalithic Europe

Megalithic constructions have been identified in numerous locations across Europe. Many megalithic monuments are located in Atlantic regions, such as Denmark, the western British Isles, Brittany, Portugal and Andalusia. This has fuelled speculation that the groups who erected these stones may have had contact with each other via the Atlantic Ocean.

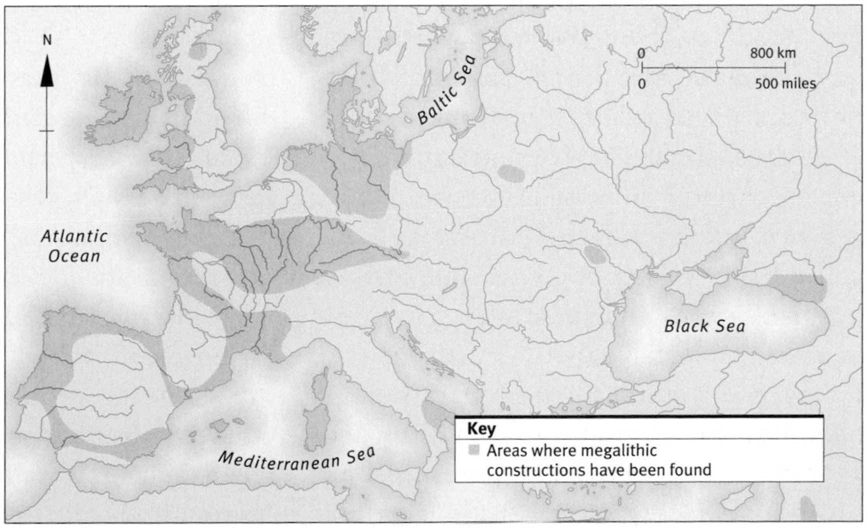

or imagine. Their modern austerity and weathered grandeur may well be misleading; great places of human resort are not like that when in use and it is more likely that the huge stones were daubed in ochres and blood, hung with skins and fetishes. They may well often have looked more like totem-poles than the solemn, brooding shapes we see today. Except for the tombs, it is not easy to say what these works were for, though it has been argued that some were giant clocks or huge solar observatories, aligned to the rising and setting of sun, moon, and stars at the major turning-points of the astronomical year. Careful observation underlay building like that, even if it fell far short in detail and precision of what was done by astronomers in Babylon and Egypt.

CONSTRUCTING THE MONUMENTS

Megalithic monuments represent huge concentrations of labour and argue for well developed social organization. Stonehenge contains several blocks weighing about fifty tons apiece and they had to be brought some eighteen miles to the site before being erected. There are some eighty pieces of stone there weighing about five tons which came 150 miles or so from the mountains of Wales. The peoples who put up Stonehenge without the help of wheeled vehicles, like those who built the carefully lined tombs of Ireland, the lines of standing stones of Brittany or the dolmens of Denmark, were capable of work on a scale approaching that of ancient Egypt, therefore, though without its fineness or any means of recording their purposes and intentions except these great constructions themselves. Such skill, coupled with the fact of the monuments' distribution in a long chain within short distances of the sea, has suggested that their explanation might lie in what was learnt from wandering stonemasons from the East, perhaps from Crete, Mycenae, or the Cyclades, where the technique of dressing and handling such masses was understood. But recent advances in dating have removed a plausible hypothesis; megaliths were being put up in Brittany and western Iberia in 4800–4000 BCE, before any significant Mediterranean or Near Eastern building, Stonehenge was probably complete before Mycenaean times, tombs in Spain and Brittany antedate the pyramids, and Malta's mysterious temples with

Europe's most extensive megalithic group was erected near Carnac, in Brittany, France. More than 3,000 menhirs (vertical stone blocks) were erected there, probably during the 2nd millennium BCE.

their huge carved blocks of building stone were there before 3000 BCE. Nor do the monuments have to form part of any one process of distribution or Atlantic phenomenon. They may all have been achieved more or less in isolation, by four or five cultures made up of relatively small and simple agricultural societies who were in touch with one another, and the motives and occasions of their building may have been very different. Like its agriculture and metallurgy, prehistoric Europe's engineering and architecture arose independently of the outside world.

THE SHORTCOMINGS OF EUROPEAN CULTURES

For all their considerable achievements, the Europeans of ancient times seem strangely passive and unresisting when they finally appear in regular contact with advanced civilization. Their hesitations and uncertainties may have resembled those of other primitive peoples meeting advanced societies at later dates – eighteenth-century Africans, for example. But, in any case, regular contact only began shortly before the Common Era.

The Ile de Gavrinis dolmen, the interior of which is shown here, was constructed between 4000 and 3000 BCE in the Morbihan Gulf in Brittany, France. A dolmen is a burial chamber, consisting of large vertical stones supporting a horizontal top stone. The stone chamber is usually covered by a tumulus (mound) of earth.

Before then, the European peoples seem to have exhausted their energies in grappling with an environment which, though easily worked to satisfy modest needs, required the coming of iron to make it fully exploitable. Though far more advanced than their contemporaries in America, or in Africa south of the Nile valley, they never reached the stage of urbanization. Their greatest cultural achievements were decorative and mechanical. At best, in their metallurgy, the ancient Europeans serviced other civilizations' needs. Beyond that, they would only provide the stocks which would receive the impress of civilization later.

Only one group of western barbarians had a more positive contribution to make to the future. South of the olive-line an Iron Age people of central Italy had already during the eighth century BCE established trading contacts with Greeks further south in Italy and with Phoenicia. We call them Villanovans, after one of the sites where they lived. In the next two hundred years they adopted Greek characters for writing their language. By then they were organized in city-states, producing art of high quality. These were the Etruscans. One of their city-states would one day be known as Rome.

On the small island of Malta in the western Mediterranean, a number of megalithic temples have been preserved. They were built between 3500 and 2400 BCE, which makes them the world's oldest existing stone buildings. This is a view of the Ggantija Temple.

4 THE END OF THE OLD WORLD

Of what was going on in India and China and its importance for the future, the rulers of the Mediterranean and Near Eastern peoples knew hardly anything. Some of them, listening to traders, may have had a dim perception of a barbarian northern and northwestern Europe. Of what happened beyond the Sahara and of the existence of the Americas, they knew nothing. Yet their world was to expand rapidly in the first millennium BCE and, equally and perhaps even more obviously, it was to become more integrated as its internal communications grew more complex and effective. A world of a few highly distinctive and almost independent civilizations was giving way to one where larger and larger areas shared in the same achievements of civilization literacy, government, technology, organized religion, city life and, under their influence, changed more and more rapidly as the interplay of different traditions increased. It is important not to think of this in terms too abstract or grandiose. It is not only registered by art and speculative thought, but also by much that is more down-to-earth. Small things show it as well as great. On the legs of the huge statues at Abu Simbel, seven hundred miles up the Nile, sixth-century Greek mercenaries in the Egyptian army cut inscriptions which recorded their pride in coming that far, just as two thousand five

Early civilizations in the Near East

Sumer, the oldest civilization in the Near East, emerged in the lower valley of the Euphrates and Tigris rivers and spread to the north of Mesopotamia. The Babylonian Empire encompassed the whole of Mesopotamia, while the Hittite Empire was founded in central Anatolia. In the 7th century BCE, the Assyrians controlled several of the earliest centres of civilization, from Sumer to Lower Egypt.

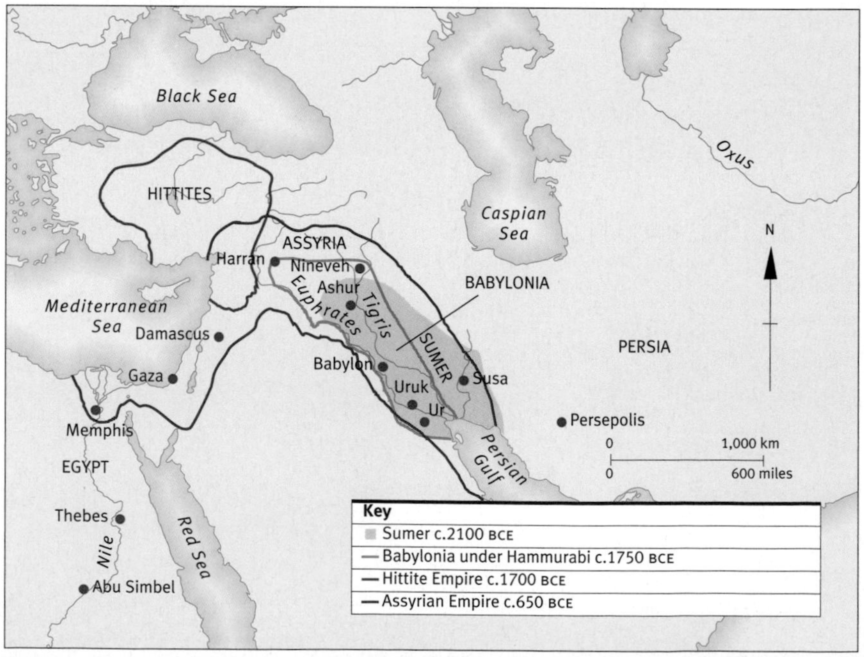

This depiction of a shroud shows that during the last stage of its existence as an independent kingdom, when it was ruled by the Ptolemaic Dynasty, Egypt was strongly influenced by Greek culture. The figures of Anubis (right) and the other gods that surround the dead man are shown according to traditional Egyptian conventions; however, Osiris (left) and the deceased (centre) are of Greek inspiration.

hundred years later English county regiments would leave their badges and names cut into the rocks of the Khyber Pass.

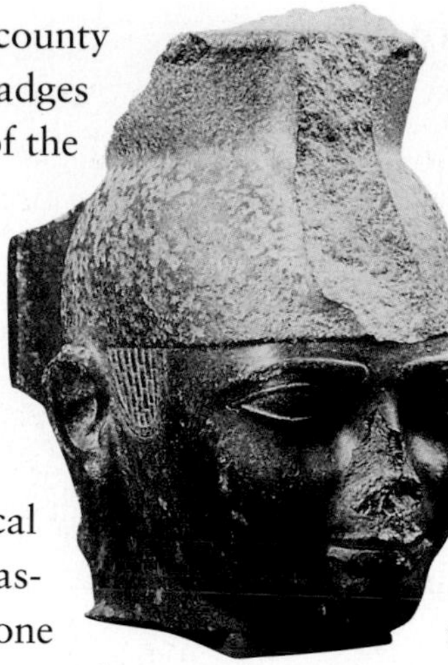

Egypt was conquered in the 8th century BCE by the Nubian kingdom of Kush. This granite head depicts one of the Nubian pharoahs, King Taharqa (690–664 BCE).

THE LEGACY OF ANTIQUITY

There is no clear chronological line to be drawn in this increasingly complicated world. If one exists it has already been crossed several times before we reach the eve of the classical age of the West. The military and economic drive of the Mesopotamians and their successors, the movements of the Indo-Europeans, the coming of iron and the spread of literacy thoroughly mixed up the once-clear patterns of the Near East well before the appearance of a Mediterranean civilization which is the matrix of our own. Nevertheless, there is a sense in which it becomes manifest that an important boundary was crossed somewhere early in the first millennium BCE. The greatest upheavals of the *Völkerwanderung* in the ancient Near East were then over. The patterns set there in the late Bronze Age would still be modified locally by colonization and conquest, but not for another thousand years by big comings and goings of peoples.

The political structures left behind from antiquity would be levers of the next era of world history in a zone which stretched from Gibraltar to the Indus. Civilization within this area would more and more be a matter of interplay, borrowing and cosmopolitanism. The framework for this was provided by the great political change of the middle of the first millennium BCE, the rise of a new power, Persia, and the final collapse of the Egyptian and Babylonian-Assyrian traditions.

EGYPT IN DECLINE

The story of Egypt is the easiest to summarize, for it records little except decline. It has been called a "Bronze Age anachronism in a world that steadily moved away from her" and its fate seems to be explained by an inability to change or adapt. Egypt survived the first attacks of the iron-using peoples and had beaten off the Peoples of the Sea at the beginning of the age of turmoil. But this was to be the last big achievement of the New Kingdom: thereafter the symptoms are unmistakably those of a machine running down. At home, kings and priests disputed power while Egypt's suzerainty beyond its borders declined to a shadow. A period of rival dynasties was briefly followed by a reunification which again took an Egyptian army to Palestine, but by the end of the eighth century

Time chart (559 BCE–323 BCE)

559–529 BCE
Reign of Cyrus II: Persian Empire founded

529–522 BCE
Reign of Cambyses II: Conquest of Egypt

522–486 BCE
Reign of Darius I: First attack on Greece

486–465 BCE
Reign of Xerxes I: Second attack on Greece

336–323 BCE
Reign of Alexander the Great: Persian Empire brought to an end

600 BCE | 500 BCE | 400 BCE | 300 BCE

a dynasty of Kushite invaders had established itself; in 671 BCE it was ejected from Lower Egypt by the Assyrians. Ashurbanipal then sacked Thebes. As Assyrian power ebbed, there was again an illusory period of Egyptian "independence".

By this time, evidence of a new world towards which Egypt had to make more than political concessions can be seen in the establishment of a school for Greek interpreters and of a Greek trading enclave with special privileges at Naucratis in the Delta. Then again, in the sixth century, Egypt went down to defeat first at the hands of the forces of Nebuchadnezzar (588 BCE) and sixty years later, before the Persians (525 BCE), to become a province of an empire which was to set boundaries for a new synthesis and would for centuries dispute world supremacy with new powers appearing in the Mediterranean. It was not quite the end of Egyptian independence, but from the fourth century BCE to the twentieth century CE, she was to be ruled by foreigners or immigrant dynasties and passes from view as an independent nation. The last bursts of Egyptian recovery show little innate vitality. They express, rather, temporary relaxations of the pressures upon her which always, in the end, were followed by their resumption. The Persian threat was the last of these and was fatal.

PERSIA

ONCE AGAIN, THE STARTING-POINT is a migration. On the high plateau which is the heart of modern Iran there were settlements in 5000 BCE, but the word "Iran" (which does not appear until about 600 CE) in its oldest form means "land of the Aryans" and it is somewhere around 1000 BCE, with an irruption of Aryan tribes from the north, that the history of the Persian Empire begins. In Iran, as in India, the impact of the Aryans was to prove ineffaceable and founded a long-enduring tradition. Among their tribes, two, especially vigorous and powerful, have been remembered further west by their biblical names as the Medes and Persians. The Medes moved west and northwest to Media; their great age came at the beginning of the sixth century, after they had overthrown Assyria, their neighbour. The Persians went south

This carved pillar stands among the ruins of the great Persian palace at Persepolis, which was built during the 5th century BCE.

towards the Gulf, establishing themselves in Khuzistan (on the edge of the Tigris valley and in the old kingdom of Elam) and Fars, the Persia of the ancients.

CYRUS

Oral tradition preserves a story of legendary kings more important for the light it throws on later Persian attitudes to kingship than as history. It was none the less from the Persian dynasty of the Achaemenids that there descended the first king of a united Persia – anachronistic though this term is. He was Cyrus, the conqueror of Babylon. In 549 BCE he humbled the last independent king of the Medes and thenceforth the boundaries of conquest rolled outwards, swallowing Babylon and advancing through Asia Minor to the sea, dropping down into Syria and Palestine. Only in the east (where he was eventually killed fighting the Scythians) did Cyrus find it difficult to stabilize his frontiers, though he crossed the Hindu Kush and set up some sort of supremacy over the region of Gandhara, north of the Jhelum.

This was the largest empire the world had seen until that time. Its style was different from its predecessors; the savagery of the Assyrians seems muted. At least brutality was not celebrated in official art and Cyrus was careful to respect the institutions and ways of his new subjects. The result was a diverse empire, but a powerful one, commanding loyalties of a kind lacking to its predecessors. There are some notable religious symptoms: the protection of Marduk was solicited for

In Pasargadae, Persia, stands the austere tomb of Cyrus the Great. The mortuary chamber, built from huge blocks, is raised on a stepped platform. According to one story, the body of Cyrus, who was killed in a border war, was never buried in the tomb.

On the rock wall of the Naqsh-i-Rustam pass, close to Persepolis, the burial places of four Persian kings have been excavated. Here, from left to right, are the tombs of Artaxerxes I, his father Xerxes I and his grandfather Darius I. The tombs' monumental façades recreate those of the great palace at Persepolis. The small entrances to the funeral chambers are located 50 ft (15 m) from the ground.

Cyrus's assumption of the Babylonian kingship and at Jerusalem he launched the rebuilding of the Temple. A Jewish prophet saw in his victories God's hand, named him the Lord's anointed and gloated over the fate of the old enemy, Babylon:

"Let now the astrologers, the stargazers, the monthly prognosticators, stand up, and save thee from these things that shall come upon thee."

Isaiah xiv, 1, xivii, 1–13

IMPERIAL GOVERNMENT

Cyrus's success owed much to the material resources of his kingdom. It was rich in minerals, above all in iron, and in the high pastures of the valleys lay a great reserve of horses and cavalrymen. Yet it is impossible to resist the conclusion that sheer personal ability also counted for much; Cyrus lives as a world-historical figure, recognized as such by other would-be conquerors who were to strive in the next few centuries to emulate

This capital from Susa, the ancient Elamite city that Darius I turned into the administrative centre of his empire, is characteristic of Persian art. The upper part is formed by two bulls, whose backs are joined together in such a way that one beam rests on their heads and the other, perpendicular to the first, rests on their backs.

him. He based his government upon provincial governors who were the forbears of the later Persian satraps, and required from his subject provinces little beyond tribute usually in gold, which replenished the treasuries of Persia – and obedience.

Thus began the empire which, though with setbacks aplenty, provided for nearly two centuries a framework for the Near East, sheltering a great cultural tradition which grew to nourish itself both from Asia and Europe. Large areas knew longer periods of peace under it than they had for centuries and it was in many ways a beautiful and gentle civilization. Greeks had already been told by Herodotus that the Persians loved flowers and there are many things we could do without more easily than the tulip, which we owe to them. Cyrus's son added Egypt to the empire; yet he died before he could deal with a pretender to the throne whose attempts encouraged Medes and Babylonians to seek to recover their independence. The restorer of Cyrus's heritage was a young man who claimed Achaemenid descent, Darius.

DARIUS

Darius (who reigned 522–486 BCE) did not achieve all he wished. His work, none the less, rivalled that of Cyrus. His own inscription on the monument recording his victories over rebels may be thought justified by what he did: "I am Darius the Great King, King of Kings, King in Persia", a recitation of an ancient title whose braggadocio he adopted. In the east the boundaries of the empire were carried further into the Indus valley. In the west they advanced to Macedonia, though they were checked there, and in the north Darius failed, as Cyrus before him, to make much headway against the Scythians. Inside the empire a remarkable work of consolidation was undertaken. Decentralization was institutionalized with the division of the empire into twenty provinces, each under a satrap who was a royal prince or great nobleman. Royal inspectors surveyed their work and their control of the machine was made easier by the institution of a royal secretariat to conduct correspondence with the provinces, and Aramaic, the old *lingua franca* of the Assyrian Empire, became the administrative language. It was well adapted to the conduct of affairs because it was not written in cuneiform but in the Phoenician alphabet. The bureaucracy rested on better communications than any yet seen, for much of the provincial tribute was invested in road-building. At their best these roads made it possible to convey messages at two hundred miles a day.

PERSEPOLIS

The great new capital at Persepolis, where Darius himself was buried in a rock tomb cut into the cliff face, was to have been a monument to his achievement. Intended as a colossal glorification of the king, it remains impressive even when it seems pompous. Persepolis was in the end a collective creation; later kings added their palaces to it and embodied in it the diversity and cosmopolitanism of the empire. Assyrian colossi, man-headed bulls and lions guarded its gates as they had done those of Nineveh. Up its staircases marched stone warriors bearing tribute; they are a little less mechanical than the regimented Assyrians of earlier sculpture, but only a little. The decorative columns recall Egypt, but it is an Egyptian device transmitted through Ionian stone-cutters and sculptors. Greek details are to be found also in the reliefs and decoration, and a similar mixture of reminiscences is to be found in the

The *apadana* (audience hall) in the palace of Persepolis was probably the citadel's largest audience chamber, with an interior of 4,300 sq yds (3,600 sq m). Its wooden ceiling was supported by 36 columns, which stood 65 ft (20 m) high and were crowned with decorated capitals.

Persepolis

A lion attacking a bull in a relief from the Persepolis citadel.

Darius I built his palace on a newly founded site, Persepolis, where his successors Xerxes I and Artaxerxes I would later add their own palaces. The remains of the city's residential district have not yet been found, but the imperial citadel has survived and is in extraordinarily good condition. There is an enormous terrace, 1640 ft (500 m) long by 985 ft (300 m) wide, which is raised 50 ft (15 m) above the ground on a brick platform. The terrace is reached by a monumental double stairway, the walls of which depict the majestic advance of long ranks of soldiers and tribute bearers. On the flat surface stand the ruins of various buildings. It took 60 years to construct this complex, between 500 and 440 BCE.

royal tombs not far away. They recall the Valley of the Kings in their conception while their cruciform entrances speak of something else. Cyrus's own tomb, at Pasargadae, had also been marked by Greek design. A new world is coming to birth.

PERSIAN CULTURE

Monuments such as those at Persepolis and Pasargadae fittingly express the continuing diversity and tolerance of Persian culture. It was one always open to influence from abroad and would continue to be. Persia took up not only the languages of those it conquered, but also sometimes their ideas. It also contributed Vedic and Persian religion mingled in Gandhara, where stood the Indian city the Greeks called Taxila, but both, of course, were Aryan. The core of Persian religion was sacrifice and centred on fire. By the age of Darius the most refined of its cults had evolved into what has been called Zoroastrianism, a dualist religion accounting for the problem of evil in terms of the struggle of a good with an evil god. Of its prophet, Zoroaster, we know little, but it seems that he taught his disciples to uphold the cause of the god of light with ritual and moral behaviour; ahead lay a messianic deliverance, the resurrection of the dead and life everlasting after judgment.

The Zoroastrian creed spread rapidly through western Asia with Persian rule, even though it was probably never more than the cult of a minority. It would influence Judaism and the oriental cults which were to be part of the setting of Christianity; the angels of Christian tradition and the notion of the hell-fire which awaited the wicked both came from Zoroaster.

THE INTERPLAY OF CIVILIZATIONS IN THE NEAR EAST

It is too early to speak of the interplay of Asia and Europe, but there are few more striking examples of the interplay of reciprocal influences which marks the end of the ancient world. We can mark an epoch. Right across the Old World, Persia suddenly pulled peoples into a common experience. Indians, Medes, Babylonians, Lydians, Greeks, Jews, Phoenicians and Egyptians were for the first time all governed by one empire whose eclecticism showed how far civilization had already come. The era of civilization embodied in distinct units of history was over in the Near East. Too much had been shared, too much diffused for the direct successors of the first civilizations to be any longer intelligible independent units of study. Indian mercenaries fought in the Persian armies; Greeks in those of Egypt. City-dwelling and literacy were widespread through the Near East. People lived in cities around much of the Mediterranean, too. Agricultural and metallurgical techniques stretched even beyond that area and were to be spread further as the Achaemenids transmitted the irrigation skill of Babylon to Central Asia and brought rice from India to be planted in the Near East. When Asian Greeks came to adopt a currency it would be based on the sexagesimal numeration of Babylon. The base of a future world civilization was in the making.

THE CLASSICAL MEDITERRANEAN: GREECE

MEASURED IN YEARS, more than half the story of civilization is already over by about 500 BCE. We are still nearer to that date than were the people who lived then to their first civilized predecessors. In the three thousand or so years between them, humanity had come a long way; however imperceptibly slow the changes of daily life in them had been, there is an enormous qualitative gap between Sumer and Achaemenid Persia. By the sixth century, a great period of foundation and acceleration was already over. From the western Mediterranean to the coasts of China a variety of cultural traditions had established themselves. Distinct civilizations had taken root in them, some firmly and deeply enough to survive into our own era. Some of them lasted, moreover, with little but superficial and temporary change for hundreds or even thousands of years. Virtually isolated, they contributed little to humanity's shared life outside their own areas. For the most part, even the greatest centres of civilization were indifferent to what lay outside their spheres for at least two thousand years after the fall of Babylon except when troubled by an occasional invasion. Only one of the civilizations already discernible by the sixth century BCE in fact showed much potential for expanding beyond its cradle – that of the eastern Mediterranean. It was the youngest of them but was to be very successful, lasting for over a thousand years without a break in its tradition. Even this is less remarkable than what it left behind, though, for it was the seedbed of almost all that played a dynamic part in shaping the world we still inhabit.

The Acropolis in Athens was badly damaged by a Persian attack in 480 BCE, but was rebuilt 40 years later under the supervision of Pericles. The Parthenon, built between 447 and 432 BCE, dominates this view of the famous ancient Greek monuments. On the left-hand side stands the Propylaia, the monumental entrance to the Acropolis, designed by Mnesicles and constructed between 437 and 432 BCE. The temple of Athene Nike, in front of the Propylaia, appears tiny in comparison to the mighty Parthenon towering above it.

1 *THE ROOTS OF ONE WORLD*

THE APPEARANCE OF a new civilization in the eastern Mediterranean owed much to older Near Eastern and Aegean traditions. From the start we confront an amalgam of Greek speech, a Semitic alphabet, ideas whose roots lie in Egypt and Mesopotamia, and reminiscences of Mycenae. Even when this civilization matured it still showed the diversity of its origins. It was never to be a simple, monolithic whole and in the end was very complex indeed. For all that integrated it and gave it unity, it was always hard to delimit, a cluster of similar cultures around the Mediterranean and Aegean, their frontier zones blurring far outwards into Asia, Africa, barbarian Europe and southern Russia. Even when its boundaries with them were clear, other traditions always played upon Mediterranean civilization and received much from it.

This civilization also varied in time. It showed greater powers of evolution than any of its predecessors. Even when they had undergone important political changes their institutions remained fundamentally intact, while Mediterranean civilization displayed a huge variety of transient political forms and experiments. In religion and ideology, whereas other traditions tended to develop without violent changes or breaks, so that civilization and religion were virtually coterminous, the one living and dying with the other, Mediterranean civilization begins in a native paganism and ends by succumbing to an exotic import, Christianity, a revolutionized Judaism which was to be the first global religion. This was a huge change and it transformed this civilization's possibilities of influencing the future.

The Greek sphinx was a fantastical creature, often depicted with a woman's head, a lion's body and the wings of a bird. The existence of this image in much Greek sculpture and pottery reveals the influence of the cultural traditions that preceded Greek civilization in the Near East and the Aegean.

THE MEDITERRANEAN CONTEXT

Of all the forces making for this culture's crystallization, the most fundamental was the setting itself, the Mediterranean basin. It was both a collecting area and a source; currents flowed easily into it from the lands of the old civilizations and from this central reservoir they also flowed back to where they came from and northwards into the barbarian lands. Though it is large and contains a variety of peoples, this basin has well-defined general characteristics. Most of its coasts are

narrow plains behind which quickly rise fairly steep and enclosing mountain ranges, broken by a few important river valleys. Those who lived on the coasts tended to look along them and outward across the sea, rather than behind them to their hinterland. This, combined with a climate they all shared, made the spreading of ideas and techniques within the Mediterranean natural for enterprising peoples.

The Romans, with reason, named the Mediterranean *Mare Magnum*, the Great Sea. It was the outstanding geographical fact of their world, the centre of classical maps. Its surface was a great uniting force for those who knew how to use it, and by 500 BCE maritime technology was advanced enough to make this possible, except in winter. Prevailing winds and currents determined the exact routes of ships whose only power was provided by sails or oars, but any part of the Mediterranean was accessible by water from any other. The upshot was a littoral civilization, with a few languages spoken widely within it. It had specialized trading centres, for exchanges of materials were easy by sea, but the economy rested firmly on the growing of wheat and barley, olives and vines, mainly for local consumption. The metals increasingly needed by this economy could be brought in from outside. The deserts to the south were held at bay further from the coast and for perhaps thousands of years North Africa was richer than it now is, more heavily wooded, better watered, and more fertile. The same sort of civilization therefore tended to appear all around the Mediterranean. The difference between Africa and Europe that we expect today did not exist until after 500 CE.

The rugged coast of the Aegean and its lack of flat land led many of the inhabitants of the ancient Greek peninsula to take to the sea. Technical prowess and knowledge of the sea currents and winds enabled them to open trade routes in the Mediterranean.

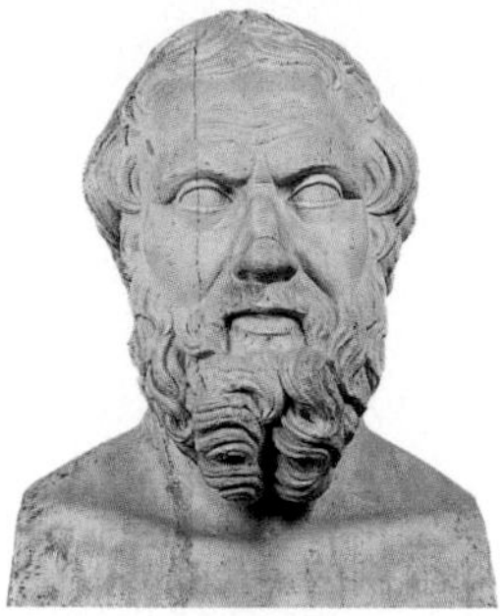

Born at the start of the 5th century BCE in Halicarnassus (a Greek colony on the coast of Asia Minor), Herodotus is considered by many to be "the father of history".

THE CULTURE OF THE CLASSICAL WORLD

THE OUTWARD-LOOKING PEOPLES of this littoral civilization created a new world. The great valley civilizations had not colonized, they had conquered. Their peoples looked inward to the satisfaction of limited aims under local despots. Many later societies, even within the classical world, were to do the same, but there is a discernible change of tempo and potential from the start, and eventually Greeks and Romans grew corn in Russia, worked tin from Cornwall, built roads into the Balkans and enjoyed spices from India and silk from China.

About this world we know a great deal, partly because it left behind a huge archaeological and monumental legacy. Much more important, though, is the new richness of written materials. With them, we enter the era of full literacy. Among other things, they include the first true works of history; important as were to be the great folk records of the Jews, the narrations of a cosmic drama built about the pilgrimage of one people through time, they are not critical history. In any case, they, too, reach us through the classical Mediterranean world. Without Christianity, their influence would have been limited to Israel; through it, the myths they presented and the possibilities of meaning they offered were to be injected into a world with four hundred years of what we can recognize as critical writing of history already behind it. Yet the work of ancient historians, important as it is, is only a tiny part of the record. Soon after 500 BCE, we are in the presence of the first complete great literature, ranging from drama to epic, lyric hymn, history and epigram, though what is left of it is only a small part – seven out of more than a hundred plays by its greatest tragedian, for example. Nevertheless, it enables us to enter the mind of a civilization as we can enter that of none earlier.

The world according to Herodotus

Herodotus, a contemporary of Pericles, visited Greece, Macedonia, Thrace, Ionia, Syria, Mesopotamia, Egypt and Cyrene, in North Africa. Everywhere he travelled, he carried out extensive research, guided by a profoundly critical attitude and a mistrust of existing fables and legends. The great wealth of knowledge that he amassed is contained in his series of nine books of history, which open with the sentence: "Herodotus of Halicarnassus here displays his inquiry, so that human achievements may not become forgotten in time, and great and marvellous deeds – some displayed by Greeks, some by barbarians – may not be without their glory; and especially to show why the two peoples fought with each other."

An extract from *The Histories* by Herodotus, translated by Aubrey de Sélincourt.

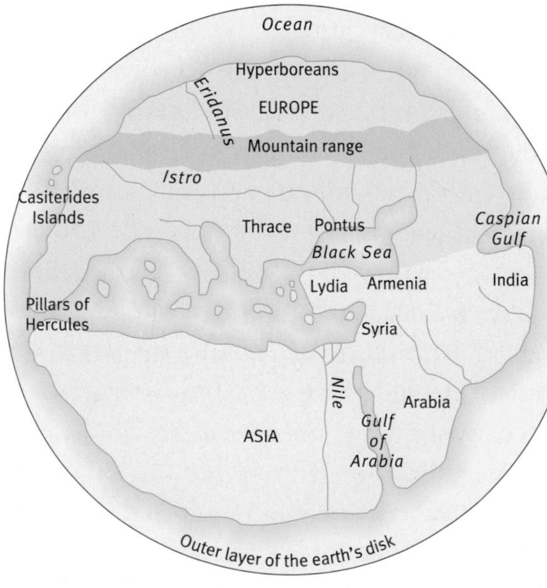

Map of the world according to Herodotus.

The laws of Gortys, carved on stone tablets on the island of Crete in the middle of the 5th century BCE, form the oldest Greek legal code. Some of the laws inscribed had been in use since the 7th century BCE.

CLASSICAL LANGUAGES

Even for Greece, of course, the source of much great literature, and *a fortiori* for other and more remote parts of the classical world, the written record is not enough on its own. The archaeology is indispensable, but it is all the more informative because literary sources are so much fuller than anything from the early past. The record they offer us is for the most part in Greek or Latin, the two languages which provided the intellectual currency of Mediterranean civilization. The persistence in English, the most widely used of languages today, of so many words drawn from them is by itself almost enough evidence to show this civilization's importance to its successors (all seven nouns in the last sentence but one, for example, are based on Latin words). It was through writings in these languages that later people approached this civilization and in them they detected the qualities which made them speak of what they found simply as "*the* classical world".

DEFINING "CLASSICAL"

"Classical" is a perfectly proper usage, provided we remember that those who coined it were heirs to the traditions they saw in it and stood, perhaps trapped, within its assumptions. Other traditions and civilizations, too, have had their "classical" phases. What it means is that people see in some part of the past an age setting standards for later times. Many later Europeans were to be hypnotized by the power and glamour of classical Mediterranean civilization. Some contemporaries who lived in it, too, thought that they, their culture and times were exceptional, though not always for reasons we should now find convincing. Yet it *was* exceptional: vigorous and

This 1st-century Roman mural from Stabiae depicts ships in a well-established harbour, probably Stabiae or Puteoli. The busy trade routes that criss-crossed the Mediterranean Sea were vital to the development of the classical civilizations that grew up around its shores.

The theatre at the sanctuary of Asclepius in Epidaurus, in modern-day Turkey, dates from the 4th century BCE and is one of the best surviving examples of an ancient Greek theatre.

restless, it provided standards and ideals, as well as technology and institutions, on which huge futures were to be built. In essence, the unity later discerned by those who admired the Mediterranean heritage was a mental one.

THE LEGACY OF THE CLASSICAL WORLD

Inevitably, there was to be much anachronistic falsification in some of the later efforts to study and utilize the classical ideal, and much romanticization of a lost age, too. Yet even when this is discounted, and when the classical past has undergone the sceptical scrutiny of scholars, there remains a big indissoluble residue of intellectual achievement which somehow places it on our side of a mental boundary, while the great empires of Asia lie beyond it. With whatever difficulty and possibility of misconstruction, the mind of the classical age is recognizable and comprehensible in a way perhaps nothing earlier can be. "This", it has been well said, "is a world whose air we can breathe."

The role of the Greeks was pre-eminent in making this world and with them its story must begin. They contributed more than any other single people to its dynamism and to its mythical and inspirational legacy. The Greek search for excellence defined for later nations what excellence was and their achievement remains difficult to exaggerate. It is the core of the process which made classical Mediterranean civilization.

The culture of classical Greece spread across the Mediterranean to Asia Minor and was eventually carried even further east by the campaigns of Alexander the Great. The ruins of this 4th-century BCE temple of Athene are in Pirene, originally an early Ionian settlement, in present-day Turkey.

2 THE GREEKS

The oldest surviving Greek inscription is on this jug found in the tomb of Dipylon. It dates from c.750 BCE and is written from right to left. A transcription of the text suggests that the jug may have been a prize in a dance competition or a dedication for a banquet.

IN THE SECOND HALF of the eighth century BCE, the clouds which had hidden the Aegean since the end of the Bronze Age begin to part a little. Processes and sometimes events become somewhat more discernible. There is even a date or two, one of which is important in the history of a civilization's self-consciousness: in 776 BCE, according to later Greek historians, the first Olympian games were held. After a few centuries the Greeks would count from this year as we count from the birth of Christ.

GREEK-SPEAKING PEOPLES

The people who gathered for the first Olympian games and for later festivals of the same sort recognized by doing so that they shared a culture. Its basis was a common language: Dorians, Ionians, Aeolians all spoke Greek. What is more, they had done so for a long time; the language was now to acquire the definition which comes from being written down, an enormously important development, making possible, for example, the recording of the traditional oral poetry which was said to be the work of Homer. Our first surviving inscription in Greek characters is on a jug of about 750 BCE. It shows how much the renewal of Aegean civilization owed to Asia. The inscription is written in an adaptation of Phoenician script; Greeks were illiterate until their traders brought home this alphabet. It seems to have been used first in the Peloponnese, Crete and Rhodes; possibly these were the first areas to benefit from the renewal of intercourse with Asia after the Dark Ages. The process is mysterious and can probably never be recovered, but somehow the catalyst which precipitated Greek civilization was contact with the East.

Who were the Greek-speakers who attended the first Olympiad? Though it is the name by which they and their descendants are still known, they were not called Greeks; that name was only given them centuries later by the Romans. The word they would have used was the one we render in English as "Hellenes". First used to distinguish invaders of the Greek peninsula from the earlier inhabitants, it became one applied to all the Greek-speaking peoples of the Aegean. This was the new conception and the new name emerging from the Dark Ages and there is more than a verbal significance to it. It expressed a consciousness of a new entity, one still emerging and one whose exact meaning would always remain uncertain. Some of the Greek-speakers had

This bronze statue is known as the Piombino Apollo and dates from the 5th century BCE. The figure's serious expression, typical of the pre-classical period, contrasts with his classical-style headdress and the soft lines of his body. His left hand probably held an offering and on his left foot, in silver letters, there is a dedication to Athene.

in the eighth century BCE already long been settled and their roots were lost in the turmoil of the Bronze Age invasions. Some were much more recent arrivals. None came as Greeks; they became Greeks by being there, all around the Aegean. Language identified them and wove new ties between them. Together with a shared heritage of religion and myth, it was the most important constituent of being Greek, always and supremely a matter of common culture.

THE AEGEAN SETTING

Yet cultural ties were never politically effective. They were unlikely to make for unity because of the size and shape of the theatre of Greek history, which was not what we now call Greece, but was, rather, the whole Aegean. The wide spread of Minoan and Mycenaean influences in earlier civilized times had foreshadowed this, for between the scores of its islands and the shores which closed about them it was easy to voyage during much of the year. The explanation of the appearance of Greek civilization at all may well be largely a matter of this geography. The past certainly counted for something, too, but Minoan Crete and Mycenae probably left less to Greece than Anglo-Saxon England left to a later Great Britain. The setting was a much more important factor than history. It offered a specially dense cluster of economically viable communities using the same language and easily accessible not only to one another but to older centres of civilization in the Near East. Like the old river valleys – but for different reasons – the Aegean was a propitious place; civilization could appear there.

Much of the Aegean was settled by Greeks as a consequence of limitations of opportunities

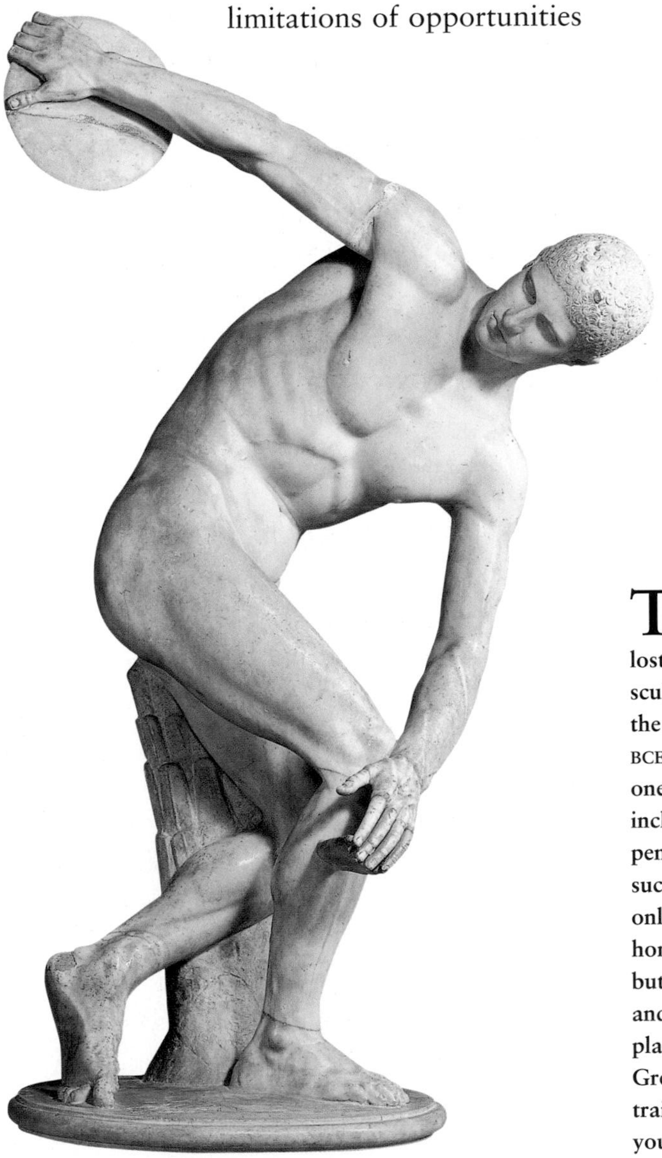

The discus thrower, a replica of the lost work of art sculpted by Myron in the mid-5th century BCE. The statue depicts one of the sports included in the ancient pentathlon. To win such a competition not only brought great honour to the athlete, but also to his family and his city. Sport played a major role in Greek culture and training prepared young men for war.

Time chart (776 BCE–404 BCE)

- 776 BCE — First Olympian games. Date from which the Greek calendar begins
- 750–700 BCE — Beginning of Greek colonization in the Mediterranean. Greek alphabet emerges
- 700 BCE
- 600 BCE
- 507 BCE — Cleisthenes' political reforms in Athens
- 500 BCE
- 500–479 BCE — Median Wars: Greek victory over Persia
- 431–404 BCE — Peloponnesian Wars between Athens and Sparta

that they found on the mainland. Only in very small patches did its land and climate combine to offer the chance of agricultural plenty. For the most part, cultivation was confined to narrow strips of alluvial plain, which had to be dry-farmed, framed by rocky or wooded hills; minerals were rare, there was no tin, copper or iron. A few valleys ran direct to the sea and communication between them was usually difficult. All this inclined the inhabitants of Attica and the Peloponnese to look outward to the sea, on the surface of which transport and communication was much easier than on land. None of them, after all, lived more than forty miles from it.

GREEK CIVILIZATION IS DIFFUSED

The region's predisposition to civilization was intensified as early as the tenth century by a growth of population which brought greater

The Greek world of the Aegean

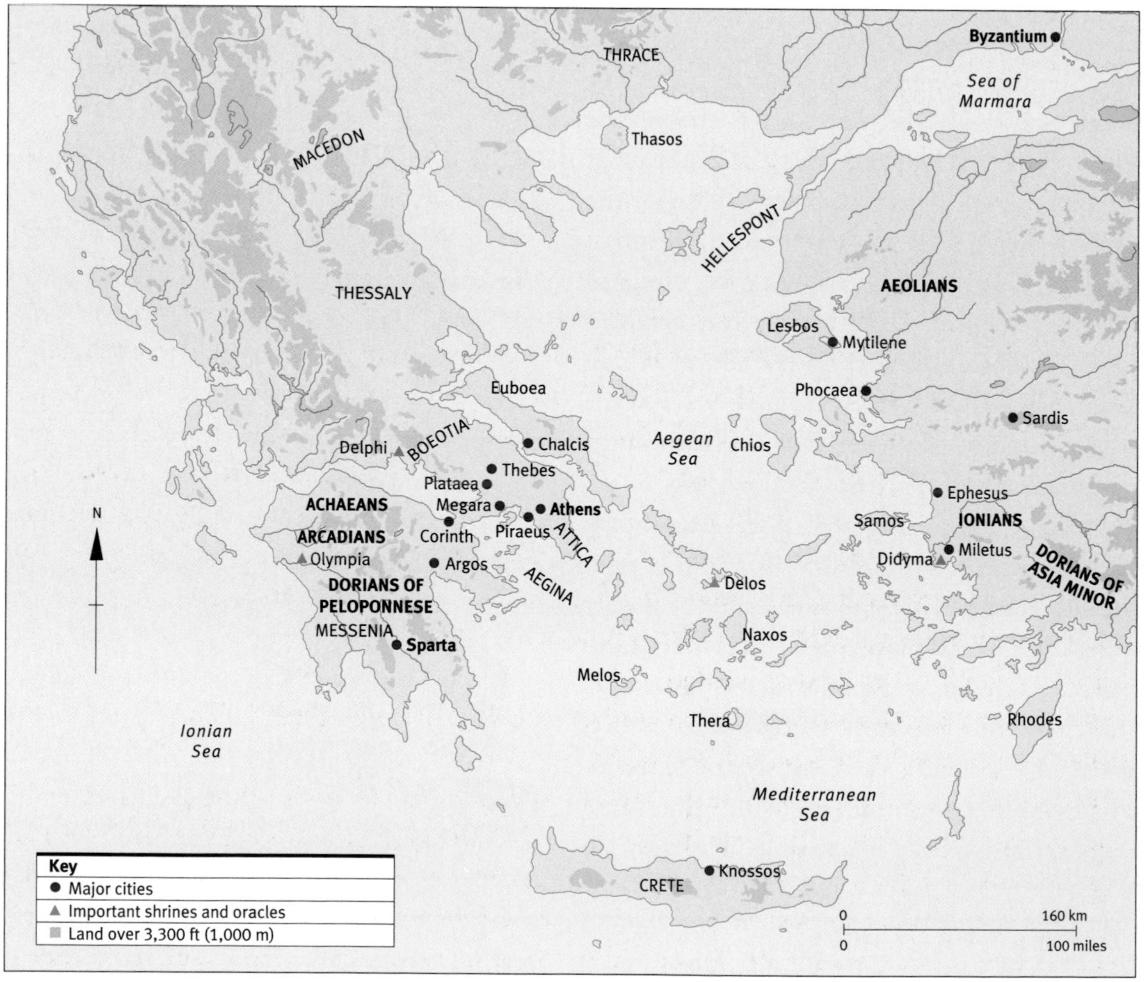

The Aegean coastline was dotted with Greek cities, most of which were involved in trading. Important settlements on the coast of Ionia, in Asia Minor, developed as a result of early emigration from mainland Greece, and Greek culture impregnated life in city-states throughout the Aegean. The remains of sanctuaries and oracles, which were attended by Greeks of all backgrounds, are scattered throughout the region.

In Greece narrow valleys and a lack of flat land made it difficult to produce large harvests. These unfavourable conditions drove many inhabitants of Peloponnesia and Attica to take to the Aegean Sea in search of new lands where they could settle.

pressure on available land. Ultimately this led to a great age of colonization; by the end of it, in the sixth century, the Greek world stretched far beyond the Aegean, from the Black Sea in the east to the Balearics, France and Sicily in the west and Libya in the south. But this was the result of centuries during which forces other than population pressure had also been at work. While Thrace was colonized by agriculturalists looking for land, other Greeks settled in the Levant or southern Italy in order to trade, whether for the wealth it would bring or for the access it offered to the metals they needed and could not find in Greece. Some Black Sea Greek cities seem to be where they are because of trade, some because of their farming potential. Nor were traders and farmers the only agents diffusing Greek ways and teaching Greece about the outside world. The historical records of other countries show us that there was a supply of Greek mercenaries available from the sixth century (when they fought for the Egyptians against the Assyrians) onwards. All these facts were to have important social and political repercussions on the Greek homeland, but before considering them there is much to be said about what kind of civilization it was which was being diffused in this way and was absorbing, by way of return, what others had to give.

LINGUISTIC IDENTITY

Despite serving in foreign armies, and quarrelling violently among themselves while cherishing the traditional and emotional distinctions of Boeotian, or Dorian, or Ionian, the Greeks were always very conscious that they were different from other peoples. This could be practically important; Greek prisoners of war, for example, were in theory not to be enslaved, unlike "barbarians". This word expressed self-conscious Hellenism in its

This 6th-century BCE amphora reproduces a scene from the *Iliad*: the Greek warrior heroes Achilles and Ajax playing a game of dice. Although both players seem absorbed in the game, they hold their spears at the ready, prepared to resume battle against the Trojan enemy at any moment.

essence but is more inclusive and less dismissive than it is in modern speech; the barbarians were the rest of the world, those who did not speak an intelligible Greek (dialect though it might be) but who made a sort of "bar-bar" noise which no Greek could understand. The great religious festivals of the Greek year, when people from many cities came together, were occasions to which only the Greek-speaker was admitted.

RELIGION

RELIGION, TOO, WAS FUNDAMENTAL to Greek identity. The Greek pantheon is enormously complex, the amalgam of a mass of myths created by many communities over a wide area at different times, often incoherent or even self-contradictory until ordered by later, rationalizing minds. Some were imports, like the Asian myth of golden, silver, bronze and iron ages. Local superstition and belief in such legends was the bedrock of the Greek religious experience. Yet it was a religious experience very different from that of other peoples in its ultimately humanizing tendency. Greek gods and goddesses, for all their supernatural standing and power, are remarkably human. They express the human-centred quality of later Greek civilization. Much as they owed to Egypt and the East, Greek mythology and art usually presents their gods as better, or worse, men and women, a world

The Greek pantheon

The Greeks were polytheists and depicted their gods as men and women, often moved by human passions. During the classical period, the twelve Olympian gods, who often had several personalities, were the most important deities. These Olympian gods were Zeus, Hera, Apollo, Artemis, Athene, Ares, Aphrodite, Demeter, Hephaestus, Poseidon, Hermes and Hestia. A large number of other lesser gods and local gods were also worshipped. Each city had a divine protector – Athene, goddess of intelligence, art and war, was the protector of Athens.

Rituals held in honour of the gods were usually carried out on open-air altars. These were placed in front of the doors of a sanctuary, in meeting places or in people's homes, rather than inside temples, which were used to house cult images of the gods.

This 5th-century BCE *marble plaque depicts the birth of Aphrodite, as described in one of Homer's poems. The goddess of love emerges from the foaming sea, assisted by her servants, the Graces and the Seasons. Wife of the god Hephaestus, Aphrodite was the lover of both Ares and Adonis, mother of Eros and protector of the Trojan Paris, who abducted Helen.*

away from the monsters of Assyria and Babylonia, or from Shiva the many-armed. Whoever is responsible, this was a religious revolution; its converse was the implication that humans could be godlike. It is already apparent in Homer; perhaps he did as much as anyone to order the Greek supernatural in this way and he does not give much space to popular cults. He presents the gods taking sides in the Trojan war in postures all too human. They compete with one another; while Poseidon harries the hero of the *Odyssey*, Athene takes his part. A later Greek critic grumbled that Homer "attributed to the gods everything that is disgraceful and blameworthy among men: theft, adultery and deceit". It was a world which operated much like the actual world.

HOMER'S THE *ILIAD* AND THE *ODYSSEY*

The *Iliad* and the *Odyssey* have already been touched upon because of the light they throw on prehistory; they were also shapers of the future. They are at first sight curious objects for a people's reverence. The *Iliad* gives an account of a short episode from a legendary long-past war; the *Odyssey* is more like a novel, narrating the wandering of one of the greatest of all literary characters, Odysseus, on his way home from the same struggle. That, on the face of it, is all. But they came to be held to be something like sacred books. If, as seems reasonable, the survival rate of early copies is thought to give a true reflection of relative popularity, they were copied more frequently than any other text of Greek literature. Much time and ink have been spent on argument about how they were composed. It now seems most likely that they took their present shape in Ionia slightly before 700 BCE. The Greeks referred to their author without qualification as "the poet" (a sufficient sign of his standing in their eyes) but some have found arguments for thinking the two poems are the work of different men. For our purpose, it is unimportant whether he was one author or not; the essential point is that someone took material presented by four centuries of bardic transmission and wove it into a form which acquired stability, and in this sense these works are the culmination of the era of Greek heroic poetry. Though they were probably written down in the seventh century, no standard version of these poems was accepted until the sixth; by then they were already regarded as the authoritative account of early Greek history, a source of morals and models, and the staple of literary education. Thus they became not only the first documents of Greek self-consciousness, but the embodiment of the fundamental values of classical civilization. Later they were to be even more than

Zeus was believed to be the father of all the gods as well as god of the sky. He used storms and lightning to show his wrath and administered justice on the earth and in heaven. He was the brother and husband of the goddess Hera and the father of countless heroes, the fruits of his relationships with goddesses and mortal women.

The *Odyssey*

"(Jove) saith, that here thou hold'st the most distrest
Of all those warriors who nine years, assail'd
The city of Priam, and, (that city sack'd)
Departed in the tenth; but, going thence,
Offended Pallas, who with adverse winds
Opposed their voyage, and with boist'rous waves.
Then perish'd all his gallant friends, but him
Billows and storms drove hither; Jove commands
That thou dismiss him hence without delay,
For fate ordains him not to perish here
From all his friends remote, but he is doom'd
To see them yet again, and to arrive
At his own palace in his native land."

An extract from Book V of the *Odyssey* by Homer, translated by William Cowper.

this: together with the Bible, they became the source of western literature.

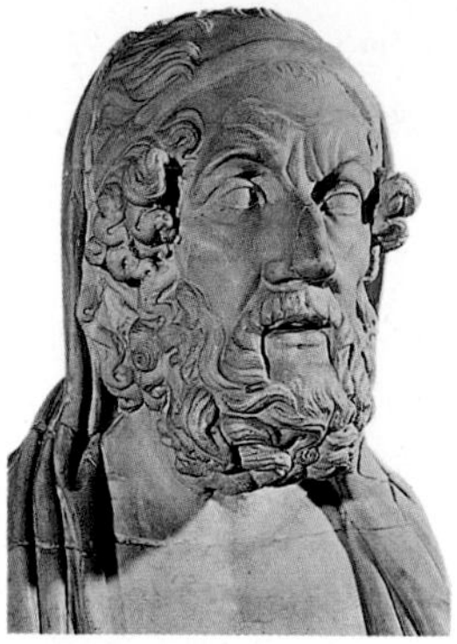

Homer, who was probably born in an Ionian city, lived between 750 and 650 BCE. The existing portraits of the poet, all of them imaginary, depict him as a blind, bearded figure. Homer's influence is omnipresent in Greek culture.

THE OCCULT

Human though Homer's gods might be, the Greek world had also a deep respect for the occult and mysterious. It was recognized in such embodiments as omens and oracles. The shrines of the oracles of Apollo at Delphi or at Didyma in Asia Minor were places of pilgrimage and the sources of respected if enigmatic advice. There were ritual cults which practised "mysteries" which reenacted the great natural processes of germination and growth at the passage of the seasons. Popular religion does not loom large in the literary sources, but it was never wholly separated from "respectable" religion. It is important to remember this irrational subsoil, given that the achievements of the Greek élite during the later classical era are so impressive and rest so importantly on rationality and logic; the irrational was always there and in the earlier, formative period with which this chapter is concerned, it loomed large.

Mount Olympus, the highest mountain in Greece, was cited by Homer as the home of the Olympian gods. It is not surprising that the ancient Greeks installed their most important deities on the northern edge of the known world, on a mountain visible from the sea.

SOCIETY AND POLITICS

The literary record and accepted tradition also reveal something, if nothing very precise, of the social and (if the word is appropriate) political institutions of early Greece. Homer shows us a society of kings and aristocrats, but one that was already anachronistic when he depicted it. The title of king sometimes lived on, and in one place, Sparta, where there were always two kings at once, it had a shadowy reality which sometimes was effective, but by historical times power had passed from monarchs to aristocracies in almost all the Greek cities. The council of the Areopagus at Athens is an example of the sort of restricted body which usurped the kingly power in many places. Such ruling élites rested fundamentally on land; their members were the outright owners of the estates, which provided not only their livelihood but the surplus for the expensive arms and horses which made leaders in war. Homer depicts such aristocrats behaving with a remarkable degree of independence of his kings; this probably reflects the reality of his own day. They were the only people who counted; other social distinctions have little importance in these poems. Thersites is properly chastized for infringing the crucial line between gentlemen and the rest.

A military aristocracy's preoccupation with courage may also explain a continuing self-assertiveness and independence in Greek public life; Achilles, as Homer presents him, was as prickly and touchy a fellow as any medieval baron. To this day a man's standing in his peers' eyes is what many Greeks care about more than anything else and their politics have often reflected this. It was to prove true during the classical age when time and time again individualism wrecked the chances of cooperative action. The Greeks were never to produce an enduring empire, for it could only have rested on some measure of subordination of the lesser to the greater good, or some willingness to accept the discipline of routine service. This may have been no bad thing, but meant that for all their Hellenic self-consciousness the Greeks could not unite even their homeland into one state.

LIBERTY AND SLAVERY IN ANCIENT GREECE

Below the aristocrats of the early cities were the other ranks of a still not very complex society. Freemen worked their own land or

The Tholos at Delphi was located outside the grounds of the main sanctuary dedicated to the god Apollo. People came to Delphi from all over the Greek world to consult the oracle of Apollo on both political and private affairs.

sometimes for others. Wealth did not change hands rapidly or easily until money made it available in a form more easily transferred than land. Homer measured value in oxen and seems to have envisaged gold and silver as elements in a ritual of gift-giving, rather than as means of exchange. This was the background of the later idea that trade and menial tasks were degrading; an aristocratic view lingered on. It helps to explain why in Athens (and perhaps elsewhere) commerce was long in the hands of metics, foreign residents who enjoyed no civic privilege, but who provided the services Greek citizens would not provide for themselves.

A 6th-century BCE Athenian hydria. The decoration – a group of women, probably slaves, filling their hydrias at the fountain – alludes to the function of this jar, which was used to collect water. A number of monumental fountains, such as those shown here, were built in Athens during the 6th century BCE.

Slavery, of course, was taken for granted, though much uncertainty surrounds the institution. It was clearly capable of many different interpretations. In archaic times, if that is what Homer reflects, most slaves were women, the prizes of victory, but the slaughter of male prisoners later gave way to enslavement. Large-scale plantation slavery, such as that of Rome or the European colonies of modern times, was unusual. Many Greeks of the fifth century who were freemen owned one or two slaves and one estimate is that about one in four of the population was a slave when Athens was most prosperous. They could be freed; one fourth-century slave became a considerable banker. They were also often well treated and sometimes loved. One has become famous: Aesop. But they were not free and the Greeks thought that absolute dependence on another's will was intolerable for a free man though they hardly ever developed this notion into positive criticism of slavery. It would be anachronistic to be surprised at this. The whole world outside Greece, too, was organized on the assumption that slavery would go on. It was the prevailing social institution almost everywhere well into Christian times and it is not yet dead. It is hardly cause for comment, therefore, that the Greeks took it for granted. There was no task that slavery did not sustain for them, from agricultural labour to teaching (our word "pedagogue" originally meant a slave who accompanied a well-born boy to school). A famous Greek philosopher later tried to justify this state of affairs by arguing that there were some human beings who were truly intended to be slaves by nature, since they had been given only such faculties as fitted them to serve the purposes of more enlightened individuals. To modern ears this does not seem a very impressive argument, but in the context of the way Greeks thought about nature and humanity

Full-size bronze mirrors such as this one became fashionable at the end of the archaic age. In this example, the figurine shows the influence of oriental art. Only members of a wealthy family could afford to purchase such a luxury.

there was more to it than simple rationalization of prejudice.

CONTACT WITH THE NEAR EAST

Slaves may and foreign residents must have been among the many channels by which the Greeks continued to be influenced by the Near East long after civilization had re-emerged in the Aegean. Homer had already mentioned the *demiourgoi*, foreign craftsmen who must have brought with them to the cities of the Hellenes not only technical skill but the motifs and styles of other lands. In later times we hear of Greek craftsmen settled in Babylon and there were many examples of Greek soldiers serving as mercenaries to foreign kings. When the Persians took Egypt in 525 BCE, Greeks fought on each side. Some of these men must have returned to the Aegean, bringing with them new ideas and impressions. Meanwhile, there was all the time a continuing commercial and diplomatic intercourse between the Greek cities in Asia and their neighbours.

GREEK ART

The multiplicity of day-to-day exchanges resulting from the enterprise of the Greeks makes it very hard to distinguish native and foreign contributions to the culture of archaic Greece. One tempting area is art; here, just as Mycenae had reflected Asian models, so the animal motifs which decorate Greek bronze work, or the postures of goddesses such as Aphrodite, recall the art of the Near East. Later, the monumental architecture and statuary of Greece was to imitate Egypt's, and Egyptian antiquities shaped the styles of the things made by Greek craftsmen at Naucratis. Although the

Most manual labour, both in the city and the countryside, was carried out by slaves, who also took care of domestic tasks. In Athenian comedies, the characters of the comic slave and servant were firm favourites. These small terracotta statuettes wearing grotesque masks were found in a 4th-century BCE Athenian tomb and depict actors dressed up for a performance.

The inside of a kylix (two-handled drinking vessel), depicting the god Dionysus who, after being captured by pirates, turned the mast of their ship into a vine and transformed the crew into dolphins.

final product, the mature art of classical Greece, was unique, its roots lie far back in the renewal of ties with Asia in the eighth century. What is not possible to delineate quickly is the slow subsequent irradiation of a process of cultural interplay which was by the sixth century working both ways, for Greece was by then both pupil and teacher. Lydia, for example, the kingdom of the legendary Croesus, richest man in the world, was Hellenized by its tributary Greek cities; it took its art from them and, probably more important, the alphabet, indirectly acquired via Phrygia. Thus Asia received again what Asia had given.

COMMERCIAL EXPANSION

Well before 500 BCE, Greek civilization was so complex that it is easy to lose touch with the exact state of affairs at any one time. By the standards of its contemporaries, early Greece was a rapidly changing society, and some of its changes are easier to see than others. One important development towards the end of the seventh century seems to have been a second and more important wave of colonization, often from the eastern Greek cities. Their colonies were a response to agrarian difficulties and population pressure at home. There followed an upsurge of commerce: new economic relationships appearing as trade with the non-Greek world became easier. Part of the evidence is an increased circulation of silver. The Lydians had been the first to strike true coins – tokens of standard weight and imprint – and in the sixth century money began to be widely used in both foreign and internal trade; only the Spartans resisted its introduction. Specialization became a possible answer to land shortage at home. Athens assured the grain imports it needed by specializing in the output of great quantities of pottery and oil; Chios exported oil and wine. Some Greek cities became notably more dependent on foreign corn, in particular, from Egypt or the Greeks colonies of the Black Sea.

THE HOPLITES

Commercial expansion meant not only that land was no longer the only important source of wealth, but also that more men could buy the land which was so important in establishing status. This began a revolution both military and political. The old Greek ideal of warfare had been single combat, a form of fighting natural to a society whose warriors were aristocrats, riding or driving to the field of battle to confront their equals, while less well-armed inferiors brawled about them. The new rich could afford the armour and arms which provided a better military instrument, the regiment of "hoplites", the heavy-armed infantry who were to be for two centuries the backbone of Greek armies and give them superiority. They would prevail by disciplined cohesion, rather than by individual derring-do.

The Greek hoplite wore helmet and body-armour and carried a shield. His main weapon was the spear, which he did not throw, but with which he thrust and stabbed in the mêlée which followed a charge by an ordered formation of spearmen whose weight gave it its effect. Such tactics could work only on relatively level ground, but it was such ground that was usually being contested in Greek wars, for the agriculture on which a Greek city depended could be devastated by seizure of the little plains of the valley floor where most of its crops were grown. On such terrain, the hoplites would charge as a mass, with the aim of sweeping away defenders by their impact. They depended completely on their power to act as a disciplined unit. This both maximized the effect of the charge and enabled them to prevail in the hand-to-hand fighting which followed, because each hoplite had to rely for protection on his right-hand side by the shield of his neighbour. To keep an ordered line was therefore crucial. The Spartans were in particular admired for their expertise in performing the preliminary evolutions which preceded such an encounter and for retaining cohesion as a group once the scrimmage had begun.

The ability to act collectively was the heart of the new warfare. Though bigger numbers now took part in battles, numbers were no longer all that counted, as three centuries of Greek success against Asian armies were to prove. Discipline and tactical skill began to matter more and they implied some sort of regular training, as well as a social widening of the warrior group. More men thus came to share in the power which comes from a near-monopoly of the means of exercising force.

This funerary stele depicts a Greek hoplite. He wears a short tunic allowing free movement of the legs. His chest is protected by a metal or leather breastplate. On his head he wears a raised Corinthian-style helmet, part of which has been lost.

CITY-STATES

The development of a highly-trained army was not the only crucial innovation of these years. It was then, too, that the Greeks invented politics; the notion of running collective concerns by discussion of possible choices in a public setting is theirs. The magnitude of what they did lives on in the language we still use, for "politics" and "political" are terms derived from the Greek word for city, *polis*. This was the framework of Greek life. It was much more than a mere agglomeration of people living in the same place for economic reasons. That it was more is shown by another Greek turn of speech:

The decoration of this 7th-century BCE Corinthian jug depicts a group of horsemen taking part in a hunt. As neither saddle nor stirrups were used in Greece, the riders are mounted bareback. The cavalry played only a small role in the army and was never significant in attack; it was used to explore the terrain, to protect the army's flanks and to hound a retreating enemy.

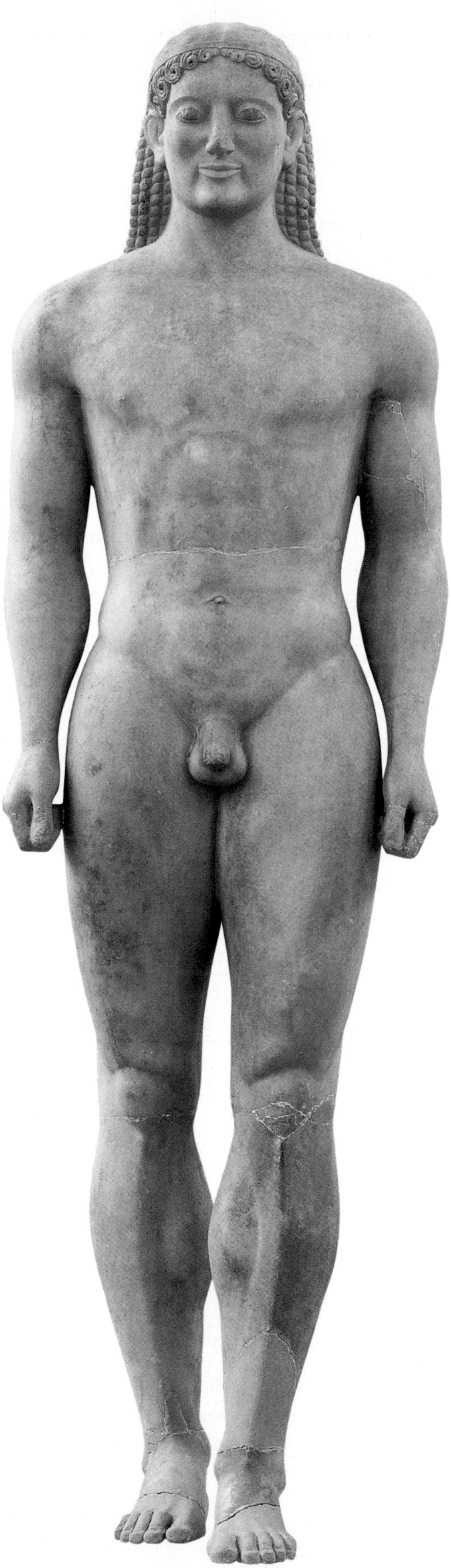

This marble statue comes from an Athenian tomb and is a grave marker, or *kouros*. Made in about 530 BCE, it is a good example of how, as late as the 6th century BCE, Greek sculpture retained features from Egyptian art, including the rigidity and marked frontality of the body.

they did not speak of Athens doing this, or Thebes doing that, but of the Athenians and the Thebans. Bitterly divided though it might often be, the *polis* – or, as for convenience it can be called, the city-state – was a community, a body of men conscious of shared interests and common goals.

Such collective agreement was the essence of the city-state; those who did not like the institutions of the one they lived in could look for alternatives elsewhere. This helped to produce a high degree of cohesiveness, but also a narrowness; the Greeks never transcended the passion for local autonomy (another Greek word) and the city-state characteristically looked outwards defensively and distrustfully. Gradually, it acquired its protecting gods, its festivals and its liturgical drama, which connected living people with the past and educated them in its traditions and laws. Thus it came to be an organism living in time, spanning generations. But at its root lay the hoplite ideal of disciplined, cooperative action in which men stood shoulder to shoulder with their neighbours, relying on them to support them in the common cause. In early days the citizen body – those, that is to say, who constituted the politically effective community – was confined to the hoplites, those who could afford to take their place in the ranks on which the defence of the city-state depended. It is not surprising that in later times Greek reformers who were worried about the results of political extremism would often turn hopefully to the hoplite class when looking for a stable, settled foundation for the *polis*.

At the roots of city-states lay also other facts: geography, economics, kinship. Many of them grew up on very ancient sites, settled in Mycenaean times; others were newer, but almost always the territory of a city-state was one of the narrow valleys which could provide just enough for its maintenance. A few

Greek Coins

The development of commerce in Greek cities stimulated the introduction of coins, probably around the mid-6th century BCE. We know that the first coins minted in Greece were made in Aegina, where silver, regularly brought from Siphnos, was used to produce the famous "silver turtles". A large variety of coins existed in the Greek world and the capacity to mint was seen as a sign of independence. Usually made of silver, the coins bore drawings and inscriptions showing the emblem of the city.

Greek coins dating from the 6th–4th centuries BCE – above: silver tetradrachma; right: silver stater from Poseidonia; far right: silver coin from Leontini.

were luckier: Sparta sat in a broad valley. A few were specially handicapped: the soil of Attica was poor and Athens would have to feed its citizens on imported grain in consequence. Dialect intensified the sense of independence latent in the mountains separating a city from its neighbours. In it was preserved a sense of common tribal origin which lived on in the great public cults.

CITIZENSHIP

By the beginning of historical times, intense feelings of community and individuality had already been generated which made it virtually impossible for Greeks to transcend the city-state: a few shadowy leagues and confederations did not count for much. Within the city the involvement of citizens in its life was close; we might find it excessive. Yet because of its scale the city-state could do without elaborate bureaucracies; the citizen body, always much smaller than the whole population, could always assemble at one meeting place. There was no likelihood that a city-state could or would aspire to a minute bureaucratic regulation of affairs; anything like this would probably have been beyond the capacity of its institutions. If we judge by the evidence of Athens, the state of which we know most because it recorded so much in stone, the distinction between administration, judgment and law-making was not as we know it; as in the Europe of the Middle Ages, an executive act might be clothed as a decision of a court interpreting established law. Law courts were, formally speaking, only sections of the assembly of the citizens.

The size and qualification of the membership of this body determined the

The wealthy city of Corinth produced an enormous amount of pottery for trade. The decoration of Corinthian pieces such as these often reflected the influence of the Near East, depicting fantastic animals, probably inspired by imported textiles.

constitutional character of the state. Upon it depended, more or less, the authorities of day-to-day government, whether magistrates or courts. There was nothing like the modern permanent civil service. True, it is still risky to generalize about such matters. There were over a hundred and fifty city-states and about many of them we know nothing; of most of the rest we know only a little. Obviously there were important differences between the ways in which they ran their affairs; in the fourth century BCE, Aristotle made a great collection of their constitutions and there would not have been much point in a political scientist doing this unless they were significantly different from one another. But the detail of what went on is hard to discern, even in the few cases where we have good information.

In the year 514 BCE, Hipparchus, son and successor of the Athenian tyrant Pisistratus, was killed by the tyrannicides Harmodius and Aristogeiton. After the fall of the Athenian tyranny in 510 BCE, their deed was extolled in this bronze sculpture.

TYRANTS

The origins of Greek political forms are usually buried in legends as informative as the story of Hengist and Horsa is to the historian of England. Even Homer is unhelpful about the city-state; he hardly mentions it because his subject is warrior bands. Yet when the historical age dawns the city-state is there, ruled by aristocracies. The forces which determined the broad lines of its later evolution have already been touched upon. New wealth meant new men, and the new men battered away at the existing élites to get admission to citizenship. The aristocracies which had supplanted the kings themselves became objects of rivalry and attack. The new men sought to replace them by governments less respectful of traditional interests; the result was an age of rulers the Greeks called tyrants. They were often moneyed, but their justification was their popularity; they were strong men who set aside the aristocracies. The later sinister connotations of the word "tyrant" did not then exist; many tyrants must have seemed benevolent despots. They brought peace after social struggles probably intensified by a new crisis arising from pressure on land. Peace favoured economic growth, as did the usually good relations the tyrants enjoyed with one another. The seventh century was their golden age. Yet the institution did not long survive. Few tyrannies lasted two generations. In the sixth century the current turned almost everywhere towards collective government; oligarchies, constitutional governments, even incipient democracies began to emerge.

ATHENS

Athens was an outstanding example of this process. For a long time it seems that Attica, though poor, had sufficient land for Athens to escape the social pressures which in other states led to the colonization movement. In other ways, too, Athens' economy early reflected a special vigour; even in the eighth century its pottery suggests that the city-state was something of a commercial and artistic leader. In the sixth, though, it too was racked by conflict between rich and poor. A soon legendary lawgiver, Solon, forbade the enslavement of debtors by wealthy creditors (which had the effect of leading men to turn to greater dependence on chattel slaves, since debt bondage could no longer guarantee a labour force). Solon also encouraged farmers to specialize. Oil and wine (and their containers) became staple Athenian exports and grain was kept at home. Simultaneously, a series of reforms (also attributed to Solon) gave to the newly enriched equality with the old landed class and provided for a new popular council to prepare business for the *ecclesia*, the general assembly of all citizens.

Such changes did not at once quiet Athens' divisions. An age of tyrants only closed with the expulsion of the last in 510 BCE. Then there at last began to operate the institutions whose paradoxical outcome was to be the most democratic government in Greece, though one over a state which held more slaves than any other. All political decisions were taken in principle by majority vote of the *ecclesia* (which also elected the important magistrates and military commanders). Ingenious arrangements provided for the organization of the citizens in units which would prevent the emergence of sectional factions representing city-dwellers as against farmers or merchants. It was the beginning of a great age, one of prosperity, when Athens would consciously foster festivals and cults looking beyond the city and offered something to all Greeks. This was something of a bid for leadership.

SPARTA

Much has been made of the contrast between Athens and its great rival, Sparta. Unlike

Every four years the Great Panathenaeas was held in Athens. This civic celebration in honour of the goddess Athene consisted of four days of athletic contests and festivities. The entire Athenian community also participated in a solemn procession to the Acropolis, bearing a new robe for the huge statue of Athene. The sculptor Phidias depicted the procession in his decorations for the frieze at the Parthenon, from which this fragment is taken.

Athens, Sparta met the pressures upon it not by modifying its institutions but by resisting change. Sparta embodied the most conservative approach to the problem, solving it for a long time by rigid social discipline at home and by conquest among its neighbours, which allowed it to meet the demand for land at others' expense. A very early consequence was a fossilizing of the social structure. So tradition-bound was Sparta that it was alleged that its legendary law-giver, Lycurgus, had even forbidden the writing down of its laws; they were driven home in the minds of the Spartiates by a rigorous training all undergone in youth, boys and girls alike.

Sparta had no tyrants. Its effective government appears to have been shared between a council of old men and five magistrates called "ephors", while the two hereditary kings had special military powers. These oligarchs were in the last resort answerable to the assembly of the Spartiates (of whom, according to Herodotus, there were early in the fifth century about five thousand). Sparta was, therefore, a large aristocracy whose origin, ancient writers agreed, was the hoplite class. Society remained agricultural; no commercial class was allowed to appear and when the rest of Greece took up the use of money, around 600 BCE, Sparta stood out and permitted only an iron currency for internal use. Spartiates were not supposed to own silver or gold until the fourth century. Sparta even stood aside from the colonizing movement, and launched only one enterprise of this sort.

This produced a sort of militarized egalitarianism often admired by later puritans, and an atmosphere strongly suggestive, for good and ill, of the aspirations of an old-

This painting of fighting warriors is from a 7th-century BCE Corinthian ceramic known as the Chigi Vase. The artist demonstrates his skill by evoking the movement and formation of the hoplites, shown advancing into battle to the sound of the flute music.

A bronze statuette of a Spartan wearing a large cloak. His long curls hang down under his helmet, to which a plume is attached. The statuette dates from approximately 500 BCE.

fashioned and high-minded boarding school. Though the passing of time and the position of kings slightly softened their practice, Spartiates knew no great distinctions of wealth or comfort. Until well into classical times they avoided dressing differently and ate at communal messes. Their conditions of life were, in a word, "spartan", reflecting the idealization of military virtues and strict discipline. The details are often strikingly unpleasant as well as curious. For the marriage ceremony, for example, the bride's hair was cropped and she was dressed as a boy. This was followed by a simulated rape, after which the couple did not live together, but the man continued to live with his companions in a male dormitory and eat in messes with them. It is interesting that Sparta exported nursemaids to other Greek states (later parallels will again occur to the reader). It had no artistic or cultural achievement to speak of and its internal politics remain mysterious.

Possibly Spartan politics were simplified or muted by Sparta's gravest problem, the division between the citizen commune and the rest. The bulk of the inhabitants of the Spartan state were not citizens. Some were freemen, but most were helots, serf-like workers, bound to the land, who shared with the free peasants the task of producing the food consumed at the Spartiates' communal meals. Originally the helot population may have been the native population enslaved by the Dorian invasions, but they were, like later serfs, tied to land rather than being the chattels of individual owners. Certainly their number was later swollen by conquest, above all by the annexation in the eighth century BCE of the plain of Messenia, which disappeared from Greek history as an independent state for more than three hundred years. As a result, a cloud hung over the Spartan achievement – the fear of a helot revolt – and it was remarked by other Greeks.

It hobbled the Spartans in their relations with other states. Increasingly they feared to have their army abroad lest its absence should tempt revolt at home. Sparta was always on the alert and the feared enemy was at home.

THE GREEK ACHIEVEMENT

Sparta and Athens were to quarrel fatally in the fifth century and this has led them to be seen always as the poles of the political world of ancient Greece. They were not, of course, the only models available, and herein lies one of the secrets of the Greek achievement. It would draw upon a richness of political experience and data far greater than anything seen in the world until this time. This experience would provide the first systematic reflections upon the great problems of law, duty, and obligation which have exercized people's minds ever since, largely in terms set by the classical Greeks. In pre-classical times, speculation on such themes is almost nonexistent. The weight of custom and the limitations of local experience sufficiently explain this.

Solon, born in about 639 BCE, was the first important reformer of the Athenian constitution. He eliminated the punishment of slavery for debt from the statute book and worked to further democratize Athenian institutions.

COLONIZATION

The city-state was the shared inheritance and experience of the Greeks, but they knew of other types of political organization through contacts made in the course of trade and because of the exposed nature of many of their own settlements. The Greek world had frontier regions where conflict was likely. In the west they once seemed to be pushing ahead in an almost limitless expansion, but two centuries of striking advance came to an end round about

Types of pottery

The earliest Greek city-states developed the manufacture of pottery for exportation, as containers for commercial goods as well as for domestic and funerary purposes. Gradually, the shapes of Greek pottery objects evolved and the style of decoration used allows archaeologists to distinguish both the period and the geographical origin of a piece.

Some of the most common types of containers: (1) Amphorae, large pieces which contained wine and oil; (2) Kraters, in which wine and water were mixed to serve at banquets; (3) Oinochoes, wine jugs with a trefoil mouth to help pouring; (4) Jugs and cups for serving wine; (5) Arybaloi, small jars of oriental origin used to contain the ointments used by athletes; and (6 and 7) Lekythoi, small oil jars used to contain offerings to the dead.

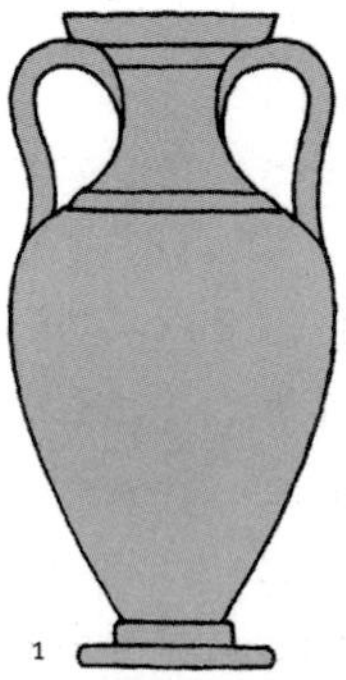

The Doric-style Temple of Concord in Agrigento, Sicily, was erected around 430 BCE. Because it was converted into a Christian church at the end of the 6th century CE, this is one of the best-preserved ancient Greek buildings.

550 BCE, when Carthaginian and Etruscan power prescribed a limit. The first settlements – once again, at sites sometimes used centuries earlier by Minoans and Mycenaeans – show that trade mattered as much as agriculture in their foundation. Their main strength lay in Sicily and in southern Italy, an area significantly to be called Magna Graecia in later classical times. The richest of these colonies was Syracuse, founded by Corinthians in 733 BCE and eventually the dominating Greek state in the west. It had the best harbour in Sicily. Beyond this colonial area, settlements were made in Corsica and southern France (at Massilia, the later Marseilles) while some Greeks went to live among the Etruscans and Latins of central Italy. Greek products have turned up even as far afield as Sweden and Greek style has been seen in sixth-century fortifications in Bavaria. More impalpable influence is hard to pin down, but a Roman historian believed that Greek example first civilized the barbarians of what was later to be France and set them not only to tilling their fields, but to cultivating the vine. If so, posterity owes Greek commerce a debt indeed.

GREEK ENEMIES

The Greeks' vigorous expansion seems to have provoked Phoenician envy and imitation. It led the Phoenicians to found Carthage and the Carthaginians to seize footholds in western Sicily. Eventually they were able to close down Greek trade in Spain. Yet they could not turn the Greek settlers out of Sicily any more than the Etruscans could drive them from Italy. The decisive battle in which the Syracusans routed a Carthaginian force was in 480 BCE.

This was a date of yet greater significance for Greek relations with Asia, where the Greek cities of Asia Minor had often been at loggerheads with their neighbours. They had suffered much from the Lydians until they came to terms with the Lydian king, Croesus of legendary wealth, and paid him tribute. Before this, Greece already influenced Lydian

The colony of Carthage in modern Tunisia was founded by Phoenicians in 814 BCE to ensure commercial domination of the western Mediterranean. The city was soon competing against the region's Greek colonies, some of which became Carthaginian strongholds. Carthage was razed by the Romans in the 2nd century BCE – ruins are all that remain of it today.

fashions; some of Croesus's predecessors had sent offerings to the shrine at Delphi. Now the Hellenization of Lydia went even more quickly ahead. None the less, a much more formidable opponent loomed up even further east: Persia.

GREECE AND PERSIA

THE GREEK STRUGGLE with Persia is the climax of the early history of Greece and the inauguration of its classical age. Because the Greeks made so much of their long conflict with the Persians it is easy to lose sight of the many ties that linked the contestants. The Persian fleets – and to a lesser extent, Persian armies – launched against the Peloponnese had thousands of Greeks, mainly from Ionia, serving in them. Cyrus had employed Greek stone-cutters and sculptors and Darius had a Greek physician. Probably the war did as much to create as to feed antagonism, however deep the emotional revulsion proclaimed by the Greeks for a country which treated its kings like gods.

The Persian Empire and the Achaemenids

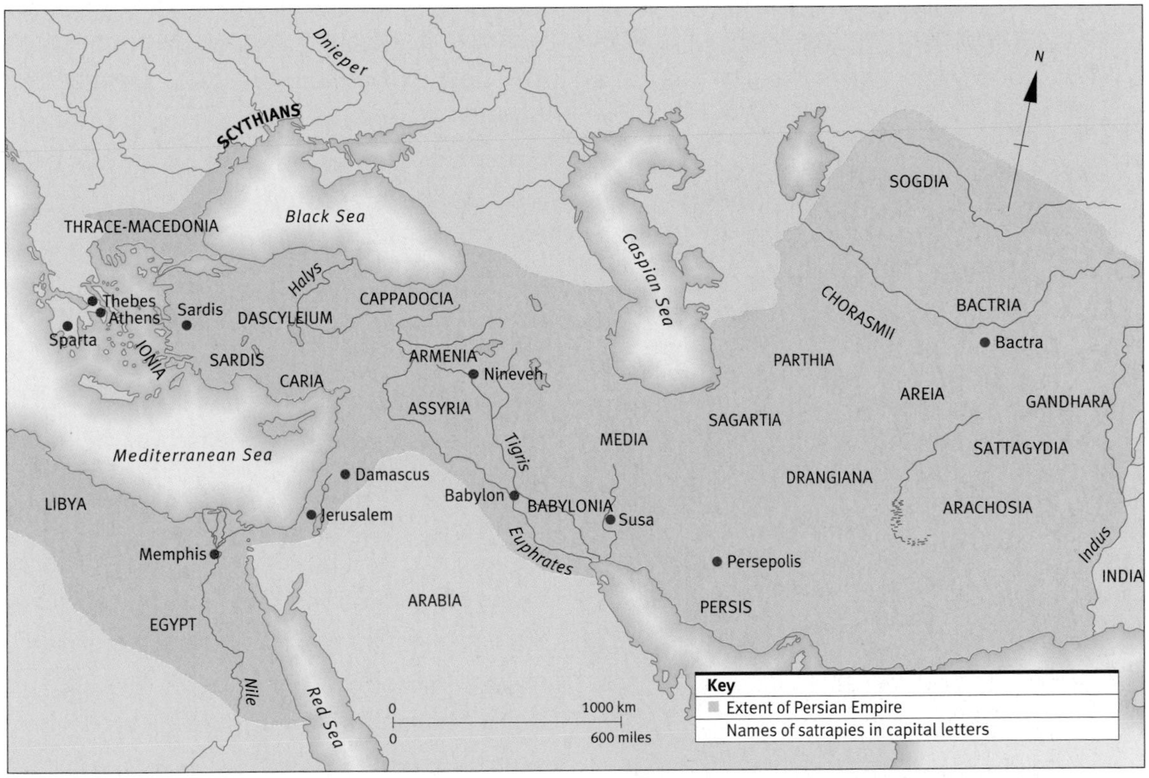

The construction of the great Persian Empire of the Achaemenids began in the middle of the 6th century BCE. In Asia Minor, the Persian king Cyrus the Great defeated the king of Lydia and subjugated the Greek cities on the coast and on a number of Aegean islands. He went on to conquer Babylonia and the lands between the Mediterranean and Mesopotamia. At the end of the 6th century BCE, his son Cambyses conquered Egypt. King Darius continued the empire's expansion to the east, in the Indus valley, and to the west, where he crossed the straits and annexed Thrace and Macedonia in 522–486 BCE. In spite of their greater numbers, however, the Persians were defeated by the Greeks at the battle of Eurymedon in 467 BCE.

THE PERSIAN WAR

The origins of the Persian war lay in the great expansion of Persia under the Achaemenids. In about 540 BCE, the Persians overthrew Lydia (and that was the end of Croesus, who was supposed to have provoked the assault by an incautious interpretation of an utterance of the Delphic oracle, which said that if he went to war with Persia he would destroy a great empire, but not which one). This brought Greeks and Persians face to face; elsewhere, the tide of Persian conquest rolled on. When the Persians took Egypt they damaged Greek traders' interests there. Next, the Persians crossed to Europe and occupied the cities of the coast as far west as Macedon; across the Danube and they failed, and soon retired from Scythia. At this point there was something of a pause. Then, in the first decade of the fifth century, the Asian Greek cities revolted against Persian suzerainty, encouraged, perhaps, by Darius's failure against the Scythians. The mainland cities, or some of them, decided to help. Athens and Eretria sent a fleet to Ionia. In the subsequent operations the Greeks burnt Sardis, the former capital of Lydia and the seat of the western satrapy of the Persian Empire. But the revolt failed in the end and left the mainland cities facing an enraged opponent.

Things did not usually happen very quickly in the ancient world, and large-scale expeditions still take a long time to prepare, but almost as soon as the Ionian revolt was crushed the Persians sent a fleet against the Greeks; it was wrecked off Mount Athos. A second attempt, in 490 BCE, sacked Eretria but then came to grief at the hands of the Athenians in a battle whose name has become legendary – Marathon.

This amphora dates from the beginning of the 5th century BCE. It illustrates one of the stories about the death of Croesus, king of Lydia, after his capture by the Persian king Cyrus. Croesus is pictured seated on a pyre, about to be burned alive by his captors. This is one of the few pottery decorations from this period whose subject is related to the Persian War.

THE PELOPONNESIAN LEAGUE

Although Marathon was an Athenian victory, the leader in the next phase of the struggle with Persia was Sparta, the strongest of the city-states on land. Out of the Peloponnesian League, an alliance whose origins had been domestic in that its aim had been to assure Sparta's future by protecting her from the need to send her army abroad, there devolved upon Sparta something like national leadership. When the Persians came again, ten years later, almost all the Greek states accepted this – even Athens, whose strengthening of her fleet had made her the preponderant power of the League at sea.

The Greeks said, and no doubt believed, that the Persians came again (in 480 BCE, through Thrace) in millions; if, as now seems more likely, there were in fact well under a

Greek triremes

The navy became increasingly important for Greece's defence during the 5th century BCE. The above bas-relief shows an Athenian trireme – a warship with three rows of oars. This invention has been attributed to the Corinthians, who developed a fleet of warships in the 7th and 6th centuries BCE to protect their merchant navy.

Although the length of a wooden boat could not exceed 125 ft (38 m), because of the risk of the keel being broken out at sea, more oars were needed if speed were to be increased. The trireme solved this problem by using three tiers of rowers, arranged in a way that allowed them sufficient space to operate their oars (see illustration, below). This was also important for the defence of the vessel, as the oars could be retracted quickly when the enemy approached, with the intention of breaking them.

The trireme was a lightweight and highly-manoeuvrable boat. With a well-trained crew of 200 men, the ship could reach a speed of up to 6 miles (10 km) per hour and could easily be steered towards enemy vessels, which it attacked using its large ram.

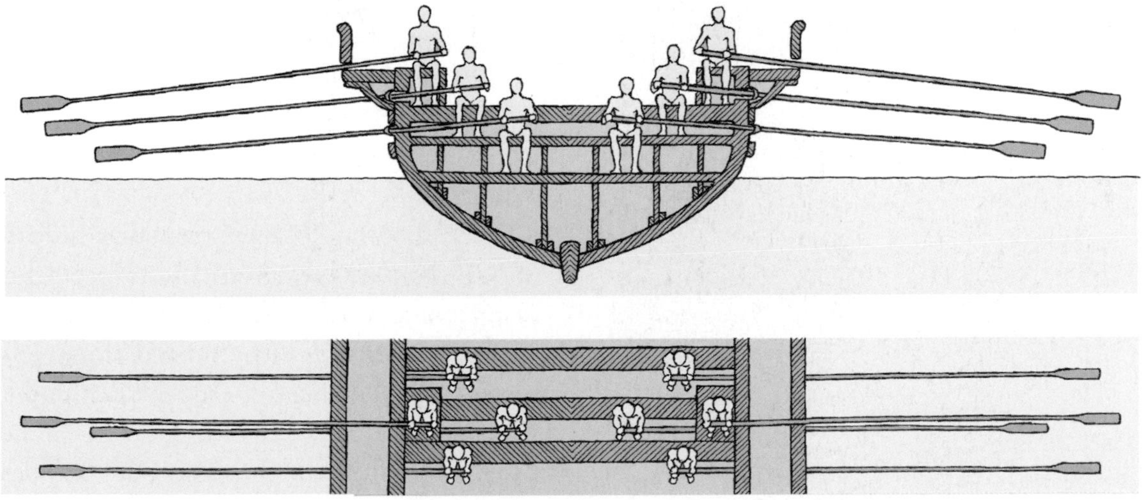

An illustration of a cross-section (above) and bird's-eye view (below) of a Greek trireme.

The Persian War: the battle for the Thermopylae Pass

"As the Persian army advanced to the assault, the Greeks under Leonidas, knowing that they were going to their deaths, went out into the wider part of the pass much further than they had done before; in the previous days' fighting they had been holding the wall and making sorties from behind it into the narrow neck, but now they fought outside the narrows. Many of the invaders fell; behind them the company commanders plied their whips indiscriminately, driving the men on. Many fell into the sea and were drowned, and still more were trampled to death by their friends. No one could count the number of the dead. The Greeks, who knew that the enemy were on their way round by the mountain track and that death was inevitable, put forth all their strength and fought with fury and desperation. By this time most of their spears were broken, and they were killing Persians with their swords.

"In the course of that fight Leonidas fell, having fought most gallantly, and many distinguished Spartans with him – their names I have learned, as those of men who deserve to be remembered..."

An extract from *The Histories* by Herodotus, translated by Aubrey de Sélincourt.

The torso of this Spartan warrior may depict the famous general Leonidas.

This Athenian Greek wine jug dates from the middle of the 5th century BCE. The red-figure painting depicts a fight between a Greek and a Persian soldier – the Greek is shown fighting in the nude, as was the custom, except for a raised Corinthian-style helmet, and is in stark contrast to his Persian enemy, who is bearded and dressed in Asian-style clothes.

hundred thousand of them (including thousands of Greeks), this was still an overwhelming disproportion for the defenders of the Greek cities. The Persian army moved slowly along the coast and down towards the Peloponnese, accompanied by a huge fleet which hung on its flanks. Yet the Greeks had important advantages in their better-armed and trained heavy infantry, a terrain which nullified the Persian cavalry superiority, and morale.

THE GREEK VICTORY OVER THE PERSIANS

The next crucial battle was at sea. It followed another legendary episode: the overwhelming of Leonidas the Spartan king and his three hundred at the pass of Thermopylae, after which Attica had to be abandoned to the Persians. The Greeks retired to the isthmus of Corinth, their fleet massed in the bay of Salamis near Athens. Time was on their side. It was autumn; a winter which would catch the Persians unprepared would soon be coming and Greek winters are severe. The Persian king threw his numerical advantage away by deciding to engage the Greek fleet in the narrow waters of Salamis. His fleet was shattered and he began a long retreat to the Hellespont. The next year the army he had left behind was defeated at Plataea and the Greeks won another great sea fight, at Mycale on the other side of the Aegean, on the same day. This was the end of the Persian War.

It was a great moment in Greek history, perhaps the greatest, and Sparta and Athens had covered themselves with glory. The liberation of Asiatic Greece followed. It opened an age of huge self-confidence for the Greeks. Their outward drive was to continue until its culmination in a Macedonian empire a century and a half later. The sense of Greek identity was at its height, and people looking back at these heroic days were to wonder later if some great chance to unite Greece as a

Poseidonia, which was later known as Paestum, was founded in the 8th century BCE in the Bay of Naples. The western façade of the Temple of Poseidon, built in around 450 BCE, is a good example of the simplicity of the Doric style that developed in Magna Graecia. The temple's architect was directly inspired by the Temple of Zeus in Olympia.

nation had not then been missed for ever. Perhaps, too, it was something more, for in the repulse of an Asian despot by Greek freemen lay the seed of a contrast often to be drawn by later Europeans, though in the fifth century BCE it existed only in the minds of a few Greeks. But myths breed future realities and centuries later other men and women would look back anachronistically to Marathon and Salamis, seeing them as the first of many victories in which Europe confronted barbarism and won.

The red-figure painting on this Attic vase depicts an armed hoplite wearing armour and leg shields and a raised Attic helmet. The vase was found in Caere and dates from c.480 BCE.

3 GREEK CIVILIZATION

Today the Temple of Hephaestus is known as the Theseum, after the images of the hero Theseus that decorate its interior. The temple, which stands on a hill above the Agora of Athens, was converted into a Christian church in the 5th century CE.

VICTORY OVER THE PERSIANS launched the greatest age of Greek history. Some have even spoken of a "Greek miracle", so high do the achievements of classical civilization appear. Yet those achievements had as their background a political history so embittered and poisoned that it ended in the extinction of the institution which sheltered Greek civilization – the city-state. Complicated though it is in detail, the story can easily be summarized.

THE DELIAN LEAGUE

For thirty years after the Greek victories at Plataea and Mycale the war with Persia dragged on, but as a background to a more important theme, a sharpening rivalry between Athens and Sparta. Survival assured, the Spartans had gone home with relief, anxious about their helots. This left Athens the undisputed leader of those states which wanted to press ahead with the liberation of other cities from the Persians. A confederation called the Delian League was formed which was to support a common fleet to fight the Persians and command of it was given to an Athenian. As time passed, the members contributed not ships but money. Some did not wish to pay up as the Persian danger declined. Athenian intervention to make sure that they did not default increased and grew harsher. Naxos, for example, which tried to leave the alliance, was besieged back into it. The League was turning gradually into an Athenian empire and the signs were the removal of its headquarters from Delos to Athens, the use of the tribute money for Athenian purposes, the imposition of resident Athenian magistrates and the transfer of important legal cases to Athenian courts. When peace was made with Persia in 449 BCE, the League continued, though its excuse had gone. At its peak, over one hundred and fifty states were paying tribute to Athens.

THE COALITION AGAINST ATHENS

Sparta had welcomed the first stages of the transfer of responsibility to Athens, happy to see others take up commitments outside its own borders. Like other states, Sparta only gradually became aware of a changing situation. When it did, this had much to do with the fact that Athenian hegemony increasingly affected the internal politics of the Greek states. They were often divided about the League, the richer, tax-paying citizens resenting the tribute, while the poorer did not; they did not have to find the money to pay it. When Athenian interventions occurred they were sometimes followed by internal revolution, the result of which was often imitation of Athenian institutions. Athens was itself living through struggles which steadily drove her in the direction of democracy. By 460 BCE, the issue at home was really settled, so that irritation over its diplomatic behaviour soon came to have an ideological flavour. Other things, too, may have added to an irritation with Athens. It was a great trading state and another big trading city, Corinth, felt itself threatened. The Boeotians were directly the subjects of Athenian aggression, too. The

The Athenian treasury in the sanctuary of Delphi was built to hold valuable offerings to Apollo from the city of Athens. These gifts were intended as a sign of the Athenians' gratitude to the god following their victory over Persia in the battle of Marathon in the year 490 BCE.

This sculpture of a dying warrior is from the sanctuary of Aphaia, Aegina. It dates from the early 5th century BCE and is one of many figures illustrating the deeds of the heroes described in Homer's accounts of the Trojan War.

materials thus accumulated for a coalition against Athens, and Sparta eventually took the lead in it by joining in a war against Athens begun in 460. Fifteen years of not very determined fighting followed and then a doubtful peace. It was only after almost another fifteen years, in 431 BCE, that there began the great internal struggle which was to break the back of classical Greece: the Peloponnesian War.

THE PELOPONNESIAN WAR

THE WAR LASTED, with interruptions, twenty-seven years, until 404 BCE. Essentially it was a struggle of land against sea. On one side was the Spartan league, with Boeotia, Macedon (an unreliable ally) and Corinth as Sparta's most important supporters; they held the Peloponnese and a belt of land separating Athens from the rest of Greece. Athens' allies were scattered around the Aegean shore, in the Ionian cities and the islands, the area it had dominated since the days of the Delian League. Strategy was dictated by the means available. Sparta's army, clearly, was best used to occupy Athenian territory and then exact submission. The Athenians could not match their enemies on land. But they had the better navy. This was in large measure the creation of a great Athenian statesman and patriot, the demagogue Pericles. On the fleet he based a

The columns of a great Doric temple constructed in about 500 BCE were incorporated into the nave walls of Syracuse cathedral, Sicily, by the builders of the later Christian church.

strategy of abandoning the Athenian countryside to annual invasion by the Spartans – it was in any case never capable of feeding the population – and withdrawing the inhabitants to the city and its port, the Piraeus, to which it was linked by two walls some five miles long, two hundred yards apart. There the Athenians could sit out the war, untroubled by bombardment or assault, which were beyond the capacities of Greek armies. Their fleet, still controlling the sea, would assure they were fed in war as in peace, by imported corn, so that blockade would not be effective.

Things did not work as well as this, because of plague within the city and the absence of leadership after Pericles's death in 429 BCE, but the basic sterility of the first ten years of the war rests on this strategical deadlock. It brought peace for a time in 421 BCE, but not a lasting one. Athenian frustrations found an outlet in the end in a scheme to carry the war further afield.

THE DEFEAT OF ATHENS

In Sicily lay the rich city of Syracuse, the most important colony of Corinth, herself the greatest of Athens' commercial rivals. To seize Syracuse would deeply wound an

The Peloponnesian War

During the war, the two most powerful Greek city-states, Sparta and Athens, created such complex alliance systems against each other that every state in the Greek world was drawn into the destructive conflict. The war was largely a battle between ground forces and naval forces. Sparta and her allies had solid and well-equipped armies, whereas Athens and the city-states on the Aegean coast had the best fleet. Although the war ended when Athens was forced to capitulate in 404 BCE, there was no true victor – the two states (and their respective allies) had torn each other apart and neither would ever fully recover from the struggle.

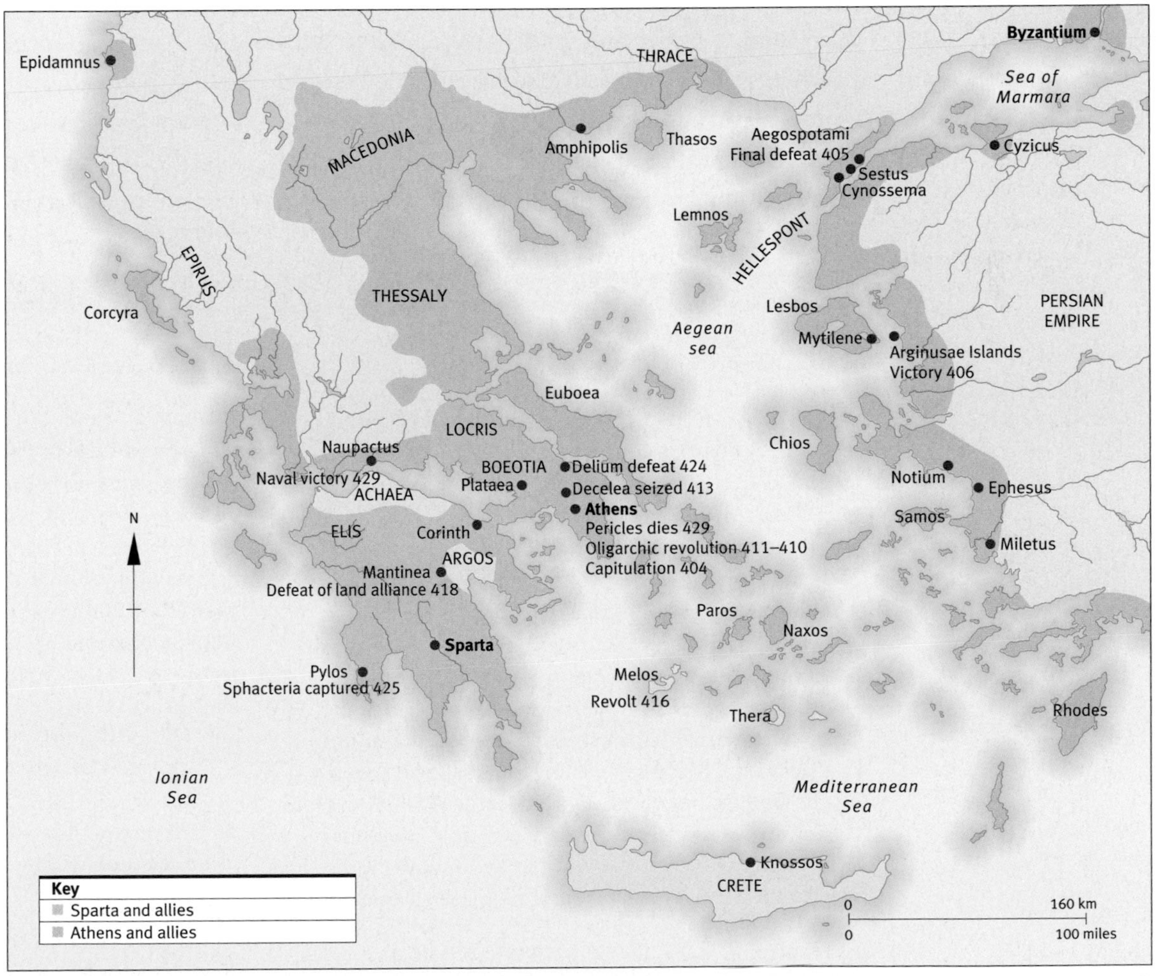

Political divisions in the Greek world during the Peloponnesian War.

The Athenian historian Thucydides (460–c.400 BCE) fought in the Peloponnesian War and narrated the conflict. His meticulous account of the war constitutes a surprisingly objective historical record. Thucydides persistently sought to expose the causes of events and to explain their outcomes.

enemy, finish off a major grain-supplier to the Peloponnese, and provide immense booty. With this wealth Athens could hope to build and man a yet bigger fleet and thus achieve a final and unquestioned supremacy in the Greek world – perhaps the mastery of the Phoenician city of Carthage and a western Mediterranean hegemony, too. The result was the disastrous Sicilian Expedition of 415–413 BCE. It was decisive, but as a death-blow to the ambitions of Athens. Half her army and all her fleet were lost; a period of political upheaval and disunion began at home. Finally, the defeat once more crystallized the alliance of Athens' enemies.

The Spartans now sought and obtained Persian help in return for a secret undertaking that the Greek cities of mainland Asia should again become vassals of Persia (as they had been before the Persian War). This enabled them to raise the fleet which could help the Athenian subject cities who wanted to shake off its imperial control. Military and naval defeat undermined morale in Athens. In 411 BCE an unsuccessful revolution replaced the democratic régime briefly with an oligarchy. Then there were more disasters, the capture of the Athenian fleet and, finally, blockade. This time starvation was decisive. In 404 BCE Athens made peace and her fortifications were slighted.

THE CONCLUSION OF THE PELOPONNESIAN WAR

Formally the story ends in 404 BCE, for what followed was implicit in the material and psychological damage the leading states of Greece had done to one another in these bitter years. There followed a brief Spartan hegemony during which she attempted to prevent the Persians cashing the promissory note on the Greek Asian cities, but this had to be conceded after a war which brought a revival of Athenian naval power and the rebuilding of the Long Walls. In the end, Sparta and Persia had a common interest in

Thucydides' *History of the Peloponnesian War*

"In peace and prosperity, states and individuals have better sentiments because they do not find themselves suddenly confronted with imperious necessities; but war takes away the easy supply of daily wants, and so proves a rough master that brings most men's characters to a level with their fortunes. Revolution thus ran its course from city to city, and the places which it arrived at last, from having heard what had been done before, carried to a still greater excess the refinement of their inventions, as manifested in the cunning of their enterprises and the atrocity of their reprisals ... Reckless audacity came to be considered the courage of a loyal ally; prudent hesitation, specious cowardice; moderation was held to be a cloak for unmanliness; ability to see all sides of a question, inaptness to act on any. Frantic violence became the attribute of manliness; cautious plotting, a justifiable means of self-defence ... Oaths of reconciliation, being only proffered on either side to meet an immediate difficulty, only held good so long as no other weapon was at hand; but when opportunity offered, he who first ventured to seize it and to take his enemy off his guard thought this perfidious vengeance sweeter than an open one, since, considerations of safety apart, success by treachery won him the palm of superior intelligence ... Thus every form of iniquity took root in the Hellenic countries by reason of the troubles ..."

An extract from Book III of the *History of the Peloponnesian War* by Thucydides, translated by Richard Crawley.

preventing a renaissance of Athenian power and made peace in 387 BCE. The settlement included a joint guarantee of all the other Greek cities except those of Asia. Ironically, the Spartans soon became as hated as the Athenians had been. Thebes took the leadership of their enemies. At Leuctra, in 371 BCE, to the astonishment of the rest of Greece, the Spartan army was defeated. It marked a psychological and military epoch in something of the same way as the battle of Jena in Prussian history over two thousand years later. The practical consequences made this clear, too; a new confederation was set up in the Peloponnese as a counterweight to Sparta on her very doorstep and the foundation of a revived Messenia in 369 BCE was another blow. The new confederation was a fresh sign that the day of the city-state was passing. The next half-century would see it all but disappear, but 369 BCE is far enough to take the story for the moment.

Such events would be tragic in the history of any country. The passage from the glorious days of the struggle against Persia to the Persians' almost effortless recouping of their losses, thanks to Greek divisions, is a rounded drama which must always grip the imagination. Another reason why such intense interest has been given to it is that it was the subject-matter of an immortal book, Thucydides' *History of the Peloponnesian War*, the first work of contemporary as well as of scientific history. But the fundamental explanation why these few years should fascinate us when greater struggles do not is because we feel that at the heart of the jumble of battles, intrigues, disasters and glory still lies an intriguing and insoluble puzzle: was there a squandering of real opportunities after Mycale, or was this long anti-climax simply a dissipation of an illusion, circumstances having for a moment seemed to promise more than in fact was possible?

This suit of armour, consisting of a bronze Corinthian-style helmet and breastplate, is similar to those that were worn by Greek soldiers during the Peloponnesian War.

FIFTH-CENTURY GREEK CIVILIZATION

THE WAR YEARS have another startling aspect, too. During them there came to fruition the greatest achievement in civilization the world had ever seen. Political and military events then shaped that achievement in certain directions and in the end limited it and determined what should continue to the future. This is why the century or so of this small country's history, whose central decades are those of the war, is worth as much attention as the millennial empires of antiquity.

At the outset we should recall how narrow a plinth supported Greek civilization. There were many Greek states, certainly,

The minting of coins continued to demonstrate the independence of the *polis*. Some coins, such as the Athenian silver tetradrachma, with its image of Athene and owl symbol, remained practically unchanged from the 6th to the 2nd century BCE.

and they were scattered over a large expanse of the Aegean, but even if Macedonia and Crete were included, the land-surface of Greece would fit comfortably into England without Wales or Scotland – and of it only about one-fifth could be cultivated. Of the states, most were tiny, containing not more than 20,000 souls at most; the biggest might have had 300,000. Within them only a small élite took part in civic life and the enjoyment of what we now think of as Greek civilization.

The other thing to be clear about at the outset is the essence of that civilization. The Greeks were far from underrating comfort and the pleasures of the senses. The physical heritage they left behind set the canons of beauty in many of the arts for two thousand years. Yet in the end the Greeks are remembered as poets and philosophers; it is an achievement of the mind that constitutes their major claim on our attention. This has been recognized implicitly in the idea of classical Greece, a creation of later ages rather than of the Greeks themselves. Certainly some Greeks of the fifth and fourth centuries BCE saw themselves as the bearers of a culture which was superior to any other available, but the force of the classical ideal lies in its being a view from a later age, one which looked back to Greece and found there standards by which to assess itself.

Later generations saw these standards above all in the fifth century, in the years following victory over the Persians, but there is a certain distortion in this. There is also an Athenian bias in such a view, for the fifth century was the apogee of Athenian cultural success. Nevertheless, to distinguish classical Greece from what went before – usually named "archaic" or "pre-classical" – makes sense. The fifth century has an objective unity because it saw a special heightening and

An Attic krater from the first half of the 5th century BCE portraying two great archaic poets from Lesbos, Sappho and Alcaeus. Both became hugely popular in Athens and their poems about love and politics were often recited at gatherings, accompanied by the music of lyres.

This krater depicts a banquet. Apart from the dancers and musicians who entertained the revellers, such festive dinners were attended exclusively by men.

intensification of Greek civilization, even if that civilization was ineradicably tied to the past, ran on into the future and spilled out over all the Greek world.

ECONOMIC FOUNDATIONS

Greek civilization was rooted still in relatively simple economic patterns; essentially, they were those of the preceding age. No great revolution had altered it since the introduction of money and for three centuries or so there were only gradual or specific changes in the direction or materials of Greek trade. Some markets opened, some closed and the technical arrangements grew slightly more elaborate as the years went by, but that was all. And trade between countries and cities was the most advanced economic sector. Below this level, the Greek economy was still nothing like as complicated as would now be taken for granted. Barter, for example, persisted for everyday purposes well into the era of coinage. It also speaks for relatively simple markets, with only limited demands made on them by the consumer. The scale of manufacture, too, was small. It has been suggested that at the height of the craze for the best Athenian pottery not more than 150 craftsmen were at work making and painting it. We are not dealing with a world of factories; most craftsmen and traders probably worked as individuals with a few employees and slaves. Even great building projects, such as the embellishment of Athens, reveal subcontracting to small groups of workers. The only exception may have been in mining, where the silver mines of Laurium in Attica might have been worked by thousands of slaves, though the arrangements under which this was done – the mines belonged to the state and were in some way sublet – remain obscure. The heart of the economy almost everywhere was subsistence agriculture. In spite of the specialized demand and production of an Athens or a Miletus (which had something of a name as a producer of woollens) the typical community depended on the production by small farmers of grain, olives, vines and timber for the home market.

A black-figure Corinthian plaque dating from the beginning of the 6th century BCE. Baked-clay plaques such as this one were offered as *ex votos*: some showed gods, others portrayed simple work scenes. Here, clay is being extracted from a pit. This was the first stage in the production of pottery – a vitally important commodity for Corinthian trade.

The decoration on this 5th-century BCE ceramic depicts preparations for a nuptial ceremony. The seated young woman is waiting for a slave to put her necklace on.

GREEK MEN

Men who worked small farms were the typical Greeks. Some were rich, most of them were probably poor by modern standards, but even now the Mediterranean climate makes a relatively low income more tolerable than it would be elsewhere. Commerce on any scale, and other kinds of entrepreneurial activity, were likely to be mainly in the hands of metics. They might have considerable social standing and were often rich men, but, for example in Athens, they could not acquire land without special permission, though they were liable for military service (which gives us a little information about their numbers, for at the beginning of the Peloponnesian War there were some 3000 who could afford the arms and armour needed to serve as hoplite infantry). The other male inhabitants of the city-state who were not citizens were either freemen or slaves.

GREEK WOMEN

Women, too, were excluded from citizenship, though it is hazardous to generalize any further about their legal rights. In Athens, for example, they could neither inherit nor own property, though both were possible in Sparta, nor could they undertake a business transaction if more than the value of a bushel of grain was involved. Divorce at the suit of the wife was, it is true, available to Athenian women, but it seems to have been rare and was probably practically much harder to

Euripides' *Trojan Women*

"All the accomplishments that bring credit to a woman I strove to put into practice in the house of Hector. In the first instance, in the matter where a woman gets a bad reputation (whether she attracts criticism or not), namely, not remaining indoors, I suppressed my longing and stayed in the house. And inside the home I would not tolerate the idle gossip of women but was content to have in my own mind a teacher I could trust. I kept a quiet tongue in my husband's presence and let no clouds pass over my face. I knew in which matters I should be superior to my husband and when it was right for me to let him prevail. And it was because my reputation for this reached the ears of the Greek army that my doom was sealed. For once I was a captive, Achilles' son wished to take me as his wife. I shall be a slave in a murderer's house.

"Now if I dismiss any thought of my beloved Hector and open my heart to my new husband, it will seem that I have betrayed the dead ..."

An extract from Andromache's speech from *Trojan Women* by Euripides, translated by John Davie.

obtain than it was by men, who seem to have been able to get rid of wives fairly easily. Literary evidence suggests that wives other than those of rich men lived, for the most part, the lives of drudges. The social assumptions that governed all women's behaviour were very restrictive; even women of the upper classes stayed at home in seclusion for most of the time. If they ventured out, they had to be accompanied; to be seen at a banquet put their respectability in question. Entertainers and courtesans were the only women who could normally expect a public life; they could enjoy a certain celebrity, but a respectable woman could not. Significantly, in classical Greece girls were thought unworthy of education. Such attitudes suggest the primitive atmosphere of the society out of which they grew, one very different from, say, Minoan Crete among its predecessors, or later Rome.

SEXUALITY IN ANCIENT GREEK CULTURE

So far as sexuality is revealed by literature, Greek marriage and parenthood could produce deep feeling and as high a mutual regard between individual men and women as in our own societies. One element in it, which is nowadays hard to weigh up exactly, was a tolerated and even romanticized male homosexuality. Convention regulated this. In many Greek cities, it was acceptable for young upper-class males to have love-affairs with older men (interestingly, there is much less evidence in Greek literature of homosexual love between men of the same age). This was not thought to disqualify them for subsequent heterosexual marriage. Something must be allowed for fashion in this, but all societies can provide examples of homosexual relationships which suit many men at one

This *kore* (a statue of a woman), dates from the beginning of the 5th century BCE and marks the move from the archaic style to classicism. *Korai* statues, many of which bear traces of polychromatism, were usually placed in sanctuaries as offerings to the gods. Male *kouroi* figures were often made as grave-markers.

Athenian education

Until they were six or seven years old, Athenian children lived at home in separate apartments inhabited exclusively by women and other children. The boys then attended school, while girls remained secluded in the house and were not given a formal education. Sons of wealthy citizens were accompanied to school by a slave, who was known as the "pedagogue".

Teachers were independent and charged parents directly for their services; they taught pupils how to read, write and count and had them learn verses by Homer and Hesiod by rote. Music lessons were also important, as were gymnastics classes, which took place in the *palestras*, where the boys were taught the main athletic exercises.

At the age of 15, youths began to attend gymnasiums where they frequented discussions with philosophers and practised athletics in preparation for military service. After the two-year course that constituted an *ephebe*, young men began their military training, often continuing to visit the gymnasium.

An illustration entitled "The poet Linos tutoring the young Mousaios" from a 5th-century BCE *dish.*

stage of their lives; those of the ancient Greeks have attracted undue attention, perhaps because of the absence of inhibitions and controls which made the expression of homosexual affection improper in other societies and because the general prestige of their civilization has rubbed off on even its minor embodiments. At root, it may only have been a function of the restrictions which segregated and circumscribed the lives of free women.

GREEK SOCIETY

In sexual matters as in everything else we know much more about the behaviour of an élite than about that of most Greeks. Citizenship, which must often have spanned very different social levels in practice, is a category too big to permit generalizations. Even in democratic Athens the kind of man who rose in public life and of whom, therefore, we read in the records, was usually a landowner; he was not likely to be a businessman, far less a craftsman. A craftsman might be important as a member of his group in the assembly, but he could hardly make his way to leadership. Businessmen may have been handicapped by the long-engrained conviction of upper-class Greeks that trade and industry were no proper occupations for a gentleman, who should ideally live a life of cultivated leisure based on the revenues of his own lands. This was a view which was to pass into European tradition with important effect.

Social history therefore blurs into politics. The Greek preoccupation with political life – the life of the *polis* – and the fact that classical Greece is neatly delimited by two distinct epochs (that of the Persian wars and that of a new, Macedonian, empire) makes it easy to

A parade of riders from one of the friezes that decorated the Parthenon of Athens. These young men, depicted taking part in a procession in honour of Athene, represented the vitality of the Athenian élite. It is likely that they commemorated the young men killed fighting for Athens and Greece against Persia at Marathon.

appreciate the importance of Greek political history to civilization. Yet to reconstruct it in any complete sense is impossible. Many, perhaps most, English parishes have records richer than those we can recover for most of the city-states of Greece. What can be discovered from the evidence is much of the history of Athens, quite a lot of that of a few other states, almost nothing of many, and a fairly full narrative of their relations with one another. Together, these facts provide us with a pretty clear picture of the political context of classical Greek civilization, but uncertainty about many of its details.

Athens dominates this picture and so there are considerable risks in arguing too readily from Athens to what was typical. What we know most about we often tend to think most important and because some of the greatest of fifth-century Greeks were Athenians and Athens is one pole of the great story of the Peloponnesian War, scholars have long given its history enormous attention. Yet we also know that Athens was – to take only two points – both big and a commercial centre; it was, therefore, untypical in very important ways.

ATHENIAN PRIMACY

THE TEMPTATION TO OVER-VALUE Athens' cultural importance is less dangerous. Such a primacy was, after all, recognized at the time. Though many of the greatest Greeks were not Athenians, and many Greeks rejected the Athenians' claims to superiority, Athenians saw themselves as leaders of Greece. Only a few of the most scrupulous among them hesitated to use the tribute of the Delian League for embellishing its leading city. Thus were built the buildings whose

The Acropolis of Athens

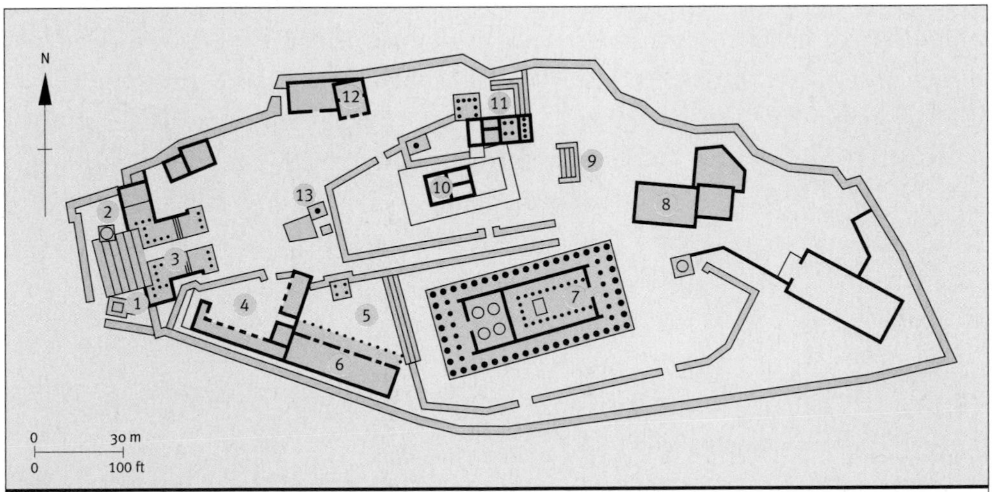

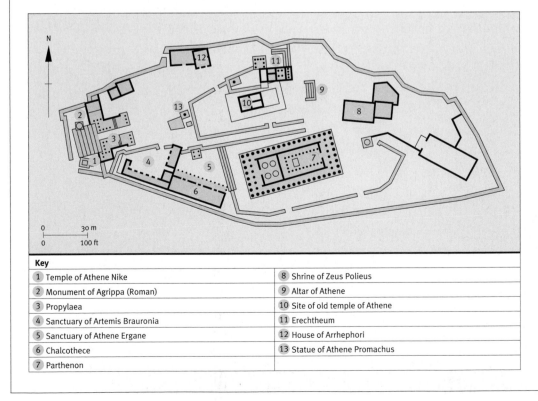

Key	
1 Temple of Athene Nike	8 Shrine of Zeus Polieus
2 Monument of Agrippa (Roman)	9 Altar of Athene
3 Propylaea	10 Site of old temple of Athene
4 Sanctuary of Artemis Brauronia	11 Erechtheum
5 Sanctuary of Athene Ergane	12 House of Arrhephori
6 Chalcothece	13 Statue of Athene Promachus
7 Parthenon	

Athens' Acropolis crowned a steep-sided, easily defensible rock, upon which various ancient buildings had once stood, including a Bronze Age Mycenaean palace. During the Classical Age, the city's main religious sanctuaries and temples were located at the site. The Acropolis was reduced to ruins during the war with Persia in the first half of the 5th century BCE. After the end of the war, the Athenian general and statesman Pericles oversaw an extensive rebuilding programme and initiated the construction of several magnificent monuments and temples, some of which were completed after his death in 429 BCE. The Romans later added to the complex.

A plan showing the main buildings in the Athenian Acropolis.

A view of the western façade of the Ionic-style temple on the Acropolis at Athens known as the Erechtheum (it originally housed the tomb of the hero Erechtheus). Building work on the temple began in 421 BCE. The olive tree in the foreground is the sacred tree of the goddess Athene, patroness of the city. On the southern façade is the famous porch of six caryatids (statues of female figures used as columns).

ruins still crown the Acropolis, the Parthenon and Propylaea, but, of course, the money spent on them was available just because so many Greek states recognized Athens' paramountcy. This reality is what the tribute lists record. When on the eve of the Peloponnesian War Pericles told his countrymen that their state was a model for the rest of Greece he was indulging in propaganda, but there was also conviction in what he said.

ATHENS' GEOGRAPHICAL ADVANTAGES

Solid grounds for the importance traditionally given to Athens ought, indeed, to be suggested *a priori* by the basic facts of geography. Her position recalls the tradition that she played an ill-defined but seemingly important role in the Ionian plantation of the Aegean and Asia Minor. Easy access to this region, together with poor agricultural resources, made her a trading and maritime power early in the sixth century. Thanks to this she was the richest of the Greek cities; at the end of it the discovery of the silver deposits of Laurium gave her the windfall with which to build the fleet of Salamis. From the fleet came her undisputed pre-eminence in the Aegean and thence, eventually, the tribute which refreshed her treasury in the fifth century. The peak of her power and wealth was reached just before the Peloponnesian War, in the years when creative activity and patriotic inspiration reached their height. Pride in the extension of empire was then linked to a cultural achievement which was truly enjoyed by the people.

THE ATHENIAN NAVY

Commerce, the navy, ideological confidence and democracy are themes as inseparably and traditionally interwoven in the history of fifth-century Athens as of late nineteenth-century England, though in very different ways. It was widely recognized at the time that a fleet of ships whose movement depended ultimately upon about two hundred paid oarsmen apiece was both the instrument of imperial power and the preserve of the democracy. Hoplites were less important in a naval state than elsewhere, and no expensive armour was needed to be an oarsman, who would be paid by the tribute of the League or the proceeds of successful warfare – as it was hoped, for example, the Sicilian Expedition would prove. Imperialism was genuinely popular among Athenians who would expect to share its profits, even if only indirectly and collectively, and not to have to bear its burdens. This was an aspect of Athenian democracy which was given much attention by its critics.

This red-figure Attic cup was painted by Brygos at the beginning of the 5th century BCE and depicts an Athenian democratic voting session. Athene presides over the scene, wearing her emblematic helmet and surrounded by citizens who are about to vote.

ATHENIAN DEMOCRACY

ATTACKS ON ATHENIAN DEMOCRACY began in early times and have continued ever since. They have embodied as much historical misrepresentation as have over-zealous and idealizing defences of the same institutions. The misgivings of frightened conservatives who had never seen anything like it before are understandable, for democracy emerged at Athens unexpectedly and at first almost unobserved. Its roots lay in sixth-century constitutional changes which replaced the organizing principle of kinship with that of locality; in theory and law, at least, local attachment came to be more important than the family you belonged to. This was a development which appears to have been general in Greece and it put democracy on the localized institutional basis which it has usually

Basic institutions and democracy at work in Athens

ECCLESIA: An assembly composed of all Athenian citizens, which met at least 40 times per year. Only those who were 18 years old or over, male, free and of Athenian parents could be citizens, which meant that a large portion of the population was excluded from public life. The *ecclesia* took decisions concerning important affairs – decrees were voted on following a public discussion.
BOULE: A council formed by 500 citizens, all over 30 years old and generally with public experience, chosen by a draw. The *boule* prepared the work to be carried out by the *ecclesia*, studying the drafts for laws. It also controlled foreign policy and the administration of the city. The *boule* was divided into ten sections, called *prytaneas*, which rotated during the year. The acting councillors were called *prytaneans*.
MAGISTRATES: Magistrates wielded considerable power. Candidates underwent a detailed interrogation by the *boule* about their morality. Most posts were assigned by a draw. The magistrates' work consisted of guaranteeing the administration of the various public services and making sure that the decisions taken by the *ecclesia* and the *boule* were carried out. Among the elected magistrates, the strategists were extremely powerful because they were heads of the army and the navy and intervened in matters concerning war and peace. Although magistrates could only stay in office for one year, there was no limit to the number of times they could be re-elected and, if they had exceptional administrative abilities or oratory skills, individuals were often able to prolong their term of office. The famous general Pericles, for example, served as a magistrate for 30 years.
DIKASTERIA: A popular tribune formed by 6,000 jurists. The jurists were assigned annually by a draw from candidates who were more than 30 years old.

These pieces of pottery are *ostrakas*, on which voters wrote the name of a citizen to be ostracized (exiled from Athens) for 10 years. Intended to restrict the power of individuals in 5th-century BCE Athens, ostracism could be misused – it became evident that intrigue limited its effectiveness.

had ever since. Other changes followed from this. By the middle of the fifth century all adult males were entitled to take part in the assembly and through it, therefore, in the election of major administrative officers. The powers of the Areopagus were steadily reduced; after 462 BCE it was only a law court with jurisdiction over certain offences. The other courts were at the same time rendered more susceptible to democratic influence by the institution of payment for jury service. As they also conducted much administrative business, this meant a fair amount of popular participation in the daily running of the city. Just after the Peloponnesian War, when times were hard, pay was also offered for attendance at the assembly itself. Finally, there was the Athenian belief in selecting by lot; its use for the choice of magistrates told against hereditary prestige and power.

POLITICIANS

At the root of the Athenian constitution lay distrust of expertise and entrenched authority and confidence in collective common sense. From this derived, no doubt, the relative lack of interest Athenians showed in rigorous jurisprudence – argument in an Athenian court was occupied much more with questions of motive, standing and substance, than with questions of law – and the importance they gave to the skills of oratory. The effective political leaders of Athens were those who could sway their fellow citizens by their words. Whether we call them demagogues or orators does not matter; they were the first politicians seeking power by persuasion.

Towards the end of the fifth century, though even then by no means usually, some such men came from families outside the traditional ruling class. The continuing importance of old political families was nevertheless an important qualification of the democratic system. Themistocles at the beginning of the century and Pericles when the war began were members of old families, their birth making it proper for them even in the eyes of conservatives to take the lead in affairs; the old ruling classes found it easier to accept democracy because of this practical qualification of it. There is a rough parallel in the grudging acceptance of Whig reform by nineteenth-century English aristocrats; government in Athens as in Victorian England remained for a long time in the hands of men whose forefathers might have expected to rule the state in more aristocratic days.

Another tempering qualification was provided by the demands of politics on time and money. Though jurors and members of the assembly might be paid, the fee for attendance was small; it seems to have been prompted, too, by the need to make sure of a quorum, which does not suggest that the assembly found it easy to get the mass of the citizens to attend. Many of them must have lived too far away and it has been calculated that not

Athenian democracy

"Our constitution does not copy the laws of neighbouring states; we are rather a pattern to others than imitators ourselves. Its administration favours the many instead of the few; this is why it is called a democracy. If we look to the laws, they afford equal justice to all in their private differences; if to social standing, advancement in public life falls to reputation for capacity, class considerations not being allowed to interfere with merit; nor again does poverty bar the way, if a man is able to serve the state, he is not hindered by the obscurity of his condition. The freedom which we enjoy in our government extends also to our ordinary life. There, far from exercising a jealous surveillance over each other, we do not feel called upon to be angry with our neighbour for doing what he likes, or even to indulge in those injurious looks which cannot fail to be offensive, although they inflict no positive penalty. But all this ease in our private relations does not make us lawless as citizens. Against this, fear is our chief safeguard, teaching us to obey the magistrates and the laws, particularly such as regard the protection of the injured, whether they are actually on the statute book, or belong to that code which, although unwritten, yet cannot be broken without acknowledged disgrace."

An extract from the funeral oration by Pericles from Book II of the *History of Peloponnesian War* by Thucydides, translated by Richard Crawley.

more than about one in eight of them were present at the usual statutory meetings, of which some forty were held each year. These facts tend to be lost to sight both in the denunciation and the idealization of Athenian democracy and they go some way to explaining its apparent mildness. Taxation was light and there was little discriminatory legislation against the rich, such as we would now associate with democratic rule and such as Aristotle said would be the inevitable result of the rule of the poor.

FOREIGN POLICY

Even in its emergent period Athenian democracy was identified with adventure and enterprise in foreign policy. Popular demand lay behind support for the Greek cities of Asia in their revolt against Persia. Later, for understandable reasons, it gave foreign policy an anti-Spartan bias. The struggle against the Areopagus was led by Themistocles, the builder of the Athenian fleet of Salamis, who had sensed a potential danger from Sparta from the moment the Persian War was over. Thus the responsibility for the Peloponnesian War, and for its exacerbation of the factions and divisions of all the other cities of Greece, came to be laid at the door of democracy. It not only brought disaster upon Athens itself, its critics pointed out, but exported to or at least awoke in all the Greek cities the bitterness of faction and social conflict. Oligarchy was twice restored in Athens – not that it helped matters – and by the end of the century faith in Athenian decmocracy was grievously weakened. Thucydides could take his history only down to 411 BCE but it closes in misgiving and disillusion over his native city – which had exiled him – and Plato was to imprint for ever upon the Athenian democrats the stigma of the execution of his teacher Socrates in 399 BCE.

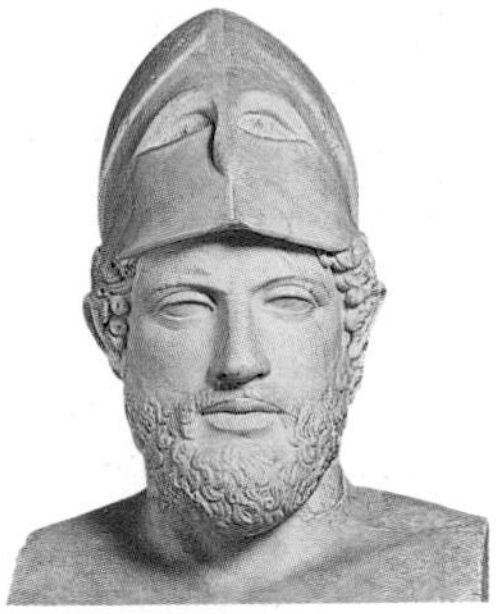

The Athenian politician Pericles was a decisive force in democratic Athenian politics for 30 years. This bust of Pericles is a Roman copy of an original by Cresilas made at the end of the 5th century BCE. The helmet alludes to Pericles' strategic skills and his regular features recall the idealized portrayal of classical figures.

To cast their votes, the Athenians used small bronze pieces or clay tablets such as these. The tiny handles on each piece were hollow or solid, depending on whether the vote was for an acquittal or a conviction.

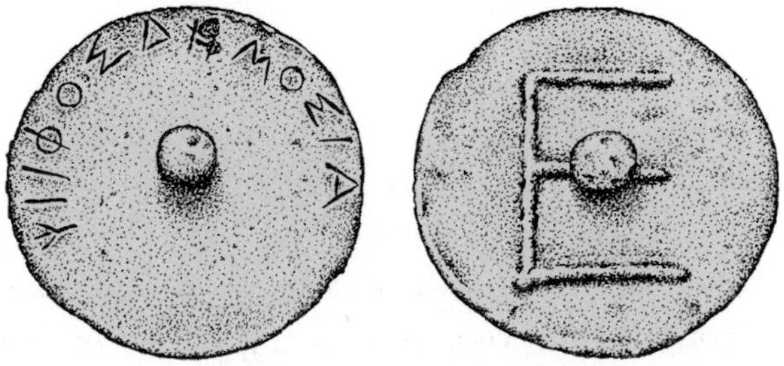

THE ACHIEVEMENTS OF ATHENIAN DEMOCRACY

If Athenian democracy's exclusion of women, metics and slaves is also placed in the scale, the balance against it seems heavy; to modern eyes, it looks both narrow and disastrously unsuccessful. Yet it should not disqualify Athens for the place she later won in the regard of posterity. Anachronistic and invalid comparisons are too easy; Athens is not to be compared with ideals still imperfectly realized after two thousand years, but with her contemporaries. For all the survival of the influence of the leading families and the practical impossibility that even a majority of its members would turn up to any particular meeting of the assembly, more Athenians were engaged in self-government than was the case in any other state. Athenian democracy more than any other institution brought about the liberation of men from the political ties of kin which is one of the great Greek achievements. Many who could not have contemplated office elsewhere could experience in Athens the political education of taking responsible decisions which is the heart of political culture. Men of modest means could help to run the institutions which nurtured and protected Athens' great civilized achievement. They listened to arguments of an elevation and thoughtfulness which makes it impossible to dismiss them as mere rhetoric; they must surely have weighed them seriously *sometimes*. Just as the physical divisions between the old Greek communities fostered a variety of experience which led in the end to a break with the world of god-given rulers and a grasp of the idea that political arrangements could be consciously chosen, so the stimulus of participation in affairs worked on unprecedentedly large numbers of men in classical Athens, not only in the assembly, but in the daily meetings of the people's council which prepared its business. Even without the eligibility of all citizens to office Athenian democracy would still have been the greatest instrument of political education contrived down to that time.

A fragment of the Parthenon's east frieze, sculpted in 442–432 BCE, depicting Hephaestus, Apollo and Artemis. This group of divinities is one of those which, together with the frieze on the Parthenon's main façade, greeted the long procession of the Panathenaea, in which the whole city of Athens took part.

It is against that background that the errors, vanities and misjudgments of Athenian politics must be seen. We do not cease to treasure the great achievements of British political culture because of the shallowness and corruptness of much of modern democracy. Athens may be judged, like any political system, by its working at its best; under the leadership of Pericles it was outstanding. It left to posterity the myth of the individual's responsibility for his own political fate. We need myths in politics and have yet to find a better.

THE CONCEPT OF "VIRTUE"

The Athenians, in any case, would have been uninterested in many modern criticisms of their democracy. Its later defenders and attackers have both often fallen into another sort of anachronism, that of misinterpreting the goals Greeks thought worth achieving. Greek democracy, for example, was far from being dominated, as is ours, by the mythology of cooperativeness, and cheerfully paid a larger price in destructiveness than would be welcomed today. There was a blatant competitiveness in Greek life apparent from the Homeric poems onwards. Greeks admired men who won and thought men should strive to win. The consequent release of human power was colossal, but also dangerous. The ideal expressed in the much-used word which we inadequately translate as "virtue" illustrates this. When Greeks used it, they meant that people were able, strong, quick-witted, as much as they were just, principled, or virtuous in a modern sense. Homer's hero, Odysseus, frequently behaved like a rogue, but he is brave and clever and he succeeds; he is therefore admirable. To show such quality was good; it did not matter that the social cost might sometimes be high. The Greek was concerned with image; his culture taught him to avoid shame rather than guilt and the fear of shame was never far from the fear of public evidence of guilt. Some of the explanation of the bitterness of faction in Greek politics lies here; it was a price willingly paid.

When all is said, Athenian democracy must be respected above all for what it cradled, a series of cultural triumphs which are peaks even in the history of Greek civilization. These were public facts. The art of Athens was applauded and sustained by many people; the tragedies were tested not by the takings of a box office but by

This bronze statue is known as the Ephebe of Anticiterea because it was found among the cargo of a boat that was shipwrecked off this small island, northeast of Crete. The piece dates from the 4th century BCE. The figure's raised right arm has given rise to a number of interpretations: a winning athlete, a ball player, maybe Paris with the apple, or Perseus with the Medusa's head.

judges interpreting a public taste vigorously expressed. The sculptor Phidias worked to beautify the city and not for an individual patron. And as democracy degenerated, so it seems, there was a waning of artistic nerve. This was a loss to the whole of Greece.

PHILOSOPHICAL QUESTIONING

The achievement which made Greece teacher of Europe (and through it of the world) is too rich and varied to generalize about even in long and close study; it is impossible to summarize in a page or so. But there is a salient theme which emerges in it: a growing confidence in rational, conscious enquiry. If civilization is advance towards the control of mentality and environment by reason, then the Greeks did more for it than any of their predecessors. They invented the philosophical question as part and parcel of one of the great intuitions of all time, that a coherent and logical explanation of things could be found, that the world did not ultimately rest upon the meaningless and arbitrary fiat of gods or demons. Put like that, of course, it is not an attitude which could be or was grasped by all, or even most, Greeks. It was an attitude which had to make its way in a world permeated with irrationality and superstition. Nevertheless, it was a revolutionary and beneficial idea. It looked forward to the possibility of a society where such an attitude would be generalized; even Plato, who thought it impossible that most people could share it, gave to the rulers of his ideal state the task of rational reflection as the justification both of their privileges and of the discipline laid upon them. The Greek challenge to the weight of irrationality in social and intellectual activity tempered its force as it had never been tempered before. For all the subsequent exaggeration and myth-making about it, the liberating effect of this emphasis was felt again and again for thousands of years. It was the greatest single Greek achievement.

The work of the dramatic poet Aeschylus (525–456 BCE), including the famous Oresteia Trilogy, explored his belief that humanity's destiny was decided by supernatural forces.

POPULAR SUPERSTITION

The enormity of the revolution in modes of thought in the Aegean means that it now obscures its own scale. So remarkable are the works of the Greek intellectuals and so large have they loomed that it requires effort to penetrate through them to the values of the world from which they emerged. It is made a little easier because no such revolution is ever complete. A look at the other side of the coin reveals that most Greeks continued to live in cocoons of traditional irrationality and superstition; even those who were in a position to understand something of the speculations which were opening new mental worlds rarely accepted the implications. A continuing respect was shown to the old public orthodoxies. It was impiety in late fifth-century Athens, for example, to deny belief in the gods. One philosopher believed that the sun was a red-hot disc; it did not protect him that he had been the friend of Pericles when he said so, and he had to flee. It was at Athens, too, that public opinion was convulsed, on the eve of the Sicilian Expedition, by the mysterious and ominous mutilation of certain public statues, the "Hermae", or busts of Hermes. The disasters which followed were attributed by some to this sacrilege. Socrates, the Athenian philosopher who became, thanks to his pupil

Plato, the archetypal figure of the man of intellect, and left as a maxim the view that "the unexamined life is not worth living", offended the pieties of his state and was condemned to die for it by his fellow citizens; he was also condemned for questioning received astronomy. It does not seem that similar trials took place elsewhere, but they imply a background of popular superstition which must have been more typical of the Greek community than the presence of a Socrates.

GREEK THOUGHT

In spite of important historical residues, Greek thought, more than that of any earlier civilization, reflected changes of emphasis and fashion. They arose from its own dynamism and did not always lead to a greater ability to grapple with nature and society rather than surrender to them, but sometimes to dead ends and blind alleys, to exotic and extravagant fantasies. Greek thought is not monolithic; we should think not of a bloc with a unity pervading all its parts, but of a historical continuum extending across three or four centuries, in which different elements are prominent at different times and which is hard to assess.

One reason for this is that Greek categories of thought – the way, so to speak, in which they laid out the intellectual map before beginning to think about its individual components in detail at all – are not our own, though often deceptively like them. Some of those we use did not exist for the Greeks and their knowledge led them to draw different boundaries between fields of enquiry from those which we take for granted. Sometimes this is obvious and presents no difficulties; when a philosopher, for example, locates the

The ruins of the temple of Apollo and its foundations in the sanctuary at Delphi. The temple's altar was situated in front of these restored columns. The details of the inner design, where the famous oracle of the god Apollo was consulted, can still be discerned.

Miletus

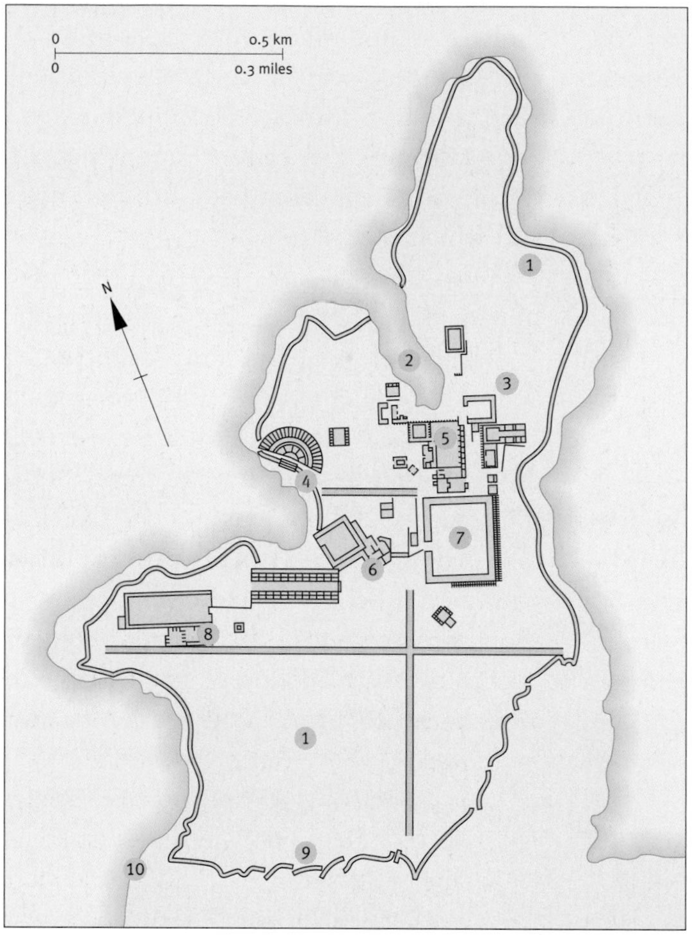

Key
1 Residential quarters
2 Lion Bay
3 Delphinium
4 Theatre
5 North Agora
6 Baths
7 South Agora
8 Temple of Athene
9 City walls
10 Ancient coastline

Located at the mouth of the Maeander River on the Aegean coast, Miletus was once the most important Greek city in Asia. Its remains also testify to the fact that it was a major centre of philosophical and scientific thought in the 6th century BCE.

A plan of the classical city of Miletus.

Today the theatre at Miletus, built in the Hellenistic period and altered on many occasions, preserves the appearance that it was given by the Romans. It was the largest theatre in Asia and could seat 15,000 spectators.

The Great Gate of the south Agora of Miletus, of which this is a detail, was built in the 1st century CE. This is a good example of Hellenistic architecture – the monumental façade is organized independently from the structure and floor plan of the building.

A Roman bust of the philosopher Socrates, who was born in 470 BCE in Athens. Socrates' teachings are known to us through the work of his disciple Plato.

management of the household and its estate (economics) as a part of a study of what we should call politics, we are not likely to misunderstand him. In more abstract topics it can cause trouble.

GREEK SCIENCE

FOR US, SCIENCE SEEMS TO BE an appropriate way of approaching the understanding of the physical universe, and its techniques are those of empirical experiment and observation. Greek thinkers found the nature of the physical universe just as approachable through abstract thought, as through metaphysics, logic and mathematics. It has been said that Greek rationality actually came in the end to stand in the way of scientific progress, because enquiry followed logic and abstract deduction, rather than the observation of nature. Among the great Greek philosophers, only Aristotle gave prominence to collecting and classifying data, and he did this for the most part only in his social and biological studies. This is one reason for not separating the history of Greek science and philosophy too violently. They are a whole, the product of scores of cities and developing across four centuries or so in time.

THE MILETAN SCHOOL

The beginnings of Greek science and philosophy constitute a revolution in human thought and it has already taken place when there appear the earliest Greek thinkers of whom we have information. They lived in the Ionian city of Miletus in the seventh and sixth centuries BCE. Important intellectual activity went on there and in other Ionian cities right down to the remarkable age of Athenian speculation which begins with Socrates. No doubt the stimulus of an Asian background was important here as in so many other ways

A view of the ruins of Miletus, in present-day Turkey. In the background stands the Nymphaion, which dates from the 2nd century CE. In the foreground lie the remains of Corinthian capitals, decorated with acanthus leaves.

in getting things started; it may also have been significant that Miletus was a rich place; early thinkers seem to have been rich men who could afford the time to think. None the less, the early emphasis on Ionia gives way before long to a spectrum of intellectual activity going on all over the Greek world. The western settlements of Magna Graecia and Sicily were crucial in many sixth- and fifth-century developments and primacy in the later Hellenistic age was to go to Alexandria. The whole Greek world was involved in the success of the Greek mind and even the great age of Athenian questioning should not be given exaggerated standing within it.

In the sixth century BCE Thales and Anaximander launched at Miletus the conscious speculation about the nature of the universe which shows that the crucial boundary between myth and science has been crossed. Egyptians had set about the practical manipulation of nature and had learned much inductively in the process, while Babylonians had made important measurements. The Miletan school made good use of this information, and possibly took more fundamental cosmological notions from the old civilizations, too; Thales is said to have held that the earth had its origin in water. Yet the Ionian philosophers soon went beyond their inheritance. They set out a general view of the nature of the universe which replaced myth with impersonal explanation. This is more impressive than the fact that the specific answers they put forward were in the end to prove unfruitful. The Greek analysis of the nature of matter is an example. Although an atomic theory was adumbrated which was over two thousand years before its time, this was by the fourth century rejected in favour of a view, based on that of the early Ionian thinkers, that all matter was composed of four "elements" – air, water, earth, fire – which combined in different proportions in different substances. This theory subsequently shaped western science down to the Renaissance. It was of enormous historical importance because of the boundaries it set and the possibilities it opened. It was also, of course, erroneous.

LEGACY OF IONIAN TRADITION

The fear that the theory of the elements was wrong should be firmly kept in place as a secondary consideration at this point. What mattered about the Ionians and the school they founded was what has rightly been called their "astonishing" novelty. They pushed aside gods and demons from the understanding of nature. Time was to overwhelm some of what they had done, it is true. In Athens in the late fifth century more than a temporary alarm in the face of defeat and danger has been seen in the condemnation as blasphemous of views far less daring than those of Ionian thinkers two centuries before. One of them had said "If the ox could paint a picture, his god would look like an ox"; a few centuries later, classical Mediterranean civilization has lost much of such perceptiveness. Its early appearance is the most striking sign of the vigour of Greek civilization.

Not only popular superstition swamped such ideas. Other philosophical tendencies also played a part. One coexisted with the Ionian tradition for a long time and was to have much longer life and influence. Its crux was the view that reality was immaterial, that, as Plato later put it in one of its most persuasive expressions, in life we experience only the images of pure Form and Ideas, which are the heavenly embodiments of true reality. That reality was only to be apprehended by thought, though not only by systematic speculation, but by intuition too. For all its immateriality, this kind of thinking also had its roots in Greek science, though not in the speculations of the Ionians about matter but in the activities of mathematicians.

The philosopher Pythagoras was born in the 6th century BCE in Samos. He later settled in the Sicilian city of Crotone, where he founded a philosophical school that operated in a similar way to a religious sect.

MATHEMATICS

Some of the Greek mathematicians' greatest advances were not to be made until long after Plato's death, when they would round off what is the single biggest triumph of Greek thought, its establishment of most of the arithmetic and geometry which served western civilization down to the seventeenth century. Every schoolboy used to know the name of Pythagoras, who lived at Crotone in southern Italy in the middle of the sixth century and may be said to have founded the deductive proof. Fortunately or unfortunately, he did more than this. He discovered the mathematical basis of harmonics by studying a vibrating string and he became especially interested in the relationship of numbers and geometry. His approach to them was semi-mystical; Pythagoras, like many mathematicians, was a religiously minded man who is said to have celebrated the satisfactory conclusion of his famous proof by sacrificing an ox. His school – there was a secret Pythagorean "Brotherhood" – later came to hold that the ultimate nature of the universe was mathematical and numerical. "They fancied that the principles of mathematics were the principles of all things," reported Aristotle, somewhat

Hippocrates

Hippocrates was born into a family of doctors on the island of Cos in around 460 BCE. At a time when the treatment of illnesses was mainly governed by superstition, Hippocrates claimed that medicine was a science that should be taught and discussed openly. The teachers from the medical school he established at Cos published a large number of texts, of which around 70 have survived, under the name of Hippocrates. Although none of the published works are believed actually to have been written by Hippocrates, their contents are clearly influenced by his scientific research and teaching. Topics covered include women and children's illnesses, dietary and drug treatments, surgery and medical ethics. Although the texts attributed to him have now been scientifically surpassed, the work of Hippocrates still contains a lucid analysis of contemporary medicine and medical practice.

A detail from the Roman fresco "Galenus and Hippocrates" from the crypt of a church in Anagni, Latium, depicting Hippocrates – the "father of medicine".

disapprovingly, yet his own teacher, Plato, had been greatly influenced by this belief, and by the scepticism of Parmenides, an early fifth-century Pythagorean, about the world known to the senses. Numbers seemed more attractive than the physical world; they possessed both the defined perfection and the abstraction of the Idea which embodied reality.

ASTRONOMY

Pythagorean influence on Greek thought is an immense subject; fortunately, it need not be summarized. What matters here is its ultimate repercussions in a view of the universe which, because it was constructed on mathematical and deductive principles, rather than from observation, fixed astronomy on the wrong lines for nearly two thousand years. From it came the vision of a universe built up of successively enclosing spheres on which moved sun, moon and planets in a fixed and circular pattern about the earth. The Greeks noticed that this did not seem to be the way the heavens moved in practice. But, to summarize crudely, appearances were saved by introducing more and more refinements into the basic scheme while refusing to scrutinize the principles from which it was deduced. The final elaborations were not achieved until work in the second century CE by a famous Alexandrian, Ptolemy. These efforts were remarkably successful, and only a few dissentients demurred (which shows that other intellectual outcomes were possible in Greek science). For all the inadequacies of Ptolemy's system, predictions of planetary movement could be made which would still serve as adequate guides for oceanic navigation in the age of Columbus, even if they rested on misconceptions which sterilized cosmological thinking until his day.

Both the theory of the four elements

List of the major Greek philosophers

Pre-Socratic
Thales of Miletus (6th century BCE, first half)
Anaximander of Miletus (6th century BCE, first half)
Anaximenes of Miletus (6th century BCE, second half)
Xenophanes of Colophon (6th century BCE, second half)
Pythagoras of Samos (6th century BCE, second half)
Parmenides of Elea (5th century BCE, first half)
Heraclitus of Ephesus (5th century BCE, first half)
Empedocles of Acragas (5th century BCE, middle)
Anaxagoras of Clazomenae (5th century BCE, middle)
Leucippus (5th century BCE, middle)
Democritus (5th century BCE, middle)
Zeno of Elea (5th century BCE, middle)
Hippasus of Metapontum (5th century BCE, middle)
Sophists
Protagoras of Abdera (5th century BCE, middle)
Gorgias of Leontini (5th century BCE, middle)
Thrasymachus of Challedon (5th century BCE, second half)

Classical
Socrates (470–399 BCE)
Plato (c.427–c.347 BCE)
Aristotle (384–322 BCE)
Hellenistic
Stoics
Zeno of Citium (c.335–c.264 BCE)
Cleanthes (304–233 BCE)
Chrysippus (c.281–c.205 BCE)
Epicureans
Epicurus (341–270 BCE)
Skeptics
Pyrrho of Elis (c.365–c.275 BCE)
Sextus Empiricus (3rd century CE, first half)

The philosopher Plato (c.427–347 BCE) was one of Socrates' disciples. Plato disseminated his philosophy through his writing. He also gave classes at a gymnasium dedicated to the hero Academus, on the outskirts of Athens, from which his school, the Academy, took its name.

and the development of Greek astronomy illustrate the deductive bias of Greek thought and its characteristic weakness, its urge to set out a plausible theory to account for the widest possible range of experience without submitting it to the test of experiment. It affected most fields of thought which we now think to be covered by science and philosophy. Its fruits were on the one hand argument of unprecedented rigour and acuteness and on the other an ultimate scepticism about sense-data. Only the Greek doctors, led by the fifth-century Hippocrates, made much of empiricism.

PLATO

IN THE CASE of Plato – and, for good or ill, philosophical discussion has been shaped more by him and his pupil Aristotle than by any other two men – this bias may have been reinforced by his low opinion of what he observed. By birth an aristocratic Athenian, Plato turned away from the world of practical affairs in which he had hoped to take part, disillusioned with the politics of the Athenian democracy and, in particular, with its treatment of Socrates, whom it had condemned to death. From Socrates Plato had learnt not only his Pythagoreanism but an idealist approach to ethical questions, and a technique of philosophical enquiry. The Good, he thought, was discoverable by enquiry and intuition; it was reality. It was the greatest of a series of "ideas" – Truth, Beauty, Justice were others – which were not ideas in the sense that at any moment they had shape in anyone's mind (as one might say "I have an idea about that"), but were real entities, enjoying a real existence in a world fixed and eternal, of which such ideas were the elements. This world of changeless reality, thought Plato, was hidden from us by the senses, which deceived us and misled us. But it was accessible to the soul, which could understand it by the use of reason.

Such ideas had a significance going far

beyond technical philosophy. In them (as in the doctrines of Pythagoras) can be found, for example, traces of a familiar later idea, fundamental to puritanism, that a human being is irreconcilably divided between the soul, of divine origin, and the body which imprisons it. Not reconciliation, but the victory of one or another, must be the outcome. It was an idea which would pass into Christianity with enormous effect. Immediately, Plato had an intensely practical concern since he believed that knowledge of the Ideal world of universals and reality could be helped or hindered by the arrangements under which people lived.

THE REPUBLIC

Plato set out his views in a series of dialogues between Socrates and people who came to argue with him. They were the first textbooks of philosophical thinking and the one we call *The Republic* was the first book in which anyone had ever set out a scheme for a society directed and planned to achieve an ethical goal. It describes an authoritarian state (reminiscent of Sparta) in which marriages would be regulated to produce the best genetic results, families and private property would not exist, culture and the arts would be censored and education carefully supervised. The few who ruled this state would be those of sufficient intellectual and moral stature to fit them for the studies which would enable them to realize the just society in practice by apprehending the Ideal world. Like Socrates, Plato held that wisdom was the understanding of reality and he assumed that to see truth ought to make it impossible not to act in accordance with it. Unlike his teacher, he held that for most people education and the laws should impose exactly that unexamined life which Socrates had thought not worth living. *The Republic* and its arguments were to provoke centuries of discussion and imitation, but this was true of almost all Plato's work. As a twentieth-century English philosopher put it, practically all subsequent

Plato's *The Republic*

"... it is obvious that the elder must govern, and the younger be governed."
"That is obvious."
"And again that those who govern must be the best of them."
"That's equally obvious."
"And the best farmers are those who have the greatest skill at farming, are they not?"
"Yes."
"And so if we want to pick the best Guardians, we must pick those who have the greatest skill in watching over the community."
"Yes."
"For that shan't we need men who, besides being intelligent and capable, really care for the community?"
"True."
"But we care most for what we love."
"Inevitably."
"And the deepest affection is based on identity of interest, when we feel that our own good and ill fortune is completely bound up with that of something else."
"That is so."
"So we must choose from among our Guardians those who appear to us on observation to be most likely to devote their lives to doing what they judge to be in the interest of the community, and who are never prepared to act against it."

An extract from Book III of *The Republic* by Plato, translated by Desmond Lee.

philosophy in the West was a series of footnotes to Plato. In spite of Plato's distaste for what he saw about him and the prejudice it engendered in him, he anticipated almost all the great questions of philosophy, whether they concerned morals, aesthetics, the basis of knowledge, or the nature of mathematics, and he set out his ideas in great works of literature, which have always been read with pleasure and excitement.

Aristotle (384–322 BCE) founded a philosophical school, the Lyceum, which was attended by a large number of followers. He was also Alexander the Great's tutor.

ARISTOTLE

THE ACADEMY which Plato founded has some claim to be the first university. From it emerged his pupil Aristotle, a thinker more comprehensive and balanced, less sceptical of the possibilities of the actual, and less adventurous than he. Aristotle never altogether rejected his master's teaching but he departed from it in fundamental ways. He was a great classifier and collector of data (with a special interest in biology) and did not reject sense experience as did Plato. Indeed, he sought both firm knowledge and happiness in the world of experience, rejecting the notion of universal ideas and arguing inductively from facts to general laws. Aristotle was so rich a thinker and interested in so many sides of experience that his historical influence is as hard to delimit as that of Plato. What he wrote provided a framework for the discussion of biology, physics, mathematics, logic, literary criticism, aesthetics, psychology, ethics and politics for two thousand years. He provided ways of thinking about these subjects and approaches to them which were elastic and capacious enough eventually to contain Christian philosophy. He also founded a science of deductive logic which was not displaced until the end of the nineteenth century. It is a vast achievement, different in kind but not less important than that of Plato.

THE MEAN

Aristotle's political thinking was in one sense in agreement with Plato's: the city-state was the best conceivable social form, but required reform and purification to work properly, he thought. But beyond this point he diverged greatly from his master. Aristotle saw the proper working of the *polis* as being that which would give each of its parts the role appropriate to it and that was essentially for him a matter of understanding what led in most existing states to happiness. In formulating an answer, he made use of a Greek idea to which his teaching was to give long life, that of the Mean, the idea that excellence lay in a balance between extremes. The empirical facts seemed to confirm this and Aristotle assembled greater quantities of such evidence in a systematic form than any predecessor, it seems; but in stressing the importance of facts about society, he had been anticipated by another Greek invention, that of history.

The decoration on this ceramic piece depicts an imaginary dialogue between the great philosopher Plato and his student Aristotle.

This scene illustrates an episode from the War of the Titans, a struggle which, according to Greek mythology, was held at the beginning of time between the gods of Olympus and the giants, sons of the Earth. This is one of the most glorious myths related in Hesiod's poetry. Here, it is used as a theme to decorate this frieze from the Great Altar of Zeus and Athene at Pergamum, erected in the 2nd century BCE.

GREEK HISTORIANS

The invention of history was another major achievement. In most countries, chronicles or annals which purport simply to record successions of events precede history. In Greece, this was not so. Historical writing in Greek emerged from poetry. Amazingly, it at once reached its highest level in its first embodiments – two books by masters who were never equalled by their successors.

HERODOTUS

The first Greek historian, Herodotus, has reasonably been termed "the father of history". The word – *historie* – existed before him; it meant enquiry. Herodotus gave it an added meaning, that of enquiry about events in time, and in putting down the results wrote the first prose work of art in a European language which survives. His stimulus was a wish to understand a near-contemporary fact, the great struggle with Persia. He accumulated information about the Persian Wars and their antecedents by reading a huge mass of the available literature and by interrogating people on his travels and assiduously recording what he was told and read. For the first time, these things became the subject of more than a chronicle. The result is his *Histories*, a remarkable account of the Persian Empire, with, built into it, much information about early Greek history and a sort of world survey, followed by an account of the Persian Wars down to Mycale. He spent much of his life travelling, having been born (it was traditionally said) in the Dorian town of Helicarnassus in southwest Asia Minor in 484 BCE. At one point he came to Athens where he remained for a few years living as a metic, and while there he may have been rewarded for public recitations of his work.

He went later to a new colony in southern Italy; there he completed his work and died, a little after 430 BCE. He therefore knew something by experience of the whole spread of the Greek world and travelled in Egypt and elsewhere as well. Thus wide experience lay behind his great book, an account scrupulously based on witnesses, even if Herodotus sometimes treated them somewhat credulously.

THUCYDIDES

It is usually conceded that one of the superiorities of Thucydides, Herodotus's greater successor, was his more rigorous approach to reports of fact and his attempts to control them in a critical way. The result is a more impressive intellectual achievement, though its austerity throws into even stronger relief the charm of Herodotus's work. Thucydides' subject was even more contemporary – the Peloponnesian War. The choice reflected deep personal involvement and a new conception. Thucydides was a member of a leading Athenian family (he served as a general until disgraced for an alleged failure in command) and he wanted to discover the causes which had brought his city and Greece into their dreadful plight. He shared with Herodotus a practical motive, for he thought (as most Greek historians were to do after him) that what he found out would have practical value, but he sought not merely to describe, but to explain.

The result is one of the most striking pieces of historical analysis ever written and the first ever to seek to penetrate through different levels of explanation. In the process he provided a model of disinterested judgment to future historians, for his Athenian loyalties rarely obtrude. The book was not completed – it takes the story only to 411 BCE – but the overall judgment is concise and striking: "the growth of Athens' power and Sparta's fear was, in my view, the cause which compelled them to go to war".

The invention of history is itself evidence of the new intellectual range of the literature created by the Greeks. It is the first complete one known to humanity. The Jewish is almost as comprehensive, but contains neither drama nor critical history, let alone the lighter genres. But Greek literature shares with the Bible a primacy shaping the whole of subsequent western writing. Besides its positive content,

The Great Sphinx of Giza represents a creature with a human head and a lion's body and was constructed in the 3rd millennium BCE. The precise religious significance of the Sphinx when it was erected, during ancient Egypt's Old Empire, remains a mystery. It was linked with the sun god and later came to be identified with the god Horus.

it imposed the major forms of literature and the first themes of a criticism by which to judge them.

POETRY AND DRAMA

FROM THE BEGINNING, as Homer shows, Greek literature was closely linked to religious belief and moral teaching. Hesiod, a poet who probably lived in the late eighth century and is usually considered to be the first Greek poet of the post-epic age, consciously addressed himself to the problem of justice and the nature of the gods, thus confirming the tradition that literature was for more than enjoyment and setting out one of the great themes of Greek literature for the next four centuries. For the Greeks, poets were always likely to be seen as teachers, their work suffused with mystical overtones, inspiration. Yet there were to be many poets, many styles of poetry in Greek. The first which can be distinguished is writing in a personal vein which was to the taste of aristocratic society. But as private patronage became concentrated during the era of the tyrants, so it passed slowly into the collective and civic area. The tyrants deliberately fostered the public festivals which were to be vehicles of the greatest specimens of Greek literary art, the tragedies. The drama's origins lie everywhere in religion and its elements must have been present in every civilization. The ritual of worship is the first theatre. Yet there, too, the Greek achievement was to press this towards conscious reflection on what was going forward; more was to be expected of the audience than passive resignation or orgiastic possession. The didactic impulse emerges in it.

TRAGEDY

The first form of the Greek drama was the dithyramb, the choral song recited at the festivals of Dionysus, together with dance and mime. In 535 BCE, we are told, this was

Greek theatre

The origin of Greek tragedy can be found in the Dionysian dithyramb – performances in which choruses sang hymns in honour of the god. The role of the chorus in early Greek drama was very important: plays consisted of a dialogue between one actor and the chorus. Later, the action became more complicated; the number of actors was increased and, in Euripides' plays, the chorus was reduced to separating the main episodes of the tragedy. The range of theatrical effects also widened.

Increasingly, playwrights made an effort to expose the characters' emotions through oratory duels between the protagonists, thus fostering the interest and empathy of the audience. The number of ancient Greek theatres that have survived to the present day suggest that the theatre-going public must have been very large and in Athens annual drama festivals were held, at which writers competed for prizes. Among the greatest of the Greek tragic writers were the famous poets Aeschylus, Sophocles and Euripides.

Comedy developed simultaneously to tragedy and in Athens the genre was eventually taken over by the state. The most significant 5th-century BCE comedy writer, Aristophanes, was followed in the next century by the highly popular comic poet, Menander.

A krater depicting a group of Greek comic actors.

The amphitheatre at Delphi, pictured here, is one of the best-preserved in Greece.

the subject of a crucial innovation, when Thespis added to it an individual actor whose speech was some kind of antiphone to the chorus. Further innovation and more actors followed and within a hundred years we have reached the full, mature theatre of Aeschylus, Sophocles and Euripides. Of their work thirty-three plays survive (including one complete trilogy), but we know that more than three hundred different tragedies were performed in the fifth century. In this drama the religious undertone is still there, though not so much in the words as in the occasions at which they would have been performed. The great tragedies were sometimes performed in trilogies at civic festivals attended by citizens who were already familiar with the basic stories (often mythological) they had come to see. This, too, suggests the educational effect. Probably most Greeks never saw a play by Aeschylus; certainly an infinitesimally small number by comparison with the number of modern English people who have seen a play of Shakespeare. None the less, those who were not too busy on their farms, or too far away, provided a large audience.

More human beings than in any other ancient society were thus able and encouraged to scrutinize and reflect upon the content of their own moral and social world. What they expected was a revealing emphasis in familiar rites, a new selection from their meaning. This is what the great dramatists mostly gave them, even if some plays went beyond this and some even, at favourable moments, satirized social pieties. It was not, of course, a naturalistic picture that was presented, but the operation of the laws of a heroic, traditional world and their agonizing impact on individuals caught in their working. In the

A 4th-century BCE bronze votive mask of the kind worn by actors performing in tragedies.

This detail is taken from a 4th-century BCE vase by the Greek painter Python. The scene depicts a performance of the *Eumenides*, the third play of the *Oresteia* trilogy, written by the tragic poet Aeschylus.

second half of the fifth century Euripides had even begun to use the conventional tragic form as a vehicle for questioning conventional assumptions; thus he inaugurated a technique to be exploited in the Western theatre by authors as late and as different as Gogol and Ibsen. The framework provided by plot, though, was familiar, and at its heart lay a recognition of the weight of inexorable law and *nemesis*. The acceptance of this setting may be thought, in the last resort, to be testimony to the irrational rather than the rational side of the Greek mind. Yet it was a long way from the state of mind in which the congregation of an eastern temple fearfully or hopefully witnessed the round of unchanging ritual and sacrifice.

COMEDY

In the fifth century the scope of the theatre was broadening in other ways. This was when Attic comedy developed as a form in its own right, and found in Aristophanes its first great manipulator of people and events for others' amusement. His material was often political, almost always highly topical, and frequently scurrilous. His survival and success is the most striking evidence we possess of the tolerance and freedom of Athenian society. A hundred years later, we have almost reached the modern world in a fashion for plays about the intrigues of slaves and troubled love-affairs. It has not the impact of Sophocles, but it can still amuse and remains a near-miracle, for there had been nothing like it two hundred years before. The rapidity with which Greek literature grew after the age of epic poetry and its enduring power is evidence of Greek powers of innovation and mental development which, even when we cannot explain it, we can still appreciate today.

These baked-clay figurines represent actors from a Greek comedy.

THE VISUAL ARTS

LITERATURE AT THE END of the classical age still had a long and important life ahead when the city-states disappeared. It had a growing audience, for Greek was to become both *lingua franca* and an official language over all the Near East and much of the Mediterranean. It was not to reach again the heights of Athenian tragedy, but it was still to show us masterpieces. The sense of decline in the visual arts is more apparent. Here, above all in monumental architecture and the nude, Greece had again set standards for the future. From the first borrowings from Asia a wholly original architecture was evolved, the classical style whose elements are still consciously evoked even by the austerities of modern builders. Within a few hundred years it spread over much of the world from Sicily to India; in this art, too, the Greeks were cultural exporters.

MONUMENTAL ARCHITECTURE

The Greeks were in one respect favoured by geology, for Greece contained much high-quality stone. Its durability is attested by the magnificence of the relics we look at today. Yet there is an illusion in this. The purity and austerity with which fifth-century Athens speaks to us in the Parthenon conceals its image in Greek eyes. We have lost the garish statues of gods and goddesses, the paint and ochre and the clutter of monuments, shrines and *stelae* that must have encumbered the Acropolis and obscured the simplicity of its temples. The reality of many great Greek centres may have been more like, say, modern Lourdes; in approaching, for example, the Temple of Apollo at Delphi, the impression gained can easily be of a jumble of untidy little shrines cluttered by traders, booths, and the rubbish of superstition (though we must also make allowances for the contribution made by the archaeologist to this).

None the less, this qualification made,

Greek architecture

The remains of temples are the most impressive surviving examples of classical Greek architecture. Although each temple tends to have a standard ground plan, the elevation usually belongs to one of the two main orders of Greek architecture, the Doric and the Ionic. At first, the two orders were unevenly distributed in geographical terms: the Doric in mainland Greece, Sicily and southern Italy, and the Ionic in Anatolia and the Aegean islands. Later, from the 5th century BCE onwards, the movement of populations and political affinities between cities allowed greater exchange.

The Doric style, which is more severe, can be primarily distinguished by its baseless columns, which are thinner at the top than at the bottom with very simple capitals. Metope panels above the architrave were sometimes embellished with reliefs. In contrast, the Ionic style is more flamboyant. Columns are set in a decorative base and are more slender with more marked vertical fluting. The main difference can be seen in the capital, which has a double volute, on which rests the architrave, and then a frieze, usually adorned by sculptures.

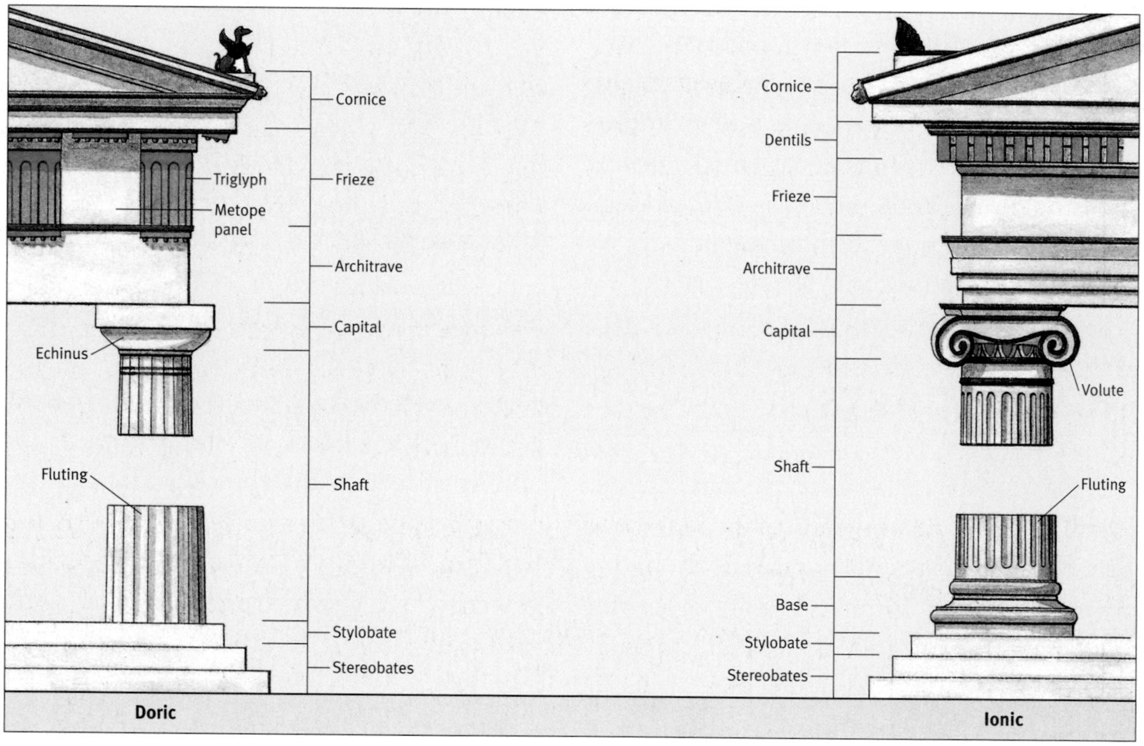

the erosion of time has allowed a beauty of form which is almost unequalled to emerge from the superficial experience. There is no possibility here of discounting the interplay of judgment of the object with standards of judgment which derive ultimately from the object itself. It remains simply true that to have originated an art that has spoken so deeply and powerfully to the human mind across such ages is itself not easily interpreted except as evidence of an unsurpassed artistic greatness and an astonishing skill in giving it expression.

SCULPTURE

Great artistic quality is also present in Greek sculpture. Here, too, the presence of good stone was an advantage, and the original influence of oriental, often Egyptian, models important. Like pottery, the eastern models once absorbed, sculpture evolved towards greater naturalism. The supreme subject of the Greek sculptors was the human form, portrayed no longer as a memorial or cult object, but for its own sake. Again it is not always possible to be sure of the finished statue the Greeks saw; these figures were often gilded, painted or decorated with ivory and precious stones. Some bronzes have undergone looting or melting down, so that the preponderance of stone may itself be misleading. Their evidence, though, records a clear evolution. We begin with statues of gods and of young men and women whose identity is often unknown, simply and symmetrically presented in poses not too far removed from those of the Orient. In the classical figures of the fifth century, naturalism begins to tell in an uneven distribution of weight and the abandonment of the simple frontal stance and to evolve towards the mature, human style of Praxiteles and the fourth century in which the body – and for the first time the female nude – is treated.

THE CULTURAL LEGACY

A great culture is more than a mere museum and no civilization can be reduced to a catalogue. For all its élite quality, the achievement and importance of Greece comprehended all sides of life; the politics of the city-state, a tragedy of Sophocles and a statue by Phidias are all part of it. Later ages grasped this intuitively, happily ignorant of the conscientious discrimination which historical scholarship was eventually to make possible between periods and places. This was a fruitful error, because in the end what Greece was to be thought to be was as important to the future as what she was. The meaning of the Greek experience was to be represented and reinterpreted, and ancient Greece was to be rediscovered and reconsidered and, in different ways, reborn and re-used, for more than two thousand years. For all the ways in which reality had fallen short of later idealization and for all the strength of ties with past, Greek civilization was quite simply the most

The Parthenon in the Acropolis of Athens is a good example of the Doric order in Greek architecture. It was constructed from Pentelic marble and was built in the middle of the 5th century BCE. Great care was taken over every detail of the structure – for example, the columns lean inward slightly to create an impression of strength and harmony.

important extension of humanity's grasp of its own destiny down to that time. Within four centuries, Greece had invented philosophy, politics, most of arithmetic andgeometry, and the categories of western art. It would be enough, even if her errors too had not been so fruitful. Europe has drawn interest on the capital Greece has laid down ever since, and through Europe the rest of the world has traded on the same account.

This classical bronze statue of Zeus, god of the sky and supreme deity, was recovered from the sea off Cape Artemisium and was probably made around 460 BCE. The god is preparing to launch a thunderbolt (now missing) from his right hand.

This tombstone, found at Thasos, depicts a dead woman holding a small box which contains a writing scroll. Bas-reliefs carved on tombstones have provided us with a great deal of information about life in ancient Greece.

4 THE HELLENISTIC WORLD

THE HISTORY OF GREECE rapidly becomes less interesting after the fifth century. It is also less important. What remains important is the history of Greek civilization and the shape of this, paradoxically, was determined by a kingdom in northern Greece which some said was not Greek at all: Macedon. In the second half of the fourth century it created an empire bigger than any yet seen, the legatee of both Persia and the city-states. It organized the world we call Hellenistic because of the preponderance and uniting force within it of a culture, Greek in inspiration and language. Yet Macedon was a barbarous place, perhaps centuries behind Athens in the quality of its life and culture.

This gold casket was found in a royal tomb in the ancient capital of Macedonia, Aegas, now called Vergina. The casket's decoration includes the star emblem of the Macedonian Dynasty and dates from the 4th century BCE.

THE DECLINE OF PERSIA

The story begins with the decline of Persian power. Persian recovery in alliance with Sparta had masked important internal weaknesses. One of them is commemorated by a famous book, the *Anabasis* of Xenophon, the story of the long march of an army of Greek mercenaries back up the Tigris and across the mountains to the Black Sea after an unsuccessful attempt on the Persian throne by a brother of the king. This was only a minor and subsidiary episode in the important story of Persian decline, an offshoot of one particular crisis of internal division. Throughout the fourth century that empire's troubles continued, with province after province (among them Egypt, which won its independence as early as 404 BCE and held it for sixty years) slipping out of control. A major revolt by the western satraps took a long time to master and though in the end imperial rule was restored the cost had been great. When at last reimposed, Persian rule was often weak.

PHILIP OF MACEDON

ONE RULER TEMPTED by the possibilities of the Persian decline was Philip II of Macedon, a not very highly regarded northern kingdom whose power rested on a warrior aristocracy; it was a rough, tough society, its rulers still somewhat like the warlords of Homeric times, their power resting more on personal ascendancy than institutions. Whether this was a state which was a part of the world of the Hellenes was disputed; some Greeks thought Macedonians barbarians. On the other hand, their kings claimed descent from Greek houses (one going back to Heracles) and their claim was generally recognized. Philip himself sought status; he wanted Macedon to be thought of as Greek. When he became regent of Macedon in 359 BCE he began a steady acquisition of territory at the expense of other Greek states. His ultimate argument was an army which became by the end of his reign the best-trained and organized in Greece. The Macedonian military tradition had emphasized heavy, armoured cavalry, and this continued to be a major arm. Philip added to this tradition the benefit of lessons about infantry he had drawn while a hostage at Thebes in his youth. From hoplite tactics he evolved a new weapon, the sixteen-deep phalanx of pikemen. The men in its ranks carried pikes twice as long as a hoplite spear and they operated in a more open formation, pike shafts from the second and third ranks running between men in the front to present a much denser array of weapons for the charge. Another advantage of the Macedonians was a grasp of siege-warfare techniques not shown by other Greek armies; they had catapults which made it possible to force a besieged town's defenders to take cover while battering-rams, mobile towers and mounds of earth were brought into play. Such things had previously been seen only in the armies of Assyria and their Asian successors. Finally, Philip ruled a fairly wealthy state, its riches much increased once he had acquired the goldmines of Mount Pangaeum, though he spent so much that he left huge debts.

This small ivory head is thought to be a portrait of Philip II of Macedon. The right eye appears to show one of the king's battle scars, said to have resulted from an arrow wound.

He used his power first to ensure the effective unification of Macedon itself. Within a few years the infant for whom he was regent was deposed and Philip was elected king. Then he began to look to the south and northeast. In these areas expansion sooner or later meant encroachment upon the interests and position of Athens. Her allies in Rhodes, Cos, Chios and Byzantium placed themselves under Macedonian patronage. Another, Phocis, went down in a war in which Athens had egged her on but failed to give effective support. Although Demosthenes, the last great agitator of Athenian democracy, made himself a place in history, still recalled by the word "philippic", by warning his countrymen of the dangers they faced, he

Time chart (359–30 BCE)

359–336 BCE
Reign of Philip II of Macedon

148–145 BCE
Rome annexes Macedonia and Greece

88–64 BCE
Roman dominion in Asia Minor

300 BCE — 200 BCE — 100 BCE

336–323 BCE
Reign of Alexander the Great

315–301 BCE
Division of Alexander's empire

30 BCE
Rome annexes Egypt, the last Hellenistic kingdom

The entrance to the Acrocorinth, the great fortress that towered above the ancient city of Corinth, is one of the best surviving examples of Greek military architecture, built in an age when the demise of the *polis* meant that outer defences were necessary. The fortress was connected to the city by long walls in the 4th century BCE.

could not save them. When the war between Athens and Macedon (355–346 BCE) at last ended, Philip had won not only Thessaly, but had established himself in central Greece and controlled the pass of Thermopylae.

THE LEAGUE OF CORINTH

Philip's situation favoured designs on Thrace and this implied a return of Greek interests towards Persia. One Athenian writer advocated a Hellenic crusade to exploit Persia's weakness (in opposition to Demosthenes, who continued to denounce the Macedonian "barbarian"), and once more plans were made to liberate the Asian cities, a notion attractive enough to bear fruit in a reluctant League of Corinth formed by the major Greek states other than Sparta in 337 BCE. Philip was its president and general, but the apparent independence of its members was a sham, for they were Macedonian satellites. Though the culmination of Philip's work and reign (he was assassinated the following year), it had only come into being after Macedon had defeated the Athenians and Thebans again in 338 BCE. The terms of peace imposed by Philip were not harsh, but the League had to agree to go to war with Persia under Macedonian leadership. There was one more kick of Greek independence after Philip's death, but his son and successor Alexander crushed the Greek rebels as he did others in other parts of his kingdom. Thebes was then razed to the ground and its population enslaved (335 BCE).

The Macedonian army

Philip reorganized Macedonia's army, which had been based on a cavalry made up of noblemen. The king increased the number of infantry soldiers, took pains to arm them well and provided them with a new weapon: the *sarissa*, a 20-ft (6-m) long pike (one and a half times as long as the Greek spears). He also created the phalanx, a concentrated infantry group consisting of 16 rows of soldiers. The soldiers in the front five rows lowered their *sarissas* to go into battle. This mass of soldiers was more manoeuvrable than the Greek formations of the day and its weapons easier to handle. Its flanks and rearguard were protected by cavalry.

Reconstruction of a Macedonian phalanx ready to go into battle.

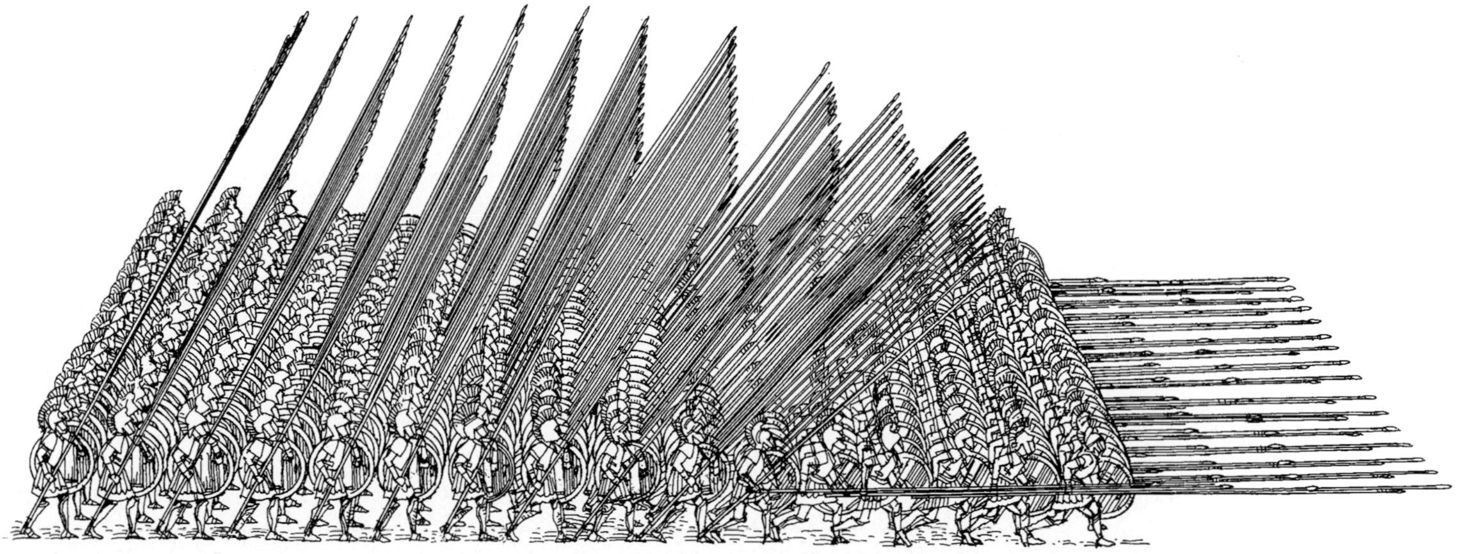

The legendary Alexander

Born in 356 BCE, Alexander studied under the philosopher Aristotle, who instructed him in classical Greek culture and told him stories about the revered heroes of Greek mythology. In 336 BCE, at the age of twenty, Alexander succeeded his father, Philip II. Macedon's new king was a battle-hardened soldier who had already taken part in the conquest of Greece.

The Egyptians' willingness to treat Alexander as a deity had a huge influence on the young man's behaviour. He cultivated his image as a divine being deserving of worship, although it is not known whether he believed himself to be a god. Alexander used carefully orchestrated propaganda techniques to control his public image – he allowed himself to be portrayed only by his own official sculptors.

This typically idealized portrait of Alexander the Great, which was made in Miletus in the first half of the 2nd century BCE, *depicts him as a handsome and heroic leader.*

ALEXANDER THE GREAT

THE DEFEAT OF THEBES was the real end of four centuries of Greek history. During this period civilization had been created and sheltered by the city-state, one of the most successful political forms the world has ever known. Now, not for the first time nor the last, the future seemed to belong to the bigger battalions, the bigger organizations. Mainland Greece was from this time a political backwater under Macedonian governors and garrisons.

Like his father, Alexander sought to conciliate the Greeks by giving them a large measure of internal self-government in return for adherence to his foreign policy. This was always to leave some Greeks, notably the Athenian democrats, unreconciled. When Alexander died, Athens once more tried to organize an anti-Macedonian coalition. The results were disastrous. A part of the price of defeat was the replacement of democracy by oligarchy at Athens (322 BCE); Demosthenes fled to an island off the coast, seeking sanctuary in the temple of Poseidon there, but poisoned himself when the Macedonians came for him. A Macedonian governor henceforth ruled the Peloponnese.

Alexander's reign had thus begun with difficulties, but once they were surmounted, he could turn his attention to Persia. In 334 BCE he crossed to Asia at the head of an army of which a quarter was drawn from Greece. There was more than idealism in this; aggressive war might also be prudent, for the fine army left by Philip had to be paid if it was not to present a threat to a new king, and conquest would provide the money. He was twenty-two years old and before him lay a short career of conquest so brilliant that it would leave his name a myth down the ages and provide a setting for the widest expansion of Greek culture. He drew the city-states into a still wider world.

CONQUESTS

The story of Alexander's success is simple to summarize. Legend says that after crossing to Asia Minor he cut the Gordian Knot. He then defeated the Persians at the battle of Issus. This was followed by a campaign which swept south through Syria, destroying Tyre on the way, and eventually to Egypt, where Alexander founded the city still bearing his name. In every battle he was his own best soldier and he was wounded several times in the mêlée. He pushed into the desert, interrogated the oracle at Siwah and then went back into Asia to inflict a second and decisive defeat on Darius III in 331 BCE. Persepolis was sacked and burnt and Alexander proclaimed successor to the Persian throne; Darius was murdered by one of his satraps the next year. On went Alexander, pursuing the Iranians of the northeast into Afghanistan (where Kandahar, like many cities elsewhere, commemorates his name) and penetrating a hundred miles or so beyond the Indus into the Punjab. Then he turned back because his army would go no further. It was tired and having defeated an army with two hundred elephants may have been disinclined to face the further five thousand reported to be waiting for it in the Ganges valley. Alexander returned to Babylon. There he died in 323 BCE, thirty-two years old and just ten years after he had left Macedon.

ALEXANDER THE GREAT'S ACHIEVEMENTS

Both Alexander's conquests and their organization in empire bear the stamp of individual genius; the word is not too strong, for

Alexander's march to the east

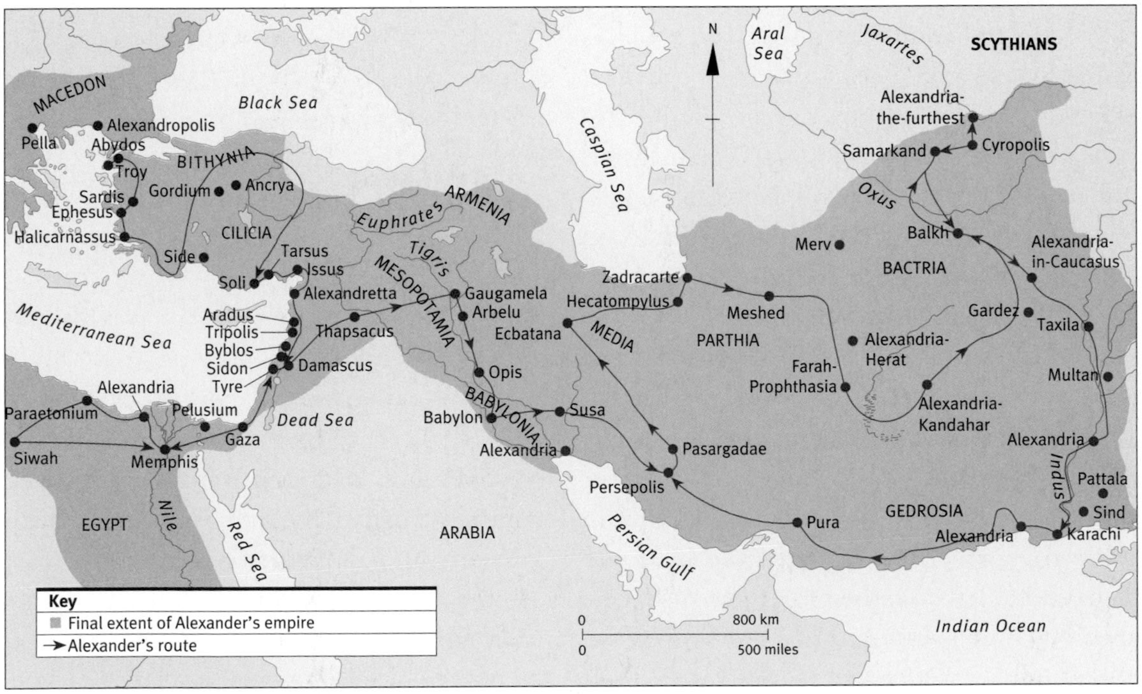

In 334 BCE, Alexander and his army crossed the Dardanelles with the aim of crushing the Persian empire. After crossing Asia Minor and marching along the Mediterranean coast to Egypt, he headed eastwards. When his army finally mutinied in 323 BCE, Alexander decided to return westwards. However, his journey only took him as far as Babylon, where he died at the age of 32, possibly the victim of a plague.

achievement on this scale is more than the fruit of good fortune, favourable historical circumstance or blind determinism. Alexander was a creative mind and something of a visionary, even if self-absorbed and obsessed with his pursuit of glory. With great intelligence he combined almost reckless courage; he believed his mother's ancestor to be Homer's Achilles and strove to emulate the hero. He was ambitious as much to prove himself in men's eyes – or perhaps those of his forceful and repellent mother – as to win new lands. The idea of the Hellenic crusade against Persia undoubtedly had reality for him, but he was also, for all his admiration of the Greek culture of which he had learnt from his tutor Aristotle, too egocentric to be a missionary, and his cosmopolitanism was grounded in an appreciation of realities. His empire had to be run by Persians as well as Macedonians. Alexander himself married first a Bactrian and then a Persian princess, and accepted – unfittingly, thought some of his companions – the homage which the East rendered to rulers it thought to be godlike. He was also at times rash and impulsive; it was his soldiers who finally made him turn back at the Indus, and the ruler of Macedon had no business to plunge into battle with no attention for what would happen to the monarchy if he should die without a successor. Worse still, he killed a friend in a drunken brawl and he may have arranged his father's murder.

Alexander lived too short a time either to ensure the unity of his empire in the future or to prove to posterity that even he could not have held it together for long. What he did in this time is indubitably impressive. The foundation of twenty-five "cities" is by itself a considerable matter, even if some of them were only spruced-up strongpoints; they were keys to the Asian land routes. The integration of east and west in their government was still more difficult, but Alexander took it a long way in ten years. Of course, he had little choice; there were not enough Greeks and Macedonians to conquer and govern the huge empire. From the first he ruled through Persian officials in the conquered areas and after coming back from India he began the reorganization of the army in mixed regiments of Macedonians and Persians. His adoption of Persian dress and his attempt to exact prostration – an obligatory kow-tow like that which so many Europeans in recent times found degrading when it was asked for by Chinese rulers – from his compatriots as

This detail of the so-called Alexander mosaic from Pompeii depicts a battle between Alexander the Great and the Persian king Darius III. Dating from the 2nd century BCE, the mosaic is a replica of a late 4th-century BCE Greek fresco. The figure represents Alexander entering the fray.

well as from Persians, also antagonized his followers, for they revealed his taste for oriental manners. There were plots and mutinies; they were not successful, and his relatively mild reprisals do not suggest that the situation was ever very dangerous for Alexander. The crisis was followed by his most spectacular gesture of cultural integration when, taking Darius's daughter as a wife (in addition to his Bactrian princess, Roxana), he then officiated at the mass wedding of 9,000 of his soldiers to eastern women. This was the famous "marriage of East and West", an act of state rather than of idealism, for the new empire had to be cemented together if it was to survive.

What the empire really meant in cultural interplay is more difficult to assess. There was certainly a wider physical dispersal of Greeks. But the results of this were only to appear after Alexander's death, when the formal framework of empire collapsed and yet the cultural fact of a Hellenistic world emerged from it. We do not in fact know very much about life in Alexander's empire and it must be unlikely, given its brief duration, the

This bas-relief comes from the famous so-called Alexander sarcophagus, made in 305 BCE in painted marble, and decorated on this side with battle scenes that are much more realistic than usual for the classical period. Alexander is shown on the left on horseback, wearing a lion-scalp helmet.

An effigy of Ptolemy I (305–282 BCE) is displayed on this coin. A Greek general in Alexander the Great's army, Ptolemy Soter later became King Ptolemy I of Egypt. He founded the Ptolemaic Dynasty, which ruled until the Roman conquest of Egypt at the end of the 1st century BCE.

limitations of ancient government and a lack of will to embark upon fundamental change, that most of its inhabitants found things very different in 323 BCE from what they had known ten years before.

ALEXANDER'S LEGACY

Alexander's impact was made in the east. He did not reign long enough to affect the interplay of the western Greeks with Carthage, which was the main preoccupation of the later fourth century in the west. In Greece itself things stayed quiet until his death. It was in Asia that he ruled lands no Greeks had ruled before. In Persia he had proclaimed himself heir to the Great King and rulers in the northern satrapies of Bithynia, Cappadocia and Armenia did him homage.

Weak as the cement of the Alexandrine Empire must have been, it was subjected to intolerable strain when he died without a competent heir. His generals fell to fighting for what they could get and keep, and the empire was dissolving even before the birth of his posthumous son by Roxana. She had already murdered his second wife, so when she and her son died in the troubles any hope of direct descent vanished. In forty-odd years of fighting it was settled that there would be no reconstitution of Alexander's empire. There emerged instead a group of big states, each of them a hereditary monarchy. They were founded by successful soldiers, the *diadochi*, or "Successors".

THE HELLENISTIC STATES

PTOLEMY SOTER, one of Alexander's best generals, had at once seized power in Egypt on his master's death and to it he subsequently conveyed the valuable prize of Alexander's body. Ptolemy's descendants were to rule the province for nearly three hundred years until the death of Cleopatra in 30 BCE. Ptolemaic Egypt was the longest-lived and richest of the successor states. Of the Asian Empire, the Indian territories and some of Afghanistan passed out of Greek hands altogether, being ceded to an Indian ruler in return for military help. The rest of it was by 300 BCE a huge kingdom of one and a half million square miles and perhaps thirty million subjects, stretching from Afghanistan to Syria, the site of its capital, Antioch. This vast domain was ruled by the descendants of Seleucus, another Macedonian general. Attacks by migrating Celts from northern Europe (who had already invaded Macedonia itself) led to its partial disruption early in the third century BCE and part of it thenceforth formed the kingdom of Pergamon, ruled by a dynasty called the Attalids, who pushed the Celts further into Asia Minor. The Seleucids kept the rest, though they were to lose Bactria in 225 BCE, where descendants of Alexander's soldiers set up a remarkable Greek kingdom. Macedon, under another dynasty, the Antigonids, strove to retain a control of the Greek states contested in the Aegean by the Ptolemaic fleet and in Asia Minor by the Seleucids. Once again, about 265 BCE, Athens made a bid for independence but failed.

These events are complicated, but not very important for our purpose. What

The Hellenistic world soon after 200 BCE

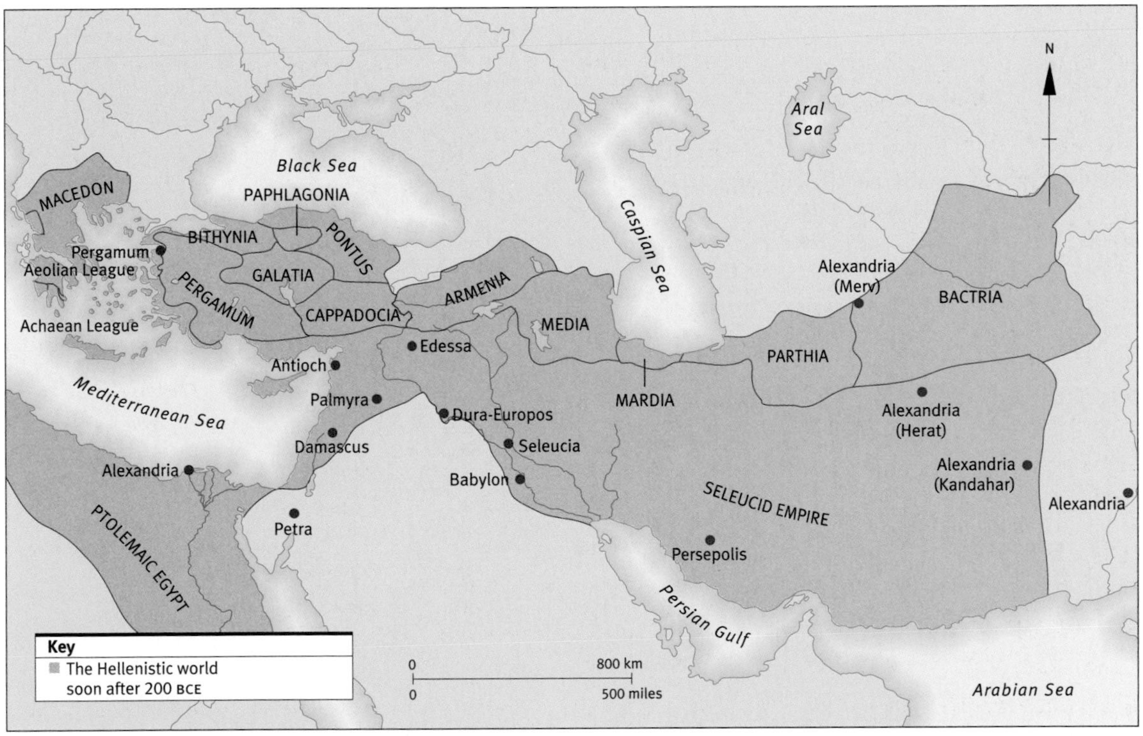

When Alexander the Great died, his generals began to fight for control of his empire's different regions. These disputes left the empire fragmented, making way for the Hellenistic kingdoms. At the beginning of the 3rd century BCE, three large kingdoms were consolidated: Egypt under the Ptolemaic Dynasty; Syria, Mesopotamia and part of Persia under the Seleucids; and Macedonia under the Antigonid Dynasty. Later, the borders of these kingdoms were altered and some minor kingdoms appeared. All of them later succumbed to pressure from the Romans and the Parthians in the 2nd century BCE.

Hellenism and the city of Pergamum

The Hellenistic period began when Alexander the Great died and ended with the Roman conquest of Asia Minor, which took place throughout the 2nd and 1st centuries BCE. Through the Hellenistic kingdoms founded after Alexander's death, Greek culture spread across the Near East and Egypt, and shifted its main focus outside Greece for the first time. The main centres of Hellenism were generally new Greek colonies and cities, such as Pergamum. In these colonies, a busy cultural life developed and considerable advances were made in the fields of science and art. Greek culture itself was enriched in many ways by oriental influences, notably in politics, art and religion.

The kingdom of Pergamum on the Asian coast became independent from the Seleucid state in the 3rd century BCE and during the following century its capital was a major centre of Hellenistic art and culture. The city was redesigned and adapted to steep, uneven mountainside terrain, its buildings and open spaces linked by a network of stairways and terraces.

Key
1 Arsenal
2 Temple of Trajan
3 Library
4 Palace
5 Sanctuary of Athene
6 Theatre
7 Great Altar
8 Stoa
9 Upper Agora
10 Sanctuary of Demeter
11 Baths
12 Upper gymnasium
13 Middle gymnasium
14 Lower gymnasium
15 Lower Agora
16 Town wall

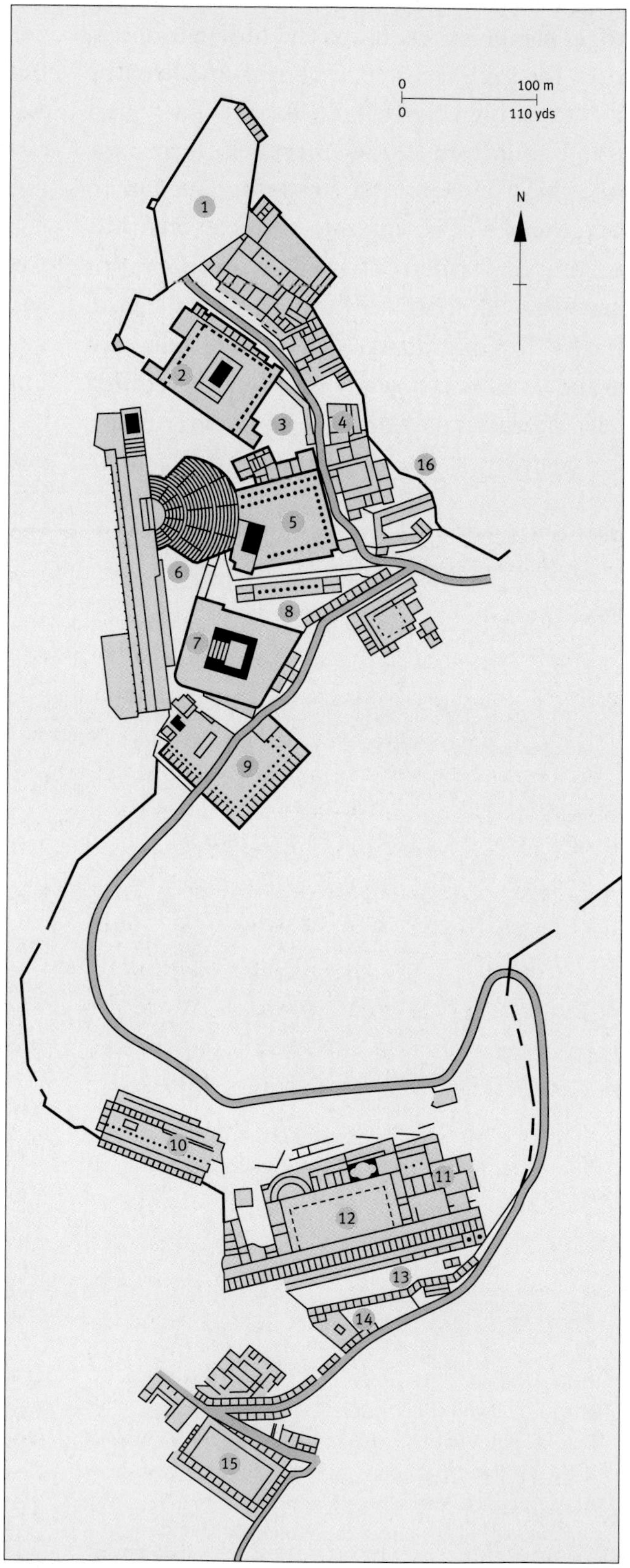

(Right) A plan of the Hellenistic city of Pergamum.

(Below) From the year 400 BCE, Pergamum had one of the main sanctuaries dedicated to Asclepius, the Greek god responsible for curing the sick.

mattered more was that for about sixty years after 280 BCE the Hellenistic kingdoms lived in a rough balance of power, preoccupied with events in the eastern Mediterranean and Asia and, except for the Greeks and Macedonians, paying little attention to events further west. This provided a peaceful setting for the greatest extension of Greek culture and this is why these states are important. It is their contribution to the diffusion and growth of a civilization that constitute their claim on our attention, not the obscure politics and unrewarding struggles of the *diadochi*.

THE HELLENISTIC CITIES

Greek was now the official language of the whole Near East; even more important, it was the language of the cities, the foci of the new world. Under the Seleucids the union of Hellenistic and oriental civilization to which Alexander may have aspired began to be a reality. They urgently sought Greek immigrants and founded new cities wherever they could as a means of providing some solid framework for their empire and of hellenizing the local population. The cities were the substance of Seleucid power, for beyond them stretched a heterogeneous hinterland of tribes, Persian satrapies, vassal princes. Seleucid administration was still based fundamentally upon the satrapies; the theory of absolutism was inherited by the Seleucid kings from the Achaemenids just as was their system of taxation. Yet it is not certain what this meant in practice and the east seems to have been less closely governed than Mesopotamia and Asia Minor, where Hellenistic influence was strongest and where the capital lay. The size of the Hellenistic cities here far surpassed those of the older Greek emigrations; Alexandria, Antioch and the new capital city, Seleucia, near Babylon, quickly achieved populations of between one and two hundred thousand.

This reflected economic growth as well as conscious policy. The wars of Alexander and his successors released an enormous booty, much of it in bullion, accumulated by the Persian Empire. It stimulated economic life all over the Near East, but also brought the evils of inflation and instability. Nevertheless, the overall trend was towards greater wealth. There were no great innovations, either in manufacture or in the tapping of new natural resources. The Mediterranean economy remained much what it had always been except in scale, but Hellenistic civilization was richer than its predecessors and population growth was one sign of this.

Its wealth sustained governments of some magnificence, raising large revenues and spending them in spectacular and

In this late 2nd-century BCE bas-relief, known as *The Apotheosis of Homer*, the poet appears at the bottom left, seated on a throne. Led by Myth and History and accompanied by Physics and Nature, the dramatic genres advance towards Homer to make a sacrifice in his honour, while in the upper section, Zeus and Apollo are depicted with the muses. Sculpted by Archilochus of Pirene, the bas-relief reflects the developing interest in literature in the Hellenistic kingdoms.

A detail from the western part of a frieze that decorates the Great Altar at Pergamum. These dynamic sculptures depict the battle between the gods and the giants.

sometimes commendable ways. The ruins of the Hellenistic cities show expenditure on the appurtenances of Greek urban life; theatres and gymnasia abound, games and festivals were held in all of them. This probably did not much affect the native populations of the countryside who paid the taxes and some of them resented what would now be called "westernization". None the less, it was a solid achievement. Through the cities the east was Hellenized in a way which was to mark it until the coming of Islam. Soon they produced their own Greek literature.

Yet though this was a civilization of Greek cities, in spirit it was unlike that of the past, as some Greeks noted sourly. The Macedonians had never known the life of the city-state and their creations in Asia lacked its vigour; the Seleucids founded scores of cities but maintained the old autocratic and centralized administration of the satrapies above that level. Bureaucracy was highly developed and self-government languished. Ironically, besides having to bear the burden of disaster in the past, the cities of Greece itself, where a flickering tradition of independence lived on, were the one part of the Hellenistic world that actually underwent economic and demographic decline.

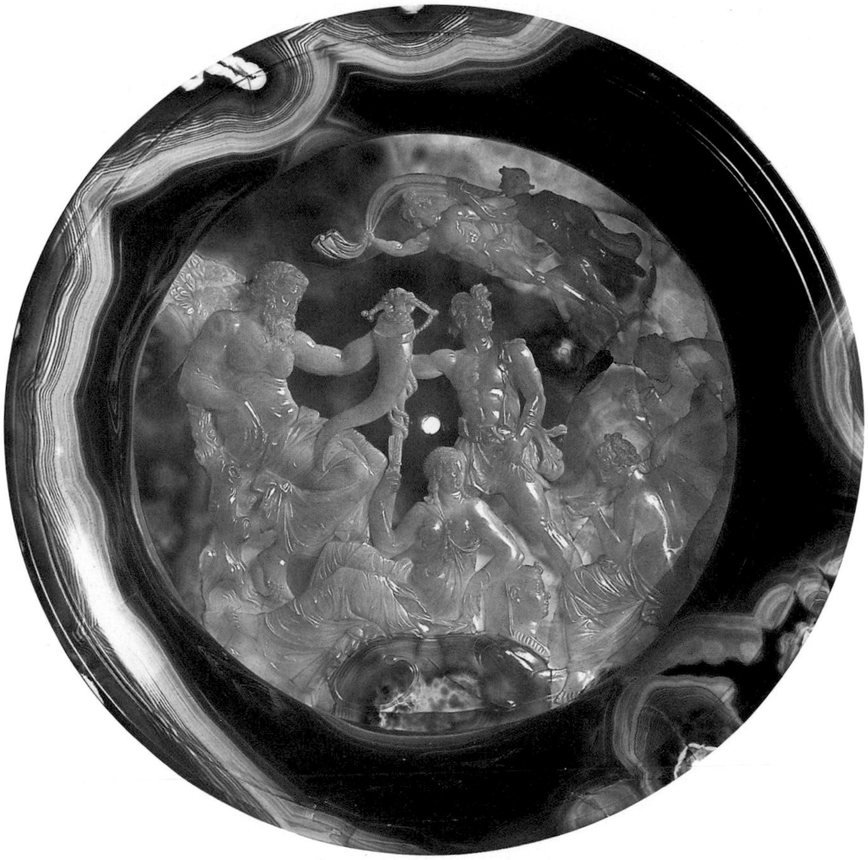

Dating from 172 BCE, this Alexandrian cameo is one of the few surviving examples of the cultural confluence of Greece and Egypt. It represents the fertility of the Nile. At the bottom of the cameo, the sphinx of Osiris, the Egyptian god of agriculture, appears with the facial features of Ptolemy V.

Archimedes

One of the greatest of the Greek mathematicians, Archimedes (c.287–212 BCE) was born in Syracuse and studied in Alexandria. He invented siege engines for use against the Romans and the Archimedean screw, which was used for raising water. He also formulated the famous principle according to which a body submerged in a liquid undergoes an apparent loss of weight equal to the weight of the displaced liquid. Archimedes made many contributions to geometry, calculating the approximate value of *pi*, as well as formulae for working out the area and volume of various figures, including cylinders, spheres and parabolas.

Archimedes was killed by a Roman soldier during the siege of Syracuse, as depicted in this copy of a 2nd-century Roman mosaic.

HELLENISTIC ACADEMIC LIFE

Although the political nerve had gone, city culture still served as a great transmission system for Greek ideas. Large endowments provided at Alexandria and Pergamum the two greatest libraries of the ancient world. Ptolemy I also founded the Museum, a kind of institute of advanced study. In Pergamum a king endowed schoolmasterships and it was there that people perfected the use of parchment (*pergamene*) when the Ptolemies cut off supplies of papyrus. In Athens the Academy and the Lyceum survived, and from such sources the tradition of Greek intellectual activity was everywhere refreshed. Much of this activity was academic in the narrow sense that it was in essence commentary on past achievement, but much of it was also of high quality and now seems lacking in weight only because of the gigantic achievements of the fifth and fourth centuries. It was a tradition solid enough to endure right through the Common Era, though much of its content has been irretrievably lost. Eventually, the world of Islam would receive the teaching of Plato and Aristotle through what had been passed on by Hellenistic scholars.

HELLENISTIC SCIENCE

Hellenistic civilization preserved the Greek tradition most successfully in science, and here Alexandria, the greatest of all Hellenistic cities, was pre-eminent. Euclid was the greatest systematizer of geometry, defining it until the nineteenth century, and Archimedes, who is famous for his practical achievements in the construction of war-machines in Sicily, was probably Euclid's pupil. Another Alexandrian, Eratosthenes, was the first man to measure the size of the earth, and yet another, Hero, is said to have invented a steam engine and certainly used steam to transmit energy. It is inconceivable that the state of contemporary metallurgy could ever have made the widespread application of this discovery practicable, which probably explains why we hear no more of it. The point is of general relevance; the intellectual achievements of the ancient world (and of European medieval civilization later) often pushed up to the limits of existing technical skills but could not be expected to go beyond them; further progress had to wait for better instrumentation. Another Hellenistic Greek, Aristarchus of Samos, got so far as to say that the earth moved around the sun, though his views were set aside by contemporaries and posterity because they could not be squared with Aristotelian physics which stated the contrary; the truth or falsity of both views remained untested experimentally. In hydrostatics, it is true, Archimedes made great strides (and invented the windlass, too) but the central achievement of the Greek tradition was always mathematical, not practical, and in Hellenistic times it reached its apogee with the theory of conic sections and ellipses and the founding of trigonometry.

CHANGING POLITICAL STRUCTURES

Such scientific discoveries were important additions to humanity's toolkit. Yet they were less distinct from what went before than was Hellenistic moral and political philosophy. It is tempting to find the reason for this in the political change from the city-state to larger units. It was still in Athens that the philosophy of the age found its greatest centre and Aristotle had hoped to reinvigorate the city-state; in the right hands, he thought, it could still provide the framework for the good life. The unhappy last age of the city-state after the Peloponnesian War and the size and impersonality of the new monarchies must have soon sapped such confidence. In them, the old patriotic impulse of the city-states had dried up. Efforts were made to find other ways of harnessing public loyalty and

The 3rd-century BCE philosopher Chrysippus was a disciple of Zeno and one of the founders of the Stoic school, which became highly influential in the Hellenistic world and later in Rome.

Situated to the southeast of the Athenian Acropolis is the temple of the Olympian, Zeus. Building work on the structure began under Antiochus IV in about 174 BCE and was completed under the Roman emperor Hadrian in the 2nd century CE. The original building had eight columns on its façades, three rows deep, and twenty columns on each side.

emotion. Perhaps because of the need to impress non-Greeks, perhaps because they felt the positive attraction of the world beyond Greek culture, the new monarchs buttressed themselves more and more with oriental cults attached to the person of the ruler whose origins went back into the Mesopotamian and Egyptian past. Extravagant titles were employed but perhaps much of this was flattery: "Soter", as Ptolemy I was called, meant "Saviour". The Seleucids allowed themselves to be worshipped, but the Ptolemies outdid them; they took over the divine status and prestige of the pharaohs (and practice, too, to the extent of marrying their sisters). Meanwhile, the real basis of the Hellenistic states was bureaucracy unchecked by traditions of civic independence – since the Seleucids had founded or refounded most of the Greek cities in Asia, what they had given they could take back – and armies of Greek and Macedonian mercenaries which relieved them of dependence on native troops. Powerful and awe-inspiring though they might be, there was little in such structures to capture their very mixed subjects' loyalties and emotions.

HELLENISTIC RELIGION

Probably the erosion of Hellenistic loyalties had gone too far even before Alexander. The triumph of Greek culture was deceptive. Language went on being used, but with a different meaning. Greek religion, for example, a great force for unity among Hellenes, rested not on ecclesiastical institutions but on respect for the Homeric gods and goddesses and the behaviour they exemplified. Beyond this, there were the city cults and official mysteries. This had already begun to change, possibly as early as the fifth century, when, under the impact of the prolonged war, the Olympian gods began to lose the respect paid to them. There was more than one cause of this. The rationalism of much Greek fourth-century philosophy is as much a part of the story as the rise of new fears. With the Hellenistic age another influence is felt, that of a pervasive irrationality, of the pressure of fortune and fate. People sought reassurance in new creeds and faiths. The popularity of astrology was one symptom. All this only came to its climax in the first century BCE, "the period", says one scholar, "when the tide of rationalism, which for the past hundred years had flowed ever more sluggishly, has finally expended its force and begins to retreat". This is perhaps further ahead than we need look at this point in the story, but one thing about this reversal is striking at an early date. Swamped as the Hellenistic world was with mysteries and crazes of all kinds, from the revival of Pythagorean mysticism to the raising of altars to dead philosophers, traditional Greek religion was not a beneficiary. Its decay had already gone too far. The decline of Delphi, remarked from the third century, was not arrested.

A bust of the philosopher Epicurus, who was born on the island of Samos in 341 BCE.

THE CYNICS AND STOICS

THE COLLAPSE OF A TRADITIONAL religious framework of values was the background to philosophical change. The study of philosophy was still vigorous in Greece itself and even there its Hellenistic development suggests that men were falling back upon personal concerns, contracting out of societies they could not influence, seeking shelter from the buffets of fate and the strain of daily life. It seems somewhat familiar. One example was Epicurus, who sought the good in an essentially private experience of pleasure. Contrary to later misinterpretations, he

This coin bears the portrait of the Parthian king, Mithridates I (171–138 BCE). He captured Iran from the Seleucids and established the frontier with the Hellenistic kingdom along the Euphrates River.

meant by this something far from self-indulgence. For Epicurus, pleasure was psychological contentment and the absence of pain – a view of pleasure somewhat austere to modern eyes. But symptomatically its importance is considerable because it reveals a shift in people's preoccupations towards the private and personal. Another form of this philosophic reaction advocated the ideals of renunciation and non-attachment. The school known as the Cynics expressed contempt for convention and sought release from dependence on the material world. One of them, Zeno, a Cypriot, who lived at Athens, began to teach a doctrine of his own in a public place, the *stoa Poikile*. The place gave its name to those he taught, the Stoics. They were to be among the most influential of philosophers because their teaching was readily applicable to daily life. Essentially the Stoics taught that life should be lived to fit the rational order they discerned running through the universe. Man could not control what happened to him, they said, but he could accept what was sent by fate, the decree of the divine will in which the Stoics believed. Virtuous acts, accordingly, should not be performed for their likely consequences, which might well be unfortunate or thwarted, but for their own sake, because of their intrinsic value.

THE SUCCESS OF STOICISM

In stoicism, which was to have great success in the Hellenistic world, lay doctrine which gave the individual a new ground for ethical confidence at a time when neither *polis* nor traditional Greek religion retained their authority. Stoicism also had the potential for a long life, because it applied to all men, who, it taught, were all alike: this was the seed of an ethical universalism which gradually transcended the old distinction between Greek and barbarian, as it would any other distinction between reasonable men. It spoke to a common humanity and actually produced a condemnation of slavery, an amazing step in a world built by forced labour. It was to be a fecund source for thinkers for two thousand years. Soon its ethic of disciplined common sense was to have great success at Rome.

The seven wonders of the ancient world

The 30-m (100-ft) high Colossus of Rhodes was an impressive example of the influence that the monumental statues of the East had on Greek sculpture. One Hellenistic citizen considered the Colossus to be one of "the seven things worthy of being seen". Sadly, of these seven ancient "wonders", only the pyramids of Giza survive today.

Key
1 Statue of Zeus at Olympia
2 Temple of Artemis at Ephesus
3 Mausoleum of Halicarnassus
4 Colossus of Rhodes
5 Pharos of Alexandria
6 Pyramids of Giza
7 Hanging Gardens of Babylon

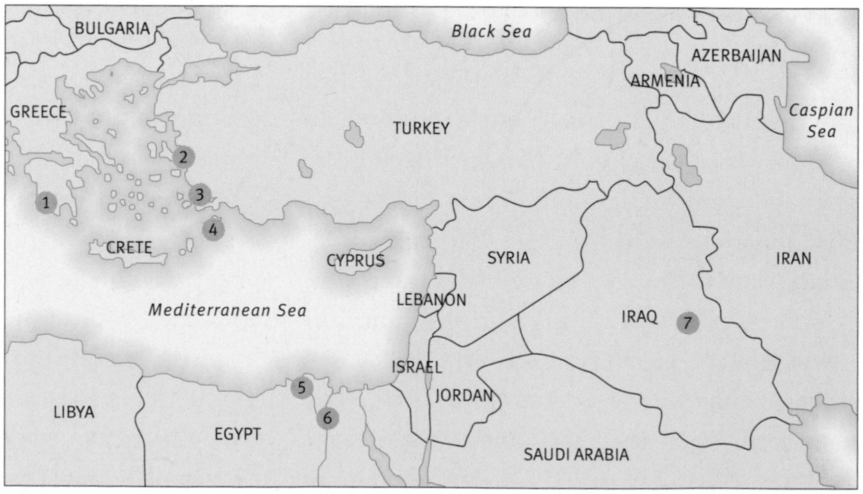

Philosophy thus showed the eclecticism and cosmopolitanism which strike the eye in almost every aspect of Hellenistic culture. Perhaps their most obvious expression was the adaptation of Greek sculpture to the monumental statuary of the East, which produced such monsters as the hundred-foot-high Colossus of Rhodes; yet in the end eclecticism and cosmopolitanism appeared everywhere, in the aspirations of the Stoics just as in the oriental cults which displaced the Greek gods. It was the scientist Eratosthenes who said that he saw all good men as fellow countrymen and the remark expresses the new spirit which was Hellenism at its best.

PARTHIA

THE POLITICAL FRAMEWORK of the Hellenistic world was bound in the end to change, because sources of change grew up beyond its circumference. One early omen was the appearance of a new threat in the east, the kingdom of Parthia. By the middle of the third century BCE the weakness imposed by the Seleucid kingdom's concentration of population and wealth in its western half was leading to over-preoccupation with relations with the other Hellenistic states. The northeast was threatened – as always – by nomads from the steppes, but government was distracted from this danger by the need to supply money and resources for quarrels with Ptolemaic Egypt. The temptation to a remote satrap to strike out on his own as a warlord was often irresistible.

Scholars contest the details, but one of the satrapies in which this happened was Parthia, an important area to the southeast of the Caspian. It was to become more important still as the centuries passed for it lay across the caravan route to Central Asia by which the western classical world and

These monumental heads belonged to statues of divinities which spread over the terraces marking the tumulus of Nimrud Dagh. Antiochus I ordered the monument to be built in the first half of the 1st century BCE to house the tomb of his father, Mithridates I, who founded the small Commagene kingdom (present-day Turkey).

China came to be remotely in touch – the Silk Road.

PARTHIAN ORIGINS

Who were the Parthians? They were originally the Parni, one of those Indo-European nomadic peoples who emerged from Central Asia to create and re-create a political unity in the highlands of Iran and Mesopotamia. They became a byword for a military skill then peculiar to them: the discharging of arrows by mounted horsemen. They did not build nearly five hundred years of political continuity only on this, though. They also inherited an administrative structure left to the Seleucids by Alexander, who had taken it from the Persians. Indeed, in most things the Parthians seemed inheritors, not originators; their great dynasty used Greek for its official documents, and they seem to have had no law of their own but to have readily accepted existing practice, whether Babylonian, Persian or Hellenistic.

THE PARTHIAN STATE

Much about the Parthians' early history remains obscure. There was a kingdom, whose centre remains undiscovered, in Parthia in the third century BCE, but the Seleucids do not seem to have reacted strongly to it. In the second century, when the Seleucid monarchy was much more disastrously engaged in the west, two brothers, the younger of whom was Mithridates I, established a Parthian empire, which at his death stretched from Bactria (another fragment of the Seleucid inheritance which had been finally separated from it at about the same time as Parthia) in the east to Babylonia in the west. Consciously reminiscent of those who had gone before, Mithridates described himself on his coins as the "great king". There were setbacks after his death but his namesake Mithridates II recovered lost ground and went even further. The Seleucids were now confined to Syria. In Mesopotamia the frontier of his empire was the Euphrates and the Chinese opened diplomatic relations with him. The coins of the second Mithridates

Syracuse, which became the most powerful Sicilian city, was a Corinthian colony founded in 733 BCE. This theatre probably dates from the 3rd century BCE and has an enormous stage cut into the rock.

bore the proud Achaemenid title, "King of Kings", and the inference is reasonable that the Arsacid Dynasty to which Mithridates belonged was now being consciously related to the great Persian line. Yet the Parthian state seems a much looser thing than the Persian. It is more reminiscent of a feudal grouping of nobles about a warlord than a bureaucratized state.

In order to demonstrate that he is of noble birth, this Roman patrician is depicted holding busts of his forefathers. The statue dates from the late 1st century BCE.

THE GREEK WEST

On the Euphrates, Parthia was eventually to meet a new power from the West. Less remote from it than Parthia, and therefore with less excuse, even the Hellenistic kingdoms had been almost oblivious of the rise of Rome, this new star of the political firmament, and went their way almost without regard for what was happening in the West. The western Greeks, of course, knew more about it, but they long remained preoccupied with the first great threat they had faced, Carthage, a mysterious state which almost may be said to have derived its being from hostility to the Greeks. Founded by Phoenicians somewhere around 800 BCE, perhaps even then to offset Greek commercial competition on the metal routes, Carthage had grown to surpass Tyre and Sidon in wealth and power. But she remained a city-state, using alliance and protection rather than conquests and garrisons, her citizens preferring trade and agriculture to fighting. Unfortunately, the native documentation of Carthage was to perish when, finally, the city was razed to the ground and we know little of its own history.

Yet it was clearly a formidable commercial competitor for the western Greeks. By 480 BCE they had been confined commercially to little more than the Rhône valley, Italy and, above all, Sicily. This island, and one of its cities, Syracuse, was the key to the Greek west. Syracuse for the first time protected Sicily from the Carthaginians when she fought and beat them in the year of Salamis. For most of the fifth century Carthage troubled the western Greeks no more and the Syracusans were able to turn to supporting the Greek cities of Italy against the Etruscans. Then Syracuse was the target of the ill-fated Sicilian Expedition from Athens (415–413 BCE) because she was the greatest of the western Greek states. The Carthaginians came back after this, but Syracuse survived defeat to enjoy soon afterwards her greatest period of power, exercised not only in the island, but in

The Mediterranean in 600 BCE

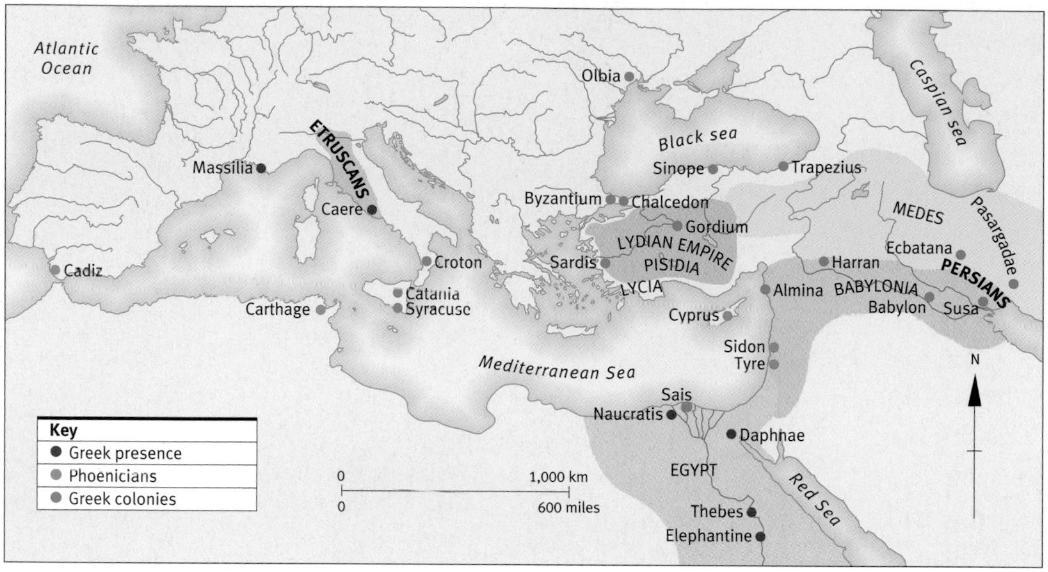

The movement of colonists from the Greek *polis* and the Phoenician cities in search of lands in the central and western Mediterranean encouraged the creation of new colonies, which in turn became important trade centres. The Phoenician settlement in Carthage is a good example of this.

A map showing the main Mediterranean colonies in 600 BCE.

southern Italy and the Adriatic. During most of it she was at war with Carthage. There was plenty of vigour in Syracuse; at one moment she all but captured Carthage, and another expedition added Corcyra (Corfu) to her Adriatic possessions. But soon after 300 BCE it was clear that Carthaginian power was growing while Syracuse had also to face a Roman threat in mainland Italy. The Sicilians fell out with a man who might have saved them, Pyrrhus of Epirus, and by mid-century the Romans were masters of the mainland.

THE POWER OF HELLENIZATION

There were now three major actors in the arena of the West, yet the Hellenistic east seemed strangely uninterested in what was going forward (though Pyrrhus was aware of it). This was perhaps short-sighted, but at this time the Romans did not see themselves as world conquerors. They were as much moved by fear as by greed in entering on the Punic Wars with Carthage, from which they would emerge victors. Then they would turn east. Some Hellenistic Greeks were beginning to be aware by the end of the century of what might be coming. A "cloud in the west" was one description of the struggle between Carthage and Rome viewed from the Hellenized east. Whatever its outcome, it was bound to have great repercussions for the whole Mediterranean. None the less, the East was to prove in the event that it had its own strengths and powers of resistance. As one Roman later put it, Greece would take her captors captive, Hellenizing yet more barbarians.

This 1st-century BCE sculpture, *Laocoön and his Sons*, shows the story of the lapsed priest of Apollo at Troy, who advised the Trojans not to bring the Greeks' wooden horse into the city. While the priest was preparing to sacrifice to Poseidon, two serpents strangled him and his children.

ROME AND THE CLASSICAL WEST

For all the enterprise of the Phoenicians and the early vigour of Greek colonization there, the western half of the Mediterranean basin can reasonably be judged during several centuries to have been of only marginal importance to world history. This ceased to be true because of the actions and decisions of the ruling class of what had been at first a numerically insignificant Italian people barely distinguishable from several other agglomerations of tribes and kinship groups. Barely known about by their Greek neighbours in, say, the age of Solon, they have gone down in history to be remembered as Romans, taking their name from what began as only a tiny city-state. When they became involved, much later and as the third century BCE was drawing to a close, in the affairs of Greece and the East, the Romans opened the way to a new era of world history. They forged in the next two centuries a unique institutional structure, eventually embracing the whole Hellenistic world as well as much of western Europe, making of them for the first time a single entity. The Roman Empire, as it is now remembered, was in a sense the last of the successor states of the Alexandrian world, but it embraced much more than they had ever done. Accordingly, it was to shape much more. It was, above all, to shelter the infancy of a new world religion and put political power behind it. It was to transform economic and ethnic relationships over wide areas. It was to ensure the transmission of much of the Greek classical heritage to the future. In the longest run of all, too, it was to nourish the seeds of something not to be born until long after the Roman Empire in the West had crumbled away, the civilization of Europe, which it would continue to feed not only directly through its cultural and institutional legacy, but, through example and myth, the idea of empire itself.

Set in the small valley between the Capitoline, Palatine and Esquiline hills, the Forum in the city of Rome has been the site of political, religious and commercial buildings since the 7th century BCE. The square's monumental appearance is mainly due to the work of Julius Caesar, Augustus and Tiberius. Although its basilicas, temples and triumphant arches now stand in ruins, the Forum was once the hub of the great Roman Empire.

1 *ROME*

ALL AROUND the western Mediterranean shores and across wide tracts of western Europe, the Balkans and Asia Minor, relics can still be seen of a great achievement, the empire of Rome. In some places – Rome itself, above all – they are very plentiful. To explain why they are there takes up a thousand years of history. If we no longer look back on the Roman achievement as our ancestors often did, feeling dwarfed by it, we can still be puzzled and even amazed that people could do so much. Of course, the closer the scrutiny historians give to those mighty remains, and the more scrupulous their sifting of the documents which explain Roman ideals and Roman practice, the more we realize that Romans were not, after all, superhuman. The grandeur that was Rome sometimes looks more like tinsel and the virtues its publicists proclaimed can sound as much like political cant as do similar slogans today. Yet when all is said and done, there remains an astonishing and solid core of creativity. In the end, Rome remade the setting of Greek civilization. Thus Romans settled the shape of the first civilization embracing all the West. This was a self-conscious achievement. Romans who looked back on it when it was later crumbling about them still felt themselves to be Romans like those who had built it up. They were, though only in the sense that they believed it. That was what mattered, though for all its material impressiveness and occasional grossness, the core of the explanation of the Roman achievement was an idea, the idea of Rome itself, the values it embodied

This bronze Etruscan sculpture represents a Chimaera, a mythological fire-breathing monster, which has the body and head of a lion, a serpent for a tail, and a goat's head emerging from its back. Pieces such as this demonstrate the masterly skill of the Etruscan metalworkers.

Southern Italy 509–272 BCE

In 509 BCE, according to legend, the Romans drove the last king of the Etruscan Tarquin Dynasty out of Rome and established a republican system. Roman expansion towards southern Italy began in the 5th century BCE. Rome maintained control over the neighbouring towns by allowing her "allies" the freedom of self-government, while at the same time imposing Roman foreign policy on them and forcing them to supply soldiers for the powerful Roman army.

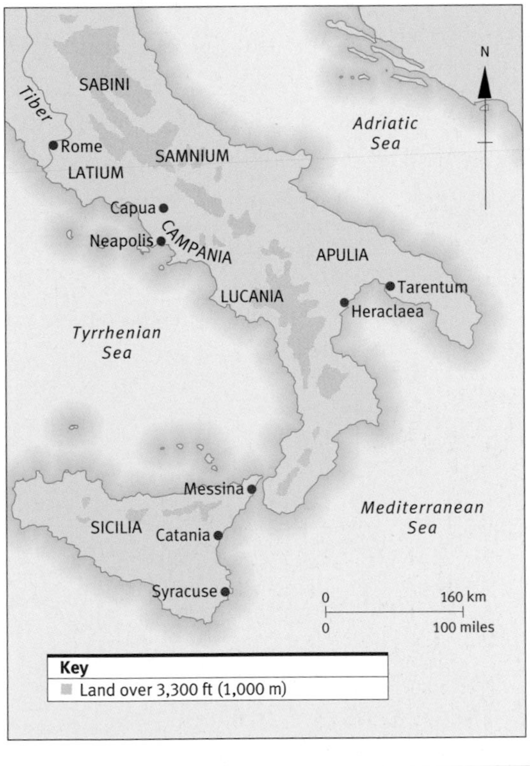

The Capitoline She-Wolf, a 5th-century BCE Etruscan sculpture. Legend has it that the abandoned twins Romulus and Remus were saved by a she-wolf. They went on to found the city of Rome, but Romulus killed his brother and ruled as sole king.

and imposed, the notion of what was one day to be called *romanitas*.

It was believed to have deep roots. Romans said their city was founded by one Romulus in 753 BCE. We need not take this seriously, but the legend of the foster-mother wolf which suckled both Romulus and his twin, Remus, is worth a moment's pause; it is a good symbol of early Rome's debt to a past that was dominated by the people called Etruscans, among whose cults has been traced a special reverence for the wolf.

THE ETRUSCANS

In spite of a rich archaeological record, with many inscriptions and much scholarly effort to make sense of it, the Etruscans remain a mysterious people. All that has so far been delineated with some certainty is the general nature of Etruscan culture, not its history or chronology. Different scholars have argued that Etruscan civilization came into existence at a wide range of different times, stretching from

Time chart (753 BCE–44 BCE)

700 BCE | 600 BCE | 500 BCE | 400 BCE | 300 BCE | 200 BCE | 100 BCE | 0

- 753 BCE Foundation of Rome, according to legend
- 509 BCE Establishment of the Roman Republic
- c.450 BCE Law of the Twelve Tables
- 264–241 BCE First Punic War
- 218–201 BCE Second Punic War
- 149–146 BCE Third Punic War
- 88–82 BCE Civil War between the armies of Marius and Sulla
- 49–45 BCE Civil War between the armies of Caesar and Pompey
- 44 BCE Assassination of Julius Caesar

Both sides of this gold tablet bear Etruscan inscriptions and abbreviated versions in Phoenician. The tablet originates from the Etruscan port of Pyrgi and probably dates from the early 5th century BCE. It forms part of a treaty between Rome and Carthage, which was signed during the first year of the republic, confirming the relationship that had been established when Rome was an Etruscan city.

The lifestyle and beliefs of the Etruscans

Little is known about the origins of the Etruscan people, although many historians now believe that they came from the Villanovan culture, which developed in the Po valley, and that they were also strongly influenced by ancient Greek culture. Etruscan civilization reached its peak during the 7th and 6th centuries BCE, when the Etruscans controlled a region that encompassed most of central Italy, including Rome, extending to the north as far as the Po, and to the south as far as Campania. They maintained strong trade links with Greece, based mainly on the exportation of metals, which added to the prosperity of the noble families who inhabited the Etruscan cities to the north of the Tiber.

It seems, from the opulence of the large private tombs they built on the outskirts of their cities, that the Etruscans believed in the existence of life after death. They filled their tombs with furniture and fabrics, weapons and cooking utensils – objects that, together with a number of well-preserved tomb frescoes, tell us a great deal about certain aspects of their lives and culture. It appears that the Etruscans thought their world to be ordered and regulated by the gods. Communication between the gods and human beings was believed to take place through omens. These were then interpreted by seers, whose powers of divination meant that they played an important role in Etruscan society.

A married couple, probably the master and mistress of a large household, is depicted on the lid of a 6th-century BCE sarcophagus discovered in the Etruscan burial ground at Cerveteri. The husband and wife, shown reclining on a low couch, are guests at a banquet. Unlike the Greeks, the Etruscans did not forbid women from attending such feasts.

Several colourful tomb murals have been found in the Etruscan burial ground at Tarquinia. This scene depicts servants and musicians, probably at a banquet, and is thought to date from the first half of the 5th century BCE.

the tenth to the seventh century BCE. Nor have they been able to agree about where the Etruscans came from; one hypothesis points to immigrants from Asia just after the end of the Hittite Empire, but several other possibilities have their supporters. All that is obvious is that they were not the first Italians. Whenever they came to the peninsula and wherever from, Italy was then already a confusion of peoples.

There were probably still at that time some aboriginal natives among them whose ancestors had been joined by Indo-European invaders in the second millennium BCE. In the next thousand years some of these Italians developed advanced cultures. Iron-working was going on in about 1000 BCE. The Etruscans probably adopted the skill from the peoples there before them, possibly from a culture which has been called Villanovan (after an archaeological site near modern Bologna). They brought metallurgy to a high level and vigorously exploited the iron deposits of Elba, off the coast of Etruria. With iron weapons, they appear to have established an Etruscan hegemony, which at its greatest extent covered the whole central peninsula, from the valley of the Po down to Campania. Its organization remains obscure, but Etruria was probably a loose league of cities governed by kings. The Etruscans were literate, using an alphabet derived from Greek which may have been acquired from the cities of Magna Graecia (though little of their writing can be understood at present), and they were relatively rich.

THE ROMAN REPUBLIC

IN THE SIXTH CENTURY BCE the Etruscans were installed in an important bridgehead on the south bank of the River Tiber. This was the site of Rome, one of a number of small cities of the Latins, an old-established people of the Campania. Through this city something of the Etruscan legacy was to survive to flow into and eventually be lost in the European tradition. Near the end of the sixth century BCE Rome broke away from Etruscan dominion when it took part in a revolt of the Latin cities against their masters. Until then, the city had been ruled by kings, the last of whom, tradition would later hold, was expelled in 509 BCE. Whatever the exact date, this was certainly about the time at which Etruscan power, which was over-strained by struggle with the western Greeks, was successfully challenged by the Latin peoples, who thereafter went their own ways.

Nevertheless, Rome was to retain much from its Etruscan past. It was through Etruria that Rome first had access to the Greek civilization with which it continued to live in contact both by land and sea. Rome was a focus of important land and water routes, high enough up the Tiber to bridge it, but not so high that the city could not be reached by sea-going vessels. Fertilization by Greek influence was perhaps its most important inheritance, but Rome also preserved much else from its Etruscan past. One was the way its people were organized into "centuries" for military purposes; more superficial but striking instances were its gladiatorial games, civic triumphs and reading of auguries – a consultation of the entrails of sacrifices in order to discern the shape of the future.

The Romans imitated the Greek custom of erecting statues in honour of their leaders in public spaces and dedicating votive statues to them in the sanctuaries. This bronze bust of the Roman aristocrat Brutus dates from the end of the 4th century BCE.

EARLY REPUBLICAN GOVERNMENT

The republic was to last for more than four hundred and fifty years and even after that its institutions survived in name. Romans always harped on continuity and their loyal adherence (or reprehensible non-adherence) to the good old ways of the early republic. This was not just historical invention. There was some reality in such claims, much as there is, for example, in the claims made for the continuity of parliamentary government in Great Britain or for the wisdom of the founding fathers of the United States in agreeing a constitution which still operates successfully. Yet, of course, great changes took place as the centuries passed. They eroded the institutional and ideological continuities and historians still argue about how to interpret them. Yet for all these changes Rome's institutions made possible a Roman Mediterranean and a Roman empire stretching far beyond it which was to be the cradle of Europe and Christianity. Thus Rome, like Greece (which reached many later peoples only through Rome), shaped much of the modern world. It is not just in a physical sense that we still live among its ruins.

THE CHANGING REPUBLIC

Broadly speaking, the changes of republican times were symptoms and results of two main processes. One was of decay; gradually the republic's institutions ceased to work. They

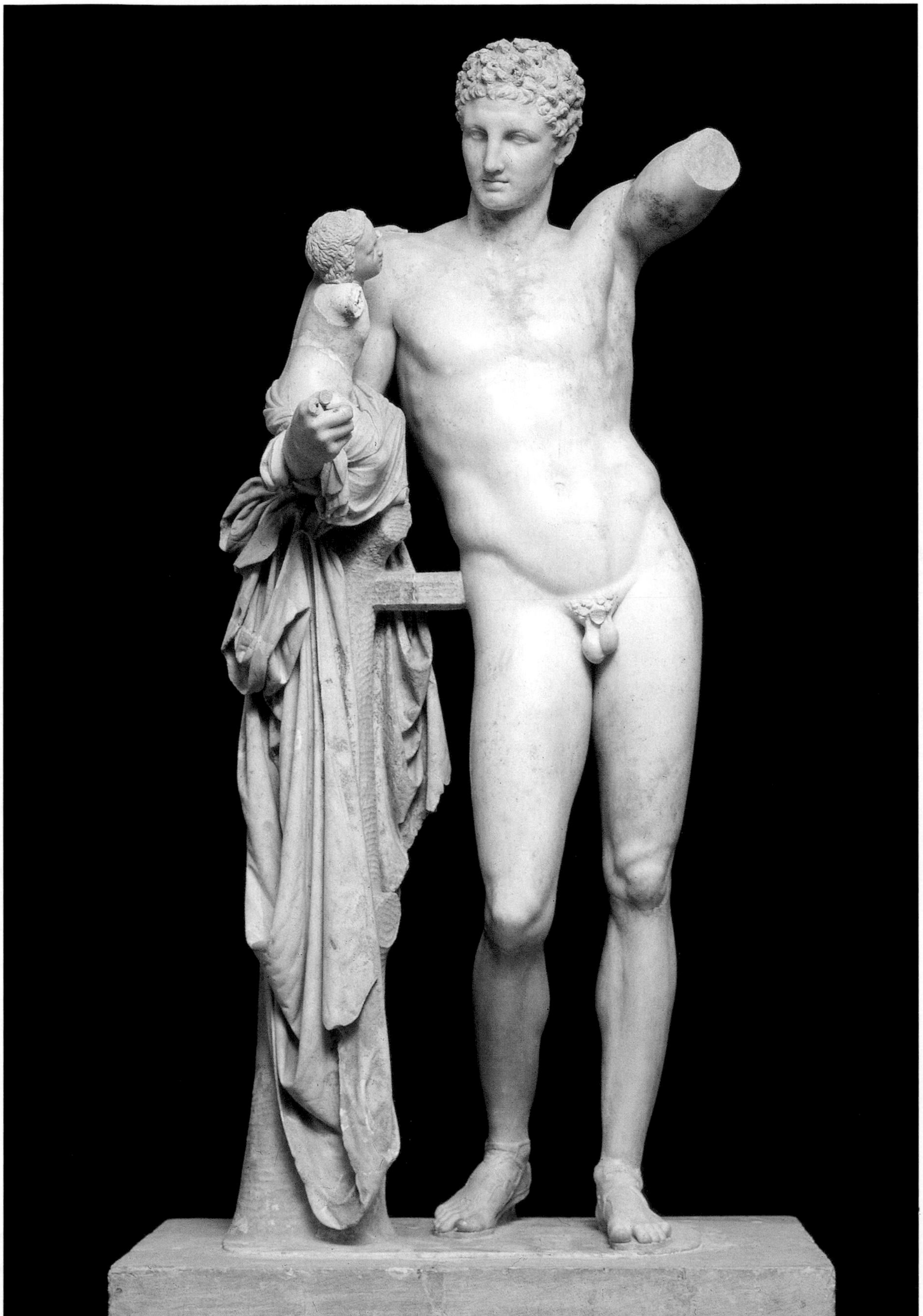

Roman civilization was greatly influenced by the Greek example and it is through Rome that much of what we know about Greek culture has been preserved. This statue of Hermes with the infant Dionysus is believed to be a Roman copy of a piece by the 4th-century BCE Greek sculptor Praxiteles. The Romans copied large numbers of Greek statues.

could no longer contain political and social realities and, in the end, this destroyed them, even when they survived in name. The other was the extension of Roman rule first beyond the city and then beyond Italy. For two centuries both processes went on rather slowly.

Internal politics were rooted in arrangements originally meant to make impossible the return of monarchy. Constitutional theory was concisely expressed in the motto carried by the monuments and standards of Rome until well into imperial times: SPQR, the abbreviation of the Latin words for "the Roman Senate and People". Theoretically, ultimate sovereignty always rested with the people, which acted through a complicated set of assemblies attended by all citizens in person (of course, not all inhabitants of Rome were citizens). This was similar to what went on in many Greek city-states. The general conduct of business was the concern of the Senate; it made laws and regulated the work of elected magistrates. It was in the form of tensions between the poles of Senate and people that the most important political issues of Roman history were usually expressed.

The Curia Julia, the building that once housed the Senate's meeting room, can be seen in the foreground of this picture of the Roman Forum. There was originally an altar outside the entrance, at which members of the Senate offered sacrifices to the gods. At the beginning of the 4th century CE the Curia Julia was rebuilt by Diocletian.

OLIGARCHY AT WORK

Rather surprisingly, the internal struggles of the early republic seem to have been comparatively bloodless. Their sequence is complicated and sometimes mysterious, but their general result was that they gave the citizen body as a whole a greater say in the affairs of the republic. The Senate, which concentrated political leadership, had come by 300 BCE or so to represent a ruling class which was an amalgamation of the old patricians of pre-republican days with the wealthier members of the *plebs*, as the rest of the citizens were termed. The Senate's members constituted an oligarchy, self-renewing though some were usually excluded from each census (which took place once every five years). Its core was a group of noble families whose origins might be plebeian, but among whose ancestors were men who had held the office of consul, the highest of the magistracies.

Two consuls had replaced the last of the kings at the end of the sixth century BCE. Appointed for a year, they ruled the state through the Senate and were its most important officers. They were bound to be men of experience and weight, for they had to have passed through at least two subordinate levels of elected office, as *quaestores* and *praetores*, before they were eligible. The *quaestores* (of whom there were twenty elected each year) also automatically became members of the Senate. These arrangements gave the Roman ruling élite great cohesiveness and competence; for progress to the highest office was a matter of selection from a field of candidates who had been well tested and trained in office. That this constitution worked well for a long time is indisputable. Rome was never short of able men. What it masked was the natural tendency of oligarchy to decay into faction, for whatever victories were won by the plebs, the working of the system ensured that it was the rich who ruled and the rich who disputed the right to office among themselves. Even in the electoral college, which was supposed to represent the whole people, the *comitia centuriata*, organization gave an undue proportion of influence to the wealthy.

SOCIAL FOUNDATIONS

Plebs IS A MISLEADINGLY simple term. The word stood for different social realities at different times. Conquest and enfranchisement slowly extended the boundaries of citizenship. Even in early times they ran well beyond the city and its environs as other cities were incorporated in the republic. At that time, the typical citizen was a countryman. The basis of Roman society was always agricultural and rural. It is significant that the Latin word for money, *pecunia*, is derived from the word for a flock of sheep or herd of cattle, and that the Roman measure of land was the *iugerum*, the extent that could be ploughed in a day by two oxen. Land and the society it supported were related in changing ways during the republic, but always its base was the rural population. The later preponderance in popular memory of the image of imperial Rome, the great parasitic city, obscures this.

THE CITIZEN CLASS

The free citizens who made up the bulk of the population of the early republic were peasants, some much poorer than others. They were legally grouped in complicated arrangements whose roots were sunk in the Etruscan past. Such distinctions were economically insignificant, though they had constitutional importance for electoral purposes, and tell us less about the social realities of republican Rome than distinctions made by the Roman census between those able to equip themselves with the arms and armour

The Rostrum was the platform from which political speakers addressed the Roman public in the Forum. Its name comes from the prows, or *rostra*, of six ships (captured in the war against the Latins in 338 BCE) which adorned the front section.

This funerary bas-relief, which dates from the 1st century CE, depicts a scene from the grape harvest – a very important moment in the Roman agricultural year. Workers are shown here treading grapes to extract the juice from which wine was produced.

needed to serve as soldiers, those whose only contribution to the state was to breed children (the *proletarii*) and those who were simply counted as heads, because they neither owned property nor had families. Below them all, of course, were the slaves.

There was a persistent tendency, accelerating rapidly in the third and second centuries BCE, for many of the *plebs* who in earlier days had preserved some independence through possession of their own land to sink into poverty. Meanwhile, the new aristocracy increased its relative share of land as conquest brought it new wealth. This was a long-drawn-out process, and while it went on, new subdivisions of social interest and political weight appeared. Furthermore, to add another complicating factor, there grew up the practice of granting citizenship to Rome's allies. The republic in fact saw a gradual enlargement of the citizen class but a real diminution of its power to affect events.

This Roman floor mosaic shows the use of oxen and horses in the harvesting and threshing of wheat. A country villa is depicted in the background.

THE PLEBEIANS

The decrease of the influence of the citizen class did not only occur because wealth came to count for so much in Roman politics. It was also because everything had to be done at Rome, though there were no representative arrangements which could effectively reflect the wishes of even those Roman citizens who lived in the swollen city, let alone those scattered all over Italy. What tended to happen instead was that threats to refuse military service or to withdraw altogether from Rome and found a city elsewhere enabled the *plebs* to restrict somewhat the powers of the Senate and magistrates. After 366 BCE, too, one of the two consuls had to be a plebeian and in 287 BCE the decisions of the plebeian assembly were given overriding force of law. But the main restriction on the traditional rulers lay in the ten elected Tribunes of the People, officers chosen by popular vote, who could initiate legislation or veto it (one veto was enough) and were available night and day to citizens who felt themselves unjustly treated by a magistrate. The tribunes had most weight when there was great social feeling or personal division in the Senate, for then they were courted by the politicians. In the earlier republic and often thereafter, the tribunes, who were members of the ruling class and might be nobles, worked for the most part easily enough with the consuls and the rest of the Senate. The administrative talent and experience of this body and the enhancement

A street in the ruined city of Pompeii, which was buried in lava when Mount Vesuvius erupted in 79 BCE. The city's wealthy inhabitants lived in huge houses that were often lavishly decorated. Poorer residents lived in tiny dwellings or in shops that opened on to the pavement. The stones seen here set in the centre of the road made it easier for pedestrians to cross the street.

of its prestige because of its leadership in war and emergency could hardly be undermined until there were social changes grave enough to threaten the downfall of the republic itself.

THE CONSTITUTION

The constitutional arrangements of the early republic were thus complicated, but effective. They prevented violent revolution and permitted gradual change. Yet they would be no more important to us than those of Thebes or Syracuse, had they not made possible and presided over the first phase of victorious expansion of Roman power. The story of the republic's institutions is important for even later periods, too, because of what the republic itself became. Almost the whole of the fifth century BCE was taken up in mastering Rome's neighbours and her territory was doubled in the process. Next, the other cities of the Latin League were subordinated; when some of them revolted in the middle of the fourth century they were forced back into it on harsher terms. It was a little like a land version of the Athenian Empire a hundred years before; Roman policy was to leave her "allies" to govern themselves, but they had to subscribe to Roman foreign policy and supply contingents to the Roman army. In addition, Roman policy favoured established dominant groups in the other Italian communities, and Roman aristocratic families multiplied their personal ties with them. The citizens of those communities were also admitted to rights of citizenship if they migrated to Rome. Etruscan hegemony in central Italy, the richest and most developed part of the peninsula, was thus replaced by Roman.

THE EXPANSION OF ROMAN POWER

ROMAN MILITARY POWER GREW, as did the number of subjected states. The republic's own army was based on conscription. Every male citizen who owned property was obliged to serve if called, and the obligation was

A small bronze statue of a 4th-century BCE Samnite warrior. He is wearing armour and would also have held a shield and a spear. The southern Italian Samnite people continued to oppose the Romans for almost three centuries after their defeat.

heavy, sixteen years for an infantryman and ten for cavalry. The army was organized in legions of 5,000, which fought at first in solid phalanxes with long pike-like spears. It not only subdued Rome's neighbours, but also beat off a series of fourth-century incursions by Gauls from the north, though on one occasion they sacked Rome itself (390 BCE). The last struggles of this formative period came at the end of the fourth century when the Romans conquered the Samnite peoples of the Abruzzi. Effectively, the republic could now tap allied manpower from the whole of central Italy.

Rome was now at last face to face with the western Greek cities. Syracuse was by far the most important of them. Early in the third century the Greeks asked the assistance of a great military leader of mainland Greece, Pyrrhus, King of Epirus, who campaigned against both the Romans and the Carthaginians (280–275 BCE), but achieved only the costly and crippling victories to whose type he gave his name. He could not destroy the Roman threat to the western Greeks. Within a few years they were caught up willynilly in a struggle between Rome and Carthage in which the whole western Mediterranean was at stake – the Punic Wars.

THE PUNIC WARS

The Punic Wars form a duel of more than a century. Their name comes from the Roman rendering of the word Phoenician and, unfortunately, we have only the Roman version of what happened. There were three bursts of fighting, but the first two settled the question of preponderance. In the first (264–241 BCE),

This bone tablet, found in Palestrina and dating from the first half of the 3rd century BCE, shows a Roman soldier during the time of the republic.

the Romans began naval warfare on a large scale for the first time. With their new fleet they took Sicily and established themselves in Sardinia and Corsica. Syracuse abandoned an earlier alliance with Carthage, and western Sicily and Sardinia became the first Roman provinces, a momentous step, in 227 BCE.

This was only round one. As the end of the third century approached, the final outcome was not yet discernible and there is still argument about which side, in this touchy situation, was responsible for the outbreak of the Second Punic War (218–201 BCE), the greatest of the three. It was fought in a greatly extended theatre, for when it began the Carthaginians were established in Spain. Some of the Greek cities there had been promised Roman protection. When one of them was attacked and sacked by a Carthaginian general, Hannibal, the war began. It is famous for Hannibal's great march to Italy and passage of the Alps with an army including elephants, and for its culmination in the crushing Carthaginian victories of Lake Trasimene and Cannae (217 and 216 BCE), where a Roman army twice the size of Hannibal's was destroyed. At this point Rome's grasp on Italy was badly shaken; some of her allies and subordinates began to look at Carthaginian power with a new respect. Virtually all the south changed sides, though central Italy remained loyal. With no resources save her own exertions and the great advantage that Hannibal lacked the numbers needed to besiege Rome, Rome hung on and saved herself. Hannibal campaigned in an increasingly denuded countryside far from his base. The Romans mercilessly destroyed Capua, a rebellious ally, without Hannibal coming to help her, and then boldly embarked upon a strategy of striking at Carthage in her own possessions, especially in Spain. In 209 BCE "New Carthage" (Cartagena) was taken by the Romans. When an attempt by Hannibal's younger brother to reinforce him was beaten off in 207 BCE the Romans transferred their offensives to Africa itself. There, at last, Hannibal had to follow them to meet his defeat at Zama in 202 BCE, the end of the war.

The defeat of Pyrrhus, King of Epirus, by the Romans in 275 BCE was a blow to the Greek world.

Carthage, a colony founded in the 9th century BCE by the Phoenicians of Tyre, was destroyed by the Roman general Scipio Aemilianus in 146 BCE, at the end of the Third Punic War. The surviving ruins, such as these, date from the new city that was founded by Julius Caesar in the Roman period. Recent excavations have revealed traces of the original Phoenician city and its port.

Roman gains in the Punic Wars

The outbreak of hostilities between Rome and Carthage in 264 BCE was the beginning of a long period of fighting known as the Punic Wars. The battleground was enormous, extending as far as New Carthage on the Iberian peninsula and throughout Italy. During the wars, Rome also began incursions into the eastern Mediterranean, which led to the eventual conquest of the Greek territories. The conflict ended in 146 BCE when the city of Carthage was totally destroyed by the Romans. In just over one century, they had unquestionably become the masters of the Mediterranean, a situation reflected in their use of the term *Mare nostrum* – "our sea".

Publius Cornelius Scipio, depicted in this bust, was known as "Africanus" because of his African campaigns during the Second Punic War. He came from the aristocratic Cornelius family, which was renowned for its military achievements in the long struggle against Carthage.

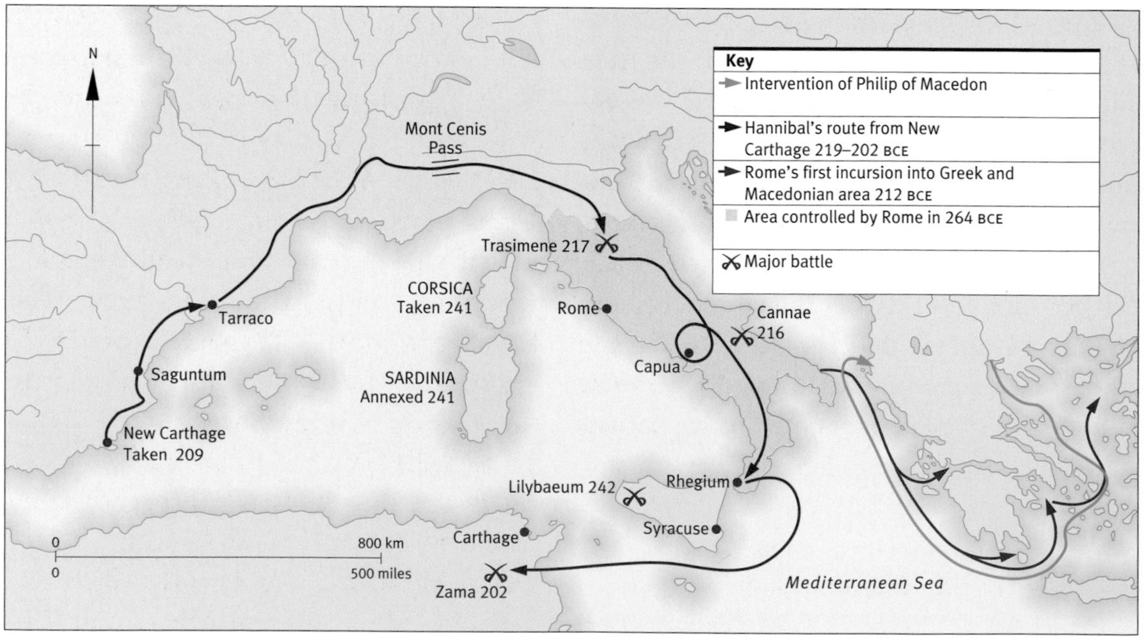

The above map shows the area affected by the Punic Wars, as well as the dates of all the major battles and of the Roman successes.

A Roman warship is depicted on this bas-relief found at the site of the Oracle of Fortuna Primigenia in Praeneste, near Rome. The bas-relief is probably from a memorial dedicated to Mark Antony (c.83–30 BCE).

This battle settled more than a war; it decided the fate of the whole western Mediterranean. Once the Po valley was absorbed early in the second century BCE, Italy was, whatever the forms, henceforth a single state ruled from Rome. The peace imposed on Carthage was humiliating and crippling. Roman vengeance pursued Hannibal himself and drove him to exile at the Seleucid court. Because Syracuse had once more allied with Carthage during the war, her presumption was punished by the loss of her independence; she was the last Greek state in the island. The whole of Sicily was now Roman, as was southern Spain, where another province was set up.

ROME TURNS EAST

Roman expansion was not limited to the western Mediterranean. Events there opened the way to the East. At the end of the Second Punic War it is tempting to imagine Rome at a parting of the ways. On the one hand lay the alternative of moderation and the maintenance of security in the West, on the other that of expansion and imperialism in the East. Yet this over-simplifies reality. Eastern and Western issues were already too entangled to sustain so simple an antithesis. As early as 228 BCE the Romans had been admitted to the Greek Isthmian games; it was a recognition, even if only formal, that for some Greeks they were already a civilized power and part of the Hellenistic world. Through Macedon, that world had already been involved directly in the wars of Italy, for Macedon had allied with Carthage; Rome had therefore taken the side of Greek cities opposed to Macedon and thus begun to dabble in Greek politics. When a direct appeal for help against Macedon and the Seleucids came from Athens, Rhodes and a king of Pergamon in 200 BCE, the Romans were already psychologically ready to commit themselves to Eastern enterprise. It is unlikely,

This sarcophagus is from the Scipio family tomb and dates from the 3rd century BCE, although the inscription is later.

though, that any of them saw that this could be the beginning of a series of adventures from which would emerge a Hellenistic world dominated by the republic.

Another change in Roman attitudes was not yet complete, but was beginning to be effective. When the struggle with Carthage began, most upper-class Romans probably saw it as essentially defensive. Some went on fearing even the crippled enemy left after Zama. The call of Cato in the middle of the next century – "Carthage must be destroyed" – was to be famous as an expression of an implacable hostility arising from fear. None the less, the provinces won by war had begun to awake Romans' minds to other possibilities and soon supplied other motives for its continuation. Slaves and gold from Sardinia, Spain and Sicily were soon opening the eyes of Romans to what the rewards of empire might be. These countries were not treated like mainland Italy, as allies, but as resource pools to be administered and tapped. A tradition grew up under the republic, too, of generals distributing some of the spoils of victory to their troops.

THE GROWTH OF THE ROMAN EMPIRE

THE TWISTS AND TURNS are complicated, but the main stages of Roman expansion in the East in the second century BCE are obvious enough. The conquest and reduction of Macedon to a province was accomplished in a series of wars ending in 148 BCE; the phalanxes were not what they had been, nor was Macedonian generalship. On the way, the cities of Greece had also been reduced to vassalage and forced to send hostages to Rome. An intervention by a Syrian king led to the first passage of Roman forces to Asia Minor; next came the disappearance of the kingdom of Pergamon, Roman hegemony in the Aegean, and the establishment of the new province of Asia in 133 BCE. Elsewhere, the conquest of the remainder of Spain, except the northwest, the organization of a tributary confederacy in Illyria, and the provincial organization of southern France in 121 BCE,

The octagonal Tower of the Winds was constructed in Athens in the 1st century BCE, when the ancient city was part of the Roman Empire. Bas-reliefs representing the eight winds embellish the upper part of the tower. The structure, which was originally crowned by a weather vane, housed a 24-hour clock run by hydraulic power.

At the beginning of the 6th century BCE, the Greeks founded Emporiae on the northern Catalan coast. In the 3rd century BCE the city's port played a significant role in the Second Punic War. Emporiae later became part of the Roman Empire and enjoyed a period of great economic splendour, during which a new Roman city was built next to the original Greek one.

meant that the coasts from Gibraltar to Thessaly were all under Roman rule. Finally, the chance long sought by the enemies of Carthage came in 149 BCE with the start of the third and last Punic War. Three years later the city was destroyed, ploughs were run over its site and a new Roman province covering western Tunisia – Africa – existed in its stead.

The Roman expansion into southern France left a considerable mark on the architecture of the region. This commemorative arch in Saint-Rémy in Provence stands at what was once the entrance to the Roman city of Glanum.

This 1st-century BCE frieze was probably a monument to Gelio Publicola, who was censor in 70 BCE. The scene depicts the census being carried out in Rome. On the left, a citizen is being registered at a counter. The figures on the right are preparing to perform sacrifices.

THE IMPERIAL ADMINISTRATION

Thus was the empire made by the republic. Like all empires, but perhaps more obviously than any earlier one, its appearance owed as much to chance as to design. Fear, idealism and eventually cupidity were the mingled impulses which sent the legions further and further afield. Military power was the ultimate basis of the Roman Empire, and it was kept up by expansion. Numbers were decisive in overcoming Carthaginian experience and tenacity and the Roman army was large. It could draw upon an expanding pool of first-class manpower available from allies and satellites, and republican rule brought order and regular government to new subjects. The basic units of the empire were its provinces, each ruled by a governor with proconsular powers whose posting was formally for one year. Beside him stood a taxing officer.

Empire inevitably had political consequences at home. In the first place it made it even more difficult to ensure popular participation – that is, the participation of poor citizens – in government. Prolonged warfare reinforced the day-to-day power and the moral authority of the Senate, and it must be said that its record was a remarkable one. Yet the expansion of territory carried even further shortcomings already apparent in the extension of Roman rule over Italy. Serious and novel problems arose. One was posed by the new opportunities war and empire gave to generals and provincial governors. The fortunes to be made, and made quickly, were immense; not until the days of the Spanish *conquistadores* or the British East India Company were such prizes so easily available to those in the right

This beautiful silver dish dates from the 4th century CE. It is part of the Mildenhall Treasure – the household silver of a rich Roman family – found in a field in Suffolk, England, in 1942. The treasure, which was probably buried to save it from Saxon raiders, demonstrates the great wealth of some of the Romans who settled in the conquered territories.

place at the right time. Much of this was legal; some was simply looting and theft. Significantly, in 149 BCE a special court was created to deal with illegal extortion by officials. Whatever its nature, access to this wealth could only be obtained through participation in politics, for it was from the Senate that governors were chosen for the new provinces and it was the Senate which appointed the tax-gatherers who accompanied them from among the wealthy but non-noble class of *equites*, or knights.

CONSTITUTIONAL PROBLEMS

One constitutional weakness arose because the principle of annual election of magistrates had more and more frequently to be set aside in practice. War and rebellion in the provinces provided emergencies which consuls elected for their political skill might well find beyond them. Inevitably, proconsular power fell into the hands of those who could deal with emergencies effectively, usually proven generals. It is a mistake to think of the republic's commanders as professional soldiers in the modern sense; they were members of the ruling class who might expect in a successful career to be civil servants, judges, barristers, politicians and even priests. One key to the administrative proficiency of Rome was its acceptance of the principle of non-specialization in its rulers. None the less, a general who stayed years with his army became a different sort of political animal from the proconsuls of the early republic who commanded an army for one campaign and then returned to Rome and politics. Paradoxically, it was a weakness that the provincial governorships were themselves annual. In that lay a temptation to make hay while the sun shone. If this was one way by which irresponsibility crept into the administrative structure, there was a corresponding tendency for successful generals in the field for longer to draw to themselves the loyalty soldiers owed to the republic. Finally, there was even a kind of socialized corruption, for all Roman citizens benefited from an empire which made possible their exemption from any direct taxation; the provinces were to pay for the homeland. Awareness of such evils lay behind much moralizing condemnation and talk of decline which arose in the first century BCE, when their impact became fatal.

CONTINUING HELLENIZATION

Another change brought by empire was a further spread of Hellenization. Here there are difficulties of definition. In some measure,

The Romans loved Greek art, particularly statuary. This statue of Venus Genetrix is a Roman copy of a 5th-century BCE Greek statue attributed to the sculptor Callimachus.

Roman culture was already Hellenized before conquest went beyond Italy. The republic's conscious espousal of the cause of the Greek cities' independence of Macedon was a symptom. On the other hand, whatever Rome already possessed, there was much that could be won only after more direct contact with the Hellenized world. In the last resort, Rome looked to many Greeks like another barbarian power, almost as bad as Carthage. There is symbolism in the legend of the death of Archimedes, struck down while pondering geometrical problems in the sand, by the sword of a Roman soldier who did not know who he was.

HELLENISTIC INFLUENCES

With empire contact with the Hellenized world became direct and the flow of Hellenistic influence manifold and frequent. Later ages were to wonder at the Roman passion for baths; the habit was one they had learnt from the Hellenized East. The first Roman literature was translated Greek drama and the first Latin comedies were imitations of Greek models. Art began to flow to Rome through pilfering and looting, but Greek style – above all its architecture – was already familiar from the western cities. There was a movement of people, too.

One of the thousand hostages sent to Rome from the Greek cities in the middle of the second century BCE was Polybius, who provided Rome with its first scientific history in the tradition of Thucydides. His history of the years 220–146 BCE was a conscious exploration of a phenomenon which he felt would mark a new epoch: Rome's success in overthrowing Carthage and conquering the Hellenistic world. He was first among historians to recognize a complement to the earlier civilizing work of Alexander in the new unity given to the Mediterranean by Rome. He also admired the disinterested air Romans appeared to bring to imperial government – a reminder to be set against the Romans' own denunciation of their wickednesses under the late republic.

STABILITY

Rome's greatest triumph rested on the bringing of peace. In a second great Hellenistic age, travellers could move from one end to another of the Mediterranean without hindrance. The essential qualities of the structure which sustained the *Pax Romana* were already there under the republic, above all in the cosmopolitanism encouraged by Roman administration, which sought not to impose a uniform pattern of life but only to collect taxes, keep the peace and regulate the quarrels of men by a common law. The great achievements of Roman jurisprudence still lay far ahead, but the early republic in about 450 BCE launched Roman law on its history of definition by the consolidation of the Twelve Tables which little Roman boys, lucky enough to go to school, had still to get by heart hundreds of years later. On them was eventually built a framework within which many cultures might survive to contribute to a common civilization.

THE DECLINE OF THE REPUBLIC

IT IS CONVENIENT to finish the story of the spread of the rule of the republic to its limits before considering how such success in the end proved fatal. Transalpine Gaul (southern France) was a province in 121 BCE but (like north Italy) it remained troubled from time to time by the incursions of Celtic tribes. The Po valley was given provincial status as Cisalpine Gaul in 89 BCE and nearly forty years later (51 BCE) the rest of Gaul – roughly northern France and Belgium – was conquered and with that the Celtic danger effectively came to an end. Meanwhile there had been further conquests in the East. The last king of Pergamon had bequeathed his kingdom to Rome in 133 BCE. There followed the acquisition of Cilicia in the early first century BCE, and then a series of wars with Mithridates, King of Pontus, a state on the Black Sea. The outcome was the reorganization of the Near East, Rome being left with possession of a coast running from Egypt to the Black Sea, all of which was divided between client kingdoms or provinces (one was named "Asia"). Finally, Cyprus was annexed in 58 BCE.

DOMESTIC CRISIS

Ironically, the counterpoint of continuing and apparently irresistible success abroad was

The heads of four dead Gallic warriors are depicted on a stone stele found in Provence, France. The piece is thought to date from the 3rd to 1st centuries BCE.

growing strife at home. The crux of the matter was the restriction of access to office to members of the ruling class. Electoral institutions and political conventions had come to work differently because of two grave long-term problems. The first was the gradual impoverishment of the Italian peasant who had been the typical figure of the early republic. It had several causes, but the root of the matter was the terrible cost of the Second Punic War. Not only had conscripted soldiers been absent for long years of almost continuous campaigns, but the physical damage to southern Italy was enormous. Meanwhile, those who were lucky enough to amass wealth in imperial enterprise laid it out in the only good investment available, land. The effect in the long run was to concentrate property in large estates usually worked by slaves made cheaper by the wars; there was no place on them for the smallholder, who now had to make his way to the city and fend for himself as best he could, a Roman citizen in name, but a proletarian in the making. Yet as a citizen he still had a vote. To those with wealth and political ambition he became someone to buy or to intimidate. Since the road to lucrative office lay through popular elections, the politics of the republic could hardly fail increasingly to reflect the power of money. This, too, had repercussions far and wide in Italy. Once votes had a price, the citizen proletariat of Rome was unlikely to welcome their continual devaluation by extending civic rights to other Italians, even though Rome's allies had to put up with conscription.

Marcus Tullius Cicero, born in 106 BCE, enjoyed a brilliant political career. He was a great orator who also composed philosophical and historical treatises. His prolific writing has given historians a valuable insight into the political and social issues of his time. Cicero was assassinated in 43 BCE.

Hannibal, who used elephants in his army during the Second Punic War, was not the first enemy of Rome to do so. Indian elephants, such as the one depicted on this 3rd-century BCE Campanian dish, were first used in battle against the Romans by Pyrrhus, King of Epirus.

MILITARY SERVICE

Another problem was change in the army. The legions had more than four hundred years' history under the republic and their evolution can hardly be condensed in a simple formula, but if one is to be sought, it is perhaps best to say that the army became increasingly professional. After the Punic Wars it was impossible any longer to rely solely on soldiers fighting in such time as they could spare from farming. The burden of conscription had always been heavy and became unpopular. When campaigns carried men further and further afield for year after year, and as garrisons had sometimes to remain for decades in conquered provinces, even the Roman pool of manpower showed signs of drying up. In 107 BCE a formal change registered what was happening: the property qualification for service was abolished. This was the work of a consul called Marius, who thus solved the problem of recruitment, for after this there were usually enough poor volunteers for conscription to be unnecessary. Military service still continued to be restricted to citizens, but there were many of these; in the end, though, service itself was to confer citizenship. Another innovation of Marius was to give the legions their "eagles", the standards so important to their *esprit de corps*, something between an idol and a modern regimental badge. Such changes gradually turned the army into a new kind of political force, available to a man like Marius who was an able general and much called upon for service in the provinces. He actually exacted a personal oath of allegiance from one army under his own command.

The widening gap of rich and poor in central Italy as peasant farming gave way to large estates bought (and stocked with slaves) with the spoils of empire, and the new possibilities open to political soldiers, proved fatal to the republic in the end. At the end of the second century BCE, the Gracchi brothers, Tribunes of the People, sought to do something about the social problem in the only way open to an agrarian economy, by land reform, reduction of senatorial power and a bigger role for the *equites* in government. They tried, in effect, to spread the wealth of empire, but their attempts only ended in their deaths. This itself marked the raising of the stakes in politics; in the last century of the republic factional bitterness reached its peak because politicians knew their lives might be forfeit. It also saw the beginning of what has been called the Roman revolution, for the

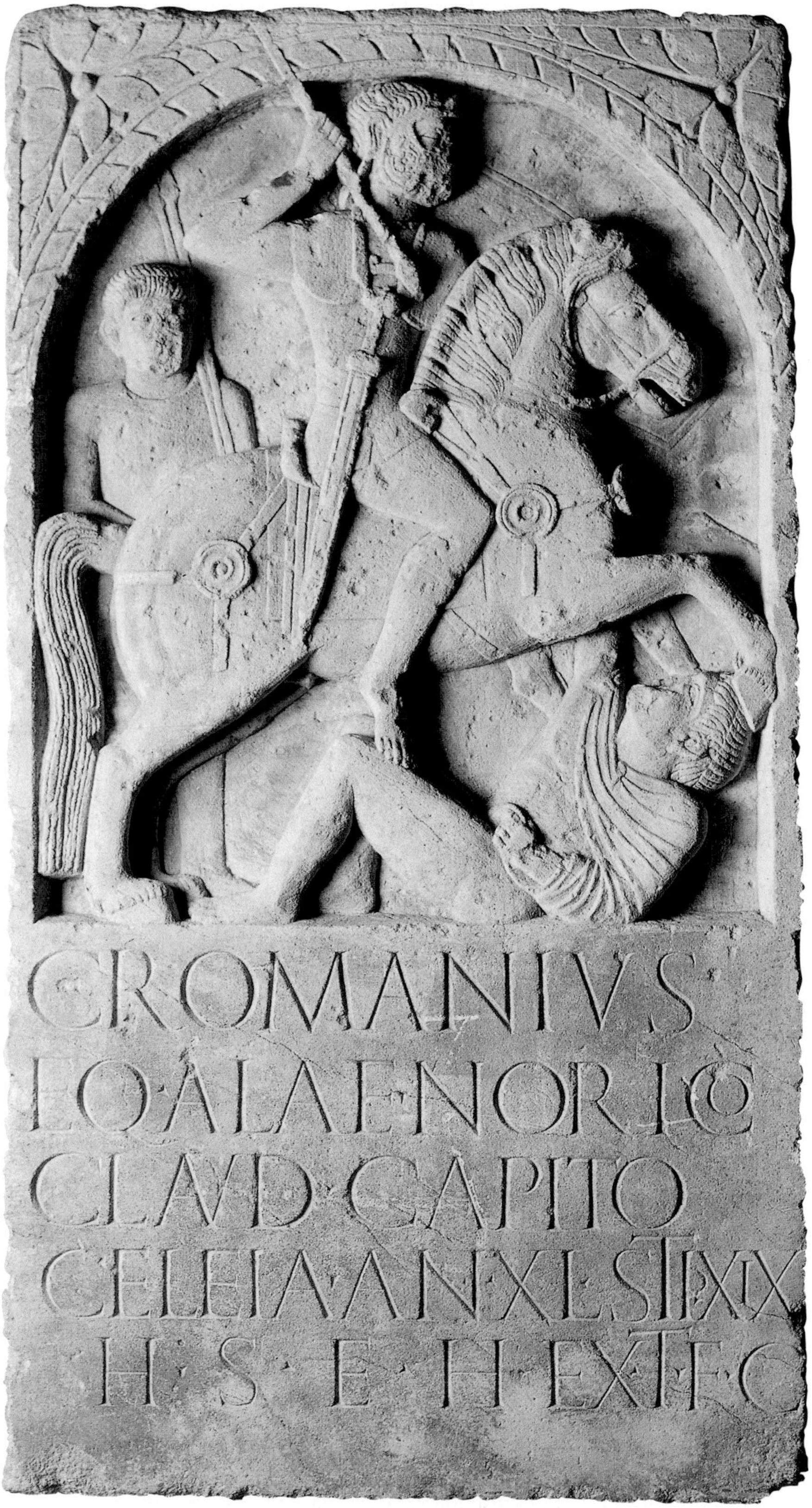

This funerary stele commemorates the death of a Roman soldier called Gaius Romanius Capitus. He was born in Slovenia in the 1st century CE and died at the age of 40.

Horse-drawn carriages were a common sight on the busy streets of Rome, as depicted on this Gallo-Roman bas-relief.

conventions of Roman politics were set aside when Tiberius Gracchus (the elder brother), then consul, persuaded the plebs to unseat the tribune who had vetoed his land-bill and thus announced that he would not accept the traditional circumvention of the popular will by the prerogative of a tribune to use his veto.

MARIUS SEIZES POWER

The final plunge of the republic into confusion was precipitated in 112 BCE by a new war when a north African king massacred a great number of Roman businessmen. Not long afterwards a wave of barbarian invaders in the north threatened Roman rule in Gaul. The emergency brought forward the consul Marius, who dealt successfully with the enemies of the republic, but at the cost of further constitutional innovation, for he was elected to the consulship for five years in succession. He was, in fact, the first of a series of warlords who were to dominate the last century of the republic, for other wars rapidly followed. Demand grew for the extension of Roman citizenship to the other Latin and Italian states. In the end these allies (*socii*) revolted in what is somewhat misleadingly called the "Social War" in 90 BCE. They were only pacified with concessions which made nonsense of the notion that the Roman popular assemblies were the ultimate sovereign; citizenship was extended to most of Italy. Then came new Asian wars – from which emerged another general with political ambitions, Sulla. There was civil war, Marius died after once more being consul, and Sulla returned to Rome in 82 BCE to launch a dictatorship (voted by the Senate) with a ruthless "proscription" of his opponents (a posting of their names which signified that anyone who could do so was entitled to kill them), an assault on the popular powers of the

Plutarch describes Gaius Marius

"It was a hard war, but he [Gaius Marius] was not afraid of any undertaking, however great, and was not too proud to accept any task, however small. The advice he gave and his foresight into what was needed marked him out among the officers of his own rank, and he won the affection of the soldiers by showing that he could live as hard as they did and endure as much. Indeed it seems generally to be the case that our labours are eased when someone goes out of his way to share them with us; it has the effect of making the labour not seem forced. And what a Roman soldier likes most to see is his general eating his ration of bread with the rest, or sleeping on an ordinary bed, or joining in the work of digging a trench or a raising a palisade. The commanders whom they admire are not so much those who distribute honours and riches as those who take a share in their hardships and their dangers; they have more affection for those who are willing to join in their work than for those who indulge them in going easy.

"By these actions and in this way Marius won the hearts of the soldiers. First Libya and then Rome were soon full of his name and of his glory, and the men in the army wrote in their letters home that the African war could never be brought to a proper conclusion unless Marius were elected consul."

The republican general Gaius Marius.

An extract from "Gaius Marius", from *Fall of the Roman Republic: Six Lives* by Plutarch (c.46–c.120 CE), translated by Rex Warner.

constitution and an attempted restoration of those of the Senate.

POMPEY

One former supporter and protégé of Sulla was a young man whose name has passed into English as Pompey. Sulla had advanced his career by giving him posts normally held only by consuls and in 70 BCE he was elected to that office, too. He left for the East three years later to eliminate piracy from the Mediterranean and went on to conquer huge Asian territories in the wars against Pontus. Pompey's youth, success and outstanding ability began to make him feared as a potential dictator. But the interplay of Roman politics was complicated. As the years passed, disorder increased in the capital and corruption in ruling circles. Fears of dictatorship were intensified, but the fears were those of one oligarchic faction among several and it was less and less clear where the danger lay. Moreover one danger went long disregarded before people awoke to it.

Mithridates VI (132–63 BCE), King of Pontus, tried to weaken the Roman presence in Asia Minor and the Aegean, taking advantage of the Greeks' hatred of the Romans. Defeated by Pompey, he committed suicide.

JULIUS CAESAR

In 59 BCE another aristocrat, the nephew of Marius's wife, had been elected consul. This was the young Julius Caesar. For a time he had cooperated with Pompey. The consulship led him to the command of the

Lucius Cornelius Sulla (138–78 BCE) was a Roman general and statesman in the last era of the republic. From 82 to 79 BCE, he assumed the role of dictator, appointed by the Senate. He is remembered for his ruthless leadership style.

army of Gaul and a succession of brilliant campaigns in the next seven years, ending in its complete conquest. Though he watched politics closely, these years kept Caesar away from Rome where gangsterism, corruption and murder disfigured public life and discredited the Senate. After them he was enormously rich and had a loyal, superbly experienced and confident army looking to him for the leadership, which would give them pay, promotion and victory in the future. He was also a cool, patient and ruthless man. There is a story of him joking and playing at dice with some pirates who captured him. One of his jokes was that he would crucify them when he was freed. The pirates laughed, but crucify them he did.

Some senators suddenly became alarmed when this formidable man wished to remain in Gaul in command of his army and the province, although its conquest was complete, retaining command until the consular election. His opponents strove to get him recalled to face charges about illegalities during his consulship. Caesar then took the step which, though neither he nor anyone else knew it, was the beginning of the end of the republic. He led his army across the Rubicon, the boundary of his province, beginning a march which brought him in the end to Rome. This was in January 49 BCE. It was an act of treason, though he claimed to be defending the republic against its enemies.

Julius Caesar in Gaul

"On learning of his [Caesar's] arrival and the Roman preparations, the Veneti and the other tribes ... began to make ready for war on a scale commensurate with the seriousness of their peril. ... Their hopes of success were increased by the confidence they placed in the natural strength of their country. They knew that the roads were intersected by tidal inlets, and that sailing would be difficult for us on account of our ignorance of the waterways and the scarcity of harbours. ... And even if all their expectations were disappointed, they had a strong fleet, while we had no ships available and were unacquainted with the shoals, harbours, and islands of the coast on which we should have to fight. ... Having resolved to fight, they fortified their strongholds, stocked them with corn from the fields, and assembled as many ships as possible on the coast of Venetia, where it was ... thought that Caesar would open hostilities. They secured the alliance of various tribes in the neighbourhood ... and summoned reinforcements from Britain, which faces that part of Gaul.

"In spite of the difficulties, Caesar had several strong reasons for undertaking this campaign: the unlawful detention of Roman knights, the revolt and renewal of hostilities by enemies who had submitted and given hostages, the large number of tribes leagued against him, and above all the danger that if these were left unpunished others might think themselves entitled to follow their example. Knowing, too, that nearly all the Gauls were fond of political change and quickly and easily provoked to war, and that all men naturally love freedom and hate servitude, he thought it advisable to divide his forces and distribute them over a wider area before more tribes could join the coalition."

An extract from Book III of *The Conquest of Gaul* by Julius Caesar, translated by S. A. Handford.

Gaius Julius Caesar (100–44 BCE) came from a well-known aristocratic family and was the main protagonist in the collapse of the Roman Republic. He also had a gift for self-promotion, which is demonstrated in his historical writing.

The Roman army

The emperor Marcus Aurelius celebrates his victories over the barbarians in the Danube region with a triumphal march. Growing pressure from the Germanic peoples posed a serious threat to the empire's northern frontier at the end of the 2nd century BCE. *This meant that most imperial soldiers were stationed in camps near the empire's borders, where distance from the cities and from their families tended to encourage cohesion among the troops.*

In the time of the republic, there was little difference between civil and military powers. However, after the Punic Wars, it was clearly not viable for the army to continue to depend on soldiers who had to tend their land for part of each year. From the end of the 2nd century BCE, army recruits were no longer required to be landowners. This made it possible to abolish conscription – there were enough eager, poor volunteers to form a professional army. Later, non-Roman citizens were allowed to join the army, and military service became a means of earning citizenship. These reforms greatly increased the power of the army's generals, who depended on their troops' loyalty.

During the imperial era, the army was divided into three separate bodies: the imperial guard, known as the praetorians (9,000 élite soldiers, with their headquarters in Rome); the 30 legions (180,000 soldiers who were Roman citizens); and the auxiliary troops (200,000 soldiers who could apply for citizenship at the end of their service).

CAESAR TAKES POWER

In its extremity the Senate called Pompey to defend the republic. Without forces in Italy, Pompey withdrew across the Adriatic to raise an army. The consuls and most of the Senate went with him. Civil war was now inevitable. Caesar marched quickly to Spain to defeat seven legions there which were loyal to Pompey; they were then mildly treated in order to win over as many of the soldiers as possible. Ruthless and even cruel though he could be, mildness to his political opponents was politic and prudent; he did not propose to imitate Sulla, said Caesar. Then he went after Pompey, chasing him to Egypt, where he was murdered. Caesar stayed long enough to dabble in an Egyptian civil war and became, almost incidentally, the lover of the legendary Cleopatra. Then he went back to Rome, to embark almost at once for Africa and defeat a Roman army there which opposed him. Finally, he returned again to Spain and destroyed a force raised by Pompey's sons. This was in 45 BCE, four years after the crossing of the Rubicon.

Brilliance like this was not just a matter of winning battles. Brief though Caesar's recent visits to Rome had been, he had organized his political support carefully and packed the Senate with his men. The victories brought him great honours and real power. He was voted dictator for life and became in effect a monarch in all but name. His power he used without much regard for the susceptibilities of politicians and without showing an imaginativeness which suggests his rule would have been successful in the long term, although he

The town of Orange (Arausio), in southern France, was originally founded as a colony for Roman military veterans by Julius Caesar. This triumphal arch, which is decorated with battle scenes, was erected in Caesar's honour to commemorate the event.

The expansion of the Roman Empire

By the end of the 1st century BCE, the Roman Empire extended throughout most Mediterranean countries in the south and reached as far as the Rhine in the north. In order to make such impressive expansion possible, it had been necessary to eliminate Carthage, Rome's greatest opponent in the western Mediterranean, and to push further into the lands of the ancient Hellenistic kingdoms. The conquest of these new territories greatly enriched Rome, both materially and culturally. The burgeoning empire's immense size also challenged the capacities of her military and political organizations, which were obliged to adapt quickly to the new situation.

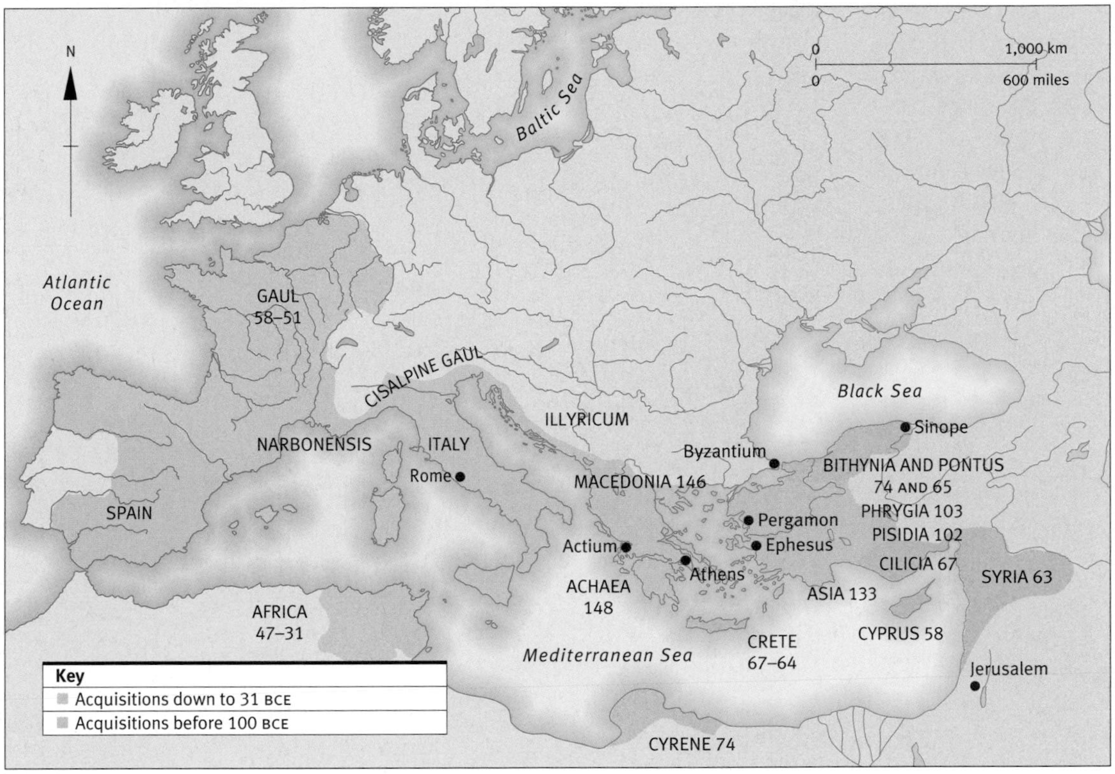

imposed order in the Roman streets, and undertook steps to end the power of the money-lenders in politics. To one reform in particular the future of Europe was to owe much – the introduction of the Julian calendar. Like much else we think of as Roman, it came from Hellenistic Alexandria, where an astronomer suggested to Caesar that the year of 365 days, with an extra day each fourth year, would make it possible to emerge from the complexities of the traditional Roman calendar. The new calendar began on 1 January 45 BCE.

THE END OF THE REPUBLIC

Fifteen months after the beginning of the new calendar, Caesar was dead, struck down in the Senate on 15 March 44 BCE at the height of his success. His assassins' motives were complex. The timing was undoubtedly affected by the knowledge that he planned a great Eastern campaign against the Parthians. Were he to join his army, it might be to return again in triumph, more unassailable than ever. There had been talk of a kingship; a Hellenistic despotism was envisaged by some. The complicated motives of his enemies were given respectability by the distaste some felt for the flagrant affront to republican tradition in the *de facto* despotism of one man. Minor acts of disrespect for the constitution antagonized others and in the end his assassins were a mixed bag of disappointed soldiers, interested oligarchs and offended conservatives.

His murderers had no answer to the problems which Caesar had not had the time, and their predecessors had so conspicuously

As well as reorganizing the ancient Forum, Julius Caesar built a new one next to it. The original Forum had become rather small for a city now at the head of a vast empire. Before construction work could begin, Caesar had to expropriate an area of private houses, at great expense. His new Forum was rectangular in shape and was surrounded by porticos lined with shops, the ruins of which can be seen here behind the double colonnade.

failed, to solve. Nor could they protect themselves for long. The republic was pronounced restored, but Caesar's acts were confirmed. There was a revulsion of feeling against the conspirators, who soon had to flee the city. Within two years they were dead and Julius Caesar was proclaimed a god. The republic was moribund, too. Damaged fatally long before the crossing of the Rubicon, the heart had gone out of its constitution whatever attempts were made to restore it. Yet its myths, its ideology and forms lived on in a romanized Italy. Romans could not bring themselves to turn their backs on the institutional heritage and admit that they had done with it. When eventually they did, they had already ceased in all but name and aspiration to resemble the Romans of the republic.

This statue represents Julius Caesar, the great general and statesman who defeated his rival Pompey to become the ruler of Rome. Caesar is famous for conquering Gaul and for his remarkable literary accounts of his military campaigns. All the subsequent Roman emperors took the official title of Caesar, perhaps in the hope that their predecessor's glory would be reflected on them.

2 *THE ROMAN ACHIEVEMENT*

If the Greek contribution to civilization was essentially mental and spiritual, that of Rome was structural and practical; its essence was the empire itself. Though no man is an empire, not even the great Alexander, its nature and government were to an astonishing degree the creation of one man of outstanding ability, Julius Caesar's great-nephew and adopted heir, Octavian.

THE AUGUSTAN AGE

Later Octavian was to be known as Caesar Augustus. An age has been named after him; his name gave an adjective to posterity. Sometimes one has the feeling that Octavian invented almost everything that characterized imperial Rome, from the new Praetorian Guard, which was the first military force stationed permanently in the capital, to the taxation of bachelors. One reason for this impression (though only one) is that he was a master of public relations; significantly, more representations of him than of any other Roman emperor have come down to us.

Minted in 32 BCE, this coin bears Mark Antony's portrait (top). The Armenian tiara in the background symbolizes his military conquests in the East. On the reverse side (bottom) is a portrait of Cleopatra, the Egyptian queen with whom Mark Antony allied himself.

Though a Caesar, Octavian came of a junior branch. From Julius (whom he succeeded at the age of eighteen) he inherited aristocratic connections, great wealth and military support. For a time he cooperated with one of Caesar's henchmen, Mark Antony, in a ferocious series of proscriptions to destroy the party which had murdered the great dictator. Mark Antony's departure to win victories in the East, failure to do so and injudicious marriage to Cleopatra, Julius Caesar's sometime mistress, gave Octavian further opportunities. He fought in the name of the republic against a threat that Antony might make a proconsular return, bringing oriental monarchy in his baggage-train. The victory of Actium (31 BCE) was followed by the legendary suicides of Antony and Cleopatra; the kingdom of the Ptolemies came to an end and Egypt too was annexed as a province of Rome.

Time chart (32 BCE–193 CE)

32–31 BCE	Octavian's war against Antony and Cleopatra
27 BCE–14 CE	Reign of Octavian (Augustus)
14–68 CE	Julio-Claudian Dynasty: Tiberius, Caligula, Claudius and Nero
68–69 CE	Year of the Four Emperors
69–96 CE	Flavian Dynasty: Vespasian, Titus and Domitian
96–192 CE	Adoptive emperors: Nerva, Trajan, Hadrian, Antoninus Pius, Marcus Aurelius and Commodus
117 CE	Empire reaches its maximum extent with Trajan's conquests
193 CE	Septimius Severus founds Severan Dynasty

Timeline scale: 50 BCE · 25 BCE · 0 · 50 CE · 100 CE · 150 CE · 200 CE

The Gemma Augustae is a cameo from c.10 CE in which Augustus is shown, enthroned as Jupiter, beside the goddess Roma. In front of the emperor, Germanicus is preparing for his next expedition, while Tiberius alights from a chariot driven by Victoria. In the lower section, Roman soldiers are raising a monument to Victoria and auxiliaries are leading their barbarian captives away.

AUGUSTUS AS CONSUL

The annexation of Egypt signalled the end of civil war. Octavian returned to become consul. He had every card in his hand and judiciously refrained from playing them, leaving it to his opponents to recognize his strength. In 27 BCE he carried out what he called a republican restoration with the support of a Senate whose republican membership, purged and weakened by civil war and proscription, he reconciled to his real primacy by his careful preservation of forms. He re-established the reality of his great-uncle's power behind a facade of republican piety. He was *imperator* only by virtue of his command of the troops of the frontier provinces – but that was where the bulk of the legions were. As old soldiers of his and his great-uncle's armies returned to retirement, they were duly settled on smallholdings and were appropriately grateful. His consulship was prolonged from year to year and in 27 BCE he was given the honorific title of Augustus, the name by which he is remembered. At Rome, though, he was formally and usually called by his family name, or was identified as *princeps*, first citizen. As the years passed Augustus's power still grew. The Senate accorded him a right of interference in those provinces which it formally ruled (that is, those where there was no need to keep a garrison army). He was voted the tribunician power. His special status was enhanced and formalized by a new recognition of his state or *dignitas*, as the Romans called it; he sat between the two consuls after his resignation from that office in 23 BCE and his business was given precedence in the agenda of the Senate. Finally, in 12 BCE he became *pontifex maximus*, the head of the official cult, as his great-uncle had been. The forms of the republic with their popular elections and senatorial elections were maintained, but Augustus said who should be elected.

THE BENEVOLENT DESPOT

The political reality masked by the ascendancy enjoyed by Augustus was the rise to domination within the ruling class of men who owed their position to the Caesars. But the new élites were not to be allowed to behave like the old. The Augustan benevolent despotism regularized the provincial administration and army by putting them into obedient and

This marble statue of Augustus is a copy of a bronze piece that was made around 20 BCE. The emperor is portrayed as both a triumphant general and a god – his bare feet symbolize his divinity. At his side is Cupid on a dolphin, respresenting Augustus' descent from Venus.

The Ara Pacis Augustae is a monument dedicated to the peace established by the emperor Augustus. This fragment from the frieze shows a procession that includes members of the royal family. Augustus' son-in-law Agrippa is seen walking behind the servants. Behind Agrippa are his young son Gaius Caesar and his wife Julia (the daughter of Augustus).

salaried hands. The conscious resuscitation of republican tradition and festivals had a part to play in this, too. Augustan government was heavily tinged with concern for moral revival; the virtues of ancient Rome seemed to some to live again. Ovid, a poet of pleasure and love, was packed off to exile in the Black Sea when a sexual scandal at the edge of the imperial family provided an excuse. When to this official austerity is added the peace which marked most of the reign and the great visible monuments of the Roman architects and engineers, the reputation of the Augustan age is hardly surprising. After his death in 14 CE Augustus was deified, as Julius Caesar had been.

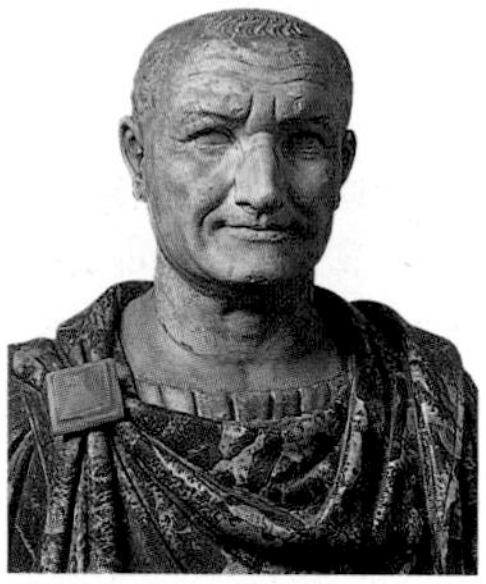

Vespasian (9–81 CE) enjoyed a brilliant military career. On the death of the emperor Vitellius in 69, during the civil war, the Eastern legions proclaimed Vespasian emperor. He reestablished order in the empire and secured its borders by creating permanent military encampments on the Danube and the Rhine.

MONARCHY AND CIVIL WAR

Augustus intended to be succeeded by a member of his own family. Although he respected republican forms (and they were to endure with remarkable tenacity) Rome was now really a monarchy. This was demonstrated by the succession of five members of the same family. Augustus's only child was a daughter; his immediate successor was his adopted stepson, Tiberius, one of his daughter's three husbands. The last of his descendants to reign, Nero, died in 68 CE.

The rulers of the classical world did not usually live easy lives. Some Roman emperors had great mirrors installed at the corners of the corridors of their palaces so that would-be assassins could not lurk around them. Tiberius himself may have not have died a natural death, and none of his four successors did. The fact is significant of the weaknesses inherent in Augustus' legacy. There was still scope for pinpricks from a Senate which formally continued to appoint the first magistrate, and always room for intrigue and cabal about the court and imperial household. Yet the Senate could never hope to recover authority, for the ultimate basis of power was always military. If there was confusion and indecision at the centre, then the soldiers would decide. This was what happened in the first great burst of civil war to shake the empire, in the year of the Four Emperors, 69 CE, from which there emerged Vespasian, the grandson of a centurion and far from an aristocrat. The first magistracy had passed out of the hands of the great Roman families.

Army officer Mucianus appeals to Vespasian

"I call upon you, Vespasian, to assume the position of emperor and so perform an act which is beneficial to our country and does honour to yourself. ... There is no need for you to fear what might seem mere flattery: it is perhaps as much an insult as a compliment to be chosen to succeed Vitellius. We are not rising in revolt against the subtle statesmanship of Augustus, nor against the elaborate precautions of the elderly Tiberius, nor even against Gaius or Claudius or Nero, whose power was firmly based on a long dynasty. ... Further passivity in the face of a process in which our country suffers defilement and decay would smack of sloth and feebleness. ... The time has gone and is now long past when it was possible for you to pretend to be indifferent to power. ...

"Besides, the lesson that an army can create an emperor is one that Vitellius can learn from his own accession. ... Vitellius has now made his predecessor seem a great emperor whose loss is regretted. ... You, Vespasian, can draw on Judaea, Syria and Egypt for nine legions. ... Your troops are in good training and have successfully fought a foreign foe; and to these must be added other powerful resources in the shape of fleets, cavalry regiments and cohorts, devoted native kings and your own unrivalled experience."

An extract from Book II, v. 76, of *The Histories* by Tacitus (c.56–c.120 CE), translated by Kenneth Wellesley.

THE ANTONINES

When Vespasian's younger son was murdered in 96 CE this upstart house came to an end. Its successor was an elderly senator, Nerva. He solved the problem of succession by breaking with attempts to ensure natural dynastic continuity. Instead, he institutionalized the practice of adoption to which Augustus had been driven. The result was a succession of four emperors, Trajan, Hadrian, Antoninus Pius and Marcus Aurelius, who gave the empire a century of good government; it has been named (after the third of them) the age of the Antonines. All of them came of families with provincial roots; they were evidence of the degree to which the empire was a cosmopolitan reality, the framework of the post-Hellenistic world of the West, and not merely the property of the Italian-born. Adoption made it easier to find candidates upon whom army, provinces and Senate could agree, but this golden age came to an end with a reversion to the hereditary principle, the succession of Commodus, son of Marcus Aurelius. He was murdered in 192 CE, and there appeared to be a repetition of 69 CE when, in the following year, there were again four emperors, each acclaimed by his own army. The Illyrian army prevailed in the end, imposing an African general. Other and later emperors were to be the nominees of soldiers too; bad times lay ahead.

THE LIMITS OF EMPIRE

The emperors now ruled a far larger area than had Augustus. In the north Julius

This is the only bronze equestrian statue known to have survived from the classical era. It depicts the emperor Marcus Aurelius (161–180 CE), who prided himself on his love of culture. His own writings include the *Soliloquies*, which strongly reflect his Stoic philosophy.

Augustus and the Roman Empire

"Augustus kept for himself all the more vigorous provinces – those that could not be safely administered by an annual governor; the remainder went to proconsuls chosen by lot. Yet, as occasion arose, he would change the status of provinces from imperial to senatorial, or contrariwise, and paid frequent visits to either sort. Finding that certain city-states which had treaties of alliance with Rome were ruining themselves through political irresponsibility, he took away their independence; but also granted subsidies to others crippled by public debts, rebuilt some cities which had been devastated by earthquakes, and even awarded Latin rights or full citizenship to states that could show a record of faithful service in the Roman cause. So ... Augustus inspected every province of the Empire, except Sardinia and North Africa. ... He nearly always restored the kingdoms which he had conquered to their defeated dynasties, or combined them with others, and followed a policy of linking together his royal allies by mutual ties of friendship or intermarriage, which he was never slow to propose. Nor did he treat them otherwise than as integral parts of the Empire, showing them all consideration and finding guardians for those who were not yet old enough to rule, until they came of age. ... He also brought up many of their children with his own, and gave them the same education."

An extract from "Augustus", v. 47–8, from *The Twelve Caesars* by Suetonius (c.69–c.150 CE), translated by Robert Graves.

Caesar had carried out reconnaissances into Britain and Germany, but had left Gaul with the Channel and the Rhine as its frontiers. Augustus pressed into Germany, and also up to the Danube from the south. The Danube eventually became the frontier of the empire, but incursions beyond the Rhine were less successful and the frontier was not stabilized on the Elbe as Augustus had hoped. Instead, a grave shock had been given to Roman confidence in 9 CE when the Teutonic tribes led by Arminius (in whom later Germans were to see a national hero) destroyed three legions. The ground was never recovered, nor the legions, for their numbers were thought so ill-omened that they never again appear in the army lists. Eight remained stationed along the Rhine, the most strongly held part of the frontier because of the dangers which lay beyond it.

Elsewhere, Roman rule still advanced. In 43 CE Claudius began the conquest of Britain, which was carried to its furthest enduring limit when Hadrian's Wall was built across the north as an effective boundary eighty or so years later. In 42 CE Mauretania had become a province. In the East, Trajan conquered Dacia, later Romania, in 105 CE, but this was more than a century and a half after a quarrel, which was to be long-lasting, had begun in Asia.

ROME AND PARTHIA

Rome had first faced Parthia on the Euphrates when Sulla's army campaigned there in 92 BCE. Nothing of importance followed until thirty years later when Roman armies began to advance against Armenia. Two spheres of influence overlapped there and Pompey at one moment arbitrated between the Armenian and Parthian kings in a boundary dispute. Then, in 54 BCE, the Roman politician Crassus launched an invasion of Parthia across the Euphrates. Within a few weeks he was dead and a Roman army of forty thousand destroyed. It was one of the worst military disasters of Roman history. Evidently there was a new great power in Asia. The Parthian army consisted of more than good mounted archers by this time. It also had heavy cavalry of unrivalled quality, the cataphracts, mail-clad horsemen with their mounts mailed too, charging home with heavy lances. The fame of their great horses even awoke the envy of the distant Chinese.

Hadrian's Wall was built to defend the empire's northern frontier in Britain during the reign of Hadrian (117–138 CE). The wall was 75 miles (120 km) long and relied on 17 heavily guarded fortresses, at which infantry units were garrisoned. Between the fortresses, smaller "milecastles" were built, and between each of these stood two lookout towers, allowing close observation of the surrounding terrain.

After this, the eastern frontier on the Euphrates was to remain undisturbed for a century, but the Parthians did not endear themselves to Rome. They dabbled in the politics of the civil war, harassing Syria and encouraging unrest among the Palestinian Jews. Mark Antony had to retreat in disgrace and distress to Armenia after losing thirty-five thousand men in a disastrous campaign against them. But Parthia suffered from internal divisions too, and in 20 BCE Augustus was able to obtain the return of the Roman standards taken from Crassus and thankfully set aside any need to attack Parthia for reasons of honour. Yet the likelihood of conflict persisted, both because of the sensitivity with which each power regarded Armenia and because of the instability of Parthia's dynastic politics. One emperor, Trajan, conquered the Parthian capital of Ctesiphon and fought his way down to the Persian Gulf, but his successor Hadrian wisely conciliated the Parthians by handing back much of his conquest.

THE *PAX ROMANA*

It was the Roman boast that their new subjects all benefited from the extension to them of the *Pax Romana*, the imperial peace which removed the threats of barbarian incursion or international strife. The claim has to be qualified by recognition of the violence with which many subject peoples resisted Roman rule, and the bloodshed this cost, but there is something in it. Within the frontiers there was order and peace as never before. In some places this permanently changed the patterns of settlement as new cities were founded in the East or descendants of Caesar's soldiers

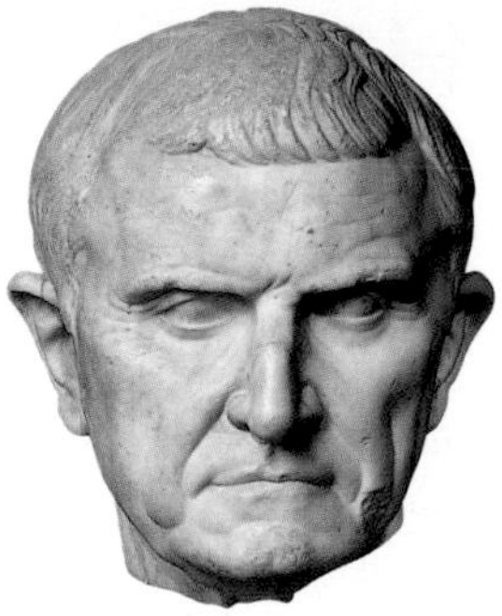

Marcus Licinius Crassus (115–53 BCE) was one of the richest men in Rome in his day. A member of the first Triumvirate with Caesar and Pompey, Crassus was responsible for Asia Minor and Syria. In 53 BCE, in one of the greatest military disasters in Roman history, he was defeated by the Parthian army.

These detailed bas-reliefs decorate Trajan's Column, constructed in his Forum in Rome. The column commemorates the Romans' victory over the Dacians, which led to the annexation of Dacia (now Romania) to the empire at the beginning of the 2nd century CE. Various events from the campaign are depicted in the above scenes, including the emperor delivering speeches to his troops, the building of fortifications, and battles.

The imperial residences on the Palatine Hill

At the end of the 1st century CE, the emperor Domitian ordered that a large residential complex be built next to Tiberius' palace, extending throughout the central part of the Palatine Hill. The Domus Flavia was comprised of official buildings, each one huge: the throne room, the advisory chamber or *basilica*, the dining room and the libraries. It also had a large patio surrounded by marble columns. The Domus Augustia – a luxurious villa with several patios – was the emperor's private residence. To this, Domitian later added a stadium and thermal baths. The Domus Severiana, built in the time of Septimius Severus, in the late 2nd century CE, stands partly on a large platform jutting out from the hillside.

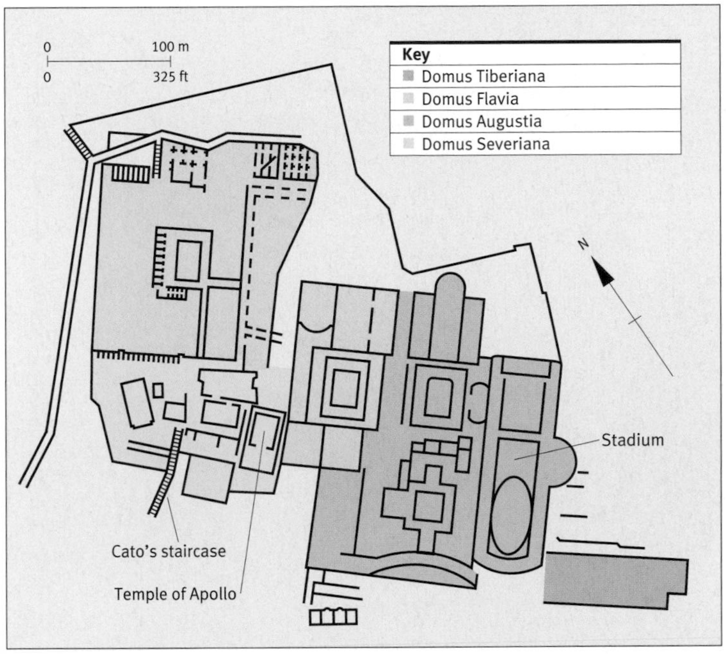

The Domus Tiberiana was built during the reign of Tiberius in the 1st century CE, *above the Roman Forum. It was the first of the imperial buildings on the Palatine Hill, hence the word* palatium *(palace). In the 16th century* CE, *the Farnesian Orchards were established over this area, obscuring a large part of the remains.*

The Porta Nigra in the Roman city of Treveri (now Trier, or Trèves) dates from the end of the 2nd century CE. The city became a major centre, as its favourable geographical situation allowed easy access to the military encampments along the Rhine. Treveri was the headquarters of the procurator of Belgium and the Two Germanias and, from the end of the 3rd century, it was one of the most important cities in the Western Empire.

were settled in new military colonies in Gaul. Sometimes there were even more far-reaching results. The adoption of the Rhine frontier permanently affected the history of Europe by its division of the Germanic peoples. Meanwhile, there took place everywhere, as things settled down, a gradual romanization of the local notables. They were encouraged to share a common civilization whose spread was made easier by the new swiftness of communication along the roads whose main purpose was the movement of the legions. Napoleon could not move couriers faster from Paris to Rome than could the emperors of the first century CE.

IMPERIAL ORGANIZATION

The empire was a huge area and required the solution of problems of government which had not been faced by Greeks or solved by Persians. A complex bureaucracy appeared, with remarkable scope. To cite one small example, the records of all officers of centurion rank and above (company commanders upwards, as it were) were centralized at Rome. The corps of provincial civil servants was the administrative armature, sustained by a practical reliance for many places upon the army, which did much more than merely fight. Bureaucracy was controlled by the adoption of fairly limited aims. These were above all fiscal; if the taxes came in, then Roman rule did not want to interfere in other ways with the operation of local custom. Rome was tolerant. It would provide the setting within which the example of its civilization would wean barbarians from their native ways. The reform of the administrators had begun under Augustus. The Senate still appointed to many posts on an annual basis, but the emperor's *legati* who acted for him in the frontier provinces held office at his pleasure. All the evidence is that, whatever the means were by which it was achieved, the administration underwent a notable improvement under the empire by comparison with the corruption of the last century of the republic. It was much more centralized and integrated than the satrapy system of Persia.

The cooperation of the subject peoples was tempted with a bait. First the republic and then the empire had been extended by granting citizenship to wider and wider numbers of Rome's subjects. It was an important privilege; among other things, as the Acts of the Apostles remind us, it carried with it rights of appeal from local courts to the emperor at Rome. On the granting of citizenship could be based the winning of the loyalties of local notables; more and more non-Romans make their appearance in the Senate and at Rome as the centuries pass. Finally, in 212 CE, citizenship was granted to all free subjects of the empire.

COSMOPOLITANISM

The enlargement of the citizen class was an outstanding instance of the Roman power of assimilation. The empire and the civilization it carried were unashamedly cosmopolitan. The administrative framework contained an astonishing variety of contrasts and diversities. They were held together not by an impartial despotism exercised by a Roman élite or a professional bureaucracy, but by a constitutional system which took local élites and romanized them. From the first century CE the senators themselves included only a dwindling number of men of Italian descent. Roman tolerance in this was diffused among other peoples. The empire was never a racial unity whose hierarchies were closed to non-Italians. Only one of its peoples, the Jews, felt strongly about the retention of their distinction within it, and

In 312 BCE, the censor Appius Claudius gave orders for the Appian Way (below) to be paved, making it the first paved road in Rome. A vast network of similar roads was eventually constructed, enabling the empire's capital city to be connected to even its most remote provinces.

that distinction rested on religion and the practices associated with it.

ROME'S GREEK HERITAGE

Already Hellenistic civilization had achieved a remarkable mixing of East and West; now Rome continued the process over an even wider area. The element in the new cosmopolitanism which was most obvious was, indeed, the Greek, for the Romans themselves made much of their inheritance from the Greeks, though it was the Greeks of the Hellenistic era with whom they were most at home. All educated Romans were bilingual and this illustrates the tradition upon which they drew. Latin was the official language and always remained the language of the army; it was spoken widely in the West and to judge by the military records, literacy in it was high. Greek was the *lingua franca* in the Eastern provinces, understood by all officials and merchants, and used in the courts if the litigants wished. Educated Romans grew up to read the Greek classics and drew from them their standards; the creation of a literature which could stand on an equal footing with the older was the laudable ambition of most Roman writers. In the first century CE they got nearest to this and the coincidence of a cultural and an imperial achievement is striking in Virgil, the conscious renewer of the epic tradition who was also the poet of imperial mission.

It may be that in this lies one clue to the peculiar tenor of Roman culture. Perhaps it is the obviousness and pervasiveness of the Greek background which does much to deprive it of the air of novelty. Its weight was accentuated by the static, conservative concern of Roman thinkers. Between them, their attention was absorbed almost exclusively by the two foci provided by the Greek inheritance and the

The Roman Empire owed its cosmopolitanism to its great size. This detail from a 3rd-century CE mosaic floor comes from a villa in the port of Hadrumetum (now Sousse) in the Roman province of Africa Proconsularis. Though the animals depicted are clearly inspired by African wildlife, the scene is quintessentially Roman, showing the triumphal procession of Dionysus, lord of the beasts and god of wine and ecstasy.

Latin language and literature

Latin, the official language throughout the empire, constitutes one of Roman civilization's greatest legacies. Evidence suggests that written Latin was in use as early as the 4th century BCE. Literary Latin, the earliest evidence of which dates from the 3rd century BCE, was to remain relatively unchanged for centuries. During the Middle Ages and the Renaissance, the principal philosophical or scientific works continued to be written in Latin, which had become an international cultural language. However, spoken Latin evolved much more quickly and became the basis of the various Romance languages.

Countless authors have been inspired by Roman literature over the centuries and its profound influence on later European literature is undeniable. The Romans cultivated literary genres that had already been established by the Greeks – drama, poetry and historic narrative. They also developed new genres, including satire, and placed great importance on the art of rhetoric.

This 4th-century mosaic, found in a house in northern Africa, is a testament to the veneration that the Romans felt for the poet Virgil, who lived in the 1st century BCE. Virgil is shown flanked by Calliope, Muse of Epic Poetry, and Melpomene, Muse of Tragedy. In his lap is a scroll of the Aeneid *displaying Book 8, in which the poet invokes the Muses.*

moral and political traditions of the republic. Both lived on curiously and somewhat artificially in a material setting, which more and more ceased to fit them. Formal education changed little in practice and content from century to century, for example. Livy, the great Roman historian, sought again to quicken republican virtues in his history, but not to criticize and reinterpret them. Even when Roman civilization was irreversibly urban the (almost extinct) virtues of the independent peasant continued to be celebrated and rich Romans longed (they said) to get away from it all to the simple life of the countryside. Roman sculpture only provided again what Greeks had already done better. The philosophies of Rome were Greek, too. Epicureanism and Stoicism held the centre of the stage; neo-Platonism was innovatory, but came from the East, as did the mystery religions which were eventually to provide Roman men and women with something their culture could not give them.

Discovered in the villa in Boscoreale, this fresco dates from 10 BCE and is an example of the pastoral style of painting that became highly popular in Rome from the time of Augustus. Nature was idealized and the virtues and simplicity of rural life were glorified while being portrayed in decidedly urban surroundings.

LAW, ENGINEERING AND TOWN PLANNING

The Romans were only great innovators in two practical fields, law and engineering. The achievements of the lawyers were relatively late; it was in the second and early third centuries CE that the jurisconsults began the accumulation of commentary which would be so valuable a legacy to the future when codification passed their work to medieval Europe. In engineering – and Romans did not distinguish it from architecture – the quality of their achievement is more immediately impressive. It was a source of pride to the Romans and one of the few things in which they were sure they outstripped the Greeks. It was based on cheap labour: in Rome it was slaves and in the provinces often the unemployed legions on garrison duty in peaceful times who carried out the great works of

A tutor is depicted giving instruction to children from a rich family in this scene from a Roman tomb. Teaching methods in Rome were reformed during the 1st and 2nd centuries CE and education was divided into three grades: primary school, grammar school and rhetoric school.

Engineering and architecture

The Romans' engineering skills were outstanding. Great Roman monuments are surprising not only for their grandeur but also for the strength of their walls and vaults – a tribute to the expert construction techniques of their builders.

Until the 3rd century BCE, Roman buildings were made of wood and clay-brick and only city walls were built with superimposed blocks of cut stone. The use of cement, from the 3rd century BCE, revolutionized building methods. When a cement facade was not decorated with stone bas-reliefs or tiles the surface was usually covered with stucco and whitewashed.

From the 1st century BCE, the Romans used baked tiles, which, because of their refractory properties, were ideal for the construction of thermal baths.

The Greek tradition of huge columns and cut stone was upheld in the decoration of large public buildings. For the first time, interior areas were treated as more than just rooms to decorate: space and lighting were taken into account. Civil engineering projects, however, such as bridges and aqueducts, were designed to meet technical and functional rather than decorative needs.

This marble funerary bas-relief dates from the year 100 CE and, in memory of one of the building contractors for the project, represents the construction of a temple. The crane on the left was powered by slaves inside the enormous tread-wheel.

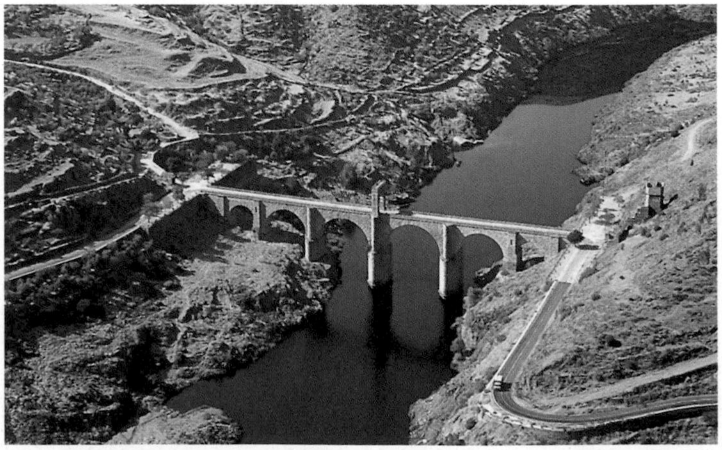

The road bridge across the Tagus River at Alcántara in Spain dates from the 1st century CE and is an example of the Roman administration's efforts to provide the provinces with an efficient communication system. The architect left an inscription, proudly declaring that the bridge "will last for always throughout time".

Work on the Pantheon in Rome was begun by Agrippa, Augustus' son-in-law, in 27 BCE. Agrippa's temple was later destroyed by fire and then rebuilt by Hadrian c.118–128 CE. Brick and six different types of concrete were used in the construction of the Pantheon, as well as coloured marble from many parts of the empire. Although the exterior of the structure is unremarkable, the interior is a large, impressive circular space surmounted by a huge hemispherical dome. A central hole, or oculus (eye), is the sole internal source of light. Seven niches, which originally contained statues of the planetary gods, ring the vestibule; as the sun moved round each was illuminated in turn by the ray of light from the roof, representing the sky god Jupiter. The Pantheon was a triumph of Roman engineering, as well as an important symbolic and religious building; the dome itself, made of concrete, weighs 5,000 tons and is carried on walls that are nearly 20 ft (6 m) thick.

Roman law

The first attempt to collate the laws that were in use in Rome took place c.450 BCE, when the *Twelve Tables* were inscribed and erected in the Roman Forum. As Roman law evolved, it covered mainly personal issues, such as obligations, property, possessions and succession. Although the first emperors created new laws by *senatus consultatum* (resolutions passed by the Senate), later emperors simply passed *constitutiones principium* (decrees). The emperor Justinian's *Codex constitutionum* of 529 CE collated all valid laws, and constitutes the basis of most of the legal systems in Western civilization.

The Tabula Claudina is the inscription in bronze of a speech given by the emperor Claudius in 48 CE. In his address to the Senate, the emperor recognized the right of the Gauls to be members of that ancient Roman institution.

hydraulic engineering, bridging and road-building. But more was involved than material factors. The Romans virtually founded town-planning as an art and administrative skill west of the Indus, and their inventions of concrete and the vaulted dome revolutionized the shapes of buildings. For the first time the interiors of buildings became more than a series of surfaces for decoration. Volumes and lighting became part of the subject-matter of architecture; the later Christian basilicas were to be the first great expressions of a new concern with the spaces inside buildings.

Roman technical accomplishment was stamped on an area stretching from the Black Sea in the east to Hadrian's Wall in the north and the Atlas mountains in the south. The capital, of course, contained some of its most spectacular relics. There, the wealth of empire

Roman roads

The Romans built 50,000 miles (80,000 km) of roads, constituting a transport network that united the most far-flung points of the empire. The majority of the routes, which were constructed mainly for military purposes, led to provincial cities that were islands of Graeco-Roman culture set in the middle of regions that had been scarcely romanized at all.

Roman roads were built to last: they had solid foundations topped with hard-wearing paving stones. Because the roads' surfaces were slightly higher in the middle than at the edges, water drained away – a feature that allowed the network to be relied on all year round. Many Roman roads were still in use during the Middle Ages.

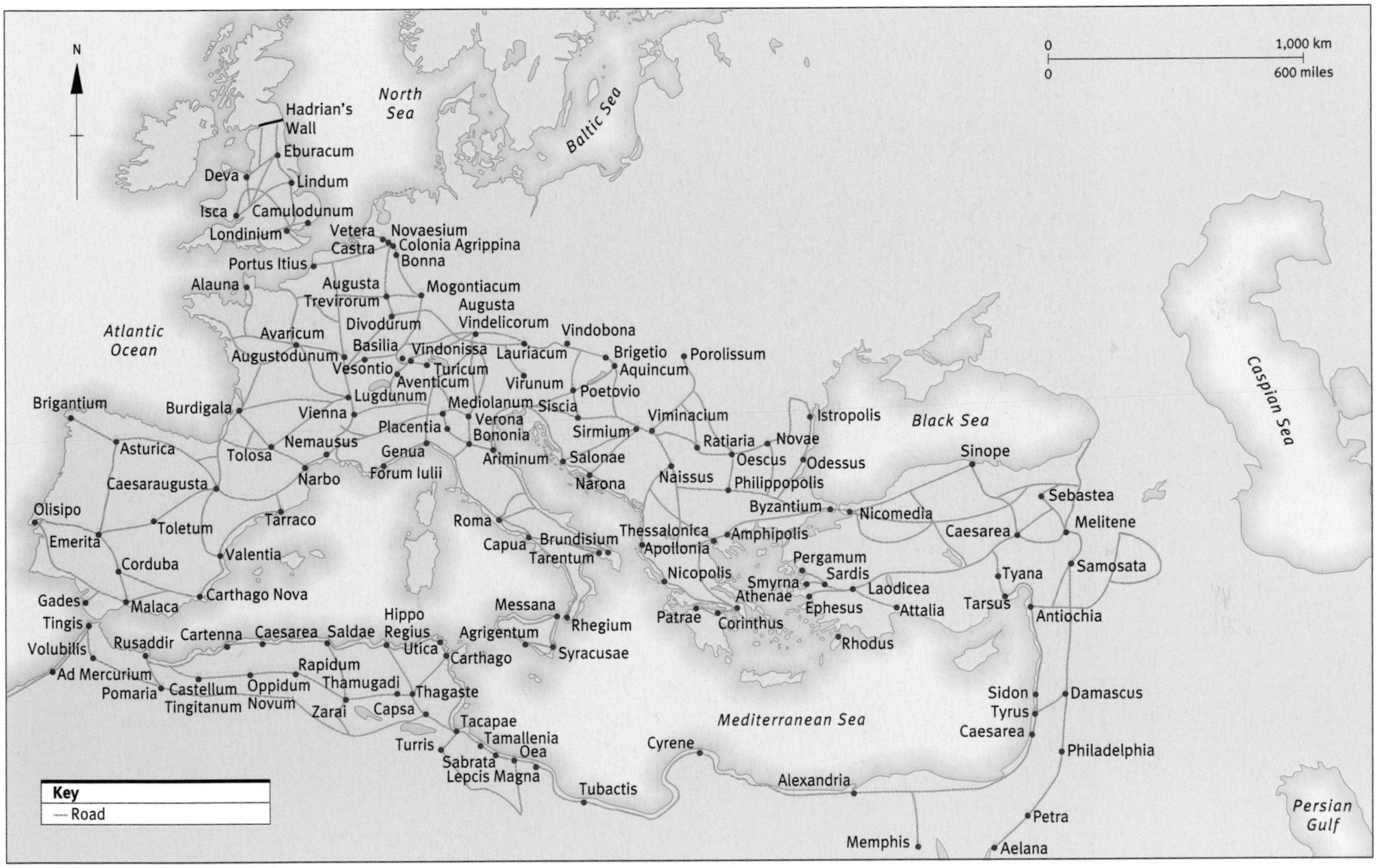

expressed itself in a richness of finish and decoration nowhere else so concentrated. When the marble facings were intact, and paint and stucco moulding relieved the sheer mass of stone, Rome must have had some of the appeal to the imagination earlier possessed by Babylon. There was an ostentation about it which spoke of a certain vulgarity, too, and in this again it is not hard to sense a difference of quality between Rome and Greece; Roman civilization has a grossness and materiality inescapable in even its greatest monuments.

SOCIAL DIVISIONS

Roman materialism was, in part, the simple expression of the social realities on which the empire rested: Rome, like all the ancient

Many wealthy Romans lived in magnificent villas, expensively furnished and lavishly decorated. This mural adorned the bedroom wall of the Roman villa found at Boscoreale, just north of Pompeii. Dating from c.35 BCE, it depicts an idealized classical garden.

A Roman fresco depicting an urban villa. Of note is the elegant portico, which protected the villa's wealthy residents from the heat and the glare of the sun, as well as from the rain.

world, was built on a sharp division of rich and poor, and in the capital itself this division was an abyss not concealed but consciously expressed. The contrasts of wealth were flagrant in the difference between the sumptuousness of the houses of the new rich, drawing to themselves the profits of empire and calling on the services of perhaps scores of slaves on the spot and hundreds on the estates which maintained them, and the swarming tenements in which the Roman proletariat lived. Romans found no difficulty in accepting such divisions as part of the natural order; for that matter, few civilizations have ever much worried about them before our own, though few displayed them so flagrantly as imperial Rome. Unfortunately, though easy to recognize, the realities of wealth in Rome still remain curiously opaque to the historian. The finances of only one senator, the younger Pliny, are known to us in any detail.

MUNICIPAL LIFE

The Roman pattern was reflected in all the great cities of the empire. It was central to the

The atrium, or vestibule, of a house was the main room. An opening in the roof provided light and a rectangular pond in the floor collected rain water, as can be seen in this house in Pompeii. Surrounding the atrium were the bedrooms. Luxurious homes such as this one would have belonged to wealthy families, while the majority of the urban population lived in tiny rooms in houses containing several apartments.

civilization that Rome sustained everywhere. The provincial cities stood like islands of Graeco-Roman culture in the aboriginal countrysides of the subject-peoples. Due allowance made for climate, they reflected a pattern of life of remarkable uniformity, displaying Roman priorities. Each had a forum, temples, a theatre, baths, whether added to old cities or built as part of the basic plan of those which were refounded. Regular grid-patterns were adopted as ground plans. The government of the cities was in the hands of local bigwigs, the *curiales* or city-fathers who at least until Trajan's time enjoyed a very large measure of independence in the conduct of municipal affairs, though later a tighter supervision was to be imposed on them. Some of these cities, such as Alexandria or Antioch, or Carthage (which the Romans refounded), grew to a very large size. The greatest of all cities was Rome itself, eventually containing more than a million people.

This portrait was found in Pompeii. It lay in the ruins between the houses of an aristocrat and a baker, which makes it difficult to establish the identities of the people portrayed. The writing boards and papyrus are symbols of a good education, suggesting that the figures are aristocrats, although their rustic appearance could also mean that they are commoners.

Martial on life in Rome

"Do you ask why I often visit my bit of land near dry Nomentum and my villa's dingy hearth? Sparsus, there's no place in Rome for a poor man to think or rest. Schoolmasters deny you life in the morning, bakers at night, the hammers of the coppersmiths all day. On one hand the idle money-changer rattles his grubby counter with Nero's metal, on the other the pounder of Spanish gold dust beats his well-worn stone with shining mallet; neither does Bellona's frenzied throng give up, nor the garrulous castaway with his swaddled trunk, nor the Jew that his mother taught to beg, nor the blear-eyed pedlar of sulphurated wares. Who can count up the losses of lazy sleep? He will tell us how many pots and pans the hands of the City clash when the moon is cut and beaten by the magic wheel of Colchis. You, Sparsus, know nothing of all this, nor can you know, leading your life of luxury in your Petilian domain, where your ground floor looks down on the hill tops ... where there's ... quiet that no tongues disturb, and no daylight save by admission. As for me, the thrusting of the passing crowd awakes me and Rome is at my bedside. Whenever I'm sick and tired of it and want to go to sleep, I go to my villa."

An extract from Book XII, v. 57, of the *Epigrams* by Martial (c.40–c.104 CE), translated by D. R. Shackleton Bailey.

In this civilization the omnipresence of the amphitheatre is a standing reminder of the brutality and coarseness of which it was capable. It is important not to get this out of perspective, just as it is important not to infer too much about "decadence" from the much-quoted works of would-be moral reformers. One disadvantage under which the repute of Roman civilization has laboured is that it is one of the few before modern times in which we have very much insight into the popular

The Roman city

Roman civilization was centred on city life. In the provinces the Romans founded, or developed from existing nuclei, many imperial cities, where the political organizations and cultural activities for each province were based. Many of today's European cities have Roman origins, which are evident not only from the ruins that have been preserved but also from their street plans.

Typical Roman town plans are orthogonal in design, with two main axes and streets crossing each other at right angles. The origin of this type of plan is Greek, but evidence of the design can also be found in the ruins of Roman military encampments. Each city contained several open squares and various public buildings dedicated to religious, administrative or economic life, or to popular entertainment. Triumphal arches and gateways allowed access to the city, which was sometimes surrounded by fortified walls, particularly in the later stages of the empire, when the danger of attack from outside was very real.

Roman cities also had an advanced infrastructure. Water, for example, was carried to them via elaborate systems of pipes and aqueducts and then stored in central reserves, from which water supplies were distributed. At the end of the 3rd century CE, Rome had 11 free public baths and more than 800 private ones. (The Caracalla Baths, which were opened in 216 CE by the emperor Caracalla himself, could accommodate up to 1,600 bathers.) Many Roman cities even had sewerage networks.

From the 4th century CE onwards, Rome's Caracalla Baths fell into disuse and were eventually dismantled to provide stone for other buildings, reducing them to their present state (above).

mind through its entertainments, for the gladiatorial games and the wild-beast shows were emphatically mass entertainment in a way in which the Greek theatre was not. Popular relaxation is in any era hardly likely to be found edifying by the sensitive, and the Romans institutionalized its least attractive aspects by building great centres for their shows, and by permitting the mass-entertainment industry to be used as a political device; the provision of spectacular games was one of the ways in which a rich man could bring to bear his wealth to secure political advancement.

Nevertheless, when all allowances are made for the fact that we cannot know how, say, the ancient masses of Egypt or Assyria amused themselves, we are left with the uniqueness of the gladiatorial spectacle; it was an exploitation of cruelty as entertainment on a bigger scale than ever before and one unrivalled until the twentieth century. It was made possible by the urbanization of Roman culture, which could deliver larger mass audiences than ever. The ultimate roots of the "games" were Etruscan, but their development sprang from a new scale of urbanism and the exigencies of Roman politics.

Public entertainment

The inhabitants of Roman cities often enjoyed free entertainment, paid for by local dignatories, senators or sometimes the emperor himself. For the sponsors, staging public performances in theatres, amphitheatres or circuses was a method of demonstrating their wealth and social prestige and increasing their popularity.

These terracotta figurines represent two gladiators in combat. Most gladiators were prisoners of war or convicts condemned to death; some were free men who were paid to fight. They underwent gruelling training at Rome's imperial school of gladiators.

The performances that the Romans loved best were the gladiator fights, the wild animal fights and the chariot races. Success or failure in the games could be a matter of life or death for the participants – these were often exceptionally cruel and bloody spectacles. Even outside the arena, rivalry between supporters of opposing individuals or teams could frequently lead to violent confrontations.

Although, to modern-day students of Roman civilization, this use of violence for the entertainment of the masses may seem horrible, the games played a very important part in city life in the empire. They served as a powerful outlet for social tensions and instilled a sense of cultural identity. The free food that was often distributed during the performances also went some way to lessening the misery of the urban poor.

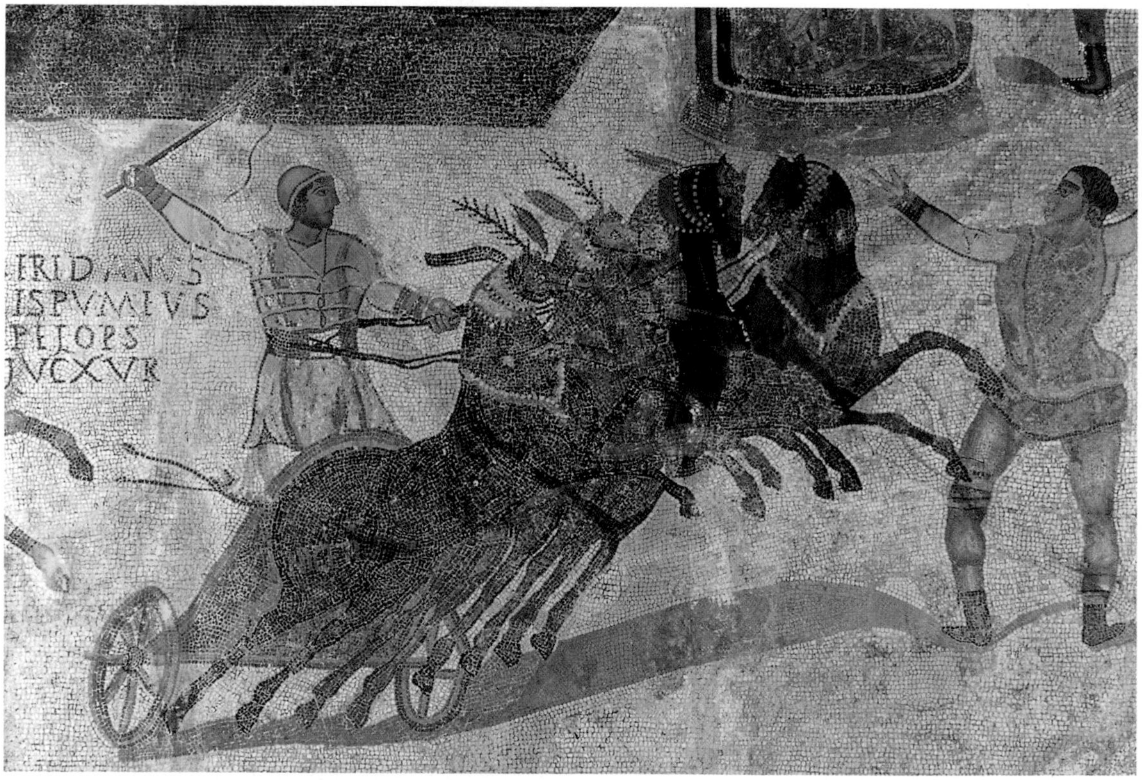

Chariot racing was the oldest kind of public performance. Races took place in the circuses, and the participating teams of charioteers were distinguished from each other by the colour of their clothes. This detail from a 4th-century mosaic, from a villa near Barcelona, shows a quadriga *(a chariot drawn by four horses). Several important centres for the breeding and exportation of horses were located in Hispania (Spain) towards the end of the imperial era.*

Although, owing to an economic crisis, it was never finished, this amphitheatre in El Djem (Tunisia) was the largest in the Roman province of Africa. Built at the beginning of the 3rd century CE, its structure and decoration are based on Rome's Colosseum.

SLAVERY

Another aspect of the brutality at the heart of Roman society was, of course, far from unique: the omnipresence of slavery. As in Greek society, slavery was so varied in its forms that it cannot be summarized in a generalization. Many slaves earned wages, some bought their freedom, and the Roman slave had rights at law. The growth of large plantation estates, it is true, provided examples of a new intensification of it in the first century or so, but it would be hard to say Roman slavery was worse than that of other ancient societies. A few who questioned the institution were very untypical: moralists reconciled themselves to slave-owning as easily as later Christians were to do.

RELIGION

Much of what we know about popular mentality before modern times is known through religion. Roman religion was a very obvious part of Roman life, but that may be misleading if we think in modern terms. It had nothing to do with individual salvation and not much with individual behaviour; it was above all a public matter. It was a part of the *res publica*, a series of rituals whose maintenance was good for the state, whose neglect would bring retribution. There was no priestly caste set apart from other people (if we exclude one or two

This 1st-century funerary bas-relief is from the tomb of a slave couple who had gained their freedom – denoted by the letter L (*libertus*) written after their names. The fact that they are depicted holding hands confirms that their marriage was recognized by law.

The Temple of Hadrian in Ephesus in Asia Minor was founded in the 2nd century CE by a local noble family. On the façade, two pilasters frame columns crowned with Corinthian capitals. The cornice would have continued in an arch and would have been finished off by a triangular pediment, now lost. In the keystone of the arch is an image of the goddess of Ephesus.

antiquarian survivals in the temples of a few special cults) and priestly duties were the task of the magistrates, who found priesthood a useful social and political lever. Nor was there creed or dogma. What was required of Romans was only that the ordained services and rituals should be carried out in the accustomed way; for proletarians this meant little except that they should not work on a holiday. The civic authorities were everywhere responsible for the rites, as they were responsible for the maintenance of the temples. The proper observances had a powerfully practical purpose: Livy reports a consul saying the gods "look kindly on the scrupulous observance of religious rites which has brought our country to its peak". People genuinely felt that the peace of Augustus was the *Pax deorum*, a divine reward for a proper respect for the gods which Augustus had reasserted. Somewhat more cynically, Cicero had remarked that the gods were needed to prevent chaos in society. This, if different, was also an expression of the Roman's practical approach to religion. It was not insincere or disbelieving; the recourse to diviners for the interpretation of omens and the acceptance of the decisions of the augurs about important acts of policy would alone establish that. But it was unmysterious and down-to-earth in its understanding of the official cults.

RELIGIOUS CULTS

The content of the official cults was a mixture of Greek mythology and festivals and rites derived from primitive Roman practice and therefore heavily marked by agricultural preoccupations. One which lived to deck itself out in the symbols of another religion was the December Saturnalia, which is with us still as Christmas. But the religion practised by Romans stretched far beyond official rites. The most striking feature of the Roman approach to religion was its eclecticism and cosmopolitanism. There was room in the empire for all manner of belief, provided it did not contravene public order or inhibit adherence to the official observances. For the most part, peasants everywhere pursued the timeless superstitions of their local nature cults, townspeople took up new crazes from time to time, and the educated professed some acceptance of the classical pantheon of Greek gods and led the people in the official observances. Each clan and household, finally, sacrificed to its own god with appropriate special rituals at the great moments of human life: childbirth, marriage, sickness and death. Each household had its shrine, each street-corner its idol.

THE IMPERIAL CULT

Under Augustus there was a deliberate attempt to reinvigorate old belief, which had been somewhat eroded by closer acquaintance with the Hellenistic East and about which a few sceptics had shown cynicism even in the second century BCE. After Augustus, emperors always held the office of chief priest (*pontifex maximus*) and political and religious primacy were thus combined in the same person. This began the increasing importance and definition of the imperial cult itself. It fitted well the Romans' innate conservatism, their respect for the ways and customs of their ancestors. The imperial cult linked respect for traditional patrons, the placating or invoking of familiar deities and the commemoration of outstanding personalities and events, to the ideas of divine kingship which came from the East, from Asia. It was there that altars were first raised to Rome or the Senate, and there that they were soon reattributed to the emperor. The

Built at the end of the 2nd century BCE, the circular temple of Hercules Victor is the oldest marble temple in Rome. Although it was consecrated to Hercules, it is often called the Temple of Vesta because it once housed the sacred fire of Vesta, goddess of the household.

This 1st-century CE statue represents Claudius as the god Jupiter, emphasizing the emperor's unlimited power and magnifying his glory.

This detail from a bas-relief shows a great sacrificial procession, part of festivities that were held in memory of the emperor Augustus during the 1st century CE. The figures in the foreground are *ministri*, slaves specially chosen to carry small statues of the *lares* gods.

cult spread through the whole empire, though it was not until the third century CE that the practice was wholly respectable at Rome itself, so strong was republican sentiment. But even there the strains of empire had already favoured a revival of official piety which benefited the imperial cult.

EXTERNAL INFLUENCES

The deification of rulers was not the only external influence that came from the East. By the second century, the distinction of a pure Roman religious tradition from others within the empire is virtually impossible. The Roman pantheon, like the Greek, was absorbed almost indistinguishably into a mass of beliefs and cults, their boundaries blurred and fluid, merging imperceptibly over a scale of experience running from sheer magic to the philosophical monotheism popularized by the stoic philosophies. The intellectual and religious world of the empire was omnivorous, credulous and deeply irrational. It is important here not to be over-impressed by the visible practicality of the Roman mind; practical people are often superstitious. Nor was the Greek heritage understood in an altogether rational way; its philosophers were seen by the first century BCE as men inspired, holy men whose mystical teaching was the most eagerly studied part of their works, and even Greek civilization had always rested on a broad basis of popular superstition and local cult practice. Tribal gods swarmed throughout the Roman world.

All this boils down to a large measure of practical criticism of the ancient Roman ways. Obviously, they were no longer enough for an urban civilization, however numerically preponderant the peasants on which it rested. Many of the traditional festivals were pastoral or agricultural in origin, but occasionally even the god they invoked was forgotten. City-dwellers gradually came to need more than piety in a more and more puzzling world. People grasped desperately at anything which could give meaning to the world and some degree of control over it. Old superstitions and new crazes benefited. The evidence can be seen in the appeal of the Egyptian gods, whose cults flooded through the empire as its security made travel and intercourse easier (they were even patronized by an

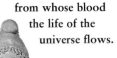

Roman soldiers first came into contact with the Persian god Mithras in Asia Minor. The Mithraic cult, which offered hope of life after death, became immensely popular in the Roman army and quickly spread throughout the empire. This sculpture represents Mithras killing the bull from whose blood the life of the universe flows.

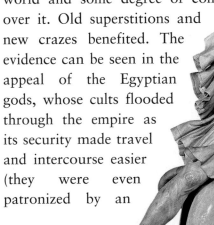

emperor, the Libyan Septimius Severus). A civilized world of greater complexity and unity than any earlier was also one of greater and greater religiosity and a curiousness almost boundless. One of the last great teachers of pagan antiquity, Apollonius of Tyana, was said to have lived and studied with the *Brahmans* of India. Men and women were looking about for new saviours long before one was found in the first century CE.

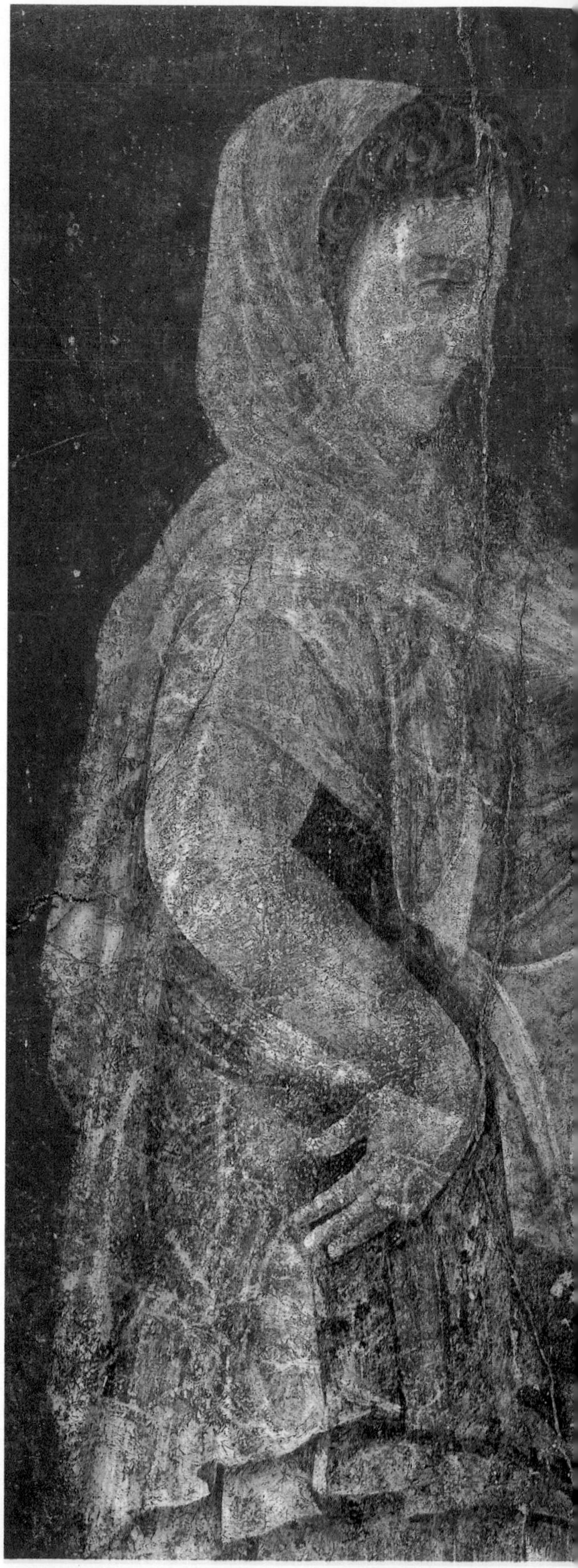

MYSTERY CULTS

Another symptom of Eastern influence was the popularization of mysteries, cults which rested upon the communication of special virtues and powers to the initiated by secret rites. The sacrificial cult of Mithras, a minor Zoroastrian deity especially favoured by soldiers, was one of the most famous. Almost all the mysteries register impatience with the constraints of the material world, an ultimate pessimism about it and a preoccupation with (and perhaps a promise of survival after) death. In this lay their power to provide a psychological satisfaction no longer offered by the old gods and never really possessed by the official cult. They drew individuals to them; they had some of the appeal that was later to draw converts to Christianity, which in its earliest days was often seen, significantly, as another mystery.

UNREST IN THE EMPIRE

That Roman rule did not satisfy all Roman subjects all the time was even true in Italy itself as late as 73 BCE when, in the disorderly last age of the republic, a great slave revolt required three years of military campaigning and was punished with the crucifixion of 6,000 slaves along the roads from Rome to

This detail from a 1st-century BCE painting is from the Villa of the Mysteries in Pompeii. The woman wearing a veil is acting as an initiator in a Dionysiac mystic ritual. Initiation ceremonies for various cults, including Mithraism, took place throughout the Mediterranean region during the Hellenistic era. Only the initiated were allowed to know the cults' "mysteries", or secrets, hence the label. Mystic rituals were banned in Rome, on the grounds of the extreme emotional state to which the participants were often reduced and because of the leaders' alleged excesses. But the rituals continued in secret celebrations shrouded in an aura of religious fervour, prohibition and occultism.

Roman religion

Traditional Roman religion was essentially a combination of rituals performed either publicly by representatives of the state or privately by the members of a family. The relationship between the gods and human beings was considered to be a kind of contract – Romans fulfilled their obligations, by performing rituals and offering sacrifices, in the hope that the gods would fulfill theirs, by providing protection and good fortune.

Roman gods adopted the human form in the 3rd century BCE, when Rome incorporated the Greek pantheon. The divinities of Hellenic origin that received the most attention were the Capitoline Triad, consisting of Jupiter (the Greek Zeus), Juno (Hera) and Minerva (Athene). In private religion, the *penates* (household gods), the *lares* (ancestors' spirits) and the goddess Vesta were revered.

After the conquest of Greece, philosophers and intellectuals from around the Hellenistic world arrived in Rome. Especially popular amongst the masses were the religious mysteries dedicated to Dionysus, Cybele, Isis and Osiris, and Mithras. These cults shared similar initiation rights and the belief that a judgment after death would decide whether the deceased was to be saved or damned.

Rome's domed Pantheon, which is among the buildings represented by this model, was constructed in the 1st century BCE as a temple dedicated to all the Roman gods.

the south. In the provinces revolt was endemic, always likely to be provoked by a particular burst of harsh or bad government. Such was the famous rebellion of Boadicea in Britain, or the earlier Pannonian revolt under Augustus. Sometimes such troubles could look back to local traditions of independence, as was the case at Alexandria where they were frequent. In one particular instance, that of the Jews, they touched chords not unlike those of later nationalism. The spectacular Jewish record of disobedience and resistance goes back beyond Roman rule to 170 BCE, when they bitterly resisted the "westernizing" practices of the Hellenistic kingdoms which first adumbrated policies later to be taken up by Rome. The imperial cult made matters worse. Even Jews who did not mind Roman tax-gatherers and thought that Caesar should have rendered unto him what was Caesar's were bound to draw the line at the blasphemy of sacrifice at his altar. In 66 CE came a great revolt; there were others under Trajan and Hadrian. Jewish communities were like powder-kegs; their sensitivity makes somewhat more understandable the unwillingness of a procurator of Judaea in about 30 CE to press hard for the strict observance of the legal rights of an accused man when Jewish leaders demanded his death.

TAXATION AND THE ECONOMY

Taxes kept the empire going. Although not heavy in normal times, when they paid for administration and police quite comfortably, they were a hated burden and one augmented, too, from time to time, by levies in kind, requisitioning and forced recruiting. For a long time, they drew on a prosperous and growing economy. This was not only a matter of such lucky imperial acquisitions as the gold-mines of Dacia. The growth in the circulation of trade and the stimulus provided by the new markets of the great frontier encampments also favoured the appearance of new industry and suppliers. The huge numbers of wine jars found by archaeologists are only an indicator of what must have been a vast commerce – of foodstuffs, textiles, spices – which have left fewer traces. Yet the economic base of empire was always agriculture. This was not rich by modern standards, for its techniques were primitive; no Roman farmer ever saw a windmill and watermills were still rare when the empire ended in the West. For all its idealization, rural life was a harsh and laborious thing. To it too, therefore, the *Pax Romana* was essential: it meant that taxes could be found from the small surplus produced and that lands would not be ravaged.

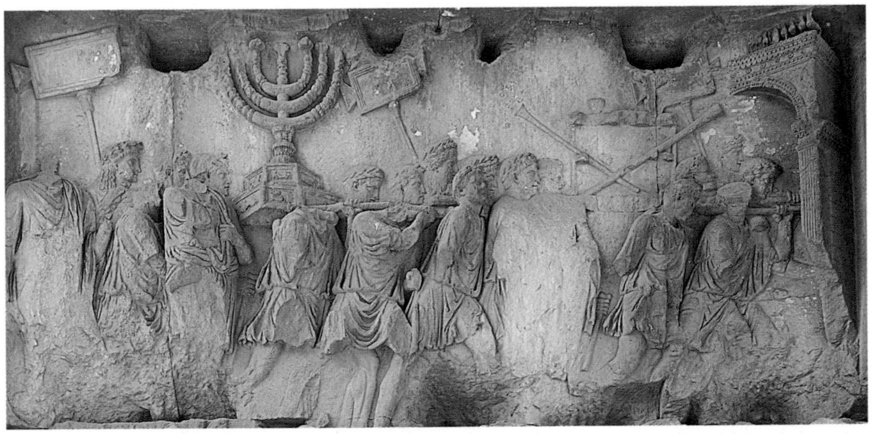

This bas-relief from the arch of Titus celebrates the emperor's conquest of Judaea in the year 70 CE. The scene represents a procession of Roman soldiers carrying spoils from the destroyed Temple of Jerusalem.

THE ROLE OF THE ARMY IN THE ROMAN STATE

In the last resort almost everything seems to come back to the army, on which the Roman peace depended; yet it was an instrument which changed over six centuries as much as did the Roman state itself. Roman society and

Judaism in the ancient world

Jewish communities have existed in a number of European cities since ancient times, when there were large Jewish populations in the eastern Mediterranean, to the north of Gaul and along the Rhine.

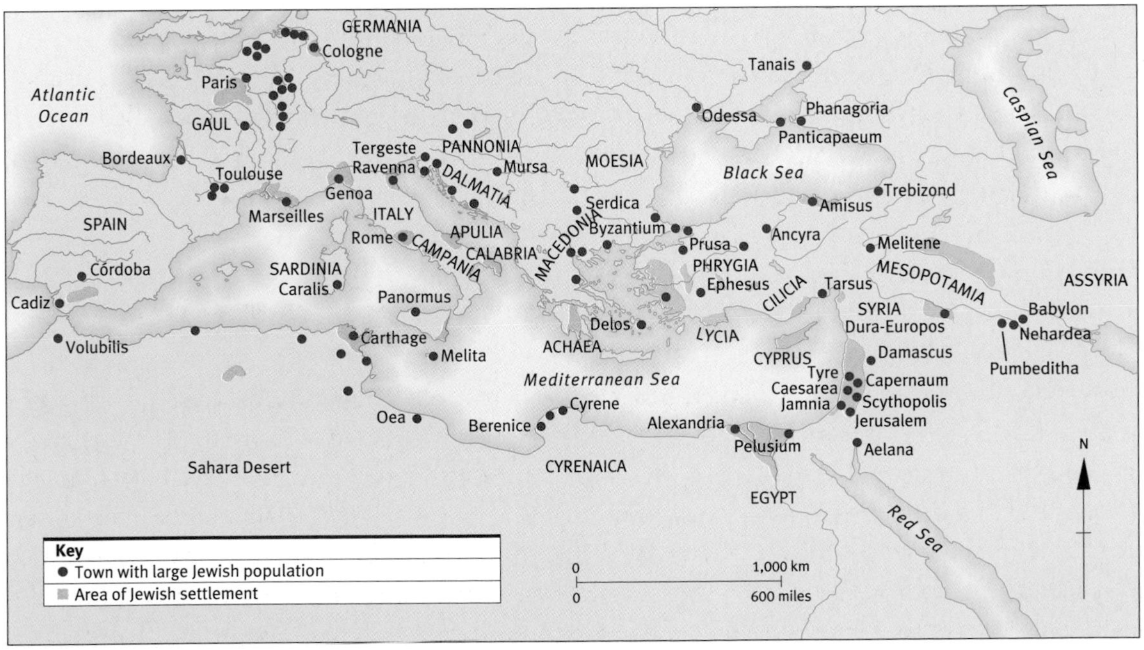

These amphoras, which were used for the transportation of wine, are from a trade vessel found in a Ligurian port. Wine was an indispensable part of the Roman diet and an important commercial product. Together with oil, it had to be transported from the Mediterranean countries to all the parts of the empire where Roman legions were stationed.

culture were always militaristic, yet the instruments of that militarism changed. From the time of Augustus the army was a regular long-service force, no longer relying even formally upon the obligation of all citizens to serve. The ordinary legionary served for twenty years, four in reserve, and increasingly came from the provinces as time went by. Surprising as it may seem, given the repute of Roman discipline, volunteers seem to have been plentiful enough for letters of recommendation and the use of patrons to be resorted to by would-be recruits. The twenty-eight legions which were the normal establishment after the defeat in Germany were distributed along the frontiers, about 160,000 men in all. They were the core of the army, which contained about as many men again in the cavalry, auxiliaries and other arms. The legions continued to be commanded by senators (except in Egypt) and the central issue of politics at the capital itself was still access to opportunities such as this. For, as had become clearer and clearer as the centuries passed, it was in the camps of the legions that the heart of the empire lay, though the Praetorian Guard in Rome sometimes contested their right to choose an emperor. Yet the soldiers comprised only part of the history of the empire. Quite as much impact was made on it, in the long run, by the handful of people who were the followers and disciples of the man the procurator of Judaea had handed over for execution.

A group of Praetorian soldiers is depicted in this marble bas-relief from the 2nd century CE. The Praetorian Guard was created by Augustus to maintain public order and enforce the law. Its most important duty was to protect the person of the emperor, upon whom it was dependent.

3 JEWRY AND THE COMING OF CHRISTIANITY

This mosaic from the 6th-century CE church of Saints Cosmas and Damian in Rome depicts Christ as the Pantocrator (a Byzantine term meaning omnipotent God).

FEW READERS OF THIS BOOK are likely to have heard of Abgar, far less of his east Syrian kingdom, Osrhoene; both were unknown to the writer until he was well embarked upon this book. Yet this little-known and obscure monarch is a landmark: he was long believed to be the first Christian king. In fact, the story of his conversion is a legend; it seems to have been under his descendant, Abgar VIII (or IX, so vague is our information), that Osrhoene became Christian at the end of the second century CE. The conversion may not even have included the king himself, but this did not trouble hagiographers. They placed Abgar at the head of a long and great tradition; in the end it was to incorporate virtually the whole history of monarchy in Europe. From there, in turn, it was to spread to influence rulers in other parts of the world.

THE IMPACT OF CHRISTIANITY

All these later monarchs would behave differently because they saw themselves as Christian, yet, important though it was, this is only a tiny part of the difference Christianity has made to history. Until the coming of industrial society, in fact, it is the only historical phenomenon we have to consider whose implications, creative power and impact are comparable with the great determinants of prehistory in shaping the world we live in. Christianity grew up within the classical world of the Roman Empire, fusing itself in the end with its institutions and spreading through its social and mental structures to become our most important legacy from that civilization. Often disguised or muted, its influence runs through all the great creative processes of the last fifteen hundred years; almost incidentally, it defined Europe. We are what we are today because a handful of Jews saw their teacher and leader crucified and believed he rose again from the dead.

CHRISTIANITY'S JEWISH ORIGINS

THE JEWISHNESS of Christianity is fundamental and was probably its salvation (to speak in worldly terms), for the odds against the historical survival, let alone worldwide success, of a small sect centred upon a holy man in the Roman Eastern Empire were enormous. Judaism was a matrix and protecting environment for a long time as well as the source of the most fundamental Christian ideas. In return, Jewish ideas and myths were to be generalized through Christianity to become world forces. At the heart of these was the Jewish view that history was a meaningful story, providentially ordained, a cosmic drama of the unfolding design of the one omnipotent God for His chosen people. Through His covenant with that people could be found guidance for right action, and it lay in adherence to His law. The breaking of that law had always brought punishment, such as had come by the waters of Babylon. In its keeping lay the promise of salvation for the whole community. This great drama was the inspiration of Jewish historical writing, in which the Jews of the Roman Empire discerned the pattern which made their lives meaningful.

JEWISH HISTORY

That very relevant mythological pattern was deeply rooted in Jewish historical experience, which, after the great days of Solomon, had been bitter, fostering an enduring distrust of the foreigner and an iron will to survive. Few things are in fact more remarkable in the life of this remarkable people than the simple fact of its continued existence. The Exile which began in 587 BCE when Babylonian conquerors took many of the Jews away after the destruction of the Temple was the last crucial experience in the moulding of their national identity before modern times. It finally crystallized the Jewish vision of history. The exiles heard prophets like Ezekiel promise a renewed covenant; Judah had been punished for its sins by exile and the Temple's destruction, now God would turn His face again to Judah, who would return again to Jerusalem, delivered out of Babylon as Israel had been delivered out of Ur, out of Egypt. The Temple would be rebuilt. Perhaps only a minority of the Jews of the Exile heeded this, but it was a significant one and it

The Dura-Europos synagogue was built c.200 BCE. These remarkably well-preserved frescoes from the synagogue's walls depict scenes from the Hebrew Bible.

Time chart (587 BCE–70 CE)

600 BCE — 500 BCE — 50 BCE — 0 — 25 CE — 50 CE — 75 CE

- 587 BCE Destruction of Jerusalem by Babylonians
- 538 BCE Exiled Jews return to Jerusalem
- 63 BCE Pompey imposes Roman rule on Judaea
- 37–4 BCE Reign of Herod the Great, during which Christ is thought to have been born
- 26–36 CE Governorship of Pontius Pilate, during which Christ dies
- 49 CE Apostolic Council of Jerusalem
- 66–70 CE Jewish uprising against Rome

The beliefs of Judaism

The term Judaism refers to the religious tradition of the Jewish people, whose most ancient texts are those collected in the Hebrew Bible, or the Christian Bible's Old Testament. In accordance with biblical tradition, the basic idea of the Covenant between the god Yahweh and his people was determined in the time of Moses, the legendary patriarch who is thought to have lived in the 13th century BCE. Exclusive loyalty to Yahweh was the feature that distinguished the Jews from the polytheistic peoples among whom they lived. Yahweh was the all-powerful eternal god, creator of all things. He was a strictly fair god, who brought death to the impious and destroyed his enemies but had mercy on the faithful. He severely punished those who disobeyed his laws, but was also the loving and compassionate father of his chosen people, the Jews, to whom he had promised to send a Messiah who would lead them to victory against their enemies.

From the 8th century BCE, successive prophets affirmed the belief that the misfortunes of Israel, including its subjection to foreign conquerors, were a punishment from Yahweh for not having honoured the Covenant. They also stated, however, that Israel's sufferings would purify the Jews and prepare them for future glory, which would culminate in Yahweh being recognized by all the world's peoples.

The Jews' loss of independence and their subjection to successive empires (Persian, Macedonian and Roman) led to the growth of nuclei of Jewish exiles in various parts of the Mediterranean and the Near East: this process of dispersal was known as the *diaspora*, literally meaning "scattering". In Palestine itself, the Jewish presence was practically eliminated following the failure of the nationalist revolts against Rome in the 1st and 2nd centuries CE, but, under the guidance of the rabbis, Judaism would survive the diaspora. At the beginning of the 3rd century CE, the oral tradition of Jewish law was set down in the Mishna, which later became the first part of the Talmud, the body of Jewish law and legend.

conciliatory policy was resumed by the Seleucid kings. It did not satisfy many Jews, who in 142 BCE were able to take advantage of a favourable set of circumstances to win an independence which was to last for nearly eighty years. Then, in 63 BCE, Pompey imposed Roman rule and there disappeared the last independent Jewish state in the Near East for nearly two thousand years.

Independence had not been a happy experience. A succession of kings drawn from the priestly families had thrown the country into disorder by innovation and high-handedness. They and the priests who acquiesced in their policies excited opposition. They were challenged in their authority by a new, more austere school of interpreters, who clung to the Law, rather than the cult, as the heart of Judaism and gave it new and searchingly rigorous interpretation. These were the Pharisees, the representatives of a reforming strain which was time and time again to express itself in Jewry in protest against the danger of creeping Hellenization. They also accepted proselytism among non-Jews, teaching a belief in the resurrection of the dead and a divine Last Judgment; there was a mixture in their stance of national and universal aspiration and they drew out further the implications of Jewish monotheism.

THE SPREAD OF JUDAISM

Most of the Pharisees' activity took place in Judaea, the tiny rump of the once great kingdom of David; fewer Jews lived there in the time of Augustus than in the rest of the empire. From the seventh century onwards they had spread over the civilized world. The armies of Egypt, Alexander and the Seleucids all had Jewish regiments. Others had settled abroad in the course of trade. One of the greatest Jewish colonies was at Alexandria, where they had gathered from about 300 BCE. The Alexandrian Jews were Greek-speakers; there the Old Testament was first translated into Greek and when Jesus was born there were probably more Jews there than in Jerusalem. In Rome there were approximately another 50,000. Such agglomerations increased the opportunities to proselytize and therefore the danger of friction between communities.

THE ATTRACTIONS OF JUDAISM

Judaism offered much to a world in which traditional cults had waned. Circumcision and dietary restraints were obstacles, but were far outweighed for many a proselyte by the attractions of a code of behaviour of great minuteness, a form of religion not dependent on temples, shrines or priesthood for its exercise, and, above all, the assurance of salvation. A prophet whose teaching was ascribed by the Old Testament compilers to Isaiah, but who is almost certainly of the Exile, had already announced a message to bring light to the gentiles, and many of them had responded to that light long before the Christians, who were to promote it in a new sense. The proselytes could identify themselves with the chosen people in the great story which inspired Jewish historical writing, the only achievement in this field worthy of comparison with the Greek invention of scientific history, and one which gave meaning to the tragedies of the world. In their history the Jews discerned an unfolding pattern by which they were being refined in the fire for the Day of Judgment. A fundamental contribution of Judaism to Christianity would be its sense of the people apart, its eyes set on things not of this world; Christians were to go on to the idea of the leaven in the lump, working to redeem the world. Both myths were deeply rooted in Jewish historical experience and in the remarkable though simple fact of this people's survival at all.

The Bible contains several stories about the extraordinary protection that Yahweh was believed to offer his followers. One of the best known is that of the three young Jews who were thrown into a burning oven by King Nebuchadnezzar for refusing to prostrate themselves before his statue. This 3rd-century CE mural painting from the Priscilla catacomb in Rome depicts the three Jews emerging from the oven unhurt.

THE JEWS UNDER ROMAN RULE

The big communities of Jews and Jewish proselytes were important social facts to Roman governors, standing out not only because of their size but because of their tenacious separateness. Archaeological evidence of synagogues as distinct and separate buildings does not appear until well into the Common Era, but Jewish quarters in cities were distinct, clustering about their own synagogues and courts of law. While proselytizing was widespread and even some Romans were attracted by Jewish belief, there were also early signs of popular dislike of Jews in Rome itself. Rioting was frequent in Alexandria and easily spread to other towns of the Near East. This led to distrust on the part of authorities and (at least at Rome) to the dispersal of Jewish communities when things became difficult.

Jerusalem

Though little of what he did survives, Herod the Great (74–4 BCE), who was put on the throne of Judaea by the Romans in 37 BCE, constructed many buildings in Jerusalem. In particular, he began work to rebuild the Temple – a project that took 46 years to complete – including raising it on a huge platform and adding the Temple square, where money-lenders and merchants could do business. Herod also constructed a new fortress, Antonia, to protect the Temple.

Between 66 and 74 CE, the Jews rebelled against Roman rule in the Judaean War. In March 70 CE the Roman army laid siege to Jerusalem, and the two outer city walls fell in May. Four months later, the Romans broke through the inner defences. They devastated the city, killing or enslaving its inhabitants and destroying the Temple, more than six centuries after the Babylonians' destruction, in 587 BCE, of the first Temple, built by Solomon on the same spot. Only the western wall (or Wailing Wall) of the Temple platform remains today.

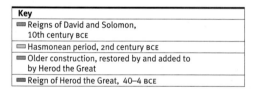

Key
Reigns of David and Solomon, 10th century BCE
Hasmonean period, 2nd century BCE
Older construction, restored by and added to by Herod the Great
Reign of Herod the Great, 40–4 BCE

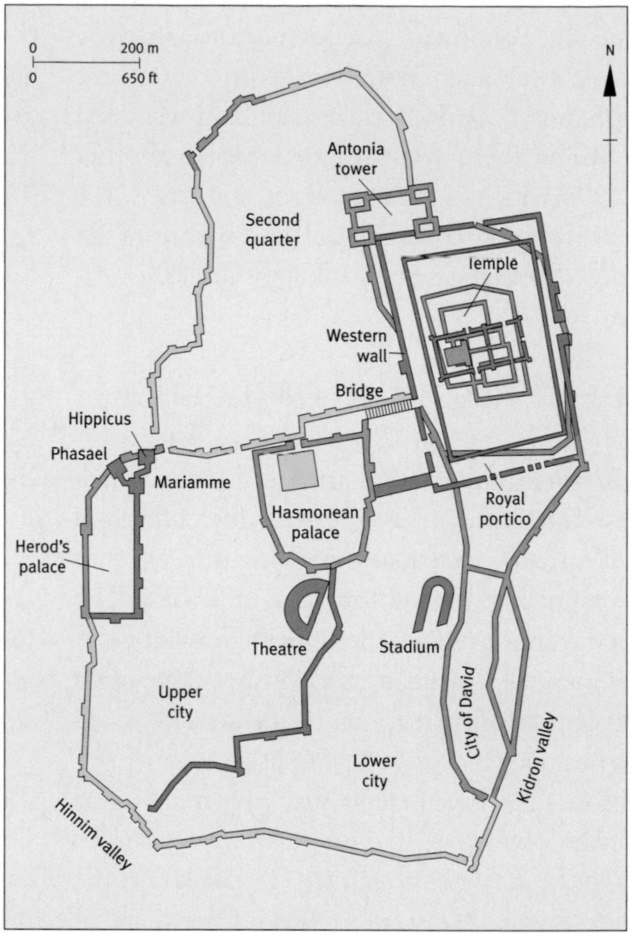

A plan of Jerusalem (top) in the time of Herod the Great, and a view of the city today (above), looking westwards. The walls in the foreground follow those of the Temple platform built by Herod the Great. On the right is the Dome of the Rock – a 7th-century CE mosque built on the site of Solomon's Temple and the third most holy place in Islam.

KING HEROD

Judaea itself was regarded as a particularly ticklish and dangerous area and to this the religious ferment of the last century and a half BCE had greatly contributed. In 37 BCE the Senate appointed a Jew, Herod the Great, King of Judaea. He was an unpopular monarch. No doubt there was popular distaste for a Roman nominee and a ruler anxious – with reason – to preserve the friendship of Rome. Herod earned further dislike, though, by the Hellenistic style of life at his court (though he was careful to display his loyalty to the Jewish religion) and by the heavy taxes which he raised, some of them for grandiose building. Even if it were not for the legendary Massacre of the Innocents and his place in Christian demonology, Herod would not have had a good historical press. At his death, in 4 BCE, his kingdom was divided between his three sons, an unsatisfactory arrangement which was superseded in 6 CE, when Judaea became part of the Roman province of Syria governed from Caesarea. In 26 CE Pontius Pilate became procurator, the taxing officer, or, effectively, governor, an uncomfortable and exacting post he was to hold for ten years.

JEWISH UNREST

The end of the first century BCE was a bad moment in the history of a turbulent province. Something of a climax to the excitements of nearly two centuries was being reached. The Jews were at loggerheads with their Samaritan neighbours and resented an influx of Greek-Syrians noticeable in the coastal towns. They detested Rome as the latest of a long line of conquerors and also because of its demands for taxes; tax-gatherers – the "publicans" of the New Testament – were unpopular not just because of what they took but because they took it for the foreigner. But worse still, the Jews were also bitterly divided between themselves. The great religious festivals were often stained by bloodshed and rioting. Pharisees,

Herodium, the citadel that Herod the Great built close to Jerusalem, is seen in this aerial view. Herod was buried in his citadel in 4 BCE, which, according to most modern historians, was shortly after the birth of Christ.

In caves at Qumran, close to the Dead Sea, 1st-century BCE scrolls have been found. The scrolls, some of which had been preserved in urns such as this one, are thought to have been written by members of the Jewish ascetic community of the Essenes.

for instance, were bitterly divided from Sadducees, the formalizing representatives of the aristocratic priestly caste. Other sects rejected them both. One of the most interesting has become known to us only in recent years, through the discovery and reading of the Dead Sea Scrolls, in which it can be seen to have promised its adherents much that was also offered by early Christianity. It looked forward to a last deliverance which would follow Judaea's apostasy and would be announced by the coming of a Messiah. Jews attracted by such teaching searched the writings of the Prophets for the prefigurings of these things. Others sought a more direct way. The Zealots looked to the nationalist resistance movement as the way ahead.

JESUS OF NAZARETH

INTO THIS ELECTRIC ATMOSPHERE Jesus was born in about 6 BCE, into a world in which thousands of his countrymen awaited the coming of a Messiah, a leader who would lead them to military or symbolic victory and inaugurate the last and greatest days of Jerusalem. The evidence for the facts of his life is contained in the records written down after his death in the Gospels, the assertions and traditions which the early Church based on the testimony of those who had actually known Jesus. The Gospels are not by themselves satisfactory evidence but their inadequacies can be exaggerated. They were no doubt written to demonstrate the supernatural authority of Jesus and the confirmation provided by the events of his life for the prophecies which had long announced the coming of Messiah. This interested and hagiographical origin does not demand scepticism about all the facts asserted; many have inherent plausibility in that they are what might be expected of a Jewish religious leader of the period. They need not be rejected; much more inadequate evidence about far more intractable subjects has often to be employed. There is no reason to be more austere or rigorous in our canons of acceptability for early Christian records than for, say, the evidence in Homer which illuminates Mycenae. Nevertheless, it is very hard to find corroborative evidence of the facts stated in the Gospels in other records.

THE GOSPELS' STORY OF JESUS

The picture of Jesus presented in the Gospels is of a man of modest though not destitute family, with a claim to royal lineage. Such a claim would no doubt have been denied by his opponents if there had not been something in it. Galilee, where Jesus grew up, was something of a frontier area for Judaism, where it was most exposed to the contact

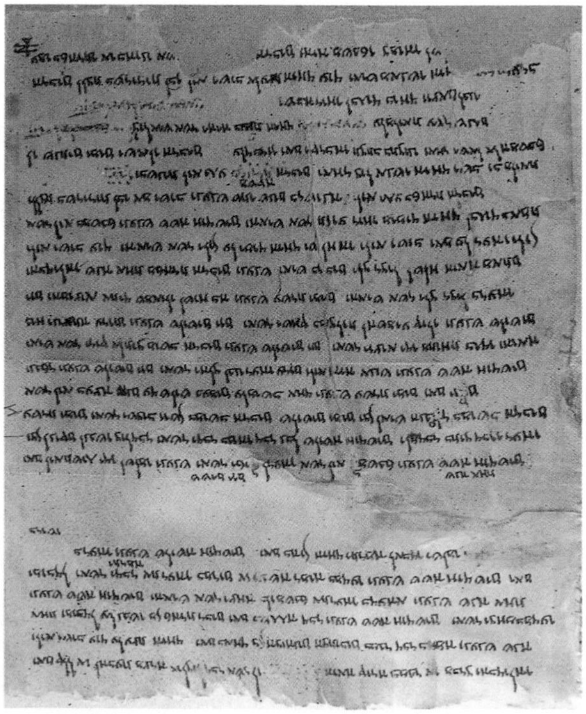

This is one of the Dead Sea Scrolls that were found at Qumran. It reproduces a fragment of the Bible from the Book of Isaiah.

This mosaic, which embellishes the central dome of the Neonian baptistry in Ravenna, dates from the 5th century CE. John the Baptist is shown baptizing Christ, who is immersed in the waters, in the presence of the Holy Spirit.

with Greek-Syrians, which often irritated religious sensibilities. There preached in the neighbourhood a man called John, a prophet to whom crowds had flocked in the days before his arrest and execution. Scholars have tried to link John with the Qumran community, which left behind the Dead Sea Scrolls; he appears, though, to have been a solitary, highly individual figure, a teacher modelling himself on the Prophets. One evangelist tells us that he was the cousin of Jesus; this is possibly true, but less important than the agreement of all the Gospels that John baptized Jesus as he baptized countless others who came to him fearing the approach of the Last Day. He is also said to have recognized in Jesus a teacher like himself and perhaps something more: "Art thou He that cometh, or look we for another?"

Jesus knew himself to be a holy man; his teaching and the evidence of his sanctity, which was seen in miracles, soon convinced

the excited multitude to Jerusalem. His triumphal entry to the city was based on their spontaneous feeling. They followed him as they followed other great teachers in the hope of the Messiah that was to come.

The end came with a charge of blasphemy before the Jewish court and the relaxation of the letter of Roman law by Pilate in order to avoid further trouble in a violent city. Jesus was not a Roman citizen and for such men the extreme penalty was crucifixion after scourging. The inscription on the cross on which he was nailed said: "Jesus of Nazareth, King of the Jews"; this was political irony by a Roman governor, and that the significance of it should not go unmissed was ensured by posting the words in Latin, Greek and Hebrew. This was probably in 33 CE, though 29 CE and 30 CE have also been put forward as possible dates.

Shortly after his death, Jesus's disciples believed that he had risen from the dead, that they had seen him and his ascension into heaven, and that they had received a divine gift of power from him at Pentecost which would sustain them and their adherents until the Last Day. That would soon come, they also believed, and would bring back Jesus as the judge sitting at the right hand of God. All this the Gospels tell us.

This tomb was dug into a rocky wall in the Kidron valley in the 1st century BCE. The body of Christ may have been placed in a similar tomb.

The Sermon on the Mount

"And seeing the multitudes, he went up into a mountain, and when he had sat, his disciples came unto him; and he opened his mouth and taught them, saying:

"Blessed are the poor in spirit, for theirs is the kingdom of heaven. Blessed are they that mourn, for they shall be comforted. Blessed are the meek, for they shall inherit the earth. Blessed are they which do hunger and thirst after righteousness, for they shall be filled. Blessed are the merciful, for they shall obtain mercy. Blessed are the pure in heart, for they shall see God. Blessed are the peacemakers, for they shall be called the children of God. Blessed are they which are persecuted for righteousness' sake, for theirs is the kingdom of heaven.

"Blessed are ye, when men shall revile you, and persecute you, and shall say all manner of evil against you falsely, for my sake. Rejoice, and be exceeding glad, for great is your reward in heaven, for so persecuted they the prophets which were before you."

An extract from Matthew, 5: 1–12.

JESUS'S TEACHING

If this was what the first Christians saw in Christ (as he came to be called, from the Greek word meaning "the anointed one") there were also in his teaching other elements capable of far wider application. The reported devotional ideas of Jesus do not go beyond custom; Jewish service in the Temple and observance of traditional holy days and feasts, together with private prayer, were all that he indicated. In this very real sense, he lived and died a Jew. His moral teaching, though, focused upon repentance and deliverance from sin, and upon a deliverance available to all, and not just to Jews. Retribution had its part in Jesus's teaching (on this the Pharisees agreed with him); strikingly, most of the more terrifying things said in the New Testament are attributed to him. Fulfilment of the Law was essential. Yet it was not enough; beyond observance lay the duties of repentance and restitution in the case of wrong done, even of self-sacrifice. The law of love was the proper guide to action. Emphatically, Jesus rejected the role of the political leader. A political quietism was one of the meanings later discerned in a dictum which was to prove to be of terrible ambiguity: "My kingdom is not of this world."

Yet a Messiah who would be a political leader was expected by many. Others sought a leader against the Jewish religious establishment and therefore were potentially a danger to order even if they aimed only at religious purification and reform. Inevitably, Jesus, of the house of David, became a dangerous man in the eyes of the authorities. One of his disciples was Simon the Zealot, an alarming associate because he had been a member of an extremist sect. Many of Jesus's teachings encouraged feeling against the dominant Sadducees and Pharisees, and they in their turn strove to draw out any anti-Roman implication which could be discerned in what he said.

THE FOLLOWERS OF CHRIST

Political facts provide the background to Jesus's destruction and the disappointment of the people; they do not explain the survival of his teaching. He had appealed not only to the politically dissatisfied but to Jews who felt that the Law was no longer guide

A 4th-century CE Christian sarcophagus is decorated with scenes from the Old and New Testaments, including, in the middle of the lower register, Christ's triumphal entry into Jerusalem.

The figure of Christ surrounded by the Apostles is depicted on a marble bas-relief from a 4th-century CE sarcophagus (subsequently used in the pulpit of the church of St Ambrose in Milan). The image of Christ, beardless and dressed as a Roman, is typical of early Christian art.

enough and to non-Jews who, though they might win second-class citizenship of Israel as proselytes, wanted something more to assure them of acceptance at the Last Day. Jesus had also attracted the poor and outcast; they were many in a society which offered enormous contrasts of wealth and no mercy to those who fell by the wayside. These were some of the appeals and ideas which were to yield in the end an astonishing harvest. Yet though they were effective in his own lifetime, they seemed to die with him. At his death his followers were only one tiny Jewish sect among many. But they believed that a unique thing had happened. They believed that Christ had risen from the dead, that they had seen him, and that he offered to them and those that were saved by his baptism the same overcoming of death and personal life after God's judgment. The generalization of this message and its presentation to the civilized world was achieved within a half-century of Jesus's death.

The conviction of the disciples led them to remain at Jerusalem, an important centre of pilgrimage for Jews from all over the Near East, and therefore a seminal centre for a new doctrine. Two of Jesus's disciples, Peter and Jesus's brother, James, were the leaders of the tiny group which awaited the imminent return of the Messiah, striving to prepare for it by penitence and the service of God in the Temple. They stood emphatically within the Jewish fold; only the rite of baptism, probably, distinguished them. Yet other Jews saw in them a danger; their contacts with Greek-speaking Jews from outside Judaea led to questioning of the authority of the priests. The first martyr, Stephen, one of this group, was lynched by a Jewish crowd. One of those who witnessed this was a Pharisee from Tarsus of the tribe of Benjamin, named Paul. It may have been that as a Hellenized Jew of the dispersion he was especially conscious of the need for orthodoxy. He was proud of his own. Yet he is the greatest influence in the making of Christianity after Jesus himself.

Christ is depicted handing the keys of the Christian Church to St Peter in this 5th or 6th century CE mosaic from the church of Santa Costanza in Rome.

Dating from the 4th century CE, this mural from the catacomb of Domitilla in Rome shows Christ among the Apostles.

St Paul, depicted in this mosaic from the crypt of St Peter's in Rome, is thought to have been preaching during the 1st century CE. Through Paul's teaching, Christianity began to move away from its original Jewish roots and take on its own identity.

THE TEACHINGS OF ST PAUL

Somehow, Paul underwent a change of heart. From being a persecutor of the followers of Christ, he became one himself: it seems to have followed a sojourn of meditation and reflection in the deserts of eastern Palestine. Then, in 47 CE (or perhaps earlier; dating

Paul's life and travels is a very uncertain business), he began a series of missionary journeys which took him all over the eastern Mediterranean. In 49 CE an apostolic council at Jerusalem took the momentous decision to send him as a missionary to gentiles, who would not be required to undergo the circumcision, which was the most important act of submission to the Jewish faith; it is not clear whether he, the council, or both in agreement were responsible. There were already little communities of Jews following the new teaching in Asia Minor, where it had been carried by pilgrims. Now these were given a great consolidation by Paul's efforts. His especial targets were Jewish proselytes, gentiles to whom he could preach in Greek and who were now offered full membership of Israel through the new covenant. The doctrine that Paul taught was new. He rejected the Law (as Jesus had never done), and strove to reconcile the essentially Jewish ideas at the heart of Jesus's teaching with the conceptual world of the Greek language. He continued to emphasize the imminence of the coming end of things, but offered all nations, through Christ, the chance of understanding the mysteries of creation and, above all, of the relationship of things seen and things invisible, of the spirit and the flesh, and of the overcoming of the second by the first. In the process, Jesus became more than a human deliverer who had overcome death, and was God Himself – and this was to shatter the mould of Jewish thought within which the faith had been born. There was no lasting place for such an idea within Jewry, and Christianity was now forced out of the Temple. The intellectual world of Greece was the first of many new resting-places it was to find over the centuries. A colossal theoretical structure was to be built on this change.

The Acts of the Apostles give plentiful evidence of the uproar which such teaching could cause and also of the intellectual tolerance of the Roman administration when public order was not involved. But it often was. In 59 CE, Paul had to be rescued from the Jews at Jerusalem by the Romans. When put on trial in the following year, he appealed to the emperor and to Rome he went, apparently with success. From that time he is lost to history; he may have perished in a persecution by Nero in 67 CE.

Paul writes to the Christians at Corinth

"For I delivered unto you first of all that which I also received, how that Christ died for our sins according to the scriptures; And that he was buried, and that he rose again the third day according to the scriptures: And that he was seen of Cephas, then of the twelve: After that, he was seen of above five hundred brethren at once; of whom the greater part remain unto this present, but some are fallen asleep. After that he was seen of James; then of all the Apostles. And last of all he was seen of me also, as of one born out of due time. For I am the least of the Apostles, that am not meet to be called an Apostle, because I persecuted the church of God. But by the grace of God I am what I am: And his grace which was bestowed upon me was not in vain; But I laboured more abundantly than they all: Yet not I, but the grace of God that was with me. Therefore whether it were I or they, so we preach, and so ye believed.

"Now if Christ be preached that he rose from the dead, how say some among you that there is no resurrection of the dead? But if there be no resurrection of the dead, then is Christ not risen: And if Christ be not risen, then is our preaching vain, and your faith is also vain."

An extract from 1 Corinthians, 15: 3–14.

THE SPREAD OF CHRISTIANITY

The first age of Christian missions permeated the civilized world by sinking roots everywhere

St Paul's journeys

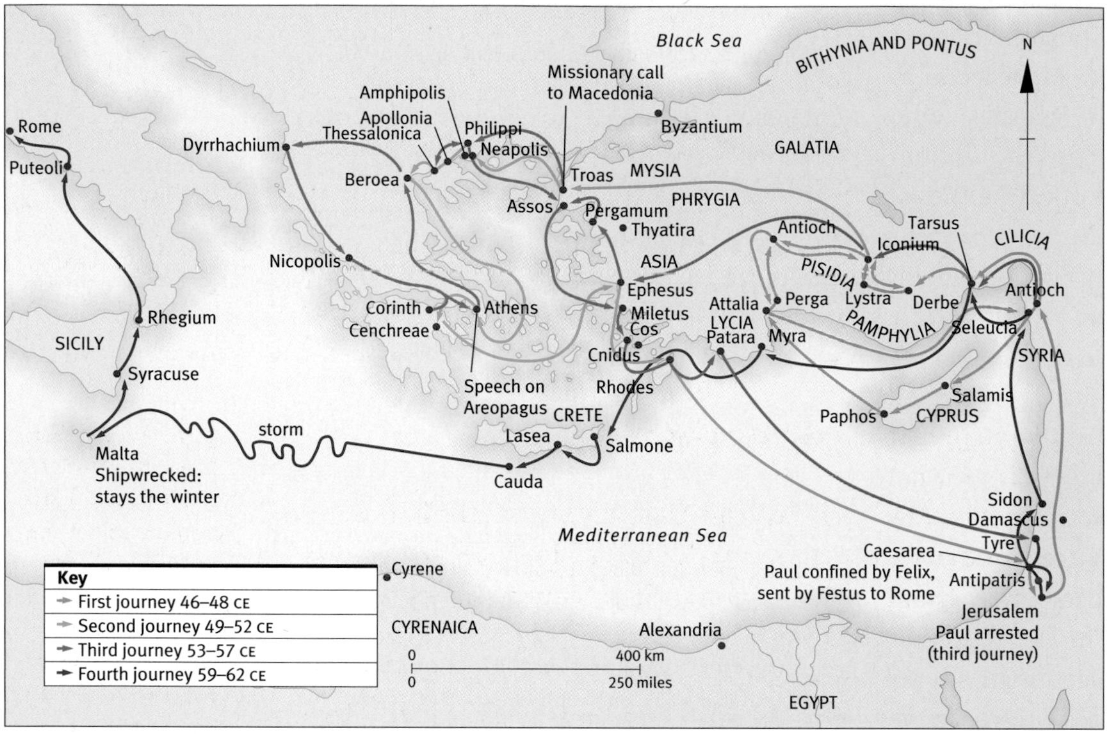

This map shows the routes St Paul is believed to have followed on his journeys, as described in the Acts of the Apostles. It appears that he visited numerous cities in the eastern Mediterranean, where he preached to Jews and non-Jews, with the aim of converting them to Christianity. St Paul taught that the Church should partly renounce its Jewish roots in order to allow gentiles also to hear the word and become Christians.

Through personal visits and long didactic letters, St Paul also spread his concept of the Church among the Christian communities that were already established in the region.

in the first place in the Jewish communities. The "Churches" which emerged were administratively independent of one another, though the community at Jerusalem was recognized to have an understandable primacy. There were to be found those who had seen the risen Christ and their successors. The only links of the Churches other than their faith were the institutional one of baptism, the sign of acceptance in the new Israel, and the ritual practice of the eucharist, the re-enactment of the rites performed by Jesus at his last supper with his disciples, the evening before his arrest. It has remained the central sacrament of the Christian Churches to this day.

The local leaders of the Churches exercised independent authority in practice, therefore, but this did not cover much. There was nothing except the conduct of the affairs of the local Christian community to be decided upon, after all. Meanwhile, Christians expected the Second Coming. Such influence as Jerusalem had flagged after 70 CE, when a Roman sack of the city dispersed many of the Christians there; after this time Christianity had less vigour within Judaea. By the beginning of the second century the communities outside Palestine were clearly more numerous and more important and had already evolved a hierarchy of officers to regulate their affairs. These identified the three later orders of the Church: bishops, presbyters and deacons. Their sacerdotal functions were at this stage minimal, and it was their administrative and governmental role which mattered.

JEWISH EXTREMISTS REBEL

The response of the Roman authorities to the rise of a new sect was largely predictable; its

governing principle was that unless specific cause for interference existed, new cults were tolerated unless they awoke disrespect or disobedience to the empire. There was a danger at first that the Christians might be confounded with other Jews in a vigorous Roman reaction to Jewish nationalist movements which culminated in a number of bloody encounters, but their own political quietism and the announced hostility of other Jews saved them. Galilee itself had been in rebellion in 6 CE (perhaps a memory of it influenced Pilate's handling of the case of a Galilean among whose disciples was a Zealot) but a real distinction from Jewish nationalism came with the great Jewish rising of 66 CE. This was the most important in the whole history of Jewry under the empire, when the extremists gained the upper hand in Judaea and took over Jerusalem. The Jewish historian Josephus has recorded the atrocious struggle which followed, the final storming of the Temple, the headquarters of resistance, and its burning after the Roman victory. Before this, the unhappy inhabitants had been reduced to cannibalism in their struggle to survive. Archaeology has recently revealed at Masada, a little way from the city, what may well have been the site of the last stand of the Jews before it, too, fell to the Romans in 73 CE.

THE DISPERSION

The Roman crushing of the rebellion was not the end of Jewish turbulence, but it was a turning-point. The extremists never again enjoyed such support and must have been discredited. The Law was now more than ever the focus of Jewishness, for the Jewish scholars and teachers (after this time, they are more and more designated as "rabbis") had continued to unfold its meaning in centres

This detail is from a 6th-century CE Roman sarcophagus decorated with scenes from the Passion. A symbolic representation of the Resurrection appears in the centre: a cross, upon which a monogram of Christ is held up by two doves. At the base of the cross are two Roman soldiers.

One of the most impressive examples of early Christian art, this mural from the catacomb of Priscilla in Rome dates from the middle of the 3rd century CE. The praying figure represents the deceased.

Jonah is depicted being thrown from a ship and about to be swallowed by the whale in this bas-relief on a 3rd-century CE sarcophagus. The biblical story of Jonah, who spent three days in the belly of the whale and emerged safe and sound, can be seen as an allegory of the resurrection that Christ promised his followers.

other than Jerusalem while the revolt was in progress. Their good conduct may have saved these Jews of the dispersion. Later disturbances were never so important as had been the great revolt, though in 117 CE Jewish riots in Cyrenaica developed into full-scale fighting, and in 132 CE the last "Messiah", Simon Bar Kochba, launched another revolt in Judaea. But the Jews emerged with their special status at law still intact. Jerusalem had been taken from them (Hadrian made it an Italian colony, which Jews might enter only once a year), but their religion was granted the privilege of having a special officer, a patriarch, with sovereignty over it, and they were allowed exemption from the obligations of Roman law which might conflict with their religious duties. This was the end of a volume of Jewish history. For the next eighteen hundred years Jewish history was to be the story of communities of the diaspora (dispersion), until a national state was again established in Palestine among the debris of another empire.

HOSTILITY TO CHRISTIANITY

The nationalists of Judaea apart, Jews elsewhere in the empire were for a long time thereafter safe enough during the troubled years. Christians did less well, though their religion was not much distinguished from Judaism by the authorities; it was, after all, only a variant of Jewish monotheism with, presumably, the same claims to make. It was the Jews, not the Romans, who first persecuted it, as the Crucifixion itself, the martyrdom of Stephen and the adventures of Paul have shown. It was a Jewish king, Herod Agrippa, who, according to the author of the Acts of the Apostles, first persecuted the community at Jerusalem. It has even appeared plausible to some scholars that Nero, seeking a scapegoat for a great fire at Rome in 64 CE, should have had the Christians pointed out to him by hostile Jews. Whatever the source of this persecution, in which, according to popular Christian tradition, St Peter and St Paul both perished, and which was accompanied by horrific and bloody scenes in the arena, it seems to have been for a long time the end of any official attention by Rome to the Christians. They did not take up arms against the Romans in the Jewish revolts, and this must have soothed official susceptibilities with regard to them.

When they emerge in the administrative records as worth notice by government it is in the early second century CE. This is because of the overt disrespect which Christians were by then showing in refusing to sacrifice to the emperor and the Roman deities. This was their distinction. Jews had a right to refuse; they had possessed a historic cult which the Romans respected – as they always respected such cults – when they took Judah under their rule. The Christians were now clearly seen as distinct from other Jews and were a recent creation. Yet the Roman attitude was that although Christianity was not legal it should not be the subject of general persecution. If, on the other hand, breaches of the law were alleged – and the refusal to sacrifice might be one – then the authorities should punish when the allegations were specific and shown in court to be well founded. This led to many martyrdoms, as Christians refused the well-intentioned attempts of Roman civil servants to persuade them to sacrifice or abjure their god, but there was no systematic attempt to eradicate the sect.

Nero (54–68 CE) was the first Roman emperor to persecute the Christians.

PERSECUTION

The authorities' hostility was, indeed, much less dangerous than that of the Christians' fellow subjects. As the second century passed, there is more evidence of pogroms and popular attacks on Christians, who were not protected by the authorities since they followed

The Christian message

The Christian religion grew out of the preaching of Jesus of Nazareth, known as Christ, who transformed the monotheist tradition, exclusive to the Jewish people, into a message aimed at all of humankind regardless of social or ethnic differences. Some time after his death, various accounts of Christ's life and teachings were collected in the Gospels, which are included in the New Testament. Together with the earlier biblical writings (the Hebrew Bible, or Old Testament), this came to form the Christian Bible. For Christians, Christ represents the Son, the Father and the Holy Spirit which, combined, are the one and only God.

Christ's first followers were all Jews, like himself, but Christianity soon spread among other peoples, particularly through the work of Paul of Tarsus, for whom Jesus' death was the redeeming act that atoned for the sins of the whole of humanity and with which he surpassed the Law of Moses. Christ's resurrection was seen as an example of the eternal life that could be attained by all those who obeyed the law of God, the law of justice and love.

Christian communities grew up all over the Roman Empire, their cohesion assured by a hierarchical system headed by the bishops. Christianity is currently the most widespread religion in the world.

This Roman mosaic represents a spectacle, held in the amphitheatre, in which people were set on and killed by wild animals. Early Christians who refused to renounce their faith were often condemned to this terrible fate.

an illegal religion. They may sometimes have been acceptable scape-goats for the administration or lightning-conductors diverting dangerous currents. It was easy for the popular mind of a superstitious age to attribute to Christians the offences to the gods which led to famine, flood, plague and other natural disasters. Other equally convincing explanations of these things were lacking in a world with no other technique for explaining natural disaster. Christians were alleged to practise black magic, incest, even cannibalism (an idea no doubt explicable in terms of misleading accounts of the Eucharist). They met secretly at night. More specifically and acutely, though we cannot be sure of the scale of this, the Christians threatened by their control of their members the whole customary structure which regulated and defined the proper relations of parents and children, husbands and wives, masters and slaves. They proclaimed that in Christ there was neither bond nor free and that he had come to bring not peace but a sundering sword to families and friends. It is not hard, therefore, to understand the violent outbursts

in the big provincial towns, such as that at Smyrna in 165 CE, or Lyons in 177 CE. They were the popular aspect of an intensification of opposition to Christianity which had an intellectual counterpart in the first attacks on the new cult by pagan writers.

THE CHURCH'S SURVIVAL

Persecution was not the only danger facing the early Church. Possibly it was the least grave. A much more serious one was that it might develop into just another cult of the kind of which many examples could be seen in the Roman Empire and, in the end, be engulfed like them in the magical morass of ancient religion. All over the Near East could be found examples of the "mystery religions", whose core was the initiation of the believer into the occult knowledge of a devotion centred on a particular god (the Egyptian Isis was a popular one, the Persian Mithras another). Almost always believers were offered the chance to identify themselves with the divine being in a ceremony

The Eucharist could be misinterpreted as a cannibalistic rite by those who mistrusted the Christians. This 3rd-century CE mural showing a Eucharistic banquet is from the catacomb of Priscilla in Rome.

Rome's Colosseum was opened in 80 CE. Many Christian martyrs died in the savage events that were staged there.

which involved a simulated death and resurrection, thus to overcome mortality. Such cults offered, through their impressive rituals, the peace and liberation from the temporal which many craved. They were very popular.

THE GNOSTICS

The real danger that Christianity might develop into just another "mystery religion" is shown by the importance in the second

century of the Gnostics. Their name derives from the Greek word *gnosis*, meaning "knowledge": the knowledge the Christian Gnostics claimed was an esoteric tradition, not revealed to all Christians but only to a few (one version said only to the Apostles and the sect to which it had subsequently descended). Some of their ideas came from Zoroastrian, Hindu and Buddhist sources which stressed the conflict of matter and spirit in a way which distorted the Judaeo-Christian tradition; some came from astrology and even magic. There was always a temptation in such a dualism, the attribution of evil and good to opposing principles and entities and the denial of the goodness of the material creation. The Gnostics were haters of this world and in some of their systems this led to the pessimism typical of the mystery cults; salvation was only possible by the acquisition of arcane knowledge, secrets of an initiated elect. A few Gnostics even saw Christ not as the saviour who confirmed and renewed a covenant but as one who delivered humanity from Yahweh's error. It was a dangerous creed in whatever form it came, for it cut at the roots of hopefulness which was the heart of the Christian revelation. It turned its back on the redemption of the here and now, of which Christians could never wholly despair, since they accepted the Judaic tradition that God made the world and that it was good.

In the second century, with its communities scattered throughout the diaspora and their organizational foundations fairly firmly settled, Christianity thus seems to stand at a parting of ways, either of which could prove fatal to it. Had it turned its back on the implications of Paul's work and remained merely a Jewish heresy, it would at best have been reabsorbed eventually into the Judaic tradition; on the other hand, a flight from a Jewry which rejected it might have driven Christians into the Hellenistic world of the mystery cults or the despair of the Gnostics. Thanks to a handful of men, it escaped both and became a promise of salvation to the individual.

THE FATHERS OF THE CHURCH

THE ACHIEVEMENT of the Fathers of the Church who navigated these perils was, for all its moral and pietistic content, above all intellectual. They were stimulated by their danger. Irenaeus, who succeeded the martyred Bishop of Lyons in 177 CE, provided the first

The Christians considered their doctrine to be the true philosophy, which explains the appearance of philosopher figures on several Christian sarcophagi. This marble relief from a 3rd-century CE sarcophagus shows a young Roman girl listening attentively to the teachings of a philosopher.

This mural painting is from the Teotecno family hypogeum (underground vault) in a 6th-century CE catacomb in Naples. Surrounded by lighted candles, members of the family are shown praying, waiting faithfully for the moment of resurrection. The scene presents a moving image of the peaceful approach to death that Christianity offers.

great outline of Christian doctrine, a creed and definition of the scriptural canon. All of these set off Christianity from Judaism. But he wrote also against the background of the challenge of heretical beliefs. In 172 CE the first Council had met to reject Gnostic doctrines. Christian doctrine was squeezed into intellectual respectability by the need to resist the pressures of competitors. Heresy and orthodoxy were born twins. One of the pilots who steered an emerging Christian theology through this period was the prodigiously learned Clement of Alexandria, a Christian Platonist (perhaps born in Athens), through whom Christians were brought to an understanding of what the Hellenistic tradition might mean apart from the mysteries. In particular, he directed Christians to the thought of Plato. To his even greater pupil, Origen, he transmitted the thought that God's truth was a reasonable truth, a belief which could attract those educated in the Stoic view of reality.

THE DIFFUSION OF CHRISTIANITY IN THE CLASSICAL WORLD

The intellectual drive of the early Fathers and the inherent social appeal of Christianity made it possible for it to utilize the huge possibilities of diffusion and expansion inherent in the structure of the classical and later Roman world. Its teachers could move freely and talk and write to one another in Greek. It had the great advantage of emerging in a religious age; the monstrous credulousness of the second century cloaks deep longings. They hint that the classical world is already running out of vigour; the Greek capital needed replenishment and one place to look for it was in new religions. Philosophy had become a religious quest and rationalism or scepticism appealed only to an infinitesimally small

THEOTECNUS

minority. Yet this promising setting was also a challenge to the Church; early Christianity has to be seen always in the context of thriving competitors. To be born in a religious age was a threat as well as an advantage. How successfully Christianity met the threat and seized its opportunity was to be seen in the crisis of the third century, when the classical world all but collapsed and survived only by colossal, and in the end mortal, concession.

Christianity was to spread far beyond its birthplace and far beyond Rome in the centuries following the deaths of the Fathers of the Church. This Christian manuscript is from the Irish MacDurnan Gospels. Dating from the 9th century CE, it depicts St Luke holding a crozier and a book.

4 THE WANING OF THE CLASSICAL WEST

After 200 CE there are many signs that Romans were beginning to look back on the past in a new way. Men and women had always talked of golden ages in the past, indulging in a conventional, literary nostalgia. But the third century brought something new for many inhabitants of the Roman Empire – a sense of conscious decline.

An image of Christ from the St Ermite catacomb in Rome. The figure's gestures and expression are reminiscent of Byzantine painting, which was developed by artists in the Eastern Roman Empire.

CRISIS AND CHANGE

Historians have spoken of a "crisis", but its most obvious expressions were in fact surmounted. The changes Romans carried out or accepted by the year 300 CE gave a new lease of life to much of classical Mediterranean civilization. They may even have been decisive in ensuring that it would in the end transmit so much of itself to the future. Yet the changes themselves took a toll, for some of them were essentially destructive of the spirit of that civilization. Restorers are often unconscious imitators. Somewhere around the beginning of the fourth century we can sense that the balance has tipped against the Mediterranean heritage. It is easier to feel it than to see what was the crucial moment. The signs are a sudden multiplication of ominous innovations – the administrative structure of the empire is rebuilt on new principles, its ideology is transformed, the religion of a once-obscure Jewish sect becomes established orthodoxy, and physically, large tracts of territory are given up to settlers from outside, alien immigrants. A century later still, and the consequence of these changes is apparent in political and cultural disintegration.

THE LAST EMPERORS' ROLES

The ups and downs of imperial authority mattered a lot in this process of disintegration. Classical civilization had come by the end of the second century CE to be coterminous with the empire. It was dominated by the conception of *romanitas*, the Roman way of doing things. Because of this, the weaknesses of the structure of government were fundamental to what was going wrong. The imperial office had long since ceased to be held, as Augustus had carefully pretended, by the agent of the Senate and people; the reality was a despotic monarch, his rule tempered only by such practical considerations as the placating of the Praetorian Guard on which he depended. A round of civil wars which followed the accession of the last, inadequate, Antonine emperor in 180 opened a terrible era. This wretched man, Commodus, was strangled by a wrestler at the bidding of his concubine and chamberlain in 192, but that solved nothing. From the struggles of four "emperors" in the months following his death there finally emerged an African, Septimius Severus, married to a Syrian, who strove to base the empire again on heredity, attempting to link his own family with the Antonine succession and thus to deal with one fundamental constitutional weakness.

THE IMPORTANCE OF THE ARMY

The emphasis Severus placed on hereditary succession was really to deny the fact of his own success. Like his rivals, he had been the candidate of a provincial army. Soldiers were the real emperor-makers throughout the third century and their power lay at the root of the empire's tendency to fragment. Yet the

Time chart (212 CE–476 CE)

212 CE
Roman citizenship is granted to all free inhabitants of the empire

313 CE
Edict of Milan: tolerance of Christianity within the Roman Empire

325 CE
Council of Nicaea (first ecumenical council): condemnation of Arianism

391 CE
Theodosius campaigns to Christianize the Roman Empire

395 CE
Roman Empire is divided between East and West

406 CE
Vandals cross the Roman border on the Rhine

419 CE
Establishment of the Visigoth kingdom of Toulouse

476 CE
Last Western Roman emperor is deposed

200 CE · 250 CE · 300 CE · 350 CE · 400 CE · 450 CE · 500 CE

Roman emperors wanted to be perceived as having the characteristics of heroes and of gods. This statue of Commodus portrays him in the guise of Hercules, with whom the 2nd-century CE emperor wished to be identified in order to magnify his authority.

In the 3rd century CE, the emperor Septimius Severus ordered the construction of what was to be the last imperial residence on the Palatine Hill. These magnificent arcades were part of the artificial terrace upon which the palace was built.

soldiers could not be dispensed with; indeed, because of the barbarian threat, now present on several frontiers simultaneously, the army had to be enlarged and pampered. Here was a dilemma to face emperors for the next century. Severus's son Caracalla, who prudently began his reign by bribing the soldiers heavily, was none the less murdered by them in the end.

In theory the Senate still appointed the emperor. In fact it had little effective power except in so far as it could commit its prestige to one of a number of contending candidates. This was not much of an asset but still had some importance so long as maintaining the old forms had some moral effect. It was inevitable, though, that the arrangements should intensify the latent antagonism of Senate and emperor. Severus gave more power to officers drawn from the equestrian class and socially inferior to the senatorial families; Caracalla inferred that a purge of the Senate would help and took this further step towards autocratic rule. More military emperors followed him; soon there was for the first time one who did not come from the senatorial ranks, though he was from the *equites*. Worse was to follow. In 235 Maximinus, a huge ex-ranker from the Rhine legions, contested the prize with an octogenarian from Africa who had the backing of the African army and, eventually, of the Senate. Many emperors were murdered by their troops; one died fighting his own commander-in-chief in battle (his conqueror subsequently being slain by the Goths after his betrayal to them by one of his other officers). It was a dreadful century; altogether, twenty-two emperors came and went and that number does not include mere pretenders (or such semi-emperors as Postumus, who for a while maintained himself in Gaul, thus pre-figuring a later division of the empire).

Septimius Severus, depicted on this tablet with his family, left the empire to his sons Caracalla and Geta. However, when Severus died in 211 CE, Caracalla seized power, and had Geta assassinated and all images of him defaced, including this one.

During the 1st and 2nd centuries CE, under the emperors Septimius Severus and Caracalla, a new Roman theatre and forum were built in Lepcis Magna in the province of Africa.

ECONOMIC WEAKNESS

Though Severus's reforms had for a time improved matters, the fragility of his successors' position accelerated a decline in administration. Caracalla was the last emperor to try to broaden the basis of taxation by making all free inhabitants of the empire Roman citizens and thus liable to inheritance taxes, but no fundamental fiscal reform was attempted. Perhaps decline was inevitable, given the emergencies to be faced and the resources available. With irregularity and extemporization went growing rapacity and corruption as those with power or office used it to protect themselves. This reflected another problem, the economic weakness which the empire was showing in the third century.

Few generalizations are safe about what this meant to the consumer and supplier. For all its elaboration and organization around a network of cities, the economic life of the empire was overwhelmingly agrarian. Its bedrock was the rural estate, the *villa*, large or small, which was the basic unit both of production and also, in many places, of society. Such estates were the source of subsistence for all those lived on them (and that meant nearly all the rural population). Probably, therefore, most people in the countryside were less affected by the long-term swings of the economy than by the requisitioning and heavier taxation which resulted from the

The Boscoreale Roman villa, a luxurious residence on the outskirts of Pompeii, was covered in lava when Mount Vesuvius erupted in 79 CE. This mural, which depicts an urban landscape framed by a pedestal and marble columns, was found in one of the villa's rooms.

This detail is from a fresco found in the Boscoreale villa. It dates from the mid-1st century BCE, when Hellenistic-style art was very fashionable. This scene may be an attempt to recreate the atmosphere of the Macedonian court.

empire ceasing to expand; the armies had to be supported from a narrower base. Sometimes, too, the land was devastated by fighting. But peasants lived at subsistence level, had always been poor, and continued to be so, whether bond or free. As times got worse, some sought to bind themselves as serfs, which suggests an economy in which money was in retreat before payment in goods and services. It also probably reflects another impact of troubled times such as drove peasants to the towns or to banditry; the population everywhere sought protection.

Requisitioning and higher taxation may in some places have helped to produce depopulation – though the fourth century provides more evidence of this than the third – and to this extent were self-defeating. In any case, they were likely to be inequitable, for many of the rich were exempt from taxation and the

owners of the estates cannot have suffered much in inflationary times unless they were imprudent. The continuity of many of the great estate-owning families in antiquity does not suggest that the troubles of the third century bit deeply into their resources.

One of the signs of crisis within the 3rd-century CE empire was inflation – the value of money decreased while the price of goods on the market rose. Soldiers, and others who lived on fixed wages, were hard hit.

INFLATION AND INCREASING TAXATION

The administration and the army felt most of the effects of economic troubles, and particularly the major ill of the century, inflation. Its sources and extent are complex and still disputed. In part it derived from an official debasement of the coinage which was aggravated by the need to pay tribute in bullion to barbarians who from time to time were best placated by this means. But barbarian incursions themselves often helped to disrupt supply, and this again told against the cities, where prices rose. Because the soldiers' pay was fixed it fell in real value (this made them, of course, more susceptible to generals who offered lavish bribes). Although the overall impact is hard to assess, it has been suggested that money may have fallen during the century to about one-fiftieth of its value at the beginning.

The damage showed both in the towns and in imperial fiscal practice. From the third century onwards many towns shrank in size and prosperity; their early medieval successors were only pale reflections of the important places they once had been. One cause was the increasing demands of the imperial tax-collectors. From the beginning of the fourth century the depreciation of coin led imperial officials to levy taxes in kind – they could often be used directly to supply local garrisons but were also the means of payment to civil servants – and this not only made the government more unpopular, but also the *curiales* or municipal office-holders who had the task of raising these impositions. By 300 they often had to be forced to take office, a sure sign that a once sought-after dignity had become a strenuous obligation. Some towns suffered from actual physical damage, too, especially those in the frontier regions. Significantly, as the third century wore on, towns well within the frontier began to rebuild (or build for the first time) walls for their protection. Rome began again to fortify itself soon after 270.

CONFRONTATION WITH PARTHIA

The army steadily grew bigger. If the barbarians were to be kept out it had to be paid, fed and equipped. If the barbarians were not kept out there would be tribute to pay to them instead. And there was not only the barbarian to contend with. Only in Africa was the imperial frontier reasonably secure against Rome's neighbours (because there

Rome's city walls were begun c.271 CE, at the time of the emperor Aurelian. The brick walls, intended to protect the city from Germanic incursions, incorporated defence towers and 14 main gates, which were later modified.

Palmyra, in present-day Syria, was an independent oasis city that lay between the Roman and Parthian empires. As a major caravan town, Palmyra enjoyed great wealth, of which its monumental buildings, now ruined, are the evidence.

were no neighbours there who mattered). In Asia things were much grimmer. Ever since the days of Sulla a cold war with Parthia had flared up from time to time into full-scale campaigning. Two things prevented the Romans and Parthians from ever really settling down peacefully. One was the overlapping of their spheres of interest. This was most obvious in Armenia, a kingdom which was alternately a buffer and shuttlecock between them for a century and a half, but the Parthians also dabbled in the disturbed waters of Jewish unrest, another sensitive matter for Rome. The other factor making for disturbance was the temptation presented to Rome time and time again by Parthia's own internal dynastic troubles.

Such facts had already led in the second century CE to intense fighting over Armenia, its details often obscure. Severus eventually penetrated Mesopotamia but had to withdraw; the Mesopotamian valleys were too far away. The Romans were trying to do too much and faced the classic problem of over-extended imperialism. But their opponents were tiring and at low ebb, too. Parthian written records are fragmentary, but the tale of exhaustion and growing incompetence emerges from a coinage declining into unintelligibility and blurred derivations from earlier Hellenized designs.

THE PERSIAN THREAT

In the third century Parthia disappeared, but the threat to Rome from the East did not. A turning-point was reached in the history of the old area of Persian civilization. In about 225 a king called Ardashir (later known in the West as Artaxerxes) killed the last king of Parthia and was crowned in Ctesiphon. He was to re-create the Achaemenid Empire of Persia under a new dynasty, the Sassanids; it would be Rome's greatest antagonist for more than four hundred years. There was much continuity here; the Sassanid Empire was Zoroastrian, as Parthia had been, and evoked the Achaemenid tradition as Parthia had done.

Within a few years the Persians had invaded Syria and opened three centuries of struggle with the empire. In the third century there was not a decade without war. The Persians conquered Armenia and took one emperor (Valerian) prisoner. Then they were driven from Armenia and Mesopotamia in 297. This gave the Romans a frontier on the Tigris, but it was not one they could keep for ever. Neither could the Persians keep their conquests. The outcome was a long-drawn-out and ding-dong contest. A sort of equilibrium grew up in the fourth and fifth centuries and only in the sixth did it begin to break down. Meanwhile, commercial ties appeared. Though trade at the frontier was officially limited to three designated towns, important colonies of Persian merchants came to live in the great cities of the empire. Persia, moreover, lay across trade routes to India and China which were as vital to Roman exporters as to those who wanted

The Sassanid Empire c.400 CE

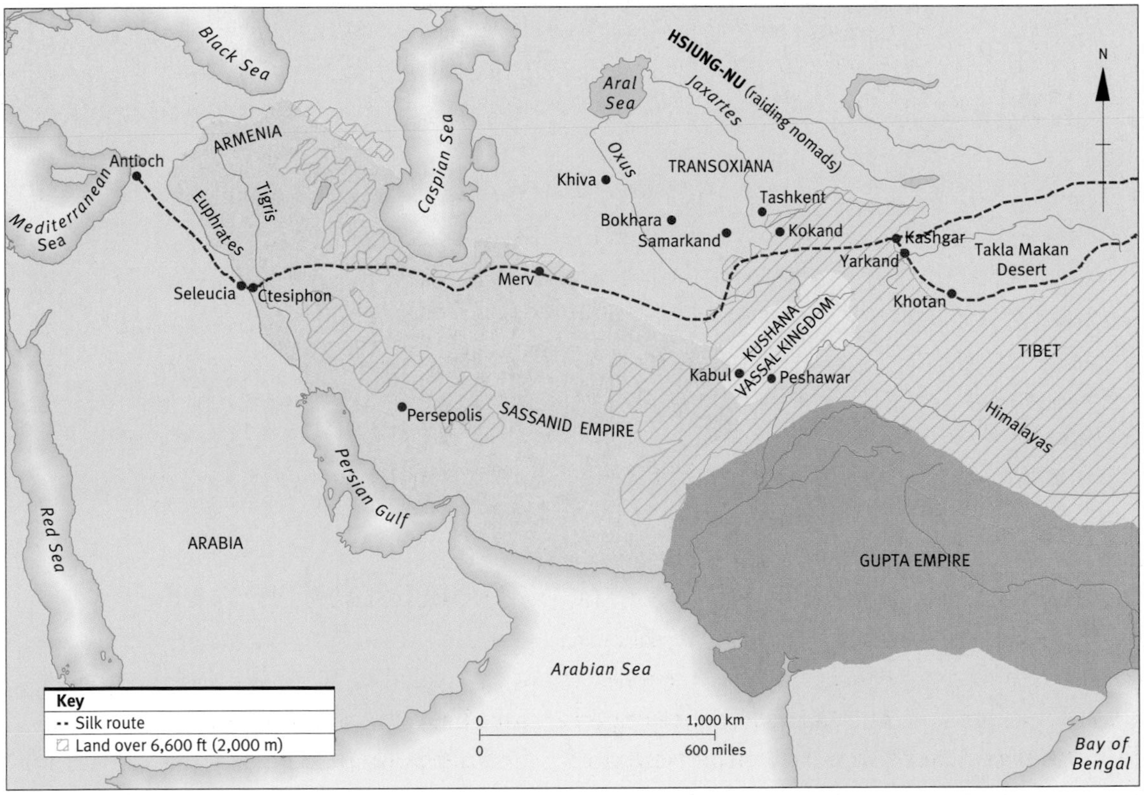

Around 225 CE, Ardashir, conqueror of the last Parthian king, re-created the ancient Persian kingdom under the new Sassanid Dynasty. The Persians quickly launched an invasion of Syria and attempted to increase their hold on the Near East. Many of the main commercial trading routes to the India and the Far East crossed Persian territory, including the famous Silk Route that made it possible for the Roman Empire to import valuable goods such as spices, gems and silk from China. From the late 3rd century CE, the Romans and the Persians began to hold negotiations concerning the silk trade.

The arch built in 203 CE in honour of Septimius Severus and his children dominates the western end of the Roman Forum. It is decorated with bas-reliefs portraying the emperor's military campaigns against the Parthians and the Arabs.

oriental silk, cotton and spices. Yet these ties did not offset other forces. When not at war, the two empires tended to co-exist with cold and cautious hostility; their relations were complicated by communities and peoples settled on both sides of the frontier, and there was always the danger of the strategic balance being upset by a change in one of the buffer kingdoms – Armenia, for instance. The final round of open struggle was put off, but came at last in the sixth century.

This is to jump too far ahead for the present; by then huge changes had taken place in the Roman Empire which have still to be explained. The conscious dynamism of the Sassanid monarchy was only one of the pressures encouraging them. Another came from the barbarians along the Danube and Rhine frontiers. The origins of the folk movements which propelled them forward in the third century and thereafter must be sought in a long development and are less important than the outcome. These peoples grew more insistent, acted in larger groupings and had, in the end, to be allowed to settle inside Roman territory. Here they were first engaged as soldiers to protect the empire against other barbarians and then, gradually, began to take a hand in running the empire themselves.

A Roman military camp

This plan of a Roman encampment is based on descriptions of such camps given in a military treatise drawn up between the 1st and 3rd centuries CE. A typical Roman army camp was designed to accommodate 40,000 men. The complex was surrounded by a wall of earth, peat or stone and had a moat. Inside, two main roads running parallel across the minor axis of the camp divided the space into three principal sections.

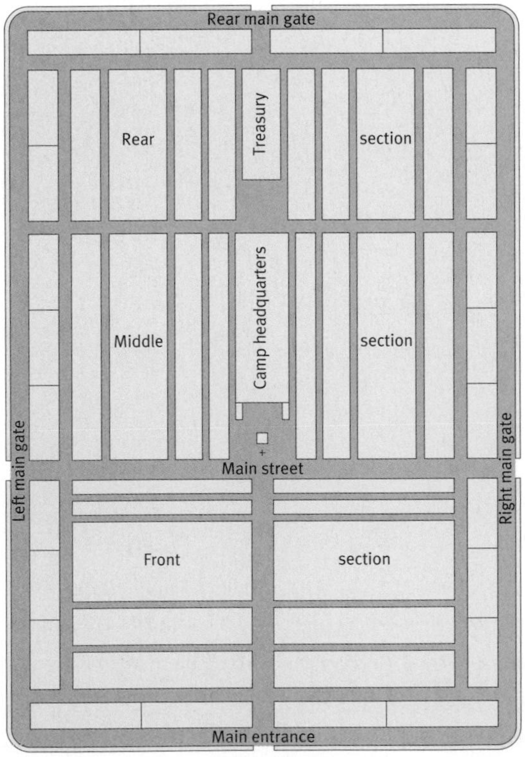

This scene is from a Sassanid rock relief in the Naqsh-i-Rustam pass, north of Persepolis. It represents the mounted forces of King Ardashir, following his victory over the last Parthian king c.225. Ardashir, on the left, is depicted receiving a diadem from the god Mazda. Defeated Parthians lie trampled beneath the horses' hooves.

THE EUROPEAN THREAT

In 200 the assimilation of barbarians into the empire still lay in the future; all that was clear then was that new pressures were building up. The most important barbarian peoples involved were the Franks and Alamanni on the Rhine and the Goths on the lower Danube. From about 230 the empire was struggling to hold them off but the cost of fighting on two fronts was heavy; his Persian entanglements soon led one emperor to make concessions to the Alamanni. When his immediate successors added their own quarrels to their Persian burdens, the Goths took advantage of a promising situation and invaded Moesia, the province immediately south of the Danube, killing an emperor there *en passant* in 251. Five years later, the Franks crossed the Rhine. The Alamanni followed and got as far as Milan. Gothic armies invaded Greece and raided Asia and the Aegean from the sea. Within a few years the European dams seemed to give way everywhere at once.

The scale of these incursions is not easy to establish. Perhaps the barbarians could never field an army of more than twenty or thirty thousand. But this was too much at any one

Daily life in Roman cities

From the 3rd century BCE, more and more Romans took to city life. As the cities expanded, artisanal and commercial activities within them became increasingly important. Numerous funeral monument decorations give us a good idea of the kind of trades that existed. Most businesses were on a small scale: the artisans' workshops were often family-run, perhaps employing a few slaves and apprentices, and also serving as a shop for the mainly local clientele. Tools were simple, except in the large-scale construction industry, where more complex machinery was occasionally used.

Many of the shops in and around the crowded markets sold foodstuffs, competing with pedlars.
Some taverns offered ready-prepared food to travellers. Most city-dwellers spent a great deal of time in the streets and did not eat at fixed times.

Ordinary people cooked very little. In houses belonging to wealthy Romans, however, slaves often prepared lavish meals. Meat and fish dishes were rarely eaten without some kind of sauce. These sauces were based on aromatic herbs, pepper, pickles, oil, vinegar, wine and honey.

Trajan's Markets were constructed by the emperor Trajan on the western side of the Forum in the 2nd century CE. Paid for by the gains from the Dacian wars, this large vaulted structure housed shops and commercial properties. The six-storey complex was bounded by a semicircular public space, the exedra.

place for the imperial army. Its backbone was provided by recruits from the Illyrian provinces; appropriately, it was a succession of emperors of Illyrian stock who turned the tide. Much of what they did was simple good soldiering and intelligent extemporization. They recognized priorities; the main dangers lay in Europe and had to be dealt with first. Alliance with Palmyra helped to buy time against Persia. Losses were cut; trans-Danubian Dacia was abandoned in 270. The army was reorganized to provide effective

Barrels of wine were often transported by boat. This bas-relief depicts men on a river bank hauling a boat along by pulling on thick ropes attached to a pivot.

mobile reserves in each of the main danger areas. This was all the work of Aurelian, whom the Senate significantly called "Restorer of the Roman Empire". But the cost was heavy. A more fundamental reconstruction was implicit if the work of the Illyrian emperors was to survive and this was the aim of Diocletian. A soldier of proven bravery, he sought to restore the Augustan tradition but revolutionized the empire instead.

THE AGE OF DIOCLETIAN

DIOCLETIAN HAD an administrator's genius rather than a soldier's. Without being especially imaginative, he had an excellent grasp of organization and principles, a love of order and great skill in picking and trusting men to whom he could delegate. He was also energetic. Diocletian's capital was wherever the imperial retinue found itself; it moved about the empire, passing a year here, a couple of months there, and sometimes only a day or two in the same place. The heart of the reforms which emerged from this court was a division of the empire intended to deliver it both from the dangers of internal quarrels between pretenders in remote provinces and from the over-extension of its administrative and military resources. In 285 Diocletian appointed a co-emperor, Maximian, with responsibility for the empire west of a line running from the Danube to Dalmatia. The two *augusti* were subsequently each given a *caesar* as coadjutor; these were to be both their assistants and their successors, thus making possible an orderly transfer of power. In fact, the machine of succession only once operated as Diocletian intended, at his own abdication and that of his colleague, but the practical separation of administration in two imperial structures was not reversed. After this time all emperors had to accept a large measure of division even when there was nominally still only one of them.

There also now emerged explicitly a new conception of the imperial office. No longer was the title *princeps* employed; the emperors were the creation of the army, not the Senate, and were deferred to in terms recalling the semi-divine kingship of oriental courts. Practically, they acted through pyramidal bureaucracies. "Dioceses", responsible directly to the emperors through their "vicars", grouped provinces much smaller and about twice as numerous as the old ones had been. The senatorial monopoly of governmental power had long since gone; senatorial rank now meant in effect merely a social distinction (membership of the wealthy land-owning class) or occupation of one of the important bureaucratic posts. Equestrian rank disappeared.

THE TETRARCHY

The military establishment of the Tetrarchy, as it was called, was much larger (and therefore more expensive) than that laid down originally by Augustus. The theoretical mobility of the legions, deeply dug into long-occupied garrisons, was abandoned. The army of the frontiers was now broken up into units, some of which remained permanently in the same place while others provided new mobile forces smaller than the old legions. Conscription was reintroduced. Something like a half-million men were under arms. Their direction was wholly separated from the civilian government of the provinces with which it had once been fused.

The results of this system do not seem to have been exactly what Diocletian envisaged. They included a considerable measure of military recovery and stablization, but its cost was enormous. An army whose size doubled in a century had to be paid for by a population which had probably already begun to shrink. Heavy taxation not only compromised the loyalty of the empire's subjects and encouraged corruption; it also required a close control of social arrangements so that the tax base should not be eroded. There was great administrative pressure against social mobility; the peasant, for example, was obliged to stay where he was recorded at the census. Another celebrated (though so far as can be seen totally unsuccessful) example was the attempt to regulate wages and prices throughout the empire by a freeze. Such efforts, like those to raise more taxation, meant a bigger civil service, and as the number of administrators increased so, of course, did the overheads of government.

Diocletian and Maximian were the two emperors who, together with their respective *caesars*, formed the first government within the tetrarchic system organized by Diocletian at the end of the 3rd century CE. This porphyry sculpture, which dates from c.300 CE, symbolizes the tetrarchs' solidarity.

THE IDEOLOGICAL CRISIS

In the end Diocletian probably achieved most by opening the way to a new view of the imperial office itself. The religious aura which it acquired was a response to a real problem. Somehow, under the strain of continued usurpation and failure the empire had ceased to be unquestioningly accepted. This was not merely because of dislike of higher taxation or fear of its growing numbers of secret police. Its ideological basis had been eroded and it could not focus loyalties. A crisis of civilization was going on as well as a crisis of government. The spiritual matrix of the classical world was breaking up; neither state nor civilization was any longer to be taken for granted and they needed a new ethos before they could be.

An emphasis on the unique status of the emperor and his sacral role was one early response to this need. Consciously, Diocletian acted as a saviour, a Jupiter-like figure holding back chaos. Something in this recalled affinities with those thinkers of the late classical world who saw life as a perpetual struggle of good and evil. Yet this was a vision not Greek or Roman at all, but oriental. The acceptance of a new vision of the emperor's relation to the gods, and therefore of a new conception of the official cult, did not bode well for the traditional practical tolerance of the Greek world. Decisions about worship might now decide the fate of the empire.

THE GROWTH OF THE CHRISTIAN CHURCH

Changes in the attitudes of successive Roman emperors were now to shape the history of the Christian Churches for both good and ill. In the end Christianity was to be the legatee of Rome. Many religious sects have risen from the position of persecuted minorities to become establishments in their own right. What sets the Christian Church apart is that this took place within the uniquely comprehensive structure of the late Roman Empire, so that it both attached itself to and strengthened the lifeline of classical civilization, with enormous consequences not only for itself but for Europe and ultimately the world.

At the beginning of the third century missionaries had already carried the faith to the non-Jewish peoples of Asia Minor and North Africa. Particularly in North Africa, Christianity had its first mass successes in the towns; it long remained a predominantly urban phenomenon. But it was still a matter of minorities. Throughout the empire, the old gods and the local deities held the peasants' allegiance. By the year 300 Christians may have made up only about a tenth of the population of the empire. But there had already been striking signs of official favour and even concession. One emperor had been

The St Simeon basilica in Qalaat Semaan, Syria, was constructed c.480 CE. Its impressive remains, such as this section from the central octagon, testify to the robustness of Christian churches built in the Near East during the 4th and 5th centuries.

Paul of Tarsus was a Greek-speaking Roman citizen and a Pharisee from Cilicia. Following his conversion to Christianity, he became a key figure in the early Church, spreading his belief that Christianity was not a religion exclusive to the Jews.

nominally a Christian and another had included Jesus Christ among the gods honoured privately in his household. Such contacts with the court illustrate an interplay of Jewish and classical culture which is an important part of the story of the process by which Christianity took root in the empire. Perhaps Paul of Tarsus, the Jew who could talk to Athenians in terms they understood, had launched this. Later, early in the second century, Justin Martyr, a Palestinian Greek, had striven to show that Christianity had a debt to Greek philosophy. This had a political point; cultural identification with the classical tradition helped to rebut the charge of disloyalty to the empire. If a Christian could stand in the ideological heritage of the Hellenistic world he could also be a good citizen, and Justin's rational Christianity (even though he was martyred for it in about 165) envisaged a revelation of the Divine Reason in which all the great philosophers and prophets had partaken, Plato among them, but which was only complete in Christ. Others were to follow similar lines, notably the learned Clement of Alexandria, who strove to integrate pagan scholarship with Christianity, and Origen (though his exact teaching is still debated because of the disappearance of many of his writings). A North African Christian, Tertullian, had contemptuously asked what the Academy had to do with the Church; he was answered by the Fathers who deliberately employed the conceptual armoury of Greek philosophy to provide a statement of the faith which anchored Christianity to rationality as Paul had not done.

This relief from a sarcophagus, probably of Christian origin, dates from the 2nd or 3rd century CE. A philosopher is depicted, book in hand, with a man and a woman. The classical and monumental style is reminiscent of compositions that were often used to decorate pagan sarcophagi.

THE PERSECUTION OF CHRISTIANS

When coupled to its promise of salvation after death and the fact that the Christian life could be lived in a purposeful and optimistic way, such developments might lead us to suppose that Christians were by the third century confident about the future. In fact, favourable portents were much less striking than the persecutions so prominent in the history of the early Church. There were two great outbreaks. That of the middle of the century expressed the spiritual crisis of the establishment. It was not only economic strain and military defeat that were troubling the empire, but a dialectic inherent in Roman success itself: the cosmopolitanism which had been so much the mark of the empire was, inevitably, a solvent of the *romanitas*, which was less and less a reality and more and more a slogan. The emperor Decius seems to have been convinced that the old recipe of a return to traditional Roman virtue and values could still work; it implied the revival of service to the gods whose benevolence would then be once more deployed in favour of the empire. The Christians, like others, must sacrifice to the Roman tradition, said Decius, and many did, to judge by the certificates

Constantine, Roman emperor in the years 306–337 CE, was, in the eyes of some, the "thirteenth Apostle", due to what he did for the Christian Church. His effigy appears on this gold coin.

issued to save them from persecution; some did not, and died. A few years later, Valerian renewed persecution on the same grounds, though his proconsuls addressed themselves rather to the directing personnel and the property of the Church – its buildings and books – than to the mass of believers. Thereafter, persecution ebbed, and the Church resumed its shadowy, tolerated existence just below the horizon of official attention.

Persecution had shown, nevertheless, that it would require great efforts and prolonged determination to eradicate the new sect; it may even have been already beyond the capacities of Roman government to carry out such an eradication. The exclusiveness and isolation of early Christianity had waned. Christians were increasingly prominent in local affairs in the Asian and African provinces. Bishops were often public figures with whom officials expected to do business; the development of distinct traditions within the faith (those of the Churches of Rome, Alexandria and Carthage being the most important) spoke for the degree to which it was rooted in local society and could express local needs.

Outside the empire, too, there had been signs that better times might lie ahead for Christianity. The local rulers of the client states under the shadow of Persia could not afford to neglect any source of local support. Respect for widely held religious views was at least prudent. In Syria, Cilicia and Cappadocia, Christians had been very successful in their missionary work and in some towns they formed a social élite. Simple superstition, too, helped to convince kings; the Christian god might prove powerful and it could hardly be damaging to insure against his ill-will. Thus Christianity's political and civic prospects improved.

Christians noted with some satisfaction that their persecutors did not prosper; the Goths slew Decius, and Valerian was said to have been skinned alive by the Persians (and stuffed). But Diocletian did not appear to draw any conclusions from this and in 303 launched the last great Roman persecution. It was not at first harsh. The main targets were Christian officials, clergy and the books and buildings of the Church. The books were to be handed over for burning, but for some time there was no death penalty for failing to sacrifice. (Many Christians none the less did sacrifice, the bishop at Rome among them.) Constantius, the *caesar* of the West, did not enforce the persecution after 305, when Diocletian abdicated, though his Eastern colleague (Diocletian's successor, Galerius) felt strongly about it, ordering a general sacrifice on pain of death. This meant that persecution was worst in Egypt and Asia where it was kept up a few years longer. But before this it had been cut across by the complicated politics which led to the emergence of the emperor Constantine the Great.

CONSTANTINE THE GREAT

The father of Constantine the Great was Constantius, who died in Britain in 306, a year after his accession as *augustus*. Constantine was there at the time and although he had not been his father's *caesar* he was hailed as emperor by the army at York. A troubled period of nearly two decades followed. Its intricate struggles demonstrated the failure of Diocletian's arrangements for the peaceful transmission of the empire and only ended in 324, when Constantine reunited the empire under one ruler.

By this time he had already addressed himself vigorously and effectively to its

Constantinople

In 324 CE Constantine, having become sole emperor with his defeat of Licinius, decided to build a new imperial capital on the site of Byzantium in the Eastern Empire. On 11 May 330 CE, the "new Rome" – a Christian city from the outset – was inaugurated and a column of porphyry crowned with a statue of Constantine was erected at its centre. During the whole Byzantine era, this column was the symbol of the foundation and perpetuity of the capital.

It was only from the end of the 4th century that Constantinople became the definitive headquarters of the Eastern Empire – the city in which the emperor showed himself in public and asserted his divine and imperial power. During the Middle Ages, the city again assumed the name of Byzantium, which it retained until its conquest by the Turks in 1453 CE.

Constantinople's enviable strategic position between Europe and Asia, with control of the Bosphorus Straits, meant that it enjoyed rapid economic growth. A large number of artisans and tradespeople set up their businesses in the capital, where they were able to obtain materials and products from all over the East and export them to the Western Roman Empire.

The city's expansion was accompanied by a public building programme, during which churches, squares and municipal offices were constructed. In the 5th century, according to a contemporary survey, Constantinople had 14 churches, 11 imperial palaces, 5 markets, 8 public baths and 153 private ones, 20 public bakeries and 120 private ones, 322 streets and a total of 4,388 houses.

This French miniature of Constantinople by Péronet Lamy dates from 1436 CE and depicts the capital of the Eastern Roman Empire less than 20 years before its downfall.

problems, though with more success as a soldier than as an administrator. Often with barbarian recruits, he built up a powerful field army distinct from the frontier guards; it was stationed in cities within the empire. This was a strategically sound decision which proved itself in the fighting power the empire showed in the East for the next two centuries. Constantine also disbanded the Praetorian Guard and created a new, German bodyguard. He restored a stable gold currency and paved the way to the abolition of payments of taxes in kind and the restoration of a money economy. His fiscal reforms had more mixed results but attempted some readjustment of the weight of taxation so that more should be borne by the rich. None of these things, though, struck contemporaries as much as his attitude to Christianity.

CONSTANTINE AND THE CHURCH

Constantine gave the Church official houseroom. He thus played a more important part in shaping its future than any other Christian layman and was to be called the "thirteenth Apostle". Yet his personal relationship to

Rome's mausoleum of St Constance, the interior of which is shown here, was built in the 4th century CE during the reign of Constantine. The domed central room is encircled by 12 pairs of twin columns with composite capitals supporting large arches. Originally, the sarcophagus of Constantina, the emperor's daughter, stood beneath one of these arches.

Christianity was complicated. He grew up intellectually with the monotheistic predisposition of many late classical men and women and was in the end undoubtedly a convinced believer (it was not then unusual for Christians to do as he did and postpone baptism until their deathbed). But he believed out of fear and hope, for the god he worshipped was a god of power. His first adherence was to the sun-god whose sign he bore and whose cult was already officially associated with that of the emperor. Then, in 312, on the eve of battle and as a result of what he believed to be a vision he ordered his soldiers to put on their shields a Christian monogram. This showed a willingness to show suitable respect to whatever gods there might be. He won the battle, and thenceforth, though continuing publicly to acknowledge the cult of the sun, he began to show important favours to the Christians and their god.

THE EDICT OF MILAN

One manifestation of the emperor's new enthusiasm for Christianity was an edict the following year, which was issued by another of the contenders for the empire, after agreement with Constantine at Milan. It restored to Christians their property, and granted them the toleration that other religions enjoyed. The justification may reveal Constantine's own thinking as well as his wish to arrive at a satisfactory compromise formula with his colleague, for it explained its provisions by the hope "that whatever divinity dwells in the heavenly seat may be appeased and be propitious towards us and to all who are placed under our authority". Constantine went on to make considerable gifts of property to the churches, favouring, in particular, that of Rome. Besides providing important tax concessions to the clergy, he conferred an unlimited right to receive bequests on the Church. Yet for years his coins continued to honour pagan gods, notably the "Unconquered Sun".

The lack of individuality in this bronze bust of Constantine represents his divine authority. It marks the birth of a new style, emphasizing the superiority of emperors who saw themselves as guardians of the Church.

CHURCH AND STATE

Constantine gradually came to see himself as having a quasi-sacerdotal role, and this was of the first importance in the further evolution of the imperial office. He saw himself as responsible to God for the well-being of the Church, to which he more and more publicly and unequivocally adhered. After 320 the sun no longer appeared on his coins and soldiers had to attend church parades. But he was always cautious of the susceptibilities of his pagan subjects. Though he later despoiled temples of their gold while building splendid Christian churches and encouraging converts by preferment, he did not cease to tolerate the old cults.

In some of Constantine's work (like that of Diocletian) there was the development of things latent and implicit in the past, an extension of earlier precedents. This was true of his interventions in the internal affairs of the Church. As early as 272, the Christians of Antioch had appealed to the emperor to remove a bishop and in 316 Constantine himself tried to settle a controversy in North Africa by installing a bishop of Carthage against the will of a local sectarian group known as Donatists. Constantine came to believe that the emperor owed to God more than a grant of freedom to the Church or even an endowment. His conception of his role evolved towards that of the guarantor and, if need be, the imposer of the unity which God required as the price of His continuing favour. When he turned on the Donatists it was this view of his duty which gave them the unhappy distinction of being the first schismatics to be persecuted by a Christian government. Constantine was the creator of Caesaropapism, the belief that the secular ruler has divine authority to settle religious belief, and of the notion of established religion in Europe for the next thousand years.

Dura-Europos, built as a fortress by the Hellenistic Seleucid monarchy, was a Roman stronghold from 165 CE. The fortress incorporated elements from both Eastern and Western culture. Archaeological findings suggest that near the temples to the Roman gods there stood a synagogue, a sanctuary dedicated to Mithras and a Christian church.

This mosaic from the dome of the Arian Baptistry in Ravenna dates from c.500 CE. The baptism of Christ is depicted in the centre, with John the Baptist on the right and a personification of the river Jordan on the left. The scene is surrounded by the 12 Apostles and a throne, upon which a cross is raised.

THE COUNCIL OF NICAEA

Constantine's greatest act in the ordering of religion came just after he had formally declared himself a Christian in 324 (a declaration preceded by another victory over an imperial rival who had, interestingly, been persecuting Christians). This was the calling of the first ecumenical council, the Council of Nicaea. It met for the first time in 325, nearly 300 bishops being present, and Constantine presided over it. Its task was to settle the response of the Church to a new heresy, Arianism, whose founder, Arius, taught that the Son did not share the divinity of the Father. Though technical and theological, the nice issues to which this gave rise prompted enormous controversy. Grave scandal was alleged by Arius's opponents. Constantine sought to heal the division and the Council laid down a Creed which decided against the Arians, but went on in a second reunion to re-admit Arius to communion after suitable declarations. That this did not satisfy all the bishops (and that there were few from the West at Nicaea) was less important than the fact that Constantine had presided at this crucial juncture of proclaiming the emperor's enjoyment of special authority and responsibility. The Church was clothed in the imperial purple.

Constantine is shown being crowned by the hand of God on this 4th-century CE gold medal. The emperor's children are at his side, receiving crowns from Victoria.

CHRISTIANITY DIVIDED

There were other great implications, too. Behind the hair-splitting of the theologians lay a great question both of practice and of principle: in the new ideological unity given to the empire by the official establishment of Christianity, what was to be the place of diverging Christian traditions which were social and political, as well as liturgical and theological, realities? The churches of Syria and Egypt, for example, were strongly tinctured by their inheritance of thought and custom both from the Hellenistic culture and the popular religion of those regions. The importance of such considerations helps to explain why the practical outcome of Constantine's ecclesiastical policy was less than he had hoped. The Council did not produce an emollient formula to make easier a general reconciliation in a spirit of compromise. Constantine's own attitude to the Arians soon relaxed (in the end, it was to be an Arian bishop who baptized him as he lay dying) but the opponents of Arius, led by the formidable Athanasius, bishop of Alexandria, were relentless. The quarrel remained unsettled when Arius died, and Constantine's own death followed not long after. Yet Arianism was not to prosper in the East. Its last successes, instead, were won by Arian missionaries to the Germanic tribes of southeast Russia; borne by these barbarian nations, Arianism was to survive until the seventh century in the West.

CONSTANTINE'S LEGACY

How much of the Church's rise was in the end inevitable it is hardly profitable to consider. Certainly – in spite of a North African

Arius was a 3rd-century CE Christian priest from Alexandria. His teaching, which spread among the Germanic peoples, also reached Ravenna, where an Arian baptistry, shown below, still stands. In 325 Arianism was condemned as heresy at the Council of Nicaea, which was presided over by Constantine.

Scenes on the triumphal arch dedicated to the emperor Galerius in Thessalonica depict his 4th-century CE military campaigns. In this detail, Galerius is shown taking part in a triumphal procession.

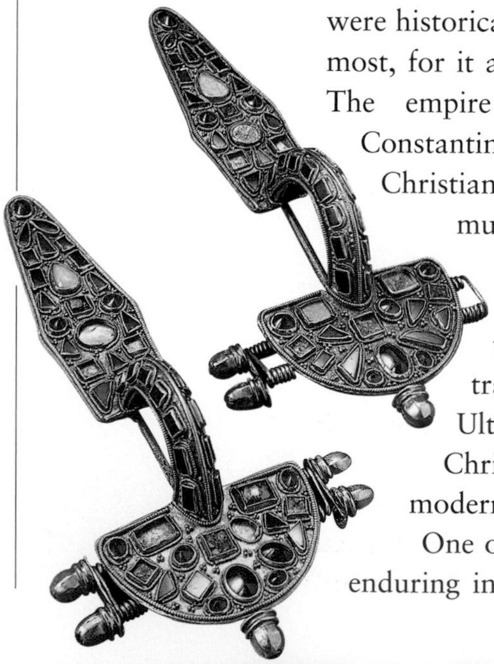

These elaborate clasps were found in the tomb of a 5th-century CE Germanic princess. They were probably brought to the West from the Pontus region.

Christian tradition which saw the state as an irrelevancy – something so positively important as Christianity could hardly have remained for ever unrecognized by the civil power. Yet someone had to begin. Constantine was the man who took the crucial steps which linked Church and empire for so long as the empire should last. His choices were historically decisive. The Church gained most, for it acquired the charisma of Rome. The empire seemed less changed. Yet Constantine's sons were brought up as Christians and even if the fragility of much in the new establishment was to appear soon after his death in 337, he had registered a decisive break with the tradition of classical Rome. Ultimately, unwittingly, he founded Christian Europe and, therefore, the modern world.

One of his decisions only slightly less enduring in its effects was his foundation, "on the command of God", he said, of a city to rival Rome on the site of the old Greek colony of Byzantium at the entrance to the Black Sea. It was dedicated in 330 as Constantinople. Though his own court remained at Nicomedia and no emperor was to reside there permanently for another fifty years, Constantine was again shaping the future. For a thousand years Constantinople would be a Christian capital, unsullied by pagan rites. After that, for five hundred years more, it would be a pagan capital and the constant ambition of would-be successors to its traditions.

DISUNITY IN THE EMPIRE

The empire as Constantine left it was, in Roman eyes, still coterminous with civilization. Its frontiers ran for the most part along natural features which recognized, more or less, the demarcations of distinct geographical or

The two parts of the Roman Empire

After the 3rd century CE, the differences between the Eastern and Western Roman Empires became increasingly noticeable. There was a sharp fall in the populations of many Western cities around this time, accompanied by a decrease in trade and reduced rates of production. This decline contrasted sharply with the dynamism of the Eastern Mediterranean cities, which continued to reap the benefits of their commercial and diplomatic relationships with the Far East.

Moreover, the Eastern Empire's geographical position meant that most of the principal invasion routes did not cross her territories – the rampaging barbarian hordes tended to move westward from the vast plains of central Europe.

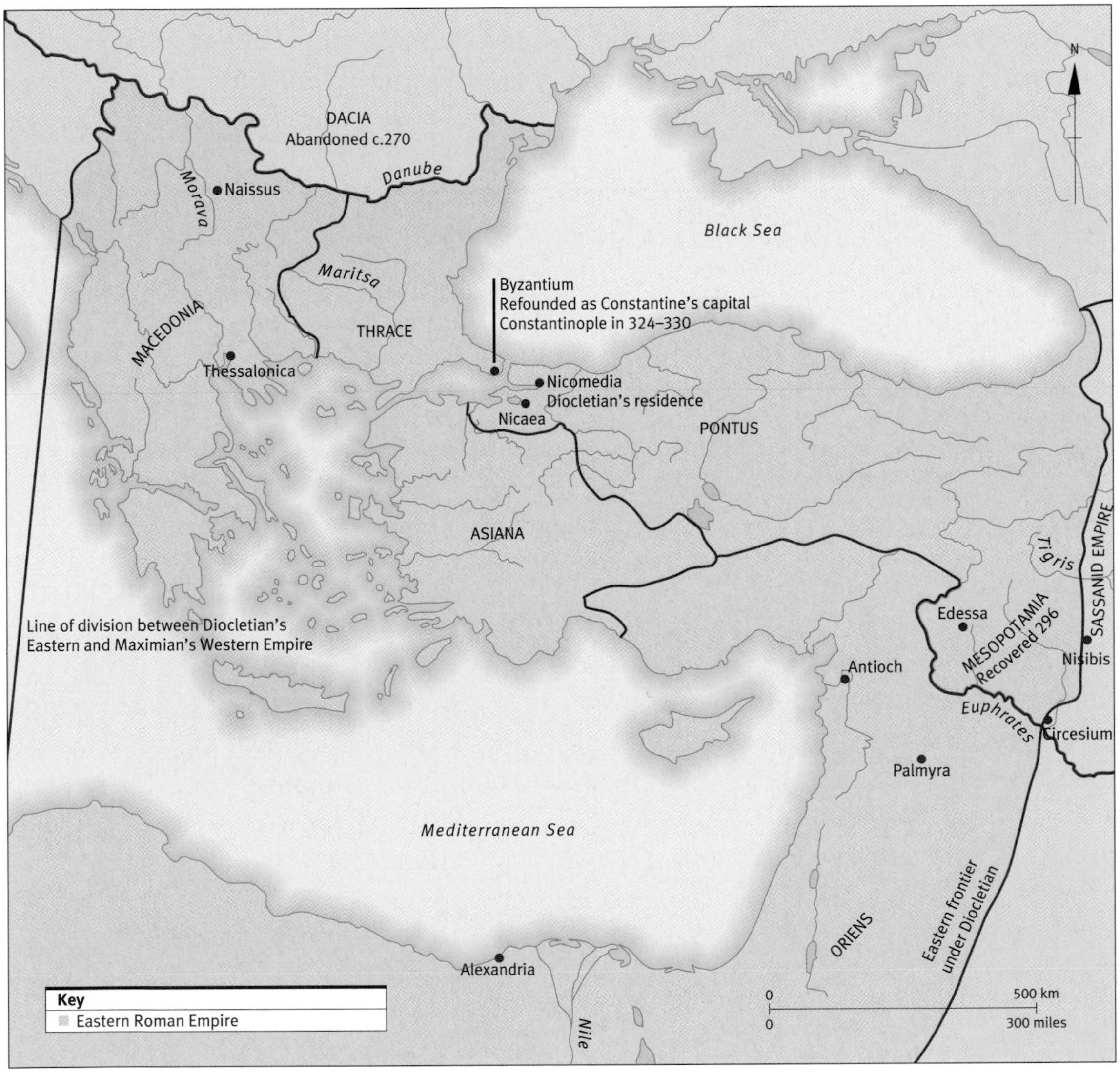

historical regions. Hadrian's Wall in Britannia was their northern limit; in continental Europe they followed the Rhine and Danube. The Black Sea coasts north of the mouths of the Danube had been lost to barbarians by 305 BCE, but Asia Minor remained in the empire; it stretched as far east as the shifting boundary with Persia. Further south, the Levant coast and Palestine lay within a frontier which ran to the Red Sea. The lower Nile valley was still held by the empire and so was the North African coast; the African frontiers were the Atlas and the desert.

This unity was, for all Constantine's great work, in large measure an illusion. As the first experiments with co-emperors had shown, the world of Roman civilization had grown too big for a unified political structure, however desirable the preservation of the myth of unity might be. Growing cultural differentiation between a Greek-speaking East and a Latin-speaking West, the new importance of Asia Minor, Syria and Egypt (in all of which there were large Christian communities) after the establishment of Christianity and the continuing stimulus of direct contact with Asia in the East all drove the point home. After 364 the two parts of the old empire were only once more and then only briefly ruled by the same man. Their institutions diverged further and further. In the East the emperor was a theological as well as a juridical figure; the identity of empire and Christendom and the emperor's standing as the expression of divine intention were unambiguous. The West, on the other hand, had by 400 already

The migration of the Germanic peoples

The great population movements that affected the Roman Empire during the 4th and 5th centuries CE transformed the cultural map of Europe and dealt the decadent Western Empire its death-blow. The barbarian invasions differed in their effects: some tribes were determined to occupy territories and property by force, others destroyed everything they found in their path, while others made an effort to settle more peacefully, looking for recognition from the Romans. The invaders were often not very numerous, but the local populations offered little or no resistance. As a result, several independent kingdoms emerged, such as the Visigothic kingdom in Hispania and the Frankish kingdom in Gaul, both former Roman provinces.

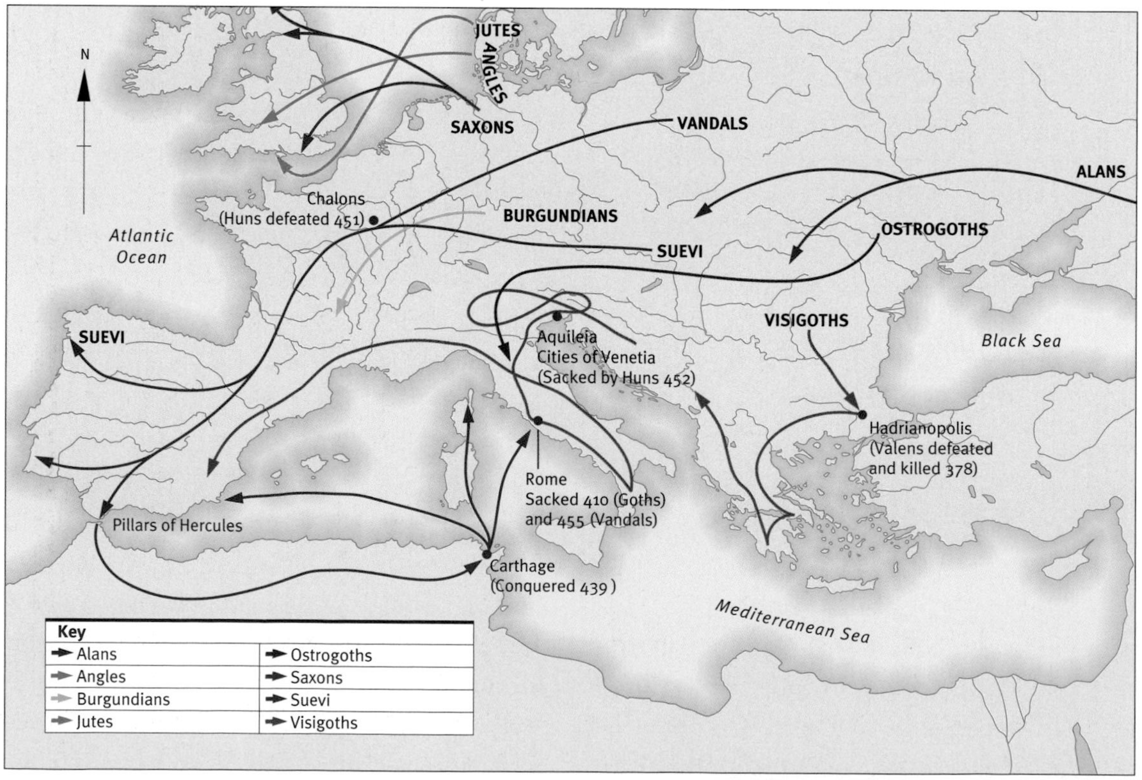

Djemila, a Christian enclave in present-day Algeria, was built in brick in the 5th and 6th centuries CE.

seen adumbrated the distinction of the roles of Church and State which was to father one of the most creative arguments of European politics. There was an economic contrast, too: the East was populous and could still raise great revenues, while the West was by 300 unable to feed itself without Africa and the Mediterranean islands. It now seems obvious that two distinct civilizations were to emerge, but it was a long time before any of the participants could see that.

THE DECLINE OF THE WEST

In the event, something much more appalling came about before the emergence of two civilizations: the Western Empire simply disappeared. By 500, when the boundaries of the Eastern Empire were still much what they had been under Constantine, and his successors were still holding their own against the Persians, the last Western emperor had been deposed and his *insignia* sent to Constantinople by a barbarian king who claimed to rule as the Eastern emperor's representative in the West.

This is striking: what, actually, had collapsed? What had declined or fallen? Fifth-century writers bewailed it so much that it is easy to have the impression, heightened by such dramatic episodes as sackings of Rome itself, that the whole of society fell apart. This was not so. It was the state apparatus which collapsed, some of its functions ceasing to be carried out, and some passing into other hands. This was quite enough to explain the alarm. Institutions with a thousand years of history behind them gave way within a half-century. It is hardly surprising that people have asked why ever since.

One explanation is cumulative: the state

A rider in Germanic-style dress is shown setting out to go hunting in this mosaic from 6th-century CE Carthage. He may be a Vandal landowner who has adopted the customs of North Africa's romanized territory, captured from the empire in the 5th century.

apparatus in the West gradually seized up after the recovery of the fourth century. The whole concern became too big for the demographic, fiscal and economic base which carried it. The main purpose of raising revenue was to pay for the military machine, but it became more and more difficult to raise enough. There were no more conquests after Dacia to bring in new tribute. Soon the measures adopted to squeeze out more taxes drove rich and poor alike to devices for avoiding them. The effect was to make agricultural estates rely more and more upon meeting their own needs and becoming self-supporting, rather than producing for the market. Parallel with this went a crumbling of urban government as trade languished and the rich withdrew to the countryside.

The military result was an army recruited from inferior material, because better could not be paid for. Even the reform of dividing it into mobile and garrison forces had its defects, for the first lost their fighting spirit by being stationed at the imperial residence and becoming used to the pampering and privileges that went with city postings, while the second turned into settled colonists, unwilling to take risks which would jeopardize their homesteads. Another descent in the unending spiral of decline logically followed. A weaker army drove the empire to rely still more on the very barbarians the army was supposed to keep at bay. As they had to be recruited as mercenaries, soothing and conciliatory politics were needed to keep them sweet. This led the Romans to concede more to the barbarians just when the pressure of the Germanic folk movements was reaching a new climax. Migration and the attractive prospect of paid service with the empire probably counted for much more in the barbarian contribution to imperial collapse than the simple desire for loot. The prospect of booty might animate a raiding-party but could hardly bring down an empire.

These are the decorated hilts of two swords found in the tomb of the Merovingian king Childeric, who died in 481 CE. Elaborately designed swords were used in Frankish countries until the 6th century. Gold inlay was characteristic of ornamental art from the East and was introduced to the West by the Germanic peoples.

THE GERMANIC THREAT

At the beginning of the fourth century Germanic peoples were stretched along the whole length of the frontier from the Rhine to the Black Sea, but it was in the south that the most formidable concentration was at that moment assembled. These were the Gothic peoples, Ostrogoth and Visigoth, who waited beyond the Danube. Some of them were already Christian, though in the Arian form. Together with Vandals, Burgundians and Lombards, they made up an east Germanic group. To the north were the west Germans: Franks, Alamanni, Saxons, Frisians and Thuringians. They would move into action in the second phase of the *Völkerwanderung* of the fourth and fifth centuries.

THE VISIGOTHS

The crisis began in the last quarter of the fourth century. The pressure of the Huns, a formidable nomadic people from central Asia, on more western barbarians was mounting

The bas-reliefs on the Ludovisi sarcophagus, which dates from the 3rd century CE, depict scenes from battles between Romans and barbarians. The style is reminiscent of Hellenistic art: the sculptors' great skill and the theatricality of the composition serve to glorify the Roman legions' dead.

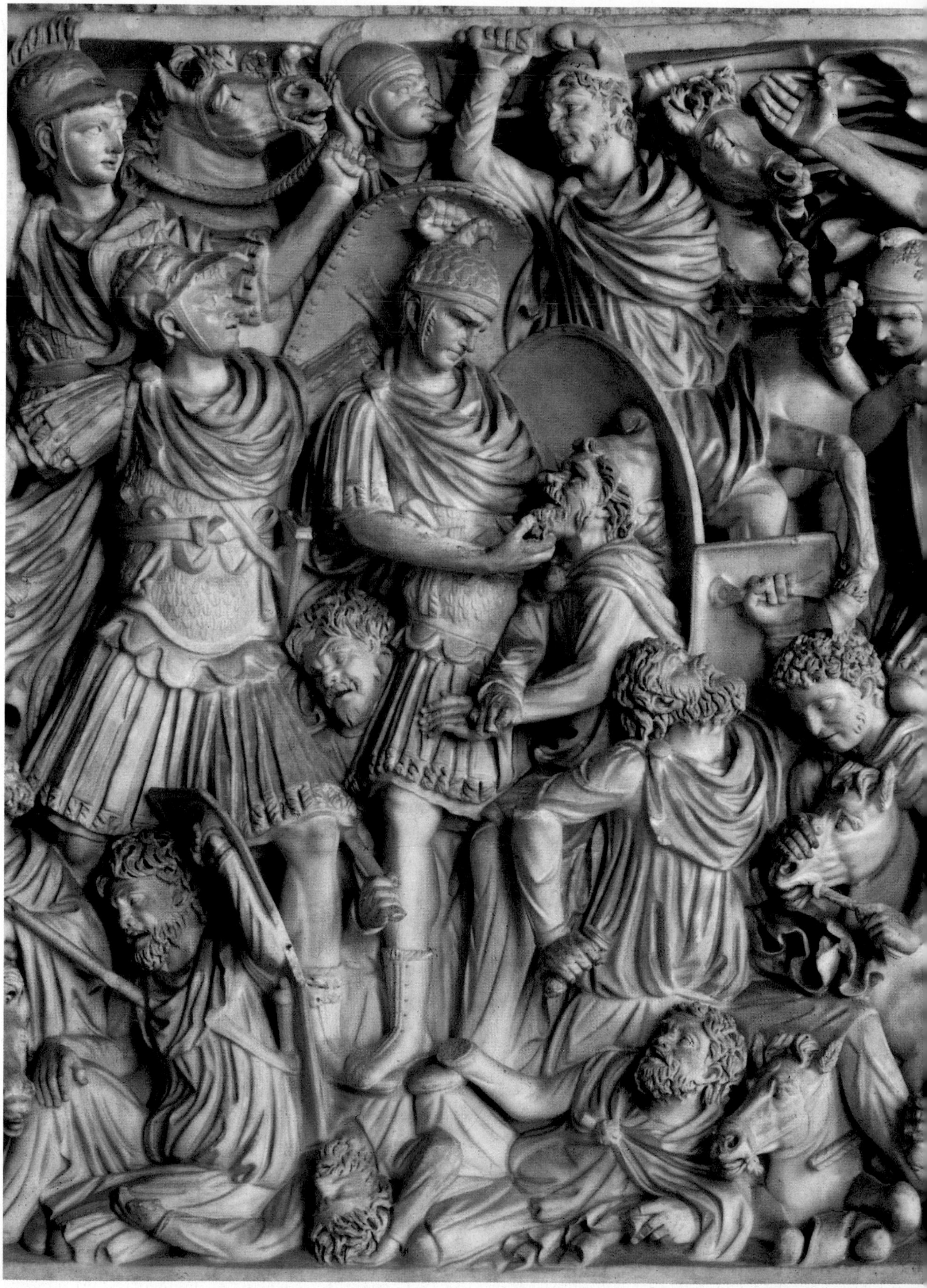

after 370. They overran the Ostrogothic territory, defeated the Alans and then turned on the Visigoths near the Dniester. Unable to hold them, the Visigoths fled for refuge to the empire. In 376 they were allowed to cross the Danube to settle within the frontier. This was a new departure. Earlier barbarian incursions had been driven out or absorbed. Roman ways had attracted barbarian rulers and their followers had joined Rome's army. The Visigoths, though, came as a people, perhaps 40,000 strong, keeping their own laws and religion and remaining a compact unit. The emperor Valens intended to disarm them; it was not done and instead there was fighting. At the battle of Adrianople in 378 the emperor was killed and a Roman army defeated by the Visigoth cavalry. The Visigoths ravaged Thrace.

This was in more than one way a turning-point. Now whole tribes began to be enrolled as confederates – *foederati*, a word first used in 406 – and entered Roman territory to serve against other barbarians under their own chiefs. A temporary settlement with the Visigoths could not be maintained. The Eastern Empire was helpless to protect its European territories outside Constantinople, though when the Visigothic armies moved north towards Italy early in the fifth century, they were checked for a while by a Vandal general. By now the defence of Italy, the old heart of the empire, was entirely dependent on barbarian auxiliaries and soon even this was not enough; Constantinople might be held, but in 410 the Goths sacked Rome.

After an abortive move to the south, with a view to pillaging Africa as they had pillaged Italy, the Visigoths again turned north, crossed the Alps into Gaul and eventually settled as the new kingdom of Toulouse in 419 CE, a Gothic state within the empire,

Tacitus describes the German tribal warriors

"On the field of battle it is a disgrace to a chief to be surpassed in courage by his followers, and to the followers not to equal the courage of their chief. And to leave a battle alive after their chief has fallen means lifelong infamy and shame. To defend and protect him, and to let him get the credit for their own acts of heroism, are the most solemn obligations of their allegiance. The chiefs fight for victory, the followers for their chief. Many noble youths, if the land of their birth is stagnating in a long period of peace and inactivity, deliberately seek out other tribes which have some war in hand. For the Germans have no taste for peace; renown is more easily won among the perils, and a large body of retainers cannot be kept together except by means of violence and war. They are always making demands on the generosity of their chief, asking for a coveted war-horse or a spear stained with the blood of a defeated enemy. Their meals, for which plentiful if homely fare is provided, count in lieu of pay. The wherewithal for this openhandedness comes from war and plunder. A German is not so easily prevailed upon to plough the land and wait patiently for harvest as to challenge a foe and earn wounds for his reward. He thinks it tame and spiritless to accumulate slowly by the sweat of his brow what can be got quickly by the loss of a little blood."

An extract from *The Germania*, para 14, by Tacitus (c.56–c.120 CE), translated by H. Mattingly.

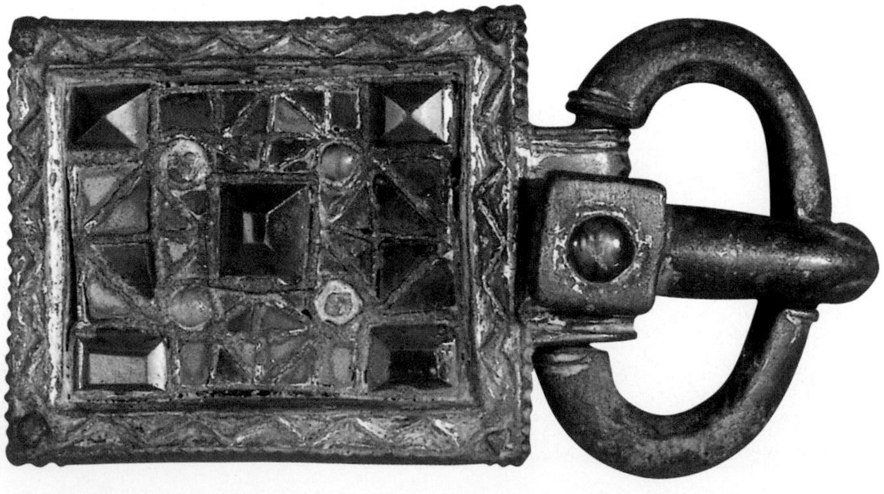

This 6th-century CE belt buckle, made of gilded bronze and precious stones, is from the Visigothic kingdom in Spain.

The Eastern emperor Valens, depicted on this 4th-century CE gold coin, was far less talented than his brother, the Western emperor Valentinian I. Valens' poor judgment resulted in his army's defeat by the Visigoths – two-thirds of his troops died and the emperor was killed by a Visigothic arrow.

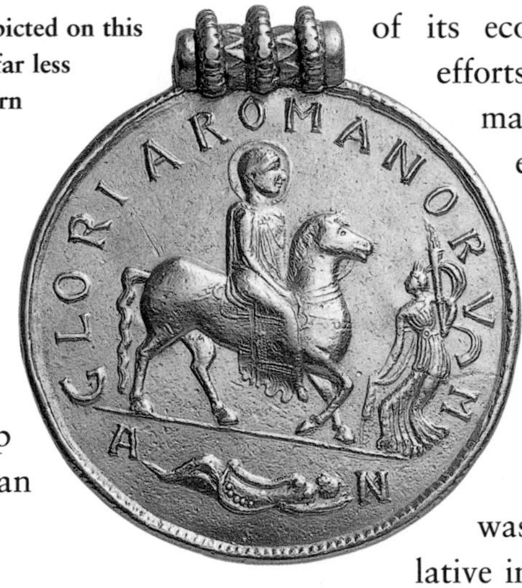

where a Gothic aristocracy shared its over-lordship with the old Gallo-Roman landlords.

THE GROWTH OF THE VANDAL KINGDOM

One other major movement of peoples still needs notice in order to explain the fifth-century remaking of the European racial and cultural map. In return for their settlement in Aquitania, the Western emperor had succeeded in getting the Visigoths to promise that they would help him to clear Spain of other barbarians. Of these the most important were the Vandals. In 406 the Rhine frontier, denuded of soldiers sent to defend Italy against the Visigoths, had given way too and the Vandals and Alans had broken into Gaul. From there they made their way southward, sacking and looting as they went and crossing the Pyrenees to establish a Vandal state in Spain. Twenty years later they were tempted to Africa by a dissident Roman governor who wanted their help. Visigoth attacks encouraged them to leave Spain. By 439 they had taken Carthage. The Vandal kingdom of Africa now had a naval base. They were to stay there for nearly a century, and in 455 they, too, crossed to sack Rome and leave their name to history as a synonym for mindless destructiveness. Terrible as this was, it was less important than the seizure of Africa, the mortal blow to the old Western Empire. It had now lost much of its economic base. Though great efforts could and would still be made in the West by Eastern emperors, Roman rule there was on its last legs. Even in 402, the western emperor and the Senate had already fled from Rome to Ravenna, the last imperial capital in Italy. The dependence on barbarian against barbarian was a fatal handicap. The cumulative impact of fresh pressure made recovery impossible. The protection of Italy had meant abandoning Gaul and Spain to the Vandals; their invasion of Africa had meant the loss of Rome's grain-growing provinces.

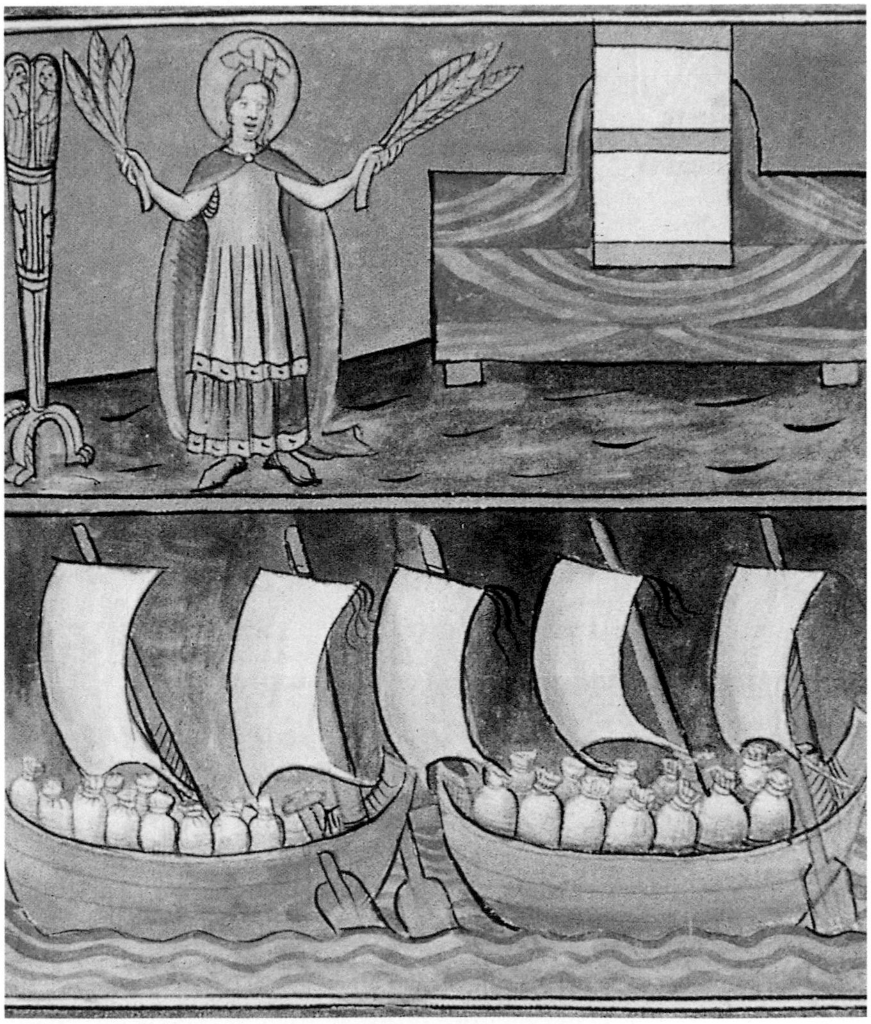

This detail is taken from an illustration in the "Register of military and civil dignitaries", which was compiled in 390 CE. Africa is represented as the romanized granary of the empire: a woman is depicted holding ears of wheat and boats are shown transporting sacks of cereal.

This 396 CE diptych by Euquerius represents the Vandal Stilicho, the West's most important general. Stilicho exercised a kind of protectorate over the two emperors, Arcadius and Honorius, whose busts appear on his shield.

THE HUNS

The Western Empire's collapse was completed in Europe in the third quarter of the century. It followed the greatest of the Hun assaults. These nomads had followed the Germanic tribes into the Balkans and central Europe after a preliminary diversion to ravage Anatolia and Syria. By 440 the Huns were led by Attila, under whom their power was at its height. From Hungary, where the steppe corridor of Asia peters out, he drove west for the last time with a huge army of allies, but was defeated near Troyes in 451 by a "Roman" army of Visigoths under a commander of barbarian origin. This was the end of the Hun threat; Attila died two years later, apparently scheming to marry the Western emperor's sister and perhaps become emperor himself. A great revolt the following year by the Huns' subjects in Hungary finally broke them and they are thenceforth almost lost to sight. In Asia, their home, new confederations of nomads were forming to play a similar part in the future, but their story can wait.

THE COLLAPSE OF THE WESTERN EMPIRE

The Huns had all but delivered the *coup de grâce* in the West; one emperor had sent the pope to intercede with Attila. The last Western emperor was deposed by a Germanic warlord, Odoacer, in 476 and formal sovereignty passed to the Eastern emperors. Though Italy, like the rest of the former Western provinces, was henceforth a barbarian kingdom, independent in all but name, Italians regarded the emperor as their sovereign, resident in Constantinople though he might be.

THE BARBARIANS' RISE TO POWER

The structure which had finally given way under these blows has in its last decades something of the Cheshire cat about it. It was fading away all the time; it is not particularly meaningful to pick one date rather than another as its end. It is unlikely that 476 seemed especially remarkable to contemporaries. The barbarian kingdoms were only a logical development of the reliance upon barbarian troops for the field army and their settlement as *foederati* within the frontiers. The barbarians themselves usually wanted no more, unless it was simple loot. Certainly they did not plan to replace imperial authority with their own. It is a Goth who is reported as saying, "I hope to go down to posterity as the restorer of Rome, since it is not possible that I should be its supplanter." Other dangers were greater and more fundamental than barbarian swagger.

Socially and economically, the tale of the third century had been resumed in the fifth. Cities decayed and population fell. The civil service slid deeper into disorder as officials sought to protect themselves against inflation by taking payment for carrying out their duties. Though revenue declined as provinces were lost, the sale of offices somehow kept up the lavish expenditure of the court. But independence of action was gone. From being emperors whose power rested on their armies, the last emperors of the West declined through the stage of being the equals in negotiation with barbarian warlords whom they had to placate, to being their puppets, cooped up in the last imperial capital, Ravenna. Contemporaries had been right in this sense to see the sack of Rome in 410 as the end of an age, for then it was revealed that the empire could no longer preserve the very heart of *romanitas*. By then, there had been many other signs, too, of what was going on. The last emperor of Constantine's house had tried during a brief reign (361–3) to restore the pagan cults; this had earned him historical fame (or, in Christian eyes, infamy) and, revealingly, the title "the Apostate", but he was not successful. Believing that a restoration of the old sacrifices would ensure the return of prosperity, he had too little time to test the proposition. What is now perhaps more striking is the unquestioned assumption that religion and public life were inseparably

This statue portrays Julian the Apostate, Roman emperor from 361 to 363 CE. Julian, who tried to revive paganism in the empire, wrote "We openly worship the gods and the bulk of the army which has followed me is full of piety. We sacrifice oxen in public; we have given thanks to the gods in numerous hecatombs. These gods order me to purify everything as much as possible and I devotedly obey." (Julian, *Letters*, XXVI)

This imposing silver plate, found in Spain, dates from the end of the 4th century CE and represents the court of Theodosius. The emperor, shown as a larger figure in the centre, is surrounded by the *caesars* and his sons Arcadius and Honorius, future emperors of the East and West respectively.

intertwined, on which his policy was based and which commanded general agreement; it was an assumption whose origins were Roman, not Christian. Julian did not threaten Constantine's work and Theodosius, the last ruler of a united empire, at last forbade the public worship of the ancient gods in 380.

THE REPRESSION OF PAGANISM

What the outlawing of ancient gods meant in practice is hard to say. In Egypt it seems to have been the final landmark in the process of overcoming the ancient civilization which had been going on for eight centuries or so. The victory of Greek ideas first won by the philosophers of Alexandria was now confirmed by the Christian clergy. The priests of the ancient cults were to be harried as pagans. Roman paganism found outspoken defenders still in the fifth century and only at the end of it were pagan teachers expelled from the universities at Athens and Constantinople. Nonetheless a great turning-point had been reached; in principle the closed Christian society of the Middle Ages was now in existence.

THE PERSECUTION OF THE JEWS

Christian emperors soon set about developing it in a particular direction, which became only too familiar, by depriving Jews, the most easily identifiable of groups alien to the closed society, of their juridical equality with other citizens. Here was another turning-point. Judaism had long been the only monotheistic representative in the pluralistic religious world of Rome and now it was ousted by its derivative, Christianity. A prohibition on proselytizing was the first blow and others soon followed. In 425 the patriarchate under which Jews had enjoyed administrative autonomy was abolished. When pogroms occurred, Jews began to withdraw to Persian territory. Their growing alienation from the empire weakened it, for they could soon call upon Rome's enemies for help. Jewish Arab states which lay along trade routes to Asia through the Red Sea were able to inflict damage on Roman interests in support of their co-religionists too. Ideological rigour came at a high price.

THEODOSIUS

Theodosius's reign is also notable in Christian history because of his quarrel with St Ambrose, Bishop of Milan. In 390, after an insurrection at Thessalonica, Theodosius pitilessly massacred thousands of its inhabitants. To the amazement of contemporaries, the emperor was soon seen standing in

In a bas-relief from the obelisk in Constantinople's hippodrome, the emperor Theodosius and his family are shown attending chariot races.

Many beautiful Christian mosaics can be found in the city of Ravenna in Italy. This 5th-century CE mosaic is from the Mausoleum Galla Placidia and depicts Christ as the Good Shepherd watching over his flock.

This 4th-century CE Christian mosaic, which was originally a coffin cover, was found in a basilica in Tabarca, Tunisia. It features a representation of the basilica, surrounded by floral motifs and images of birds to symbolize paradise.

penance for the deed in a Milan church. Ambrose had refused him communion. Superstition had won the first round of what was to prove a long battle for humanity and enlightenment. Other men of might were to be tamed by excommunication or its threat, but this was the first time the spiritual arm had been so exercised and it is significant that it happened in the Western Church. Ambrose had alleged a higher duty for his office than that owed to the emperor. It is the inauguration of a great theme of western European history, the tension of spiritual and secular claims, which was time and time again to pull it back into a progressive channel, the conflict of Church and State.

THE CHRISTIANIZATION OF THE EMPIRE

By the time St Ambrose refused to give communion to Theodosius, a glorious century for Christianity was almost over. It had been a great age of evangelization, in which missionaries had penetrated as far afield as Ethiopia, a brilliant age of theology and, above all, the age of establishment. Yet the Christianity of the age has about it much which now seems repellent. Establishment gave Christians power they did not hesitate to use. "We look on the same stars, the same heavens are above us all," pleaded one pagan to St Ambrose, "the same universe surrounds us. What matters it by what method each of us arrives at the truth?" But Symmachus asked in vain. East and West, the temper of the Christian Churches was intransigent and enthusiastic; if there was a distinction between the two, it lay between the Greeks' conviction of the almost limitless authority of a Christianized empire, blending spiritual and secular power, and the defensive, suspicious hostility to the whole secular world, state included, of a Latin tradition which taught Christians to see themselves as a saving remnant, tossed on the seas of sin and paganism in the Noah's Ark of the Church. Yet to be fair to the Fathers, or to understand their anxieties and fears, a modern observer has to recognize the compelling power of superstition and mystery in the whole late classical world. Christianity acknowledged and expressed it. The demons among whom Christians walked their earthly ways were real to them and to pagans alike, and a fifth-century pope consulted the augurs in order to find out what to do about the Goths.

RIVAL RELIGIONS

The power of superstition is part of the explanation of the bitterness with which heresy and schism were pursued. Arianism had not been finished off at Nicaea; it flourished among the Gothic peoples and Arian Christianity was dominant over much of Italy, Gaul and Spain. The Catholic Church was not persecuted in the Arian barbarian kingdoms, but it was neglected there and when everything depended on the patronage of rulers and the great, neglect could be dangerous. Another threat was the Donatist schism in Africa, which had taken on a social content and broke out in violent conflicts of town and country. In Africa, too, the old threat of Gnosticism lived again in Manichaeism which came to the West from Persia; another heresy, Pelagianism, showed the readiness of some Christians in Latinized Europe to welcome a version of Christianity which subordinated mystery and sacramentalism to the aim of living a good life.

St Ambrose, Bishop of Milan in the late 4th century CE, was one of the original four Doctors of the Church and had an enormous influence on the development of the Church.

THE LIFE OF ST AUGUSTINE OF HIPPO

Few men were better fitted by temperament or education to discern, analyse and combat such dangers than was St Augustine, the greatest of the Fathers. It was important that he came from Africa – that is to say, the Roman province of that name, which corresponded roughly to Tunisia and eastern Algeria – where he was born in 354. African Christianity had more than a century's life behind it by then but was still a minority affair. The African Church had had a special temper of its own since the days of Tertullian, its great founding figure. Its roots did not lie in the Hellenized cities of the East, but in soil laid down by the religions of Carthage and

Numidia which lingered on amid the Berber peasantry. The humanized deities of Olympus had never been at home in Africa. The local traditions were of remote gods dwelling in high places, worshipped in savage and ecstatic rituals (the Carthaginians are supposed to have practised child sacrifice).

AUGUSTINE'S SPIRITUALITY

The intransigent, violent temper of the African Christianity which grew up against this background was reflected to the full in Augustine's own personality. He responded to the same psychological stimuli and felt the

Among the many diverse early Christian cults that were in existence around the time of St Augustine, the Copts were an important group. This Coptic linen cloth was produced in Egypt in the 4th or 5th century CE. The figure is wearing a pointed cap – a style imported to the region from western Asia – to symbolize his divinity or heroism.

The church of San Lorenzo in Milan was built in the 4th and 5th centuries CE on a square base, with a central dome and four elevated towers on the corners. The building, the interior of which is seen here, was probably originally used to house the imperial family's tombs.

need to confront the fact of an evil lurking in himself. One answer was available and popular. The stark dualism of Manichaeism had a very wide appeal in Africa; Augustine was a Manichee for nearly ten years. Characteristically, he then reacted against his errors with great violence.

Before adulthood and Manichaeism, Augustine's education had orientated him towards a public career in the Western Empire. That education was overwhelmingly Latin (Augustine probably spoke only that language and certainly found Greek difficult) and very selective. Its skills were those of rhetoric and it was in them that Augustine first won prizes, but as for ideas, it was barren. Augustine taught himself by reading; his first great step forward was the discovery of the works of Cicero, probably his first contact, though at secondhand, with the classical Athenian tradition.

BAPTISM

Augustine's lay career ended in Milan (where he had gone to teach rhetoric) with his baptism as a Catholic by St Ambrose himself in 387. At that time Ambrose exercised an authority which rivalled that of the empire itself in one of its most important cities. Augustine's observation of this relation between religion and secular power confirmed him in views very different from those of Greek churchmen, who welcomed the conflation of lay and religious authority in the emperor which followed establishment. Augustine then returned to Africa, first to live as a monk at Hippo and then, reluctantly, to become its bishop. There he remained until his death in 430, building up Catholicism's position against the Donatists and, thanks to a huge literary output, becoming a dominant personality of the Western Church.

These are the ruins of a Roman Christian enclave in Tebessa, in present-day Algeria. The settlement dates from the 5th and 6th centuries CE.

AUGUSTINE AND THEOLOGY

In his lifetime Augustine was best known for his attacks on the Donatists and the Pelagians. The first was really a political question: which of two rival Churches was to dominate Roman Africa? The second raised wider issues. They must seem remote to our non-theologically minded age but on them turned much future European history. Essentially, the Pelagians preached a kind of Stoicism; they were part of the classical world and tradition, dressed up in Christian theological language though it might be. The danger this presented – if it was a danger – was that the distinctiveness of Christianity would be lost and the Church simply become the vehicle of one strain in classical Mediterranean civilization, with the strengths and weaknesses which that implied. Augustine was uncompromisingly other-worldly and theological; for him the only possibility of redemption for humanity lay in the Grace which God conferred and no human being could command by his or her works. In the history of the human spirit Augustine deserves a place for having laid out more comprehensively than any predecessor the lines of the great debate between predestination and free will, Grace and Works, belief and motive, which was to run for so long through European history. Almost incidentally, he established Latin Christianity firmly on the rock of the Church's unique power of access to the source of Grace through the sacraments.

AUGUSTINE'S WRITINGS

The detail of the voluminous writing of St Augustine (as he came to be) is now largely neglected except by specialists. Instead, he now enjoys instead some notoriety as one of the most forceful and insistent exponents of a distrust of the flesh which was long especially to mark Christian sexual attitudes and thereby the whole of Western culture. He stands in strange company – with Plato, for example – as a founding father of puritanism. But his intellectual legacy was far richer than this suggests. In his writings can also be seen the foundations of much medieval political thinking, in so far as they are not Aristotelian or legalistic, and a view of history which would long dominate Christian society in the West and would affect it as importantly as the words of Christ himself.

The book now called *The City of God*

This is an illuminated page from St Augustine's manuscript *The City of God*. Augustine (354–430 CE) converted to Christianity when he was 32 years old and was baptized in Milan by St Ambrose.

contains the writing of Augustine which had most future impact. It is not so much a matter of specific ideas or doctrines – there is difficulty in locating his precise influence on medieval political thinkers, perhaps because there is much ambiguity about what he says – as of an attitude. He laid out in this book a way of looking at history and the government of the human race which became inseparable from Christian thinking for a thousand years and more. The subtitle of the book is *Against the Pagans*. This reveals his aim: to refute the reactionary and pagan charge that the troubles crowding in on the empire were to be blamed on Christianity. He was inspired to write by the Gothic sack of

The chair of Archbishop Maximian was made in the 6th century for the church of St Vitale in Ravenna. On the front St John the Baptist appears with the four Evangelists.

Rome in 410; his overriding aim was to demonstrate that the understanding of even such an appalling event was possible for a Christian and, indeed, could only be understood through the Christian religion, but his huge book swoops far and wide over the past, from the importance of chastity to the philosophy of Thales of Miletus, and expounds the civil wars of Marius and Sulla as carefully as the meaning of God's promises to David. It is impossible to summarize: "It may be too much for some, too little for others," said Augustine wryly in his last paragraph. It is a Christian interpretation of a whole civilization and what went to its making. Its most remarkable feature is its own central judgment: that the whole earthly tissue of things is dispensable, and culture and institutions – even the great empire itself – of no final value, if God so wills.

THE TWO CITIES

That God did so will was suggested by Augustine's central image of two cities. One was earthly, founded in human beings' lower nature, imperfect and made with sinful hands, however glorious its appearance and however important the part it might from time to time have to play in the divine scheme. Sometimes its sinful aspect predominates and it is clear that humanity must flee the earthly city – but Babylon, too, had had its part in the divine plan. The other city was the heavenly city of God, the community founded on the assurance of God's promise of salvation, a goal towards which the human race might make a fearful pilgrimage from the earthly city, led and inspired by the Church. In the Church was to be found both the symbol of the City of God and the means of reaching it. History had changed with the appearance of the Church: from that moment the struggle of good and evil was clear in the world and human salvation rested upon its defence. Such arguments would be heard long into modern times.

The two cities sometimes make other appearances in Augustine's argument too. They are sometimes two groups of men, those who are condemned to punishment in the next world and those who are making the pilgrimage to glory. At this level the cities are divisions of the actual human race, here and now, as well as of all those since Adam who have already passed to judgment. But Augustine did not think that membership of the Church explicitly defines one group, the rest of humanity being the other. Perhaps the power of Augustine's vision was all the greater because of its ambiguities, dangling threads of argument and suggestion. The state was not *merely* earthly and wicked: it had its role in the divine scheme and government, in its nature, was divinely given. Much was later to be heard about that; the state would be asked to serve the Church by preserving it from its carnal enemies and by using its own power to enforce the purity of the faith. Yet the mandate of heaven (as another civilization might put it) could be withdrawn and, when it was, even an event like the sack of Rome was only a landmark in the working of judgment on sin. In the end the city of God would prevail.

The above coin bears the effigy of Romulus Augustus, the last Western Roman emperor to be officially recognized. He was deposed by the barbarian general Odoacer in 476 CE, signalling the end of the classical age in the West.

The sides and lid of this marble shrine are decorated with exquisite bas-reliefs portraying biblical scenes. Medallions depicting Christ and the Apostles line the edge of the lid. The shrine was probably produced in a Milanese workshop in the mid-4th century CE.

THE LEGACY OF ST AUGUSTINE

St Augustine escapes simple definition in his greatest book but perhaps he escapes it in every sense. Much remains to be said about him for which there is little room here. He was, for example, a careful and conscientious bishop, the loving pastor of his flock; he was also a persecutor with the dubious distinction of having persuaded the imperial government to use force against the Donatists. He wrote a fascinating spiritual study which, though profoundly misleading on the facts of his early life, virtually founded the literary genre of romantic and introspective autobiography. He could be an artist with words – Latin ones, not Greek (he had to ask St Jerome for help with Greek translation) – and a prize-winning scholar, but his artistry was born of passion rather than of craftsmanship and his Latin is often poor. Yet he was soaked in the classical Roman past. It was from the high ground of his mastery of this tradition that he looked out with the eyes of Christian faith to a cloudy, uncertain and, in others' eyes, frightening future. He embodied two cultures more completely, perhaps, than any other man of those divided times and perhaps this is why, fifteen hundred years later, he still seems to dominate them.

St Augustine's disciples are depicted in this illustration from an Anglo-Saxon manuscript of the saint's greatest work, *The City of God*.

5 THE ELEMENTS OF A FUTURE

Britain's many surviving Roman ruins serve as reminders of its time under the rule of the empire. This lighthouse, which overlooks the English Channel at Dover in Kent, was built by the Romans in the 1st or 2nd century CE.

IN THE GERMANIC INVASIONS lie the origins of the first nations of modern Europe, though when the Western Empire disappeared the barbarian peoples did not occupy areas that looked much like later states. They fall clearly into four major and distinctive groups. The northernmost, the Saxons, Angles and Jutes, were moving into the old Roman province of Britain from the fourth century onwards, settling there well before the island was abandoned to its inhabitants when the last emperor to be proclaimed there by his soldiers crossed with his army to Gaul in 407. Britain was then contested between successive bands of invaders and the Romano-British inhabitants until there emerged from it at the beginning of the seventh century a group of seven Anglo-Saxon kingdoms fringed by a Celtic world consisting of Ireland, Wales and Scotland.

THE END OF ROMANO-BRITISH CIVILIZATION

Although the first British still lived on in communities which seem to have survived sometimes to the tenth century, and perhaps longer, Romano-British civilization disappeared more completely than its equivalents anywhere else in the Western Empire. Even the language was to go; a Germanic tongue almost completely replaced it. We may have a fleeting glimpse of the last spasms of Romano-British resistance in the legend of King Arthur and his knights, which could be a reminiscence of the cavalry-fighting skills of the late imperial army, but that is all. Of administrative or cultural continuity between

Time chart (419 CE–604 CE)

419 CE	The Visigoth kingdom of Toulouse is founded
493 CE	The Italian Ostrogoth kingdom is founded
496 CE	The Frankish king Clovis converts to Catholicism
507 CE	The Visigoth kingdom in Spain is founded
526 CE	The Ostrogoth king Theodoric dies
527–565 CE	Reign of the emperor Justinian; codification of Roman law. Temporary reunification of large part of the old Roman Empire
529 CE	St Benedict of Nursia establishes his monastic order in the West
587 CE	The Visigoth king Recared converts to Catholicism
590–604 CE	Gregory the Great is pope

400 CE · 450 CE · 475 CE · 500 CE · 525 CE · 550 CE · 600 CE

The Roman city of Bath in England, founded in the 1st century CE, owed much of its prosperity to its thermal springs. These 2nd-century baths remained hidden for hundreds of years, until they were rediscovered during the 18th and 19th centuries.

this imperial province and the barbarian kingdoms there is virtually no trace. The imperial heritage of the future England was purely physical. It lay in the ruins of towns and villas, occasional Christian crosses, or the great constructions like Hadrian's wall, which were to puzzle newcomers until they came at last to believe that they were the work of giants of superhuman power. Some of these relics, like the complex of baths built upon the thermal springs at Bath, disappeared from sight for hundreds of years until rediscovered by the antiquaries of the eighteenth and nineteenth centuries. The roads remained, sometimes serving for centuries as trade routes even when their engineering had succumbed to time, weather and pillage. Finally, there were the natural immigrants who had come with the Romans and stayed: animals like ferrets, or plants like mustard, which was to spice the roast beef that became a minor national mythology over a thousand years later. But of the things of the mind left by the Romans we have hardly a trace. Romano-British Christianity, whatever it may have been, disappeared and the keepers of the faith retired for a time to the misty fastnesses where there brooded the monks of the Celtic Church. It was another Rome which was to convert the English nation, not the empire. Before that, Germanic tradition would be the preponderant formative influence as nowhere else within the old imperial territory.

THE FRANKS

ACROSS THE CHANNEL, things were very different. Much survived. After its devastation by the Vandals, Gaul continued to lie in the shadow of the Visigoths of Aquitaine. Their share in repelling the Huns gave them greater importance than ever. To the north-east of Gaul, nevertheless, lay German tribes which were to displace them from this superiority, the Franks. Unlike the Visigoths, the Franks had not been converted by the Arian clergy, in part because of this the future was to belong to them. They were to have a bigger impact on the shaping of Europe than any other barbarian people.

The graves of the first Franks reveal a warrior society, divided into a hierarchy of

The growth of the Frankish kingdom

Of all the Germanic peoples, the Franks had the greatest influence on the formation of the future Europe. In the 4th century, they were already established in the region of present-day Belgium, where many of them became federal Roman soldiers. Some Franks eventually emigrated southward and established themselves in Gaul itself. One group, based in Tournai, founded the Merovingian Dynasty – their third king, Clovis, expanded the kingdom's territory and moved the capital to Paris. He was married to a princess from Burgundy and converted to Catholicism in 496 – a decision that gained him the support of the Roman Church and the friendship of the Gallo-Roman people. At the end of the 6th century, the Frankish kingdom included former Germanic lands such as Austrasia, the centre of which was located in the Rhine valley, where most of the Franks now lived.

Having become one of the most powerful peoples in the empire, the Franks also began to conquer romanized lands, mainly inhabited by Latin-speaking people. They took Neustria in the Seine valley in the 5th century and Burgundy in the Rhône valley in the middle of the 6th century. At this time, the Frankish kingdom was already a Latinized state, with a settled population and a large number of noble landowners.

Dating from the 7th century, this Frankish stone funerary monument features a stylized figure of Christ.

This engraved wooden writing desk was commissioned by Queen Radegunda in the 6th century. Radegunda, who was later canonized, was married to the Frankish king Chlotar I but left him to become a nun.

ranks. More willing to settle than some other barbarians, they were established in the fourth century in modern Belgium, between the Scheldt and the Meuse, where they became Roman *foederati*. Some of them moved on into Gaul. One group, settled at Tournai, threw up a ruling family subsequently called Merovingians; the third king (if this is the correct word) of this line was Clovis. His is the first great name in the history of the country known as Francia after the peoples which Clovis put together.

CLOVIS

Clovis became ruler of the western Franks in 481. Though formally the subject of the emperor, he soon turned on the last Roman governors of Gaul and conquered lands far to the west and down to the Loire. Meanwhile the eastern Franks defeated the Alamanni and when Clovis had been elected their king, too, a Frankish realm straddled the lower Rhine valley and northern France. This was the heartland of the Frankish state which in due course appeared as the heir to Roman supremacy in north Europe. Clovis married a princess from another Germanic people, the Burgundians, who had settled in the Rhône valley and the area running southeast to modern Geneva and Besançon. She was a Catholic, though her people were Arians, and at some time after their marriage (traditionally in 496), and after a battlefield conversion which is reminiscent of Constantine's, Clovis himself embraced Catholicism. This gave him the support of the Roman Church, the most important power still surviving from the empire in the barbarian lands, in what it now chose to regard as a religious war against the other Germanic peoples of Gaul. Catholicism was also the way to friendship with the Romano-Gaulish population. No doubt the conversion was political; it was also momentous. A new Rome was to rule in Gaul.

The Burgundians were Clovis's first victims, though they were not subjugated completely until after his death, when they were given Merovingian princes but kept an independent state structure. The Visigoths were tackled next; they were left only the southeastern territories they held north of the Pyrenees (the later Languedoc and Roussillon and Provence). Clovis was now the successor of the Romans in all Gaul;

the emperor recognized it by naming him a consul.

The Frankish capital was moved to Paris by Clovis and he was buried in the church he had built there, the first Frankish king not to be buried as a barbarian. But this was not the start of the continuous history of Paris as a capital. A Germanic kingdom was not what later times would think of as a state nor what a Roman would recognize. It was a heritage composed partly of lands, partly of kinship groups. Clovis's heritage was divided among his sons. The Frankish kingdom was not reunited until 558. A couple of years later it broke up again. Gradually, it settled down in three bits. One was Austrasia, with its capital at Metz and its centre of gravity east of the Rhine; Neustria was the western equivalent and had its capital at Soissons; under the same ruler, but distinct, was the kingdom of Burgundy. Their rulers tended to quarrel over the lands where these regions touched.

A bearded head of Christ is the centrepiece of this round silver clasp, decorated with small garnet incrustations. Frankish in origin, it dates from the 6th or 7th century.

THE EARLY FRANKISH NATION

In this tripartite structure there begins to appear a Frankish nation no longer a collection of barbarian war bands, but peoples belonging to a recognizable state, speaking a Latin vernacular, and with an emerging class of landowning nobles. Significantly, from it there also comes a Christian interpretation of the barbarian role in history, the *History of the Franks*, by Gregory, Bishop of Tours, himself from the Romano-Gaulish aristocracy. Other barbarian peoples would produce similar works (the greatest, perhaps, is that written for England by the Venerable Bede) which sought to reconcile traditions in which paganism was still strong to Christianity and the civilized heritage. It must be said that Gregory presented a picture of the Franks after the death of his hero Clovis which was pessimistic; he thought the Frankish rulers had behaved so badly that their kingdom was doomed.

KING THEODORIC

The Merovingians kept other barbarians out of Gaul, and took their lands north of the Alps from the Ostrogoths, where their greatest king was Theodoric. His right to rule in Italy, where he fought off other Germans, was recognized by the emperor in 497. He was utterly convinced of Rome's authority; he had an emperor as godfather and had been brought up at Constantinople until he was eighteen. "Our royalty is an imitation of yours, a copy of the only empire on earth," he once wrote to the emperor in Constantinople from his capital in Ravenna. On his coins appeared the legend "Unvanquished Rome" (*Roma invicta*), and when he went to Rome, Theodoric held games in the old style in the circus. Yet

Anicius Manlius Severinus Boethius, consul in 510, is depicted on this marble diptych. Boethius lived during the reign of Theodoric and made significant contributions to the fields of theology, philosophy, science and music.

technically he was the only Ostrogoth who was a Roman citizen; his personal authority was accepted by the Senate but his countrymen were merely the mercenary soldiers of the empire. To civil offices he appointed Romans. One of them was his friend and adviser, the philosopher Boethius, who was to be possibly the most important single thinker through whom the legacy of the classical world passed to medieval Europe.

Theodoric seems to have been a judicious ruler, maintaining good relations with other barbarian peoples (he married Clovis's sister) and enjoying some sort of primacy among them. But he did not share his own people's Arian faith, and religious division told against Ostrogothic power in the long run. Unlike the Franks, and in spite of their ruler's example,

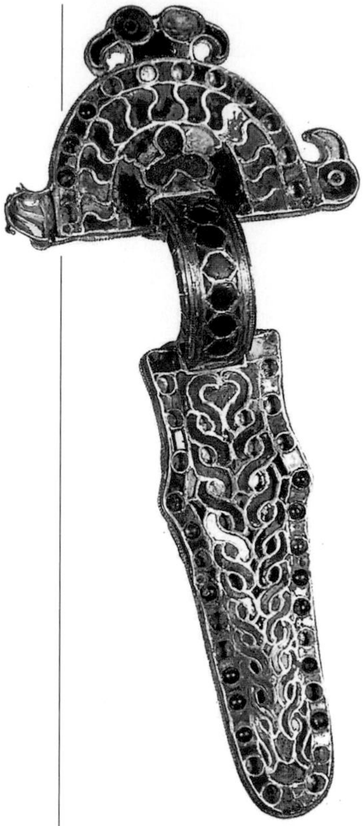

The Ostrogoths, having established themselves in northern Italy in 488, introduced a highly colourful style of gold- and silverwork. This clasp, dating from 500, is made of gold studded with emeralds and other small stones. The upper part is decorated with four eagles' heads.

they were not to ally with the Roman past; and after Theodoric the Ostrogoths were expelled from Italy and history by generals from the Eastern Empire. They left a ruined Italy, soon to be invaded by yet another barbarian people, the Lombards.

VISIGOTHIC SPAIN

In the west Clovis had left the Visigoths virtually confined to Spain, from which they had driven the Vandals. Other Germanic peoples were already settled there. Its terrain presented quite special problems – as it has continued to do to all invaders and governments – and the Visigothic kingdom of Spain was not able to resist much more romanization than its founders had undergone in Gaul, where they had fused much less with existing society than had the Franks.

The Visigoths – and there were not so very many of them, less than 100,000 at most – clustered about their leaders who spread out from Old Castile through the provinces; they then quarrelled so much that imperial rule was able to re-establish itself for more than a half-century in the south. Finally, the Visigothic kings turned to Catholicism and thus enlisted the authority of the Spanish bishops. In 587 begins the long tradition of Catholic monarchy in Spain.

ROMAN AND BARBARIAN WESTERN EUROPE

What the flux of peoples in Europe adds up to is hard to say. Generalization is hazardous. Simple duration alone almost explains this; the Visigoths underwent three centuries of evolution between the creation of the kingdom of Toulouse and the end of their ascendancy in Spain. Much changed in so long a time. Though

Theodoric, King of the Ostrogoths, was buried in 526 in this mausoleum outside the city walls of Ravenna. The stone building is crowned with a huge monolith and is similar in style to many Roman funerary monuments.

economic life and technology hardly altered except for the worse, mental and institutional forms were undergoing radical, if slow, transformations in all the barbarian kingdoms. Soon it is not quite right to think of them still as merely such (except, perhaps, the Lombards). The Germanic population were a minority, often isolated in alien settings, dependent on routines long established by the particular environment for their living and forced into some sort of understanding with the conquered. The passage of their invasions must sometimes have seemed at close quarters like a flood tide, but when it had passed there were often only tiny, isolated pools of invaders left behind, here and there replacing the Roman masters, but often living alongside them and with them.

Marriage between Roman and barbarian was not legal until the sixth century, but that was not much of a check. In Gaul the Franks took up its Latin, adding Frankish words to it. By the seventh century, western European

The Visigoths

The presence of the Visigoth Germanic people was first recorded in Gaul. There they founded a kingdom, with its capital at Toulouse, which lasted from 419 to 457, the year in which the Franks seized southern Gaul. From this time the Visigoths, who probably numbered only 100,000 in total, moved to establish themselves in the centre of the Iberian peninsula, between the Ebro and the Tagus rivers, where the population of Hispano-Roman people was least dense. At the end of the 6th century, they conquered the Swabian kingdom in the northwest of the country, which had been established at the beginning of the previous century, and made Toledo their capital. Lengthy internal disputes in the middle of the 6th century led to the establishment of imperial Byzantine control in the south, as a result of the campaign by the emperor Justinian to restore the old Roman Empire.

The Visigoths, like many of the Germanic peoples who had been Christianized in early times, were Arians. In the year 587, however, their king, Recared, converted to Roman Catholicism, as the Frankish king Clovis had done almost a century earlier. The Visigoth kingdom assimilated many aspects of Roman culture and tradition and, at the end of the 7th century, a Romano-Visigoth code was set up – clear evidence of the cultural changes that had taken place within the kingdom. Visigoth power in the old Hispania disappeared in 711 with the arrival of the Muslims.

A capital from the church of San Pedro de la Nave near Zamora, Spain. Carved by skilful stonemasons in the 7th century, the scene represents the biblical story of Daniel in the lions' den. In the abacus, top, the intricate decoration with plant-like spirals includes images of birds and fruit.

This marble diptych depicts a Roman consul in the Ostrogoth kingdom in 530, Rufus Genadius Probus Orestes. He appears in his consular garments, seated on a throne and accompanied by two figures representing Rome and Constantinople. Above his head are the busts of the Ostrogoth king Athalaric and his mother Amalasuntha. The piece symbolizes the Ostrogoth leaders' goodwill towards Rome and their desire that there should be harmony between East and West.

society has already a very different atmosphere from that of the turbulent fifth.

GERMANIC CULTURAL LEGACY

The barbarian past left its imprint. In almost all the barbarian kingdoms society was long and irreversibly shaped by Germanic custom. This sanctioned a hierarchy reflected in the characteristic Germanic device for securing public order, the blood feud. Men – and women, and cattle, and property of all sorts – had in the most literal sense their price; wrongs done were settled by interesting a whole clan or family in the outcome if customary compensation were not forthcoming. Kings more and more wrote down and thus in a sense "published" what such customs were. Literacy was so rare that there can have been no point in imagining devices such as the stele of Babylon or the white boards on which the decrees of Greek city-states were set out. Recording by a scribe on parchment for future consultation was the most that could be envisaged. None the less, in this Germanic world lie the origins of a jurisprudence one day to be carried across oceans to new cultures of European stock. The first institution to open the way to this was the acceptance of kingly or collective power to declare what was to be recorded. All the Germanic kingdoms moved towards the writing down and codification of their law.

THE BARBARIANS AND THE ROMAN TRADITION

Where the early forms of public action are not religious or supernatural, they are usually judicial, and it is hardly surprising that, for example, the Visigothic court of Toulouse should have sought the skills of Roman legal experts. But this was only one form of a respect which almost every barbarian aristocracy showed for Roman tradition and forms. Theodoric saw himself as the representative of the emperor; his problem did not lie in identifying his own role, but in the need to avoid irritating his followers who could be provoked by any excess of romanization. Perhaps similar considerations weighed with Clovis before his conversion, which was an act of identification with empire as well as with Church. At the level just below such heroic figures, both Frankish and Visigothic noblemen seem to have taken pleasure in showing themselves the heirs of Rome by writing to one another in Latin and patronizing light literature. There was a tie of interest with the Romans, too; Visigothic warriors

Ravenna was captured from the Ostrogoths by Justinian's armies in 540. To mark the city's return to the imperial fold, the emperor built two magnificent churches: St Vitale in Ravenna itself and a basilica at Classe (a port on the outskirts of the town). The Classe basilica is dedicated to St Apollinaris, who appears at the centre of the decoration of the apse, shown here.

sometimes found employment in putting down the revolts of peasants who menaced the Romano-Gaulish landowner as well as the invaders. Yet so long as Arianism stood in the way, there was a limit to the identification with *romanitas* possible for the barbarians. The Church, after all, was the supreme relic of empire west of Constantinople.

The Eastern emperors had not seen these changes with indifference. But troubles in their own domains hamstrung them and in the fifth century their barbarian generals dominated them too. They watched with apprehension the last years of the puppet emperors of Ravenna but recognized Odoacer, the deposer of the last of them. They maintained a formal claim to rule over a single empire, east and west, without actually questioning Odoacer's independence in Italy until an effective replacement was available in Theodoric, to whom the title of patrician was given. Meanwhile, Persian wars and the new pressure of Slavs in the Balkans were more than enough to deal with. It was not until the accession of the emperor Justinian in 527 that it seemed at all likely that reality would be restored to imperial government.

JUSTINIAN

IN RETROSPECT JUSTINIAN SEEMS something of a failure. Yet he behaved as people thought an emperor should; he did what most people still expected that a strong emperor would one day do. He boasted that Latin was his native tongue; for all the wide sweep of the empire's foreign relations, he could still think plausibly of reuniting and restoring the old empire, centred on Constantinople though it now had to be. We labour under the handicap of knowing what happened, but he reigned a long time and his contemporaries were more struck by his temporary successes. They expected them to herald a real restoration. After all, no one could really conceive a world without the empire. The barbarian kings of the West gladly deferred to Constantinople and accepted titles from it;

Justinian's empire 527–565 CE

On his accession to the imperial throne in 527, Justinian embarked on a series of military campaigns, with the objective of reunifying and restoring the former Roman Empire. For a few years, as a result of Justinian's conquests, the Byzantine dominions were extended to North Africa, southern Spain and Italy: once again, large areas of the Mediterranean coast were united to form a single state. However, the unity restored by Justinian was destroyed again at the end of the 6th century by the unstoppable advances of the Germanic and Slavic peoples, and in the 7th century by the expansion of Islam.

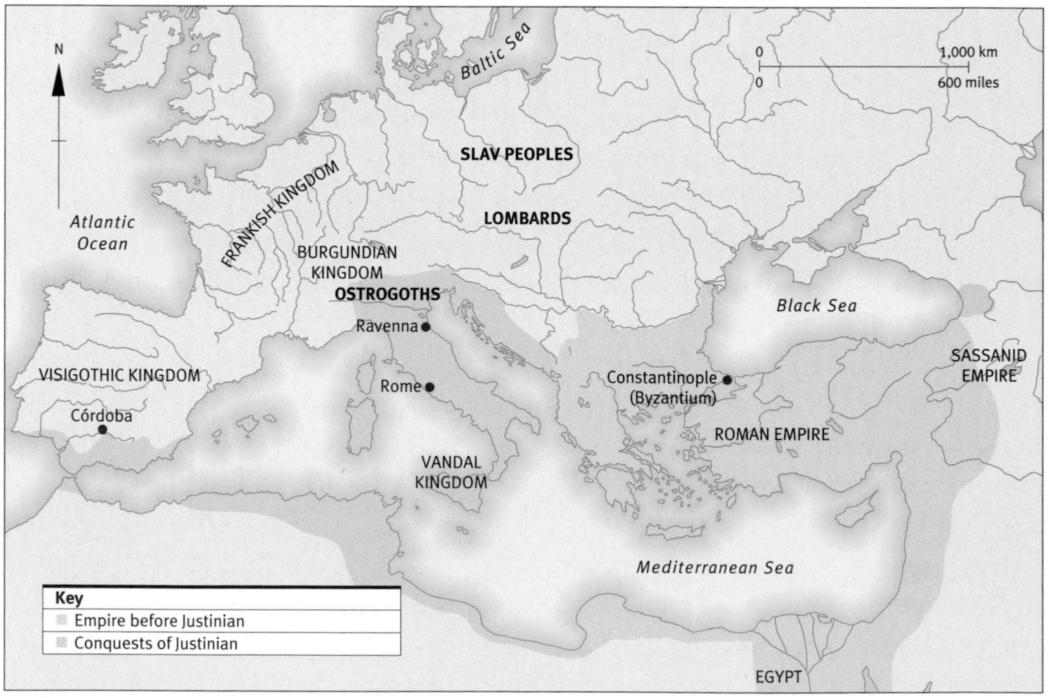

The above map shows the extent of the Byzantine Empire at the time of Justinian's accession and the territories he added during his long reign.

In a mosaic from the church of St Vitale in Ravenna, Justinian is shown with his retinue of ecclesiastical dignitaries and courtiers. The halo around Justinian's head is a reminder of the emperor's sacred status. While the figures' faces are individual and expressive, their bodies give the impression of floating in space, emphasizing their spirituality.

they did not grasp at the purple themselves. Justinian sought autocratic power, and his contemporaries found the goal both comprehensible and realistic. There is a certain grandeur about his conception of his role; it is a pity that he should have been so unattractive a man.

Justinian was almost always at war. Often he was victorious. Even the costly Persian campaigns (and payments to the Persian king) were successful in the limited sense that they did not lose the empire much ground. Yet they were a grave strategic handicap; the liberation of his resources for a policy of recovery in the West, which had been Justinian's aim in his first peace with the Persians, always eluded him. Nevertheless, his greatest general, Belisarius, destroyed Vandal Africa and recovered that country for the empire (though it took ten years to reduce it to order). He went on to invade Italy and begin the struggle which ended in 554 with the final eviction of the Ostrogoths from Rome and the unification once more of all

This is the front of a 7th-century helmet that is thought to have belonged to Agilulf, who was King of the Lombards between 590 and 615. In spite of the crudeness of the reliefs, the Roman influence is evident in the warriors' appearance and in the figures of winged victories watching over the monarch.

Justinian, Emperor of the East from 527 to 565, did everything in his power to reunite the old Roman Empire. Although his success was short-lived, Justinian left a remarkable legacy, including numerous civic and religious buildings and the codification of Roman law (a major contribution to the development of the modern idea of the state).

Byzantine architecture

The people of the Byzantine Empire inherited their taste for grandiose architecture from ancient Rome. The Byzantines also developed an ever-greater passion for decorative richness and the use of polychromy through their close contact with the East. Amid the rigidity and pomp of court ceremonies, the emperor's public appearances were carefully and elaborately staged to set him apart from ordinary mortals and make him seem nearer to the divine world. This sumptuous theatricality had an important influence on the artistic tastes of the period and inspired the magnificence of Byzantine buildings. The Eastern Roman Empire's architectural style was not totally formed until the time of Justinian, in the 6th century. The emperor adapted the region's existing vaulted architecture and sought to create a new architectural style suitable for his holy realm, leaving a legacy of sumptuous imperial palaces and beautiful churches.

The major features of Byzantine architecture were the prominence of domes and capitals and the use of mosaics as a decoration for the walls rather than the floors, as had been the Roman custom. The Byzantines managed to build domes of huge proportions, such as that of St Sophia in Constantinople, which is more than 100 ft (30 m) in diameter. Byzantine capitals, based on the Roman Corinthian style, were converted into truncated structures decorated with luxuriant foliage. Highly skilled Byzantine artists covered the churches' walls and vaults with brightly coloured mosaics depicting emperors, saints and ecclesiastical dignitaries or scenes from the Bible.

The major Byzantine monuments to have been preserved can be found in Constantinople itself (now Istanbul) and in Ravenna, capital of the exarchate, which included the imperial domain that Justinian restored in Italy, Spain and North Africa.

Depicting the port of Classe, this mosaic from the St Apollinaris basilica near Ravenna dates from the 6th century. As in many Byzantine mosaics, the use of gold creates an impression of grandeur.

Italy under imperial rule, albeit an Italy devastated by the imperial armies as it had never been by the barbarians. These were great achievements, though badly followed up. More were to follow in southern Spain, where the imperial armies exploited rivalry between Visigoths and again set up imperial government in Córdoba. Throughout the western Mediterranean, too, the imperial fleets were supreme; for a century after Justinian's death, Byzantine ships moved about unmolested.

It did not last. By the end of the century most of Italy was gone again, this time to the Lombards, another Germanic people and the final extinguishers of imperial power in the peninsula. In eastern Europe, too, in spite of a vigorous diplomacy of bribery and missionary ideology, Justinian had never been successful in dealing with the barbarians.

The magnificent church of St Sophia in Constantinople, which later became a mosque, was consecrated in 537. It has a large central dome supported by pillars, arches and secondary vaulting. This immense space is enhanced by the play of light through the building's many windows.

Perhaps enduring success there was impossible. The pressure from behind on these migrant peoples was too great and, besides, they could see great prizes ahead; "the barbarians," wrote one historian of the reign, "having once tasted Roman wealth, never forgot the road that led to it." By Justinian's death, in spite of his expensive fortress-building, the ancestors of the later Bulgars were settled in Thrace and a wedge of barbarian peoples separated West and East Rome.

JUSTINIAN'S LEGACY

Justinian's conquests, great as they were, could not be maintained by his successors in the face of the continuing threat from Persia, the rise of Slav pressure in the Balkans and, in the seventh century, of a new rival, Islam. A terrible time lay ahead. Yet even then Justinian's legacy would be operative through the diplomatic tradition he founded, the building of a network of influences among the barbarian peoples beyond the frontier, playing off one against another, bribing one prince with tribute or a title, standing god-parent to the baptized children of another. If it had not been for the client princedoms of the Caucasus who were converted to Christianity in Justinian's day, or his alliance with the Crimean Goths (which was to last seven centuries), the survival of the Eastern Empire would have been almost impossible. In this sense, too, the reign sets out the ground-plan of a future Byzantine sphere.

Within the empire, Justinian left an indelible imprint. At the time of his accession the monarchy was handicapped by the persistence of party rivalries which could draw upon popular support, but in 532 this led to a great insurrection which made it possible to strike at the factions and, though much of the city was burned, this was the end of domestic threats to Justinian's autocracy. It showed itself henceforth more and more consistently and nakedly.

Its material monuments were lavish; the greatest is the basilica of St Sophia itself (532–537 CE), but all over the empire public buildings, churches, baths and new towns mark the reign and speak for the inherent wealth of the Eastern Empire. The richest and most civilized provinces were in Asia and Egypt; Alexandria, Antioch and Beirut were their great cities. A nonmaterial, institutional monument of the reign was Justinian's codification of Roman law. In four collections a thousand years of Roman jurisprudence was put together in a form which gave it deep influence across the centuries and helped to shape the modern idea of the state.

St Catherine's Monastery on Mount Sinai was founded by Justinian in 527. It is one of the best-preserved of many churches and monasteries commissioned by the emperor throughout the Byzantine Empire's extensive territories.

Justinian's efforts to win administrative and organizational reform were far less successful. It was not difficult to diagnose ills known to be dangerous as long before as the third century. But given the expense and responsibilities of empire, permanent remedies were hard to find. The sale of offices, for example, was known to be an evil and Justinian abolished it, but then had to tolerate it when it crept back.

The main institutional response to the empire's problem was a progressive regimentation of its citizens. In part, this was in the tradition of regulating the economy which he

This 16th-century fresco is one of the few surviving representations of a session of the Church Council. The painting depicts the emperor at the Council of Ephesus in 431. He is banishing Nestor, patriarch of Constantinople, and another heretic.

had inherited. Just as peasants were tied to the soil, craftsmen were now attached to their hereditary corporations and guilds; even the bureaucracy tended to become hereditary. The resulting rigidity was unlikely to make imperial problems easier to solve.

RELIGION IN THE EASTERN EMPIRE

It was unfortunate that a quite exceptionally disastrous series of natural calamities fell on the East at the beginning of the sixth century: they go far to explain why it was hard for Justinian to leave the empire in better fettle than he found it. Earthquake, famine and plague devastated the cities and even the capital itself, where people saw phantoms in the streets. The ancient world was a credulous place, but tales of the emperor's capacity to take off his head and then put it on again, or to disappear from sight at will, suggest that under these strains the mental world of the Eastern Empire was already slipping its moorings in classical civilization. Justinian was to make the separation easier by his religious outlook and policies, another paradoxical outcome, for it was far from what he intended. After it had survived for eight hundred years, he abolished the academy of Athens; he wanted to be a Christian emperor, not a ruler of unbelievers, and decreed the destruction of all pagan statues in the capital. Worse still, he accelerated the demotion of the Jews in civic status and the reduction of their freedom to exercise their religion. Things had already gone a long way by then. Pogroms had long been connived at and synagogues destroyed; now Justinian went on to alter the Jewish calendar and interfere with the Jewish order of worship. He even encouraged barbarian rulers to persecute Jews. Long before the cities of western Europe, Constantinople had a ghetto.

Justinian was all the more confident of the rightness of asserting imperial authority in ecclesiastical affairs because (like the later James I of England) he had a real taste for theological disputation. Sometimes the consequences were unfortunate; such an attitude did nothing to renew the loyalty to the empire of the Nestorians and Monophysites, heretics who had refused to accept the definitions of the precise relationship of God the Father to God the Son laid down in 451 at a council at Chalcedon. The theology of such deviants mattered less than the fact that their symbolic tenets were increasingly identified with important linguistic and cultural groups. The empire began to create its Ulsters. Harrying heretics intensified separatist feeling in parts of Egypt and Syria. In the former,

In the upper part of this fresco from the Coptic convent of St Apollinaris in Bauit, Egypt, Christ is depicted blessing the world. In the lower part, the Virgin Mary is shown sitting on a throne with the infant Jesus in her arms, surrounded by the Apostles.

the Coptic Church went its own way in opposition to Orthodoxy in the later fifth century, and the Syrian Monophysites followed, setting up a "Jacobite" church. Both were encouraged and sustained by the numerous and enthusiastic monks of those countries. Some of these sects and communities, too, had important connections outside the empire, so that foreign policy was involved. The Nestorians found refuge in Persia, and, though not heretics, the Jews were especially influential beyond the frontiers; Jews in Iraq supported Persian attacks on the empire and Jewish Arab states in the Red Sea interfered with the trade routes to India when hostile measures were taken against Jews in the empire.

This plaque, which represents an Evangelist or an Apostle, is thought to originate from the 6th-century early Christian abbey of Mettlach in Egypt.

DIVERGENCE OF EAST AND WEST

Justinian's hopes of reuniting the Western and Eastern Churches were to be thwarted in spite of his zeal. A potential division between them had always existed because of the different cultural matrices in which each had been formed. The Western Church had never accepted the union of religious and secular authority which was the heart of the political theory of the Eastern Empire; the empire would pass away as others had done (and the Bible told) and it would be the Church which would prevail against the gates of hell. Now such doctrinal divergences became more important, and separation had been made more likely by the breakdown in the West. A Roman pope visited Justinian and the emperor spoke of Rome as the "source of priesthood", but in the end the two Christian communions were first to go their own ways and then violently to quarrel. Justinian's own view, that the emperor was supreme, even on matters of doctrine, fell victim to clerical intransigence on both sides.

This seems to imply (as do so many others of his acts) that Justinian's real achievement was not that which he sought and temporarily achieved, the re-establishment of the imperial unity, but a quite different one, the easing of the path towards the development of a new, Byzantine civilization. After him, it was a reality, even if not yet recognized. Byzantium was evolving away from the classical world towards a style clearly related to it, but

The Egyptian Copts, who became Monophysites, formed a strong cult within Eastern Christianity. This Egyptian painting on wood depicts the Coptic abbot, Menas, with Christ, and is thought to date from the 6th or 7th century.

independent of it. This was made easier by contemporary developments in both Eastern and Western culture, by now overwhelmingly a matter of new tendencies in the Church.

THE ROLE OF THE BISHOPS IN THE LATE CLASSICAL AGE

As often in later history, the Church and its leaders had not at first recognized or welcomed an opportunity in disaster. They identified themselves with what was collapsing and understandably so. The collapse of empire was for them the collapse of civilization; the Church in the West was, except for municipal authority in the impoverished towns, often the sole institutional survivor of *romanitas*. Its bishops were men with experience of administration, at least as likely as other local notables to be intellectually equipped to grapple with new problems. A semi-pagan population looked to them with superstitious awe and attributed to them near-magical power. In many places they were the last embodiment of authority left when imperial

The Bishoi Coptic Monastery is situated in Wadi-al-Natrun in Egypt.

armies went away and imperial administration crumbled, and they were lettered men among a new unlettered ruling class which craved the assurance of sharing the classical heritage. Socially, they were often drawn from the leading provincial families; that meant that they were sometimes great aristocrats and proprietors with material resources to support their spiritual role. Naturally, new tasks were thrust upon them.

CHRISTIAN MONASTICISM

THE END OF THE CLASSICAL WORLD also saw two new institutions emerge in the western Church, which were to be lifelines in the dangerous rapids between a civilization which had collapsed and one yet to be born. The first was Christian monasticism, a phenomenon first appearing in the East. It was about 285 that a Copt, St Anthony, retired to a hermit's life in the Egyptian desert. His example was followed by others who watched, prayed and strove with demons or mortified the flesh by fasting and more dubious disciplines. Some of them drew together in communities. In the next century this new form of spirituality established itself in a communal form in the Levant and Syria. From there, the idea spread to the West, to the Mediterranean coast of France. In a crumbling society such as fifth-century Gaul the monastic ideal of undistracted worship and service to God in prayer, within the discipline of an ascetic rule, was attractive to many men and women of intellect and character. Through it they could assure personal salvation. The communities attracted many from among the well-born who sought a refuge from a changing world. Unfriendly critics who hankered after the old Roman ideal of service to the state condemned them for shirking their proper responsibilities to society by withdrawing from it. Nor did churchmen always welcome what they saw as the desertion of some of the most zealous among their congregations. Yet many of the greatest churchmen of the age were monks and the institution prospered. Landowners founded communities or endowed existing ones with lands. There were some scandals and no doubt many compromises of principle in grappling with patrons and men of power.

ST BENEDICT

One Italian monk, of whom we know little except his achievement and that he was believed to work miracles, found the state of monasticism shocking. This was St Benedict, one of the most influential men in the Church's history. In 529 he set up a monastery at Monte Cassino in central Italy, giving it a new rule which he had compiled by sifting and selecting among others available. It is a seminal document of Western Christianity and therefore of Western civilization. It directed the attention of the monk to the community, whose abbot was to have complete authority. The community's purpose was not merely to provide a hotbed for the cultivation or the salvation of individual souls but that it should worship and live as a whole. The individual monk was to contribute to its task in the framework of an ordered routine of worship, prayer and labour. From the individualism of traditional monasticism a new human instrument was forged; it was to be one of the main weapons in the armoury of the Church.

This mosaic, which is from the 5th-century Mausoleum of Costantina in Rome, shows Christ delivering the law to St Peter and St Paul.

St Benedict and the founding of his monastic Rule

St Benedict was born c.480, in Nursia, central Italy. After studying in Rome, he was attracted by the solitary lifestyle of hermits, who devoted themselves to prayer and penitence, following the example of the Desert Fathers. Benedict retired to a grotto near Subiaco in the Abruzzi foothills where, over the next three years, he became famous among the local people because of the miracles he performed. As his reputation spread, he was invited to become abbot of a nearby monastery. However, Benedict found this an unrewarding experience, and soon returned to his refuge in Subiaco, where his followers established 12 communities of 12 monks under his leadership.

Legend has it that a scheming local priest, jealous of Benedict's fame, forced him to flee Subiaco in 529 by inciting a group of women to attack his communities. Benedict moved to Monte Cassino, between Rome and Naples, and founded the monastery where he was to spend the rest of his life. It was there that he composed the 73 chapters of his Rule. After his death in 543, the monastery was razed by the Lombards, but the monks found refuge in Rome. They received strong papal support, particularly from Gregory I (later canonized), whose *Dialogues* (Book 2) is the only recognized source to provide the details of St Benedict's life (Gregory's information came from four of the saint's disciples).

St Benedict's character can only be discovered from his Rule. Although he insisted that his monks take vows of chastity, poverty and obedience and of absolute loyalty to the monastery where they had taken those vows, St Benedict was also moderate and paternal, allowing the monks warm clothing and adequate sleep. The Rule specifies precise times for services and prayer, yet makes special provisions for the treatment of the sick and elderly. The enduring success of the Benedictine Rule is no doubt due to this blend of practicality and spirituality.

St Benedict of Nursia, known as the father of Western monasticism, is depicted in this fresco from the Cluniac monastery in Subiaco, Italy. St Benedict's motto "Pray and work" still governs the daily life of every Benedictine monk.

St Benedict did not set his sights too high and this was one secret of his success; the Rule was within the powers of ordinary men who loved God and his monks did not need to multilate either body or spirit. Its success in estimating their need was demonstrated by its rapid spread. Benedictine monasteries quickly appeared everywhere in the West. They became the key sources of missionaries and teaching for the conversion of pagan England and Germany. In the West, only the Celtic Church at its fringe clung to the older, eremitical model of the monkish life.

THE EARLY PAPACY

Besides the Benedictine monasteries, the Church's other new great support was the papacy. The prestige of St Peter's see and the legendary guardianship of the Apostle's bones always gave Rome a special place among the bishoprics of Christendom. It was the only one in the West to claim descent from one of the Apostles. But in principle it had little else to offer; the Western Church was a junior branch and it was in the Churches of Asia that the closest links with the apostolic age

Many Benedictine monks dedicated themselves to producing religious manuscripts. In this illuminated manuscript from a 15th-century collection of writings on St Benedict, four of the saint's disciples are depicted assisting Pope Gregory the Great (540–604) with the compilation of his *Dialogues* or *Lives of the Saints*.

could be asserted. Something more was required for the papacy to begin its rise to the splendid pre-eminence which was taken for granted by the medieval world.

To begin with there was the city. Rome had been seen for centuries as the capital of the world, and for much of the world that had been true. Its bishops were the business colleagues of Senate and emperor and the departure of the imperial court only left their eminence more obvious. The arrival in Italy of alien civil servants from the eastern empire, whom the Italians disliked as much as they did the barbarians, directed new attention to the papacy as the focus of Italian loyalties. It was, too, a wealthy see, with an apparatus of government commensurate with its possessions. It generated administrative skill superior to anything to be found outside the imperial administration itself. This distinction, too, stood out all the more clearly in times of trouble, when the barbarians lacked these skills. The see of Rome had the finest records of any; already in the fifth century papal apologists were exploiting them. The characteristically conservative papal stance, the argument that no new departures are being made but that old positions are being defended, is already present and was wholly sincere; popes did not see themselves as conquerors of new ideological and legal ground; but as men desperately trying to keep the small foothold the Church had already won.

St Gregory the Great (540–604) is shown dictating a manuscript to two scribes in this 9th-century illustration. Gregory was recognized as a Father of the Church, in the Latin tradition.

This was the setting of the papacy's emergence as a great historical force. The fifth-century Leo the Great was the first pope under whom the new power of the bishop of Rome was clearly visible. An emperor declared papal decisions to have the force of law and Leo vigorously asserted the doctrine that the popes spoke in the name of St Peter. He assumed the title *pontifex maximus*, discarded by the emperors. It was believed that his intervention by visiting Attila had staved off the Hun attack on Italy; bishops in the West who had hitherto resisted claims for Rome's primacy became more willing to accept them in a world turned upside-down by barbarians. Still, though, Rome was a part of the state church of an empire whose religion Justinian saw as above all the emperor's concern.

GREGORY THE GREAT

The pope in whom the future medieval papacy is most clearly revealed was also the first pope who had been a monk. In Gregory

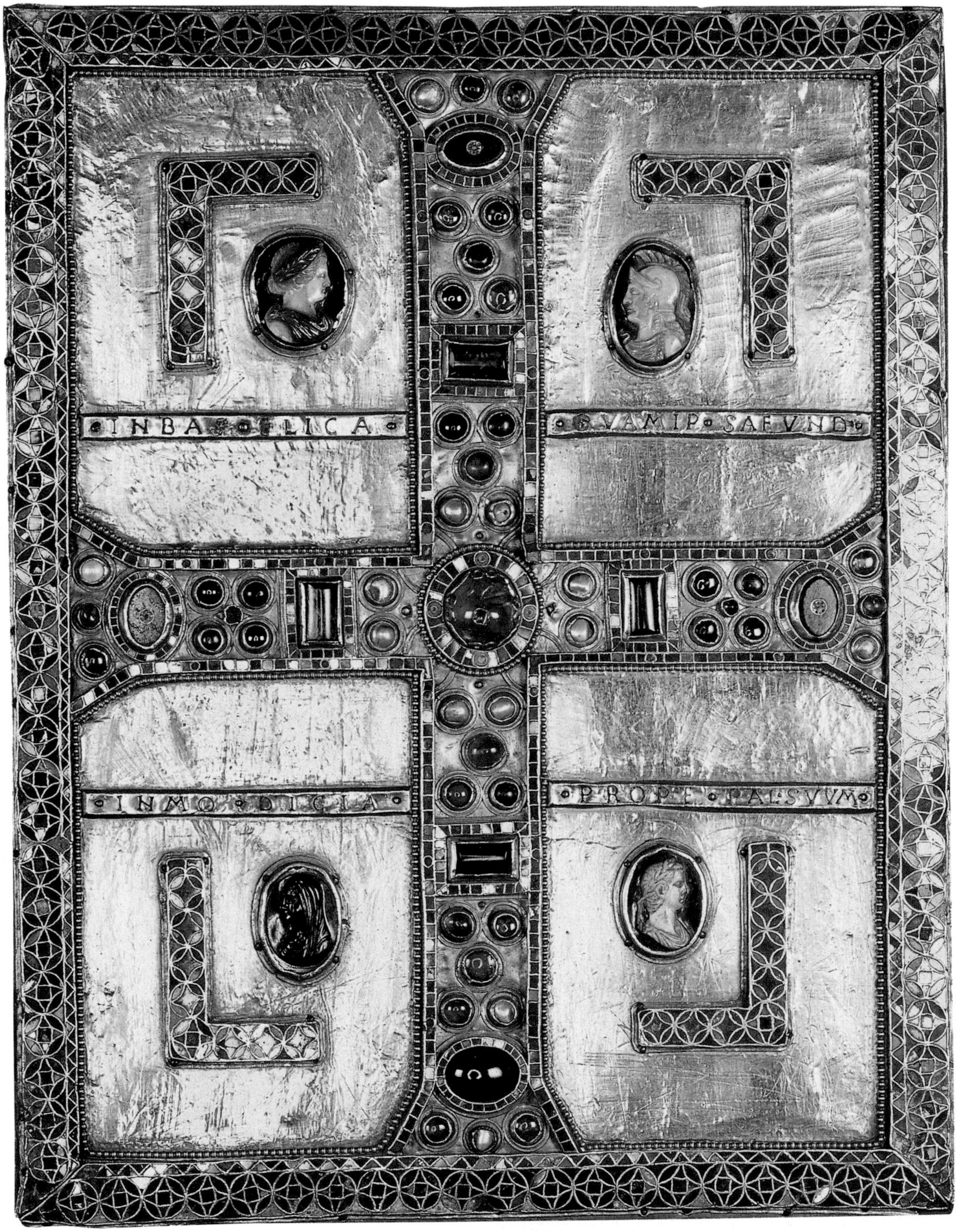

This is the cover from a copy of the Gospels belonging to the Lombardian queen Theodelinda. It dates from 600 and was probably among the gifts sent to the queen by Pope Gregory the Great to thank her for helping to re-establish harmony between himself and her people. Theodelinda had used her influence to convince her husband and his subjects to renounce Arianism.

the Great, who reigned from 590 to 604, there thus came together the two great institutional innovations of the early Church. He was a statesman of great insight. A Roman aristocrat, loyal to the empire and respectful of the emperor, he was nevertheless the first pope who fully accepted the barbarian Europe in which he reigned; his pontificate at last reveals a complete break with the classical world. He saw as his duty the first great missionary campaign, one of whose targets was pagan England, to which he sent Augustine of Canterbury in 596. He struggled against the Arian heresy and was delighted by the conversion of the Visigoths to Catholicism. He was as much concerned with the Germanic kings as with the emperor in whose name he claimed to act, but was also the doughtiest opponent of the Lombards; for help against them he turned both to the emperor and, more significantly, to the Franks. Yet the Lombards also made the pope, of necessity, a political power. Not only did they cut him off from the imperial representative at Ravenna but he had to negotiate with them when they stood before the walls of Rome. Like other bishops in the West who inherited civilian authority, he had to feed his city and govern it. Slowly Italians came to see the pope as successor to Rome as well as to St Peter.

This votive crown, which belonged to the Visigoth king Recesvinto, dates from the second half of the 7th century. It is made of gold and precious stones and was found in the province of Toledo, Spain, along with other similar pieces that had been buried c.670.

AN EMERGING EUROPE

In Gregory the classical-Roman heritage and the Christian are subsumed; he represented something new though he can hardly have seen it like that. Christianity had been a part of the classical heritage, yet it was now turning away from much of it and was distinct from it. Significantly, Gregory did not speak Greek; nor did he feel he needed to. There had already been signs of transformation in the Church's relations with the barbarians. With Gregory, one focus of this story has come at last to be Europe, not the Mediterranean basin. There were already sown in it the seeds of the future, though not of the near future; for most of the world's people the existence of Europe for the next thousand years or so is almost irrelevant. But a Europe is at last discernible, unimaginably different though it may be from what was to come and limited to the west of the continent.

It was also decisively different from the past. The ordered, literate, unhurried life of the Roman provinces had given way to a fragmented society with, encamped in it, a warrior aristocracy and their tribesmen, sometimes integrated with the earlier inhabitants, sometimes not. Their chiefs were called kings and were certainly no longer merely chiefs, any more than their followers, after nearly two centuries of involvement with what Rome had left behind, were mere barbarians. It was in 550 that a barbarian king – a Goth – for the first time represented himself on his coins decked in the imperial insignia. Through the impression wrought on their imaginations by the relics of a higher culture, through the efficacy of the idea of Rome itself and through the conscious and unconscious work of the Church, above all, these peoples were on their way to civilization and their art remains to prove it.

The 7th-century Gospels from which this miniature is taken were produced at the Abbey of Durrow, in Ireland. The figure symbolizes St Matthew.

THE MINGLING OF CHRISTIANITY AND PAGANISM

Of formal culture, the barbarians brought nothing with them to compare with antiquity. There was no barbarian contribution to the civilized intellect. Yet the cultural traffic was not all in one direction at less formal levels. The extent to which Christianity, or at least the Church, was still an elastic form must not be underrated. Everywhere Christianity had to flow in the channels available and these were defined by layers of paganism, Germanic upon Roman upon Celtic. The conversion of a king like Clovis did not mean that his people made at once even a formal adherence to Christianity; some were still pagan after generations had passed, as their graves showed. But this conservatism presented opportunities as well as obstacles. The Church could utilize the belief in folk magic, or the presence of a holy site which could associate a saint with respect for age-old deities of countryside and forest. Miracles, knowledge of which was assiduously propagated in the saints' lives read aloud to pilgrims to their shrines, were the persuasive arguments of the age. People were used to the magical interventions of the old Celtic deities or manifestations of Woden's power. For most men and women, as it has been for most of human history, the role of religion was not the provision of moral guidance or spiritual insight, but the propitiation of the unseen.

Only over blood-sacrifice did Christianity draw the line between itself and the pagan past unambiguously; much other pagan practice and reminiscence it simply christened.

The process by which this came about has often been seen as one of decline and there are certainly reasonable arguments to be made to that effect. In material terms, barbarian Europe was an economically poorer place than the empire of the Antonines; all over Europe tourists gape still at the monuments of Rome's builders as our barbarian predecessors must have done. Yet out of this confusion something quite new and immeasurably more creative than Rome would emerge in due course. It was perhaps impossible for contemporaries to view what was happening in anything but apocalyptic terms. But some may have seen just a little beyond this, as the concerns of Gregory suggest.

From the manuscript of the *Homilies* of St Gregory, this miniature on parchment was produced in northern Italy in around 800. St Gregory, giving his blessing, sits beneath an arch adorned with geometric motifs and supported by two richly decorated columns.

THE AGE OF DIVERGING TRADITIONS

The "Romans" of Justinian's day knew they were very different from other people and were proud of it. They belonged to a particular civilization; some of them, at least, thought it was the best conceivable. They were not unique in this. Undoubtedly there would have been people belonging to other civilizations who felt much the same, and there were, long before the birth of Christ, well-developed civilizations everywhere except in the Americas and Australasia. Because of this, the differences which had already appeared between patterns of life in different parts of the world in prehistoric times were to deepen and become richer and more complex.

Yet though civilizations were at work and dominant for long periods of time in certain parts of the globe, they tended before the age of modern history to be confined to them. From two or three centuries before the birth of Christ, the civilizations of different parts of the Eurasian landmass survived largely independently of one another. Though there were occasional and restricted contacts between them, they tended to occur because of the travels of enterprising merchants, wandering scholars, ambitious diplomats or enthusiastic missionaries, and such dependence on individuals meant that intercommunication between cultures was slight. Such sporadic contact could hardly be expected to overcome the great distances which separated some of them. Only when civilizations were actually contiguous – as were the Christian cultures of the Latin and Catholic West and the Greek and Orthodox East, for example – were there really possibilities of influencing one another profoundly.

Yet for all the differences of style and detail between them, in certain fundamental and shaping ways all civilizations were for a long time much alike. All civilizations until very recent times relied on subsistence agriculture for the most part; similarly, all of them had to find their energy supplies in wind, running water and human and animal muscle-power. None of them had for a long time any outstanding advantage over the others. As a result, technological sophistication or lack of it mattered less than in later times, when advantages would be deployed across huge distances to impose the ways of one civilization on another. Yet the insulation of one civilization from another was never absolute; there was always just a little interaction going on, some sharing of knowledge or techniques, even if merely those of war-making.

The major impact of civilizations on one another came about when migration actually changed the location of peoples and gave them new neighbours, or when nomadic peoples broke into settled societies. Then, sometimes, first a clash and then a symbiosis of civilizations might take place. These could be stimulating. Often, though, the effects of incursions by alien and barbarian peoples were destructive and negative. Such, for the most part, was the impact on the Middle East and eastern Europe of the Mongol peoples who poured out more than once from their Central Asian fastnesses to harry both Asia and Europe. Sometimes, though, the effects were more positive and enduring, as was the case when one of the Turkish peoples from the heart of Asia established itself in Anatolia and built on it a new empire which was to replace that of Byzantium. But the most important of all these world-historical clashes was one with which the story contained in this volume has to begin. It was to disturb peoples from Spain to Indonesia, and from the Niger basin to China, but it was also to be one of the first great carriers of cultural fertilization between civilizations.

During the Middle Ages, civilized society consisted of and was determined by three cultures: Christianity, Islam and Judaism. This Christian manuscript illustration is from 9th-century Spain. It is taken from the "Codex of the Council of Abelda", which forms part of a collection of manuscripts held at the El Escorial Monastery related to the Roman Catholic Councils of Toledo.

1 ISLAM AND THE RE-MAKING OF THE NEAR EAST

WITH RELATIVELY BRIEF interruptions, the great empires based in Iran hammered away at the West for a thousand years before 500. Wars sometimes bring civilizations closer, and in the Near East two cultural traditions had so influenced one another that their histories, though distinct, are inseparable. Through Alexander and his successors, the Achaemenids had passed to Rome the ideas and style of a divine kingship whose roots lay in ancient Mesopotamia; from Rome they went on to flower in the Byzantine Christian empire which fought the Sassanids. Persia and Rome fascinated and, in the end, helped to destroy one another; their antagonism was a fatal commitment to both of them when their attention and resources were urgently needed elsewhere. In the end both succumbed.

THE SASSANIDS

THE FIRST SASSANID, Ardashir, or Artaxerxes, had a strong sense of continuing Persian tradition. He deliberately evoked memories of the Parthians and the Great King, and his successors followed him in cultivating them by sculpture and inscription. Ardashir claimed all the lands once ruled by Darius and went on himself to conquer the oases of Merv and Khiva, and invade

The survival of the Sassanid monarchy depended on its control of the army and of religion. The latter was used to sanction the divine status of royal authority. In this Persian bas-relief from Naqsh-i-Rustam, the gods Mithras and Ahura Mazda are depicted offering a crown to King Ardashir II (379–383).

The Sassanid Empire at the time of Khusrau I

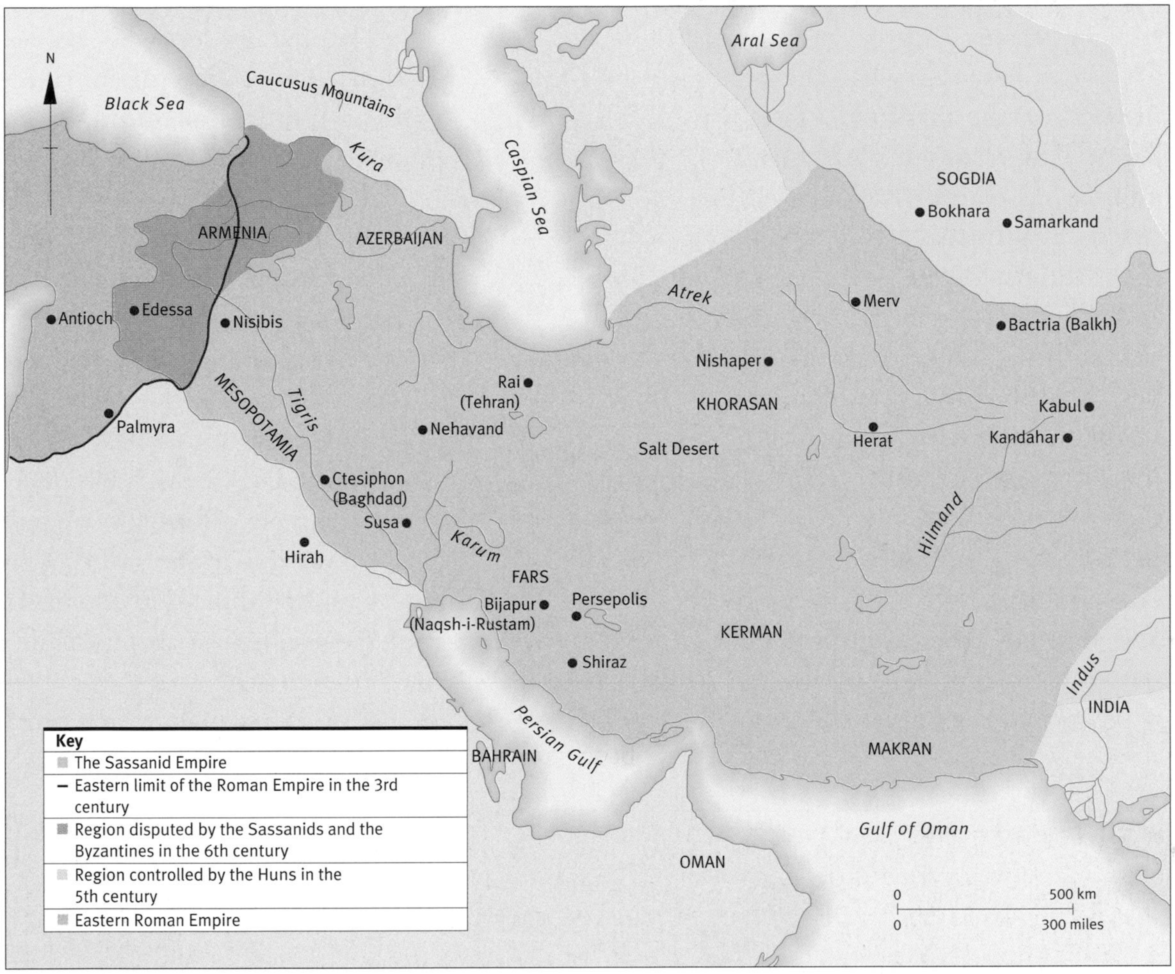

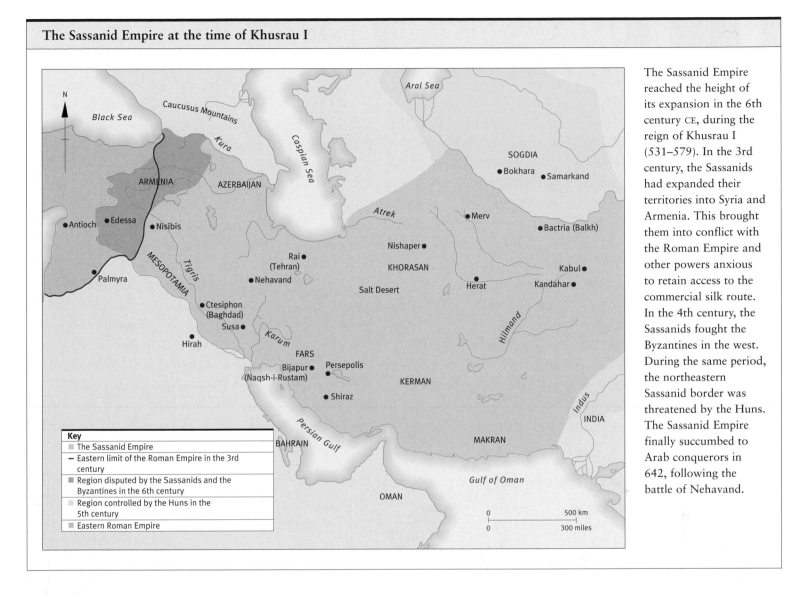

The Sassanid Empire reached the height of its expansion in the 6th century CE, during the reign of Khusrau I (531–579). In the 3rd century, the Sassanids had expanded their territories into Syria and Armenia. This brought them into conflict with the Roman Empire and other powers anxious to retain access to the commercial silk route. In the 4th century, the Sassanids fought the Byzantines in the west. During the same period, the northeastern Sassanid border was threatened by the Huns. The Sassanid Empire finally succumbed to Arab conquerors in 642, following the battle of Nehavand.

the Punjab; the conquest of Armenia took another hundred and fifty years to confirm but most of it was in the end brought under Persian hegemony. This was the last reconstitution of the ancient Iranian Empire and in the sixth century it even stretched south as far as the Yemen.

SASSANID GOVERNMENT

Geographical and climatic variety always threatened this huge sprawl of territory with disintegration, but for a long time the Sassanids solved the problems of governing it. There was a bureaucratic tradition running

Time chart (224–651)

224
Ardashir I defeats Artabanus V, the last Parthian emperor, marking the birth of the Sassanid Empire

260
Shapur I defeats the Roman emperor Valerian

363
Shapur II defeats the Roman emperor Julian

578
Sassanid expedition against Ceylon

591
Khusrau II wins back the throne, with the help of Roman emperor Maurice

651
Yazdigird III, the last Sassanid emperor, is murdered and the Arabs conquer Persia

200 300 400 500 600 700

back to Assyria to build on and a royal claim to divine authority. The tension between these centralizing forces and the interests of great families was what the political history of the Sassanid state was about. The resultant pattern was of alternating periods of kings encumbered or unsuccessful in upholding their claims. There were two good tests of this. One was their ability to appoint their own men to the major offices of state and resist the claims on them of the nobility. The other was their retention of control over the succession. Some Persian kings were deposed and though the kingship itself formally passed by nomination by the ruler, this gave way at times to a semi-electoral system in which the leading officers of state, soldiers and priests made a choice from the royal family.

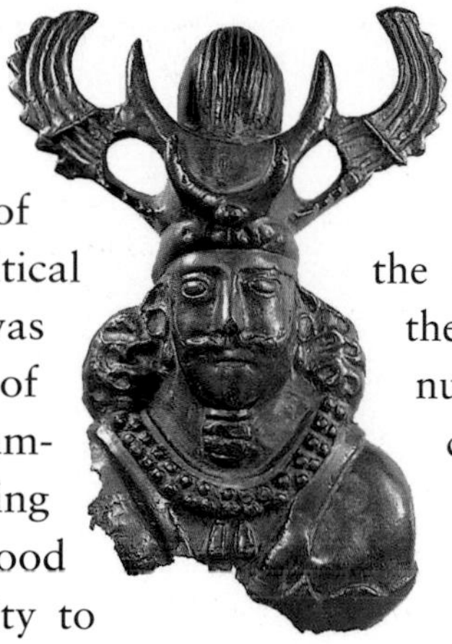

This bronze represents the emperor Khusrau I, who carried out several important economic and military reforms. The splendour that the Sassanid Empire enjoyed during his reign has made Khusrau I an idealized figure in Eastern mythology.

The dignitaries who contested the royal power and often ruled in the satrapies came from a small number of great families which claimed descent from the Parthian Arsacids, the paramount chiefs of that people. They enjoyed large fiefs for their maintenance but their dangerous weight was balanced by two other forces. One was the mercenary army, which was largely officered by members of the lesser nobility, who were thus given some foothold against the greater. Its corps d'élite, the heavy-armed household cavalry, was directly dependent on the king. The other force at work to counteract the dignitaries' power was that of the priesthood.

As well as providing fresh meat, a hunt was a means of demonstrating the king's strength and skill to the court. The decoration on this Sassanid plate portrays Khusrau II taking part in a hunt.

ZOROASTRIANISM

Sassanid Persia was a religious as well as a political unity. Zoroastrianism had been formally restored by Ardashir, who gave important privileges to its priests, the *magi*. They led in due course to political power as well. Priests confirmed the divine nature of the kingship, had important judicial duties, and came, too, to supervise the collection of the land-tax which was the basis of Persian finance. The doctrines they taught seem to have varied considerably from the strict monotheism attributed to Zoroaster but focused on a creator, Ahura Mazda, whose viceroy on earth was the king. The Sassanids' promotion of the state religion was closely connected with the assertion of their own authority.

THE EMERGENCE OF MANICHAEISM

The ideological basis of the Persian state became even more important when the Roman Empire became Christian. Religious differences began to matter much more; religious disaffection came to be seen as political. The wars with Rome made Christianity treasonable. Though Christians in Persia had at first been tolerated, their persecution became logical and continued well into the fifth century. Nor was it only Christians who were tormented. In 276 a Persian religious teacher called Mani was executed – by the particularly agonizing method of being flayed alive. He was to become known in the West under the Latin form of his name, Manichaeus, and the teaching attributed to him had a future as a Christian heresy. Manichaeism brought together Judaeo-Christian beliefs and Persian mysticism and saw the whole cosmos as a great drama in which the forces of light and darkness struggled for domination. Those who apprehended this truth sought to participate in the struggle by practising austerities which would open to them the way to perfection and to harmony with the cosmic drama of salvation. Manichaeism sharply differentiated good and evil, nature and God; its fierce dualism appealed to some Christians who saw in it a doctrine coherent with what Paul had taught. St Augustine was a Manichee in his youth and Manichaean traces have been detected much later in the heresies of medieval Europe. Perhaps an uncompromising dualism has always a strong appeal to a certain cast of mind. However that may be, the distinction of being persecuted both by a Zoroastrian and a Christian monarchy preceded the spread of Manichaean ideas far and wide. Their adherents found refuge in Central Asia and China, where Manichaeism appears to have flourished as late as the thirteenth century.

Ahura Mazda was the ancient Persians' principal deity. He later became known as Ormazd, sole creator and god of good. In this stone bas-relief Ahura Mazda is represented by a symbol depicting the winged spirit of light.

ORTHODOX CHRISTIANS IN PERSIA

As for orthodox Christians in Persia, although a fifth-century peace stipulated that they should enjoy toleration, the danger that they might turn disloyal in the continual wars

St Augustine, who is depicted in this miniature, was one of a number of distinguished Christians to be influenced by Mani, the son of an important Sassanid family. Before Mani was executed for his beliefs, he had spread his teachings in the East (where he visited China, India and Tibet) as well as in the West (he went to Spain and southern Italy).

This cameo represents the defeat at Edessa in 260 of the Roman emperor Valerian (seen here on the left) at the hands of Shapur I. The victorious Sassanids took Valerian prisoner and went on to plunder 36 cities in the territory abandoned by the Romans.

with Rome made this a dead letter. Only at the end of the century did a Persian king issue an edict of toleration and this was merely to conciliate the Armenians. It did not end the problem; Christians were soon irritated by the vigorous proselytizing of Zoroastrian enthusiasts. Further assurances by Persian kings that Christianity was to be tolerated do not suggest that they were very successful or vigorous in seeing that it was. Perhaps it was impossible against the political background: the exception which proves the rule is provided by the Nestorians, who *were* tolerated by the Sassanids, but this was just because they were persecuted by the Romans. They were, therefore, thought likely to be politically reliable.

THE PERSIAN-ROMAN WARS

Though religion and the fact that Sassanid power and civilization reached their peak under Khusrau I in the sixth century both help to give the rivalry of the empires something of the dimensions of a contest between civilizations, the renewed wars of that century are not very interesting. They offer for the most part a dull, ding-dong story, though they were the last round but one of the struggle of East and West begun by the Greeks and Persians a thousand years earlier. The climax to this struggle came at the beginning of the seventh century in the last world war of antiquity. Its devastations may well have been the fatal blow to the Hellenistic urban civilization of the Near East.

Khusrau II, the last great Sassanid, then ruled Persia. His opportunity seemed to have come when a weakened Byzantium – Italy was already gone and the Slavs and Avars were pouring into the Balkans – lost a good emperor, murdered by mutineers. Khusrau owed a debt of gratitude to the dead Maurice, for his own restoration to the Persian throne had been with his aid. He seized on the crime as an excuse and said he would avenge it. His armies poured into the Levant, ravaging the cities of Syria. In 615 they sacked Jerusalem, bearing away the relic of the True Cross which was its most famous treasure. The Jews, it may be remarked, often welcomed the Persians and seized the chance to carry out pogroms of Christians no doubt all the more delectable because the boot had for so long been on the other foot. The next year Persian armies went on to invade Egypt; a year later still, their advance-guards paused only a mile from Constantinople. They even put to sea, raided Cyprus and seized Rhodes from the empire. The empire of Darius seemed to be restored almost at the moment when, at the other end of the Mediterranean, the Roman Empire was losing its last possessions in Spain.

HERACLIUS

This was the blackest moment for Rome in her long struggle with Persia, but a saviour was at hand. In 610 the imperial viceroy of Carthage, Heraclius, had revolted against

Maurice's successor and ended that tyrant's bloody reign by killing him. In his turn he received the imperial crown from the Patriarch. The disasters in Asia could not at once be stemmed but Heraclius was to prove one of the greatest of the soldier emperors. Only sea-power saved Constantinople in 626, when the Persian army could not be transported to support an attack on the city by their Avar allies. Next year, though, Heraclius broke into Assyria and Mesopotamia, the old disputed heartland of Near Eastern strategy. The Persian army mutinied, Khusrau was murdered and his successor made peace. The great days of Sassanid power were over. The relic of the True Cross – or what was said to be such – was restored to Jerusalem. The long duel of Persia and Rome was at an end and the focus of world history was to shift at last to another conflict.

Following Khusrau II's defeat by the emperor Heraclius, who is represented on this coin, the descendants of the Sassanid Empire's last king fled to China.

THE ASIAN NOMADS

The Sassanids went under in the end because they had too many enemies. The year 610 had brought a bad omen: for the first time an Arab force defeated a Persian army. But for centuries Persian kings had been much more preoccupied with enemies on their northern frontiers than with those of the south. They had to contend with the nomads of Central Asia who have already made their mark on this narrative, yet the history of these peoples is hard to make out. None the less, one salient fact is clear – for nearly fifteen centuries Central Asia was the source of an impetus in world history which, though spasmodic and confused, produced results ranging from the Germanic invasions of the West to the revitalizing of Chinese government in East Asia.

The best starting-point is geography. The place from which the nomads came, "Central Asia", is not very well named. The term is imprecise. "Land-locked Asia" might be better, for it is its remoteness from oceanic contact which distinguishes the crucial area. In the first place, this remoteness produced a distinctive and arid climate; secondly, it ensured until modern times an almost complete seclusion from external political pressure, though Buddhism, Christianity and Islam all showed that it was open to cultural influence from the outside.

One way to envisage the zone is in a combination of human and topographic terms. It is that part of Asia which is suitable for nomads and it runs like a huge corridor from east to west for four thousand miles or so.

Caravanserais, which were large inns built around internal courtyards, provided accommodation for the many caravans that passed through the trade cities in Asia's oases. This elaborately decorated portal formed the entrance to the Rabati-Malik caravanserai near Bokhara in Uzbekistan.

Its northern wall is the Siberian forest mass; the southern is provided by deserts, great mountain ranges, and the plateaux of Tibet and Iran. For the most part it is grassy steppe, whose boundary with the desert fluctuates. That desert also shelters important oases, which have always been a distinctive part of its economy. They had settled populations whose way of life both aroused the antagonism and envy of the nomads and also complemented it. The oases were most frequent and richest in the region of the two great rivers known to the Greeks as the Oxus and the Jaxartes. Cities rose there which were famous for their wealth and skills – Bokhara, Samarkand, Merv – and the trade-routes which bound distant China to the West passed through them.

NOMADIC CULTURE

No one knows the ultimate origins of the peoples of Central Asia. They seem distinctive at the moment they enter history, but more for their culture than for their genetic stock. By the first millennium BCE they were specialists in the difficult art of living on the move, following pasture with their flocks and herds and mastering the special skills this demanded. It is almost completely true that until modern times they remained illiterate and they lived in a mental world of demons and magic except when converted to the higher religions. They were skilled horsemen and especially adept in the use of the composite bow, the weapon of the mounted archer, which took extra power from its construction not from a single piece of wood but from strips of wood and horn. They could carry out elaborate weaving, carving and decoration, but of course, did not build, for they lived in their tents.

When a Scythian leader died, a funeral ceremony was held beside his tomb. The rituals performed included the sacrifice of his wives, servants and horses, as depicted in the decoration of this 5th- or 4th-century BCE gold comb, found in a royal tomb.

THE SCYTHIANS

The first among these peoples who require mentioning were the Scythians, though it is not easy to say very precisely who they were. The term is a catch-all that includes several peoples; "Scythians" have been identified by archaeologists in many parts of Asia and Russia, and as far into Europe as Hungary. They seem to have had a long history of involvement in the affairs of the Near East. Some of them are reported harrying the Assyrian borders in the eighth century BCE. Later they attracted the attention of Herodotus, who had much to say about a people who fascinated the Greeks. Possibly they were never really one people, but a group of related tribes. Some of them seem to have settled in south Russia long enough to build up regular relations with the Greeks as farmers, exchanging grain for the beautiful gold objects made by the Greeks of the Black Sea coasts, which have been found in Scythian graves. But they also most impressed the Greeks as warriors, fighting in the way which was to be characteristic of the Asian

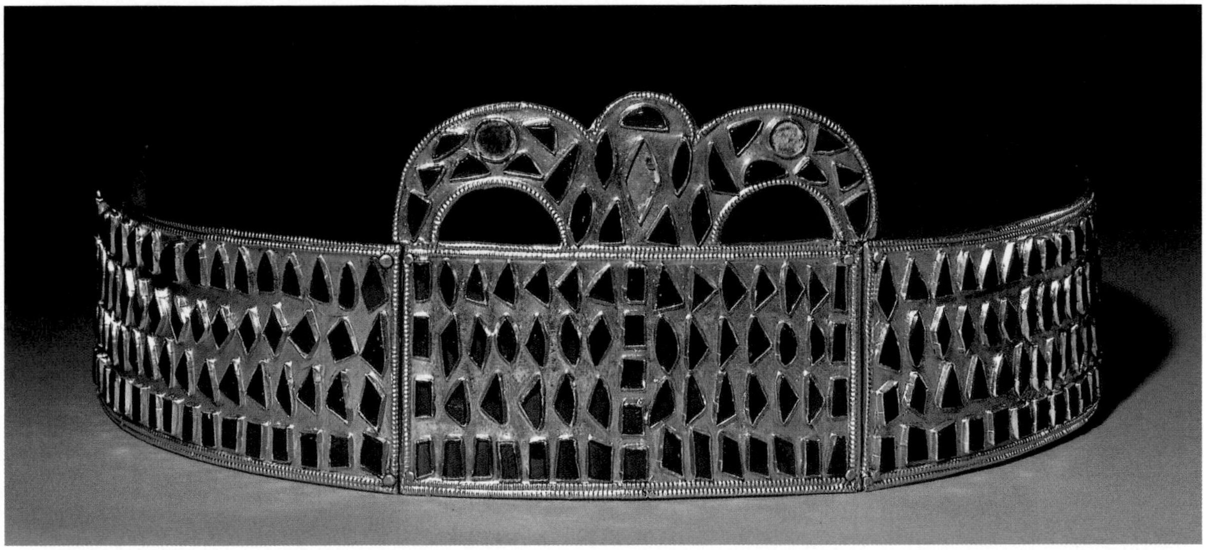

This stunning gold crown, decorated with precious stones, is thought to have belonged to the Hun people. It was found in Hungary.

nomads, using bow and arrow from horseback, falling back when faced with a superior force. They harassed the Achaemenids and their successors for centuries and shortly before 100 BCE overran Parthia.

The Scythians can serve as an example of the way in which such peoples are set in motion, for they were responding to very distant impulses. They moved because other peoples were moving them. The balance of life in Central Asia was always a nice one; even a small displacement of power or resources could deprive a people of its living-space and force it to long treks in search of a new livelihood. Nomads could not travel fast with flocks and herds, but seen from a background of long immunity their irruptions into settled land could seem dramatically sudden. Through its large-scale periodic upheavals by such peoples, rather than the more or less continuous frontier raiding and pillaging, Central Asia has made its impact on world history.

THE HSIUNG-NU

In the third century BCE another nomadic people was at the height of its power in Mongolia, the Hsiung-Nu, in whom some recognize the first appearance on the historical stage of those more familiar as Huns. For centuries they were a byword; all sources agree at least that they were most unpleasant opponents, ferocious, cruel and, unfortunately, skilled warriors. It was against them that the Chinese emperors built the Great Wall, a fourteen-hundred-mile-long insurance policy. Later Chinese governments none the less found it inadequate protection and suffered at the Huns' hands until they embarked on a forward policy, penetrating Asia so as to outflank the Hsiung-Nu. This led to a Chinese occupation of the Tarim basin up to the foothills of the Pamirs and the building on its north side of a remarkable series of frontier works. It was an early example of the generation of imperialism by suction; great powers can be drawn into areas of no concern to them except as sources of trouble. Whether or not this Chinese advance was the primary cause, the Hsiung-Nu now turned on their fellow nomads and began to push west. This drove before them another people, the Yueh-chih, who in turn pushed out of their way more Scyths. At the end of the line stood the post-Seleucid Greek state of Bactria; it disappeared towards 140 BCE and the Scythians then went on to invade Parthia.

The Huns advanced determinedly towards western Europe from the 4th century. In the year 451, led by Attila, they reached Gaul, where they were detained by an alliance of Franks and Romans. The following year, Attila attempted to invade Italy – Pope Leo I is widely believed to have begged him not to do so. The scene is depicted in this 16th-century fresco by Raphael.

They also pushed into south Russia, and into India, but that part of the story may be set aside for a moment. The history of the Central Asian peoples quickly takes non-specialists out of their depth; experts are in much disagreement, but it is clear that there was no comparable major upheaval such as that of the third century BCE for another four hundred years or so. Then about 350 CE came the re-emergence of the Hsiung-Nu in history, when Huns began to invade the Sassanid Empire (where they were known as Chionites). In the north, Huns had been moving westwards from Lake Baikal for centuries, driven before more successful rivals as others had been driven before them. Some were to appear west of the Volga in the next century; we have already met them near Troyes in 451. Those who turned south were a new handicap to Persia in its struggle with Rome.

THE TURKS

Only one more major people from Asia remains to be introduced, the Turks. Again, the first impact on the outside world was indirect. The eventual successors of the Hsiung-Nu in Mongolia had been a tribe called the Juan-Juan. In the sixth century its survivors were as far west as Hungary, where they were called Avars; they are noteworthy for introducing a revolution in cavalry warfare to Europe by introducing there the stirrup, which had given them an important advantage. But they were only in Europe because in about 550 they had been displaced in Mongolia by the Turks, a clan of iron-workers who had been their slaves. Among them were tribes – Khazars, Pechenegs, Cumans – which played important parts in the later history of the Near East and Russia.

The Khazars were Byzantium's allies against Persia, when the Avars were allies of the Sassanids. What has been called the first Turkish empire seems to have been a loose dynastic connection of such tribes running from the Tamir river to the Oxus. A Turkish khan sent emissaries to Byzantium in 568, roughly nine centuries before other Turks were to enter Constantinople in triumph. In the seventh century the Turks accepted the nominal suzerainty of the Chinese emperors, but by then a new element had entered Near Eastern history, for in 637 Arab armies overran Mesopotamia.

This follow-up to the blows of Heraclius announced the end of an era in Persian

The Euro-Asiatic nomadic peoples

This detail from a fresco at the Moldovita Monastery in Romania shows Turkish warriors slaughtering Christians during a siege of the Byzantine capital, Constantinople.

In the 4th century there was already a number of various "barbarian" peoples living in the Euro-Asiatic region who were to play an important role in its future political and economic structure. These peoples all shared a nomadic way of life and an economy based on animal husbandry or rudimentary trade.

At the end of the 4th century there was a huge population explosion among the region's nomadic peoples. This encouraged many of them, including the notorious Huns, to break through the frontiers of the great empires of the time – Chinese, Indian (Gupta), Persian (Sassanid) and Roman – all of which offered cities to sack and peoples to enslave. When, in around 550, the Turks from Alta (near present-day Mongolia) started to move westwards, it was the culmination of centuries of often aggressive migration by the Euro-Asiatic nomads. By the 10th century, the Turks had arrived at the frontiers of Byzantium.

Numerous legends surround the birth of the prophet Muhammad, depicted in this manuscript – it is even said that the baby was washed by the angels themselves. Tradition also tells how Muhammad's grandfather, al-Muttalib, noticed that his grandson's footprint was identical to that of the patriarch Abraham, supposedly preserved in the shrine of the Kaaba at Mecca.

history. In 620 Sassanid rule stretched from Cyrenaica to Afghanistan and beyond; just thirty years later it no longer existed. The Sassanid Empire was gone, its last king murdered by his subjects in 651. More than a dynasty passed away, for the Zoroastrian state went down before a new religion as well as before the Arab armies and it was one in whose name the Arabs would go on to yet greater triumphs.

ISLAM

ISLAM HAS SHOWN greater expansive and adaptive power than any other religion except Christianity. It has appealed to peoples as different and as distant from one another as Nigerians and Indonesians; even in its heartland, the lands of Arabic civilization between the Nile and India, it encompasses huge differences of culture and climate. Yet none of the other great shaping factors of world history was based on fewer initial resources, except perhaps the Jewish religion. Perhaps significantly, the Jews' own nomadic origins lay in the same sort of tribal society, barbaric, raw and backward, which supplied the first armies of Islam. The comparison inevitably suggests itself for another reason, for Judaism, Christianity and Islam are the great monotheistic religions. None of them, in their earliest stages, could have been predicted to be world-historical forces, except perhaps by their most obsessed and fanatical adherents.

THE PROPHET MUHAMMAD

The history of Islam begins with Muhammad, but not with his birth, for its date is one of many things which are not known about him. His earliest Arabic biographer did not write until a century or so after he died and even his account survives only indirectly. What is known is that around 570 Muhammad was born in the Hejaz of poor parents, and was soon an orphan. He emerges as an individual in young manhood preaching the message that there is one God, that He is just and will judge all men, who may assure their salvation by following His will in their religious observance and their personal and social behaviour. This God had been preached before, for he was the God of Abraham and the Jewish prophets, of whom the last had been Jesus of Nazareth.

Muhammad belonged to a minor clan of an important Bedouin tribe, the Quraysh. It was one of many in the huge Arabian peninsula, an area six hundred miles wide and over a thousand long. Those who lived there were subjected to very testing physical conditions; scorched in its hot season, most of Arabia was desert or rocky mountain. In much of it even survival was an achievement. But around its fringes there were little ports, the homes of Arabs who had been seafarers even in the second millennium BCE. Their enterprise linked the Indus valley to Mesopotamia and brought the spices and gums of East Africa up the Red Sea to Egypt. The origins of these peoples and those who lived inland is disputed, but both language and the traditional genealogies which go back to Old Testament patriarchs suggest ties with other early Semitic pastoralists who were also ancestors of the Jews, however disagreeable such a conclusion may be to some today.

Arabia had not always been so uninviting. Just before and during the first centuries of the Common Era it contained a group of prosperous kingdoms. They survived until, possibly, the fifth century CE; both Islamic tradition and modern scholarship link their disappearance with the collapse of the irrigation arrangements of southern Arabia. This produced migration from south to north, which created the Arabia of Muhammad's day. None of the great empires had penetrated more than briefly and fairly superficially into the peninsula, and Arabia had undergone little sophisticating fertilization from higher civilizations. It declined swiftly into a tribal society based on nomadic pastoralism. To regulate its affairs, patriarchal and kinship arrangements were enough so long as the Bedouin remained in the desert.

MECCA

At the end of the sixth century new changes can be detected. At some oases, population was growing. There was no outlet for it and this was straining traditional social practice. Mecca, where the young Muhammad lived, was such a place. It was important both as an oasis and as a pilgrim centre, for people came to it from all over Arabia to venerate a black meteoric stone, the Kaaba, which had for centuries been important in Arab religion. But Mecca was also an important junction of caravan routes between the Yemen and Mediterranean ports. Along them came foreigners and strangers. The Arabs were polytheists, believing in nature gods, demons and spirits, but as intercourse with the outside world increased, Jewish and Christian

The Great Mosque at Mecca is shown in this Persian gouache by Mustafa-al-Shukri. Pilgrims still flock to Mecca to worship at the Kaaba shrine – seen here in the centre of the image.

Arabia in the 7th century

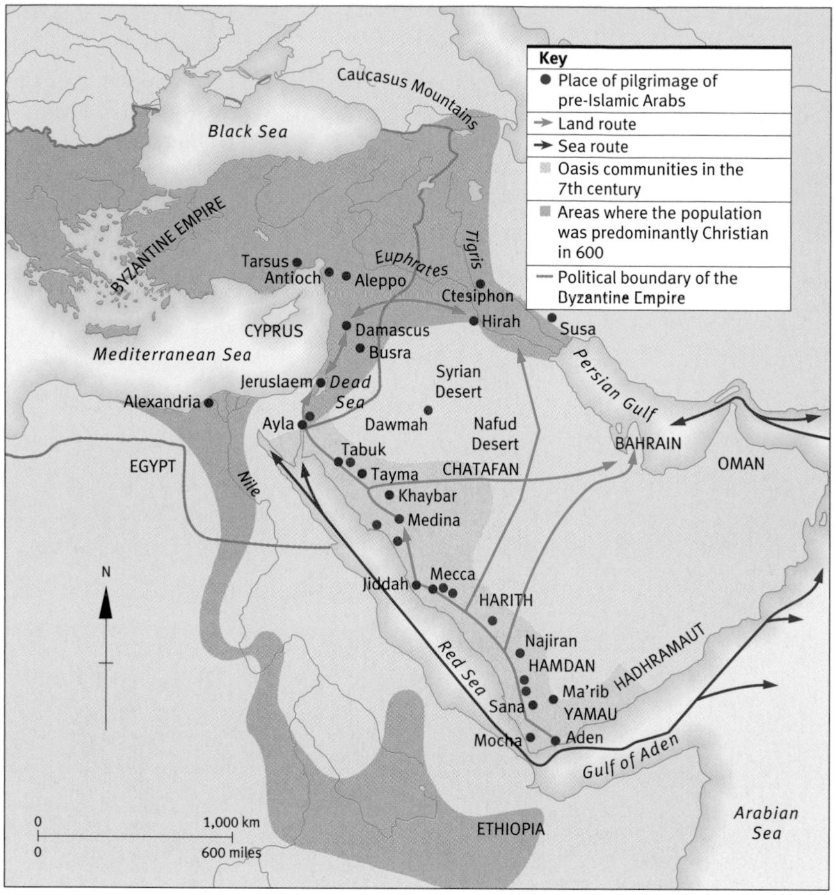

For hundreds of years, the two main commercial routes through Arabia were the Nile passage and the Tigris-Euphrates route to the Persian Gulf. At the end of the 6th century, as a result of the conflicts threatening to engulf the Persian and Byzantine empires, these routes fell into disuse. The route through the oasis city of Mecca soon replaced them. Mecca itself became one of the greatest trade centres of its time and a powerful economic oligarchy emerged there. Several smaller but prosperous commercial towns also lined the route between the Yemen and the Mediterranean ports.

communities appeared in the area; there were Christian Arabs before there were Muslims.

At Mecca some of the Quraysh began to go in for commerce (another of the few early biographical facts we know about Muhammad is that in his twenties he was married to a wealthy Qurayshi widow who had money in the caravan business). But such developments brought further social strains as the unquestioned loyalties of tribal structure were compromised by commercial values. The social relationships of a pastoral society assumed noble blood and age to be the accepted concomitants of wealth and this was no longer always the case. Here were some of the formative psychological pressures working on the tormented young Muhammad. He began to ponder the ways of God to man. In the end he articulated a system which helpfully resolved many of the conflicts arising in his disturbed society and gave it a set of beliefs still alive today.

THE KORAN AND MUHAMMAD'S TEACHING

The roots of Muhammad's achievement lay in the observation of the contrast between the Jews and Christians who worshipped the God familiar also to his own people as Allah, and the Arabs; Christians and Jews had a scripture for reassurance and guidance, and Muhammad's people had none. One day while he contemplated in a cave outside Mecca a voice came to him revealing his task:

"Recite, in the name of the Lord, who created,
Created man from a clot of blood."

For twenty-two years Muhammad was to recite and the result is one of the great formative books of humankind, the Koran. Its narrowest significance is still enormous and, like that of Luther's Bible or the Authorized Version, it is linguistic; the Koran crystallized a language. It was the crucial document of Arabic culture not only because of its content but because it was to propagate the Arabic tongue in a written form. But it is much more: it is a visionary's book, passionate in its conviction of divine inspiration; vividly conveying Muhammad's spiritual genius and vigour. Though not collected in his lifetime, it was taken down by his entourage as delivered by him in a series of revelations; Muhammad saw himself as a passive instrument, a mouthpiece of God. The word *Islam* means submission or surrender. Muhammad believed he was to convey God's message to the Arabs as other messengers had earlier brought His word to other peoples. But Muhammad was sure that his position was special; though there had been prophets before him, their revelations heard (but falsified) by Jew and Christian, he was the final Prophet. Through him, Muslims were to believe, God spoke his last message to his creation.

The message demanded exclusive service for Allah. Tradition says that Muhammad on one occasion entered the Kaaba's shrine and struck with his staff all the images of the other deities which his followers were to wash out, sparing only that of the Virgin and Child (he retained the stone itself). His teaching began with the uncompromising preaching of monotheism in a polytheistic religious centre. He went on to define a series of observances necessary to salvation and a social and personal code which often conflicted with current ideas, for example in its attention to the status of the individual believer, whether man, woman or child. It can readily be understood that such teaching was not always welcome. It seemed yet another disruptive and revolutionary influence – as it was – setting its converts against those of their tribe who worshipped the old gods and would certainly go to hell for it. It might damage the pilgrim business, too (though in the end it improved it, for Muhammad insisted strictly on the value of pilgrimage to so holy a place). Finally, as a social tie Muhammad's teaching placed blood second to belief; it was the brotherhood of believers which was the source of community, not the kinship group.

The Koran

"Give thou good tidings to those who believe
and do deeds of righteousness, that for them
await gardens underneath which rivers flow;
whensoever they are provided with fruits therefrom
they shall say, 'This is that wherewithal
we were provided before'; that they shall be
given in perfect semblance; and there
for them shall be spouses purified; therein
they shall dwell forever.

"God is not ashamed to strike a similitude
even of a gnat, or aught above it.
As for the believers, they know it is the truth
from their Lord; but as for unbelievers,
they say, 'What did God desire by this
for a similitude?' Thereby He leads
many astray, and thereby He guides
many; and thereby He leads none astray
save the ungodly such as break the covenant of
God after its solemn binding, and such as cut
what God has commanded should be joined,
and such as do corruption in the land –
they shall be the losers."

An extract from v. 23/25, Book II ("The Cow") of the Koran, translated by Arthur J. Arberry.

Muhammad's marriage to Khadijah, which is represented in this manuscript illustration, took place in the year 595. Khadijah was a wealthy widow who had been married twice previously. She bore Muhammad four daughters and two sons, although both the boys died in infancy.

The five pillars of the Islamic faith

The Islamic religion has five precepts, known as the pillars of the faith. The first, the *shahada*, is summarized in the phrase "there is no god but God and Muhammad is His messenger." The recitation of this phrase in the presence of another Muslim, preceded by the words "I testify", is sufficient to join the faith.

The second pillar of Islam involves compulsory formal prayers (*salat*), which must be said at least five times a day – at dawn, noon, mid-afternoon, evening and night. The faithful pray facing in the direction of their most holy city, Mecca. This is considered to be Muslims' most important duty and is their way of paying homage to God.

The third pillar of the Muslim religion is the giving of alms. There are two types of alms: the *sadaqa*, which is given voluntarily, and the *zakat*, which is obligatory and is collected by the state in Islamic countries as a portion of each person's income.

Fasting (*sawm*) constitutes the fourth precept. The fasting takes place during Ramadan, the ninth month in the Muslim calendar, during which it is believed the Koran was first revealed to Muhammad. All Muslims, with the exception of children, pregnant women and the sick, must fast from dawn until sunset.

The last precept is the pilgrimage to Mecca (*hajj*), which every Muslim who is able to has to undertake at least once during his or her lifetime.

The *jihad*, although not one of the five pillars, is considered equally important by many Muslims. Often translated as "holy war", *jihad* signifies the individual's duty to defend the faith – for example, by protecting fellow Muslims who are persecuted for their beliefs.

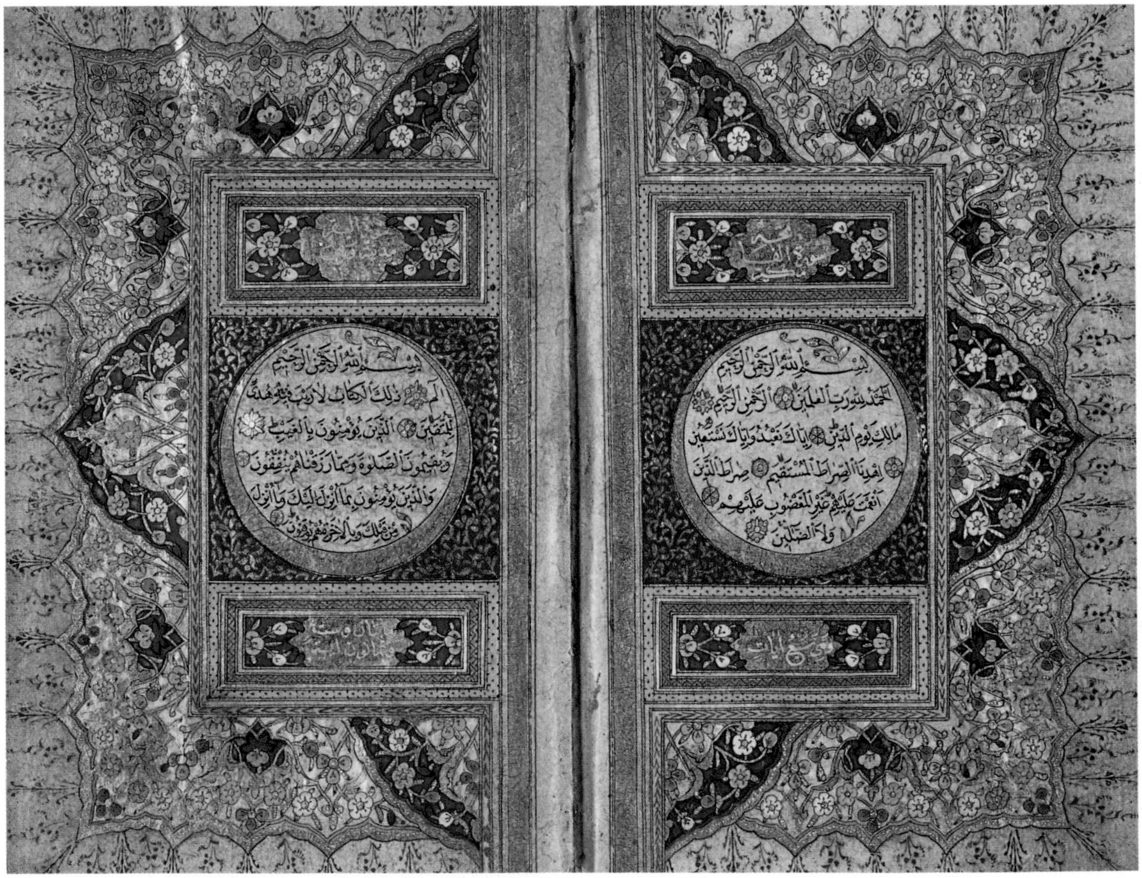

The sacred book of the Islamic religion is the Koran, the text of which is believed to have been revealed to Muhammad by God. Throughout its 114 chapters, or suras, *the beliefs and duties to which all good Muslims must adhere are detailed. The above pages are taken from a copy of the Koran that was produced in Damascus in the 18th century.*

Muhammad's flight to Yathrib, depicted on this 16th-century Turkish manuscript, marks the start of the Muslim calendar. Although the representation of human figures is forbidden in Islamic religious art, the work from which this image is taken (*The Life of the Prophet* from the Topkapi Palace in Istanbul) is one of three manuscripts that are an exception to this rule. The face of Muhammad, however, can never be shown and in this illustration, as in others from the same source, the Prophet's head is covered.

THE *HEGIRA*

It is not surprising that the leaders of his tribe turned on Muhammad. Some of his followers emigrated to Ethiopia, a monotheistic country already penetrated by Christianity. Economic boycott was employed against the recalcitrant who stayed. Muhammad heard that the atmosphere might be more receptive at another oasis about two hundred and fifty miles further north, Yathrib. Preceded by some two hundred followers, he left Mecca and went there in 622. This *Hegira*, or emigration, was to be the beginning of the Muslim calendar and Yathrib was to change its name, becoming the "city of the prophet", Medina.

It, too, was an area unsettled by economic and social change. Unlike Mecca, though, Medina was not dominated by one powerful tribe, but was a focus of competition for two; moreover, there were other Arabs there who adhered to Judaism. Such divisions favoured Muhammad's leadership. Converted families gave hospitality to the immigrants. The two groups were to form the future élite of Islam, the "Companions of the Prophet". Muhammad's writings for them show a new direction in his concerns, that of organizing a community. From the spiritual emphasis of his Mecca revelations he turned to practical, detailed statements about food, drink, marriage, war. The characteristic flavour of Islam, a religion which was also a civilization and a community, was now being formed.

THE ISLAMIC BROTHERHOOD

Medina was the base for subduing first Mecca and then the remaining tribes of Arabia. A unifying principle was available in Muhammad's idea of the *umma*, the brotherhood of believers. It integrated Arabs (and, at first, Jews) in a society which maintained much of the traditional tribal framework, stressing the patriarchal structure in so far as it did not conflict with the new brotherhood of Islam, even retaining the traditional primacy of Mecca as a place of pilgrimage. Beyond this it is not clear how far Muhammad wished to go. He had made approaches to Jewish tribesmen at Medina, but they had refused to accept his claims; they were therefore driven out, and a Muslim community alone remained, but this need not have implied any enduring conflict with either Judaism or its continuator, Christianity. Doctrinal ties existed in their monotheism and their scriptures even if Christians were believed to fall into polytheism with the idea of the Trinity. Nevertheless, Muhammad enjoined the conversion of the infidel and for those who wished there was a justification here for proselytizing.

MUHAMMAD'S LEGACY

Muhammad died in 632. At that moment the community he had created was in grave danger of division and disintegration. Yet on it two Arab empires were to be built, dominating successive historical periods from two different centres of gravity. In each the key institution was the caliphate, the inheritance of Muhammad's authority as the head of a community, both its teacher and its ruler. From the start, there was no tension of religious and secular authority in Islam, no "Church and State" dualism such as was to shape Christian policies for a thousand years and more. Muhammad, it has been well said, was his own Constantine – prophet and sovereign in one. His successors would not prophesy as he had done, but they were long to enjoy his legacy of unity in government and religion.

Following the death of Muhammad, Abu-Bakr, the father of one of the Prophet's nine wives, became the first caliph and initiated the expansion of Islam to Chaldea, Palestine and Trans-Jordan. His successor, Umar, continued the territorial conquests through Syria, Iraq, Mesopotamia, Egypt and Persia. Umar was replaced by Uthman, Muhammad's son-in-law, who was assassinated and succeeded by Ali, the Prophet's cousin. These caliphs are all depicted surrounding Muhammad in this illustration.

THE CALIPHS

The first "patriarchal" caliphs were all Quraysh, most of them related to the Prophet by blood or marriage. Soon, they were criticized for their wealth and status and were alleged to act as tyrants and exploiters. The last of them was deposed and killed in 661 after a series of wars in which conservatives contested what they saw as the deterioration of the caliphate from a religious to a secular office. The year 661 saw the beginning of the Umayyad caliphate, the first of the two major chronological divisions of Arab empire, focused on Syria, with its capital as Damascus. It did not bring struggle within the Arab world to an end for in 750 the Abbasid caliphate displaced it. The new caliphate lasted longer. After moving to a new location, Baghdad, it would survive nearly two centuries (until 946) as a real power and even longer as a puppet régime. Between them the two dynasties gave the Arab peoples three centuries of ascendancy in the Near East.

ISLAMIC CONQUESTS

The first and most obvious expression of Arab ascendancy was an astonishing series of conquests in the first century of Islam which remade the world map from Gibraltar to the Indus. They had in fact begun immediately after the Prophet's death with the assertion of the first caliph's authority. Abu-Bakr set about conquering the unreconciled tribes of southern and eastern Arabia for Islam. But this led to fighting which spread to Syria and Iraq. Something analogous to the processes by which barbarian disturbances in Central Asia rolled outward in their effects was at work in the overpopulated Arabian peninsula; this time there was a creed to give it direction as well as a simple love of plunder.

The spread of early Islam

When Muhammad died in 632, members of the new faith were centred around the Arabian cities of Mecca and Medina. The early Muslims quickly began the long campaign of Islamic expansion: in 655 Muslim armies arrived in Samarkand to the east and in Tripoli to the west. Although they defeated Sassanid Persia, the Muslims were prevented from expanding into eastern Europe by the Byzantine defensive. However, between 634 and 650, they did take control of Libya, Syria, Palestine, Iraq and Egypt, among others, recruiting soldiers from new converts to the faith. In 711, the caliph's armies conquered Spain at the same time as arriving in India and China. The European conquests ended in 732 when the Franks defeated the Muslims at Poitiers.

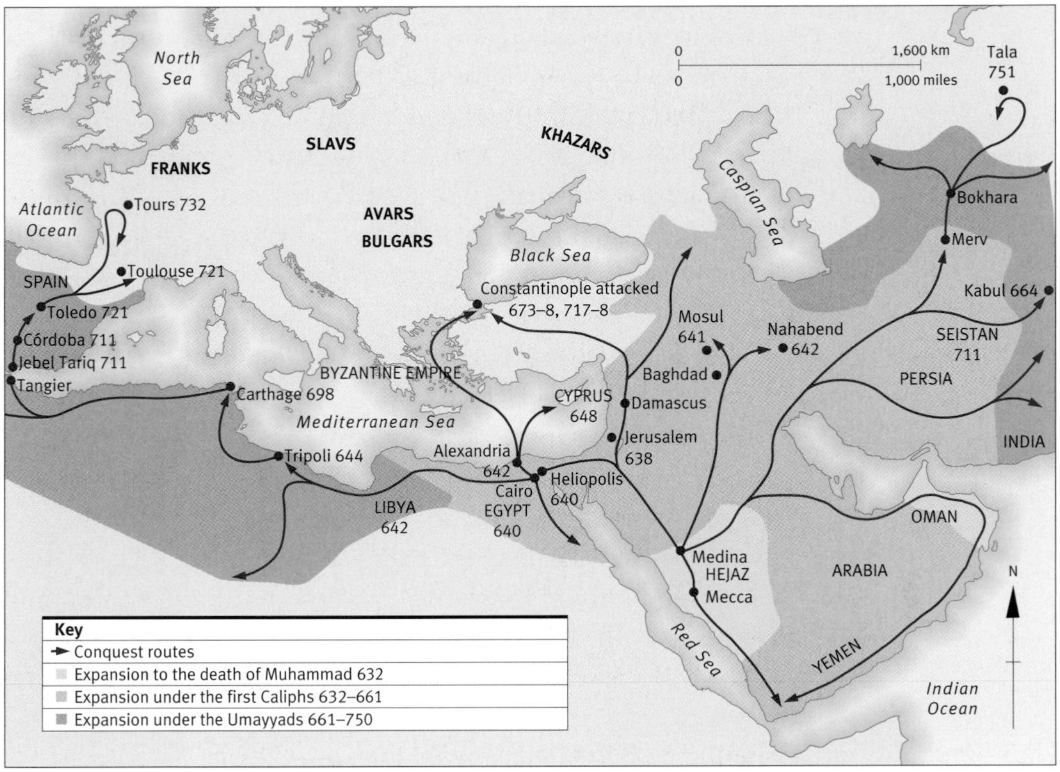

Once beyond the peninsula, the first victim of Islam was Sassanid Persia. The challenge came just as it was under strain at the hands of the Heraclian emperors who were likewise to suffer from this new scourge. In 633 Arab armies invaded Syria and Iraq. Three years later the Byzantine forces were driven from Syria and in 638 Jerusalem fell to Islam. Mesopotamia was wrested from the Sassanids in the next couple of years, and at about the same time Egypt was taken from the empire. An Arab fleet was now created and the absorption of North Africa began. Cyprus was raided in the 630s and 640s; later in the century it was divided between the Arabs and the empire. At the end of the century the Arabs took Carthage, too. Meanwhile, after the Sassanids' disappearance the Arabs had conquered Khurasan in 655, Kabul in 664; at the beginning of the eighth century they crossed the Hindu Kush to invade Sind, which they occupied between 708 and 711. In the latter year an Arab army with Berber allies crossed the Straits of Gibraltar (its Berber commander, Tariq, is commemorated in that name, which means *Jebel Tariq*, or mount of Tariq) and advanced into Europe, shattering at last the Visigothic kingdom. Finally, in 732, a hundred years after the death of the Prophet, a Muslim army, deep in France, puzzled by over-extended communications and the approach of winter, turned back near Poitiers. The Franks who faced them and killed their commander claimed a victory; at any rate, it was the high-water mark of Arab conquest, though in the next few years Arab expeditions raided into France as far as the upper Rhône. Whatever brought it to an end (and possibly it was just because the Arabs were not much interested in European conquest, once away from the warm lands of the Mediterranean littoral), the Islamic onslaught in the West remains an astonishing achievement, even if Gibbon's vision of Oxford teaching the Koran was never remotely close to realization.

The Arab armies were at last stopped in the East, too, although only after two sieges of Constantinople and the confining of the eastern empire to the Balkans and Anatolia. From eastern Asia there is a report that an Arab force reached China in the early years of the eighth century; even if questionable, such a story is evidence of the conquerors' prestige. What is certain is that the frontier of Islam settled down along the Caucasus mountains and the Oxus after a great Arab defeat at the hands of the Khazars in Azerbaijan, and a victory in 751 over a Chinese army commanded by a Korean general on the river Talas, in the high Pamirs. On all fronts, in western Europe, Central Asia, Anatolia and in the Caucasus, the tide of Arab conquest at last came to an end in the middle of the eighth century.

FAVOURABLE CONDITIONS FOR ISLAM

The Arab drive to conquer had not been uninterrupted. There had been something of a lull in Arab aggressiveness during the internecine quarrelling just before the establishment of the Umayyad caliphate, and there had been bitter fighting of Muslim against Muslim in the last two decades of the seventh century. But for a long time circumstances favoured the Arabs. Their first great enemies, Byzantium and Persia, had both had heavy commitments on other fronts and had been for centuries one another's fiercest antagonists. After Persia went under, Byzantium still had to contend with enemies in the west and to the north, fending them off with one hand while grappling with the Arabs with the other. Nowhere did the Arabs face an opponent comparable to the Byzantine Empire nearer than China. Because of this, they pressed their conquests to the limit of geographical possibility or attractiveness, and sometimes their defeat showed they had overstretched themselves. Even when they met formidable opponents, though, the Arabs still had great military advantages. Their armies were recruited from hungry fighters to whom the Arabian desert had left small alternative; the spur of overpopulation was behind them. Their assurance in the Prophet's teaching that death on the battlefield against the infidel would be followed by certain removal to paradise was a huge moral advantage. They fought their way, too, into lands whose peoples were often already disaffected with their rulers; in Egypt, for example, Byzantine religious orthodoxy had created dissident and alienated minorities. Yet when all such influences have been totted up, the Arab success remains amazing. The fundamental explanation must lie in the movement of large numbers of individuals by a religious ideal. The Arabs thought they were doing God's will and creating a new brotherhood in the process; they generated an excitement in themselves like that of later revolutionaries. And conquest was only the beginning of the story of the impact of Islam on the world. In its range and complexity it can only be compared to that of Judaism or Christianity. At one time it looked as if Islam might be irresistible everywhere. That was not to be, but one of the great traditions of civilization was to be built on its conquests and conversions.

This illustration, dating from the 13th century, depicts the Islamic warrior Maqamat de al-Hariri and his troops going into battle.

2 THE ARAB EMPIRES

This image, which dates from 1237, illustrates a poem by the 10th-century writer Al-Mutanabbi about the Muslim conquest of Spain.

IN 661 THE ARAB GOVERNOR OF SYRIA, Mu-Awiyah, set himself up as caliph after a successful rebellion and the murder (though not at his hands) of the caliph Ali, cousin and son-in-law of the Prophet. This ended a period of anarchy and division, and so, thought many Muslims, excused what Ali did. It was also the foundation of the Umayyad caliphate.

THE UMAYYAD CALIPHATE

THIS USURPATION gave political ascendancy among the Arab peoples to the aristocrats of the Quraysh, the very people who had opposed Muhammad at Mecca. Mu-Awiyah set up his capital at Damascus and later named his son crown prince, an innovation which introduced the dynastic principle. This was also the beginning of a schism within Islam, for a dissident group, the Shi'ites, henceforth claimed that the right of interpreting the Koran was confined to Muhammad's descendants. The murdered caliph, they said, had been divinely designated as *imam* to transmit his office to his descendants and was immune from sin and error. The Umayyad caliphs, correspondingly, had their own party of supporters, called Sunnites, who believed that doctrinal authority changed hands with the caliphate. Together with the creation of a regular army and a system of supporting it by taxation of the unbelievers, a decisive movement was thus made away from an Arab world solely of tribes. The site of the Umayyad capital, too, was important in changing the style of Islamic culture, as were the personal tastes of the first caliph. Syria was a Mediterranean state, but

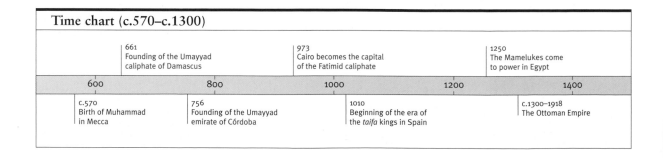

Time chart (c.570–c.1300)

- c.570 Birth of Muhammad in Mecca
- 661 Founding of the Umayyad caliphate of Damascus
- 756 Founding of the Umayyad emirate of Córdoba
- 973 Cairo becomes the capital of the Fatimid caliphate
- 1010 Beginning of the era of the *taifa* kings in Spain
- 1250 The Mamelukes come to power in Egypt
- c.1300–1918 The Ottoman Empire

600 — 800 — 1000 — 1200 — 1400

Mu-Awiyah seized power in 661. He established the capital of Islam in Damascus, the seat of his political and military power, where buildings such as the Great Mosque still serve as reminders of the city's Umayyad past. The last caliph of the Umayyad Dynasty was overthrown in 750.

Damascus was roughly on the border between the cultivated land of the Fertile Crescent and the barren expanses of the desert; its life was fed by two worlds. To the desert-dwelling Arabs, the former must have been the more striking. Syria had a long Hellenistic past and both the caliph's wife and his doctor were Christians. While the barbarians of the West looked to Rome, Arabs were to be shaped by the heritage of Greece.

UMAYYAD GOVERNMENT

The first Umayyad speedily reconquered the East from dissidents who resisted the new régime and the Shi'ite movement was driven underground. There followed a glorious century whose peak came under the sixth and seventh caliphs between 685 and 705. Unfortunately we know little about the detailed and institutional history of Umayyad times. Archaeology sometimes throws light on general trends and reveals something of the Arabs' impact on their neighbours. Foreign records and Arab chroniclers log important events. Nevertheless, early Arab history produces virtually no archive material apart from an occasional document quoted by an Arab author. Nor did Islamic religion have a bureaucratic centre of ecclesiastical government. Islam had nothing remotely approaching the records of the papacy in scope, for example, though the analogy between the popes and the caliphs might reasonably arouse similar expectations. Instead of administrative records throwing light on continuities there are only occasional collections preserved almost by chance, such as a mass of papyri from Egypt, special

The internal courtyard of the Great Mosque in Damascus, Syria, is shown here with the fountain of ablutions on the left. The mosque dates from 705, the last year of the seventh caliph's reign, and bears testament to the wealth and ambition of the early Umayyad caliphate.

accumulations of documents by minority communities such as the Jews, and coins and inscriptions. The huge body of Arabic literature in print or manuscript provides further details, but it is much more difficult to make general statements about the government of the caliphates with confidence than, say, similar statements about Byzantium.

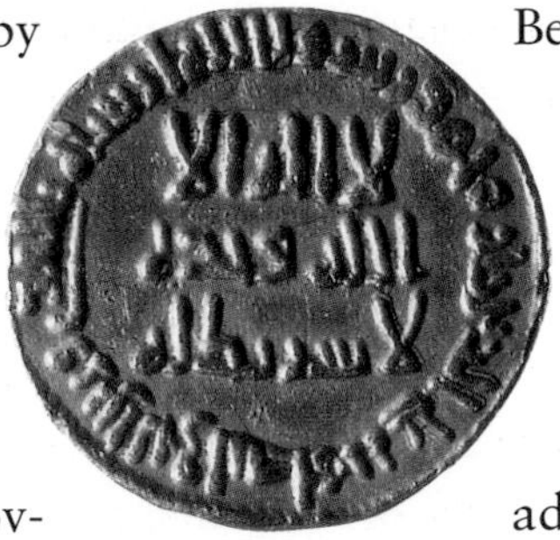

The characteristic feature of Arab coins is the absence of any figurative decoration. Only religious inscriptions, the name of the mint where the coin was produced, the date and the name of the ruler appear.

TAXATION AND COMMERCE

It seems, none the less, that the early arrangements of the caliphates, inherited from the orthodox caliphs, were loose and simple – perhaps too loose, as the Umayyad defection showed. Their basis was conquest for tribute, not for assimilation, and the result was a series of compromises with existing structures. Administratively and politically, the early caliphs took over the ways of earlier rulers. Byzantine and Sassanid arrangements continued to operate; Greek was the language of government in Damascus, Persian in Ctesiphon, the old Sassanid capital, until the early eighth century. Institutionally, the Arabs left the societies they took over by and large undisturbed except by taxation. Of course, this does not mean that they went on just as before. In northwestern Persia, for example, Arab conquest seems to have been followed by a decline in commerce and a drop in population, and it is hard not to associate this with the collapse of a complex drainage and irrigation system successfully maintained in Sassanid times. In other places, Arab conquest had less drastic effects. The conquered were not antagonized by having to accept Islam, but took their places in a hierarchy presided over by the Arab Muslims. Below them came the converted neo-Muslims of the tributary peoples, then the *dhimmi*, or "protected persons" as the Jewish and Christian monotheists were called. Lowest down the scale came unconverted pagans or adherents of no revealed religion. In the early days the Arabs were segregated from the native population and lived as a military caste in special towns paid by the taxes raised locally, forbidden to enter commerce or own land.

ARAB INTEGRATION

Segregation could not be kept up. Like the Bedouin customs brought from the desert, it was eroded by garrison life. Gradually the Arabs became landowners and cultivators, and so their camps changed into new, cosmopolitan cities such as Kufa or Basra, the great *entrepôt* of the trade with India. More and more Arabs mixed with the local inhabitants in a two-way relationship, as the indigenous élites underwent an administrative and linguistic arabization. The caliphs appointed more and more of the officials of the provinces and by the mid-eighth century Arabic was almost everywhere the language of government. Together with the standard coinage bearing Arabic inscriptions it is the major evidence of Umayyad success in laying the foundations of a new, eclectic civilization. Such changes were effected fastest in Iraq, where they were favoured by prosperity as trade revived under the Arab peace.

The assertion of their authority by the Umayyad caliphs was one source of their troubles. Local bigwigs, especially in the eastern half of the empire, resented interference with their practical independence. Whereas many of the aristocracy of the former Byzantine territories emigrated to Constantinople, the élites of Persia could not; they had nowhere to go and had to remain, irritated by their subordination to the Arabs who left them much of their local authority. Nor did it help that the later Umayyad caliphs were men of poor quality, who did not command the respect won by the great men of the dynasty. Civilization softened them. When they sought to relieve the tedium of life in the towns they governed, they moved out into the desert, not to live again the life of the Bedouin, but to enjoy their new towns and palaces, some of them remote and luxurious, equipped as they were with hot baths and great hunting enclosures and supplied from irrigated plantations and gardens.

THE SHI'A

Umayyad government created opportunities for the disaffected, among whom the Shi'a, the party of the Shi'ites, were especially notable. Besides their original political and religious appeal, they increasingly drew on social grievances among the non-Arab converts to Islam, particularly in Iraq. From the start, the Umayyad régime had distinguished sharply between those Muslims who were and those who were not by birth members of an Arab tribe. The numbers of the latter class grew rapidly; the Arabs had not sought to convert (and sometimes even tried to deter from conversion in early times) but the attractiveness of the conquering creed was powerfully reinforced by the fact that adherence to it might bring tax relief. Around the Arab garrisons, Islam had spread rapidly among the non-Arab populations which grew up to service their needs. It was also very successful among the local élites who maintained the day-to-day administration. Many of these neo-Muslims, the *mawali*, as they were called, eventually became soldiers, too. Yet they increasingly felt alienated and excluded from the aristocratic society of the pure Arabs. The puritanism and orthodoxy of the Shi'ites, equally alienated from the same society for political and religious reasons, made a great appeal to them.

THE UMAYYAD CALIPHATE LOSES POWER

Increasing trouble in the east heralded the breakdown of Umayyad authority. In 749 a new caliph, Abu-al-Abbas, was hailed publicly in the mosque at Kufa in Iraq. This was the beginning of the end for the Umayyads. The pretender, a descendant of an uncle of the Prophet, announced his intention of restoring the caliphate to orthodox ways; he appealed to a wide spectrum of opposition including the Shi'ites. His full name was promising: it meant "Shedder of Blood". In 750 he defeated and executed the last Umayyad caliph. A dinner-party was held for the males of the defeated house; the guests were murdered before the first course, which was then served to their hosts. With this clearing of the decks began nearly two centuries during which the Abbasid caliphate ruled the Arab world, the first of them the most glorious.

THE ABBASID CALIPHATE

THE SUPPORT THE ABBASIDS ENJOYED in the eastern Arab dominions was reflected by the shift of the capital to Iraq, to Baghdad, until then a Christian village on the Tigris. The change had many implications. Hellenistic influences were weakened; Byzantium's prestige seemed less unquestionable. A new

General disorder, resulting from poor economic and social policies, eventually led to a loss of support for the Umayyad régime. Several insurrections took place, one of which was instigated by the Abbasid party and led by Abu-al-Abbas, who was appointed caliph by his followers in 749 in the mosque at Kufa (Iraq), shown here.

weight was given to Persian influence, which was both politically and culturally to be very important. There was a change in the ruling caste, too, and one sufficiently important to lead some historians to call it a social revolution. They were from this time Arabs only in the sense of being Arabic-speaking; they were no longer Arabian. Within the matrix provided by a single religion and a single language the élites which governed the Abbasid Empire came from many peoples right across the Middle East. They were almost always Muslims but they were often converts or children of convert families. The cosmopolitanism of Baghdad reflected the new cultural atmosphere. A huge city, rivalling Constantinople, with perhaps a half-million inhabitants, it was a complete antithesis of the ways of life brought from the desert by the first Arab conquerors. A great empire had come again to the whole Middle East. It did not break with the past ideologically, though, for after dallying with other possibilities the Abbasid caliphs confirmed the Sunnite orthodoxy of their predecessors. This was soon reflected in the disappointment and irritation of the Shi'ites who had helped to bring them to power.

ABBASID RULE

The Abbasids were a violent lot and did not take risks with their success. They quickly and ruthlessly quenched opposition and bridled former allies who might turn sour. Loyalty to the dynasty, rather than the brotherhood of Islam, was increasingly the basis of the empire

This coin was minted during the era of the Abbasid caliphs, who claimed to be descendants of the prophet Muhammad. Their power lasted until the middle of the 11th century, when they were deposed by the Seljuk Turks.

and this reflected the old Persian tradition. Much was made of religion as a buttress to the dynasty, though, and the Abbasids persecuted nonconformists. The machinery of government became more elaborate. Here one of the major developments was that of the office of vizier (monopolized by one family until the legendary caliph Haroun-al-Raschid wiped them out). The whole structure became somewhat more bureaucratized, the land taxes raising a big revenue to maintain a magnificent monarchy. Nevertheless, provincial distinctions remained very real. Governorships tended to become hereditary, and, because of this, central authority was eventually forced on to the defensive. The governors exercised a greater and greater power in appointments and the handling of taxation. It is not easy to say what was the caliphate's real power, for it regulated a loose collection of provinces whose actual dependence was related very much to the circumstances of the moment. But of Abbasid wealth and prosperity at its height there can be no doubt. They rested not only on its great reserves of manpower and the large areas where agriculture was untroubled during the Arab peace, but also upon the favourable conditions it created for trade. A wider range of commodities circulated over a larger area then ever before. This revived commerce in the cities along the caravan routes which passed through the Arab lands from east to west. The riches of Haroun-al-Raschid's Baghdad reflected the prosperity they brought.

ISLAMIC CIVILIZATION

ISLAMIC CIVILIZATION in the Arab lands reached its peak under the Abbasids. Paradoxically, one reason for this was the movement of its centre of gravity away from Arabia and the Levant. Islam provided a political organization which, by holding together a huge area, cradled a culture which was essentially synthetic, mingling, before it was done, Hellenistic, Christian, Jewish, Zoroastrian and Hindu ideas. Arabic culture under the Abbasids had closer access to the Persian tradition and a new contact with India which brought to it renewed vigour and new creative elements.

One aspect of Abbasid civilization was a great age of translation into Arabic, the new lingua franca of the Middle East. Christian and Jewish scholars made available to Arab readers the works of Plato and Aristotle, Euclid and Galen, thus importing the categories of Greek thought into Arab culture. The tolerance of Islam for its tributaries made this possible in principle from the moment when Syria and Egypt were conquered, but it was under the early Abbasids that the most important translations were made. So much it is possible to chart fairly confidently. To say what this meant, of course, is more difficult, for though the texts of Plato might be available, it was the Plato of late Hellenistic culture, transmitted through interpretations by Christian monks and Sassanid academics.

The astrolabe is a navigational instrument used for observing the position of the stars and for establishing their distance from the horizon. This astrolabe, made by Ibrahim ibn Said al-Sahli in Toledo, Spain, has a very important feature: it indicates the duration of the longest and shortest diurnal arcs of the year for various Eastern, North African and Spanish cities.

The Thousand Nights and One Night

"Then she fell silent, and King Shahryar cried, 'O Shahrazad, that was a noble and admirable story! O wise and subtle one, you have taught me many lessons, letting me see that every man is at the call of Fate; you have made me consider the words of kings and peoples passed away; you have told me some things which were strange, and many that were worthy of reflection. I have listened to you for a thousand nights and one night, and now my soul is changed and joyful, it beats with an appetite for life. I give thanks to Him Who has perfumed your mouth with so much eloquence and has set wisdom to be a seal upon your brow! ... O Shahrazad, I swear by the Lord of Pity that you were already in my heart before the coming of these children. He had given you gifts with which to win me; I loved you in my soul because I had found you pure, holy, chaste, tender, straightforward, unassailable, ingenious, subtle, eloquent, discreet, smiling, and wise. May Allah bless you, my dear, your father and mother, your root and race! O Shahrazad, this thousand and first night is whiter for us than the day!'"

An extract from the epilogue of *The Book of the Thousand Nights and One Night* by Haroun-al-Raschid (766–809), translated by Powys Mathers from the French rendering by Dr J. C. Mardrus.

Also known as *The Arabian Nights, The Book of the Thousand Nights and One Night* is probably the best-known literary work from the Arab world. This illustration from an 18th-century Persian manuscript shows a scene from one of the tales about Sinbad the Sailor.

LITERARY CULTURE

Abbasid culture was predominantly literary; Arabic Islam produced beautiful buildings, lovely carpets, exquisite ceramics, but its great medium was the word, spoken and written. Even the great Arab scientific works are often huge prose compendia. The accumulated bulk of this literature is immense and much of it simply remains unread by western scholars. Large numbers of its manuscripts have never been examined at all. The prospect is promising; the absence of archive material for early Islam is balanced by a huge corpus of literature of all varieties and forms except the drama. How deeply it penetrated Islamic society remains obscure, though it is clear that educated people expected to be able to write verses and could enjoy critically the performances of singers and bards. Schools were widespread; the Islamic world was probably highly literate by comparison, for example, with medieval Europe. Higher learning, more closely religious in so far as it

Astronomy was a fundamental part of Islamic science. This 16th-century Ottoman illustration shows astronomers using various instruments to study the celestial bodies.

Arab science: the writing of Maimonides

"You have to know that as far as the spheres of Venus and Mercury are concerned there are differences of opinion amongst the ancient mathematicians, of whether they are found above the Sun or below, for the position of these two spheres has not been proved. These ancient people were of the opinion that the two spheres of Venus and Mercury are above the Sun. ... Then came Ptolemy, who asserted that they were underneath, alleging that it is more natural to place the Sun in the centre, with three planets above and three below. Later on, there appeared men in El-Andalus ... who proved that Venus and Mercury were found above the Sun, in accordance with the principles of Ptolemy.

"Ibn Aflah of Seville ... wrote a famous book on the subject; and later the eminent philosopher Abu Bakr ibn Al-Sa'ig ... examined the question and formulated some arguments ... by virtue of which the theory that Venus and Mercury lie above the Sun was revoked. But the argument that Abu Bakr cites suggests the improbability and not the impossiblity. So, as it turns out, all the ancient mathematicians placed Venus and Mercury above the Sun, and for this reason they counted five spheres: the Moon, which is undoubtedly near us; the Sun, which has to be above it; the other five planets; the fixed stars and the sphere which surrounds it all, in which there are no stars."

An extract from Chapter 9 of the *Guide for the Perplexed* by Maimonides (1135–1204).

This 13th-century Turkish illustration shows two astrologers in the "House of Wisdom".

was institutionalized in the mosques or special schools of religious teachers, is more difficult to assess. How much, therefore, the potentially divisive and stimulating effect of ideas drawn from other cultures was felt below the level of the leading Islamic thinkers and scientists is hard to say, but potentially many seeds of a questioning and self-critical culture were there from the eighth century onwards. They seem not to have ripened.

SCIENCE AND MATHEMATICS

Judged by its greatest men, Arabic culture was at its height in the East in the ninth and tenth centuries and in Spain in the eleventh and twelfth. Although Arab history and geography are both very impressive, its greatest triumphs were scientific and mathematical; we still employ the "arabic" numerals which made possible written calculations with far

The prohibition of the use of the human form in Islamic art led to the development of a decorative style based on calligraphy and abstract or floral shapes, as shown in this detail of the mosaics in Córdoba's Great Mosque.

greater simplicity than did Roman numeration and which were set out by an Arab arithmetician (though in origin they were Indian). This transmission function of Arabic culture was always important and characteristic but must not obscure its originality. The name of the greatest of Islamic astronomers, Al-Khwarizmi, indicates Persian Zoroastrian origins; it expresses the way in which Arabic culture was a confluence of tributaries. His astronomical tables, none the less, were an Arabic achievement, an expression of the synthesis made possible by Arab empire.

The translation of Arabic works into Latin in the later Middle Ages, and the huge repute enjoyed by Arab thinkers in Europe, testify to the quality of this culture. Of the works of Al-Kindi, one of the greatest of Arab philosophers, more survive in Latin than in Arabic, while Dante paid Ibn-Sina (Avicenna in Europe) and Averroës the compliment of placing them in limbo (together with Saladin, the Arab hero of the crusading epoch) when he allocated great men to their fate after death in his poem, and they were the only men of the Common Era whom he treated thus. The Persian practitioners who dominated Arabic medical studies wrote works which remained for centuries standard textbooks of western training. European languages are still marked by Arabic words which indicate the special importance of Arabic study in certain areas: "zero", "cipher", "almanac", "algebra" and "alchemy" are among them. The survival of a technical vocabulary of commerce, too – tariff, *douane*, magazine – is a reminder of the superiority of Arab commercial technique; the Arab merchants taught Christians how to keep accounts.

Strikingly, this cultural traffic with Europe was almost entirely one way. Only one Latin text, it appears, was ever translated into Arabic during the Middle Ages, at a time when Arabic scholars were passionately interested in the cultural legacies of Greece, Persia and India. A single fragment of paper bearing a few German words with their Arabic equivalents is the only evidence from eight hundred years of Islamic Spain of any interest in western languages outside the peninsula. The Arabs regarded the civilization of the cold lands of the north as a meagre, unsophisticated affair, as no doubt it was. But Byzantium impressed them.

ARCHITECTURE

An Arabic tradition in visual art founded under the Umayyads also flourished under the Abbasids, but it was narrower in its scope than Islamic science. Islam came to forbid the making of likenesses of the human form or face; this was not scrupulously enforced, but it long inhibited the appearance of naturalistic painting or sculpture. Of course, it did not restrict architects. Their art developed very far within a style whose essentials had appeared at the end of the seventh century; it was at once in debt to the past and unique to Islam. The impression produced upon the Arabs by Christian building in Syria was the catalyst; from it they learnt, but they sought to surpass it, for believers should, they were sure, have places of worship better and more beautiful than the Christians' churches. Moreover, a distinctive architectural style could visibly serve as a separating force in the non-Muslim world which surrounded the first Arab conquerors of Egypt and Syria.

The Arabs borrowed Roman techniques and Hellenistic ideas of internal space, but what resulted was distinctive. The oldest architectural monument of Islam is the Dome of the Rock built at Jerusalem in 691. Stylistically, it is a landmark in architectural history, the first Islamic building with a dome. It appears to have been built as a monument to victory over Jewish and Christian belief, but unlike the congregational mosques which were to be the great buildings of the next three centuries, the Dome of the Rock was a shrine glorifying and sheltering one of the most sacred places of Jew and Muslim alike; men believed that on the hill-top it covered Abraham had offered up his son Isaac in sacrifice and that from it Muhammad was taken up into heaven.

Soon afterwards came the Umayyad mosque at Damascus, the greatest of the classical mosques of a new tradition. As so often in this new Arab world, it embodied much of the past; a Christian basilica (which had itself replaced a temple of Jupiter) formerly stood on its site, and it was itself decorated with Byzantine mosaics. Its novelty was that it established a design derived from the pattern of worship initiated by the Prophet in his house at Medina; its essential was the *mihrab*, or alcove in the wall of the place of worship, which indicated the direction of Mecca.

Built on the site of the Christian basilica of St Vicente, the Great Mosque in Córdoba is one of the most magnificent edifices of western Islamic architecture. The mosque was begun by Abd-ar-Rahman I in 785 and was enlarged over the following two centuries. Its most striking feature is this prayer hall – a forest of marble columns supporting superimposed arches.

THE ARTS

Architecture and sculpture, like literature, continued to flourish and to draw upon elements culled from traditions all over the Near East and Asia. Potters strove to achieve the style and finish of the Chinese porcelain which came to them down the Silk Road. The

The Dome of the Rock in Jerusalem was built during the caliphate of Abd-al-Malik (685–705). He had several motives for its construction. Rebellions in Medina and Mecca, where an "anti-caliph" had ruled for a decade, had prevented Muslims from making their pilgrimages to those cities' holy sites. A great Islamic shrine in Jerusalem, which was firmly in the control of the Damascus-based caliphate, could provide a secure focus for Muslim pilgrims. Abd-al-Malik also knew that, by attracting Muslim pilgrims as well as Jews and Christians, Jerusalem would grow in status and wealth. Perhaps most importantly, however, the caliph wanted to create an Islamic building that would rival any Christian church in splendour and size.

performing arts were less cultivated and seem to have drawn little on other traditions, whether Mediterranean or Indian. There was no Arab theatre, though the storyteller, the poet, the singer and the dancer were esteemed. Arabic musical art is commemorated in European languages through the names of lute, guitar, and rebec; its achievements, too, have been seen as among the greatest of Arabic culture, though they were to remain less accessible to Western sensibility than those of the plastic and visual arts.

Many of the greatest names of this civilization were writing and teaching when its political framework was already in decay, even visibly collapsing. In part this was a matter of the gradual displacement of Arabs within the caliphate's élites, but the Abbasids in their turn lost control of their empire, first of the peripheral provinces and then of Iraq itself. As an international force they peaked early; in 782 an Arab army appeared for the last time before Constantinople. They were never to get so far again. Haroun-al-Raschid might have been treated with respect by Charlemagne but the first signs of an eventually irresistible tendency to fragmentation were already there in his day.

UMAYYAD SPAIN

In Spain, in 756, an Umayyad prince, who had not accepted the fate of his house, had proclaimed himself emir, or governor, of Córdoba, the first breach of its unity. Others were to follow in Morocco and Tunisia. Meanwhile, El-Andalus acquired its own caliph only in the tenth century (until then its rulers remained emirs) but long before that was independent de facto. This did not mean that Umayyad Spain was untroubled. Islam had never conquered the whole peninsula and the Franks recovered the northeast by the tenth century.

El-Andalus: Islamic Spain

In 711 the Muslim armies' invasion of Visigoth Spain marked the beginning of one of the most important eras in the history of the Iberian peninsula. For almost eight centuries, until 1492, El-Andalus (the name given to Muslim Spain by Arab writers) was a cultural centre of great importance – its Islamic inheritance has had a deep and lasting effect on the Western world. Muslim Spain enjoyed a level of urban civilization unequalled in the Christian world. It boasted a society with an original and enriching culture that was both polyglot (Arabic, Romance and Hebrew) and tolerant (the Muslims granted Christians and Jews the freedom to practise their religions openly).

During the early years of Muslim rule El-Andalus was the most westerly province of the Islamic Abbasid Empire and was governed by a representative sent from Damascus. This period came to an end in 756 when Abd-ar-Rahman I, an Umayyad prince who was the only member of his family to have avoided assassination, set up the Umayyad emirate of Córdoba, with the aim of turning the city into the new Damascus. In 929 the Córdoba caliphate was established: Abd-ar-Rahman III was declared caliph and prince of the faithful, making way for the era of greatest political, economic and cultural development that El-Andalus was ever to see.

However, the caliphs' authority slowly diminished. During the 11th century, increasing political fragmentation led to the foundation of "cantons", also known as *taifas*, which were governed by various local dynasties. On two occasions these *taifas* came under the control of African warriors – the Almoravids and the Almohads – who attempted to impose a fierce, centralized power. Their failure resulted in the reduction of Muslim Spain to the small kingdom of Granada, which survived until 1492, when it was conquered by the Catholic Monarchs, thus putting an end to a unique period in the history of Spain.

An aerial view of the ruins of the 10th-century caliphate palace of Madinat-al-Zahara, in the province of Córdoba.

There were by then Christian kingdoms in northern Iberia and they were always willing to help stir the pot of dissidence within Arab Spain where a fairly tolerant policy towards Christians did not end the danger of revolt.

Yet El-Andalus prospered as the centre of a Muslim world. The Umayyads developed their sea-power and contemplated imperial expansion not towards the north, at the expense of the Christians, but into Africa, at the expense of Muslim powers, even negotiating for alliance with Byzantium in the process. It was not until the eleventh and twelfth centuries, when the caliphate of Córdoba was in decline, that Spain's Islamic civilization reached its greatest beauty and maturity in a golden age of creativity which rivalled that of Abbasid Baghdad. This left behind great monuments as well as producing great learning and philosophy. The seven hundred mosques of tenth-century Córdoba numbered among them one which can still be thought the most beautiful building in the world, the Mezquita. Arab Spain was of enormous importance to Europe, a door to the learning and science of the East, but one through which were also to pass more material goods as well: through it Christendom received knowledge of agricultural and irrigation techniques, oranges and lemons, sugar. As for Spain itself, the Arab stamp went very deep, as many students of the later, Christian, Spain have pointed out, and can still be observed in language, manners and art.

THE DECLINE OF THE CALIPHS' POWER

Another important breakaway within the Arab world came when the Fatimids from Tunisia set up their own caliph and moved their capital to Cairo in 973. The Fatimids were Shi'ites and maintained their government of Egypt until a new Arab invasion destroyed it in the twelfth century. Less conspicuous examples could be found elsewhere in the Abbasid dominions as local governors began to term themselves emir and sultan. The power base of the caliphs narrowed more and more rapidly; they were unable to reverse the trend. Civil wars among the sons of Haroun led to a loss of support by the religious teachers and the devout. Bureaucratic corruption and embezzlement alienated the subject populations. Recourse to tax-farming as a way around these ills only created new examples of oppression. The army was increasingly recruited from foreign mercenaries and slaves; even by the death of Haroun's successor it was virtually Turkish. Thus, barbarians were

Islamic Iberia

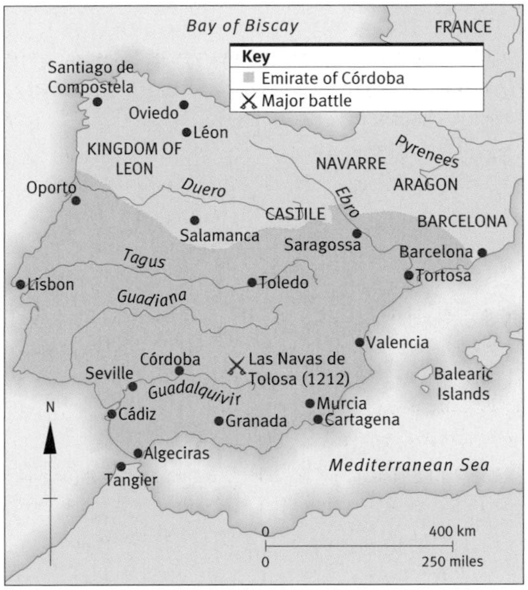

In the middle of the 11th century there were two quite distinct political entities in the Iberian peninsula. One – the Christians – continually advancing towards the south, was comprised of the kingdoms of Castile and León, Navarre, Aragon and the county of Barcelona. The other – the Muslim world – suffered a gradual break-up, until the arrival in 1086 of the Almoravids, who halted the Christian "conquest".

This chess piece dates from the Fatimid era. The Fatimids, who were named after Muhammad's daughter Fatima, founded a new caliphate in Tunisia. In 973 they moved the capital to Cairo, making the city one of the period's most important economic centres. Unlike other believers, who maintained that Allah was the one and only god, the Fatimids deified Fatima and her husband Ali.

A Muslim man may cast out his wife, and then wait three months for the dissolution of the marriage to be definitive. This 13th-century picture shows a *qadi* (judge) listening to a man whose wife is standing behind him.

incorporated within the structure of the caliphates as had been the western barbarians within the Roman Empire. As time went by they took on a praetorian look and increasingly dominated the caliphs. And all the time popular opposition was exploited by the Shi'ites and other mystical sects. Meanwhile, the former economic prosperity waned. The wealth of Arab merchants was not to crystallize in a vigorous civic life such as that of the late medieval West.

Abbasid rule effectively ended in 946 when a Persian general and his men deposed a caliph and installed a new one. Theoretically, the line of Abbasids continued, but in fact the change was revolutionary; the new Buwayhid dynasty lived henceforth in Persia. Arab Islam had fragmented; the unity of the Near East was once more at an end. No empire remained to resist the centuries of invasion which followed, although it was not until 1258 that the last Abbasid was slaughtered by the Mongols. Before that, Islamic unity had another revival in response to the crusades, but the great days of Islamic empire were over.

"The Women" from the Koran

"O believers, it is not lawful for you
to inherit women against their will;
neither debar them, that you may go off
with part of what you have given them,
except when they commit a flagrant indecency.
Consort with them honourably; or if
you are averse to them, it is possible
you may be averse to a thing, and God see
in it much good.
And if you desire to exchange a wife
in place of another, and you have given
to one a hundredweight, take of it nothing.
What, will you take it by way of calumny
and manifest sin?
How shall you take it, when each of you has been
privily with the other, and they have taken from
you a solemn compact?
And do not marry women that your fathers
married, unless it be a thing of the past;
surely that is indecent and hateful, an evil way."

An extract from Book IV ("The Women") of the Koran, translated by Arthur J. Arberry.

THE ISLAMIC REVOLUTION

The peculiar nature of Islam meant that religious authority could not long be separated from political supremacy; the caliphate was eventually to pass to the Ottoman Turks, therefore, when they became the makers of Near Eastern history. They would carry the frontier of Islam still farther afield and once again deep into Europe. But their Arab predecessors' work was awe-inspiringly vast for all its ultimate collapse. They had destroyed both the old Roman Near East and Sassanid Persia, hemming Byzantium in to Anatolia. In the end, though, this would call Western Europeans back into the Levant. The Arabs had also implanted Islam ineradicably from Morocco to Afghanistan. Its coming was in many ways revolutionary. It kept women, for example, in an inferior position, but gave them legal rights over property not available to women in many European countries until the nineteenth century. Even the slave had rights and inside the community of the believers there were no castes nor inherited status. This revolution was rooted in a religion which – like that of the Jews – was not distinct from other sides of life, but embraced them all; no words exist in Islam to express the distinctions of sacred and profane, spiritual and temporal, which our own tradition takes for granted. Religion *is* society for the Muslims, and the unity this has provided has outlasted centuries of political division. It was a unity both of law and of a certain attitude; Islam is not a religion of miracles (though it claims some), but of practice and intellectual belief.

THE DISPERSION OF ISLAM WORLDWIDE

Besides having a great political, material and intellectual impact on Christendom, Islam also spread far beyond the world of Arab hegemony, to Central Asia in the tenth century, India between the eighth and eleventh, and in the eleventh beyond the Sudan and to the Niger. Between the twelfth and sixteenth centuries still more of Africa would become Muslim; Islam remains today the fastest-growing faith of that continent. Thanks to the conversion of Mongols in the thirteenth century, Islam would also reach China. In the fifteenth and sixteenth centuries it spread across the Indian Ocean to Malaya and Indonesia. Missionaries, migrants and merchants carried it with them, the Arabs above all, whether they moved in caravans into Africa or took

Islam beyond the Arabic world until 1800

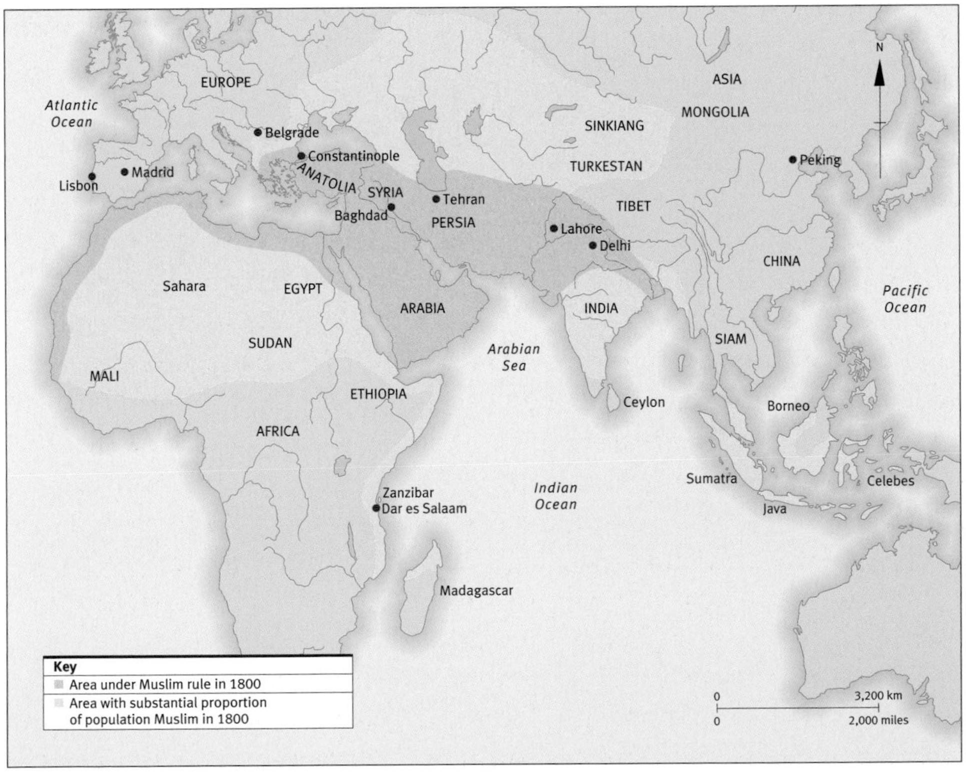

Over the centuries since the death of the prophet Muhammad, Islam has spread through most parts of the world. Regions in which the Islamic religion was already particularly well established in 1800 include the Middle East, a large part of Asia and much of northern Africa, as this map shows.

their dhows from the Persian Gulf and Red Sea to the Bay of Bengal. There would even be a last, final extension of the faith in southeastern Europe in the sixteenth and seventeenth centuries. It was a remarkable achievement for an idea at whose service there had been in the beginning no resources except those of a handful of Semitic tribes. But in spite of its majestic record no Arab state was ever again to provide unity for Islam after the tenth century. Even Arab unity was to remain only a dream, though one cherished still today.

The *mihrab* is a highly decorated arched niche oriented towards Mecca, indicating the direction in which worshippers must face when praying. It is usually situated in the centre of the main part of the mosque and was first seen in Islamic architecture in the mosque at Medina, which dates from the beginning of the 8th century. Decorated with beautiful mosaics, this example is from the Great Mosque in Córdoba, Spain.

3 BYZANTIUM AND ITS SPHERE

IN 1453, NINE HUNDRED YEARS after Justinian, Constantinople fell to an infidel army. "There has never been and there never will be a more dreadful happening," wrote one Greek scribe. It was indeed a great event. No one in the West was prepared; the whole Christian world was shocked. More than a state, Rome itself was at an end. The direct descent from the classical Mediterranean civilization had been snapped at last; if few saw this in quite so deep a perspective as the literary enthusiasts who detected in it retribution for the Greek sack of Troy, it was still the end of two thousand years' tradition. And if the pagan world of Hellenistic culture and ancient Greece were set aside, a thousand years of Christian empire at Byzantium itself was impressive enough for its passing to seem an earthquake.

The troops of the Ottoman sultan Mehmet II, who is depicted in this portrait, took Constantinople by storm on 29 May 1453. The last Byzantine emperor, Constantine XI, died defending his capital. This event marked the end of the Eastern Roman Empire.

This is one of those subjects where it helps to know the end of the story before beginning it. Even in their decline Byzantine prestige and traditions had amazed strangers who felt through them the weight of an imperial past. To the end its emperors were *augusti* and its citizens called themselves "Romans". For centuries, St Sophia had been the greatest of Christian churches, the Orthodox religion it enshrined needing to make fewer and fewer concessions to religious pluralism as previously troublesome provinces were swallowed by the Muslims. Though in retrospect it is easy to see the inevitability of decline and fall, this was not how the people who lived under it saw the Eastern Empire. They knew, consciously or unconsciously, that it had great powers of evolution. It was a great conservative *tour de force* which had survived many extremities and its archaic style was almost to the end able to cloak important changes.

THE IMPERIAL OFFICE

A THOUSAND YEARS brought great upheavals in both East and West; history played upon Byzantium, modifying some elements in its heritage, stressing others, obliterating others, so that the empire was in the end very different from Justinian's while never becoming wholly distinct from it. There is no clear dividing line between antiquity and Byzantium. The centre of gravity of the

In this 6th-century mosaic from the church of St Vitale in Ravenna, the empress Theodora is depicted with her entourage. Theodora's head is encircled by a nimbus – a pagan solar symbol adapted to serve the purposes of Byzantine imperial ambition.

empire had begun to shift eastwards before Constantine and when his city became the seat of world empire it was the inheritor of the pretensions of Rome. The office of the emperors showed particularly sharply how evolution and conservatism could combine. Until 800 there was no formal challenge to the theory that the emperor was the secular ruler of all humanity. When a Western ruler was hailed as an "emperor" in Rome that year, the uniqueness of the imperial purple of Byzantium was challenged, whatever might be thought and said in the East about the exact status of the new régime. Yet Byzantium continued to cherish the fantasy of universal empire; there would be emperors right to the end and their office was one of awe-inspiring grandeur. Still theoretically chosen by Senate, army and people, they had none the less an absolute authority. While the realities of his accession might determine for any particular emperor the actual extent of his power – and

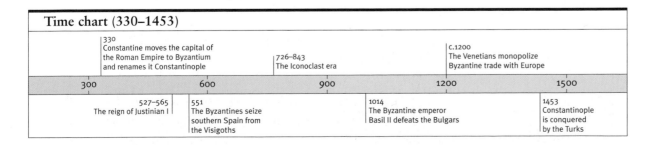

Time chart (330–1453)

- 330 Constantine moves the capital of the Roman Empire to Byzantium and renames it Constantinople
- 527–565 The reign of Justinian I
- 551 The Byzantines seize southern Spain from the Visigoths
- 726–843 The Iconoclast era
- 1014 The Byzantine emperor Basil II defeats the Bulgars
- c.1200 The Venetians monopolize Byzantine trade with Europe
- 1453 Constantinople is conquered by the Turks

300 600 900 1200 1500

The Byzantine emperors, unlike their Western counterparts, had absolute political and religious power – they saw themselves as God's representatives on earth. This is clearly illustrated in this mosaic from the church of St Sophia (now a mosque) in Constantinople (now Istanbul): the figure on the left represents the emperor Justinian, who is holding a model of a church in his hands, while the figure on the right is that of the emperor Constantine holding a model of a city – no doubt symbolizing Constantinople, which he founded.

sometimes the dynastic succession broke under the strains – he was *autocrat* as a Western emperor never was. Respect for legal principle and the vested interests of bureaucracy might muffle the emperor's will in action, but it was always supreme in theory. The heads of the great departments of state were responsible to no one but him. This authority explains the intensity with which Byzantine politics focused at the imperial court, for it was there, and not through corporate and representative institutions such as evolved slowly in the West, that authority could be influenced.

RELIGION AND EMPERORS

Autocracy had its harsh side. The *curiosi* or secret police informers who swarmed through the empire were not there for nothing. But the nature of the imperial office also laid obligations on the emperor. Crowned by the Patriarch of Constantinople, the emperor had the enormous authority, but also the responsibilities, of God's representative upon earth. The line between lay and ecclesiastical was always blurred in the East where there was nothing like the Western opposition of Church and State as a continuing challenge to unchecked power. Yet in the Byzantine scheme of things there was a continuing pressure upon God's vice-regent to act appropriately, to show *philanthropia*, a love of humanity, in his acts. The purpose of the autocratic power was the preservation of the human race and of the conduits by which it drew the water of life – orthodoxy and the Church. Appropriately most of the early Christian emperors were canonized – just as pagan emperors had been deified. Other traditions than the Christian also affected the office, as this suggested. Byzantine emperors were to receive the ritual prostrations of oriental tradition and the images of them which look down from their mosaics show their heads surrounded by the nimbus in which the last pre-Christian emperors were depicted, for it was part of the cult of the sun god. (Some representations of Sassanid rulers have it, too.) It was, none the less, above all as a Christian ruler that the emperor justified his authority.

ORTHODOX TRADITION

The imperial office itself thus embodied much of the Christian heritage of Byzantium. That heritage also marked the Eastern Empire off sharply from the West at many other levels. There were, in the first place, the ecclesiastical peculiarities of what came to be called the Orthodox Church. Islam, for example, was sometimes seen by the Eastern clergy less as a pagan religion than a heresy. Other differences lay in the Orthodox view of the relationship of clergy to society; the coalescence of spiritual and lay was important at many levels below the throne. One symbol of it was the retention of a married clergy; the Orthodox priest, for all his presumed holiness, was never to be quite the man apart his Western and Catholic colleague became. This suggests the great role of the Orthodox Church as a cementing force in society down to modern times. Above all, no sacerdotal authority as great as that of the papacy would

Byzantium – the great empire of the East

By the early 4th century, the Romans were desperate to ensure the protection of their eastern border against Slav and Persian attack. This was one of the factors that motivated Constantine to transfer the capital of the Eastern half of the Roman Empire to the small city of Byzantium, which the emperor officially named Constantinople in the year 330. As the capital of the Eastern Roman Empire, Constantinople was to become the only power that could claim the title of Roman Empire after the collapse of the West in 476. The most important of the early Byzantine emperors was Justinian I (527–565), who reconquered the western Mediterranean basin, built the magnificent church of St Sophia in Constantinople and published the legal code that took his name.

The beginning of the end for Byzantium came in 1204 when the crusaders conquered Constantinople. The empire was lost in 1453, conquered by the Ottoman Turks, although the Greek Orthodox Trebizond Empire, the last bastion of Byzantium, survived until 1461.

Justinian I is depicted in this mosaic in St Vitale, Ravenna.

emerge. The focus of authority was the emperor, whose office and responsibility towered above the equally ranked bishops. Of course, so far as social regulation went, this did not mean that Orthodoxy was more tolerant than the Church of the medieval West. Bad times were always liable to be interpreted as evidence that the emperor had not been doing his Christian duty – which included the harrying of such familiar scapegoats as Jews, heretics and homosexuals.

EAST AND WEST GROW APART

Distinction from the West was in part a product of political history, of the gradual loosening of contact after the division of the empires, in part a matter of an original distinction of style. The Catholic and Orthodox traditions were on divergent courses from early times, even if at first the divergence was only slight. At an early date Latin Christianity was somewhat estranged by the concessions the Greeks had to make to Syrian and Egyptian practice. Yet such concessions had also kept alive a certain polycentrism within Christendom. When Jerusalem, Antioch and Alexandria, the other three great patriarchates of the East, fell into Arab hands, the polarization of Rome and Constantinople was accentuated. Gradually, the Christian world was ceasing to be bilingual; a Latin West came to face a Greek East. It was at the beginning of the seventh century that Latin finally ceased to be the official language of the army and of justice, the two departments where it had longest resisted Greek. That the bureaucracy was Greek-speaking was to be very important. When the Eastern Church failed among Muslims, it opened a new missionary field and won much ground among the pagans to the north. Eventually, south-eastern Europe and Russia were to owe their

evangelizing to Constantinople. The outcome – among many other things – was that the Slav peoples would take from their teachers not only a written language or script based on Greek, but many of their most fundamental political ideas. And because the West was Catholic, its relations with the Slav world were sometimes hostile, so that the Slav peoples came to view the Western half of Christendom with deep reservations. This lay far in the future and takes us further afield than we need to go for the present.

The distinctiveness of the Eastern Christian tradition could be illustrated in

Constantinople's cathedral of St Sophia is probably the most impressive surviving example of Byzantine architecture. Its design is attributed to Anthemius of Tralles and Isidore of Miletus and work on its construction began in 532 by order of the emperor Justinian I. St Sophia was consecrated in 537. On the night of 28–29 May 1453 – the last night of Byzantium – a final Christian service was held in the great cathedral, attended by a congregation of thousands. Four days later, having converted the building into a mosque, the Turkish conquerors held the first Muslim service there. The four minarets seen in this picture are later Islamic additions.

many ways. Monasticism, for example, remained closer to its original forms in the East and the importance of the holy man has always been greater there than in the more hierarchically aware Roman Church. The Greeks, too, seem to have been more disputatious than the Latins; the Hellenistic background of the early Church had always favoured speculation and the Eastern Churches were open to oriental trends, always susceptible to the pressures of many traditional influences. Yet this did not prevent the imposition of dogmatic solutions to religious quarrels.

THEOLOGICAL DISPUTES

Some religious quarrels were about issues which now seem trivial or even meaningless. Inevitably, a secular age such as our own finds even the greatest of them difficult to fathom simply because we lack a sense of the mental world lying behind them. It requires an effort to recall that behind the exquisite definitions and logic-chopping of the theologians lay a concern of appalling importance, nothing less than that humanity should be saved from damnation. A further obstacle to understanding arises for the diametrically opposed reason that theological differences in Eastern Christianity often provided symbols and debating forms for questions about politics and society, about the relationship of national and cultural groups to authority, much as hair-splitting about the secular theology of Marxist-Leninism was to mask practical differences between twentieth-century communists. There is more to these questions than appears at first sight and much of it affected world history just as powerfully as the movements of armies or even peoples. The slow divergence of the two main Christian traditions is of enormous importance; it may not have originated in any sense in theological division, but theological disputes propelled divergent traditions yet further apart. They created circumstances which make it more and more difficult to envisage an alternative course of events.

The image of Christ Pantocrator was common in the iconography of Byzantine coins such as this one.

THE ISSUE OF MONOPHYSITISM

One episode provides an outstanding example, the debate on Monophysitism, a doctrine which divided Christian theologians from about the middle of the fifth century. The significance of the theological issue is at first sight obscure to our post-religious age. It originated in an assertion that Christ's nature while on earth was single; it was wholly divine, instead of dual (that is, both divine and human), as had generally been taught in the early Church. The delicious subtleties of the long debates which this view provoked must, perhaps regrettably, be bypassed here. It is sufficient only to notice that there was an important non-theological setting of the uproar of Aphthartodocetists, Corrupticolists and Theopaschitists (to name a few of the contesting schools). One element in it was the slow crystallization of three Monophysite Churches separated from Eastern Orthodoxy and Roman Catholicism. These were the Coptic Church of Egypt and Ethiopia, and the Syrian Jacobite and the Armenian Churches; they became, in a sense, national churches in their countries. It was in an endeavour to reconcile such groups and consolidate the unity of the empire in the face of first the Persian and then the Arab threat that the emperors were drawn into theological dispute; there was more to it, that is to say, than the special responsibility of the office first revealed by Constantine's presiding at the Council of Nicaea. The emperor Heraclius, for example, did his best in the early seventh century to produce a compromise formula to reconcile the disputants over Monophysitism. It took the form of a new theological definition soon called Monothelitism, and on it, for a time, agreement seemed likely, though it was in the end condemned as Monophysitism under a new name.

Meanwhile, the issue had pushed East and West still further apart in practice. Though, ironically, the final theological outcome was agreement in 681, Monophysitism had produced a forty-year schism between Latins and Greeks as early as the end of the fifth century. This was healed, but then came the further trouble under Heraclius. The empire had to leave Italy to its own devices when threatened by the Arab onslaught but both pope and emperor were now anxious to show a common front. This partly explains the pope's endorsement of Monothelitism (on which Heraclius had asked his view so as to quieten the theological misgivings of the Patriarch of

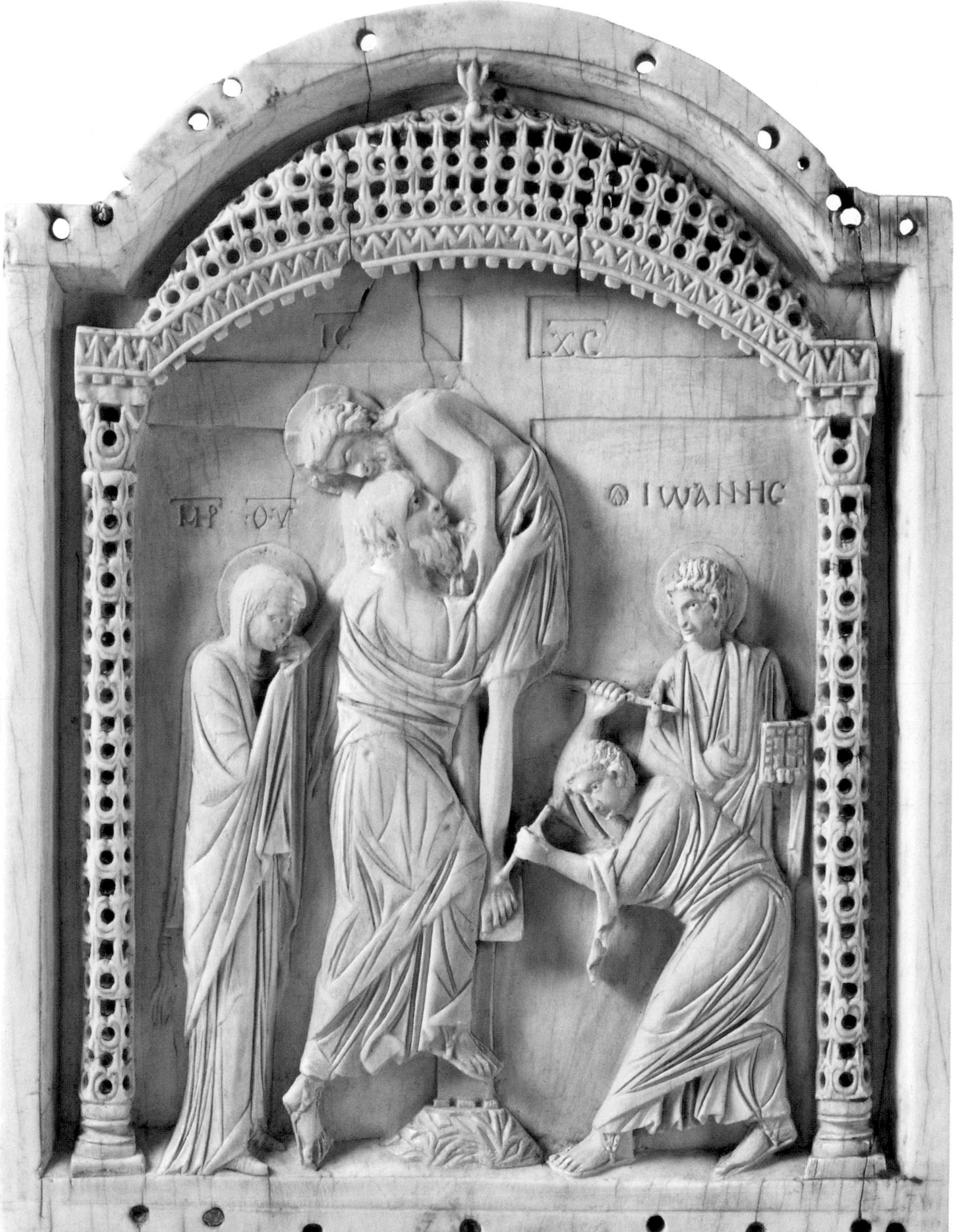

Unlike Nestorianism and Arianism, in which the human nature of Christ is of foremost importance, the Monophysitic doctrine emphasizes the divine nature of Christ. Monophysitism had many followers in Egypt within the early Coptic Church. This Monophysitic marble plaque shows Christ being taken down from the cross.

Jerusalem). Pope Honorius, successor of Gregory the Great, supported Heraclius and so enraged the anti-Monophysites that almost half a century later he achieved the distinction (unusual among popes) of being condemned by an ecumenical council at which even the Western representatives at the council joined in the decision. At a crucial moment of danger Honorius had done much damage. The sympathies of many Eastern churchmen in the early seventh century had been alienated still further from Rome by his imprudent action.

In the many naval battles they fought against the Arabs, the Byzantines deployed a highly effective secret weapon. Known as "Greek fire" (a compound of petroleum, saltpetre, quicklime and sulphur), it was a substance that ignited on impact and could be sprayed or shot in projectiles at enemy vessels, as depicted in this 11th-century manuscript illustration.

BYZANTIUM AND ASIA

The Byzantine inheritance was not only imperial and Christian. It also owed debts to Asia. These were not merely a matter of the direct contacts with alien civilizations symbolized by the arrival of Chinese merchandise along the Silk Road, but also of the complex cultural inheritance of the Hellenistic East. Naturally, Byzantium preserved the prejudice which confused the idea of "barbarians" with that of peoples who did not speak Greek, and many of its intellectual leaders felt they stood in the tradition of Hellas. Yet the Hellas of which they spoke was one from which the world had long been cut off except through the channels of the Hellenistic East. When we look at that cultural region it is hard to be sure how deep Greek roots went there and how much nourishment they owed to Asiatic sources. The Greek language, for example, seems in Asia Minor to have been used mainly by the few who were city-dwellers. Another sign comes from the imperial bureaucracy and leading families, which reveal more and more Asian names as the centuries go by. Asia was bound to count for more after the losses of territory the empire suffered in the fifth and sixth centuries, for these pinned it increasingly into only a strip of mainland Europe around the capital. Then the Arabs hemmed it in to Asia Minor, bounded in the north by the Caucasus and in the south by the Taurus. On the edges of this, too, ran a border always permeable to Muslim culture. The people who lived on it naturally lived in a sort of marcher world, but sometimes there are indications of deeper external influence than this upon Byzantium. The greatest of all the Byzantine ecclesiastical disputes, that over iconoclasm, had its parallels almost contemporaneously within Islam.

MEDIEVAL BYZANTIUM

The most characteristic features of a complicated inheritance were set in the seventh and eighth centuries: an autocratic tradition of government, the Roman myth, the guardianship of Eastern Christianity and practical confinement to the East. There had by then begun to emerge from the late Roman Empire the medieval state sketched under Justinian. Yet of these crucial centuries we know little. Some say that no adequate history of Byzantium in that era can be written, so poor are the sources and so skimpy the present state of archaeological knowledge. Yet at the start of this disturbed period the empire's assets are clear enough. It had at its disposal a great accumulation of diplomatic and bureaucratic skills, a military tradition and enormous prestige. Once its commitments could be reduced in proportion, its potential tax resources were considerable and so were its reserves of manpower. Asia Minor was a recruiting ground which relieved the Eastern Empire of the need to rely upon Germanic barbarians as had been necessary in the West. It had a notable war-making technology; the "Greek fire", which was its secret weapon, was used powerfully against ships which might attack the capital. The situation of Constantinople, too, was a military asset. Its great walls, built in the fifth century, made it hard to attack by land without heavy weapons that were unlikely to be available to barbarians; at sea the fleet could prevent a landing.

What was less secure in the long run was the social basis of the empire. It was always to be difficult to maintain the smallholding peasantry and prevent powerful provincial landlords from encroaching on their properties. The law courts would not always protect the small man. He, too, was under economic pressure from the steady expansion of church estates. These forces could not easily be offset by the imperial practice of making land grants to smallholders on condition that they supplied military service. But this was a problem whose dimensions were only to be revealed with the passage of centuries; the short-term prospects gave the emperors of the seventh and eighth centuries quite enough to think about.

Umayyad Arabs laid siege to the city walls of Constantinople between 674 and 678. This illustration shows the Persian attack on the Byzantine capital.

To create mosaics, small cubes of glass or stone, known as *tesserae*, were set into a plaster surface. It was in the Byzantine Empire, mainly during the 10th and 11th centuries, that mosaic decoration reached the height of technical and artistic perfection. The famous "Entourage of Virgins" is one of a number of mosaics that embellish the church of St Apollinare the New in Ravenna.

THE PROBLEMS OF EMPIRE

The emperors' resources were over-extended. In 600 the empire still included the North African coast, Egypt, the Levant, Syria, Asia Minor, the far coast of the Black Sea beyond Trebizond, the Crimean coast and that from Byzantium up to the mouths of the Danube. In Europe there were Thessaly, Macedonia and the Adriatic coast, a belt of territory across central Italy, enclaves in the toe and heel of the peninsula, and finally the islands of Sicily, Corsica and Sardinia. Given the empire's potential enemies and the location of its resources, this was a strategist's nightmare. The story of the next two centuries was to be of the return again and again of waves of invaders. Persians, Avars, Arabs, Bulgars and Slavs tormented the main body of the empire, while in the West the territories won back by the generals of Justinian were almost all soon taken away again by Arabs and Lombards. Eventually, the West, too, was to reveal itself as a predator; that the Eastern Empire for centuries absorbed much of the punishment which might otherwise have fallen on the West would not save it. The result of this was that the Eastern Empire faced continual warfare. In Europe it meant fighting up to the very walls of Constantinople; in Asia it meant wearisome campaigning to dispute the marches of Asia Minor.

Such challenges from the outside world were offered to a state which, even at the beginning of the seventh century, already had only a very loose control over its domain and depended for much of its power on a penumbra of influence, diplomacy, Christianity and military prestige. Its relations to its neighbours might be seen in more than one way; what looks to a later eye like blackmail paid by every emperor from Justinian to Basil II to menacing barbarians was in the Roman

SCA PELAGIA
SCA EVFIMIA

This detail from an illustration in the 15th-century "Madrid Bible" represents a Jewish menorah (sacred candelabrum) housed in a Khazar tent. In spite of the Byzantines' attempts to convert them to Christianity, the Khazars turned to Judaism.

tradition bounty to subject allies and *foederati*. Its diversity of peoples and religions was masked by official ideology. Its Hellenization was often superficial. The reality was expressed in the willingness with which many of the Christian communities of Syria welcomed the Arab, as, later, many of those in Anatolia were to welcome the Turk. Here, religious persecution came home to roost. Moreover, Byzantium numbered no great power among her allies. In the troubled seventh and eighth centuries the most important friendly power was the Khanate of Khazaria, a huge, but loose, state founded by nomads who by 600 dominated the other peoples of the Don and Volga valleys. This established them across the Caucasus, the strategic land bridge which they thus barred to Persians and Arabs for two centuries. At its widest the Khazar state ran around the Black Sea coast to the Dniester and northwards to include the Upper Volga and Don. Byzantium made great efforts to keep the goodwill of the Khazars and seems to have tried, but failed, to convert them to Christianity. What happened exactly is a mystery, but the Khazar leaders, while tolerating Christianity and several other cults, were apparently converted to Judaism in about 740, possibly as a result of Jewish immigration from Persia after the Arab conquest and probably as a conscious act of diplomacy. As Jews they were not likely to be sucked into either the spiritual and political orbit of the Christian empire, or into that of the caliphs. Instead they enjoyed diplomatic relations and trade with both.

A SHRINKING EMPIRE

The first great hero of the Byzantine struggle for survival was Heraclius, who strove to balance the threats in Europe with alliances and concessions so that he could campaign vigorously against the Persians. Successful though he eventually was, the Persians had by then done appalling damage to the empire in the Levant and Asia Minor before their expulsion. They have been believed by some scholars to be the real destroyers of the Hellenistic world of great cities; the archaeology is mysterious still, but after Heraclius's victory there are signs that once-great cities lay in ruins, that some were reduced to little more than the acropolis which was their core and that population fell sharply. It was, then, on a structure much of which was already badly

The Byzantine Empire

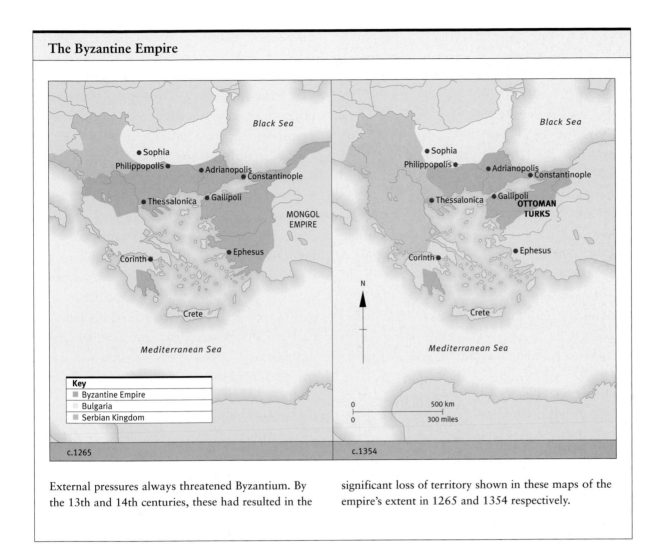

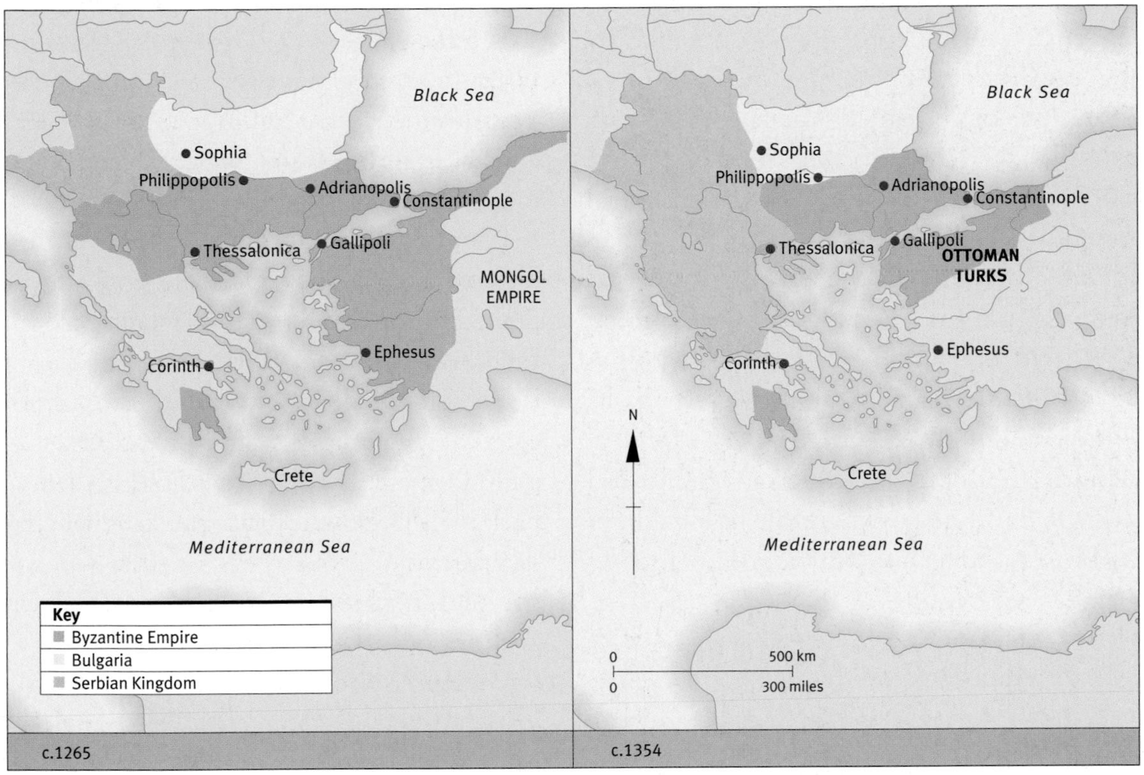

External pressures always threatened Byzantium. By the 13th and 14th centuries, these had resulted in the significant loss of territory shown in these maps of the empire's extent in 1265 and 1354 respectively.

shaken that the Arab onslaughts fell – and they were to continue for two centuries. Before Heraclius died in 641 virtually all his military achievements had been overturned. Some of the emperors of his line were men of ability, but they could do little more than fight doggedly against a tide flowing strongly against them.

In 643 Alexandria fell to the Arabs and that was the end of Greek rule in Egypt. Within a few years they had lost North Africa and Cyprus. Armenia, that old battleground, went in the next decade and finally the high-water mark of Arab success came with the five years of attacks on Constantinople (673–678); it may have been Greek fire that saved the capital from the Arab fleet. Before this, in spite of a personal visit by the emperor to Italy, no progress had been made in recovering the Italian and Sicilian lands taken by Arabs and Lombards. And so the century went on, with yet another menace appearing in its last quarter as Slavs pressed down into Macedonia and Thrace and another race, the Bulgars, themselves one day to be Slavicized, crossed the Danube.

THE ISAURIAN RECOVERY

The seventh century ended with a revolt in the army and the replacement of one emperor by another. All the symptoms suggested that the Eastern Empire would undergo the fate of

This miniature portrays Basil II (976–1025) as a triumphant emperor with defeated Bulgarian princes grovelling at his feet. During Basil's reign, the Byzantine Empire enjoyed a period of great wealth and power, following the conquest of Bulgaria in 1014 and victory over the Arabs.

the West, the imperial office becoming the prize of the soldiers. A succession of beastly or incompetent emperors at the beginning of the eighth century let the Bulgars come to the gates of Constantinople and finally brought about a second siege of the capital by the Arabs in 717. But this was a true turning-point, though it was not to be the last Arab appearance in the Bosphorus. In 717 there had already come to the throne one of the greatest Byzantine emperors, the Anatolian Leo III. He was a provincial official who had successfully resisted Arab attacks on his territory and who had come to the capital to defend it and force the emperor's abdication. His own elevation to the purple followed and was both popular and warmly welcomed by the clergy. This was the foundation of the Isaurian Dynasty, so-called from their place of origin; it was an indication of the way in which the élites of the Eastern Roman Empire were gradually transformed into those of Byzantium, an oriental monarchy.

The eighth century brought the beginning of a period of recovery, though with setbacks. Leo himself cleared Anatolia of the Arabs and his son pushed back the frontiers to those of Syria, Mesopotamia and Armenia. From this time, the frontiers with the caliphate had rather more stability than hitherto, although each campaigning season brought border raids and skirmishes. From this achievement – in part attributable, of course, to the relative decline in Arab power – opened out a new period of progress and expansion which lasted until the early eleventh century. In the West little could be done. Ravenna was lost and only a few toeholds remained in Italy and Sicily. But in the East the empire expanded again from the base of Thrace and Asia Minor, which was its heart. A chain of "themes", or administrative districts, was established along the fringe of the Balkan peninsula; apart from them, the empire had no foothold there for two centuries. In the tenth century Cyprus, Crete and Antioch were all recovered. Byzantine forces at one time crossed the Euphrates and the struggle for northern Syria and the Taurus continued. The position in Georgia and Armenia was improved.

BULGAROCTONOS AND THE LATE ISAURIAN DYNASTY

In eastern Europe the Bulgar threat was finally contained after reaching its peak at the beginning of the tenth century, when the Bulgars had already been converted to Christianity. Basil II, who has gone down in history as *Bulgaroctonos*, the "slayer of Bulgars", finally destroyed their power in a great battle in 1014 which he followed up by blinding 15,000 of his prisoners and sending them home to encourage their countrymen. The Bulgar ruler is said to have died of shock. Within a few years Bulgaria was a Byzantine province, though it was never to be successfully absorbed. Shortly afterwards the last conquests of Byzantium were made when Armenia passed under its rule.

The overall story of these centuries is therefore one of advance and recovery. It was also one of the great periods of Byzantine culture. Politically there was an improvement in domestic affairs in that, by and large, the dynastic principle was observed between 820 and 1025. The Isaurian Dynasty had ended badly in an empress who was followed by another series of short reigns and irregular successions until Michael II, the founder of the Phrygian Dynasty, succeeded a murdered emperor in 820. His house was replaced in 867 by the Macedonian Dynasty, under whom Byzantium reached its summit of success. Where there were minorities the device of a co-emperor was adopted to preserve the dynastic principle.

The consecration of icons

Ever since the Byzantine era, priests in Orthodox churches around the world have conducted the same ceremony for the consecration of icons. During the ceremony, the priest, after singing the *Hymn to the Holy Trinity* and the *Kyrie Eleison*, recites:

"Lord, God, you have created Man in your image, which has been blemished by the fall, but by the incarnation of your Christ made Man, you have restored it and thus have restored your saints to their original dignity. Worshipping them, we worship your image and your likeness, and through them, we glorify your Archetype."

ICONOCLASM

One major source of division and difficulty for the empire in the earlier part of this period was, as so often before, religion. This plagued the empire and held back its recovery because it was so often tangled with political and local issues. The outstanding example was a controversy which embittered feelings for over a century, the campaign of the Iconoclasts.

The Iconoclast Byzantine emperor Constantine V (741 and 743–775), who is depicted on this coin, launched a bloody campaign of persecution against the Iconophiles.

The depicting of the saints, the Blessed Virgin and God Himself had come to be one of the great devices of Orthodox Christianity for focusing devotion and teaching. In late antiquity such images, or icons, had a place in the West too, but to this day they occupy a special place in Orthodox churches, where they are displayed in shrines and on special screens to be venerated and contemplated by the believer. They are much more than mere decoration, for their arrangement conveys the teachings of the Church and (as one authority has said) provides "a point of meeting between heaven and earth", where the faithful amid the icons can feel surrounded by the whole invisible Church, by the departed, the saints and angels, and Christ and His mother themselves. It is hardly surprising that something concentrating religious emotion so intensely should have led in paint or mosaic to some of the highest achievements of Byzantine (and, later, Slav) art.

Icons had become prominent in Eastern churches by the sixth century. There followed two centuries of respect for them and in many places a growing popular devotion to them, but then their use came to be questioned. Interestingly, this happened just after the caliphate had mounted a campaign against

This 11th- or 12th-century plaque is probably part of an ornate cover for a religious manuscript. It is dedicated to St Michael and the materials used in its decoration include enamels, precious stones, pearls and gold.

the use of images in Islam, but it cannot be inferred that the Iconoclasts took their ideas from Muslims. The critics of the icons claimed that they were idols, perverting the worship due to God towards the creations of human beings. They demanded their destruction or expunging and set to work with a will with whitewash, brush and hammer.

THE PERSECUTION OF THE ICONOPHILES

Leo III favoured the Iconoclasts. There is still much that is mysterious about the reason why imperial authority was thrown behind them, but Leo acted on the advice of bishops and other ecclesiastes, and Arab invasions and volcanic eruptions were no doubt held to indicate God's disfavour. In 730, therefore, an edict forbade the use of images in public worship. A persecution of those who resisted followed; enforcement was always more marked at Constantinople than in the provinces. The movement reached its peak under Constantine V and was ratified by a council of bishops in 754. Persecution became fiercer, and there were martyrs, particularly among monks, who usually defended icons more vigorously than did the secular clergy. But Iconoclasm was always dependent on imperial support; there were ebbings and flowings in the next century. Under Leo IV and Irene, his widow, persecution was relaxed and the "Iconophiles" (lovers of icons) recovered ground, though this was followed by renewed persecution. Only in 843, on the first Sunday of Lent, a day still celebrated as a feast of Orthodoxy in the Eastern Church, were the icons finally restored.

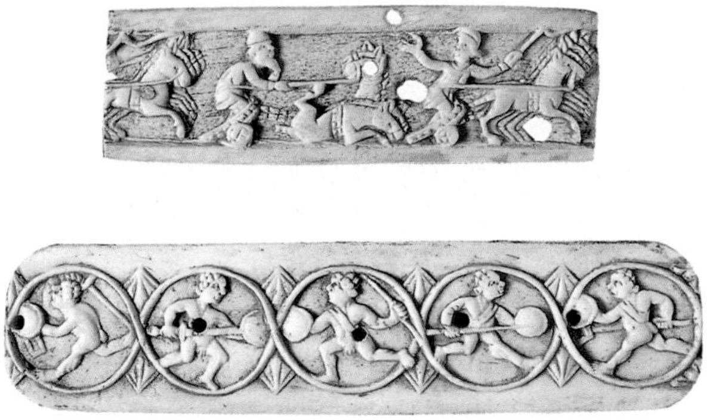

These plaques depict soldiers from the Byzantine army, an institution in which Iconoclasm was held in high regard.

THE SOURCES OF ICONOCLASM

What was the meaning of this strange episode? There was a practical justification, in that the conversion of Jews and Muslims was said to be made more difficult by Christian respect for images, but this does not take us very far. Once again, a religious dispute cannot be separated from factors external to religion, but the ultimate explanation probably lies in a sense of religious precaution, and given the passion often shown in theological controversy in the

The two figures who most clearly personified the disagreement over image worship are depicted in this manuscript illustration: the Iconoclast emperor Leo V (813–820) is shown receiving the anti-Iconoclast patriarch Nicephorus I at court, while on the right an icon is being coated in whitewash.

During the 7th and 8th centuries, some icons, such as the above image of the Virgin and Child, were created using the encaustic technique. The use of a combination of colour pigment and molten wax meant that the icon had to be painted while the mixture was still warm.

Eastern Empire, it is easy to understand how the debate became embittered. No question of art or artistic merit arose: Byzantium was not like that. What was at stake was the feeling of reformers that the Greeks were falling into idolatry in the extremity of their (relatively recent) devotion to icons and that the Arab disasters were the first rumblings of God's thunder; a pious king, as in the Israel of the Old Testament, could yet save the people from the consequences of sin by breaking the idols. This was easier in that the process suited the mentalities of a faith which felt itself at bay. It was notable that Iconoclasm was particularly strong in the army. Another fact which is suggestive is that icons had often represented local saints and holy men; they were replaced by the uniting, simplifying symbols of eucharist and cross, and this says something about a new, monolithic quality in Byzantine religion and society from the eighth century onwards. Finally, Iconoclasm was also in part an angry response to a tide which had long flowed in favour of the monks who gave such prominence to icons in their teaching. As well as a prudent step towards placating an angry God, therefore, Iconoclasm represented a reaction of centralized authority, that of emperor and bishops, against local pieties, the independence of cities and monasteries, and the cults of holy men.

THE INCREASING DIVISIONS BETWEEN EAST AND WEST

Iconoclasm offended many in the Western Church but it showed more clearly than anything yet how far Orthodoxy now was from Latin Christianity. The Western Church had been moving, too; as Latin culture was taken over by the Germanic peoples, it drifted away in spirit from the churches of the Greek East. The Iconoclast synod of bishops had been an affront to the papacy, which had already condemned Leo's supporters. Rome viewed with alarm the emperor's pretensions to act in spiritual matters. Thus Iconoclasm drove deeper the division between the two halves of Christendom. Cultural differentiation had now spread very far – not surprisingly when it could take two months by sea to go from Byzantium to Italy and by land a wedge of Slav peoples soon stood between the two languages.

The Iconoclast movement

In Byzantium, representations of Christ, the Virgin, certain saints or scenes from the Bible were used as subjects for icons. Iconoclasm, the movement for the prohibition of this type of image, had a significant impact on the principal trends of European thought. According to some specialists, the movement's origins can be found in Muslim Iconoclasm, which spread through the army and the Byzantine clergy based in Asia Minor, although other historians of Byzantium believe that the prohibition of images was part of an anti-monastic movement or an attempt to strengthen the emperor's absolute power.

Iconoclasm was at its most ferocious and pervasive during the reign of Constantine V, when hundreds of religious icons and mosaics were destroyed. However, the Iconophiles never gave up the fight to keep their holy images and by the 9th century icons were once more at the centre of Byzantine religious life.

Long before Iconoclasm reached its height, Byzantine artists used emblematic designs in religious mosaics, often incorporating images of plants and animals as Christian symbols alongside portraits of saints and emperors, as in the decoration of the 6th-century church of St Vitale in Ravenna. This style became the only one acceptable during the Iconoclastic period. After the ravages of Iconoclasm, artists showed a greater tendency than before to concentrate on imperial and holy figures.

This Byzantine icon represents the archangels Michael and Gabriel and dates from the 10th or 11th century – the early post-Iconoclastic period.

Contact between East and West could not be altogether extinguished at the official level. But here, too, history created new divisions, notably when the Pope crowned a Frankish king "emperor" in 800. This was a challenge to the Byzantine claim to be the legatee of Rome. Distinctions within the Western world did not much matter in Constantinople; the

Byzantine art and architecture

During the 7th and 8th centuries, wars against the Muslims and Slavs were a constant drain on the resources of the Byzantine Empire. This in turn meant that Byzantine art suffered a serious decline, which worsened during the Iconoclastic period.

When the Macedonian Dynasty came to power, all the fine arts underwent a renaissance, principally due to the patronage of Basil II (976–1025). Architecture also enjoyed a period of great splendour. The origins of the architectural style that was to become characteristic of this era can be seen in the monasteries of Mount Athos, particularly in the beauty of the Grand Lavra Monastery.

During the 13th century, Byzantine artists produced a large number of outstanding mosaics and paintings – the mosaics of Pammakaristos (Constantinople) and the paintings of Mistra form part of the legacy of this brilliant creative period. Another centre of artistic interest was the Greek city of Trebizond, where the dome of St Eugene's church is considered by many to be of great note.

Byzantine art had a remarkable influence on cultures far beyond the empire's political borders. Byzantium's distinct style left a lasting mark in states such as Armenia, Georgia and Serbia, as this detail from a 13th-century fresco in a Belgrade church demonstrates.

Byzantine officials identified a challenger in the Frankish realm and thereafter indiscriminately called all westerners "Franks", a usage which was to spread as far as China. The two states failed to cooperate against the Arab and offended one another's susceptibilities. The Roman coronation may itself have been in part a response to the assumption of the title of emperor at Constantinople by a woman, Irene, an unattractive mother who had blinded her own son. But the Frankish title was only briefly recognized in Byzantium; later emperors in the West were regarded there only as kings. Italy divided the two Christian empires, too, for the remaining Byzantine lands there came to be threatened by Frank and Saxon as much as they had ever been by Lombards. In the tenth century

Byzantine coins often depict two or more people. The emperors Heraclius, Constantine and Heraclonas appear on this *solidus*.

the manipulation of the papacy by Saxon emperors made matters worse.

THE SPLENDOUR OF BYZANTIUM

Of course the two Christian worlds could not altogether lose touch. One German emperor of the tenth century had a Byzantine bride and German art of the tenth century was much influenced by Byzantine themes and techniques. But it was just the difference of two cultural worlds that made such contacts fruitful, and, as the centuries went by, the difference became more and more palpable. The old aristocratic families of Byzantium were replaced gradually by others drawn from Anatolian and Armenian stocks. Above all, there was the unique splendour and complication of the life of the imperial city itself, where religious and secular worlds seemed completely to interpenetrate one another. The calendar of the Christian year was inseparable from that of the court; together they set the rhythms of an immense theatrical spectacle in which the rituals of both Church and State displayed to the people the majesty of the empire. There was some secular art, but the art constantly before the people's eyes was overwhelmingly religious. Even in the worst times it had a continuing vigour, expressing the greatness and omnipresence of God, whose vice-regent was the emperor. Ritualism sustained the rigid etiquette of the court about which there proliferated the characteristic evils of intrigue and conspiracy. The public appearance of even the Christian emperor could be like that of the deity in a mystery cult, preceded by the raising of several curtains from behind which he dramatically emerged. This was the apex of an astonishing civilization, which showed half the world for perhaps half a millennium what true empire was. When a mission of pagan Russians came to Byzantium in the tenth century to examine its version of the Christian religion, as they had examined others, they could only report that what they had seen in Hagia Sophia had amazed them. "There God dwells among men," they said.

This clasp belonged to a lady from the Visigoth aristocracy and was found in a tomb in Tureñuelo in Spain. The fact that the clasp is clearly Eastern in style – it appears to have Syrian influences – has caused speculation about its origin. One theory is that the lady may have brought the jewel back to the Iberian peninsula as a souvenir of a trip to the holy sites of Jerusalem.

THE BYZANTINE ECONOMY

What was happening at the base of the empire is not easy to say. There are strong indications that population fell in the seventh and eighth centuries; this may be connected both with the disruptions of war and with plague. At the same time there was little new building in the provincial cities and the circulation of the coinage diminished. All these things suggest a flagging economy, as does more and more interference with it by the state. Imperial officials sought to ensure that its primary needs would be met by arranging for direct levies of produce, setting up special organs to feed the cities and by organizing artisans and tradesmen bureaucratically in guilds and corporations. Only one city of the empire retained its economic importance throughout, and that was the capital itself, where the spectacle of Byzantium was played out at its height. Trade never dried up altogether in the empire and right down to the twelfth century there was still an important transit commerce in luxury goods from Asia to the West; its position alone guaranteed Byzantium a great commercial role and stimulation for the artisan industries which

Representing St Gregory, this miniature is one of the most important surviving examples of Byzantine art. It was commissioned by the emperor Basil I the Macedonian (867–886).

The style of this buckle, which originates from the Byzantine city of Trebizond, was much copied in workshops throughout western Europe.

provided other luxuries to the West. Finally, there is evidence across the whole period of the continuing growth in power and wealth of the great landowners. The peasants were more and more tied to their estates and the later years of the empire see something like the appearance of important local economic units based on the big landholdings.

INTERNAL POWER STRUGGLES

The economy was able to support both the magnificence of Byzantine civilization at its height and the military effort of recovery under the ninth-century emperors. Two centuries later an unfavourable conjuncture once more overtaxed the empire's strength and opened a long era of decline. It began with a fresh burst of internal and personal troubles. Two empresses and a number of short-lived emperors of poor quality weakened control at the centre. The rivalries of two important groups within the Byzantine ruling class got out of hand; an aristocratic party at court whose roots lay in the provinces was entangled in struggles with the permanent officials, the higher bureaucracy. In part this reflected also a struggle of a military with an intellectual élite. Unfortunately, the result was that the army and navy were starved of the funds they needed by the civil servants and were left incapable of dealing with new problems.

During most of the 11th century, the Normans and the Arabs were a constant source of problems for the Byzantine Empire. This manuscript illustration depicts a battle between Byzantine and Arab armies.

NEW ENEMIES

At one end of the empire new problems were provided by the last barbarian migrants of the West, the Christian Normans, now moving into south Italy and Sicily. In Asia Minor they arose from Turkish pressure. Already in the eleventh century a Turkish sultanate of Rum was established inside imperial territory (hence its name, for "Rum" signified "Rome"), where Abbasid control had slipped into the hands of local chieftains. After a shattering defeat by the Turks at Manzikert in 1071 Asia Minor was virtually lost, and this was a terrible blow to Byzantine fiscal and manpower resources. The caliphates with which the emperors had learnt to live were giving way to fiercer enemies. Within the empire there was a succession of Bulgarian revolts in the eleventh and twelfth centuries and there spread widely in that province the most powerful of the dissenting movements of medieval Orthodoxy, the Bogomil heresy, a popular movement drawing upon hatred of the Greek higher clergy and their Byzantinizing ways.

A new dynasty, the Comneni, once again rallied the empire and managed to hold the line for another century (1081–1185). They pushed back the Normans from Greece and they fought off a new nomadic threat from

Emperor John II Comnenus (1118–1143) is portrayed in this mosaic in St Sophia in Constantinople. The Comneni Dynasty's policies concentrated on finding the solutions to three major problems: the control of the Slav peoples in the Balkans, the expulsion of the Normans and the halting of the onslaught of the Seljuk Turks.

south Russia, the Pechenegs, but could not crack the Bulgars or win back Asia Minor and had to make important concessions to do what they did. Some concessions were to their own magnates; some were to allies who would in turn prove dangerous.

THE GROWTH OF VENETIAN POWER

To one of Byzantium's allies, the Republic of Venice, once a satellite of the empire, concessions were especially ominous, for her whole

The growth of Venice as a Mediterranean power

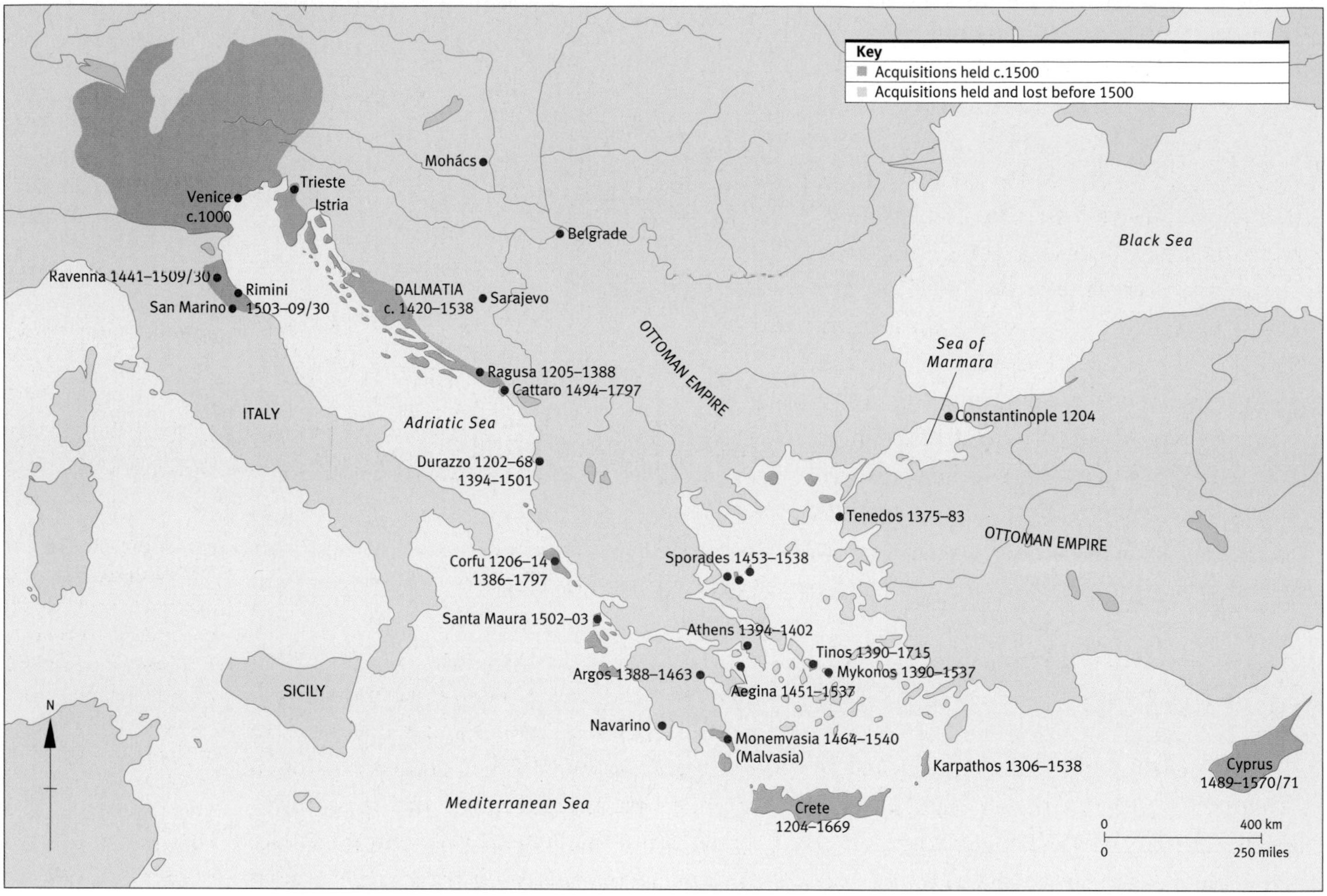

The city of Venice was formally a Byzantine dependency and run by a *magister militum* appointed by Constantinople. From the 11th century, however, it was virtually independent and came to almost monopolize trade between East and West. In 1082 the emperor Alexius I Comnenus (1081–1118) conceded considerable commercial privileges to Venice. Together with the freedom of trade with Germany, this led to the city's enormous growth. After taking part in the Fourth Crusade and the storming of Constantinople in 1204, the Venetians were also able to take control of most of the Greek islands, as well as part of Thrace and the Peloponnese.

Venice's greatest rival was Genoa. The two cities fought for the domination of eastern Mediterranean trade for most of the 13th and 14th centuries, including the "War of Chioggia" (1378–1381), which ended in defeat for Genoa. The commercial supremacy of Venice was now undeniable: for three centuries the Venetian ducat was the standard monetary unit for the eastern Mediterranean world.

raison d'être had come to be aggrandizement in the eastern Mediterranean. She was the major beneficiary of Europe's trade with the East and at an early time had developed a specially favoured position. In return for help against the Normans in the eleventh century, the Venetians were given the right to trade freely throughout the empire; they were to be treated as subjects of the emperor, not as foreigners. Venetian naval power grew rapidly and, as the Byzantine fleet fell into decline, it was more and more dominant. In 1123 the Venetians destroyed the Egyptian fleet and thereafter were uncontrollable by their former suzerain. One war was fought with Byzantium, but Venice did better from supporting the empire against the Normans and from the pickings of the crusades. Upon these successes followed commercial concessions and territorial gains and the former mattered most; Venice, it may be said, was built on the decline of the empire, which was an economic host of huge potential for the Adriatic parasite – in the middle of the twelfth century there were said to be 10,000 Venetians living at Constantinople, so important was their trade there. By 1204 the Cyclades, many of the other Aegean islands, and much of the Black Sea coasts belonged to them: hundreds of communities were to be added to those and Venetianized in the next three centuries. The first commercial and maritime empire since ancient Athens had been created.

THE CRUSADERS' THREAT TO THE BYZANTINE EMPIRE

The appearance of the Venetian challenge and the persistence of old ones would have been embarrassing enough for the Byzantine emperors had they not also faced new trouble at home. In the twelfth century revolt became more common. This was doubly dangerous when the West was entering upon enterprise in the East in the great and complex movement which is famous as the crusades. The Western view of the crusades need not detain us here; from Byzantium these irruptions from the West looked more and more like new barbarian invasions. In the twelfth century they left behind four crusading states in the former Byzantine Levant as a reminder that there was now another rival in the field in the Near East. When the Muslim forces rallied under Saladin, and there was a resurgence of Bulgarian independence at the end of the twelfth century, the great days of Byzantium were finally over.

St Mark's in Venice, the domes of which are visible here behind the city's waterfront buildings, was inspired by the Byzantine churches of St Irene in Constantinople and St John in Ephesus. Work on St Mark's began in 829. It is constructed in the shape of a Greek cross and is crowned by four Byzantine domes surrounding a larger dome.

THE "FRANKS" SACK CONSTANTINOPLE

The fatal blow came in 1204, when Constantinople was at last taken and sacked, but by Christians, not by the pagans who had threatened it so often. A Christian army which had gone east to fight the infidel in a fourth crusade was turned against the empire by the Venetians. It terrorized and pillaged the city (this was when the bronze horses of the Hippodrome were carried off to stand, as they did until lately, in front of St Mark's Cathedral in Venice), and enthroned a prostitute in the patriarch's seat in St Sophia. East and West could not have been more brutally distinguished; the sack, denounced by the pope, was to live in Orthodox memory as one of infamy. The "Franks", as the Greeks called them, all too evidently did not see Byzantium as a part of their civilization, nor, perhaps, as even a part of Christendom, for a schism had existed in effect for a century and a half. Though they were to abandon Constantinople and the emperors would be restored in 1261 the Franks would not again be cleared from the old Byzantine territories until a new conqueror

In 1204 the crusaders entered Constantinople and created the new Latin Empire of the East, which lasted until 1261. The event is portrayed in this painting by Delacroix, which dates from 1840.

came along, the Ottoman Turk. Meanwhile, the heart had gone out of Byzantium, though it had still two centuries in which to die. The immediate beneficiaries were the Venetians and Genoese to whose history the wealth and commerce of Byzantium was now annexed.

THE SLAVS

THE LEGACY OF BYZANTIUM – or a great part of it – was on the other hand already secured to the future, though not, perhaps, in a form in which the Eastern Roman would have felt much confidence or pride. It lay in the rooting of Orthodox Christianity among the Slav peoples. This was to have huge consequences, many of which we still live with. The Russian state and the other modern Slav nations would not have been incorporated into Europe and would not have been reckoned as part of it, if they had not been converted to Christianity in the first place.

Much of the story of how this happened is still obscure, and what is known about the Slavs before Christian times is even more debatable. Though the ground-plan of the Slav peoples of today was established at roughly the same time as that of western Europe, geography makes for confusion. Slav Europe covers a zone where nomadic invasions and the nearness of Asia still left things very fluid long after barbarian society had settled down in the west. Much of the central and southeastern European landmass

The political situation in western Europe during the 12th and 13th centuries

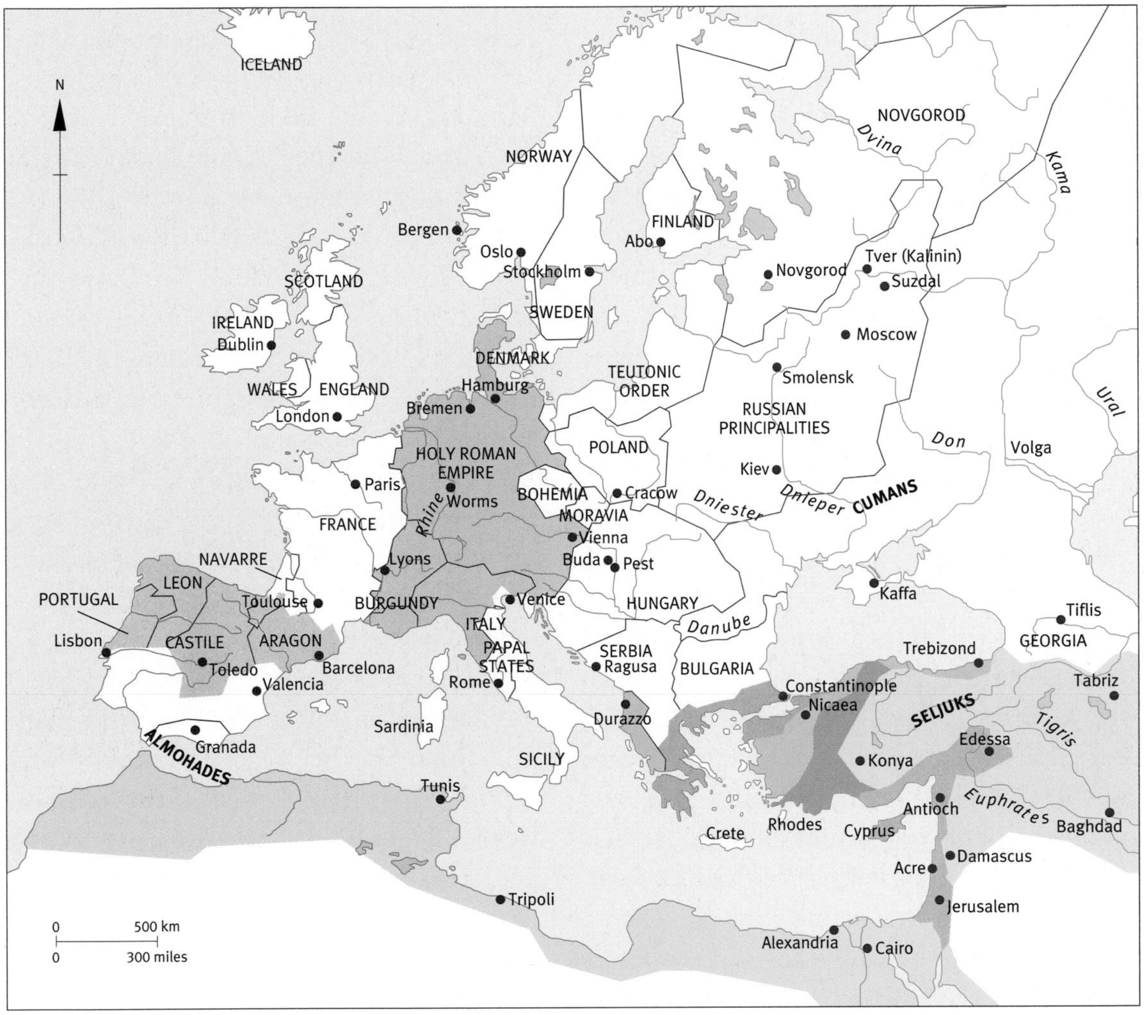

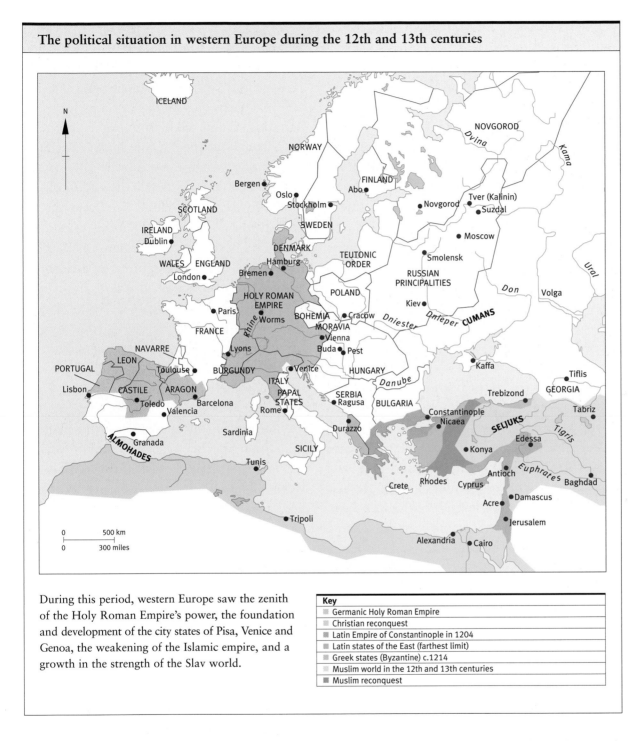

During this period, western Europe saw the zenith of the Holy Roman Empire's power, the foundation and development of the city states of Pisa, Venice and Genoa, the weakening of the Islamic empire, and a growth in the strength of the Slav world.

Key
- Germanic Holy Roman Empire
- Christian reconquest
- Latin Empire of Constantinople in 1204
- Latin states of the East (farthest limit)
- Greek states (Byzantine) c.1214
- Muslim world in the 12th and 13th centuries
- Muslim reconquest

is mountainous. There, river valleys channelled the distribution of stocks. Most of modern Poland and European Russia, on the other hand, is a vast plain. Though for a long time covered in forests, it provided neither obvious natural lodgements nor insuperable barriers to settlements. In its huge spaces, rights were disputed for many centuries. By the end of the process, at the beginning of the thirteenth century, there had emerged in the East a number of Slav peoples who would have independent historical futures. The pattern thus set has persisted down to our own day.

There had also come into existence a characteristic Slav civilization, though not all Slavs belonged wholly to it and in the end the peoples of Poland and modern Slovakia and the Czech Republic were to be more closely tied by culture to the West than to the East. The state structures of the Slav world would come and go, but two of them, those evolved by the Polish and Russian nations, proved particularly tenacious and capable of survival in organized form. They would have much to survive, for the Slav world was at times – notably in the thirteenth and twentieth centuries – under pressure as much from the West as from the East. Western aggressiveness is another reason why the Slavs retained a strong identity of their own.

SLAV ORIGINS

The story of the Slavs has been traced back at least as far as 2000 BCE when this ethnic group appears to have been established in the eastern Carpathians. For two thousand years they spread slowly both west and east, but especially to the east, into modern Russia. From the fifth to the seventh century CE Slavs from both the western and eastern groups began to move south into the Balkans. Perhaps their direction reflects the power of the Avars, the Asiatic people who, after the ebbing of the Hun invasions, lay like a great barrier across the Don, Dnieper and Dniester valleys, controlling south Russia as far as the Danube and courted by Byzantine diplomacy.

Throughout their whole history the Slavs have shown remarkable powers of survival. Harried in Russia by Scythians and Goths, in Poland by Avars and Huns, they none the less stuck to their lands and expanded them; they must have been tenacious agriculturists. Their early art shows a willingness to absorb the culture and techniques of others; they learnt from masters whom they outlasted. It was important, therefore, that in the seventh century there stood between them and the dynamic power of Islam a barrier of two peoples, the Khazars and the Bulgars. These strong peoples also helped to channel the gradual movement of Slavs into the Balkans and down to the Aegean. Later it was to run up the Adriatic coast and was to reach Moravia and central Europe, Croatia, Slovenia and Serbia. By the tenth century Slavs must have been numerically dominant throughout the Balkans.

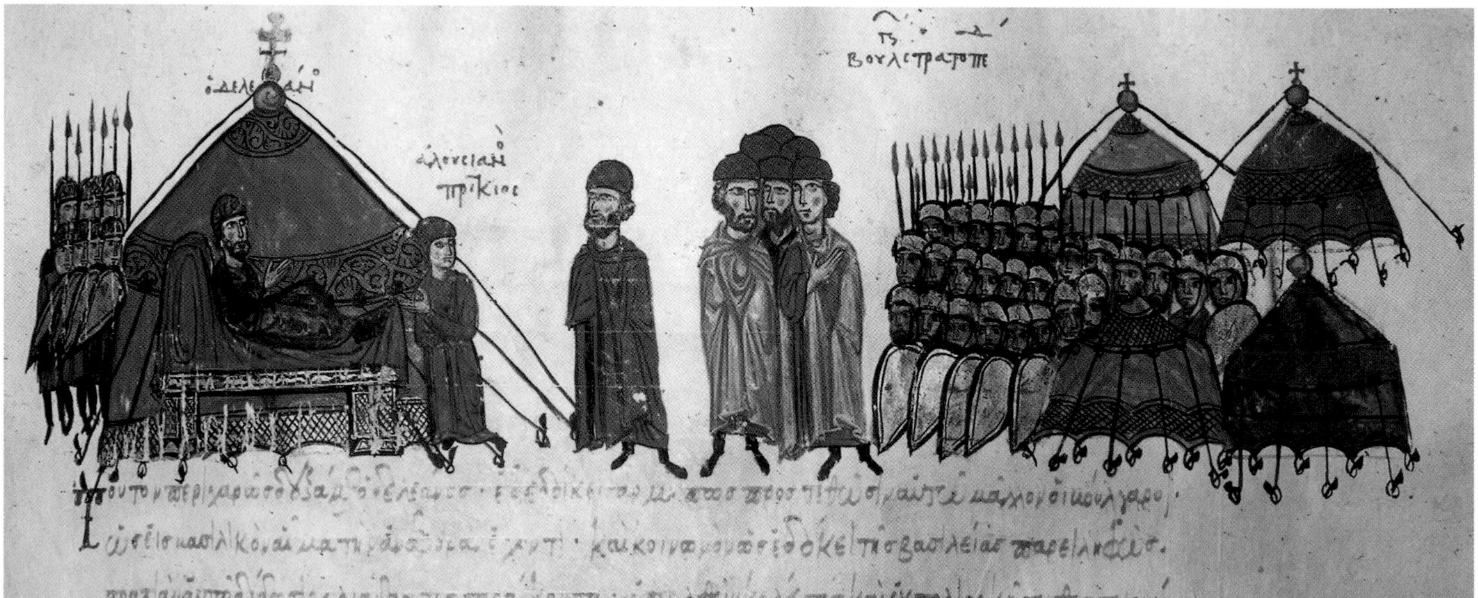

This illustration from an 11th-century historical manuscript portrays a scene from the Bulgar siege of Thessaloniki. Deleanos, the Bulgar leader, is about to receive one of his army commanders, while some of his soldiers watch from their tented encampment.

THE BULGARS

THE FIRST SLAV STATE to emerge was Bulgaria, though the Bulgars were not Slavs, but stemmed from tribes left behind by the Huns. Some of them gradually became Slavicized by intermarriage and contact with Slavs; these were the western Bulgars, who were established in the seventh century on the Danube. They cooperated with the Slav peoples in a series of great raids on Byzantium; in 559 they had penetrated the defences of Constantinople and camped in the suburbs. Like their allies, they were pagans. Byzantium exploited differences between Bulgar tribes and a ruler from one of them was baptized in Constantinople, the Emperor Heraclius standing godfather. He used the Byzantine alliance to drive out the Avars from what was to be Bulgaria. Gradually, the Bulgars were diluted by Slav blood and influence. When a Bulgar state finally appears at the end of the century we can regard it as Slav. In 716 Byzantium recognized its independence; now an alien body existed on territory long taken for granted as part of the empire. Though there were alliances, this was a thorn in the side of Byzantium which helped to cripple her attempts at recovery in the West. At the beginning of the ninth century the Bulgars killed an emperor in battle (and made a cup for their king from his skull); no emperor had died on campaign against the barbarians since 378.

THE BULGARS CONVERT TO CHRISTIANITY

A turning-point – though not the end of conflict – was reached when the Bulgars were converted to Christianity. After a brief period during which, significantly, he dallied with Rome and the possibility of playing it off against Constantinople, another Bulgarian prince accepted baptism in 865. There was opposition among his people, but from this time Bulgaria was Christian. Whatever diplomatic gain Byzantine statesmen may have hoped for, it was far from the end of their Bulgarian problem. None the less, it is a landmark, a momentous step in a great process, the Christianizing of the Slav peoples. It was also an indication of how this would happen: from the top downwards, by the conversion of their rulers.

The Bulgars could prove formidable enemies for Byzantium. Here, the skull of the Byzantine emperor Nicephorus I (802–811) – turned into a bowl or cup – is shown being offered to the Bulgar king Krum by his subjects.

THE CYRILLIC ALPHABET

What was at stake was a great prize, the nature of the future Slav civilization. Two great names dominate the beginning of its

The brothers Cyril and Methodius, who set out to Christianize the Slav territories during the 9th century, are represented in this fresco from the church of St Clement in Rome. The two saints are just visible kneeling before the figure of Christ, who is accompanied by angels and by saints Andrew and Clement.

shaping, those of the brothers St Cyril and St Methodius, priests still held in honour in the Orthodox communion. Cyril had earlier been on a mission to Khazaria and their work must be set in the overall context of the ideological diplomacy of Byzantium; Orthodox missionaries cannot neatly be distinguished from Byzantine diplomatic envoys, and these churchmen would have been hard put to recognize such a distinction. But they did much more than convert a dangerous neighbour. Cyril's name is commemorated still in the name of the Cyrillic alphabet which he devised. It was rapidly diffused through the Slav peoples, soon reaching Russia, and it made possible not only the radiation of Christianity but the crystallization of Slav culture. That culture was potentially open to other influences, for Byzantium was not its only neighbour, but Eastern Orthodoxy was in the end the deepest single influence upon it.

KIEV AND BYZANTIUM

From the Byzantine point of view a still more important conversion than that of the Bulgars was to follow, though not for more than a century. In 860 an expedition with 200 ships raided Byzantium. The citizens were terrified. They listened tremblingly in St Sophia to the prayers of the patriarch: "A people has crept down from the north ... the people is fierce and has no mercy, its voice is as the roaring sea ... a fierce and savage tribe ... destroying everything, sparing nothing." It might have been the voice of a Western monk invoking divine protection from the sinister longships of the Vikings, and understandably so, for Viking in essence these raiders were. But they were known to the Byzantines as Rus (or Rhos) and the raid marks the tiny beginnings of Russia's military power.

As yet, there was hardly anything that could be called a state behind it. Russia was still in the making. Its origins lay in an amalgam to which the Slav contribution was basic. The east Slavs had over the centuries dispersed over much of the upper reaches of the river valleys which flow down to the Black Sea. This was probably because of their agricultural practice, a primitive matter of cutting and burning, exhausting the soil in two or three years and then moving on. By the eighth century there were enough of them for there to be signs of relatively dense inhabitation, perhaps of something that could be called town life, on the hills near Kiev. They lived in tribes whose economic and social arrangements remain obscure, but this was the basis of future Russia. We do not know who their native rulers were, but they seem to have lived in the defended stockades which were the first towns, exacting tribute from the surrounding countryside.

VIKING RUSSIA

On to the Slav tribes in the Kiev hills fell the impact of Norsemen who became their overlords or sold them as slaves in the south. These Scandinavians combined trade, piracy and colonization, stimulated by land-hunger. They brought with them important commercial techniques, great skills in navigation and the management of their longships, formidable fighting power and, it seems, no women. Like

This ceramic icon from the Patleina Monastery, close to Preslav, is the oldest surviving Bulgarian icon. It dates from the end of the 9th century, around the time that Bulgaria adopted Christianity as its official religion.

their Viking cousins in the Humber and the Seine, they used the Russian rivers, much longer and deeper, to penetrate the country which was their prey. Some went right on; by 846 we hear of the "Varangians", as they were called, at Baghdad. One of their many sallies in the Black Sea was that to Constantinople in 860. They had to contend with the Khazars to the east and may have first established themselves in Kiev, one of the Khazar tributary districts, but Russian traditional history begins with their establishment in Novgorod, the Holmgardr of Nordic saga. Here, it was said, a prince called Rurik had established himself with his brothers in about 860. By the end of the century another Varangian prince had taken Kiev and transferred the capital of a new state to that town.

The appearance of a new power caused consternation but provoked action in Byzantium. Characteristically, its response to a new diplomatic problem was cast in ideological terms; there seems to have been an attempt to convert some Rus to Christianity and one ruler may have succumbed. But the Varangians retained their northern

The Vikings made their much-feared raids by boat, crossing oceans and navigating rivers for thousands of miles. This detail from a mythological scene, taken from an 8th-century Norse picture stone, shows men at sea and gives an impression of the form of the Viking longboat with its large, square sail.

paganism – their gods were Thor and Odin – while their Slav subjects, with whom they were increasingly mingled, had their own gods, possibly of very ancient Indo-European origins; in any case, these deities tended to merge as time passed. Soon there were renewed hostilities with Byzantium. Oleg, a prince of the early tenth century, again attacked Constantinople while the fleet was away. He is said to have brought his own ships ashore and to have put them on wheels to outflank the blocked entrance to the Golden

Viking mythology

The Vikings worshipped a pantheon of gods who had their origins in Indo-European culture. The most significant of these gods was Odin, the All-Father and Lord of Magic. He was associated with the underworld and the dead and his followers were called Berserks. Odin is sometimes portrayed accompanied by two ravens and mounted on an eight-legged horse known as Sleipnir.

Odin's son, Thor, although less powerful than his father, was more popular. He was usually portrayed carrying a hammer and travelling across the skies in a chariot pulled by two goats. Thor was known for his enormous appetite, his fearful temper and his extraordinary strength.

The Scandinavian god of fertility and plenty was Freyr, who was the son of Njörd, god of ships and the sea. Freyr and Njörd belonged to the Vanir – a group of gods associated with the land and water, symbolized by a golden boar and a ship. The Vanir were in direct opposition to the Aesir, the gods of the sky.

A 19th-century painting by M. Ewinge, in which the Nordic god Thor, whose name means "thunder", is depicted fighting giants.

Horn. However he did it, he was successful in extracting a highly favourable treaty from Byzantium in 911. This gave the Russians unusually favourable trading privileges and made clear the enormous importance of trade in the life of the new principality. Half a century or so after the legendary Rurik, it was a reality, a sort of river-federation centred on Kiev and linking the Baltic to the Black Sea. It was pagan, but when civilization and Christianity came to it, it would be because of the easy access to Byzantium which water gave to the young principality, which was first designated as Rus in 945. Its unity was still very loose. An incoherent structure was made even less rigid by the Vikings' adoption of a Slav principle which divided an inheritance. Rus princes tended to move around as rulers among the centres, of which Kiev and Novgorod were the main ones. Nevertheless, the family of Kiev became the most important.

CONFLICT AND DIPLOMACY

During the first half of the tenth century the relation between Byzantium and Kiev Rus was slowly ripening. Below the level of politics and trade a more fundamental re-orientation was taking place as Kiev relaxed its links with Scandinavia and looked more and more to the south. Varangian pressure seems to have been diminishing, and this may have had something to do with the success of Norsemen in the West, where one of their

Art in Christian Russia was strongly influenced by its Byzantine inheritance, as this 12th-century gold Gospel cover demonstrates.

rulers, Rollo, had been granted in 911 land later to be known as the duchy of Normandy. Yet it was a long time before there were closer ties between Kiev and Byzantium. One obstacle was the caution of Byzantine diplomacy, still quite as concerned in the early tenth century to fish in troubled waters by negotiating with the wild tribes of the Pechenegs as to placate the Rus whose territories they harried. The Pechenegs had already driven to the west the Magyar tribes, which had previously formed a buffer between the Rus and the Khazars, and more trouble could be expected there. Nor did Varangian raids come to an end, though there was something of a turning-point when the Rus fleet was driven off by Greek fire in 941. A treaty followed which significantly reduced the trading privileges granted thirty years earlier. But the reciprocity of interests was emerging more clearly as Khazaria declined and the Byzantines realized that Kiev might prove to be a valuable ally against Bulgaria. Signs of contact multiplied; Varangians appeared in the royal guard at Constantinople and Rus merchants came there more frequently. Some are believed to have been baptized.

EARLY RUSSIAN CHRISTIANITY

Christianity, though sometimes despising the merchant, has often followed the trader's wares. There was already a church in Kiev in 882, and it may have been there for foreign merchants. But nothing seems to have followed from this. There is little evidence of Russian Christianity until the middle of the next century. Then, in 945, the widow of a Kievan prince assumed the regency on behalf of his successor, her son. This was Olga. Her son was Sviatoslav, the first prince of Kiev to bear a Slav and not a Scandinavian name. In due course, Olga made a state visit to Constantinople. She may have been secretly baptized a Christian before this, but she was publicly and officially converted on this visit in 957, the emperor himself attending the ceremonies in St Sophia. Because of its diplomatic overtones it is difficult to be sure exactly how to understand this event. Olga had, after all, also sent to the West for a bishop, to see what Rome had to offer. Furthermore, there was no immediate practical sequel. Sviatoslav, who reigned from 962 to 972, turned out to be a militant pagan, like

This miniature from a 15th-century Russian manuscript, the Radziwill Chronicle, depicts a momentous event for Russia – the baptism of Vladimir. The ceremony took place in 988 in Cherson, a Byzantine outpost in the Crimea, and immediately preceded Vladimir's marriage to a Byzantine princess.

other Viking military aristocrats of his time. He clung to the gods of the north and was doubtless confirmed in his belief by his success in raiding Khazar lands. He did less well against the Bulgars, though, and was finally killed by the Pechenegs.

This was a crucial moment. Russia existed but was still Viking, poised between Eastern and Western Christianity. Islam had been held back at the crucial period by Khazaria, but Russia might have turned to the Latin West. Already the Slavs of Poland had been converted to Rome and German bishoprics had been pushed forward to the east in the Baltic coastlands and Bohemia. The separation, even hostility, of the two great Christian Churches was already a fact, and Russia was a great prize waiting for one of them.

VLADIMIR

In 980 a series of dynastic struggles ended with the victorious emergence of the prince who made Russia Christian, Vladimir. It seems possible that he had been brought up as a Christian, but at first he showed the ostentatious paganism which became a Viking warlord. Then he began to enquire of other religions. Legend says that he had their

During the 11th century, Kiev was one of the most important cities in Europe. The cathedral of St Sophia, the interior of which is shown here, was built in Kiev between 1018 and 1037. It was one of the first of many great Russian churches to have clear Byzantine features.

Several artistic schools for the production of icons were founded in Russia from the beginning of the 12th century. However, the most revered icon of all, the "Virgin of Vladimir" (so-called because it was housed in a church in the city of Vladimir for a while) was made in Constantinople in the early 12th century. It is one of the earliest examples of the exaltation of the Virgin Mary as the Mother of God and it inspired countless copies by Russian artists, who sought to recapture the tenderness of the image.

different merits debated before him; Russians treasure the story that Islam was rejected by him because it forbade alcoholic drink. A commission was sent to visit the Christian Churches. The Bulgarians, they reported, smelt. The Germans had nothing to offer. But Constantinople had won their hearts. There, they said in words often to be quoted, "we knew not whether we were in heaven or earth, for on earth there is no such vision nor beauty, and we do not know how to describe it; we know only that there God dwells among men". The choice was accordingly made. Around about 986–8 Vladimir accepted Orthodox Christianity for himself and his people.

It was a turning-point in Russian history and culture, as Orthodox churchmen have recognized ever since. "Then the darkness of idolatry began to leave us, and the dawn of orthodoxy arose," said one, eulogizing Vladimir a half-century or so later. Yet for all the zeal Vladimir showed in imposing baptism on his subjects (by physical force if necessary), it was not only enthusiasm which influenced him. There were diplomatic dimensions to the choice, too. Vladimir had been giving military help to the emperor and now he was promised a Byzantine princess as a bride. This was an unprecedented acknowledgment of the standing of a prince of Kiev. The emperor's sister was available because Byzantium needed the Rus alliance against the Bulgars. When things did not go smoothly, Vladimir put on the pressure by occupying Byzantine possessions in the Crimea. The marriage then took place. Kiev was worth a nuptial mass to Byzantium, though Vladimir's choice was decisive of much more than diplomacy. Two hundred years later his countrymen acknowledged this: Vladimir was canonized. He had made the single decision which, more than any other, determined Russia's future.

SOCIETY IN KIEV RUS

Probably tenth-century Kiev Rus had in many ways a richer culture than most of western Europe could offer. Its towns were important trading centres, channelling goods into the Near East where Russian furs and beeswax were prized. This commercial emphasis reflects another difference: in western Europe the self-contained, subsistence economy of the manor had emerged as the institution bearing the strain of the collapse of the classical economic world. Without the western manor, Russia would also be without the western feudal nobleman. A territorial aristocracy would take longer to emerge in Russia than in Catholic Europe; Russian nobles were for a long time to remain very much the companions and followers of a war-leader. Some of them opposed Christianity and paganism hung on in the north for decades. As in Bulgaria, the adoption of Christianity was a political act with internal as well as external dimensions and though the capital of a Christian principality, Kiev was not yet the centre of a Christian

Russia's conversion to Orthodox Christianity, at the end of the 10th century, resulted in an influx of artistic influences from Byzantium, although Russian Orthodox art and architecture also developed their own characteristics. The cathedral of St Sophia in Novgorod, pictured here, was built during the reign of Yaroslav the Wise (1019–1054).

nation. The monarchy had to assert itself against a conservative alliance of aristocracy and paganism. Lower down the social scale, in the towns, the new faith gradually took root, at first thanks to Bulgarian priests, who brought with them the liturgy of the south Slav Church and the Cyrillic alphabet which created Russian as a literary language. Ecclesiastically, the influence of Byzantium was strong and the Metropolitan of Kiev was usually appointed by the Patriarch of Constantinople.

From 1157, Vladimir became the centre of the Russian principality of Vladimir-Suzdal. It was later to become an important religious centre – the church of St Dmitri (shown here) was built there between 1193 and 1197.

THE APOGEE OF KIEV RUS

Kiev became famous for the magnificence of its churches; it was a great time of building in a style showing Greek influence. Unhappily, being of wood, few of them have survived. But the repute of this artistic primacy reflects Kiev's wealth. Its apogee came under Yaroslav "the Wise", when one western visitor thought it rivalled Constantinople. Russia was then culturally as open to the outside world as it was ever to be for centuries. In part this reflected Yaroslav's military and diplomatic standing. He exchanged diplomatic missions with Rome while Novgorod received the merchants of the German Hanse. Having himself married a Swedish princess, he found husbands for the womenfolk of his family in kings of Poland, France and Norway. A harried Anglo-Saxon royal family took refuge at his court. Links with western courts were never to be so close again. Culturally, too, the first fruits of the Byzantine implantation on Slav culture were being gathered. Educational foundation and legal creation reflected this. From this reign comes also one of the first great Russian works of literature, *The Primary Chronicle*, an interpretation of Russian history with a political purpose. Like much other early Christian history, it sought to provide a Christian and historical argument for what had already been done by Christian princes, in this case the unification of Russia under Kiev. It stressed the Slav heritage and offered an account of Russian history in Christian terms.

THE NORTHERN PRINCEDOMS

The weaknesses of Kiev Rus lay in the persistence of a rule of succession, which almost guaranteed division and dispute at the death of the major prince. Though one other

Kiev Rus

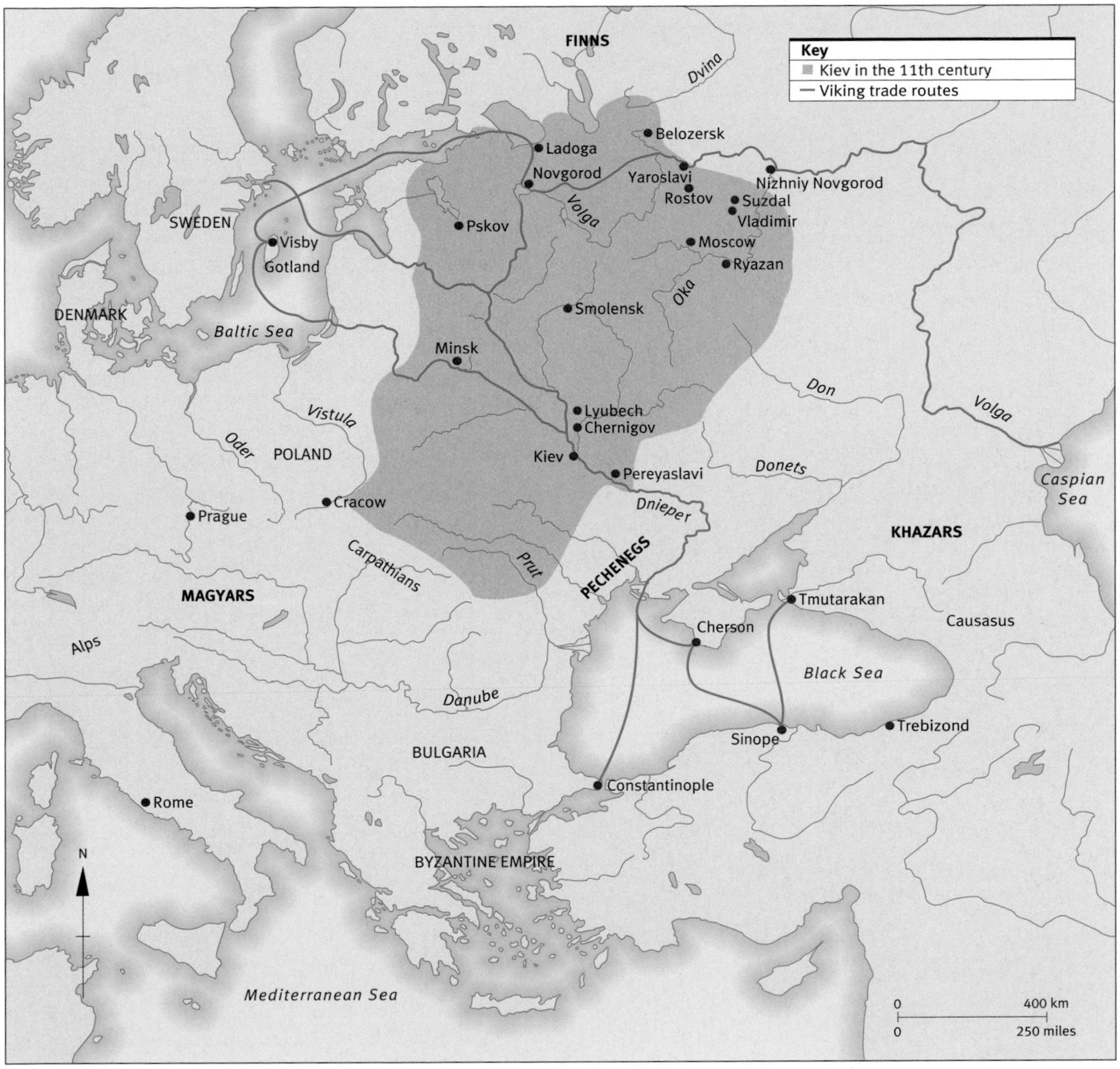

According to Russian legend, Rurik arrived in eastern Europe in around 860 and established himself in Novgorod as a "Varangian" prince (the name that the Russians and Greeks gave to the Vikings). During the 9th century, the name Rus or Rhos came to denote all the eastern Slavs. Rurik's descendants gradually became Slavicized, although they maintained some contact with their place of origin, Scandinavia, until the 12th century. The above map shows Viking trade routes into Russia and the territory that belonged to Kiev at the height of the principality's power in the 11th century.

eleventh-century prince managed to assert his authority and hold foreign enemies at bay, the Kiev supremacy waned after Yaroslav. The northern princedoms showed greater autonomy; Moscow and Novgorod were, eventually, the two most important among them, though another "grand" princedom to match Kiev's was established at Vladimir in the second half of the thirteenth century. In part this shift of the centre of gravity of Russia's history reflects a new threat to the south in the pressure of the Pechenegs, now

Long after the apogee of Kiev Rus and after the conquest of Constantinople by the Ottoman Turks in the mid-15th century, icons continued to be venerated in the Slav countries that had converted to Orthodox Christianity. This Bulgarian icon depicting the crucifixion dates from 1541.

This early 14th-century Byzantine icon, from the church of St Saviour in Constantinople's Chora Monastery, portrays the "Fathers of the Eastern Church": St Basil, St Gregory and St Cyril. All three are holding copies of the Gospels.

reaching its peak.

This was a momentous change. In these northern states, the beginnings of future trends in Russian government and society can be discerned. Slowly, grants from the princes were transforming the old followers and boon-companions of the warlord kings into a territorial nobility. Even settled peasants began to acquire rights of ownership and inheritance. Many of those who worked the land were slaves, but there was no such pyramid of obligations as shaped the territorial society of the medieval West. Yet these changes unrolled within a culture whose major direction had been settled by the Kiev period of Russian history.

THE EMERGENCE OF POLAND

Another enduring national entity, which began to crystallize at about the same time as Russia, was Poland. Its origins lay in a group of Slav tribes who first appear in the historical record in the tenth century, struggling against pressure from the Germans in the west. It may well have been politics, therefore, that dictated the choice of Christianity as a religion by Poland's first historically recorded ruler, Mieszko I. The choice was not, as in Russia's case, the Eastern Orthodox Church. Mieszko plumped for Rome. Poland, therefore, would be linked throughout her history to the West as Russia would be to the

The name Bohemia comes from the Boios, early occupants of this central European region. Later the area was inhabited by various Slav tribes. According to legend, the founder of the first Bohemian dynasty was Premysl. This statue portrays Premysl's grandson, Ottokar I, and was made in around 1373 for his tomb in the cathedral of St Vitus in Prague.

East. This conversion, in 966, opened a half-century of rapid consolidation for the new state. A vigorous successor began the creation of an administrative system and extended his lands to the Baltic in the north and through Silesia, Moravia and Cracow in the west. One German emperor recognized his sovereignty in 1000 and in 1025 he was crowned King of Poland as Boleslav I. Political setbacks and pagan reactions dissipated much of what he had done and there were grim times to come, but Poland was henceforth a historical reality. Moreover, three of the dominating themes of her history had also made their appearance: the struggle against German encroachment from the west, the identification with the interests of the Roman Church, and the factiousness and independence of the nobles towards the Crown. The first two of these do much to account for Poland's unhappy history, for they tugged her in different directions. As Slavs, Poles guarded the glacis of the Slav world; they formed a breakwater against the tides of Teutonic immigration. As Catholics, they were the outposts of Western culture in its confrontation with the Orthodox East.

RELIGIOUS DIFFERENCES BETWEEN SLAV PEOPLES

During these confused centuries other branches of the Slav peoples had been pushing on up the Adriatic and into central Europe. From them emerged other nations with important futures. The Slavs of Bohemia and Moravia had in the ninth century been converted by Cyril and Methodius, but were then reconverted by Germans to Latin Christianity. The conflict of faiths was important, too, in Croatia and Serbia, where another branch settled and established states separated from the eastern Slav stocks first by Avars, and then by Germans and Magyars, whose invasions from the ninth century were especially important in cutting off central European Orthodoxy from Byzantine support.

SLAV EUROPE UNDER STRAIN

A Slav Europe therefore existed at the start of the twelfth century. It was divided, it is true, by religion and into distinct areas of settlement. One of the peoples settled in it, the

Yaroslav the Wise, who is shown in this fresco with his family, carried out a policy of expansion that extended the Russian territories as far as the Baltic. He also tried to strengthen Christianity through an extensive building programme. The churches of St Sophia in Kiev and Novgorod are among the many that were constructed during his reign.

Magyars, who had crossed the Carpathians from south Russia, were not Slav at all. The whole of the area was under growing pressure from the West, where politics, crusading zeal and land-hunger all made a drive to the East irresistibly attractive to Germans. The greatest Slav power, Kievan Russia, developed less than its full potential; it was handicapped by political fragmentation after the eleventh century and harried in the next by the Cumans. By 1200 it had lost its control of the Black Sea river route; Russia had retreated to the north and was becoming Muscovy. Bad times for the Slavs lay ahead. A hurricane of disasters was about to fall upon Slav Europe, and for that matter on Byzantium. It was in 1204 that the crusaders sacked Constantinople and the world power which had sustained Orthodoxy was eclipsed. Worse still was to come. Thirty-six years later the Christian city of Kiev fell to a terrible nomadic people. These were the Mongols.

Russian icons, although clearly influenced by the style of Byzantium, gained renown across the Christian East for their great beauty and spirituality. This 12th-century icon, known as *The Annunciation of Ustjug*, was painted by a Russian artist of the Novgorod school.

4 THE DISPUTED LEGACIES OF THE NEAR EAST

BYZANTIUM WAS NOT the only temptation to the predators prowling about the Near East; indeed, it survived their attentions longer than its old enemy the Abbasid caliphate. The Arab empire slipped into decline and disintegration and from the tenth century we enter an age of confusion, which makes any brief summary of what happened a despairing exercise. There was no take-off into sustained growth such as the flowering of commerce and the emergence of moneyed men outside the ruling and military hierarchies might have seemed to promise. Rapacious and arbitrary expectations by government may be the basic explanation. In the end, for all the comings and goings of rulers and raiders, nothing disturbed the foundations of Islamic society. The whole area from the Levant to the Hindu Kush was pervaded for the first time in history by a single religion and it was to endure. Within that zone, the Christian inheritance of Rome hung on as a major cultural force only until the eleventh century, bottled up beyond the Taurus in Asia Minor. After that, Christianity declined in the Near East to become only a matter of the communities tolerated by Islam.

This carved ivory casket, known as the Jar of Zamora, dates from 964 – the era of the Umayyad Córdoba caliphate. It bears the following inscription: "God's blessing for Iman Abd-Allah al-Hakim al-Mustansir Billah, Prince of the Faithful. This was ordered to be made by the Lady Mother of Abd-ar-Rahman III and given to the care of Durri the Boy."

THE CALIPHATE DYNASTIES

The stability and deep-rootedness of Islamic social and cultural institutions were enormously important. They far transcended the weaknesses – which were mainly political and administrative – of the semi-autonomous states which emerged to exercise power under the formal supremacy of the caliphate in its decadent period. About them little need be said. Interesting to Arabists though they are, they need be noted here rather as convenient landmarks than for their own sake. The most important and strongest of them was ruled by the Fatimid Dynasty which controlled Egypt, most of Syria and the Levant, and the Red Sea coast. This territory included the great shrines of Mecca and Medina and therefore the profitable and important pilgrim trade. On the borders of Anatolia and northern Syria another dynasty, the Hamdanid, stood between the

The famous mosque of al-Azhar in Cairo was built by the Fatimid caliph al-Muizz (953–975). Its construction, begun in 970, took just two years to complete. During the reign of the next caliph, al-Aziz (975–996), a school was installed in the mosque and took its name. Part of the building still serves as an Islamic university.

Fatimids and the Byzantine Empire, while the heartland of the caliphate, Iraq and western Iran, together with Azerbaijan, was ruled by the Buwayhid. Finally, the north-eastern provinces of Khurasan, Sijistan and Transoxiana had passed to the Samanids. Listing these four groupings of power far from exhausts the complexity of the unsettled Arab world of the tenth century, but it provides all the background now needed to narrate the unrolling of the process by which two new empires appeared within Islam, one based on Anatolia and one on Persia.

THE TURKISH PEOPLES

THE THREAD is provided by a Central Asian people already introduced into this story, the Turks. Some of them had been granted a home by the Sassanids in their last years in

Time chart (909–1453)

909 Founding of the Fatimid Dynasty

1055 The Seljuk Turks take Baghdad

1096–1099 The First Crusade

1250 Founding of the Mameluke Sultanate

900 1000 1100 1200 1300 1400 1500

1071 The Seljuk Turks destroy Byzantine power in Asia Minor

1099 The crusades establish the Latin kingdom of Jerusalem

1237 Chinghis Khan's Mongol armies enter Europe

1453 Constantinople is conquered by the Turks

The Mamelukes, four of whom are shown in this 13th-century illustration, were famed for their courage and horsemanship and were much in demand as mercenaries.

return for help. In those days the Turkish "empire", if that is the right word for their tribal confederation, ran right across Asia; it was their first great era. Like that of other nomadic peoples, this ascendancy soon proved to be transient. The Turks faced at the same time inter-tribal divisions and a resurgence of Chinese power and it was on a divided and disheartened people that there had fallen the great Arab onslaught. In 667 the Arabs invaded Transoxiana and in the next century they finally shattered the remains of the Turkish empire in western Asia. They were only stopped at last in the eighth century by the Khazars, another Turkish people. Before this the eastern Turkish confederation had broken up.

In spite of this collapse what had happened was very important. For the first time a nomadic polity of sorts had spanned Asia and it had lasted for more than a century. All four of the great contemporary civilizations, China, India, Byzantium, and Persia, had felt bound to undertake relations with the Turkish khans, whose subjects had learned much from these contacts. Among other things, they acquired the art of writing; the first surviving Turkish inscription dates from the early eighth century. Yet in spite of this, for long stretches of Turkish history we must rely upon other people's accounts and records, for no Turkish authority seems to go back beyond the fifteenth century and the archaeological record is sporadic.

THE MUSLIM TURKS

This lack of documentary evidence, combined with the fragmentation of the Turkish tribes, makes for obscurity until the tenth century. Then came the collapse of the T'ang Dynasty in China, a great event which offered important opportunities to the eastern and Sinicized Turks, just at the moment when signs of weakness were multiplying in the Islamic world. One was the emergency of the Abbasid successor states. Turkish slaves or "Mamelukes" had long served in the caliphates' armies; now they were employed as mercenaries by the dynasties which tried to fill their vacuum of power. But the Turkish peoples themselves were again on the move by the tenth century.

In the middle of it a new dynasty re-established Chinese power and unity; perhaps it was this which provided the decisive impetus for another of the long shunting operations by which Central Asian peoples jostled one another forward to other lands. Whatever the cause, a people called the Oghuz Turks were in the van of those who pressed into the northeastern lands of the old caliphate and set up their own new states there. One clan among them were the Seljuks. They were notable because they were already Muslim. In 960 they had been converted by the assiduous missionary efforts of the Samanids, when still in Transoxiana.

Many of the leaders of the new Turkish régimes were former slave soldiers of the Arab-Persians; one such group were the Ghaznavids, a dynasty who briefly built a huge dominion which stretched into India (this was also the first post-Abbasid régime to choose its generals as sultans, or heads of state). But they were in their turn pushed aside as new nomadic invaders arrived. The

During the Seljuk era a restoration of Islamic culture took place, particularly in the field of architecture. The style that developed during that time – of which the famous 12th-century Friday Mosque in Isfahan, Iran, pictured here, is an example – is still influential today.

The Seljuk poet Khoja Dehhani wrote, "In describing your lips, my poetry ... is sweet, because pure distilled sugar sweetens the water." This 17th-century painting of lovers is by Riza-i Abbasi of Isfahan.

Oghuz came in sufficient numbers to produce a major change in the ethnic composition of Iran and also in its economy. In another way, too, their arrival means a deeper change than any preceding one and opened a new phase of Islamic history. Because of what the Samanids had done, some of the Oghuz Turks were already Muslim and respected what they found. There now began the translation into Turkish of the major works of Arabic and Persian scholarship which was to give the Turkish peoples access to Arab civilization as never before.

THE SELJUK EMPIRE

Early in the eleventh century the Seljuks crossed the Oxus, too. This was to lead to the creation of a second Turkish empire, which lasted until 1194, and, in Anatolia, to 1243. After evicting the Ghaznavids from eastern Iran, the Seljuks turned on the Buwayhids and seized Iraq, thus becoming the first Central Asian invaders of historical times to penetrate further than the Iranian plateau. Perhaps because they were Sunnites they seem to have been readily welcomed by many of the former subjects of the Shi'ite Buwayhid. They went on, though, to much greater deeds than this. After occupying Syria and Palestine they invaded Asia Minor, where they inflicted on the Byzantines one of the worst defeats of their history at Manzikert in 1071. Significantly, the Seljuks called the sultanate they set up there the Sultanate of Rum, for they saw themselves henceforth as the inheritors of the old Roman territories. That Islam should have a foothold inside the old Roman Empire touched off crusading zeal in the West; it also opened Asia Minor to the settlement of Turks.

In many ways, then, the Seljuks played an outstanding historic role. Not only did they begin the conversion of Asia Minor from Christianity to Islam, but they provoked the crusades and long bore the brunt of resisting them, too. This cost them heavily on other fronts. By the mid-twelfth century Seljuk power was already dwindling in the Iranian lands. Nevertheless, the Seljuk Empire lasted long enough to make possible a final crystallization over the whole Islamic heartlands of a common culture and of institutions which this time included Turkish peoples.

THE STRUCTURE OF THE SELJUK EMPIRE

A kind of Islamic hegemony was achieved, less because Seljuk government innovated than because it recognized social (and in Islam that meant religious) realities. The essence of the Seljuk structure was tribute rather than administrative activity. It was something of a confederation of tribes and localities and was no more capable of standing up to long-term stress than its predecessors. The central apparatus of the empire was its armies and what was necessary to maintain them; locally, the notables of the *ulema*, the teachers and religious leaders of Islam, ruled. They provided a consolidation of authority and social custom which would survive the caliphates and become the cement of Islamic society all over the Middle East. They would run things until the coming of nationalism in the twentieth century. For all the divisions of schools within the *ulema*, it provided at local levels a common cultural and social system, which ensured that the loyalty of the masses would be available to new régimes which replaced one another at the top and might have alien origins. It provided political spokesmen who could assure satisfaction at the local level and legitimize new régimes by their support.

This produced one of the most striking differences between Islamic and Christian society. Religious élites were the key factor in the *ulema*; they organized the locally, religiously based community, so that bureaucracy, in the Western sense, was not needed. Within the political divisions of the Islamic world in the age of the caliphates' decadence these élites provided its social unity. The Seljuk pattern spread over the Arabic world, and was maintained under the successor empires. Another basic institution was the use of slaves, a few as administrators, but many in the armies. Though the Seljuks granted some great fiefs in return for military service, it was the slaves – often Turkish – who provided the real force on which the régime rested, its armies. Finally, it relied also on the maintenance, where possible, of the local grandee, Persian or Arab.

In the late 11th century, the Seljuk Empire split into three parts from which the Sultanate of Rum, or Iconium (the name given to the Byzantine territories), was formed. The mosque of Ala-al-Din, completed in 1220, was built in Konya, the capital of the new sultanate.

THE THREAT OF THE CRUSADES

The declining years of the Seljuk régime exposed the weaknesses in this structure. It depended heavily for its direction upon the availability of able individuals supported by tribal loyalties. But the Turks were thin on the ground and could not keep their subjects' loyalties if they did not succeed. When the first wave of Muslim settlement in Anatolia was spent, that area was still only superficially Turkish, and Muslim towns stood in the middle of a countryside linguistically distinct; local language was not Arabized as it was further south and the submergence of the Greek culture of the area was only very slowly achieved. Further east, the first Muslim lands to be lost went to pagans in the twelfth century; a nomad ruler (widely supposed in the West to be a Christian king, Prester John, on his way from Central Asia to help the crusaders) took Transoxiana from the Seljuks.

The crusading movement was in part a response to the establishment of Seljuk power. The Turks, perhaps because of their late conversion to Islam, were less tolerant than the Arabs. They began to trouble Christian pilgrims going to the holy places. The other causes which promoted the crusades belong rather to European than to Islamic history and can be dealt with elsewhere, but by 1100 the Islamic world felt itself on the defensive even though the Frankish threat was not yet grave. Still, the reconquest of Spain had begun, and the Arabs had already lost Sicily. The First Crusade (1096–9) was favoured by Muslim divisions which enabled the invaders to establish four Latin states in the Levant: the kingdom of Jerusalem, and its three fiefs, the county of Edessa, the principality of Antioch and the county of Tripoli. They were not to have much of a future, but in the early twelfth century their presence seemed ominous to Islam. The crusaders' success provoked Muslim reaction and a Seljuk general seized Mosul as a centre from which he built up a new state in northern Mesopotamia and Syria. He recaptured Edessa (1144); his son saw the possibilities of exploiting the Christians' alienation of the local Muslim population by bad treatment. It was a nephew of this prince, Saladin, who seized power in Egypt in 1171, declaring the Fatimid caliphate at an end.

On 4 July 1187 the battle of the Horns of Hattin took place between the armies of Saladin and those of Guy de Lusignan, the king of Jerusalem. This manuscript illustration depicts a scene from the battle in which the victorious Saladin is smashing a reliquary carried by King Guy.

The confrontation between Richard the Lionheart, king of England (1189–1199), and Saladin, sultan of Egypt and Syria (1174–1193), has been a recurrent theme in the iconography dedicated to the crusades.

SALADIN

Saladin was a Kurd. He came to be seen as the hero of the Muslim reconquest of the Levant and he remains a captivating figure even after strenuous efforts by unromantic and sceptical scholars to cut through the image of the *beau idéal* of Saracenic chivalry. The fascination he exercised over the minds of his Christian contemporaries was rooted in paradoxes which must have had real educational force. He was indisputably a pagan, yet he was said to be good, a man of his word and just in his dealings; he was chivalrous, yet of a world that did not know the knightly ideal. (This puzzled some Frenchmen so much that they were forced to believe he had in fact been knighted by a Christian captive and that he baptized himself on his deathbed.) On a more mundane level, Saladin's first great triumph was the recapture of Jerusalem (1187), which provoked a new, and third, crusade (1189–92). This could achieve little against him, though it further intensified the irritation of Muslims who now began to show a quite new and unprecedented bitterness and ideological hostility towards Christianity. Persecution of Christians followed and with it began the slow but irreversible decline of the formerly large Christian populations of the Muslim lands.

Saladin founded a dynasty, the Abbuyid sultans, which ruled the Levant (outside the crusader enclaves), Egypt and the Red Sea coast. It lasted until it was replaced by rulers drawn from its own palace guards, the Turkish Mamelukes. These were to be the destroyers of the remaining crusader conquests in Palestine. The revival of the caliphate which followed at Cairo (it was given to a member of the Abbasid house) is of small significance in comparison with this. It registered, nevertheless, that so far as Islam still had a preponderant power and a cultural focus, both were now to be found in Egypt. Baghdad was never to recover.

THE MONGOLS AND TATARS

THE MAMELUKES were to have another, greater, achievement to their credit in the thirteenth century. It was they who finally halted the tide of a conquest far more threatening than that of the Franks, when it had been rising for more than half a century. This was the onslaught of the Mongols, whose history makes nonsense of chronological and

This miniature depicts Chinghis Khan sitting in his tent. He is shown giving arrows to his sons, who are accompanied by a male servant.

territorial divisions. In an astonishingly short time this nomadic people drew into their orbit China, India, the Near East and Europe and left ineffaceable marks behind them. Yet there is no physical focus for their history except the felt tents of their ruler's encampment; they blew up like a hurricane to terrify half a dozen civilizations, slaughtered and destroyed on a scale the twentieth century alone has emulated, and then disappeared almost as suddenly as they came. They demand to be considered alone as the last and most terrible of the nomadic conquerors.

Twelfth-century Mongolia is as far back as a search for their origins need go. A group of peoples speaking the languages of the family called Mongol, who had long demanded the attention of Chinese governments, then lived there. Generally, China played off one of them against another in the interests of its own security. They were barbarians, not much different in their cultural level from others who have already crossed these pages. Two tribes among them, the Tatars and that which became known as the Mongols, competed and on the whole the Tatars had the best of it. They drove one young Mongol to extremes of bitterness and self-assertion. The date of his birth is uncertain, but in the 1190s he became khan to his people. A few years later he was supreme among the Mongol tribes and was acknowledged as such by being given the title of Chinghis Khan. By an Arabic corruption of this name he was to become known in Europe as Genghis Khan. He extended his power over other peoples in Central Asia and in 1215 defeated (though he did not overthrow) the Chin state in northern China and Manchuria. This was only the beginning. By the time of his death, in 1227, he had become the greatest conqueror the world has ever known.

CHINGHIS KHAN

Chinghis Khan seems unlike all earlier nomad warlords. He genuinely believed he had a mission to conquer the world. Conquest, not booty or settlement, was his aim and what he conquered he often set about organizing in a systematic way. This led to a structure which deserves the name "empire" more than do most of the nomadic polities. He was superstitious, tolerant of religions other than his own paganism and, said one Persian historian, "used to hold in esteem beloved and respected sages and hermits of every tribe, considering this a procedure to please God". Indeed, he seems to have held that he was himself the recipient of a divine mission. This

The Great Khan of the Mongols

Chinghis Khan, the Mongols' first "Great Khan", is one of the most important historical figures of all time. Probably born in 1162 or 1167, he unified all of the Mongol and Turkish-Mongol tribes who, after having defeated the Merkit clan, proclaimed him king in 1196. Chinghis proclaimed himself *jagan* (supreme khan or universal sovereign) in a popular assembly held in 1206, following which he embarked on a campaign of conquests. In order to maximize the efficiency of the troops, he carried out a number of military reforms and strong discipline, based on the *yasa* (strict law), became one of the Mongol army's most important features.

The first Mongol incursion into China was carried out against the Chin Dynasty. This was settled with the conquest of Peking in 1215, which opened the way to Bokhara and Samarkand. Seven years later, Chinghis Khan's troops penetrated southern Russia, defeating the Prince of Kiev on 31 May 1223. To these conquests he added Burma (now known as Myanmar), Central Asia, Iran and the Near East, forming an enormous Mongol empire.

Chinghis Khan also carried out reforms of the civil service, creating a series of institutions to render it more efficient, including a postal service. In spite of his intransigence in many respects, the Mongol leader showed a great tolerance of other religions, with the exception of Islam. He became a legendary figure in medieval Europe where, at one time, he was identified with the mysterious Prester John.

Chinghis Khan's power lay in his remarkable ability to bring together under his control the diverse Mongol tribes, who led nomadic lives between northern China and southern Siberia.

Chinghis Khan died on 18 August 1227, leaving his three heirs, Ogoday (1229–1241), Güyük (1246–1248) and Möngke (1251–1259), with the task of continuing his conquests. However, rivalry amongst the Great Khan's descendants eventually led to the empire's division into khanates.

religious eclecticism was of the first importance, as was the fact that he and his followers (except for some Turks who joined them) were not Muslim, as the Seljuks had been when they arrived in the Near East. Not only was this a matter of moment to Christians and Buddhists – there were both Nestorians and Buddhists among the Mongols – but it meant that the Mongols were not identified with the religion of the majority in the Near East.

In 1218 Chinghis Khan turned to the west and the era of Mongol invasions opened in Transoxiana and northern Iran. He never acted carelessly, capriciously, or without premeditation, but it may well be that the attack was provoked by the folly of a Muslim prince who killed his envoys. From there Chinghis went on to a devastating raid into Persia followed by a swing northward through the Caucasus into southern Russia, and returned, having made a complete circuit of the Caspian.

All this was accomplished by 1223. Bokhara and Samarkand were sacked with massacres of the townspeople which were meant to terrify others who contemplated resistance. (Surrender was always the safest course with the Mongols and after it several minor peoples were to survive with nothing

Chinghis Khan's Mongol Empire

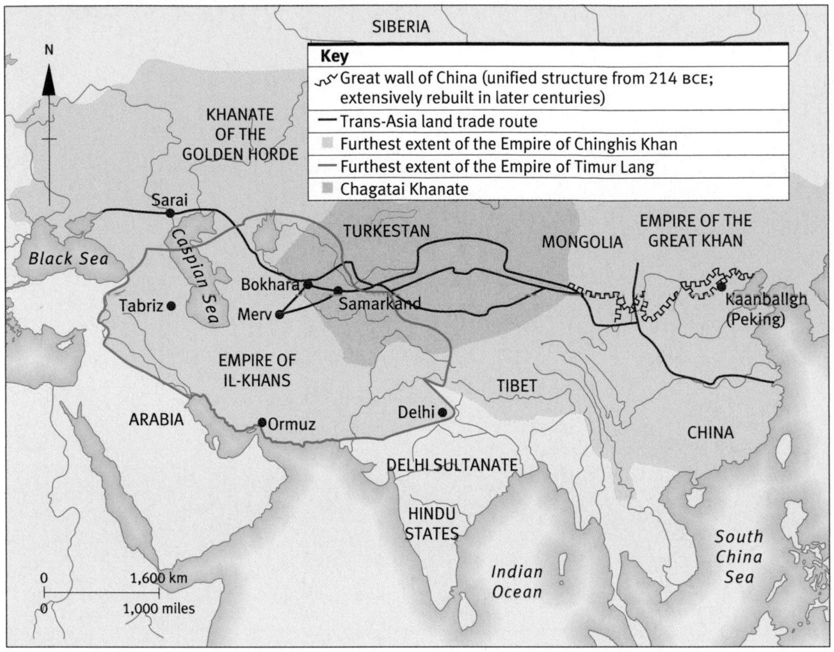

Throughout its history, the Mongol Empire experienced a series of major political and geographical transformations. Continual expansion occurred during the reign of Chinghis Khan as his conquests accumulated. In the second half of the 13th century, however, the empire broke up into khanates, which soon became mutual enemies. In the 14th century Timur Lang tried, although unsuccessfully, to rebuild Chinghis Khan's empire.

worse than the payment of tribute and the arrival of a Mongol governor.) Transoxiana never recovered its place in the life of Islamic Iran after this. Christian civilization was given a taste of Mongol prowess by the defeat of the Georgians in 1221 and of the southern Russian princes two years later. Even these alarming events were only the overture to what was to follow.

THE MONGOLS IN EUROPE

Chinghis died in the East in 1227, but his son and successor returned to the West after completing the conquest of northern China. In 1236 his armies poured into Russia. They took Kiev and settled on the lower Volga, from where they organized a tributary system for the Russian principalities they had not occupied. Meanwhile they raided Catholic Europe. The Teutonic knights, the Poles and the Hungarians all went down before them. Cracow was burnt and Moravia devastated. A Mongol patrol crossed into Austria, while the pursuers of the king of Hungary chased him through Croatia and finally reached Albania before they were recalled.

The Mongols left Europe because of dissensions among their leaders and the arrival of the news of the death of the khan. A new one was not chosen until 1246. A Franciscan friar attended the ceremony (he was there as an emissary of the pope); so did a Russian grand duke, a Seljuk sultan, the brother of the Abbuyid sultan of Egypt, an envoy from the Abbasid caliph, a representative of the king of Armenia, and two claimants to the Christian throne of Georgia. The election did not solve the problems posed by dissension among the Mongols and it was not until another Great Khan was chosen (after his predecessor's death had ended a short reign) that the stage was set for another Mongol attack.

THE MONGOL ONSLAUGHT ON ISLAM

This time the force of Mongol aggression fell almost entirely upon Islam, and provoked unwarranted optimism among Christians who noted also the rise of Nestorian influence at the Mongol court. The area nominally still subject to the caliphate had been in a state of disorder since Chinghis Khan's campaign. The Seljuks of Rum had been defeated in 1243 and were not capable of asserting authority. In this vacuum, relatively small and local Mongol forces could be effective and the Mongol Empire relied mainly upon vassals among numerous local rulers.

The campaign was entrusted to the younger brother of the Great Khan and began with the crossing of the Oxus on New Year's Day 1256. After destroying the notorious sect of the Assassins en route, he moved on Baghdad, summoning the caliph to surrender. The city was stormed and sacked and the last Abbasid caliph murdered – because there were superstitions about shedding his blood he is supposed to have been rolled up in a carpet and trampled to death by horses. It was a black moment in the history of Islam as, everywhere, Christians took heart and anticipated the overthrow of their Muslim overlords. When, the following year, the Mongol offensive was launched against Syria, Muslims were forced to bow to the cross in the streets of a surrendered Damascus and a mosque was turned into a Christian church. The Mamelukes of Egypt were next on the list for conquest when the Great Khan died. The Mongol commander in the West favoured the succession of his younger brother, Kubilai, far away in China. But he was distracted and withdrew many of his men to Azerbaijan to wait on events. It was on a weakened army that the Mamelukes fell at the Goliath Spring near Nazareth on 3 September 1260. The Mongol general was killed, the legend of Mongol invincibility was shattered and a turning-point in world history was reached. For the Mongols the age of conquest was over and that of consolidation had begun.

THE KHANATES

The unity of Chinghis Khan's empire was at an end. After civil war the legacy was divided among the princes of his house, under the nominal supremacy of his grandson Kubilai, Khan of China, who was to be the last of the Great Khans. The Russian khanate was divided into three: the khanate of the Golden Horde ran from the Danube to the Caucasus and to the east of it lay the "Cheibanid" khanate in the north (it was named after its first khan) and that of the White Horde in the south. The khanate of Persia included much of Asia Minor, and stretched across Iraq and Iran to the Oxus. Beyond that lay the khanate of Turkestan. The quarrels of these states left the Mamelukes free to mop up the crusader enclaves and to take revenge upon the Christians who had compromised themselves by collaboration with the Mongols.

In retrospect it is still far from easy to understand why the Mongols were so successful for so long. In the west they had the advantage that there was no single great power such as Persia or the Eastern Roman Empire had been, to stand up to them, but in

An illustration from a later era portrays a scene from the Mongol court, in which two dancers are depicted entertaining the khan while he dines. The painting gives an impression of the great opulence that was perceived to have been at the heart of the Mongol Empire.

This illustration is taken from a 15th-century edition of Marco Polo's *The Book of the Wonders of the World*, in which the Venetian traveller described Kubilai Khan's palace in Peking. The building, he wrote, was made of marble, the interior walls were covered in gold and silver and the dining halls could seat 6,000 people.

the east they defeated China, undeniably a great imperial state. It helped, too, that they faced divided enemies; Christian rulers toyed with the hope of using Mongol power against the Muslim and even against one another, while any combination of the Christian civilizations of the West with China against the Mongols was inconceivable given Mongol control of communication between the two. Their tolerance of religious diversity, except during the period of implacable hatred of Islam, also favoured the Mongols; those who submitted peacefully had little to fear. Would-be resisters could contemplate the ruins of Bokhara or Kiev, or the pyramids of skulls where there had been Persian cities; much of the Mongol success must have been a result of the sheer terror which defeated many of their enemies before they ever came to battle. In the last resort, though, simple military skill explained their victories. The Mongol soldier was tough, well-trained and led by generals who exploited all the advantages which a fast-moving cavalry arm could give them. Their mobility was in part the outcome of the care with which reconnaissance and intelligence work was carried out before a campaign. The discipline of their cavalry and their mastery of the techniques of siege warfare (which, none the less, the Mongols preferred to avoid) made them much more formidable than a horde of nomadic freebooters. As conquests continued, too, the Mongol army was recruited by specialists among its captives; by the middle of the thirteenth century there were many Turks in its ranks.

MONGOL RULE

Though his army's needs were simple, the empire of Chinghis Khan and, in somewhat less degree, of his successors was an administrative reality over a vast area. One of the first innovations of Chinghis was the reduction of Mongol language to writing, using the Turkish script. This was done by a captive. Mongol rule always drew willingly upon the skills made available to it by its conquests. Chinese civil servants organized the conquered territories for revenue purposes; the Chinese device of paper money, when introduced by the Mongols into the Persian economy in the thirteenth century, brought about a disastrous collapse of trade, but the failure does not make the example of the use of alien techniques less striking.

In so great an empire, communications were the key to power. A network of post-houses along the main roads looked after rapidly moving messengers and agents. The roads helped trade, too, and for all their ruthlessness to the cities which resisted them, the Mongols usually encouraged rebuilding and the revival of commerce, from the taxation of which they sought revenue. Asia knew a sort of *Pax Mongolica*. Caravans were protected against nomadic bandits by the policing of the Mongols, poachers turned gamekeepers. The most successful nomads of all, they were not going to let other nomads spoil their game. Land trade was as easy between China and Europe during the Mongol era as at any time; Marco Polo is the most famous of Europe's travellers to the Far East in the thirteenth century and by the time he went there the Mongols had conquered China, but before he was born his father and uncle had begun travels in Asia which were to last years. They were both Venetian merchants and were sufficiently successful to set off again almost as soon as they got back, taking the young Marco with them. By sea, too, China's trade was linked with Europe, through the port of Ormuz on the Persian Gulf, but it was the land-routes to the Crimea and Trebizond which carried most of the silks and spices westward and provided the bulk of Byzantine

In this 14th-century Mongol illustration a wealthy nobleman, who is seated on the right, waits for his servants to bring his meal.

Marco Polo's travels

Marco Polo was born in 1254 to a family of Venetian nobles. In 1271 his merchant father Niccolò and his uncle Mafio, who had already visited the court of Kubilai Khan (1259–1294), decided to return to China. Taking Marco with them, they passed through Armenia, Tabriz and Keman, reaching Ormuz in the Persian Gulf. From Ormuz they followed a dangerous route through Persia, Pamir and the Gobi desert, finally arriving in Peking in 1275. Marco Polo stayed in the Far East for two decades, in the service of Kubilai Khan. He was put in charge of Mongol embassies in Yunan, Cochin China, Tibet and India.

In 1291 the Polos were requested to accompany an imperial princess to Persia. They then returned to Europe via Sumatra and the southern coasts of Asia, as far as the Persian Gulf and, from there, across Persia and Armenia. They reached Constantinople and later their home port of Venice, where they were received with great honours. They had made their fortunes in the East and returned as very wealthy men.

In 1298, during the war between Venice and Genoa, Marco Polo was imprisoned by the Genoese. Upon his returned to Venice in 1299 he was made a member of the Great Council. He remained in the city until his death in 1324.

Marco Polo's memoirs, which he entitled *The Book of Marco*, gained international renown. Later editions were called *The Book of the Wonders of the World* and *The Discovery of the World*.

Marco Polo is depicted kneeling before an idealized Kubilai Khan in this illustration from a 15th-century edition of his memoirs. The khan's servant is handing the Venetian a passport to enable him to travel to distant Mongolia.

trade in its last centuries. The land-routes depended on the khans, and, significantly, the merchants were always strong supporters of the Mongol régime.

MONGOL ARROGANCE

In its relations with the rest of the world, the Mongol Empire came to show the influence of China in its fundamental presuppositions. The khans were the representatives on earth of the one sky god, Tengri; his supremacy had to be acknowledged, though this did not mean that the practice of other religions would not be tolerated. But it did mean that diplomacy in the Western sense was inconceivable. Like the Chinese emperors whom they were to replace, the khans saw themselves as the upholders of a universal monarchy;

Mongol armies are shown besieging a fortress defended by archers in this illustration from *The History of the Conquest of the World* by Ala-al-din.

those who came to it had to come as suppliants. Ambassadors were the bearers of tribute, not the representatives of powers of equal standing. When in 1246 emissaries from Rome conveyed papal protests against the Mongol treatment of Christian Europe and a recommendation that he should be baptized, the new Great Khan's reply was blunt: "If you do not observe God's command, and if you ignore my command, I shall know you as my enemy. Likewise I shall make you understand." As for baptism, the pope was told to come in person to serve the khan. It was not an isolated message, for another pope had the same reply from the Mongol governor of Persia a year later: "If you wish to keep your land, you must come to us in person and thence go on to him who is master of the earth. If you do not, we know not what will happen: only God knows."

MONGOL CULTURE

The cultural influences playing upon the Mongol rulers and their circle were not only Chinese. There is much evidence of the importance of Nestorian Christianity at the Mongol court and it encouraged European hopes of a rapprochement with the khans. One of the most remarkable Western visitors to the khan, the Franciscan William of Roebruck, was told just after New Year 1254, by an Armenian monk, that the Great Khan would be baptized a few days later, but nothing came of it. William went on, however, to win a debate before him, defending the Christian faith against Muslim and Buddhist representatives and coming off best. This was, in fact, just the moment at which Mongol strength was being gathered for the double assault on world power, against Sung China and the Muslims, which was finally checked in Syria by the Mamelukes in 1260.

Marco Polo in the East

"In that region there were many monks dedicated to the worship of idols. There is a large monastery there, which because of its size seems more like a small city, in which nearly two thousand monks live and worship idols. In contrast to the custom of the layman they shave their heads and beards and wear clothes more in tune with their religious role. They sing great canticles in the celebration of their gods and light an incredible number of candles in their temple."

An extract describing a Buddhist temple in Nepal, from the *The Book of the Wonders of the World* by Marco Polo.

PERSIA UNDER THE IL-KHANS

Their defeat in Syria did not put an end to Mongol attempts to conquer the Levant. None was successful, though; the Mongols' quarrels among themselves had given the Mamelukes a clear field for too long. Logically, Christians regretted the death of Hulugu, the last khan to pose a real threat to the Near East for decades. After him a succession of Il-khans, or subordinate khans, ruled in Persia, preoccupied with their quarrels with the Golden and White Hordes. Gradually Persia recovered under them from the invasions it had suffered earlier in the century. As in the east, the Mongols ruled through locally recruited administrators and were tolerant of Christians and Buddhists, though not, at first, of Muslims. There was a clear sign of a change in the relative positions of Mongol and European when the Il-khans began to suggest to the pope that they should join in an alliance against the Mamelukes.

The mausoleum of Oljeyetu (1302–1317) stands close to the city of Sultaniya (in present-day Iran), which was founded by the Mongol king Arghun in 1290. Oljeyetu was the successor of Ghazan, the first Mongol ruler to convert to Islam.

PERSIA TURNS TO ISLAM

When Kubilai Khan died in China in 1294 one of the few remaining links that held together the Mongol Empire had gone. In the following year an Il-khan called Ghazan made a momentous break with the Mongol tradition; he became a Muslim. Since then the rulers of Persia have always been Muslim. But this did not do all that might have been hoped and the Il-khan died young, with many problems unsolved. To embrace Islam had been a bold stroke, but it was not enough. It had offended many Mongols and in the last resort the khans depended upon their captains. Nevertheless, the contest with the Mamelukes was not yet abandoned. Though in the end unsuccessful, Ghazan's armies took Aleppo in 1299; he was prayed for in the Umayyad mosque at Damascus the next year. He was the last khan to attempt to realize the plan of Mongol conquest of the Near East set out a half-century before, but was frustrated in the end when the Mamelukes defeated the last Mongol invasion of Syria in 1303. The Il-khan died the following year.

As in China, it soon appeared in Persia that Mongol rule had enjoyed only a brief Indian summer of consolidation before it began to crumble. Ghazan was the last Il-khan of stature. Outside their own lands, his successors could exercise little influence; the

Mamelukes terrorized the old allies of the Mongols, the Christian Armenians, and Anatolia was disputed between different Turkish princes. There was little to hope for from Europe, where the illusion of the crusading dream had been dissipated. Though Mongol power ebbed away, there came one last flash of the old terror in the West as a conqueror appeared who rivalled even Chinghis.

TIMUR LANG

In 1369 Timur Lang, or Timur the lame, became ruler of Samarkand. For thirty years the history of the Il-khans had been one of civil strife and succession disputes; Persia was conquered by Timur in 1379. Timur (who has passed into English literature, thanks to Marlowe, as Tamberlane) aspired to rival Chinghis. In the extent of his conquests and the ferocity of his behaviour he did; he may even have been as great a leader of men. None the less, he lacked the statesmanship of his predecessors. Of creative art he was barren. Though he ravaged India and sacked Delhi (he was as hard on his fellow-Muslims as on Christians), thrashed the khans of the Golden Horde, defeated Mameluke and Turk alike and incorporated Mesopotamia as well as Persia in his own domains, he left little behind. His historic role was, except in two respects, almost insignificant. One negative achievement was the almost complete extinction of Asiatic Christianity in its Nestorian and Jacobite form. This was hardly in the Mongol tradition, but Timur was as much a Turk by blood as a Mongol and knew nothing of the nomadic life of Central Asia from which Chinghis came, with its willingness to indulge Christian clergy. His sole positive achievement was unintentional and temporary: briefly, he prolonged the life of Byzantium. By a great defeat of an Anatolian Turkish people, the Ottomans, in 1402, he prevented them for a while from going in to the kill against the Eastern Empire.

This was the direction in which Near Eastern history had been moving ever since the Mongols had been unable to keep their grip on Seljuk Anatolia. The spectacular stretch of Mongol campaigning – from Albania to Java – makes it hard to sense this until Timur's death, but then it was obvious. Before that, the Mongols had already been overthrown in China. Timur's own legacy crumbled, Mesopotamia eventually becoming the emirate of the attractively named Black Sheep Turks, while his successors for a while still hung on to Persia and Transoxiana. By the middle of the fifteenth century, the Golden Horde was well advanced in its break-up. Though it could still terrorize Russia, the Mongol threat to Europe was long over.

THE END OF BYZANTIUM

BY THE FIFTEENTH CENTURY, Byzantium was at her last gasp. For more than two centuries it had fought a losing battle for survival, and not merely with powerful Islamic neighbours. It was the West which had first reduced Byzantium to a tiny patch of territory and had sacked its capital. After the mortal wound of 1204 it became merely a small Balkan state. A Bulgarian king had seized the opportunity of that year to assure his country's independence as one of several ephemeral successor states which made their appearance. Furthermore, on the ruins of Byzantine rule there was established the new western European maritime empire of Venice, the cuckoo in the nest which had been in the first place bribed to enter it. This former client had by the middle of the fourteenth century taken for itself from the Byzantine heritage the whole Aegean complex of islands, with

Having occupied the Byzantine throne for seven years, John VI Cantacuzenus abdicated in 1354 to become a monk. He spent the remaining 29 years of his life in a remote monastery, where he wrote *Histories*, an account of his reign, and studied theology. His dual roles, as an emperor and as a monk, are represented in this manuscript illustration, which dates from 1347–1354.

During the era of the Palaeologus Dynasty, Byzantine art, particularly fresco painting and mosaics, reached new heights, rarely surpassed since. This 14th-century mosaic, entitled *The Dormition of the Virgin*, is from the church of the Chora Monastery in Istanbul. The Virgin lies surrounded by the apostles. In the centre, Christ is depicted with an infant in his arms, representing the rebirth of Mary's soul in heaven.

Rhodes, Crete, Corfu and Chios. During this time, too, Venice had kept up a bitter commercial and political struggle with her rival, Genoa, which had itself by 1400 acquired control of the southern corner of the Crimea and its rich trade with Russia.

In 1261 the Byzantines had won back their own capital from the Franks. They did so with the help of a Turkish power in Anatolia, the Osmanlis. Two factors might still benefit the empire; the crucial phase of Mongol aggression was past (though this could hardly have been known and Mongol attacks continued to fall on peoples who cushioned her from them), and in Russia there existed a great Orthodox power which was a source of help and money. But there were also new threats and these outweighed the positive factors. Byzantine recovery in Europe in the later thirteenth century was soon challenged by a Serbian prince with aspirations to empire. He died before he could take Constantinople, but he left the empire with little but the hinterland of the capital and a fragment of Thrace. Against the Serbs, the empire once more called on Osmanli help. Already firmly established on the Asian shores of the Bosphorus, the Turks took a toehold in Europe at Gallipoli in 1333.

THE SHRINKING EMPIRE

The best that the last eleven emperors, the Palaeologi, could manage in these circumstances was a rearguard action. They lost what was left of Asia Minor to the Osmanlis in 1326 and it was there that the fatal danger lay. In the eastern Black Sea they had an ally in the Greek empire of Trebizond, a great trading state which was just to outlive Byzantium itself, but in Europe they could hope for little. The ambitions of the Venetians and Genoese (who by now dominated even

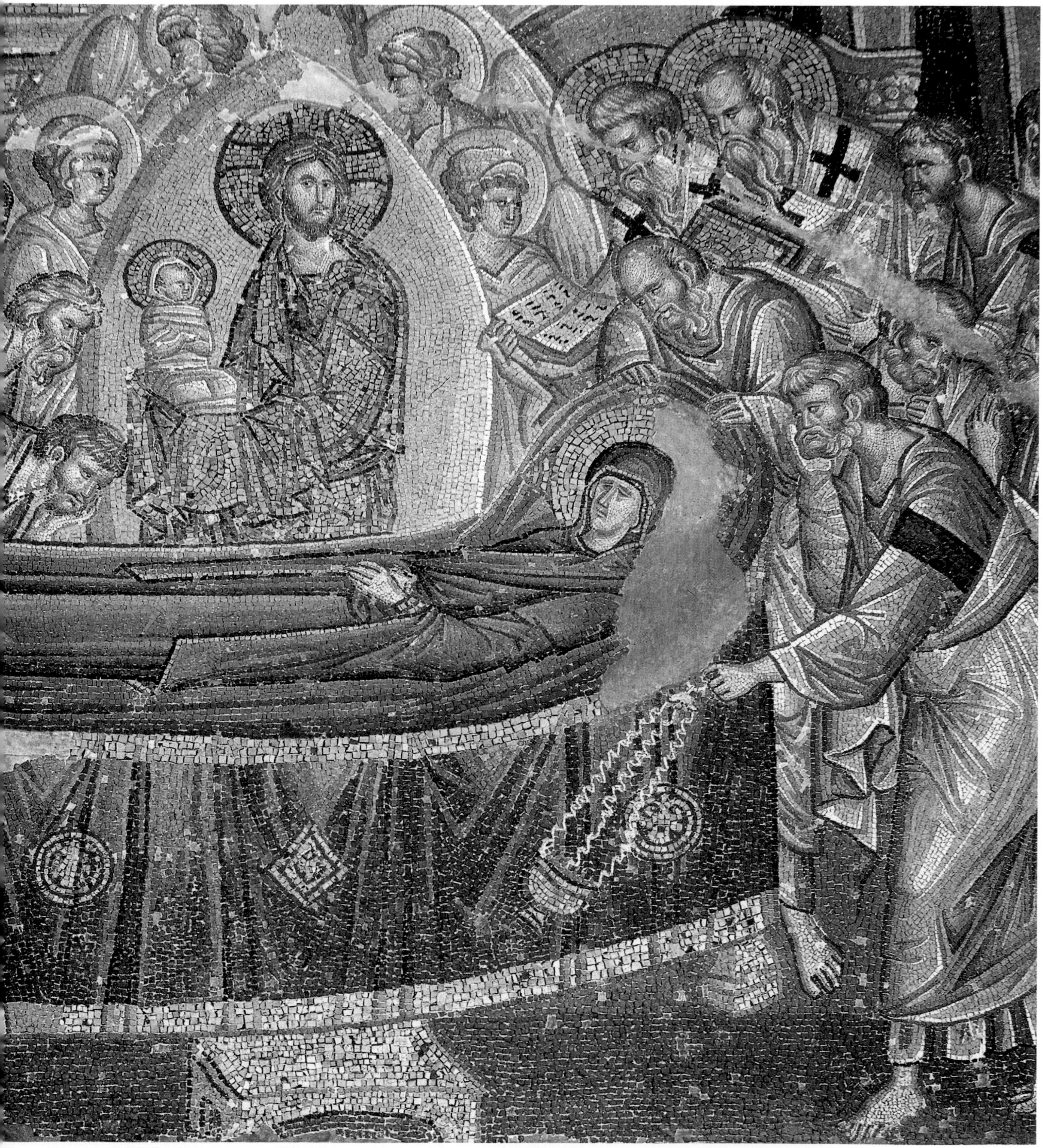

This 15th-century manuscript illustration depicts the troops of John II Kalojan, King of Bulgaria (1197–1207), defeating the army of Baldwin I (1171–1205), Count of Flanders and Latin Emperor of the East, near Adrianopolis in 1205.

the trade of the capital city itself), and the King of Naples, gave Byzantium little respite. One emperor desperately accepted papal primacy and reunion with the Roman Church; this policy did little except antagonize his own clergy and his successor abandoned it. Religion still divided Christendom.

As the fourteenth century wore on, the Byzantines had a deepening sense of isolation. They felt abandoned to the infidel. An attempt to use Western mercenaries from Catalonia only led to their attacking Constantinople and setting up yet another breakaway state, the Catalan duchy of Athens, in 1311. Occasional victories when an island or a province was retaken did not offset the general tendency of these events, nor the debilitating effect of occasional civil war within the empire. True to their traditions, the Greeks managed even in this extremity to invest some of these struggles with a theological dimension. On top of all this, the plague in 1347 wiped out a third of what was left of the empire's population.

CHRISTIANITY DIVIDED

In 1400, when the emperor travelled the courts of western Europe to drum up help (a little money was all he got) he ruled only Constantinople, Salonica and the Morea. Many in the West now spoke of him, significantly, as "emperor of the Greeks", forgetting he was still titular emperor of the Romans. The Turks surrounded the capital on all sides, and had already carried out their first attack on it. There was a second in 1422. John VIII made a last attempt to overcome the strongest barrier to cooperation with the West. He went in 1439 to an ecumenical council sitting in Florence and there accepted papal primacy and union with Rome. Western Christendom rejoiced; the bells were rung in all the parish churches of England. But the Orthodox East scowled. The council's formula ran headlong against its tradition; too much stood in the way – papal authority, the equality of bishops, ritual and doctrine. The most influential Greek clergy had refused to attend the council; the large number who did all signed the formula of union except one (he, significantly, was later canonized) but many of them recanted when they went home. "Better," said one Byzantine dignitary, "to see in the city the power of the Turkish turban than that of the Latin tiara." Submission to the pope was for most Greeks a renegade act; they were denying the true Church, whose tradition Orthodoxy had conserved. In Constantinople itself priests known to accept the council were shunned; the emperors were loyal to the agreement but thirteen years passed before they dared to proclaim the union publicly at Constantinople. The only benefit from the submission was the pope's support for a last crusade (which ended in disaster in 1441). In the end the West and East could not make common cause. The infidel was, as yet, battering only at the West's outermost defences. France and Germany were absorbed in their own affairs; Venice and Genoa saw their interest might lie as much in conciliation of the Turk as in opposition to him. Even the Russians, harried by Tatars, could do little to help Byzantium, cut off as they were from direct contact with it. The imperial city, and little else, was left alone and divided within itself to face the Ottomans' final effort.

THE OTTOMANS

WHO WERE THE OSMANLIS, or, as they became known in Europe, the Ottomans? They were one of the Turkish peoples who had emerged from the collapse of the sultanate of Rum. When the Seljuks arrived there they found on the borderlands between the dissolved Abbasid caliphate and the Byzantine Empire a number of Muslim marcher lords, petty princes called *ghazis*, sometimes Turkish by race, lawless, independent and the inevitable beneficiaries of the ebbing of paramount power. Their existence was precarious, and the Byzantine Empire had absorbed some of them in its tenth-century recovery, but they were hard to control. Many survived the Seljuk era and benefited from the Mongol destruction of the Seljuks at a time when Constantinople was in the hands of the Latins. One of these *ghazis* was Osman, a Turk who may have been an Oghuz. But his appeal lay in his leadership and enterprise, and men gathered to him. His quality is shown by the transformation of the world *ghazi*: it came to mean "warrior of the faith". Fanatical frontiersmen, his followers seem to have been distinguished by a certain spiritual *élan*. Some of them were influenced by a particular mystical tradition within Islam. They also developed highly characteristic institutions of their own. They had a military organization somewhat like that of merchant guilds or religious orders in medieval Europe and it has been suggested that the West learnt in these matters from the Ottomans. Their situation on a curious borderland of cultures, half-Christian, half-Islamic, must also have been provoking. Whatever its ultimate source, their staggering record of conquest rivals that of Arab and

After its conquest by the sultan Orkhan (1326–1359), son of the founder of the Ottoman Dynasty, Bursa (Turkey) became the Ottoman Empire's first capital. Most of the sultans are buried there. The Green Mausoleum, pictured here, was built in 1421 and houses the remains of the sultan Mehmet I.

Mongol. They were in the end to reassemble under one ruler the territory of the old Eastern Roman Empire and more.

THE OTTOMAN SULTANS

The first Ottoman to take the title of Sultan did so in the early fourteenth century. This was Orkhan, Osman's son. Under him began the settlement of conquered lands which was eventually to be the basis of Ottoman military power. Like his foundation of the "Janissaries", the new infantry corps which he needed to fight in Europe, the change marked an important stage in the evolution of Ottoman empire away from the institutions of a nomadic people of natural cavalrymen. Another sign that things were settling down was Orkhan's issue of the first Ottoman coinage. At his death he ruled the strongest of the post-Seljuk states of Asia Minor as well as some European lands. Orkhan was important enough to be three times called upon by the Byzantine emperor for help and he eventually married one of the emperor's daughters.

His two successors steadily ate up the Balkans, conquering Serbia and Bulgaria. They defeated another "crusade" against them in 1396 and went on to take Greece. In 1391 they began their first siege of Constantinople, which they maintained successfully for six years. Meanwhile, Anatolia was absorbed by war and diplomacy. There was only one bad setback, the defeat by Timur which brought on a succession crisis and almost dissolved the Ottoman Empire. The advance was then resumed and the Venetian Empire now began to suffer, too. But for Byzantine and Turk alike, the struggle was essentially a religious one and its heart was the possession of the thousand-year-old Christian capital, Constantinople.

THE FALL OF CONSTANTINOPLE

It was under Mehmet II, named the Conqueror, that in 1453 Constantinople fell to the Turks and the Western world shuddered. It was a great victory, depleted though the resources of Byzantium were, and Mehmet's personal achievement, for he had persisted against all obstacles. The age of gunpowder was now well under way and he had a Hungarian engineer build him a gigantic cannon, whose operation was so cumbersome that it could only be moved by a hundred oxen and fired only seven times a day (the Hungarian's assistance had been turned down by the Christians though the fee he asked was a quarter of what Mehmet gave him). It was a failure. Mehmet did better with orthodox methods, driving his soldiers forward ruthlessly, cutting them down if they flinched from the assault. Finally, he carried seventy ships overland to get them behind the imperial squadron guarding the Horn.

The last attack began early in April 1453. After nearly two months, on the evening of 28 May, Roman Catholics and Orthodox alike gathered in St Sophia and the fiction of the religious reunion was given its last parade. The emperor Constantine XI, eightieth in succession since his namesake, the great first Constantine, took communion and then went out to die worthily, fighting. Soon afterwards, it was all over. Mehmet entered the city, went straight to St Sophia and there set up a triumphant throne. The church which had been the heart of Orthodoxy was made a mosque.

OTTOMAN EXPANSION

The conquest of Constantinople was only a step, great as it was; the banner of Ottoman success was to be raised yet higher. The invasion of Serbia in 1459 was almost at once

During the mandate of Sultan Orkhan, the Janissaries, an élite body of soldiers, was formed. Its ranks were initially made up of Christians who were abducted from their families as children and brought up as Muslims. From the 17th century, recruitment to the Janissaries was carried out from among the Turks themselves.

followed by the conquest of Trebizond. Unpleasant though this may have been for the inhabitants, it would merit only a footnote to the roll of Turkish conquest were it not also the end of Hellenism. At this remote spot on the southeastern coast of the Black Sea in 1461 the world of Greek cities made possible by the conquest of Alexander the Great gave its last gasp. It marked an epoch as decisively as the fall of Constantinople, which a humanist pope bewailed as "the second death of Homer and Plato". From Trebizond, Turkish conquest rolled on. In the same year the Turks occupied the Peloponnese.

Two years later they took Bosnia and Herzegovina. Albania and the Ionian islands followed in the next twenty years. In 1480 they captured the Italian port of Otranto and held it for nearly a year. In 1517 Syria and Egypt were conquered. They took longer to pick up the remainder of the Venetian Empire, but at the beginning of the sixteenth century Turkish cavalry were near Vicenza. Belgrade fell to them in 1521, and a year later Rhodes was seized. In 1526 at Mohács the Turks wiped out the army of the Hungarian king in a defeat which is remembered still as the black day of Hungarian history. Three years later they besieged Vienna for the first time. In 1571 Cyprus fell to them and nearly a century later Crete. By this time they were deep into Europe. They again besieged Vienna in the seventeenth century; their second failure to take it was the high-water mark of Turkish conquest. But they were still conquering new territory in the Mediterranean as late as 1715. Meanwhile, they had taken Kurdistan from Persia, with whom they had hardly ceased to quarrel since the appearance of a new dynasty there in 1501, and had sent an army as far south as Aden.

THE CONSEQUENCES OF OTTOMAN VICTORY

The Ottoman Empire was to be of unique importance to Europe. It is one of the big differences marking off the history of its eastern from that of its western half. It was crucial that the Church survived and was tolerated in the Ottoman Empire. That preserved the heritage of Byzantium for its Slav subjects (and, indeed, ended any threat to the supremacy of the patriarch at Constantinople either from the Catholics or from ethnic Orthodox churches in the Balkans). Outside the former empire, only one important focus of Orthodoxy remained; it was crucial that the Orthodox Church was now the heritage of Russia. The establishment of the Ottoman Empire for a time sealed off Europe from the Near East and the Black Sea and, therefore, in large measure from the land routes to Asia. The Europeans had really only themselves to blame; they had never been (and were never to be) able to unite effectively against the Turks. Byzantium had been left to her fate. "Who will make the English love the French? Who will unite Genoese and Aragonese?" asked one pope despairingly; not long after, one of his successors was sounding out the possibilities of Turkish help against France. Yet the challenge had awoken another sort of response, for even before the fall of Constantinople Portuguese ships were

Ottoman expansion in the 14th and 15th centuries

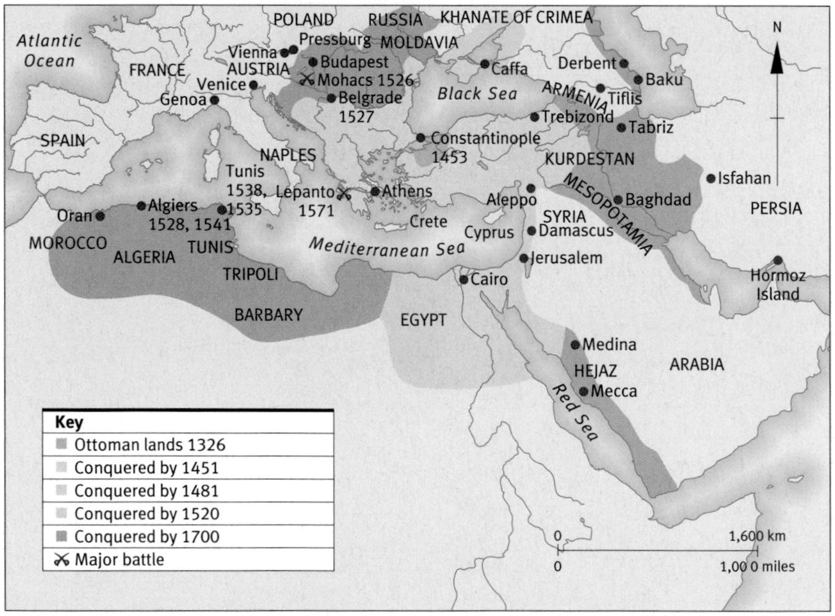

The above map shows the expansion and decline of the Ottoman Empire and gives the dates of its major campaigns. The Ottomans first entered Europe in 1345; by 1520 they controlled most of southeastern Europe, as well as parts of the Middle East and North Africa. The tide of conquest was largely stemmed in Europe with the Turkish defeat at Lepanto in 1571. Tunis was successfully captured in 1574, but the Ottoman army's second siege of Vienna in 1683 was a disaster for the Turks – the days of great Ottoman expansion were over, although there were still conquests to come.

picking their way southwards down the African coast to look for a new route to the spices of the East and, possibly, an African ally to take the Turk in the flank from the south. People had mused over finding a way around the Islamic barrier since the thirteenth century, but the means had long been inadequate. By one of history's ironies they were just about to become available as Ottoman power reached its menacing peak.

RELIGIOUS TOLERANCE UNDER MEHMET

Behind the Ottoman frontiers a new multiracial empire was organized. Mehmet was a man of wide, if volatile, sympathies; later Turks found it hard to understand his forbearance to the infidel. He was a man who could slaughter a boy, the godson of the emperor, because his sexual advances were refused, but he allowed a band of Cretans who would not surrender to sail away after the fall of Constantinople because he admired their courage. He seems to have wanted a multireligious society. He brought back Greeks to Constantinople from Trebizond and appointed a new patriarch under whom the Greeks were eventually given a kind of self-government. The Turkish record towards Jew and Christian was better than that of Spanish Christians towards Jew and Muslim. Constantinople remained a great cosmopolitan city (and with a population of 700,000 in 1600, one far larger than any other in geographical Europe).

Thus the Ottomans reconstructed a great power in the eastern Mediterranean. While they rebuilt something like the Byzantine Empire, another power was emerging in

The Sulaimaniye Mosque in Istanbul was built between 1550 and 1557, during the reign of Sulaiman the Magnificent. The famous Ottoman architect, Sinan, based the design of the mosque on that of the former church of St Sophia. The new mosque, however, was intended to surpass its rival in size and beauty and thus assert the superiority of Islam over Christianity.

This view of the interior of the great Byzantine church of St Sophia, which now houses a museum, shows one of the two half-domed apses. From the Ottoman conquest of Constantinople in 1453, when it was converted into a mosque, the building's interior was gradually Islamicized. Additions have included a *mihrab*, Koranic inscriptions, chandeliers and railings. In 1623, the original baptistry was transformed into a mausoleum to the sultan Mustafa I; and under Ahmed III (1703–1730), a pulpit, or *minbar*, was erected.

The origins of the Persian Safavid Dynasty can be traced to the members of a ruling Turkish family who were natives of Ardabil. This bowl was produced during the Safavid era.

Persia which was also reminiscent of the past, this time of the empire of the Sassanids.

SAFAVID PERSIA

BETWEEN 1501 AND 1736 the Safavid Dynasty ruled Persia. Like their predecessors, the Safavids were not themselves Persian. Since the days of the Sassanids, conquerors had come and gone. The continuities of Persian history were meanwhile provided by culture and religion. Persia was defined by geography, by its language and by Islam, not by the maintenance of national dynasties. The Safavids were originally Turk, *ghazis* like the Osmanlis, and succeeded, like them, in distancing possible rivals. The first ruler they gave to Persia was Ismail, a descendant of the fourteenth-century tribal ruler who had given his name to the line.

At first, Ismail was only the most successful leader of a group of warring Turkish tribes, rather like those further west, exploiting similar opportunities. The Timurid inheritance had been in dissolution since the middle of the fifteenth century. In 1501 Ismail defeated the people known as the White Sheep Turks, entered Tabriz and proclaimed himself shah. Within twenty years he had carved out an enduring state and had also embarked upon a long rivalry with the Ottomans.

This rivalry had a religious dimension, for the Safavids were Shi'ites and they made Persia Shi'ite, too. When in the early sixteenth century the caliphate passed to the Ottomans they became the leaders of Sunnite Muslims who saw the caliphs as the proper interpreters and governors of the faith. The Shi'ites were therefore automatically anti-Ottoman. Ismail's establishment of the sect in Persia thus gave a new distinctiveness to Persia's civilization and this was to prove of great importance in preserving it.

SHAH ABBAS THE GREAT

Ismail's immediate successors had to fight off the Turks several times before a peace

Under the Safavids, Isfahan regained the splendour it had enjoyed during the 11th and 12th centuries when it had been ruled by the Seljuk Dynasty. Shah Abbas the Great instigated an ambitious building programme designed to convert Isfahan into a great imperial capital. Here, a view from the Royal Mosque towards the dome of the Lutfullah Mosque takes in the Maidan – a rectangular public space that served both as a marketplace and as a sportsfield.

This Persian bathing scene is taken from a 15th-century Safavid miniature.

was made in 1555, which left Persia intact and opened Mecca and Medina to Persian pilgrims. There were domestic troubles too, and fighting for the throne, but in 1587 there came to it one of the most able of Persian rulers, Shah Abbas the Great. Under his rule the Safavid Dynasty was at its zenith. Politically and militarily he was very successful, defeating the Uzbeks and the Turks and taming the old tribal loyalties which had weakened his predecessors. He had important advantages: the Ottomans were distracted in the west, the potential of Russia was sterilized by internal troubles and Moghul India was past its peak. He was clever enough to see that Europe could be enrolled against the Turk. Yet a favourable conjuncture of international forces did not lead to schemes of world conquest. The Safavids did not follow the Sassanid example. They never took the offensive against Turkey except to recover earlier loss and they did not push north through the Caucasus to Russia, or beyond Transoxiana.

Persian culture enjoyed a spectacular flowering under Shah Abbas, who built a new capital at Isfahan. Its beauty and luxury astounded European visitors. Literature flourished. The only ominous note was religious. The shah insisted on abandoning the religious toleration which had until now characterized Safavid rule and imposed conversion to Shi'ite views.

This did not at once mean the imposition of an intolerant system; that would only come later. But it did mean that Safavid Persia had taken a significant step towards decline and towards the devolution of power into the hands of religious officials.

SAFAVID DECLINE

After Shah Abbas's death in 1629 events rapidly took a turn for the worse. His unworthy successor did little about this, preferring to withdraw to the seclusion of the harem and its pleasures, while the traditional splendour of the Safavid inheritance cloaked its actual collapse. The Turks took Baghdad again in 1638. In 1664 came the first portents of a new threat: Cossack raids began to harry the Caucasus and the first Russian mission arrived in Isfahan. Western Europeans had already long been familiar with Persia. In 1507 the Portuguese had established themselves in the port of Ormuz where Ismail levied tribute on them. In 1561 an English merchant reached Persia overland from Russia and opened up Anglo-Persian trade. In the early seventeenth century his connection was well established and by then Shah Abbas had Englishmen in his service. This was the result of his encouragement of relations with the West, where he hoped to find support against the Turk.

The Safavid ruler Shah Abbas the Great (1587–1629) lowered taxes, improved the road network, encouraged the development of trade and supported craftsmen and artists. This brazier dates from the Safavid era.

The growing English presence was not well received by the Portuguese. When the East India Company opened operations they attacked its agents, but unsuccessfully. A little later the English and Persians joined forces to eject the Portuguese from Ormuz. By this time other European countries were becoming interested, too. In the second half of the seventeenth century the French, Dutch and Spanish all tried to penetrate the Persian

Safavid poetry

"I have made my grandparents glorious by my own hand!
If I should ever flee, cut short my life if it is long!
May my grandparents put the envious to shame by my hand.
Do not allow them to spit in my face,
but rather only over my dead body!
Make my adversaries thirty thousand heroes,
and may each one of them be a Rustam!
I will go to the battlefield when I feel inclined
and then they will see I will fight all of them!
I will put them all to the edge of my sword.
They will neither be able to agree or to attack.
And do heroes worry about dying?
Should I let a sack of bran rot?"

A poem by Ismail I (1486–1524), the founder of the Persian Safavid Dynasty.

trade. The shahs did not rise to the opportunity of playing off one set of foreigners against another.

At the beginning of the eighteenth century Persia was suddenly exposed to a double onslaught. The Afghans revolted and established an independent Sunnite state; religious antagonism had done much to feed their sedition. From 1719 to 1722 the Afghans were at war with the last Safavid shah. He abdicated in that year and an Afghan, Mahmud, took the throne, thus ending Shi'ite rule in Persia. The story must none the less be taken a little further forward, for the Russians had been watching with interest the progress of Safavid decline. The Russian ruler had sent embassies to Isfahan in 1708 and 1718. Then, in 1723, on the pretext of intervention in the succession, the Russians seized Derbent and Baku and obtained from the defeated Shi'ites promises of much more. The Turks decided not to be left out and, having seized Tiflis, agreed in 1724 with the Russians upon a dismemberment of Persia. That once great state seemed to be ending in nightmare. In Isfahan a massacre of possible Safavid sympathizers was carried out by orders of a shah who had now gone mad. There was, before long, to be a last Persian recovery by the last great Asiatic conqueror, Nadir Kali. But though he might restore Persian empire, the days when the Iranian plateau was the seat of a power which could shape events far beyond its borders were over until the twentieth century, and then it would not be armies which gave Iran its leverage.

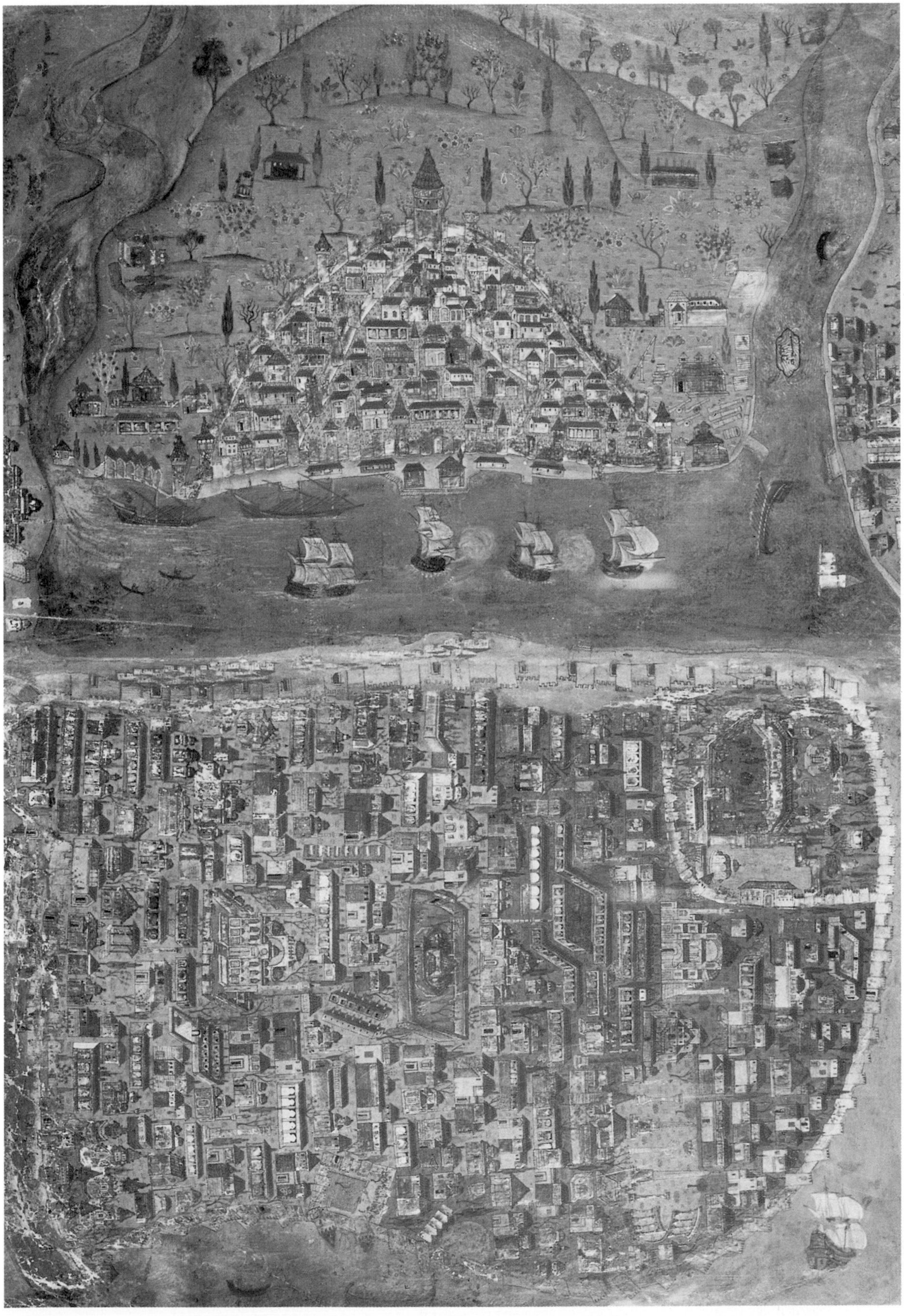

The arrival of the Ottoman Turks in Constantinople was to radically change the appearance of the ancient Christian city. Building fever gripped successive sultans – the personal ambitions of each one live on in an array of mosques and minarets. Many of the city's new Islamic buildings can be seen in this illustration, dated 1537.

5 THE MAKING OF EUROPE

During the 11th century, Saragossa was one of the most important Islamic centres in the Western world. This frieze embellishes the so-called Marble Room in the city's enormous Aljaferia Palace, which was built during the reign of al-Muqtadir.

If the comparison is with Byzantium or the caliphate, then Europe west of the Elbe was for centuries after the Roman collapse an almost insignificant backwater of world history. The cities in which a small minority of its people lived were built among and of the ruins of what the Romans had left behind; none of them could have approached in magnificence Constantinople, Córdoba, Baghdad or Ch'ang-an. A few of the leading individuals of its peoples felt themselves a beleaguered remnant and so, in a sense, they were. Islam cut them off from Africa and the Near East. Arab raids tormented their southern coasts. From the eighth century the seemingly inexplicable violence of the Norse peoples we call Vikings fell like a flail time and time again on the northern coasts, river valleys and islands. In the ninth century the eastern front was harried by the pagan Magyars. Europe had to form itself in a hostile, heathen world.

THE CONSOLIDATION OF EUROPE

The foundations of a new civilization had to be laid in barbarism and backwardness, which only a handful of men was available to tame and cultivate. Europe would long be a cultural importer. It took centuries before its architecture could compare with that of the classical past, of Byzantium or the Asian empires, and when it emerged it did so by borrowing the style of Byzantine Italy and the pointed arch of the Arabs. For just as long, no science, no school in the West could match those of Arab Spain or Asia. Nor could the West produce an effective political unity or theoretical justification of power such as the Eastern Empire and the caliphates; for centuries even the greatest European kings were hardly more than barbarian warlords to whom the population clung for protection and in fear of something worse.

Had it come from Islam, that something might well have been better. At times, such an outcome must have seemed possible, for the

Arabs established themselves not only in Spain but in Sicily, Corsica, Sardinia and the Balearics; people long feared they might go further. They had more to offer than the Scandinavian barbarians, yet in the end the northerners left more of a mark on the kingdoms established by earlier migrants. As for Slavic Christendom and Byzantium, both were culturally sundered from the West and able to contribute little to it. Yet they were a cushion which just saved Europe from the full impact of Eastern nomads and of Islam. A Muslim Russia would have meant a very different history for the West.

GEOGRAPHICAL LIMITS

Roughly speaking, Western Christendom before 1000 CE meant half the Iberian peninsula, all modern France and Germany west of the Elbe, Bohemia, Austria, the Italian mainland and England. At the fringes of this area lay barbaric, but Christian, Ireland, Scotland and the Scandinavian kingdoms. To this area the word "Europe" began to be applied in the tenth century; a Spanish chronicle even spoke of the victors of 732 as "European". The area they occupied was all but landlocked; though the Atlantic was wide open, there was almost nowhere to go in that direction once Iceland was settled by the Norwegians, while the western Mediterranean, the highway to other civilizations and their trade, was an Arab lake. Only a thin channel of seaborne communication with an increasingly alien Byzantium brought Europe some relief from its introverted, narrow existence. Its people grew used to privation rather than opportunity. They

This dish is one of many similar glazed ceramic pieces that are characteristic of Islamic art. Known as "green and manganese", the technique used consists of covering plaster in varnished tin and decorating it with copper and manganese oxides.

Found in the medieval cemetery of St Mary's church in Llugo de Llanera, Spain, this tablet dates from between the 8th and 10th centuries. It features the ancient symbol of the tree of life, upon which two lions appear to be feeding. The tree's roots are immersed in water, represented by a line of half moons. Appropriated by Christian, and particularly Byzantine, symbolism, this motif was common all over Europe.

Time chart (711–962)

- 711 The Muslims invade the Iberian peninsula
- 751 Pepin the Short founds the Carolingian Dynasty
- 771 Charlemagne becomes sole ruler of the Frankish kingdoms
- 843 The Treaty of Verdun results in the three-way division of the Carolingian Empire
- 871–899 Alfred the Great is king of Wessex
- 910 Foundation of the Abbey of Cluny
- 962 Otto I is crowned Holy Roman Emperor by the pope

700 750 800 850 900 950 1000

As the end of the 1st millennium approached, some Christians believed that the Kingdom of God was about to be established on earth, freeing the poor of the world from their bonds. Others believed in the prophecy, contained in the Book of Revelation, that the Devil would be set free from his chains and rule on earth. This miniature comes from the "Apocalypse of St Sever" (a manuscript named after the French church in which it was originally housed) and depicts the "fifth plague": the Angel of Hell (Satan) watches gleefully as locusts torment human beings.

huddled together under the rule of a warrior class whose protection they needed.

In fact, the worst was over in the tenth century. The Magyars were checked, the Arabs were beginning to be challenged at sea, and the northern barbarians were on the road to Christianity. The approach of the year 1000 was no portentous fact for most Europeans; many were unaware of it, for counting by years from the supposed birth of Christ was by no means yet the norm. That year can serve, none the less, very approximately, as the marker of an epoch. Not only had the pressures upon Europe begun to relax, but the lineaments of a later, expanding Europe were already hardening. Much of its basic political and social structure was set and the Christian culture had already much of its peculiar flavour. The eleventh century was to begin an era of revolution and adventure, for which the centuries sometimes called the Dark Ages had provided raw materials. As a way to understand how this happened, a good starting-point is the map.

Well before this, three great changes began the making of the European map we know. One was a cultural and psychological shift away from the Mediterranean, the focus of classical civilization. Between the fifth and eighth centuries, the centre of European life, in so far as there was one, moved to the valley

The Western world in the year 1000

Key

- Holy Roman Empire under Otto III (996–1002)
- Anglo-Saxon reconquest in the 10th century
- State of Kiev in 912
- Expansion of the State of Kiev from 912 to 1054
- Byzantine Empire in the 10th century
- Western extent of Byzantine Empire on the death of Basil II, 1025
- Bulgarian Empire of Tsar Samuel in around 996
- Muslim world at the end of the 10th century
- Christian kingdoms in the Iberian Peninsula

of the Rhine and its tributaries. By preying on the sea-lanes to Italy and by its distraction of Byzantium in the seventh and eighth centuries, Islam, too, helped to throw back the West upon this heartland of a future Europe. The second change was more positive, a gradual advance of Christianity and settlement in the East. Though far from complete by 1000, the advance guards of Christian civilization had by then long been pushed out well beyond the old Roman frontier. The third change was the slackening of barbarian pressure. The Magyars were checked in the tenth century; the Norsemen who were eventually to provide rulers in England, northern France, Sicily and some of the Aegean came from the last wave of Scandinavian expansion, which was in its final phase in the early eleventh century. Western Europe was no longer to be just a prey to others. True, even two hundred years later, when the Mongols menaced her, it must have been difficult to feel this. None the less, by 1000 she was ceasing to be wholly plastic.

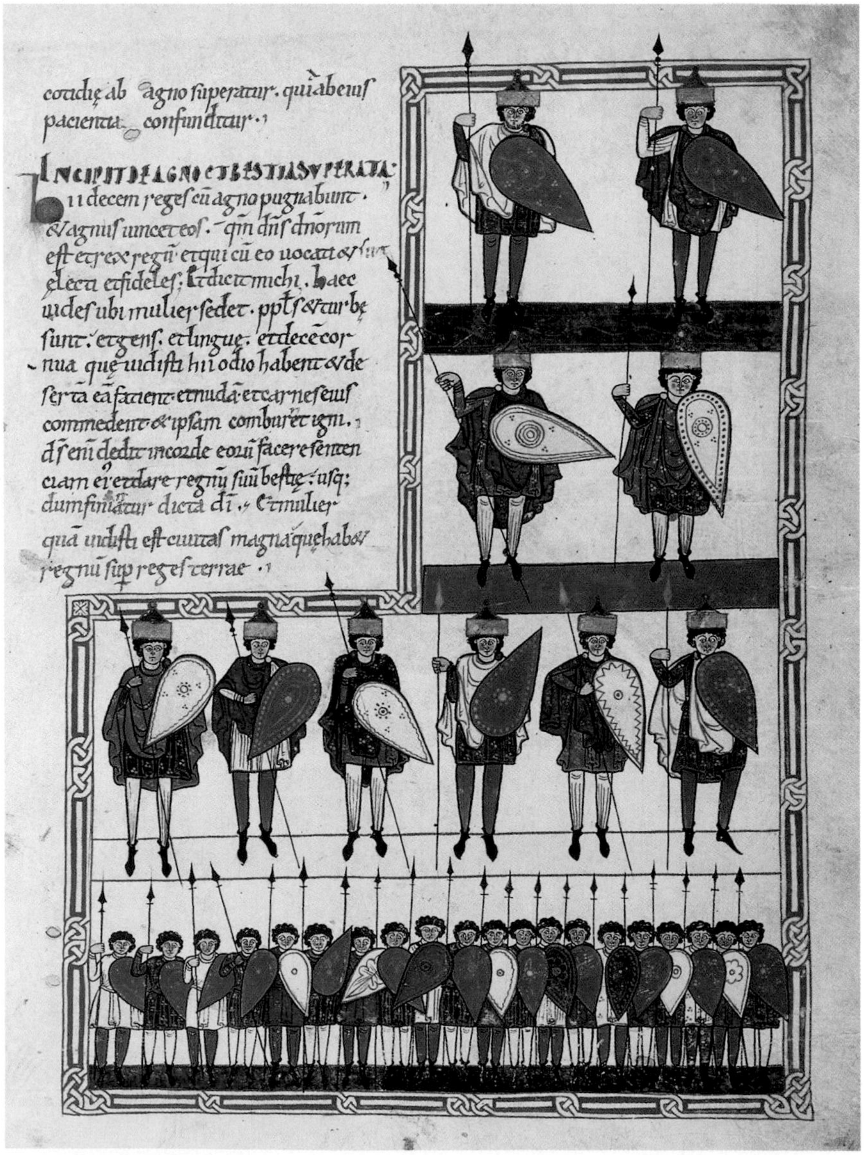

Frankish warriors, such as the ones depicted in this 11th-century miniature, rendered military service to the Romans in exchange for permission to settle on the empire's frontiers.

WESTERN CHRISTENDOM

Western Christendom can be considered in three big divisions. In the central area, built around the Rhine valley, the future France and the future Germany were to emerge. Then there was a west Mediterranean littoral civilization, embracing at first Catalonia, the Languedoc and Provence. With time and the recovery of Italy from the barbarian centuries, this extended itself further to the east and south. A third Europe was the somewhat varied periphery in the west, northwest and north where there were to be found the first Christian states of northern Spain, which emerged from the Visigothic period; England, with its independent Celtic and semi-barbarous neighbours, Ireland, Wales and Scotland; and lastly the Scandinavian states. We must not be too categorical about such a picture. There were areas one might allocate to one or the other of these three regions, such as Aquitaine, Gascony and sometimes Burgundy. Nevertheless, these distinctions are real enough to be useful. Historical experience, as well as climate and race, made these regions significantly different, yet of course most people living in these areas would not have known in which one they lived; they would certainly have been more interested in differences between them and their neighbours in the next village than of those between their region and its neighbour. Dimly aware that they were a part of Christendom, very few of them would have had even an approximate conception of what lay in the awful shadows beyond that comforting idea.

THE FRANKISH HERITAGE

The origin of the heartland of the medieval West was the Frankish heritage. It had fewer towns than the south and they mattered little; a settlement like Paris was less troubled by the collapse of commerce than, say, Milan. Life centred on the soil, and aristocrats were successful warriors turned landowners. From this base, the Franks began the colonization of Germany, protected the Church and hardened and passed on a tradition of kingship whose origins lay somewhere in the magical powers of Merovingian rulers. But for centuries, state structures were fragile things, dependent on strong kings. Ruling was a very personal activity.

Frankish ways and institutions did not help. After Clovis, though there was dynastic continuity, a succession of impoverished and therefore feeble kings led to more independence for landed aristocrats, who warred with one another; they had the wealth which could buy power. One family from Austrasia came to overshadow the Merovingian royal line. It produced Charles Martel, the soldier who turned the Arabs back at Tours in 732 and the supporter of St Boniface, the evangelizer of Germany. This is a considerable double mark to have left on European history (St Boniface said he could not have succeeded without Charles's support) and it confirmed the alliance of Martel's house with the Church. His second son, Pepin the Short, was chosen king by the Frankish nobles in 751. Three years later, the pope came to France and anointed him king as Samuel had anointed Saul and David.

The conversion to Roman Catholicism of the Merovingian monarch Clovis (this illustration shows his baptism in 496), was a political measure. It was a means of drumming up the support of the Gallo-Roman people for the Franks against other Germanic peoples such as the Visigoths, Ostrogoths and Burgundians, who advocated Arian heresy.

PAPAL RECOGNITION

The papacy needed a powerful friend. The pretensions of the emperor in Constantinople were a fiction and in Roman eyes he had fallen into heresy, in any case, through taking up Iconoclasm. To confer the title of Patrician on Pepin, as Pope Stephen did, was really a usurpation of imperial authority, but the Lombards were terrorizing Rome. The papacy drew the dividend on its investment almost at once. Pepin defeated the Lombards and in 756 established the Papal States of the future by granting Ravenna "to St Peter". This was the beginning of eleven hundred years of the Temporal Power, the secular authority enjoyed by the pope over his own dominions as a ruler like any other ruler. A Romano-Frankish axis was created, too. From it stemmed the reform of the Frankish Church, further colonization and missionary conversion in Germany (where wars were waged against the pagan Saxons), the throwing back of the Arabs across the

Pyrenees and the conquest of Septimania and Aquitaine. These were big gains for the Church. It is hardly surprising to find Pope Hadrian I no longer dating official documents by the regnal year of the emperor at Byzantium, and minting coins in his own name. The papacy had a new basis for independence. Nor did the new magic of anointing benefit only kings. Though it could replace or blur mysteriously with the old Merovingian thaumaturgy and raise kings above common men in more than their power, the pope gained the subtle implication of authority latent in the power to bestow the sacral oil.

Charlemagne's churches

"With the gold that Charlemagne gave to the kings and princes of Spain, he enriched the Basilica of Santiago, in whose lands he had stayed for three years; he established a bishop and canons, according to the Order of St Isadore, bishop and confessor, and with great dignity furnished it with bells, tapestries, books and other ornaments. With the rest of the gold and the endless amount of silver that he had taken out of Spain having returned from there, he built many churches, namely: the Church of the Virgin Mary in Aquisgranum (Aachen) and the Basilica of Santiago in the same city; the Church of Santiago in Béziers; the Basilica of Santiago in Toulouse and in Gascony, between the city which is popularly known as Aix and St Jean de Sorde on the Jacobean route; the church that is in the city of Paris between the River Seine and Montmartre, and innumerable abbeys throughout the world."

An extract from Chapter V, Book IV of the "Pseudo-Turpin Chronicle", from the *Liber Santi Jacobi* or *Codex Calistinus*, thought to be the work of Turpin, Archbishop of Reims (died c.794).

CHARLEMAGNE

PEPIN, LIKE ALL FRANKISH KINGS, divided his land at his death but the whole Frankish heritage was united again in 771 in his elder son. This was Charlemagne, crowned emperor in 800. The greatest of the Carolingians, as the line came to be called, he was soon a legend. This increases the difficulties, always great in medieval history, of penetrating an individual's biography. Charlemagne's actions speak for certain continuing prepossessions. He was obviously still a traditional Frankish warrior-king; he conquered and his business was war. What was more novel was the seriousness with which he took the Christian sanctification of this role. He took his duties seriously, too, in patronizing learning and art; he wanted to magnify the grandeur and prestige of his court by filling it with evidence of Christian learning.

Scenes from the life of Charlemagne (742–814) are shown in these illustrations from a 15th-century manuscript of the emperor's biography.

The achievements of Charlemagne's reign

One of the most significant figures in European history is, without a doubt, Charlemagne (also known as Charles the Great). The son of Pepin the Short and Bertha, daughter of Cariberto, Count of Lyons, Charlemagne ruled a unified Carolingian kingdom from 771 to 814.

Although Charlemagne's empire lacked centralized organization, it did achieve a remarkable ascendancy over the political and warrior class, of a kind that had not been seen in Europe since the fall of the Western Roman Empire. One of his important achievements as emperor was the enforcement throughout the imperial territories of a general code of law, issued through a series of instructions. Charlemagne also initiated a cultural renaissance and the use of Latin as the official language. He carried out monetary reform, imposing an imperial monopoly on the minting of coins. Even such cohesion as his empire achieved, however, was to be short-lived: it did not survive the reign of his son, Louis the Pious (814–831 and 835–840).

Charlemagne's dreams are depicted in this miniature from a 15th-century manuscript entitled "The Great Chronicles of France".

Territorially, Charlemagne was a great builder, overthrowing the Lombards in Italy and becoming their king; their lands, too, passed into the Frankish heritage. For thirty years he hammered away in campaigns on the Saxon March and achieved the conversion of the

Legend has it that this sword, with its elaborate hilt, once belonged to the emperor Charlemagne. It was customary for a small relic of a saint to be carried in the hilt of such swords: this was thought to render the user invincible.

Saxon pagans by force. Fighting against the Avars, Wends and Slavs brought him Carinthia and Bohemia and, perhaps as important, the opening of a route down the Danube to Byzantium. To master the Danes, the Dane Mark (March) was set up across the Elbe. Charlemagne pushed into Spain early in the ninth century and instituted the Spanish March across the Pyrenees down to the Ebro and the Catalonian coast. But he did not put to sea; the Visigoths had been the last western European sea-power.

CHARLEMAGNE AND THE IMPERIAL TITLE

Charlemagne put together a realm bigger than anything in the West since Rome. Historians have been arguing almost ever since about what its reality was and about what Charlemagne's coronation by the pope on Christmas Day, 800, and his acclamation as emperor, actually meant. "Most pious Augustus, crowned by God, the great and peace-giving Emperor" ran the chart at the service but there already was an emperor whom everybody acknowledged to be such: he lived in Constantinople. Did a second ruler with the title mean that there were two emperors of a divided Christendom, as in later Roman times? Clearly, it was a claim to authority over many peoples; by this title, Charlemagne said he was more than just a ruler of Franks. Perhaps Italy mattered most in explaining it, for among the Italians a link with the imperial past might be a cementing factor as nowhere else. An element of papal gratitude – or expediency – was involved, too;

"La Chanson de Roland"

A number of "epic poems" – tales of heroic deeds recounted by minstrels – have survived from the Carolingian era and give us a fascinating insight into the feudal society and culture of the time. The epics appear to have been written by poets who turned certain historic or legendary deeds into "songs", to which they then added epic characteristics with a strong ethical content.

The oldest of the French songs is "La Chanson de Roland". The identity of the author is unknown, although some specialists believe that the monk Turoldus may have composed the song. Written in the early 12th century, it has 4,002 verses and tells of the death of Count Roland, Charlemagne's nephew. The poem is loosely based on real events – Roland was the warden of the Breton March. He and his troops, who had been left behind in Spain as a rear-guard by Charlemagne in 778, were killed by Basques. The poem tells how Roland, having been betrayed by his stepfather Ganelon, was killed in Roncesvalles by the soldiers of Marsilius, King of Spain. It recounts how, before he died, Roland had managed to alert Charlemagne's troops, who rushed in vain to his aid. They then pursued Marsilius' armies, defeating them at Baligant and conquering Saragossa.

Leo III had just been restored to his capital by Charlemagne's soldiers. Yet Charlemagne is reported to have said that he would not have entered St Peter's had he known what the pope intended to do. He may have disliked the pope's implied arrogation of authority. He may well have foreseen the irritation the coronation would cause at Constantinople. He must have known that to his own people, the Franks, and to many of his northern subjects he was more comprehensible as a traditional Germanic warrior-king than as the successor of Roman emperors, yet before long his Seal bore the legend *Renovatio Romani imperii*, a conscious reconnection with a great past.

Charlemagne's Europe

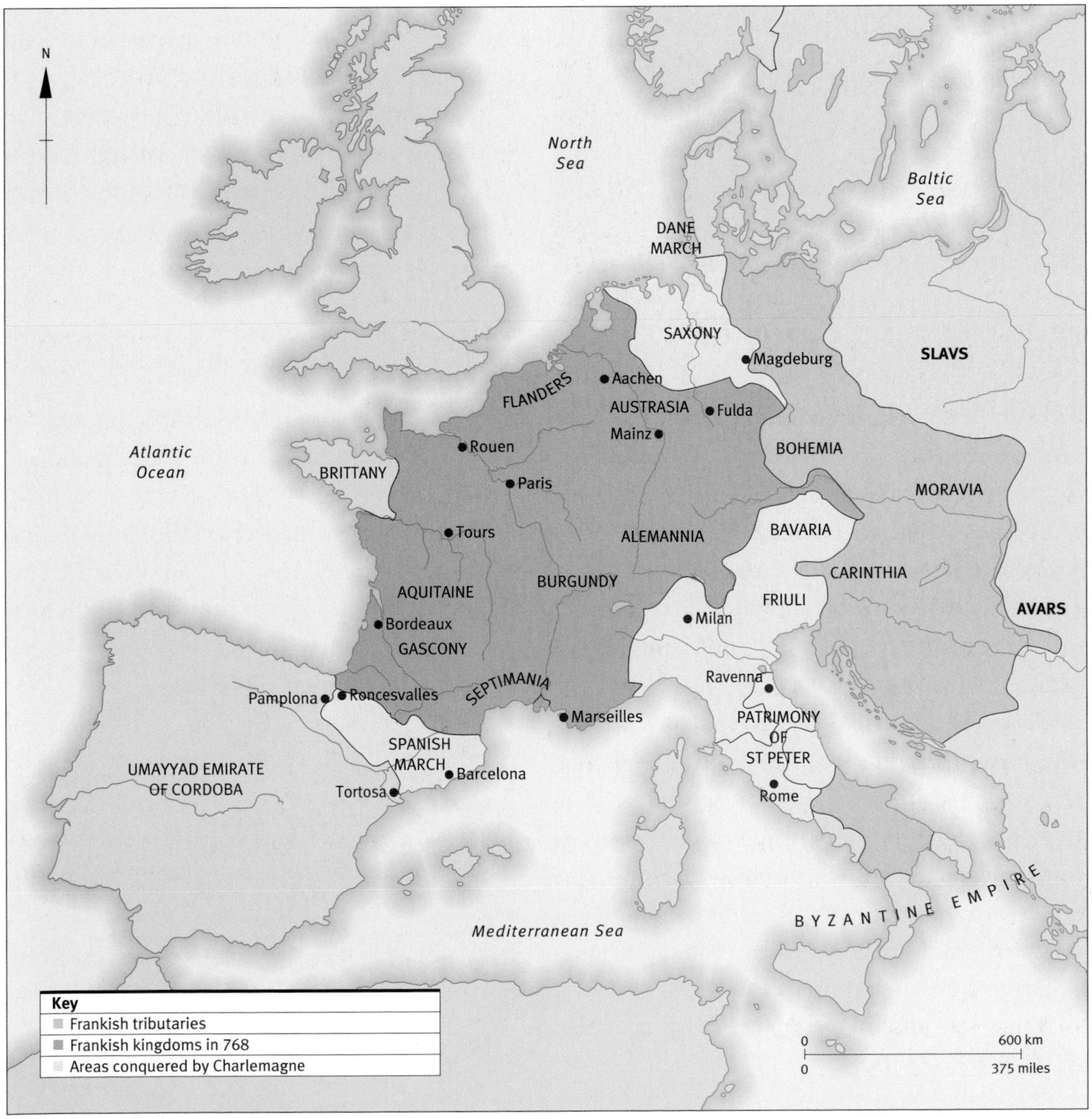

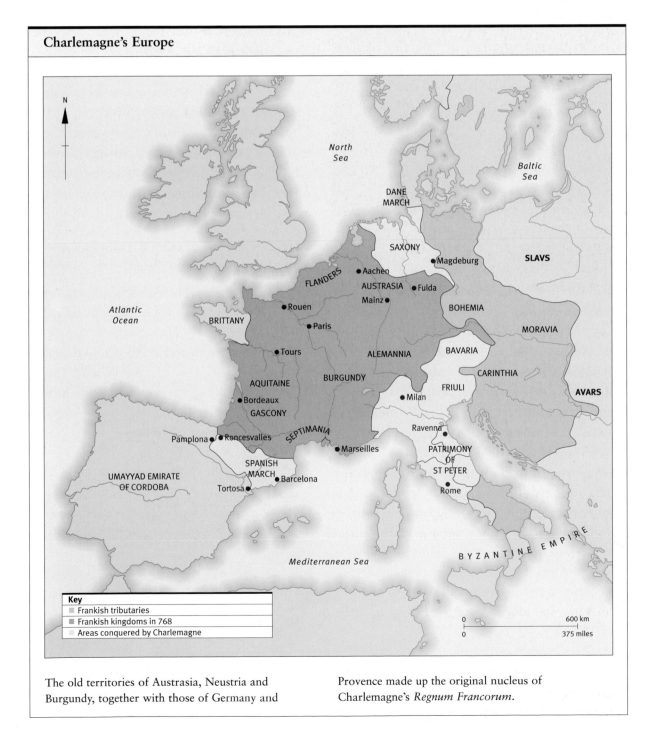

The old territories of Austrasia, Neustria and Burgundy, together with those of Germany and Provence made up the original nucleus of Charlemagne's *Regnum Francorum*.

Taken from the "Chronicle of St Denis", which was written in 1497, this illustration depicts the emperor Charlemagne surveying progress in the construction of a church he commissioned at Aachen, now Aix-la-Chapelle.

CHARLEMAGNE'S RULE

Charlemagne's relations with Byzantium were troubled, though his title was a few years later recognized as valid in the West in return for a concession to Byzantium of sovereignty over Venice, Istria and Dalmatia. With another great state, the Abbasid caliphate, Charlemagne had somewhat formal but not unfriendly relations; Haroun-al-Raschid is said to have given him a cup bearing a portrait of Khusrau I, the king under whom Sassanid power and civilization was at its height (perhaps it is significant that it is from Frankish sources that we learn of these contacts; they do not seem to have struck the Arab chroniclers as important enough to mention). The Umayyads of Spain were different; they were marked down as the enemies of a Christian ruler because near enough to be a threat. To protect the faith from pagans was a part of Christian kingship. For all his support and protection, though, the Church was firmly subordinate to Charlemagne's authority. He presided over the Frankish synods, pronouncing upon dogmatic questions as authoritatively as had Justinian, and seems to have hoped for an integrated reform of the Frankish Church and the Roman, imposing upon them both the Rule of St Benedict. In such a scheme there is the essence of the later European idea that a Christian king is responsible not only for the protection of the Church but for the quality of the religious life within his dominions. Charlemagne also used the Church as an instrument of government, ruling through bishops.

THE CAROLINGIAN RENAISSANCE

Further evidence of religion's special importance to Charlemagne lies in the tone of the life of his court at Aachen. He strove to beautify its physical setting with architecture and decorative treasures. There was, of course, much to be done. The ebbing of economic life and of

According to legend, the famous "Cup of Solomon" was given to Charlemagne by the Abbasid caliph Haroun-al-Raschid. At the centre of the cup, the Sassanid king Khusrau I is depicted.

The Four Evangelists are depicted in this illustration from a 9th-century manuscript called "The Coronation Gospels". The manuscript was produced at Charlemagne's court school in Aachen during the great creative period known as the "Carolingian Renaissance".

In the period of cultural splendour that occurred during Charlemagne's reign, the familiar traditions of Roman and Byzantine art were merged with characteristics from other cultures, including Celtic and Viking. This renaissance also influenced architecture – Gerona cathedral's 9th-century tower, known as "the Charlemagne Tower", dates from this period.

literacy meant that a Carolingian court was a primitive thing by comparison with Byzantium and possibly even in comparison with those of some of the early barbarian kingdoms which were open to influence from a more cultivated world, as the appearance of Coptic themes in early barbarian art attests. When Charlemagne's men brought materials and ideas to beautify Aachen from Ravenna, Byzantine art, too, moved more freely into the north European tradition and classical models still influenced his artists. But it was its scholars and scribes who made Charlemagne's court most spectacular. It was an intellectual centre. From it radiated the impulse to copy texts in a new refined and reformed hand called Carolingian minuscule which was to be one of the great instruments of culture in the West (and, in the end, a model for modern typefaces). Charlemagne had hoped to use it to supply an authentic copy of the Rule of St Benedict to every monastery in his realm, but the major expression of a new manuscript potential was first evident in the copying of the Bible. This had a more than religious aim, for the scriptural story was to be interpreted as a justification of Carolingian rule. The Jewish history of the Old Testament was full of examples of pious and anointed warrior-kings. The Bible was the major text in the monastic libraries which now began to be assembled throughout the Frankish lands.

Copying and the diffusion of texts went on for a century after the original impulse had been given at Aachen and were the core of what modern scholars have called "the Carolingian Renaissance". It had none of the pagan connotations of that word as it was used of a later revival of learning which focused attention on the classical

His relationship with the papacy played an important role in Charlemagne's politics. This illustration, dated 1499, depicts the emperor receiving Pope Leo III (795–816), who had fled to the Frankish court after being forced to leave Rome. Charlemagne's soldiers escorted Leo back to Rome, where the papacy was restored to him.

past, for it was emphatically Christian. Its whole purpose was the training of clergy to raise the level of the Frankish Church and carry the faith further to the east. The leading men in the beginnings of this transmission of sacred knowledge were not Franks. There were several Irishmen and Anglo-Saxons in the palace school at Aachen and among them the outstanding figure was Alcuin, a cleric from York, a great centre of English learning. His most famous pupil was Charlemagne himself, but he had several others and managed the palace library. Besides writing books of his own he set up a school at Tours, where he became abbot, and began to expound Boethius and Augustine to the men who would govern the Frankish church in the next generation.

Although it was actually made for the coronation of Otto I the Great (936–973), the fact that this beautiful object is known as "Charlemagne's Crown" is indicative of the legendary status that the Carolingian emperor achieved in medieval Europe. The enamel plaque, one of four that decorate the crown, represents King Solomon as the symbol of wisdom.

CHARLEMAGNE'S PERSONAL AUTHORITY

Alcuin's pre-eminence is as striking a piece of evidence as any of the shift in the centre of cultural gravity in Europe, away from the classical world and to the north. But others than his countrymen were involved in teaching, copying and founding the new monasteries which spread outwards into East and West Francia; there were Franks, Visigoths, Lombards and Italians among them, too. One of these, a layman called Einhard, wrote a life of the emperor from which we learn such fascinating human details as the facts that he could be garrulous, that he was a keen hunter and that he passionately loved swimming and bathing in the thermal springs, which explain his choice of Aachen as a residence. Charlemagne comes to life in Einhard's pages as an intellectual, too, speaking Latin as well, we are told, as Frankish, and understanding Greek. This is made more credible because we hear also of his attempts to write, keeping notebooks under his pillow so that he could do so in bed, "but", Einhard says, "although he tried very hard, he had begun too late in life".

From this account and from his work a remarkably vivid picture can be formed of a dignified, majestic figure, striving to make the transition from warlord to ruler of a great Christian empire, and having remarkable success in his own lifetime in so doing. Clearly his physical presence was impressive (he probably towered over most of his entourage), and others saw in him the image of a kingly soul, gay, just and magnanimous, as well as that of the heroic paladin of whom poets and minstrels would be singing for centuries. His authority was a more majestic spectacle than anything seen to that time in barbarian lands. When his reign began, his

This illustration, from the Bible of Count Vivian, dates from 851. It shows Charles the Bald (840–877), one of the three grandsons of Charlemagne who succeeded him in a partitioned empire, enthroned and surrounded by his courtiers.

court was still peripatetic, it normally ate its way from estate to estate throughout the year. When Charlemagne died, he left a palace and a treasury established at the place where he was to be buried. He had been able to reform weights and measures, and had given to Europe the division of the pound of silver into 240 pennies (*denarii*) which was to survive in the British Isles for eleven hundred years. But his power was also very personal. This may be inferred from the efforts he made to prevent his noblemen from replacing tribal rulers by settling down into hereditary positions of their own, and from the repeated issuing of "capitularies" or instructions to his servants (a sign that his wishes were not carried out). In the last resort, even a Charlemagne could only rely on personal rule, and that meant a monarchy based on his own domain and its produce and on the big men close enough to him for supervision. These vassals were bound to him by especially solemn oaths, but even they began to give trouble as he grew older.

THE SUCCESSORS

Charlemagne thought in traditional Frankish terms of his territorial legacy. He made plans to divide it and only the accident of sons dying before him ensured that the empire passed undivided to the youngest, Louis the Pious, in 814. With it went the imperial title (which Charlemagne gave to his son) and the alliance of monarchy and papacy; two years after his succession the pope crowned Louis at a second coronation. Partition was only delayed by this. Charlemagne's successors had neither his authority nor his experience, nor perhaps an interest in controlling fissiparous forces. Regional loyalties were forming around individuals and a series of partitions finally culminated in one between three of Charlemagne's grandsons, the Treaty of Verdun of 843, which had great consequences. It gave a core kingdom of Frankish lands centred on the western side of the Rhine valley and containing Charlemagne's capital, Aachen, to Lothair, the reigning emperor (thus it was called Lotharingia) and added to this the kingdom of Italy. North of the Alps, this united Provence, Burgundy, Lorraine and the lands between the Scheldt, Meuse, Saône and Rhône. To the east lay a second block of lands of Teutonic speech between the Rhine and the German Marches; it went to Louis the German. Finally, in the west, a tract of

Louis the Pious, who is pictured here, was Charlemagne's sole heir. Dethroned by his son Lothair in 831, he was reinstated as emperor by his other sons in 835, but died five years later.

The Eastern Frankish kingdom came to be made up of a mixture of peoples, including the Saxons, Bavarians, Swabians and Franconians. This initial, framed by images of the Four Evangelists, is from a 9th-century Franco-Saxon gospel.

territory including Gascony, Septimania and Aquitaine, and roughly the equal of the rest of modern France, went to a half-brother of these two, Charles the Bald.

THE WEST AND EAST FRANKS

The Treaty of Verdun settlement was not long untroubled, but it was decisive in a broad and important way; it effectively founded the political distinction of France and Germany, whose roots lay in West and East Francia. Between them it set up a third unit with much less linguistic, ethnic, geographical and economic unity. Lotharingia was there in part because three sons had to be provided for. Much future Franco-German history was going to be about the way in which it could be divided between neighbours bound to covet it and therefore likely to grow apart from one another in rivalry.

CAROLINGIAN DECLINE

No royal house could guarantee a constant flow of able kings, nor could they for ever buy loyalty from their supporters by giving away lands. Gradually, and like their predecessors, the Carolingians declined in power. The signs of break-up multiplied, an independent kingdom of Burgundy appeared and people began to dwell on the great days of Charlemagne, a significant symptom of decay and dissatisfaction. The histories of West and East Franks diverged more and more.

In West Francia the Carolingians lasted just over a century after Charles the Bald. By the end of his reign Brittany, Flanders, and Aquitaine were to all intents and purposes independent. The West Frankish monarchy thus started the tenth century in a weak position and it had the attacks of Vikings to deal with as well. In 911 Charles III, unable to expel the Norsemen, conceded lands in what was later Normandy to their leader, Rollo. Baptized the following year, Rollo set to work to build the duchy for which he did homage to the Carolingians; his Scandinavian countrymen continued to arrive and settle there until the end of the tenth century, yet somehow they soon became French in speech and law. After this, the unity of the West Franks fell even more rapidly apart. From confusion over the succession there emerged a son of a count of Paris who steadily built up his family's power around a domain in the Ile de France. This was to be the core of France. When the last Carolingian ruler of the West Franks died in 987, this man's son, Hugh Capet, was elected king. His family was to rule France for nearly four hundred years. For the rest, the West Franks were divided into a dozen or so territorial units ruled by magnates of varying standing and independence.

CONRAD OF FRANCONIA

Among the supporters of Hugh's election was the ruler of the East Franks. Across the Rhine, the repeated division of their heritage had quickly proved fatal to the Carolingians. When the last Carolingian king died in 911 there emerged a political fragmentation which was to characterize Germany down to the nineteenth century. The assertiveness of local magnates combined with stronger tribal loyalties than in the west to produce a half-dozen powerful dukedoms. The ruler of one of these, Conrad of Franconia, was chosen as king by the other dukes, somewhat surprisingly. They wanted a strong leader against the Magyars. The change of dynasty made it advisable to confer some special standing on the new ruler; the bishops therefore anointed Conrad at his coronation. He was the first ruler of the East Franks so to be treated and perhaps this is the moment at which there emerges a German state distinct from Carolingian Frankia. But Conrad was not successful against the Magyars; he lost and could not win back Lotharingia and he strove, with the support of the Church, to exalt his own house and office. Almost automatically, the dukes gathered their peoples about them to safeguard their own independence. The four whose distinction mattered most were the Saxons, the Bavarians, the Swabians and the Franconians (as the East Franks became known). Regional differences, blood and the natural pretensions of great nobles stamped on Germany in Conrad's reign the pattern of its history for a thousand years: a tug-of-war between central authority and local power not to be resolved in the long run in favour of the centre as elsewhere, though in the tenth century it looked otherwise for a while. Conrad faced ducal rebellion but nominated one of the rebels his successor and the dukes agreed. In 919, Henry "the Fowler" (as he was called), Duke of Saxony, became king. He and his descendants, the "Saxon emperors", or Ottonians, ruled the East Franks until 1024.

THE OTTONIANS

Henry the Fowler avoided the ecclesiastical coronation. He had great family properties and the tribal loyalties of the Saxons on his side and brought the magnates into line by proving himself a good soldier. He won back Lotharingia from the West

This 11th-century illustration, depicting St Peter receiving the keys of the Church, is from one of the many religious manuscripts commissioned by the Ottonian king Henry II.

The emperor Otto II (973–1002) is depicted on this marble plaque with his wife Theophano, who is holding their son (the future Otto III) in her arms. The couple are shown kneeling at the feet of the enthroned figure of Christ.

Franks, created new Marches on the Elbe after victorious campaigns against the Wends, made Denmark a tributary kingdom and began its conversion, and, finally, he defeated the Magyars. His son, Otto I, thus had a substantial inheritance and made good use of it. In disciplining the dukes, he continued his father's work. In 955 he inflicted on the Magyars a defeat which ended for ever the danger they had presented. Austria, Charlemagne's east March, was recolonized. Though he faced some opposition, Otto made a loyal instrument out of the German Church; it was an advantage of the Saxon emperors that in Germany churchmen tended to look with favour to the monarchy for protection against predatory laymen. A new archiepiscopal province, Magdeburg, was organized to direct the bishoprics established among the Slavs. With Otto ends, it has been said, the period of mere anarchy in central Europe; under him, certainly, we have the first sense of something we might call Germany. But Otto's ambition did not stop there.

In 936 Otto had been crowned at Aachen, Charlemagne's old capital. Not only did he accept the ecclesiastical service and anointing which his father had avoided, but he afterwards held a coronation banquet at which the German dukes served him as his vassals. This was in the old Carolingian style. Fifteen years later he invaded Italy, married the widow of a claimant to the crown of Italy, and assumed it himself. Yet the pope refused him an imperial coronation. Ten years later, in 962, Otto was back in Italy again in response to an appeal by the pope for help, and this time the pope crowned him.

EMPIRE REVIVED

Through Otto's coronation, the Roman and the Carolingian ideal of empire was revived. The German and Italian crowns were united again in what would one day be known as the Holy Roman Empire and would last nearly a thousand years. Yet it was not so wide an empire as Charlemagne's, nor did Otto dominate the Church as Charlemagne had done. For all his strength (and he deposed two popes and nominated two others) Otto was the Church's protector who thought he knew what was best for it, but he was not its governor. Nor was the structure of the empire very solid; it rested on the political manipulation of local magnates rather than on administration.

Nevertheless, the Ottonian Empire was a remarkable achievement. Otto's son, the future Otto II, married a Byzantine princess. Both he and Otto III had reigns troubled by revolt, but successfully maintained the tradition established by Otto the Great of exercising power south of the Alps. Otto III made a cousin pope (the first German to sit in the chair of St Peter) and followed him by appointing the first French pope. Rome seemed to captivate him and he settled down there. Like both his immediate predecessors, he called himself *augustus* but in addition his seals revived the legend "Renewal of the Roman Empire" which he equated with the Christian empire. Half Byzantine by birth, he saw himself as a new Constantine. A diptych of a gospel-book painted nearly at the end of the tenth century shows him in state, crowned and orb in hand, receiving the homage of four crowned women: they are Sclavonia (Slavic Europe), Germany, Gaul and Rome. His notion of a Europe organized as a hierarchy of kings serving under the emperor was Eastern. In this there was megalomania as well as genuine religious conviction; the real basis of Otto's power was his German kingship, not the Italy which obsessed and detained him. Nevertheless, after his death in 1002, his body was taken to Aachen, as he had ordered, to be buried beside Charlemagne.

The medieval Empire

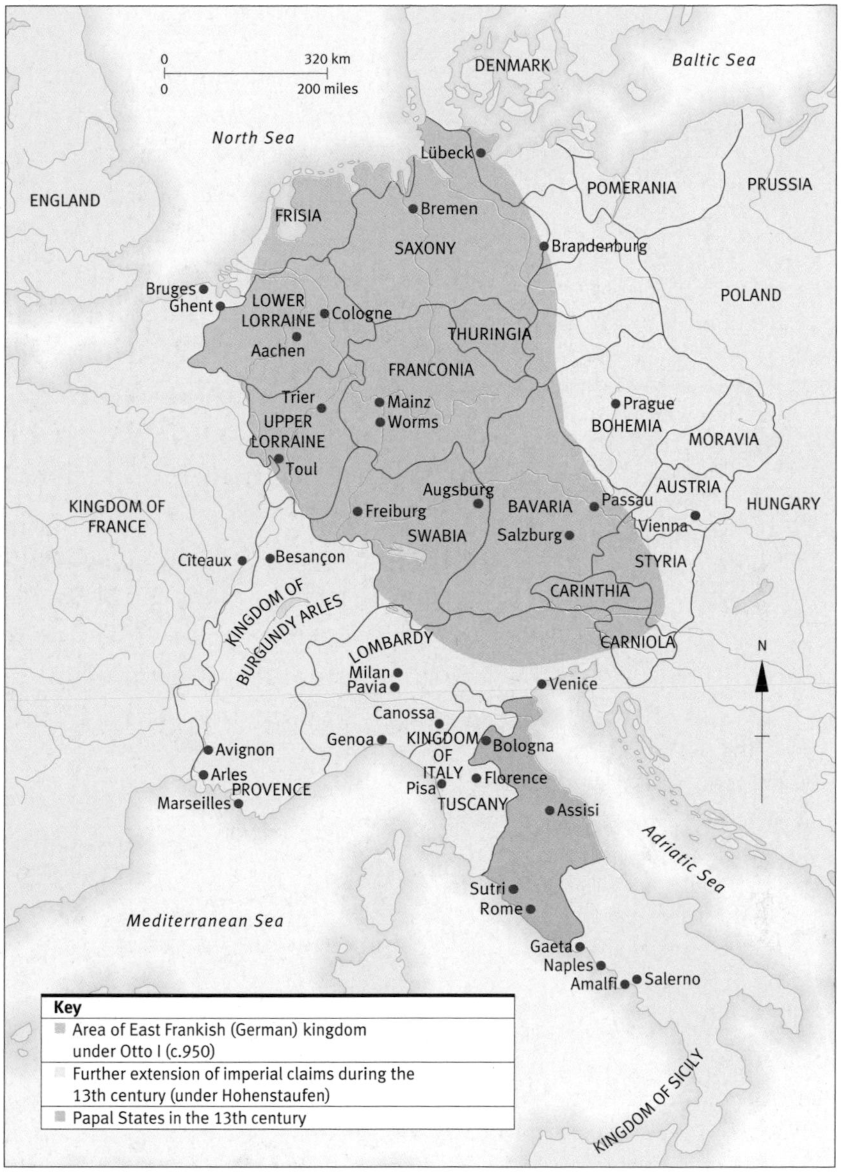

Otto I reunified two-thirds of the Carolingian Empire, redirecting its focus from France to the German regions. Only the western part of France remained outside his control.

During the 13th century, the rulers of the Hohenstaufen Dynasty expanded the territories of the empire, but 200 years of conflict with the papal monarchy had fatally weakened it.

THE DECLINE OF THE OTTONIANS

Otto III left no heir, but the direct Saxon line was not exhausted; Henry II, who was elected after a struggle, was a great-grandson of Henry the Fowler. But his coronation at Rome hardly hid the reality; he was a German ruler, not emperor of the West, at heart. His seal's inscription read "Renewal of the kingdom of the Franks" and his attention was focused on pacification and conversion in the German east. Though he made three expeditions to Italy, Henry relied there not on government but on politics, the playing off of factions against one another. With him the Byzantine style of the Ottonian Empire began to wane.

Thus the eleventh century opened with the idea of Western empire still capable of beguiling monarchs, but with the Carolingian inheritance long since crumbled into fragments. They set out the lines of European history for ages to come. The idea of Germany barely existed but a political reality did, even if it was still inchoate. The curious federal structure which was to emerge from the German Middle Ages was to be the last refuge of the imperial idea in the West, the Holy Roman Empire.

Meanwhile, in France, too, the main line of the future was settled, though it could not have been discerned at the time. West Francia had dissolved into a dozen or so major units over which the suzerainty of the Capetians was for a long time feeble. But they had on their side a centrally placed royal domain, including Paris and the important diocese of Orleans, and the friendship of the Church. These were advantages in the hands of able kings, and able kings would be forthcoming in the next three centuries.

This is the title page of a copy of "The Edict of Rothari", a codification of Lombard customs that was still observed as law in Italy as late as the 11th century.

ITALY AND SOUTHERN EUROPE

The other major component of the Carolingian heritage had been Italy. It had gradually become more and more distinct from the territories north of the Alps; since the seventh century it had been evolving away from the possibility of integration with northern Europe and back towards re-emergence as a part of Mediterranean Europe. By the middle of the eighth century, much of Italy had been subjugated by the Lombards. This barbarian people had settled down in the peninsula and had adopted an Italianate speech, but they remained an aggressive minority, whose social tensions demanded release in frequent wars of conquest, and they had shaped the Catholicism they had adopted to their own needs and institutions. In spite of the theoretical survival of the legal claims of the Eastern emperors, the only possible balancing power to them in Italy until the eighth century was the pope. When the Lombard principalities began to consolidate under a vigorous monarchy, this was no longer enough; hence the evolution of papal diplomacy towards alliance with the Carolingians. Once the Lombard kingdom had been destroyed by Charlemagne, there was no rival in the peninsula to the Papal States, though after the waning of the Carolingians' power the popes had to face both the rising power of the Italian magnates and their own Roman aristocracy. The Western Church was at its lowest ebb of cohesion and unity

The Lombards' early relationship with the Church was not always a friendly one. This painting from the Theodolinda Chapel in Monza, near Milan, shows a Christian hermit (the blond figure to the left of the central rider), about to go into battle against the Lombard troops.

and the Ottonians' treatment of the papacy showed how little power it had. An anarchic Italian map was another result of this situation. The north was a scatter of feudal statelets. Only Venice was very successful; for two hundred years she had been pushing forward in the Adriatic and her ruler had just assumed the title of duke. She is perhaps better regarded as a Levantine and Adriatic rather than a Mediterranean power. City-states which were republics existed in the south, at Gaeta, Amalfi, Naples. Across the middle of the peninsula ran the Papal States. Over the whole fell the shadow of Islamic raids as far north as Pisa, while emirates appeared at Taranto and Bari in the ninth century. They were not to last, but the Arabs completed the conquest of Sicily in 902 and went on to rule it for a century and a half with profound effects.

The Arabs shaped the destiny of the other west Mediterranean coasts of Europe, too. Not only were they established in Spain, but even in Provence they had more or less permanent bases (one of them being St Tropez). The inhabitants of the European coasts of the Mediterranean had, perforce, a complex relationship with the Arabs, who appeared to

We know that the Lombard architects tended to concentrate on restoration. Although few examples of original Lombard building and sculpture survive today, these stucco sculptures have been preserved in a small oratory in the church of St Mary of the Valley in Cividale, near Rome.

The discovery of this gilt bronze helmet of Swedish type in a Saxon royal burial ground at Sutton Hoo, England, demonstrates the strong Nordic influence that pervaded 7th-century Saxon England. The helmet was part of a mainly pagan treasure which was buried with a ship, possibly in honour of the East Anglian king Redwald (599–625).

them both as free-booters and as traders; the mixture was not unlike that observable in the Viking descents except that the Arabs showed little tendency to settle. Southern France and Catalonia were areas in which Frankish had followed Gothic conquest, but many factors differentiated them from the Frankish north. The physical reminiscences of the Roman past were plentiful in these areas and so was a Mediterranean agriculture. Another distinctive characteristic was the appearance of a family of Romance languages in the south, of which Catalan and Provençal were the most enduring.

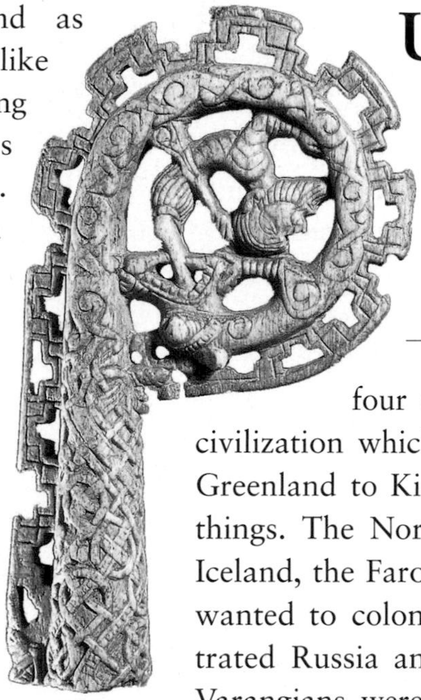

Until the 9th century, the Viking raids on England and Ireland were relentless and the violence and pillaging with which they were carried out were sometimes devastating. This staff originally belonged to an English bishop and was probably stolen during a raid: it was found in Helgö in Sweden.

SCANDINAVIA

IN 1000 CE, the peripheral Europe of the north barely included Scandinavia, if Christianity is the test of inclusion. Missionaries had been at work for a long time but the first Christian monarchs only appear there in the tenth century and not until the next were all Scandinavian kings Christian. Long before that, pagan Norsemen had changed the history of the British Isles and the northern fringe of Christendom.

For reasons which, as in the case of many other folk-movements, are by no means clear, but are possibly rooted in over-population, the Scandinavians began to move outwards from the eighth century onwards. Equipped with two fine technical instruments, a longboat which oars and sails could take across seas and up shallow rivers and a tubby cargo-carrier which could shelter large families, their goods and animals for six or seven days at sea, they thrust out across the water for four centuries, and left behind a civilization which in the end stretched from Greenland to Kiev. Not all sought the same things. The Norwegians who struck out to Iceland, the Faroes, Orkney and the far west wanted to colonize. The Swedes who penetrated Russia and survive in the records as Varangians were much busier in trade. The Danes did most of the plundering and piracy the Vikings are remembered for. But all these themes of the Scandinavian migrations wove in and out of one another. No branch of these peoples had a monopoly of any one of them.

The Viking colonization of remote islands was their most spectacular achievement. They wholly replaced the Picts in the Orkneys and the Shetlands and from them extended their rule to the Faroes (previously uninhabited except for a few Irish monks and their sheep) and the Isle of Man. Offshore, the Viking lodgement was more lasting and profound than on the mainland of Scotland and Ireland, where settlement began in the ninth century. Yet the Irish language records their importance by its adoption of Norse words in commerce, and the Irish map marks it by the situation of Dublin, founded by the Vikings and soon turned into an important trading-post. The most successful colony of all was Iceland. Irish hermits had anticipated Vikings there, too, and it was not until the end of the ninth century that they came in large numbers. By 930 there may have been 10,000 Norse Icelanders, living by farming and fishing, in part for their own subsistence, in part to produce commodities such as salt fish which they might trade. In that year the Icelandic state was founded and the *Thing* (which romantic antiquarians later saw as the first European "parliament") met for the first time. It was more like a council of the big men of the community than a modern representative body and it followed earlier Norwegian practice, but Iceland's continuous historical record is in this respect a remarkable one.

Colonies in Greenland followed in the tenth century; there were to be Norsemen there for five hundred years. Then they disappeared, probably because the settlers were wiped out by Eskimos pushed south by an advance of the ice. Of discovery and settlement further west we can say much less. The Sagas, the heroic poems of medieval Iceland, tell us of the exploration of "Vinland", the land where Norsemen found the wild vine growing, and of the birth of a child there (whose mother subsequently returned to Iceland and went abroad again as far as Rome as a pilgrim before settling into a highly sanctified retirement in her native land). There are reasonably good grounds to believe that a settlement discovered in Newfoundland is Norse. But we cannot at present go much further than this in uncovering the traces of the predecessors of Columbus.

This chalice, which dates from the beginning of the 8th century, was found in Ardagh in 1868 and constitutes one of the masterpieces of Irish gold and silver work. Treasures such as this were often seized by Viking raiders as booty.

VIKING RAIDS

In western European tradition, the colonial and mercantile activities of the Vikings were from the start obscured by their horrific impact as marauders. Certainly, they had some very nasty habits, but so did most barbarians. Some exaggeration must therefore be allowed for, especially because our main evidence comes from the pens of churchmen doubly appalled, both as Christians and as victims, by attacks on churches and monasteries; as pagans, of course, Vikings saw no special sanctity in the concentrations of precious metals and food so conveniently provided by such places, and found them especially attractive targets. Nor were the Vikings the first people to burn monasteries in Ireland.

None the less, however such considerations are weighed, it is indisputable that the Viking impact on northern and western Christendom was very great and very terrifying. They first attacked England in 793, the monastery of Lindisfarne being their victim; the attack shook the ecclesiastical world (yet the monastery lived on another eighty years). Ireland they raided two years later. In the first half of the ninth century the Danes began a harrying of Frisia which went on regularly year after year, the same towns being repeatedly plundered. The French coast was then attacked; in 842 Nantes was sacked with a great massacre. Within a few years a Frankish chronicler bewailed that "the endless flood of Vikings never ceases to grow". Towns as far inland as Paris, Limoges, Orleans, Tours and Angoulême were attacked. The Vikings had become professional pirates. Soon Spain suffered and the Arabs, too, were harassed; in 844 the Vikings stormed Seville. In 859 they even raided Nîmes and plundered Pisa, though they suffered heavily at the hands of an Arab fleet on their way home.

One of the first victims of the Vikings in England was the 7th-century monastery of Lindisfarne. The Lindisfarne monks produced intricate miniatures, of which this Hiberno-Saxon-style page from the so-called Lindisfarne Gospels (c.696–698) is an example.

THE CONSEQUENCES OF THE VIKING CAMPAIGNS

At its worst, think some scholars, the Viking onslaught came near to destroying civilization in West Francia; certainly the West Franks had to endure more than their cousins in the east and the Vikings helped to shape the differences between a future France and a future Germany. In the west their ravages threw new responsibilities on local magnates, while central and royal control crumbled away and men looked more and more towards their local lord for protection. When Hugh Capet came to the throne, it was very much as *primus inter pares* in a recognizably feudal society.

Not all the efforts of rulers to meet the Viking threat were failures. Charlemagne and Louis the Pious did not, admittedly, have to face attacks as heavy and persistent as their successors, but they managed to defend the vulnerable ports and river-mouths with some effectiveness. The Vikings could be (and were) defeated if drawn into full-scale field engagements and, though there were dramatic exceptions, the main centres of the Christian West were on the whole successfully defended. What could not be prevented were repeated small-scale raids on the coasts. When the Vikings learnt to avoid pitched battles, the only way to deal with them was to buy them off and Charles the Bald began paying them tribute so that his subjects should be left in peace.

This was the beginning of what the English called Danegeld. Their island had soon become a major target, to which Vikings began to come to settle as well as to raid. A small group of kingdoms had emerged there from the Germanic invasions; by the seventh century many of Romano-British descent were living alongside the communities of the new settlers, while others had been driven back to the hills of Wales and Scotland. Christianity continued to be diffused by Irish missionaries from the Roman mission which had established Canterbury. It competed with the older Celtic Church until 664, a crucial date. In that year a Northumbrian king at a synod of churchmen held at Whitby pronounced in favour of adopting the date of Easter set by the Roman Church. It was a symbolic choice, determining that the future England would adhere to the Roman traditions, not the Celtic.

Alfred the Great, King of Wessex (871–899), is depicted on this 9th-century Anglo-Saxon penny.

ALFRED THE GREAT

From time to time, one or other of the English kingdoms was strong enough to have some sway over the others. Yet only one of them could successfully stand up to the wave of Danish attacks from 851 onwards, which led to the occupation of two-thirds of the country.

This was Wessex and it gave England its first national hero who is also an historical figure, Alfred the Great.

As a child of four, Alfred had been taken to Rome by his father and was given consular honours by the pope. The monarchy of Wessex was indissolubly linked with Christianity and Carolingian Europe. As the other English kingdoms succumbed to invaders, it defended the faith against paganism as well as England against an alien people. In 871 Alfred inflicted the first decisive defeat on a Danish army in England. Significantly, a few years later the Danish king agreed not only to withdraw from Wessex but to accept conversion as a Christian. This registered that the Danes were in England to stay (they had settled in the north) but also that they might be divided from one another. Soon Alfred was leader of all the surviving English kings; eventually, he was the only one left. He recovered London and when he died in 899 the worst period of Danish raids was over and his descendants were to rule a united country. Even the settlers of the Danelaw, the area marked to this day by Scandinavian place-names and fashions of speech as that of Danish colonization defined by Alfred, accepted their rule. Nor was this all. Alfred had also founded a series of strongholds ("burghs") as a part of a new system of national defence by local levies. They not only gave his successors bases for the further reduction of the Danelaw but set much of the pattern of early medieval urbanization in England; on them were built towns whose sites are still inhabited today. Finally, with tiny resources, Alfred deliberately undertook the cultural and intellectual regeneration of his people. The scholars of his court, like those of Charlemagne, proceeded by way of copying and translation: the Anglo-Saxon

The Nordic Sagas

The Sagas are legendary tales – transcriptions of traditional oral stories from ancient Nordic literature in narrative or verse form. The Sagas, many of which are about about heroic deeds and great Nordic warriors, fall into two groups: the family Sagas and the historical Sagas. The latter cover the period of Scandinavian expansion in the 9th to 11th centuries. Later historical Sagas recounted the lives of kings and queens and, following the arrival of Christianity in the 11th century, of bishops.

The tradition of writing and story-telling was extremely widespread in Scandinavia (and in the lands conquered by the Vikings) until the 13th century, when its popularity appears to have waned.

The Viking gods Thor, Odin and Freyr are represented in this 12th-century tapestry from the church of Skog in Halringland, Sweden.

This Thor's hammer amulet dates from the 10th century. Although Christianity became important in Sweden from this time, objects such as this are evidence of the co-existence, at least until the 10th century, of ancient Nordic religion and Christianity.

Canute I, King of England, Denmark and Norway, and his wife, Queen Emma of Normandy, are depicted on this 11th-century manuscript. The couple are installing an altar cross in the Abbey of Newminster (which originally belonged to Canute's enemy Ethelred II).

nobleman and cleric were intended to learn of Bede and Boethius in their own tongue, the vernacular English.

THE SCANDINAVIAN LEGACY

Alfred's innovations were a creative effort of government unique in Europe. They marked the beginning of a great age for England. The shire structure took shape and boundaries were established which lasted until 1974. The English Church was soon to experience a remarkable surge of monasticism, the Danes were held in a united kingdom through a half-century's turbulence. It was only when ability failed in Alfred's line that the Anglo-Saxon monarchy came to grief and a new Viking offensive took place. Colossal sums of Danegeld were paid until a Danish king (this time a Christian) overthrew the English king and then died, leaving a young son to rule his conquest. This was the celebrated Canute, under whom England was briefly part of a great Danish empire (1016–35). There was a last great Norwegian invasion of England

The destruction of Barcelona in 985 by Al-Mansur's troops made it possible for the Counts of Barcelona to gain independence from the Carolingian monarch. Here, one of the counts, Ramón Berenguer I (1024–1076), is portrayed with his third wife, Almodis de la Marca, who was said to wield great influence over him.

in 1066, but it was shattered at the battle of Stamford Bridge. By that time, all the Scandinavian monarchies were Christian and Viking culture was being absorbed into Christian forms. It left many evidences of its individuality and strength in both Celtic and continental art. Its institutions survive in Iceland and other islands. The Scandinavian legacy is strongly marked for centuries in English language and social patterns, in the emergence of the duchy of Normandy, and, above all, in the literature of the Sagas. Yet where they entered settled lands, the Norsemen gradually merged with the rest of the population. When the descendants of Rollo and his followers turned to the conquest of England in the eleventh century they were really Frenchmen and the war-song they sang at Hastings was about Charlemagne the Frankish paladin. They conquered an England where the people of the Danelaw were by then English. Similarly, the Vikings lost their distinctiveness as an ethnic group in Kiev Rus and Muscovy.

CHRISTIAN SPAIN

The only other Western peoples of the early eleventh century who call for remark because of the future that lay before them were those of the Christian states of northern Spain. Geography, climate and Muslim division had all helped Christianity's survival in the peninsula and in part defined its extent. In the Asturias and Navarre Christian princes or chieftains still hung on early in the eighth century. Aided by the establishment of the Spanish March by Charlemagne and its subsequent growth under the new Counts of Barcelona, they nibbled away successfully at Islamic Spain while it was distracted by civil war and religious schism. A kingdom of León emerged in the Asturias to take its place beside a kingdom of Navarre. In the tenth century, however, it was the Christians who fell out with one another and the Arabs who again

The Iberian city of León in the Asturias was re-established in the reign of Ordoño II (914–924), the monarch who restored Christian unity in the region. He is depicted in this manuscript illustration.

Pagan and Christian imagery are combined in the decoration on this whalebone chest. The pagan scene on the left depicts Wayland the Smith awaiting his daughter Beadohild, after having murdered Nidhad's children. On the right, a Christian scene portrays the Adoration of the Three Kings.

made headway against them. The blackest moment came at the very end of the century when a great Arab conqueror, Al-Mansur, took Barcelona, León, and in 998 the shrine of Santiago de Compostela itself, where St James the Apostle was supposed to be buried. The triumph was not long-lived, for here, too, what had been done to found Christian Europe proved ineradicable. Within a few decades Christian Spain had rallied as Islamic Spain fell into disunion. In the Iberian peninsula as elsewhere, the age of expansion which this inaugurated belongs to another historical era, but was based on long centuries of confrontation with another civilization. For Spain, above all, Christianity was the crucible of nationhood.

THE CHURCH IN THE WEST

The Iberian example suggests just how much of the making of the map of Europe is the making of the map of the Faith, but an emphasis only on successful missions and ties with powerful monarchs is misleading. There was much more to early Christian Europe and the Christian life than this. The Western Church provides one of the great success stories of history, yet its leaders between the end of the ancient world and the eleventh or twelfth century long felt isolated and embattled in a pagan or semi-pagan world. Increasingly at odds with, and finally almost cut off from, Eastern Orthodoxy, it is hardly surprising that Western Christianity developed an aggressive intransigence almost as a defensive reflex. It was another sign of its insecurity. Nor was it threatened merely by enemies without. Inside Western Christendom, too, the Church felt at bay and beleaguered. It strove in the middle of still semi-pagan populations to keep its teaching and practice intact while christening what it could of a culture with which it had to live, judging nicely the concession which could be made to local practice or tradition and distinguishing it from a fatal compromise of principle. All this it had to do with a body of clergy of whom many, perhaps most, were men of no learning, not much discipline and dubious spirituality. Perhaps it is not surprising that the leaders of the Church sometimes overlooked the enormous asset they enjoyed in being faced by no spiritual rival in western Europe after Islam was turned back by Charles Martel; they had to contend only with vestigial paganism and superstition, and

Christendom before the Islamic conquest

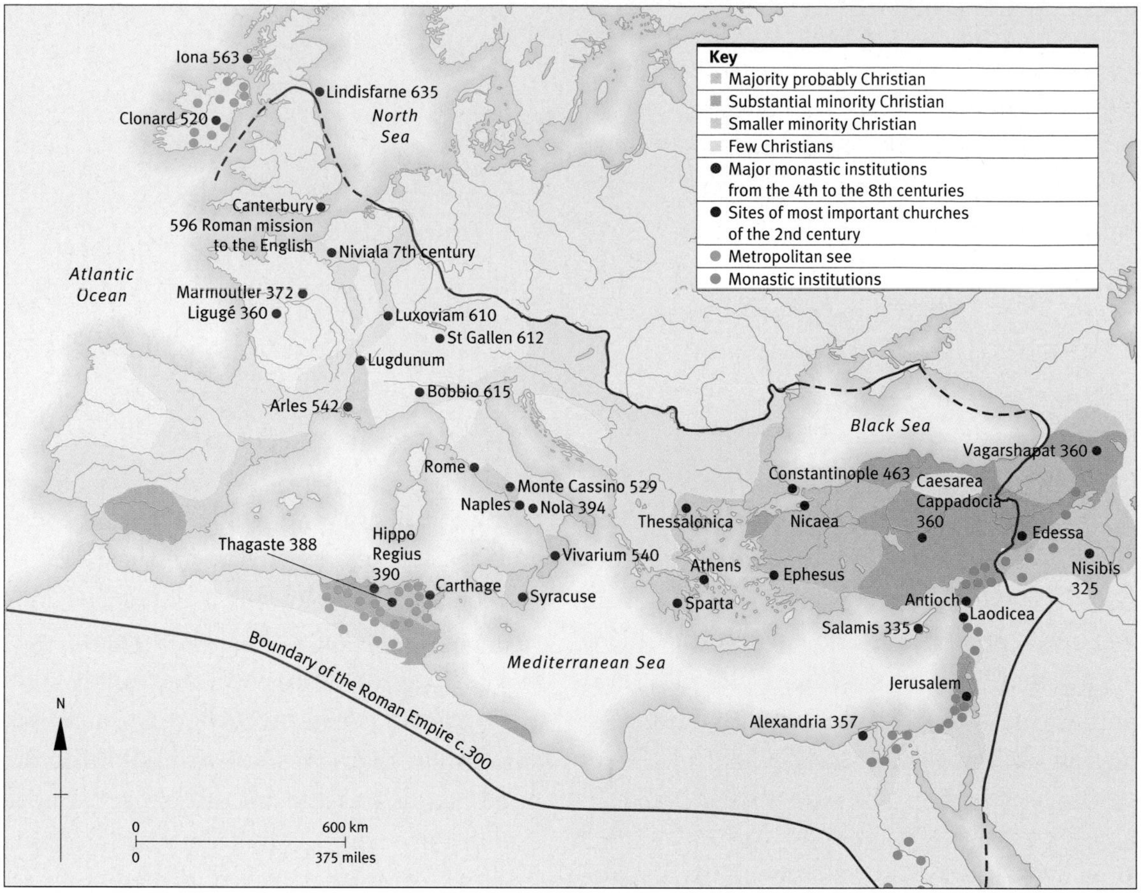

Before the period of Islamic expansion, Christianity had already taken possession of most of western Europe and the Near East. The above map shows the locations of the great metropolitan sees and the most important monastic institutions and gives the years in which they were established.

these the Church knew how to use. Meanwhile, the great men of this world surrounded it, sometimes helpfully, sometimes hopefully, always a potential and often a real threat to the Church's independence of the society it had to strive to save.

THE PAPACY

INEVITABLY, MUCH OF THE HISTORY which resulted is the history of the papacy. It is the central and best-documented institution of Christianity. Its documentation is part of the reason why so much attention has been given to it, a fact that should provoke reflection about what can be known about religion in these centuries. Though papal power had alarming ups and downs, the division of the old empire meant that if there was anywhere in the West a defender of the interests of religion, it was Rome, for it had no ecclesiastical rival. After Gregory the Great it was obviously implausible to maintain the theory of one Christian Church in one empire, even if the imperial exarch resided at Ravenna. The last emperor who came to Rome did so in 663 and the last pope to go to Constantinople went there in 710. Then came Iconoclasm, which brought further ideological division. When Ravenna fell to the renewed advance of the Lombards, Pope Stephen set out for Pepin's court, not that of Byzantium. There was no desire to break with the Eastern Empire, but Frankish armies could offer protection no longer available from the East. Protection was needed, too, for the Arabs menaced Italy from the beginning of the eighth century, and, increasingly, the native Italian magnates became obstreperous in the ebbing of Lombard hegemony.

THE VULNERABILITY OF THE PAPACY

There were some very bad moments in the two and a half centuries after Pepin's coronation. Rome seemed to have very few cards in its hands and at times only to have exchanged one master for another. Its claim to primacy was a matter of the respect due to the guardianship of St Peter's bones and the fact that the see was indisputably the only apostolic one in the West: a matter of history rather than of practical power. For a long time the popes could hardly govern effectively even within the temporal domains, for they had neither adequate armed forces nor a civil administration. As great Italian property-owners, they were exposed to predators and blackmail. Charlemagne was only the first, and perhaps he was the most high-minded, of several emperors who made clear to the papacy their views of the respective standing of pope and emperor as guardians of the Church. The Ottonians were great makers and unmakers of popes. The successors of St Peter could not welcome confrontations, for they had too much to lose.

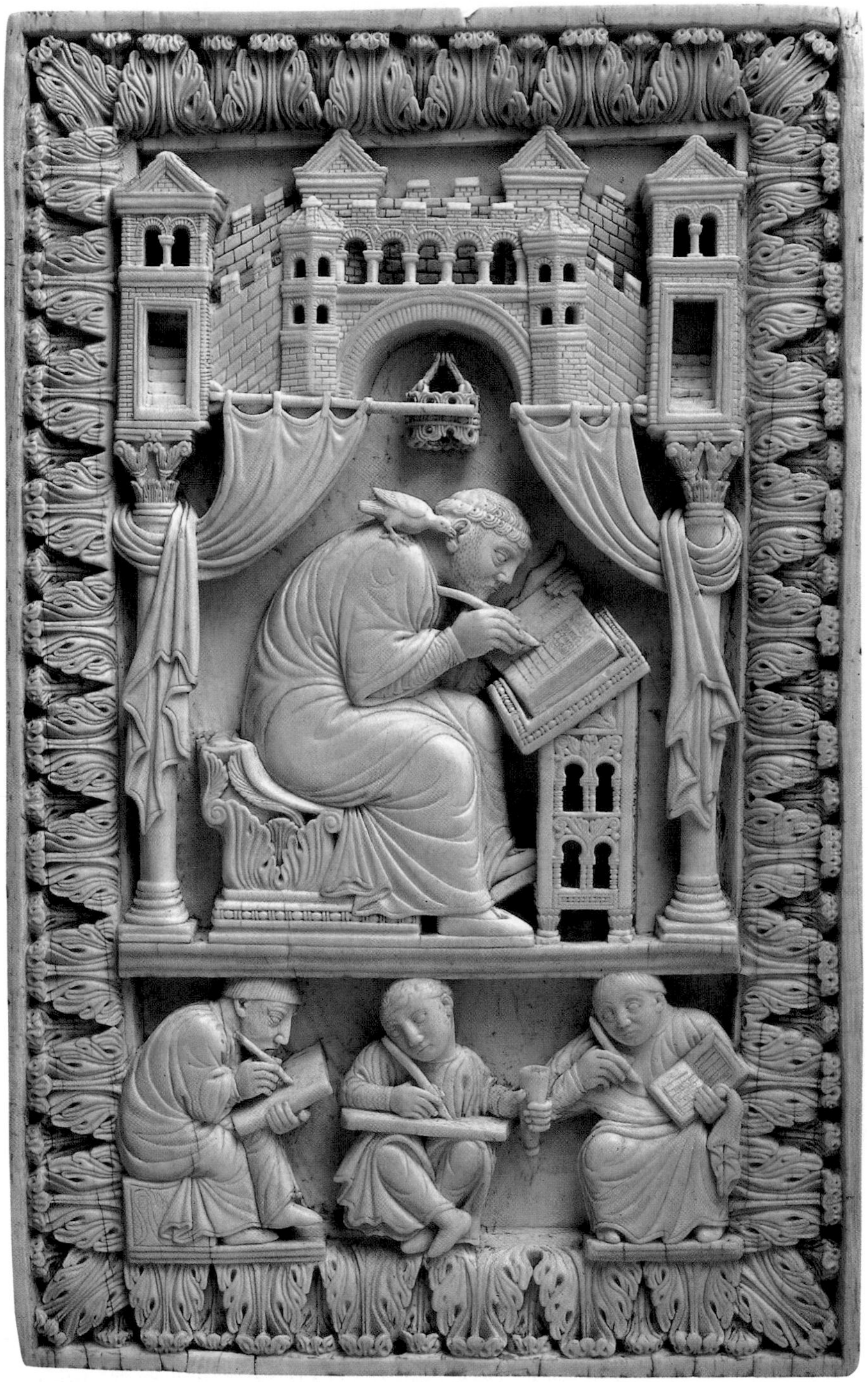

St Gregory the Great (540–604) is portrayed here working on one of his manuscripts. According to legend, the divine word was dictated to St Gregory by a dove (which is shown perched on his shoulder).

PAPAL PRETENSIONS

There was another side to the balance sheet, even if it was slow to reveal its full implications. Pepin's grant of territory to the papacy would in time form the nucleus of a powerful Italian territorial state. In the pope's coronation of emperors there rested veiled claims, perhaps to the identification of rightful emperors. Significantly, as time passed, popes withdrew from the imperial coronation ceremony (as from that of English and French kings) the use of the chrism, the specially sacred mixture of oil and balsam for the ordination of priests and the coronation of bishops, substituting simple oil. Thus was expressed a reality long concealed but easily comprehensible to an age used to symbols: the pope conferred the crown and the stamp of God's recognition on the emperor. Perhaps, therefore, he could do so conditionally. Leo's coronation of Charlemagne, like Stephen's of Pepin, may have been expedient, but it contained a potent seed. When, as often happened, personal weaknesses and succession disputes disrupted the Frankish kingdoms, Rome might gain ground.

More immediately and practically, the support of powerful kings was needed for the reform of local Churches and the support of missionary enterprise in the East. For all the jealousy of local clergy, the Frankish Church changed greatly; in the tenth century what the pope said mattered a great deal north of the Alps. From the *entente* of the eighth century there emerged gradually the idea that it was for the pope to say what the Church's policy should be and that the individual bishops of the local Churches should not pervert it. A great instrument of standardization was being forged. It was there in principle when Pepin used his power as a Frankish king to reform his countrymen's Church and did so on lines which brought it into step with Rome on questions of ritual and discipline, and further away from Celtic influences.

NICHOLAS I

The balance of advantage and disadvantage long tipped to and fro, the boundaries of the effective powers of the popes ebbing and flowing. Significantly, it was after a further subdivision of the Carolingian heritage so that the crown of Italy was separated from Lotharingia that Nicholas I pressed most successfully the papal claims. A century before, a famous forgery, the "Donation of Constantine", purported to show that Constantine had given to the Bishop of Rome the former dominion exercised by the empire in Italy; Nicholas addressed kings and emperors as if this theory ran everywhere in the West. He wrote to them, it was said, "as though he were lord of

the world", reminding them that he could appoint and depose. He used the doctrine of papal primacy against the emperor of the East, too, in support of the Patriarch of Constantinople. This was a peak of pretension which the papacy could not long sustain in practice, for it was soon clear that force at Rome would decide who should enjoy the imperial power the pope claimed to confer. Nicholas's successor, revealingly, was the first pope to be murdered. None the less, the ninth century laid down precedents, even if they could not yet be consistently followed.

Especially in the collapse of papal authority in the tenth century, when the throne became the prey of Italian factions whose struggles were occasionally cut across by the interventions of the Ottonians, the day-to-day work of safeguarding Christian interests could only be in the hands of the bishops of the local Churches. They had to respect the powers that were. Seeking the cooperation and help of the secular rulers, they often moved into positions in which they were all but indistinguishable from royal servants. They were under the thumbs of their secular rulers just

For the Roman Catholic Church, the papacy is a divine institution. In this fresco by Perugino (c.1450–1523) in the Vatican's Sistine Chapel, Christ is shown giving the keys of the Church to Peter, Bishop of Rome. The Catholic tradition recognizes the bishops of Rome as successors to St Peter and as the guardians of all authority over the universal Church.

Pope Nicholas I (c.858–867), who was determined to maintain papal authority, opposed the divorce of Lothair II, king of Lorraine, and his wife Theutberga. The famous crystal of Lothair (above), one of the best-known examples of engraving on rock crystal, tells the story of Theutberga.

as, often, the parish priest was under the thumb of the local lord and had to share his ecclesiastical proceeds in consequence. This humiliating dependency was later to lead to some of the sharpest papal interventions in the local Churches.

BISHOPS AND MONASTERIES

The bishops also did much good; in particular, they encouraged missionaries. This had a political side to it. In the eighth century the Rule of St Benedict was well-established in England. A great Anglo-Saxon missionary movement, whose outstanding figures were St Willibrord in Frisia and St Boniface in Germany, followed. Largely independent of the East Frankish bishops, the Anglo-Saxons asserted the supremacy of Rome; their converts tended therefore to look directly to the throne of St Peter for religious authority. Many made pilgrimages to Rome. This papal emphasis died away in the later phases of evangelizing the East, or, rather, became less conspicuous because of the direct work of the German emperors and their bishops. Missions were combined with conquest and new bishoprics were organized as governmental devices.

Another great creative movement, that of reform in the tenth century, owed something to the episcopate but nothing to the papacy. It was a monastic movement which enjoyed the support of some rulers. Its essence was the renewal of monastic ideals; a few noblemen founded new houses which were intended to recall a degenerate monasticism to its origins. Most of them were in the old central Carolingian lands, running down from Belgium to Switzerland, west into Burgundy and east into Franconia, the area from which the reform impulse radiated outwards. At the end of the tenth century it began to enlist the support of princes and emperors. Their patronage in the end led to fear of lay dabbling in the affairs of the Church but it made possible the recovery of the papacy from a narrowly Italian and dynastic nullity.

CLUNIAC MONASTICISM

The most celebrated of the new foundations was the Burgundian Abbey of Cluny, founded in 910. For nearly two and a half centuries it was the heart of reform in the Church. Its monks followed a revision of the Benedictine rule and evolved something quite new, a religious order resting not simply on a uniform way of life, but on a centrally disciplined organization. The Benedictine monasteries had all been independent communities, but the new Cluniac houses were all subordinate to the abbot of Cluny itself; he was the

Romanesque architecture

During the 19th century the term "Romanesque", previously used only by philologists to denote languages derived from Latin, began to be used by art historians and archaeologists to define an 11th-, 12th- and 13th-century architectural style which had clear links with Roman art. Early specialists studied Romanesque architecture as something homogeneous, although today it is recognized that there are variations in the Romanesque style found in different regions and historical periods.

Romanesque architecture – broadly recognizable by its round arches, thick walls with small windows, and massive vaulting – dates back to the first part of the 11th century in areas of southern Europe, first appearing in the Lombardy region and later spreading towards central Europe (the Ottonian Empire), the kingdom of France (Burgundy) and Catalonia. This early style, which is known as "First Romanesque", is characterized by vaulted spaces, devoid of sculpture or any other kind of decoration. Floor plans vary in Romanesque churches of this period: some constructions have only one aisle while larger basilicas may have three or five aisles. Some small buildings are circular in shape, although these are less common. A large bell-tower, adjacent to the main part of the church, is also typical of this style.

From the last quarter of the 11th century until the middle of the 12th, there emerged a style often called "Full Romanesque", which was influenced by the great monastic institutions, mainly the Abbey of Cluny, and by Pope Gregory VII's reforms. Full Romanesque churches are often vaulted buildings in which the use of a large amount of monumental sculpture is important. Although the sculpture has various motifs, the great theophanies were common in churches of this period.

The last stage, called "Late Romanesque", corresponds to the end of Romanesque art and many of its characteristics, such as the flying buttress, also form part of the early Gothic style. Pointed arches, substituting half-pointed arches, appeared during this phase.

The Church of St Martin Fromista, one of the most beautiful Romanesque buildings in northern Spain, is an example of the Full Romanesque architectural style.

This miniature from a Bible belonging to Charles the Bald (840–877) depicts scenes from the story of St Paul: his conversion to Christianity, his baptism and his subsequent role as a preacher. Most medieval art and literature was produced under the patronage of the Church, creating a rich legacy of religious material.

general of an army of (eventually) thousands of monks who only entered their own monasteries after a period of training at the mother house. At the height of its power, in the middle of the twelfth century, more than three hundred monasteries throughout the West and even some in Palestine looked for direction to Cluny, whose abbey contained the greatest church in Western Christendom after St Peter's at Rome.

CHRISTIAN CULTURE

Even in its early days, though, Cluniac monasticism was disseminating new practices and ideas throughout the Church. This takes us beyond questions of ecclesiastical structure and law, though it is not easy to speak with certainty of all aspects of Christian life in the early Middle Ages. Religious history is especially liable to be falsified by records which sometimes make it very difficult to see spiritual dimensions beyond the bureaucracy. They make it clear, though, that the Church was unchallenged, unique, and that it pervaded the whole fabric of society. It had something like a monopoly of culture. The classical heritage had been terribly damaged and curtailed by the barbarian invasions and the intransigent other-worldliness of early Christianity: "What has Athens to do with Jerusalem?" Tertullian had asked, but such intransigence had subsided. By the tenth century, what had been preserved of the classical past had been preserved by churchmen, above all by the Benedictines and the copiers of the palace schools who transmitted not only the Bible but Latin compilations of Greek learning. Through their version of Pliny and Boethius a slender line connected early medieval Europe to Aristotle and Euclid.

Literacy was virtually coterminous with the clergy. The Romans had been able to post their laws on boards in public places, confident that enough literate people existed to read them; far into the Middle Ages, even kings were normally illiterate. The clergy controlled virtually all access to such writing as there was. In a world without universities, only a court or church school offered the chance of letters beyond what might be offered, exceptionally, by an individual cleric-tutor. The effect of this on all the arts and intellectual activity was profound; culture was not just related to religion but took its rise only in the setting of overriding religious assumptions. The slogan "art for art's sake" could never have made less sense than in the early Middle Ages. History, philosophy, theology, illumination, all played their part in sustaining a sacramental culture, but, however narrowed it might be, the legacy they transmitted, in so far as it was not Jewish, was classical.

CHURCH AND COMMUNITY

In danger of dizziness on such peaks of cultural generalization, it is salutary to remember that we can know very little directly about what must be regarded both theologically and statistically as much more important than this and, indeed, as the most important of all the activities of the Church. This is the day-to-day business of exhorting, teaching, marrying, baptizing, shriving and praying, the whole religious life of the secular clergy and laity which centred about the provision of the major sacraments. The Church was in these centuries deploying powers which often cannot have been distinguished clearly by the faithful from those of magic. It used them to drill a barbaric world into civilization. It was enormously successful and yet we have

The rise of Cluny, under the patronage of Rome, led to diverse local liturgies being substituted by Roman ones. In Spain's Christian kingdoms, this led to the emergence of new artistic trends and the abandonment of the Hispanic artistic tradition. One example of this can be found in the Bible of 960, now in the collegiate church of St Isadore of León. Self-portraits of the calligraphers who contributed to the work appear on the last page, which is shown here.

almost no direct information about the process except at its most dramatic moments, when a spectacular conversion or baptism reveals by the very fact of being recorded that we are in the presence of the untypical.

Of the social and economic reality of the Church we know much more. The clergy and their dependants were numerous and the Church controlled much of society's wealth. The Church was a great landowner. The

The monastic orders often received large donations of land or property, and many monasteries came to wield considerable economic power. The monastery of Santo Domingo de Silos in Spain, the 12th-century cloisters of which are pictured here, was an example of this trend.

revenues which supported its work came from its land and a monastery or chapter of canons might have very large estates. The roots of the Church were firmly sunk in the economy of the day and to begin with that implied something very primitive indeed.

ECONOMIC RECESSION IN THE WEST

Difficult though it is to measure exactly, there are many symptoms of economic regression in the West at the end of antiquity. Not everyone felt the setback equally. The most developed economic sectors went under most completely. Barter replaced money and a money economy emerged again only slowly. The Merovingians began to coin silver, but for a long time there was not much coin, particularly coin of small denominations, in circulation. Spices disappeared from ordinary diet; wine became a costly luxury; most people ate and drank bread and porridge, beer and water. Scribes turned to parchment, which could be obtained locally, rather than papyrus, now hard to get; this turned out to be an advantage, for minuscule was possible on parchment, and had not been on papyrus, which required large, uneconomical strokes, but none the less it reflects difficulties within the old Mediterranean economy. Though recession often confirmed the self-sufficiency of the individual estate, it ruined the towns. The universe of trade also disintegrated from time to time because of war. Contact was maintained with Byzantium and further Asia, but the western Mediterranean's commercial activity dwindled during the seventh and eighth centuries as the Arabs seized the North African coast. Later, thanks again to the Arabs, it was partly revived (one sign was a brisk trade in slaves, many of whom came from eastern Europe, from the Slav peoples who thus gave their name to a whole category of forced labour). In the north, too, there was a certain amount of exchange with the Scandinavians, who were great traders. But this did not matter to most Europeans, for whom life rested on agriculture.

FARMING

Subsistence was for a long time to be almost all that most Europeans could hope for. That it was the main concern of the early medieval economy is one of the few safe generalizations about it. Animal manure or the breaking of new and more fertile ground were for a long time virtually the only ways of improving a yield on seed and labour which was by modern standards derisory. Only centuries of laborious husbandry could change this. The animals who lived with the stunted and scurvy-ridden human tenants of a poverty-stricken landscape were themselves undernourished and undersized, yet for fat, the luckier peasant depended upon the pig, or, in the south, on the olive. Only with the introduction in the tenth century of plants yielding food of higher protein content did the energy return from the soil begin to improve. There were some technological innovations, notably the diffusion of mills and the adoption of a better plough, but when production rose it did so for the most part because new land was brought into cultivation. And there was much to exploit. Most of France and Germany and England was still covered with forest and waste.

URBAN LIFE

The economic relapse at the end of antiquity left behind few areas where towns thrived. The main exception was Italy, where some commercial relations with the outside world always persisted. Elsewhere, towns did not begin much to expand again until after 1100; even then, it would be a long time before western Europe contained a city comparable with the great centres of the classical Islamic and Asian civilizations. Almost universally in the West the self-sufficient agricultural estate was for centuries the rule. It fed and maintained a population probably smaller than that of the ancient world in the same area, though even approximate figures are almost impossible to establish. At any rate, there is no evidence of more than a very slow growth of population until the eleventh century. The population of western Europe may then have stood at about forty million – fewer than live in the United Kingdom today.

FEUDALISM

In this world, possession of land or access to it was the supreme determinant of the social order. Somehow, slowly but logically, the great men of Western society, while continuing to be the warriors they had always been in barbarian societies, became landowners too. With the dignitaries of the Church and their kings, they were the ruling class. From the possession of land came not only revenue by rent and taxation, but jurisdiction and labour service, too. Landowners were the lords, and gradually their hereditary status was to loom larger and their practical prowess and skill as warriors was to be less emphasized (though in theory it long persisted) as the thing that made them noble.

The lands of some of these men were granted to them by a king or great prince. In return they were expected to repay the favour by turning out when required to do him military service. Moreover, administration had to be decentralized after imperial times; barbarian kings did not have the bureaucratic and literate resources to rule directly over great areas. Thus the grant of exploitable economic goods in return for specific obligations of service was very common, and this idea was what lay at the

These pictures illustrate an 11th-century copy of a text written by Beatus of Liebana, a monk who lived in late 8th-century Spain. Warriors are depicted in combat while their feudal overlord sits in state.

Feudalism

The word "feudal", from the Latin word *feudum*, meaning "fief", did not appear until the early 17th century. At the height of feudalism, the fief was a possession (usually a piece of land) granted by a lord (a noble of high standing) to a vassal (a noble generally of lesser standing than the lord) in exchange for a number of services – this was usually marked by an investiture ceremony.

The origins of the feudal system lie in 8th-century Frankish society, following the decline of the Carolingian Dynasty. The emergence of feudalism has been linked with the new military importance of heavy cavalry. The expense and level of expertise required by cavalry resulted in the emergence of a military élite, which gradually developed into a social élite and then a feudal nobility. From the Frankish lands, the feudal system was dispersed through Frankish conquests into northern Italy, Spain and Germany. In 1066 the Norman Conquest introduced it to England, and from there it spread to Ireland and Scotland. From the 12th century, however, the feudal system was threatened by the growth of the centralized state and the increasing power of towns. Feudalism's importance declined in the 14th century.

Various definitions of the term feudalism have been proposed. Some historians claim that it involved no more than the relationship between two free men – the lord and his vassal. This definition, however, is unsatisfactory, as it wrongly implies that the majority of the population were excluded from feudalism. Some medievalists see the feudal system as the precursor of

Agriculture was the basis for economic and social development under the feudal system. This manuscript illustration depicts a peasant harvesting grapes.

later socio-economic systems that favoured slavery and preceded capitalism.

Most experts agree, none the less, that the feudal system helped prevent absolutism and encouraged the development of increasingly powerful councils – one of the vassal's obligations was to provide counsel to the lord. Feudalism, therefore, formed the basis for the growth of the modern parliamentary system.

heart of what later lawyers, looking back at the European Middle Ages, called feudalism. It was a widespread but not universal phenomenen.

Many tributaries flowed into this stream. Both Roman and Germanic custom favoured the elaboration of such an idea. It helped, too, that in the later days of the empire, or in the troubled times of Merovingian Gaul, it had become common for men to "commend" themselves to a great lord for protection; in return for his protection they offered him a special loyalty and service. This was a usage easily assimilated to the practices of Germanic society. Under the Carolingians, the practice began of "vassals" of the king doing him homage; that is to say, they acknowledged with distinctive ceremonies, often public, their special responsibilities of service to him. He was their lord; they were his men. The old loyalties of the blood-brotherhood of the warrior-companions of the barbarian chief began to blend with notions of commendation in a new moral ideal of loyalty, faithfulness and reciprocal obligation. Vassals then bred vassals and one lord's man was another man's lord. A chain of obligation and personal service might stretch in theory from the king down through his great men and their retainers to the lowest of the free. And, of course, it might produce complicating and conflicting demands. A king could be another king's vassal in respect of some of his lands. Below the free were the slaves, more numerous perhaps in southern Europe than in the north and everywhere showing a tendency to evolve marginally upwards in status to that of the serf – the unfree man, born tied to the soil of his manor, but nevertheless, not quite without rights of any kind.

SOCIAL ORGANIZATION

Some students of medieval history later spoke as if the relationship of lord and man could explain the whole of medieval society. This was never so. Though much of the land of Europe was divided into fiefs – the *feuda* from which "feudalism" takes its name – which were holdings bearing obligation to a lord, there were always important areas, especially in southern Europe, where the "mix" of Germanic overlay and Roman background did not work out in the same way. Much of

Christendom in the 11th century

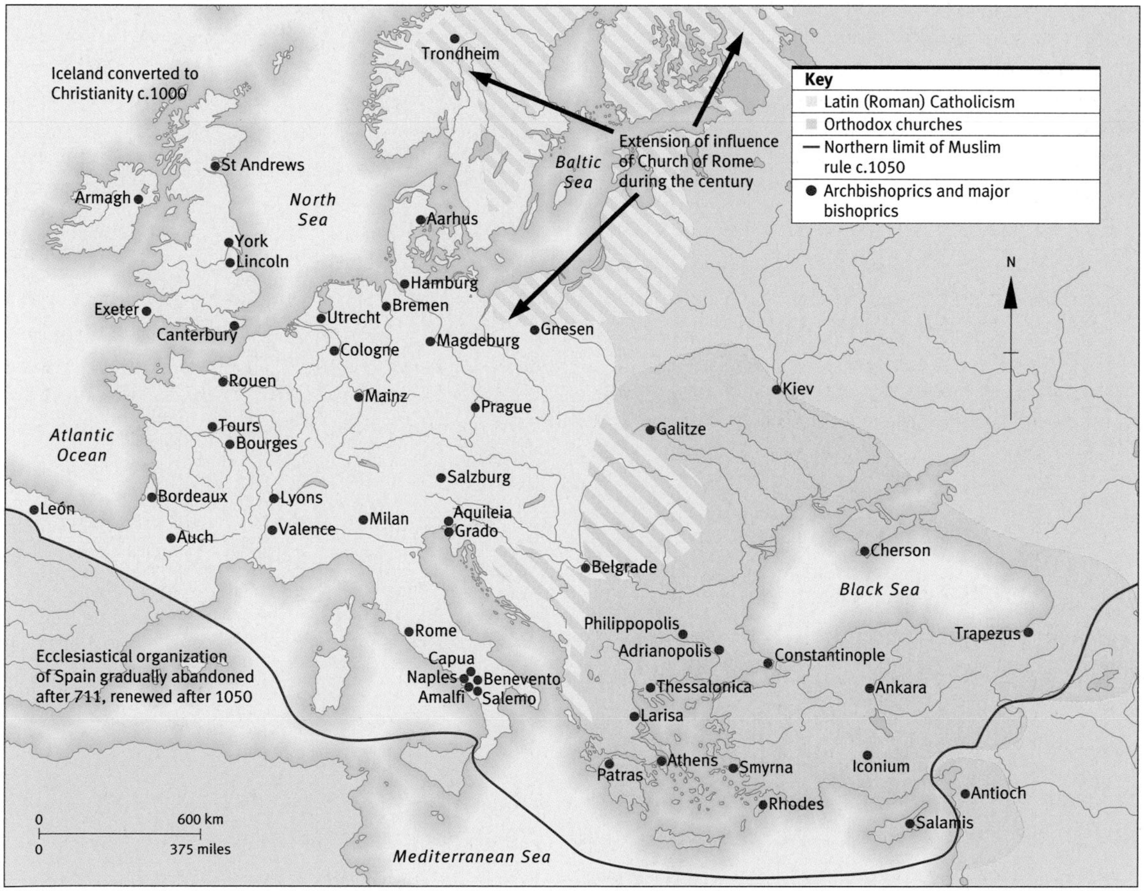

At the beginning of the 11th century important events took place which were to have considerable repercussions for the future of medieval Europe: Islam was dispersed (the Fatimids in Egypt, the Abbasids in Baghdad and the Umayyads in Córdoba); the Byzantine Empire, Bulgaria and, finally, the legacy of the empire created by Charlemagne, all began to disintegrate and evolve into separate principalities.

A nobleman's commitment to vassalage was signified by two symbolic acts, usually performed in public. First the vassal, kneeling, would place his hands, clasped together, between those of his lord. This signified the establishment of a bond of peace between the vassal and the lord, as well as a mutual tie of friendship and fidelity. The vassal would then stand holding his hands above a sacred object and make an oath of loyalty to the lord. In this illustration from a 12th-century Spanish manuscript, Ramón Caldes and other noblemen pay homage to Alfonso II (791–842).

Italy, Spain and southern France was not "feudal" in this sense. There were also always some freeholders even in more "feudal" lands, an important class of men, more numerous in some countries than others, who owed no service for their lands but owned them outright.

For the most part, nevertheless, contractual obligations based on land set the tone of medieval European civilization. Corporations, like men, might be lords or vassals; a tenant might do homage to the abbot of a monastery (or the abbess of a nunnery) for the manor he held of its estates, and a king might have a cathedral chapter or a community of monks as one of his vassals. There was much room for complexity and ambiguity in the "feudal order". But the central fact of an exchange of obligations between superior and inferior ran through the whole structure and does more than anything else to make it intelligible to modern eyes. Lord and man were bound to one another reciprocally: "Serfs, obey your temporal lords with fear and trembling; lords, treat your serfs according to justice and equity" was a French cleric's injunction, which concisely summarized a principle in a specific case. On this rationalization rested a society of growing complexity, which it long proved able to interpret and sustain.

MILITARY ARISTOCRACIES

Mutual obligation also justified the extraction from the peasant of the wherewithal to maintain the warrior and build his castle. From this grew the aristocracies of Europe. The military function of the system which supported them long remained paramount. Even when personal service in the field was not required, that of the vassal's fighting-men (and later of his money to pay fighting-men) would be. Of the military skills, that which was most esteemed (because it was the most effective) was that of fighting in armour on horseback. At some point in the seventh or eighth century the stirrup was adopted; from that time the armoured horseman had it for the most part his own way on the battlefield until the

The investiture of two feudal knights is depicted in this 14th-century Castilian manuscript illustration. The English legal writer Henry de Bracton recorded one of the vows used in investiture ceremonies in his book *De Legibus Angliae*: "Hear this, lord, I promise my fidelity to your life and your limbs and your body and your possessions and your worldly honour, if God and these holy relics help me."

A "Tournament of English Knights before Richard II" is represented in this 15th-century illustration from the St Alban's Chronicle. In the tournament, military skills were perfected in what was intended to be a friendly and honourable encounter, although fatalities were not unusual.

coming of weapons which could master him. From this technical superiority emerged the knightly class of professional cavalrymen, maintained by the lord either directly or by a grant of a manor to feed them and their horses. They were the source of the warrior aristocracy of the Middle Ages and of European values for centuries to come. Yet for a long time, the boundaries of this class were ill-defined and movement into (and out of) it was common.

KINGS

Political realities often militated against theory. In the intricate web of vassalage, a king might have less control over his own vassals than they over theirs. The great lord, whether lay magnate or local bishop, must always have loomed larger and more important in the life of the ordinary person than the remote and probably never-seen king or prince. In the tenth and eleventh centuries there are everywhere examples of kings obviously under pressure from great men. The country where this seemed to present the least trouble was Anglo-Saxon England, whose monarchical tradition was the strongest of any. But pressure was not always effective against even a weak king if he were shrewd. He had, after all, other vassals, and if wise he would not antagonize all of them at once. Furthermore, his office was unique. The anointing of the Church confirmed its sacred, charismatic authority. Kings were set apart in the eyes

The Bayeux Tapestry (in fact an embroidery), dating from c.1077, tells the story of the events leading up to the Battle of Hastings of 1066 and the Norman conquest of England. In this detail, the Englishman Harold is depicted swearing an oath of loyalty to William, Duke of Normandy. In Norman eyes, Harold later broke his oath by usurping the English throne after the death of Edward the Confessor.

of most by the special pomp and ceremony which surrounded them and which played as important a part in medieval government as does bureaucratic paper in ours. If in addition a king had the advantage of large domains of his own, then he stood an excellent chance of having his way.

RESTRICTED LIVES

Not always in the technical and legal sense, but in the common sense, kings and great magnates were the only people who enjoyed much freedom in early medieval society. Yet even they led lives cramped and confined by

This scene from the Bayeux Tapestry represents the Battle of Hastings.

the absence of much that we take for granted. There was nothing much to do, after all, except pray, fight, hunt and run your estate; there were no professions for men to enter, except that of the Church, and small possibility of innovation in the style or content of daily life. Women's choices were even more restricted, and so they were for men as one went further down the social scale. Only with the gradual revival of trade and urban life as the economy expanded was this to change. Obviously, dividing lines are of almost no value in such matters, but it is not really until after 1100 that important economic expansion begins, and only then that we have the sense of moving out of a society still semi-barbarous, whose pretensions to civilization are sometimes negligible.

Edward II, whose coronation ceremony is depicted here, was the first English heir-apparent to bear the title of Prince of Wales. His reign (1307– 1327) was plagued with ill-advised favouritism, intrigue and constitutional conflicts, which ultimately resulted in his forced abdication and, a year later, his murder.

Fferrat G. de gorjas alcalde de burgos guarda de nro señor el Rey.
Fferrat G. de ayelça.
Iohn G. de ayelça.
Alffon G. de camargo el moço,

THE FAR EAST AND A NEW EUROPE

PATTERNS OF BEHAVIOUR still vigorously alive when the twentieth century began had been established in China and the Chinese sphere of civilization long before what Europeans think of as their Middle Ages. This was also true for the Indian subcontinent, whose first civilizations collapsed in circumstances still mysterious, but whose only slightly later and less remote Aryan cultures provide patterns and influences there and over much of South Asia and Indonesia which have set frameworks for the lives of hundreds of millions of people. In Asia, societies (some of considerable complexity, some until recently almost barbaric) were long to live within traditions deriving from these sources which were to remain largely unchanged for thousands of years until the coming of others vigorous enough first to threaten, sometimes to overturn and, occasionally, to invigorate them.

Europe, by contrast is a late-comer to the ranks of distinctive civilizations. For a long time after the "Dark Ages", she was, indeed, hardly discernible at all as a cultural entity; rooted as she was in the larger reality of Christendom. By the end of the first millennium of the Common Era, though, there are observable at least the beginnings of the construction of a distinctive European tradition. Based on Christianity and a selection from the classical past, the role of religion in it was of overwhelming importance (but so was that of more material forces, geographical position, for instance, or of circumstance, such as the threat perceived in the alien world of Islam). Somehow, in a huge and complex process, an idea of Europe and of what it might mean to be a European, was evolving, though very slowly, and it was to emerge in the end as a dominant fact of nearly three centuries of world history.

The Eastern world was hardly aware of western Europe as a coherent force before the First Crusade at the end of the 11th century, when stories of Muslim attacks on Christian pilgrims visiting the Holy Places of the Near East were used to justify Pope Urban II's call to liberate the Holy Sepulchre in Jerusalem. This manuscript illustration depicts equestrian knights from the Spanish Order of Santiago, who fought, alongside knights from other military orders, in the crusades.

1 *INDIA*

THOUGH ACCOMPANIED and advised by scholars and savants, Alexander the Great had only hazy ideas of what he would find in India; he seems to have thought that the Indus was part of the Nile and that beyond it lay more of Ethiopia. A fair amount had long been known by the Greeks about the Indian northwest, the seat of the Persian satrapy of Gandhara. But beyond that all was darkness. So far as political geography is concerned, the obscurity has remained; the relations between and, for that matter, the nature of the states of the Ganges valley at the time of Alexander's invasion are still hard to get at. A kingdom of Magadha, based on the lower river and exercising some sort of hegemony over the rest of the valley, had been the most important political unit in the subcontinent for two centuries or more, but not much is known about its institutions or history. Indian sources say nothing of Alexander's arrival in India and, as the great conqueror

Hindu art flourished in India's Gupta Empire. This detail is from a 6th-century cave painting in Ajanta representing a woman from the court of Prince Gautama.

Megasthenes on India

"To prove the Indians' artistic abilities, he recounts that they imitated the sponges that the Macedonians had seen, sewing wool with hairs with fine twine and cords and, after having matted them together, they took out the threads and dyed the wool; that many of them also learnt how to make scrubbing brushes and little jars of salves. Moreover, he says, they write letters on thickly woven cotton material, although others say that they do not know how to write at all; he also says that they use smelted bronze, but they do not decorate it. Another item in the report about India says that it is customary to stand upright to petition kings and everyone who has power and majesty, instead of throwing oneself at their feet. What is more, the country also produces precious gems as well as crystals and all types of carbuncles and pearls."

An extract from Book XV of *Geographica* by Strabo (c.60 BCE–20 CE), in which the author writes about Megasthenes' report.

Alexander the Great (356–323 BCE), who is portrayed on this 4th-century BCE silver coin, invested considerable energy in his attempt to conquer India. Although Alexander was to leave India without achieving his goal, Hellenistic culture penetrated a few settlements in the country's northwestern borderlands.

never penetrated beyond the Punjab, we can learn from Greek accounts of his day only of his disruption of the petty kingdoms of the northwest, not about the heartland of Indian power.

THE MAURYA EMPIRE AND MEGASTHENES

UNDER THE SELEUCID DYNASTY more reliable information became available in the West about what lay beyond the Punjab. This new knowledge roughly coincides with the rise of a new Indian power, the Maurya Empire, and here the India of historical record really begins. One of our informants is a Greek ambassador, Megasthenes, sent to India by the Seleucid king in about 300 BCE. Fragments of his account of what he saw were preserved long enough for later writers to quote him at length. As he travelled as far as Bengal and Orissa and was respected both as a diplomat and as a scholar, he met and interrogated many Indians. Some later writers found him a credulous and unreliable reporter; they dwelt upon his tales of people who subsisted on odours instead of food and drink, of others who were Cyclopean or whose feet were so large that they used them to shelter from the sun, of pygmies and creatures without mouths. Such tales were, of course, nonsense. But they were not necessarily without foundation. They may well represent only the highly developed awareness shown by Aryan Indians of the physical differences which marked them off from neighbours or remote acquaintances from central Asia or the jungles of Burma. Some of these must have looked very strange indeed, and some of their behaviour was, no doubt, also very strange in Indian eyes. Others among these tales may dimly reflect the curious ascetic practices of Indian religion

Time chart (c.563 BCE–1605 CE)

c.563–c.483 BCE	The life of the Buddha
327–325 BCE	Alexander the Great's expedition to India
268–232 BCE	The reign of Asoka
c.78–c.101 CE	The reign of King Kanishka, the greatest of the Kushana rulers
320–c.335 CE	The reign of Chandra Gupta, founder of the Gupta Dynasty
1206 CE	Foundation of the Delhi Sultanate
1526–1530 CE	The reign of Babur
1526–1858 CE	The Moghul Empire in India
1556–1605 CE	The reign of Akbar

0 — 1000 CE — 1500 CE

which have never ceased to impress outsiders and usually improve in the telling. Such tales need not discredit the teller; therefore they do not mean that other things he reports must be wholly untrue. They may even have a positive value if they suggest something of the way in which Megasthenes' Indian informants saw the outside world.

Muslim India

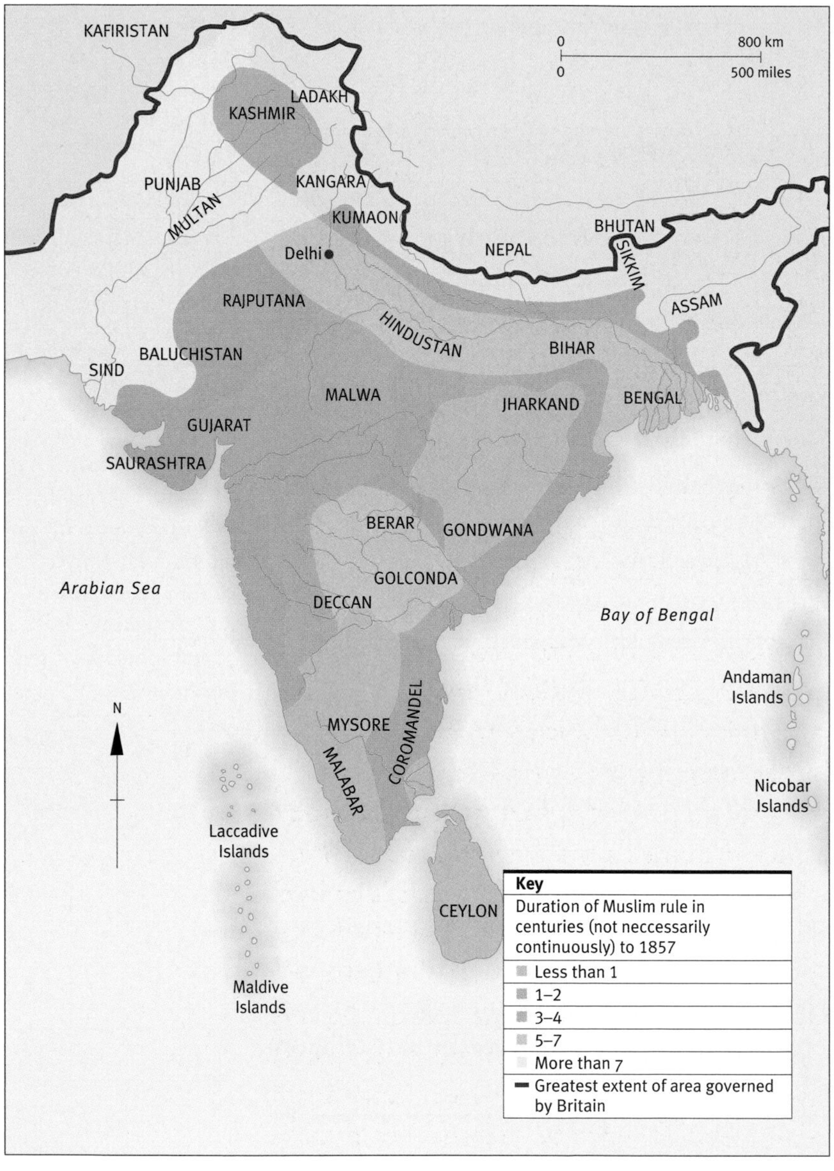

The Muslim conquest of India started in the Punjab in the 11th century. It was led by various Islamic dynasties, some of which were known as the "northern" (Pala, Sena, Lohara, etc.) or "southern" (Rasthrakuta, Chola, etc.) dynasties. Other ruling powers included the Ghaznavids, the Guries, the Delhi Sultanate, the Turkish dynasties and, finally, the Moghul Empire.

CHANDRAGUPTA

Megasthenes describes the India of a great ruler, Chandragupta, founder of the Maurya line. Something is known about him from other sources. The ancients believed that he had been inspired to conquest by having as a youth seen Alexander the Great during his invasion of India. However this may be, Chandragupta usurped the Magadha throne in 321 BCE and on the ruins of that kingdom built a state which encompassed not only the two great valleys of the Indus and Ganges, but most of Afghanistan (taken from the Seleucids) and Baluchistan. His capital was at Patna, where Chandragupta inhabited a magnificent palace. It was made of wood; archaeology still cannot help us much at this stage of Indian history. From Megasthenes' account it might be inferred that Chandragupta exercised a sort of monarchical presidency but Indian sources seem to reveal a bureaucratic state, or at least something that aspired to be one. What it was like in practice is hard to see. It had been built from political units formed in earlier times, many of which had been republican or popular in organization, and many of these were connected to the emperor through great men who were his officers; some of these, nominally subjects, must often have been very independent in practice.

About the empire's inhabitants, too, Megasthenes is informative. Besides providing a long list of different peoples, he distinguished two religious traditions (one the Brahmanical and the other apparently Buddhist), mentioned the rice-eating habits of Indians and their abstention from wine except for ritual purposes, said much about the domestication of elephants, and remarked on the fact (surprising to Greek eyes) that in India there were no slaves. He was wrong, but excusably so. Though Indians were not bought and sold in absolute servitude, there were those bound to labour for their masters and legally incapable of removal. Megasthenes also reported that the king diverted himself by hunting, which was done from raised platforms, or from the backs of elephants – much as tigers were shot in the twentieth century.

Chandragupta is said to have spent his last days in retirement with Jains, ritually starving himself to death in a retreat near Mysore. His son and successor turned the expansive course of empire already shown by his father to the south. Maurya power began to penetrate the dense rain-forests east of Patna, and to push down the eastern coast. Finally, under the third Maurya, the conquest of Orissa gave the empire control of the land and sea routes to the south and the subcontinent acquired a measure of political unity not matched in extent for over two thousand years. The conqueror who achieved this was Asoka, the ruler under whom a documented history of India at last begins to be possible.

Asoka's precepts reflected a moral code of behaviour greatly influenced by Buddhism, the religion to which the emperor had converted in 260 BCE. The precept that is inscribed on this rock pillar, which is from the Buddhist site at Sarnath in northern India, refers to the expulsion of dissenting monks.

ASOKA

From Asoka's era survive many inscriptions bearing decrees and injunctions to his subjects. The use of this means of propagating official messages and the individual style of the inscriptions both suggest Persian and Hellenistic influence, and India under the Mauryas was certainly more continually in touch with the civilizations to the West than ever before. At Kandahar, Asoka left inscriptions in both Greek and Aramaic.

Such evidence reveals a government capable of much more than that sketched by Megasthenes. A royal council ruled over a society based on caste. There was a royal army and a bureaucracy; as elsewhere, the coming of literacy was an epoch in government as well as in culture. There seems also to have been a large secret police, or internal intelligence service. Besides raising taxes and maintaining communication and irrigation services, this machine, under Asoka, undertook the promotion of an official ideology. Asoka had himself been converted to Buddhism early in his reign. Unlike Constantine's conversion, his did not precede but followed a battle whose cost in suffering appalled Asoka. Be that as it may, the result of his conversion was the abandonment of the pattern of conquest which had marked his career until then. Perhaps this is why he felt no temptation to campaign outside the subcontinent – a limitation which, however, he shared with most Indian rulers, who never aspired to rule over barbarians, and one which, of course, was only evident when he had completed the conquest of India.

The 16th-century Adinatha temple at Ranakpur in Rajasthan is the biggest Jain temple in India. Founded by Mahavira (c.599–527 BCE), Jainism was the product of attempts to reform the Brahmanical system. It enjoyed offical patronage from the time of the 4th-century BCE emperor Chandragupta and is still an important religious force in India today.

DHAMMA

The philosophy of Asoka's Buddhism is expressed in the recommendations he made to his subjects in the rock inscriptions and pillars dating from this part of his reign (roughly after 260 BCE). The consequences are remarkable – they amounted to a complete new social philosophy. Asoka's precepts have the overall name of *Dhamma*, a variant of a Sanskrit word meaning "Universal Law", and their novelty led to much anachronistic admiration of Asoka's modernity by twentieth-century Indian politicians. Asoka's ideas are, none the less, striking. He enjoined respect for the dignity of all people, and, above all, religious toleration and non-violence. His precepts were general rather than precise and they were not laws. But their central themes are unmistakable and they were intended to provide principles of action. While Asoka's own bent and thinking undoubtedly made such ideas agreeable to him, they suggest less a wish to advance the ideas of Buddhism (this is something Asoka did in other ways) than a wish to allay differences; they look very much like a device of government for a huge, heterogeneous and religiously divided empire. Asoka was seeking to establish some focus for a measure of political and social unity spanning all India, which would be based on its people's interests as well as upon force and spying. "All men", said one of his inscriptions, "are my children."

This may also explain his pride in what might be called his "social services", which sometimes took forms appropriate to the climate: "on the roads I have had banyan trees planted," he proclaimed, "which will give shade to beasts and men." The value of this apparently simple device would have been readily apparent to those who toiled and travelled in the great Indian plains. Almost incidentally, improvements also smoothed the path of trade, but like the wells he dug and the rest-houses he set up at nine-mile intervals, the banyan trees were an expression of *Dhamma*. Yet *Dhamma* does not appear to have succeeded, for we hear of sectarian struggles and the resentment of priests.

THE SPREAD OF BUDDHISM

Asoka did better in promoting simple Buddhist evangelization. His reign brought the first great expansion of Buddhism, which had prospered, but had remained hitherto confined to northeastern India. Now Asoka sent missionaries to Burma who did well; in Ceylon others did better still, and from his day the island was predominantly Buddhist. Those sent, more optimistically, to Macedonia and Egypt were less successful, though Buddhist teaching left its mark on some of the philosophies of the Hellenistic world and some Greeks were converted.

The vitality of Buddhism under Asoka may in part explain signs of reaction in the Brahmanical religion. It has been suggested that a new popularization of certain cults, which dates from about this time, may have been a conscious Brahman response to challenge. Notably, the third and second centuries BCE brought a new prominence to the cults of two of the most popular avatars of Vishnu. One is the proteiform Krishna, whose legend offers vast possibilities of psychological identification to the worshipper, and the other Rama, the embodiment of the benevolent king, good husband and son, a family god. It was in the second century BCE, too, that the two great Indian epics, the *Mahabharata* and the *Ramayana*, began to take their final form. The first of these was extended by a long passage, which is now the most famous work of Indian literature and its greatest poem, the *Bhagavad Gita*, or "Song of the lord". It was to become the central testament of Hinduism, weaving around the figure of Vishnu/Krishna the ethical doctrine of duty in the performance of the obligations laid upon one by membership of one's class (*dharma*) and the recommendation that works of devotion, however meritorious, might be less efficacious than love of Krishna as a means to release into eternal happiness.

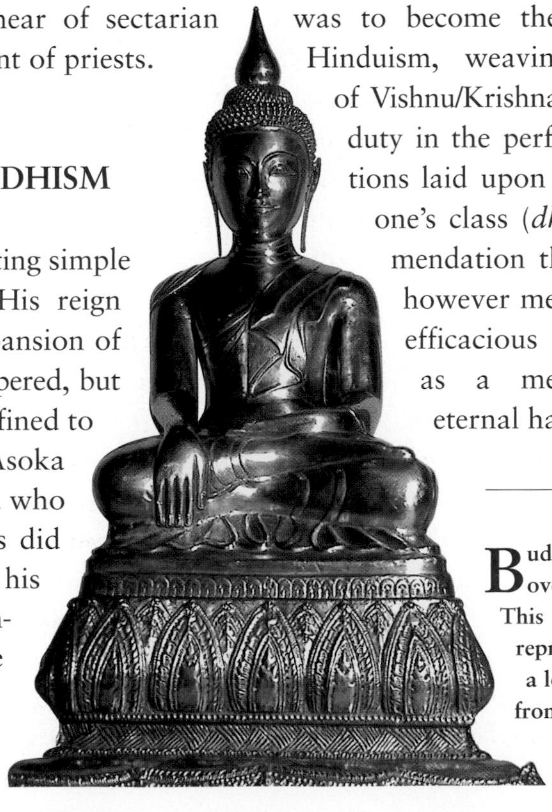

Buddhism eventually spread over almost the whole of Asia. This 19th-century statue, which represents the Buddha seated on a lotus-flower throne, comes from Burma, where Buddhism is still the most popular religion today.

MAURYA DECLINE

Mounted archers were the shock troops of the Parthian Empire, which harassed the western border of the Punjab region. Above are the obverse and reverse of a Parthian coin dating from the 2nd century BCE.

These were important facts for the future of Hinduism, but were to develop fully only over a period which ran on far past the crumbling of the Maurya Empire, and this began soon after Asoka's death. Such a disappearance is so dramatically impressive – and the Maurya Empire had been so remarkable a thing – that, though we are tempted to look for some special explanation, yet perhaps there is only a cumulative one. In all ancient empires except perhaps the Chinese, the demands made on government eventually outgrew the technical resources available to meet them: when this happened, they broke up. The Mauryas had done great things. They conscripted labour to exploit large areas of wasteland, thereby both feeding a growing population and increasing the tax base of the empire. They undertook great irrigation works which survived them for centuries. Trade prospered under Maurya rule, if we may judge from the way northern pottery spread throughout India in the third century BCE. They kept up a huge army and a diplomacy which ranged as far afield as Epirus. The cost, however, was great. The government and army were parasitical upon an agricultural economy which could not be indefinitely expanded. There was a limit to what it could pay for. Nor, though bureaucracy seems at this distance to have been centralized in principle, was it likely to have been very effective, let alone flawless. Without a system of control and recruitment to render it independent of society, it fell at one end into the hands of the favourites of the monarch on whom all else depended and at the other into the gift of local élites who knew how to seize and retain power.

One political weakness was rooted deep in pre-Maurya times. Indian society had already sunk its anchors in the family and the institutions of caste. Here, in social institutions rather than in a dynasty or an abstract notion of a continuing state (let alone a nation) was the focus of Indian loyalties. When an Indian empire began to crumble under economic, external or technical pressures, it had no unthinking popular support to fall back upon. This is a striking indication of the lack of success of Asoka's attempts to provide ideological integument for his empire. What is more, India's social institutions, and especially caste, in its elaborated forms, imposed economic costs. Where functions were inalterably allocated by birth, economic aptitude was held back. So was ambition. India had a social system which was bound to cramp the possibilities of economic growth.

POLITICAL DISUNITY RETURNS

THE ASSASSINATION of the last Maurya was followed by a Ganges dynasty of Brahmanical origin and thereafter the story of India for five hundred years is once more one of political disunity. References in Chinese sources become available from the end of the second century BCE, but it cannot be said that they have made agreement between scholars about what was happening in India any easier:

even the chronology is still largely conjectural. Only the general processes stand out.

The most important of these is a new succession of invasions of India from the historic northwestern routes. First came Bactrians, descendants of the Greeks left behind by Alexander's empire on the upper Oxus, where by 239 BCE they had formed an independent kingdom standing between India and Seleucid Persia. Our knowledge of this mysterious realm is largely drawn from its coins and has grave gaps in it, but it is known that a hundred years later the Bactrians were pushing into the Indus valley. They were the foremost in a current which was to flow for four centuries. A complex series of movements was in train whose origins lay deep in the nomadic societies of Asia. Among those who followed the Indo-Greeks of Bactria and established themselves at different times in the Punjab were Parthians and Scythians. One Scythian king, according to legend, received St Thomas the apostle at his court.

THE KUSHANAS

One important people came all the way from the borders of China and left behind them the memory of another big Indian empire, stretching from Benares beyond the mountains to the caravan routes of the steppes. These were the Kushanas. Historians still argue about how they are related to other nomadic peoples, but two things about them seem clear enough. The first is that they (or their rulers) were both enthusiastically Buddhist and also patronized some Hindu sects. The second was that their political interests were focused in central Asia, where their greatest king died fighting.

The Kushana period brought fresh foreign influences once more into Indian culture, often from the West, as the Hellenistic flavour of its sculpture, particularly of the Buddha, shows. It marks an epoch in another way, for the depicting of the Buddha was something of an innovation in Kushana times. The Kushanas carried it very far and the Greek models gradually gave way to the forms of Buddha familiar today. This was one expression of a new complicating and developing of Buddhist religion. One thing which was

This stucco head of the Buddha dates from the Kushana period (c.50–240 CE). Although the Buddha's face is clearly influenced by the Hellenistic style of earlier sculpture, the Indian features are quite pronounced.

happening was that Buddhism was being popularized and materialized; Buddha was turning into a god. But this was only one among many changes. Millenarianism, more emotional expressions of religion and more sophisticated philosophical systems were all interplaying with one another. To distinguish Hindu or Buddhist "orthodoxy" in this is somewhat artificial.

THE ASSIMILATION OF INVADERS

In the end the Kushanas succumbed to a greater power: Bactria and the Kabul valley were taken by Artaxerxes early in the third century CE. Soon after, another Sassanid king took the Kushana capital of Peshawar – and such statements make it easy to feel impatient with the narrative they provide. Contemplating them, the reader may well feel with Voltaire: "What is it to me if one king replaces another on the banks of the Oxus and Jaxartes?" It is like the fratricidal struggles of Frankish kings, or of the Anglo-Saxon kingdoms of the Heptarchy, on a slightly larger scale. It is indeed difficult to see much significance in this ebb and flow beyond its registration of two great constants of Indian history, the importance of the northwestern frontier as a cultural conduit and the digestive power of Hindu civilization. None of the invading peoples could in the end resist the assimilative power India always showed. New rulers were before long ruling Hindu kingdoms (whose roots went back possibly beyond Maurya times to political units of the fourth and fifth centuries BCE), and adopting Indian ways.

Invaders never penetrated far to the south. After the Maurya break-up, the Deccan long remained separate and under its own Dravidian rulers. Its cultural distinction persists even today. Though Aryan influence was stronger there after the Maurya era and Hinduism and Buddhism were never to disappear, the south was not again truly integrated politically with the north until the coming of the British Raj.

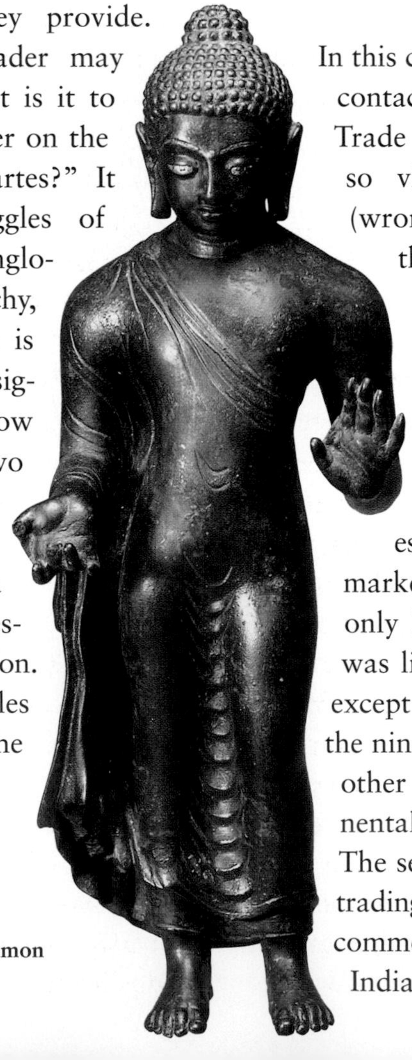

A 6th-century bronze statue of the Buddha, made during the Gupta period. Many of the Gupta emperors were known as patrons of the arts and numerous Indian artistic styles still common today were established during that era.

TRADE

In this confusing period not all India's contacts with outsiders were violent. Trade with Roman merchants grew so visibly that Pliny blamed it (wrongly) for draining gold out of the empire. We have little hard information, it is true, except about the arrival of embassies from India to negotiate over trade but the remark suggests that one feature of India's trade with the West was already established; what Mediterranean markets sought were luxuries which only India could supply and there was little they could offer in return except bullion. This pattern held until the nineteenth century. There are also other interesting signs of intercontinental contacts arising from trade. The sea is a uniter of the cultures of trading communities; Tamil words for commodities turn up in Greek, and Indians from the south had traded

with Egypt since Hellenistic times. Later, Roman merchants lived in southern ports where Tamil kings kept Roman bodyguards. Finally, it seems likely that whatever the truth may be about the holy apostle Thomas, Christianity appeared in India first in the western trading ports, possibly as early as the first century CE.

THE GUPTA EMPIRE

POLITICAL UNITY DID NOT APPEAR again even in the north until hundreds of years had passed. A new Ganges valley state, the Gupta Empire, was then the legatee of five centuries of confusion. Its centre was at Patna, where a dynasty of Gupta emperors established itself. The first of these, another Chandra Gupta, began to reign in 320 CE, and within a hundred years north India was once more for a time united and relieved of external pressure and incursion. It was not so big an empire as Asoka's, but the Guptas preserved theirs longer. For some two centuries north India enjoyed under them a sort of Antonine age, later to be imagined with nostalgia as India's classical period.

ART IN THE GUPTA ERA

The Gupta age brought the first great consolidation of an Indian artistic heritage. From the earlier times little has survived from before the perfection of stone-carving under the Mauryas. The columns which are its major monuments were the culmination of a native tradition of stonework. For a long time stone-carving and building still showed traces of styles evolved in an age of wood construction, but techniques were well advanced before the arrival of Greek influence, once thought to be the origin of Indian stone sculpture. What the Greeks brought were new artistic motifs and techniques from the West. If we are to judge by what survives, the major deployment of these influences was found in Buddhist sculpture until well into the Common Era. But before the Gupta era, a rich and indigenous tradition of Hindu sculpture had also been established, and from this time India's artistic life is mature and self-sustaining. In Gupta times there began to be built the great numbers of stone temples (as distinct from excavated and embellished caves), which are the great glories of both Indian art and architecture before the Muslim era.

Gupta-period stone temples, with their smooth and supple carvings, profoundly influenced the development of Indian art for hundreds of years. This 5th-century stone bas-relief, which depicts lovers enjoying a dance performance, was found among the ruins of a Gupta temple in Deogarh in Rajasthan.

LITERATURE

Gupta civilization was also remarkable for its literary achievement. Again, the roots are deep. The standardization and systematization of Sanskrit grammar just before Maurya times opened the path to a literature which could be shared by the élite of the whole subcontinent. Sanskrit was a tie uniting north and south in spite of their cultural differences. The great epics were given their classical form in Sanskrit (though they were also available in translations into local languages) and in it wrote the greatest of Indian poets, Kalidasa. He was also a dramatist, and in the Gupta era there emerged from the shadowy past the Indian theatre whose traditions have been maintained and carried into the popular Indian film industry of the present day.

Intellectually, too, the Gupta era was a great one. It was in the fifth century that Indian arithmeticians invented the decimal system. A layman can perhaps glimpse the importance of this more readily than he can that of the Indian philosophical resurgence of the same period. The resurgence was not confined to religious thought, but what can be gathered from it about general attitudes or the direction of culture seems highly debatable. In a literary text such as the *Kama Sutra*, a western observer may be most struck by the prominence given in it to the acquisition of techniques whose use, however stimulating to the individual, can at most have absorbed only a small fraction of the interest and time of a tiny élite. A negative point is perhaps safest: neither the emphasis on *dharma* of the Brahmanical tradition, nor the ascetic severities of some Indian teachers, nor the frank acceptance of sensual pleasure suggested by many texts beside the *Kama Sutra* have anything in common with the striving, militant puritanism so strong in both the Christian and Islamic traditions. Indian civilization moved to very different rhythms from those further west; here, perhaps, lay its deepest strength and the explanation of its powers of resistance to alien cultures.

Kalidasa's poetry

"You are not the only one to feel sad when you leave the village;
even the trees are touched by the sadness
that your separation produces.
You only have to look: the deer
they can hardly eat the grass,
the cherry trees stop their dance
and the reeds drop their pale leaves on the earth
as if they were tears."

An extract from *Sakuntala* by the Indian poet Kalidasa.

These fragments of manuscripts form part of a collection of more than 100 similar pieces, all of which are thought to have belonged to the Buddhist school of Mahasangika-Lokottaravadin. Although some of the texts have been dated to as early as the 2nd century, most of the fragments found date from the Gupta period (4th and 5th centuries).

HINDU SOCIETY

IN THE GUPTA ERA Indian civilization came to its mature, classical form. Chronology derived from politics is a hindrance here; important developments flow across the

The caste system

Although the term caste comes from the Latin *castus*, meaning "pure", the Indians use the word *varna*, which means "colour", demonstrating the system's racial origins. The caste system has been present in many cultures throughout history, but nowhere has it taken root to the same extent as in India. Most researchers believe that it emerged after the conquest of India by the Aryans in around 1500 BCE. The Aryans probably imposed their strongly hierarchical social structure – consisting of a religious and judicial body, a military class and a merchant class – on the rest of Hindu society. This social structure was then consolidated during the Brahman period.

Theoretical concepts, taken from the *Rig-Veda*, suggest that there were originally four Indian castes: the Brahmans (priests), the Kshatriyas (warriors), the Vaishyas (farmers and merchants) and the Shudras (labourers). Each of the main castes has been gradually subdivided into innumerable layers, which are known as *jatis*. A further group, the Untouchables, are considered so impure that they are outside the caste system. Despite modern legislation outlawing discrimination against them, Untouchables are still often treated as less than human and are obliged to carry out "unclean" tasks such as those of "sweepers": cleaning lavatories and collecting manure.

The castes to which individuals belong govern every facet of their lives, including the job they do, the food they eat and whom they are permitted to marry. Caste should not, however, be confused with social class, since paradoxes abound: poverty-stricken Brahmans and wealthy Untouchables are not uncommon.

Between the 3rd and 2nd centuries BCE*, the Brahman priests reacted against the threat to Hinduism posed by the arrival of Buddhism, making their own rituals ever more elaborate and exclusive. As a result, ordinary Hindus increasingly turned to the more open* bhakti *(devotion) movement, which was at its height between the 6th and 16th centuries.* Bhakti *cults emphasized the worshipper's personal relationship with a deity and often rejected the intermediary role of the priest, proclaiming that direct contact with the divine was available to men and women of every caste. In this 19th-century painting, Krishna's love for Rada is represented, symbolizing* bhakti *devotion.*

boundaries of any arbitrary period. Nevertheless, in Gupta culture we can sense the presence of the fully evolved Hindu society. Its outstanding expression was a caste system which by then had come to overlay and complicate the original four-class division of Vedic society. Within castes which locked them into well-defined groups for marriage and, usually, into their occupations, most Indians lived a life close to the land. The cities were for the most part great markets or great centres of pilgrimage. Most Indians were, as they are now, peasants, whose lives were lived within the assumptions of a religious culture already set in its fundamental form in pre-Maurya times. Some of its later developments have been mentioned already; others run on past the Gupta period and will have to be discussed elsewhere. Of their vigour and power there can be no doubt; with centuries of further elaboration ahead, they were already expressed in Gupta times in a huge development of carving and sculpture which manifest the power of popular religion and

Hinduism and the Ganges river

The Ganges river rises on the southern slopes of the Himalayas and after flowing for a total of 1,680 miles (2,700 km) enters the Bay of Bengal. The great river passes across the plains of northeastern India and into Bangladesh, where it is joined by the waters of the Brahmaputra.

For Hindus, the Ganges has been a sacred river from time immemorial – they believe that the goddess Ganga was born in Mount Meru, where the gods reside. The god Shiva's hair served as a pathway down from the holy mountain to the earth.

The banks of the Ganges are lined with countless temples, sanctuaries and Hindu holy places. These include Hardwar, one of the seven sacred cities and home every 12 years to the important Kumba Mela religious festival. During the festival thousands of Hindu pilgrims immerse themselves in the Ganges' waters, which they believe will purify their *karma* from their former and current lives, with the hope of achieving a perfect reincarnation.

Another important pilgrimage centre is the city of Allahabad (also known as Prayag, meaning "Place of Sacrifice"), where, legend has it, the invisible Sarasvati river joins the Ganges and the Yamuna.

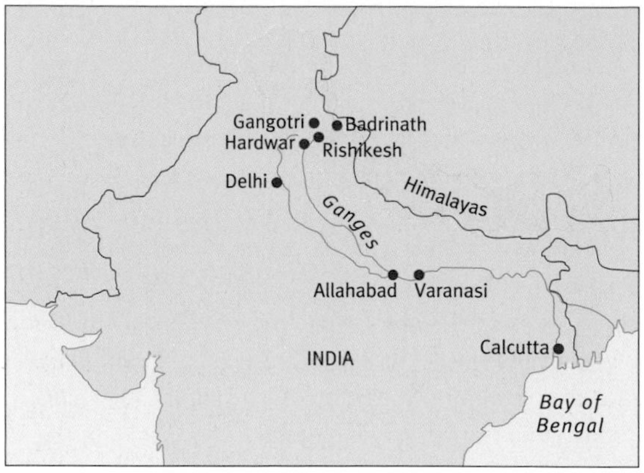

This map shows the route of the Ganges, from its source in the Himalayas to its estuary in the Bay of Bengal.

Varanasi, another of the sacred cities, is a place of pilgrimage not only for Hindus, but also for Buddhists and Jains. According to tradition, the Buddha, Siddhartha Gautama, gave his first sermon (on "The Foundation of Righteousness") in Sarnath, near Varanasi, and Mahavira, the founder of Jainism, lived in the historic city.

take their place alongside the *stupa*s and Buddhas of pre-Gupta times as enduring features of the Indian landscape.

Paradoxically, India, largely because of its religious art, is a country where we have perhaps more evidence about the minds of the people of the past than we have about their material lives. We may know little about the precise way in which Gupta taxation actually weighed on the peasant (though we can guess), but in the contemplation of the endless dance of the gods and demons, the forming and dissolving patterns of animals and symbols, we can touch a world still alive and visible in the village shrines and juggernauts of our own day. In India as nowhere else, there is some chance of access to the life of the uncounted millions whose history should be recounted in such books as this, but which usually escapes us.

RELIGIOUS CHANGES

In the climax of Hindu civilization, between Gupta times and the coming of Islam, the fertility of Indian religion, the soil of Indian culture, was hardly troubled by political change. One symptom was the appearance by 600 or thereabouts of an important new cult which quickly took a place it was never to lose in the Hindu worship, that of the mother-goddess Devi. Some have seen in her an expression of a new sexual emphasis which marked both Hinduism and Buddhism. Her cult was part of a general effervescence of religious life, lasting a couple of centuries or more, for a new popular emotionalism is associated with the cults of Shiva and Vishnu at about the same time. Dates are not very helpful here; we have to think of continuing change during the whole of the centuries corresponding to those of the early Common Era whose result was the final evolution of the old Brahmanical religion into Hinduism.

From it there emerged a spectrum of practice and belief offering something for all needs. The philosophic system of the *Vedanta* (which stressed the unreality of the factual and material and the desirability of the winning of disengagement in true knowledge of reality, *brahma*) was at one end of a spectrum which ran at the other into the village superstitions which worshipped local deities long assimilated into one of the many cults of Shiva or Vishnu. Religious effervescence thus found expression antithetically in the simultaneous growth of image worship and the rise of new austerity. Animal sacrifice had never stopped. It was one of the things now endorsed by a new strictness of conservative religious practice. So was a new rigidity of attitudes towards women and their intensified subordination. The religious expression of this was an upsurge of child marriage and the practice called *suttee*, or self-immolation of Indian widows on their husbands' funeral pyres.

MAHAYANA BUDDHISM

The richness of Indian culture is such that this coarsening of religion was accompanied also by the development to their highest pitch of the philosophical tradition of the *Vedanta*, the culmination of Vedic tradition, and the new development of *Mahayana* Buddhism, which asserted the divinity of the Buddha. The roots of the latter went back to early deviations from the Buddha's teaching on contemplation, purity and non-attachment. These deviations had favoured a more ritualistic and popular religious approach and also stressed a new interpretation of the Buddha's role. Instead of merely being understood as a teacher and an example, Buddha was now seen as the greatest of *bodhisattvas*, saviours who, entitled to the bliss of self-annihilation themselves, nevertheless rejected it to remain in the world and teach people the way to salvation.

To become a *bodhisattva* gradually became the aim of many Buddhists. In part, the efforts of a Buddhist council summoned by the Kushan ruler Kanishka had been directed towards re-integrating two tendencies in Buddhism which were increasingly divergent. This had not been successful. *Mahayana* Buddhism (the word means "great vehicle") focused upon a Buddha who was effectively a divine saviour who might be worshipped and followed in faith, one manifestation of a great, single heavenly Buddha who begins to look somewhat like the undifferentiated soul behind all things found in Hinduism. The disciplines of austerity and contemplation Gautama had taught were now increasingly confined to a minority of orthodox Buddhists, the followers of *Mahayana* winning conversions among the masses. One sign of this was the proliferation in the first and second centuries CE of statues and representations of the

This 12th-century statue represents Devi, the goddess of the Hindu pantheon, portrayed as Sadasiva's consort, with four arms. Devi takes on various forms, sometimes appearing as Bhu (the ancient earth goddess) or Parvati (daughter of the Himalayas), among others. She is generally associated with fertility and with the earth.

Buddha, a practice which had been hitherto restrained by the Buddha's prohibition of idol-worship. *Mahayana* Buddhism eventually replaced earlier forms in India, and spread also along the central Asian trade routes through Central Asia to China and Japan. The more orthodox tradition did better in Southeast Asia and Indonesia.

INDIAN PHILOSOPHY

Hinduism and Buddhism were thus both marked by changes which broadened their appeal. The Hindu religion prospered better, though there is a regional factor at work here; since Kushan times, the centre of Indian Buddhism had been the northwest, the region most exposed to the devastations of the Hun raiders. Hinduism prospered most in the south. Both the northwest and the south, of course, were zones where cultural currents intermingled most easily with those from the classical Mediterranean world, in the one across land and in the other by sea.

These changes provoke a sense of culmination and climax. They matured only shortly before Islam arrived in the subcontinent, but early enough for a philosophical outlook to have solidified, one which has marked India

Buddhist *bodhisattvas*, such as the one portrayed in this *Mahayana* stone bas-relief, were masters of the "six perfections": energy, generosity, meditation, morality, patience and wisdom.

ever since and has shown astonishing invulnerability to competing views. At its heart was a vision of endless cycles of creation and reabsorption into the divine, a picture of the cosmos which predicated a cyclic and not a linear history. What difference this made to the way Indians have actually behaved – right down to the present day – is a huge subject, and almost impossible to grasp. It might be expected to lead to passivity and scepticism about the value of practical action, yet this is very debatable. Few Christians live lives that are logically wholly coherent with their beliefs and there is no reason to expect Hindus to be more consistent. The practical activity of sacrifice and propitiation in Indian temples survives still. Yet the direction of a whole culture may none the less be determined by the emphasis of its distinctive modes of thought, and it is difficult not to feel that much of India's history has been determined by a world outlook which stressed the limits rather than the potential of human action.

Mahayana Buddhism created a new anthropomorphic configuration of the Buddha in the Kushana period: the upright posture and monastic wrap became the defining characteristics of the statuary of the Buddha, as is demonstrated by this 8th- or 9th-century bronze.

THE IMPACT OF ISLAM ON INDIA

FOR THE BACKGROUND to Islam in India we must return to 500 CE or so. From about that time, northern India was once again divided in obedience both to the centrifugal tendencies which afflicted early empires and to the appearance of a mysterious invasion of "Hunas". Were they perhaps Huns? Certainly they behaved like them, devastating much of the northwest, sweeping away many of the established ruling families. Across the mountains, in Afghanistan, they mortally wounded Buddhism, which had been strongly established there. In the subcontinent itself, this anarchic period did less fundamental damage. Though the northern plains had broken up again into warring kingdoms, Indian cities do not seem to have been much disturbed and peasant life recovers quickly from all but the worst blows. Indian warfare appears rapidly to have acquired important and effective conventional limits on its potential for destructiveness. The state of affairs over much of the north at this time seems in some ways rather like that of some European countries during the more anarchic periods of the Middle Ages, when feudal relationships more or less kept the peace between potentially competitive grandees but could not completely contain outbreaks of violence which were essentially about different forms of tribute.

Meanwhile, Islam had come to India. It did so first through Arab traders on the western coasts. Then, in 712 or thereabouts, Arab armies conquered Sind. They got no further, gradually settled down and ceased to trouble the Indian peoples. A period of calm followed which lasted until a Ghaznavid ruler broke deep into India early in the eleventh century with raids which were destructive, but again did not produce radical change. Indian religious life for another two centuries moved still to its own rhythms, the most striking changes being the decline of Buddhism and the rise of Tantrism, a semi-magical and superstitious growth of practices promising access to holiness by charms and ritual. Cults centred

In 1192 the Turkish leader Muhammad Ghur defeated the Hindu alliance. His successor, a slave and loyal general, Qutb ud-Din Aibvak, built the Qutb-Minar in Delhi. This victory tower, 240 ft (73 m) high, was erected to proclaim the victory of Islam over the infidel and became a potent symbol of the Muslim domination of India.

on popular festivals at temples also prospered, no doubt in the absence of a strong political focus in post-Gupta times. Then came a new invasion of central Asians.

MUSLIM INVADERS

The new invaders were Muslims and were drawn from the complex of Turkish peoples. Theirs was a different sort of Islamic onslaught from earlier ones, for they came to stay, not just to raid. They first established themselves in the Punjab in the eleventh century and then launched a second wave of invasions at the end of the twelfth century, which led within a few decades to the establishment of Turkish sultans at Delhi who ruled the whole of the Ganges valley. Their empire was not monolithic. Hindu kingdoms survived within it on a tributary basis, as Christian kingdoms survived to be tributaries of Mongols in the West. The Muslim rulers, perhaps careful of their material interests, did not always support their co-religionists of the *Ulema* who sought to proselytize and were willing to persecute (as the destruction of Hindu temples shows).

The heartland of the first Muslim empire in India was the Ganges valley. The invaders rapidly overran Bengal and later established themselves on the west coast of India and the tableland of the Deccan. Further south they did not penetrate and Hindu society survived there largely unchanged. In any case, their rule was not to last long even in the north. In 1398 Timur Lang's army sacked Delhi after a devastating approach march which was made all the speedier, said one chronicler, because of the Mongols' desire to escape from the stench of decay arising from the piles of corpses they left in their wake. In the troubled waters after this disaster, generals and local potentates struck out for themselves and Islamic India fragmented again. None the less, Islam was by now established in the subcontinent, the greatest challenge yet seen to India's assimilative powers, for its active, prophetic, revelatory style was wholly antithetical both to Hinduism and to Buddhism (though Islam, too, was to be subtly changed by them).

THE DELHI SULTANATE: BABUR

New sultans emerged at Delhi but long showed no power to restore the former Islamic empire. Only in the sixteenth century was it revived by a prince from outside, Babur of Kabul. On his father's side he descended from Timur and on his mother's from Chinghis, formidable advantages and a source of inspiration to a young man schooled in adversity. He quickly discovered he had to fight for his inheritance and there can have been few monarchs who, like Babur, conquered a city of the importance of Samarkand at the age of fourteen (albeit to lose it again almost at once). Even when legend and anecdote are separated, he remains, in spite of cruelty and duplicity, one of the most attractive figures among great rulers: munificent, hardy, courageous, intelligent and sensitive. He left a remarkable autobiography, written from notes made throughout his life, which was to be treasured by his descendants as a source of inspiration and guidance. It displays a ruler who did not think of himself as Mongol in culture, but Turkish in the tradition of those peoples long settled in the former eastern provinces of the Abbasid caliphate. His taste and culture were formed by the inheritance of the Timurid princes of Persia; his love of gardening and poetry came from that country and fitted easily into the setting of an Islamic India whose courts were already much influenced by Persian models. Babur was a bibliophile, another Timurid trait; it is reported that when he took Lahore he went at once to his defeated adversary's library to choose texts from it to send as gifts to his sons. He himself wrote, among other things, a forty-page account of his conquests in Hindustan, noting its customs and caste structure and, even more minutely, its wildlife and flowers.

This 16th-century illustration depicts the troops of Timur Lang, one of Babur of Kabul's ancestors, sacking the city of Isfahan.

THE MOGHUL EMPIRE

Babur was called in to India by Afghan chiefs, but had his own claims to make to the inheritance of the Timurid line in Hindustan. This was to prove the beginning of Moghul India; Moghul was the Persian word for Mongol, though it was not a word Babur applied to himself. Originally, those whose discontent and intrigue called him forward had only aroused in him the ambition of conquering the Punjab, but he was soon drawn further. In 1526 he took Delhi after the sultan had fallen in battle. Soon Babur was subduing those who had invited him to come to India while at the same time conquering the infidel Hindu princes who had seized an opportunity to renew their own independence.

In his famous memoirs Babur expresses his great love of gardening and natural history. This 16th-century painting depicts Babur in a palace garden.

The result was an empire which in 1530, the year of his death, stretched from Kabul to the borders of Bihar. Babur's body, significantly, was taken, as he had directed to Kabul, where it was buried in his favourite garden with no roof over his tomb in the place he had always thought of as home.

The reign of Babur's son, troubled by his own instability and inadequacy and by the presence of half-brothers anxious to exploit the Timurid tradition which, like the Frankish, prescribed the division of a royal inheritance, showed that the security and consolidation of Babur's realm could not be taken for granted. For five years of his reign he was driven from Delhi, though he returned there to die in 1555. His heir, Akbar, born during his father's distressed wanderings (but enjoying the advantages of a very auspicious horoscope and the absence of rival brothers), thus came to the throne as a boy. He inherited at first only a small part of his grandfather's domains, but was to build from them an empire recalling that of Asoka, winning the awed respect of Europeans, who called him "the Great Moghul".

AKBAR

AKBAR HAD MANY kingly qualities. He was brave to the point of folly – his most obvious weakness was that he was headstrong – enjoying as a boy riding his own fighting elephants and preferring hunting and hawking to lessons (one consequence was that, uniquely in Babur's line, he was almost illiterate). He once killed a tiger with his sword in single combat and was proud of his marksmanship with a gun (Babur had introduced firearms to the Moghul army). Yet he was also, like his predecessors, an admirer of learning and all things beautiful. He collected books, and in his reign Moghul architecture

From "The Life of Akbar", this 16th-century illustration depicts the celebrations that followed the birth in 1569 of Salim, son of Akbar and Mariam Uz-Zamani Begum, who can be seen in the top left of the picture. Prince Salim would eventually inherit his father's throne as Emperor Jahangir (1605–1627).

Akbar was a skilled and experienced military leader. At the age of 15 he had conquered Ajmer and a large part of central India. In 1567–1568 the emperor brought most of present-day Rajasthan under his control when his armies took Chittoor and Ranthambor; Akbar is shown leading the siege of the latter in this illustration.

and painting came to their peak, a department of court painters being maintained at his expense. Above all, he was statesmanlike in his handling of the problems posed by religious difference among his subjects.

Akbar reigned for almost half a century, until 1605, thus just overlapping at each end the reign of his contemporary, Queen Elizabeth I of England. Among his first acts on reaching maturity was to marry a Rajput princess who was, of course, a Hindu. Marriage always played an important part in Akbar's diplomacy and strategy, and this lady (the mother of the next emperor) was the daughter of the greatest of the Rajput kings and therefore an important catch. None the less, something more than policy may be seen in the marriage. Akbar had already permitted the Hindu ladies of his harem to practise the rites of their own religion within it, an unprecedented act for a Muslim ruler. Before long, he abolished the poll tax on non-Muslims; he was going to be the emperor of all religions, not a Muslim fanatic. Akbar even went on to listen to Christian teachers; he invited the Portuguese who had appeared on the west coast to send missionaries learned in their faith to his court and three Jesuits duly arrived there in 1580. They disputed vigorously with Muslim divines before the emperor and received many marks of his favour, though they were disappointed in their long-indulged hope of his conversion. He seems, in fact, to have been a man of genuine religious feeling and eclectic mind; he went so far as to try to institute a new religion of his own, a sort of mishmash of Zoroastrianism, Islam and Hinduism. It had little success except among prudent courtiers and offended some.

IMPERIAL EXPANSION

However Akbar's religious tolerance is interpreted, it is evident that the appeasement of non-Muslims would ease the problems of government in India. Babur's advice in his memoirs to conciliate defeated enemies pointed in this direction too, for Akbar launched himself on a career of conquest and added many new Hindu territories to his empire. He rebuilt the unity of northern India from Gujarat to Bengal and began the conquest of the Deccan. The empire was governed by a system of administration much of which lasted well into the era of the British Raj, though Akbar was less an innovator in government than the confirmer and establisher of institutions he inherited. Officials ruled in the emperor's name and at his pleasure; they had the primary function of providing soldiers as needed and raising the land tax, now reassessed on an empire-wide

India's Moghul Empire was at its most splendid under Akbar. This miniature from "The Life of Akbar" gives an impression of the elegance of the imperial court. The emperor, seated on his throne, is depicted receiving Prince Abdur Rahin in the city of Agra in 1562.

and more flexible system devised by a Hindu finance minister. This seems to have had an almost unmatched success in that it actually led to increases in production which raised the standard of living in Hindustan. Among other reforms, which were notable in intention, if not in effect was the discouragement of *suttee*.

Moghul India

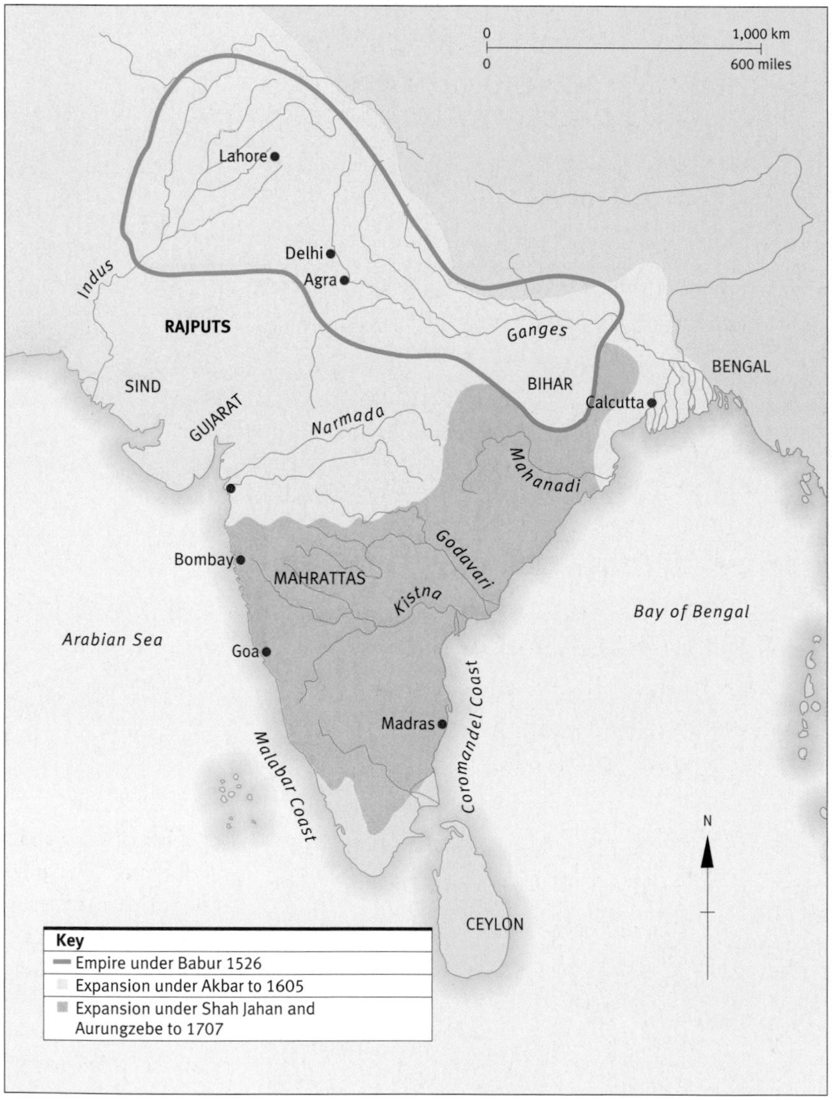

During the reign of Akbar, the Moghul Empire conquered all of northern India and a large part of the Deccan States, which were later totally annexed by Emperor Aurungzebe (1658–1707). By the late 17th century, however, the days of imperial expansion were over and the empire began to decline.

RELIGIOUS ASSIMILATION

Above all, Akbar stabilized the régime. He was disappointed in his sons and quarrelled with them, yet the dynasty was solidly based when he died. There were revolts nevertheless. Some of them seem to have been encouraged by Muslim anger at Akbar's apparent falling-away from the faith. Even in the "Turkish" era the sharpness of the religious distinction between Muslim and non-Muslim had somewhat softened as invaders settled down in their new country and took up Indian ways. One earlier sign of assimilation was the appearance of a new language, Urdu, the tongue of the camp. It was the *lingua franca* of rulers and ruled, with a Hindi structure and a Persian and Turkish vocabulary. Soon there were signs that the omnivorous power of Hinduism would perhaps even incorporate Islam; a new devotionalism in the fourteenth and fifteenth centuries had spread through popular hymns an abstract, almost monotheistic, cult, of a God whose name might be Rama or Allah, but who offered love, justice and mercy to all. Correspondingly, some Muslims even before Akbar's reign had shown interest in and respect for Hindu ideas. There was some absorption of Hindu ritual practice. Soon it was noticeable that converts to Islam tended to revere the tombs of holy men: these became places of resort and pilgrimage which satisfied the scheme of a subordinate focus of devotion in a monotheistic religion and thus carried out the functions of the minor and local deities who had always found a place in Hinduism.

RELATIONS WITH EUROPE

An important development before the end of Akbar's reign was the consolidation of India's

Akbar is described by a Western visitor

"Akbar was imbued with a spirit which enabled him to perceive and judge things rapidly, as well as a strict sense of duty. He was intelligent, pleasant and generous; to these characteristics were added the courage of a brave and very enterprising person. He could be friendly and be in a good mood, without losing any of his dignity as king. He recognized virtue and was well-disposed to foreigners, particularly towards Christians, some of whom he always wanted near him. Impressed and eager to learn, he had a profound knowledge not only of political and military matters, but also of technical things."

An extract from the *History of memorable things that happened in the East Indies and in the countries discovered by the Portuguese* by Jarric.

first direct relations with Atlantic Europe. Links with Mediterranean Europe may already have been made slightly easier by the coming of Islam; from the Levant to Delhi a common religion provided continuous, if distant, contact. European travellers had turned up from time to time in India and its rulers had been able to attract the occasional technical expert to their service, though they were few after the Ottoman conquests. But what was now about to happen was to go much further and would change India for ever. The Europeans who now arrived would be followed by others in increasing numbers and they would not go away.

The process had begun when a Portuguese admiral reached Malabar at the end of the fifteenth century. Within a few years his countrymen had installed themselves as traders – and behaved sometimes as pirates at Bombay and on the coast of Gujarat. Attempts to dislodge them failed in the troubled years following Babur's death, and in the second half of the century the Portuguese moved around to found new posts in the Bay of Bengal. They made the running for Europeans in India for a long time. They were liable, none the less, to attract the hostility of good Muslims because they brought with them pictures and images of Christ, Mary and the saints, which smacked of idolatry. Protestants were to prove less irritating to religious feeling when they arrived. The British age in India was still a long way off, but with rare historical neatness the first British East India Company was founded on 31 December 1600, the last day of the sixteenth century. Three years later the Company's first emissary arrived at Akbar's court at Agra and by then Elizabeth I, who had given the merchants

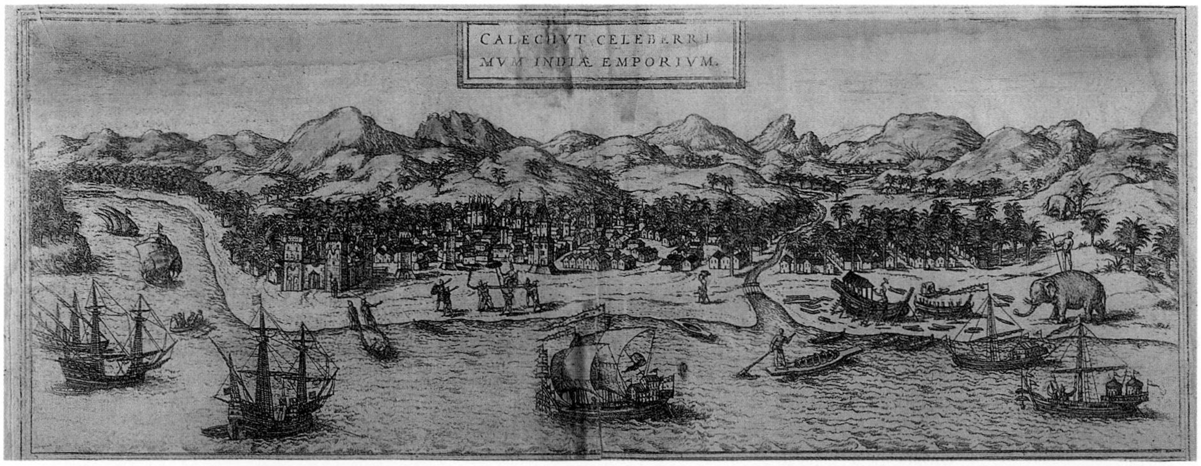

Calicut (Kozhikode) was the first place where the Portuguese landed on the Indian mainland (on 21 May 1498). They were eventually given trading rights and allowed to build a fort at the site. The Calicut trading station, depicted in this engraving, was a centre of Portuguese commerce for more than 100 years.

their charter of incorporation, was dead. Thus at the end of the reigns of two great rulers came the first contact between two countries whose historical destinies were to be entwined so long and with such enormous effect for them both and for the world. At that moment no hint of such a future could have been sensed. The English then regarded trade in India as less interesting than that with other parts of Asia. The contrast between the two realms, too, is fascinating: Akbar's empire was one of the most powerful in the world, his court one of the most sumptuous, and he and his successors ruled over a civilization more glorious and spectacular than anything India had known since the Guptas, while Queen Elizabeth's kingdom, barely a great power, even in European terms, was crippled by debt and contained fewer people than modern Calcutta. Akbar's successor was contemptuous of the presents sent to him by James I a few years later. Yet the future of India lay with the subjects of the queen.

SHAH JAHAN

The Moghul emperors continued in Babur's line in direct descent, though not without interruption, until the middle of the nineteenth century. After Akbar, so great was the dynasty's prestige that it became fashionable in India to claim Mongol descent. Only the three rulers who followed Akbar matter here, for it was under Jahangir and Shah Jahan that the empire grew to its greatest extent in the first half of the seventeenth century and under Aurungzebe that it began to decay in the second. The reign of Jahangir was not so glorious as his father's, but the empire survived his cruelty and alcoholism, a considerable test of its administrative structure. The religious toleration established by Akbar also survived intact. For all his faults, though, Jahangir was a notable promoter of the arts, above all of painting. During his reign there becomes visible for the first time the impact of European culture in Asia, through artistic motifs drawn from imported pictures and prints. One of these motifs was the halo or nimbus given to Christian saints and, in Byzantium, to emperors. After Jahangir all Moghul emperors were painted with it.

COURT LIFE

Shah Jahan began the piecemeal acquisition of the Deccan sultanates though he had little success in campaigns in the northwest and failed to drive the Persians from Kandahar. In domestic administration there was a weakening of the principle of religious toleration, though not sufficiently to place Hindus at a disadvantage in government service; administration remained multi-religious. Although the emperor decreed that all newly built Hindu temples should be pulled down, he patronized Hindu poets and musicians. At Agra, Shah Jahan maintained a lavish and exquisite court life. It was there, too, that he built the most celebrated and the best-known of all Islamic buildings, the Taj Mahal, a tomb for his favourite wife; it is the only possible rival to the mosque of Córdoba for the title of the most beautiful building in the world. She had died soon after Shah Jahan's accession and for over twenty years his builders were at work. It is the culmination of the work with arch and dome which is one of the most conspicuous Islamic legacies to Indian art and the greatest monument of Islam in India. The waning of Indian representational sculpture after the Islamic invasions had its compensations. Shah Jahan's court also brought to its culmination a great tradition of miniature painting.

The reign of the Moghul emperor Shah Jahan, who is shown seated on his peacock throne in this 18th-century painting, lasted from 1628 until 1658.

TAXATION

Beneath the level of the court, the picture of life in Moghul India is far less attractive. Local officials had to raise more and more money to support not only the household expenses and campaigns of Shah Jahan but also the social and military élites who were

Emperor Aurungzebe built the Bibika Maqbara mausoleum in Aurangabad for his wife, Rabia Daurani. Modelled on the Taj Mahal, which had been completed 25 years earlier, the Bibika Maqbara was half the size of its predecessor. The construction of elaborate tombs in the Moghul period reflects the Islamic nature of the dynasty: unlike Hindus, who believe in cremation and reincarnation, Muslims believe in burial and eternal life.

essentially parasitic on the producing economy. Without regard for local need or natural disaster, a rapacious tax-gathering machine may at times have been taking from the peasant producers as much as half their incomes. Virtually none of this was productively invested. The flight of peasants from the land and rise of rural banditry are telling symptoms of the suffering and resistance these exactions provoked. Yet even Shah Jahan's demands probably did the empire less damage than the religious enthusiasm of his third son, Aurungzebe, who set aside three brothers and imprisoned his father to become emperor in 1658. He combined, disastrously, absolute power, distrust of his subordinates and a narrow religiosity. To have succeeded in reducing the expenses of his court is not much of an offsetting item in the account. New conquests were balanced by revolts against Moghul rule which were said to owe much to Aurungzebe's attempt to prohibit the Hindu religion and destroy its temples, and to his restoration of the poll tax on non-Muslims. The Hindu's advancement in the service of the state was less and less likely; conversion became necessary for success. A century of religious toleration was cancelled and one result was the alienation of many subjects' loyalties.

HINDU OPPOSITION

Among other results, the alienation of Hindus helped to make it impossible finally to conquer the Deccan, which has been termed the ulcer which ruined the Moghul Empire. As under Asoka, north and south India could not be united. The Mahrattas, the hillmen who were the core of Hindu opposition, constituted themselves under an independent ruler in 1674. They allied with the remains of the Muslim armies of the Deccan sultans to resist the Moghul armies in a long struggle which threw up a heroic figure who has become something of a paladin in the eyes of modern Hindu nationalists. This was Shivagi, who built from fragments a Mahratta political identity which soon enabled him to exploit the tax-payer as ruthlessly as the Moghuls had done. Aurungzebe was continuously campaigning against the Mahrattas down to his death in 1707. There followed a grave crisis for the régime, for his three sons disputed the succession. The empire almost at once began to break up and a much more formidable legatee than the Hindu or local prince was waiting in the wings – the European.

MOGHUL DECLINE

Perhaps the negative responsibility for the eventual success of the Europeans in India is Akbar's, for he did not scotch the serpent in the egg. Shah Jahan, on the other hand, destroyed the Portuguese station on the Hooghly, though Christians were later tolerated at Agra. Strikingly, Moghul policy never seems to have envisaged the building of a navy, a weapon used formidably against the Mediterranean Europeans by the Ottomans. One consequence was already felt under Aurungzebe, when coastal shipping and even the pilgrim trade to Mecca were in danger from the Europeans. On land, the Europeans had been allowed to establish their toeholds and bridgeheads. After beating a Portuguese squadron, the English won their first west-coast trading concession early in the seventeenth century. Then, in 1639, on the Bay of Bengal and with the permission of the local ruler, they founded at Madras the settlement which was the first territory of British India, Fort St George. The headstones over their graves in its little cemetery still commemorate the first English who lived and died in India. Thousands more would do the same in the next three centuries.

The English later fell foul of Aurungzebe, but got further stations at Bombay and Calcutta before the end of the century. Their ships had maintained the paramountcy in trade won from the Portuguese, but a new European rival was also in sight by 1700. A French East India Company had been founded in 1664 and soon established its own settlements.

Aurungzebe, the son of Shah Jahan and the last of the great Moghul emperors, is portrayed in this 17th-century painting.

A century of conflict lay ahead, but not only between the newcomers. Europeans were already having to make nice political choices because of the uncertainties aroused when Moghul power was no longer as strong as it once had been. Relations had to be opened with his opponents as well as with the emperor, as the English in Bombay discovered, looking on helplessly while a Mahratta squadron occupied one island in Bombay harbour and a Moghul admiral the one next to it. In 1677 an official sent back a significant warning to his employers in London: "the times now require you to manage your general commerce with your sword in your hands." By 1700 the English were well aware that much was at stake.

After the arrival of the Portuguese, the Malabar coastal region became an important financial centre where several commercial routes converged. This French miniature shows the harvest of local pepper for export to Europe.

THE EUROPEAN LEGACY

By 1700 we are into the era in which India is increasingly caught up in events not of her own making, the era of world history, in fact. Little things show it as well as great; in the sixteenth century the Portuguese had brought with them chillies, potatoes and tobacco from America. Indian diet and agriculture were already changing. Soon maize, pawpaws and pineapple were to follow. The story of Indian civilizations and rulers can be broken once this new connection with the larger world is achieved. Yet it was not the coming of the European which ended the great period of Moghul Empire; that was merely coincidental, though it was important that newcomers were there to reap the advantages. No Indian empire had ever been able to maintain itself for long. The diversity of the subcontinent and the failure of its rulers to find ways to tap indigenous popular loyalty are probably the main explanations. India remained a continent of exploitative ruling élites and productive peasants upon whom they battered. The "states", if the term can be used, were only machinery for transferring resources from producers to parasites. The means by which they did this destroyed the incentive to save – to invest productively.

India was, by the end of the seventeenth century, ready for another set of conquerors. They were awaiting their cue, already on stage, but as yet playing hardly more than bit parts. Yet in the long run the European tide would recede as well. Unlike early conquerors, though Europeans were to stay a long time, they were not to be overcome by India's assimilative power as their predecessors had been. They would go away defeated, but would not be swallowed. And when they went they would leave a deeper imprint than any of their predecessors because they would leave true state structures behind.

The Taj Mahal is one of the most enchanting buildings in the world. It was constructed by the grief-stricken Shah Jahan as a tomb for his wife Mumtaz Mahal (which means "Jewel of the Palace"), who died in 1631 while giving birth to her 14th child. The Moghul Empire, which was already in decline, could hardly afford such an extravagant project; the shah almost bankrupted the state to create his monument to love. It is said that 1,000 elephants were used to carry white marble the 185 miles (300 km) from the quarry at Makrana. Precious stones for the inlays were brought from as far away as Russia and China.

2 IMPERIAL CHINA

The lettering (top left) on this Ch'ing-era painting of Chinese nobles means "Chart of the ancestors of the Honourable Madame Wu".

ONE EXPLANATION of the striking continuity and independence of Chinese civilization is its remoteness: China seemed inaccessible to alien influence, far from sources of disturbance in other great civilizations. Empires came and went in both countries, but Islamic rule made more difference to India than any dynasty's rise or fall made to China. It was also endowed with an even greater capacity to assimilate alien influence, probably because the tradition of civilization rested on different foundations in each country. In India the great stabilizers were provided by religion and a caste system inseparable from it. In China stability rested on the culture of an administrative élite which survived dynasties and empires and kept China on the same course.

OFFICIAL RECORDS

One thing we owe to this élite is the maintenance of written records from very early times. Thanks to them, Chinese historical accounts provide an incomparable documentation, crammed with often reliable facts, though the selection of them was dominated by the assumptions of a minority, whose preoccupations they reflect, and they still leave us uninformed about many things. The Confucian scholars who kept up the historical records had a utilitarian and didactic aim: they wanted to provide a body of examples and data which would make easier the maintenance of traditional ways and values. Their histories emphasize continuity and the smooth flow of events. Given the needs of administration in so huge a country this is perfectly understandable; uniformity and regularity were clearly to be desired. Yet such a record leaves much out. It remains very difficult even in historical times – and much more difficult than in the classical Mediterranean world – to recover the concerns and life of the vast majority of Chinese. Moreover, official history may well give a false impression, both of the unchanging nature of Chinese administration and of the permeation of society by Confucian values. For a long time, the assumptions behind the Chinese administrative machine can only have been those of a minority, even if they came in the end to be shared by many Chinese and accepted, unthinkingly and even unknowingly, by most.

With the Ch'in Dynasty (221–206 BCE), all China's feudal kingdoms were united for the first time. Shih-Huang-ti, who designated himself First Emperor in 221 BCE, was the best-known of the Ch'in rulers. These infantry men are part of the famous terracotta army that guarded his tomb.

GEOGRAPHICAL ISOLATION

Chinese official culture was extraordinarily self-sufficient. Such outside influences as played upon it did so with little effect and this remains impressive. The fundamental explanation, again, is geographic isolation. China was much further removed from the classical West than the Maurya and Gupta empires. She had little intercourse with it even indirectly, although until the beginning of the seventh century Persia, Byzantium and the Mediterranean depended upon Chinese silk and valued her porcelain. Always, too, China had complicated and close relations with the people of Central Asia; yet, once unified, she had for many centuries on her borders no great states with whom relations had to be carried on. This isolation was, if anything, to increase as the centre of gravity of Western civilization moved west and north and as the Mediterranean was more and more cut off from East Asia first by the inheritors of the Hellenistic legacy (the last and most important of which was Sassanid Persia), and then by Islam.

DYNASTIC RULE

CHINA'S HISTORY between the end of the period of Warring States and the beginning of the T'ang in 618 has a chronological backbone of sorts in the waxing and waning of dynasties. Dates can be attached to these, but there is an element of the artificial, or at least a danger of being over-emphatic, in using them. It could take decades for a dynasty to make its power a reality over the whole empire and

Time chart (c.1523 BCE–1912 CE)

c.1523–1027 BCE The Shang Dynasty

221–206 BCE The unification of China by the Ch'in Emperor Shih-Huang-ti

618–907 CE The T'ang Dynasty

1368–1644 CE The Ming Dynasty

1644–1912 CE The Manchu Ch'ing Dynasty

1000 BCE | 0 | 500 CE | 1000 CE | 1500 CE | 2000 CE

551–479 BCE The life of Confucius

c.110 BCE The Silk Route opens up

c.150 CE Buddhism is introduced to China

1206–1227 CE Chinghis Khan is Mongol emperor

1557 CE The Portuguese settle in Macao

This bas-relief, on the flagstone of a sarcophagus from the Han era, depicts typical scenes from palace life.

even longer to lose it. With this reservation, the dynastic reckoning can still be useful. It gives us major divisions of Chinese history down to the twentieth century, which are called after the dynasties which reached their peaks during them. The first three which concern us are the Ch'in, the Han and the Later Han.

THE CH'IN

The Ch'in ended the disunity of the period of Warring States. They came from a western state still looked upon by some as barbarous as late as the fourth century BCE. Nevertheless, the Ch'in prospered, perhaps in part because of a radical reorganization carried out by a legalist-minded minister in about 356 BCE; perhaps also because of their soldiers' use of a new long iron sword. After swallowing Szechuan, the Ch'in claimed the status of a kingdom in 325 BCE. The climax of Ch'in success was the defeat of their last opponent in 221 BCE and the unification of China for the first time under an emperor, and the dynasty which gives the country its name.

Although the empire was to last only fifteen years after this, it was a great achievement. China from this time may be considered the seat of a single, self-conscious civilization. There had been earlier signs that such an outcome was likely. Given the potential of their own Neolithic cultures, the stimuli of cultural diffusion and some migration from the north, the first shoots of civilization had appeared in several parts of China before 500 BCE. By the end of the Warring States period some of them showed marked similarities which offset the differences between them. The political unity achieved by Ch'in conquest over a century was in a sense the logical corollary of a cultural unification already well under way. Some have even claimed that a sense of Chinese nationality can be discerned before 221 BCE; if so, it must have made conquest itself somewhat easier.

THE TWO HAN DYNASTIES

Fundamental administrative innovations by the Ch'in were to survive that dynasty's displacement by the Han, who ruled for two hundred years (206 BCE–9 CE), to be followed after a brief interlude by the almost equally

The principal Chinese dynasties

Shang ?1523–?1027 BCE
Chou ?1027–?256 BCE
Ch'in 21–206 BCE (*having annihilated Chou in 256* BCE *and other rival states afterwards*)

Former Han 206 BCE–9 CE
Hsin 9–23
Later Han 25–220
Wei 220–265
Shu 221–263
Wu 222–280
Western Chin 265–316
Sixteen Kingdoms 304–439

Eastern Chin 317–420
Liu Sung 420–479
Southern Ch'i 479–502
Liang 502–557
Ch'en 557–589

Northern Wei 386–581
Western Wei 535–557
Eastern Wei 534–550

Northern Chou 557–581
Northern Ch'i 550–577

Sui 581–618
T'ang 618–907

Five Dynasties 906–960
Ten Kingdoms 907–979
Northern Han 951–979 (*reckoned as one of the Ten Kingdoms*)

Sung 960–1126
(*the extreme north of China being ruled by the Liao 947–1125*)

Chin 1126–1234
Southern Sung 1127–1279
Yuan 1279–1368 (*having succeeded the Chin in North China in 1234*)
Ming 1368–1644
Ch'ing 1644–1912

creative Later Han dynasty (25–220 CE). Though they had their ups and downs, the Han emperors showed unprecedented strength. Their sway extended over almost the whole of modern China, including southern Manchuria and the southeastern province of Yueh. The Later Han, indeed, went on to create an empire as big as that of their Roman contemporaries. They faced an old threat from Mongolia and a great opportunity towards the south. They handled both with skill aided by the tactical superiority given their armies by the new crossbow. This weapon was probably invented soon after 200 BCE and was both more powerful and more accurate than the bows of the barbarians, who did not for a long time have the ability to cast the bronze locks required. It was the last major achievement of Chinese military technology before the coming of gunpowder.

EXPANSION

In Mongolia at the beginning of Han times lived the Hsiung-Nu, whom we have already met as the forerunners of the Huns. The Ch'in had sought to protect their domain on the frontier by unifying a number of existing earthworks into a new Great Wall, to be further elaborated by later dynasties. The Han emperors drove the Hsiung-Nu north of the Gobi desert and then seized control of the caravan routes of Central Asia, sending armies far west into Kashgaria in the first century BCE. They even won tribute from the Kusharas, whose own power straddled the Pamirs. To the south, they occupied the coasts as far as the Gulf of Tonkin; Annam accepted their suzerainty and Indo-China has been regarded by Chinese statesmen as part of their proper sphere ever since. To the north-east they penetrated Korea. All this was the work of the Later, or "Eastern", Han whose capital was at Loyang. From there they continued to press forward in Turkestan and raised tribute from the oases of Central Asia. One general in 97 CE may have got as far as the Caspian.

Tentative diplomatic encounters with Rome in Han times suggest that expansion gave China much more contact with the rest of the world. Until the nineteenth century this was in the main by land, and besides the silk trade which linked her regularly with the Near East (caravans were leaving for the West with silk from about 100 BCE), China also developed more elaborate exchanges with her nomadic neighbours. Sometimes this was within the fictional framework of tribute acknowledged in turn by gifts, sometimes within official monopolies which were the foundation of great merchant families. Nomadic contacts may explain one of the most astonishing works of Chinese art, the great series of bronze horses found in tombs at Wu-Wei. These were only one among many fine works of Han bronze-workers; they evidently broke more readily with tradition than the Han potters, who showed more antiquarian respect for past forms. At a different level, though, Han pottery provides evidence of some of the earliest exploitations in art of the subject-matter of the daily life of most Chinese, in the form of collections of tiny figures of peasant families and their livestock.

During the excavations of a tomb thought to be that of a general from the Later Han period, a series of artifacts were found. Among them was this famous figure of a flying horse. One of the horse's hooves rests on a swallow, instilling the figure with a sense of speed and dynamism.

CHINESE CIVILIZATION

A brilliant culture flourished in Han China, centred on a court with huge, rich palaces built in the main of timber – unhappily, for the result is that they have disappeared, like the bulk of the Han collections of paintings on silk. Much of this cultural capital was dissipated or destroyed during the fourth and fifth centuries, when the barbarians returned to the frontiers. Failing at last to provide China's defence from her own manpower, the Han emperors fell back on a policy tried elsewhere, that of bringing within the Wall some of the tribes who pressed on it from outside and then deploying them in its defence. This raised problems of relations between the newcomers and the native Chinese. The Han emperors could not prolong their empire for ever, and after four hundred years China once more dissolved into a congeries of kingdoms.

Some of these had barbarian dynasties, but in this crisis there is observable for the first time China's striking powers of cultural digestion. Gradually the barbarians were swallowed by Chinese society, losing their own identity and becoming only another kind of Chinese. The prestige which Chinese civilization enjoyed among the peoples of Central Asia was already very great. There was a disposition among the uncivilized to see China as the centre of the world, a cultural pinnacle, somewhat in the way in which the Germanic peoples of the West had seen Rome. One Tatar ruler actually imposed Chinese customs and dress on his people by decree in 500. The Central Asian threat was

Under the T'ang Dynasty emperors became increasingly powerful. This painting on silk, which dates from the later Ming era, shows the lavish procession that accompanied an emperor and his entourage leaving the palace.

not over; far from it, there appeared in Mongolia in the fifth century the first Mongol Empire. Nonetheless, when the T'ang, a northern dynasty, came to receive the mandate of heaven in 618 China's essential unity was in no greater danger than it had been at any time in the preceding two or three centuries.

THE T'ANG DYNASTY

Political disunity and barbarian invasion had not damaged the foundations of Chinese civilization, which entered its classical phase under the T'ang. Among those foundations, the deepest continued to lie in kinship. Throughout historical times the clan retained its importance because it was the mobilized power of many linked families, enjoying common institutions of a religious and sometimes of an economic kind. The diffusion and ramification of family influence were all the easier because China did not have primogeniture; the paternal inheritance was usually divided at death. Over a social ocean in which families were the fish that mattered presided one Leviathan, the state. To it and to the family the Confucians looked for authority; those institutions were unchallenged by others, for in China there were no entities such as Church or communes which confused questions of right and government so fruitfully in Europe.

The state's essential characteristics were all in place by T'ang times. They were to last until the twentieth century and the attitudes they built up linger on still. In their making, the consolidating work of the Han had been especially important, but the office of the emperor, holder of the mandate of heaven, could be taken for granted even in Ch'in times. The comings and goings of dynasties did not compromise the standing of the office since they could always be ascribed to the withdrawal of the heavenly mandate. The emperor's liturgical importance was, if anything, enhanced by the inauguration under the Han of a sacrifice only he could make. Yet his position also changed in a positive sense. Gradually, a ruler who was essentially a great feudal magnate, his power an extension of that of the family or

Chinese civil servants, such as the two portrayed in these drawings, wore special clothes to denote their rank.

the manor, was replaced by one who presided over a centralized and bureaucratic state. Three hundred prefectures provided its administrative armature.

THE GREAT CHINESE STATE

CENTRALIZATION HAD BEGUN a long way back. Already in Chou times a big effort was made to build canals for transport. Great competence in organization and large human resources were required for this and only a potent state could have deployed them. A few centuries later the first Ch'in emperor had been able to link together the existing sections of the Great Wall in 1,400 miles of continuous barrier against the barbarians (legendarily, his achievement cost a million lives and, true or not, the story is revealing of the way the empire was seen). His dynasty went on to standardize weights and measures and impose a degree of disarmament on its subjects while itself putting in the field perhaps a million soldiers. The Han were able to impose a monopoly of coining and standardized the currency. Under them, too, entry to the civil service by competitive examination began; though it was to fade out again, not to be resumed until T'ang times, it was very important. Territorial expansion had required more administrators. The resulting bureaucracy was to survive many periods of disunion (a proof of its vigour) and remained to the end one of the most striking and characteristic institutions of imperial China. It was probably the key to China's successful emergence from the era when collapsing dynasties were followed by competing petty and local states which broke up the unity already achieved. It linked China together by an ideology as well as by administration. The civil servants were trained and examined in the Confucian classics; under the Han, legalism finally lost its grip after a lively ideological struggle. Literacy and political culture were thus wedded in China as nowhere else.

SCHOLARSHIP AND THE BUREAUCRACY

Chinese scholars had been deeply offended by the Ch'in. Though a few of them had been favoured and gave the dynasty advice, there had been a nasty moment in 213 BCE when the emperor turned on scholars who had criticized the despotic and militaristic character of his régime. Books were burned and only "useful" works on divination, medicine or agriculture were spared; more than four hundred scholars perished. What was really at stake is not clear; some historians have seen this attack as an offensive aimed at "feudal" tendencies opposed to Ch'in centralization. If so, it was far from the end of the confusion of cultural and political struggle with which China has gone on mystifying foreign observers even in the last one hundred years. Whatever the sources of this policy, the Han took a different tack and sought to conciliate the intellectuals.

This led first to the formalization of Confucian doctrine into what quickly became an orthodoxy. The canonical texts were established soon after 200 BCE. True, Han Confucianism was a syncretic matter; it had absorbed much of legalism. But the important fact was that Confucianism had been the absorbing force. Its ethical precepts remained dominant in the philosophy which formed China's future rulers. In 58 CE sacrifices to Confucius were ordered in all government schools. Eventually, under the T'ang, administrative posts were confirmed to those trained in this orthodoxy. For more than a thousand years it provided China's governors with a set of moral principles and a literary culture doggedly acquired by rote-learning. The

Confucianism

Confucianism represents a way of life that has been followed by the Chinese and other neighbouring peoples for more than 2,000 years. The doctrine systematized by Confucius in the 6th century BCE, which was designed with the aim of creating an ideal society led by an élite, states that:

Each individual has a duty to behave with virtue (*te*), integrity (*yi*) and benevolence (*jen*).

The family is the basis of society and the state represents "the Great Family" – the emperor is mother and father to his people.

The clearly defined relationships between "superiors and inferiors" (sovereign and subject, father and son, husband and wife, older and younger brothers, etc.) must be respected.

These hierarchical principles and the organized structures of the state should be preserved through the observance of a minutely detailed set of ceremonies and rituals known as *li*.

This stone rubbing portraying Confucius (551–479 BCE) is a somewhat idealized representation of the great teacher.

examinations they underwent were designed to show which candidates had the best grasp of the moral tradition discernible in the classical texts as well as to test mechanical abilities and the capacity to excel under pressure. It made them one of the most effective and ideologically homogeneous bureaucracies the world has ever seen and also offered great rewards to those who successfully made the values of Confucian orthodoxy their own.

The official class was in principle distinguished only by educational qualification (the possession of a degree, as it were) from the rest of society. Most civil servants came from the land-owning gentry, but they were set apart from them. Their office once achieved by success in the test of examination, they enjoyed a status only lower than that of the imperial family, and great material and social privileges besides. Officials' duties were general rather than specific, but they had two crucial annual tasks, the compilation of the census returns and the land registers on which Chinese taxation rested. Their other main work was judicial and supervisory, for local affairs were very much left to local gentlemen acting under the oversight of about two thousand or so district magistrates from the official class. Each of these lived in an official compound, the *yamen*, with his clerks, runners and household staff about him.

The gentry undertook a wide range of quasi-governmental and public-service activities, which were both an obligation of the privileged class and also an insurance of much of its income. Local justice, education, public works were all part of this. The gentry also often organized military forces to meet local emergencies and even collected the taxes, from which it might recoup its own expenses. Over the whole of these arrangements and the official class itself, there watched a state apparatus of control, checking and reporting on a bureaucracy bigger by far than that of the Roman Empire and, at its greatest extent, ruling a much larger area.

SOCIAL ORGANIZATION

The structure of imperial China had huge conservative power. Crisis only threatened legal authority, rarely the social order. The permeation of governmental practice by the agreed ideals of Confucian society was rendered almost complete by the examination system. Moreover, though it was very hard for anyone not assured of some wealth to support himself during the long studies necessary for the examination – writing in the traditional literary forms itself took years to master – the principle of competition ensured that a continuing search for talent was not quite confined to the wealthier and established gentry families; China was a meritocracy in which learning always provided some social mobility. From time to time there were corruption and examples of the buying of places, but such signs of decline usually appear towards the end of a dynastic period. For the most part, the imperial officials showed remarkable independence of their background. They were not supposed to act on such assumptions of obligation to family and connection as characterized the public servants drawn from the eighteenth-century English gentry. The civil servants were the emperor's men; they were not allowed to own land in the province where they served, serve in their own provinces, or have relatives in the same branch of government. They were not the representatives of a class, but a selection from it, an independently recruited élite, renewed and promoted by competition. They made the state a reality.

Imperial China is thus not best seen as an aristocratic polity; political power did not pass by descent within a group of noble families, though noble birth was socially important. Only in the small closed circle of the court was hereditary access to office possible, and there it was a matter of prestige, titles and standing, rather than of power. To the imperial counsellors who had risen through the official hierarchy to its highest levels and had become more than officials, the only rivals of importance were the court eunuchs. These creatures were often trusted with great authority by the emperors because, by definition, they could not found families. They were thus the only political force escaping the restraints of the official world.

Two young noblewomen are depicted with their tutor in this detail from a 4th-century hand scroll (red and black ink on silk). Chinese society was divided into two clearly differentiated groups: the ruling classes, made up of the nobility and the civil servants, and the peasants, who made up 90 per cent of the population.

Buddhism first arrived in China during the Later Han period and gradually spread all over the country, becoming the dominant religion. The Ch'an school of Chinese Buddhism emerged in the late 6th century and was linked to a period of great artistic creativity during the T'ang Dynasty. This gigantic Ch'an sculpture of the Buddha of Leshan, in Szechwan, dates from 713–722.

The ideas which inspired it were profoundly conservative; the predominant administrative task was seen to be the maintenance of the established order; the aim of Chinese government was to oversee, conserve and consolidate, and occasionally to innovate in practical matters by carrying out large public works. Its overriding goals were regularity and the maintenance of common standards in a huge and diverse empire, where many district magistrates were divided from the people in their charge even by language. In achieving its conservative aims, the bureaucracy was spectacularly successful and its ethos survived intact across all the crises of the dynasties.

CONFUCIAN VALUES AND RIVAL CREEDS

Clearly, in the Chinese state there was little sense of the European distinction between government and society. Official, scholar and gentleman were usually the same man, combining many roles which in Europe were increasingly to be divided between governmental specialists and the informal authorities of society. He combined them, too, within the framework of an ideology which was much more obviously central to society than any to be found elsewhere than perhaps in Islam. The preservation of Confucian values was not a light matter, nor satisfiable by lip-service. The bureaucracy maintained those values by exercising a moral supremacy somewhat like that long exercised by the clergy in the West – and in China there was no Church to rival the state.

The best-known figures of popular Taoist mythology are the Eight Immortals, who are depicted in this painting.

Below the Confucian orthodoxy of the officials and gentry, it is true, other creeds were important. Even some who were high in the social scale turned to Taoism or Buddhism. The latter was to be very successful after the Han collapse, when disunity gave it an opportunity to penetrate China. In its *Mahayana* variety it posed more of a threat to China than any other ideological force before Christianity, for, unlike Confucianism, it posited the rejection of worldly values. It was never to be eradicated altogether, in spite of persecution under the T'ang; attacks on it were, in any case, probably mounted for financial rather than ideological reasons. Unlike the persecuting Roman Empire, the Chinese state was more interested in property than in the correction of individual religious eccentricity. Under the fiercest of the persecuting emperors (who is said to have been a Taoist) over four thousand monasteries were dissolved, and over a quarter of a million monks and nuns dispersed from them. Nevertheless, in spite of such material damage to Buddhism, Confucianism had to come to terms with it. No other foreign religion influenced China's rulers so strongly until Marxism in the twentieth century; even some emperors were Buddhists.

PEASANT REVOLTS

Taoism developed into a mystical cult (borrowing something from Buddhism in the process), appealing both to those who sought personal immortality and to those who felt the appeal of a quietistic movement as an outlet from the growing complexity of Chinese life. As such it would have enduring significance. Its recognition of the subjectivity of human thought gives it an appearance of humility which some people in different cultures with more aggressive intellectual attitudes find attractive today. Such religious and philosophical traditions, important as they were, touched the lives of the peasants directly only a little more than Confucianism, except in debased forms. A prey to the insecurities of war and famine, a peasant's outlet lay in magic or superstition. What little can be discerned of peasant life suggests that it was often intolerable, sometimes terrible. A significant symptom is the appearance under the Han of peasant rebellion, a phenomenon which became a major theme of Chinese history, punctuating it almost as rhythmically as the passing of dynasties. Oppressed by officials acting either on behalf of an imperial government seeking taxes for its campaigns abroad or in their own interest as grain speculators, the peasants turned to secret societies, another recurrent theme. Their revolts often took religious forms. A millenarian, Manichaean strain has run through Chinese revolution, bursting out in many guises, but always positing a world dualistically divided into good and evil, the righteous and the demons. Sometimes this threatened the social fabric, but the peasants were rarely successful for long.

Chinese society changed very slowly. In spite of some important cultural and administrative innovations, the lives of most Chinese were for centuries little altered in style, appearance or reality. The comings and goings of the dynasties were accounted for by the notion of the mandate of heaven and although great intellectual achievements were possible, China's civilization already seemed self-contained, self-sufficient, stable to the point of immobility. No innovation compromised the fundamentals of a society more closely woven into a particular governmental structure than anything in Europe. This structure proved quite competent to contain such changes as did take place and to regulate them so as not to disturb the traditional forms.

URBANIZATION AND TAXATION

One visibly important change was a continuing growth of commerce and towns which made it easier to replace labour service by taxation. Such new resources could be tapped by government both to rule larger areas effectively and to provide a series of great material monuments. They had already permitted the Ch'in to complete the Great Wall, which later dynasties were further to extend, sometimes rebuilding portions of it. It still astonishes the observer and far outranks the walls of Hadrian and Antoninus. Just before the inauguration of the T'ang, too, at the other end of this historical epoch, a great system of canals was completed which linked the lower Yangtze valley with the Yellow river valley to the north, as far as Hangchow to the south. Millions of labourers were employed on this and on other great irrigation schemes. Such works are comparable in scale with the Pyramids and surpass the great cathedrals of medieval Europe. They imposed equally heavy social costs, too, and there were revolts against conscription for building and guard duties.

POPULATION PRESSURE

It was a state with great potential and a civilization with impressive achievements already to its credit which entered its mature phase in 618. For the next thousand years, as for the previous eight hundred, its formal development can be linked to the comings and goings of the dynasties which provide a chronological structure (T'ang, 618–907; Sung, 960–1126; Mongol ascendancy, 1234–1368; Ming, 1368–1644; Manchu or

This illustration from a Ch'ing-era scroll shows workmen building a dyke.

Ch'ing, 1644–1912). Many historical themes overrun these divisions. One is the history of population. There was an important shift of the demographic centre of gravity towards the south during the T'ang period; henceforth most Chinese were to live in the Yangtze valley rather than the old Yellow river plain. The devastation of the southern forests and exploitation of new lands to grow rice fed them, but new crops became available, too. Together they made possible an overall growth of population which accelerated under the Mongols and the Ming. Estimates have been made that a population of perhaps eighty million in the fourteenth century more than doubled in the next two hundred years, so that in 1600 there were about 160 million subjects of the empire. This was a huge number, given populations elsewhere, but there was still great increase to come.

In this detail from an illustration on a Ming-Dynasty vase, tea workers are shown in the process of drying tea leaves in order to preserve them.

The weight of this fact is great. Apart from the enormous importance it gives to China in world population history, it puts in perspective the great manifestations of Chinese culture and imperial power, which rested on the huge mass of desperately poor peasants utterly unconcerned with such things. For the most part their lives were confined to their villages; only a few could hope to escape from this, or can have envisaged doing so. Most could have dreamed only of obtaining the precarious, but best, security available to them: the possession of a little land. Yet this became more and more difficult as numbers grew and gradually all available land was occupied. It was farmed more and more intensively in smaller and smaller plots. The one way out of the trap of famine was rebellion. At a certain level of intensity and success this might win support from the gentry and officials, whether from prudence or sympathy. When that happened, the end of a dynasty was probably approaching, for Confucian principles taught that, though rebellion was wrong if a true king reigned, a government which provoked rebellion and could not control it ought to be replaced for it was *ipso facto* illegitimate. At the *very* end of this road lay the success of a twentieth-century Chinese revolution based on the peasants.

AN OVERLONG FRONTIER

For many centuries population pressure, a major fact of modern China's history, made itself felt to the authorities only in indirect and obscured ways, when, for instance, famine or hunger drove people to rebellion. A much more obvious threat came from the outside. Essentially the problem was rather like that of Rome, an overlong frontier beyond which lay barbarians. T'ang influence over them was weakened when Central Asia succumbed to Islam. Like their Roman predecessors, too, the later T'ang emperors found that reliance on soldiers could be dangerous. There were hundreds of military rebellions by local warlords under the T'ang and any rebellion's success, even if short-lived, had a multiplier effect, tending to disrupt administration and damage the irrigation arrangements on which food (and therefore internal peace) depended. A régime thought of as a possible ally by Byzantium, which had sent armies to fight the Arabs and received ambassadors from Haroun-al-Raschid, was potentially a great world power. In the end, though, unable to police their frontier effectively, the T'ang went under in the tenth century, and China collapsed again into political chaos. The Sung empire which emerged from it had to face an even graver external threat, the Mongols, and were in due course swallowed after the barbarian dynasty which had evicted them from north China had itself been engulfed by the warriors of Chinghis Khan.

SOCIAL STABILITY AND DYNASTIC CHANGE

During the whole of this time, the continuity and recuperative power of the bureaucracy and the fundamental institutions of society kept China going, and were particularly exploited by the first Sung emperors. As after earlier dynastic change, the inheritors of power continued to turn to existing officialdom (an estimate for the eighteenth century gives less than 30,000 civil and military officers actually

Li Po (701–762), who is portrayed in this drawing, was one of the most important poets of the T'ang era, often considered to be the golden age of classical Chinese poetry. His poems, the central themes of which were always wine, music or women, were renowned for their beauty.

in post). They thus drew into the service of each new government the unchanging values of the Confucian system, which were strengthened, if narrowed, by disaster. Only a small number of especially crucial matters were ever expected to be the reserved province of the imperial government. Confucian teaching supported this distinction of spheres of action and made it easy for a dynasty to be displaced without compromising the fundamental values and structure of society. A new dynasty would have to turn to the officials for its administration and to the gentry for most of its officials who, in their turn, could get some things done only on the gentry's terms.

T'ANG CULTURE

Recurrent disunity did not prevent China's rulers, sages and craftsmen from bringing Chinese civilization to its peak in the thousand years after the T'ang inauguration. Some have placed the classical age as early as the seventh and eighth centuries, under the T'ang themselves, while others discern it under the Sung. Such judgments usually rest on the art forms considered, but even Sung artistic achievement was in any case a culmination of development begun under the T'ang, between whom and the Han much more of a break in style had been apparent. It was in fact the most important break in the continuity of Chinese art until the twentieth century.

T'ang culture reflects the stimulus of contacts with the outside world, but especially with Central Asia, unprecedentedly close under this dynasty. The capital was then at Ch'ang-an, in Shensi, a western province. Its name means "long-lasting peace" and to this city at the end of the Silk Route came Persians, Arabs and Central Asians who made it one of the most cosmopolitan cities in the world. It contained Nestorian churches, Zoroastrian temples, Muslim mosques, and was probably the most splendid and luxurious capital of its day, as the objects which remain to us show. Many of them reflect Chinese recognition of styles other than their own – the imitation of Iranian silverware, for example – while the flavour of a trading entrepôt is preserved in the pottery figures of horsemen and loaded camels which reveal the life of Central Asia swirling in the streets of Ch'ang-an. These figures were often finished with the new polychromatic glazes achieved by T'ang potters; their style was imitated in places as far away as Japan and Mesopotamia. The presence of the court was as important in stimulating such craftsmanship as the visits of merchants from abroad, and from tomb paintings something of the life of the court aristocracy can be seen. The men relax in hunting, attended by Central Asian retainers; the women, vacuous in expression, are luxuriously dressed and, if servants, elaborately equipped with fans, cosmetic boxes, back-scratchers and other paraphernalia of the boudoir. Great ladies, too, favour Central Asian styles borrowed from their domestic staff.

UNOFFICIAL CULTURE

The history of women, though, is the history of one of those other Chinas always obscured by the bias of the documentation towards the official culture. We hear little of them, even in literature, except in sad little poems and love stories. Yet presumably they must have made up about half of the population, or perhaps slightly less, for in hard times girl babies were exposed by poor families to die. That fact, perhaps, characterizes women's place in China until very recent times even better than the more familiar and superficially striking practice of foot-binding, which produced grotesque deformations and could leave a

From "The Thirteen Emperors", this illustration depicts the 7th-century T'ang emperor Yen Li-Pen.

The building of the Great Wall

"In olden times, the Chou ordered Nan Zhong to build a wall in that northern region and Prince Ling Wu and Ch'in Shih-Huang-ti built the Great Wall and the emperor Han Wu Ti eagerly imitated those ancient feats … . The reason why the heroic sovereigns took on these difficult tasks was not a lack of tactical capacity or political intelligence, nor a military weakness, but rather it was inspired by the principle that it is extremely important to take measures against the barbarians. This is why they had to build, then, a Great Wall … as a protection against the barbarians from the north. Although a great effort had to be made and hard work undertaken for some time, afterwards we will be able to enjoy the advantage of a long period of peace."

An extract from the *History of the Northern Dynasties*.

high-born lady almost incapable of walking. Another China still all but excluded from the historical evidence by the nature of the established tradition was that of the peasants. They become shadowly visible only as numbers in the census returns and as eruptions of revolt; after the Han pottery figures, there is little in Chinese art to reveal them, and certainly nothing to match the uninterrupted (and often idealized) recording of the life of the common worker in the fields, which runs from medieval European illumination, through the vernacular literature to the Romantics, and into the peasant subjects of the early Impressionists.

Official culture also excluded the tenth or so of the Chinese population who lived in the cities, some of which grew as time passed to become the biggest in the world. Ch'ang-an, when the T'ang capital, is said to have had two million inhabitants. No eighteenth-century European city was as big as contemporary Canton or Peking, which

Surviving classical Chinese documents tend to deal only with official culture, glossing over the aspects of daily life that could have given us an insight into women's lives. This wall painting, from the tomb of a T'ang princess called Yongtai, shows some ladies of her court.

were even larger. Such huge cities housed societies of growing complexity. Their development fostered a new commercial world; the first Chinese paper money was issued in 650. Prosperity created new demands, among other things for a literature which did not confine itself to the classical models and in colloquial style far less demanding than the elaborate classical Chinese. City life thus gradually secreted a literate alternative to the official culture, and because it was literate, it is the first part of unofficial China to which we have some access. Such popular demand could be satisfied because of two enormously important inventions: that of paper in the second century BCE, and of printing before 700 CE. The latter derived from the taking of rubbed impressions from stone under the Han. Printing from wood blocks was taking place under the T'ang and movable type appeared in the eleventh century CE. Soon after this, large numbers of books were published in China, long before they appeared anywhere else. In the cities, too, flourished popular poetry and music which abandoned the classical tradition.

The culture of Ch'ang-an never recovered from its disruption by rebellion in 756, only two years after the foundation of an Imperial Academy of Letters (about nine hundred years before any similar academy in Europe). After this the T'ang dynasty was in decline. The Sung ascendancy produced more great pottery; the earlier, northern phase of Sung history was marked by work still in the coloured, patterned tradition, while southern Sung craftsmen came to favour monochromatic, simple products. Significantly, they attached themselves to another tradition: that of the forms evolved by the great bronze-casters of earlier China. For all the beauty of its ceramics, though, Sung is more notable for some of the highest achievements of Chinese painting, their subject-matter being, above all, landscape. As a phase of Chinese development, though, the Sung era is more remarkable still for a dramatic improvement in the economy.

SUNG INDUSTRIALIZATION

In part this can be attributed to technological innovation – gunpowder, movable type and the sternpost all can be traced to the Sung

The origins of Chinese printing

At the beginning of the 8th century BCE the first bronze tablets appeared engraved with Chinese characters alongside drawings. However, archaeological research has indicated that the characters were placed in moulds separately.

Another printing system used by the Chinese during the 2nd century CE involved using carved stones stamped with ink. Later came stencilling, which consisted of punching very fine holes onto a piece of paper to create an image that was revealed when the paper was pressed onto a blank sheet and ink was applied to it. This system was widely used by the Buddhists.

The printing press first came into use in classical China in the 7th century, long before it was used in Europe. Text was reproduced by means of a polished wooden tablet, on which the words were written by cutting away the wood surrounding the characters, leaving the inscription in relief. The tablet was then covered in ink and pressed on to a sheet of rice-paper. The substitution, in the 11th century, of engraved tablets by independent movable characters was an enormous step forward.

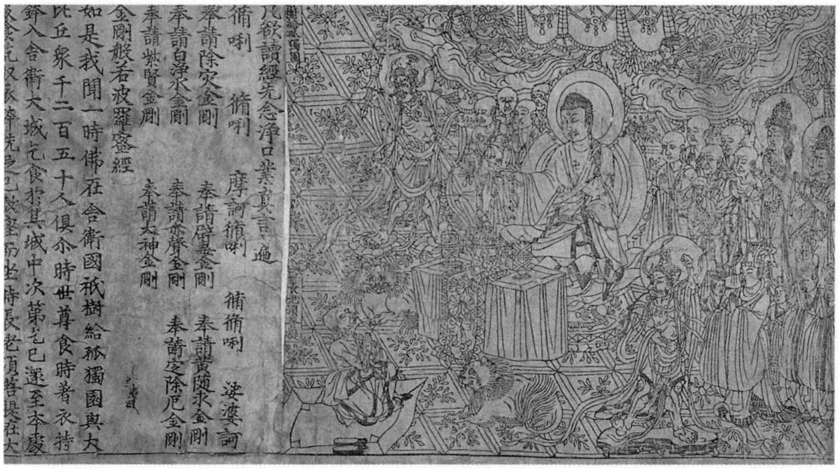

The earliest-known printed book is the Diamond Sutra, *which dates from 858. It comprises a scroll that is 16 ft (5 m) long and 11 in (27 cm) wide. The cover, shown here, is illustrated with a drawing of the Buddha talking to his disciple Subhuti.*

Technological advances are evident in many aspects of productive life in imperial China, such as in spinning. This illustration, which dates from the 12th or 13th century, shows various stages in the processes of spinning and weaving hemp.

era – but it was also linked to the exploitation of technology already long available. Technological innovation may indeed have been as much a symptom as a cause of a surge in economic activity between the tenth and thirteenth centuries which appears to have brought most Chinese a real rise in incomes in spite of continuing population growth. For once in the pre-modern world economic growth seems for a long period to have outstripped demographic trends. One change making this possible was certainly the discovery and adoption of a rice variety which permitted two crops a year to be taken from well-irrigated land and one from hilly ground only watered in the spring. The evidence of rising production in a different sector of the economy has been dramatically distilled into one scholar's calculation that within a few years of the battle of Hastings, China was producing nearly as much iron as the whole of Europe six centuries later. Textile production, too, underwent dramatic development (notably through the adoption of water-driven spinning machinery) and it is possible to speak of Sung "industrialization" as a recognizable phenomenon.

It is not easy (the evidence is still disputed) to say why this remarkable burst of growth took place. Undoubtedly there was a real input to the economy by public – that is, governmental – investment in public works, above all, communications. Prolonged periods of freedom from foreign invasion and domestic disorder also must have helped, though the second benefit may be explained as much by economic growth as the other way around. The main explanation, though, seems likely to be an expansion in markets and the rise of a money economy which owed something to factors already mentioned, but which rested fundamentally on a great expansion in agricultural productivity. So long as this kept ahead of population increase, all was well. Capital became available to utilize more labour, and to tap technology by investment in machines. Real incomes rose.

A RELATIVE LACK OF INNOVATION IN CHINA

It is hard to say why, after temporary and local regression at the end of the Sung era, and the resumption of economic growth, this intensive growth, which made possible rising consumption by greater numbers, came to an end. Nonetheless, it did, and was not resumed. Instead, average real incomes in China stabilized for something like five centuries, as production merely kept pace with population growth. (After that time, incomes began to fall, and continued to do so to a point at which the early twentieth-century Chinese peasant could be described as a man standing neck-deep in water, whom even ripples could drown.) But the economic relapse after Sung times is not the only factor to be taken into account in explaining why China did not go on to produce a dynamic, progressive society. In spite of printing, the mass of Chinese remained illiterate down to the twentieth century. China's great cities, for all their growth and commercial vitality, produced neither the freedom and immunities which sheltered people and ideas in Europe, nor the cultural and intellectual life which in the end revolutionized European civilization, nor effective questioning of the established order. Even in technology, where China achieved so much so soon, there is a similar strange gap between intellectual fertility and revolutionary change. The Chinese could invent (they had a far more efficient wheelbarrow than other civilizations), but once Chou times were over, it was the use of new land and the introduction of new crops rather than technical change which raised production. Other examples of a low rate of innovation are even more striking. Chinese sailors already had the magnetic compass in Sung times, but though naval expeditions were sent to Indonesia, the Persian Gulf, Aden and East Africa in the fifteenth century, their aim was to impress those places with the power of the Ming, not to accumulate information and experience for further voyages of exploration and discovery. Masterpieces had been cast in bronze in the second millennium BCE and the Chinese knew how to cast iron fifteen hundred years before Europeans, yet much of the engineering potential of this metallurgical tradition was unexplored even when iron production rose so strikingly. What he called "a sort of black stone" was burnt in China when Marco Polo was there; it was coal, but there was to be no Chinese steam engine.

This list could be much lengthened. Perhaps the explanation lies in the very success of Chinese civilization in pursuit of a different goal, the assurance of continuity and the prevention of fundamental change. Neither officialdom nor the social system favoured the innovator. Moreover, pride in the Confucian tradition and the confidence generated by great wealth and remoteness made it difficult to learn from the outside. This was not because the Chinese were intolerant. Jews, Nestorian Christians, Zoroastrian Persians, and Arab Muslims long practised their own religion freely, and the last even made some converts, creating an enduring Islamic minority. Contacts with the West multiplied, too, later under Mongol rule. But what has been called a "neo-Confucian" movement was by then already manifesting tendencies of defensive hostility, and formal tolerance had never led to much receptivity in Chinese culture.

MONGOL CHINA

INVASION BY THE MONGOLS showed China's continuing seductive power over its conquerors. By the end of the thirteenth century, all China had been overrun by them – and this may have cost the country something like thirty million lives, or well over a quarter of its whole population in 1200 – but the centre of gravity of the Mongol Empire had moved from the steppes to Peking, Kubilai's capital. This grandson of Chinghis was the last of the Great Khans and after his time Mongol China can be considered Chinese, not Mongol; Kubilai adopted a dynastic life in 1271 and the remainder of the Mongol era is recorded as that of the dynasty. China changed the Mongols more than the Mongols changed China, and the result was the magnificence reported by the amazed Marco Polo. Kubilai made a break with the old conservatism of the steppes, the distrust of civilization and its works, and his followers slowly succumbed to Chinese culture in spite of their initial distrust of the scholar officials. They were, after all, a tiny minority of rulers in an ocean of Chinese subjects; they needed collaborators to survive. Kubilai spent nearly all his life in China, though his knowledge of Chinese was poor.

But the relationship of Mongol and Chinese was long ambiguous. Like the British in nineteenth-century India, who set up social conventions to prevent their assimilation by their subjects, so the Mongols sought by positive prohibition to keep themselves apart. Chinese were forbidden to learn the Mongol language or marry Mongols. They were not allowed to carry arms. Foreigners, rather than Chinese, were employed in administration where possible, a device paralleled in the western khanates of the Mongol Empire: Marco Polo was for three years an official of the Great Khan; a Nestorian presided over the imperial bureau of astronomy; Muslims from Transoxiana administered Yunan. For some years the traditional examination system was also suspended. Some of the persistent Chinese hostility to the Mongols may be explained by such facts, especially in the south. When Mongol rule in China collapsed, seventy years after Kubilai's death, there appeared an, if possible, even more exaggerated respect for tradition and

This portrait of the Mongol emperor Kubilai Khan (1259–1294) is from a collection entitled "Portraits of Famous Chinese Figures", which dates from the 18th century.

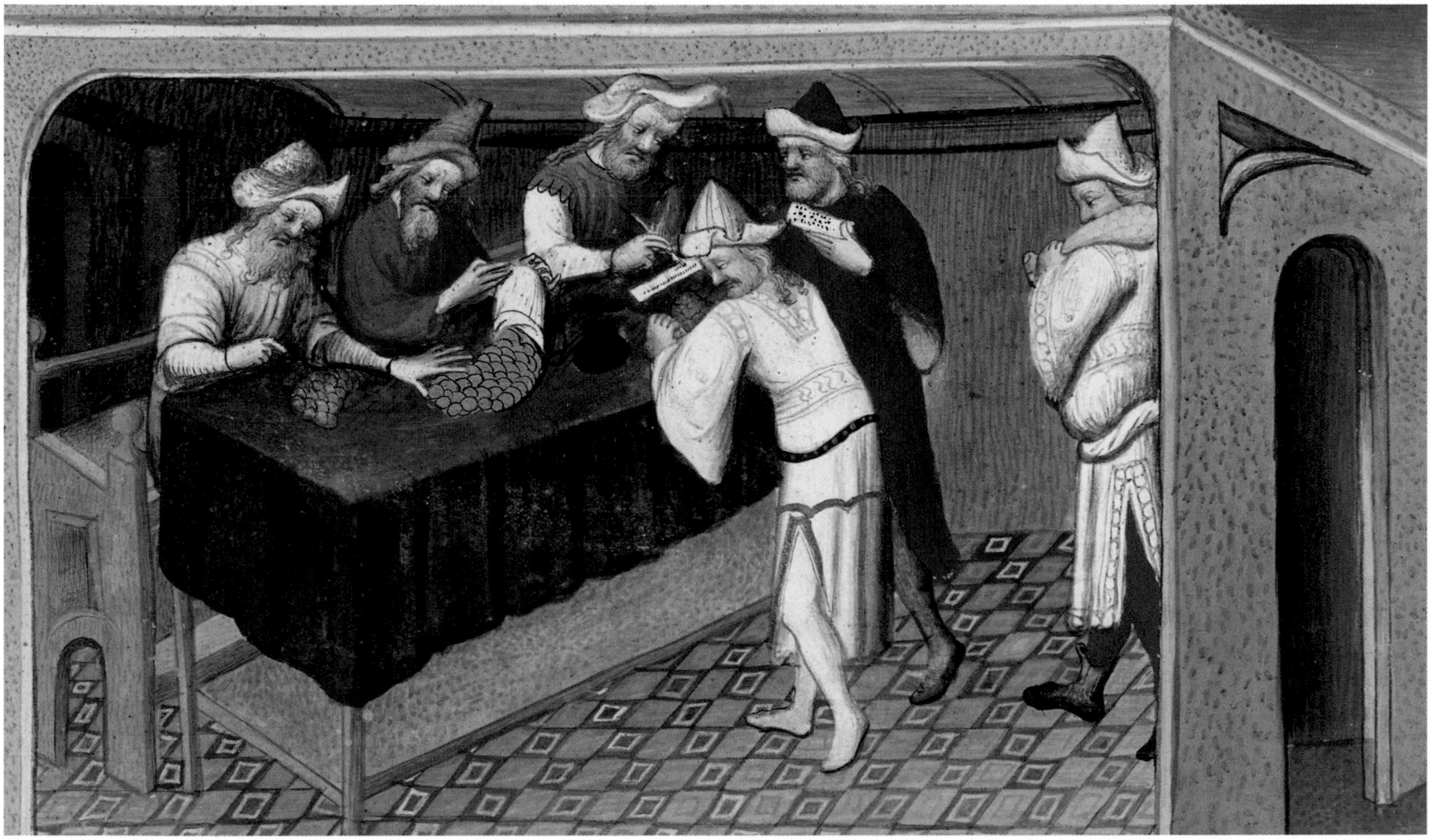

From the *Book of the Wonders of the World* by Marco Polo (1254–1324), this Italian illustration depicts Kubilai Khan's tax collectors at work. Some of the Mongols' heaviest taxes were imposed on salt, sugar and coal.

a renewed distrust of foreigners among the Chinese ruling class.

THE ACHIEVEMENTS OF MONGOL RULE

The short-run achievement of the Mongols was very impressive. It was most obvious in the re-establishment of China's unity and the realization of its potential as a great military and diplomatic power. The conquest of the Sung south was not easy, but once it was achieved (in 1279) Kubilai's resources were more than doubled (they included an important fleet) and he began to rebuild the Chinese sphere of influence in Asia. Only in Japan was he totally unsuccessful. In the south, Vietnam was invaded (Hanoi was captured three times) and after Kubilai's death Burma was occupied for a time. These conquests were not, it is true, to prove long-lasting and they resulted in tribute rather than prolonged occupation. In Java, too, success was qualified; a landing was made there and the capital of the island taken in 1292, but it proved impossible to hold. There was also further development of the maritime trade with India, Arabia and the Persian Gulf, which had been begun under the Sung.

Since it failed to survive, the Mongol régime cannot be considered wholly successful, but this does not take us far. Much that was positive was done in just over a century. Foreign trade flourished as never before. Marco Polo reports that the poor of Peking were fed by the largesse of the Great Khan, and it was a big city. A modern eye finds something attractive, too, about the Mongols' treatment of religion. Only Muslims were hindered in the preaching of their doctrine; Taoism and Buddhism were positively encouraged, for example by relieving

The Forbidden City in Peking was founded by the Ming emperor Yung-lo (1403–1424).

Buddhist monasteries of taxes (this, of course, meant heavier impositions on others, as any state support for religion must; the peasants paid for religious enlightenment).

REVOLT AND THE MING DYNASTY

In the fourteenth century natural disasters combined with Mongol exactions to produce a fresh wave of rural rebellions – the telling symptom of a dynasty in decline. They may have been made worse by Mongol concessions to the Chinese gentry. Giving landlords new rights over their peasants can hardly have won the régime popular support. Secret societies began to appear again and one of them, the "Red Turbans", attracted support from gentry and officials. One of its leaders, Chu Yuan-chang, a monk, seized Nanking in 1356. Twelve years later he drove the Mongols from Peking and the Ming era began. Yet like many other Chinese revolutionary leaders Chu Yuan-chang gradually became an upholder of the traditional order. The dynasty he founded, though it presided over a great cultural flowering and managed to maintain the political unity of China which was to last from Mongol times to the twentieth century, confirmed China's conservatism and isolation. In the early fifteenth century the maritime expeditions by great fleets came to an end. An imperial decree forbade Chinese ships to sail beyond coastal waters or individuals to travel abroad. Soon, Chinese shipyards lost the capacity to build the great ocean-going junks; they did not even retain their specifications. The great voyages of the eunuch Cheng Ho, a Chinese Vasco da Gama, were almost forgotten. At the same time, the merchants who had prospered under the Mongols were harassed.

In the end the Ming Dynasty ran to seed. A succession of emperors virtually confined to their palaces while favourites and imperial princes disputed around them the enjoyment of the imperial estates registered the decline, and eunuchs emerged as the dominant figures in government. Except in Korea, where the Japanese were beaten off at the end of the sixteenth century, the Ming could not maintain the peripheral zones of Chinese empire. Indo-China fell away from the Chinese sphere, Tibet went more or less out of Chinese control and in 1544 Mongols burnt the suburbs of Peking.

Under the Ming, too, came the first Europeans to seek more than a voyage of trade or discovery. In 1557 Portuguese established themselves at Macao. They had little to offer that China wanted, except silver; but Jesuit missionaries followed and the official tolerance of Confucian tradition gave them opportunities they successfully exploited. They became very influential at the Ming court after one of them, Matteo Ricci, established himself there in 1602. But while he and other Jesuits were admired for their learning by some Chinese officials, others began to feel alarmed. By then, though, besides the mechanical toys and clocks which the missionaries added to the imperial collections, their scientific and cosmographical learning had begun to interest Chinese intellectuals. The correction of the Chinese calendar, which one Jesuit carried out, was of great importance, for the authenticity of the emperor's sacrifices depended on accurate dating. From the Jesuits the Chinese learnt also to cast heavy cannon, another useful art.

THE MANCHU CONQUEST

Early in the seventeenth century, the Ming needed any military advantages they could procure. They were threatened from the north by a people living in Manchuria, a province to which they later gave its name, but who were not known as Manchu until after their conquest of China. The way was opened to them in the 1640s by peasant revolt and an attempted usurpation of the Chinese throne. An imperial general asked the Manchu to help him and they came through the Wall, but only to place their own dynasty, the Ch'ing, on the throne in 1644 (and incidentally wipe out the general's own clan). Like other

This Ch'ing-era painting depicts a scene from Emperor K'ang-hsi's tour of Kiang-Han in 1699. The imperial troops are shown marching through the city gates, watched by the townspeople.

The Sui emperor Yang Kuang (1605–1617), who was canonized as Yang-ti, is shown on a boat on the Grand Canal in this 18th-century painting on silk. Yang Kuang was responsible for an ambitious construction programme that included reinforcing the Great Wall, dredging canals, and building huge palaces. Thousands of Chinese labourers died working on his extravagant projects.

barbarians and semi-barbarians, the Manchu had long been fascinated by the civilization they threatened and were already somewhat sinicized before their arrival. They were familiar with the Chinese administrative system, which they had imitated at their own capital of Mukden, and found it possible to cooperate with the Confucian gentry as they extended their grip on China. The attachment of Manchu inspectors stimulated the bureaucracy who needed to change little in their ways except to conform to the Manchu practice of wearing pigtails (thus was introduced what later struck Europeans as one of the oddest features of Chinese life).

THE EMPEROR K'ANG-HSI

The cost of Manchu conquest was high: some twenty-five million people perished. Yet recovery was rapid. China's new power was already spectacularly apparent under the Emperor K'ang-hsi, who reigned from 1662 to 1722. This roughly corresponded to the reign of Louis XIV of France, whose own exercises in magnificence and aggrandizement took different forms but showed curious parallels on the other side of the world. K'ang-hsi was capable of a personal violence which the Sun King would never have permitted himself (he once attacked two of his sons with a dagger) but for all the difference in the historical backgrounds which formed them, there is a similarity in their style of rule. Jesuit observers speak of K'ang-hsi's "nobility of soul" and the description seems to have been prompted by more than the desire to flatter, and justified by more than his patronage. He was hardworking, scrutinizing with a close eye the details of business (and its manner, for he would painstakingly correct defective calligraphy in the memorials placed before him), and like Louis, he refreshed himself by indulging his passion for hunting.

Characteristically, though K'ang-hsi was a foreigner and unusual among the Chinese emperors in admiring European skill (he patronized the Jesuits for their scientific knowledge), the merits of his reign were set firmly within accepted tradition; he identified himself with the enduring China. He rebuilt Peking, destroyed during the Manchu invasion, carefully restoring the work of the Ming architects and sculptors. It was as if Versailles had been put up in the Gothic style or London rebuilt in Perpendicular after the Great Fire. K'ang-hsi's principles were Confucian and he had classical works translated into Manchu. He sought to respect ancient tradition and assured his Chinese subjects their usual rights; they continued to rise to high office in the civil service in spite of its opening to Manchus, and K'ang-hsi appointed Chinese generals and viceroys. In the style of his personal life the emperor was, if not austere, at least moderate. He enjoyed the bracing life of the army and on campaigns lived simply; in Peking the pleasures of the palace were deliberately reduced and the emperor relaxed from the burdens of state with a harem of a mere three hundred girls.

EXTERNAL RELATIONS

K'ang-hsi extended imperial control to Formosa, occupied Tibet, mastered the Mongols and made them quiescent vassals. This was something of a turning-point, as final as anything can be in history; from this time the nomadic peoples of Central Asia at last begin gradually to recede before the settler. Further north, in the Amur valley, another new historical chapter opened when, in 1685, a Chinese army attacked a Russian post at Albazin. There had been earlier clashes in Manchuria. Negotiations now led to the withdrawal of the Russians and the razing of their fort. The treaty of Nershinsk which settled matters conceded by implication that Russia was recognized as an independent entity, and not as a vassal kingdom. Among its clauses one prescribed that boundary posts should be set up with inscriptions not only in Russian, Manchu, Chinese and Mongolian, but also in Latin. The suggestion had been made by a French Jesuit who was a member of the Chinese delegation and, like the establishment of a frontier line at all, was a symptom of changing Chinese relationships with the outside world, relationships developing faster, perhaps, than any Chinese knew. The treaty was far from being the final settlement of accounts between China and the only European power with which she shared a land frontier but it quietened things for a time. Elsewhere, Manchu conquest continued to unroll; later in the eighteenth century Tibet was again invaded and vassal status reimposed on Korea, Indo-China and Burma. These were major feats.

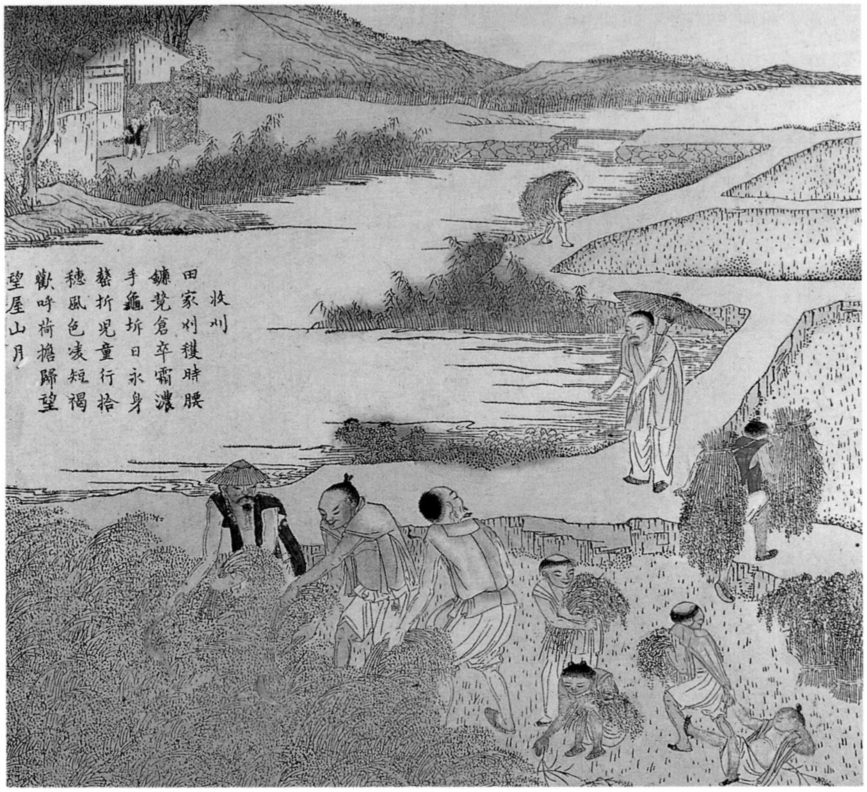

This woodcut, which dates from 1696, is one of a series commissioned by the emperor K'ang-hsi. It depicts peasants involved in rice cultivation.

MANCHU CULTURE

At home, peace and prosperity marked the last years of Manchu success. It was a silver age of the high classical civilization which some scholars believe to have reached its peak under the later Ming. If it did, it could still produce much beauty and scholarship under the Manchu. Great efforts of compilation and criticism, initiated and inspired by K'ang-hsi himself, opened a hundred years of transcription and publication which not only spawned such monsters as a five-thousand-volume encyclopedia, but also collections of classical editions now given canonical form. In K'ang-hsi's reign, too, the imperial kilns began a century of technical advance in enamelling which produced exquisite glazes.

Yet however admirable – and however the emphasis is distributed between its various expressions in different arts – Manchu China's civilization was still, like that of its predecessors, the civilization of an élite. Although there was at the same time a popular culture of great vigour, the Chinese civilization which Europeans were struck by was as much the property of the Chinese ruling class as it always had been, a fusion of artistic, scholarly and official activity. Its connection with government still gave it a distinctive tone and colour. It remained profoundly conservative, not only in social and political matters but even in its aesthetic. The art it esteemed was based on a distrust of innovation and originality; it strove to imitate and emulate the best, but the best was always past. The traditional masterpieces pointed the way. Nor was art seen as the autonomous expression of aesthetic activity. Moral criteria were brought to the judgment of artistic work and these criteria were, of course, the embodiments of Confucian values. Restraint, discipline, refinement and respect for the great masters were the qualities admired by the scholar-civil servant who was also artist and patron.

ART

Whatever appearances might suggest at first sight, Chinese art was no more directed towards escape from conventional life and values than that of any other culture before the European nineteenth century. This was also paradoxically apparent in its traditional exaltation of the amateur and the disapprobation it showed towards professionals. The man most esteemed was the official or landowner who was able to execute with sureness and apparent lack of effort works of painting, calligraphy or literature. Brilliant amateurs were greatly admired and in their activities, Chinese art escapes from its anonymity; we often know such artists' names. Its beautiful ceramics and textiles, on the other hand, are the products of tradesmen whose names are lost, often working under the direction of civil servants. Artisans were not esteemed for originality; craftsmen were encouraged to develop their skills not to the point of innovation but towards technical perfection. Central direction of large bodies of craftsmen within the precincts of the imperial palace only imposed upon these arts all the more firmly the stamp of traditional style. Even a brilliant explosion of new technical masteries at the imperial kilns during the reign of K'ang-hsi still expressed itself within the traditional canons of restraint and simplicity.

This water buffalo, which dates from c.1400 CE, was carved from green jade during the early Ming Dynasty. The animal's shape means that as little of the stone as possible is wasted.

THE LIMITATIONS OF CHINESE SUCCESS

The final Chinese paradox is the most obvious and by the eighteenth century it seems starkly apparent. For all her early technological advances China never arrived at a mastery of nature which could enable her to resist Western intervention. Gunpowder is the most famous example; the Chinese had it before anyone else, but could not make guns as good as those of Europe, nor even employ effectively those made for them by European craftsmen. Chinese sailors had long had the use of the mariner's compass and a cartographical heritage which produced the first grid map, but they were only briefly exploring navigators. They neither pushed across the Pacific like the more primitive Melanesians, nor did they map it, as did later the Europeans. For six hundred years or so before Europe had them, the Chinese made mechanical clocks fitted with the escapement which is the key to successful time-keeping by machines, yet the Jesuits brought with them an horological technology far superior to the Chinese when they arrived in the sixteenth century. The list of unexploited intellectual triumphs could be much lengthened, by important Chinese innovations in hydraulics, for example, but there is no need to do so. The main point is clear. Somehow, a lack of interest in the utilization of invention was rooted in a Confucian social system which, unlike that of Europe, did not regard as respectable any association between the gentleman and the technician.

NEW THREATS TO STABILITY

Pride in a great cultural tradition long continued to make it very hard to recognize

The *Atlas of China*, which was produced by the monk Martini Martini in 1655, was based on Chinese maps.

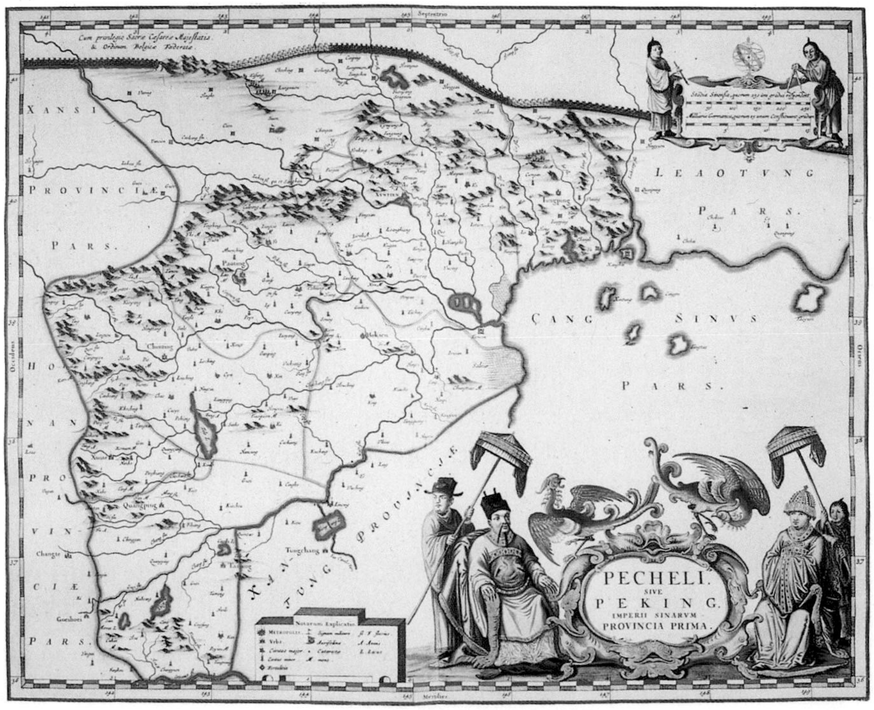

its inadequacies. This made learning from foreigners – all barbarians, in Chinese eyes – very difficult. To make things worse, Chinese morality prescribed contempt for the soldier and for military skills. In a period when external threats would multiply, China was therefore dangerously cramped in her possibilities of response. Even under K'ang-hsi there were signs of new challenges ahead. In his old age he had to restore Manchu power in Tibet, when Mongol tribes had usurped it. The Russians were by 1700 installed in Kamchatka, were expanding their trade on the caravan routes and were soon to press on into the Trans-Caspian region. Even peace and prosperity had a price, for they brought faster population growth. Here, unsolved because unrecognized and perhaps insoluble, was another problem to upset the stability of the order authorized by the mandate of heaven. By 1800 there were over three hundred, perhaps even four hundred, million Chinese, and already signs were appearing of what such an increase might portend.

During the Ming era (1368–1644), the first European traders appeared in China. The arrival of a Dutch vessel off the coast of China is represented in this detail from a 17th-century Coromandel screen.

3 *JAPAN*

There was a time when the English liked to think of Japan as the Great Britain of the Pacific. The parallel was developed at many levels; some were less plausible than others, but there was an indisputable hard nugget of reality in the facts of geography. Both are island kingdoms whose people's destinies have been shaped deeply by the sea. Both, too, live close to neighbouring land masses whose influence on them could not but be profound. The Straits of Tsushima which separate Korea from Japan are about five times as wide as the Straits of Dover, it is true, and Japan was able to maintain an isolation from the Asian *terra firma* far more complete than any England could hope for from Europe. Nevertheless, the parallel can be pressed a good way and its validity is shown by the excitement which the Japanese have always shown about the establishment of a strong power in Korea; it rivals that of the British over the danger that the Low Countries might fall into unfriendly hands.

EMERGING JAPANESE CIVILIZATION

The Japanese proper probably arrived from Korea in about 300 BCE, and when Japan emerges in her own historical records, in the eighth century CE, there was Japanese-held territory in the Korean peninsula. In those days, Japan was a country divided up among a number of clans, presided over by an emperor with an ill-defined supremacy and an ancestry traced back to the Sun Goddess. The Japanese did not occupy the whole of the territory of modern Japan, but lived in the

This 19th-century Japanese triptych shows the Sun Goddess Amaterasu emerging from her cave to bathe the world in sunlight once more. The scene has been interpreted by some as representing the return of spring after winter. It may also have been inspired by a solar eclipse.

In Japanese mythology Izanagi ("the August Male") and his sister and wife Izanami ("the August Female"), shown in this 19th-century print, immersed a jewelled spear in the waters of the High Plains of Heaven. The drops that fell when they withdrew the spear became the island of Onogoro – the first solid land.

main on the southern and central islands. Here were the mildest climate and the best agricultural prospects. In prehistoric times the introduction of rice growing and the fishing potential of Japanese waters had already made it possible for this mountainous country to feed a disproportionately large population, but pressure on land was to be a recurrent theme of Japanese history.

In 645 CE a political crisis in the dominant clan brought about its downfall and a new one arose, the Fujiwara. It was to preside over a great age of Japanese civilization and to dominate the emperors. There was more than political significance in the change. It also marked a conscious effort to redirect Japanese life along paths of renewal and reform. The direction could only be sought from the guidance offered by the highest example of civilization and power of which the Japanese were aware, and possibly the finest in the world at that time, that of imperial China, which was also an example of expanding, menacing power.

JAPAN'S RELATIONSHIP WITH CHINA

Its continuing and often changing relationship with China is another theme of Japanese history. Both peoples were of Mongoloid stock, though some Caucasoids whose presence it is difficult to account for also form a part of the Japanese ethnic heritage (these, the Ainus, were, at the beginning of the historical era, mainly to be found in the northeast). In prehistoric times Japan appears to have followed in the wake of the civilization of the mainland; bronze artifacts, for example, appear in the islands only in the first century or so BCE. Such innovations in the last millennium BCE may owe something

The arrival of Buddhism in Japan resulted in the introduction of the Chinese T'ang culture, which enriched Japanese art and science. The architecture of the Nara period (710–784), for example, imitated T'ang models, as seen in the Buddha Hall of the Todaiji shrine in Nara. The construction dates from the mid-8th century, but was largely rebuilt in 1709.

to immigrants displaced by the Chinese as they moved southwards on the mainland. But the first references to Japan in the Chinese records (in the third century CE) still depict a country not much affected by mainland events and Chinese influence was not very marked until the centuries following the Han collapse. Then, a vigorous Japanese intervention in Korea seems to have opened the way to closer contact. It was subsequently fostered by the movement of Buddhist students. Confucianism, Buddhism, and iron technology all came to Japan from China. There were attempts to bring about administrative changes on Chinese lines. Above all, Chinese writing had been brought to Japan and its characters were used to provide a written form of the native language. Yet cultural attraction and dependence had not meant political submission.

This 18th-century Japanese scroll depicts the death of the Buddha, a scene known in Japan as *nehanzu* or *parinirvana*. The dying Buddha is shown lying on his right side, facing north.

Shintoism

Shintoism has its origins in the animistic beliefs of early Japan. At the core of the Shinto religion are the cults of deities, which personify natural phenomena, including human beings, and who are called *kami*. Among these are the Sun Goddess (Amaterasu), the Moon God (Tsuki-yomi) and the Storm God (Susano).

Primitive Shinto ceremonies were simple and comprised ablutions and purification rituals. The arrival of Buddhism, however, produced a mutual influence that was to change both religions substantially, resulting in a syncretism known as Ryobu-Shinto (double Shinto). Some Shinto gods, such as Hachiman, the God of War, who is also called Bosatsu (Bodhisattva), have been adapted to Buddhist forms. Other important Shinto gods include Amida, Kannon and Jizo, the latter being closely linked with children, the souls of the dead and those who withstand pain.

The torii *(ceremonial gateway) at the Miyajima Shinto sanctuary, which is dedicated to Susano's three daughters.*

THE IMPORTANCE OF THE CLAN

The Japanese central administration was already well developed in scope and scale at the beginning of the period of centralization and major efforts of reform were made in the seventh and eighth centuries. Yet, in the end, Japan evolved not in the direction of a centralized monarchy but of what might be termed, in a Western analogy, feudal anarchy. For almost nine hundred years it is hard to find a political thread to Japanese history. Its social continuity is much more obvious. From the beginnings of the historical era, even down to the present day, the keys to the continuity and toughness of Japanese society have been the family and the traditional religion. The clan was an enlarged family, and the nation the most enlarged family of all. In patriarchal style, the emperor presided over the national family as did a clan leader over his clan or, even, the small farmer over his family. The focus of family and clan life was participation in the traditional cult known as Shinto. Its ritual essence was the worship at the proper times of certain local or personal deities. This religious tradition upheld

Time chart (794–1867)

646
The Taika reforms aim to create a centralized state based on Chinese Sui and T'ang models

1185–1333
The Kamakura period of military feudalism. Shintoism is at its most splendid

1603–1867
The Tokugawa shogunate

500 | 1000 | 1500 | 2000

794–1185
The Heian period, characterized by the influence of Buddhism and Chinese culture

1274 and 1281
Mongol attempts to invade Japan

The *shogun* Yorimoto (1147–1199) made the city of Kamakura the Japanese capital, situated on a bay to the south of present-day Tokyo. Kamakura is famous for its 12th-century statue, the Great Buddha, which is 45 ft (14 m) high.

certain values and cosmological views, but it has no fixed doctrine, canonical scriptures, or even an identified founder. When Buddhism came to Japan in the sixth century it was easily conjoined with this traditional way.

THE ECLIPSE OF THE EMPERORS

The institutional coherence of old Japan was less marked than its social unity. The emperor was its focus. From the beginning of the eighth century, though, the emperor's power was more and more eclipsed and so, in spite of the efforts of an occasional vigorous individual, it remained until the nineteenth century. This eclipse arose in part from the activities of the would-be reformers of the seventh century, for one of them was the founder of the great Fujiwara clan. In the next hundred years or so, his family tied itself closely to the imperial household by marriage. As children were frequently brought up in the household of their mother's family, the clan could exercise a crucial influence upon future emperors while they were children. In the ninth century the chief of the Fujiwara was made regent for the emperor – who was an adult – and for most of what is called the Heian period (794–1185: the name comes from that of the capital city, the modern Kyoto), that clan effectively controlled central government through marriage alliances and court office, its leaders acting in the emperor's name. The power of the Fujiwara did something to disguise the decline of the royal authority, but in fact the imperial clan was tending to become simply one among several which existed in the shade of the Fujiwara, each of them governing its own estates more or less independently.

THE KAMAKURA PERIOD

The displacement of the emperor became much more obvious after the passing of the power of the Fujiwara. The Kamakura period (1185–1333) was so called because power passed to a clan whose estates were in the area of that name, and the bypassing of the imperial court, which remained at Heian, became much more obvious. It was early in the Kamakura period that there appeared the first of a series of military dictators who bore the title of *shogun*. They ruled in the emperor's name but in fact with a large independence. The emperor lived on the revenues of his own estates, and as long as he acquiesced in the *shogun*'s intentions he would have military power behind him; when he did not, he would be overruled.

CENTRAL AUTHORITY FADES

The eclipse of the imperial power was so different from what had occurred in China, the model of the seventh-century reformers, that the explanation is not easy to see. It was complex. There was a progression through the centuries from the exercise of a usurped central authority in the emperor's name to the virtual disappearance of any central authority at all. No doubt there was a fundamental bias in the traditional clan loyalties of Japanese society and the topography of Japan which would have told against any central power; remote valleys provided lodgements for great magnates. But other countries have met these problems successfully: the Hanoverian governments of eighteenth-century Great Britain tamed the Scottish highlands with punitive expeditions and military roads. A more specific explanation can be seen in the way in which the land reforms of the seventh century, which were the key to political change, were in practice whittled away by the clans with influence at court. Some of these exacted privileges and exemptions, as did some land-holding religious institutions. The most common example of the abuses which resulted from this was the granting of tax-free manors to noblemen who were imperial court officials by way of payment for carrying out their duties. The Fujiwara themselves were unwilling to check this practice. At a lower level, smaller proprietors would then seek to commend themselves and their land to a powerful clan in order to get assured tenure in return for rent and an obligation to provide service. The double result of such developments was to create a solid base for the power of local magnates while starving the central administrative structure of support from taxation. Taxes (in the form of a share of the crops) went not to the imperial administration but to the person to whom a manor had been granted.

GOVERNMENTAL STRUCTURES

Such a civil service as existed, unlike the Chinese, was firmly restricted to the aristocracy. Not being recruited by competition, it could not provide a foothold for a group whose interests might be opposed to the hereditary noble families. In the provinces, posts just below the highest level tended to go to the local notables, only the most senior appointments being reserved to civil servants proper.

No one planned that this should happen. Nor did anyone plan a gradual transition to military rule, whose origins lay in the need to make some of the families of the frontier districts responsible for defence against the still unsubdued

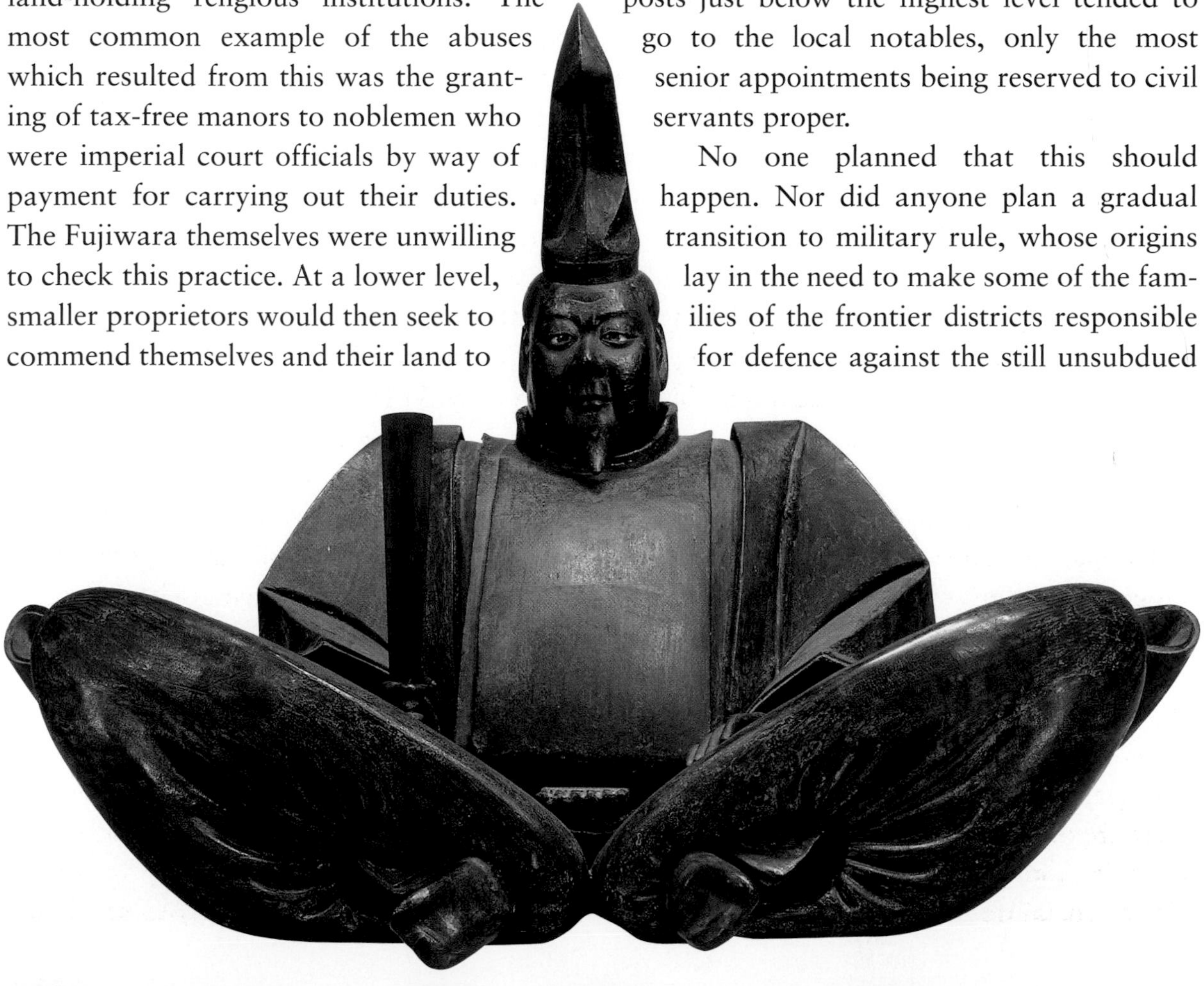

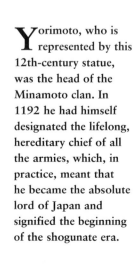

Yorimoto, who is represented by this 12th-century statue, was the head of the Minamoto clan. In 1192 he had himself designated the lifelong, hereditary chief of all the armies, which, in practice, meant that he became the absolute lord of Japan and signified the beginning of the shogunate era.

Ainu peoples. Slowly the prestige of the military clans drew to their leaders the loyalties of people seeking security in troubled times. And, indeed, there was a need for such security. Provincial dissidence began to express itself in outbreaks in the tenth century. In the eleventh there was clearly discernible an emerging class of manorial officers on the great estates. They enjoyed the real management and use of the lands of their formal masters and felt loyalties to the warrior clans in an elementary tie of service and loyalty. In this situation the Minamoto clan rose to a dominance which recreated central government in the early Kamakura period.

ISOLATION AND SECURITY

In one way internal power struggles were a luxury. The Japanese could indulge them because they lived in an island-state where no foreign intruder was ever more than occasionally threatening. Among other things, this meant that there was no need for a national army which might have mastered the clans. Although she came near to it in 1945, Japan has never been successfully invaded, a fact which has done much to shape the national psychology. The consolidation of the national territory was for the most part achieved in the ninth century when the peoples of the north were mastered and, after this, Japan rarely faced any serious external threat to her national integrity, though her relations with other states underwent many changes.

THE OUTSIDE WORLD

In the seventh century the Japanese had been ousted from Korea and this was the last time for many centuries that they were physically installed there. It was the beginning of a phase of cultural subservience to China which was matched by an inability to resist her on the mainland. Japanese embassies were sent to China in the interests of trade, good relations and cultural contact, the last one in the first half of the ninth century. Then, in 894, another envoy was appointed. His refusal to serve marks something of an epoch, for he

Kubilai Khan's ferocious armies met with defeat on the two occasions on which they tried to conquer Japan. This illustration, from *The Mongol Invasions Picture Scroll*, which dates from c.1293, shows a small Japanese vessel attacking a large Mongol ship during the second invasion.

gave it as his reason that China was too much disturbed and distracted by internal problems and that she had, in any case, nothing to teach the Japanese. Official relations were not resumed until the Kamakura period.

There were exploratory gestures in the thirteenth century. They did not prevent the expansion of irregular and private trade with the mainland in forms some of which looked much like freebooting and piracy. It may have been this which did much to provoke the two attempted Mongol invasions of 1274 and 1281. Both retired baffled, the second after grievous losses by storm – the *Kamikaze*, or "divine wind", which came to be seen in much the same light as the English saw the storms which shattered the Armada – and this was one of the greatest moments in strengthening the belief which the Japanese came to hold in their own invincibility and national greatness. Officially, the Mongols' motive had been the Japanese refusal to recognize their claim to inherit the Chinese pretensions to empire and to receive tribute from them. In fact, this conflict once more killed off the recently revived relations with China; they were not taken up again until the coming of Ming rule. By then the reputation of the Japanese as pirates was well established. They ranged far and wide through the Asian seas, just as Drake and his companions ranged the Spanish Main. They had the support of many of the feudal lords of the south and it was almost impossible for the *shoguns* to control them even when they wished (as they often did) to do so for the sake of good relations with the Chinese.

One of the best-known symbols of the Japanese landscape and culture is Mount Fuji, which has inspired countless artists. This painting is by So-Ami, one of the finest artists of the *suibokuga* style, who lived in the middle of the 16th century.

JAPANESE CULTURE

THE COLLAPSE of the Kamakura shogunate in 1333 brought a brief and ineffective attempt to restore real power to the emperor, which ended when confronted with the realities of the military power of the clans. In the ensuing period neither *shogun* nor emperor often enjoyed assured power. Until the end of the sixteenth century civil warfare was almost continuous. Yet these troubles did not check the consolidation of a Japanese cultural achievement which remains across the centuries a brilliant and moving spectacle and still shapes Japanese life and attitudes even in an era of industrialism. It is an achievement notable for its power to borrow and adopt from other cultures without sacrificing its own integrity or nature.

Even at the beginning of the historical era, when the prestige of T'ang art makes the derivative nature of what is done in Japan very obvious, there was no merely passive acceptance of a foreign style. Already in the first of the great periods of high Japanese culture, in the eighth century, this is apparent in Japanese painting and a poetry already written in Japanese, though people for centuries still wrote works of art or learning in Chinese (it had something of the status long held by Latin in Europe). At this time, and still more during the climax of the Fujiwara ascendancy, Japanese art other than religious architecture was essentially a court art, shaped by the court setting and the work and enjoyment of a relatively narrow circle. It was hermetically sealed from the world of ordinary Japan by its materials, subject-matter and standards. The great majority of Japanese would never even see the products of what can now be discerned as the first great peak of Japanese culture. The peasant wove hemp and cotton; his womenfolk would be no more likely to touch the fine silks whose careful gradations of colour established the taste displayed by a great court lady's twelve concentric sleeves than he would be to explore the psychological complexities of the Lady Murasaki's subtle novel, the *Tale of Genji*, a study as compelling as Proust and almost as long. Such art had the characteristics to be expected of the art of an élite insulated from society by living in the compound of the imperial palace. It was beautiful, refined, subtle and sometimes brittle, insubstantial and frivolous. But it already found a place for an emphasis which was to become traditional in Japan, that of simplicity, discipline, good taste and love of nature.

Much Kamakura art aimed to aggrandize the military classes, who had substituted the old nobility. This 14th-century illustration depicts the sea battle of Dannoura at which the Minamoto crushed the rival Taira clan in 1185.

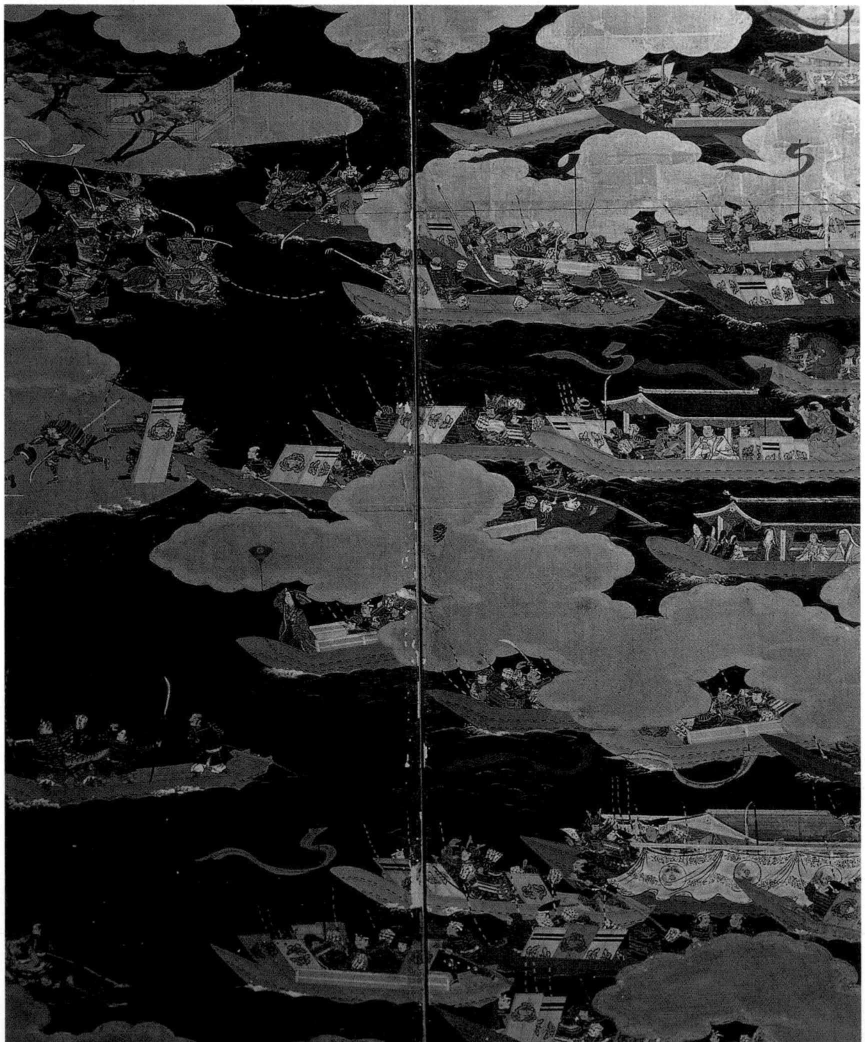

The culture of the Heian court attracted criticism from provincial clan leaders who saw in it an effete and corrupting influence, sapping both the independence of the court nobles and their loyalty to their own clans. From the Kamakura period, a new subject-matter – the warrior – appears in both literature and painting. Yet, as the centuries passed, a hostile attitude to traditional arts changed into one of respect, and during the troubled centuries the warring magnates showed by their own support for them that the central canons of Japanese culture were holding fast. It was protected more and more by an insularity and even a cultural arrogance confirmed by the defeat of the Mongol invasions. A new military element was also added to this culture during the centuries of war, in part originating in criticism of the apparently effete court circles but then blending with their traditions. It was fed by the feudal ideal of loyalty and self-sacrificing service, by the warrior ideals of discipline and austerity, and by an aesthetic arising out of them. One of its characteristic expressions was an offshoot of Buddhism, Zen. Gradually there emerged a fusion of the style of the high nobility with the austere virtues of the *samurai* warrior, which was to run through Japanese life down to the present day. Buddhism also left a visible mark on the Japanese landscape in its temples and great statues of the Buddha himself. Overall, the anarchy was the most creative of all periods of Japanese culture, for in it there appeared the greatest landscape painting, the culmination of the skill of landscape gardening and the arts of flower arrangement, and the *No* drama.

THE ECONOMY

In particular areas, the lawlessness of these centuries often inflicted grave social and economic damage. As was long to be the case, most Japanese were peasants: they might suffer terribly from an oppressive lord, banditry, or the passage of an army of retainers from a rival fief. Yet such damage was nationally insignificant, it seems. In the sixteenth century a great burst of castle-building testifies to the availability of substantial resources, there was a prolonged expansion of the circulation of copper coinage, and Japanese exports – particularly the exquisite examples of the work of the swordsmiths – began to appear in the markets of China and Southeast Asia. By 1600 Japan's population stood at about eighteen million. Both its slow growth (it had somewhat more than trebled in five centuries) and its substantial urban component rested on a steady improvement in agriculture, which had been able to carry the costs of civil strife and lawlessness as well. It was a healthy economic position.

EUROPEAN INTEREST

Sooner or later the Europeans were bound to come to find out more about the mysterious islands which produced such beautiful things. The first were the Portuguese who stepped ashore from Chinese ships, probably in 1543. Others followed in the next few years and in their own ships. It was a promising situation. Japan was virtually without a central government to undertake the regulation of intercourse with foreigners and many of the southern magnates were themselves highly interested in competing for foreign trade. Nagasaki, then a little village, was opened to the newcomers by one of them in 1570. This nobleman was a zealous Christian and had already built a church there; in 1549 the first Christian missionary had arrived, St Francis Xavier. Nearly forty years later Portuguese missionaries were forbidden, so much had the situation changed, though the ban was not at once enforced.

Among other things brought by the Portuguese to Japan were new food crops originally from the Americas – sweet potatoes, maize, sugar cane. They also brought muskets. The Japanese soon learnt to make them. This new weapon played an important part in assuring that the baronial wars of "feudal" Japan came to an end, as did those of medieval Europe, with the emergence of a preponderant power, a brilliant, humbly born soldier-dictator, Hideyoshi. His successor, Ieyasu, was one of his henchmen, a member of the Tokugawa family. In 1603 he revived

Several jars like this one, which dates from the 15th-century Muramachi shogunate, have been found in central Japan. Most served as vessels for saké, although some were used as funerary urns.

and assumed the old title of *shogun* and so inaugurated a period of Japanese history known as the "great peace", which lasted until a revolutionary change in 1868 but was itself an immensely creative period, in which Japan changed significantly.

THE TOKUGAWA SHOGUNATE

During the Tokugawa shogunate, for two and a half centuries, the emperor passed even further into the wings of Japanese politics and was firmly kept there. Court gave way to camp; the shogunate rested on a military overlordship. The *shoguns* themselves changed from being outstandingly important feudal lords to being in the first place hereditary princes and in the second the heads of a stratified social system over which they exercised viceregal powers in the name of the emperor and on his behalf. This régime was called the *bakufu* – the government of the camp. The *quid pro quo* provided by Ieyasu, the first Tokugawa *shogun*, was order and the assurance of financial support for the emperor.

The key to the structure was the power of the Tokugawa house itself. Ieyasu's origins had been pretty humble, but by the middle of the seventeenth century the clan appears to have controlled about one-quarter of Japan's rice-growing land. The feudal lords became in effect vassals of the Tokugawa, linked to the clan by a variety of ties. The term "centralized feudalism" has been coined to label this system. Not all the lords, or *daimyo*, were connected to the *shogun* in the same way. Some were directly dependent, being vassals with a hereditary family attachment to the Tokugawa family. Others were related to it by marriage, patronage or business. Others, less reliable, formed an outer category of those families which had only at length submitted. But all were carefully watched. The lords lived alternately at the *shogun*'s court or on their estates; when they were on their estates, their families lived as potential hostages of the *shogun* at Edo, the modern Tokyo, his capital.

The Jesuit St Francis Xavier was sent as a missionary to Portugal's Eastern colonies by King John III. In 1549 St Francis arrived in Japan, where he travelled widely and founded a mission that was to flourish for 100 years. On the right in this illustration two Jesuit priests from one of the early Japanese missions are depicted.

SOCIAL RIGIDITY

Below the lords was a society strictly and legally separated into hereditary classes and the maintenance of this structure was the primary goal of the régime. The noble *samurai* were the lords and their retainers, the warrior rulers who dominated society and gave it its tone as did the gentry bureaucrats of China. They followed a spartan, military ideal symbolized by the two swords they carried, and were allowed to use on commoners guilty of disrespect. *Bushido*, their creed, stressed above all the loyalty owed by a person to his or her lord. The original links of the retainers with the land were virtually gone by the seventeenth century and they lived in the castle towns of their lords. The other classes were the peasants, the artisans and the merchants (the lowest in the social hierarchy because of their non-productive character); the self-assertive ethos of the merchant which emerged in Europe was unthinkable in Japan, in spite of the vigour of Japanese trade. As the aim of the whole system was stability, attention to the duties of one's station and confinement to them was determinedly enforced. Hideyoshi himself had supervised a great sword hunt whose aim was to take away these weapons from those who were not supposed to have them – the lower classes. Whatever the equity of this, it must have told in favour of order. Japan wanted stability and her society accordingly came to emphasize the things that could ensure it: knowing one's place, discipline, regularity, scrupulous workmanship, stoical endurance. At its best it remains one of humanity's most impressive social achievements.

THE EUROPEANS ARE EXPELLED

The Japanese system shared one particular weakness with the Chinese; it presumed effective insulation from external stimuli to change. It was for a long time threatened by the danger of a relapse into internal anarchy; there were plenty of discontented *daimyo* and restless swordsmen about in seventeenth-century Japan. By then, one obvious external danger came from Europeans. They had already brought to Japan imports which would have profound effects. Among them the most obvious were firearms, whose

This detail of part of a folding screen depicts *samurai* warriors taking part in the siege of the castle of Osaka in 1615.

powerfully disruptive impact went beyond that which they achieved on their targets, and Christianity. This faith had at first been tolerated and even welcomed as something tempting traders from outside. In the early seventeenth century the percentage of Japanese Christians in the population was higher than it has ever been since. Soon, it has been estimated, there were over half a million of them. Nevertheless, this state of affairs did not last. Christianity has always had great subversive potential. Once this was grasped by Japan's rulers, a savage persecution began. It not only cost the lives of thousands of Japanese martyrs, who often suffered cruel deaths, but brought trade with Europe almost to an end. The English left and the Spanish were excluded in the 1620s. After the Portuguese had undergone a similar expulsion they rashly sent an embassy in 1640 to argue the toss; almost all of its members were killed. Japanese had already been forbidden to go abroad, or to return if they were already there, and the building of large ships was banned. Only the Dutch, who promised not to proselytize and were willing as a symbolic act to trample on the cross, kept

From a 17th-century folding screen, this detail shows Portuguese sailors unloading their merchandise in a Japanese port.

up Japan's henceforth tiny contact with Europe. They were allowed a trading station on a tiny island in Nagasaki harbour.

After this, there was no real danger of foreigners exploiting internal discontent. But there were other difficulties. In the settled conditions of the "great peace", military skill declined. The *samurai* retainers sat about in the castle towns of their lords, their leisure broken by little except the ceremonial parade in outdated armour which accompanied a lord's progress to the city of Edo. When the Europeans came back in the nineteenth century equipped with up-to-date weapons, Japan's military forces would be technically unable to match them.

A CHANGING ECONOMY

The external military threat could, perhaps, hardly have been foreseen. Nor could another result of the general peace in which internal trade prospered. The Japanese economy became more dependent on money. Old relationships were weakened by this and new social stresses appeared. Payment in cash forced lords to sell most of the tax rice which was their subsistence to pay for their visits to the capital. At the same time, the market became a national one. Merchants did well: some of them soon had money to lend their rulers. Gradually the warriors became dependent on the bankers. Besides feeling a shortage of cash, those rulers found themselves sometimes embarrassed by their inability to deal with economic change and its social repercussions. If retainers were to be paid in coin, they might more easily transfer loyalty to another paymaster. Towns were growing, too, and by 1700 Osaka and Kyoto both had more than 300,000 inhabitants, while Edo may have had 800,000. Other changes were bound to follow such growth. Price fluctuations in the rice market of the towns sharpened hostility towards the wealthy dealers.

ECONOMIC GROWTH

In this changing economy we face one great paradox of Tokugawa Japan. While its rulers slowly came to show less and less ability to contain new challenges to traditional ways, those challenges stemmed from a fundamental fact – economic growth – which in historical perspective now appears the dominant theme of the era. Under the Tokugawa, Japan was developing fast. Between 1600 and 1850 agricultural production approximately doubled, while the population rose by less than half. Since the régime was not one which was able to skim off the new wealth for itself, it remained in society as savings for investment by those who saw opportunities, or went into a rising standard of living for many Japanese.

Dispute continues about the explanation of what seems to have been a successful stride to self-sustaining economic growth of a kind which was elsewhere to appear only in Europe. Some are obvious and have been touched upon: the passive advantages conferred by the seas around Japan, which kept out invaders such as the steppe-borne nomads who time and again harried the wealth-producers of mainland Asia. The shogunate's own "great peace" ended feudal warfare and was another bonus. Then there were positive improvements to agriculture which resulted from more intensive cultivation, investment in irrigation, the exploitation of the new crops brought (originally from the Americas) by the Portuguese. But at this point the enquiry is already touching on reciprocal effects: the improvement of agriculture was possible because it became profitable to the producer, and it was profitable because social and governmental conditions were of a certain kind. Enforced residence of noblemen and their families at Edo not only put rice on the market (because the nobles had to find cash), but created a new huge urban market at the capital which sucked in both labour (because it supplied employment) and goods which it became more and more profitable to produce. Regional specialization (in textile manufacture, for example) was favoured by disparities in the capacity to grow food: most of Japanese industrial and handicraft production was, as in early industrial Europe, to be found in rural areas. Government helped, too; in the early years of the shogunate there was organized development of irrigation, standardizing of weights and currency. But for all its aspirations to regulate society, the government of the *bakufu* in the end probably favoured

Two Japanese ferry boats are shown lowering their sails in this 19th-century woodcut from Kuwana.

economic growth because it lacked power. Instead of an absolute monarchy, it came to resemble a balance-of-power system of the great lords, and was able to maintain itself only so long as there was no foreign invader to disturb it. As a result it could not obstruct the path to economic growth and divert resources from producers who could usefully employ them. Indeed, the economically quasi-parasitical *samurai* actually underwent a reduction in their share of the national income at a time when producers' shares were rising. It has been suggested that by 1800 the *per capita* income and life expectancy of the Japanese was much the same as that of their British contemporaries.

THE CONSEQUENCES OF ISOLATION

Much has been obscured by the more superficial but strikingly apparent features of the Tokugawa era. Some of these, of course, were important, but at a different level. The new prosperity of the towns created a clientèle for printed books and the coloured wood-block prints which were later to excite European artists' admiration. It also provided the audiences for the new *kabuki* theatre. Yet brilliant though it often was, and successful, at the deepest economic level (if undesignedly) as it was, it is not clear that the Tokugawa system could have survived much longer even without the coming of a new threat from the West in the nineteenth century. Towards the end of the period there were signs of uneasiness. Japanese intellectuals began to sense that somehow their isolation had preserved them from Europe but also had cut them off from Asia. They were right. Japan had already made for herself a unique historical destiny and it would mean that she faced the West in a way very different from the subjects of Manchu or Moghul.

In the Edo period a new artistic movement, which involved the production of xylographs or woodcuts with a purely popular character, emerged as a reaction against the traditional élitist painting. In these popular paintings women began to be represented as courtesans (*yujo* women) rather than geishas, who were the subject of traditional art. In this 18th-century piece three girls are depicted paddling in a river.

4 WORLDS APART

AFRICA AND THE AMERICAS moved towards civilization to rhythms very different from those operating elsewhere. Of course, this was not quite so true of Africa as of the Americas, which were cut off by the oceans from all but fleeting contacts with the other continents. The Africans, by contrast, lived in a continent much of which was gradually Islamicized, and for a long time had at least peripheral encounters with first Arab and then European traders. These were of growing importance as time went by, though they did not suck Africa completely into the mainstream of world history until the late nineteenth century. This isolation, combined with an almost complete dependence for much of the story on archaeological evidence, makes much African and American history an obscure business.

This illustration, which depicts the arrival of Ethiopian legatees in ancient Rome to sue for peace, gives an idea of how Europeans living in the 15th century imagined Africans to look.

AFRICA

AFRICAN HISTORY BEFORE the coming of European trade and exploration is largely a matter of an internal dynamic we can barely discern, but we may presume folk-movements to have played a large part in it. There are many legends of migration and they always speak of movement from the north to the south and west. In each case, scholars have to evaluate the legend in its context, and with help from reference in Egyptian records, travellers' tales and archaeological discovery, but the general tendency is striking. It seems to register a general trend, the enrichment and elaboration of African culture in the north first and its appearance in the south only much later.

METALLURGICAL SKILLS

The kingdom of Kush, which had connections with ancient Egypt, is a convenient place to begin the story of these cultural changes. By the fifth century BCE the Kushites had lost control of Egypt and retreated once more to Meroe, their capital in the south, but they had centuries of flourishing culture still ahead of them. From Egypt, probably, they had brought with them a hieroglyph (claims are now being made to have deciphered it). Certainly they diffused their knowledge to the south and west in the Sudan, where notable metallurgical skills were later to flourish among the Nubians and Sudanese. In the last few centuries BCE iron-working appears south of the Sahara, in central Nigeria. Its importance was recognized by its remaining the closely guarded secret of kings, but so valuable a skill slowly travelled southwards. By about the twelfth century CE it had penetrated the south-east, and the pygmies and the San people (previously known as Bushmen) of the south were the only Africans then still living in the Stone Age.

AGRICULTURE

Probably the greatest difference made by the spread of iron-working was to agriculture. It made possible a new penetration of the forests and better tilling of the soil (which may be connected with the arrival of new food-crops from Asia in the early Common Era), and so led to new folk-movements and population growth. Hunting and gathering areas were broken up by the coming of herdsmen and farmers who can be discerned already by about 500 CE in much of east and southeast Africa, in modern Zimbabwe and the Transvaal. Yet those Africans did not acquire the plough. Possibly the reason lies in the lack in most of the continent south of Egypt of an animal resistant enough to African diseases to draw one. One area where there were ploughs was Ethiopia, and there animals could be bred successfully, as the early use of the horse indicates. Horses were also bred for riding in the southern Sahara.

This suggests once again the important limiting factor of the African environment. Most of the continent's history is the story of response to influences from the outside – iron-working and new crops from the Near East, Asia, Indonesia and the Americas; steam engines and medicine from nineteenth-century Europe. These made it possible gradually to grapple with African nature. Without them, Africa south of the Sahara seems almost inert under the huge pressures exercised upon it by geography, climate and disease. It remained (with some exceptions) for the most part tied to a shifting agriculture, not achieving an intensive one; this was a positive response to difficult conditions but could not sustain more than a slow population growth. Nor did southern Africa arrive at the wheel, so it lagged behind in transport, milling and pottery.

CHRISTIAN AND ISLAMIC AFRICA

The story was different north of the Equator. Much Kushite history waits, in the most literal sense, to be uncovered, for few of the major cities have yet been excavated. It is known that in about 300 CE Kush was overthrown by Ethiopians. They were not then the unique people they were to become, with kings claiming descent from Solomon and for centuries the only Christian people in Africa outside Egypt. They were converted to Christianity by Copts only later in the fourth

From the 11th century to the 14th century the Nigerian Ife culture was created by the Yoruba tribe, to which this bronze head of a king is attributed. The outstanding terracotta and bronze sculptures produced by the Yoruba have become a milestone in Africa's cultural history.

Time chart (500 BCE–900 CE)

Africa:	500 BCE	The beginning of the Nox culture in northern Nigeria
	c.300 CE	The Kush kingdom is overthrown by Ethiopians
	c.700 CE	The Empire of Ghana enjoys great economic development and growth in trade
	900 CE	The Hausa settle in the Daura Kingdom of northern Nigeria
The Americas:	c.400 BCE	The decline of the Olmec civilization
	c.300 CE	The Teotihuacán civilization
	600 CE	The apogee of the Maya civilization in Mesoamerica

500 BCE — 0 — 500 CE — 1000 CE

century; at that time they were still in touch with the classical Mediterranean world. But the Islamic invasions of Egypt placed between them and it a barrier which was not breached for centuries, during which the Ethiopians battled for survival against pagan and Muslim, virtually isolated from Rome or Byzantium. An Amharic-speaking people, they were the only literate non-Islamic African nation.

The only other place in Africa where Christianity established itself was in the Roman north. Here it had been a vigorous, if minority, cult. The violence of its dissensions and the pursuit of the Donatists as heretics probably explain its weakness when the Arab invasions brought it face to face with Islam. Except in Egypt, Christianity was extinguished in the Africa of the Arab states. Islam, on the other hand, was and has remained enormously successful in Africa. Borne by Arab invasion, it spread in the eleventh century right across to the Niger and western Africa. Arab sources therefore provide our main information about the non-literate African societies which stretched across the Sudan and Sahara after the passing of Kush. They were often trading communities and may reasonably be thought of as city-states; the most famous was Timbuctoo, impoverished by the time Europeans finally got there, but in the fifteenth century important enough to be the site of what has been described as an Islamic university. Politics and economics are still as closely intertwined in Africa as in any part of the world, and it is not surprising that the early kingdoms of black Africa should have appeared and prospered at the end of important trade routes where there was wealth to tap. Merchants liked stability.

Timbuctoo was founded by Tuareg nomads in c.1100 CE. It was absorbed into the Mali Empire in the late 13th century and became the main trading centre in Africa. Emperor Mansa Musa, the most famous of Mali's rulers, who reigned in the early 14th century, built palaces and mosques there, the best-known of which is the Great Mosque (Djingereyber). It is constructed of adobe and rubble and covered with clay.

GHANA

Another African state, the earliest recorded by the Arabs, had a name later taken by a modern nation: Ghana. Its origins are obscure, but may well have lain in the assertion of its supremacy by a people in the late pre-Common Era, who had the advantage of iron weapons and horses. However this may be, the Ghana recorded by Arab chroniclers and geographers is already an important kingdom when it appears in the records in the eighth century CE. At its greatest extent, Ghana spanned an area about five hundred miles across the region framed to the south by the upper reaches of the Niger and Senegal and protected to the north by the Sahara. The Arabs spoke of it as "the land of gold"; the gold came from the upper Senegal and the Ashanti, and was passed by Arab traders by trans-Saharan routes or through Egypt up to the Mediterranean, where it lubricated

Christianity had already been prevalent in Egypt for more than 100 years when this 5th-century Coptic tapestry, clearly inspired by the art of the Eastern Roman Empire, was made. In the 7th century Egypt was conquered by the Arabs. At first the Christians were protected by their new overlords, but later they were enslaved until well into the 19th century.

European trade. In this way, Africa for a time exercised a positive influence on the outside world. The most important other commodities traded across the Sahara were salt and slaves. Ghana collapsed during the twelfth and thirteenth centuries.

MALI

Ghana's eclipse was followed by the preeminence of Mali, a kingdom whose ruler's wealth caused a sensation when in 1307 he made a pilgrimage to Mecca. It, too, gave its name to an African state in the twentieth century. Mali was even bigger than Ghana, taking in the whole Senegal basin and running about a thousand miles inland from the coast at the beginning of the fourteenth century. The Mali ruler is said to have had ten thousand horses in his stables. This empire broke up in dynastic wars in the late fourteenth century and finally went under after defeat by the Moroccans. Other African states were to follow. But, although in some cases the Arab records speak of African courts attended by men of

Mali's huge economic growth was a result of its trade with Arab merchants, who, at the end of the 12th century, had begun to exploit African gold. Legend has it that, as Emperor Mansa Musa travelled through Egypt during his pilgrimage to Mecca, he gave away so much gold that its value in Cairo dropped by 12 per cent. Musa's fame soon reached the Western world, as the Great Catalan Atlas (shown here), dated 1375, demonstrates.

letters, there is no native documentation which enables us to reach these peoples. Clearly they remained pagan while their rulers belonged to the Islamic world. It may be that the dissolution of Ghana owed something to dissent caused by conversions to Islam. Arab reports make it obvious that the Islamic cult was associated with the ruler in the Sudanese and Saharan states but had also still to accommodate traditional practice from the pagan past – rather as early Christianity in Europe accepted a similar legacy. Nor did social custom always adapt itself to Islam: Arabic writers expressed shocked disapproval of the public nakedness of Mali girls.

SUB-SAHARAN AFRICA

Africa further south of the Sahara is even harder to get at. At the roots of the history which determined its structure on the eve of its absorption into world events was a folk-migration of the negroid peoples who speak languages of the group called Bantu. This is a term somewhat like "Indo-European", referring to identifiable linguistic characteristics, not a genetic strain. The detailed course of this movement is, of course, still highly obscure but its beginnings lie in eastern Nigeria, where there were early Bantu-speakers. From there they took their language and agriculture south, first into the Congo basin. There followed a rapid spread, round about the beginning of the Common Era, over most of southern Africa. This set the ethnic pattern of modern Africa.

Some peoples, speaking the language the Arabs called "Swahili" (from the Arabic word meaning "of the coast"), established towns on the east African coasts which were linked to mysterious kingdoms in the interior. This was before the eighth century CE, when the Arabs began to settle in these towns and turn them into ports. The Arabs called the region the land of the Zanz (from which was later to come the name of Zanzibar) and said that its peoples prized iron above gold. It is probable that these polities had some kind of trading relations with Asia even before Arab times; who the intermediaries were it is not possible to say, but they may have been Indonesians such as those who colonized Madagascar. The Africans had gold and iron to offer for luxuries and they also began the implantation of new crops from Asia, cloves and bananas among them.

RULING STRUCTURES

Even a vague picture of the working of the African states is hard to arrive at. Monarchy was by no means the rule in them and a sense of the importance of ties of kin seems to have been the only widespread characteristic shared by the black African polities. Organization must have reflected the needs of particular environments and the possibilities presented by particular resources. Yet kingship was widely diffused. Again, the earliest signs are northern, in Nigeria and Benin. By the fifteenth century there were kingdoms in the region of the great eastern lakes and we hear of the kingdom of the Kongo, on the lower Congo river. There are not many signs of organization on this scale and African states were for a long time not to produce bureaucratized administration or standing armies. The powers of kings must have been limited, not only by custom and respect for tradition, but by the lack of resources to bind people's allegiance beyond the ties imposed by kinship and respect. No doubt this accounts for the transitory and fleeting nature of many of these "states". Ethiopia was an untypical African country.

ZIMBABWE

Some remarkable traces remain of these dim and shadowy kingdoms. A high level of culture in the east African interior in about the twelfth century is demonstrated by the remains of mine-workings, roads, rock paintings,

In the late 15th century the Portuguese established trade relations with Benin in western Africa: their collaboration was to prove highly profitable for both kingdoms. African craftsmen began to work for the Portuguese, combining motifs from the two cultures in their work. This ivory salt-cellar is an example of this syncretic influence.

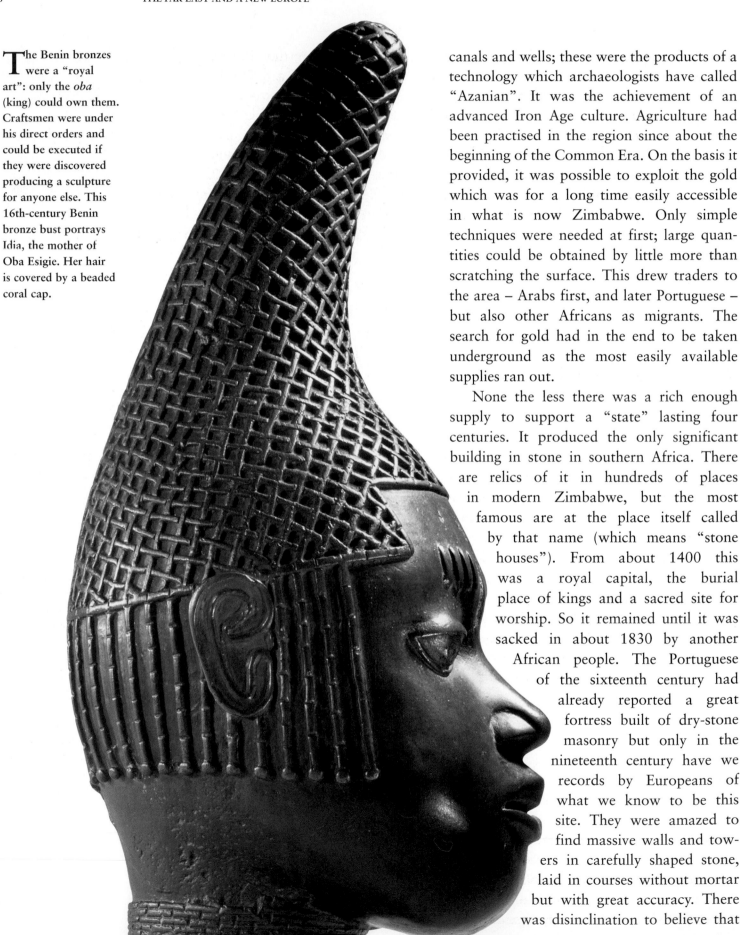

The Benin bronzes were a "royal art": only the *oba* (king) could own them. Craftsmen were under his direct orders and could be executed if they were discovered producing a sculpture for anyone else. This 16th-century Benin bronze bust portrays Idia, the mother of Oba Esigie. Her hair is covered by a beaded coral cap.

canals and wells; these were the products of a technology which archaeologists have called "Azanian". It was the achievement of an advanced Iron Age culture. Agriculture had been practised in the region since about the beginning of the Common Era. On the basis it provided, it was possible to exploit the gold which was for a long time easily accessible in what is now Zimbabwe. Only simple techniques were needed at first; large quantities could be obtained by little more than scratching the surface. This drew traders to the area – Arabs first, and later Portuguese – but also other Africans as migrants. The search for gold had in the end to be taken underground as the most easily available supplies ran out.

None the less there was a rich enough supply to support a "state" lasting four centuries. It produced the only significant building in stone in southern Africa. There are relics of it in hundreds of places in modern Zimbabwe, but the most famous are at the place itself called by that name (which means "stone houses"). From about 1400 this was a royal capital, the burial place of kings and a sacred site for worship. So it remained until it was sacked in about 1830 by another African people. The Portuguese of the sixteenth century had already reported a great fortress built of dry-stone masonry but only in the nineteenth century have we records by Europeans of what we know to be this site. They were amazed to find massive walls and towers in carefully shaped stone, laid in courses without mortar but with great accuracy. There was disinclination to believe that

Africans could have produced anything so impressive; some suggested the Phoenicians should have the credit and a few romantics toyed with the idea that Zimbabwe had been put there by the masons of the Queen of Sheba. Today, remembering the world of other Iron Age peoples in Europe and the civilizations of America, such hypotheses do not seem necessary. The Zimbabwe ruins may reasonably be attributed to the Africans of the fifteenth century.

AFRICAN CULTURE

Advanced as East Africa was, its peoples failed to achieve literacy for themselves; like the early Europeans, they were to acquire it from other civilizations. Perhaps the absence of a need for careful records of land, or of crops which could be stored, is a part of the explanation. Whatever the reason, the absence of literacy was a handicap in acquiring and diffusing information and in consolidating government. It was also a cultural impoverishment: Africa would not have a native tradition of learned sages from whom would come scientific and philosophical skill. On the other hand, the artistic capacity of black Africa was far from negligible, as the achievement of Zimbabwe, or the bronzes of Benin, which captivated later Europeans, show.

THE AMERICAS

ISLAM HAD BEEN AT WORK in Africa for nearly eight hundred years (and before that there had been the influence of Egypt on its neighbours) by the time the Europeans arrived in America, to discover civilizations which had achieved much more than those of Africa and appeared to have done so without stimuli from the outside. This has seemed so improbable to some people that much time has been spent investigating and discussing the possibility that the elements of civilization were implanted in the Americas by trans-Pacific voyagers a very long time ago. Most scholars find the evidence inconclusive. If there was such a contact in remote times, it had long since ceased. There is no unequivocal trace of connection between the Americas and any other continent between the time when the first Americans crossed the Bering Straits and the landings of Vikings. There is then none thereafter until the Spanish arrived at the end of the fifteenth century. To an even greater degree than Africa, and for a longer time, we must assume the Americas to have been cut off from the rest of the world.

Representing a king, this piece is one of the remarkable Benin bronze plaques, most of which were taken to England in 1897 by members of a British expedition. The kingdom of Benin, which was founded in the 12th century, reached its heyday in the 15th century, when Lagos (now the capital of Nigeria) was founded.

The pre-imperialist Americas

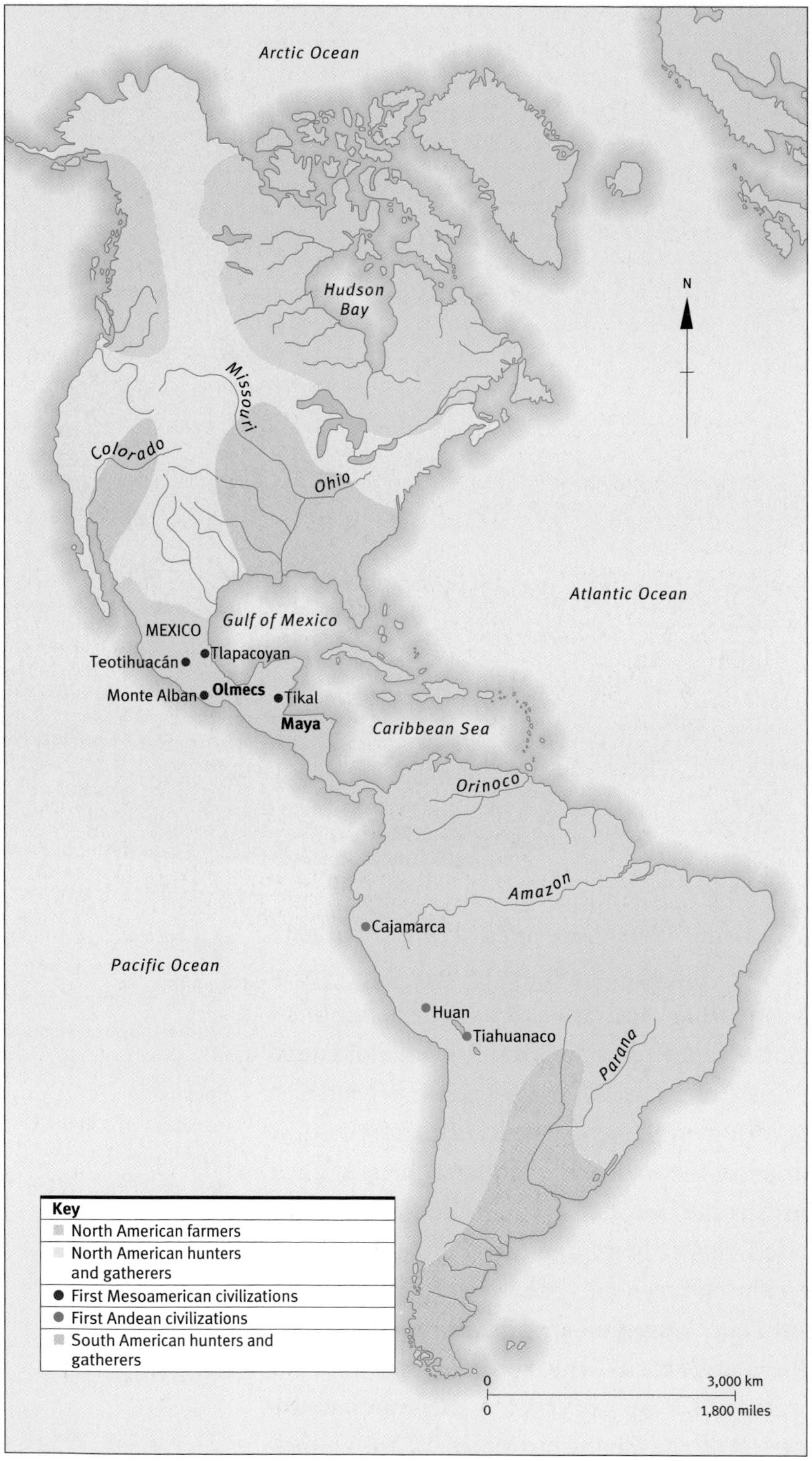

This map shows the empires that ruled in the Americas before Spanish explorers and imperialists landed there.

NORTH AMERICAN PEOPLES

Their isolation accounts for the fact that, even in the nineteenth century, pre-agricultural peoples still survived in North America. On the eastern plains of the modern United States there were "Indians" (as Europeans later came to call them) practising agriculture before the arrival of Europeans, but further west other communities were then still hunting and gathering. They would go on doing so, though with important changes of techniques as first the horse and metal, brought by Europeans, and then firearms were added to their technical equipment. Further west still, there were peoples on the west coast who fished or collected their subsistence on the seashore, again in ways fixed since time immemorial. Far to the north, a *tour de force* of specialization enabled the Eskimos to live with great efficiency in an all but intolerable environment; this pattern survives in its essentials even today. Yet although the native cultures of North America are respectable achievements in their overcoming of environmental challenge, they are not civilization. For the American achievement in indigenous civilization it is necessary to go south of the Rio Grande. Here were to be found a series of major civilizations linked by common dependence on the cultivation of maize and by possessing pantheons of nature gods, but strikingly different in other ways.

MESOAMERICAN CIVILIZATIONS

IN MESOAMERICA the Olmec foundation proved very important. The calendars, hieroglyphics and the practice of building large ceremonial sites which mark so much of the region in later times may all be ultimately derived from it; the gods of Mesoamerica were already known in Olmec times, too. Between the beginning and the fourth century of the Common Era the successors of the Olmecs built the first great American city, Teotihuacán, in what is now Mexico. It was for two or three centuries a major trading centre and probably of outstanding religious importance, for it contained a huge complex of pyramids and great public buildings. Mysteriously, it was destroyed in about the seventh century, possibly by one of a series of waves of invaders moving southwards into the valley of central Mexico. These movements began an age of migration and warfare which was to last until the coming of the Spaniards, and produced several brilliant regional societies.

Teotihuacán

One of the most impressive ancient ceremonial centres in Latin America is, without a doubt, Teotihuacán (City of the Gods), located in a valley near the present-day city of Mexico. Mythology stated that the gods had convened at the site to create the world for the fifth time. The city's most famous buildings, the Pyramids of the Sun and the Moon, were founded around the year 100 CE. Many temples, squares and houses were constructed around them – the houses are believed to have provided lodgings for the priests who made up the most important social class.

Between the middle of the 4th century and the end of the 5th century CE, the city reached the height of its glory: the Avenue of the Dead, a thoroughfare lined with the ruins of more than 75 temples, dates from this time. Next to it stands the Temple of Quetzalcoatl, the exterior of which is decorated with the famous heads of winged serpents.

All this splendour was probably made possible by improvements in agricultural techniques. The resulting increased harvests then led to population growth, and to the expansion of commerce. This in turn gave rise to the appearance of extensive trade networks, established to discover new sources of raw materials.

The Avenue of the Dead, seen here from the Pyramid of the Sun, leads to the smaller Pyramid of the Moon.

THE MAYA

THE MOST REMARKABLE Mesoamerican societies were those formed by the Maya cultures of Yucatán, Guatemala and northern Honduras. Their setting was extraordinary, given its appearance today. Virtually all the great Maya sites lie in tropical rain-forest, whose animals and insects, climate and diseases demand great efforts if its resources are to be tapped by agriculture. Yet the Maya not only maintained huge populations for many centuries with rudimentary agricultural techniques (they had no ploughs or metal tools and long depended on burning and clearing land to use it for a couple of seasons before moving on), but also raised stone buildings comparable to those of ancient Egypt.

Many Maya sites may remain undiscovered in the jungle, but enough have now been found to reconstruct an outline of Maya history and society, both of which have in the past few decades been shown to have been much more complex than was once thought. The earliest traces of Maya culture have been discerned in the third and fourth centuries BCE; it blossomed into its greatest period between the sixth and ninth centuries CE, when its finest buildings, sculpture and pottery were produced. Maya cities of that era contained great ceremonial complexes, combinations of temples, pyramids, tombs and ritual courts, often covered with hieroglyphic writing which has only in the last twenty years begun to yield to investigation. Religion played an important part in the government of this culture, endorsing the dynastic rulers of the cities in ceremonies in which bloodshed and sacrifice played a signal part.

THE MAYA CALENDAR

Maya religious practice consisted of the performance of regular acts of intercession and worship in a cycle calculated from a calendar derived from astronomical observation. Many scholars have found this the only Maya achievement worthy of comparison with the buildings, and it was indeed a great feat of mathematics. Through the calendar, enough of Maya thinking can be grasped to make it evident that this people's religious leaders had an idea of time much vaster than that of any other civilization of which we have knowledge; they calculated an antiquity of hundreds of thousands of years. They may even have arrived at the idea that time has no beginning.

The stone hieroglyphs and three surviving books tell us something of this calendar and have provided a chronology for Maya dynasties. The Maya of the classical era used to put up dated monuments every twenty years to record the passage of time, the last of them dated to 928. By then, Maya civilization was past its peak. For all the skill of its builders and craftsmen in jade and obsidian, it had considerable limitations. The makers of the great temples never achieved the arch, nor could they employ carts in their operations, for the Maya never discovered the wheel, while the religious world in whose shadows they lived was peopled by two-headed dragons, jaguars and grinning skulls. As for its political achievement, Maya society had long been based on patterns of alliances tying together the cities in two dynastic agglomerations whose history is set out in the hieroglyph of the monuments. At its greatest extent, the largest Maya city may have had as many as 40,000 inhabitants, with a dependent rural population far greater than that of Maya America today.

THE DECLINE OF THE MAYA

Maya civilization was highly specialized. Like the Egyptian, it required a huge investment of

The Maya codices

The Maya codices constitute one of the most splendid expressions of Maya art. These documents consist of folded leaves of paper (made from tree bark covered with whitewash), on which representations of the gods, leaders and hieroglyphs were drawn. Most of the codices vanished when the Spanish arrived; some Spaniards, such as the first Bishop of Yucatán, Diego de Landa, gave orders that the Maya documents should be systematically destroyed.

Only four pre-conquest codices survive today, three of which are named after the cities in which they are now held. The 13th-century Dresden Codex contains articles about astronomy and astrology. The Paris Codex, only a fragment of which has been found, contains information about divination and ceremonial rituals. The Madrid Codex, also known as the Trocortesian Codex, was found in two fragments. It is made up of 56 sheets of text describing the various rituals that the Maya priests used to predict the future.

The Madrid Codex, from which this detail is taken, shows a large number of gods, priests and Maya nobles.

labour in unproductive building, but the Egyptians had done much more. Perhaps Maya civilization was overloaded at an early date. Soon after its beginning a people from the valley of Mexico, probably Toltec, seized Chichen Itza, the greatest Maya site, and from this time the jungle centres of the south began to be abandoned. The invaders brought metal with them and also the Mexican practice of sacrificing prisoners of war. Their gods begin to appear in sculpture at the Maya sites. Seemingly, there was also a shift of power from priests to secular rulers among the Maya, and there was a contemporaneous cultural recession marked by cruder pottery and sculpture and a decline in the quality of the hieroglyph, too. By the end of the eleventh century the Maya political order had collapsed, though a few cities were to flicker back to life at a lower level of cultural and material existence during the next couple of centuries. Chichen Itza was finally abandoned in the thirteenth century and the centre of Maya culture shifted to another site, sacked in its turn, possibly after a peasant rising in about 1460. With that, the Maya story goes into eclipse until the twentieth century. In the sixteenth century Yucatán passed into the hands of the Spanish, though only in 1699 did the last Maya stronghold fall to them.

The Spaniards were only in the most formal sense the destroyers of Maya civilization. It had already collapsed from within by the time they arrived. Explanation is not easy, given our information, and it is tempting to fall back on metaphor: Maya civilization was the answer to a huge challenge and could meet it for a time, but only with a precarious political structure vulnerable to outside influence, and at the cost of narrow specialization and burdens which were huge in relation to the resources available to support them. Even before foreign invasion, as political

The Maya used two calendars. One was ritual and consisted of a combination of 13 numerals and 20 named days, resulting in 260-day cycles. The solar calendar, however, was made up of 365 days, divided into 18 months of 20 days each, with five days added to the end. Every 52 solar calendar years, the two types of calendar coincided on one day. This bas-relief, from the city of Palenque, bears a hieroglyph referring to a unit of time that is equivalent to 7,200 days.

fragmentation occurred, the irrigation arrangements of which the archaeologists have discovered the remains were falling into desuetude and decay. As decisively as elsewhere in the Americas, the native culture left behind no living style, no technology of note, no literature, no political or religious institution of significance. Only in the language of the Maya peasantry did the past retain some foothold. What the Maya left behind were wondrous ruins, which would long bemuse and fascinate those who had later to try to explain them.

THE AZTECS

WHILE MAYA SOCIETY was in its final decay, one of the last peoples to arrive in the valley of Mexico won an hegemony there which amazed the Spanish more than anything they later found in Yucatán. These were the Aztecs, who had entered the valley in about 1350 CE, overthrowing the Toltecs who then exercised supremacy there. They

This illustration from the Axcatitlán Codex represents the Aztecs' long journey from their nomadic origins in northern Mexico to their definitive settlement at Tenochtitlán, the city from which they ruled a huge empire.

settled in two villages on marshy land at the edge of Lake Texcoco; one of these was called Tenochtitlán and it was to be the capital of an Aztec empire which expanded in less than two centuries to cover the whole of central Mexico. Aztec expeditions went far south into what was later the republic of Panama, but showed no diligence in settlement. The Aztecs were warriors and preferred an empire of tribute: their army gave them the obedience of some thirty or so minor tribes or states which they left more or less alone, provided the agreed tribute was forthcoming. The gods of these peoples were given the compliment of inclusion in the Aztec pantheon.

The centre of Aztec civilization was Tenochtitlán, the capital they had built up from the village. It stood in Lake Texcoco on a group of islands connected to the lake shores by causeways, one of which was five miles long and took eight horsemen abreast. The Spanish left excited descriptions of this city: its magnificence, said one, exceeded that of Rome or Constantinople. It probably contained about 100,000 inhabitants at the beginning of the sixteenth century and to its maintenance went what was received from the subject peoples. By comparison with European cities it was an astonishing place, filled with temples and dominated by huge artificial pyramids, yet its magnificence seems to have been derivative, for the Aztecs exploited the skills of their subjects. Not a single important invention or innovation of Mexican culture can confidently be assigned to the post-Toltec period. The Aztecs controlled, developed and exploited the civilization that they found.

AZTEC CULTURE

When the Spanish arrived in the early sixteenth century, the Aztec Empire was still expanding. Not all of its subject peoples were completely subdued, but Aztec rule ran from coast to coast. At its head was a semi-divine but elected ruler, chosen from a royal family. He directed a highly ordered and centralized society, making heavy demands on its members for compulsory labour and military service, but also providing them with an annual subsistence. It was a civilization pictographically literate, highly skilled in agriculture and the handling of gold, but knowing nothing of the plough, iron-working or the wheel. Its central rituals – which greatly shocked the Spaniards – included human sacrifice; no less than 20,000 victims were killed at the dedication of the great pyramid of Tenochtitlán. Such holocausts re-enacted a cosmic drama which was at the heart of Aztec mythology; it taught that the gods had been obliged to sacrifice themselves to give the sun the blood it needed as food.

RELIGION AND WEAKNESS

Aztec religion struck Europeans by its revolting details – the tearing out of victims' hearts, the flayings and ceremonial decapitations – but its bizarre and horrific accompaniments were less significant than its profound political and social implications. The importance of sacrifice meant that a continual flow of victims was needed. As these were usually supplied by prisoners of war – and because death in battle was also a route to the paradise of the sun for the warrior – a state of peace in the Aztec Empire would have been disastrous from a religious point of view. Hence the Aztecs did not really mind that their dependencies were only loosely controlled and that revolts were frequent. Subject tribes were allowed to keep their own rulers and governments so that punitive raids could be made upon them at the slightest excuse. This ensured that the empire could not win the loyalty of the subject peoples; they were bound to welcome the Aztec collapse when it came. Religion was also to affect in other ways the capacity to respond to the threat from Europeans, notably in the Aztecs' desire to take prisoners for sacrifice rather than to kill their enemies in battle, and in their belief that one day their great god, Quetzalcoatl, white-skinned and bearded, would return from the east, where he had gone after instructing his people in the arts.

Altogether, for all its aesthetic impressiveness and formidable social efficiency, the feel of Aztec civilization is harsh, brutal and unattractive. Few civilizations of which we know much have pressed so far their demands on their members. It seems to have lived always in a state of tension, a pessimistic civilization, its people uneasily aware that collapse was more than a possibility.

PERU

TO THE SOUTH OF MEXICO and Yucatán lay several other cultures, distinct enough in their degree of civilization but none of them were so remarkable as the most distant, the Andean civilization of Peru. The Mexican peoples still lived for the most part in the Stone Age; the Andeans had got much further than this. They had also created a true state. If the Maya excelled among the American cultures in the elaborate calculations of their calendar, the Andeans were far ahead of their neighbours in the complexity of their government. The imagination of the Spaniards was captured by Peru even more than by Mexico, and the reason was not simply its

This 15th-century bas-relief, known as the "Sun Stone", represents the Aztec solar calendar. In the central circle is the face of the Sun God. The second circle shows the fifth sun and the talons of the solar god. The third circle comprises 20 hieroglyphs representing the days. Eight solar rays alternate with eight hieroglyphs of stylized feathers and "precious water" (representing blood) in 40 blocks to make up the next circle. Finally, the outer ring shows the sun disc surrounded by two enormous serpents.

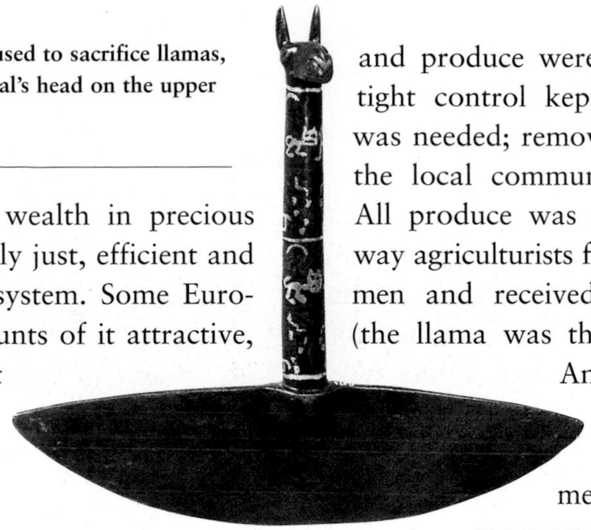

This ceremonial knife was used to sacrifice llamas, as the carving of the animal's head on the upper part of the handle indicates.

immense and obvious wealth in precious metals, but its apparently just, efficient and highly complex social system. Some Europeans soon found accounts of it attractive, for it required an almost total subordination of the individual to the collective.

INCA GOVERNMENT

Andean society was ruled by the Incas. In the twelfth century a people from Cuzco began to extend its control over earlier centres of civilization in Peru. Like the Aztecs, they began as neighbours of those longer civilized than themselves; they were barbarians who soon took over the skills and fruits of higher cultures. At the end of the fifteenth century the Incas ruled a realm extending from Ecuador to central Chile, their conquest of the coastal areas being the most recent. This was an astonishing feat of government, for it had to contend with the natural obstacles provided by the Andes. The Inca state was held together by about ten thousand miles of roads passable in all weathers by chains of runners who bore messages either orally or recorded in *quipu*, a code of knots in coloured cords. With this device elaborate records were kept. Though pre-literate, the Andean Empire was formidably totalitarian in the organization of its subjects' lives. The Incas became the ruling caste of the empire, its head becoming *Sapa Inca* – the "only Inca". His rule was a despotism based on the control of labour. The population was organized in units, of which the smallest was that of ten heads of families. From these units, labour service and produce were exacted. Careful and tight control kept population where it was needed; removal or marriage outside the local community was not allowed. All produce was state property; in this way agriculturists fed herdsmen and craftsmen and received textiles in exchange (the llama was the all-purpose beast of Andean culture, providing wool as well as transport, milk and meat). There was no commerce. Mining for precious metals and copper resulted in an exquisite adornment of Cuzco which amazed the Spaniards when they came to it. Tensions inside this system were not dealt with merely by force, but by the resettlement of loyal populations in a disaffected area and a strict control of the educational system in order to inculcate the notables of conquered peoples with the proper attitudes.

INCA CULTURE

Like the Aztecs, the Incas organized and exploited the achievements of culture which they found already to hand, though less brutally. Their aim was integration rather than obliteration and they tolerated the cults of conquered peoples. Their own god was the sun. The absence of literacy makes it hard to penetrate the mind of this civilization, but it is noticeable that, though in a different way, the Peruvians seem to have shared the Aztecs' preoccupation with death. Accidents of climate, as in Egypt, favoured its expression in rites of mummification; the dry air of the high Andes was as good a preservative as the sand of the desert. Beyond this it is not easy to say what divisions among the conquered peoples persisted and were expressed in the survival of tribal cults. When a challenge appeared from

On a high mountain ridge, around 45 miles (70 km) northwest of Cuzco, stand the ruins of the Inca city of Machu Picchu. A large rectangular plaza, surrounded by small stone houses, lies at the heart of the settlement. Terraces that were used for farming line the mountainside down to the Urubamba river, which flows along the valley floor 2,000 ft (600 m) below the city.

Europe it became apparent that Inca rule had not eliminated discontent among its subjects, for all its remarkable success.

THE LOST CIVILIZATIONS

All the American civilizations were in important and obvious ways very different from those of Asia or Europe. A complete literacy escaped them, though the Incas had good enough record-keeping processes to run complex governmental structures. Their technologies, though they had certain skills at a high level, were not so developed as those already known elsewhere. Though these civilizations provided satisfactory settings and institutions for cultures of intense (but limited) power, the contribution of the indigenous Americans to the world's future was not to be made through them, therefore. It had in fact already been made before they appeared, through the obscure, unrecorded discoveries of primitive cultivators who had first discovered how to exploit the ancestors of tomatoes, maize, potatoes and squash. In so doing they had unwittingly made a huge addition to the resources of humanity and were to change economies around the world. The glittering civilizations built on that in the Americas, though, were fated in the end to be no more than beautiful curiosities in the margin of world history, ultimately without progeny.

5 EUROPE: THE FIRST REVOLUTION

FEW TERMS HAVE SUCH misleading connotations as the "Middle Ages". A wholly Eurocentric usage meaning nothing in the history of other traditions, the phrase embodies the negative idea that no interest attaches to certain centuries except for their position in time. They were first singled out and labelled by people in the fifteenth and sixteenth centuries, seeking to recapture a classical antiquity long cut off from them. In that remote past, they thought, people had done and made great things; a sense of rebirth and quickening of civilization upon them, they could believe that in their own day great things were being done once more. But in between two periods of creativity they saw only a void – *Medio Evo*, *Media Aetas* in the Latin they used – defined just by falling in between other ages, and in itself dull, uninteresting, barbaric. Thus they invented the Middle Ages.

The Church tried to fill the economic, social and ideological vacuum created in the West by the collapse of the Roman Empire in Europe. Pope Urban VI (1378–1389), portrayed in this engraving, was a key figure in one of the major religious conflicts of the Middle Ages: the Great Schism.

THE "MIDDLE AGES"

It was not long before people could see that there was a little more in this period of a thousand or so years of European history than a mere void. One way in which they gained perspective was by looking for the origins of what they knew; in the seventeenth century the English talked about a "Norman Yoke" supposedly laid on their ancestors and in the eighteenth century the French idealized their aristocracy by attributing its origins to Frankish Conquest. Such reflections, nonetheless, were very selective; in so far as the Middle Ages were thought of as a whole it was still, even

Time chart (711–1558)

711–1492 The Spanish Reconquest
1000–1300 Europe's first universities are founded
1066 The Norman conquest of England
1122 The Concordat of Worms (the Investiture Contest)
c.1200 The beginning of Venetian commercial and military power
1337–1558 The Hundred Years' War

500 — 1000 — 1500

two hundred years ago, often with mild contempt. Then, quite suddenly, came a great change. Men and women started to idealize those lost centuries as vigorously as their forebears had ignored them. Europeans began to fill out their picture of the past with historical novels about chivalry and their countryside with mock baronial castles inhabited by cotton-spinners and stock-brokers. More important, a huge effort of scholarship was then brought to bear on the records of these times, which still continues. In its earlier phases it encouraged some romanticized and over-enthusiastic responses to them. People came to idealize the unity of medieval Christian civilization and the seeming stability of its life, but in so doing blurred the huge variety within it.

AN AGE OF CHANGE

It is still very hard to be sure we understand the European Middle Ages. One crude distinction in this great tract of time nevertheless seems obvious enough: the centuries between the end of antiquity and the year 1000 or so now look very much like an age of foundation. Certain great markers then laid out the patterns of the future, though change was slow and its staying power still uncertain. Then, in the eleventh century, a change of pace can be sensed. New developments quicken and become discernible. It becomes clear, as time passes, that they are opening the way to something quite different. An age of adventure and revolution is beginning in Europe, and it will go on until European

The continent of Europe was personified in Greek myth as the youthful beauty Europa. She is seized and carried over the sea by Zeus in the form of a bull in this version depicted by François Boucher's *Rape of Europa*, which was painted in 1747.

history merges with the first age of global history.

This makes it hard to say when the Middle Ages "end". In many parts of Europe, they were still going strong at the end of the eighteenth century, the moment at which Europe's first independent offshoot had just come into existence across the Atlantic. Even in the new United States, there were many people who, like millions of Europeans, were still gripped by a supernatural view of life, and traditional religious views about it, much as medieval men and women had been five hundred years earlier. Many Europeans then lived lives which in their material dimensions were still those of their medieval forerunners. Yet at that moment, in many places the Middle Ages were long over in any important sense. Old institutions had gone or were crumbling, taking unquestioned traditions of authority with them. Here and there, something we can recognize as the life of the modern world was already going on. This became first possible, then likely, and finally unavoidable in what can now be seen as Europe's second major formative phase, and the first of her revolutionary eras.

Leo IX was appointed pontiff at the Council of Worms in 1048. His papacy was marked by a determined attempt to reform the Church. Leo's efforts to win over Byzantium, however, failed and led to the excommunication of Cerularius, the patriarch of Constantinople; both are portrayed in this 15th-century manuscript illustration.

THE CHURCH

THE CHURCH is a good place to begin the story of Europe's first revolutionary era. By "the Church" as an earthly institution, Christians mean the whole body of the faithful, lay and cleric alike. In this sense, in Catholic Europe, the Church came to be the same thing as society during the Middle Ages. By 1500 only a few Jews, visitors and slaves stood apart from the huge body of people who (at least formally) shared Christian beliefs. Europe was Christian. Explicit paganism had disappeared from the map between the Atlantic coasts of Spain and the eastern boundaries of Poland. This was a great qualitative as well as a quantitative change. The religious beliefs of Christians were the deepest spring of a whole civilization which had matured for hundreds of years and was not yet threatened seriously by division or at all by alternative mythologies. Christianity had come to define Europe's purpose and to give its life a transcendent goal. It was also the reason why a few Europeans first became conscious of themselves as members of a particular society, Christendom.

Nowadays, non-Christians are likely to think of something else as "the Church". People use the word to describe ecclesiastical institutions, the formal structures and organizations which maintain the life of worship and discipline of the believer. In this sense, too, the Church had come a long way by 1500. Whatever qualifications and ambiguities hung about it, its successes were huge; its failures might be great, too, but within the Church there were plenty of men who confidently insisted on the Church's power (and duty) to put them right. The Roman Church which had been a backwater of ecclesiastical life in late antiquity was, long before the fall of Constantinople, the possessor and focus of unprecedented power and influence. It had not only acquired new independence and importance but also had given a new temper to the Christian life since the eleventh century. Christianity then had become both more disciplined and more aggressive. It had also become more rigid: many doctrinal and liturgical practices dominant until our day are less than a thousand years old.

ECCLESIASTICAL REFORMS

The most important changes took roughly from 1000 to 1250, and they constituted a revolution. Their beginnings lay in the Cluniac movement. Four of the first eight abbots of Cluny were later canonized: seven of them were outstanding men. They advised popes, acted as their legates, served emperors as ambassadors. They were men of culture, often of noble birth, sprung from the greatest families of Burgundy and the West Franks (a fact which helped to widen Cluny's influence) and they threw their weight behind the moral and spiritual reform of the Church. Leo IX, the pope with whom papal reform really begins, eagerly promoted Cluniac ideas. He spent barely six months of his five years' pontificate at Rome; instead, he visited synods in France and Germany, correcting local practice, checking interference with the Church by lay magnates, punishing clerical impropriety, imposing a new pattern of ecclesiastical discipline. Greater standardization of practice within the Church was one of the first results. It began to look more homogeneous.

Another outcome was the founding of a second great monastic order, the Cistercians (so named after the place of their first house, at Cîteaux), by monks dissatisfied with Cluny and anxious to return to the original strictness of the Benedictine rule, in particular by resuming the practical and manual labour Cluny had abandoned. A Cistercian monk, St Bernard, was to be the greatest leader and preacher of both Christian reform and crusade in the twelfth century, and his order had widespread influence both on monastic discipline and upon ecclesiastical architecture. It, too, pushed the Church towards greater uniformity and regularity.

INVESTITURE

The success of reform was also shown in the fervour and moral exaltation of the crusading movement, often a genuinely popular manifestation of religion. But new ways also aroused opposition, some of it among churchmen themselves. Bishops did not

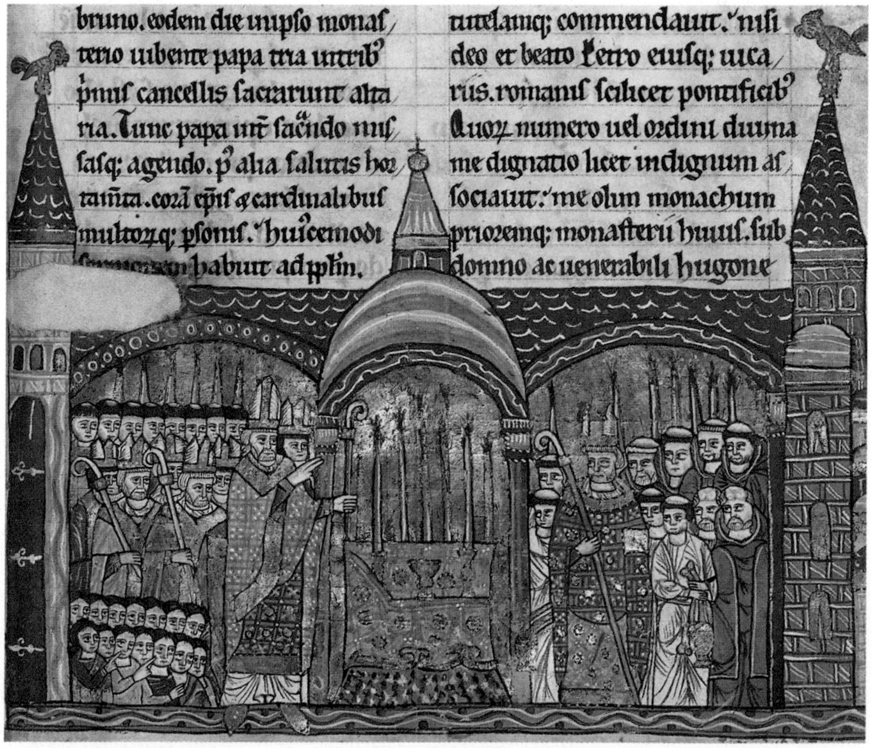

Pope Urban II is depicted consecrating one of the churches at Cluny in this 12th-century miniature.

always like papal interference in their affairs and parochial clergy did not always see a need to change inherited practices which their flock accepted (clerical marriage, for example). The most spectacular opposition to ecclesiastical reform came in the great quarrel which has gone down in history as the Investiture Contest. The attention given to it has been perhaps slightly disproportionate and, some would say, misleading. The central episodes lasted only a half-century or so and the issue was by no means clear-cut. The very distinction of Church and State implicit in some aspects of the quarrel was in anything like the modern sense still unthinkable to medieval people. The specific administrative and legal practices at issue were by and large quite soon the subject of agreement and many clergy felt more loyalty to their lay rulers than to the Roman Pope. Much of what was at stake, too, was very material. What was in dispute was the sharing of power and wealth within the ruling classes who supplied the personnel of both royal and ecclesiastical government in Germany and Italy, the lands of the Holy Roman Empire. Yet other countries were touched by similar quarrels – the French in the late eleventh century, the English in the early twelfth – because there was a transcendent question of principle at stake which did not go away: what was the proper relationship of lay and ecclesiastical authority?

HILDEBRAND

The most public battle of the Investiture Contest was fought just after the election of Pope Gregory VII in 1073. Hildebrand (Gregory's name before his election: hence the adjective "Hildebrandine" sometimes used of his policies and times) was a far from attractive person, but a pope of great personal and moral courage. He had been one of Leo IX's advisers and fought all his life for the independence and dominance of the papacy within western Christendom. He was an Italian, but not a Roman, and this, perhaps, explains why before he was himself pope he played a prominent part in the transfer of papal election to the college of cardinals, and the exclusion from it of the Roman lay nobility. When reform became a matter of politics and law rather than morals and manners (as it did during his twelve years' pontificate) Hildebrand was likely to provoke rather than avoid conflict. He was a lover of decisive action without too nice a regard for possible consequences.

Perhaps strife was already inevitable. At the core of reform lay the ideal of an independent Church. It could only perform its task,

Henry IV, accompanied by Hugo, abbot of Cluny, is depicted here imploring Countess Matilda of Tuscany to intercede on his behalf with Pope Gregory VII.

thought Leo and his followers, if free from lay interference. The Church should stand apart from the state and the clergy should live lives different from laymen's lives: they should be a distinct society within Christendom. From this ideal came the attacks on simony (the buying of preferment), the campaign against the marriage of priests, and a fierce struggle over the exercise of hitherto uncontested lay interference in appointment and promotion. This last gave its name to the long quarrel over lay "investiture": who rightfully appointed to a vacant bishopric – the temporal ruler or the Church? The right was symbolized in the act of giving his ring and staff to the new bishop when he was invested with his see.

Further potential for trouble lay in more mundane issues. Perhaps the emperors were bound to find themselves in conflict with the papacy sooner or later, once it ceased to be in need of them against other enemies, for they inherited big, if shadowy claims of authority from the past which they could hardly abandon without a struggle. In Germany the Carolingian tradition had subordinated the Church to a royal protection which easily blurred into domination. Furthermore, within Italy the empire had allies, clients and interests to defend. Since the tenth century, both the emperors' practical control of the papacy and their formal authority had declined. The new way of electing popes left the emperor with a theoretical veto and no more. The working relationship, too, had deteriorated in that some popes had already begun to dabble in troubled waters by seeking support among the emperor's vassals.

Scenes from the life of Pope Gregory VII, who was born c.1020 in the Italian region of Tuscany. Having worked in the service of the papal *curia* for more than 20 years, notably as an emissary to France and Germany, he was elected pope on 22 April 1073.

THE CLASH WITH HENRY IV

The temperament of Gregory VII was no emollient in this delicate situation. Once elected, he took his throne without imperial assent, simply informing the emperor of the fact. Two years later he issued a decree on lay investiture. Curiously, what it actually said has not survived, but its general content is known: Gregory forbade any layman to invest a cleric with a bishopric or other ecclesiastical office, and excommunicated some of the emperor's clerical councillors on the grounds that they had been guilty of simony in purchasing their preferment. To cap matters, Gregory summoned Henry IV, the Holy Roman Emperor, to appear before him and defend himself against charges of misconduct.

Henry responded at first through the Church itself; he got a German synod to declare Gregory deposed. This earned him excommunication, which would have mattered less had he not faced powerful enemies in Germany who now had the pope's support. The result was that Henry had to give way.

This illustration graphically encapsulates the resolution of the confrontation between pope and emperor. God is shown handing St Peter's keys, the symbol of spiritual power, to the pope and a sword, the symbol of secular power, to the emperor.

To avoid trial before the German bishops presided over by Gregory (who was already on his way to Germany), Henry came in humiliation to Canossa, where he waited in the snow barefoot until Gregory would receive his penance in one of the most dramatic of all confrontations of lay and spiritual authority. But Gregory had not really won. Not much of a stir was caused by Canossa at the time. The pope's position was too extreme: he went beyond canon law to assert a revolutionary doctrine, that kings were but officers who could be removed when the pope judged them unfit or unworthy. This was almost unthinkably subversive to people whose moral horizons were dominated by the idea of the sacredness of oaths of fealty; it foreshadowed later claims to papal monarchy but was bound to be unacceptable to any king.

Investiture ran on as an issue for the next fifty years. Gregory lost the sympathy he had won through Henry's bullying and it was not until 1122 that another emperor agreed to a concordat which was seen as a papal victory, though one diplomatically disguised. Yet Gregory had been a true pioneer; he had differentiated clerics and laymen as never before and had made unprecedented claims for the distinction and superiority of papal power. More would be heard of them in the next two centuries. Though his immediate successors acted less dramatically than he, they steadily pressed papal claims to papal advantage. Urban II used the first crusade to become the diplomatic leader of Europe's lay monarchs; they looked to Rome, not the empire. Urban also built up the Church's administrative machine; under him emerged the *curia*, a Roman bureaucracy which corresponded to the household administrations of the English and French kings. Through it the papal grip on the Church itself was strengthened. In 1123, a historic date, the first ecumenical council was held in the West and its decrees were promulgated in the pope's own name. And all the time, papal jurisprudence and jurisdiction ground away; more and more legal disputes found their way from the local church courts to papal judges, whether resident at Rome, or sitting locally.

St Thomas à Becket (1118–1170) was appointed chancellor of England by Henry II in 1154. In 1162 he was chosen as archbishop of Canterbury, being ordained as a priest only the day before his consecration. As a consequence of his actions in defence of the independence of the Church, Becket was exiled to France in 1164, from where he threatened to excommunicate the English king. In 1170 Becket returned to England, where he was murdered in Canterbury Cathedral by the king's knights – an event depicted in this 14th-century manuscript illustration.

THE PAPAL MONARCHY

Prestige, dogma, political skill, administrative pressure, judicial practice and the control of more and more benefices all buttressed the new ascendancy of the papacy within the Church. By 1100 the groundwork was done for the emergence of a true papal monarchy. As the investiture contest receded, secular princes were on the whole well disposed to Rome and it appeared that no essential ground had been lost by the papacy. There was indeed a spectacular quarrel in England over the question of clerical privilege and immunity from the law of the land which would be an issue of the future; immediately, it provoked the murder (and then the canonization) of Becket, the archbishop of Canterbury. But on the whole, the large legal immunities of clergy were not much challenged. Under Innocent III papal pretensions to monarchical authority reached a new theoretical height. True, Innocent did not go quite so far as Gregory. He did not claim an absolute plenitude of temporal power everywhere in western Christendom, but he said that the papacy had by its authority transferred the empire from the Greeks to the Franks. Within the Church his power was limited by little but the inadequacies of the bureaucratic machine through which he had to operate. Yet papal power was still often deployed in support of the reforming ideas – which shows that much remained to be done.

Clerical celibacy became more common and more widespread. Among new practices which were pressed on the Church in the thirteenth century was that of frequent individual confession, a powerful instrument of control in a religiously minded and anxiety-ridden society. Among doctrinal innovations, the theory of transubstantiation, that by a mystical process the body and blood of Christ were actually present in the bread and wine used in the communion service, was imposed from the thirteenth century onwards.

THE GREAT GOTHIC CATHEDRALS

The final christening of Europe in the central Middle Ages was a great spectacle. Monastic reform and papal autocracy were wedded to

Gothic architecture

The term Gothic, first used by the Florentine writer Giorgio Vasari, defines an architectural style which developed in Europe at the beginning of the 12th century and lasted until the end of the 15th century. It originated in France where, during the 12th and 13th centuries, the most notable Gothic cathedrals were constructed, including Chartres (built on the site of the old Romanesque cathedral), Amiens, Paris (the true centre of Gothic culture) and Reims.

Chartres Cathedral was built between 1195 and 1240 and has been referred to as an incarnation of medieval thought. With its 10,000 painted and sculpted figures, it represents one of the greatest endeavours ever carried out in the name of Christian education.

The emergence of the Gothic style heralded an architectural and artistic revolution. Some of the most representative elements of this impressive architectural style include pointed arches, the disappearance of partition walls, windows divided up by columns and curved-stone decorations, pinnacles on buttresses, and finials on towers and spires.

Gothic art spread throughout Europe and had clearly differentiated phases: the "classic Gothic" style, the best examples of which can be found in France; the "late Gothic" style, which developed in the 14th century (the most important characteristic of which was the recognition of artistic individuality); and a final "flamboyant" period, characterized partly by its asymmetry.

The ambulatory around the sanctuary of Chartres Cathedral.

In this 14th-century Gothic mural from the Cerco church in Artajona (northeastern Spain), various scenes from the life of St Saturnin are depicted. The saint was the first bishop of the French city of Toulouse during the 3rd century.

intellectual effort and the deployment of new wealth in architecture to make this the next peak of Christian history after the age of the Fathers. It was an achievement whose most fundamental work lay, perhaps, in intellectual and spiritual developments, but it became most visible in stone. What we think of as "Gothic" architecture was the creation of this period. It produced the European landscape which, until the coming of the railway, was dominated or punctuated by a church tower or spire rising above a little town. Until the twelfth century the major buildings of the Church were usually monastic; then began the building of the astonishing series of cathedrals, especially in northern France and England, which remains one of the great glories of European art and, together with castles, constitutes the major architecture of the Middle Ages. There was great popular enthusiasm, it seems, for these huge investments, though it is difficult to penetrate to the mental attitudes behind them. Analogies might be sought in the feeling of twentieth-century enthusiasts for space exploration, but this omits the supernatural dimension of these great buildings. They were both offerings to God and an essential part of the instrumentation of evangelism and education on earth. About their huge naves and aisles moved the processions of relics and the crowds of pilgrims who had come to see them. Their windows were filled with the images of the biblical story which was the core of European culture; their façades were covered with the didactic representations of the fate awaiting just and unjust. Christianity achieved in them a new publicity and collectiveness. Nor is it possible to assess the full impact of these great churches on the imagination of medieval Europeans without reminding ourselves how much greater was the contrast their splendour presented to the reality of everyday life than any imaginable today.

THE FRANCISCANS

The power and penetration of organized Christianity were further reinforced by the appearance of new religious orders. Two were outstanding: the mendicant Franciscans and Dominicans, who in England came to be called respectively the Grey and Black Friars, from the colours of their habits. The Franciscans were true revolutionaries: their founder, St Francis of Assisi, left his family to lead a life of poverty among the sick, the needy and the

St Francis of Assisi

St Francis of Assisi was born into a noble family in 1181. In 1206 he enlisted in the pontifical army, which was fighting against the emperor. Before going into combat, however, St Francis had a vision that prompted him to leave the army and dedicate himself to prayer and charity. After two years of living as a hermit, he began to attract disciples and in 1210 Pope Innocent III approved the Franciscan Rule.

The new rule's key element was its ideal of poverty, in imitation of Christ's own rejection of material wealth, described in the New Testament. In 1212, with his sister Clare, St Francis founded the female branch of his rule, later known as the Poor Clares. Between 1213 and 1214, after a thwarted trip to the Holy Land, St Francis settled in Spain where he tried to evangelize the Muslims. In 1219 he undertook a journey to Palestine and Egypt, where he attempted to convert the sultan. In 1221, in collaboration with Cardinal Ugolino of Conti, the first written rule of the Franciscan Order was compiled.

An illness contracted on his journey to the East was the cause of St Francis' death on 3 October 1226. He was canonized by Pope Gregory IX in 1228. In 1980 St Francis was designated patron saint of ecology.

Giotto (1266–1336) painted three huge cycles of frescos representing the life of St Francis of Assisi. This mural from Santa Croce in Florence shows St Francis trying to convert the Egyptian sultan.

leprous. The followers who soon gathered about him eagerly took up a life directed towards the imitation of Christ's poverty and humility. There was at first no formal organization and Francis was never a priest, but Innocent III, shrewdly seizing the opportunity of patronizing this potentially divisive movement instead of letting it escape from control, bade them elect a Superior. Through him the new fraternity owed and maintained rigorous obedience to the Holy See. They could provide a counterweight to local episcopal authority because they could preach without the licence of the bishop of the diocese. The older monastic orders recognized a danger and opposed the Franciscans, but the friars prospered, despite internal quarrels. In the end they acquired a substantial administrative structure of their own, but they always remained peculiarly the evangelists of the poor and the mission field.

THE DOMINICANS AND THE PERSECUTION OF HERETICS

The Dominicans were founded to further a narrower end. Their founder was a Castilian priest who went to preach in the Languedoc to heretics, the Albigensians. From his companions grew a new preaching order; when Dominic died in 1221 his seventeen followers had become over five hundred friars. Like the Franciscans, they were mendicants vowed to poverty, and like them, too, they threw themselves into missionary work. But their impact was primarily intellectual and they became a great force in a new institution of great importance, just taking shape: the first universities. Dominicans came also to provide many of the personnel of the Inquisition, an organization to combat heresy, which appeared in the early thirteenth century. From the fourth century onwards, churchmen had urged the persecution of heretics. Yet the first papal condemnation of them did not come until 1184. Only under Innocent III did persecution come to be the duty of Catholic kings. The Albigensians were certainly not Catholic, but there is some doubt whether they should really be regarded even as Christian heretics. Their beliefs reflect Manichaean doctrines. They were dualists, some of whom rejected all material creation as evil. Like those of many later heretics, heterodox religious views were taken to imply aberration or at least nonconformity in social and moral practices. Innocent III seems to have decided to persecute the Albigensians after the murder of a papal legate in the Languedoc, and in 1209 a crusade was launched against them. It attracted many laymen (especially from northern France) because of the chance it offered for a quick grab at the lands and homes of the Albigensians, but it also marked a great innovation: the joining of State and Church in Western Christendom to crush by force dissent which

In this painting by the Spanish artist Pedro Berruguete (c.1450–1504), St Dominic is depicted overseeing the burning of the Albigensians' books, a fate only the Holy Bible was spared.

might place either in danger. It was for a long time an effective device, though never completely so.

In judging the theory and practice of medieval intolerance it must be remembered that the danger in which society was felt to stand from heresy was appalling: its members might face everlasting torment. Yet persecution did not prevent the appearance of new heresies again and again in the next three centuries, because they expressed real needs. Heresy was, in one sense, an exposure of a hollow core in the success which the Church had so spectacularly achieved. Heretics were living evidence of dissatisfaction with the outcome of a long and often heroic battle. Other critics would also make themselves heard in due course and different ways. Papal monarchical theory provoked counter-doctrinc; thinkers would argue that the Church had a defined sphere of activity which did not extend to meddling in secular affairs. As individuals became more conscious of national communities and respectful of their claims, this would seem more and more appealing. The rise of mystical religion was yet another phenomenon always tending to slip outside the ecclesiastical structure. In movements like the Brethren of the Common Life, following the teachings of the mystic Thomas à Kempis, laymen created religious practices and devotional forms which sometimes escaped from clerical control.

THE WORLDLINESS OF THE MEDIEVAL CHURCH

Mystical religious movements expressed the great paradox of the medieval Church. It had risen to a pinnacle of power and wealth. It deployed vast estates, tithes, and papal taxation in the service of a magnificent hierarchy, whose worldly greatness reflected the glory of God and whose lavish cathedrals, great monastic churches, splendid liturgies, learned foundations and libraries embodied the devotion and

Lincoln Cathedral in England was constructed between 1123 and 1233. This view down the central aisle gives an impression of the grandeur of this building and of the many other similar cathedrals that were erected in Europe in the Gothic period.

sacrifices of the faithful. Yet the point of this huge concentration of power and grandeur was to preach a faith at whose heart lay the glorification of poverty and humility and the superiority of things not of this world.

The worldliness of the Church drew increasing criticism. It was not just that a few ecclesiastical magnates lolled back upon the cushion of privilege and endowment to gratify their appetites and neglect their flocks. There was also a more subtle corruption inherent in power. The identification of the defence of the faith with the triumph of an institution had given the Church an increasingly bureaucratic and legalistic face. The point had arisen as early as the days of St Bernard; even then, there were too many ecclesiastical lawyers, it was said. By the mid-thirteenth century legalism was blatant. The papacy itself was soon criticized. At the death of Innocent III the Church of comfort and of the sacraments was already obscured behind the granite face of centralization. The claims of religion were confused with the assertiveness of an ecclesiastical monarchy demanding freedom from constraint of any sort. It was already difficult to keep the government of the Church in the hands of men of spiritual stature; Martha was pushing Mary aside, because administrative and legal gifts were needed to run a machine which more and more generated its own purposes.

The claim to papal supremacy

"The faith commands us to recognize only one and holy Church, which has only one body and one head: it has two swords, a spiritual one and a material one; both swords, the spiritual and the material, are under the power of the Church and must be used for the Church; one for the priests, the other for the kings and warriors, but according to the priest's instructions and when he permits it ... . He represents spiritual power sent to instruct man on earth, and correct him when he is not good. Consequently, when the earthly power is led astray it should be put back on the right path by the spiritual, as should be the inferior spiritual power by the superior, but the supreme power can only be corrected by God and not by any man. Therefore whoever opposes this power established by God opposes the order of God."

An extract from Boniface VIII's papal bull, *Unam Sanctam* (November, 1302).

BONIFACE VIII

In 1294 a hermit of renowned piety was elected pope. The hopes this roused were quickly dashed. Celestine V was forced to resign within a few weeks, seemingly unable to impose his reforming wishes on the *curia*. His successor was Boniface VIII. He has been called the last medieval pope because he embodied all the pretensions of the papacy at its most political and its most arrogant. He was by training a lawyer and by temperament far from a man of spirituality. He quarrelled violently with the kings of both England and France and in the Jubilee of 1300 had two swords carried before him to symbolize his possession of temporal as well as spiritual power. Two years later he asserted that a belief in the sovereignty of the pope over every human being was necessary to salvation.

Under him the long battle with kings came to a head. Nearly a hundred years before, England had been laid under interdict by the pope; this terrifying sentence forbade the administration of any of the sacraments while the king remained unrepentant and unreconciled. Men and women could not have their children baptized or obtain absolution for their own sins, and those were fearful

A 16th-century portrait of the humanist Italian writer Francesco Petrarch (1304–1374), who spent much of his life in papal Avignon.

deprivations in a believing age. King John had been forced to yield. A century later, things had changed. Bishops and their clergy were often estranged from Rome, which had undermined their authority, too. They could sympathize with a stirring national sense of opposition to the papacy whose pretensions reached their peak under Boniface. When the kings of France and England rejected his authority they found churchmen to support them. They also had resentful Italian noblemen to fight for them. In 1303 some of them (in French pay) pursued the old pope to his native city and there seized him with, it was said, appalling physical indignity. His fellow townsmen released Boniface and he was not (like Celestine, whom he had put in prison) to die in confinement, but die he did, no doubt of shock, a few weeks later.

This was only the beginning of a bad time for the papacy and, some would claim, for the Church. For more than four centuries it was to face recurrent and mounting waves of hostility which, though often heroically met, ended by calling Christianity itself in question. Even by the end of Boniface's reign, the legal claims he had made were almost beside the point; no one stirred to avenge him. Now spiritual failure increasingly drew fire; henceforth the papacy was to be condemned more for standing in the way of reform than for claiming too much of kings. For a long time, though, criticism had important limits. The notion of autonomous, self-justified criticism was unthinkable in the Middle Ages: it was for failures in their traditional religious task that churchmen were criticized.

THE AVIGNON PAPACY

In 1309 a French pope brought the papal *curia* to Avignon, a town belonging to the king of Naples but overshadowed by the power of the French kings whose lands overlooked it. There was to be a preponderance of French cardinals, too, during the papal residence at Avignon (which lasted until 1377). The English and Germans soon believed the popes had become the tool of the French kings and took steps against the independence of the Church in their own territories. The imperial electors declared that their vote required no approval or confirmation by the pope and that the imperial power came from God alone.

At Avignon the popes lived in a huge palace, whose erection was a symbol of their decision to stay away from Rome, and whose luxury was a symbol of growing worldliness. The papal court was of unexampled magnificence, attended by a splendid train of servitors and administrators paid for by ecclesiastical taxation and misappropriation. Unfortunately the fourteenth century was a time of economic disaster; a much-reduced population was being asked to pay more for

The Great Schism at Avignon

In 1309 Pope Clement V fixed his residence in Avignon at the request of the French king Philip the Fair. The reasons for this papal exodus from Rome were complex. The role of the pope as the visible head of Christianity and as arbiter in conflicts between the various monarchies was in decline. The burgeoning power of the national monarchies and the appearance of new social sectors were making it impossible for the pope to control European politics.

In 1377 Gregory XI moved the pontifical headquarters back to Rome; he died one year later in the Eternal City. In the campaign to choose his successor, two factions emerged, one pro-Italian and the other formed mainly by French cardinals. Urban VI was elected but then rejected by the French cardinals, who, on 20 September 1378, appointed Robert of Geneva as pope, under the name of Clement VII. This brought about the Great Schism of Avignon.

This imposing palace-fortress was the headquarters of the popes during the years they spent in Avignon. Its construction, begun by Benedict XII (1333–1342), was continued by Clement VI and completed in the time of Innocent VI (1352–1366).

a more costly (and, some said, extravagant) papacy. Centralization continued to breed corruption – the abuse of the papal rights to appoint to vacant benefices was an obvious instance – and accusations of simony and pluralism had more and more plausibility. The personal conduct of the higher clergy was more and more obviously at variance with apostolic ideals. A crisis arose among the Franciscans themselves, some of the brothers, the "spirituals", insisting that they take seriously their founder's rule of poverty, while their more relaxed colleagues refused to give up the wealth which had come to their order. Theological issues became entangled with this dispute. Soon there were Franciscans preaching that Avignon was Babylon, the scarlet whore of the Apocalypse, and that the papacy's overthrow was at hand, while a pope, asserting that Christ Himself had respected property, condemned the ideal of apostolic poverty and unleashed the Inquisition against the "spirituals". They were burned for their preachings, but not before they had won audiences.

THE GREAT SCHISM

The exile in Avignon fed a popular anticlericalism and anti-papalism different from that of kings exasperated against priests who would not accept their jurisdiction. Many of the clergy themselves felt that rich abbeys and worldly bishops were a sign of a Church that had become secularized. This was the irony that tainted the legacy of Gregory VII. Criticism eventually rose to the point at which the papacy returned to Rome in 1377, only to face the greatest scandal in the history of the Church, a "Great Schism". Secular monarchs set on having quasi-national churches in their own realms, and the college of twenty or so cardinals, manipulating the papacy so as to maintain their own revenues and position, together brought about the election of two popes, the second by the French cardinals alone. For thirty years popes at Rome and Avignon simultaneously claimed the headship of the Church. Eight years afterwards there was a third contender as well. As the schism wore on, the criticism directed against the papacy became more and more virulent. "Antichrist" was a favourite term of abuse for the claimant to the patrimony of St Peter. It was complicated by the involvement of secular rivalries, too. For the Avignon pope, broadly, there stood as allies France, Scotland, Aragon and Milan; the Roman was supported by England, the German emperors, Naples and Flanders.

THE CONCILIAR MOVEMENT

The schism at one moment seemed to promise renovation and reformation. The instrument to which reformers turned was an ecumenical or general council of the Church; some claimed for it an authority over-riding that of the pope. In any case, to return to the days of the apostles and the Fathers for a way of putting the papal house in order sounded good sense to many Catholics. Unfortunately, the idea did not turn out well. Four councils were held. The first, held at Pisa in 1409, struck out boldly, proclaiming the deposition of both popes and choosing another. This meant there were now three pretenders to the chair of St Peter; moreover, when the new one died after a few months, another was elected whose choice was said to be tainted by simony (this was the first John XXIII, now no longer recognized as an authentic pope and the victim of one of Gibbon's most searing judgments). The next council (Constance, 1414–18) removed John (though he had summoned it), got one of his competitors to abdicate and then deposed the third pretender. At last there could be a fresh start; the schism was healed. In 1417 a new pope was elected, Martin V. This was a success, but some people had hoped for more; they had sought reform and the council had been diverted from that. Instead it had devoted its time to heresy, and support for reform dwindled once the unity of the papacy was restored. After another council (Siena, 1423–4) had been dissolved by Martin V for urging reform ("that the Supreme Pontiff should be called to account was perilous," he declared), the last met at Basle (1431–49), but was ineffective long before its dissolution. The conciliar movement had not achieved the desired reform and papal power was restored. The principle that there existed an alternative conciliar source of authority inside the Church was for the next four hundred years regarded with suspicion at Rome. Within a few years it was declared heresy to appeal from the pope to a general council.

PAPAL AUTHORITY WEAKENED

The Church had not risen to the level of the crisis now upon it. The papacy had maintained its superiority, but its victory was only partial; secular rulers had reaped the benefits of anti-papal feeling in new freedoms for national Churches. As for the moral authority of Rome, that had clearly not been restored and one result would be a more damaging movement for reform three-quarters of a century later. The papacy had already begun to look more and more Italian, and so it was to remain. There were some dismal popes to come in the next two centuries, but that did less damage to the Church than the evolution of their See towards becoming just one more Italian state.

WYCLIF AND HUS

Heresy, always smouldering, had burst out in a blaze of reforming zeal during the conciliar period. Two outstanding men, Wyclif in England and Hus in Bohemia, focused the discontents to which schism had given rise. They were first and foremost ecclesiastical reformers, although Wyclif was a teacher and thinker rather than a man of action. Hus became the leader of a movement which involved national as well as ecclesiastical issues; he exercised huge influence as a preacher in Prague. He was condemned by the council of Constance for heretical views on predestination and property and was burned in 1415. The great impulse given by Wyclif and Hus flagged as their criticisms were muffled, but they had tapped the vein of national anti-papalism which was to prove so destructive of the unity of the Western Church. Catholics and Hussites were still disputing Bohemia in bitter civil wars twenty years after Hus's death. Meanwhile, the papacy itself made concessions in its diplomacy with the lay monarchies of the fifteenth century.

CHANGES IN POPULAR RELIGION

Religious zeal in the fifteenth century more and more appeared to bypass the central apparatus of the Church. Fervour manifested itself in a continuing flow of mystical writing and in new fashions in popular religion. A new obsession with the agony of the Passion appears in pictorial art; new devotions to saints, a craze for flagellation, outbreaks of dancing frenzy all show a heightened excitability. An outstanding example of the appeal and power of a popular preacher can be seen in Savonarola, a Dominican, whose immense success made him for a time moral dictator of Florence in the 1490s. But religious fervour often escaped the formal and ecclesiastical structures.

In the fourteenth and fifteenth centuries much of the emphasis of popular religion was individual and devotional. Another impression of the inadequacy of both vision and machinery within the hierarchies is also to be found in a neglect of missionary work outside Europe.

The execution of the convicted heretic John Hus is depicted in this 15th-century drawing. The accused had been paraded through the streets of Constance wearing a hat decorated with two devils arguing over which one would get his soul. The last words Hus spoke were: "I will die today in the light of the truth of the Gospel which I have preached and taught."

A RELIGIOUS CIVILIZATION

All in all, the fifteenth century leaves a sense of withdrawal, an ebbing after a big effort which had lasted nearly two centuries. Yet to leave the medieval Church with that impression uppermost in our minds would be to risk a grave misunderstanding of a society made

The central panel of *The Last Judgment*, a triptych by the German artist Stephan Lochner. Painted between 1435 and 1440, this was originally an altarpiece for the church of St Lawrence in Cologne.

more different from our own by religion than by any other factor. Europe was still Christendom and was so even more consciously after 1453. Within its boundaries, almost the whole of life was defined by religion. All power flowed ultimately from God. The Church was for most men and women the only recorder and authenticator of the great moments of their existence – their marriages, their children's births and baptisms, their deaths. Many of them wholly gave themselves up to it: a much greater proportion of the population became monks and nuns than is the case today, but though they might think of withdrawal to the cloister from a hostile everyday existence, what they left behind was no secular world such as ours, wholly distinct from and indifferent to the Church. Learning, charity, administration, justice and huge stretches of economic life all fell within the ambit and regulation of religion. Even when laymen attacked churchmen, they did so in the name of the standards the Church had itself taught them and with appeals to the knowledge of God's purposes it had given to them. Religious myth was not only the deepest spring of a civilization, it was still the life of everyone. It defined human purpose and did so in terms of a transcendent good. Outside the Church, the community of all believers, lay only paganism. The devil – conceived in a most material form – lay in wait for those who strayed from the path of grace. If there were some bishops and even popes among the errant, so much the worse for them. Human frailty could not compromise the religious view of life. God's justice would be shown and He would divide sheep from goats on the Day of Wrath when all things would end.

PRINCIPALITIES AND POWERS

MOST PEOPLE TODAY are used to the idea of the State. It is generally agreed that the world's surface is divided up between impersonal organizations working through officials marked out in special ways, and that such organizations provide the final public

Europe in the Middle Ages

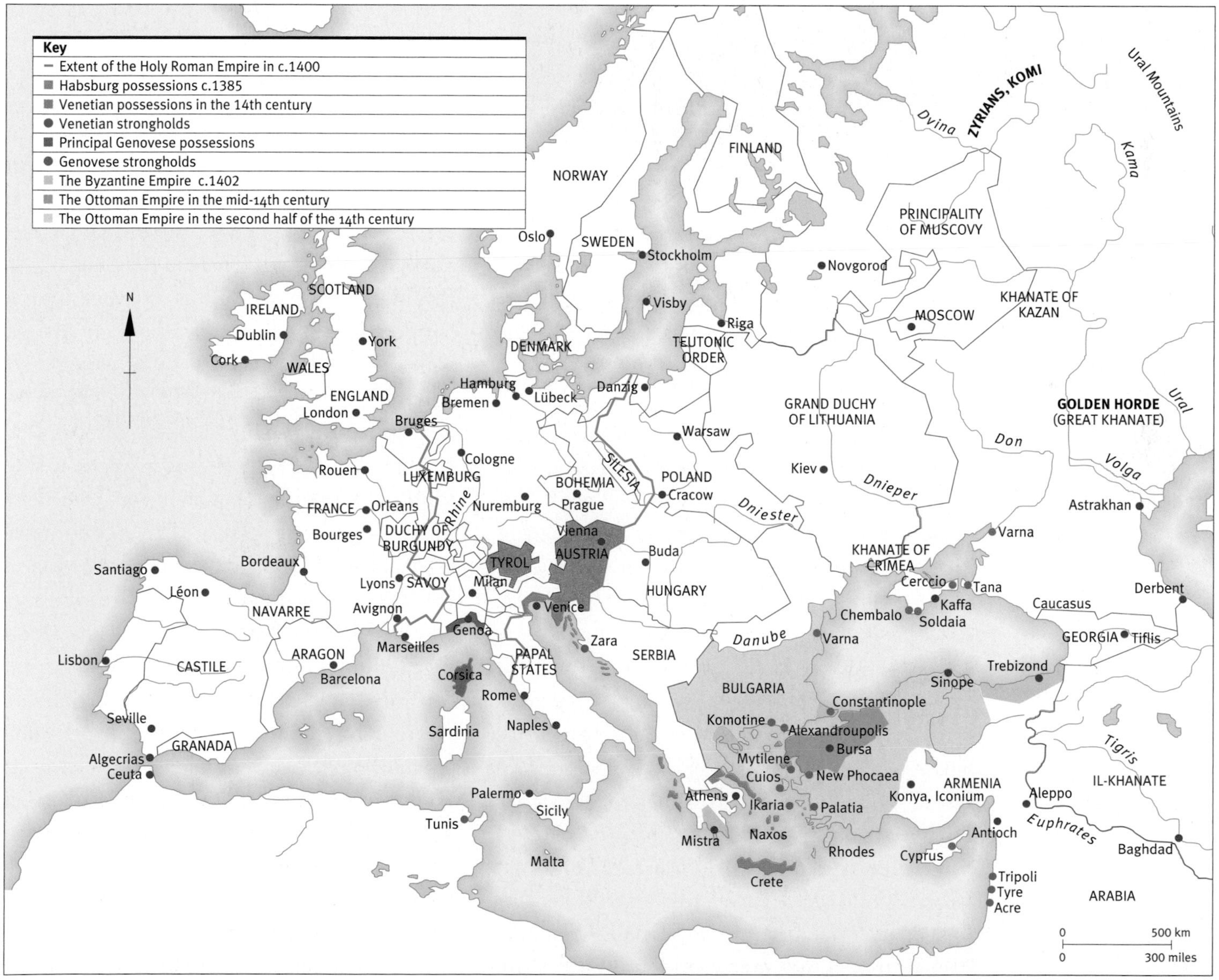

This map shows European political divisions between the 13th and 15th centuries.

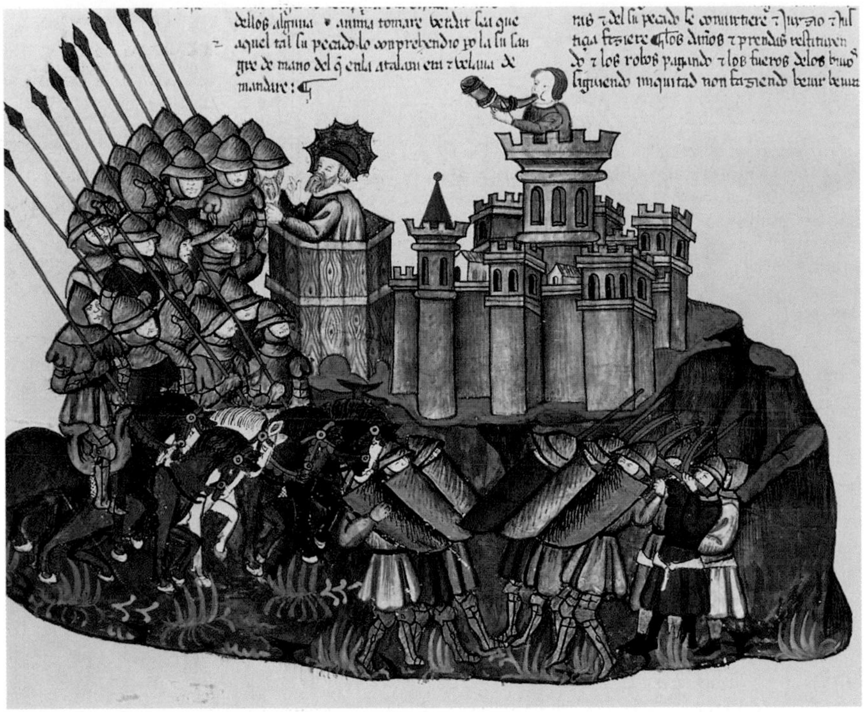

This 16th-century miniature depicts an attack on a castle. Medieval castles were not merely military establishments: they also served as centres of political power and social organization, and were often crucial to the local economy.

authority for any given area. Often, states are thought to represent people or nations. But whether they do or not, states are the building blocks from which most of us would construct a political account of the modern world.

None of this would have been intelligible to a European in 1000; five hundred years later much of it might well have been, depending on who the European was. The process by which the modern state emerged, though far from complete by 1500, is one of the markers which delimit the modern era of history. The realities had come first, before principles and ideas. From the thirteenth century onwards many rulers, usually kings, were able for a variety of reasons to increase their power over those they ruled. This was often because they could keep up large armies and arm them with the most effective weapons. Iron cannons were invented in the early fourteenth century; bronze followed, and in the next century big cast-iron guns became available. With their appearance, great men could no longer brave the challenges of their rulers from behind the walls of their castles. Steel crossbows, too, gave a big advantage to those who could afford them. Many rulers were by 1500 well on the way to exercising a monopoly of the use of armed force within their realms. They were arguing more, too, about the frontiers they shared, and this expressed more than just better techniques of surveying. It marked a change in emphasis within government, from a claim to control persons who had a particular relationship to the ruler to one to control people who lived in a certain area. Territorial was replacing personal dependence.

ROYAL BUREAUCRACIES

Over territorial agglomerations, royal power was increasingly exercised directly through officials who, like weaponry, had to be paid for. A kingship which worked through vassals known to the king, who did much of his work for him in return for his favours and who supported him in the field when his needs went beyond what his own estates could supply, gave way to one in which royal government was carried out by employees, paid for by taxes (more and more in cash, not kind), the raising of which was one of their most important tasks. The parchment of charters and rolls began by the sixteenth century to give way to the first trickles and rivulets of what was to become the flood of modern bureaucratic paper.

Such a sketch hopelessly blurs this immensely important and complicated change. It was linked to every side of life: to religion and the sanctions and authority it embodied; to the economy, the resources it offered and the social possibilities it opened or closed; to ideas and the pressure they exerted on still plastic institutions. But the upshot is not in doubt. Somehow, Europe was beginning by 1500 to organize itself differently from the Europe of Carolingians and Ottonians. Though personal and local ties were to remain for centuries overwhelmingly the most important ones for most Europeans, society was institutionalized in a different way from that of the days when even tribal loyalties still counted. The relationship of lord and vassal which, with the vague claims of pope and emperor in the background, so long seemed to exhaust political thought, was beginning to give way to an idea of princely power over all the inhabitants of a domain which, in extreme assertions (such as that of Henry VIII of England that a prince knew no external superior save God) was really quite new.

THE APPEAL OF MONARCHY

Necessarily, changes in political thinking neither took place everywhere in the same way nor at the same pace. By 1800 France and England would have been for centuries unified in a way that Germany and Italy were still not. But wherever it happened, the centre of the process was usually the steady aggrandizement of royal families. Kings enjoyed great advantages. If they ran their affairs carefully they had a more solid power base in their usually large (and sometimes very large) domains than had noblemen in their smaller estates. The kingly office had a mysterious aura about it, reflected in the solemn circumstances of coronations and anointings. Royal courts seemed to promise a more independent, less expensive justice than could be got from the local feudal lords. In the twelfth century, too, a new consciousness of the need for law began to appear and kings were in a powerful position to say what law was to run in their courts. They could therefore appeal not only to the resources of the feudal structure at whose head – or somewhere near it – they stood, but also to other forces outside. One of these, which was of growing importance, was the sense of nationhood.

Under the newly empowered monarchs, medieval society's institutions were very different from those that had existed when tribal loyalties still held sway. This manuscript illustration, dated c.1460, shows the judges of "The King's Bench", who made up England's highest court, and one which had originally sat only in the presence of the king himself.

NATIONHOOD

The idea of nationhood is another concept taken for granted nowadays, but we must be careful not to antedate it. No medieval state was national in our sense. Nevertheless, by 1500 the subjects of the kings of England and France could think of themselves as different from aliens who were not their fellow-subjects, even if they might also regard people who lived in the next village as virtually foreigners. Even two hundred years earlier this sort of distinction was being made between those born within and those born outside the realm and the sense of community of the native-born was steadily enhanced. One symptom was the appearance of belief in national patron saints; though churches had been dedicated to him under the Anglo-Saxon kings, only in the fourteenth century did

His tripartite *Divine Comedy* is the best-known work by the poet Dante Alighieri (1265–1321). This illustration depicts a scene described in verse 33 of the poem's first section, the *Inferno*.

St George's red cross on a white background became a kind of uniform for English soldiers when he was recognized as official protector of England (his exploit in killing the dragon had only been attributed to him in the twelfth century and may be the result of mixing him up with a legendary Greek hero, Perseus). Others were the writing of national histories (already foreshadowed by the Dark Age histories of the Germanic peoples) and the discovery of national heroes. In the twelfth century a Welshman more or less invented the mythological figure of Arthur, while an Irish chronicler of the same period built up an unhistorical myth of the High King Brian Boru and his defence of Christian Ireland against the Vikings. Above all, there was more vernacular literature. First Spanish and Italian, then French and English began to break through the barrier set about literary creativity by Latin. The ancestors of these tongues are recognizable in twelfth-century romances such as the Song of Roland, which transformed a defeat of Charlemagne by Pyrenean mountaineers into the glorious stand of his rearguard against the Arabs, or the Poem of the Cid, the epic of a Spanish national hero. With the fourteenth century came Dante, Langland and Chaucer, each of them writing in a language which we can read with little difficulty.

THE IMPORTANCE OF LOCAL COMMUNITIES

We must not exaggerate the immediate impact of the growing sense of nationhood. For centuries yet, family, local community, religion or trade were still to be the focus of most people's loyalties. Such national institutions as they could have seen growing among them would have done little to break into this conservatism; in few places was it more than a matter of the king's justices and the king's tax gatherers – and even in England, in some ways the most national of late medieval states, many people might never have seen either. The rural parishes and little towns of the Middle Ages, on the other hand, were real communities, and in ordinary times provided enough to think about in the way of social responsibilities. We really need another word than "nationalism" to suggest the occasional and fleeting glimpses of a community of the realm which might once in a while touch a medieval man, or even the irritation which might suddenly burst out in a riot against the presence of foreigners, whether workmen or merchants. (Medieval anti-Semitism, of course, had different roots.) Yet such hints of national feeling occasionally reveal the slow consolidation of support for new states in western Europe.

THE ANGLO-NORMANS

The first western European states to cover anything like the areas of their modern successors were England and France. A few thousand Normans had come over from France after the invasion of 1066 to Anglo-Saxon England to form a new ruling class. Their leader, William the Conqueror, gave them lands, but retained more for himself (the royal estates were larger than those of his Anglo-Saxon predecessors) and asserted an ultimate lordship over the rest: he was to be lord of the land and all men held what they held either directly or indirectly of him. He inherited the prestige and machinery of the old English monarchy, too, and this was important, for it raised him decisively above his fellow Norman warriors. The greatest of them became William's earls and barons, the lesser ones among them knights, ruling England at first from the wooden and earth castles which they spread over the length of the land.

They had conquered one of the most civilized societies in Europe, which went on under the Anglo-Norman kings to show unusual vigour. A few years after the Conquest, the English government carried out one of the most remarkable administrative

The legend of King Arthur, which clearly follows in the Celtic tradition, made its first literary appearance in the 12th-century tale *The History of the Kings of England* by Geoffrey of Monmouth. A scene from the legend is evoked in this illustration from a 14th-century manuscript of *The Quest for the Holy Grail*: while King Arthur is dying, Sir Bedivere flings the king's sword (Excalibur) into the water, where it is seized by the Lady of the Lake.

Chaucer's *Canterbury Tales*

"A KNIGHT ther was, and that a worthy man,
That fro the tyme that he first bigan
To riden out, he loved chivalrie,
Trouthe and honour, fredom and curteisie.
Ful worthy was he in his lordes werre,
And therto hadde he riden, no man ferre,
As wel in cristendom as in hethenesse,
And evere honoured for his worthynesse.
At Alisaundre he was whan it was wonne.
Ful ofte tyme he hadde the bord bigonne
Aboven alle nacions in Pruce;
In Lettow hadde he reysed and in Ruce,
No Cristen man so ofte of his degree.
In Gernade at the seege eek hadde he be
Of Algezir, and riden in Belmarye.
At Lyeys was he and at Satalye,
Whan they were wonne; and in the Grete See
At many a noble armee hadde he be."

An extract from the "General Prologue" to *The Canterbury Tales* (c.1387–c.1400) by Geoffrey Chaucer, edited by A. C. Spearing.

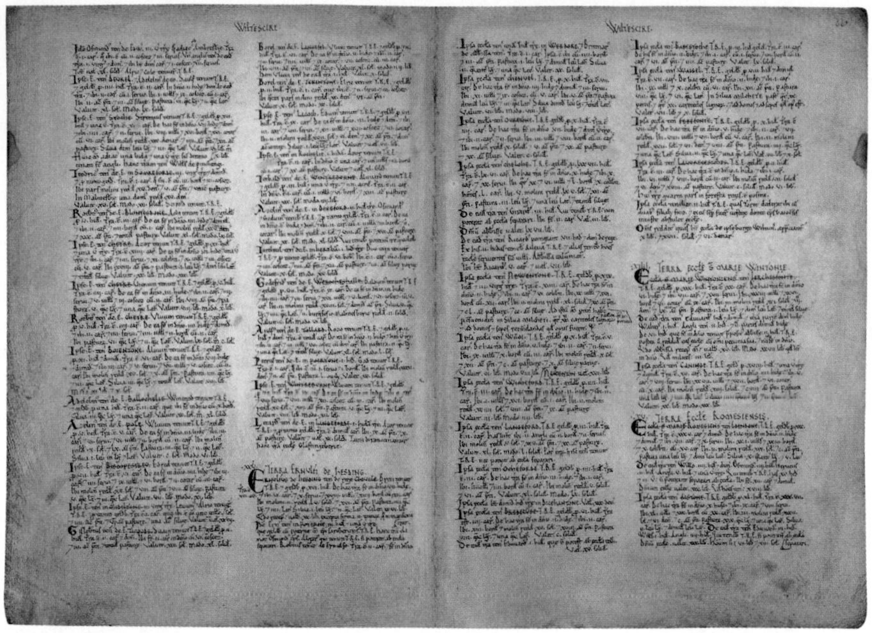

William the Conqueror commissioned the Domesday Book in 1085 and it was completed three years later. The book, of which two of the Wiltshire folios are shown here, listed the kingdom's taxable wealth and resources in great detail.

acts of the Middle Ages, the compilation of the Domesday Book, a huge survey of England for royal purposes. The evidence was taken from juries in every shire and hundred, and its minuteness deeply impressed the Anglo-Saxon chronicler who bitterly noted ("it is shameful to record, but did not seem shameful for him to do") that not an ox, cow or pig escaped the notice of William's men. In the next century there was rapid, even spectacular, development in the judicial strength of the Crown. Though minorities and weak kings from time to time led to royal concessions to the magnates, the essential integrity of the monarchy was not compromised. The constitutional history of England is for five hundred years the story of the authority of the Crown – its waxing and waning. This owed much to the fact that England was separated from possible enemies, except to the north, by water; it was hard for foreigners to interfere in her domestic politics and the Normans were to remain her last successful invaders.

For a long time, though, the Anglo-Norman kings were more than kings of an island state. They were heirs of a complex inheritance of possessions and feudal dependencies which at its furthest stretched far into southwestern France. Like their followers, they still spoke Norman French. The loss of most of their "Angevin" inheritance (the name came from Anjou) at the beginning of the twelfth century was decisive for France as well as for England. A sense of nationhood was further nurtured in each of them by their quarrels with one another.

THE CAPETIANS

The Capetians had hung on grimly to the French crown. From the tenth century to the fourteenth their kings succeeded one another in unbroken hereditary succession. They added to the domain lands which were the basis of royal power. The Capetians' lands were rich, too. They fell in the heartland of modern France, the cereal-growing area round Paris called the Ile de France, which was for a long time the only part of the country bearing the old name of Francia, thus commemorating the fact that it was a fragment of the old kingdom of the Franks. The domains of the first Capetians were thus distinguished from the other west Carolingian territories, such as Burgundy; by 1300 their vigorous successors had expanded "Francia" to include Bourges, Tours, Gisors and Amiens. By then the French kings had also acquired Normandy and other feudal dependencies from the kings of England.

THE HUNDRED YEARS' WAR

In the fourteenth century (and later) the great fiefs and feudal principalities existing in what is now France make it improper to think of the Capetian kingdom as a monolithic unity. Yet it was a unity of sorts, though much rested on the personal tie. During the fourteenth century that unity was greatly enhanced by a long struggle with England, remembered by the misleading name of the Hundred Years' War. In fact, English and French were only sporadically at war between 1337 and 1453. Sustained warfare was difficult to keep up – it was too expensive. Formally, though, what was at stake was the maintenance by the kings of England of territorial and feudal claims on the French side of the Channel; in 1350 Edward III had quartered his arms with those of France. There were therefore always likely to be specious grounds to start fighting again, and the opportunities it offered to English noblemen for booty and ransom money made war seem a plausible investment to many of them.

For England, these struggles supplied new elements to the infant mythology of nationhood (largely because of the great victories won at Crécy and Agincourt) and generated a long-lived distrust of the French. The Hundred Years' War was important to the French monarchy because it did something to check feudal fragmentation and broke down somewhat the barriers between Picard and Gascon, Norman and French. In the long run, too, French national mythology benefited; its greatest acquisition was the story and example of Joan of Arc whose astonishing career accompanied the turning of the balance of the long struggle against the English, though few of the French of the day knew she existed. The two long-term results of the war which mattered most were that Crécy soon led to the English conquest of Calais, and that England was the loser in the

In 1429 Joan of Arc (1412–1431) led the French armies to victory against the English in Orleans. The following year Joan fell into the hands of the English, who had her declared guilty of heresy and burned her at the stake, as depicted in this 15th-century illustration. "La Pucelle", as she was affectionately known, was canonized in 1920.

The main events of the Hundred Years' War

The name is conventionally applied to a period of intermittent Anglo-French struggle in pursuit of English claims to the French crown. After performing homage for his lands in Aquitaine to the King of France, the English king Edward III quarrelled with his overlord, which led to open hostilities:

1337 Edward III proclaims himself King of France, in right of his mother.

1340–47 The English are victors at Sluys (naval, 1340) and Crécy (1346), and Calais is captured (1347).

1355–6 Raids by the Black Prince across France from the southwest; the French are defeated at Poitiers.

1360 The Treaty of Brétigny ends the first phase of the war. Edward is given an enlarged, sovereign duchy of Aquitaine.

1369–72 The French re-open the conflict, the English fleet is defeated at La Rochelle (1372) and the loss of Aquitaine begins a steady decline of the English position.

1399 The deposition of Richard II (who was married in 1396 to a daughter of Charles VI of France) renews French hostility.

1405–6 The French arrive in Wales and attack English lands in Guienne.

1407 The outbreak of civil war in France is exploited by the English.

1415–19 Henry V reasserts the claim to the French throne. Alliance with Burgundy and the defeat of the French at Agincourt are followed by the English re-conquest of Normandy (1417–19).

1420 The Treaty of Troyes confirms the conquest of Normandy. Henry V marries the daughter of the King of France and is recognized as the regent of France.

1422 The death of both Henry V and Charles VI of France. The infant Henry VI succeeds to the English throne; the war is successfully continued by the English with Burgundian help.

1429 The intervention of Joan of Arc saves Orleans; Charles VII is crowned at Reims.

1430 Henry VI has himself crowned King of France.

1436 The English lose Paris after the collapse of the Anglo-Burgundian alliance.

1444 The Treaty of Tours: England concedes the Duchy of Maine.

1449 The Treaty of Tours is broken by the English, resulting in the collapse of English resistance under concerted French pressure.

1453 The English defeat at Castillon ends their effort to reconquer Gascony; the English are left with only Calais and the Channel Islands and the struggle peters out in their abortive expeditions of 1474 and 1492.

1558 Calais is lost to France (but the title of King of France is retained by English kings down to George III – and the French coat of arms is displayed in *The Times* newspaper's device until 1932).

long run. Calais was to be held by the English for two hundred years and opened Flanders (where a cluster of manufacturing towns was ready to absorb English wool and later cloth exports), to English trade. England's ultimate defeat meant that her territorial connection with France was virtually at an end by 1500 (though in the eighteenth century George III was still entitled "King of France"). Once more, England became almost an island. After 1453 French kings could push forward with the consolidation of their state undisturbed by the obscure claims of England's kings, from which the wars had sprung. They could settle down to establish their sovereignty over their rebellious magnates at their leisure. In each country, war in the long run strengthened the monarchy.

A depiction of the Battle of Crécy, the most important of the early English victories in the Hundred Years' War.

SPAIN

Progress towards a future national consolidation was also to be seen in Spain. She achieved a measure of unity by the end of the fifteenth century which was mythologically underpinned by the Reconquest. The long struggle against Islam gave Spanish nationhood a quite special flavour from the start because of its intimate connection with Christian faith and fervour; the Reconquest was a crusade uniting men of different origins. Toledo had been a Christian capital again in the mid-twelfth century. A hundred years later,

Ferdinand II of Aragon and Isabella I of Castile, whose marriage had united their two kingdoms, were supporters of the great Genoese explorer, Christopher Columbus. Three scenes from the journey during which Columbus discovered America are depicted in this tapestry. In the left-hand section Queen Isabella is shown giving the navigator her jewels to help finance the voyage. In the right-hand section he is portrayed about to set sail on the *Santa Maria*. The central section of the tapestry depicts Columbus at the Spanish court, having just returned from his first journey.

Seville belonged to the kingdom of Castile and the crown of Aragon ruled the great Arab city of Valencia. In 1340, when the last great Arab offensive was defeated, success brought the threat of anarchy as the turbulent nobles of Castile strove to assert themselves. The monarchy took the burghers of the towns into alliance. The establishment of stronger personal rule followed the union of the crowns of Aragon and Castile by the marriage in 1479 of *Los Reyes Católicos*, "the Catholic monarchs", Ferdinand of Aragon and Isabella of Castile. This made easier both the final expulsion of the Moors and the eventual creation of one nation, though the two kingdoms long remained formally and legally separate. Only Portugal in the peninsula remained outside the framework of a new Spain; she clung to an independence often threatened by her powerful neighbour.

GERMANY

Little sign of the groundplans of future nations was to be found in Germany. Potentially, the claims of the Holy Roman Emperors were an important and broad base for political power. Yet after 1300 they had lost virtually all the special respect due to their title. The last German to march to Rome and force his coronation as emperor did so in 1328, and it proved an abortive effort. A long thirteenth-century dispute between rival emperors was one reason for this. Another was the inability of the emperors to consolidate monarchical authority in their diverse dominions.

In Germany the domains of successive imperial families were usually scattered and disunited. The imperial election was in the hands of great magnates. Once elected, emperors had no special capital city to provide a centre for a nascent German nation.

Political circumstances led them more and more to devolve such power as they possessed. Important cities began to exercise imperial powers within their territories. In 1356 a document traditionally accepted as a landmark in German constitutional history (though only a registration of established fact), the Golden Bull, named seven electoral princes who acquired the exercise of almost all the imperial rights in their own lands. Their jurisdiction, for example, was henceforth absolute; no appeals lay from their courts to the emperor. What persisted in this situation of attenuated imperial power was a reminiscence of the mythology which would still prove a temptation to many vigorous princes.

An Austrian family, the house of Habsburg, eventually succeeded to the imperial throne. The first Habsburg to be emperor was chosen in 1273, but he remained a solitary example for a long time. The imperial greatness of the house lay ahead, for the Habsburgs were to provide emperors almost without a break from the accession of Maximilian I, who became emperor in 1493, to the end of the empire in 1806. And even then they were to survive another century as the rulers of a great state. They began with an important advantage: as German princes went, they were rich. But their major resources only became available to them after a marriage which, in the end, brought them the inheritance of the duchy of Burgundy, the most affluent of all fifteenth-century European states and one including much of the Netherlands. Other inheritances and marriages would add Hungary and Bohemia to their possessions. For the first time since the thirteenth century, it seemed possible that an effective political unity might be imposed on Germany and central Europe; Habsburg family interest in uniting the scattered dynastic territories now had a possible instrument in the imperial dignity.

German eastward expansion

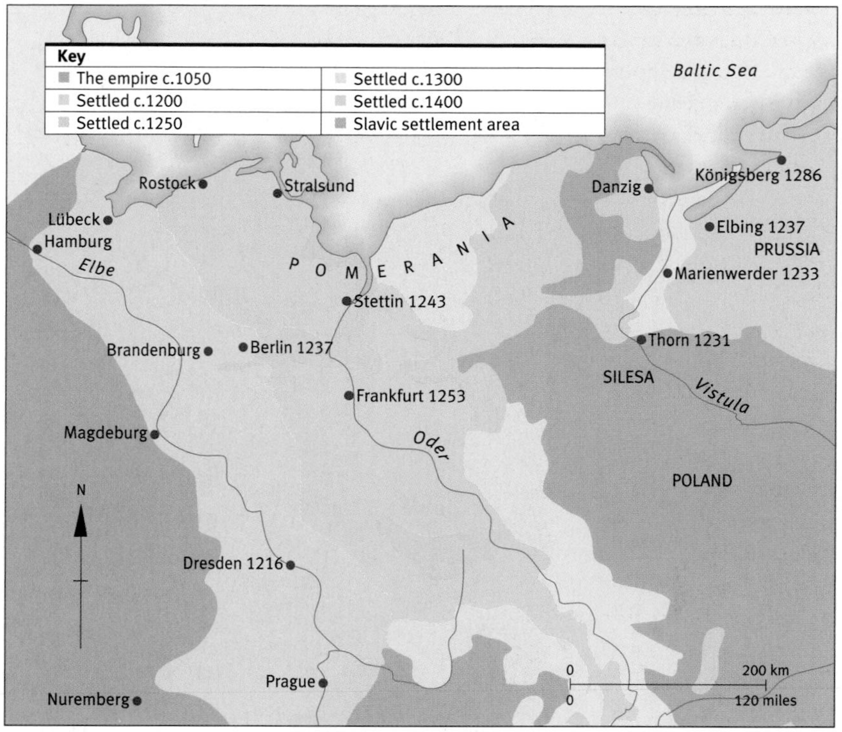

From the 12th to the 15th centuries the territories of Germany expanded eastwards. Its borders eventually shaped the kingdom of France to the west and the kingdoms of Burgundy, Italy and the Papal States to the south, as well as the territories of the Polish Slavic peoples and the kingdom of Hungary to the east.

ITALY

By the fifteenth century the empire had virtually ceased to matter south of the Alps. The struggle to preserve it there had long been tangled with Italian politics: the contestants in feuds which tormented Italian cities called themselves Guelph and Ghibelline long after those names ceased to mean, as they formerly did, allegiance respectively to pope or emperor. After the fourteenth century there was no imperial domain in Italy and emperors hardly went there except to be crowned with the Lombard crown. Imperial authority was delegated to "vicars" who made of their vicariates units almost as independent as the electorates of

Italian cities became thriving centres of trade and industry during the Middle Ages. Many banks, such as the one depicted in this 14th-century illustration, enjoyed great prosperity.

Germany. Titles were given to these rulers and their vicariates, some of which lasted until the nineteenth century; the duchy of Milan was one of the first. But other Italian states had different origins. Besides the Norman south, the "kingdom of the two Sicilies", there were the republics, of which Venice, Genoa and Florence were the greatest.

The city republics represented the outcome of two great trends sometimes interwoven in early Italian history, the "communal" movement and the rise of commercial wealth. In the tenth and eleventh centuries, in much of north Italy, general assemblies of the citizens had emerged as effective governments in many towns. They described themselves sometimes as *parliamenta* or, as we might say, town meetings, and represented municipal oligarchies who profited from a revival of trade beginning to be felt from 1100 onwards. In the twelfth century the Lombard cities took the field against the emperor and beat him. Thereafter they ran their own internal affairs.

VENICE

The greatest beneficiary of the revival of trade after 1100 was Venice, and it contributed much to it. Formally a dependency of Byzantium, Venice was long favoured by the detachment from the troubles of the European mainland accorded by its position on a handful of islands in a shallow lagoon. Refugees had already fled to the city from the Lombards. Besides offering security, geography also imposed a destiny; Venice, as its citizens loved later to remember, was wedded to the sea, and a great festival of the republic long commemorated it by the symbolic act of throwing a ring into the waters of the Adriatic. Venetian citizens were forbidden to acquire estates on the mainland and instead turned their energies to commercial empire overseas. Venice became the first west European city to live by trade. It was also the most successful of those who pillaged and battered on the Eastern Empire after winning a long struggle with Genoa for commercial supremacy in the East. There was plenty to go around: Genoa, Pisa and the Catalan ports all prospered with the revival of Mediterranean trade with the East.

LIMITED MONARCHICAL POWER

Much of the political groundplan of modern Europe was in being by 1500. Portugal, Spain, France and England were recognizable in their modern form, but although in Italy and Germany the vernacular had begun to define nationhood, there was no correspondence in them between nation and state. State institutions, too, were still far from enjoying the firmness and coherence they later acquired. The kings of France were not kings of Normandy but dukes. Different titles symbolized different legal and practical powers in different provinces. There were many such complicated survivals; constitutional relics everywhere cluttered up the idea of monarchical sovereignty, and they could provide excuses for rebellion. One explanation of the success of Henry VII, the first of the Tudors, was that by judicious marriages he drew much of the remaining poison from the bitter struggle of great families which had bedevilled the English crown in the fifteenth-century Wars of the Roses. Yet there were still to be feudal rebellions to come.

REPRESENTATION

One limitation on monarchical power had appeared which has a distinctly modern look. In the fourteenth and fifteenth centuries can be found the first examples of the representative, parliamentary bodies which are so characteristic of the modern state. The most famous of them all, the English parliament, was the most mature by 1500. Their origins are complex and have been much debated. One root is Germanic tradition, which imposed on a ruler the obligation of taking

This engraving of the English parliament depicts representatives at the House of Commons in Westminster on 13 April 1640. The assembly is presided over by King Charles I.

counsel from his great men and acting on it. The Church, too, was an early exponent of the representative idea, using it, among other things, to obtain taxation for the papacy. It was a device which united towns with monarchs, too: in the twelfth century representatives from Italian cities were summoned to the diet of the empire. By the end of the thirteenth century most countries had seen examples of representatives with full powers being summoned to attend assemblies which princes had called to find new ways of raising taxation.

This was the nub of the matter. New resources had to be tapped by the new (and more expensive) state. Once summoned, princes found representative bodies had other advantages. They enabled voices other than those of the magnates to be heard. They provided local information. They had a propaganda value. On their side, the early parliaments (as we may loosely call them) of Europe were discovering that the device had advantages for them, too. In some of them the thought arose that taxation needed consent and that someone other than the nobility had an interest and therefore ought to have a voice in the running of the realm.

WORKING AND LIVING

FROM AROUND THE YEAR 1000 another fundamental change was under way in Europe: it began to get richer. As a result, more Europeans slowly acquired a freedom of choice almost unknown in earlier times; society became more varied and complicated. Slow though it was, this was a revolution; society's wealth at last began to grow a little faster than population. This was by no means obvious everywhere to the same degree and was punctuated by a bad setback in the fourteenth century. Yet the change was decisive and launched Europe on a trajectory of economic growth lasting to our own day.

POPULATION GROWTH

One crude but by no means misleading index is the growth of population. Only approximate estimates can be made but they are based on better evidence than is available for any earlier period. The errors they contain are unlikely much to distort the overall trend. They suggest that a Europe of about forty million people in 1000 grew to sixty million or so in the next

This detail is from a mural painted by Ambrogio Lorenzetti in Siena's Palazzo Pubblico in around 1338. It is part of an allegory representing the effects of good government on a city and depicts Siena as a peaceful, prosperous town, whose people are shown trading and dancing in the streets.

two centuries. Growth then seems to have further accelerated to reach a peak of about seventy-three million around 1300, after which there is indisputable evidence of decline. The total population is said to have gone down to about fifty million by 1360 and only to have begun to rise in the fifteenth century. Then it began to go up again, and overall growth has been uninterrupted ever since.

Of course, the rate of increase varied even from village to village. The Mediterranean and Balkan lands did not succeed in doubling their population in five centuries and by 1450 had relapsed to levels only a little above those of 1000. The same appears to be true of Russia, Poland and Hungary. Yet France, England, Germany and Scandinavia probably trebled their populations before 1300 and after bad setbacks in the next hundred years still had twice the population of the year 1000. Contrasts within countries could be made, too, sometimes between areas very close to one another, but the general effect is indisputable: population grew overall as never before, but unevenly, the north and west gaining more than the Mediterranean, the Balkans and eastern Europe.

AGRICULTURAL DEVELOPMENT

The explanation for population growth lies in food supply, and therefore in agriculture. It was for a long time the only possible major source of new wealth. More food was obtained by bringing more land under cultivation and by increasing its productivity. Thus began the rise in food production which has gone on ever since. Europe had great natural advantages in her moderate temperatures and good rainfall, and these, combined with a physical relief whose predominant characteristic is a broad northern plain, have always given her a large area of potentially productive agricultural land. Huge areas of it still wild and forested in 1000 were brought into cultivation in the next few centuries.

Land was not short in medieval Europe and a growing population provided the labour to clear and till it. Though slowly, the landscape changed. The huge forests were gradually cut into as villages pushed out their fields. In some places, new colonies were deliberately established by landlords and rulers. The building of a monastery in a remote spot – as many were built – was often the beginning of a new nucleus of cultivation or stock-raising in an almost empty desert of scrub and trees. Some new land was reclaimed from sea or marsh. In the east, much was won in the colonization of the first German *Drang nach Osten*. Settlement there was promoted as consciously as it was later to be promoted in Elizabethan England in the first age of North American colonization.

By about 1300 the breaking in of fresh land slowed down. There were even signs of over-population. Symptoms of rural dislocation such as smaller holdings, shortage of livestock and manure and pressure on pasture became more obvious. The first big increase in Europe's cultivated and grazed areas was over after underpinning an indispensable increase in production. Some have argued that in parts of western Europe output had doubled. Besides having brought more land under cultivation, this also owed something to better husbandry – increased use of regular fallows and cropping, the gradual enrichment of the soil, and even the introduction of some new crops. Although grain-growing was still the main business of the cultivator in northern Europe, the appearance of beans and peas of various sorts in larger quantities from the tenth century onwards meant that more nitrogen was being returned to the soil. Cause and effect are difficult to disentangle in economic history; other suggestive signs of change go along with these. In the thirteenth century

This illustration, from a French 15th-century Book of Hours, shows work to be done on the land in March. A farmer is using the new symmetrical plough, which increased yields by digging more deeply than had previously been possible.

the first manuals of agricultural practice appear and the first agricultural book-keeping, a monastic innovation. More specialized cultivation brought a tendency to employ wage labourers instead of serfs carrying out obligatory work. By 1300 it is likely that most household servants in England were recruited and paid as free labour, and probably a third of the peasants as well. The bonds of servitude were relaxing and a money economy was spreading slowly into the countryside.

THE HARDSHIP OF PEASANT LIFE

Some peasants benefited from the emerging fiscal economy, but increased wealth usually went to the landlord who took most of the profits. Most still lived poor and cramped lives, eating coarse bread and various grain-based porridges, seasoned with vegetables and only occasionally fish or meat. Calculations suggest each peasant consumed about two thousand calories daily (the average daily intake of a Sudanese in the late twentieth century), and this had to sustain him or her for very laborious work. If peasants grew wheat they did not eat its flour, but sold it to the better-off, keeping barley or rye for their own food. They had little elbow-room to better themselves. Even when their lord's legal grip through bond labour became less firm, the lord still had practical monopolies of mills and carts, which the peasants needed to work the land. "Customs", or taxes for protection, were levied without regard to distinctions between freeholders and tenants and could hardly be resisted.

URBAN GROWTH

More cash crops for growing markets gradually changed the self-sufficient manor into a unit producing for sale. Its markets were to be found in towns which grew steadily between 1100 and 1300; urban population increased faster than rural. This is a complicated phenomenon. The new town life was in part a revival going hand in hand with the revival of trade, in part a reflection of growing population. It is a chicken-and-egg business to decide which came first. A few new towns grew up around a castle or a monastery. Sometimes this led to the establishment of a market. Many new towns, especially in Germany, were deliberately settled as colonies. On the whole, long-established towns grew bigger – Paris may have had about eighty thousand inhabitants in 1340 and Venice, Florence and Genoa were probably comparable – but few were so big. Fourteenth-century Germany had only fifteen towns of more than ten thousand inhabitants, and London, with about thirty-five thousand, was then by far the biggest English city. Of the great medieval towns, only those in the south had been important Roman centres (though many in the north, of course, had, like London, Roman nuclei). New cities tended to be linked distinctively to economic possibilities. They were markets, or lay on great trade-routes such as the Meuse and Rhine, or were grouped in an area of specialized production such as Flanders, where already in the late twelfth century Ypres, Arras and Ghent were famous as textile towns, or Tuscany, another cloth-producing, cloth-finishing region. Wine was one of the first agricultural commodities to loom large in international trade and this underpinned the early growth of Bordeaux. Ports often became the metropolitan centres of maritime regions, as did Genoa and Bruges.

Grain merchants are portrayed trading their wares in Florence, Italy, in this 14th-century painting.

TRADE

The commercial revival was most conspicuous in Italy, where trade with the outside world was resumed, above all by Venice. In that great commercial centre banking for the first time separated itself from the changing of money. By the middle of the twelfth century, whatever the current state of politics, Europeans enjoyed continuing trade not only with Byzantium but with the Arab Mediterranean. Beyond those limits, an even wider world was involved. In the early fourteenth century trans-Saharan gold from Mali relieved a bullion shortage in Europe. By then, Italian merchants had long been at work in Central Asia and China. They sold slaves from Germany and central Europe to the Arabs of Africa and the Levant. They bought Flemish and English cloth and took it to Constantinople and the Black Sea. In the thirteenth century the first voyage was made from Italy to Bruges; before this the Rhine, Rhône and overland routes had been used.

European trade in the 13th century

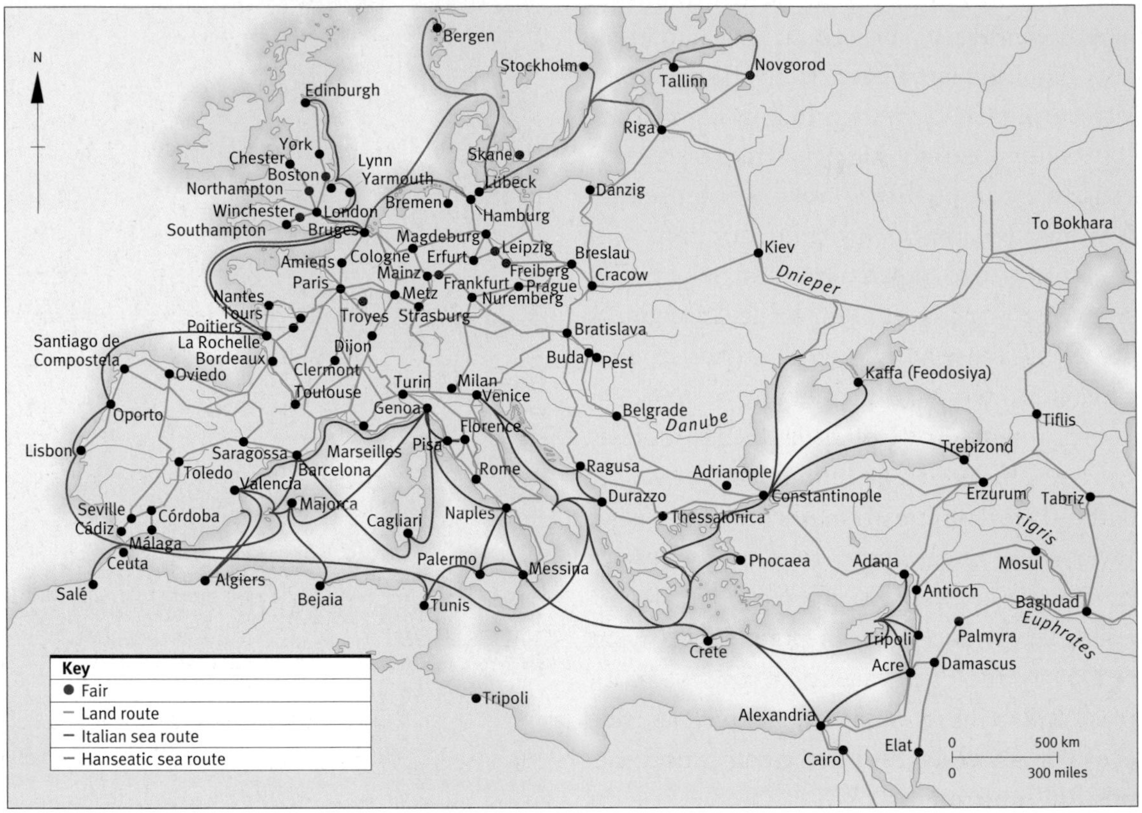

This map represents the most important trade routes and commercial fairs in 13th-century Europe.

Roads were built across Alpine passes. Trade fed on trade and the northern European fairs drew other merchants from the northeast. The German towns of the Hanse, the league which controlled the Baltic, provided a new outlet for the textiles of the West and the spices of the East. But transport costs on land were always high; to move goods from Cracow to Venice quadrupled their price.

TECHNOLOGY

Through the expansion of trade, European economic geography was revolutionized. In Flanders and the Low Countries economic revival soon began to generate a population big enough to stimulate new agricultural innovation. Everywhere, towns which could escape from the cramping monopolies of the earliest manufacturing centres enjoyed the most rapid new prosperity. One visible result was a great wave of building. It was not only a matter of the houses and guildhalls of newly prosperous cities; it left a glorious legacy in Europe's churches, not just in the great cathedrals, but in scores of magnificent parish churches of little English towns.

Building was a major expression of medieval technology. The architecture of a cathedral posed engineering problems as complex as those of a Roman aqueduct; in solving them, the engineer was slowly to emerge from the medieval craftsman. Medieval technology was not in a modern sense science-based, but achieved much by the accumulation of experience and reflection on it. Possibly its most important achievement was the harnessing of other forms of energy to do the work of muscles and, therefore, to deploy muscle-power more effectively and productively. Winches, pulleys and inclined planes thus eased the shifting of heavy loads, but change was most obvious in agriculture, where metal tools had been becoming more common since the tenth century. The iron plough had made available the heavier soils of valley lands; since it required oxen to pull it, the evolution of a more efficient yoke followed and with it more efficient traction. The whipple-tree and the shoulder collar for the horse also made possible bigger loads. There were not many such innovations, but they were sufficient to effect a considerable increase in the cultivators' control of the land. They also imposed new demands. Using horses meant that more grain had to be grown to feed them, and this led to new crop rotations.

Another innovation was the spread of milling; both windmills and watermills, first known in Asia, were widely spread in Europe even by 1000. In the centuries to come they were put to more and more uses. Wind often replaced muscle-power in milling foodstuffs, as it had already done in the evolution of better ships; water was used when possible to provide power for other industrial operations. It drove hammers both for cloth-fulling and for forging (here the invention of the crank was

Long-distance trade was increasingly common from the 12th century. This 15th-century miniature shows a trade ship's merchandise being unloaded in a European port.

Leonardo da Vinci

As well as being one of the greatest artists of all time, Leonardo da Vinci was one of the founders of modern scientific thought – he solved many of the important technical problems of his time. Leonardo's designs (from flying machines to an early concept for the automobile) have come down to us through thousands of drawings, notes and sketches found on loose sheets of paper and in notebooks. Leonardo reflected a new empiricism: he was educated in an artisan's workshop and never learnt Latin (the language of official culture).

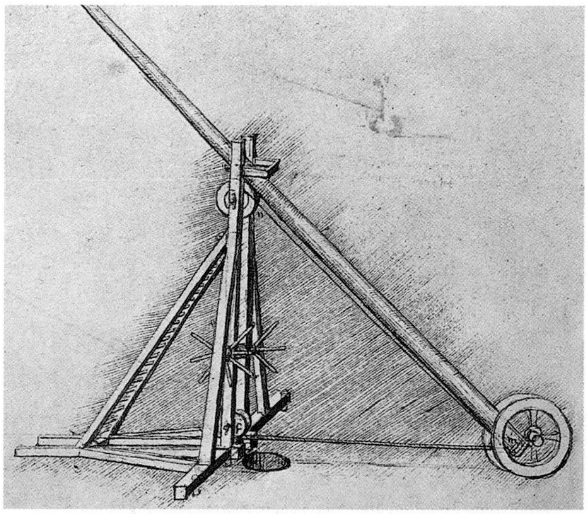

A drawing by Leonardo da Vinci of a machine to manufacture files for working metal or wood.

This 15th-century illustration is a detail from the altarpiece of the church of St Michael in Avila, in the Spanish region of Old Castile. It shows the church under construction.

of the greatest importance), an essential element in a great expansion of Europe's metallurgical industry in the fifteenth century, and one closely connected with rising demand for an earlier technological innovation of the previous century, artillery. Water-driven hammers were also used in paper-making. The invention of printing soon gave this industry an importance which may even have surpassed that of the new metal-working of Germany and Flanders. Print and paper had their own revolutionary potential for technology, too, because books made the diffusion of techniques faster and easier in the growing pool of craftsmen and artificers able to use such knowledge. Some innovations were simply taken over from other cultures; the spinning-wheel came to medieval Europe from India (though the application of a treadle to it to provide drive with the foot seems to have been a European invention of the sixteenth century).

EARLY BANKING

Whatever qualifications are needed, it is clear that by 1500 a technology was available which was already embodied in a large capital investment. It was making the accumulation of further capital for manufacturing enterprises easier than ever before. The availability of this capital must have been greater, moreover, as new devices eased business. Medieval Italians invented much of modern accountancy as well as new credit instruments for the financing of international trade. The bill of exchange appears in the thirteenth century, and with it and the first true bankers we are at the edge of modern capitalism. Limited liability appears in Florence in 1408. Yet though such a change from the past was by implication colossal, it is easy to get it out of proportion if we do not recall its scale. For all the magnificence of its palaces, the goods shipped by medieval Venice in a year could all have fitted comfortably into one large modern ship.

A FRAGILE ECONOMY

Nonetheless, the ground won over long, slow improvement and growth was precarious. For centuries, economic life was fragile, never far from the edge of collapse. Medieval agriculture, in spite of such progress as had been made, was appallingly inefficient. It abused the land and exhausted it. Little was consciously put back

Large-scale commercial trade generated a great deal of wealth for the major medieval cities such as Bristol, London, Bruges and, above all, Venice and Genoa. Genoese bankers and money-changers are shown at work in this 14th-century miniature.

The burial of some of the victims of the Black Death at Tournai in 1349 is depicted in this manuscript illustration.

into it except manure. As population rose and new land became harder to find, family holdings got smaller; probably most European households farmed less than eight acres in 1300. Only in a few places (the Po valley was one) were there big investments in collective irrigation or improvement. Above all, agriculture was vulnerable to weather; two successive bad harvests in the early fourteenth century reduced the population of Ypres by a tenth. Local famine could rarely be offset by imports. Roads had broken down since Roman times, carts were crude and for the most part goods had to be carried by packhorse or mule. Water transport was cheaper and swifter, but could rarely meet the need. Commerce could have its political difficulties, too; the Ottoman onslaught brought a gradual recession in Eastern trade in the fifteenth century. Demand was small enough for a very little change to determine the fate of cities: cloth production in Florence and Ypres fell by two-thirds in the fourteenth century.

DEPOPULATION AND DISORDER

It is very difficult to generalize but about one thing there is no doubt: a great and cumulative setback occurred during the fourteenth century. There was a sudden rise in mortality, not occurring everywhere at the same time, but notable in many places after a series of bad harvests around 1320. This started a slow decline of population which suddenly became a disaster with the onset of attacks of epidemic disease. These are often called by the name of one of them, the "Black Death" of 1348–50 and the worst single attack. It was of bubonic plague, but no doubt it masked many other killing diseases which swept Europe with it and in its wake. Europeans died of typhus, influenza and smallpox, too; all contributed to a great demographic disaster. In some areas a half or a third of the population may have died; over Europe as a whole the total loss has been calculated as a quarter. A papal enquiry put the figure at more than forty million. Toulouse was a city of thirty thousand in 1335 and a century later only eight thousand lived there; fourteen hundred died in three days at Avignon.

There was no universal pattern, but all Europe shuddered under these blows. In extreme cases a kind of collective madness broke out. Pogroms of Jews were a common expression of a search for scapegoats or those guilty of spreading the plague; the burning of witches and heretics was another. The European psyche bore a scar for the rest of the Middle Ages, which were haunted by the imagery of death and damnation in painting, carving and literature. The fragility of settled order illustrated the precariousness of the balance of food and population. When disease killed enough people, agricultural production would collapse; then the inhabitants of the towns would die of famine if they were not already dying of plague. Probably a plateau of productivity had already been reached by about 1300. Both available techniques and easily accessible new land for cultivation had reached a limit and some have seen signs of

This miniature shows a penitential procession of the Dutch Flagellants of Doonik in 1349. The Flagellants were one of the many fanatical groups that emerged as a result of the horrors of the plague epidemic.

population pressure treading close upon resources even by that date. From this flowed the huge setback of the fourteenth century and then the slow recovery in the fifteenth.

PEASANT RISINGS AND GAINS

It is scarcely surprising that an age of such colossal dislocations and disasters should have been marked by violent social conflicts. Everywhere in Europe the fourteenth and fifteenth centuries brought peasant risings. The French *jacquerie* of 1358 which led to over thirty thousand deaths, and the English Peasants' Revolt of 1381, which for a time captured London, were especially notable. The roots of rebellion lay in the ways in which landlords had increased their demands under the spur of necessity and in the new demands of royal tax collectors. Combined with famine, plague and war they made an always miserable existence intolerable. "We are made men in the likeness of Christ, but you treat us like savage beasts," was the complaint of English peasants who rebelled in 1381. Significantly, they appealed to the Christian standards of their civilization; the demands of medieval peasants were often well formulated and effective but it is anachronistic to see in them a nascent socialism.

Demographic disaster on such a scale paradoxically made things better for some of the poor. One obvious and immediate result was a severe shortage of labour; the pool of permanently under-employed had been brutally dried up. A rise in real wages followed. Once the immediate impact of the fourteenth-century disasters had been absorbed the standard of living of the poor may have risen slightly, for the price of cereals tended to fall. The tendency for the economy, even in the countryside, to move on to a money basis was speeded up by the labour shortage. By the sixteenth century, serf labour and servile status had both receded a long way in western Europe, particularly in England. This weakened the manorial structure and the feudal relationships clustered about it. Landlords were also suddenly confronted with a drop in their rent incomes. In the previous two centuries the habits of consumption of the better-off had become more expensive. Now property-owners suddenly ceased to grow more prosperous. Some landlords could adapt. They could, for example, switch from cultivation which required much labour to sheep-running which required little. In Spain there were still even possibilities of taking in more land and living directly off it. Moorish estates were the reward of the soldier of the Reconquest. Elsewhere, many landlords simply let their poorer land go out of cultivation.

RANK AND STATUS

The results are very hard to pin down, but they were bound to stimulate further and faster social change. Medieval society changed dramatically, and sometimes in oddly assorted ways, between the tenth century and the sixteenth. Even at the end of that age, though, it seems still almost unimaginably remote. Its obsession with status and hierarchy is one index of this. Medieval European men and women were defined by their legal status. Instead of being an individual social atom, so to speak, each person was the point at which a number of coordinates met. Some of them were set by birth, and the most obvious expression of this was the idea of nobility. The noble society, which was to remain a reality in some places until the twentieth century, was already present in its essentials in the thirteenth. Gradually, warriors had turned into landowners. Descent then became important because there were inheritances to argue about. One indicator was the rise of the sciences of heraldry and genealogy, which have since had a profitable life right down to our own day. New titles appeared as distinctions within the nobility ripened. The first English duke was created in 1337, an expression of the tendency to find ways of singling out the greater magnates

Hunting was a favourite occupation of European noblemen and landowners. This oil painting, which dates from 1529, is entitled *Elector Frederick the Wise's Deerhunt*. Among the figures in the foreground are Elector Frederick III of Saxony, the Holy Roman Emperor (Maximilian I of Habsburg), and Elector John the Constant of Ernestine Saxony.

from among their peers. Symbolic questions of precedence became of intense interest; rank was at stake. From this rose the dread of disparagement, the loss of status which might follow for a woman from an unequal marriage or for a man from contamination by a lowly occupation. For centuries most noblemen took it for granted that only arms, the Church or the management of their own estates were fit occupations for their like in northern Europe. Trade, above all, was closed to them except through agents. Even when, centuries later, this barrier gave way, hostility to retail trade was the last thing to be abandoned by those who cared about these things. When a sixteenth-century French king called his Portuguese cousin "the grocer king" he was being rude as well as witty and no doubt his courtiers laughed at the sneer.

The investiture of a medieval knight is portrayed in this 14th-century illustration.

CHIVALROUS VALUES

The values of the nobility were, at bottom, military. Through their gradual refinement there emerged slowly the notions of honour, loyalty and disinterested self-sacrifice, which were to be held up as models for centuries to well-born boys and girls. The ideal of chivalry articulated these values and softened the harshness of a military code. It was blessed by the Church, which provided religious ceremonies to accompany the bestowal of knighthood and the knights' acceptance of Christian duties. The heroic figure who came supremely to embody the notion was the mythological English King Arthur, whose cult spread to many lands. It was to live on in the ideal of the gentleman and gentlemanly conduct, however qualified in practice.

Of course, it never worked as it should have done. But few great creative myths do; neither did the feudal theory of dependence, nor does democracy. The pressures of war and, more fundamentally, economics, were always at work to fragment and confuse social obligations. The increasing unreality of the feudal concept of lord and vassal was one factor favouring the growth of kingly power. The coming of a money economy made further inroads, service had increasingly to be paid for in cash, and rents became more important than the services that had gone with them. Some sources of feudal income remained fixed in terms made worthless by changes in real prices. Lawyers evolved devices which enabled new aims to be realized within a "feudal" structure more and more unreal and worm-eaten.

MERCHANTS

Medieval nobility was for a long time very open to new entrants, but usually this became

Urban growth led to an increase in the number of private businesses in medieval Europe. A butcher's shop is represented in this Italian manuscript dating from the 14th century.

less and less true as time passed. In some places attempts were actually made to close for ever a ruling caste. Yet European society was all the time generating new kinds of wealth and even of power which could not find a place in the old hierarchies and challenged them. The most obvious example was the emergence of rich merchants. They often bought land; it was not only the supreme economic investment in a world where there were few, but it might open the way to a change of status for which landownership was either a legal or a social necessity. In Italy merchants sometimes themselves became the nobility of trading and manufacturing cities. Everywhere, though, they posed a symbolic challenge to a world which had, to begin with, no theoretical place for them. Soon they evolved their own social forms, guilds, mysteries and corporations, which gave new definitions to their social role.

The rise of the merchant class was almost a function of the growth of towns; the appearance of merchants was inseparably linked with the most dynamic element in medieval European civilization. Unwittingly, at least at first, towns and cities held within their walls much of the future history of Europe. Though their independence varied greatly in law and practice, there were parallels in other countries to the Italian communal movement. Towns in the German east were especially independent, which helps to explain the appearance there of the powerful Hanseatic League of more than a hundred and fifty free cities. The Flemish towns also tended to enjoy a fair degree of freedom: French and English towns usually had less. Yet lords everywhere sought the support of cities against kings, while kings sought the support of townsmen and their wealth against overmighty subjects. They gave towns charters and privileges. The walls which surrounded the medieval city were the symbol as well as a guarantee of its immunity. The landlords' writ did not run in them and sometimes their anti-feudal implication was even more explicit: villeins, for example, could acquire their freedom in some towns if they lived in them for a year and a day. "The air of the town makes men free," said a German proverb. The communes, and within them the guilds were associations of free men for a long time isolated in a world unfree. The burgher – the *bourgeois*, the dweller in *bourg* or borough – was a man who stood up for himself in a universe of dependence.

THE DIFFERENTIATION OF EUROPEAN HISTORY

Much of the history behind the emergence of the *bourgeoisie* remains obscure because it is for the most part the history of obscure individuals. The wealthy merchants who became the typically dominant figures of the new town life and fought for their corporate privileges are visible enough, but their humbler predecessors are usually not. In earlier times a

The Hanseatic League

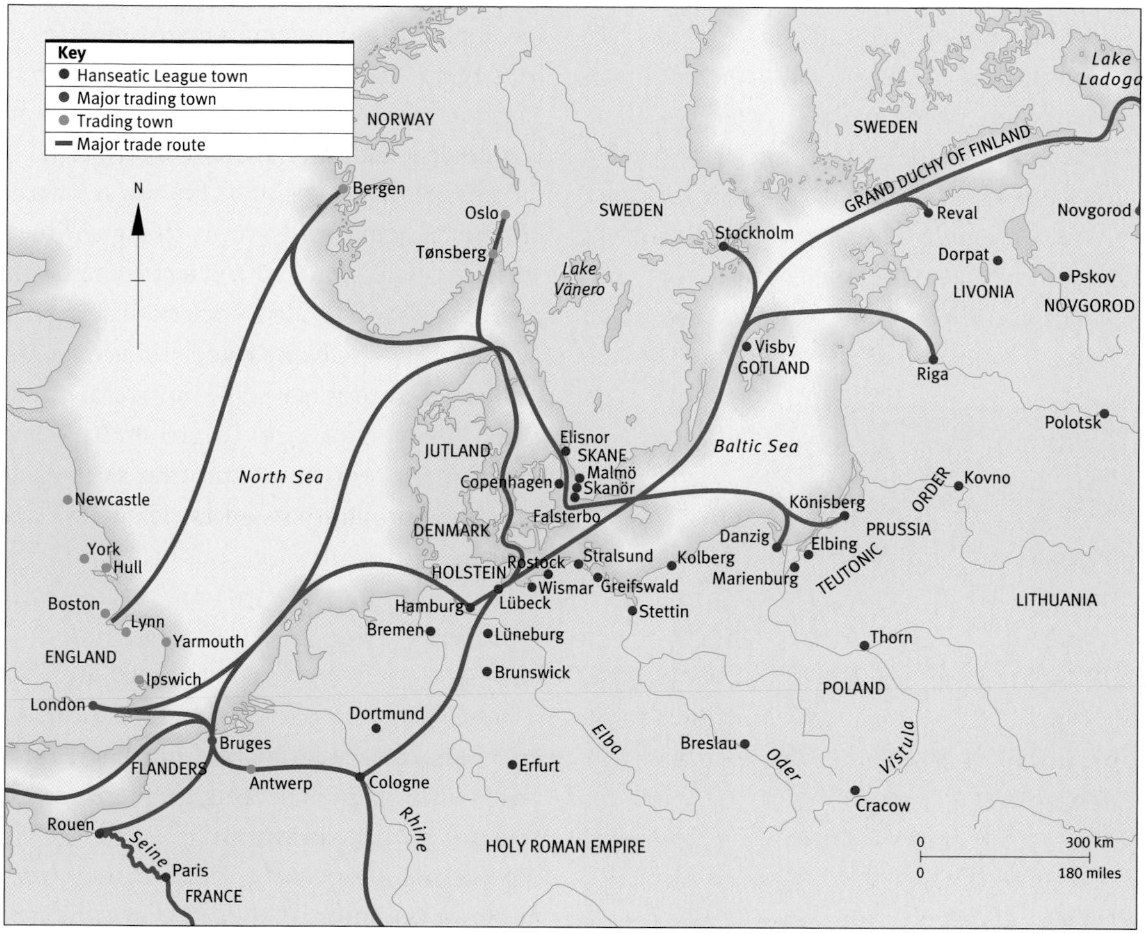

The economic community of the Teutonic Hanse appeared in the middle of the 14th century, although its origins date back to the 11th century. The attempt by the Danish king Valdemar IV (1340–1375) to monopolize trade in the Baltic resulted in the union of several cities and, consequently, the foundation of the Hanseatic League. In 1375 Emperor Charles IV recognized the Hanse's economic monopoly in the coastal territories of the Baltic. The League's "capital" was in the city of Lübeck and the great master of the Teutonic Order was its only prince. The Hanse of the Seventeen Cities (an organization set up by various merchants in the Netherlands and northern France) had similar characteristics, as did the Hanse of London.

merchant can have been little but the pedlar of exotica and luxuries which the medieval European estate could not provide for itself. Ordinary commercial exchange for a long time hardly needed a middleman: craftsmen sold their own goods and cultivators their own crops. Yet somehow in the towns there emerged traders who dealt between them and the countryside, and their successors were to be those who used capital to order in advance the whole business of production for the market.

In the blossoming of its urban life lies buried much which made European history different from that of other continents. Neither in the ancient world (except, perhaps, classical Greece) nor in Asia or America, did

Nuns usually came from privileged backgrounds – the working classes could not afford to pay the large dowry required to enter into a convent. On this panel from a 15th-century polyptych, Blessed Humility (a beatified nun) is portrayed reading aloud from the Bible in a convent refectory.

city life develop the political and social power it came to show in Europe. One reason was the absence of destructively parasitic empires of conquest to eat away at the will to betterment; Europe's enduring political fragmentation made rulers careful of the geese which laid the golden egg they needed to compete with their rivals. A great sack of a city was a noteworthy event in the European Middle Ages; it was the inescapable and recurrent accompaniment of warfare in much of Asia. This, of course, could not be the whole story. It also must have mattered that, for all its obsession with status, Europe had no caste system such as that of India, no ideological homogeneity so intense and stultifying as China's. Even when rich, the city-dwellers of other cultures seem to have acquiesced in their own inferiority. The merchant, the craftsman, the lawyer and the doctor had roles in Europe, though, which at an early date made them more than simple appendages of landed society. Their society was not closed to change and self-advancement; it offered routes to self-improvement other than the warrior's or the court favourite's. Townsmen were equal and free, even if some were more equal than others.

WOMEN

It need not surprise us that practical, legal and personal freedom was much greater for men than for women (though there were still those of both sexes who were legally unfree at the bottom of society). Whether they were of noble or common blood, medieval European women suffered, by comparison with their menfolk, from important legal and social disabilities, just as they have done in every civilization which has ever existed. Their rights of inheritance were often restricted; they could inherit a fief, for example, but could not enjoy personal lordship, and had to appoint men to carry out the obligations that went with it. In all classes below the highest there was much drudgery to be done by women; even in the twentieth century there were European peasant women who worked on the land as women still do in Africa and Asia today.

There were theoretical elements in the subjection of women and a large contribution was made to them by the Church. In part this was a matter of its traditionally hostile stance towards sexuality. Its teaching had never been able to find any justification for sex except for its role in the reproduction of the species. Woman being seen as the origin of Man's fall and a standing temptation to concupiscence, the Church threw its weight behind the domination of society by men. Yet this is not all there is to be said. Other societies have done more to seclude and oppress women than Christendom, and the Church at least offered women the only respectable alternative to domesticity available until modern times; the history of the female religious is studded with outstanding women of learning, spirituality and administrative gifts. The position of at least a minority of well-born women, too, was marginally bettered by the idealization of women in the chivalric codes of behaviour of the thirteenth and fourteenth centuries. There lay in this a notion of romantic love, and an entitlement to service, a stage towards a higher civilization. Nevertheless, no Christian Church could ever deny to women so much as was denied in some other cultures. The deepest roots of what later generations were to think of as the "liberation" of women lie, for this reason, in Western culture, whose role in so many places was to be disturbing, exotic and revolutionary.

Yet such ideas can in the Middle Ages have had little impact even on the lives of European women. Among themselves, medieval European women were more equal before death than would be rich and poor women in Asia today, but then so were men. Women lived less long than men, it seems, and frequent confinements and a high mortality rate no doubt explain this. Medieval obstetrics remained, as did other branches of medicine, rooted in Aristotle and Galen; there was nothing better available. But men died young, too. Aquinas lived only to forty-seven and philosophy is not nowadays thought to be physically exacting. This was about the age to which a man of twenty in a medieval town might normally expect to survive: he was lucky to have got as far already and to have escaped the ferocious toll of infant mortality which imposed an average life of about thirty-three years and a death rate about twice that of modern industrial countries. Judged by the standards of antiquity, so far as they can be grasped, this was of course by no means bad.

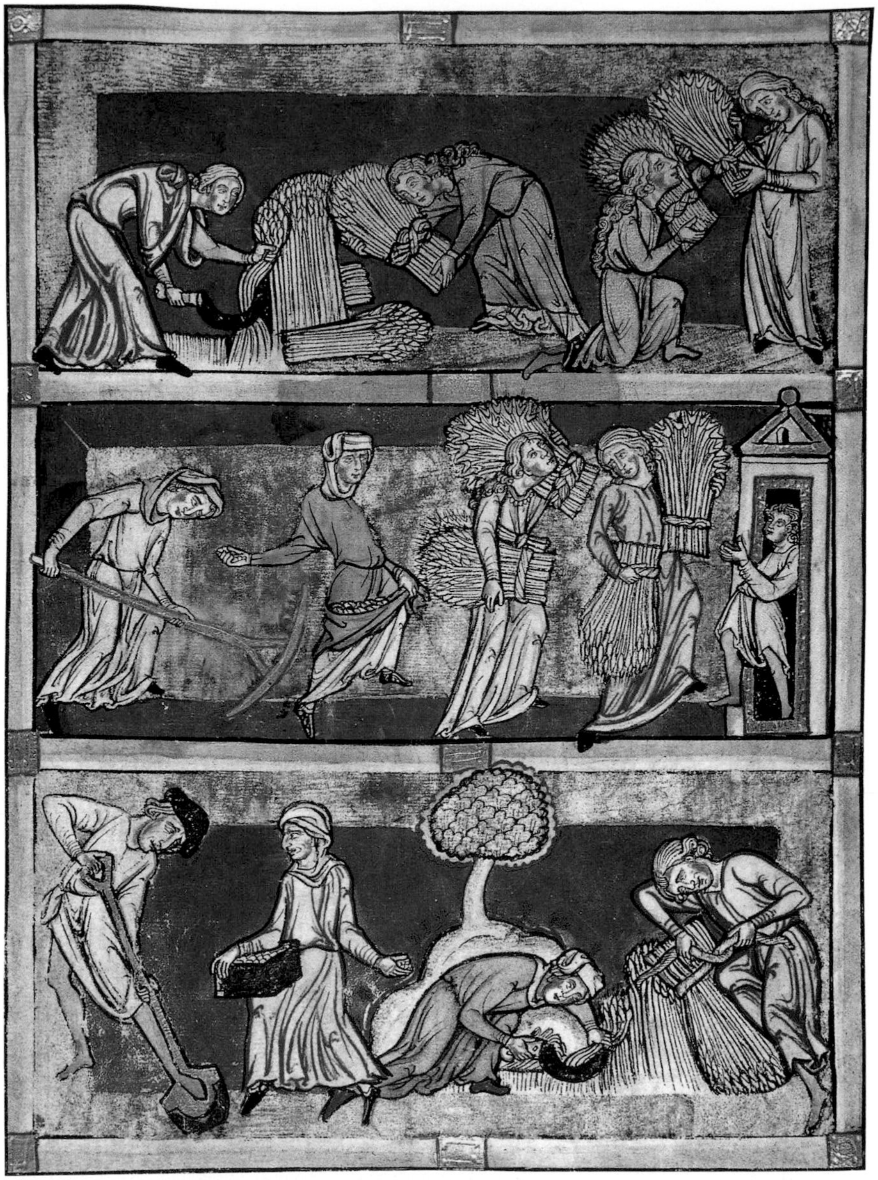

Women often helped their husbands in their work, although there are many examples of women who had jobs or businesses of their own. Unmarried women generally did the same work as men. This 7th-century illustration shows men and women toiling together in the fields.

INFORMATION GATHERING

This reminds us of one last novelty in the huge variety of the Middle Ages; they left behind

The *Triumph of Death* is portrayed by an anonymous 15th-century Sicilian artist. Death could never be far from the thoughts of medieval Europeans, ill-equipped as they were to combat disease.

the means for us to measure just a little more of the dimensions of human life. From these centuries come the first collections of facts upon which reasoned estimates can be made. When in 1085 William the Conqueror's officers rode out into England to interrogate its inhabitants and to record its structure and wealth in the Domesday Book, they were unwittingly pointing the way to a new age. Other collections of data, usually for tax purposes, followed in the next few centuries. Some have survived, together with the first accounts which reduce farming and business to quantities. Thanks to them, historians can talk with a little more confidence about late medieval society than about that of any earlier time.

In this painting, which is dated 1434, Jan Van Eyck portrayed the rich Italian merchant Arnolfini and his betrothed, members of the growing urban bourgeoisie.

6 NEW LIMITS, NEW HORIZONS

IN THE NEAR EAST Europeans were until very recently called "Franks", a word first used in Byzantium to mean Western Christians. It caught on elsewhere and was still being used in various distortions and mispronunciations from the Persian Gulf to China a thousand years later. This is more than just a historical curiosity; it is a helpful reminder that non-Europeans were struck from the start by the unity, not the diversity, of the Western peoples and long thought of them as one.

EUROPE LOOKS OUTWARDS

THE ROOTS OF THE IDEA of European unity can be seen even in the remote beginnings of Europe's long and victorious assault on the world, when a relaxation of pressure on her eastern land frontier and northern coasts at last began to be felt. By 1000 CE or so, the barbarians were checked; then they began to be Christianized. Within a short space of time Poland, Hungary, Denmark and Norway came to be ruled by Christian kings. One last great threat, the Mongol onslaught, still lay ahead, it is true, but that was unimaginable at that time. By the eleventh century, too, the rolling back of Islam had already begun. The Islamic threat to southern Europeans diminished because of the decline into which the Abbasid caliphate had fallen in the eighth and ninth centuries.

THE CRUSADES

THE STRUGGLE WITH ISLAM was to continue vigorously until the fifteenth century. It was given unity and fervour by Christianity, the deepest source of European self-consciousness,

The participants of the People's Crusade set off for Jerusalem ahead of the armies of the First Crusade in 1096. They were massacred by the Seljuk Turks in Anatolia, as this contemporary illustration shows.

which bound people together in a great moral and spiritual enterprise. (Similar fervour came to be generated among Muslims, at times proclaimed as a *Jihad* or Holy War, but its effects seemed less far-reaching.) Christian crusading also provided a licence for the predatory appetites of the military class which dominated lay society. They could despoil the pagans with clear consciences. The Normans, always great predators, were in the vanguard, taking south Italy and Sicily from the Arabs, a task effectively complete by 1100. (Almost incidentally they swallowed the last Byzantine possessions in the West as well.) The other great struggle in Europe against Islam was the epic of Spanish history, the Reconquest, whose climax came in 1492, when Granada, the last Muslim capital of Spain, fell to the armies of the Catholic monarchs.

The Spaniards had come to see the Reconquest as a religious cause, and as such it had drawn warriors from all over Europe since its beginnings in the eleventh century. It had benefited from the same religious revival and quickening of vigour in the West which expressed itself in a succession of great enterprises in Palestine and Syria. The earliest and most successful crusade was launched in 1096. Within three years the crusaders recaptured Jerusalem, where they celebrated the triumph of the Gospel of Peace by an appalling massacre of their prisoners, women and children included. The Second Crusade (1147–9), in contrast, *began* with a successful massacre (of Jews in the Rhineland), but thereafter, though the presence of an emperor and a king of France gave it greater importance than its predecessor, it was a disaster. It failed to recover Edessa, the city whose loss had largely provoked it, and did much to discredit St Bernard, its most fervent advocate (though it had a by-product of some importance when an English fleet took Lisbon from the Arabs and it passed into the hands of the King of Portugal). Then in 1187 Saladin recaptured Jerusalem for Islam. The Third Crusade which followed (1189–1192) was socially the most spectacular. A German emperor (drowned in the course of it) and the kings of England and France all took part. They quarrelled and the

Richard the Lionheart was one of the main protagonists in the Third Crusade, together with Philip II of France and Emperor Frederick I Barbarossa. One of its most significant achievements was the taking of Acre in 1191 (the illustration shows a scene from the siege), although Jerusalem, the crusaders' prime objective, remained in the hands of Saladin.

Time chart (1095–1498)

1120 Order of the Knights Templar is founded

1453 Constantinople falls to the Turks

1492 Columbus crosses the Atlantic and discovers the New World

1000 — 1200 — 1400 — 1600

1095 Urban II proclaims the First Crusade at the Council of Clermont

1309 The papacy is transferred to Avignon

1498 Vasco da Gama circumnavigates the Cape of Good Hope and reaches India

The Crusades

Conventionally, the Crusades were the series of expeditions directed from Western Christendom to the Holy Land whose aim was to recover the Holy Places from their Islamic rulers. Those who took part were assured by papal authority of certain spiritual rewards including indulgences (remission of time spent in purgatory after death) and the status of martyr in the event of death on the expedition. The first four expeditions were the most important and made up what is usually thought of as the crusading era.

1095 Urban II proclaims the First Crusade at the Council of Clermont.

1099 The capture of Jerusalem and foundation of the Latin Kingdom.

1144 The Seljuk Turks capture the (Christian) city of Edessa, whose fall inspires St Bernard's preaching of a new crusade (1146).

1147–9 The Second Crusade is a failure (its only significant outcome is the capture of Lisbon by an English fleet – and its transfer to the King of Portugal).

1187 Saladin reconquers Jerusalem for Islam.

1189 The launch of the Third Crusade, which fails to recover Jerusalem.

1192 Saladin allows pilgrims access to the Holy Sepulchre.

1202 The Fourth Crusade, the last of the major crusades, which culminates in the capture and sack of Constantinople by the crusaders (1204) and the establishment of a "Latin Empire" there.

1212 The so-called "Children's Crusade".

1216 The Fifth Crusade captures Damietta in Egypt, soon lost again.

1228–9 The emperor Frederick II (excommunicate) undertakes a crusade and recaptures Jerusalem, crowning himself king.

1239–40 Crusades by Theobold of Champagne and Richard of Cornwall.

1244 Jerusalem is retaken for Islam.

1248–54 Louis IX of France leads a crusade to Egypt where he is taken prisoner, ransomed and sets out on a pilgrimage to Jerusalem.

1270 Louis IX's second crusade, against Tunis, where he dies.

1281 Acre, the last Christian foothold in the Levant, falls to Islam.

There were many other expeditions to which the title of "crusade" was given, sometimes formally. Some were directed against non-Christians (Moorish Spain and the Slav peoples), some against heretics (such as the Albigensians), some against monarchs who had offended the papacy. There were also further futile expeditions to the Near East. In 1464 Pius II failed to obtain support for what proved to be a last attempt to mount a further crusade to that region.

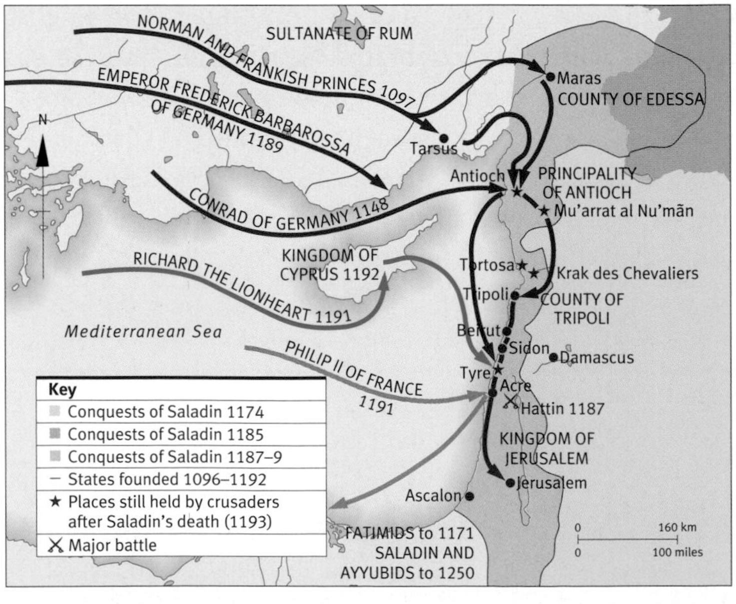

This map shows the routes of the first four crusades.

crusaders failed to recover Jerusalem. No great monarch answered Innocent III's appeal to go on the next crusade, though many land-hungry magnates did. The Venetians financed the expedition, which left in 1202. It was at once diverted by interference in the dynastic troubles of Byzantium, which suited the Venetians, who helped to recapture Constantinople for a deposed emperor. There followed the terrible sack of the city in 1204 and that was the end of the Fourth Crusade, whose monument was the establishment of a "Latin Empire" at Constantinople, which survived there for only a half-century.

One of the crusaders' most famous possessions was Krak des Chevaliers, a castle located in Syria near Tripoli, which was used as a surveillance centre. From 1142 the castle was held by the Knights Hospitallers, who managed to resist Muslim assaults until 1271, when the castle was taken by Sultan Baybars I.

THE CRUSADERS AND THE EUROPEAN OUTLOOK

Several more crusades set out in the thirteenth century, but though they helped to put off a little longer the dangers which faced Byzantium, crusading to the holy land was dead as an independent force. Its religious impulse could still move people, but the first four crusades had too often shown the unpleasant face of greed. They were the first examples of European overseas imperialism, both in their characteristic mixture of noble and ignoble aims, and in their abortive settler colonialism. Whereas in Spain, and on the

The crusaders take Jerusalem

"Our pilgrims, once in the city, chased and killed the Saracens as far as the Temple of Solomon, where they had regrouped and from where they confronted our people in the fiercest fighting of the day, to the point where the whole temple glistened with their blood. In the end, after having defeated the pagans, our people took possession in the temple of a large number of women and children, whom they killed or spared as they pleased. In the upper level of the temple of Solomon, a large group of pagans of both sexes had taken refuge, to whom Tancred and Gaston de Bearn had given their standards as safe-keeping. The crusaders immediately spread all over the city, making off with gold, silver, horses, mules and pillaging the houses that overflowed with riches. Afterwards, absolutely ecstatic and crying with joy, they went to worship at the Sepulchre of our Saviour Jesus and paid their debt with Him. The next morning, our people scaled the roof of the temple and attacked the Saracens, both men and women, and drawing their swords, they beheaded them. Some of them threw themselves off the Temple roof. On seeing this spectacle, Tancred became very indignant."

An anonymous chronicler recounts the taking of Jerusalem by the crusaders on 15 July 1099, during the First Crusade.

This illustration shows the French king Louis IX (1215–1270) setting out on his ill-fated final crusade, which culminated in the surrender of his troops. The captured crusaders were taken to Cairo. In the peace treaty negotiated there the Christians had to give up Damietta.

pagan marches of Germany, Europeans were pushing forward a frontier of settlement, they tried in Syria and Palestine to transplant Western institutions to a remote and exotic setting as well as to seize lands and goods no longer easily available in the West. They did this with clear consciences because their opponents were infidels who had by conquest installed themselves in Christianity's most sacred shrines. "Christians are right, pagans are wrong," said the Song of Roland and that probably sums up well enough the average crusader's response to any qualms about what he was doing.

THE CRUSADERS

The brief successes of the First Crusade had owed much to a passing phase of weakness and anarchy in the Islamic world. The feeble transplants of the Frankish states and the Latin Empire of Constantinople would not last. But there were to be more enduring results, above all in the relations of Christianity and Islam, creating for centuries a sense of unbridgeable ideological separation between the two faiths. What one scholar has well called a "flood of misrepresentation" of Islam was well under way in western Christendom early in the twelfth century. Among other things it ended the possibility of the two religions living side by side, as they had often done in Spain, as well as halting the corrosion of Christian culture there by Muslim learning. But the division of Christendom was embittered, too, by the crusades; the sack of Constantinople had been the work of crusaders. The crusaders had a legacy, moreover, in a new temper in western Christianity, a militant tone and an aggressiveness which would often break out in centuries to come (when it would also be able to exploit technological superiority). In it lay the roots of a mentality which, when secularized, would power the world-conquering culture of the modern era. The Reconquest was scarcely to be complete before the Spanish would look to the Americas for the battlefield of a new crusade.

Yet Europe was not impervious to Islamic influence. In these struggles she imported and invented new habits and institutions. Wherever they encountered Islam, whether in the crusading lands, Sicily or Spain, western Europeans found things to admire. Sometimes they took

The early military orders and the Knights Templar

From the time of St Augustine, the Catholic Church supported the idea of using arms in its defence. Hundreds of knights from all over Europe took part in the Spanish Reconquest, many of whom later went on to spearhead the Christian armies which travelled to the Near East with the intention of liberating the Holy Places. It is in this context that the military orders were born, combining the religious spirit of the monastic order with the warrior ideal of the knightly order.

Many medievalists believe that the origins of the military orders lie in the Muslim world, in the famous *ribats* – frontier castles where the faithful offered temporary military service. Some experts hold that there are parallels between the Christian idea of Holy War and the Islamic *jihad*. Other scholars reject these theories, in the belief that the military orders had Latin origins and emerged from the internal transformations which were taking place within the Catholic Church during that period.

The first military orders – the Hospitallers and the Templars – were founded at the beginning of the 12th century. The Order of the Knights of the Temple, or Templars, was established in 1120 by Hugh of Payns, a French knight, who had long dreamed of creating a new religious order of knights whose role would be to protect pilgrims. From the foundation of their order, the Templars received substantial donations, making it one of the best-funded orders in Christendom. The Templar Rule was approved at the Council of Troyes in 1129, having been enthusiastically defended by St Bernard of Clairvaux.

This picture by the Spanish painter Casado de Alisal depicts Pope Alexander III confirming the foundation of the Order of Santiago in 1170.

up luxuries not to be found at home: silk clothes, the use of perfumes and new dishes. One habit acquired by some crusaders was that of taking more frequent baths. This may have been unfortunate, for it added the taint of religious infidelity to a habit already discouraged in Europe where bath-houses were associated with sexual licence. Cleanliness had not yet achieved its later quasi-automatic association with godliness.

MILITARY ORDERS

One institution crystallizing the militant Christianity of the high Middle Ages was the military order of knighthood. It brought together soldiers who professed vows as members of a religious order and of an accepted discipline to fight for the faith. Some of these orders became very rich, owning endowments in many countries. The Knights of St John of Jerusalem (who are still in existence) were to be for centuries in the forefront of the battle against Islam. The Knights Templar rose to such great power and prosperity that they were destroyed by a French king who feared them, and the Spanish military orders of Calatrava and Santiago were in the forefront of the Reconquest.

Another military order operated in the

north, the Teutonic Knights, the warrior monks who were the spearhead of Germanic penetration of the Baltic and Slav lands. There, too, missionary zeal combined with greed and the stimulus of poverty to change both the map and the culture of a whole region. The colonizing impulse which failed in the Near East had lasting success further north. German expansion eastwards was a huge folk-movement, a centuries-long tide of men and women clearing forest, planting homesteads and villages, founding towns, building fortresses to protect them and monasteries and churches to serve them. When the crusades were over, and the narrow escape from the Mongols had reminded Europe that it could still be in danger, this movement went steadily on. Out on the Prussian and Polish marches, the soldiers, among whom the Teutonic Knights were outstanding,

This painting, which dates from c.1600, represents a 13th-century battle between Turkish troops and the Knights of the Teutonic Order. One of the German knights in the foreground is carrying a flag bearing the emblem of the Teutonic cross.

provided its shield and cutting edge at the expense of the native peoples. This was the beginning of a cultural conflict between Slav and Teuton which persisted down to the twentieth century. The last time that the West threw itself into the struggle for Slav lands was in 1941: many Germans saw "Barbarossa" (as Hitler's attack on Russia was named in memory of a medieval emperor) as another stage in a centuries-old civilizing mission in the East. In the thirteenth century a Russian prince, Alexander Nevsky, Grand Duke of Novgorod, had to beat off the Teutonic Knights (as Russians were carefully reminded by a great film in 1937) at a moment when he also faced the Tatars on another front.

THE SHAPING OF THE RUSSIAN STATE

While the great expansion of the German East between 1100 and 1400 made a new economic, cultural and racial map, it also raised yet another barrier to the union of the two Christian traditions. Papal supremacy in the West made the Catholicism of the late medieval period more uncompromising and more unacceptable than ever to Orthodoxy. From the twelfth century onwards Russia was more and more separated from western Europe by her own traditions and special historical experience. The Mongol capture of Kiev in 1240 had been a blow to Eastern Christianity as grave as the sack of Constantinople in 1204. It also broke the princes of Muscovy. With Byzantium in decline and the Germans and Swedes on their backs, they were to pay tribute to the Mongols and their Tatar successors of the Golden Horde for centuries. This long domination by a nomadic people was another historical experience sundering Russia from the West.

Tatar domination had its greatest impact on the southern Russian principalities, the area where the Mongol armies had operated. A new balance within Russia appeared; Novgorod and Moscow acquired new importance after the eclipse of Kiev, though both paid tribute to the Tatars in the form of silver, recruits and labour. Their emissaries, like other Russian princes, had to go to the Tatar capital at Sarai on the Volga, and make their separate arrangements with their conquerors. It was a period of the greatest dislocation and confusion in the succession patterns of the Russian states. Both Tatar policy and the struggle to survive favoured those which were most despotic. The future political tradition of Russia was thus now shaped by the Tatar experience as it had been by the inheritance of imperial ideas from Byzantium. Gradually Moscow emerged as the focus of a new centralizing trend. The process can be discerned as early as the reign of Alexander Nevsky's son, who was prince of Muscovy. His successors had the support of the Tatars, who found them efficient tax gatherers. The Church offered no resistance and the metropolitan archbishopric was transferred from Vladimir to Moscow in the fourteenth century.

Meanwhile, a new challenge to Orthodox Christianity had arisen in the West. A Roman Catholic but half-Slav state had emerged which was to hold Kiev for three centuries. This was the medieval duchy of Lithuania, formed in 1386 in a union by marriage which incorporated the Polish kingdom and covered much of modern Poland, Prussia, the Ukraine and Moldavia. Fortunately for the Russians, the Lithuanians fought the Germans, too; it was they who shattered the Teutonic Knights at Tannenberg in 1410. Harassed by the Germans and the Lithuanians to the west, Muscovy somehow survived by exploiting divisions within the Golden Horde.

Ivan IV, known as Ivan the Terrible, ruled over Russia from 1533 to 1584. He ruthlessly eliminated his enemies, making full use of the despotic powers with which his grandfather, Ivan the Great, had invested the Russian monarchy.

The fall of Constantinople brought a great change to Russia; Eastern Orthodoxy had now to find its centre there, and not in Byzantium. Russian churchmen soon came to feel that a complex purpose lay in such awful events. Byzantium, they believed, had betrayed its heritage by seeking religious compromise at the Council of Florence. "Constantinople has fallen", wrote the metropolitan of Moscow, "because it has deserted the true Orthodox faith ... There exists only one true Church on earth, the Church of Russia." A few decades later, at the beginning of the sixteenth century, a monk could write to the ruler of Muscovy in a quite new tone: "Two Romes have fallen, but the third stands and a fourth will not be. Thou art the only Christian sovereign in the world, the lord of all faithful Christians."

IVAN THE GREAT

The end of Byzantium came when other historical changes made Russia's emergence from confusion and Tatar domination possible and likely. The Golden Horde was rent by dissension in the fifteenth century. At the same time, the Lithuanian state began to crumble. These were opportunities, and a ruler who was capable of exploiting them came to the throne of Muscovy in 1462. Ivan the Great (Ivan III) gave Russia something like the definition and reality won by England and France from the twelfth century onwards. Some have seen him as the first national ruler of Russia. Territorial consolidation was the foundation of his work. When Muscovy swallowed the republics of Pskov and Novgorod, his authority stretched at least in theory as far as the Urals. The oligarchies which had ruled them were deported, to be replaced by men who held lands from Ivan in return for service. The German merchants of the Hanse who had dominated the trade of these republics were expelled, too. The Tatars made another onslaught on Moscow in 1481 but were beaten off, and two invasions of Lithuania gave Ivan much of White Russia and Little Russia in 1503. His successor took Smolensk in 1514.

Ivan the Great was the first Russian ruler to take the title of "Tsar". It was a conscious evocation of an imperial past, a claim to the heritage of the Caesars, the word from which it originated. In 1472 Ivan married a niece of the last Greek emperor. He was called "autocrat by the grace of God" and during his reign the double-headed eagle was adopted, which was to remain part of the insignia of Russian rulers until 1917. This gave a further Byzantine colouring to Russian monarchy and Russian history, which became still more unlike that of western Europe. By 1500 western Europeans already recognized a distinctive kind of monarchy in Russia; Basil, Ivan's successor, was acknowledged to have a despotic power over his subjects greater than that of any other Christian rulers over theirs.

EUROPE TURNS TO THE OCEANS

Much of Europe's future seems already discernible by 1500. A great process of definition and realization had been going on for centuries. Europe's land limits were now filled up; in the East further advance was blocked by the consolidation of Christian Russia, in the Balkans by the Ottoman Empire of Islam. The first, crusading, wave of overseas expansion was virtually spent by about 1250. With the onset of the Ottoman threat in the fifteenth century, Europe was again forced on the defensive in the eastern Mediterranean and Balkans. Those unhappy states with exposed territories in the East, such as Venice, had to look after them as best they could. Meanwhile, others were taking a new look at their oceanic horizons. A new phase of western Europe's relations with the rest of the world was about to open.

In 1400 it had still seemed sensible to see Jerusalem as the centre of the world. Though the Vikings had crossed the Atlantic, Europeans could still think of a world which, though spherical, was made up of three continents, Europe, Asia and Africa, around the shores of one land-locked sea, the Mediterranean. A huge revolution lay just ahead, which for ever swept away such views, and the route to it lay across the oceans because elsewhere advance was blocked. Europe's first direct contacts with the East had been on land rather than on water. The caravan routes of Central Asia were their main channel and brought goods west to be shipped from Black Sea or Levant ports. Elsewhere, ships rarely ventured far south of Morocco until the fifteenth century. Then, a mounting wave of maritime enterprise becomes noticeable. With it, the age of true world history was beginning.

The Portuguese galleons and caravels represented in this manuscript were in use during the late 16th century.

ADVANCES IN MARITIME TECHNOLOGY

One explanation of the boom in maritime enterprise was the acquisition of new tools and skills. Different ships and new techniques of long-range navigation were needed for oceanic sailing and they became available from the fourteenth century onwards, thus making possible the great effort of exploration which has led to the fifteenth century being called "the Age of Reconnaissance". In ship design there were two crucial changes. One was specific, the adoption of the sternpost rudder; though we do not know exactly when this happened, some ships had it by 1300. The other was a more gradual and complex process of improving rigging. This went with a growth in the size of ships. A more complex maritime trade no doubt spurred such developments. By 1500 the tubby medieval "cog" of northern Europe, square-rigged with a single sail and mast, had developed into a ship carrying up to three masts, with mixed sails. The main-mast still carried square-rigging, but more than one sail; the mizzen-mast had a big lateen sail borrowed from the Mediterranean tradition; a fore-mast might carry more square-rigged sails, but also newly invented fore-and-aft jib sails attached to a bowsprit. Together with the lateen sail aft, these head-sails made vessels much more manoeuvrable; they could be sailed much closer to the wind.

Once these innovations were absorbed, the design of ships which resulted was to remain essentially unchanged (though refined) until the coming of steam propulsion. Though he would have found them small and cramped, Columbus's ships would have been perfectly comprehensible machines to a nineteenth-century clipper captain. Since they carried guns, though tiny ones by comparison with what was to come, they would equally have been comprehensible to Nelson.

Prince Henry of Portugal (1394–1460), portrayed in this detail from a triptych panel, was known as "the Navigator". One of his main contributions to navigation was his establishment at Sagres of a settlement where he gathered together mathematicians, shipbuilders and cartographers. At this nautical think-tank, the combination of classical and Arabic knowledge produced significant advances in ship design.

NAVIGATIONAL INNOVATIONS

By 1500 some crucial navigational developments had also taken place. The Vikings had first shown how to sail an oceanic course. They had better ships and navigational skill than anything previously available in the West. Using the Pole Star and the sun, whose height above the horizon in northern latitudes at midday had been computed in tables by a tenth-century Irish astronomer, they had crossed the Atlantic by running along a line of latitude. Then, with the thirteenth century, there is evidence of two great innovations. At that time the compass came to be commonly used in the Mediterranean (it already existed in China, but, though it seems likely, it is not known if or how it was transmitted from Asia to the West), and in 1270 there appears the first reference to a chart, one used in a ship engaged on a crusading venture. The next two centuries gave birth to modern geography and exploration. Spurred by the thought of commercial prizes, by missionary zeal and diplomatic possibilities, some princes began to subsidize research. In the fifteenth century they came to employ their own cartographers and hydrographers. Foremost among these princes was the brother of the King of Portugal, Henry, "the Navigator" as English-speaking scholars were later to call him (unsuitably, for he never navigated anything).

PORTUGUESE EXPLORATION

The Portuguese had a long Atlantic coast. They were land-locked by Spain, and increasingly barred from the Mediterranean trade by the experience and armed force with which the Italians guarded it. Almost inevitably, it seems, they were bound to push out into the Atlantic. They had already started to familiarize themselves with northern waters when Prince

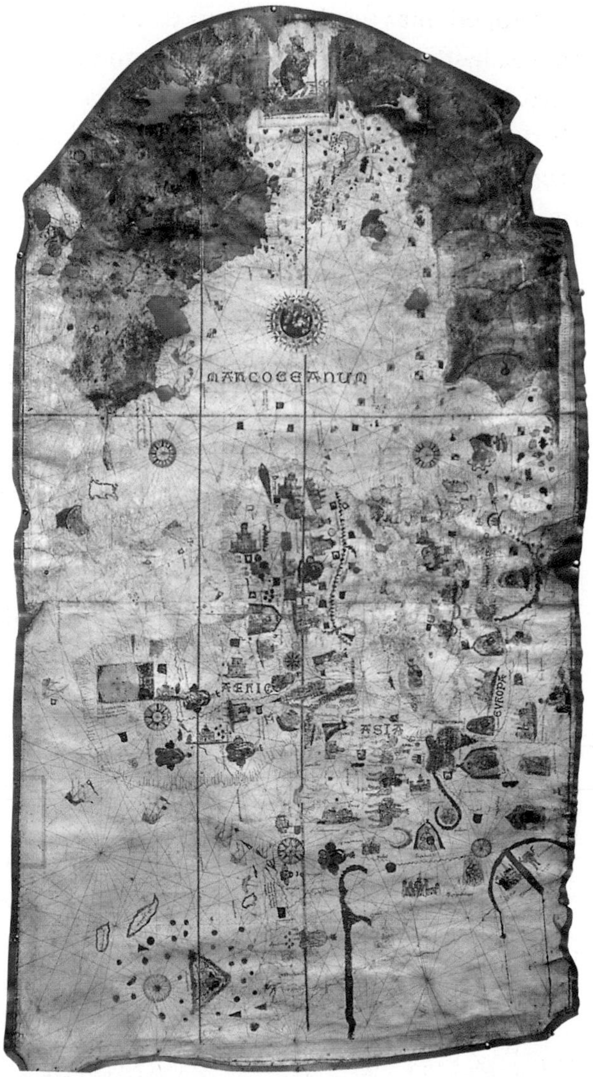

Spanish cartographer Juan de Cosa drew up this first general map of the New World around 1500.

Henry began to equip and launch a series of maritime expeditions. His initiative was decisive. From a mixture of motives, he turned his countrymen southwards. Gold and pepper, it was known, were to be found in the Sahara; perhaps the Portuguese could discover where. Perhaps, too, there was a possibility of finding an ally here to take the Turk in the flank, the legendary Prester John. Certainly there were converts, glory and land to be won for the Cross. Henry, for all that he did so much to launch Europe on the great expansion which transformed the globe and created one world, was a medieval man to the soles of his boots. He cautiously sought papal authority and approval for his expeditions. He had gone crusading in North Africa, taking with him a fragment of the True Cross, and had taken part in the Portuguese capture of Ceuta in 1415 which ended the Islamic stranglehold on west Mediterranean sea lanes. He dominated the start of the age of discovery, whose heart was systematic, government-subsidized research. Yet its spirit was rooted in the world of chivalry and crusade which had shaped Henry's thinking. He is an outstanding example of a man who wrought much more than he knew.

The Portuguese pushed steadily south. They began by hugging the African coast, but some of the bolder among them reached the Madeiras and had begun to settle there already in the 1420s. In 1434 one of their captains passed Cape Bojador, an important psychological obstacle whose overcoming was Henry's first great triumph; ten years later they rounded Cape Verde and established themselves in the Azores. By then they had perfected the caravel, a ship which used new rigging to tackle head winds and contrary currents on the home voyage by going right out into the Atlantic and sailing a long semicircular course home. In 1445 they reached Senegal. Their first fort was built soon after. Henry died in 1460, but by then his countrymen were ready to continue further south. In 1473 they crossed the Equator and in 1487 they were at the Cape of Good Hope. Ahead lay the Indian Ocean; Arabs had long traded across it and pilots were available. Beyond it lay even richer sources of spices. In 1498 Vasco da Gama dropped anchor at last in Indian waters.

COLUMBUS AND THE NEW WORLD

By the time Vasco da Gama ventured into the Indian Ocean, another sailor, the Genoese Columbus, had crossed the Atlantic to look for Asia, confident in the light of Ptolemaic geography that he would soon come to it. He failed. Instead he discovered the Americas for the Catholic monarchs of Spain. In the name of the "West Indies" the modern map commemorates his continuing belief that he had accomplished the discovery of islands off Asia by his astonishing venture, so different from the cautious, though brave, progress of the Portuguese towards the East around Africa. Unlike them, but unwittingly, he had in fact discovered an entire continent, though even on the much better-equipped second voyage which he made in 1493 he explored only its islands. The Portuguese had reached a known continent by a new route. Soon (though to his dying day Columbus refused to admit it, even after two more voyages and arrival on the mainland) it began to be realized that what he had discovered might not be Asia after all. In 1494 the historic name "New World" was first applied to what had been found in the western hemisphere. (Not until 1726, though, was it to be realized that Asia and America were not joined together in the region of the Bering Straits.)

THE IMPORTANCE OF THE ATLANTIC

The two enterprising Atlantic nations tried to come to understandings about their respective interests in a world of widening horizons. The first European treaty about trade outside European waters had been made by Portugal and Spain in 1479; now they went on to delimit spheres of influence. The pope made a temporary award, based on a division of the world between them along a line a hundred leagues west of the Azores, but this was overtaken by the treaty of Tordesillas in 1494, which gave to Portugal all the lands east of a line of longitude running 370 leagues west of Cape Verde and to Spain all those lands west of it. In 1500 a Portuguese squadron on the way to the Indian Ocean ran out into the Atlantic to

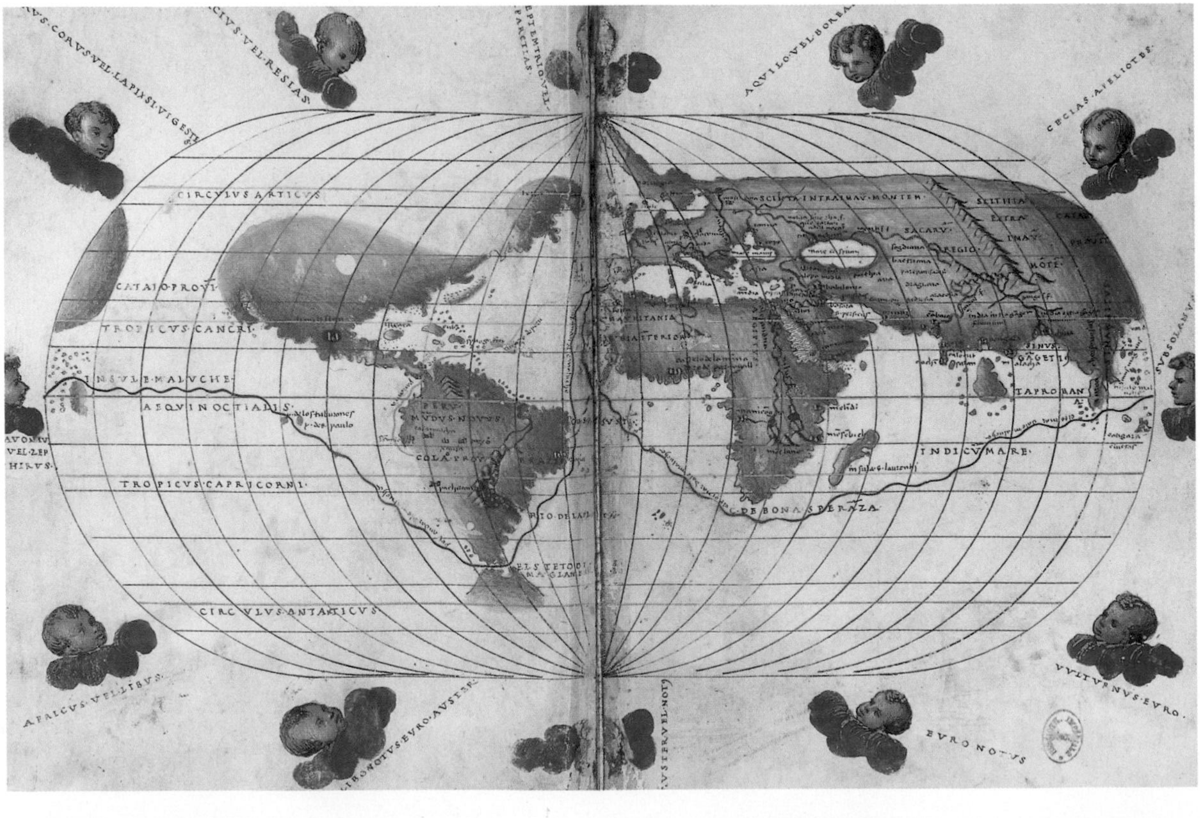

This map of the world, drawn up by Battista Agnese in 1540, shows the route Magellan followed in the first circumnavigation of the globe.

avoid adverse winds and to its surprise struck land which lay east of the treaty line and was not Africa. It was Brazil. Henceforth Portugal had an Atlantic as well as an Asian destiny. Though the main Portuguese effort still lay to the east, an Italian in Portuguese service, Amerigo Vespucci, soon afterwards ran far enough to the south to show that not merely islands but a whole new continent lay between Europe and Asia by a western route. Before long it was named after him – America – the name of the southern continent later being extended to the northern, too.

THE FIRST CIRCUMNAVIGATION OF THE GLOBE

In 1522, thirty years after Columbus's landfall in the Bahamas, a ship in the Spanish service completed the first voyage around the world. The commander under whom it sailed was Magellan, a Portuguese; he got as far as the Philippines, where he was killed, having discovered and sailed through the straits named after him. With this voyage and its demonstration that all the great oceans were interconnected, the prologue to the European age can be considered over. Just about a century of discovery and exploration had changed the shape of the world and the course of history. From this time the nations with access to the Atlantic would have opportunities denied to the land-locked powers of central Europe and the Mediterranean. In the first place this meant Spain and Portugal, but they would be joined and surpassed by France, Holland and, above all, England, a collection of harbours incomparably placed at the centre of the newly enlarged hemisphere, all of them easily accessible from their shallow hinterland, and within easy striking distance of all the great European sea routes of the next two hundred years.

The voyages undertaken by Italian, Portuguese and Spanish sailors during the 15th century brought about great improvements in map-making. This "Mappamundi" (Map of the World) by Fra Mauro dates from 1459.

PROGRESS IN CARTOGRAPHY

The enterprise behind these changes had only been possible because of a growing substratum of maritime skill and geographical knowledge. The new and characteristic figure of this movement was the professional explorer and navigator. Many of the earliest among them were, like Columbus himself, Italian. New knowledge, too, underlay not only the conception of these voyages and their successful technical performance, but also allowed Europeans to see their relationship with the world in a new way. To sum the matter up, Jerusalem ceased to be centre of the world; the maps men began to draw, for all their crudity, are maps which show the basic structure of the real globe.

In 1400 a Florentine had brought back from Constantinople a copy of Ptolemy's *Geography*. The view of the world it contained had been virtually forgotten for a thousand years. In the second century CE Ptolemy's world already included the Canaries, Iceland and Ceylon, all of which found a place on his maps, along with the misapprehension that the Indian Ocean was totally enclosed by land. Translation of his text, misleading as it was, and the multiplication of copies first in manuscript and then in print (there were six editions between 1477, when it was first printed, and 1500) was a great stimulus to better map-making. The atlas – a collection of engraved and printed maps bound in a book – was invented in the sixteenth century; more Europeans than ever could now buy or consult a picture of their world. With better projections, navigation was simpler, too. Here the great figure was a Dutchman, Gerhard Kremer, who is remembered as Mercator. He was the first man to print on a map the word "America" and he invented the projection which is still today the most familiar – a map of the world devised as if it were an unrolled cylinder, with Europe at its centre. This solved the problem of providing a flat surface on which to read direction and courses without distortion, even if it posed problems in the calculation of distances. The Greeks of the fourth century BCE had known the world was a globe and the making of terrestrial and celestial globes was another important branch of the geographical revolution (Mercator made his first globe in 1541).

An allegory of Amerigo Vespucci's famous voyage, carried out in the service of the Portuguese monarchy. Vespucci first discovered the bay of Rio de Janeiro, then, on reaching the south of Patagonia, he realized that he was not sailing along the coastline of southern Asia, as he had thought, but along the shores of a new continent – America.

A NEW CONFIDENCE

The most striking thing about this progression is its cumulative and systematic nature. European expansion in the next phase of world history would be conscious and directed as it had never been before. Europeans had long wanted land and gold; the greed which lay at the heart of enterprise was not new. Nor was the religious zeal which sometimes inspired them and sometimes cloaked their springs of action even from the actors themselves. What was new was a growing confidence derived from knowledge and success. Europeans stood in 1500 at the beginning of an age in which their energy and confidence would grow seemingly without limit. The world did not come to them, they went out to it and took it.

The scale of such a break with the past was not to be seen at once. In the Mediterranean and Balkans, Europeans still felt threatened and defensive. Navigation and seamanship still had far to go – not until the eighteenth century, for example, would there be available a timekeeper accurate enough for exact sailing. But the way was opening to new relationships between Europe and the rest of the world, and between European countries themselves. Discovery would be followed by conquest, and then, in due time, by the exploitation of vast new overseas resources by Europeans. A world revolution was beginning. An equilibrium which had lasted a thousand years was dissolving. As the next two centuries unrolled, thousands of ships would put out year after year, day after day, from Lisbon, Seville, London, Bristol,

This imaginary portrait of the Graeco-Egyptian astronomer and geographer Ptolemy was painted in the 15th century by Justus of Ghent.

This 16th-century portrait depicts Francisco de Almeida (1450–1510), who was a soldier and explorer and the first viceroy of Portuguese India.

Nantes, Antwerp and many other European ports, in search of trade and profit in other continents. They would sail to Calicut, Canton, Nagasaki. In time, they would be joined by ships from places where Europeans had established themselves overseas – from Boston and Philadelphia, Batavia and Macao. And during all that time, not one Arab dhow was to find its way to Europe; it was 1848 before a Chinese junk was brought to the Thames. Only in 1867 would a Japanese vessel cross the Pacific to San Francisco, long after the great sea-lanes had been established by Europeans.

THE EUROPEAN MIND

IN 1500 EUROPE IS CLEARLY recognizable as the centre of a new civilization; before long that civilization was to spread to other lands, too. Its heart was still religion. The institutional implications of this have already been touched upon; the Church was a great force of social regulation and government, whatever vicissitudes its central institution had suffered. But it was also the custodian of culture and the teacher of all, the vehicle and vessel of civilization itself.

THE FIRST EUROPEAN UNIVERSITIES

Since the thirteenth century the burden of recording, teaching and study so long borne by the monks had been shared by friars and, more important still, by a new institution, in which friars sometimes played a big part – the universities. Bologna, Paris and Oxford were the first of them; by 1400 there were fifty-three more. They were new devices both for concentrating and directing intellectual activity and for education. One result was the revivifying of the training of the clergy. Already in the middle of the fourteenth century half the English bishops were graduates. But this was not the only reason why universities had been set up. The Emperor Frederick II founded the University of Naples to supply administrators for his south Italian kingdom; and when in 1264 Walter de Merton, an English bishop and royal servant, founded the first college at Oxford, among his purposes was that of providing future servants for the crown.

The universities' importance for the future of Europe, though, was greater than this, yet it could not have been foreseen and proved in one respect incalculable. Their existence

Students are portrayed attending a class at the Sorbonne in this 16th-century illustration. The Maison de la Sorbonne was founded in 1257 by Robert de Sorbon as a theological college, and soon became the central institution of the University of Paris.

Medieval universities

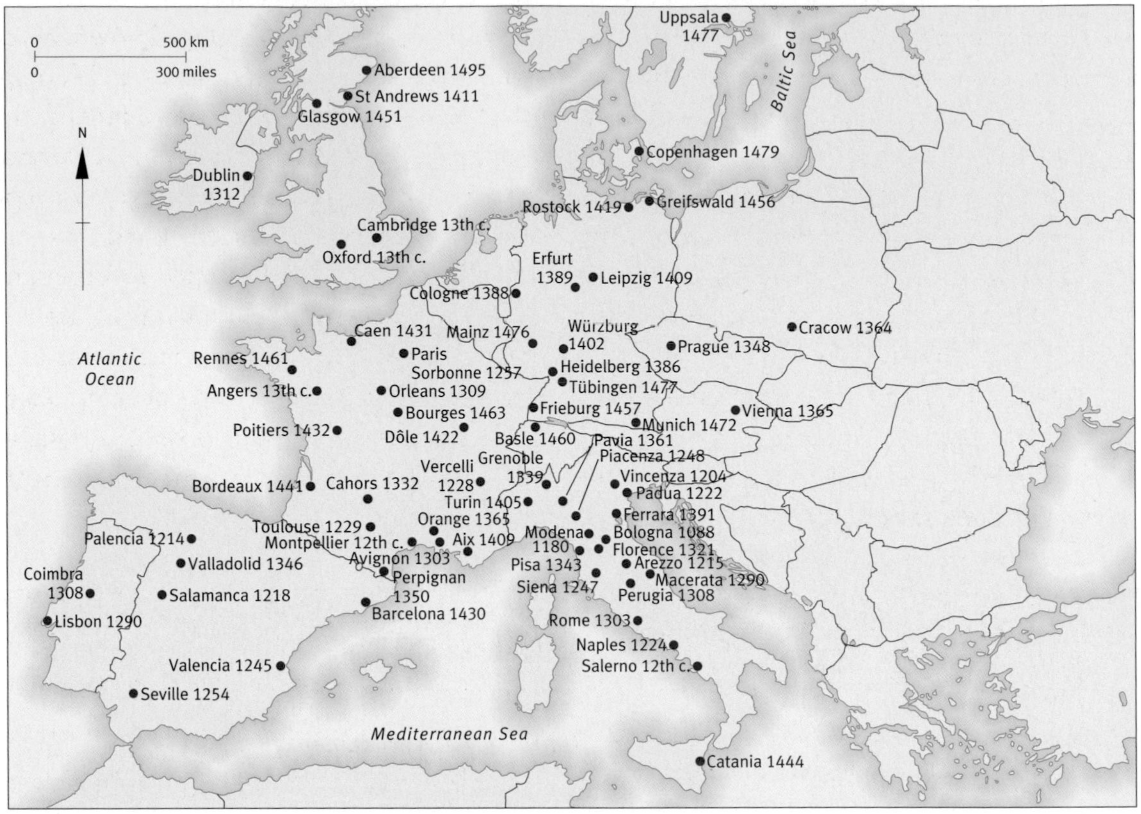

This map indicates medieval Europe's major universities and the dates when they were founded.

assured that when laymen came to be educated in substantial numbers, they, too, would long be formed by an institution under the control of the Church and suffused with religion. Furthermore, universities would be a great uniting, cosmopolitan cultural force. Their lectures were given in Latin, the language of the Church and the lingua franca of educated men. Its former pre-eminence is still commemorated today in the vestigial Latin of university ceremonies and the names of degrees.

THE CLASSICAL HERITAGE

Law, medicine, theology and philosophy all benefited from the new institution. Philosophy had all but disappeared into theology in the early medieval period. Only one important figure stands out, John Scotus Erigena, an Irish thinker and scholar of the ninth century. Then, as direct translation from Greek to Latin began in the twelfth century, European scholars could read for themselves works of classical philosophy. The texts became available from Islamic sources. As the works of Aristotle and Hippocrates were turned into Latin they were at first regarded with suspicion. This persisted until well into the thirteenth century, but gradually a search for reconciliation between the classical and Christian accounts of the world got under way and it became clear – above all because of the work of two Dominicans, Albertus Magnus and his pupil Thomas Aquinas – that reconciliation and synthesis were indeed possible. So it came about that the classical heritage was recaptured and rechristened in western Europe. Instead of providing a contrasting and critical approach to the theocentric culture of Christendom, it was incorporated within it. The classical world began to be seen as the forerunner of the Christian. For centuries men and women would turn for authority in matters intellectual to religion or to the classics. Of the latter it was Aristotle who enjoyed unique prestige. If it could not make him a saint, the Church at least treated him as a kind of prophet.

The immediate evidence was the remarkable systematic and rationalist achievement of medieval scholasticism, the name given to the intellectual effort to penetrate the meaning of Christian teaching. Its strength lay in its embracing sweep, displayed nowhere more brilliantly than in the *Summa Theologica* of Aquinas, which has been judged, contrastingly, for both its crowning achievement and a brittle synthesis. It strove to account for all phenomena. Its weakness lay in its unwillingness to address itself to observation and experiment. Christianity gave the medieval mind a powerful training in logical thinking, but only a few people, isolated and untypical, could dimly see the possibility of breaking through authority to a truly experimental method.

St Thomas Aquinas

The teacher and theologian Thomas Aquinas was born into a noble family in Roccasecca, near Aquino, in around 1225. At the age of six he was sent as an oblate to the well-known monastery of Monte Cassino. He went on to study at the University of Naples and was admitted, against his family's wishes, to the Dominican order of mendicants in 1243. Aquinas obtained his Master's degree in Paris in 1257, at which point he began to have his work published; the most notable product of his early years was Book I of *Summa contra gentiles*. It was in the Vatican in Italy, however, that Aquinas began work in 1266 on the treatise which would eventually make him famous: his *Summa Theologica*. This influential work was still incomplete when Aquinas died in 1274.

The aim of all of Aquinas' work, which is collectively known as "Thomism", was to adapt and reconcile Aristotle's writings to Christian thinking, using arguments based on reasoning as well as faith. *Summa Theologica* includes the "five ways", which claim to offer proof of God's existence. Although his writing caused divisions within the Church – the Dominicans supported his theories, while the Franciscans opposed them – in time, the philosophy of Thomas Aquinas was to become the official doctrine of the Catholic Church.

This 14th-century fresco, from the church of St Maria Novella in Florence, represents the triumph of St Thomas Aquinas.

During the reign of Alfonso X, the Iberian peninsula enjoyed a time of fruitful cooperation between the Christian, Muslim and Jewish cultures which coexisted there. From a manuscript entitled *The Book of Chess, Dice and Boards*, written by the king himself, this illustration represents a Christian and a Muslim playing chess.

ISLAM AND EUROPE

Nevertheless, within the Christian culture the first signs of liberation from the enclosed world of the early Middle Ages can be seen. Paradoxically, Christendom owed them to Islam, though for a long time there was deep suspicion and fear in the attitudes of ordinary people towards Arab civilization. There was also ignorance (before 1100, one medievalist has pointed out, there is no evidence that anyone in northern Europe had ever heard the name of Muhammad). Not until 1143 was a Latin translation of the Koran available. Easy and tolerant relationships between the faithful and the infidel (both sides thought in the same terms) were possible only in a few places. In Sicily and Spain, above all, the two cultures could meet. There the great work of translation of the twelfth and thirteenth centuries took place. The Emperor Frederick II was regarded with the deepest suspicion because, although he persecuted heretics, he was known to welcome Jews and Saracens to his court at Palermo. Toledo, the old Visigothic capital, was another especially important centre. In such places scribes copied and recopied the Latin texts of the bestsellers of the next six centuries. Euclid's works began a career of being copied, recopied and then printed, which may well have meant that in the end they surpassed the success of any book except the Bible – at least until the twentieth century – and became the foundation of mathematics teaching in western Europe until the nineteenth century. In such ways the Hellenistic world began again to irrigate the thought of the West.

NEW LINKS WITH ANTIQUITY

Roughly speaking, the Islamic transmission of antiquity began with astrology, astronomy and mathematics, subjects closely linked to one another. Ptolemy's astronomy reached the West by this route and was found a satisfactory basis for cosmology and navigation until the sixteenth century. Islamic cartography was in fact more advanced than European for most of the Middle Ages, and Arab sailors used the magnet for navigation well before their European counterparts (though it was the latter who were to carry through the great oceanic discoveries). The astrolabe had been a Greek invention, but its use was spread in the West by Arab writings. When Chaucer wrote his treatise on its use, he took as his model an earlier Arab one. The arrival from Arab sources of a new numeration and the decimal point (both of Indian origin) was perhaps most important of all; the latter's usefulness in simplifying calculation can be easily tested by trying to write sums in Roman numerals.

Of the sciences of observation other than astronomy, the most important to come to the West from Islam was medicine. Besides providing access to the medical works of Aristotle, Galen and Hippocrates (direct translation from the Greek was not begun until after 1100), Arabic sources and teachers also brought into European practice a huge body of therapeutic, anatomical and pharmacological knowledge built up by Arab physicians. The prestige of Arab learning and science made easier the acceptance of more subtly dangerous and subversive ideas; Arab philosophy and theology, too, began to be studied in the West. In the end, even European art seems to have been affected by Islam, for the invention of perspective, which was to transform painting, is said to have come from thirteenth-century Arab Spain. Europe offered little in exchange except the technology of gunnery.

In the Middle Ages Europe owed more to Islam than to any other contemporary source. For all their dramatic and exotic interest, the travels of a Marco Polo or the missionary wanderings of friars in Central Asia did little to change the West. The quantity of goods exchanged with other parts of the world was still tiny, even in 1500. Technically, Europe owed for certain to the Far East only the art of making silk (which had reached her from the Eastern Empire) and paper which, though made in China in the second century CE, took until the thirteenth to reach Europe and then did so again by way of Arab Spain. Nor did ideas reach Europe from nearer Asia, unless like Indian mathematics they had undergone refinement in the Arabic crucible. Given the permeability of Islamic culture, it seems less likely that this was because, in some sense, Islam insulated Europe from the Orient by imposing a barrier between them, than because China and India were simply too far away. They had hardly been accessible, after all, in pre-Christian antiquity, when communications had been no more difficult.

Great advances were made in the fields of astronomy and medicine in medieval times, largely thanks to knowledge that came from the Islamic world. This 13th-century illustration shows a scene in an Arab pharmacy.

DANTE AND ERASMUS

The reintegration of classical and Christian, though manifested in work like that of Aquinas, was an answer, ten centuries late, to Tertullian's jibing question about what Athens had to do with Jerusalem. In one of the supreme works of art of the Middle Ages – some would judge *the* supreme – the *Divine Comedy* of Dante, the importance of the re-attachment of the world of Christendom to its predecessor is already to be seen. Dante describes his journey through Hell, Purgatory and Paradise, the universe of Christian truth. Yet his guide is not a Christian, but a pagan, the classical poet Virgil. This role is much more than decorative; Virgil is an authoritative guide to truth, for before Christ, he foretold Him. The Roman poet has become a prophet to stand beside those of the Old Testament. Though the notion of a link with

Erasmus of Rotterdam

"Such practices of princes have long been zealously adopted by supreme pontiffs, cardinals, and bishops, and indeed, have almost been surpassed. Yet if any of these were to reflect on the meaning of his linen vestment, snow-white in colour to indicate a pure and spotless life; ... of his crozier, a reminder of his watchful care of the flock entrusted to his keeping ... . But as things are, they think they do well when they're looking after themselves, and responsibility for their sheep they either trust to Christ himself or delegate to their vicars and those they call brothers. They don't even remember that the name 'Bishop', which means 'overseer', indicates work, care, and concern. Yet when it comes to netting their revenues into the bag they can play the overseer well enough – no 'careless look-out' there.

"Similarly, the cardinals might consider how they are the successors of the apostles and are expected to follow the example of their predecessors, and that they are not the lords but the stewards of the spiritual riches for every penny of which they will soon have to render an exact account."

An extract from *Praise of Folly* (1511) by Desiderius Erasmus (1466–1536), translated by Betty Radice.

antiquity had never quite disappeared (as attempts by enthusiastic chroniclers to link the Franks or the Britons to the descendants of the Trojans had shown) there is in Dante's attitude something marking an epoch. The acceptance of the classical world by Christendom, for all the scholastic clutter of its surroundings, had made possible a change which has usually been seen as more radical: the great revival of humanistic letters of the fourteenth to sixteenth centuries. It was a revival long dominated by Latin; only in 1497 did the first Greek grammar to be printed appear.

One emblematic figure of that passage in cultural history was Erasmus of Rotterdam, a sometime monk and later, as the foremost exponent of classical studies of his day, the correspondent of most of the great humanists. Yet he still saw his classics as the entrance to the supreme study of scripture and his most important book was an edition of the Greek New Testament. The effects of printing a good text of the Bible were, indeed, to be revolutionary, but Erasmus had no intention of overthrowing religious order, for all the vigour and wit with which he had mocked and teased puffed-up churchmen, and for all the provocation to independent thought which his books and letters provided. His roots lay in the piety of a fifteenth-century mystical movement in the Low Countries called the *devotio moderna*, not in pagan antiquity.

THE RENAISSANCE IN EUROPE

SOME OF THOSE WHO BEGAN to cultivate the study of classical authors, and to invoke explicitly pagan classical ideals, invented the notion of the "Middle Ages" to emphasize their sense of novelty. They in their turn were later seen as the agents of a "rebirth" of a lost tradition, a "Renaissance" of classical antiquity. Yet they were formed in the culture which the great changes in Christian civilization from the twelfth century onwards had made possible. To speak of Renaissance may be helpful if we keep in mind the limitations of the context in which we use the word, but it falsifies history if we take it to imply a transformation of culture marking a radical break with medieval Christian civilization. The Renaissance is and was a useful myth, one of those ideas which help human beings to master their own bearings and therefore to act more effectively. Whatever the Renaissance may be, there is no clear line in European history which separates it from the Middle Ages – however we like to define them.

What can be noticed almost everywhere, though, is a change of emphasis. It shows especially in the relation of the age to the past. Artists of the thirteenth century, like those of the sixteenth, portrayed the great figures of antiquity in the garb of their own day. Alexander the Great at one time looks like a medieval king; later, Shakespeare's Caesar wears not a toga but doublet and hose. There is, that is to say, no real historical sense in either of these pictures of the past, no awareness of the immense differences between past and present human beings. Instead, history was seen at best as a school of examples. The difference between the two attitudes is that in the medieval view antiquity could also be scrutinized for the signs of a divine plan, evidence of whose existence once more triumphantly vindicated the teachings of the Church. This was St Augustine's legacy and what Dante accepted. But by 1500 something else was also being discerned in the past, equally unhistorical, but, some felt, more helpful to their age and predicament. Some saw a classical inspiration, possibly even pagan, distinct from the Christian, and the new attention to classical writings was one result.

RENAISSANCE ART AND LITERATURE

The idea of Renaissance is especially linked to innovation in art. Medieval Europe had seen much of this; it seems more vigorous and creative than any of the other great centres of

One of the most representative and best-known works of the Renaissance era is *The Birth of Venus*, by Sandro Botticelli (1444–1510). The model for the figure of Venus was Giulio de' Medici's beautiful mistress, Simonetta Cattaneo.

civilized tradition from the twelfth century onwards. In music, drama and poetry new forms and styles were created which move us still. By the fifteenth century, though, it is already clear that they can in no sense be confined to the service of God. Art is becoming autonomous. The eventual consummation of this change was the major aesthetic expression of the Renaissance, transcending by far its stylistic innovations, revolutionary though these were. It is the clearest sign that the Christian synthesis and the ecclesiastical monopoly of culture are breaking up. The slow divergence of classical and Christian mythology was one expression of it; others were the appearance of the Romance and Provençal love poetry (which owed much to Arabic influence), the deployment of the Gothic style in secular building such as the great guildhalls of the new cities, or the rise of a vernacular literature for educated laymen of which perhaps the supreme example is Chaucer's *Canterbury Tales*.

Workers at a medieval printing house, including the proofing corrector and, beside him, the printer.

Such changes are not easily dated, because acceptance did not always follow rapidly on innovation. In literature, there was a particularly severe physical restriction on what could be done because of a long-enduring shortage of texts. It was not until well into the sixteenth century that the first edition of Chaucer's complete works was printed and published. By then a revolution in thinking was undoubtedly under way, of which all the tendencies so far touched on form parts, but which was something much more than the sum of them and it owes almost everything to the coming of the printed book. Even a vernacular text such as the *Canterbury Tales* could not reach a wide public until printing made large numbers of copies easily available. When this happened, the impact of books was vastly magnified. This was true of all classes of book – poetry, history, philosophy, technology and, above all, the Bible itself. The effect was the most profound change in the diffusion of knowledge and ideas since the invention of writing; it was the greatest cultural revolution of these centuries. With hindsight it can be seen as the start of an acceleration of the diffusion of information which is still ongoing.

THE PRINTING REVOLUTION

Although already used there in a different form, the new technique owed nothing to

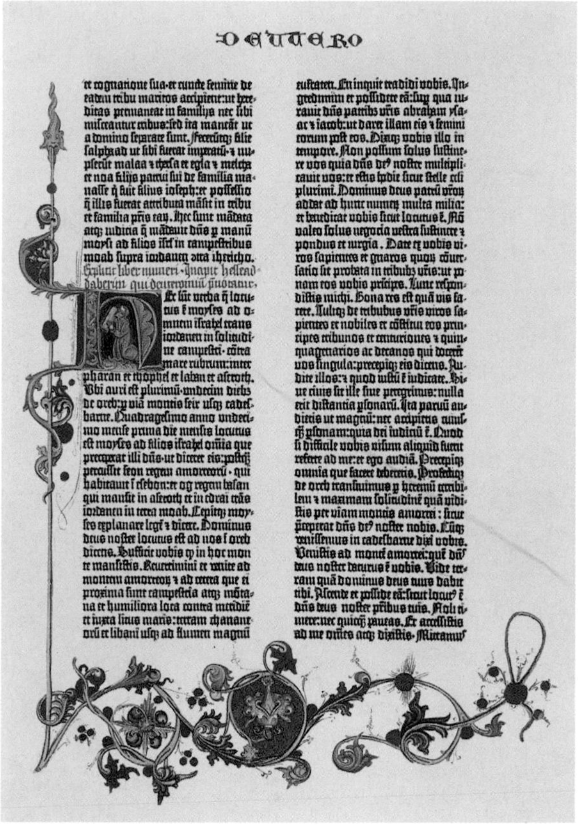

Only 300 copies of the first edition of the Gutenberg Bible were printed. Around 50 copies of the book survive today – a page from one of them is shown here.

stimulus from China, except very indirectly, through the availability of paper. From the fourteenth century, rags were used in Europe to make paper of good quality and this was one of the elements which contributed to the printing revolution. Others were the principle of printing itself (the impressing of images on textiles had been practised in twelfth-century Italy), the use of cast metal for typefaces instead of wood (already used to provide blocks for playing-cards, calendars and religious images), the availability of oil-based ink, and, above all, the use of movable metal type. It was the last invention which was crucial. Although the details are obscure, and experiments with wood letters were going on at the beginning of the fifteenth century in Haarlem, there seems to be no good reason not to credit it to the man whose name has traditionally been associated with it, Johannes Gutenberg, the diamond polisher of Mainz. In about 1450 he and his colleagues brought the elements of modern printing together, and in 1455 there appeared what is agreed to be the first true book printed in Europe, the Gutenberg Bible.

Gutenberg's own business career was by then a failure; something prophetic of a new age of commerce appears in the fact that he was probably under-capitalized. The accumulation of equipment and type was an expensive business and a colleague from whom he borrowed money took him to court for his debts. Judgment went against Gutenberg, who lost his press, so that the Bible, when it appeared, was not his property. (Happily, the story does not end there; Gutenberg was in the end ennobled by the archbishop of Mainz, in recognition of what he had done.) But he had launched a revolution. By 1500, it has been calculated, some thirty-five thousand separate editions of books – *incunabula*, as they were called – had been published. This probably means between fifteen and twenty million copies; there may well have been already at that date fewer copies of books in manuscript in the whole world. In the following century there were between a hundred and fifty and two hundred thousand separate editions and perhaps ten times as many copies printed. Such a quantitative change merges into one which is qualitative; the culture which resulted from the coming of printing with movable type was as different from any earlier one as it is from one which takes radio and television for granted. The modern age was the age of print.

THE DIFFUSION OF PRINTED BIBLES

It is interesting, but unsurprising, that the first printed European book should have been the Bible, the sacred text at the heart of medieval civilization. Through the printing press, knowledge of it was to be diffused as never before and with incalculable results. In 1450 it would have been very unusual for a parish priest to own a Bible, or even to have easy access to one. A century later, it was becoming likely that he had one, and in 1650 it would have been remarkable if he had not. The first printed Bibles were texts of the Latin Vulgate, but vernacular texts soon followed. A German Bible was printed in 1466; Catalan, Czech, Italian and French translations followed before the end of the century, but the English had to wait for a New Testament printed in their language until 1526. Into the diffusion of sacred texts – of which the Bible was only the most important – pious laymen and churchmen alike poured resources for fifty to sixty years; presses were even set up in monastic houses. Meanwhile, grammars, histories and, above all, the classical authors now edited by the humanists, also appeared in increasing numbers. Another innovation from Italy was the introduction of simpler, clearer typefaces modelled upon the manuscript of Florentine scholars, who were themselves copying Carolingian minuscule.

From the end of the 14th century, science entered an era of increased specialization. Technological advances, however, did not mean that religion became less omnipresent: the great clock being inaugurated in this 14th-century manuscript illustration is crowned with a crucifix.

The impact could not be contained. The domination of the European consciousness by printed media would be the outcome. With some prescience the pope suggested to bishops in 1501 that the control of printing might be the key to preserving the purity of the faith. But more was involved than any specific threat to doctrine, important as that might be. The nature of the book itself began to change. Once a rare work of art, whose mysterious knowledge was accessible only to a few, it became a tool and artifact for the many. Print was to provide new channels of communication for governments and a new medium for artists (the diffusion of pictorial and architectural style in the sixteenth century was much more rapid and widespread than ever before because of the growing availability of the engraved print) and would give a new impetus to the diffusion of technology. A huge demand for literacy and therefore education would be stimulated by it. No single change marks so clearly the ending of one era and the beginning of another.

A DAWNING MODERNITY

It is very hard to say exactly what all this meant for Europe's role in the coming era of world history. By 1500, there was certainly much to give confidence to the few Europeans who were likely to think at all about these things. The roots of their civilization lay in a religion which taught them they were a people voyaging in time, their eyes on a future made a little more comprehensible and perhaps a little less frightening by contemplation of past perils navigated and awareness of a common goal. As a result Europe was to be the first civilization aware of time not as endless (though perhaps cyclical) pressure, but as continuing change in a certain direction, as progress. The chosen people of the Bible, after all, were going somewhere; they were not simply a people to whom inexplicable things happened which had to be passively endured. From the simple acceptance of change soon sprang the will to live with constant change – which was to be the peculiarity of modern human beings. Secularized and far away from their origins, such ideas could be very important; the advance of science soon provided an example. In another sense, too, the Christian heritage was decisive for, after the fall of Byzantium, Europeans believed that they alone possessed it (or in effect alone, for there was little sense among ordinary folk of what Slav, Nestorian or Coptic Christianity might be). It was an encouraging idea for those who stood at the threshold of centuries of unfolding power, discovery and conquest. Even with the Ottomans to face, Europe in 1500 was no longer just the beleaguered fortress of the Dark Ages, but a stronghold from which men were beginning to sally forth in counter-attack. Jerusalem had been abandoned to the infidel, Byzantium had fallen. Where should be the new centre of the world?

The men of the Dark Ages, who had somehow persevered in adversity and had built a Christian world from the debris of the past and the gifts of the barbarians, had thus wrought infinitely more than they could have anticipated. Yet such implications required time for their development; in 1500 there was still little to show that the future belonged to the Europeans. Such contacts as they had with other peoples by no means demonstrated the clear superiority of their own way. Portuguese in West Africa might manipulate black people to their own ends and relieve them of their gold dust and slaves, but in Persia or India they stood in the presence of great empires whose spectacle often dazzled them. The Europeans of 1500 were thus, and in many other ways, far from modern. We cannot – without some effort understand them – even when they speak Latin, for their Latin had overtones and associations we are bound to miss; it was not only the language of educated men (and a few women) but the language of religion.

THE OMNIPRESENCE OF RELIGION

In the half-light of a dawning modernity the weight of religion remains the best clue to

Written in Galician-Portuguese, the "Songs of the Virgin Mary" are attributed to Alfonso X, who is thought to have based them on various manuscripts sent to him by Louis XI of France. Here, a musician is shown performing one of the songs, accompanied by a lady playing two idiophones (a type of castanet).

the reality of Europe's first civilization. Religion was one of the most impressive reinforcements of the stability of a culture which has been considered in this book almost entirely from an important but fundamentally anachronistic perspective, that of change. Except in the shortest term, change was not something most Europeans would have been aware of in the fifteenth century. The deepest determinant of the lives of all of them was still the slow but ever-repeated passage of the seasons, a rhythm which set the pattern of work and leisure, poverty and prosperity, of the routines of home, workshop and study. English judges and university teachers still work to a year originally divided by the need to get in the harvest. On this rhythm were imposed those of religion itself. When the harvest was in, the Church blessed it and the calendar of the Christian year provided the more detailed timetable to which life was lived. Some of it was very old, even pre-Christian; it had been going on for centuries and could hardly be imagined otherwise. It even regulated many people's days, for every three hours the religious were called to worship and prayer in thousands of monasteries and convents by the bell of their house. When it could be heard outside the walls, laymen set the pattern of their day by it, too. Before there were striking clocks, only the bell of the parish church, cathedral or monastery supplemented the sun or the burning of a candle as a record of passing time, and it did so by announcing the hour of another act of worship.

CHRISTIANITY'S DUALISM

It is only in a very special, long perspective that we can rightly speak of the centuries during which this went on and on as ones of "revolutionary" changes. Truly revolutionary as some changes were, even the most obvious of them – the growth of a town, an onset of plague, the displacement of one noble family by another, the building of a cathedral or the collapse of a castle – all took place in a remarkably unchanged setting. The shapes of the fields tilled by English peasants in 1500 were often still those visited by the men who wrote them down in Domesday Book, over four hundred years before, and when men went to visit the nuns of Lacock in order to wind up their house in the 1530s, they found, to their amazement, these aristocratic ladies still speaking among themselves the Norman-French commonly used in noble families three centuries earlier.

Such immense inertia must never be forgotten; it was made all the more impressive and powerful by the fleeting lives of most men and women of the Middle Ages. Only very deep in the humus of this society did there lie a future. Perhaps the key to that future's relationship with the past can be located in the fundamental Christian dualism of this life and the world to come, the earthly and the heavenly. This was to prove an irritant of great value, secularized in the end as a new critical instrument, the contrast of what is and what might be, of ideal and actual. In it, Christianity secreted an essence to be utilized against itself, for in the end it would make possible the independent critical stance, a complete break with the world Aquinas and Erasmus both knew. The idea of autonomous criticism would only be born very gradually, though; it can be traced in many individual adumbrations between 1300 and 1700, but they only go to show that, once again, sharp dividing lines between medieval and modern are matters of expository convenience, not of historical reality.

In this painting by Bonifacio de' Pitati (1487–1553) God as the "Eternal Father" appears to be protecting the city of Venice from the advance of a mass of threatening black storm clouds.

B

H

M

T

U

PARTS 1 and 2 Chapters and Contents

BEFORE HISTORY

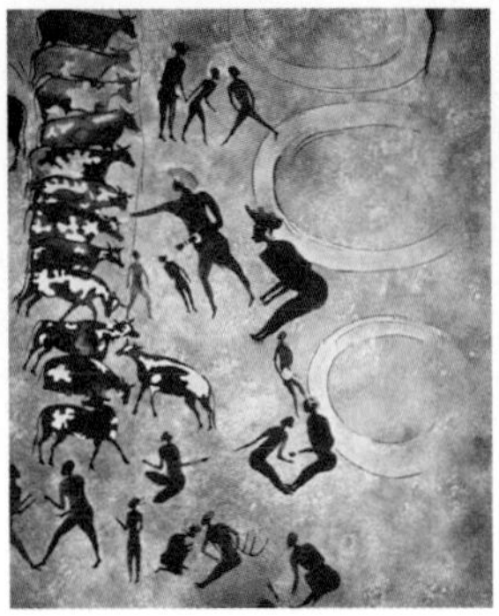

Chapter 1

The Foundations

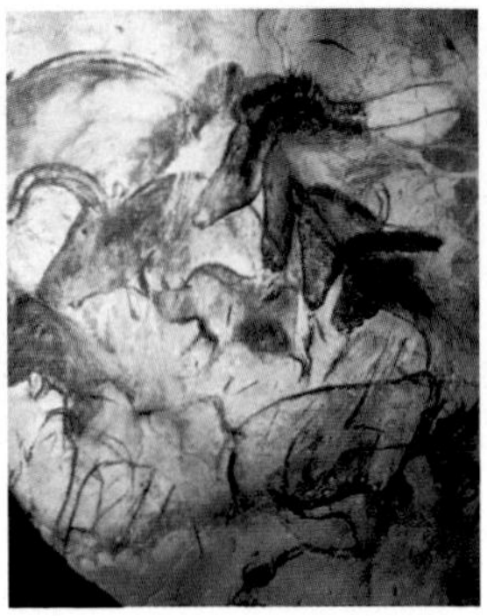

Chapter 2

Homo sapiens

Chapter 3

The Possibility of Civilization

THE FIRST CIVILIZATIONS

Chapter 1

Early Civilized Life

Chapter 2

Ancient Mesopotamia

Chapter 3

Ancient Egypt

Chapter 4

Intruders and Invaders: the Dark Ages of the Ancient Near East

PARTS 3 and 4 Chapters and Contents

THE BEGINNINGS OF CIVILIZATION IN EASTERN ASIA

Chapter 1

Ancient India

Chapter 2

Ancient China

Chapter 3

The Other Worlds of the Ancient Past

Chapter 4

The End of the Old World

THE CLASSICAL MEDITERRANEAN: GREECE

Chapter 1

The Roots of One World

Chapter 2

The Greeks

Chapter 3

Greek Civilization

Chapter 4

The Hellenistic World

PART 5 Chapters and Contents

ROME AND THE CLASSICAL WEST

Chapter 1

Rome

Chapter 2

The Roman Achievement

Chapter 3

Jewry and the Coming of Christianity

Chapter 4

The Waning of the Classical West

Chapter 5

The Elements of a Future

PART 6 Chapters and Contents

THE AGE OF DIVERGING TRADITIONS

Chapter 1

Islam and the Re-making of the Near East

Chapter 2

The Arab Empires

Chapter 3

Byzantium and its Sphere

Chapter 4

The Disputed Legacies of the Near East

Chapter 5

The Making of Europe

PART 7 Chapters and Contents

THE FAR EAST AND A NEW EUROPE

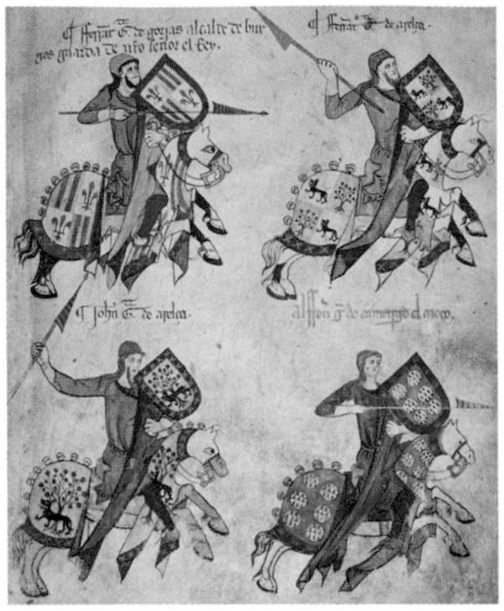

Chapter 1

India

Chapter 2

Imperial China

Chapter 3

Japan

Chapter 4

Worlds Apart

Chapter 5

Europe: the First Revolution

Chapter 6

New Limits, New Horizons

ACKNOWLEDGMENTS

PICTURE CREDITS

The publishers would like to thank the following people and photographic libraries for permission to reproduce their material. Every care has been taken to trace copyright holders. However, if we have omitted anyone we apologize for this and will, if informed, make corrections in any future edition

AA: Art Archive, London
AAA: Ancient Art and Architecture Collection Ltd
ADO Agence Dagli Orti, Paris
AGE: A.G.E. Fotostock, Barcelona
AISA: Archivo Iconografico SA, Barcelona
AKG: AKG-images London
AMH: Archaeological Museum, Heraklion
BAL: Bridgeman Art Library, London
BL: British Library, London
BM: British Museum, London
BN: Bibliothèque Nationale, Paris
BNM: Biblioteca Nacional, Madrid
BPK: Bildarchiv Preussischer Kulturbesitz, Berlin
CP: Catacombe di Priscilla, Rome
CSIC: Consejo Superior de Investigaciones Cientificas, Madrid
EM: Egyptian Museum, Cairo
KM: Kunsthistorisches Museum, Vienna
MAN: Museo Arqueológico Nacional, Madrid
MANN: Museo Archeologico Nazionale, Naples
MC: Musei Capitolini, Rome
MGP: Museo Gregoriano Profano, Vatican
MH: Michael Holford, Loughton, Essex
MVG: Museo di Villa Giulia, Rome
NAM: National Archaeological Museum, Athens
NHPA: Natural History Photographic Agency
NMI: National Museum of India, New Delhi
ON: Osterreichische Nationalbibliothek, Vienna
RHPL: Robert Harding Picture Library, London
RMN: Réunion des Musées Nationaux, Paris
SAG: Staatliche Antikensammlungen und Glypothek, Munich
SG: Scala Group, Florence
SHM: Statens Historiska Museum, Stockholm
SHP Sonia Halliday Photographs, Weston Turville, England
SK: Studio Kopperman, Munich
SMPK: Staatliche Museen zu Berlin-Preussischer Kulturbesitz
SPL: Science Photo Library, London
V&A: Victoria and Albert Museum, London
VM: Vorderasiatisches Museum, Berlin
WFA: Werner Forman Archive, London

5 National Gallery, London
6 John Lawrence
7 AKG
10 Magnum / Erich Lessing
17 AGE / Fritz Pölking
18t NHPA / Steve Robinson
20 AGE / SPL / John Reader
21t MAN
21b AGE / SPL / John Reader
25 Zardoya, Barcelona / Erich Lessing
28 MAN
31b AGE
31tl MAN
31tr MAN
32tl Santos Cid
32tr Santos Cid
33 Javier Trueba / Diario El Pais, SA
34 SPL / James King-Holmes
35 Comstock, London
36 Musée de l'homme, Paris
38 MAN
39b RS Soleski
39t SPL / John Reader
40 SPL / John Reader
44c MAN
44tl MAN
45 Frank Spooner / Sygma
46 Musée de l'homme, Paris
48b MAN
49t Godo-Foto, Barcelona
51b AGE
52 Oronoz, Madrid
53b CSIC
53t CSIC
54t MAN
54b AAA / Brian Wilson
55c MAN
56tl MAN
56tc MAN
58t MAN
58b MAN
59t Zardoya, Barcelona / Erich Lessing
59b Magnum / Erich Lessing
60 MAN
61t MAN
61b Rätisches Museum, Chur, Switzerland
62 SHP
63b AA / Hittite Museum, Ankara
65 AGE
67 Carmen Redondo
69 BAL / BM
70 SG / The Iraq Museum, Baghdad
71t Godo-Foto, Barcelona
71b RHPL
72bl BPK / Jürgen Liepe / VM
72br AGE
73 WFA / BL
75c BAL / NMI
77 MH
78 RHPL
79b SG / The Iraq Museum, Baghdad
80 RHPL
81t BPK / Jürgen Liepe / VM
81b Jürgen Liepe, Berlin / Staatliche Museum, Berlin
83b RMN / Louvre, Paris
84tl BPK / Jürgen Liepe / VM
84b RMN / Louvre, Paris
85 Erwin Böhm, Mainz
86t AAA/ G Tortoli / BM
86b AISA
88t SG / The Iraq Museum, Baghdad
88b AISA
89t RMN / Chuzeville / Louvre, Paris
89b MH / BM
90 RHPL / Richard Ashworth
91t Debate
91b BAL / BM
92t SG / The Iraq Museum, Baghdad
92b RMN / Louvre, Paris
93t AAA / R Sheridan / BM
93b RMN / Louvre, Paris
94 RMN / Louvre, Paris
95l RMN / Chuzeville / Louvre, Paris
95r BPK / Jürgen Liepe / VM
96 RMN / Louvre, Paris
97 RMN / Louvre, Paris
98 Firoexpress-Firo Foto
99t RMN / Louvre, Paris
99b RMN / Louvre, Paris
100 Hirmer Fotoarchiv, Munich
101 AAA / GT Garvey
102 Jürgen Liepe, Berlin / EM
103b Jose Angel Gutiérrez
104t BAL / Giraudon / EM
104b Jose Angel Gutiérrez
106 Jürgen Liepe, Berlin / EM
108 RHPL / John Ross / EM
109 RHPL / FL Kennett
110 RMN / Chuzeville / Louvre, Paris
111 AISA / EM
113 AGE
114 BAL / Stapleton Collection
115 RHPL / FL Kennett
116 Jose Angel Gutiérrez
117 MAN
118 Debate
119 AAA / Mary Jelliffe
120 WFA / BM
121 BAL / Giraudon
122 AKG / Erich Lessing
123 Debate
124t Jose Angel Gutiérrez / BM
124b Jose Angel Gutiérrez
125 AISA / BM
126 BAL / BM
127 Jürgen Liepe, Berlin / EM
128t BAL / Giraudon / EM
128b Jose Angel Gutiérrez
129 SG
130 BAL / Giraudon
131 AAA / Eric Hobhouse
132 RMN / Louvre, Paris
133 RMN / Chuzeville / Louvre, Paris
134 AAA / R Sheridan / BM
135 BPK / Jürgen Liepe / VM
136 AAA / R Sheridan
137 BM
138 BPK / Jürgen Liepe / VM
139 Magnum / Erich Lessing
140 BAL / Giraudon / EM
141 WFA / E Strouhal
142 AAA / R Sheridan
144 RHPL / FL Kennett
145 AISA
146 AAA / R Sheridan
147 SG / AMH
148 Jose Angel Gutiérrez
150 SG / NAM
151 Petros M Nomikos / Idryma Theras, Athens
152 SG / AMH
153b SG / AMH
154 Debate
155 AAA
156t Jose Angel Gutiérrez
156b Jose Angel Gutiérrez
157t Jose Angel Gutiérrez
157b Jose Angel Gutiérrez
158 BM
159 BAL / BM
160 AA / Archaeological Museum, Cagliari
161 MAN
162b Jose Angel Gutiérrez
163 BAL / Giraudon / Louvre, Paris
164 AA
166 Stockmarket, London
167 BAL / Basilica San Marco, Venice
169 AGE
171 BM
172 AISA / BM
173 Jose Angel Gutiérrez / BM
174 RMN / Chuzeville / Louvre, Paris
175 Jose Angel Gutiérrez / BM
177 Jose Angel Gutiérrez / BM
178 WFA / BM
179 AKG / Erich Lessing / BM
180 AKG / Pergamon Museum, Berlin
179 BPK / Jürgen Liepe / VM
182 AGE
185 RHPL
186 Godo-foto, Barcelona
187 AAA / Bruce Norman
188t RHPL / NMI
188b BAL / NMI
189tl AGE
189tr AGE
190t RHPL / NMI
190b RHPL / NMI
191 RHPL / S Sassoon
192t AAA / R Sheridan
192b AAA / R Sheridan
193 AAA / R Sheridan
194 Angelo Hornak, London / NMI
195 MH / Sarnath Museum, Varanasi
196 AAA
197 BAL / NMI
198 MH / BM
199 BAL / NMI
200t V&A
200b AAA / R Sheridan

201 V&A
202 AGE / Alain Evrard
203 AGE / Alain Evrard
204 Panos Pictures, London / Cliff Venner
205 RHPL
206 AGE
208 China Photo Library, Hong Kong
210t WFA / Yang-tzusshan, Szechwan
210b RHPL
211 AA
212 By courtesy of the Cultural Relics Bureau and the Metropolitan Museum of Art, New York
213l AISA
213r AAA / R Sheridan
214 BN
215 BN
216 BM
217 The Times, London / Ray Main
218-9 RHPL
220 BAL / BM
222 AISA
223tc AISA
223tr AAA / R Sheridan
224 AAA / R Sheridan
225 AISA
227 BAL / Oriental Museum, Durham University
228l Zardoya, Barcelona / Magnum / Erich Lessing
228r BAL / BM
229 MH, / Staatliches Museum für Völkerkunde, Munich
231 By courtesy of the Cultural Relics Bureau and the Metropolitan Museum of Art, New York
232 Godo-foto, Barcelona
233 AGE
235 AGE
236-7 Zardoya, Barcelona / Magnum / Erich Lessing
238t AISA
238b Godo-foto, Barcelona / Natural History Museum, New York
239t AISA
239b AISA / Archaeological Museum, Lima
240 AA / BM
241 AISA
244–5 Zardoya, Barcelona / Magnum / Erich Lessing
246 AKG / Erich Lessing
247 RHPL
249 Zardoya, Barcelona / Magnum / Erich Lessing
250 Jurgen Liepe, Berlin
251 Erwin Böhm, Mainz
252 AISA
253 AGE
254 Zardoya, Barcelona / Magnum / Erich Lessing
255 AISA
256 RHPL
258 AISA
260 BAL / Freud Museum, London
261 AGE
262 SG / MANN
263t RHPL
263b AKG / Erich Lessing
264 SG
265 AA
266t Kostas Kontos, Athens / NAM
266b RMN / Chuzeville / Louvre, Paris
267 SG / Museo delle Terme, Rome
269 AGE
270t SG / Museo Gregoriano Etrusco, Vatican
270b SG / Museo delle Terme, Rome
271 SG / Museo Pio Clementino, Vatican
272l AISA
272r AAA / R Sheridan
273 AGE
274 BM
275t SK / SAG
275b Metropolitan Museum of Art, New York (Rogers Fund)
276 SK / SAG
277t AAA / R Sheridan
277b SG / Museo Nazionale di Villa Giulia, Rome
278 Zardoya, Barcelona
279t MAN
279bl MAN
279br Jose Angel Gutiérrez
280 SG / MANN
281 AAA / R Sheridan
282 SG / Museo Nazionale di Villa Giulia, Rome
283 Wadsworth Atheneum, Hartford, Conneticut (Gift of J. Pierpont Morgan)
284 AGE
285 AGE
286 AGE
288 BAL / Louvre, Paris
289 AISA / BN
290t AKG / Erich Lessing / Louvre, Paris
290b SHP
291 AGE
293 AKG / KM
294 AAA / R Sheridan
295 AGE
296t SK / SAG
296b SG / Il Duomo, Syracuse
298 SG / MANN
299 Zardoya, Barcelona / Magnum / Erich Lessing
300t MAN
300b AAA / R Sheridan
301t MAN
301b AKG / Antikensammlung, Berlin
302 BM
303t SG / Acropolis Museum, Athens
303b RMN / Louvre, Paris
304 BM
306 Jose Angel Gutiérrez
307 BM
308 SG / Agora Museum, Athens
309t SG / Museo Pio Clementino, Vatican
310 SG / Acropolis Museum, Athens
311 Kostas Kontos, Athens / NAM
312 SG / Archaeological Museum, Olympia
313 AGE
314b AGE
315tl Jose Angel Gutiérrez
315tr SG / Museo Pio Clementino, Vatican
316 SHP
317 AISA / MC
318 AKG / Il Duomo di Anagni, Lazio
319 SG / Museo Pio Clementino, Vatican
321t SG / MANN
321b ADO / Louvre, Paris
322 Zardoya, Barcelona / Magnum / Erich Lessing
323 Firo-foto
324 MAN
325 AGE
326l AAA / R Sheridan
326r BM
327 Zardoya, Barcelona / Magnum / Louvre, Paris
329 SG
330 Kostas Kontos, Athens / NAM
331 AKG / Erich Lessing / Louvre, Paris
332 BAL / Archaeological Museum, Thessoloniki
333 Kostas Kontos, Athens / Archaeological Museum, Thessoloniki
334 SHP
336 SG / Acropolis Museum, Athens
338-9 SG / MANN
340t SG / Archaeological Museum, Istanbul
340c AAA / R Sheridan
342l AGE
343 WFA / BM
344 AKG / Pergamon Museum, Berlin
345t SG / MANN
345b AKG / Erich Lessing / Liebighaus, Frankfurt-am-Main
347 Zardoya, Barcelona / Magnum
348 AGE
349 SG / MC
350 BAL / BN
351 AGE
352 AGE
353 SG / MC
355 SG / Museo Pio Clementino, Vatican
356 RHPL / Simon Harris
358 AKG / MC
359 AISA / MANN
360tl AISA / MVG
360b Jose Angel Gutiérrez
361 AKG / Tomb of Leopardi, Tarquinia
362 Jose Angel Gutiérrez
363 BAL / Archaeological Museum, Olympia
364 ADO
365 SG
366t AISA / Museo Archeologico Nazionale, Venice
366b Corbis / Roger Wood
367 SG
368tl RMN / Louvre, Paris
368r AA / MVG
369t Ny Carlsberg Glyptotek, Copenhagen
369b AGE
370t SG / MC
371 AKG / Musei Pontificie, Vatican
372t SG
372b AGE
373t AGE
373b RHPL / Robert Cundy
374–5t RMN / Louvre, Paris
374b BAL / BM
376 BAL / Giraudon / Louvre, Paris
377 Zardoya, Barcelona / Erich Lessing / Musée Granet, Aix-en-Provence
378t AISA / MC
378b SG / MVG
379 Landesmuseum, Mainz
380 Zardoya, Barcelona / Erich Lessing / Maria Saal, Carinthia
381t ADO
381b BM
382t SG / Museo Archeologico Nazionale, Venice
382b Jose Angel Gutiérrez
383 SG / MC
384 MH
386 AISA
387 RHPL / Adam Woolfitt
388t BM
388c BM
389t KM
389b Oronoz, Madrid / Musei Pontificie, Vatican
390t AISA
390cl AISA / MC
391 Zardoya, Barcelona / Erich Lessing
393 AGE
394tl RMN / H Lewandowski / Louvre, Paris
394r Fiorepress-Firo Foto
395 Oronoz, Madrid
396 Stockmarket
397 AGE
398–9 ADO / Musée Archéologique de Sousse
400 AISA / Musée National du Bardo, Tunis
401t CM Dixon, Canterbury
401b BAL / Lauros-Giraudon / Landesmuseum, Trier
402b AGE
402t SG / MGP
403 Axiom, London / James Morris
404 AISA / Museo della Civiltà Romana, Rome
406 AKG / Metropolitan Museum of Art, New York
407t AISA / MANN
407b AKG / Erich Lessing
408 AKG
409 SG
410t AISA / Museo Archeologico, Taranto
410b Museo Arqueológico, Barcelona
411t Juan Avilés
411b Jürgen Liepe, Berlin/ Staatliche Museum, Berlin
412 AGE
413 Angelo Hornak, London
414 SG / Museo Pio Clementino, Vatican
415t SG / MGP
415b BM
416–7 AISA
418 SG / Museo della Civiltà Romana, Rome
419t SG
420 SG / Museo Civico, Albega
421 BAL / Louvre, Paris
422 SG / SS Cosma e Damiano, Rome
423 AKG / Erich Lessing / National Museum, Damascus
424t Werner Braun
424b SG / Ipogeo di via Latina, Rome
425t BN
425b ADO / National Museum, Damascus
427 SG / CP
428b AGE
429 Oronoz, Madrid
430tl AISA / Museo Egizio, Turin
430b Zardoya, Barcelona / F Mayer
431 BAL / Battistero Neroniano, Ravenna
432 AAA / R Sheridan
433 SG / S Prieto, Vatican
434 Iberpress / Giordano / S Ambrose, Milan
435t AA / S Constanza, Rome
435b Zardoya, Barcelona / Erich Lessing / Catacombe di S Domitilla, Rome
436 SG / S Prieto, Vatican
439t SG / Museo Pio Cristiano, Vatican
439b SG / CP
440 AAA / R Sheridan
441 SG / Galleria degli Uffizi, Florence
442–3 SG / Galleria Borghese, Rome
444t SG / CP
444b AGE
445 Oronoz, Madrid / Palazzo Rondanini, Rome
446-7 SG / Catacombe di S Gennaro, Naples

449 BAL / Lambeth Palace Library, London (Ms.1370, f.115v)
1450 SG / Catacombe di S Ermete, Rome
452 AISA / MC
453t AISA / Xavier Navarro
453b Jürgen Liepe, Berlin / Staatliche Museum, Berlin
454 AISA
455 BAL /Giraudon
456 AISA / Museo Archeologico Nazionale, Naples
457b Jose Angel Gutiérrez
457t MAN
458 AISA
460 AISA
461 Fiorepress-Firo Foto / S Fiore
462 Jose Angel Gutiérrez
463 AISA / Musée Calvet, Avignon
464 SG / Biblioteca Apostolica, Vatican
465 BAL
466 SHP / Battistero degli Ariani, Ravenna
467 SG / MGP
468 BAL / Private Collection
469 Bodleian Library, Oxford (Ms.378, f.84r)
470 SG / S Costanza, Rome
471t AISA / MC
471b AAA / G Tortoli
472 AISA / Battistero degli Ariani, Ravenna
473t KM
473b SG / Battistero degli Ariani, Ravenna
474t AAA
474b KM
477 RHPL
478 BAL / Giraudon / BM
479 BN
480–1 SG / Museo delle Terme, Rome
482 MAN
483t KM
483b Bodleian Library, Oxford (Rol.159.2/83)
484 AISA
485 RMN / H Lewandowski / Louvre, Paris
486 AISA
487 BAL / Giraudon
488–9 AA / Mausolo di Gàlla Placidia, Ravenna
490 ADO / Musée National du Bardo, Tunis
491 Oronoz, Madrid / Capilla S Vittore, Milan
492 MH / BM
493 SG / S Lorenzo Maggiore, Milan
494 RHPL / F Jackson
495 SG / Biblioteca Medicea Laurenziana, Florence (Ms.Plut.12; 17, f.3v)
496 Zardoya, Barcelona / Erich Lessing / Museo de Arcivescovado, Ravenna
497t BAL / Private Collection
497b SG / Museo Civico de "Eta" Cristiana, Brescia
499 BAL / Biblioteca Medicea-Laurenziana, Florence (Ms.Plut.12.17, f.4r)
500 MH
501 MH
502 AA / Rheinisches Landesmuseum, Bonn
503 BAL / Lauros-Giraudon
504 BN
505 BAL / Giraudon
506l Iberpress
506r AGE
507 AISA
508 V&A / Ian Thomas
509 SG / S Apollinare in Classe, Ravenna
511t BAL / Giraudon / Ainari / S Vitale, Ravenna
511b AISA / Museo Bargello, Florence
512 Zardoya, Barcelona / Erich Lessing / S Apollinare Nuovo, Ravenna
513 SG / S Apollinare Nuovo, Ravenna
514 AISA
515 AISA
516 SHP / St Sozomenus, Galata, Cyprus
517 CM Dixon, Canterbury
518 Metropolitan Museum of Art, New York (Gift of George Blumenthal, 1941)
519 BAL / Louvre, Paris
1520 Axiom, London / James Morris
521 AISA / S Constanza, Rome
522 SG / Sacro Speco, Subiaco
523 BAL / Giraudon / Musée Condé, Chantilly
524 SHP / BN
525 SG / Duomo, Monza
526 MAN
527 Trinity College Library, Dublin (Ms.57, f.21v)
529 Corpus Christi College, Cambridge (Ms.286, f.129v)
530 AKG / Real Monasterio, El Escorial
532 AISA
534t RMN / Chuzeville / Louvre, Paris
534b AISA
535b BAL / Giraudon / Bibliothèque Sainte-Geneviève, Paris
536 BN
537t MAN
537b RHPL
538 AAA
539 Römisch-Germanisches Museum, Cologne
540 Alinari-Giraudon / Pina Coteca Vaticana, Vatican
541 AA / Sucevita Monastery, Moldovita, Romania
542 Topkapi Palace Museum, Istanbul (Ms.H.1221)
543 BAL / Fitzwilliam Museum, Cambridge
545 Topkapi Palace Museum, Istanbul (Ms.1222)
546 BAL / Giraudon-Index / Museé Condé, Chantilly
547 Spencer Collection / The New York Public Library (Astor, Lenox and Tilden Foundations)
548 Reproduced by kind permission of the Trustees of the Chester Beatty Library, Dublin
551 BN (Ar.5847, f.94v)
552 Oronoz, Madrid / BN
553 Oronoz, Madrid
554 ADO
555 MAN
557 Corbis / Nik Wheeler
558t MAN
558b MAN
559 AISA / BN
560 BAL / Giraudon-Dost Yayinlari / University Central Library, Istanbul
561 AISA / BN
562 WFA
563 AISA
564 AISA
566 Corbis / Sheldan Collins
567 MAN
568 BN (Ar.5847, f.125)
571 AISA / BN
572 Oronoz, Madrid / Topkapi Palace Museum, Istanbul
573 AISA / Ravenna
574 AISA / Ravenna
575 Oronoz, Madrid
576 AISA
578 MAN
579 1997 Dumbarton Oaks, Trustees of Harvard University, Washington DC
580 BNM (Vit.26.2, f.34v)
581 Index, Barcelona / Biblioteca Apostolica, Vaticana
582 SG / S Apollinare Nuovo, Ravenna
584 Oronoz, Madrid / Colección Duques de Alba, Madrid
586 WFA / Biblioteca Nazionale Marcuana, Venice (Gr.Z17)
587 MAN
588 BAL / Lauros-Giraudon / Basilica San Marco, Venice
589b Biblioteca Vaticana (Gr.372-43v)
589t MAN
590 SG / S Francesca Romana, Rome
591 SG / Art Resource, New York / S Vitale, Ravenna
592 BAL / Richardson & Kailas Icons, London
593 SG / Galleria Fresaka, Belgrade
594t MAN
594b MAN
595 BN (Gr.510, f.438v)
596t MAN
596b BNM (Vit.26.2, f.97v)
597 Oronoz, Madrid
599 AISA
600 BAL / Giraudon / Louvre, Paris
602 WFA / BNM (f.217r)
603 Biblioteca Apostolica Vaticana (Vat. Slavo 2, f.145v)
604 SG / San Clemente, Rome
605 National Archaeological Museum, Sofia
606 MH / SHM
607 Nationalmuseum, Stockholm
608 BAL / Kremlin Museum, Moscow
609t AKG / Erich Lessing / Academy of Science, St Petersburg
609b Marco Polo / J de Vergara
610 SG / State Tretyakov Gallery, Moscow
611 AGE
612 AISA
614 BAL / Lauros-Giraudon / National Art Gallery, Sofia
615 CM Dixon, Canterbury
616 AKG / Erich Lessing
617 Corbis / Dean Conger / Santa Sofia, Kiev
619 RHPL / State Tretyakov Gallery, Moscow
620 MAN
621 AAA / B Norman
622 BL (Add.18866, f.140r)
623 Fiorepress-Firo Foto
624 Metropolitan Museum of Art, New York (Francis M Weld Fund, 1950)
625 AGE
626 Corpus Christi College, Cambridge (Ms.26, f.279)
627 BL (Cot. Faust B, f.72v)
628 BN (Per.1113, f.44v)
629 AAA / R Sheridan
631 BN
632 BN
633 BN (Pers.1113, f.107v)
634 Oronoz, Madrid
635 AISA / BN
637 Corbis / Roger Wood
639 BN (Grec.2144, f.11)
640 AISA / Kariye Camii, Istanbul
642 The John Work Garrett Library, Johns Hopkins University, Baltimore
643 SHP
645 ON (Cod.8.626, f.63)
648 BAL / Hagia Sophia, Istanbul
649 MAN
650t AISA
650b Spencer Collection / The New York Public Library (Astor, Lenox and Tilden Foundations)
651 MAN
653 BAL / Giraudon-Dost Yanyinlari / Topkapi Palace Museum, Istanbul
654 MAN
655t MAN
655b Imagen Mas / Museo Arqueológico, Oviedo
656 BN (Lat.8878, f.145v)
658 BN (Lat.8878, f.193)
659 Bibliothèque Municipale, Castres, France
660 BAL / Giraudon / Museé Condé, Chantilly
661 Bibliothèque Municipale, Castres, France
662 RMN / Willi / Louvre, Paris
664t BAL / Giraudon / BN
664b BAL / Giraudon / BN
665 AKG /Schatzkammer, Aachen
666b Index, Barcelona / Biblioteca Nazionale, Turin
666t Oronoz, Madrid
667 BAL / KM
668 BN (Lat.1, f.423)
669 BON (Cod.908, f.3v)
670 Bibliothèque Municipale d'Arras (Ms.1045, f.8)
671 Bayerische Staatsbibliothek, Munich (Nr.335, Css.4452, f.152v)
672 SG / Castello Sforzesco, Milan
674 BNM (Ms.413, f.16r)
675t AISA
675b SG
676 BM
677 BAL / SHM
678 National Museum of Ireland, Dublin
679l BL (Cott Nero)
679r BM
680 SHM
681l SHM
681r BAL / BL
682t AISA / Archivo de la Corona de Aragón, Barcelona
682b Oronoz, Madrid
683 BM
685 KM
686 SG / Pinoteca Vaticana
688 BM
689 Imagen Mas
690 BAL / BN (Lat., f.386v)
692 Oronoz, Madrid / San Isidoro, León
693 AISA
695 BNM
696 Oronoz, Madrid / San Isidoro, León
698 Oronoz, Madrid / Archivo de la Corona de Aragón, Barcelona
699 BN (Esp.36, f.72v)
700 BAL / Lambeth Palace Library, London
701d BAL / Giraudon / Musée Bayeux
701t MH / Musée Bayeux
703 Corpus Christi College, Cambridge (Ms.20, f.68r)
704 Oronoz, Madrid / Archivo Municipal, Burgos
706 Corbis / Charles and Janette Lenars
707 MAN
709 Oronoz, Madrid
710 AISA
711 AAA / R Sheridan

712 MAN
713 V&A
714 BAL / NMI
715 Angelo Hornak, London / NMI
716 Sam Fogg Rare Books, London
717 WFA / Philip Goldman Collection
719 BAL / NMI
720 Museum für Indische Kunst, SMPK, Berlin / Jürgen Liepe (I10198)
721 Museum für Indische Kunst, SMPK, Berlin / Iris Papadollos (I10148)
722 AISA
723 BAL / BL (Add. 22703, f.52v)
724 V&A
725 BAL / V&A
726 V&A
727 V&A
729 Mary Evans Picture Library, London
731 AA / V&A
732 AISA
733 BL (J.2.2)
734 BN (Fr.2810, f.84)
735 Index, Barcelona / HA Rayner-TCL
736 Metropolitan Museum of Art, New York
737 Index, Barcelona / Freston-TPS
738 Museum für Völkerkunde, SMPK, Berlin
740 RHPL / FL Kennett
741 National Palace Museum, Taipei
742 Museum für Völkerkunde, SMPK, Berlin
743 CM Dixon, Canterbury
744 AISA / BM
745tl Index, Barcelona / C Milne-Masterfile
745b Museo Oriental, Valladolid
747 AA / Musée Guimet, Paris
748 AISA / Golestan Palace, Teheran
749 University of California, Berkeley Art Museum / Benjamin Blackwell
751 Museum of Fine Arts, Boston (Denman Waldo Ross Collection)
752 AISA
753 BL (Or8210 / P2)
754 National Palace Museum, Taipei
756 BN (Fr.2810, f.54)
757 BN (Fr. 2810, f.69)
758 WFA
759 BAL / BL
760 AA / BN
762 Gutenberg-Museum, Mainz / Studio Popp
763t BAL / Fitzwilliam Museum, University of Cambridge
763b Herzog August Bibliothek, Wolfenbüttel (1.2.2. Geogr. 2°)
765 WFA / Christies's
766 Japanese Gallery, London
766 Japanese Gallery, London
768t AGE
768b MH
769 Index, Barcelona / Massonori
770 Index, Barcelona / PA Thompson
771 Tokyo National Museum
772 Museum of Imperial Collections, Sannomaru Shozokan / International Society for Education and Information, Tokyo
773 Tokyo Fuji Art Museum
774 AISA / Museo d'Arte Orientale, Eduardo Chissone, Genoa
775 Idetmitsu Museum of Arts, Tokyo
776 WFA / MH de Young Memorial Museum, San Francisco
777 WFA / Kuroda Collection, Japan
778 AISA / Museo dos Reis, Porto
779 AAA
781 BAL/ Private Collection
782 BAL / Giraudon / Musée Condé, Chantilly
783 BM
784 Index, Barcelona
785 BAL / Giraudon / Musée Historique des Tissus, Lyons
786 BN (Esp. 30, f.5v)
787 National Museum of Denmark / Kitt Wess
789 BM
791 AISA
792 Museo de América, Madrid
793 Museo de América, Madrid
794 BN (Mex. 59–64, f.1)
795 Index, Barcelona / Museo Nácional de Antropología, Mexico
796 Museo de América, Madrid
797 AISA
798 AISA / BNM
799 RMN / Louvre, Paris
800 Biblioteca Centrale della Regione Siciliana, Palermo (Ms. I.E.8, c.8r)
801 BN (Latin 17716, f. 91)
802 AISA / Biblioteca Apostolica Vaticana, Rome
803 Thüringer Universitäts und Landesbibliotek, Jena (Ms. Boc. q6, f.79r)
804 BN (Ms. Latin 3893, f.1)
805 BL (Harl.5102, f.32)
806 Firo-Foto / R de Seynes
807 Museo de Navarra, Pamplona / Luis Prieto Saenz de Tejada
808 SG / Santa Croce, Florence
809 Museo del Prado, Madrid
810 AKG / Erich Lessing
812 BAL / Lauros-Giraudon
813 Firo-Foto
815 AISA / Národní knihovna, Prague
816 Rheinisches Bildarchiv / Wallraf-Richartz-Museum, Cologne
818 Oronoz, Madrid / Coleccion Duques de Alba, Madrid
819 AA / Honourable Society of the Inner Temple
820 SG / Biblioteca Nazionale Centrale, Florence
821 Index, Barcelona / BAL / BL
822 Public Record Office, London
823 BN (Fr.5054, f.71)
825 BN (Fr 87, f.117)
826 FotoBox / Rafael Sámano
828 BL (Add.27695, f.8)
829 AA
830 Index, Barcelona / Fabbri
832 AAA
833 AISA / Biblioteca Medicea-Laurenziana, Florence
835t The Bodleian Library, Oxford (Ms. Douce 208, f. 120v)
835b Oronoz, Madrid / BNM
836 Oronoz, Madrid / Museo de la Catedral, Avila
837 BL (Add.27695, f.8)
838 Bibliothèque Royale Albert 1e, Brussels (Ms 13076-77, f.24v)
839 AKG / Bibliothèque Royale Albert 1e, Brussels
840 AKG / Erich Lessing / KM
841 AISA
842 Firo Foto/ S Fiore / Biblioteca Nazionale Universitaria, Turin
844 SG / Galleria degli Uffizi, Florence
845 Rheinisches Landesmuseum, Bonn
846 BAL / Lauros-Giraudon / Galleria Regionale della Sicilia, Palermo
847 National Gallery, London
848 BN (Fr. 2829, f.39v)
849 BL (Egerton 1500, f.45v)
851 AISA
852 BL (Royal 16b vi, fol.404v)
853 Oronoz, Madrid
854 AKG / Stadtmuseum, Sterzing
856 AAA
857 AA / Academia das Ciências, Lisbon
858 BAL / Giraudon / Museu Nacional de Arte Antiga, Lisbon (Inv. 1361)
859 Museo Naval, Madrid
860 BN (Pl.12)
861 Oronoz, Madrid / Biblioteca Nazionale Marciana, Venice
862 Oronoz, Madrid / Museo Naval, Madrid
863 RMN / Louvre, Paris / Arnaudet
864 AA / Museu Etnográfico da Sociedade de Geografia, Lisbon
865 AA / BN
867 SG / S Maria Novella, Florence
868 Oronoz, Madrid / Biblioteca del Monasterio de El Escorial
869 The Metropolitan Museum of Art, New (Bequest of Cora Timken Burnett, 1956 / photo: Schecter Lee)
871 SG / Galleria degli Uffizi, Florence
872 BN (Fr.1537, f.29v)
873 Staatsbibliotek zu Berlin – Preussischer Kulturbesitz, Abteilung, Jahr und Urheber (Inc. 1511 Bd 1, c.84r)
874 BN (Fr. 455, f. 9)
875 Oronoz, Madrid / Biblioteca del Monasterio de El Escorial
877 SG / Accademia, Venice

Text credits

The publishers wish to thank the following for their kind permission to reproduce the translations and copyright material in this book. Every effort has been made to trace copyright owners, but if anyone has been omitted we apologize and will, if informed, make corrections in any future edition.

p.201 extract from "The Chandogya Upanishad" from The Upanishads, translated by Eknath Easwaran (Arkana, 1988) copyright © The Blue Mountain Center of Meditation, 1987. Reproduced by permission of Penguin Books Ltd.; p.202 extract from "Vigilance" from *The Dammapadha: the Sayings of the Buddha* by Thomas Cleary. Copyright © 1994 by Thomas Cleary. Reproduced by permission of Bantam Books, a division of Random House, Inc.; pp.262 and 290, extracts from *The Histories* by Herodotus, translated by Aubrey de Sélincourt, revised by John Marincola (Penguin Classics 1954, Second revised edition 1996). Translation copyright © 1954 by Aubrey de Sélincourt. Revised edition copyright © John Maricola, 1996. Reproduced by permission of Penguin Books Ltd.; p.302, extract from "Trojan Women" from *Electra and Other Plays* by Euripides, translated by John Davie, (Penguin Classics, 1988) copyright © John Davie, 1988. Reproduced by permission of Penguin Books Ltd.; p.320 extract from *The Republic* by Plato, translated by Desmond Lee (Penguin Classics 1955, Third revised edition 1987) copyright © Penguin Classics H. D. P. Lee, 1953, 1974, 1987. Reproduced by permission of Penguin Books Ltd. p.381 extract from *Fall of the Roman Republic: Six Lives* by Plutarch, translated by Rex Warner (Penguin Classics 1958) copyright © Rex Warner, 1958. Reproduced by permission of Penguin Books Ltd.; p.382 extract from *The Conquest of Gaul* by Julius Caesar, translated by S. A. Handford (Penguin Classics 1951) copyright © S. A. Handford, 1951. Reproduced by permission of Penguin Books Ltd.; p.391 extract from *The Histories* by Tacitus, translated by Kenneth Wellesley (Penguin Classics 1964, Revised edition 1975) copyright © 1964, 1972. Reproduced by permission of Penguin Books Ltd.; p.392 extract from *The Twelve Caesars* by Suetonius, translated by Robert Graves, revised by Michael Grant (Penguin Classics 1957, Second revised edition 1979). Translation copyright © Robert Graves, 1957. Revised edition copyright © Michael Grant Publications Ltd., 1979. Reproduced by permission of A. P. Watt Ltd. on behalf of the Robert Graves Copyright Trust; p.408 extract from *Martial: Epigrams, Vol. III* translated by D. R. Shackleton Bailey, Cambridge, Mass., Harvard University Press, 1993. Reproduced by permission of the publishers and the Loeb Classical Library; p.482 extract from *The Agricola and the Germania* by Tacitus, translated by H. Mattingly, revised by S. A. Handford (Penguin Classics 1948, Revised edition 1970) copyright © the Estate of H. Mattingly, 1948, 1970 copyright © S. A. Handford, 1970. Reproduced by permissionof Penguin Books Ltd. pp.545 and 568 extracts from the Koran translated by Arthur J. Arberry (Oxford University Press 1964) copyright © 1955. Reproduced by permission of HarperCollins Publishers Ltd.; p.559 extract from *The Book of the Thousand Nights and One Night* by Haroun-al-Raschid, rendered into English from the literal and complete French translation of Dr J. C. Mardrus by Powys Mathers (Routledge & Kegan Paul 1986) copyright © 1964. Reproduced by permission of Routledge. p.821 extract from *The Canterbury Tales* by Geoffrey Chaucer, edited by A.C. Spearing (Cambridge University Press 1995) copyright © 1966. Reproduced by permission of Cambridge University Press; p.870 extract from *Praise of Folly* by Desiderius Erasmus, translated by Betty Radice (Penguin Classics 1971, revised edition 1993) translation copyright © Betty Radice, 1971. Reproduced by permission of Penguin Books Ltd.